12/92

P9-CJC-898

DATE DUE

DEMCO 38-296

12/92

DICTIONARY OF OCCUPATIONAL TITLES

Fourth Edition, Revised 1991

Volume II
Glossary • Appendixes • Indexes

U.S. Department of Labor
Employment and Training Administration

≣BERNAN PRESS
Lanham, MD

Riverside Community College
Library
4800 Magnolia Avenue
Riverside, California 92506

DEC '92

REF
H B
2581
U 5
1991

Bernan Press
4611-F Assembly Drive
Lanham, MD 20706

Printed in the United States of America.

The binding on this edition is Library quality, Smyth sewn, and
designed to withstand heavy use for a number of years.

ISBN 0-89059-003-6 (Volume II)
ISBN 0-89059-000-1 (2 Volume Set)

Library of Congress Catalog Card Number: 91-76504

CONTENTS

VOLUME I

VOLUME II

GLOSSARY

The Glossary contains technical or special uses of words, which are not ordinarily found in a standard desk dictionary. These words are *italicized* when they appear in an occupational definition.

ABSORPTION TOWER

Tank used to form acidic bisulfate-active agent in digesting wood, from ingredients such as sulfur dioxide, lime, manganese, and ammonia.

AGATE BEARING

A bearing made of agate used in small scales or precision balances where resistance to corrosion is essential.

AIRGAP

The gap between the rotor and stator of an electric machine.

AIR LANCE

A long metal rod that carries compressed air to its tip. It is used for cleaning purposes.

ALODIZE

A process for bathing metal in hot alodine solution to give it protective coating and surface for painting.

BACK-ROLL LATHE

A veneer lathe equipped with knives mounted on impression roller that rotates counter to rotation of log. The knives score log lengthwise causing veneer to be peeled from log in narrow stave and hoop widths.

BACK SHEET

A veneer sheet, usually of slightly inferior quality than FACE SHEET, used for the bottom surface sheet of plywood panels.

BALANCE

To adjust pressure, velocity, or volume control settings in a heating, cooling, or ventilating system to attain performance indicated in system design specifications.

BALL WARP

An untwisted rope of yarn wound on core, usually for dyeing or mercerizing.

BAND

Two plies of rubberized fabric pressed together with ends joined to form endless strip used in building pneumatic tires.

BAT

A fluffy layer which is composed of interlaced and matted strands of fibrous material used for filling or insulating articles such as mattresses or comforters.

BEAT

See IN-BEAT.

BEATING MACHINE

A machine equipped with leather strips which, when revolving, beat loose hair, dust, and foreign matter from fur pelts.

BELL REAMER

An expanding bit used to enlarge bottom of holes drilled to accommodate concrete pier footings. The conical shape of resulting hole anchors footing and serves as base for pier construction.

BENCH GRINDER

A small grinding machine for shaping and sharpening cutting edges of tools. It consists of a motor, mounted on bench or floor stand, with grinding wheel at one or both ends of shaft.

BILGE OF STAVE

The difference in width between ends and middle of a barrel stave.

BLADDER

Heavy-walled rubber cylinder used in a curing press to expand uncured tires into the recesses of the tire mold.

BLINDSTITCH SEWING MACHINE

A machine equipped with a curved needle to sew stitches that do not penetrate the outer surface of fabric. Used for operations, such as hemming, lapel padding, and lining felling.

BLOCKER

One of a number of leather strips joined together for use as trimming for shoes.

BLOCKING MACHINE

An electric stove equipped with a grill on which blocks, pitch, and lenses are heated. On depressing a lever, hot pitch is forced onto block surface.

BOARD

A sheet of varnished canvas, or a lightweight wooden board, upon which rubber slabs or parts are placed for transportation or storage.

BOARDING I

The process of softening leather and developing the grain by rubbing the surfaces together.

BOARDING II

The operation of shaping and drying hosiery on heated, metal, leg-shaped forms known as hosiery boarding forms or boards.

BOAT

A supporting structure used to hold semiconductor wafers during and between processing.

BOOK

Pieces of uncured gum rubber or rubber-coated fabric placed between cloth pages or canvas sheets to prevent cohesion.

BOX BLANK

The sides, ends, and bottom of a wire-bound box in process of manufacture.

BULKING CELL

A rectangular enclosure with an open top and hinged door used to compress tobacco into a bulk.

BURLING IRON

A handtool similar to an ice pick with a slit in the pick end used to push yarn through fabric.

BURN PATTERN

The path that a fire takes from point of origin to the outermost limit of the fire.

BUS BAR

Metal conductor forming a common junction between two or more electrical circuits.

BUSHING

Heat resistant metal device with 200-400 holes through which molten glass is extruded to manufacture fiberglass sliver.

BUTTON

A steel cylinder used on knitting machine to keep links of pattern chain from engaging and turning gears that activate shafts of machine.

CAKE

Synthetic thread piled into ring shape.

CALIPER CHISEL

A chisel attached to one leg of caliper used to turn wood to specified diameter on wood lathe.

CAPTIONS

On-screen text of a television show's or a movie's dialogue shown simultaneously with the sound of the dialogue. This is usually done to provide information for the hearing-impaired, or to provide a translation from a foreign language. Captions are sometimes called subtitles, especially when providing a translation from a foreign language.

CARD CLOTHING FILLET

A long, narrow strip of foundation material studded with many fine, closely spaced, wire teeth.

CARROTING

The brushing of furs with solution of hydrogen peroxide and nitric acid. This treatment opens sheaths surrounding each fur fiber and permits matting (felting) of fibers in subsequent operations.

CASING FLUID

A flavoring solution applied to tobacco to give it distinctive taste. Usually made according to carefully guarded plant formulas from ingredients, such as tonka beans, rum, licorice, and sugar.

CAUSTICIZER

Tanks used to convert spent liquor and lime hydrate into hydroxide.

CHARGER

A cylinder, open at both ends, which is inserted in top of hogshead container to extend height of hogshead container for packing purposes.

CHARGING MANIFOLD

A hollow pipe fixture containing holes which receive and hold capillary tubes of thermostat bellows while they are being filled with gas.

CHILL-PROOF

To stabilize or eliminate protein compounds in beer to prolong shelf life.

CHOKER

A noose of wire rope hitched about a log by means of which logs are skidded overground.

CLAMP MACHINE

A stationary hand-powered or air-driven vise used to force together and hold joints of wooden assemblies in position while being reinforced by nails, screws, staples, and glue. Also known as case clamp, chair clamp, or bed clamp, depending on design or purpose.

CLARIFIERS

A machine having submerged, rotating arms with plow blades which scrape settled silt from bottom of settling basin spirally toward center of machine where silt is collected in trough and sluiced through pipes back to river. The clarifier does not clarify in the usual sense; silt is settled by gravity.

CLEARER ROLLER

A small cloth- or felt-covered roller driven by frictional contact with rollers to keep rollers clean and collect roving waste when end breaks.

CLINCHING TOOL

A device used to secure upholstery padding material to furniture frames. Wire staples held in tension in shaft of tool are released when trigger is pressed and secure padding material to frames.

COILER HEAD

An attachment on textile machines that coils sliver after it has been processed.

COIL FORM

Paper or plastic tube onto which wire coils are wound. Forms vary in length according to number of coils wound on each form. Multiple wound coil forms are cut on bandsaw into individual coils for assembly into electronic equipment.

COLOR BOX

Metal trough under each PRINTING ROLLER that contains a reservoir of printing paste. A rubber or nylon bristle-covered roller dips color paste from the COLOR BOX and forces the paste into the engravings of the PRINTING ROLLER.

COMB

Precut undipped pasteboard resembling a hair comb, used for book matches.

CONES

A set of small triangular pyramids of clay mixtures and fluxes so graded that they represent series of fusion points. The degree of heat is measured in kiln by observing which of various cones have bent over.

CONTACT PROCESS

Catalytic method of producing sulfuric acid by treatment of sulfur dioxide with catalytic agents and reaction of resulting product with water in absorbing towers.

CORE CUTTER

A modified pneumatic pavement breaker (jack-hammer) adapted to break into wall of cement building.

CORE STOCK

Cheap veneer sheets placed between glued CROSSBANDS to form the interior of plywood panel between the FACE SHEETS and BACK SHEETS.

COUNTERBORING

A machining process in which an enlarged, flat-bottomed cylindrical hole is made at opening of existing hole usually so that bolt head or nut can be seated flush with or below surface.

COVERSTITCH SEWING MACHINE

A machine that sews parallel rows of stitches with a covering thread spread between the rows on one or both surfaces. Used for coverstitching on knit fabrics.

CRACKS

The outer grooves cut in buhr stones.

CRIMPING ATTACHMENT

Two feed rolls and a stuffer box into which yarn is overfed, then folded or bent at a sharp angle and then heat-set during compression by attached heating element.

CROSSBANDS

Cheap veneer sheets glued between CORE STOCK and surface veneer to form plywood, with the grain of the CROSSBANDS running across the grain of the CORE STOCK and surface veneer to bind and hold the veneer sheets from expansion and warping.

CRYSTAL ORIENTATION

The structural arrangement of atoms or molecules inside a semiconductor crystal or wafer.

CUP

Similar to SPREADER PAN in which it sets. Spreads molten lead around spreader pan through holes in side. Receives lead as it comes from spout.

CURING OVEN

A loop or roller-type drier through which resin treated fabrics are run in open width at high temperature to convert soluble resin into insoluble compound.

CUTLINES

Outlines of shapes of glass to be followed for cutting and leading stained-glass windows.

DEBEAKING

Removing the tip on a bird's upper beak to prevent infliction of injuries to other birds.

DECANTER

A rectangular, steel tank in which tar and ammonia are separated by settling according to their differences in specific gravity.

DEVULCANIZER

A machine used in treating ground scrap rubber with chemicals and steam to restore it as nearly possible to its original physical and chemical state for use as RECLAIM rubber.

DIAL

A flat circular plate that rotates and presents parts to machine at prescribed intervals. The worker places parts on designated spots on dial.

DIE

An individual integrated circuit also known as a chip. The term is usually used after the wafer has been scribed and sorted, although it is not limited to that use.

DOBBER

A device with serrated edge which separates strands of yarn and keeps them parallel.

DOBBY LOOM

A loom usually used for weaving goods of a nonfloral pattern in which the interlacings are complicated.

DRAWING-IN DRAFT

In weaving, a plan prepared on design paper showing how warp threads are to be drawn through the heddle to produce desired pattern. A DRAWING-IN DRAFT is prepared for all fancy patterns.

DRAWING-IN FRAME

A rack on which harnesses are hung while warp ends are being drawn through heddle eyes.

DRIFT PIN

A tapered steel pin for aligning rivet holes before inserting the rivet.

DRIP

A tank located below level of gas mains, and connected to main by pipes, for the purpose of collecting condensed water, gas, and tars which must be drained from the main continually to prevent congestion and eventual rupture of the pipe. Capacities of the tanks vary from a few gallons to as much as 500 gallons.

DROP WIRE

In textile machines, thin metal strip with an eye through which single strands of yarn are passed. If the yarn breaks, the wire drops to cut the electric circuit, thus stopping the machine.

DRYING CANS

A machine used in textile mills to dry fabric. Several large heated drums, wide enough to accommodate one or two widths of cloth, are arranged in tiers. Cloth threaded through drums contact a large area of each and are rapidly dried.

DUMPING PIVOT

A simple steel basket open at top and one side to accommodate ice freezing containers. The lower corner opposite open side is hinged to facilitate tipping and removal of ice block.

DWELL METER

An electrical meter used to measure dwell or time interval between closing cycle of distributor points of automobile ignition system. Incorrect spacing of points results in improper dwell.

EDGE ROLL

Rope-like roll of jute core covered with burlap used to build up edges of upholstered furniture before adding padding.

ELECTRICAL-DISCHARGE MACHINING

Removal of metal through action of high-energy electric sparks on surface of workpiece.

END EFFECTOR

Device attached to wrist of industrial robot arm that enables robot to perform tasks.

ESCAPE WHEEL

Wheel of escapement in clock or watch that supplies power from mainspring. It is allowed to 'escape' from pallet at rate governed by balance wheel and thereby controls motion of train.

FACE SHEET

A veneer sheet, of high quality and free from imperfections, used for the top surface sheet of plywood panels.

FACING

A machining operation that is a form of turning in which the tool is fed at right angles to axis of workpiece rotation to produce flat surface.

FAILURE MODE AND EFFECT ANALYSIS

Detailed listing of potential failures of critical parts and effects on total system operation.

FALLER

A narrow metal bar set with one or more rows of sharp, pointed pins that comb through silver to blend and align fibers.

FALLER WIRE

A device on a mule-spinning frame to keep yarn under tension during winding and to guide it onto bobbins.

FALSE SELVAGE

An extra layer of selvage woven on each edge of some looped pile fabrics. This selvage is formed by floats inserted to hold loop pile during weaving. Both FALSE SELVAGE and floats are removed after cloth is doffed from loom.

FALSE-TWIST SPINDLE

A hollow spindle with small wheel mounted in its aperture used in manufacture of stretch yarn. Yarn processed through this spindle is commonly referred to as false-twisted yarn.

FEED CUPS

A feeding mechanism on a sewing machine on which the needle operates horizontally. Two wheels or discs rotate in a horizontal plane to pull the material between them.

FEEDER TUBE

A clay tube clamped in orifice of forehearth to capture and hold gob of molten glass for delivery to bottlemaking machines.

FELLED SEAM

A stress-resistant seam formed by joining overlapped, interfolded garment-part edges with two or three parallel rows of stitching.

FELLING STITCH

A sewing stitch that does not completely penetrate the material in which it is made. Such stitching is used to fasten lining into garments so that the stitches do not show on the outside.

FESTOONS

Two banks of evenly spaced rollers in FOUR-ROLL CALENDER used for accumulating fabric to maintain continuous operations while making roll changes and for taking up slack in fabric prior to calendering.

FILLING PILE FABRIC

Fabric in which an extra set of filling yarns forms pile. Examples are corduroy and velveteen.

FILM FLAT

Group of film negatives or positives mounted on transparent plastic film, colored paper or vinyl which comprise page elements (text and illustrations) of magazine, book, or other printed material, used in preparation of lithographic printing plates.

FILTRACELL

A siliceous material that absorbs impurities and clarifies oil pressed from corn germs.

FINGER BUFF

Strips of buffing cloth used in manufacture of buffing wheels. These strips are attached to core of buffing wheel with LACING and form fingerlike projections.

FIRST-ARTICLE-CONFIGURATION INSPECTION

Detailed physical inspection by customer and company of first part or assembly of given series for conformance with authorization change and engineering drawing.

FLAGGING

Dried strips of a marsh weed, such as cattail.

FLASH

The ridge or line of excess material left on metal or plastic objects along the parting or closing line of mold. Also known as fin.

FLAT

A flat edge ground along a semiconductor crystal to denote crystal orientation and resistivity and which serves as a reference line during processing.

FLATLOCK SEWING MACHINE

A feed-off-the-arm coverstitch machine that sews a flat, nonraveling seam by joining abutted edges with a top-and-bottom covering stitch.

FLOWER NAIL

A long nail with large head that is used as base to create intricate designs with icings.

FOLDING BONE

A thin strip of fish bone used to fold and press leather edges under.

FOLLOW BOARD

See MOLDING BOARD.

FORM BOARD

A specified number of form strips fastened together side by side with long bolts.

FORMING CHUCK

A metal block shaped to contour and attached to machine spindle which serves dual purpose of holding and rotating cylindrical workpieces and as forming die to shape workpiece to contour.

FORM TOOL

A cutting tool ground to specific contour in order to machine the inverse contour in workpiece.

FOTO MAT

Linotype metal matrices with small film of letter in center.

FOUR-ROLL CALENDER

A machine which coats both sides of fabric stock with rubber simultaneously and rolls sheets to specifications. Also known as Z-calender.

FRAZING MACHINE

A machine which guides briar block against cutters to duplicate preselected pipe shape. A clamp-fitted shaft and a cam follows a master model to shape shank and lower half of bowl.

FREENESS

The quality of pulp stock that determines rate at which it parts with water when being formed into sheet on wire screen or perforated plate. The same quality is known as freeness, slowness, or wetness according to type of instrument used to estimate it.

FRENCH BINDING

A narrow strip of fabric that is stitched to edge of shoe uppers and folded over to form smooth finished edge.

FROTHING MACHINE

A mixing machine with electrically operated agitating paddles used for mixing air with latex to obtain desired density.

FULLING MILL

A machine that shrinks and felts fibers of woolen cloth through application of moisture, heat, friction, and pressure. May be used to crush and dust carbonized vegetable matter from dry woolen cloth.

FUNNEL APPROACH

A counseling technique, using open-ended questions in the early stages of counseling, to collect information, orient the individual, married couple, or family, and to establish communication. As problems become identified, questions are less open-ended and more specific to address or clarify aspects of one or more problems.

FUR MACHINE

A disk-feed sewing machine used for seaming heavy materials to make items, such as fur and fake fur garments, plush toys, and leather slippers. Layers of material are guided vertically between the two disks (cups or wheels) and sewn with a horizontal needle.

GAMB STICK

A metal or wooden rod with pointed or hooked ends which are inserted through the tendons on the hind legs of animal carcass to hold the legs apart while animal is dressed. The stick has a rind in the center for attaching to a trolley or an overhead rail.

GANG KNIFE

A set of knives, arranged to be raised and lowered by hand, used to slice fish into several pieces of predetermined length.

GARNETT MACHINE

A machine similar to a carding machine, used to open hard-twisted yarn wastes, rags, and clippings. Cylinders are covered with coarse wire teeth.

GAS CHECK

A metal cup, coated with oil or wax, that expands to form a gastight, moving seal under piston of device used to measure pressure produced within gun barrel by exploding cartridge.

GEAR CAGES

A cluster of gears, bearings, and locking devices usually attached to a shaft.

GEAR GENERATING

A gear-machining operation in which the cutter teeth have (or simulate) the shape of mating gear teeth rather than of the space between the teeth, and the cutting is done as the cutter and gear blank rotate together.

GEL-COAT

Pigmented, high purity polyester coating, catalyzed with liquid oxidizers used to form layer on boat mold prior to application of fiberglass resin layers.

GIRDLING STICK

A tool with one end threaded to hold drop, wooden middle section for hand-hold, and metal rod on the other end which is held between body and arm to support and control diamond during girdling.

GORE

An elastic insert in side, front, or panels of a shoe used to decorate or reinforce, or to allow stretching that will provide additional comfort and freedom of movement to wearer.

GROUND RACKING BOARD

Wooden boards of various lengths and widths that are placed flat on an oil well floor to form a base for tubing and pipe sections to stand on when sections are standing up-right in the derrick. Boards are used for the base to prevent sections from sinking into the ground and getting plugged with soil or mud or to prevent damage to the threaded ends of pipe and casing.

HANGER

Part of bicycle frame that holds fork assembly.

HARNESS FRAME

Two wooden laths upon which are suspended series of cords or wires called heddles.

HEAD

Part of bicycle frame that holds crank and sprocket assembly.

HEADER

A fabricated chamber to which series of tubes are joined to permit free circulation of fluid within water tube boiler.

HELICAL SPRINGS

Spiral springs used to hold rows of coil springs together in bedsprings.

HIGH LEAD

A cable-log yarding system consisting of a steel or wooden spar near the yarding machine and a circuit of cable running from the top of the spar to a block at the rear of the cutting area, which enables logs to be lifted over obstructions in rough, mountainous terrain where logging tractors cannot be used efficiently.

HOBBING

A gear-machining operation in which teeth are generated by rotating HOB and gear blank against each other with action similar to that of worm gear. See GEAR GENERATING.

HOG MILL

A power-driven machine for cutting scrap wood into fine particles suitable for blowing as fuel into fireboxes or boilers with compressed-air jet.

HOMOGENIZED LEAF

A tobacco wrapper material made from powdered tobacco and other substances that cause ingredients to stick together.

HOOKER MACHINE

A machine that folds cloth by means of blade that guides fabric back and forth across surface of table.

HORN

A device mounted on a unit similar to a sewing machine called an ULTRASONIC SEAMING MACHINE. HORN emits high-frequency sound waves that fuse thermoplastic materials.

HYDRO-SPRAYER

A tank with horizontal-in-tank agitator, motor, pumps, and piping system, mounted on truck bed, used to cover areas, such as highway median strips, hillsides, and fields with a mixture of grass seed, fertilizer, and mulch.

IMPULSE PIN

The pin mounted on the balance wheel of a clock or watch that receives impulse from pallet fork.

IN-BEAT

Characteristic of timepiece movement resulting from jewel pin being in line of center on ESCAPE WHEEL, pallet, and balance wheel when hairspring is unstressed. In this condition the strokes of the escape wheel teeth against pallet stones will occur at equal intervals. A timepiece is out of beat when strokes or ticks occur at unequal intervals.

INDEXING

Moving workpiece or toolholding device, such as a turret, to a series of regularly spaced positions to repeat an operation or to perform a series of operations at predetermined intervals.

INPOINT

The point at which editing/copying of a portion of audio, music, video, or graphics onto a videotape begins.

INVOLUTE CHECKER

A device for inspecting involute curves on teeth of gears, splines, etc.

JACQUARD LOOM

Loom equipped with device for weaving figured fabrics. The Jacquard attachment consists of mechanism controlled by perforated cards which cause warp threads to be lifted in proper succession for producing figure.

JIGGER

Small pointed metal instrument, resembling sharpened pencil, used in assembling ribs of expansion metal watch bands.

JUMPBASTING SEWING MACHINE

A basting machine that allows free movement of fabric over the work bed to produce a stitch of variable length and direction. There is no feed mechanism or presser foot. A plunger-like device (needle stripper) encloses the needle and holds the fabric down only long enough for the needle to penetrate and withdraw. Used for basting with a long, loose stitch over large areas to hold plies of fabric together, as in preliminary positioning of coat layers.

JUMP IRON

A heavy iron, supported by movable arm, designed to eject steam through holes in bottom. A pedal is depressed to lower iron and to apply pressure to article being pressed. The iron is pushed back and forth manually.

KAPLAN

A control for water turbines which varies pitch of blades in accordance with load, resulting in high efficiency over large-load range.

LACING

A circular metal strip with serrated edges used in manufacture of buffing wheels to secure buffing material to center of wheel. The serrated edges are bent outward to form groove in which material is inserted.

LAP I

A tool, usually of softer material than workpiece and of complementary shape, which is charged with LAPPING COMPOUND. See LAPPING.

LAP II

A roll of loosely matted cotton fiber.

LAP III

A horizontal wheel or disk made of cast iron, used to fine-grind flat surfaces on diamonds or other stones.

LAPPING

Smoothing, finishing, or achieving an extremely close tolerance (e.g., 0.000002 inch in gauge block manufacture) on metal surface by means of a LAP I that is charged with LAPPING COMPOUND and rubbed against workpiece in rotary and/or reciprocating motion, either by hand or machine.

Matching workpieces may be lapped against each other to assure a close fit. Sometimes used loosely to denote fine grinding or honing.

LAPPING COMPOUND

A fine abrasive material, usually mixed with oil, water, or some other vehicle in the form of paste, which becomes imbedded or "charged" in the LAP. See LAPPING.

LAP-UPS

A term used in textile industry denoting material (lap, thread, fibers, etc.) which becomes entangled in or wound about machinery.

LASTING

The operation of tacking a shoe upper and insole to a last or of turning down and sticking together the upper and sole of rubber footwear by hand or machine.

LASTING TOOL

A combination handtool usually composed of hammerhead, pincers, and tack puller used in construction of shoes. Also known as lasting pincers or shoemaker's pliers.

LAYBOY

An automatic mechanism that receives, stacks, and jogs sheets of paper into piles. It may be attached to machines, such as cutters, printing presses, or ruling machines. Generally equipped with counting and tabbing devices.

LAYOUT MACHINE

Modified vernier height gauge, having a scriber on the end of an extending arm, which when positioned next to workpiece, scribes exact locations of reference points and lines.

LEACH TANK

A tank containing hot water into which uncured balloons are dipped to remove bitter taste of coagulant.

LEAD WIRES

Soft metal wires used to take impressions between two adjoining parts to determine clearances measured by micrometers.

LEASE STRING

Strings inserted between the threads of a warp to hold the threads in the same relative position for drawing-in or tying to old warp.

LETOFF RACK

A rack that operates with braking action permitting machine to pull material from a roll.

LIGHT TABLE

A table or bench having translucent top over a light source. It is used in examining objects where it is desired that no shadow will be cast.

LITE

Flat glass cut to specified size from continuous sheet of glass.

LOADING BOX

A receptacle, usually part of, or rigidly attached to, a lever into which molten metal or equivalent may be poured to aid in balancing scale under a zero load.

LOOM BEAM

A large wood or metal cylinder on which are wound the warp threads for a loom.

LOOPING LINE

A line of stitches knitted into both sides of the open toe of seamless hose as a guide along which the looper must set the stitches to produce a straight looped toe.

LOOPING MACHINE

A machine that knits two parts of knitted garment or stocking together.

LUMBER SCALE

A ruler equipped with a calibrated scale used to measure the width of rough-sawed lumber of known thickness and length and to convert the measurement into board feet.

LUMITE

A liquid which hardens when dry to give rigidity to back of shoe.

LUMPIA

A bakery product wrapped around a filling to form lumpias (ethnic dish from the Philippines).

MASK MIRROR

A glass plate, with silvered images of facial features imprinted, used to block out portions of a photograph in preparing a montage.

MASTER STRAIGHTEDGE

A straight slender bar made of rigid material, which is placed across wide points of contact to hold the level on a structure to be leveled.

MATHEMATICAL MODEL

The general characterization of a process, object, or concept, in terms of mathematics, which enables the relatively simple manipulation of variables to be accomplished in order to determine how the process, object, or concept would behave in different situations.

MEASURING WIRES

Accurately made short wires of standard diameters, for use in precision measuring of gear or thread dimensions.

MECHANICAL PRINT

An engineering drawing that is the actual pictorial presentation of a product, part, or machine, showing dimensions, type of material, wiring, and other details.

MEGGER

An instrument used to measure insulation resistance or electrical resistance of electrical equipment, such as powerline poles.

MILL

A small, soft-steel cylinder upon surface of which a design in relief is made by rolling in contact with die.

MINERAL WOOL BLANKET

A continuous ribbon of mineral wool fibers, 2 to 4 inches thick and up to 10 feet wide, that is cut into insulation batts and felts.

MOLDING BOARD

A board on which the patterns and drag are placed when making the drag part of a mold. Also known as FOLLOW BOARD.

MOLD-PRINTING BOARD

The board on which molds are fixed in rows and which, when placed upside down over a tray of leveled starch leaves indentations into which fluid candy is introduced.

MONOTUBE

A hollow stainless-steel tube, into which enriched uranium fuel elements are loaded.

MORTAR GUIDE

A metal band that fits the edge of a stone and has a projecting side the thickness of a joint.

MOSS

A form cadmium metal takes when the molten metal drops into cold water. This bubblelike form of solidified metal enhances dissolution.

MOTHER

Nickel positive electroplate made by electrodeposition on master electroplate. Required in making stamper, which presses positive of recording into phonograph records.

MULLING

The process of heating tobacco to ferment and sweat out bitter gums, ammonia compounds, and impurities which impair flavor and color of tobacco leaves.

NARROWING

The process of contracting size of knit articles, especially a stocking, by taking two stitches in one.

NECK RING

A cast iron ring which is used in conjunction with mold to form neck of bottle.

NECKTIE-CENTRALIZING SEWING MACHINE

A machine that sews the lengthwise seam on a necktie. Two types of machines are in use: One is equipped with a hook in front of the needle and another under the bed of the machine to assist in forming an unusually stretchable single-thread stitch. The other is equipped with a feed track resembling a tractor tread in appearance, that pulls fabric edges up and down over a stationary, 55-inch, horizontal needle to simulate handstitching.

NEEDLE JACKS

Small metal pieces, fitted into grooves in needlebed of knitting machine, that transmit reciprocating motion to needles.

OPTICAL SCANNER

A device that automatically samples or verifies a number of measuring points and indicates those that have drifted from their desired values.

ORDERING MACHINE

A machine in which tobacco is brought to desired moisture content by application of water or steam spray in cylindrical device or compartment through which conveyor belt passes.

OUTFLOW QUENCH STICK

A device on spinning machine that quenches (cools) formed synthetic filaments upon ejection from spinnerette.

OUTPOINT

The point at which editing/copying of a portion of audio, music, video, or graphics onto a videotape stops.

OVERCOIL HAIRSPRING; OVERCOILING

Hairspring of a watch with its outer coil raised above plane of spring and then bent so as to terminate in a curve that is concentric with remaining coils. Purpose is to provide for concentric winding and unwinding of spring thereby eliminating side thrust against bearings. Overcoiling is the act of bending outer coil.

OVERLOCK SEWING MACHINE

A machine that sews an overedge stitch, looping over fabric edges to prevent edge fraying or to seam two or more plies.

PACK

An assembly containing a spinnerette, filter screen, gaskets, and sand through which polymer is passed to filter out impurities and form filaments by forcing polymer through spinnerette.

PACKAGE DYEING MACHINE

A dyeing machine resembling large pressure cooker. The yarn to be dyed is wound on perforated beams or tubes so that dye solution can be circulated through package.

PANTOGRAPH MECHANISM

An attachment used with conventional metal cutting machines, which allows for two (or three) dimensional duplication of a template. The exact or scalar movements of the tracer spindle over the template is transmitted to the cutter spindle which cuts the template pattern from a blank.

PAPER TAPE

A strip of paper capable of storing or recording information. Storage may be in the form of punched holes, partially punched holes, carbonization or chemical change of impregnated material, or by imprinting. Some PAPER TAPES, such as punched PAPER TAPES, are capable of being read by the input device of a computer or a transmitting device by sensing the pattern of holes which represent coded information.

PENCIL EDGE

The round or convex surface edge of glass or mirror after edges have been ground. To apply such edge by grinding.

PICAROON

A short-handled device with a pointed metal end used to move and align logs and lumber inside a sawmill or in confined areas.

PICK

One thread of filling either before weaving or in cloth. Number of picks per inch of warp is measure of fineness of fabric.

PICOT BAR

A bar on knitting machine that holds slender metal rods (picot points) used to knit a row of large, wide stitches (picot stripe) after welt is knitted.

PIECE UP

The joining or union of two or more ends of sliver, slubbing, roving, or yarn by twisting or intermingling fiber ends with fingers.

PILE WIRES

Strips of metal that are inserted into shed of looms to form pile fabrics, such as carpeting.

PILLAR PLATE

Base plate which determines size and shape of clock or watch movement. It is recessed and drilled to form foundation for assembly of various parts and pivots which comprise movement.

PINCH CLEAT

A metal cleat that fits around ends of steel bailing straps. When pinched by strapping tool cleat secures ends and keeps strap taut on bale.

PIN JACK

A cast iron pedestal, usually fastened to shoemaker's bench, on which shoe last is placed during processing operations.

PITCHED WORT

Wort (unfermented beer) with added yeast to promote fermentation.

PITCH FINGER

A metal rod mounted over journal of mill that is used to pitch design on mill in register with other portions of design during engraving process.

PIVOT

That element of conventional scale lever designed to transmit external forces through its knife edge.

PLANER GAUGE

A work aid consisting of two right-triangle ground metal blocks fastened together to enable user to adjust their outer parallel surfaces to any dimension within a given range by sliding one block on the other.

PLANETARY ACTION

A double mechanical motion in which a tool is rotated on a center, while that center is revolved in another circle at the same time.

PLATE PRESS

A filter press that removes water from gluten.

PLUG

Rubber block marked to indicate hat size.

POACHING

Process of removing acid and impurities from nitrocotton prior to processing into explosives.

POISE; POISING

Equal distribution of mass of timepiece balance wheel around axis of rotation that neutralizes effect of gravity. POISING is accomplished by removing or adding weight to balance wheel to create equal distribution of mass around axis.

POLYSOMNOGRAPH

Equipment that measures and records physiologic patterns of sleep.

POWER PRESS

A machine, used in conjunction with dies, for forming, molding, cutting, and shaping of materials under great pressure.

PREFORM RUBBER

Uncured rubber that is precut to provide specific amount of rubber necessary to fill each mold cavity.

PREROLL

The time (usually in seconds) it takes a videotape to get up to speed, i.e., the lapse time between pressing the play button and when the picture appears on the monitor for the viewing audience to see.

PRIMACORD

A flexible woven cord with an explosive core which detonates at an extremely fast velocity of over 20,000 feet per second.

PRINTING ROLLER

See PRINTING SHELL.

PRINTING SHELL

A large, engraved copper roller used to print designs in color on cloth when mounted in printing machine.

PROGRAMMABLE CONTROLLER

A device which, after being programmed by means of its keyboard and display screen, starts, stops, and coordinates one or more pieces of automated machinery.

PROGRESSIVE DIE

An integrated stamping die made up of several die units or stations through which workpiece is indexed one station at a time for a series of operations. Usually, a continuous strip of sheet metal is fed into press and completely formed workpiece is ejected from other end with each action of press.

PROJECTION (SHADOW) COMPARATOR MACHINE

Floor-mounted machine that employs intense light to project shadow of machined workpiece onto master drawing which is laid on a lighted table screen. The shadow is aligned with the master drawing to determine conformance of workpiece to specifications.

PRONGS

Scissors-like tool with three tines, one on one handle and two on other, used for gripping and twisting.

PROVER

A device for passing measured amount of gas or compressed air under constant pressure through gas meters to test accuracy of meters.

PULL-TEST MACHINE

A testing device in which pounds of pull, necessary to pull bullet out of cartridge case, are measured.

PULSATION RECORDER

An instrument equipped with a revolving drum and a pressure-sensitive pen which marks the duration and intensity of vacuum-cycle wave forms when its probe is inserted into a vacuum line. It is used to test the operation of automatic milking systems.

PUTTING-IN-BEAT

See IN-BEAT.

RACK

The standard unit of measure for lace. It is the amount of lace woven by 1,920 single motions of loom.

RADIAL DRILL PRESS

A machine tool used primarily for metal drilling, which consists of central column and horizontal radial arm to which a vertical drilling spindle is attached.

RANGE

An arrangement of machines used to perform a number of yarn- or cloth-processing operations continuously by feeding material to each unit in succession automatically and without interruption.

RAPPING

The process of removing ore dust that has accumulated on wires in the stack treater to recover the ore.

RECLAIM

Rubber material recovered from scrap rubber goods by chemical treatment.

REED HOOK

A flat metal tool, similar to crochet hook, used for drawing individual strands of yarn through reed of loom.

REEDING

Nylon monofilament or copper wire used to reinforce and shape sweatbands and brims on hats and caps.

REEF NET

A bag-like net anchored to boats or the shore to simulate a V-shaped reef in a channel.

REFLECTANCE METER

A small, bench-mounted device used to compare the whiteness of bleached paper pulp to a standard white color.

REGAUGING

Process of verifying alcoholic content of recently distilled liquor to determine quantity of diluent necessary to be added to liquor to obtain specified alcoholic content.

REGISTER WHEEL

A large indexed wheel on pantograph or engraving machine. A gross setting on larger register wheel results in precise placement of design on smaller printing roller.

RELIEVING

A machining process in which a FORM TOOL is used to cut teeth for cutting tools to specified contour.

REMELT

Pieces of crystal ingot not meeting specifications used as material to grow new ingot.

RETICLE

A photo plate on which an enlarged copy of a semiconductor circuit layer pattern is reproduced and used in the production of photomasks.

ROBOT CONTROLLER

A computerized device that provides the signals that direct the motions of the robot, so that it is both positioned and oriented correctly in space over time.

ROD TRANSFER DEVICE

A metal box-shaped device approximately eight inches tall, three inches wide, and three inches deep that is open on one side with a rectangular slot on the end. There is a swivel eye on the other end of the device where a rod hoist cable is attached. The rectangular opening at the lower end of the device is fitted on the square neck of rod to support rod sections as they are being transferred to and from holding slots and lifting clamp.

ROLLING TABLE

A heated press, the upper platen of which lowers and pivots on a shaft, to compress and roll resin impregnated fabrics onto mandrel.

ROLL PICKER

A pneumatic tool which removes lint and trash from spinning and roving frames by winding it on rapidly rotating spindle.

ROPE FORM

The form in which cloth is gathered or bunched into longitudinal folds by being drawn through a ring or series of rings. Some processing is more easily accomplished with cloth in this form.

ROTARY LATHE

A machine for cutting thin sheets of veneer from logs. The log is supported and rotated on horizontal axis as heavy steel knife is fed against its surface to slice thin sheet of wood from circumference.

ROUNDING JACK

A handtool for trimming hat brims. One end of tool is fitted with sharp blade and the other end is shaped to rest on crown of hat. The tool is drawn around hat brim, using crown as guide, to cut off excess material.

SCRATCHING TOOL

A four-pronged, long-handled tool similar to a pitch fork and used to pull up loops and uncut ends of rug pile.

SCREEN TINTS

Film used to produce shade of color or black.

SEAM

A finished edge on flat glass or mirrors on which the sharp corners are removed by an abrasive belt to form a semi-rounded edge.

SEARCHER

A notched metal strip, tooled to 0.0005 inch thickness, used to remove small particles of threads from brass bobbins.

SET POINT

A point in space, expressed in three dimensional coordinates, at which tip of cutting tool of automatic machine is set before the start of machining operations.

SHADOW LINES

Lines on power ripsaw machine table cast by wire hung between light source and table. Used as guides by saw operators in aligning boards before sawing.

SHERIFF'S SALE

A public sale of properties lawfully seized by the county as directed by a civil court order; money received reverts to county treasury.

SHOOT WIRE

Wires running short way of cloth or screen as woven.

SHORT-CYCLE SEWING MACHINE

A semi-automatic machine that sews a limited number of stitches to tack layers of fabric, attach buttons, or make buttonholes.

SHOT PAN

A pan, resembling frying pan, with equidistantly spaced holes in bottom through which molten lead is dropped to form shot pellets. Pans are numbered according to size of holes.

SHUTTLE BINDER

A wood or iron lever located at front or back of, and projecting slightly into, the shuttle box. Its purpose is to check force of shuttle as it enters the box.

SIEVE CLOTH

The fabric belts on printing machine which absorb color solutions from color trays and convey it to rollers that print designs on wallpaper.

SIGHTING RIB

Raised metal rib along entire outside length of shotgun barrel which is matted (knurled) to provide a glare-proof sighting surface.

SINKER

An elevator platform that submerges felt hat cones in tub of hot water to strengthen cohesion of fur fibers.

SKIRTLIKE UPPER

The sewn-together vamp, quarters, and counter of nonrubber upper of an article of footwear before rubber, composition, or cork sole is put on. The bottom edges of upper are cemented all around, like the hem of a skirt, for bonding with sole.

SLUBBER

The first fly frame for drawing and twisting slivers to form roving.

SPACE GAUGE

A rectangular metal piece with parallel rows of fine grooves extending across its face, used as a guide for spacing needles in the needle bar of a knitting machine.

SPINNING BOX

A device used in rayon manufacturing for piling thread into ring-shaped CAKES. The thread is drawn into spinning box through glass funnel and wound by centrifugal force.

SPOIL PILES

Earth and rock removed from coal, ore, or rock deposit in strip mine, open pit, or quarry.

SPONGE

A powder form of cadmium with a high zinc content.

SPOT-FACING

A machining process in which the area around a hole is milled to smooth, flat surface by application of a rotating tool with cutting edges on its end or face.

SPREADER PAN

A pan, resembling a frying pan, with holes around the side which sets on legs in the SHOT PAN and spreads lead evenly around shot pan.

SPRUNG OIL

Oil that has been allowed to separate from water and rise to the surface by means of gravity.

SPUR CHUCK

A stubby, pronged fork attached to driving spindle of lathe to assist in mounting and centering workpieces.

SPUTTERING

Bombarding metal surface with positive ions to form fine-grained coating on surface.

SQUEEGEE

A strip of uncured rubber, approximately tread-width, which is applied to BAND stock to reduce friction and promote adhesion between plies of completed tire.

STABILITY GAUGE

An instrument equipped with needle gauge used to indicate variation in or inadequacy of vacuum in automatic milking systems.

STANDARD SIZE SYSTEM

A system decreed by Edward II in 1324 that established a variation of one-sixth of an inch in length between half sizes and one-third of an inch in length between whole sizes of shoes.

STEAM LANCE

A long pipe attached to a steam source, through which steam under pressure is blown into boiler tubes to remove soot and sludge.

STENO-MASK

An enclosed microphone, used to record speech on tape, which renders the spoken word inaudible to other persons in the room.

STIPPLING TOOL

A small block of metal, the under surface of which is covered with small projections. It is used to make multiple indentations in wood by striking top of tool with hammer or mallet.

STIRRUP

A shackle which transmits to a connection load from only one lever.

STITCH-BONDING

A process whereby barbed needles are used to bond or entangle web fibers to produce a nonwoven fabric.

STITCHING WHEEL

A wheel mounted in the bed of an ULTRASONIC SEAMING MACHINE. STITCHING WHEEL has raised pattern that simulates sewing machine stitches. Wheels are changed to produce various decorative effects.

STRAPPING TOOL

A hand-operated device that pulls taut strip-steel straps wrapped around a bale and secures ends by pinching a cleat placed around overlapping ends of strap.

SURVEYOR

A precision instrument used to make a pencil mark around a tooth indicating its greatest circumference in any one position relative to the vertical.

SWING-FOLDING ATTACHMENT

A device, usually attached to the rear of a processing machine, to fold cloth coming from the machine. It consists of a pair of thin parallel rollers mounted between two arms that swing like a pendulum, laying cloth in loose folds.

SWING WEIGHT

The swing weight of a golf club is a measure of the leverage of the club, from beyond a fixed point, applied against the end of the handle. It is the weight felt by the golfer when he swings the club.

TAKEUP ROLL

A roller, operating continuously or intermittently, that winds long lengths of material after it has passed through a machine.

TARGET BLOCK

A tungsten block, having the same thickness as a workpiece to be welded by electron-beam system, used to substitute for workpiece during system setup.

TEACH PENDANT

A hand-held control box connected to the robot by an electrical cable used to actuate, for programming and re-programming purposes, the motions of the robot performing its prescribed task.

TELESCOPING GAUGE

A precision measuring instrument the end of which can be positioned inside hole or opening and expanded to touch walls; interior dimension can then either be read on calibrations of gauge or measured with micrometer.

TELETICKETER

An electrical device that transmits and prints transportation-routing information on passenger tickets.

TEMPERATURE POTENTIOMETER

A device to take temperature readings at any given point via transmission through thermocouples to reading device. It is equipped with a dial to select the thermocouple (point) from which to take a reading.

TENSION GUIDE

A device used as a guide to provide specified tension during winding, coning, sizing, and warping. This device contains fingers, disks, or washers that apply tension.

TENTER FRAME

A machine that dries and stretches cloth to its original width and straightens its weave after a finishing process.

THATCHER

A machine (similar to a rotary-type lawn mower with wire claws, rather than blades, on the rotating bar) used to claw and lift thatch from lawn.

THRUST END ASSEMBLY

The forward end of a turbine at which steam enters.

TIDAL PEN

Large rectangular ponds constructed on an island located in a natural shrimp growing area with screened gates at the ends to allow pens to be flushed by tidal flow. Gates can be raised for impoundment of shrimp larvae and shrimp spawners.

TIMER DRUM

A metal drum containing a series of paralleled slots extending around its circumference to hold timing buttons that trip solenoid switches, as drum revolves, to control operation of bottlemaking machine.

TOE BOARD

The portion of a board on which toe of stocking is shaped.

TRACER POINT

A metal rod placed in the chuck of the master spindle of a wood-carving machine, used to follow around the contour of a carving pattern.

TRANSFER BAR

A rectangular metal bar used to transfer knitted garment parts from one full-fashioned knitting machine onto the needle bar of another.

TRANSFER POINT

The needlelike projections on a TRANSFER BAR or transfer ring over which stitches of knitted material are hung when the material is transferred from one machine to another.

TRIBOX

Glass enclosed container housing a thermometer and a hydrometer through which distilled liquor flows, allowing the temperature and specific gravity proof of liquor to be measured.

TRIP BUTTONS

Small bolts locked in slots on TIMER DRUMS to trip solenoid switches that start and stop functions of bottlemaking machines.

TRUING I

The shaping of grinding wheel for purpose of producing consistent flatness or contour on the ground workpiece. Usually accomplished by application of diamond, abrasive, or hard-metal tool.

TRUING II

Technique used for correcting errors in timepiece balance wheels and hairsprings. Balance wheel truing is accomplished by bending the wheel rim until it lies in a single plane and is concentric with and perpendicular to the staff axis. Hairspring errors are either in the round (coils are not perfectly concentric with collet) or in the flat (coils are not in same plane as collet). Hairsprings are trued by bending coil to correct faulty colleting.

TUBE

The portion of a paper bag without a bottom.

TUNNEL HEADING

That part of a tunnel where digging operations are performed.

TURNER TUBES

A device used in turning gloves, with corresponding rods that push the finger tips of the glove into the tube, partially turning it. Turning is completed manually by worker or automatically on machine.

TYPING ELEMENT

Ball-shaped component of electric typewriters that contains raised characters, such as alpha and numeric characters, and special symbols.

ULTRASONIC HORN

A resonant bar or metal section which transfers energy from converter to workpiece.

ULTRASONIC SEAMING MACHINE

A machine that uses high-frequency sound waves to fuse layers of thermoplastic material simulating a stitchline. The machine resembles a sewing machine in appearance and operation but uses no thread and has a HORN and STITCHING WHEEL for impressing a stitch pattern. The stitching wheel can be changed to produce various decorative effects.

VENEER BLOCK

A log cut to length for peeling or slicing into veneer.

VIBRATING

Process of determining that length of timepiece hairspring will cause balance wheel to vibrate a fixed number of times per hour. Factors considered are length, width, thickness, and strength of hairspring.

WARP WIRE

Wires running the long way of the cloth or screen as woven.

WEBBING STRETCHER

A handtool used to stretch webbing across furniture seat frames.

WELD CONTROLLER

A programmable device which controls the amperage, pressure, and dwell (time) of welding guns attached to automatic machinery.

WELT BAR

A bar of a knitting machine containing a row of small steel hooks (welt points) that hold the first loops or stitch of fabric until the welt is knitted.

WELT ROD

A small metal rod used to facilitate turning of welt on full-fashioned stockings and to wind hose on takeup roller.

WHIRLING MACHINE

Machine that distributes photosensitive solution over surface of photographic printing plates by means of a rotating or whirling action.

WHITING COMPOUND

A mixture of powdered chalk and liquid glue used to form wood sealer or priming base for further application of paint.

WICK

Strands of asbestos twisted together and used for making asbestos rope, packing for steam valves, and as a seal for oven or furnace doors.

WINDUP RACK

A rack that has a continuous drive action which winds long lengths of material into a roll after material has passed through a machine.

YARN CARRIER

In flat knitting, the sliding frame above the needlebeds that hold the cams and yarn guides and carries them to and fro.

ZIGZAG SEWING MACHINE

A machine that sews with an oscillating needle. The pattern of the stitches can be varied by changing cams. Used where a decorative, stretchable stitch is needed.

APPENDIX A

REVISIONS FROM THE 4TH EDITION DOT

In this revised edition of the *Dictionary of Occupational Titles* (DOT), several format and content changes were made in an effort to make this DOT easier to use.

The most noticeable change in this revised DOT is that a profile has been appended to each definition. This profile contains the following selected occupational analysis characteristics: GOE Code; Strength rating; R, M, and L of GED; and SVP. (A detailed explanation of these characteristics can be found in Appendix C.) The last item in the trailer, the Date of Last Update (DLU), is the date of the most recent material gathered in support of that occupation. The date "1977" indicates that the occupation has not been studied since the publication of the fourth edition DOT in 1977. This entry allows the reader to identify the currency of each definition. It also identifies "new" definitions in the DOT or alerts the reader to previously published and recently updated definitions.

A new division has been added to the DOT classification structure, Division 03 COMPUTER-RELATED OCCUPATIONS, and under it there have been added five new Occupational Groups to reflect a reorganization of the DOT taxonomy to bring all of the computer-related occupations together. The five Occupational Groups are as follows:

    030 OCCUPATIONS IN SYSTEMS ANALYSIS AND PROGRAMMING
    031 OCCUPATIONS IN DATA COMMUNICATIONS AND NETWORKS
    032 OCCUPATIONS IN COMPUTER SYSTEMS USER SUPPORT
    033 OCCUPATIONS IN COMPUTER SYSTEMS TECHNICAL SUPPORT
    039 COMPUTER-RELATED OCCUPATIONS, N.E.C.

Additionally, when an updated occupational definition in this DOT contains a reference to the title of another occupation, the DOT code of the referenced occupation is listed, following the referenced DOT title. Within the definitions and the indexes, Undefined Related (UR) titles will now be shown in initial capital letters instead of all captial letters to avoid confusion between Base and UR Titles.

Also, additional appendices have been added to the revised DOT. In this revised DOT, Appendix A is new. Appendix B was the Appendix in the 1977 DOT. Appendix C, mentioned above, explains the components of the definition trailer, Appendix D explains how to use the DOT for job placement, and Appendix E explains how to submit information concerning occupations not found in the DOT. (Appendix D and Appendix E were sections in the front of the 1977 DOT).

The fourth edition DOT Industry Designations have been revised and reduced from 220 to 140 Industry Designations to more closely reflect the Standard Industrial Classification system. And finally, to facilitate its use, the Alphabetical Index of Occupational Titles appears as the last section in the DOT.

APPENDIX B

EXPLANATION OF DATA, PEOPLE, AND THINGS

Much of the information in this publication is based on the premise that every job requires a worker to function, to some degree, in relation to Data, People, and Things. These relationships are identified and explained below. They appear in the form of three listings arranged in each instance from the relatively simple to the complex in such a manner that each successive relationship includes those that are simpler and excludes the more complex. (As each of the relationships to People represents a wide range of complexity, resulting in considerable overlap among occupations, their arrangement is somewhat arbitrary and can be considered a hierarchy only in the most general sense.) The identifications attached to these relationships are referred to as Worker Functions, and provide standard terminology for use in summarizing how a worker functions on the job.

The fourth, fifth, and sixth digits of the occupational code reflect relationships to Data, People, and Things, respectively. These digits express a job's relationship to Data, People, and Things by identifying the highest appropriate function in each listing shown in the following table:

DATA (4th Digit)	PEOPLE (5th Digit)	THINGS (6th Digit)
0 Synthesizing	0 Mentoring	0 Setting Up
1 Coordinating	1 Negotiating	1 Precision Working
2 Analyzing	2 Instructing	2 Operating-Controlling
3 Compiling	3 Supervising	3 Driving-Operating
4 Computing	4 Diverting	4 Manipulating
5 Copying	5 Persuading	5 Tending
6 Comparing	6 Speaking-Signalling	6 Feeding-Offbearing
	7 Serving	7 Handling
	8 Taking Instructions-Helping	

Definitions of Worker Functions

DATA: Information, knowledge, and conceptions, related to data, people, or things, obtained by observation, investigation, interpretation, visualization, and mental creation. Data are intangible and include numbers, words, symbols, ideas, concepts, and oral verbalization.

0 Synthesizing: Integrating analyses of data to discover facts and/or develop knowledge concepts or interpretations.

1 Coordinating: Determining time, place, and sequence of operations or action to be taken on the basis of analysis of data; executing determinations and/or reporting on events.

2 Analyzing: Examining and evaluating data. Presenting alternative actions in relation to the evaluation is frequently involved.

3 Compiling: Gathering, collating, or classifying information about data, people, or things. Reporting and/or carrying out a prescribed action in relation to the information is frequently involved.

4 Computing: Performing arithmetic operations and reporting on and/or carrying out a prescribed action in relation to them. Does not include counting.

5 Copying: Transcribing, entering, or posting data.

6 Comparing: Judging the readily observable functional, structural, or compositional characteristics (whether similar to or divergent from obvious standards) of data, people, or things.

PEOPLE: Human beings; also animals dealt with on an individual basis as if they were human.

0 Mentoring: Dealing with individuals in terms of their total personality in order to advise, counsel, and/or guide them with regard to problems that may be resolved by legal, scientific, clinical, spiritual, and/or other professional principles.

1 Negotiating: Exchanging ideas, information, and opinions with others to formulate policies and programs and/or arrive jointly at decisions, conclusions, or solutions.

2 Instructing: Teaching subject matter to others, or training others (including animals) through explanation, demonstration, and supervised practice; or making recommendations on the basis of technical disciplines.

3 Supervising: Determining or interpreting work procedures for a group of workers, assigning specific duties to them, maintaining harmonious relations among them, and promoting efficiency. A variety of responsibilities is involved in this function.

4 Diverting: Amusing others, usually through the medium of stage, screen, television, or radio.

5 Persuading: Influencing others in favor of a product, service, or point of view.

6 Speaking-Signaling: Talking with and/or signaling people to convey or exchange information. Includes giving assignments and/or directions to helpers or assistants.

7 Serving: Attending to the needs or requests of people or animals or the expressed or implicit wishes of people. Immediate response is involved.

8 Taking Instructions-Helping: Attending to the work assignment instructions or orders of supervisor. (No immediate response required unless clarification of instructions or orders is needed.) Helping applies to "non-learning" helpers.

THINGS: Inanimate objects as distinguished from human beings, substances or materials; and machines, tools, equipment, work aids, and products. A thing is tangible and has shape, form, and other physical characteristics.

0 Setting Up: Preparing machines (or equipment) for operation by planning order of successive machine operations, installing and adjusting tools and other machine components, adjusting the position of workpiece or material, setting controls, and verifying accuracy of machine capabilities, properties of materials, and shop practices. Uses tools, equipment, and work aids, such as precision gauges and measuring instruments. Workers who set up one or a number of machines for other workers or who set up and personally operate a variety of machines are included here.

1 Precision Working: Using body members and/or tools or work aids to work, move, guide, or place objects or materials in situations where ultimate responsibility for the attainment of standards occurs and selection of appropriate tools, objects, or materials, and the adjustment of the tool to the task require exercise of considerable judgment.

2 Operating-Controlling: Starting, stopping, controlling, and adjusting the progress of machines or equipment. Operating machines involves setting up and adjusting the machine or material(s) as the work progresses. Controlling involves observing gauges, dials, etc., and turning valves and other devices to regulate factors such as temperature, pressure, flow of liquids, speed of pumps, and reactions of materials.

3 **Driving-Operating:** Starting, stopping, and controlling the actions of machines or equipment for which a course must be steered or which must be guided to control the movement of things or people for a variety of purposes. Involves such activities as observing gauges and dials, estimating distances and determining speed and direction of other objects, turning cranks and wheels, and pushing or pulling gear lifts or levers. Includes such machines as cranes, conveyor systems, tractors, furnace-charging machines, paving machines, and hoisting machines. Excludes manually powered machines, such as handtrucks and dollies, and power-assisted machines, such as electric wheelbarrows and handtrucks.

4 **Manipulating:** Using body members, tools, or special devices to work, move, guide, or place objects or materials. Involves some latitude for judgment with regard to precision attained and selecting appropriate tool, object, or material, although this is readily manifest.

5 **Tending:** Starting, stopping, and observing the functioning of machines and equipment. Involves adjusting materials or controls of the machine, such as changing guides, adjusting timers and temperature gauges, turning valves to allow flow of materials, and flipping switches in response to lights. Little judgment is involved in making these adjustments.

6 **Feeding-Offbearing:** Inserting, throwing, dumping, or placing materials in or removing them from machines or equipment which are automatic or tended or operated by other workers.

7 **Handling:** Using body members, handtools, and/or special devices to work, move, or carry objects or materials. Involves little or no latitude for judgment with regard to attainment of standards or in selecting appropriate tool, object, or materials.

APPENDIX C

COMPONENTS OF THE DEFINITION TRAILER

The following descriptions of the components of the Definition Trailer are in inverse order to their placement in the trailer.

I. DATE OF LAST UPDATE (DLU)

Listed as the final element in the trailer following the definition, the Date of Last Update indicates the last year in which material was gathered for that occupation. A DLU of "77" would indicate that the occupation has not been studied by an analyst since publication of the fourth edition DOT in 1977.

II. SPECIFIC VOCATIONAL PREPARATION (SVP)

Specific Vocational Preparation is defined as the amount of lapsed time required by a typical worker to learn the techniques, acquire the information, and develop the facility needed for average performance in a specific job-worker situation.

This training may be acquired in a school, work, military, institutional, or vocational environment. It does not include the orientation time required of a fully qualified worker to become accustomed to the special conditions of any new job. Specific vocational training includes: vocational education, apprenticeship training, in-plant training, on-the-job training, and essential experience in other jobs.

Specific vocational training includes training given in any of the following circumstances:

a. Vocational education (high school; commercial or shop training; technical school; art school; and that part of college training which is organized around a specific vocational objective);

b. Apprenticeship training (for apprenticeable jobs only);

c. In-plant training (organized classroom study provided by an employer);

d. On-the-job training (serving as learner or trainee on the job under the instruction of a qualified worker);

e. Essential experience in other jobs (serving in less responsible jobs which lead to the higher grade job or serving in other jobs which qualify).

The following is an explanation of the various levels of specific vocational preparation:

Level	Time
1	Short demonstration only
2	Anything beyond short demonstration up to and including 1 month
3	Over 1 month up to and including 3 months
4	Over 3 months up to and including 6 months
5	Over 6 months up to and including 1 year
6	Over 1 year up to and including 2 years
7	Over 2 years up to and including 4 years
8	Over 4 years up to and including 10 years
9	Over 10 years

Note: The levels of this scale are mutually exclusive and do not overlap.

III. GENERAL EDUCATIONAL DEVELOPMENT (GED)

General Educational Development embraces those aspects of education (formal and informal) which are required of the worker for satisfactory job performance. This is edu-

Scale of General Education Development (GED)

LEVEL	REASONING DEVELOPMENT	MATHEMATICAL DEVELOPMENT	LANGUAGE DEVELOPMENT
6	Apply principles of logical or scientific thinking to a wide range of intellectual and practical problems. Deal with nonverbal symbolism (formulas, scientific equations, graphs, musical notes, etc.) in its most difficult phases. Deal with a variety of abstract and concrete variables. Apprehend the most abstruse classes of concepts.	**Advanced calculus:** Work with limits, continuity, real number systems, mean value theorems, and implicit functions theorems. **Modern Algebra:** Apply fundamental concepts of theories of groups, rings, and fields. Work with differential equations, linear algebra, infinite series, advanced operations methods, and functions of real and complex variables. **Statistics:** Work with mathematical statistics, mathematical probability and applications, experimental design, statistical inference, and econometrics.	**Reading:** Read literature, book and play reviews, scientific and technical journals, abstracts, financial reports, and legal documents. **Writing:** Write novels, plays, editorials, journals, speeches, manuals, critiques, poetry, and songs. **Speaking:** Coversant in the theory, principles, and methods of effective and persuasive speaking, voice and diction, phonetics, and discussion and debate.
5	Apply principles of logical or scientific thinking to define problems, collect data, establish facts, and draw valid conclusions. Interpret an extensive variety of technical instructions in mathematical or diagrammatic form. Deal with several abstract and concrete variables.	**Algebra:** Work with exponents and logarithms, linear equations, quadratic equations, mathematical induction and binomial theorem, and permutations. **Calculus:** Apply concepts of analytic geometry, differentiations and integration of algebraic functions with applications. **Statistics:** Apply mathematical operations to frequency distributions, reliability and validity of tests, normal curve, analysis of variance, correlation techniques, chi-square application and sampling theory, and factor analysis.	Same as Level 6.
4	Apply principles of rational systems to solve practical problems and deal with a variety of concrete variables in situations where only limited standardization exists. Interpret a variety of instructions furnished in written, oral diagrammatic, or schedule form.	**Algebra:** Deal with system of real numbers; linear, quadratic, rational, exponential, logarithmic, angle and circular functions, and inverse functions; related algebraic solution of equations and inequalities; limits and continuity, and probability and statistical inference. **Geometry:** Deductive axiomatic geometry, plane and solid; and rectangular coordinates. **Shop Math:** Practical application of fractions, percentages, ratio and proportion, mensuration, logarithms, slide rule, practical algebra, geometric construction, and essentials of trigonometry.	**Reading:** Read novels, poems, newspapers, periodicals, journals, manuals, dictionaries, thesauruses, and encyclopedias. **Writing:** Prepare business letters, expositions, summaries, and reports, using prescribed format and conforming to all rules of punctuation, grammar, diction, and style. **Speaking:** Participate in panel discussions, dramatizations, and debates. Speak extemporaneously on a variety of subjects.

LEVEL	REASONING DEVELOPMENT	MATHEMATICAL DEVELOPMENT	LANGUAGE DEVELOPMENT
3	Apply commonsense understanding to carry out instructions furnished in written, oral, or diagrammatic form. Deal with problems involving several concrete variables in or from standardized situations.	Compute discount, interest, profit and loss; commission, markup, and selling price; ratio and proportion, and percentage. Calculate surfaces, volumes, weights, and measures. Algebra: Calculate variables and formulas; monomials and polynomials; ratio and proportion variables; and square roots and radicals. Geometry: Calculate plane and solid figures; circumference, area, and volume. Understand kinds of angles, and properties of pairs of angles.	Reading: Read a variety of novels, magazines, atlases, and encyclopedias. Read safety rules, instructions in the use and maintenance of shop tools and equipment, and methods and procedures in mechanical drawing and layout work. Writing: Write reports and essays with proper format, punctuation, spelling, and grammar, using all parts of speech. Speaking: Speak before an audience with poise, voice control, and confidence, using correct English and well-modulated voice.
2	Apply commonsense understanding to carry out detailed but uninvolved written or oral instructions. Deal with problems involving a few concrete variables in or from standardized situations.	Add, subtract, multiply, and divide all units of measure. Perform the four operations with like common and decimal fractions. Compute ratio, rate, and percent. Draw and interpret bar graphs. Perform arithmetic operations involving all American monetary units.	Reading: Passtive vocabulary of 5,000–6,000 words. Read at rate of 190–215 words per minute. Read adventure stories and comic books, looking up unfamiliar words in dictionary for meaning, spelling, and pronunciation. Read instructions for assembling model cars and airplanes. Writing: Write compound and complex sentences, using cursive style, proper end punctuation, and employing adjectives and adverbs. Speaking: Speak clearly and distinctly with appropiate pauses and emphasis, correct pronunciation, variations in word order, using present, perfect, and future tenses.
1	Apply commonsense understanding to carry out simple one- or two-step instructions. Deal with standardized situations with occasional or no variables in or from these situations encountered on the job.	Add and subtract two digit numbers. Multiply and divide 10's and 100's by 2, 3, 4, 5. Perform the four basic arithmetic operations with coins as part of a dollar. Perform operations with units such as cup, pint, and quart; inch, foot, and yard; and ounce and pound.	Reading: Recognize meaning of 2,500 (two- or three-syllable) words. Read at rate of 95–120 words per minute. Compare similarities and differences between words and between series of numbers. Writing: Print simple sentences containing subject, verb, and object, and series of numbers, names, and addresses. Speaking: Speak simple sentences, using normal word order, and present and past tenses.

cation of a general nature which does not have a recognized, fairly specific occupational objective. Ordinarily, such education is obtained in elementary school, high school, or college. However, it may be obtained from experience and self-study.

The GED Scale is composed of three divisions: Reasoning Development, Mathematical Development, and Language Development. The description of the various levels of language and mathematical development are based on the curricula taught in schools throughout the United States. An analysis of mathematics courses in school curricula reveals distinct levels of progression in the primary and secondary grades and in college. These levels of progression facilitated the selection and assignment of six levels of GED for the mathematical development scale.

However, though language courses follow a similar pattern of progression in primary and secondary school, particularly in learning and applying the principles of grammar, this pattern changes at the college level. The diversity of language courses offered at the college level precludes the establishment of distinct levels of language progression for these four years. Consequently, language development is limited to five defined levels of GED inasmuch as levels 5 and 6 share a common definition, even though they are distinct levels.

IV. PHYSICAL DEMANDS - STRENGTH RATING (Strength)

The Physical Demands Strength Rating reflects the estimated overall strength requirement of the job, expressed in terms of the letter corresponding to the particular strength rating. It represents the strength requirements which are considered to be important for average, successful work performance.

The strength rating is expressed by one of five terms: Sedentary, Light, Medium, Heavy, and Very Heavy. In order to determine the overall rating, an evaluation is made of the worker's involvement in the following activities:

a. Standing, Walking, Sitting

Standing - Remaining on one's feet in an upright position at a work station without moving about.

Walking - Moving about on foot.

Sitting - Remaining in a seated position.

b. Lifting, Carrying, Pushing, Pulling

Lifting - Raising or lowering an object from one level to another (includes upward pulling).

Carrying - Transporting an object, usually holding it in the hands or arms, or on the shoulder.

Pushing - Exerting force upon an object so that the object moves away from the force (includes slapping, striking, kicking, and treadle actions).

Pulling - Exerting force upon an object so that the object moves toward the force (includes jerking).

Lifting, pushing, and pulling are evaluated in terms of both intensity and duration. Consideration is given to the weight handled, position of the worker's body, and the aid given by helpers or mechanical equipment. Carrying most often is evaluated in terms of duration, weight carried, and distance carried.

Estimating the Strength factor rating for an occupation requires the exercise of care on the part of occupational analysts in evaluating the force and physical effort a worker must exert. For instance, if the worker is in a crouching position, it may be much more difficult to push an object than if pushed at waist height. Also, if the worker is required to lift and carry continuously or push and pull objects over long distances, the worker may exert as much physical effort as is required to similarly move objects twice as heavy, but less frequently and/or over shorter distances.

c. Controls

Controls entail the use of one or both arms or hands (hand/arm) and/or one or both feet or legs (foot/leg) to move controls on machinery or equipment. Controls include but are not limited to buttons, knobs, pedals, levers, and cranks.

Following are descriptions of the five terms in which the Strength Factor is expressed:

S-Sedentary Work - Exerting up to 10 pounds of force occasionally (Occasionally: activity or condition exists up to 1/3 of the time) and/or a negligible amount of force frequently (Frequently: activity or condition exists from 1/3 to 2/3 of the time) to lift, carry, push, pull, or otherwise move objects, including the human body. Sedentary work involves sitting most of the time, but may involve walking or standing for brief periods of time. Jobs are sedentary if walking and standing are required only occasionally and all other sedentary criteria are met.

L-Light Work - Exerting up to 20 pounds of force occasionally, and/or up to 10 pounds of force frequently, and/or a negligible amount of force constantly (Constantly: activity or condition exists 2/3 or more of the time) to move objects. Physical demand requirements are in excess of those for Sedentary Work. Even though the weight lifted may be only a negligible amount, a job should be rated Light Work: (1) when it requires walking or standing to a significant degree; or (2) when it requires sitting most of the time but entails pushing and/or pulling of arm or leg controls; and/or (3) when the job requires working at a production rate pace entailing the constant pushing and/or pulling of materials even though the weight of those materials is negligible. NOTE: The constant stress and strain of maintaining a production rate pace, especially in an industrial setting, can be and is physically demanding of a worker even though the amount of force exerted is negligible.

M-Medium Work - Exerting 20 to 50 pounds of force occasionally, and/or 10 to 25 pounds of force frequently, and/or greater than negligible up to 10 pounds of force constantly to move objects. Physical Demand requirements are in excess of those for Light Work.

H-Heavy Work - Exerting 50 to 100 pounds of force occasionally, and/or 25 to 50 pounds of force frequently, and/or 10 to 20 pounds of force constantly to move objects. Physical Demand requirements are in excess of those for Medium Work.

V-Very Heavy Work - Exerting in excess of 100 pounds of force occasionally, and/or in excess of 50 pounds of force frequently, and/or in excess of 20 pounds of force constantly to move objects. Physical Demand requirements are in excess of those for Heavy Work.

V. GUIDE FOR OCCUPATIONAL EXPLORATION (GOE)

Many youths and other jobseekers are unprepared for an effective job search because of a lack of knowledge about the kinds of jobs to look for. They have difficulty relating their interest, skills, and potentials to appropriate occupations. To be effective, vocational counselors must have sufficient information to match an individual's interest, temperaments, potential ability and other personal traits to specific career fields and work requirements.

The *Guide for Occupational Exploration* was designed by the US Employment Service to provide career counselors and other DOT users with additional information about the interests, aptitudes, entry level preparation and other traits required for successful performance in various occupations. The GOE is also useful in self-assessment and counselor-assisted settings to help people understand themselves realistically in regard to their ability to meet job requirements. Descriptive information provided for each work group assists the individual in evaluating his or her own interests and relating them to pertinent fields of work.

The GOE code assigned to a definition provides a link between the occupation defined and the GOE arrangement of occupations with similar interests, aptitudes, adaptability requirements, and other descriptors.

The GOE coding structure classifies jobs at three levels of consideration. The first level divides occupations according to twelve interest areas corresponding to interest factors identified through research conducted by the former Division of Testing in the US Employment Service. The interest factors, identified by a two-digit code, are defined in terms of broad interest requirements of occupations as well as vocational interests of individuals. The twelve interest areas are defined as follows:

01 Artistic	05 Mechanical	09 Accommodating
02 Scientific	06 Industrial	10 Humanitarian
03 Plants-Animals	07 Business Detail	11 Leading-Influencing
04 Protective	08 Selling	12 Physical Performing

The interest areas are then subdivided into work groups (the second set of two digits within the six-digit GOE code). Each work group contains occupations requiring similar worker traits and capabilities in related work settings. The GOE contains descriptive information for each work group and identifies each occupation in the group with a four-digit code and title. In many interest areas, occupations that require the most education, training, and experience are in the first group, while those requiring less formal education or experience are listed in the last group.

Work groups are then subdivided into subgroups (the third two-digit set in the GOE code) of occupations with even more homogeneous interests, aptitudes, and adaptability requirements. Each subgroup is identified by its unique six-digit code and title. Individual occupations are listed alphabetically within subgroups. Some subgroups contain occupations from more than one industry, listed within alphabetized industries.

APPENDIX D

HOW TO USE THE DOT FOR JOB PLACEMENT

Within the public Employment Service system the primary purpose for assigning a DOT code and title to a job applicant or employer job order is to facilitate the process of "finding people for jobs and jobs for people". The occupational code is a method of searching files to locate qualified applicants and to match their qualifications with available job orders. In some Employment Service offices, the Employment Service automated system provides on-line computerized access to job openings arranged in terms of DOT occupational codes making it possible for applicants to match their background and experience to job openings related to their interests.

Proper classification of both job openings and job applicants is vital to the efficient operation of the Employment Service system, and to maintain the accuracy of statistical reporting systems which are based on the DOT coding structure. The coding structure of the DOT is specifically designed to facilitate this process. The unique 9-digit code shown for each occupation allows job interviewers to perform file searches providing the linkage between an applicant's work experience and employer job orders.

The section entitled "How to Find an Occupational Title and Code" describes how to use the Occupational Group Arrangement, the Industry Arrangement, the Alphabetical Index and other DOT components to assure proper occupational coding of jobs and applicants. The occupational classification system in the revised fourth edition of the DOT arranges occupational titles within a given technology in order of work-performance complexity. It can assist in identifying occupational progression and skill transfers vertically within a technology or horizontally among closely related technologies. Each occupational definition also provides essential job placement information by indicating the industry or industries in which a given occupation is found and by describing job tasks and task variables.

The use of the DOT for job placement is summarized here in relation to the following Employment Service operations: Classifying Job Applications; Classifying Job Orders; Matching Workers to Orders; and Assisting Special Applicant Groups.

(1) Classifying Job Applicants

Job interviewers will find it useful to structure the applicant interview in accordance with the way information is provided in a DOT occupational definition. By framing specific questions to elicit detailed information concerning the jobseeker's training, experience and preferences, a job interviewer can assess the individual in terms of fields of work, job content and worker requirements for an individual occupation in the *Dictionary*. An appropriate code number and job title can then be assigned to complete the interview process. (See "How to Find an Occupational Title and Code".)

To ensure the correct occupational code and title is assigned to each application, the following steps should be followed:

(a) Using information obtained from the job seeker, make a tentative selection of an occupational code and title.
(b) Review the requirements of the particular occupation selected, and match them against past experience, training, job preferences, job interests and any test or assessment results of the applicant to verify that the occupation best fits the applicant for purposes of job placement.
(c) Supplement the data with labor market information reflecting job opportunities in the local area. Review all the information obtained and assign a final primary occupational code and title to the applicant. Be sure the assigned code reflects the jobseeker's highest level of achievement and ability.
(d) Additional codes and titles should be assigned as appropriate by repeating the steps outlined above to identify the applicant's related skills and training.

(2) Classifying Job Orders

Assigning appropriate classification codes and titles to job openings is a process complementary to that of classifying job applicants.

The order taker should review the structure content of job definitions in the *Dictionary* to assure that all of the required information needed for proper classification is obtained. The information needed is that contained in the lead statement and task element statements of each occupational definition. (See "Parts of the Occupational Definition".)

Occupational definitions in the DOT are written to reflect the most typical characteristics of a job as it occurs in the American economy. Task element statements in the definitions may not always coincide with the way work is performed in particular establishments or localities.

If the occupational code and title is not easily determined, the DOT definition finally selected should be reviewed carefully. If alternate methods of performing a job are described in the DOT definition, the order taker should review the definition with the employer to determine which description fits the firm's operation. After determining which methods described in the DOT definition are actually used in the particular establishment involved, the order taker may assign an appropriate DOT code.

Only part of the jobs contained in the DOT are found in any given labor market area. In some instances, carefully developed desk aids containing titles, codes and definitions may be useful in assigning DOT codes and titles. However, a person or job should never be forced into a code simply because it is common in the local labor market.

(3) Matching Workers to Orders

The DOT occupational definitions are the bridge in the job-matching process, linking qualified applicants with suitable job openings. Whether a placement office operates under a manual or computerized system, or is in transition, a successful job match is critically dependent upon correct input into the system.

The importance of correct input is more crucial, and reliance on the DOT classification system may be even greater, in the case of computer-assisted placement systems which include job matching.

Keep in mind that it is generally easier to find a good match when you know the following information:

- Job tasks workers are required to perform
- The purpose of the work
- Machines, tools, equipment or work aids used
- Materials, products, subject matter (academic discipline) or services involved
- Instructions received and the independent judgment that a worker exercises during job performance
- Where the work is located (outdoors: on a farm, a forest tract, on water, etc.; indoors: an office, a factory, school, etc.).

Computerized Job Service matching can improve the efficiency of placement activities in a system by allowing interviewers to use the DOT to:

(a) verify the accuracy and completeness of applications and job orders and ensure appropriate classifications are assigned;
(b) verify data on intake forms at the point of data entry and monitor the output of program or labor market information; and
(c) provide alternate search strategies using the DOT classification system within the capabilities of the computerized system.

(4) Assisting Special Applicant Groups

Entry Level Workers

Entry workers often have little or no training, education or job experience geared to specific occupational requirements. They may also lack the necessary licenses or certification for certain jobs in which they express interest. In one way or another, they may not be fully competitive with more experienced jobseekers.

An effective method of classifying such workers is to review the individual's educational background, interests, hobbies, casual or leisure time work experience, worker traits, and other indicators of potential occupational abilities and skills. For example, if the applicant had an interest in science activities in school, they might be considered for a laboratory job if such openings are available in the area. The final code assigned should allow the individual the greatest possible exposure to work or training opportunities in relation to interests, skills and abilities.

In a manual matching system, it is not usually possible to assign a 9-digit code to an entry worker, but every effort should be made to assign an appropriate 6-digit code and generalized title. One method of indicating that the individual is an entry worker is to replace the period after the third digit in the occupational code with an (x). For example, if an entry worker is assigned the job title LABORATORY TESTER (any industry), the 6-digit code assigned would be 029x261. In a computerized matching system, there is no standard method of recording entry classifications, since the recording procedures can vary from state to state.

Veterans

U.S. veterans seeking civilian jobs are usually given preference in file search and referral activities by public employment service offices. To give veterans the maximum opportunity to qualify for openings, both their civilian experience and the occupational training they received during their military careers must be fully reflected in their occupational classification and code. The inclusion of significant military occupations in the DOT assists in providing correct input and increases the chances of finding a job match.

The Department of Defense *Military Career Guide 1988-1989*, prepared in cooperation with the Department of Labor and published in 1987, is an important reference document in this area. It consolidates occupational information from all branches of the Armed Services and related military-to-DOT occupations.

Disabled Workers

The procedure for coding entry workers may also be applied to disabled or differently-abled workers and applicants with limited or nonrelevant work experience registering under various assistance or human resource development programs. The interviewer must not assume that a disability automatically precludes a worker from performing a particular job. Companies will often make special accommodations to employ disabled persons (in fact, some accommodations are legally required).

If a person has strong or special physical capabilities which would allow them to accommodate to certain tasks, these also should be taken into account. The interviewer may refer to the *Handbook for Analyzing Jobs* or his or her regional Occupational Analysis Field Center if he or she has any questions regarding the physical demands listed for a specific occupation in the DOT. Remember that additional information from testing and reinterviewing applicants may be used to review and/or revise an individual's assigned occupational classification.

Other Special Applicants

Persons in certain life situations may, based on the stressful nature of these situations, be considered in the category of special applicant. In addition to the applicant groups cited above, interviewers may be called upon to assist applicants who are difficult to place such as low-skilled youth, older workers, ex-offenders, drug abusers, seasonal or displaced reentrants to the labor market and others who need to work but challenge a counselor's placement skills. To most effectively place clients in available local jobs, interviewers must sometimes evaluate the broader needs and values of applicants including their work attitudes, personality and need for transitional support such as remedial education, medical or mental health care, transportation and day care.

The employment interviewer, to respond to this challenge, must try to determine the applicant's work resources including abilities, interests, physical capabilities, work history and experience, education and leisure activities. Use of support material such as the *Guide for Occupational Exploration* and the *Occupational Outlook Handbook* (available at most libraries) is usually advisable. These easy-to-read books, published by the Department of Labor, provide information on several job factors including specific work duties, training and education, earnings, working conditions and future opportunities.

The important thing is not the job title, but the skills and abilities required by the job. An applicant whose experience and aptitudes are matched to an occupation never considered before is a real success story. The interviewer, with effective use of the DOT, can play a pivotal role in that process.

APPENDIX E

OCCUPATIONAL CODE REQUESTS

Users of the revised fourth edition DOT may be unable to locate a specific job title, code, or definition in the DOT or the specific information for a definition in the DOT may appear to be incorrect. This situation could occur for several reasons including:

1. The job title the user seeks is new or was created as the result of recent technological changes or labor force pressures.
2. The user seeks job information that may be more specific or may be organized differently than the information provided in the composite revised DOT definition.
3. The user may not be completely familiar with the taxonomic structure of the revised DOT.
4. Job analysts may have missed occupational information due to technological advances or changes in that industry.
5. The job title may not have enough workers performing the work to facilitate data collection.

The Occupational Code Request (Form ETA-741) was developed by the OA program to allow users of the revised DOT a means to provide input to, or obtain from USES OA Field Centers, information on job titles or occupational definitions they cannot find in the DOT. Users who have searched the DOT for needed information and have been unsuccessful should contact the nearest Job Service office for assistance in locating an appropriate DOT classification for the job in question. If the Job Service office cannot supply the needed occupational information, the DOT user should submit a typed Occupational Code Request (OCR) form to the appropriate OA Field Center. A copy of the OCR showing action taken by the OAFC will be returned to the user in a timely manner.

If it is not convenient to seek the help of the local Job Service office, you may send your requests for a DOT title and code directly to an Occupational Analysis Field Center. In your correspondence, please include the OCR so that the request can be processed correctly. DOT users who find incorrect or inaccurate occupational information in the DOT may contact the nearest Occupational Analysis Field Center directly.

The OCR procedure, which has been set up to provide supplementary occupational information to users, serves as an additional method of securing job information for subsequent publications. Classifications established as a result of an OCR are usable on an interim basis until the job is studied by an occupational analyst and a definition is published in the DOT.

The Field Centers responsible for processing OCR forms for individual States are as indicated in the list on the following page:

Massachusetts Occupational Analysis Field Center   (617) 727-6718
Research and Statistics Section
Charles Hurley Building, Second Floor
Government Center
Boston, Massachusetts 02114

Connecticut	New York
Delaware	Pennsylvania
Maine	Puerto Rico
Massachusetts	Rhode Island
New Hampshire	Vermont
New Jersey	Virgin Islands

Michigan Occupational Analysis Field Center   (313) 876-5140
Michigan Employment Security Commission
7310 Woodard Avenue, Room 425
Detroit, Michigan   48202

Illinois	Ohio
Indiana	West Virginia
Michigan	Wisconsin
Minnesota	

Missouri Occupational Analysis Field Center   (314) 340-4780
Division of Employment Security
505 Washington Avenue
St. Louis, Missouri   63101

Arkansas	Nebraska
Iowa	North Dakota
Kansas	Oklahoma
Louisiana	South Dakota
Missouri	Texas

North Carolina Occupational Analysis Field Center   (919) 733-7917
Employment Security Commission of North Carolina
Post Office Box 27625
Raleigh, NC   27611

Alabama	Mississippi
District of Columbia	North Carolina
Florida	South Carolina
Georgia	Tennessee
Kentucky	Virginia
Maryland	

Utah Occupational Analysis Field Center   (801) 533-2225
Department of Employment Security
174 Social Hall Avenue
Salt Lake City, Utah   84111

Alaska	Montana
American Samoa	Nevada
Arizona	New Mexico
California	Oregon
Colorado	Utah
Guam	Washington
Hawaii	Wyoming
Idaho	

Occupational Code Request

U.S. Department of Labor
Employment and Training Administration

A. Originating Office

1. State	2. Date Transmitted

3. Local Office *(Name, LO No., Address, Phone No.)*

4. Requested By *(Name, Title, Phone No.)*

Date Received by OAFC:

OMB No. 12050137

Expires: 11/30/92

B. Information Obtained From:

1. CHECK APPROPRIATE BOX

☐ Employer ☐ Applicant ☐ Training Program

☐ Other *(specify)* . . . .

2. Establishment *(Name and Address)*

3. Establishment Contact *(Name, Title, Phone No.)*

4. Product(s)/Service(s)	5. SIC Code *(4-digits)*

C. Job Description   *(Instructions on Reverse Side)*

1. Establishment Job Title(s):

2. List Overall Purpose or Summary of this Job:

3. List Important or Regularly Performed Tasks:

4. (a) List Employer's Hiring Requirements: *(Education, vocational training, experience, other)*

4. (b) List Machines, Tools, Equipment or Work Aids the Worker Uses To Perform Duties:

D. APPROVED TITLE AND CODE:	Occupational Title	Occupational Code *(9-digits)*
	Industry	GOE Code *(6-digits)*

Public reporting burden for this collection of information is estimated to average 30 minutes per response, including the time for reviewing instructions searching existing data sources, gathering and maintaining the data needed, and completing and reviewing the collection of information. Send comments regarding this burden estimate or any other aspect of this collection of information, including suggestions for reducing this burden, to the Office of Information Management, Department of Labor, Room N–1301, 200 Constitution Avenue, N.W., Washington, DC 20210; and to the Office of Management and Budget, Paperwork Reduction Project (1205–0137), Washington, DC 20503.

E. Additional Information and Comments

List any additional information and comments not covered elsewhere. *(Use additional sheets, if necessary.)*

F. Reply to Originating Office and State Coordinator

"X" One

1. ☐   Use DOT Definition *(4th Edition Title and 9-digit Code)*

2. ☐   Use Approved O.C.R. Code *(Full 9-digit Code)*

3. ☐   Use New Code and Title *(See Item D—Approved Title and Code, on other side)*

4. ☐   Send more information *(See Attached Letter)*

G. Transmittal Action Approved By:

Name and Title	Date Returned to Originating Office
	Date Sent to DOA/ Other OAFC

Instructions for Completing Part C, Job Description

1. Summarize, in one sentence, the overall objective or purposes of the job *(such as, "Operates injection molding machine.")*

2. List the more important or regularly performed tasks. A good job description should include these five kinds of information:

    a. Worker actions (what actions a worker takes), such as "Sets-up. . . ."

    b. Machines, tools, equipment, and/or work aids (include with the task where pertinent), such as "injection molding machine."

    c. Purpose of worker actions (the results of the work, the purpose of the task), such as "to mold. . . ."

    d. Materials used, such as "granulated resin pellets," products made, such as "plastic bottles," subject matter employed, (academic discipline), such as "accounting principles," "machine shop math," etc., or service rendered, such as "hair styling."

    e. Kind of instructions received, such as "simple worksheet," "complex blue-prints;" or basis for judgments, such as "following supervisor's directions," or "according to work order and knowledge of machine operations."

NOTE: *Use more than one sentence, if necessary, to describe all important or regularly performed tasks. For example of a related published job definition using the components, see Injection-molding-machine Operator, 556.382-014 in the Dictionary of Occupational Titles.*

INDUSTRY INDEX

This index lists industries included in the section entitled "Occupational Titles Arranged by Industry Designation". The industry designations (abbreviations) and full industry titles are both listed. Entries in capital letters refer to the full industry titles and those in lower case to the industry designations.

OCCUPATIONAL TITLES ARRANGED BY INDUSTRY DESIGNATION

agric. equip.—AGRICULTURAL EQUIPMENT INDUSTRY: This designation includes occupations concerned with manufacturing and repairing implements and equipment used either exclusively or to a large extent on farms. Typical of the products included in the industry are barn and barnyard equipment, cultivators, harrows, harvesting machinery, listers, planting and fertilizing machinery, plows, rollers, tractors, and weeders. Occupations concerned with the manufacture of agricultural handtools are included in the CUTLERY, HANDTOOLS, AND HARDWARE INDUSTRY (cutlery-hrdwr.).

assembler, lawn-and-garden machinery 801.684-022
assembler, tractor 801.684-022
assembly inspector 801.381-018
ASSEMBLY INSPECTOR 706.361-014
ASSEMBLY-INSPECTOR HELPER 801.663-010
ASSEMBLY REPAIRER 624.381-010
BENCH ASSEMBLER 706.684-042
BLADE BALANCER 701.687-014
case assembler 801.684-022
Combine Inspector 624.361-010
Diesel-Mechanic, Farm 625.281-010
FARM-EQUIPMENT-MECHANIC APPRENTICE 624.281-014
FARM-EQUIPMENT MECHANIC I 624.281-010
FARM-EQUIPMENT MECHANIC II 624.381-014
FARM-MACHINERY SET-UP MECHANIC 624.381-018
farm mechanic 624.381-014
farm mechanic 624.281-010
farm-mechanic apprentice 624.281-014
field-equipment-maintenance mechanic, farm 624.381-014
finished-goods inspector 801.381-018
GREASER 624.684-010
INSPECTOR AND TESTER 624.361-010
inspector, finished machines and bundles 801.667-010
INSPECTOR, SHIPPING 801.667-010
main-line assembler 801.684-022
MAJOR-ASSEMBLY INSPECTOR 801.381-018
mechanical inspector 624.361-010
MILKING-SYSTEM INSTALLER 809.381-018
Motor-Assembly Supervisor 801.137-010
PROGRESSIVE ASSEMBLER AND FITTER 801.684-022
REEL-BLADE-BENDER FURNACE TENDER 504.685-030
Reel Fabricator 706.684-042
SPRINKLER-IRRIGATION-EQUIPMENT MECHANIC 624.361-014
subassembler 706.684-042
SUPERVISOR, ASSEMBLY 801.137-010
SUPERVISOR, FARM-EQUIPMENT MAINTENANCE 624.131-010
SUPERVISOR, INSPECTION 801.137-014
tester 624.361-010
TEST TECHNICIAN 019.261-022
Treadmill Inspector 624.361-010
Viner Mechanic 624.281-010

agriculture—AGRICULTURE AND AGRICULTURAL SERVICE: This designation includes occupations concerned with the following types of activity: (1) raising crops to be used as food, for industrial use, as in production of cotton textiles and of plastic materials and other chemicals, and for other purposes; (2) breeding and raising poultry, livestock, and other animals for food, furs, or hides, for show or utility purposes, or as pets; (3) functions related to the above that are frequently performed by persons engaged in agriculture but that are also performed as services by organizations that specialize in such activities, including functions that are characteristically performed as services to farmers and others engaged in agriculture and directly related to agriculture. Occupations of a professional character, such as agronomists, entomologists, and plant pathologists, are included in PROFESSIONAL AND KINDRED OCCUPATIONS (profess. & kin.). Occupations concerned with farming aquatic life are included in FISHING, HUNTING, AND TRAPPING (fishing & hunt.). Occupations concerned with the practice of veterinary medicine are included in MEDICAL SERVICES (medical ser.).

aerial-applicator pilot 196.263-010
AGRICULTURAL AIDE ..... term
agricultural-aircraft pilot 196.263-010
aircraft pilot 196.263-010
AIRPLANE PILOT 196.263-010
airplane pilot, crop dusting 196.263-010
AIRPLANE-PILOT HELPER 409.667-010
ANIMAL BREEDER 410.161-010
apiarist 413.161-010
Apple Checker 221.587-030
Apple Grower 403.161-010
Apple Packer 920.687-134
APPLE-PACKING HEADER 920.687-010
Apple-Picking Supervisor 409.131-010
Apple Sorter 529.687-186
Apple Washer 529.685-258
Apricot Packer 920.687-134
ARTIFICIAL-BREEDING DISTRIBUTOR 180.167-010
ARTIFICIAL-BREEDING TECHNICIAN 418.384-014
artificial-insemination technician 411.384-010
ARTIFICIAL INSEMINATOR 418.384-010
Asparagus Grader And Buncher 529.687-186
Asparagus Sorter 529.687-186
Avocado Packer 920.687-134
BALE SEWER 920.687-022
Banana Grader 529.687-186
BAND MAKER 619.685-010
BAND SALVAGER 929.686-014
Band Shover, Press 920.686-042
band splicer 619.685-010
band straightener 929.686-014
Basket Turner 920.687-134
Bean-Sprout Grower 405.161-018
Bean-Sprout Laborer 405.687-014
bee farmer 413.161-010
BEEKEEPER 413.161-010
Bee Producer 413.161-010
bee raiser 413.161-010
bee rancher 413.161-010
BEE WORKER 413.687-018
berry grower 403.161-014
BIOLOGICAL AIDE 049.364-018
Blacksmith, Farm 610.381-010
BLOOD TESTER, FOWL 411.364-010
Blueberry Grower 403.161-014
BONSAI CULTURIST 405.161-010
Boxer 920.687-134
breeding technician 418.384-014
BUDDER 405.684-010
Bulb Grower 405.161-014
Bulb Sorter 529.687-186
BUS DRIVER, DAY-HAUL OR FARM CHARTER 913.363-010
CAMP TENDER 410.137-010
CANARY BREEDER 411.161-010
CAPONIZER 411.684-010
Capper 920.687-134
Capper Picker 529.687-186
CARETAKER, FARM ..... term
Carrot Grader-Inspector 409.687-010
Carrot Washer 529.685-258
cash grain grower 401.161-010
Cat Breeder 410.161-010
Cattle Rancher 410.161-018
Cauliflower-Harvesting-And-Packing Supervisor 409.131-010
Cherry Grower 403.161-010
Cherry Packer 920.687-134
Cherry Sorter 529.687-186
chicken fancier 411.161-014
Chicken Vaccinator 411.684-014
CHICK GRADER 411.687-010
CHICK SEXER 411.687-014
Chinchilla Farmer 410.161-014
chore tender 421.687-010
Citrus-Fruit Packer 920.687-134
Citrus-Fruit-Packing Grader 529.687-186
Compress Trucker 929.687-030
Contractor, Broomcorn Threshing 409.117-010
Contractor, Field Hauling 409.117-010
Cook, Ranch 315.361-010
Corn Grower 401.161-010
COTTON BALER 920.685-114
COTTON CLASSER 429.387-010
COTTON CLASSER AIDE 429.587-010
Cotton Farmworker 404.687-010
cotton grader 429.387-010
Cotton Grower 404.161-010
COTTON SAMPLER 922.687-042
COTTON TIER 920.687-074
Cotton Weigher 221.587-030
COWPUNCHER 410.674-014
Cranberry-Farm Supervisor 403.131-014
Cranberry Grower 403.161-014
Cranberry Sorter 529.687-186
Crater 920.687-134
Crate Tier 920.687-134

agriculture

crew boss	180.167-022
crew leader	180.167-022
crew leader	180.167-050
crew manager	408.131-010
Culled-Fruit Packer	920.687-134
Cull Grader	529.687-186
cutter	404.686-010
Dairy Farmer	410.161-018
Day-Haul Youth Supervisor	913.363-010
debeaker	411.687-026
disease-and-insect-control boss	408.137-010
Dog Breeder	410.161-010
Driver	404.131-010
Duck Farmer	411.161-018
dwarf tree grower	405.161-010
Egg Packer	920.687-134
EGG PASTEURIZER	529.682-038
EGG WASHER, MACHINE	529.686-030
ELECTRIC-FORK OPERATOR	921.685-042
Face-And-Fill Packer	920.687-134
farm butcher	525.664-010
farm-crew leader	180.167-050
FARMER	term
FARMER, CASH GRAIN	401.161-010
FARMER, CONTRACT	term
FARMER, DIVERSIFIED CROPS	407.161-010
FARMER, DRY LAND	term
FARMER, FIELD CROP	404.161-010
FARMER, FRUIT CROPS, BUSH AND VINE	403.161-014
FARMER, GENERAL	421.161-010
FARMER, TENANT	term
FARMER, TREE-FRUIT-AND-NUT CROPS	403.161-010
FARMER, VEGETABLE	402.161-010
farm-labor contractor	409.117-010
farm laborer	421.687-010
FARM-MACHINE OPERATOR	409.683-010
FARM-MACHINE TENDER	409.685-010
FARMWORKER	term
Farmworker, Berry	403.687-010
Farmworker, Brooder Farm	411.584-010
FARMWORKER, BULBS	405.683-010
Farmworker, Chicken Farm	411.584-010
Farmworker, Cranberry	403.687-010
FARMWORKER, DAIRY	410.684-010
FARMWORKER, DIVERSIFIED CROPS I	407.663-010
FARMWORKER, DIVERSIFIED CROPS II	407.687-010
Farmworker, Egg-Producing Farm	411.584-010
FARMWORKER, FIELD CROP I	404.663-010
FARMWORKER, FIELD CROP II	404.687-010
FARMWORKER, FRUIT I	403.683-010
FARMWORKER, FRUIT II	403.687-010
Farmworker, Fryer Farm	411.584-010
Farmworker, Fur	410.674-010
FARMWORKER, GENERAL I	421.683-010
FARMWORKER, GENERAL II	421.687-010
FARMWORKER, GRAIN I	401.683-010
FARMWORKER, GRAIN II	401.687-010
FARMWORKER, LIVESTOCK	410.664-010
FARMWORKER, MACHINE	409.686-010
FARMWORKER, POULTRY	411.584-010
Farmworker, Pullet Farm	411.584-010
FARMWORKER, RICE	401.683-014
FARMWORKER, SEASONAL	term
Farmworker, Turkey Farm	411.584-010
FARMWORKER, VEGETABLE I	402.663-010
FARMWORKER, VEGETABLE II	402.687-010
FEED AND FARM MANAGEMENT ADVISER	096.127-018
FEED-RESEARCH AIDE	049.364-010
Fence-Post Cutter	454.684-026
FIELD HAULER	409.683-014
FIELD INSPECTOR, DISEASE AND INSECT CONTROL	408.687-010
FIELD SERVICE TECHNICIAN, POULTRY	411.267-010
field supervisor	402.131-010
FIELD SUPERVISOR, SEED PRODUCTION	180.167-014
FIG CAPRIFIER	403.687-014
Fig Sorter	529.687-186
Filbert Grower	403.161-010
fish-bait picker	413.687-010
fish-worm grower	413.161-018
FLEECE TIER	410.687-010
Flower Grader	529.687-186
Flower Grower	405.161-014
FLOWER PICKER	405.687-010
FOREST-PRODUCTS GATHERER	453.687-010
Fox Farmer	410.161-014

FRUIT DISTRIBUTOR	921.685-046
FRUIT-GRADER OPERATOR	529.665-010
Fruit Packer, Face-And-Fill	920.687-134
Fruit Packer, Wrap-And-Place	920.687-134
fruit picker	403.687-018
Fruit Sorter	529.687-186
FRUIT WORKER	term
FUR FARMER	410.161-014
GAME-BIRD FARMER	412.161-010
GAME-FARM HELPER	412.684-010
GAMEKEEPER	169.171-010
gardener-florist	406.684-018
garden farmer	402.161-010
garden worker	402.687-010
GARDEN WORKER	406.684-018
GENERAL MANAGER, FARM	180.167-018
GIN CLERK	221.467-010
GINNER	429.685-010
Ginseng Farmer	404.161-010
Goat Farmer	410.161-018
GOAT HERDER	410.687-014
GOAT-TRUCK DRIVER	term
GRADER TENDER	521.685-154
grain farmer	401.161-010
Grape Grower	403.161-014
Grass Farmer	405.161-014
Grass-Farm Laborer	405.687-014
Greenhouse Laborer	405.687-014
green house manager	405.131-010
Greenhouse Superintendent	405.131-010
Greenhouse Worker	405.684-014
GROUP LEADER	180.167-022
grove superintendent	180.167-058
GROWTH-MEDIA MIXER, MUSHROOM	405.683-014
Guinea-Pig Breeder	410.161-010
HARVEST CONTRACTOR	409.117-010
harvesting manager	405.131-010
harvest supervisor	409.131-010
HARVEST WORKER, FIELD CROP	404.687-014
HARVEST WORKER, FRUIT	403.687-018
HARVEST WORKER, VEGETABLE	402.687-014
hatchery helper	411.687-022
Hay Farmer	404.161-010
Header	920.687-134
head rose grader	405.137-010
helper, chicken farm	411.584-010
herder	410.687-022
hired worker	421.683-010
Hoer	409.687-018
HOG-CONFINEMENT-SYSTEM MANAGER	410.161-022
hoist worker	929.687-010
honey producer	413.161-010
Hop Grower	404.161-010
Hops Farmworker	404.687-010
Hop Sorter	529.687-186
Horse Rancher	410.161-018
HORSESHOER	418.381-010
HORSE TRAINER	419.224-010
HORTICULTURAL-SPECIALTY GROWER, FIELD	405.161-014
HORTICULTURAL-SPECIALTY GROWER, INSIDE	405.161-018
HORTICULTURAL WORKER I	405.684-014
HORTICULTURAL WORKER II	405.687-014
house supervisor	920.137-010
Hydroponics Grower	405.161-018
Hydroponics Worker	405.684-014
HYDRO-SPRAYER OPERATOR	408.662-010
incubator helper	411.687-022
inseminator	418.384-010
INSPECTOR-GRADER, AGRICULTURAL ESTABLISHMENT	409.687-010
interior horticulturist	408.364-010
Irrigating-Pump Operator	914.682-010
IRRIGATOR, GRAVITY FLOW	409.687-014
IRRIGATOR, HEAD	409.137-010
irrigator, overhead	409.685-014
IRRIGATOR, SPRINKLING SYSTEM	409.685-014
IRRIGATOR, VALVE PIPE	409.684-010
Kennel Attendant	410.674-010
LABORATORY TECHNICIAN, ARTIFICIAL BREEDING	040.361-010
Laborer, Brooder Farm	411.687-018
Laborer, Chicken Farm	411.687-018
laborer, dairy farm	410.684-010
Laborer, Egg-Producing Farm	411.687-018
Laborer, Fryer Farm	411.687-018
laborer, game farm	412.684-010

LABORER, HIGH-DENSITY PRESS	929.687-018
LABORER, LANDSCAPE	408.687-014
laborer, livestock	410.664-010
Laborer, Orchard	403.687-010
LABORER, POULTRY FARM	411.687-018
LABORER, POULTRY HATCHERY	411.687-022
Laborer, Pullet Farm	411.687-018
LABORER, TREE TAPPING	453.687-014
Laborer, Turkey Farm	411.687-018
laborer, vegetable farm	402.687-010
Laborer, Vineyard	403.687-010
LAMBER	410.364-010
LANDSCAPE GARDENER	408.161-010
landscaper	408.161-010
LAWN-SERVICE WORKER	408.684-010
lead rider	410.137-014
Lemon Grower	403.161-010
Lettuce Trimmer	920.687-134
Lidder	920.687-134
LIQUID-FERTILIZER SERVICER	906.683-014
livestock breeder	410.161-018
Livestock Counter	221.587-030
livestock farmer	410.161-018
LIVESTOCK RANCHER	410.161-018
Lugger	929.687-030
Make-Up Market Worker, Truck Garden	920.687-134
MANAGER, AERIAL PLANTING AND CULTIVATION	180.167-062
Manager, Chicken Hatchery	180.167-046
MANAGER, DAIRY FARM	180.167-026
Manager, Duck Hatchery	180.167-046
Manager, Game-Animal Farm	180.167-034
Manager, Game-Bird Farm	180.167-034
MANAGER, GAME BREEDING FARM	180.167-034
MANAGER, GAME PRESERVE	180.167-038
Manager, Hydroponics Nursery	180.167-042
MANAGER, NURSERY	180.167-042
MANAGER, ORCHARD	180.167-066
MANAGER, POULTRY HATCHERY	180.167-046
manager, production	180.167-058
MANAGER, PRODUCTION, SEED CORN	180.161-010
manager, regional	180.161-010
Manager, Retail Nursery	180.167-042
Manager, Turkey Hatchery	180.167-046
MEAT DRESSER	525.664-010
Medicinal-Plant Picker	453.687-010
Melon Packer	920.687-134
MIGRANT LEADER	180.167-050
MIGRANT WORKER	term
MILKER, MACHINE	410.685-010
milking-machine operator	410.685-010
MILK SAMPLER	410.357-010
Mink Farmer	410.161-014
Monkey Breeder	410.161-010
Moss Picker	453.687-010
Mouse Breeder	410.161-010
Mushroom Grower	405.161-018
Mushroom-Growing Supervisor	405.131-010
Mushroom Laborer	405.687-014
Mushroom Packer	920.687-134
mutton puncher	410.687-022
Nursery Laborer	405.687-014
Nut Orchardist	403.161-010
Nut Sorter	529.687-186
Onion Farmer	402.161-010
Onion-Harvesting Supervisor	409.131-010
Orange Grower	403.161-010
Orange-Picking Supervisor	409.131-010
Orange Washer	529.685-258
orchardist	403.161-010
Orchard Pruner	408.684-018
Orchid Grower	405.161-018
Orchid Superintendent	405.131-010
Orchid Worker	405.684-014
PACE SETTER	term
packer	920.687-134
PACKER, AGRICULTURAL PRODUCE	920.687-134
PACKING-HOUSE SUPERVISOR	920.137-010
packing-shed supervisor	920.137-010
Partridge Farmer	412.161-010
PATCH WORKER	381.687-030
Peach Grower	403.161-010
Peach Harvesting Supervisor	409.131-010
Peach Sorter	529.687-186
Peanut Farmer	404.161-010
Pear Packer	920.687-134

Pecan Grower	403.161-010
PELTER	410.687-018
Pest-Control Pilot	196.263-010
pest-control worker	408.381-010
Pheasant Farmer	412.161-010
PLANT-CARE WORKER	408.364-010
PLANTER	term
Plant Packer	920.687-134
PLANT PROPAGATOR	405.361-010
plant tender	408.364-010
Plant Wrapper	920.687-134
plater	418.381-010
Plum Packer	920.687-134
Potato Grader	529.687-186
potato-seed cutter	404.686-010
Potato Sorter	529.687-186
POULTRY BREEDER	411.161-014
poultry culler	411.687-010
POULTRY DEBEAKER	411.687-026
POULTRY DRESSER	525.687-070
POULTRY FARMER	411.161-018
Poultry Farmer, Egg	411.161-018
Poultry Farmer, Meat	411.161-018
poultry helper	411.584-010
POULTRY INSEMINATOR	411.384-010
POULTRY TENDER	411.364-014
POULTRY VACCINATOR	411.684-014
presser, cotton ginning	920.685-114
PRESS FEEDER, BROOMCORN	429.686-010
puncher	410.674-014
Quail Farmer	412.161-010
Queen Producer	413.161-010
Rabbit Breeder	410.161-010
ramrod	410.137-014
ranch hand, livestock	410.664-010
ranch manager	180.167-018
ranch rider	410.674-014
Raspberry Grower	403.161-014
Rat Breeder	410.161-010
Rattlesnake Farmer	413.161-014
Reindeer Rancher	410.161-018
REPTILE FARMER	413.161-014
Returner	920.687-074
Rice Farmer	401.161-010
rider	410.674-014
Ring Facer	920.687-134
Ring Packer	920.687-134
Roper	929.687-030
Rose-Farm Laborer	405.687-014
Rose Grader	409.687-010
Rose Grower	405.161-014
row boss	180.167-022
ROW BOSS, HOEING	409.137-014
sampler	410.357-010
sampler	922.687-042
scale clerk	221.467-010
SCOUT	408.381-010
seed cleaner	599.665-010
SEED-CLEANER OPERATOR	599.665-010
seed-cleaning-machine operator	599.665-010
SEED CUTTER	404.686-010
Seed Grower	405.161-014
Seed Packer	920.687-134
SEED PELLETER	599.685-126
SEED-POTATO ARRANGER	404.685-010
Seed Sorter	529.687-186
Segregator	929.687-030
Sewer, Head	920.687-022
SHARECROPPER	term
shed boss	404.131-014
SHED WORKER	term
sheep clipper	410.684-014
SHEEP HERDER	410.687-022
Sheep Rancher	410.161-018
SHEEP SHEARER	410.684-014
shepherd	410.687-022
SHREDDER TENDER, PEAT	599.685-086
Shrub Grower	405.161-014
skinner, pelts	410.687-018
SORTER, AGRICULTURAL PRODUCE	529.687-186
sorter, food products	529.687-186
Soybean Grower	401.161-010
SPRAYER, HAND	408.684-014
Spray Supervisor	408.131-010
Stallion Keeper	410.674-022

aircraft mfg.

STILL OPERATOR	522.685-098
stock clipper	410.684-014
Strawberry Grower	403.161-014
Suction Operator	921.662-018
Sugarcane Planter	404.161-010
SUPERINTENDENT	180.167-054
SUPERINTENDENT, PRODUCTION	180.167-058
SUPERINTENDENT, SEED MILL	599.137-010
SUPERVISOR, AREA	401.137-010
SUPERVISOR, ARTIFICIAL BREEDING RANCH	410.131-014
Supervisor, Brooder Farm	411.131-010
Supervisor, Chicken Hatchery	411.137-010
SUPERVISOR, DAIRY FARM	410.131-010
SUPERVISOR, DETASSELING CREW	401.137-014
SUPERVISOR, DIVERSIFIED CROPS	407.131-010
Supervisor, Egg-Producing Farm	411.131-010
SUPERVISOR, FIELD-CROP FARMING	404.131-010
Supervisor, Fryer Farm	411.131-010
SUPERVISOR, GAME FARM	412.131-010
supervisor, grove	403.131-010
SUPERVISOR, HORTICULTURAL-SPECIALTY FARMING	405.131-010
SUPERVISOR, INSECT AND DISEASE INSPECTION	408.137-010
supervisor, irrigation	409.137-010
SUPERVISOR, LABORATORY ANIMAL FACILITY	418.137-010
supervisor, orchard	403.131-010
SUPERVISOR, PICKING CREW	409.131-010
SUPERVISOR, POULTRY FARM	411.131-010
SUPERVISOR, POULTRY HATCHERY	411.137-010
Supervisor, Pullet Farm	411.131-010
SUPERVISOR, RESEARCH DAIRY FARM	410.134-022
SUPERVISOR, RESEARCH KENNEL	418.137-014
SUPERVISOR, ROSE-GRADING	405.137-010
SUPERVISOR, SHED WORKERS	404.131-014
SUPERVISOR, SPRAY, LAWN AND TREE SERVICE	408.131-010
SUPERVISOR, STOCK RANCH	410.131-022
SUPERVISOR, TREE-FRUIT-AND-NUT FARMING	403.131-010
Supervisor, Turkey Farm	411.131-010
Supervisor, Turkey Hatchery	411.137-010
SUPERVISOR, VEGETABLE FARMING	402.131-010
SUPERVISOR, VINE-FRUIT FARMING	403.131-010
SUPERVISOR, WOOL-SHEARING	410.134-014
Swine Rancher	410.161-018
Thorough Bred Horse Farm Manager	410.161-018
THRESHER, BROOMCORN	429.685-014
tie-out worker	920.687-074
tipper	525.687-070
TOBACCO CURER	523.682-038
Tobacco Farmworker	404.687-010
Tobacco Grader	409.687-010
Tobacco Grower	404.161-010
Tobacco Packer	920.687-134
Topper Packer	920.687-134
TOP SCREW	410.137-014
top waddy	410.137-014
TRANSPLANTER, ORCHID	405.687-018
TREE CUTTER	454.684-026
TREE PRUNER	408.684-018
Tree-Service Supervisor	408.131-010
TREE SURGEON	408.181-010
Tree-Surgeon Helper I	408.684-018
TREE-SURGEON HELPER II	408.687-018
Tree Wrapper	920.687-134
tromper	920.687-198
Truck Farmer	402.161-010
Tung-Nut Grower	403.161-010
Turkey Farmer	411.161-018
vegetable grower	402.161-010
Vegetable Sorter	529.687-186
vegetable worker	402.687-010
VETERINARIAN, POULTRY	073.101-014
VINE PRUNER	403.687-022
Vineyard Supervisor	403.131-014
wage worker see FARMWORKER, SEASONAL	
Walnut Grower	403.161-010
WASHER, AGRICULTURAL PRODUCE	529.685-258
Washing-And-Waxing-Machine Operator	529.685-258
Watermelon-Harvesting Supervisor	409.131-010
Watermelon Inspector	409.687-010
WEEDER-THINNER	409.687-018
WEED INSPECTOR	408.381-014
Wheat Grower	401.161-010
WOOL-FLEECE GRADER	589.687-054
WOOL-FLEECE SORTER	410.687-026
WOOL SACKER	920.687-198

wool shearer	410.684-014
wool tamper	920.687-198
worm-bed attendant	413.687-014
WORM-FARM LABORER	413.687-014
WORM GROWER	413.161-018
WORM PACKER	920.687-202
WORM PICKER	413.687-010
worm raiser	413.687-014
worm sorter	920.687-202
YARD SUPERVISOR, COTTON GIN	929.137-034
YARD WORKER	929.583-010

aircraft mfg.—AIRCRAFT-AEROSPACE MANUFACTURING INDUSTRY: This designation includes occupations concerned with manufacturing and repairing aerospace and aircraft vehicles, including guided missiles, spacecraft, fixed and rotary wing aircraft, gliders, helicopters, airships, balloons, and surface-effect vehicles; and manufacturing parts, such as engines, propulsion units, hydraulic and mechanical equipment, and landing gear. Occupations concerned with the manufacture of navigational, guidance, and communications systems are included in the INSTRUMENTS AND APPARATUS INDUSTRY (inst. & app.).

Abrasive Water Jet Cutter Operator	699.382-010
AERODYNAMICIST	002.061-010
aerodynamics engineer	002.061-010
AERONAUTICAL-DESIGN ENGINEER	002.061-022
AERONAUTICAL ENGINEER	002.061-014
AERONAUTICAL PROJECT ENGINEER	002.167-018
AERONAUTICAL-RESEARCH ENGINEER	002.061-026
AERONAUTICAL TEST ENGINEER	002.061-018
aerophysics engineer	002.061-010
aerospace project engineer	002.167-018
aircraft and engine electrician, field and hangar	825.261-018
Aircraft-And-Engine Mechanic, Field-And-Hangar	621.281-014
aircraft-delivery checker	222.387-010
aircraft mechanic	621.281-014
AIRCRAFT MECHANIC, ARMAMENT	806.361-030
aircraft mechanic, electrical	825.261-018
AIRCRAFT MECHANIC, ELECTRICAL AND RADIO	825.381-010
AIRCRAFT MECHANIC, ENVIRONMENTAL CONTROL SYSTEM	806.381-014
AIRCRAFT MECHANIC, PLUMBING AND HYDRAULICS	806.381-066
aircraft mechanic, rigger	806.381-018
AIRCRAFT MECHANIC, RIGGING AND CONTROLS	806.381-018
aircraft mechanic, structures	806.381-026
AIRCRAFT-SHIPPING CHECKER	222.387-010
AIRCRAFT SKIN BURNISHER	807.684-018
AIRFRAME-AND-POWER-PLANT MECHANIC	621.281-014
AIRFRAME-AND-POWER-PLANT-MECHANIC HELPER	621.684-010
AIRPLANE COVERER	849.381-010
airplane mechanic	621.281-014
airplane-mechanic helper	621.684-010
armament assembler	806.361-030
armament installer	806.361-030
assembler, aircraft, plumbing and hydraulics	806.381-066
ASSEMBLER, AIRCRAFT POWER PLANT	806.381-022
ASSEMBLER, AIRCRAFT, STRUCTURES AND SURFACES	806.381-026
assembler, bonding	806.384-030
ASSEMBLER, ELECTROMECHANICAL	828.381-018
ASSEMBLER, GROUND SUPPORT EQUIPMENT	809.261-010
assembler-installer, cable controlled systems	806.381-018
ASSEMBLER-INSTALLER, GENERAL	806.361-014
assembler-installer, structures	806.381-026
Assembler-Installer, Wing Structures	806.381-026
ASSEMBLER, METAL BONDING	806.384-030
assembler, radio and electrical	729.384-026
ASSEMBLER, SUBASSEMBLY	806.384-034
ASSEMBLER, TUBING	806.381-034
assembler, wire group	729.384-026
Assembly Line Robot Operator	606.382-026
AUTOCLAVE OPERATOR	553.362-014
AUTOMATED CUTTING MACHINE OPERATOR	699.362-010
avionics and radar technician	823.261-026
avionics mechanic	823.261-026
AVIONICS TECHNICIAN	823.261-026
Bagger	754.684-042
bench assembler, electrical	729.384-026
blacksmith, hammer operator	610.362-014
blue print control clerk	206.367-010
BONDED STRUCTURES REPAIRER	807.381-014
bonder, rework and repair	807.381-014
Bonding And Composite Fabricator	754.381-018

bonding equipment operator	553.362-014
cabin furnishings installer	806.381-078
cable assembler	806.381-042
CABLE ASSEMBLER AND SWAGER	806.381-042
cable cutter and swager	806.381-042
CALIBRATION LABORATORY TECHNICIAN	019.281-010
Checkout Mechanic, Hydraulic And Rigging	806.261-050
CHEMICAL-ETCHING PROCESSOR	704.381-014
chemical-milling processor	704.381-014
commodities requirements analyst	012.167-082
Composite Assembler	754.684-042
Composite Bond Worker	754.684-042
Composite Laminator	754.684-042
Composite Layup Worker	754.684-042
Composites Fabricator And Assembler	754.381-018
Composite Trim And Drill Worker	754.684-042
composite worker	754.684-042
computer-numerical-control nesting operator	007.362-010
CONTROLLER, REMOTELY-PILOTED VEHICLE (RPV)	196.263-026
Controls Development Mechanic	693.261-014
cost development engineer	002.167-010
Crane Operator-Hooktender	921.663-010
data acquisition laboratory technician	002.262-010
design specialist, producibility, cost and component technology	002.167-010
detail assembler	806.384-034
detail bench assembler	706.381-050
DEVELOPER PROVER, INTERIOR ASSEMBLIES	693.261-014
Developer-Prover, Mechanical	693.261-014
developer prover, upholstering	693.261-010
DEVELOPMENT MECHANIC	693.261-014
dope-and-fabric worker	849.381-010
doper	849.381-010
DRAFTER, AERONAUTICAL	002.261-014
drawing-release clerk	206.367-010
DROPHAMMER OPERATOR	610.362-010
ELECTRICAL AND RADIO MOCK-UP MECHANIC	693.381-026
ELECTRICAL ASSEMBLER	729.384-026
Electrical Checkout Mechanic	806.261-050
ELECTRICAL-EQUIPMENT TESTER	729.381-010
ELECTRICAL INSPECTOR	825.381-026
ELECTRICIAN, AIRCRAFT	825.261-018
ELECTRICIAN, RESEARCH	726.261-014
ENCAPSULATOR	556.684-014
engine buildup mechanic	806.381-014
ENGINEERING-DOCUMENT-CONTROL CLERK	206.367-010
engineering laboratory technician	019.281-010
engineering-release clerk	206.367-010
engineering test mechanic	710.361-014
engineering test pilot	196.263-042
ENGINE TESTER	621.261-014
etcher, aircraft	704.381-014
experimental aircraft and engine mechanic, field and hangar	621.261-022
EXPERIMENTAL AIRCRAFT MECHANIC	621.261-022
Experimental Electronics Developer	003.161-014
experimental flight test mechanic	621.261-022
experimental mechanic	693.261-014
Experimental Mechanic, Spacecraft	621.261-022
Experimental Plastics Fabricator	754.381-018
experimental preflight mechanic	621.261-022
EXPERIMENTAL-ROCKET-SLED MECHANIC	825.281-038
Fabrication And Structures Development Mechanic	693.261-014
FIELD-SERVICE ENGINEER	002.167-014
FIELD-SERVICE REPRESENTATIVE	621.221-010
Filament-Wound Parts Fabricator	754.381-018
Flight-Line Mechanic	621.281-014
Flight Line Service Attendant	621.684-010
FLIGHT-TEST DATA ACQUISITION TECHNICIAN	002.262-010
FLUID JET CUTTER OPERATOR	699.382-010
Form Block Maker	693.281-030
Fuel Tank Sealer And Tester	806.384-038
general helper	809.687-014
ground equipment mechanic	809.261-010
HAMMER OPERATOR	617.382-014
HELPER, MANUFACTURING	809.687-014
HELPER, METAL BONDING	806.687-022
HIGH-ENERGY-FORMING WORKER	619.380-010
Hydraulic And Plumbing Development Mechanic	693.261-014
hydraulic and plumbing installer	806.381-066
industrial robot operator	606.382-026
Inspector, Advanced Composit	806.261-046
INSPECTOR, ASSEMBLIES AND INSTALLATIONS	806.261-030
inspector, assembly	806.261-030
INSPECTOR, BENCH ASSEMBLY	806.281-026
Inspector, Electrical And Electronic Installations	806.261-030

inspector, electrical bench	825.381-026
Inspector, Engines And Components Assembly	806.261-030
Inspector, Experimental Assembly	806.261-030
INSPECTOR, FABRICATION	806.361-022
Inspector, Final Assembly	806.261-030
Inspector, Final Assembly - Electrical	806.261-030
Inspector, Final Assembly - Mechanical	806.261-030
Inspector, Machined Parts	806.361-022
INSPECTOR, MATERIAL DISPOSITION	806.261-034
INSPECTOR, MISSILE	806.261-038
Inspector, Missile Final Assembly	806.261-038
INSPECTOR, OUTSIDE PRODUCTION	806.261-042
INSPECTOR, PLASTICS AND COMPOSITES	806.261-046
Inspector, Plastics Fabrication-Developmental	806.261-046
inspector, precision electrical assembly	825.381-026
inspector, precision electrical assembly	729.381-010
INSPECTOR, PROCESSING	806.381-074
Inspector, Production Plastic Parts	806.261-046
Inspector, Radar And Electronics	722.381-014
INSPECTOR, RECEIVING	222.384-010
Inspector, Sheet Metal Parts	806.361-022
Inspector, Structural Bonding	806.261-046
Inspector, Structures	806.261-030
Inspector, Subassembly	806.261-030
Inspector, Welded Parts	806.361-022
INSTALLER, INTERIOR ASSEMBLIES	806.381-078
INSTRUMENT INSPECTOR	722.381-014
Integral Tank Sealer	806.384-038
Jig And Fixture Builder	693.281-030
Kitter	754.684-042
laboratory test mechanic	002.261-014
LIAISON ENGINEER	012.167-038
line assembler, aircraft	806.361-014
LOAD-TEST MECHANIC	929.382-010
loft patternmaker	777.281-018
Machine Tool Fixture Builder	693.281-030
material planning and acquisition analyst	012.167-082
Material Review Board Representative, Quality Control	806.261-034
MATERIAL SCHEDULER	012.167-082
MECHANIC, AIRCRAFT RIGGING AND CONTROLS	806.261-050
Mechanic, Electrical Operational Test	806.261-050
Mechanic, Experimental Structural Assembly	693.261-014
Mechanic, Field-Service	621.281-014
Mechanic, General Operational Test	806.261-050
METAL-BONDING PRESS OPERATOR	553.382-026
metal-bonding worker	806.687-022
Metal Bond Inspector	806.261-046
Missile-Control Pilot	196.263-026
Missile Inspector, Preflight	806.261-038
MOCK-UP BUILDER	693.361-014
Model Builder, Display	693.261-018
Model Builder, Wind Tunnel	693.261-018
MODEL MAKER	693.261-018
model maker, plaster and plastic	777.281-018
molder	502.381-014
MOLDER	518.361-010
MOLDER APPRENTICE	518.361-014
molder, closed molds	502.381-014
MOLDER, PUNCH	502.381-014
molder, resin	556.684-014
NESTING OPERATOR, NUMERICAL CONTROL	007.362-010
NUMERICAL-CONTROL ROUTER OPERATOR	605.382-046
Numerical-Control-Wire-Preparation-Machine-Tender	728.685-010
OVEN CURING ATTENDANT	590.685-090
Overhaul and Repair Mechanic	621.281-014
Painter, Aircraft	845.381-014
Painter, Aircraft-Production	845.381-014
PAINTER APPRENTICE, TRANSPORTATION EQUIPMENT	845.381-010
Painter, Decorative-Commercial Aircraft	845.381-014
Painter, Insignia	741.684-026
PAINTER, TRANSPORTATION EQUIPMENT	845.381-014
Paint Stocker	222.387-058
pattern data operator	007.362-010
PATTERNMAKER, PLASTER	777.281-018
patternmaker, plaster and plastic	777.281-018
planishing-hammer operator	617.382-014
Plastic Parts Fabricator	754.381-018
Plastic Parts Fabricator-Trimmer	754.684-042
plastics bench mechanic	754.381-018
PLASTICS FABRICATOR	754.381-018
plastics fabricator and assembler	754.381-018
Plastics Rework And Repair Mechanic	754.381-018
PLASTICS WORKER	754.684-042
platen operator, metal bond	553.382-026

power-hammer operator 617.382-014
PRECISION ASSEMBLER 806.381-082
PRECISION ASSEMBLER, BENCH 706.381-050
PRESSURE SEALER-AND-TESTER 806.384-038
Pressurization Mechanic 806.384-038
Pressurization Mechanic, Air Controls 806.384-038
Pressurizer 806.384-038
Primer Sprayer 741.684-026
Process Equipment Operator 704.381-014
PROCUREMENT ENGINEER 162.157-034
production control scheduler 012.167-082
proof-load mechanic 929.382-010
quality assurance calibrator 019.281-010
radio and radar technician 823.261-026
radio operator, ground 193.262-026
RADIO STATION OPERATOR 193.262-026
release and technical records clerk 206.367-010
RESEARCH MECHANIC 002.261-014
RIVETING MACHINE OPERATOR 806.380-010
Riveting Machine Operator, Programmed Control 806.380-010
Riveting Machine Operator, Tape Control 806.380-010
ROBOTIC MACHINE OPERATOR 606.382-026
ROCKET-ENGINE-COMPONENT MECHANIC 621.281-030
Rocket-Engine Mechanic, Liquid 693.261-022
ROCKET-MOTOR MECHANIC 693.261-022
ROUTER OPERATOR, HAND 806.684-150
Router Operator, Pin 605.382-034
Router Operator, Radial 605.382-034
SALES ENGINEER, AERONAUTICAL PRODUCTS 002.151-010
sand molder 518.361-010
sand-molder apprentice 518.361-014
SAW OPERATOR 607.382-014
Sealant Mixer 550.685-062
sealer, aircraft 806.384-038
sheet metal assembler 806.384-034
SHOT-PEENING OPERATOR 617.280-010
SKIN-LAP BONDER 806.684-130
Smooth And Burr Worker, Composites 754.684-042
Space Vehicle Inspector, Preflight 806.261-038
Spares Rework Mechanic 621.281-014
standards laboratory technician 019.281-010
STRESS ANALYST 002.061-030
structural test mechanic 710.361-014
structures assembler 806.381-026
SUPERVISOR, INSPECTION 806.131-038
SUPERVISOR, PRODUCTION DEPARTMENT 806.131-042
systems checkout mechanic 806.261-050
technical aide, flight test data 002.262-010
technical specialist, aircraft systems 621.221-010
TEMPLATE REPRODUCTION TECHNICIAN 976.381-022
Test Cell Technician 621.261-014
test equipment certification technician 019.281-010
TEST EQUIPMENT MECHANIC 710.361-014
tester, electrical accessories 729.381-010
tester, rocket engine 806.261-022
TESTER, ROCKET MOTOR 806.261-022
TEST PILOT 196.263-042
Thermodynamics Engineer 002.061-010
TOOL BUILDER 693.281-030
TOOL DESIGN CHECKER 007.267-014
tool-drawing checker 007.267-014
TOOLING COORDINATOR, PRODUCTION ENGINEERING 169.167-054
tooling reproduction technician 976.381-022
Tool Liaison 012.167-038
tool procurement coordinator 169.167-054
trimmer 693.261-010
tube bender-assembler 806.381-034
Undercoat Sprayer 741.687-018
UPHOLSTERER 780.384-014
VALUE ENGINEER 002.167-010
Water Router Operator 699.382-010
WIND TUNNEL MECHANIC 869.261-026
Wood-Tool Maker 693.281-030
Wrapper And Preserver 920.587-018

air trans.—AIR TRANSPORTATION INDUSTRY: This designation includes occupations concerned with operating, maintaining, and repairing aircraft; controlling and operating air transportation systems; and operating airports.

aerial navigator 196.167-014
aircraft and engine electrician, field and hangar 825.261-018
AIRCRAFT BODY REPAIRER 807.261-010
aircraft charter dispatcher 295.367-010
Aircraft-Engine Assembler 621.281-014
Aircraft-Engine-Cylinder Mechanic 621.281-014
Aircraft-Engine Dismantler 621.281-014
Aircraft-Engine Installer 621.281-014
Aircraft-Engine Mechanic 621.281-014
Aircraft-Engine Mechanic, Overhaul 621.281-014
aircraft-inspection-record clerk 221.362-010
Aircraft Instrument Repairer 710.281-026
AIRCRAFT-LOG CLERK 221.362-010
aircraft mechanic 621.281-014
aircraft mechanic, electrical 825.261-018
aircraft-time clerk 221.362-010
AIRFRAME-AND-POWER-PLANT MECHANIC 621.281-014
AIRFRAME-AND-POWER-PLANT-MECHANIC APPRENTICE 621.281-018
AIRFRAME-AND-POWER-PLANT-MECHANIC HELPER . 621.684-010
Airframe-And-Power-Plant Mechanic, Line Service 621.281-014
air-freight agent 248.367-018
AIRLINE-RADIO OPERATOR 193.262-010
AIRLINE-RADIO OPERATOR, CHIEF 193.162-022
AIRLINE SECURITY REPRESENTATIVE 372.667-010
airplane-and-engine inspector 621.261-010
airplane-cabin attendant 352.367-010
Airplane Captain 196.263-014
AIRPLANE-CHARTER CLERK 295.367-010
Airplane Cleaner 919.687-014
AIRPLANE COVERER 849.381-010
AIRPLANE-DISPATCH CLERK 248.367-010
airplane dispatcher 912.167-010
Airplane First-Officer 196.263-014
AIRPLANE-FLIGHT ATTENDANT 352.367-010
AIRPLANE INSPECTOR 621.261-010
airplane mechanic 621.281-014
airplane-mechanic apprentice 621.281-018
airplane-mechanic helper 621.684-010
airplane navigator 196.167-014
Airplane Pilot 196.263-014
airplane pilot, chief 196.167-010
AIRPLANE PILOT, COMMERCIAL 196.263-014
airplane-rental clerk 295.367-010
AIRPORT ATTENDANT 912.364-010
Airport Clerk 219.362-010
AIRPORT ELECTRICIAN 824.281-010
Airport Guide 353.367-014
AIRPORT-MAINTENANCE CHIEF 899.137-010
AIRPORT UTILITY WORKER 912.663-010
avionics and radar technician 823.261-026
avionics mechanic 823.261-026
AVIONICS TECHNICIAN 823.261-026
BAGGAGE CHECKER 357.477-010
CABIN-EQUIPMENT SUPERVISOR 869.131-010
Cabin-Service Agent 919.687-014
Carburetor Mechanic 621.281-014
CARGO AGENT 248.367-018
CHECK PILOT 196.263-022
CHIEF PILOT 196.167-010
commercial pilot 196.263-014
Commissary Agent 922.687-058
COMMUNICATION-CENTER COORDINATOR 235.132-014
COMMUNICATION-CENTER OPERATOR 235.662-014
Copilot 196.263-014
Corporate Pilot 196.263-014
CREW SCHEDULER 215.362-010
CREW SCHEDULER, CHIEF 215.137-010
customer security clerk 372.667-010
customer service agent 248.367-018
customer services instructor 099.227-018
departure clerk 912.367-014
director, airport 184.117-026
Director, Airport Operations 184.117-026
DISPATCHER 912.167-010
DOCK HAND 919.683-010
DOCUMENTATION-BILLING CLERK 214.362-014
dope-and-fabric worker 849.381-010
doper 849.381-010
ELECTRICAL INSPECTOR 825.381-026
ELECTRICIAN, AIRCRAFT 825.261-018
Electrician Supervisor, Airplane 829.131-014
ENGINE TESTER 621.261-014
equipment scheduler 221.362-010
fire fighter, airport 373.663-010
FIRE FIGHTER, CRASH, FIRE, AND RESCUE 373.663-010
FLIGHT ATTENDANT, RAMP 352.367-014
FLIGHT-CREW-TIME CLERK 215.362-018
FLIGHT ENGINEER 621.261-018

flight follower 209.367-050
FLIGHT-INFORMATION EXPEDITER 912.367-010
flight mechanic 621.261-018
flight-operations-dispatch clerk 248.367-010
flight security specialist 372.667-010
Freight-Traffic Agent 252.257-010
GATE AGENT 238.367-010
GENERAL AGENT, OPERATIONS 184.167-042
GENERAL CLAIMS AGENT 186.117-030
ground instructor, advanced 099.227-018
GUIDE, CHIEF AIRPORT 353.137-010
helicopter dispatcher 912.167-010
Helicopter Mechanic 621.281-014
HOST/HOSTESS, GROUND 352.377-010
Hydraulic Tester 621.281-014
Ignition Specialist 621.281-014
inspector, electrical bench 825.381-026
inspector, precision electrical assembly 825.381-026
INSTRUCTOR, GROUND SERVICES 099.227-018
INSTRUCTOR, PILOT 196.223-014
INSTRUMENT INSPECTOR 722.381-014
LABORER, AIRPORT MAINTENANCE 899.687-014
lead ticket-sales agent 238.137-022
LINE-SERVICE ATTENDANT 912.687-010
luggage checker 357.477-010
maintenance-planning clerk 221.362-010
MANAGER, AIRPORT 184.117-026
Manager, Airport-Property-And-Development 184.117-026
MANAGER, CARGO-AND-RAMP-SERVICES 184.167-058
Manager, Commissary Service 184.167-082
MANAGER, FLIGHT CONTROL 184.167-066
Manager, Flight Dispatching 184.167-082
MANAGER, FLIGHT OPERATIONS 184.117-038
MANAGER, FLIGHT-RESERVATIONS 184.167-070
Manager, Flight Service 184.167-082
MANAGER, OPERATIONS 184.117-050
Manager, Passenger Service 184.167-082
manager, rates and schedules 184.117-066
Manager, Reservations-And-Ticketing 184.167-082
MANAGER, SCHEDULE PLANNING 184.117-058
MANAGER, STATION 184.167-082
MANAGER, TRAFFIC 184.117-066
Manifest Clerk 214.362-014
Master Rigger 912.684-010
NAVIGATOR 196.167-014
operations agent 912.367-010
operations manager 184.117-050
Painter, Aircraft 845.381-014
PAINTER APPRENTICE, TRANSPORTATION
  EQUIPMENT 845.381-010
PAINTER, TRANSPORTATION EQUIPMENT 845.381-014
parachute packer 912.684-010
PARACHUTE RIGGER 912.684-010
Passenger-Interline Clerk 214.382-022
PASSENGER SERVICE REPRESENTATIVE 359.677-022
Passenger Traffic Agent 252.257-010
pilot 196.263-014
PORTER 357.677-010
porter, baggage 357.677-010
radio and radar technician 823.261-026
RATE ANALYST, FREIGHT 214.267-010
RECEPTIONIST, AIRLINE LOUNGE 352.677-014
redcap 357.677-010
RESERVATIONS AGENT 238.367-018
sales representative 252.257-010
screening representative 372.667-010
SENIOR-COMMISSARY AGENT 922.137-010
senior gate agent 238.137-018
senior passenger agent 238.137-022
senior radio operator 193.162-022
SENIOR RESERVATIONS AGENT 238.137-014
senior ticket-sales agent 238.137-022
service center manager 184.167-042
service coordinator 912.367-010
Skycap 357.677-010
Supercharger Mechanic 621.281-014
SUPERCHARGER-REPAIR SUPERVISOR 621.131-010
superintendent, airport 184.117-026
Superintendent, Airport-Buildings-Maintenance ... 184.117-026
Superintendent, Airport-Facilities-Repair-And-Maintenance 184.117-026
SUPERINTENDENT, MAINTENANCE 184.167-174
superintendent, maintenance, airports 899.137-010
SUPERVISOR, AIRCRAFT CLEANING 891.137-014
SUPERVISOR, AIRCRAFT MAINTENANCE 621.131-014
SUPERVISOR, AIRPLANE-FLIGHT ATTENDANT 352.137-010

SUPERVISOR, AVIONICS SHOP 823.131-018
SUPERVISOR, GATE SERVICES 238.137-018
Supervisor, Lost And Found 241.137-014
SUPERVISOR, TICKET SALES 238.137-022
telephone-sales agent 238.367-018
teleticketing agent 248.382-010
ticket agent 248.382-010
TICKETING CLERK 248.382-010
ticket sales instructor 099.227-018
Tire Changer, Aircraft 915.684-010
TRAFFIC AGENT 252.257-010
TRANSPORTATION AGENT 912.367-014
Transport Pilot 196.263-014
Traveling-Freight-And-Passenger Agent 252.257-010
TRIP FOLLOWER 209.367-050
watch supervisor 193.162-022
Waybill Clerk 214.362-014
WEATHER CLERK 248.362-014

amuse. & rec.—AMUSEMENT AND RECREATION: This designation includes occupations concerned with providing amusement and recreation facilities, and presenting commerical entertainment in the flesh, in motion pictures, and in broadcasting. Included are occupations concerned with presenting shows and athletic contests, preparing facilities for such entertainment, and training and conditioning persons and animals taking part in such entertainment. Professional entertaining jobs in all branches of the industry are included, but entertaining jobs in the production of motion pictures and radio and television broadcasts are included in the MOTION PICTURE INDUSTRY (motion picture) and the RADIO AND TELEVISION BROADCASTING INDUSTRY (radio-tv broad.). Jobs of a personal service character that typically occur in establisments primarily engaged in supplying amusement and recreation are included in PERSONAL SERVICE (personal ser.).

Accompanist 152.041-010
ACROBAT 159.247-010
Acrobatic Dancer 151.047-010
ACROBATIC RIGGER 962.684-010
ACTOR 150.047-010
Actress 150.047-010
ADVANCE AGENT 191.167-010
AERIALIST 159.247-014
amusement-equipment operator 342.663-010
AMUSEMENT PARK ENTERTAINER 159.647-010
AMUSEMENT PARK WORKER 349.664-010
animal caretaker 412.674-010
Animal Impersonator 159.047-018
ANIMAL KEEPER 412.674-010
ANIMAL KEEPER, HEAD 412.137-010
ANIMAL-NURSERY WORKER 412.674-014
ANIMAL-RIDE ATTENDANT 349.674-010
ANIMAL-RIDE MANAGER 349.224-010
ANIMAL TRAINER 159.224-010
ANNOUNCER 159.347-010
AQUARIST 449.674-010
aquarium tank attendant 449.674-010
AQUATIC PERFORMER 159.347-014
ARTIST AND REPERTOIRE MANAGER 159.167-010
artist consultant 191.117-010
Artists' Booking Representative 191.117-014
ARTIST'S MANAGER 191.117-010
artist's representative 191.117-010
ASTROLOGER 159.207-010
athletic coach 153.227-018
ATHLETIC TRAINER 153.224-010
Athletic Turf Worker 408.684-010
ATTENDANT, ARCADE 342.667-014
ATTENDANT, CAMPGROUND 329.683-010
audiovisual equipment operator 960.362-010
AUTOMOBILE RACER 153.243-010
Auto-Speedway Operator 342.663-010
Baccarat Dealer 343.464-010
Ballet Dancer 151.047-010
ball racker 340.477-010
Ballroom Dancer 151.047-010
Band Booker 191.117-014
Bareback Rider 159.344-010
BARKER 342.657-010
barker 353.363-010
Baseball Scout 153.117-018
Basketball Coach 153.227-010
Basketball Scout 153.117-018
Bat Boy/Girl 358.677-014
BEACH LIFEGUARD 379.364-014
Bear Keeper 412.674-010

Belly Dancer	151.047-010
Bet Taker	211.462-022
Bird Keeper	412.674-010
BOARD ATTENDANT	249.587-010
BOAT-RENTAL CLERK	295.467-014
boat-ride operator	342.667-010
Boat-Tank Attendant	342.667-010
BODY-MAKE-UP ARTIST	333.271-010
booker	191.117-014
bookie	187.167-014
booking agent	191.117-014
BOOKING MANAGER	191.117-014
BOOKMAKER	187.167-014
BOUNCER	376.667-010
business agent	191.117-018
BUSINESS MANAGER	191.117-018
CABANA ATTENDANT	349.677-010
CADDIE	341.677-010
CADDIE SUPERVISOR	341.137-010
Calliope Player	152.041-010
campground hand	329.683-010
card grader	343.687-010
CARD PLAYER	343.367-010
Card Reader	159.647-018
CARDROOM ATTENDANT I	343.467-010
CARDROOM ATTENDANT II	343.577-010
Caricaturist	149.041-010
carney	342.657-010
Cashier, Box Office	211.467-030
CASHIER, GAMBLING	211.462-022
Change-Booth Cashier	211.462-010
CHANGE PERSON	211.467-034
Character Actor	150.047-010
Character Actress	150.047-010
CHARTER	249.367-018
Charter-Boat Operator	911.663-010
CHILDREN'S ATTENDANT	349.677-018
children's zoo caretaker	412.674-014
chip	343.467-010
CHOREOGRAPHER	151.027-010
Chorus Dancer	151.047-010
cicerone	353.363-010
CIRCUS AGENT	191.117-022
CIRCUS LABORER	969.687-010
CIRCUS-TRAIN SUPERVISOR	910.137-018
CLERK-OF-SCALES	153.467-010
CLOCKER	153.367-010
CLOWN	159.047-010
Clubhouse Attendant	358.677-014
coach	153.227-010
Coach-Player	153.117-010
COACH, PROFESSIONAL ATHLETES	153.227-010
colors custodian	346.677-014
COMEDIAN	159.047-014
Comedy Diver	159.347-014
comic	159.047-014
COMMISSARY ASSISTANT	412.687-010
commissary helper	412.687-010
Company Manager	191.117-038
Concert Or Lecture Hall Manager	191.117-014
Contortionist	159.247-010
COUNSELOR, CAMP	159.124-010
Crystal Gazer	159.647-018
CUSTODIAN, ATHLETIC EQUIPMENT	969.367-010
DANCER	151.047-010
Defensive-Line Coach	153.227-010
DESK CLERK, BOWLING FLOOR	340.367-010
Detective, Bowling Alley	376.667-014
Dice Dealer	343.464-010
director, dance	151.027-010
DIRECTOR, FOOD AND BEVERAGE	187.167-210
DIRECTOR, STAGE	150.067-010
DIVER	349.247-010
dock attendant	342.667-010
Dramatic Reader	150.047-010
DRESSER	346.674-010
DRIVE-IN THEATER ATTENDANT	349.673-010
DRIVER, STARTING GATE	919.683-030
Drummer	152.041-010
DUDE WRANGLER	353.364-010
ELECTRIC-GOLF-CART REPAIRER	620.261-026
electrician, front	962.381-014
electrician, master	962.267-010
Elephant Keeper	412.674-010
ENTERTAINER	term

EQUESTRIAN	159.344-010
EXERCISER, HORSE	153.674-010
EXTRA	159.647-014
Fan-Mail Clerk	209.362-034
FEATURED PLAYER	term
Female Impersonator	159.047-018
Ferris-Wheel Operator	342.663-010
field attendant	349.673-010
field captain	153.267-018
Film Booker	191.117-014
Finish Judge	153.267-018
Fire Eater	159.647-010
FLAGGER	372.667-026
FLOOR ATTENDANT	343.467-014
Flume-Ride Operator	342.663-010
FLYER	962.687-018
food preparer	412.687-010
Football Coach	153.227-010
Football Scout	153.117-018
Fortune Teller	159.647-018
Fun-House Attendant	376.667-010
FUN-HOUSE OPERATOR	342.665-010
gambling broker	249.587-010
GAMBLING DEALER	343.464-010
GAMBLING MONITOR	343.367-014
GAME ATTENDANT	342.657-014
game operator	342.657-014
Gate Attendant	344.667-010
General Extra	159.647-014
GENERAL MANAGER, ROAD PRODUCTION	187.117-034
Goal Umpire	153.267-018
golf caddie	341.677-010
golf-cart mechanic	620.261-026
golf-course patroller	379.667-010
GOLF-COURSE RANGER	379.667-010
Golf-Course Starter	341.367-010
GOLF-RANGE ATTENDANT	341.683-010
GRIP	962.684-014
GROUP-SALES REPRESENTATIVE	259.357-010
Guard, Dance Hall	376.667-010
GUIDE, HUNTING AND FISHING	353.161-010
GUIDE, SIGHTSEEING	353.363-010
HANDICAPPER, HARNESS RACING	219.267-010
harness racer	153.244-014
Harpist	152.041-010
Head Animal Trainer	159.224-010
HEAD COACH	153.117-010
Head Scorer	153.387-014
HIGH RIGGER	962.664-010
high-wire artist	159.347-022
HOOF AND SHOE INSPECTOR	153.287-010
HORSE-RACE STARTER	153.267-010
HORSE-RACE TIMER	153.367-014
HOST/HOSTESS, DANCE HALL	349.667-010
HOST/HOSTESS, HEAD	349.667-014
house detective	376.667-010
Human Projectile	159.347-018
Hypnotist	159.647-010
Ice Guard, Skating Rink	376.667-010
ICE MAKER, SKATING RINK	969.687-014
IDENTIFIER, HORSE	153.387-010
imitator	159.047-018
IMPERSONATOR	159.047-018
Impresario	191.117-014
INFORMATION CLERK-CASHIER	249.467-010
Ingenue	150.047-010
INSTRUCTOR, PHYSICAL	153.227-014
INSTRUCTOR, SPORTS	153.227-018
Interpretative Dancer	151.047-010
JINRIKISHA DRIVER	349.477-010
JOCKEY	153.244-010
JOCKEY AGENT	191.117-026
JOCKEY-ROOM CUSTODIAN	346.667-010
JOCKEY VALET	346.677-010
judge	153.267-018
JUGGLER	159.341-010
Juvenile	150.047-010
keeper, head	412.137-010
KENNEL MANAGER, DOG TRACK	349.367-010
KENO WRITER	343.467-022
lap checker	153.387-014
LASERIST	159.042-010
LEAD PONY RIDER	153.674-014
LIFEGUARD	379.667-014
LIGHTING-EQUIPMENT OPERATOR	962.381-014

Line Umpire	153.267-018
MAGICIAN	159.041-010
MAKE-UP ARTIST	333.071-010
Male Impersonator	159.047-018
Mammal Keeper	412.674-010
MANAGER, AQUATIC FACILITY	187.167-054
MANAGER, ATHLETE	153.117-014
manager, athletic team	153.117-010
MANAGER, BOWLING ALLEY	187.167-222
Manager, Boxer	153.117-014
MANAGER, CAMP	329.161-010
MANAGER, CARDROOM	343.137-010
MANAGER, CASINO	187.167-070
Manager, Dance Floor	187.117-042
MANAGER, DUDE RANCH	187.167-094
manager, equipment	969.367-010
MANAGER, FISH-AND-GAME CLUB	187.167-102
MANAGER, GOLF CLUB	187.167-114
MANAGER, GUN CLUB	187.167-118
MANAGER, HANDICRAFT-OR-HOBBY SHOP	187.161-014
MANAGER, HOTEL RECREATIONAL FACILITIES	187.167-122
manager, house	187.167-154
Manager, Ice-Skating Rink	187.167-146
MANAGER, MARINA DRY DOCK	187.167-226
MANAGER, MUTUEL DEPARTMENT	187.167-134
MANAGER, POOL	153.137-010
manager, range	187.167-118
MANAGER, RECREATION ESTABLISHMENT	187.117-042
MANAGER, RECREATION FACILITY	187.167-230
Manager, Roller-Skating Rink	187.167-146
MANAGER, SKATING RINK	187.167-146
MANAGER, STAGE	159.167-018
MANAGER, THEATER	187.167-154
manager, theatrical production	191.117-038
manager, touring	191.117-038
MANAGER, TOURING PRODUCTION	191.117-038
MANAGER, WINTER SPORTS	187.167-166
Manager, Wrestler	153.117-014
MARSHALL	153.384-010
menagerie caretaker	412.674-010
Merry-Go-Round Operator	342.663-010
MIME	159.047-022
mimic	159.047-018
Mind Reader	159.647-018
MONEY COUNTER	211.467-014
money-room teller	211.467-014
Monkey Keeper	412.674-010
Monorail Operator	342.663-010
MOTION-PICTURE PROJECTIONIST	960.362-010
MOTORCYCLE RACER	153.243-014
MUSICIAN, INSTRUMENTAL	152.041-010
mutuel cashier	211.467-018
mutuel clerk	211.467-022
Narrator	139.167-010
Organ Grinder	159.647-010
Organist	152.041-010
PADDOCK JUDGE	153.167-010
Palmist	159.647-018
pantomimist	159.047-022
Parachutist	159.347-018
parimutuel cashier	211.467-018
parimutuel clerk	211.467-022
PARIMUTUEL-TICKET CASHIER	211.467-018
PARIMUTUEL-TICKET CHECKER	219.587-010
PARIMUTUEL-TICKET SELLER	211.467-022
Park Guard	372.667-034
PATROL JUDGE	153.267-014
PAYMASTER OF PURSES	211.367-010
peddler	291.457-022
performer see ENTERTAINER	
personal agent	191.117-010
personal manager	191.117-010
photo-finish photographer	143.382-014
PHOTOGRAPHER	143.457-010
PHOTOGRAPHER, FINISH	143.382-014
Photographic Double	961.364-010
Phrenologist	159.647-010
Physiognomist	159.647-010
Pianist	152.041-010
pit boss	153.167-014
Pitching Coach	153.227-010
PIT STEWARD	153.167-014
Placing Judge	153.267-014
PLASTIC-CARD GRADER, CARDROOM	343.687-010
plating inspector	153.287-010
Player-Manager	153.117-010
Pony-Ride Attendant	349.674-010
poolroom attendant	340.477-010
PRESS-BOX CUSTODIAN	344.677-010
process projectionist	960.362-010
PRODUCER	187.167-178
PROFESSIONAL ATHLETE	153.341-010
PROGRAM COORDINATOR	139.167-010
projectionist	960.362-010
promotor, group-ticket sales	259.357-010
PROMPTER	152.367-010
PROP ATTENDANT	962.684-022
PROPERTY COORDINATOR	962.167-018
PROP MAKER	962.281-010
proposition player	343.367-010
PSYCHIC READER	159.647-018
public-address announcer	159.347-010
public-relations player	343.367-010
PUPPETEER	159.041-014
QUICK SKETCH ARTIST	149.041-010
racing-board marker	249.587-010
RACING SECRETARY AND HANDICAPPER	153.167-018
RACKER	340.477-010
Railroad Operator	342.663-010
range master	187.167-118
RECEIVING-BARN CUSTODIAN	349.367-014
RECREATION-FACILITY ATTENDANT	341.367-010
referee	153.267-018
referee	153.167-014
rickshaw driver	349.477-010
RIDE ATTENDANT	342.677-010
RIDE OPERATOR	342.663-010
Riding Double	961.364-010
RIDING-SILKS CUSTODIAN	346.677-014
rigger	962.684-010
RING CONDUCTOR	159.367-010
Road Manager	191.117-038
RODEO PERFORMER	159.344-014
Roller-Coaster Operator	342.663-010
Roulette Dealer	343.464-010
scenic designer	142.061-050
SCOREBOARD OPERATOR	349.665-010
SCORER	153.387-014
SCOUT, PROFESSIONAL SPORTS	153.117-018
SECOND	346.677-018
Second-Ride-Fare Collector	211.467-030
Senior Animal Trainer	159.224-010
SET DESIGNER	142.061-050
SHEET WRITER	211.467-026
shill	343.367-010
Shooting Gallery Operator	342.657-014
SHOW GIRL	159.647-022
SHOW-HORSE DRIVER	159.344-018
Showplace Manager	191.117-014
Side-Show Entertainer	159.647-010
SIGHT-EFFECTS SPECIALIST	962.267-010
Silent Bit Extra	159.647-014
SILHOUETTE ARTIST	149.051-010
SINGER	152.047-022
SKATE-SHOP ATTENDANT	341.464-010
ski-lift operator	341.665-010
SKI PATROLLER	379.664-010
SKI-TOW OPERATOR	341.665-010
Snake Charmer	159.647-010
SNOWMAKER	969.685-010
SOUND CONTROLLER	194.262-014
Special Ability Extra	159.647-014
SPECIAL EFFECTS SPECIALIST	962.281-018
Speedboat Operator	342.663-010
spieler	353.363-010
spieler	342.657-010
Sports-Bookmaker	187.167-014
STAGE HAND	term
STAGE TECHNICIAN	962.261-014
stage technician see STAGE HAND	
stakes player	343.367-010
starter	153.267-010
STARTER	153.667-010
STEWARD, RACETRACK	153.117-022
Strip-Tease Dancer	151.047-010
STUNT PERFORMER	159.341-014
SULKY DRIVER	153.244-014
Superintendent, Circus	187.117-034
SUPERINTENDENT, GREENS	406.137-014
superintendent, menagerie	412.137-010

any industry

any industry—ANY INDUSTRY: This designation includes occupations that are not allocated to other classifications. The principal groups of jobs included under this designation are: (1) occupations that characteristically occur in practically all industries; (2) occupations that occur in a number of industries (which number is not exactly determinable) but that do not characteristically occur in most industries; and (3) occupations that are not considered to have any particular industrial attachment. The occupations included under this designation are considered to be essentially the same wherever they occur, in that they involve the same fundamental functions, and are performed for the same general purpose wherever they exist. Familiarity with a given job in one industry, however, may not permit a worker to transfer to the same job in another industry without some training period to acquaint the worker with the processes, terminology, hazards, or other factors in the industry to which he or she is being transferred that would affect the occupation in question in that industry. Many occupations that occur in various industries, and could logically fall within this group as defined above, are allocated to such classifications as CLERICAL AND KINDRED OCCUPATIONS (clerical); FOUNDRY (foundry); MACHINE SHOP (machine shop); PROFESSIONAL AND KINDRED OCCUPATIONS (profess. & kin.); and WOODWORKING (woodworking); all of which embrace occupations that cut across industry lines.

Band Tacker	787.685-042
Barber-Tool Sharpener	701.381-018
BARN BOSS	410.131-010
barnworker, groom	410.674-022
Barrel Filler, Head	920.132-010
barrel painter	599.685-070
Barrel Washer, Machine	529.685-074
Bar-Straightening-Machine Operator	613.662-022
Bar Tacker	787.685-042
Bass-Viol Repairer	730.281-050
BATTERY CHARGER	825.684-018
BATTERY REPAIRER	727.381-014
battery tester	727.381-014
bead blasting machine tender	503.685-042
Beading-Machine Operator I	617.482-014
Beading-Machine Operator II	619.685-046
beam-machine operator	699.682-022
Beer-Coil Cleaner	599.684-010
BELT REPAIRER	630.684-014
belt tender	921.685-026
bench assembler	706.684-022
BENCH GRINDER	705.684-010
bench inspector	609.684-010
bench-press operator	616.682-026
bench-press operator	690.685-014
bender, hand	709.684-090
Bending-Machine-Operator Helper	619.687-014
BENDING-MACHINE OPERATOR I	617.482-010
BENDING-MACHINE OPERATOR II	617.685-010
bending-press operator	617.260-010
bending-roll operator	619.362-014
bicycle mechanic	639.681-010
BICYCLE REPAIRER	639.681-010
BILLPOSTER	299.667-010
BINDER	787.682-010
binding-end stitcher	787.682-010
binding-machine operator	787.682-010
bit grinder	603.685-026
BIT SHARPENER	603.685-026
Blanking-Machine Operator	617.685-026
BLASTER	859.261-010
BLASTER HELPER	859.687-010
blender operator	680.685-082
Blister-Packing-Machine Tender	920.685-078
blocker	363.685-018
blower-room attendant	950.585-010
blue-line operator	979.682-014
blueprint assembler	920.687-038
BLUEPRINTING-MACHINE OPERATOR	979.682-014
blueprint maker	979.682-014
BLUEPRINT TRIMMER	920.687-038
body masker	749.687-018
Boiler Cleaner	891.687-022
boiler cleaner, chief	805.667-010
BOILER HOUSE INSPECTOR	805.667-010
BOILER HOUSE MECHANIC	805.361-010
boiler house operator	950.382-010
boiler house supervisor	950.131-014
boiler mechanic	805.361-010
BOILER OPERATOR	950.382-010
boiler operator	951.685-014
boiler-operator helper	950.685-014
boiler-room helper	699.687-018
BOILER-ROOM HELPER	950.685-014
Boiler-Shop Supervisor	809.130-014
boiler tender	951.685-010
Boiler-Tube Blower	891.687-030
Boiler-Tube Reamer	891.687-030
Bonderite Operator	599.382-010
bonding-machine operator	690.685-154
book mender	977.684-010
BOOK REPAIRER	977.684-010
BOOM-CONVEYOR OPERATOR	921.683-014
boss	899.133-010
boss see SUPERVISOR	
Bottle-Packing-Machine Cleaner	699.687-014
Bottle Washer, Machine I	529.685-074
Bottle Washer, Machine II	920.685-078
Bottling Supervisor	920.132-010
bowling-pin-machine mechanic	638.261-022
BOW MAKER	789.684-010
Bow Maker, Gift Wrapping	920.587-018
BOW REHAIRER	730.684-022
Bow Repairer	730.281-050
boxer	920.684-010

box labeler	652.682-010
box maker	669.682-058
Box Maker, Cardboard	920.587-018
BOX MAKER, PAPERBOARD	794.684-014
Box Maker, Wood	762.684-050
BOX PRINTER	652.682-010
box-printing-machine operator	652.682-010
Box Repairer	762.684-050
Box-Sealing-Machine Catcher	920.685-074
Box-Sealing-Machine Feeder	920.685-074
Box Wrapper	920.587-018
Brake Coupler, Dinkey	910.664-010
BRAKE HOLDER	932.664-010
Brake Machine Setter	616.360-022
Brake Operator, Heavy Duty	617.360-010
Brake-Operator Helper	619.687-014
BRAKE OPERATOR I	617.360-010
BRAKE OPERATOR II	619.685-026
Brake Operator, Sheet Metal I	617.360-010
Brake Operator, Sheet Metal II	619.685-026
Brasswind-Instrument Repairer	730.281-054
Bricklayer, Maintenance	861.381-018
Bridge Crane Operator	921.663-010
Brush Clearer, Surveying	869.567-010
BRUSHER	term
brusher	459.687-010
buckle-and-button maker	734.687-046
buck presser	363.682-018
Buffer, Chrome	705.684-014
Buffer, Copper	705.684-014
BUFFER I	705.684-014
Buffer II	705.687-014
Buffer, Nickel	705.684-014
BUFFING-AND-POLISHING-WHEEL REPAIRER	739.684-030
BUFFING-LINE SET-UP WORKER	603.360-010
BUFFING-MACHINE OPERATOR	603.382-010
BUFFING-MACHINE TENDER	603.665-010
buff-wheel fabricator	739.684-030
building-and-grounds supervisor	891.137-010
BUILDING CLEANER	891.684-022
Building-Maintenance Supervisor, Electrical	829.131-014
building-maintenance supervisor, mechanical	891.137-010
building repairer	899.381-010
building-service supervisor	187.167-190
building supervisor	891.137-010
bulk loader	921.667-018
BULLDOZER OPERATOR I	850.683-010
Bulldozer Operator II	617.260-010
bull-gang supervisor	899.133-010
bull riveter	800.662-010
Bundler	920.587-018
business-machine mechanic	633.281-018
business-machine-mechanic apprentice	633.281-022
BUTTON-AND-BUCKLE MAKER	734.687-046
Button-Attaching-Machine Operator	699.685-018
button bradder	699.685-018
button clamper	699.685-018
button riveter	699.685-018
BUZZSAW OPERATOR	667.685-026
BUZZSAW-OPERATOR HELPER	667.687-010
Cabinet-Abrasive Sandblaster	503.687-010
Cableway Operator	921.663-030
Cage Operator	921.663-030
Calculating-Machine Servicer	633.281-018
Camp Guard	372.667-034
camp-laundry operator	361.684-014
Can Supervisor	920.132-010
CANTEEN OPERATOR	311.674-010
CANVAS REPAIRER	782.684-010
Can Washer, Machine	529.685-074
cap-lining-machine operator	692.685-062
Capping-Machine Operator	920.685-078
CAR BLOCKER	860.684-018
CAR COOPER	910.687-014
card assembler	920.685-034
Cardboard Cutter	690.685-122
CARDER	920.685-034
carding-machine operator	920.685-034
Car Dumper	921.667-018
car-dumper operator	921.685-038
card writer, hand	970.281-022
caretaker, grounds	406.684-014
car filler	914.667-010
Car Loader	929.687-030
CARPENTER INSPECTOR	860.261-010

any industry

CARPENTER, MAINTENANCE	860.281-010
carpenter, packing	920.684-010
carpenter, repair	860.281-010
car rider	932.664-010
Cart Driver	919.664-010
carton catcher	921.686-014
Carton-Forming-Machine Adjuster	638.281-014
CARTON-FORMING-MACHINE HELPER	641.686-014
CARTON-FORMING-MACHINE OPERATOR	641.685-022
Carton-Gluing-Machine Operator	920.685-078
carton-lettering-machine operator	652.682-010
Carton Stapler	920.587-018
Carton Stenciler	920.687-178
car whacker	910.687-014
case maker	920.684-010
cash-register repairer	633.281-010
CASH-REGISTER SERVICER	633.281-010
CASTING REPAIRER	619.281-010
caulker	843.684-010
Ceiling Cleaner	381.687-018
Cellophane Sheeter	699.682-018
Cellophane Wrapper, Machine	920.685-078
cementer	795.687-014
cementer	780.684-062
Cement Mason, Maintenance	844.364-010
centrifugal-extractor operator	581.685-038
CERAMIC COATER, MACHINE	509.685-022
ceramic plater	509.685-022
chain-saw mechanic	625.281-030
CHANGE-HOUSE ATTENDANT	358.687-010
chaperon	187.167-186
CHAUFFEUR	913.663-010
check-and-transfer beader	509.687-014
CHECKROOM ATTENDANT	358.677-010
CHECKROOM CHIEF	358.137-010
chemical weigher	550.684-014
chief see SUPERVISOR	
chief clerk	169.167-034
chief engineer	959.131-010
chief technician	823.131-010
chief, vendor quality	012.167-062
child-care attendant	359.677-010
child-care leader	359.677-018
child-day-care center worker	359.677-018
chimney cleaner	891.687-010
CHIMNEY SWEEP	891.687-010
Chipper I	705.684-030
Chipper II	809.684-026
Chisel Grinder	603.664-010
CHRISTMAS-TREE CONTRACTOR	162.117-010
Chrome Cleaner	709.687-010
CIGARETTE-LIGHTER REPAIRER	709.684-034
Circular-Knife Cutter, Machine	781.684-014
Circular-Saw Filer	701.381-010
circular-shear operator	615.482-030
circulator	914.682-010
claims agent, right-of-way	191.117-046
Clamshell Operator I	921.663-058
Clamshell Operator II	921.663-062
CLAY MODELER	779.281-010
cleaner	599.684-010
cleaner	503.685-030
CLEANER AND POLISHER	709.687-010
cleaner, carpet and upholstery	389.664-010
CLEANER, COMMERCIAL OR INSTITUTIONAL	381.687-014
CLEANER, HOME RESTORATION SERVICE	389.664-010
CLEANER, HOUSEKEEPING	323.687-014
CLEANER I	master
CLEANER II	919.687-014
CLEANER III	911.687-014
CLEANER, INDUSTRIAL	381.687-018
CLEANER, LABORATORY EQUIPMENT	381.687-022
cleaner operator	503.362-010
cleaner operator	389.683-010
CLEANER, WALL	381.687-026
CLEANER, WINDOW	389.687-014
cleaning operator	891.687-010
clean-up worker	381.687-014
clean-up worker	381.687-018
clicker	699.682-022
clicker operator	699.682-022
clicking-machine operator	699.682-022
CLIPPER	789.687-030
clipper and turner	789.687-182
cloth-cutting-machine operator	781.684-014

Clothes-Drier Repairer	827.261-010
clothes wringer	581.685-038
cloth layer	781.687-058
CLOTH PRINTER	652.382-010
CLOTH-PRINTER HELPER	652.686-010
cloth spreader	781.687-058
Cloth Washer	361.685-018
coal-and-ash supervisor	921.137-010
Coal-Conveyor Operator	921.662-018
Coal Hauler	902.683-010
Coal Passer	929.687-030
Coal-Pulverizer Operator	544.582-010
COAL-YARD SUPERVISOR	921.137-010
Coat Checker	358.677-010
COATER OPERATOR	509.382-010
COATING-AND-BAKING OPERATOR	554.685-014
coating-machine operator	599.685-046
Coat Presser	363.682-018
Coffee-Maker Servicer	827.261-010
COIL SHAPER	724.684-022
coil spreader	724.684-022
COIL WINDER, REPAIR	724.381-014
Coin-Vault Guard	372.667-034
color buffer	705.684-014
color-mixer helper	550.687-018
color-shop helper	550.687-018
color weigher	550.684-014
COMMERCIAL DECORATOR	term
commercial decorator	298.381-010
COMMISSARY MANAGER	185.167-010
COMMUNICATIONS ELECTRICIAN SUPERVISOR	823.131-010
communication technician	828.261-022
Commutator Repairer	721.281-018
company laundry worker	361.684-014
company pilot	196.263-030
COMPARATOR OPERATOR	699.384-010
compressor engineer	950.685-010
compressor operator	950.685-010
Compressor Operator, Portable	950.685-010
computer-programmer, numerical control	007.167-018
Cone Spooler	681.685-154
consultant	199.251-010
Container Filler	920.587-018
Container-Maker-Filler-Packer Operator	920.685-078
container repairer	619.685-034
CONTAINER WASHER, MACHINE	529.685-074
continuous-dryout operator	503.362-010
continuous-dryout-operator helper	503.686-010
CONTRACT ADMINISTRATOR	162.117-014
Controlled-Area Checker	372.667-030
control-room operator	950.382-010
Convertible-Power-Shovel Operator	850.683-030
Conveyor-Belt Repairer	630.684-014
conveyor console operator	921.662-018
CONVEYOR FEEDER-OFFBEARER	921.686-014
CONVEYOR-MAINTENANCE MECHANIC	630.381-010
conveyor monitor	921.685-026
CONVEYOR-SYSTEM OPERATOR	921.662-018
CONVEYOR TENDER	921.685-026
COOK	315.361-010
Cook, Camp	315.361-010
Cook, Institution	315.361-010
cook, mess	315.361-010
cooler servicer	637.381-010
cooling-system operator	950.362-014
Coppersmith	804.281-010
copy-camera operator	976.361-010
COPYIST	152.267-010
corder	787.682-082
cording-machine operator	787.682-082
cordwood-cutter helper	667.687-010
CORE-DRILL OPERATOR	930.682-010
CORE-DRILL-OPERATOR HELPER	930.687-014
Cornice Upholsterer	780.381-018
corporation pilot	196.263-030
corral boss	410.131-010
cottage parent	187.167-186
COUPLE	term
coupler	932.664-010
covered button maker	734.687-046
craft supervisor	638.131-022
CRANE-CREW SUPERVISOR	921.133-010
crane engineer see CRANE OPERATOR	
crane follower	921.667-022
crane hooker	921.667-022

any industry

ELECTRICIAN, RADIO	823.281-014
ELECTRICIAN SUPERVISOR	829.131-014
Electrician Supervisor, Maintenance	829.131-014
electrician, telephone	822.281-018
Electric-Locomotive-Crane Operator	921.663-038
ELECTRIC-MOTOR ANALYST	721.261-010
ELECTRIC-MOTOR ASSEMBLER AND TESTER	721.281-014
ELECTRIC-MOTOR REPAIRER	721.281-018
ELECTRIC MOTOR REPAIRING SUPERVISOR	721.131-010
electric-organ technician	828.261-010
Electric-Power-Shovel Operator	850.683-030
Electric-Range Preparer	827.584-010
Electric-Range Servicer	827.261-010
Electric-Refrigerator Preparer	827.584-010
Electric-Refrigerator Servicer	827.261-010
ELECTRIC-SEALING-MACHINE OPERATOR	690.685-154
ELECTRIC-TOOL REPAIRER	729.281-022
Electric-Truck-Crane Operator	921.683-050
Electric-Truck Operator	921.683-050
Electrocardiograph Repairer	729.281-030
ELECTROLESS PLATER	505.684-010
Electrolytic De-Scaler	503.362-010
Electromagnet-Crane Operator I	921.663-058
Electromagnet-Crane Operator II	921.663-062
ELECTROMEDICAL-EQUIPMENT REPAIRER	729.281-030
electromedical service engineer	729.281-030
Electronic-Organ Installer	828.261-010
ELECTRONIC-ORGAN TECHNICIAN	828.261-010
electronic paint operator	599.682-010
Electronic-Piano Installer	828.261-010
ELECTRONICS ASSEMBLER, DEVELOPMENTAL	726.261-010
electronics-equipment mechanic	828.261-022
ELECTRONICS MECHANIC	828.261-022
ELECTRONICS-MECHANIC APPRENTICE	828.261-026
Electronics Mechanic, Computer	828.261-022
electronic-sound technician	823.261-010
electronics specialist	828.261-022
electronics-system mechanic	828.261-022
electronics technician	823.281-018
electronics technician	828.261-022
electronics-technician apprentice	828.261-026
ELECTRONICS TESTER	726.261-018
elevator dispatcher	388.367-010
ELEVATOR EXAMINER-AND-ADJUSTER	825.261-014
elevator inspector	825.261-014
elevator mechanic	825.281-030
ELEVATOR OPERATOR	388.663-010
ELEVATOR OPERATOR, FREIGHT	921.683-038
elevator operator, service	921.683-038
ELEVATOR REPAIRER	825.281-030
ELEVATOR-REPAIRER APPRENTICE	825.281-034
ELEVATOR-REPAIRER HELPER	825.684-014
elevator-repair mechanic	825.281-030
ELEVATOR STARTER	388.367-010
elevator supervisor	388.367-010
EMBOSSER	583.685-030
embossing-calender operator	583.685-030
embossing-machine operator	583.685-030
EMBOSSOGRAPH OPERATOR	652.682-014
EMBROIDERY-MACHINE OPERATOR	787.682-022
Enamel Dipper	599.685-026
Enamel Sprayer I	741.684-026
Enamel Sprayer II	741.687-018
engineering clerk	229.267-010
Engine-Room Cleaner	381.687-018
EQUAL OPPORTUNITY OFFICER	168.267-114
EQUIPMENT CLEANER	599.684-010
EQUIPMENT INSTALLER	828.381-010
equipment-service engineer	620.281-018
equipment washer	381.687-022
ESCORT	353.667-010
EVAPORATIVE-COOLER INSTALLER	637.381-010
EXCAVATOR	850.684-010
EXECUTIVE HOUSEKEEPER	187.167-046
EXECUTIVE PILOT	196.263-030
executive secretary	169.167-014
EXECUTIVE TRAINEE	term
exhaust tender	950.585-010
EXHIBIT-DISPLAY REPRESENTATIVE	297.367-010
EXPERIMENTAL ASSEMBLER	739.381-026
EXTERMINATOR HELPER	383.684-010
extractor	581.685-038
EXTRACTOR OPERATOR	581.685-038
EYELET-MACHINE OPERATOR	699.685-018
eyelet maker	699.685-018

eyelet riveter	699.685-018
eyeletter	699.685-018
fabricating-machine operator	616.380-018
FABRICATOR-ASSEMBLER, METAL PRODUCTS	809.381-010
FABRICATOR, FOAM RUBBER	780.684-062
Fabricator, Special Items	804.281-010
FACILITIES PLANNER	019.261-018
farmworker, animal	410.674-010
Fastener Attacher	699.685-018
FASTENER-SEWING-MACHINE OPERATOR	787.685-010
Field-Coil Enameler	599.685-030
Field-Coil Winder	724.381-014
FIELD CONTRACTOR	162.117-022
field supervisor	899.133-010
field technician	162.117-010
filer	701.381-014
Filler	920.587-018
filler-in tinter	970.381-022
Filling-Machine Operator	920.685-078
film cutter	979.681-022
FILTER OPERATOR	551.685-078
FILTER-PRESS OPERATOR	551.685-082
final-touch-up painter	749.684-038
Fine-Grade-Bulldozer Operator	850.683-010
finisher	781.687-070
finisher	705.687-014
finisher, hand	363.684-018
finisher, machine	363.682-018
finish inspector	741.687-010
finish repairer	749.684-038
fire-and-safety helper	739.687-094
fire-apparatus sprinkler inspector	379.687-010
FIRE-EQUIPMENT INSPECTOR	739.484-014
FIRE-EQUIPMENT-INSPECTOR HELPER	739.687-094
FIRE-EXTINGUISHER REPAIRER	709.384-010
FIRE-EXTINGUISHER-SPRINKLER INSPECTOR	379.687-010
FIRE FIGHTER	373.364-010
Firefighter, Marine	373.364-010
FIRE INSPECTOR	373.367-010
FIRE MARSHAL	373.167-018
firer	859.261-010
Firer, Automatic Stoker	951.685-010
firer, boiler	950.382-010
firer, boiler	951.685-010
FIRER, HIGH PRESSURE	951.685-010
Firer, Locomotive Crane	951.685-010
FIRER, LOW PRESSURE	951.685-014
Firer, Pile Driver	951.685-010
Firer, Portable Boiler	951.685-010
Firer, Powerhouse	951.685-010
Firer, Stationary Boiler	951.685-010
Firer, Steam Shovel	951.685-010
fire watcher	373.367-010
FIRST-AID ATTENDANT	354.677-010
Fishing-Tackle Repairer	732.684-122
FITTER HELPER	801.687-014
FITTER I	801.261-014
FITTER II	706.684-054
Fitter-Tacker	801.261-014
fixer	638.281-014
fixture relamper	389.687-018
FIXTURE REPAIRER-FABRICATOR	630.384-010
flame-spraying-machine operator, automatic	505.382-010
flame-spray operator	505.380-010
FLANGING-ROLL OPERATOR	619.362-010
flattening-machine operator	363.682-018
Float Builder	899.687-010
floating-labor-gang supervisor	899.133-010
Floor Cleaner	381.687-018
floor-press operator	616.682-010
floor worker	929.687-030
Flue Cleaner	891.687-030
FLUID-POWER MECHANIC	600.281-010
fluorescent lamp replacer	389.687-018
foam fabricator	780.684-062
Foil Cutter	699.685-014
folder inspector	789.587-014
FOLDER-SEAMER, AUTOMATIC	787.685-014
FOOD TESTER	029.361-014
Football-Pad Repairer	732.684-122
foreign agent	184.117-022
Fork-Lift-Truck Operator	921.683-050
FORMER, HAND	619.361-010
FORMER HELPER, HAND	619.684-010
forming-mill operator	616.685-042

Forming-Press Operator I	615.382-010
Forming-Press Operator II	615.685-030
Forming-Roll Operator, Heavy Duty	617.482-014
FORMING-ROLL OPERATOR I	617.482-014
FORMING-ROLL OPERATOR II	619.685-046
Four-Horse Hitch Driver	919.664-010
FOUR-SLIDE-MACHINE OPERATOR I	619.382-018
FOUR-SLIDE-MACHINE OPERATOR II	619.685-050
FOUR-SLIDE-MACHINE SETTER	616.380-014
Fractional-Horsepower Motor Repairer	721.281-018
frame builder, silk-screen	709.484-010
freighter	919.664-010
FRETTED-INSTRUMENT REPAIRER	730.281-026
FRONT-END LOADER OPERATOR	921.683-042
FUEL ATTENDANT	953.362-010
FUEL-INJECTION SERVICER	625.281-022
FUEL-SYSTEM-MAINTENANCE SUPERVISOR	638.131-010
FUEL-SYSTEM-MAINTENANCE WORKER	638.381-010
FURNACE CLEANER	891.687-014
FURNACE-INSTALLER-AND-REPAIRER HELPER, HOT AIR	869.687-030
FURNACE INSTALLER-AND-REPAIRER, HOT AIR	869.281-010
furnace repairer helper	869.687-030
furnace worker	869.281-010
FURNITURE UPHOLSTERER	780.381-018
FURNITURE-UPHOLSTERER APPRENTICE	780.381-022
galvanizer	503.685-030
gang leader see STRAW BOSS	
gang rider	932.664-010
Gantry Crane Operator	921.663-010
GARAGE SERVICER, INDUSTRIAL	915.687-014
gardener	406.684-014
garment finisher	782.684-058
GARMENT INSPECTOR	789.687-070
garment sewer, hand	782.684-058
GAS-APPLIANCE SERVICER	637.261-018
GAS-APPLIANCE-SERVICER HELPER	637.684-010
GAS-COMPRESSOR OPERATOR	950.382-014
GAS-ENGINE OPERATOR	950.382-018
Gas-Engine Operator, Compressors	950.382-018
Gas-Engine Operator, Generators	950.382-018
GAS-ENGINE REPAIRER	625.281-026
gas-fitter helper	637.684-010
gas-lift engineer	950.382-014
Gasoline-Dragline Operator	850.683-010
Gasoline-Locomotive-Crane Operator	921.663-038
Gasoline-Power-Shovel Operator	850.683-030
Gasoline-Tractor Operator	929.683-014
Gasoline-Truck-Crane Operator	921.663-062
Gasoline-Truck Operator	921.683-050
gas-pit specialist	638.381-010
Gas-Refrigerator Servicer	637.261-018
Gas-Stove Servicer	637.261-018
Gas-Stove-Servicer Helper	637.684-010
GAS TREATER	546.385-010
GAS-WELDING-EQUIPMENT MECHANIC	626.381-014
GATE GUARD	372.667-030
gatekeeper	372.667-030
Gate-Shear Operator I	615.685-034
Gate-Shear Operator II	615.682-018
gatherer	787.682-078
gauger	609.684-010
general-labor supervisor	899.133-010
general-maintenance helper	899.684-022
general manager, industrial organization	189.117-022
GENERAL SUPERVISOR	183.167-018
GILDER	749.381-010
GLASS CUTTER	775.684-022
GLASS-CUTTER HELPER	775.687-010
Glassine-Machine Tender	920.685-078
GLASS INSPECTOR	579.687-022
Glass Washer, Laboratory	381.687-022
GLUE MIXER	550.685-062
GLUER	795.687-014
gold charmer	749.381-010
gold-leaf gilder	749.381-010
gold-leaf printer	652.682-030
gold marker	652.682-030
gold stamper	652.682-030
grader operator	850.683-010
graduate tucker	787.682-082
GRAINER, MACHINE	652.686-014
greaser	699.687-018
greaser and oiler	699.687-018
grease remover	503.685-030

greenskeeper, head	406.137-010
GREENSKEEPER I	406.137-010
GREENSKEEPER II	406.683-010
Grinder, Belt	705.684-026
GRINDER-CHIPPER I	705.684-030
GRINDER-CHIPPER II	809.684-026
grinder-dresser	705.684-030
GRINDER I	705.684-026
Grinder II	705.684-030
Grinder III	701.381-018
Grinder IV	809.684-026
grinder, rough	809.684-026
Grinder, Wheel Or Disc	705.684-026
Gripper Attacher	699.685-018
grommet-machine operator	699.685-018
grommet maker	699.685-018
GROOVER	692.686-042
Grounds Guard, Arboretum	372.667-034
GROUNDSKEEPER, INDUSTRIAL-COMMERCIAL	406.684-014
group leader see STRAW BOSS	
GROUP LEADER see STRAW BOSS	term
group leader, river-and-harbor soundings	911.667-018
group supervisor, yard	899.133-010
guard	372.667-030
Guard, Captain	372.167-014
GUARD, CHIEF	372.167-014
Guard, Convoy	372.667-034
Guard, Lieutenant	372.167-014
GUARD, SECURITY	372.667-034
Guard, Sergeant	372.167-014
GUIDE, ESTABLISHMENT	353.367-014
GUIDE, PLANT	353.367-018
guide, tour	353.367-014
Guitar Repairer	730.281-026
GUNSMITH	632.281-010
gun striper	741.687-022
Handbill Distributor	230.687-010
hand clipper	781.687-070
Handle Attacher	690.685-014
hand luggage repairer	365.361-010
hand packager	920.587-018
hand painter	740.684-026
HAND STAMPER	709.684-042
hand stitcher	782.684-058
hand tacker	782.684-058
Harp Repairer	730.281-030
Hat Checker	358.677-010
hauler	919.664-010
head see STRAW BOSS	
heating-and-ventilating tender	950.585-010
heating-equipment repairer	805.361-010
HEATING-PLANT SUPERINTENDENT	959.131-010
heating worker	869.281-010
heat-seal operator	690.685-154
HELICOPTER PILOT	196.263-038
HELPER	master
helper, steel fabrication	619.686-022
HEMMER	787.682-026
hitcher	921.667-022
HOBBING-PRESS OPERATOR	617.682-018
HOISTING ENGINEER	921.663-030
hoisting-machine operator	921.663-030
hook-and-eye-sewing-machine operator	787.685-010
hooker	921.667-022
hook tender	921.260-010
Horse-And-Wagon Driver	919.664-010
Horse Tender	410.674-022
Hose Tender	899.664-010
HOST/HOSTESS	352.667-010
hostler	410.131-010
hostler	699.687-018
Hot-Sealing-Machine Operator	920.685-074
hot stamper	652.682-030
HOUSEHOLD-APPLIANCE INSTALLER	827.661-010
housekeeper	381.687-014
housekeeper, administrative	187.167-046
housekeeper, head	187.167-046
house manager	187.167-186
house parent	359.677-010
hydraulic-bull-riveter operator	800.662-010
hydraulic-press operator	617.260-010
HYDRAULIC REPAIRER	638.281-034
HYDRO-PNEUMATIC TESTER	862.687-018
Hydrostatic Tester	862.687-018
Ice Crusher	529.685-150

any industry

IMPERSONATOR, CHARACTER	299.647-010
IMPORT-EXPORT AGENT	184.117-022
IMPREGNATING-TANK OPERATOR	599.685-046
impregnating-tank operator	599.685-030
impregnator	599.685-026
Inclined-Railway Operator	921.663-030
Industrial-Locomotive Operator	910.363-018
INDUSTRIAL-SAFETY-AND-HEALTH TECHNICIAN	168.161-014
INDUSTRIAL-TRUCK OPERATOR	921.683-050
industrial x-ray operator	199.361-010
Industrial-Yard Brake Coupler	910.664-010
Inserter, Promotional Item	920.587-018
inserting-press operator	692.685-062
inspector and clipper	789.587-014
INSPECTOR, FABRIC	789.587-014
INSPECTOR, GENERAL	609.684-010
Inspector, Magnetic Particle	709.364-010
INSPECTOR, MAGNETIC PARTICLE AND PENETRANT	709.364-010
INSPECTOR, METAL FABRICATING	619.261-010
Inspector-Packager	920.587-018
Inspector, Penetrant	709.364-010
INSTRUCTOR, MACHINE	term
instrument maker	729.281-026
INSTRUMENT MAKER	600.280-010
INSTRUMENT-MAKER APPRENTICE	600.280-018
INSTRUMENT MECHANIC	710.281-026
instrument repairer	710.281-026
instrument repairer	729.281-026
INSTRUMENT REPAIRER	710.261-010
INSTRUMENT-REPAIRER HELPER	710.384-014
instrument repair supervisor	710.131-014
insulating-machine operator	599.685-046
insurance and risk manager	186.117-066
inter-com installer	829.281-022
inter-com servicer	829.281-022
investigator	376.367-014
ironer, hand	363.684-010
ironer, machine	363.682-018
ironworker apprentice, shop	619.361-018
Ironworker Helper, Shop	619.686-022
IRONWORKER-MACHINE OPERATOR	615.482-018
JANITOR	382.664-010
janitor	381.687-018
janitor	381.687-014
janitor, head	381.137-010
Japanner	740.684-022
jig fitter	801.261-014
JOURNEY WORKER	term
KETTLE TENDER	term
KEY CUTTER	709.684-050
key maker	709.684-050
keysmith	709.684-050
key worker	709.684-050
KICK-PRESS OPERATOR I	616.682-026
Kick-Press Operator II	690.685-014
kindergartner	359.677-026
Knife Grinder	603.664-010
LABEL CODER	920.587-014
labeler	920.687-126
Labeler, Machine	920.685-078
label marker	920.587-014
Label Sewer, Hand	782.684-058
label stamper	652.685-098
laboratory aide	381.687-022
laboratory assistant	381.687-022
laboratory helper	381.687-022
LABORATORY-SAMPLE CARRIER	922.687-054
LABORATORY TESTER	029.261-010
LABORATORY WORKER	term
LABORER, BRUSH CLEARING	459.687-010
laborer, building maintenance	381.687-014
laborer, golf course	406.683-010
LABORER, GRINDING AND POLISHING	705.687-014
LABORER, HOISTING	921.667-022
laborer, laboratory	381.687-022
LABORER, SALVAGE	929.687-022
LABORER, STORES	922.687-058
Laborer, Yard	929.687-030
Lacquer Sprayer I	741.684-026
Lacquer Sprayer II	741.687-018
lamination stacker, machine	692.682-054
larry-car operator	919.663-014
LAUNDRY WORKER I	361.684-014
LAUNDRY WORKER II	361.685-018
LAUNDRY WORKER III	369.387-010
lavatory attendant	358.677-018
Lawnmower Mechanic	625.281-034
layer up	781.685-010
Lay-Out Helper	801.687-014
Lay-Out Inspector	619.261-010
lay-out maker	809.381-014
Lay-Out Supervisor	619.130-030
LAY-OUT WORKER I	809.281-010
LAY-OUT WORKER II	809.381-014
leader see SUPERVISOR	
leader see GROUP LEADER	
lead janitor	381.137-010
leaf stamper	652.682-030
letterer	979.684-034
letterer	970.381-026
lettering-machine operator	652.682-030
Lidder	920.587-018
Lidding-Machine Operator	669.682-058
life-line attendant	899.664-010
light-bulb replacer	389.687-018
light cleaner	389.687-018
Light-Fixture Cleaner	381.687-014
LIGHT-FIXTURE SERVICER	389.687-018
LINE MAINTAINER	821.261-014
Line Maintainer, District	821.261-014
Liner Sheeter	699.682-018
line supply	929.687-030
lining-machine tender	692.685-062
Lipcoat Sprayer	741.687-018
liquid loader	914.667-010
LIVESTOCK-YARD ATTENDANT	410.674-018
load clerk	929.687-058
loader and unloader	929.687-030
loader-head operator	921.683-014
LOADER HELPER	914.687-014
LOADER I	914.667-010
Loader II	929.687-030
loader operator	921.683-042
lock expert	709.281-010
LOCKSMITH	709.281-010
LOCKSMITH APPRENTICE	709.281-014
LOCOMOTIVE-CRANE OPERATOR	921.663-038
Locomotive-Crane-Operator Helper	921.667-022
Locomotive Engineer, Gasoline	910.363-018
Locomotive-Engine Supervisor	910.137-022
Long-Haul-Sleeper Driver	904.383-010
Long-Line Teamster	919.664-010
lot boss	410.131-010
LUBRICATION-EQUIPMENT SERVICER	630.381-022
lubricator	699.687-018
LUGGAGE REPAIRER	365.361-010
Lumber Salvager	929.687-022
MACHINE ADJUSTER	term
machine-adjuster helper	638.684-018
machine brusher	699.687-014
MACHINE CLEANER	699.687-014
MACHINE FEEDER	699.686-010
MACHINE HELPER	619.687-014
machine hostler	699.687-018
machine-maintenance servicer	638.281-014
Machine-Operations Inspector	619.261-010
Machine-Operations Supervisor	619.130-030
machine-operator helper	699.587-010
MACHINE OPERATOR I	616.380-018
MACHINE OPERATOR II	619.685-062
machine operator, packaging	920.685-078
machine overhauler	638.281-014
machine repairer	638.281-014
MACHINE REPAIRER, MAINTENANCE	638.261-030
machine rubber	699.687-014
MACHINE SETTER	616.360-022
Machine Setter, Sheet Metal	616.360-022
machine sprayer	599.686-014
machine supervisor	619.130-030
MAGNETO REPAIRER	721.281-022
maid	323.687-014
Mail-Truck Driver	906.683-022
maintenance advisor	638.131-022
maintenance-and-utilities supervisor	899.131-018
maintenance associate	899.261-014
maintenance engineer	828.261-022
maintenance engineer	950.382-026
maintenance engineer	382.664-010
maintenance engineer, oil field	638.131-026
MAINTENANCE MECHANIC	638.281-014

any industry

oiler	921.667-022
oiler and greaser	699.687-018
Oil-Rag Washer	361.685-018
operating engineer	950.362-014
operating engineer	950.382-026
operating-engineer apprentice, stationary	950.382-030
operator, circuit	379.362-014
operator, direct wire	379.362-014
Orange-Peel Operator I	921.663-058
Orange-Peel Operator II	921.663-062
ORDER-DEPARTMENT SUPERVISOR	169.167-038
Order Filler	922.687-058
order picker	922.687-058
Organ Tuner, Electronic	828.261-010
ORIENTAL-RUG REPAIRER	782.381-014
ORIENTAL-RUG STRETCHER	580.687-018
Outside Trucker	929.687-030
Oven Stripper	929.687-030
Oven Unloader	929.687-030
overcasting-machine operator see SERGING-MACHINE OPERATOR	
overedge-machine operator see SERGING-MACHINE OPERATOR	
OVEREDGE SEWER	787.682-034
Overhead Cleaner	381.687-018
OVERHEAD CRANE OPERATOR	921.663-010
overlock-machine operator see SERGING-MACHINE OPERATOR	
overseaming-machine operator see SERGING-MACHINE OPERATOR	
overseer see SUPERVISOR	
overseer	899.133-010
OXIDIZED-FINISH PLATER	599.685-062
pacer see STRAW BOSS	
Package-Lift Operator	921.683-050
packager and strapper	929.687-058
PACKAGER, HAND	920.587-018
PACKAGER, MACHINE	920.685-078
PACKAGE SEALER, MACHINE	920.685-074
Packaging-Line Attendant	920.587-018
PACKAGING SUPERVISOR	920.132-010
Packer, Foamed-in-Place	920.587-018
Packing-Machine Tender	920.685-078
pack-train driver	919.687-022
Pad Attacher	795.687-014
Paint Cleaner	381.687-014
paint-coating-machine operator	599.685-046
Paint Dipper	599.685-026
PAINTER, AIRBRUSH	741.684-018
PAINTER, BRUSH	740.684-022
Painter, Drum	740.684-022
Painter, Electric Motor	741.687-018
PAINTER, ELECTROSTATIC	599.682-010
PAINTER, EMBOSSED OR IMPRESSED LETTERING	740.687-018
painter, hand	740.684-022
PAINTER, HAND	970.381-022
PAINTER HELPER, SIGN	970.664-010
PAINTER HELPER, SPRAY	741.687-014
Painter, Maintenance	840.381-010
painter, rough	741.687-018
PAINTER, SIGN	970.381-022
PAINTER, SPRAY I	741.684-026
PAINTER, SPRAY II	741.687-018
PAINTER, TOUCH-UP	749.684-038
PAINTER, TUMBLING BARREL	599.685-070
PAINTING-MACHINE OPERATOR	599.685-074
PAINT MIXER, HAND	550.684-018
PAINT MIXER, MACHINE	550.485-018
PAINT-SPRAYER OPERATOR, AUTOMATIC	599.382-010
paint-spraying-machine-operator helper	741.687-014
PAINT-SPRAY INSPECTOR	741.687-010
PALLETIZER OPERATOR I	921.682-014
Palletizer Operator II	920.685-078
Pamphlet Distributor	230.687-010
Panel-Instrument Repairer	710.281-026
Pants Presser	363.682-018
Paper Cutter	690.685-122
Paper Cutter, Hand	690.685-122
Paper Sheeter	699.682-018
PARTITION-ASSEMBLY-MACHINE OPERATOR	649.582-010
PARTS CATALOGER	229.267-010
parts data writer	229.267-010
parts inspector	609.684-010
parts mechanic	600.280-010
parts picker	922.687-058

PARTS SALVAGER	638.281-026
passenger agent	238.367-026
passenger-booking clerk	238.367-026
patcher	932.664-010
patrol guard	372.667-034
pattern cutter	775.684-022
pattern marker	781.384-014
pattern-punching-machine operator	781.684-058
PEN-AND-PENCIL REPAIRER	733.684-014
pencil striper	741.687-022
PERCUSSION-INSTRUMENT REPAIRER	730.381-042
permit agent	191.117-046
pest control worker helper	383.684-014
phone-circuit operator	193.262-034
photocopy operator	976.382-022
PHOTOGRAPHER HELPER	976.667-010
photolith operator	976.361-010
PHOTOSTAT OPERATOR	976.382-022
PHOTOSTAT-OPERATOR HELPER	979.687-014
PIANO TECHNICIAN	730.281-038
PIANO TUNER	730.361-010
PICKING-MACHINE OPERATOR	680.685-082
pickler	503.685-030
PICKLER, CONTINUOUS PICKLING LINE	503.362-010
PICKLER HELPER, CONTINUOUS PICKLING LINE	503.686-010
pickler operator	503.362-010
pickling operator	503.685-030
pickling-tank operator	503.685-030
PILOT, SUBMERSIBLE	029.383-010
Pin Inserter	920.685-034
PINSETTER MECHANIC, AUTOMATIC	638.261-022
PINSETTER-MECHANIC HELPER	829.667-014
Pin-Ticket-Machine Operator	652.685-098
Pipe Fitter, Maintenance	862.281-022
Pipe-Fitter Supervisor, Maintenance	862.131-010
PIPE-ORGAN TUNER AND REPAIRER	730.361-014
PITCH FILLER	619.687-018
Pit-Worker, Power Shovel	921.667-022
plain-goods hemmer	787.682-026
plant-maintenance worker	899.261-014
Plant-Protection Supervisor	372.167-014
plant superintendent, industrial organization	189.117-022
plant supervisor	183.117-014
plant tour guide	353.367-018
plastic-welding-machine operator	690.685-154
Plate-And-Frame-Filter Operator	551.685-082
plate-and-weld inspector	619.261-010
plater helper	599.685-062
Plate Roller	613.662-022
plate-shear operator	615.682-018
plate-shop helper	619.686-022
plate-shop inspector	619.261-010
plate stacker, machine	692.682-054
plate-worker helper	801.687-014
Platform Loader	929.687-030
Platform Supervisor	922.137-018
PLAYROOM ATTENDANT	359.677-026
pleater	787.682-082
PLEATING-MACHINE OPERATOR	583.685-082
Plumber, Maintenance	862.381-030
pneumatic-press operator see AIR-PRESS OPERATOR	
Pneumatic Tester	862.687-018
PNEUMATIC-TOOL REPAIRER	630.281-010
PNEUMATIC-TUBE REPAIRER	630.281-014
POLISHER	705.684-058
Polisher, Aluminum	705.684-058
Polisher And Buffer I	705.684-014
POLISHER AND BUFFER II	705.684-062
POLISHER APPRENTICE	705.684-066
Polisher, Brass	705.684-058
Polisher, Bronze	705.684-058
Polisher, Zinc	705.684-058
POLISHING-MACHINE OPERATOR	603.682-026
POLISHING-MACHINE-OPERATOR HELPER	603.686-010
polishing-wheel repairer	739.684-030
POLISHING-WHEEL SETTER	776.684-014
pool servicer	891.684-018
PORCELAIN-ENAMELING SUPERVISOR	590.131-010
PORCELAIN-ENAMEL LABORER	509.687-014
PORCELAIN-ENAMEL REPAIRER	741.684-030
Porcelain-Enamel Sprayer	741.684-026
Porcelain Slusher	599.685-026
portable grinder operator	705.684-010
porter	381.687-014
porter, head	381.137-010

powder carrier	859.687-010
power-brake operator	617.360-010
power-cleaner operator	389.683-010
powerhouse oiler	950.685-014
power-nut-runner operator	699.685-026
power-plant operator	950.382-026
power-plant-operator apprentice	950.382-030
power-press operator	699.682-022
POWER-PRESS OPERATOR	term
POWER-PRESS TENDER	617.685-026
POWER-SAW MECHANIC	625.281-030
POWER-SCREWDRIVER OPERATOR	699.685-026
power-shear operator	615.682-018
power-shear operator	615.685-034
POWER-SHOVEL OPERATOR	850.683-030
Power-Shovel-Operator Helper	921.667-022
Power-Sweeper Operator	919.683-022
power-tool repairer	729.281-022
power washer	503.685-030
precision-instrument and tool maker	600.280-010
precision-mechanical-instrument maker	600.280-010
precision-mechanical-instrument-maker apprentice	600.280-018
PRESIDENT	189.117-026
press-brake operator	619.685-026
press-brake operator	617.360-010
PRESS BUCKER	920.686-042
PRESSER, FORM	363.685-018
PRESSER, HAND	363.684-018
PRESSER, MACHINE	363.682-018
pressing-machine operator	363.685-018
pressing machine operator	363.682-018
press operator	920.685-010
PRESS OPERATOR, HEAVY DUTY	617.260-010
PREVENTIVE MAINTENANCE COORDINATOR	169.167-074
primary-crusher operator	570.685-022
principal see SUPERVISOR	
print applier	749.684-010
printer	652.382-010
printing-machine operator	652.382-010
private pilot	196.263-030
processor	012.167-074
process supervisor	183.167-018
process treater	503.685-030
Product-Development Worker	804.281-010
production helper	619.686-022
PRODUCTION SUPERINTENDENT	183.117-014
PRODUCTION SUPERVISOR	699.130-010
production supervisor	183.167-018
programmer, numerical control	007.167-018
PROJECT-CREW WORKER	891.687-018
projectionist	960.382-010
PROPERTY-DISPOSAL OFFICER	163.167-026
PROSPECTOR	024.284-010
protection chief, industrial plant	189.167-050
PROTECTIVE-SIGNAL OPERATOR	379.362-014
prototype assembler, electronics	726.261-010
PUBLIC-ADDRESS SERVICER	823.261-010
public-address-system operator	823.261-010
pump-and-tank servicer	620.281-018
PUMPER	914.682-010
PUMPER HELPER	914.687-018
PUMP INSTALLER	630.684-018
pump-machine operator	914.682-010
pump operator	914.682-010
pump repairer	630.281-018
pump runner	914.682-010
PUMP SERVICER	630.281-018
PUMP-SERVICER HELPER	630.684-022
PUMP-SERVICER SUPERVISOR	630.131-010
pump tender	914.682-010
Punch-Press Feeder	699.686-010
Punch-Press Offbearer	699.686-010
PUNCH-PRESS OPERATOR, AUTOMATIC	615.482-026
Punch-Press-Operator Helper	619.687-014
PUNCH-PRESS OPERATOR I	615.382-010
PUNCH-PRESS OPERATOR II	615.685-030
PUNCH-PRESS OPERATOR III	615.682-014
Punch-Press Operator IV	617.685-026
PUNCH-PRESS SETTER	619.380-014
Punch-Press Supervisor	619.130-030
pusher see STRAW BOSS	
PUTTY GLAZER	749.684-042
quality-control-assembly-test technician	726.261-018
Racker	929.687-030
RACKER, SILK-SCREEN PRINTING	659.687-014
Radar Mechanic	828.261-022
radio-communications mechanician	823.281-014
RADIOGRAPHER	199.361-010
RADIO MECHANIC	823.281-018
radio mechanic	823.281-014
radiophone operator	193.262-034
RADIO REPAIRER	720.281-010
Radio Repairer, Domestic	720.281-010
Radiotelegraph Operator-Servicer	823.281-014
RADIOTELEPHONE OPERATOR	193.262-034
radiotelephone-technical operator	193.262-034
Rag Sorter	929.687-022
railroad-crane operator	921.663-038
rapid-extractor operator	581.685-038
receiver, bulk system	921.685-026
receptionist	352.667-010
Reciprocating-Drill Operator	850.683-034
reclaimer	929.687-022
RECTIFICATION PRINTER	976.682-018
redistribution-and-marketing officer	163.167-026
REFRIGERATING ENGINEER	950.362-014
REFRIGERATING ENGINEER, HEAD	950.131-010
REFRIGERATION MECHANIC	637.261-026
REFRIGERATION-MECHANIC HELPER	637.687-014
refrigeration operator, head	950.131-010
refrigeration supervisor	950.131-010
Refrigeration-System Installer	637.261-026
RELIEF-MAP MODELER	777.381-042
repairer	632.281-010
REPAIRER, ART OBJECTS	779.381-018
REPAIRER, FINISHED METAL	809.684-034
repair helper	638.684-018
repair mechanic	638.281-014
REPRODUCTION TECHNICIAN	976.361-010
RESEARCH SUBJECT	359.677-030
reservation clerk	238.367-026
RESIDENCE SUPERVISOR	187.167-186
RESTROOM ATTENDANT	358.677-018
retoucher	740.684-026
rewinder	699.587-010
rewinder-operator helper	699.587-010
RIGGER	921.260-010
RIGGER HELPER	921.687-026
RIGHT-OF-WAY AGENT	191.117-046
RIGHT-OF-WAY SUPERVISOR	191.117-050
ring-shear operator	615.482-030
rip-machine operator	699.682-030
RISK AND INSURANCE MANAGER	186.117-066
rivet bucker	800.687-010
rivet catcher	800.687-010
RIVETER, HAND	709.684-066
RIVETER HELPER	800.687-010
RIVETER, HYDRAULIC	800.662-010
RIVETER, PNEUMATIC	800.684-014
Riveter, Portable Machine	800.662-010
RIVETER, PORTABLE PINCH	800.682-010
RIVETING-MACHINE OPERATOR I	699.482-010
RIVETING-MACHINE OPERATOR II	699.685-030
Rivet Spinner	699.685-030
rivet sticker	800.687-010
Rod-Bending-Machine Operator I	617.482-010
Rod-Bending-Machine Operator II	617.685-010
Rod-Mill Operator	599.685-058
roll attendant	570.685-022
roll-cutting operator	699.682-030
roller embosser	583.685-030
ROLLER-SKATE REPAIRER	732.684-102
roll former	619.362-014
ROLL-FORMING-MACHINE OPERATOR I	617.482-018
ROLL-FORMING-MACHINE OPERATOR II	617.685-034
ROLL-FORMING-MACHINE SET-UP MECHANIC	613.360-010
Roll-Forming Supervisor	619.130-030
Rolling-Machine Operator, Automatic	619.685-082
roll-mill operator	616.685-042
Roll-Operator Helper	619.687-014
ROLL OPERATOR I	619.362-014
ROLL OPERATOR II	term
Roll Operator, Sheet Metal	619.362-014
rope rider	932.664-010
Rotary-Rock-Drilling-Machine Operator	850.683-034
ROTARY-SHEAR OPERATOR	615.482-030
rotor-and-armature bander	724.684-010

any industry

ROUTER OPERATOR	605.382-034
RUBBER-GOODS REPAIRER	759.684-054
RUBBERIZING MECHANIC	630.281-030
ruching-machine operator	787.682-082
ruffler	787.682-078
rug stretcher	580.687-010
sack mender	782.687-046
SACK REPAIRER	782.687-046
Sack Sewer, Hand	920.587-018
Sack Sewer, Machine	920.685-078
Sack Sorter	929.687-022
Sack Stenciler	920.687-178
SAFETY INSPECTOR	168.264-014
safety technician	168.264-014
sales promotion director	164.117-010
SALES-SERVICE PROMOTER	165.167-010
salvage diver	379.384-010
salvage painter	740.684-026
salvager	929.687-022
Sample Distributor	230.687-010
sample gatherer	922.687-054
Sample Mounter	795.687-014
sampler	922.687-054
SAMPLE WORKER	920.687-154
SANDBLASTER	503.687-010
SANDBLAST-OR-SHOTBLAST-EQUIPMENT TENDER	503.685-042
SANDWICH-BOARD CARRIER	299.687-014
SANITARIAN	529.137-014
sanitation supervisor	529.137-014
sanitor	381.687-018
Santa Claus	299.647-010
Santa's Helper	299.647-010
SAW FILER	701.381-014
SCALE MECHANIC	633.281-026
Scarifier Operator	850.683-030
Scissors Grinder	701.381-018
Scrap Burner	929.687-022
SCRAP HANDLER	509.685-050
Scrap-Shear Operator	615.685-034
Scrap Sorter	929.687-022
screener	979.684-034
SCREENER OPERATOR	599.685-082
SCREEN MAKER, PHOTOGRAPHIC PROCESS	979.384-010
SCREEN PRINTER	979.684-034
screen printer	979.685-010
SCREEN PRINTER HELPER	979.687-022
scrubber	381.687-014
scrubber	381.687-018
scrubber-system attendant	950.585-010
Scrubbing-Machine Operator	381.687-014
SCUBA DIVER	379.384-010
section chief see SUPERVISOR	
section leader see SUPERVISOR	
security manager	189.167-050
SECURITY OFFICER	189.167-034
semi-truck driver	904.383-010
separator-machine operator	599.685-082
serger see SERGING-MACHINE OPERATOR	
SERGING-MACHINE OPERATOR	term
SERGING-MACHINE OPERATOR, AUTOMATIC	787.685-030
service-car operator	388.663-010
servicer	929.687-030
SERVICE SUPERVISOR, LEASED MACHINERY AND EQUIPMENT	183.167-030
service worker see MAINTENANCE WORKER	
set rider	932.664-010
Setter, Automatic-Spinning-And-Beading-Lathe	604.360-010
SETTER, AUTOMATIC-SPINNING LATHE	604.360-010
setter-up, silk-screen frame	709.484-010
SET-UP MECHANIC, CROWN ASSEMBLY MACHINE	692.362-010
SEWER, HAND	782.684-058
sewing-machine adjuster	639.281-018
SEWING-MACHINE OPERATOR	787.682-046
SEWING-MACHINE OPERATOR, AUTOMATIC	master
SEWING-MACHINE OPERATOR, REGULAR EQUIPMENT	master
SEWING-MACHINE REPAIRER	639.281-018
SEWING-MACHINE-REPAIRER HELPER	639.684-010
SEWING SUPERVISOR	787.132-010
shadowgraph operator	699.384-010
Shafting Cleaner	699.687-014
shearer	699.685-014
Shear Operator, Automatic I	615.682-018
Shear Operator, Automatic II	699.686-010
Shear-Operator Helper	619.687-014

SHEAR OPERATOR I	615.682-018
SHEAR OPERATOR II	615.685-034
SHEAR SETTER	615.380-010
sheeter operator	699.682-018
Sheet-Metal-Fabricating-Machine Operator	616.380-
Sheet-Metal Installer	804.281-010
Sheet-Metal Lay-Out Worker	809.381-010
sheet-metal mechanic	804.281-010
Sheet-Metal Production Worker	619.685-062
Sheet-Metal-Shop Helper	619.686-022
Sheet-Metal-Shop Supervisor	809.130-014
SHEET-METAL WORKER	804.281-010
SHEET-METAL-WORKER APPRENTICE	804.281-014
Sheet-Metal Worker, Maintenance	804.281-010
SHIRRING-MACHINE OPERATOR	787.682-078
shooter	859.261-010
shooter's helper	859.687-010
Shop Mechanic	804.281-010
SHOP STEWARD	term
shop supervisor	638.131-026
shop supervisor	809.130-014
Shotblaster	503.687-010
shot-blast tender	503.685-042
shot-core-drill operator	930.682-010
shot-core-drill-operator helper	930.687-014
Shot-Peen Operator	503.685-042
show-card writer	970.281-022
shower room attendant	358.687-010
shredder	680.685-082
signaler	921.667-022
signal timer	379.362-014
sign poster	299.667-010
sign printer	659.682-026
SIGN WRITER, HAND	970.281-022
SIGN WRITER, MACHINE	659.682-026
SILK-SCREEN CUTTER	979.681-022
SILK-SCREEN-FRAME ASSEMBLER	709.484-010
Silk-Screen-Layout Drafter	979.681-022
silk-screen maker	979.681-022
silk-screen operator	979.684-034
silk-screen painter	979.684-034
SILK-SCREEN PRINTER, MACHINE	979.685-010
SILK-SCREEN REPAIRER	979.684-038
siphoner	914.682-010
Six-Horse Hitch Driver	919.664-010
sizing-machine operator	599.685-046
SKEIN-WINDING OPERATOR	559.687-054
Skimmer-Scoop Operator	850.683-030
skinner	919.664-010
Skip-Hoist Operator	921.663-030
sleeve machine operator	652.682-010
slide-forming-machine operator	619.382-018
slide-forming-machine tender	619.685-050
slinger	921.260-010
slitter-and-rewinder	699.587-010
slitter-and-rewinder-machine operator	699.682-030
slitter helper	699.587-010
slitter sheeter operator	699.682-018
SLITTING-MACHINE-OPERATOR HELPER I	699.587-010
Slitting-Machine-Operator Helper II	619.687-014
SLITTING-MACHINE OPERATOR I	699.682-030
SLITTING-MACHINE OPERATOR II	615.662-010
sludge-filter operator	551.685-078
slusher	741.684-030
small-appliance repairer	723.381-010
SMALL-ENGINE MECHANIC	625.281-034
SMOKING-PIPE REPAIRER	739.484-018
Snap Attacher	699.685-018
Snap-Fastener-Machine Operator	699.685-018
SOLAR-ENERGY-SYSTEM INSTALLER	637.261-030
SOLAR-ENERGY-SYSTEM-INSTALLER HELPER	637.687-010
Solder Sprayer	505.684-014
SOUNDER	911.667-018
SOUND TECHNICIAN	829.281-022
Sound-Truck Operator	823.261-010
SPECIAL-DELIVERY DRIVER	term
Special-Lining Applier	741.687-018
special police officer	372.667-034
SPINNER, HAND	619.362-018
SPINNER, HYDRAULIC	619.362-022
spinning-lathe operator	619.362-018
SPINNING-LATHE OPERATOR, AUTOMATIC	619.685-082
spinning-lathe-operator, hydraulic	619.362-022
splitter operator	699.682-030
SPORTS-EQUIPMENT REPAIRER	732.684-122

Spot Cutter	699.682-018
spot-machine operator	692.685-062
spot sprayer	749.684-038
Spotter	215.362-022
Spout Positioner	921.667-018
Spray Blender	550.684-018
sprayer	505.685-014
sprayer helper	741.687-014
spray-gun operator	741.684-026
SPRAY-GUN REPAIRER	630.381-026
SPRAY-GUN-REPAIRER HELPER	630.684-034
spray-machine operator	599.382-010
spray-machine operator	599.685-074
SPRAY-PAINTING-MACHINE OPERATOR	741.685-010
SPRAY-UNIT FEEDER	599.686-014
SPREADER I	781.687-058
SPREADER II	term
SPREADER, MACHINE	781.685-010
Sprinkler-Truck Driver	906.683-022
Square-Shear Operator I	615.682-018
Square-Shear Operator II	615.685-034
STABLE ATTENDANT	410.674-022
stable manager	410.131-010
stacker	929.687-030
stacker attendant	921.683-014
Stacker Operator	921.683-014
STACKING-MACHINE OPERATOR I	692.682-054
STACKING-MACHINE OPERATOR II	739.685-038
Staker, Surveying	869.567-010
stamper	920.687-126
Stamper	920.587-018
stamper	652.682-030
STAMPING-PRESS OPERATOR	652.682-030
Stamping-Press Operator	617.685-026
STAPLING-MACHINE OPERATOR	692.685-202
starter	388.367-010
STATIC BALANCER	724.384-014
STATIONARY ENGINEER	950.382-026
STATIONARY-ENGINEER APPRENTICE	950.382-030
stationary engineer, refrigeration	950.362-014
STATIONARY-ENGINEER SUPERVISOR	950.131-014
station mechanic	805.361-010
station mechanic	823.281-014
station supervisor	950.131-014
STATISTICAL-MACHINE SERVICER	633.281-030
Stator Repairer	721.281-018
Steam-Fitter Supervisor, Maintenance	862.131-010
steam flattener	363.682-018
steam-power-plant operator	950.382-010
steam presser	363.682-018
steam-press operator	363.682-018
steam-station supervisor	950.131-014
steel fabricating supervisor	809.130-014
STEEL-PLATE CAULKER	843.684-010
stencil cutter	979.681-022
Stencil Cutter, Machine	920.685-078
STENCILER	920.687-178
STILL OPERATOR	term
STILL TENDER	552.685-026
stock selector	922.687-058
stock supervisor	921.133-018
stoker	951.685-010
STOKER ERECTOR-AND-SERVICER	637.281-014
stoker-installation mechanic	637.281-014
storage-battery charger	727.381-014
storekeeper	184.167-114
STOVE REFINISHER	749.684-046
straddle buggy operator	921.683-070
STRADDLE-TRUCK OPERATOR	921.683-070
straight cutter	699.685-014
straight cutter	775.684-022
straightener	617.482-026
STRAIGHTENER, HAND	709.484-014
straightener, torch	709.684-086
Straightening-Machine Feeder	699.686-010
straightening-machine operator	613.662-022
Straightening-Press-Operator Helper	619.687-014
Straightening-Press Operator I	615.382-010
STRAIGHTENING-PRESS OPERATOR II	617.482-026
STRAIGHTENING-ROLL OPERATOR	613.662-022
Straight-Knife Cutter, Machine	781.684-014
STRAW BOSS	term
Stretching-Press Operator	615.382-010
Stretch-Press Operator	617.260-010
strip cleaner	503.362-010
STRIPER, HAND	740.484-010
STRIPER, SPRAY GUN	741.687-022
STRIPPER	term
structural inspector	619.261-010
structural-metal-fabricator apprentice	619.361-018
structural-shop helper	619.686-022
Structural-Steel Lay-Out Worker	809.281-010
Structural-Steel-Shop Supervisor	809.130-014
subject, scientific research	359.677-030
submarine worker	899.261-010
superintendent	189.167-022
superintendent, automotive	184.167-226
SUPERINTENDENT, BUILDING	187.167-190
superintendent, building	382.664-010
SUPERINTENDENT, COLD STORAGE	184.167-142
superintendent, factory	183.117-014
superintendent, general	183.117-014
superintendent, institution	187.117-018
SUPERINTENDENT, LABOR UTILIZATION	189.167-042
SUPERINTENDENT, MAINTENANCE	189.167-046
superintendent, mill	183.117-014
superintendent, plant	183.117-014
SUPERINTENDENT, PLANT PROTECTION	189.167-050
superintendent, service establishment see MANAGER	
SERVICE ESTABLISHMENT	
superintendent, storage area	184.167-114
SUPERINTENDENT, TRANSPORTATION	184.167-226
superintendent, warehouse	184.167-114
SUPERVISOR	master
SUPERVISOR, AIR-CONDITIONING INSTALLER	827.131-018
SUPERVISOR, BLUEPRINTING-AND-PHOTOCOPY	979.130-010
SUPERVISOR, BOILER REPAIR	805.131-010
supervisor, building maintenance	381.137-010
supervisor, coal handling	921.137-010
SUPERVISOR, CUTTING DEPARTMENT	781.134-010
SUPERVISOR, ELECTRONICS SYSTEMS	
MAINTENANCE	828.161-010
SUPERVISOR, FITTING	801.131-014
SUPERVISOR, GRINDING	603.130-010
SUPERVISOR, HOME RESTORATION SERVICE	389.137-010
SUPERVISOR, INSTRUMENT MAINTENANCE	710.131-014
SUPERVISOR, INSTRUMENT REPAIR	710.131-022
SUPERVISOR, JANITORIAL SERVICES	381.137-010
SUPERVISOR, LABOR GANG	899.133-010
SUPERVISOR, LINE	619.130-030
SUPERVISOR, LIVESTOCK-YARD	410.134-010
SUPERVISOR, LOADING AND UNLOADING	922.137-018
Supervisor, Loading	922.137-018
SUPERVISOR, LUBRICATION	699.131-010
SUPERVISOR, MACHINE SETTER	619.130-034
SUPERVISOR, METAL FABRICATING	809.130-014
SUPERVISOR, METALIZING	505.130-010
SUPERVISOR, NETWORK CONTROL OPERATORS	031.132-010
SUPERVISOR OF COMMUNICATIONS	184.167-230
SUPERVISOR, PACKING AND WRAPPING	920.137-026
SUPERVISOR, PAINT DEPARTMENT	749.131-014
supervisor, permits, easements, and right-of-way	191.117-050
Supervisor, Photostat	979.130-010
SUPERVISOR, SHEARING	615.132-010
SUPERVISOR, SILK-SCREEN CUTTING AND PRINTING	979.131-018
Supervisor, Unloading	922.137-018
SUPERVISOR, UPHOLSTERY DEPARTMENT	780.131-014
SUPERVISOR, VACUUM METALIZING	505.130-014
SUPERVISOR, VENDOR QUALITY	012.167-062
SUPPLIES PACKER	919.687-022
surplus-property disposal agent	163.167-026
surplus sales officer	163.167-026
SURVEYOR HELPER	869.567-010
Surveyor Helper, Chain	869.567-010
Surveyor Helper, Rod	869.567-010
swamper	459.687-010
swamper	932.664-010
sweeper	381.687-018
sweeper	381.687-014
SWEEPER-CLEANER, INDUSTRIAL	389.683-010
SWIMMING-POOL SERVICER	891.684-018
Table Worker	920.587-018
table worker, sewing	782.684-058
TACKING-MACHINE OPERATOR	787.685-042
tail-end rider	932.664-010
tank-car loader	914.667-010
TANK CLEANER	891.687-022
Tank-Shop Supervisor	809.130-014
taper	787.682-010
taper	749.687-018

any industry

TAPE-RECORDER REPAIRER	720.281-014
team driver	919.664-010
TEAMSTER	919.664-010
technical release analyst	229.267-010
technician, test systems	726.261-018
telemarketer	299.357-014
telephone sales representative	299.357-014
TELEPHONE SOLICITOR	299.357-014
TELEVISION-AND-RADIO REPAIRER	720.281-018
TELEVISION INSTALLER	823.361-010
television repairer	720.281-018
Template Inspector	619.261-010
TEMPLATE MAKER	601.381-038
TEMPLATE MAKER, TRACK	809.484-014
Tennis-Racket Repairer	732.684-122
test-bore helper	930.687-014
test borer	930.682-010
TESTER, FOOD PRODUCTS	199.251-010
tester helper	381.687-022
tester, systems	726.261-018
test-hole driller	930.682-010
test technician	726.261-018
Thermospray Operator	505.380-010
THREAD CUTTER	789.684-050
three-dimensional-map modeler	777.381-042
TICKET AGENT	238.367-026
ticket clerk	238.367-026
TICKETER	652.685-098
ticket maker	652.685-098
ticket printer	652.685-098
ticket seller	238.367-026
tie puller	920.685-010
Tier-Lift-Truck Operator	921.683-050
Tinsmith	804.281-010
tipple worker	921.685-038
toggle-press operator	617.260-010
toilet attendant	358.677-018
tonal regulator	730.361-010
tool-and-machine maintainer	638.281-014
Tool Bender, Hand	619.361-010
Tool Chaser	922.687-058
TOOL DRESSER	601.682-010
TOOL GRINDER I	701.381-018
TOOL GRINDER II	603.664-010
TOOL PLANNER	012.167-074
tool programmer	007.167-018
TOOL PROGRAMMER, NUMERICAL CONTROL	007.167-018
tool sharpener	603.664-010
tool sharpener	701.381-018
Tool Straightener	709.484-014
Top-Edge Beveler	705.687-014
TORCH-STRAIGHTENER-AND HEATER	709.684-086
toter	919.664-010
TOUCH-UP PAINTER, HAND	740.684-026
Tower-Whirler Operator	921.663-010
TRACKMOBILE OPERATOR	919.683-026
tractor-crane engineer	921.663-058
TRACTOR-CRANE OPERATOR	921.663-058
TRACTOR OPERATOR	929.683-014
Tractor Operator, Laser Leveling	929.683-014
TRACTOR-TRAILER-TRUCK DRIVER	904.383-010
Trade-Show Representative	297.367-010
traffic supervisor	921.133-018
trailer	932.664-010
trailer-truck driver	904.383-010
train conductor	932.664-010
TRAINEE	term
trammer	919.663-014
transformer assembler	724.381-018
transformer rebuilder	724.381-018
TRANSFORMER REPAIRER	724.381-018
TRANSFORMER SHOP SUPERVISOR	724.131-014
transportation department head	184.167-226
TRANSPORTATION-MAINTENANCE SUPERVISOR	184.167-266
trash collector	381.687-018
trash collector	929.687-022
traveling-crane operator	921.663-010
Traveling-Maintenance Supervisor	638.131-026
TREATER	582.687-030
trimmer	789.687-070
trimmer	782.684-058
trimmer	920.687-038
TRIMMER, HAND	781.687-070
trimming-machine operator	789.684-050
TRIM-STENCIL MAKER	781.684-058

trip rider	932.664-010
trouble shooter see MAINTENANCE WORKER	
trouble shooter	726.261-018
trouble shooter, radio	720.281-010
TRUCK-CRANE OPERATOR	921.663-062
Truck-Crane-Operator Helper	921.667-022
TRUCK DRIVER	term
TRUCK DRIVER, HEAVY	905.663-014
TRUCK-DRIVER HELPER	905.687-010
TRUCK DRIVER, LIGHT	906.683-022
Trucker, Hand	929.687-030
trucker helper	905.687-010
truck loader	914.667-010
truck operator see TRUCK DRIVER	
truck repairer	620.281-050
Trunk Repairer	365.361-010
TUBE BENDER, HAND I	709.684-090
TUBE BENDER, HAND II	709.687-050
Tube-Bending-Machine Operator I	617.482-010
Tube-Bending-Machine Operator II	617.685-010
TUBE CLEANER	891.687-030
tube filler	619.687-018
Tube Winder	681.685-154
Tubing-Mill Operator I	616.685-042
Tubing-Mill Operator II	616.360-026
Tubing-Mill Setter	616.260-014
tub rider	932.664-010
Tubular-Products Fabricator	809.381-010
TUCKING-MACHINE OPERATOR	787.682-082
TUMBLER OPERATOR	599.685-110
tuner	730.361-010
TURNER	789.687-182
TURRET-PUNCH-PRESS OPERATOR	615.482-038
TURRET-PUNCH-PRESS OPERATOR, TAPE-CONTROL	615.685-042
TWISTING-MACHINE OPERATOR	619.485-014
Tying-Machine Operator	920.685-078
Typewriter Servicer	633.281-018
Ultrasonic Cleaner	503.685-030
ULTRASONIC TESTER	739.281-014
UMBRELLA REPAIRER	369.684-018
uncrater	827.584-010
upholsterer	780.381-018
upholsterer apprentice	780.381-022
UPHOLSTERER HELPER	780.687-054
UPHOLSTERY SEWER	780.682-018
UTILITIES-AND-MAINTENANCE SUPERVISOR	899.131-018
utility repairer	899.261-014
utility worker	929.687-030
vacuum cleaner	381.687-018
vacuum-cleaner operator	389.683-010
VACUUM CLEANER REPAIRER	723.381-014
vacuum-filter operator	551.685-078
vacuum-frame operator	976.361-010
VACUUM-METALIZER OPERATOR	505.685-018
vapor coater	505.685-018
Vehicle Unloader	929.687-030
VENETIAN-BLIND CLEANER AND REPAIRER	739.687-198
VENTILATION EQUIPMENT TENDER	950.585-010
ventilation mechanic	950.585-010
Vertical-Roll Operator	619.362-014
VICE PRESIDENT	189.117-034
VIOLIN REPAIRER	730.281-050
Wagon Driver	919.664-010
Walking-Dragline Operator	850.683-018
wallpaper cleaner	381.687-026
wall washer	381.687-026
Warehouse Guard	372.667-034
warehouse supervisor	184.167-114
warehouse supervisor	921.133-018
WAREHOUSE SUPERVISOR	929.137-022
warehouse worker	922.687-058
wash driller	930.682-010
wash-driller helper	930.687-014
WASHER	599.687-030
Washer-Dryer Preparer	827.584-010
WASHER, MACHINE	599.685-114
WASHING-MACHINE OPERATOR	599.685-118
Washing-Machine Servicer	827.261-010
washroom attendant	358.677-018
waste baler	920.685-010
waste collector	929.687-022
waste collector	381.687-018
WASTE-DISPOSAL ATTENDANT	955.383-010
watch engineer	950.131-014
watch engineer	950.382-026

watchguard	372.667-034
watch guard, gate	372.667-030
Water-Pumping-Station Engineer	950.382-026
Water-Pump Servicer	630.281-018
WATER TENDER	599.685-122
WAXER, FLOOR	381.687-034
Weigher, Packing	929.687-062
WEIGHER, PRODUCTION	929.687-062
welder-fitter helper	801.687-014
WHEEL-AND-CASTER REPAIRER	630.684-018
wheel loader operator	921.683-042
wheel setter	776.684-014
white-metal corrosion proofer	500.682-010
whiteprinting-machine operator	979.682-014
willower	680.685-082
Wincher	921.667-018
WIND-INSTRUMENT REPAIRER	730.281-054
WINDOW REPAIRER	899.684-042
window washer	389.687-014
wiper	699.687-014
Wire Bender, Hand	709.687-050
Wire Brusher	705.687-014
WIRE PREPARATION MACHINE TENDER	728.685-010
wirer helper	829.684-022
wire-stitcher operator	692.685-202
Wire-Straightening-Machine Operator	613.662-022
Woodwind-Instrument Repairer	730.281-054
Wrap Checker	358.677-014
Wrapper	920.587-018
Wrapper Sheeter	699.682-018
Wrapping-And-Packing-Machine Operator	920.685-078
Wrapping-Machine Operator	920.685-078
Wrapping Remover	920.587-018
wringer	581.685-038
x-ray consultant	729.281-046
X-Ray-Control-Equipment Repairer	710.281-026
x-ray equipment servicer	729.281-046
X-RAY-EQUIPMENT TESTER	729.281-046
x-ray service engineer	729.281-046
X-Ray Technician	199.361-010
yard boss see YARD SUPERVISOR	
yard-labor supervisor	899.133-010
YARD MANAGER	910.137-046
Yard Pumper	914.682-010
yard rigger	921.260-010
YARD SUPERVISOR	term
ZIPPER SETTER	787.682-086

auto. mfg.—AUTOMOBILE MANUFACTURING INDUSTRY: This designation includes occupations concerned with manufacturing automobiles and other motor vehicles, such as trucks, buses, ambulances, fire engines, taxicabs, truck and automobile bodies, and trailers. This designation also includes occupations in the manufacture of automobile parts and accessories, such as bearings, engines, brakes and brake parts, bumpers, bumperettes, bushings, carburetors, horns, piston rings, radiators, shock absorbers, and windshield wipers. Occupations concerned with the manufacture of tires and tubes are included in the RUBBER TIRE AND TUBE INDUSTRY (rubber tire). Occupations concerned with the manufacture and repair of automobile hardware are included in the CUTLERY, HANDTOOLS, AND HARDWARE INDUSTRY (cutlery-hrdwr.). Occupations concerned with the manufacture and repair of ignition apparatus, batteries, and starting systems are included in the ELECTRICAL EQUIPMENT INDUSTRY (elec. equip.). Occupations concerned with the manufacture and repair of lighting systems are included in the LIGHTING FIXTURES INDUSTRY (light. fix.). Occupations concerned with the manufacture and repair of automobile instruments and speedometers are included in the INSTRUMENTS AND APPARATUS INDUSTRY (inst. & app.). Occupations concerned with the manufacture of travel trailers are included in the MISCELLANEOUS VEHICLES AND TRANSPORTATION EQUIPMENT INDUSTRY, NOT ELSEWHERE CLASSIFIED (vehicles, nec.).

advisor	806.134-010
ASSEMBLER, AUTOMOBILE	806.684-010
Assembler, Body	806.684-010
Assembler, Chassis	806.684-010
Assembler, Engine	806.684-010
ASSEMBLER, FILTERS	739.687-026
Assembler, Final	806.684-010
Assembler, Seat	806.684-010
Assembler, Trim	806.684-010
assembler, truck-trailer	806.381-058
AUTO-DESIGN CHECKER	017.261-010
AUTO-DESIGN DETAILER	017.281-010
AUTOMOTIVE ENGINEER	007.061-010
body builder	807.281-010

BODY WIRER	829.684-014
Bonderizer	599.685-026
car driver	919.683-014
car tester	806.283-014
chassis driver	806.283-014
Chassis Inspector	806.687-018
checker	806.687-018
checker, product design	017.261-010
CLAIMS CLERK	241.387-010
coach wirer	829.684-014
Crankshaft Straightener	617.482-026
Custom-Frame Assembler	806.381-058
CUSTOM VAN CONVERTER	806.381-070
DIELECTRIC-PRESS OPERATOR	692.685-074
Differential Repairer	620.381-022
DRAFTER, AUTOMOTIVE DESIGN	017.261-042
DRAFTER, AUTOMOTIVE DESIGN LAYOUT	017.281-026
DRIVER	919.683-014
DRIVER-UTILITY WORKER	919.663-018
Dynamometer Tester, Chassis	806.281-010
DYNAMOMETER TESTER, MOTOR	806.281-010
electrician, wiring	829.684-014
Engine Repairer	620.381-022
engine tester	806.281-010
FINAL INSPECTOR	806.687-018
FINAL INSPECTOR, TRUCK TRAILER	806.361-018
Gear Straightener	617.482-026
gear tester	806.684-134
Glaze Sprayer	741.684-026
Grinder, Lead	705.684-026
group leader	806.367-018
INSPECTOR, EXHAUST EMISSIONS	806.364-010
Inspector, Filters	609.684-010
INSPECTOR, RETURNED MATERIALS	806.384-014
LABORATORY TECHNICIAN	019.261-030
LINE-UP WORKER	221.367-026
miniature-model maker	693.380-014
MODEL MAKER	693.380-014
overland driver	806.283-014
Painter, Chassis	741.687-018
Painter, Insignia	741.684-026
Primer Sprayer	741.684-026
PRODUCTION-MACHINE TENDER	699.685-050
QUALITY ASSURANCE GROUP LEADER	806.367-014
QUALITY ASSURANCE MONITOR	806.367-018
Quality Assurance Monitor, Body	806.367-018
Quality Assurance Monitor, Chassis	806.367-018
Quality Assurance Monitor, Final	806.367-018
Quality Assurance Monitor, Trim	806.367-018
QUALITY ASSURANCE SUPERVISOR	806.137-022
Quality Assurance Supervisor, Body	806.137-022
Quality Assurance Supervisor, Chassis	806.137-022
Quality Assurance Supervisor, Final	806.137-022
Quality Assurance Supervisor, Trim	806.137-022
quality worker	806.684-010
REPAIRER, GENERAL	806.684-118
REPAIRER, HEAVY	620.381-022
Rim-Roller Setter	616.260-014
ROADABILITY-MACHINE OPERATOR	806.383-010
road tester	806.283-014
Rust Proofer	599.685-026
salvage inspector	806.384-014
scheduler	221.367-026
scheduler, conveyor	221.367-026
service-claims inspector	806.384-014
service dismantler	806.384-014
SERVICE MECHANIC	807.381-022
SERVICE REPRESENTATIVE	191.167-022
Sprayer, Auto Parts	741.684-026
Supervisor, Body Assembly	806.134-010
Supervisor, Chassis Assembly	806.134-010
Supervisor, Engine Assembly	806.134-010
Supervisor, Final Assembly	806.134-010
SUPERVISOR, MOTOR VEHICLE ASSEMBLY	806.134-010
Supervisor, Seat Assembly	806.134-010
Supervisor, Trim Assembly	806.134-010
Supervisor, Truck-Trailer Assembly	806.134-010
team coordinator	806.367-014
team coordinator	806.367-018
team leader	806.134-010
team leader	806.367-014
team member	806.684-010
TEST DRIVER I	806.283-014
TEST DRIVER II	806.283-010
Thinner Sprayer	741.684-026

automotive ser.

Tinner Operator, Connecting Rods	599.685-026
TOOL, GAUGE, AND FIXTURE REPAIRER	601.281-030
TRAILER ASSEMBLER I	806.381-058
TRAILER ASSEMBLER II	806.684-082
trailer assembler, paneling	806.684-082
Trailer-Body Assembler	806.381-058
trailer-sections assembler	806.684-082
transfer and line-up worker	221.367-026
Transmission Repairer	620.381-022
TRANSMISSION TESTER	806.684-134
Trim Inspector	806.687-018
TRUCK-BODY BUILDER	807.281-010
Undercoat Sprayer	741.687-018
UPHOLSTERER, LIMOUSINE AND HEARSE	780.381-026
UTILITY WORKER, LINE ASSEMBLY	806.367-010
WATER LEAK REPAIRER	807.684-034
Wheel Filler	749.684-042
wirer	829.684-014

automotive ser.—AUTOMOTIVE SERVICES: This designation includes occupations concerned with servicing automobiles, motorcycles, trucks, and other motor vehicles. It includes such activities as automobile painting and washing; body and fender repairing, engine repairing, radiator repairing; operating parking lots and garages; renting passenger automobiles, trucks, and trailers; and selling gasoline and oil at service stations. Occupations concerned with the sale of automobiles, and of automobile parts and accessories, are included in the RETAIL TRADE INDUSTRY (retail trade).

AIR-CONDITIONING MECHANIC	620.281-010
alignment mechanic	620.281-038
Armature Winder, Automotive	724.684-018
assembler, convertible top	807.684-026
Auto-Body Painter	845.381-014
AUTO-BODY REPAIRER, FIBERGLASS	807.381-030
auto-glass worker	865.684-010
Automatic-Transmission Mechanic	620.281-062
AUTOMATIC-WINDOW-SEAT-AND-TOP-LIFT REPAIRER	825.381-014
AUTOMOBILE-ACCESSORIES INSTALLER	806.684-038
automobile-and-truck-mechanic apprentice	620.261-012
AUTOMOBILE-BODY CUSTOMIZER	807.361-010
automobile-body repair chief	807.137-010
AUTOMOBILE-BODY REPAIRER	807.381-010
Automobile-Body Repairer, Combination	807.381-010
AUTOMOBILE-BODY-REPAIRER HELPER	807.687-010
automobile-body worker	807.381-010
AUTOMOBILE-BUMPER STRAIGHTENER	807.684-010
AUTOMOBILE DETAILER	915.687-034
automobile inspector	620.261-018
AUTOMOBILE MECHANIC	620.261-010
AUTOMOBILE-MECHANIC APPRENTICE	620.261-012
automobile-mechanic assistant	620.684-014
AUTOMOBILE-MECHANIC HELPER	620.684-014
Automobile Mechanic, Motor	620.261-010
automobile mechanic, radiator	620.381-010
automobile-mechanic supervisor	620.131-014
automobile parker	915.473-010
AUTOMOBILE-RADIATOR MECHANIC	620.381-010
automobile-refrigeration mechanic	620.281-010
automobile rental agent	295.467-026
AUTOMOBILE RENTAL CLERK	295.467-026
automobile rental representative	295.467-026
AUTOMOBILE-REPAIR-SERVICE ESTIMATOR	620.261-018
AUTOMOBILE-SEAT-COVER-AND-CONVERTIBLE-TOP INSTALLER	780.384-010
AUTOMOBILE-SEAT-COVER INSTALLER	915.687-010
AUTOMOBILE-SELF-SERVE-SERVICE-STATION ATTENDANT	915.477-010
AUTOMOBILE-SERVICE-STATION ATTENDANT	915.467-010
AUTOMOBILE-SERVICE-STATION MECHANIC	620.261-030
automobile-spring repairer	619.380-018
AUTOMOBILE TESTER	620.261-014
AUTOMOBILE UPHOLSTERER	780.381-010
AUTOMOBILE-UPHOLSTERER APPRENTICE	780.381-014
automobile-upholstery-trim installer	780.384-010
Automobile Washer	919.684-014
automobile washer, steam	915.687-026
Automotive Air-Conditioner Installer	620.281-010
AUTOMOTIVE-COOLING-SYSTEM DIAGNOSTIC TECHNICIAN	620.261-034
AUTOMOTIVE-GENERATOR-&-STARTER REPAIRER	721.281-010
Automotive-Generator Repairer	721.281-010
Automotive-Starter Repairer	721.281-010
axle-and-frame mechanic	620.281-038

body builder	807.281-010
body-line finisher	807.381-010
body repairer, bus	807.381-010
Body Trimmer	780.381-010
BONDER, AUTOMOBILE BRAKES	620.685-010
BRAKE ADJUSTER	620.684-018
BRAKE-DRUM-LATHE OPERATOR	620.682-010
brake mechanic	620.281-026
BRAKE REPAIRER	620.281-026
Brake Repairer, Air	620.281-026
Brake Repairer, Bus	620.281-026
Brake Repairer, Hydraulic	620.281-026
brake-repair mechanic	620.281-026
brakeshoe repairer	620.281-026
buffer	690.685-422
bumper straightener	807.684-010
Bus Cleaner	919.687-014
BUS INSPECTOR	620.281-030
Bus Mechanic	620.261-010
Bus Upholsterer	780.381-010
CARBURETOR MECHANIC	620.281-034
carburetor repairer	620.281-034
car checker	806.361-026
car driver	919.683-014
Car Jockey	919.683-014
car rental clerk	295.467-026
CAR-WASH ATTENDANT, AUTOMATIC	915.667-010
CAR-WASH SUPERVISOR	915.137-010
cashier, automobile services	915.477-010
Cashier, Parking Lot	211.462-010
Cashier, Self-Service Gasoline	211.462-010
cementer	750.684-038
Chassis Inspector	620.281-030
chassis mechanic	620.281-038
CLUTCH REBUILDER	620.684-022
collision estimator	620.261-018
Compressor Mechanic, Bus	620.261-010
CUSTOM VAN CONVERTER	806.381-070
Cylinder-Block-Hole Reliner	616.682-010
DELIVERER, CAR RENTAL	919.663-010
dent remover	807.381-010
Diesel-Engine Mechanic, Automobile	625.281-010
Diesel-Engine Mechanic, Bus	625.281-010
Diesel-Engine Mechanic, Truck	625.281-010
Differential Repairer	620.261-010
Dispatcher, Automobile Rental	249.167-014
Dispatcher, Tow Truck	249.167-014
Door-Engine Repairer	620.281-018
door repairer, bus	807.381-010
DRIVER	919.683-014
DRIVER-UTILITY WORKER	919.663-018
Drive-Shaft-And-Steering-Post Repairer	620.261-010
Dynamometer Tuner	620.281-066
Electrical Inspector	620.281-030
Electrical Repairer, Internal Combustion Engines	825.281-022
Electrical-Unit Rebuilder	825.281-010
ELECTRIC-GOLF-CART REPAIRER	620.261-026
ELECTRICIAN, AUTOMOTIVE	825.281-022
Electrician, Bus	825.281-022
ELECTRICIAN HELPER, AUTOMOTIVE	825.684-010
Electrician Supervisor, Automotive	829.131-014
Engine-Head Repairer	620.261-010
Engine Inspector	620.281-030
Engine-Repair Mechanic, Bus	620.261-010
filling-station attendant	915.467-010
FLAME DEGREASER	503.685-022
FLOOR SERVICE WORKER, SPRING	807.684-022
Foreign-Car Mechanic	620.261-010
FRONT-END MECHANIC	620.281-038
garage mechanic	620.261-010
gasateria attendant	915.477-010
gas-station attendant	915.467-010
gas tender	915.467-010
general lot attendant	915.667-014
Giant-Tire Repairer	915.684-010
GLASS INSTALLER	865.684-010
glazier	865.684-010
golf-cart mechanic	620.261-026
greaser	915.687-018
Ignition-And-Carburetor Mechanic	825.281-022
INSTALLER, SOFT TOP	807.684-026
Limousine Rental Clerk	295.467-026
LUBRICATION SERVICER	915.687-018
lubrication technician	915.687-018
MACHINIST APPRENTICE, AUTOMOTIVE	600.280-030

MACHINIST, AUTOMOTIVE	600.280-034
machinist, brake	620.682-010
make-ready mechanic	806.361-026
MANAGER, AUTO SPECIALTY SERVICES	185.167-074
manager, service	620.261-018
MANAGER, STORAGE GARAGE	187.167-150
manager, tire service	915.134-010
MANAGER, VEHICLE LEASING AND RENTAL	187.167-162
MECHANICAL-UNIT REPAIRER	620.381-018
mechanic, chief	620.131-014
MECHANIC, ENDLESS TRACK VEHICLE	620.381-014
mechanic helper	620.684-014
mechanic, trouble-shooting	620.261-018
metal bumper	807.381-010
metal shrinker	807.381-010
metal worker	807.381-010
Motor Analyst	620.261-014
Motor Assembler	620.261-010
motorcycle mechanic	620.281-054
MOTORCYCLE REPAIRER	620.281-054
motor-inspection mechanic	620.281-030
Motor-Scooter Repairer	620.281-054
MUFFLER INSTALLER	807.664-010
NEW-CAR GET-READY MECHANIC	806.361-026
oiler	915.687-018
PAINTER APPRENTICE, TRANSPORTATION EQUIPMENT	845.381-014
Painter, Automotive	845.381-014
PAINTER HELPER, AUTOMOTIVE	845.684-014
PAINTER, TRANSPORTATION EQUIPMENT	845.381-014
parking attendant	915.473-010
PARKING-LOT ATTENDANT	915.473-010
parking-lot chauffeur	915.473-010
PARKING LOT SIGNALER	915.667-014
parking-station attendant	915.473-010
passenger-car-upholsterer apprentice	780.381-014
patcher	750.684-038
PROPULSION-MOTOR-AND-GENERATOR REPAIRER	721.281-026
radiator repairer	620.381-014
Radio Installer, Automobile	806.684-038
retreader	750.684-022
Riveter, Automobile Brakes	620.685-014
rust proofer	843.684-014
SAFETY INSPECTOR, TRUCK	919.687-018
sales associate, garage service	620.261-018
sander	845.684-014
SERVICE MANAGER	185.167-058
Service-Parts Driver	906.683-022
service-station attendant	915.467-010
service writer	620.261-018
SHOP ESTIMATOR	807.267-010
spotter	915.473-010
spring-fitter helper	620.584-010
spring-maker helper, hand	620.584-010
SPRING REPAIRER, HAND	619.380-018
SPRING-REPAIRER HELPER, HAND	620.584-010
SQUEAK, RATTLE, AND LEAK REPAIRER	620.364-010
station attendant	915.477-010
STEAM CLEANER	915.687-026
Storage-Garage Attendant	915.473-010
SUPERVISOR, AUTOMOBILE BODY REPAIR	807.137-010
SUPERVISOR, ENDLESS TRACK VEHICLE	620.131-010
SUPERVISOR, GARAGE	620.131-014
SUPERVISOR, MOTORCYCLE REPAIR SHOP	620.131-018
SUPERVISOR, PARKING LOT	915.133-010
TAXIMETER REPAIRER	710.281-038
tear-up worker, spring	620.584-010
tire-and-tube repairer	915.684-010
tire-and-tube servicer	915.684-010
TIRE BUFFER	690.685-422
TIRE BUILDER	750.684-022
Tire Changer	915.684-010
Tire Changer, Road Service	915.684-010
tire fixer	915.684-010
TIRE GROOVER	750.684-026
TIRE INSPECTOR	750.687-018
tire rebuilder	750.684-022
TIRE RECAPPER	750.685-014
TIRE-REGROOVING-MACHINE OPERATOR	690.662-010
TIRE REPAIRER	915.684-010
tire servicer	915.684-010
TIRE-SERVICE SUPERVISOR	915.134-010
TIRE VULCANIZER	750.684-038
Tire Wrapper	920.685-078
top-and-seat-cover fitter	780.384-010

Top Installer	780.381-010
top-lift and automatic-window repairer	825.381-014
touch-up finisher, metal	807.381-010
tow-car driver	919.663-026
TOW-TRUCK OPERATOR	919.663-026
TRACTOR MECHANIC	620.281-058
TRACTOR-MECHANIC HELPER	620.684-030
TRAILER-RENTAL CLERK	295.467-022
TRANSMISSION MECHANIC	620.281-062
transportation-department supervisor	620.131-014
TRUCK-BODY BUILDER	807.281-010
Truck Mechanic	620.261-010
Truck-Mechanic Helper	620.684-014
Truck-Rental Clerk	295.467-022
Truck-Repair-Service Estimator	620.261-018
TUNE-UP MECHANIC	620.281-066
UNDERCOATER	843.684-014
upholsterer apprentice	780.381-014
VEHICLE-FUEL-SYSTEMS CONVERTER	620.281-070
washer driver	919.663-010
wheel-alignment mechanic	620.281-038
WHEELWRIGHT	706.381-046
windshield installer	865.684-010
Windshield-Wiper Repairer	825.281-022
Work Coordinator, Tower Control	221.167-018
wrecker operator	919.663-026

bakery products—BAKERY PRODUCTS INDUSTRY: This designation includes occupations concerned with the production and sale of breads, biscuits, crackers, cakes, pies, pastries, and other bakery products as carried on in commercial and manufacturing bakeries. Sales occupations found in establishments with no manufacturing are included in the RETAIL TRADE INDUSTRY (retail trade).

BAKER	526.381-010
BAKER APPRENTICE	526.381-014
baker, bench	520.384-010
baker, doughnut	526.684-010
BAKER HELPER	526.686-010
baker operator, automatic	526.685-070
BAKERY-MACHINE MECHANIC	629.281-010
BAKERY-MACHINE-MECHANIC SUPERVISOR	629.131-010
BAKERY SUPERVISOR	526.131-010
Bakery Worker	920.587-018
BAKERY WORKER, CONVEYOR LINE	524.687-022
Band-Saw Operator, Cake Cutting	521.685-302
Bar-Machine Operator	520.682-034
batter depositor	526.682-010
BATTER MIXER	520.685-010
Batter-Mixer Helper	526.686-010
BATTER SCALER	526.682-010
BENCH HAND	520.384-010
Bench-Hand Helper	526.686-010
bench hand, machine	520.685-214
BLENDER	520.585-010
bolter	520.585-010
Bread-Dough Mixer	520.685-234
Bread Icer	524.684-022
Bread Icer, Machine	524.685-034
Bread-Pan Greaser	526.685-034
Bread Slicer, Machine	521.685-302
Bread Supervisor	526.131-010
Bread-Wrapping-Machine Feeder	920.685-078
BROTH MIXER	520.585-014
broth setter	520.585-014
Cake-Batter Mixer	520.685-010
Cake-Batter Scaler	526.682-010
Cake Cutter, Machine	521.685-302
CAKE DECORATOR	524.381-010
Cake Icer	524.684-022
Cake Icer, Machine	524.685-034
Cake-Pan Greaser	526.685-034
Cake Supervisor	526.131-010
CHECKER, BAKERY PRODUCTS	222.487-010
chocolate-coating-machine operator	524.685-026
Chocolate-Machine Operator	524.382-014
chocolate maker	523.685-022
chocolate-mixer operator	523.685-022
CHOCOLATE TEMPERER	523.685-022
Cone Baker, Machine	526.685-066
control-panel operator	520.462-010
Conveyorized Oven Tender	526.685-070
Cooker, Pie Filling	520.685-114
Cookie Mixer	520.685-234

beverage

Cookie-Mixer Helper	526.686-010
CRACKER-AND-COOKIE-MACHINE OPERATOR	520.682-034
Cracker-And-Cookie-Machine-Operator Helper	526.686-010
Cracker-Dough Mixer	520.685-234
CRACKER SPRAYER	524.685-022
cruller maker	526.684-010
cruller maker, machine	526.682-022
decorator	524.684-022
DECORATOR	524.684-014
decorator, hand	524.684-014
depositing-machine operator	524.682-010
DEPOSITING-MACHINE OPERATOR	524.682-010
DESSERT-CUP-MACHINE FEEDER	520.686-014
divider	526.682-010
DIVIDING-MACHINE OPERATOR	520.685-086
Dividing-Machine-Operator Helper	526.686-010
Dog-Food Dough Mixer	520.685-234
DOUGH-BRAKE-MACHINE OPERATOR	520.685-090
DOUGH MIXER	520.685-234
Dough-Mixer Helper	526.686-010
DOUGH-MIXER OPERATOR	520.462-010
dough molder, hand	520.384-010
Doughnut-Batter Mixer	520.685-010
doughnut-cooking-machine operator	526.682-022
Doughnut-Dough Mixer	520.685-234
Doughnut Icer	524.684-022
Doughnut Icer, Machine	524.685-034
DOUGHNUT-MACHINE OPERATOR	526.682-022
Doughnut-Machine-Operator Helper	526.686-010
DOUGHNUT MAKER	526.684-010
Doughnut-Maker Helper, Hand	526.686-010
dough sheeter	520.685-214
Drop-Machine Operator	520.682-034
enrober	524.685-026
ENROBING-MACHINE OPERATOR	524.685-026
ENROBING-MACHINE OPERATOR	524.382-014
Fig-Bar-Machine Operator	520.682-034
filler mixer	520.685-114
filling-machine operator	524.682-010
FILLING MACHINE TENDER	524.685-030
finisher	524.684-022
finisher, machine	524.685-034
Flour-Blender Helper	526.686-010
flour mixer	520.585-010
Fortune Cookie Maker	526.685-070
fried-cake maker	526.682-022
froster	524.684-022
froster, machine	524.685-034
Fruit Mixer	520.685-114
GRAIN-WAFER-MACHINE OPERATOR	523.685-094
ICER, HAND	524.684-022
Icer Helper, Hand	526.686-010
ICER, MACHINE	524.685-034
icing-machine operator	524.685-034
ICING MIXER	520.685-114
icing spreader	524.684-022
ingredient mixer	529.684-014
INGREDIENT SCALER	529.684-014
Ingredient-Scaler Helper	526.686-010
LABORER, PIE BAKERY	529.686-054
machine captain	520.682-034
MANAGER, BAKERY	189.117-046
marshmallow-machine worker	524.682-010
Matzo-Forming-Machine Operator	520.682-034
mill operator	520.585-010
mixing-machine attendant	520.685-234
mixing-machine attendant	520.685-010
Molding-Machine Operator	520.685-086
Molding-Machine-Operator Helper	526.686-010
order filler, bakery products	222.487-010
ornamenter	524.684-014
OVEN OPERATOR, AUTOMATIC	526.685-070
OVEN TENDER	526.685-030
Oven Tender, Bagels	526.685-030
PAN GREASER, MACHINE	526.685-034
pastry decorator	524.381-010
Pastry Mixer	520.685-234
Peel Oven Tender	526.685-030
Pie Bottomer	526.685-038
Pie-Crimping-Machine Operator	526.685-038
Pie-Crust Mixer	520.685-234
Pie-Dough Roller	526.685-038
Pie Filler	526.685-038
Pie-Filling Mixer	520.685-114
Pie Icer	524.684-022

Pie Icer, Machine	524.685-034
PIE MAKER, MACHINE	526.685-038
Pie Topper	526.685-038
PRETZEL COOKER	526.685-054
Pretzel-Dough Mixer	520.685-234
Pretzel-Stick-Machine Operator	520.685-190
PRETZEL TWISTER	520.587-010
PRETZEL-TWISTING-MACHINE OPERATOR	520.685-190
QUALITY-CONTROL INSPECTOR	529.367-018
RACKER	524.687-018
Reel Oven Tender	526.685-070
roll-dough divider	520.685-086
Roll Icer	524.684-022
Roll Icer, Machine	524.685-034
roll-machine operator	520.685-086
Rotary-Machine Operator	520.682-034
Rotary-Peel Oven Tender	526.685-030
scaling-machine operator	526.682-010
SLICING-MACHINE OPERATOR	521.685-302
spreading-machine operator	524.682-010
Sticker	524.687-018
Sugar-Wafer-Machine Operator	526.685-066
Supervisor, Bakery Sanitation	529.137-014
Supervisor, Shipping	922.137-018
Sweet-Dough Mixer	520.685-234
SWEET-GOODS-MACHINE OPERATOR	520.685-214
TROLLEY OPERATOR	524.565-010
UNLEAVENED-DOUGH MIXER	520.685-226
Wafer-Batter Mixer	520.685-010
Wafer Cutter	521.685-302
WAFER-MACHINE OPERATOR	526.685-066
waffle baker	526.685-066
waffle-machine operator	526.685-066

beverage—BEVERAGE INDUSTRY: This designation includes occupations concerned with manufacturing beverages and related ingredients and byproducts. These include such products as malt, malt byproducts, malt beverages, wines, brandy, brandy spirits, wine blends, distilled and rectified liquors, blended cordials and alcoholic cocktails, bottled and canned soft drinks and carbonated waters, flavoring extracts and syrups, and drink powders and concentrates.

BARLEY STEEPER	522.685-114
Barrel Cutter	529.687-066
BARREL-DEDENTING-MACHINE OPERATOR	617.682-010
BARREL FILLER I	522.687-010
BARREL FILLER II	914.485-010
Barrel Roller	529.687-066
Barrel Scraper	529.687-066
beer-still runner compounder	522.382-026
beverage-inspection-machine tender	529.685-026
BIN CLEANER	529.687-014
blender	520.685-030
blending-kettle tender	520.685-030
BLENDING-TANK TENDER	520.685-030
BOTTLED-BEVERAGE INSPECTOR	529.685-026
BOTTLE GAUGER	529.587-010
Bottle-House Pumper	914.665-014
BOTTLE-HOUSE QUALITY-CONTROL TECHNICIAN	029.361-010
bottle inspector	529.685-026
Bottle-Label Inspector	920.687-042
BOTTLE PACKER	920.685-026
BOTTLING-LINE ATTENDANT	920.687-042
BREWERY CELLAR WORKER	522.685-014
BREWING DIRECTOR	183.167-010
brewing superintendent	183.167-010
Bung Remover	529.687-066
can-bander operator	920.685-042
Can-Filling-Room Sweeper	381.687-018
CAN INSPECTOR	920.687-050
carbonating-stone cleaner	529.687-190
CARBONATION EQUIPMENT TENDER	522.685-026
CARBONATION TESTER	522.587-010
CAR CHASER	910.167-010
CAR-DUMPER OPERATOR	921.662-010
CAR-DUMPER-OPERATOR HELPER	921.687-010
car spotter	910.167-010
Carton Repairer	529.687-066
car unloader	921.662-010
car-unloader helper	921.687-010
CASE-LOADER OPERATOR	920.685-042
caser	920.685-026
Cellar Pumper	914.665-014
CELLAR SUPERVISOR	529.131-010
cellar worker	914.665-014

TANK PUMPER, PANELBOARD	529.685-242
tank refinisher	779.684-026
TAPPER	529.685-246
Vinegar Maker	183.161-014
WASH-HOUSE WORKER	529.685-254
Whisky Filterer	522.382-018
Whisky Inspector	522.667-010
Whisky-Proof Reader	522.382-018
Whisky-Regauger	522.382-018
wine-bottle inspector	529.687-058
WINE MAKER	183.161-014
WINE PASTEURIZER	523.685-126
WINERY WORKER	521.685-370
Wort Pumper	914.665-014
YEAST-CULTURE DEVELOPER	022.381-010
YEAST DISTILLER	522.362-010
yeast maker	522.362-010
Yeast Pumper	914.665-014
YEAST PUSHER	522.665-014

boot & shoe—BOOT AND SHOE INDUSTRY: This designation includes occupations concerned with manufacturing and repair of boots, leggings, moccasins, sandals, shoes, slippers, and allied footwear, made of canvas and other textile fabrics, man-made materials, rubber, and leather. The designation also includes the manufacture of leather soles, inner soles, and boot and shoe cutstock and findings, such as leather welting, shanks, heel and toe caps, leather shoe laces, and finished wooden heels.

anchor tacker	690.685-162
anchor-tack puller	788.687-146
ANKLE-PATCH MOLDER	692.682-010
Antiquer	788.684-066
antisqueak applier	788.687-010
antisqueak chalker	788.687-010
ANTISQUEAK FILLER	788.687-010
apex trimmer	690.685-150
Apron Trimmer	690.685-434
archer	690.682-070
Arch-Pad Cementer	788.687-030
ASSEMBLER FOR PULLER-OVER, HAND	788.684-010
ASSEMBLER FOR PULLER-OVER, MACHINE	690.685-010
assembler, rubber footwear	753.687-026
ASSEMBLER, SANDAL PARTS	788.684-014
attacher	690.685-074
Back-Seam Stitcher	690.682-082
back-shoe operator	788.667-010
BACK-SHOE WORKER	221.387-010
Backstay Stitcher	690.682-082
BACK-STRIP-MACHINE OPERATOR	690.685-018
back tacker	788.684-010
ball laster	690.685-186
Ball-Point Splitter	585.685-114
Band Splitter	585.685-114
Barrer And Tacker	690.682-082
beater	690.685-074
beater-out, leveling machine	690.685-382
BED LASTER	690.682-018
beveler	690.685-378
Binding Cementer, French Cord	690.686-018
BINDING FOLDER, MACHINE	788.684-018
Binding Nicker	690.685-298
Binding Stitcher	690.682-082
bleacher	788.687-014
BLEMISH REMOVER	788.684-022
Blind Eyeletter	699.685-018
Blind Hooker	699.685-018
BOBBIN WINDER, MACHINE	681.685-022
Boot Trimmer	690.685-434
Boot Turner	788.687-130
BOTTOM BLEACHER	788.687-014
Bottom Brusher	788.687-018
Bottom Buffer	690.685-046
Bottom Burnisher	690.685-058
Bottom Cementer I	690.686-018
Bottom Cementer II	788.687-030
BOTTOM FILLER	788.684-026
Bottoming-Room Inspector	788.384-010
Bottoming-Room Supervisor	788.131-010
bottom ironer	690.685-034
Bottom Pounder, Cement Shoes	690.685-314
BOTTOM PRESSER	690.685-034
bottom scrubber	788.687-014
bottom stainer	788.687-098
Bottom Stamper	690.685-158

BOTTOM WHEELER	788.684-030
BOW MAKER	788.684-034
Bow Stapler	690.685-162
box marker	652.685-018
box stamper, machine	652.685-018
Box-Toe Buffer	690.685-046
Box-Toe Cementer	788.687-030
Box-Toe Cutter	699.682-022
box-toe flanger, stitchdowns	690.685-426
Box-Toe Stitcher	690.682-082
braid folder	788.684-018
brander	753.687-014
Breast Buffer	690.685-046
breast finisher	788.684-126
BRUSHER	788.687-018
brusher	690.685-046
brusher	690.685-058
BUCKLER AND LACER	788.687-022
Buckle-Sewer, Machine	690.682-082
Buckle Stapler	690.685-162
Buckle-Strap Puncher	690.685-114
Buckram Cutter	699.682-022
BUFFER	690.685-046
BUFFER, AUTOMATIC	690.685-050
BUFFER, INFLATED-PAD	690.685-054
BUFFING-AND-SUEDING-MACHINE OPERATOR	753.684-010
buffing-machine operator	690.685-046
burnisher	690.685-034
BURNISHER	690.685-058
BUTTONHOLE MAKER	788.684-038
California Seamer	690.682-082
CARTON MARKER, MACHINE	652.685-018
carton stamper	652.685-018
carver	788.684-082
caser	788.687-026
CASER, SHOE PARTS	788.687-026
Casual-Shoe Inspector	788.384-010
CEMENTER AND FOLDER, MACHINE	690.685-070
Cementer For Folding, Machine	690.686-018
CEMENTER, HAND	788.687-030
CEMENTER, MACHINE	692.685-050
CEMENTER, MACHINE APPLICATOR	690.686-018
CEMENTER, MACHINE JOINER	690.685-074
chalker, soles	788.687-010
Channel Cementer, Insole, Machine	690.686-018
Channel Cementer, Outsole, Machine	690.686-018
CHANNELER, INSOLE	690.685-086
Channeler, Outsole	690.685-086
channel-lip stiffener, insoles	788.687-062
CHANNEL OPENER, OUTSOLES	690.685-082
Channel Rougher	690.685-046
channel turner	690.685-082
CHECKER-IN	221.587-014
Ciaio-Counter Molder	690.685-102
Ciaio-Lumite Injector	690.685-278
CLICKING-MACHINE OPERATOR	789.382-010
CLIPPER	753.687-010
closer	690.682-082
COBBLER	788.381-010
Cobbler, Mckay	788.381-010
Cobbler, Sole	788.381-010
Cobbler, Upper	788.381-010
COLOR MATCHER	788.687-034
color repairer	788.684-022
COMPLAINT CLERK	221.387-014
Compo-Conveyor Operator	690.685-074
compound-machine operator	690.685-278
CONCAVING-MACHINE OPERATOR	585.685-030
conformal pad former	788.687-094
cookie breaker	788.685-010
counter and upper tacker	690.685-010
Counter Buffer	690.685-046
counter caser	788.687-026
COUNTER CUTTER	690.685-094
COUNTER FORMER	690.685-098
counter maker	690.685-094
counter molder	690.685-350
COUNTER MOLDER	690.685-102
Counter-Pocket Sewer	690.682-082
COUNTER ROLLER	690.685-106
counter tacker	788.684-078
cover creaser	690.685-174
cover cutter	788.687-042
Cover Maker	690.682-082
cover remover	788.687-042

Crepe-Sole Scourer	690.685-046
Crepe-Sole Wire Brusher	690.685-046
crimper	788.687-154
Cripple Cutter	789.382-010
CRIPPLE WORKER	788.684-042
cuffer	690.685-046
cushion cementer	788.684-026
Cushion Trimmer	690.682-086
Custom-Shoe Designer And Maker	788.381-014
CUT-AND-COVER LINE WORKER	753.684-014
CUT-OUT-AND-MARKING-MACHINE OPERATOR	690.685-110
CUT-OUT-MACHINE OPERATOR	690.685-114
cut-out marker	788.584-014
cut-out-press operator	690.685-114
Cut-Out Stitcher	690.682-082
Cut-Out Worker	690.685-434
CUTTER, HOT KNIFE	751.684-018
cutter-in	690.682-046
Cutting-Room Supervisor	788.131-010
dead header	922.687-066
DEBRANDER	753.687-014
DESIGNER AND PATTERNMAKER	788.281-010
DESKIDDING-MACHINE OPERATOR	690.685-126
die-out-machine operator	690.685-114
Dope Edger	788.684-066
Double Cutter	699.682-022
Double-Needle Stitcher	690.682-082
DRESSER	788.687-038
Dress-Shoe Inspector	788.384-010
DRYING-RACK CHANGER	581.686-026
dull shoe repairer	788.684-022
edge beader	690.685-174
edge blacker, machine	690.685-234
edge burnisher	690.685-146
EDGE BURNISHER, UPPERS	690.685-138
edge dyer	690.685-234
Edge Inker	788.684-066
Edge Inker, Heels	788.684-066
Edge Inker, Uppers	788.684-066
edge kitter	690.685-146
Edge Polisher	788.687-018
edger	690.685-138
EDGE SETTER	690.685-146
Edge Setter, Heel Lift	690.685-146
edge skiver	690.685-378
edge stainer, machine	690.685-234
Edge Stitcher	690.682-082
EDGE TRIMMER	690.685-150
edge-trimming-machine operator	690.685-150
EMBOSSER	690.685-158
Eyelet-Row Marker	788.584-014
Fancy Stitcher	690.682-082
Fancy-Stitch Marker	788.584-014
fastener	690.685-162
FASTENER, MACHINE	690.685-162
featheredge-machine operator	690.685-166
FEATHEREDGER AND REDUCER, MACHINE	690.685-166
Fiber-Heel-Piece Shaper	690.685-162
filler	788.684-022
FINAL INSPECTOR	753.687-018
FINGER COBBLER	788.684-046
finisher	690.685-058
FINISHING TRIMMER	788.687-042
fitter	690.682-082
Fitting-Room Inspector	788.384-010
Fitting-Room Maintenance Mechanic	639.281-018
fitting room operator	788.685-018
Fitting-Room Supervisor	788.131-010
FLAMER	788.684-050
flamer, after lasting	788.684-130
FLARE BREAKER	788.685-010
flare chalker	788.687-010
Flare Stitcher	690.682-082
Flatbed Stitcher	690.682-082
flat folder	788.687-050
FLOORWORKER, LASTING	788.687-046
FOLDER, HAND	788.687-050
FOLDER, MACHINE	690.685-174
folding-machine operator	690.685-074
folding-machine operator	690.685-174
FOLDING-MACHINE TENDER	788.685-014
fold skiver	788.685-014
FOREPART LASTER	690.685-186
Forepart Rasper	788.684-094
forepart reducer	690.685-166
forepart rounder	690.685-334
forming-machine operator	690.685-098
FOXING CUTTER, HOT KNIFE	751.684-022
FOXING-CUTTING-MACHINE OPERATOR, AUTOMATIC	690.682-038
French-Binding Folder	788.684-018
french-binding folder	690.685-070
gang-punch operator	690.685-114
gluer	788.687-030
GOLF-SHOE-SPIKE ASSEMBLER	788.687-054
golf-stud riveter	788.687-054
Gore Inserter	690.682-082
Gore Stapler	690.685-162
goring cutter	788.687-042
GROOVER AND TURNER	690.685-198
gummer	788.687-030
gusset ripper	788.687-042
Hammerer, Tab	788.687-050
hand assembler	788.684-010
hand lacer	788.684-054
HAND SEWER, SHOES	788.684-054
hand shoe cutter	788.684-082
hand trimmer	788.684-054
HEEL ATTACHER, WOOD	788.684-058
HEEL BREASTER, LEATHER	690.682-042
Heel Brusher	788.687-018
Heel Buffer	690.685-046
Heel Builder, Hand	788.687-030
HEEL BUILDER, MACHINE	690.685-206
Heel Burnisher	690.685-058
Heel Cementer	788.687-030
Heel Cementer, Machine	690.686-018
HEEL COMPRESSOR	690.685-210
Heel Coverer	788.687-030
Heel-Cover Softener	788.687-090
Heel-Cover Splitter	585.685-114
HEEL DIPPER	788.687-058
Heel Dipper, Insole	788.687-062
Heel-Edge Inker, Machine	690.685-234
Heel-Emery Buffer	690.685-046
Heeler, Machine	690.685-162
heel finisher	788.684-126
heel fitter, machine	690.682-046
heel former	690.685-206
HEEL GOUGER	690.685-214
Heel Layer	690.685-074
Heel-Lift-Beam Cutter	699.682-022
Heel-Lift Gouger	690.685-214
Heel-Lining Paster	690.686-018
Heel Marker	788.584-014
heel molder	690.685-210
HEEL-NAILING-MACHINE OPERATOR	690.685-226
Heel-Nail Rasper	788.684-094
Heel Padder	788.687-030
HEEL PRICKER	690.685-218
Heel Reducer	690.685-166
Heel-Room Supervisor	788.131-010
Heel Sander, Rubber	690.685-046
HEEL SCORER	690.685-222
Heel-Seam Rubber	690.685-350
Heel-Seat Filler	690.685-162
HEEL-SEAT FITTER, HAND	788.684-062
HEEL-SEAT FITTER, MACHINE	690.682-046
Heel-Seat-Flap Stapler	690.685-162
HEEL-SEAT LASTER, MACHINE	690.685-230
Heel-Seat Pounder	690.685-314
Heel-Seat Sander	690.685-046
Heel-Seat Trimmer	690.685-434
Heel Slicker	690.685-046
HEEL SORTER	788.584-010
Heel Splitter	585.685-114
heel sprayer, first	788.687-034
HEEL SPRAYER, MACHINE	590.685-038
heel stainer	690.685-234
Heel-Top-Lift Splitter	585.685-114
Heel Trimmer I	690.685-434
Heel Trimmer II	690.682-086
Heel Wheeler	690.685-058
Hide Buffer	690.685-046
High-Heel Builder	690.685-206
Hole Puncher, Strap	690.685-114
HOOKER-LASTER	753.684-018
Hot-Die Picker	690.682-050
Hot-Die-Press Feeder	690.682-050
HOT-DIE-PRESS OPERATOR	690.682-050

boot & shoe

injection molder, outer sole	690.685-406
INKER	788.684-066
INKER, MACHINE	690.685-234
inner seamer	690.685-238
inseamer	690.682-078
inseam leveler	690.685-382
INSEAM TRIMMER	690.685-238
inseam-trimming-machine operator	690.685-238
INSOLE-AND-HEEL-STIFFENER	788.687-062
insole-and-outsole preparer	788.685-018
Insole-And-Outsole Splitter	585.685-114
INSOLE BEVELER	690.685-242
insole-bottom filler	788.684-026
Insole Buffer	690.685-046
insole-cloth trimmer	690.685-246
Insole Coverer	690.685-074
Insole Cutter, Machine	699.682-022
insole filler	788.684-026
insole gemmer	690.685-246
Insole-Lip Turner	690.685-074
Insole Rasper	788.684-094
INSOLE REINFORCER	690.685-246
insole rounder	690.685-338
Insole Sander	690.685-046
Insole Tacker	690.685-162
insole-tack-puller, hand	788.687-146
Insole Taper	690.685-074
Insole Tape Stitcher, Uco	690.682-082
Insole-Toe-Snipping-Machine Operator	690.685-222
INSPECTOR	788.384-010
INSTRUCTOR	788.222-010
INTERLACER	788.684-070
ironer	788.684-130
JOB PUTTER-UP AND TICKET PREPARER	788.587-010
joiner	690.682-082
joiner	690.685-074
joiner	690.685-250
JOINT CUTTER, MACHINE	690.685-250
jointer, machine	690.685-250
joint maker, machine	690.685-250
Joint Sander	690.685-046
jollier	690.685-314
Kamborian Operator	690.685-174
Label Stitcher	690.682-082
LABORER, BOOT AND SHOE	788.687-066
LACER I	788.687-070
LACER II	690.685-254
LACING-STRING CUTTER	788.687-074
LAST CHALKER	788.687-078
LAST CLEANER	788.687-082
last dipper	788.687-078
LASTER	753.684-022
laster, hand	788.684-010
LASTER, HAND	788.684-074
last greaser	788.687-078
lasting-machine operator, bed	690.682-018
LASTING-MACHINE OPERATOR, HAND METHOD	788.684-078
Lasting-Room Supervisor	788.131-010
last inserter	788.684-106
LAST PULLER	788.687-086
LAST PUTTER-AWAY	922.687-066
LAST REMODELER-REPAIRER	739.684-106
LAST REPAIRER	739.684-110
LAST-REPAIRER HELPER	739.684-114
last waxer	788.687-078
layer	690.685-074
leather grader	788.387-010
leather repairer	788.684-022
LEATHER SOFTENER	788.687-090
leveler	690.685-382
leveling-machine operator	690.685-382
lift builder, whole	690.685-206
Lining Closer	690.682-082
Lining Cutter, Machine	699.682-022
Lining Inspector	788.384-010
Lining Ironer	788.684-130
Lining Marker	788.584-014
Lining Repairer	788.381-010
lining stamper	690.685-398
Lining Stitcher	690.682-082
Lining-Strap Closer	690.682-082
Lining Vamper	690.682-082
LIP CUTTER AND SCORER	690.685-270
LIP-OF-SHANK CUTTER	690.685-274
lock-stitch channeler	690.685-086
Lockstitcher	690.682-078
Low-Heel Builder	690.685-206
LUMITE INJECTOR	690.685-278
luster repairer	788.687-038
machine assembler	690.685-010
MACHINE-MADE-SHOE UNIT WORKER	753.584-010
machine tracer	690.685-282
maker	690.682-082
MAKING-LINE WORKER	753.687-026
margin trimmer	690.685-150
margin trimmer	690.685-238
MARKER, HAND	788.584-014
MARKER, MACHINE	690.685-282
MARKING-MACHINE TENDER	783.685-026
master-pattern maker	788.281-010
material combiner	788.687-030
moccasin sewer	788.684-054
modeler	788.684-082
model maker	788.281-010
molder	690.682-070
MOLDER, LABELS	690.685-294
MOLDER, SHOE PARTS	788.687-094
MOLD FILLER AND DRAINER	753.687-030
MOLD-INSERT CHANGER	753.687-034
Multiple-Needle Stitcher	690.682-082
nailer	690.685-162
nail puller	690.685-410
Nail Welter	690.685-162
Neverslip Stitcher	690.682-082
NICKER	690.685-298
ODD-SHOE EXAMINER	788.667-010
Open-Shank Coverer	690.685-074
Ornament Stapler	690.685-162
ORTHOPEDIC-BOOT-AND-SHOE DESIGNER AND MAKER	788.261-010
OUTSIDE CUTTER, HAND	788.684-082
outside marker	690.685-398
outsole beveler	690.685-166
Outsole Cementer, Machine	690.686-018
Outsole Cutter, Machine	699.682-022
OUTSOLE FLEXER	583.686-026
outsole leveler	690.685-382
outsole or insole molder	690.682-070
outsole paraffiner	788.687-010
OUTSOLE SCHEDULER	221.587-022
outsole skiver	690.685-166
Outsole Tacker	690.685-162
outsole trimmer	690.685-150
packing inspector	753.687-018
Packing-Room Inspector	788.384-010
PAINTER, BOTTOM	788.687-098
paster	788.687-030
PEGGER	788.687-102
Perforator	690.685-114
pinker	686.685-042
PINKING-MACHINE OPERATOR	686.685-042
Piping Blocker	699.685-014
PLASTIC-DESIGN APPLIER	690.686-046
plastic insert molder	788.687-094
plastic-machine folder	690.685-070
platform beater	690.685-470
Platform Cementer	690.686-018
Platform Presser	690.685-074
Platform Stapler	690.685-162
Platform Stitcher	690.682-078
Plug Stitcher	690.682-078
polisher	690.685-046
polisher	690.685-058
Postbed Stitcher	690.682-082
Potdevin Cementer, Machine	690.686-018
POUNDER	690.685-314
Power-Hammer Operator	690.685-350
presser	788.684-130
printer	690.685-158
PULLER AND LASTER, MACHINE	788.684-086
PULLER OVER, MACHINE	788.684-090
puncher	690.685-162
puncher	690.685-114
puncher and fastener	690.685-162
push-up machine operator	690.685-206
quarter doper	788.687-038
quarter former	690.685-070
Quarter Former	690.685-098
Quarter Inspector	788.384-010
Quarter-Lining Smoother	690.685-350

Quarter-Lining Stitcher	690.682-082
quirk sander	662.685-042
rand butter	690.685-474
rand-butting-machine operator	690.685-474
Rand Cementer	690.686-018
Rand Sewer	690.682-082
Rand Tacker	690.685-162
Rapid-Outsole Stitcher	690.682-078
RASPER	788.684-094
rasper-machine operator	690.685-046
rebrander	753.687-014
reinspector	753.687-018
relaster	788.684-106
remodeler	739.684-106
remover	690.685-046
repair clerk	221.387-014
REPAIRER	753.684-026
returner, lasts	922.687-066
returns clerk	221.387-014
rib-stiffener and heel-dipper	788.687-062
riveter	690.685-162
Rolled-Seat Trimmer	690.685-434
ROLLER-STITCHER	753.684-030
ROTARY CUTTER	585.685-082
roughener	690.685-046
Rougher For Cement	690.685-046
ROUGH-ROUNDER, MACHINE	690.685-334
rounder	690.685-334
ROUNDER	690.685-338
rubber and pounder	690.685-350
ruffer	690.685-046
Russet Repairer	788.684-022
Saddle-Lining Stitcher	690.682-082
Saddle Stitcher	690.682-082
sample cutter	788.684-082
SAMPLE MAKER	690.685-506
SAMPLE SHOE INSPECTOR AND REWORKER	788.684-098
sander	690.685-046
sander and polisher	690.685-046
Sanitizer	788.687-122
scarfer	585.685-110
scarfer	690.685-378
scourer	690.685-046
SCRAP SORTER	788.687-106
SCREW REMOVER	788.684-102
seamer	690.682-082
Seam-Press Operator	690.685-350
seam roller	690.685-350
SEAM-RUBBING-MACHINE OPERATOR	690.685-350
Seam-Stay Stitcher	690.682-082
Seam Taper, Machine	690.685-414
Seat Trimmer	690.685-434
setter	690.685-074
sewer	690.685-162
sewer	690.682-082
Shank Beveler	690.685-166
Shank Burnisher	690.685-058
Shank Cementer, Hand	788.687-030
shanker	788.687-118
SHANK INSPECTOR	788.687-110
shank paperer	788.687-114
shank picker	788.687-110
SHANK-PIECE TACKER	788.687-118
Shank Sander	690.685-046
shank sorter	788.687-110
Shank Stapler	690.685-162
Shank Stitcher	690.682-082
shank tacker	788.687-118
SHANK TAPER	788.687-114
shaver	690.685-434
shaver	585.685-114
SHOE CLEANER	788.687-122
SHOE COVERER	788.687-126
shoe cutter	788.684-082
Shoe Designer	142.061-018
shoe dresser	788.687-038
shoe hammerer	690.685-350
shoe handler	920.687-166
shoe ironer	788.687-158
SHOE-LAY-OUT PLANNER	012.187-014
SHOEMAKER, CUSTOM	788.381-014
SHOE PACKER	920.687-166
Shoe-Parts Cutter	699.682-022
shoe planner	012.187-014
shoe repairer	788.684-022

shoe repairer	788.381-010
shoe singer	788.684-050
shoe stitcher, odd	788.381-010
SHOE TURNER	788.687-130
SIDE LASTER, CEMENT	690.685-358
SIDE LASTER, STAPLE	690.685-362
Side Laster, Tack	690.685-362
side stapler	690.685-362
side trimmer	690.685-238
Silk-Lining Cutter, Machine	699.682-022
singeing-torch operator	788.684-050
singer and unloader	788.684-050
Single-Beam Clicker	699.682-022
Single-Needle Stitcher	690.682-082
SKIVER, BLOCKERS	585.685-110
Skiver, Box-Toe	690.685-378
Skiver, Counter	690.685-378
Skiver, Flare	690.685-378
Skiver, Heel Tap	690.685-378
SKIVER, MACHINE	690.685-378
Skiver, Sock Linings	690.685-378
Skiver, Tuck	690.685-378
Skiver, Uppers Or Linings	690.685-378
Skiver, Welt-End	690.685-378
skiving-machine operator	690.685-378
slasher	690.685-470
SLIP LASTER	788.684-106
smoothing-machine operator	690.685-350
snipper	690.685-298
Sock Liner	788.687-030
Sock-Lining And Heel-Pad Embosser	690.685-158
Sock-Lining Examiner	788.384-010
Sock-Lining Stitcher	690.682-082
sole beater	690.685-470
sole blacker	690.685-234
Sole Buffer	690.685-046
SOLE-CONFORMING-MACHINE OPERATOR	690.682-070
sole cutter	788.685-018
Sole-Cutting-Machine Operator	699.682-022
sole dyer	690.685-234
Sole-Edge Inker, Machine	690.685-234
Sole Layer	690.685-074
Sole Layer, Hand	788.687-030
Sole-Leather-Cutting-Machine Operator	699.682-022
SOLE LEVELER, MACHINE	690.685-382
sole-leveling-machine operator	690.685-382
sole-molding-machine operator	690.682-070
sole pretrimmer	690.685-150
Sole Rougher	690.685-046
sole rounder	690.685-338
sole rounder	690.685-334
sole-rounding-machine operator	690.685-338
SOLE SCRAPER	788.687-134
SOLE SEWER, HAND	788.684-110
Sole Splitter	585.685-114
sole stainer	788.687-098
Sole Stapler, Welt	690.685-162
Sole Stitcher	690.682-078
sole stitcher, hand	788.684-110
Sole Trimmer	690.682-086
Sole Wetter	788.687-090
SORTER	753.587-010
splitter	585.685-114
SPLITTER, MACHINE	585.685-114
SPORT-SHOE-SPIKE ASSEMBLER	690.685-394
sprayer	590.685-038
Sprayer	741.687-018
squirt-machine operator	690.685-278
stamper	690.685-158
STAMPING-MACHINE OPERATOR	690.685-398
staple laster	690.685-362
stapler	690.685-162
stayer	690.685-414
stayer	690.682-082
STEEL-BOX-TOE INSERTER	788.687-138
stitchdown-thread laster	788.684-114
stitchdown-thread-lasting-machine operator	788.684-114
stitcher	690.682-082
stitcher	690.682-078
STITCHER, MACHINE	term
STITCHER, SPECIAL MACHINE	690.682-078
STITCHER, STANDARD MACHINE	690.682-082
STITCHER, TAPE-CONTROLLED MACHINE	690.685-494
Stitcher, Utility	690.682-082
stitch fudger	690.685-482

stitching-machine operator ... 690.682-082
stitch marker ... 690.685-282
Stitch Separator ... 690.685-482
stitch wheeler ... 690.685-482
STOCK FITTER ... 788.685-018
STOCKLAYER ... 753.687-042
Strap Stitcher ... 690.682-082
string cutter ... 788.687-074
STRING LASTER ... 690.685-406
stripper ... 585.685-114
STRIPPING CUTTER AND WINDER ... 585.685-118
STRIP PRESSER ... 583.685-118
sueding-and-buffing-machine operator ... 753.684-010
SUPERVISOR ... 788.131-010
SUPERVISOR, PACKING ... 788.137-010
SUPERVISOR, PLASTICS PRODUCTION ... 556.130-010
TABLE WORKER ... 788.687-142
tacker ... 690.685-162
TACK PULLER ... 788.687-146
TACK PULLER, MACHINE ... 690.685-410
taper ... 690.685-414
taper ... 690.685-074
TAPER, MACHINE ... 690.685-414
Tape Stitcher ... 690.682-082
thermo-cementing-folder operator ... 690.685-070
THREAD LASTER ... 788.684-114
TICKET SCHEDULER ... 221.587-038
Tip Burnisher ... 690.685-058
tip cementer ... 788.685-014
TIP FINISHER ... 690.685-418
Tip Puncher ... 690.685-114
Tip Stitcher ... 690.682-082
toe and heel laster ... 690.682-018
TOE FORMER, STITCHDOWNS ... 690.685-426
TOE LASTER, AUTOMATIC ... 690.685-430
toe laster, automatic ... 690.685-426
Toe-Lining Closer ... 690.682-082
Toe Pounder ... 690.685-314
Toe Stapler ... 690.685-162
TOGGLE-PRESS FOLDER-AND-FEEDER ... 690.686-066
Tongue And Quarter Stitcher ... 690.682-082
Tongue-Lining Stitcher ... 690.682-082
TONGUE PRESSER ... 788.685-022
Tongue Stitcher ... 690.682-082
TOP FORMER ... 788.685-026
top ironer ... 788.685-026
Top-Lift Compressor ... 690.685-210
Top-Lift Cutter ... 699.682-022
Top-Lift Nailer ... 690.685-162
Top-Lift Scourer ... 690.685-046
Top-Lift Trimmer ... 690.685-434
topline-beading-machine tender ... 788.685-014
Toppiece Chopper ... 699.685-014
Toppiece Cutter ... 699.682-022
Top Stitcher ... 690.682-082
Top Taper, Machine ... 690.685-414
Top Trimmer I ... 690.685-434
Top Trimmer II ... 690.682-086
TREE DRILLER ... 788.684-118
treer ... 788.687-122
trimmer ... 690.685-434
trimmer and reinforcer ... 690.685-246
TRIMMER, HAND ... 788.687-150
TRIMMER, MACHINE I ... 690.685-434
TRIMMER, MACHINE II ... 690.682-086
Trimming Cutter, Machine ... 699.682-022
Tuck-And-Insole Cementer ... 690.686-018
Twin-Beam Clicker ... 699.682-022
Underlay Stitcher ... 690.682-082
uniformer ... 788.687-034
UPPER-AND-BOTTOM LACER, HAND ... 788.684-122
Upper Cutter, Machine ... 699.682-022
upper cutter-out ... 788.684-082
Upper Doubler ... 788.687-030
upper edger ... 690.685-138
Upper Inspector ... 788.384-010
upper-leather cutter ... 788.684-082
UPPER-LEATHER SORTER ... 788.387-010
Upper-Lining Cementer ... 690.686-018
upper marker ... 788.584-014
Upper Muller ... 788.687-090
upper shaper ... 788.685-026
upper stamper ... 690.685-398
Upper Stitcher ... 690.682-082
Upper Trimmer ... 690.685-434
vamp-and-whole-shoe cutter, hand ... 788.684-082
VAMP CREASER ... 788.687-154
vamper ... 690.682-078
Vamp Marker ... 690.685-282
Vamp Presser ... 690.685-350
Vamp Stitcher ... 690.682-082
VAMP-STRAP IRONER ... 788.687-158
Vamp Wetter ... 788.687-090
VULCANIZER ... 690.685-462
VULCANIZING-PRESS OPERATOR ... 690.685-466
Waterproofer ... 741.687-018
weaver ... 788.684-070
WELT BEATER ... 690.685-470
WELT-BUTTER, HAND ... 788.687-162
WELT BUTTER, MACHINE ... 690.685-474
WELT CUTTER ... 690.685-478
welter ... 690.682-078
Welting Stitcher, Front ... 690.682-082
welt-insole channeler ... 690.685-086
welt maker ... 690.685-478
Welt Rougher ... 690.685-046
Welt-Sole Layer ... 690.685-074
Welt-Strip Cementer, Machine ... 690.686-018
Welt Treater ... 788.687-090
welt trimmer ... 690.685-238
WELT WHEELER ... 690.685-482
White-Shoe Examiner ... 788.384-010
WHITE-SHOE RAGGER ... 788.687-166
WIDTH STRIPPER ... 690.685-486
Wooden-Heel Beveler ... 690.685-198
WOOD-HEEL BACK-LINER ... 662.685-042
Wood-Heel Cementer ... 788.684-126
wood-heel cementer ... 788.684-058
Wood-Heel-Cover Ironer ... 788.684-130
WOOD-HEEL FINISHER ... 788.684-126
wood-heel fitter, machine ... 690.682-046
Wood-Heel-Flap Inserter ... 788.684-126
Wood-Heel-Flap Rubber ... 788.684-126
Wood-Heel-Flap Trimmer ... 788.684-126
wrapper laster ... 690.685-174
Wrapper Stitcher ... 690.682-082
WRAP TURNER ... 788.685-030
WRINKLE CHASER ... 788.684-130
Zig-Zag Stitcher ... 690.682-082

brick & tile—BRICK, TILE, AND NONCLAY REFRACTORIES INDUSTRY: This designation includes occupations concerned with manufacturing building and paving brick; architectural terra cotta; floor, roofing, ceramic, mosaic, enamel, faience, and wall tile; sewer pipe and drain tile; crucibles; fire brick and fire clay products; and other clay and nonclay refractories. Occupations concerned with manufacturing pottery and porcelain ware are included in the POTTERY AND PORCELAIN WARE INDUSTRY (pottery & porc.).

Adobe Maker ... 575.684-042
auger-machine offbearer ... 579.686-026
Auger-Press Operator ... 575.382-010
AUGER PRESS OPERATOR, MANUAL CONTROL ... 575.462-010
baker ... 573.682-010
BATCH MIXER ... 570.687-010
Bisque-Tile Burner ... 573.382-018
Blender Operator ... 570.382-010
blunger-machine operator ... 570.482-010
branch maker ... 862.684-010
BRICK-AND-TILE-MAKING-MACHINE OPERATOR ... 575.382-010
brick burner, head ... 573.132-010
Brick-Kiln Burner ... 573.682-010
BRICKLAYER ... 861.381-014
Brick-Molder, Hand ... 575.684-042
BRICK SETTER OPERATOR ... 579.685-058
Brick Sorter ... 573.687-034
BRICK TESTER ... 579.384-010
BRICK UNLOADER TENDER ... 579.685-062
BRIQUETTE OPERATOR ... 579.685-066
burner ... 573.682-010
BURNER ... 573.685-038
Burner, Hearth ... 573.685-038
Burner, Shaft ... 573.685-038
BURNING SUPERVISOR ... 573.132-010
CARPENTER, MOLD ... 860.381-034
castables worker ... 579.684-026
CASTER ... 579.684-026
Ceramic Saw, Tender ... 677.685-034
Ceramic Sprayer ... 741.684-026
Clay-Dry-Press Helper ... 575.686-010

Clay-Dry-Press-Mixer Operator	570.382-010
Clay-Dry-Press Operator	575.662-010
CLAY MAKER	570.482-010
CLAY MIXER	570.685-014
clay mixer	570.482-010
clay puddler	570.687-010
CLAY-STAIN MIXER	773.487-010
clay temperer	570.382-010
clay washer	570.482-010
clean-up worker	579.667-010
COLORER	773.684-010
corrugator	779.684-042
Crusher Operator	570.382-010
CUTTER	579.684-030
Cutter Operator, Brick	575.382-010
Cutter Operator, Tile	575.382-010
decorator	773.381-010
DIE TRIPPER	575.665-014
Drain-Tile-Press Operator	575.462-010
drawer	929.687-014
drier operator	573.362-010
Dry-Kiln Burner	573.682-010
DRY-KILN OPERATOR	573.362-010
DRY-KILN OPERATOR HELPER	573.687-014
dry-mill operator	570.665-010
DRY-PAN CHARGER	570.683-010
dry-pan feeder	570.683-010
DRY-PAN OPERATOR	570.665-010
DRY-PRESS OPERATOR	575.662-010
DRY-PRESS-OPERATOR HELPER	575.686-010
FETTLER	779.684-018
Field-Kiln Burner	573.682-010
finisher	779.684-042
fitting maker	862.684-010
Flue-Tile-Press Operator	575.462-010
frit burner	579.685-014
frit maker	570.685-098
FRIT-MIXER-AND-BURNER	579.685-014
GLAZE HANDLER	571.685-014
GLAZE MAKER	570.685-098
GLAZE SUPERVISOR	574.130-010
Glost-Tile Burner	573.382-018
glost-tile shader	574.367-010
glost tile sorter	573.687-038
greaser	575.665-014
green-pipe inspector	575.687-030
HACKER	573.686-022
hand decorator	773.684-010
inspector	573.687-034
JUNCTION MAKER	862.684-010
KILN BURNER	573.682-010
KILN-BURNER HELPER	573.687-026
Kiln Car Unloader	929.687-030
KILN-DOOR BUILDER	573.684-010
KILN DRAWER	929.687-014
Kiln Furniture, Saw Tender	677.685-034
kiln repairer	861.381-014
kiln setter	573.684-014
kiln-setter helper	573.687-030
kiln stacker	573.684-014
LABORER, GENERAL	579.667-010
MILLING SUPERVISOR	570.132-014
MILL OPERATOR	570.382-010
MIXER	579.685-074
Mixer Operator	570.382-010
MODEL-AND-MOLD MAKER	777.381-014
MODELER	777.081-010
MOLDER, HAND	575.684-042
molder, machine	575.662-010
mold-forms builder	860.381-034
MOLD MAKER, TERRA COTTA	575.684-038
OFFBEARER, SEWER PIPE	579.686-026
PASTER	773.684-014
PASTER SUPERVISOR	773.131-010
PASTING INSPECTOR	773.687-010
patternmaker	860.381-034
PIPE FINISHER	779.684-042
Pipe-Fittings Molder	575.684-042
PLASTIC-JOINT MAKER	590.687-014
Pot Maker	575.684-042
PRESS OFFBEARER	579.686-030
PRESS OPERATOR	575.682-018
PRESS-PIPE INSPECTOR	575.687-030
PRESS SUPERVISOR	575.130-010
pugger helper	570.685-074
Pug Mill Operator	575.382-010
PUG-MILL-OPERATOR HELPER	570.685-074
pulverizer	570.685-098
REFRACTORY-GRINDER OPERATOR	677.682-014
REPAIRER, KILN CAR	861.684-022
Retort-Kiln Burner	573.682-010
RETORT-OR-CONDENSER PRESS OPERATOR	575.382-026
Roofing-Tile Burner	573.682-010
Roofing-Tile Sorter	573.687-034
SAMPLE SAWYER	677.685-034
SAW OPERATOR	677.685-054
sealer and stripper	573.684-010
SETTER	573.684-014
SETTER HELPER	573.687-030
Sewer-Pipe-Press Operator	575.462-010
Sewer-Pipe Sorter	573.687-034
shade classifier	574.367-010
Shape-Brick Molder	575.684-042
Silica-Dry-Press Helper	575.686-010
Silica-Dry-Press Operator	575.662-010
Silica-Mixer Operator	570.382-010
slip maker	570.482-010
slip mixer	570.482-010
Soft-Mud Molder	575.684-042
SORTER	573.687-034
SORTING SUPERVISOR	920.137-014
SPRAY-DRIER OPERATOR	573.382-014
sprayer, automatic spray machine	574.682-014
SPRAY-MACHINE LOADER	574.686-010
SPRAY-MACHINE OPERATOR	574.682-014
stacker operator	579.685-058
Strapping-Machine Tender	920.685-106
SUPERVISOR	570.132-022
SUPERVISOR, EPOXY FABRICATION	579.134-014
SUPERVISOR, PIPE JOINTS	590.134-010
SUPERVISOR, REFRACTORY PRODUCTS	579.134-018
TABLE-TOP TILE SETTER	763.684-074
TERRAZZO-TILE MAKER	575.684-046
tile classifier	574.367-010
TILE DECORATOR	773.381-010
tile edger	779.684-018
TILE GRINDER	679.685-022
Tile-Molder, Hand	575.684-042
tile paster	773.684-014
TILE SHADER	574.367-010
TILE SORTER	573.687-038
Tile Sprayer	741.687-018
top-tile decorator	773.684-010
TRANSFER-CAR OPERATOR	921.683-078
TUNNEL-KILN OPERATOR	573.382-018
Tunnel-Kiln Repairer	861.381-014
turner	579.686-026
wet mixer	570.482-010
yard pipe grader	573.687-034
yard worker	

build. mat., nec—BUILDING MATERIALS INDUSTRY, NOT ELSEWHERE CLASSIFIED: This designation includes occupations concerned with manufacturing building materials not elsewhere classified, such as asphalt and tar paving mixtures, paving blocks made of asphalt creosoted wood, asphalt and other saturated felts in roll or shingle form, roofing cements and coatings, and various compositions of asphalt or tar with other materials. Excluded are occupations concerned with manufacturing material such as aluminum, wood, asbestos, and slate roofing; nails and spikes; plywood, hardboard, plasterboard, and other paneling; dimensional lumber; brick, tile, concrete, stone, and other masonry materials; wallpaper; paint and varnish; flat glass; aluminum and wood siding; and electrical and plumbing supplies. Occupations concerned with the production of mineral wood and fiberglass insulation are includedin the ABRASIVE, ASBESTOS, AND MISCELLANEOUS NONMETALLIC MINERAL PRODUCTS INDUSTRY (nonmet. min.).

blender	570.685-094
Coater, Asphalt	554.682-022
Coater, Slate	554.682-022
dry-talc racker	549.686-014
DUST BOX WORKER	574.667-010
FELT HANGER	549.686-014
INSPECTOR	549.367-010
mixer	550.382-030
MIXER HELPER	550.686-026
mixer helper	550.686-038
REELER	549.685-022
roll winder	549.685-022
ROOF-CEMENT-AND-PAINT MAKER	550.382-030

ROOF-CEMENT-AND-PAINT-MAKER HELPER 550.686-038
ROOFING-MACHINE OPERATOR 554.682-022
safety-sealer 550.686-026
SATURATOR TENDER 582.685-118
Shingle-Machine Supervisor 590.130-018
SLATE MIXER 570.685-094
STILL OPERATOR 543.682-026
SUPERVISOR, ROOFING PLANT 590.130-018
winder operator 549.685-022

business ser.—BUSINESS SERVICES: This designation includes occupations concerned with rendering services for other types of business organizations or individuals. Occupations that occur in business service establishments but also occur in other industries are excluded. Typical of the establishments in which business service occupations exist are advertising agencies, termite extermination agencies, private employment agencies, news syndicates, auctioneers' establishments, coin-machine rental agencies, armored car services, detective agencies, and bottle exchanges. Occupations concerned with personal services, including repair of personal effects, are included in PERSONAL SERVICE (personal ser.). Repairer occupations that have no other specific identification are included in ANY INDUSTRY (any industry).

ACCOUNT EXECUTIVE 164.167-010
ADVERTISING CLERK 247.387-010
Advertising-Display Rotator 869.684-054
air deodorizer servicer 389.687-010
AIRLINE-RADIO OPERATOR 193.262-010
AIRLINE-RADIO OPERATOR, CHIEF 193.162-022
Airplane-Patrol Pilot 196.263-014
AIRPLANE PILOT, PHOTOGRAMMETRY 196.263-018
AIR PURIFIER SERVICER 389.687-010
ALARM INVESTIGATOR 376.367-010
Amusement-Game Machine Coin Collector 292.483-010
APPRAISER, AUTOMOBILE DAMAGE 241.267-014
armed guard 376.367-010
ARMORED-CAR GUARD 372.567-010
ARMORED-CAR GUARD AND DRIVER 372.563-010
armored-car messenger 372.567-010
armored-car messenger 372.563-010
audio-visual-equipment-rental clerk 295.367-018
author's agent 191.117-034
automobile-damage appraiser 241.267-014
Automobile-Insurance-Claim Adjuster 241.217-010
Automobile-Insurance-Claim Examiner 241.267-018
bail bonding agent 186.267-010
BILLPOSTER 841.684-010
BONDING AGENT 186.267-010
burglar-alarm installer 822.361-018
burglar-alarm installer and servicer 822.361-022
burglar-alarm-repairer helper 822.684-014
burglar-alarm superintendent 822.131-022
business investor 189.157-010
BUSINESS-OPPORTUNITY-AND-PROPERTY-INVESTMENT BROKER 189.157-010
CALL-OUT OPERATOR 237.367-014
cashier, check-cashing agency 211.462-026
CHECK CASHIER 211.462-026
CHECKER, DUMP GROUNDS 219.367-010
CHIMNEY REPAIRER 899.364-010
CLAIM ADJUSTER 241.217-010
CLAIM EXAMINER 241.267-018
clipping marker 249.387-022
COACH DRIVER 349.677-014
COATER 503.685-010
coin-box collector 292.687-010
COIN COLLECTOR 292.483-010
COIN-MACHINE COLLECTOR 292.687-010
Construction-Machinery-And-Equipment-Rental Clerk 295.467-022
Credit Reporter 241.267-030
CREDIT REPORTING CLERK 203.362-014
crt operator 203.362-014
CUTTER-AND-PASTER, PRESS CLIPPINGS 249.587-014
detective, private eye 376.267-018
DIGITIZER OPERATOR 213.582-010
director of flight operations 184.167-026
director of photography 184.167-026
DIRECTOR, PHOTOGRAMMETRY FLIGHT OPERATIONS 184.167-026
DISPATCHER, SECURITY GUARD 372.167-010
distribution manager 163.267-010
DOCUMENT PREPARER, MICROFILMING 249.587-018
doorshaker 372.667-038
electric-sewer-cleaning-machine operator 899.664-014
estimator, automobile damage 241.267-014
EXTERMINATOR 389.684-010
EXTERMINATOR HELPER, TERMITE 383.687-010
EXTERMINATOR, TERMITE 383.364-010
Farm-Machinery-And-Equipment-Rental Clerk 295.467-022
Fidelity-And-Surety-Bonds-Claim Adjuster 241.217-010
FIELD REPRESENTATIVE 163.267-010
film booker 295.367-018
FILM-RENTAL CLERK 295.367-018
Fire-Insurance-Claim Adjuster 241.217-010
Fire-Insurance-Claim Examiner 241.267-018
FREIGHT-TRAFFIC CONSULTANT 184.267-010
FUMIGATOR 383.361-010
GOODWILL AMBASSADOR 293.357-018
guard 372.667-038
HOSPITAL-TELEVISION-RENTAL CLERK 295.467-018
income-tax-return preparer 219.362-070
installer 822.361-018
insurance adjustor 241.217-010
insurance-claim approver 241.267-018
insurance-claim auditor 241.267-018
insurance-claim representative 241.217-010
insurance investigator 241.217-010
interceptor operator 235.662-026
Inventory Transcriber 216.482-022
investigator 376.267-022
investigator operator 376.367-010
INVESTIGATOR, PRIVATE 376.267-018
Jukebox Coin Collector 292.483-010
Juke-Box Servicer 639.281-014
LAY-OUT FORMER 970.381-018
LEASING AGENT, OUTDOOR ADVERTISING 254.357-010
LITERARY AGENT 191.117-034
MANAGER, ADVERTISING AGENCY 164.117-014
MANAGER, ARMORED TRANSPORT SERVICE 372.167-022
MANAGER, CUSTOMER SERVICES 187.167-082
MANAGER, INTERNAL SECURITY 376.137-010
MANAGER, PROFESSIONAL EQUIPMENT SALES-AND-SERVICE 185.167-042
MANAGER, TEXTILE CONVERSION 185.167-050
MANAGER, TRAVEL AGENCY 187.167-158
MARINE-CARGO SURVEYOR 168.267-094
Marine-Insurance-Claim Adjuster 241.217-010
Marine-Insurance-Claim Examiner 241.267-018
MEDIA CLERK 247.382-010
MERCHANT PATROLLER 372.667-038
MICROFICHE DUPLICATOR 976.381-014
MICROFILM-CAMERA OPERATOR 976.682-022
MICROFILM PROCESSOR 976.385-010
Motor-Vehicle-Escort Driver 906.683-022
Parking-Meter-Coin Collector 292.687-010
pay-station collector 292.687-010
pest control worker 389.684-010
PETROLEUM INSPECTOR 222.367-046
PETROLEUM-INSPECTOR SUPERVISOR 222.137-026
phone-book deliverer 230.667-014
Pinball-Machine Repairer 639.281-014
press reader 249.387-022
press-service reader 249.387-022
PRICER, MESSAGE AND DELIVERY SERVICE 214.467-014
PROCESS SERVER 249.367-062
property investor 189.157-010
PROTECTIVE-SIGNAL INSTALLER 822.361-018
PROTECTIVE-SIGNAL-INSTALLER HELPER 822.664-010
PROTECTIVE-SIGNAL REPAIRER 822.361-022
PROTECTIVE-SIGNAL-REPAIRER HELPER 822.684-014
PROTECTIVE-SIGNAL SUPERINTENDENT 822.131-022
READER 249.387-022
rental clerk, tool-and-equipment 295.357-014
RENTAL MANAGER, PUBLIC EVENTS FACILITIES 186.117-062
Rodent Exterminator 389.684-010
route driver, coin machines 292.483-010
SAFE-AND-VAULT SERVICE MECHANIC 869.381-022
safe repairer 869.381-022
SALES AGENT, BUSINESS SERVICES 251.357-010
sales agent, credit services 250.357-026
sales agent, exterminating service 251.357-018
SALES AGENT, FINANCIAL-REPORT SERVICE 250.357-026
SALES AGENT, PEST CONTROL SERVICE 251.357-018
Sales Agent, Protective Service 251.357-010
SALES AGENT, PSYCHOLOGICAL TESTS AND INDUSTRIAL RELATIONS 251.257-014
Sales Agent, Trading Stamps 251.357-010
SALES REPRESENTATIVE, AUTOMOTIVE-LEASING 273.357-014
SALES REPRESENTATIVE, DATA PROCESSING SERVICES 251.157-014

SALES REPRESENTATIVE, FRANCHISE 251.357-022
SALES REPRESENTATIVE, GRAPHIC ART 254.251-010
SALES REPRESENTATIVE, HERBICIDE SERVICE 251.357-026
SALES REPRESENTATIVE, SECURITY SYSTEMS 259.257-022
SALES REPRESENTATIVE, WEATHER-FORECASTING SERVICE 259.357-030
security agent 376.367-010
SECURITY CONSULTANT 189.167-054
security guard 372.667-038
senior radio operator 193.162-022
service auditor 376.267-022
servicer, coin machines 292.483-010
SEWER-PIPE CLEANER 899.664-014
shopping inspector 376.267-022
SHOPPING INVESTIGATOR 376.267-022
SINGING MESSENGER 230.647-010
spotter 376.267-022
STORAGE-FACILITY RENTAL CLERK 295.367-026
SUPERVISOR, ADVERTISING-MATERIAL DISTRIBUTORS 230.137-010
SUPERVISOR, BILLPOSTING 841.137-010
SUPERVISOR, EXTERMINATION 389.134-010
SUPERVISOR, MICROFILM DUPLICATING UNIT 976.131-018
SUPERVISOR OF SALES 185.157-014
SUPERVISOR, PROTECTIVE-SIGNAL OPERATIONS 379.137-022
SUPERVISOR, SOUND TECHNICIAN 823.131-026
Supervisor, Telephone-Answering-Service 235.137-010
SUPERVISOR, WATER SOFTENER SERVICE 862.134-014
TANK CALIBRATOR 229.387-014
TARIFF PUBLISHING AGENT 184.167-250
tax form preparer 219.362-070
TAX PREPARER 219.362-070
tearer, press clipping 249.587-014
TELEPHONE-ANSWERING-SERVICE OPERATOR 235.662-026
TELEPHONE-DIRECTORY DELIVERER 230.667-014
TELEPHONE-DIRECTORY-DISTRIBUTOR DRIVER 906.683-018
telephone-interceptor operator 235.662-026
termite treater 383.364-010
termite-treater helper 383.687-010
TOBACCO-WAREHOUSE AGENT 259.357-038
TOOL-AND-EQUIPMENT-RENTAL CLERK 295.357-014
TOWEL-CABINET REPAIRER 709.364-014
TRAFFIC CLERK 221.367-078
transportation consultant 184.267-010
TRAVEL AGENT 252.152-010
travel counselor 252.152-010
trimmer, press clippings 249.587-014
undercover agent 376.267-018
undercover operator 376.267-018
VAULT CASHIER 222.137-050
vault mechanic 869.381-022
vault supervisor 222.137-050
VAULT WORKER 222.587-058
Vending-Machine Coin Collector 292.483-010
vermin exterminator 389.684-010
watch supervisor 193.162-022
WATER-SOFTENER SERVICER-AND-INSTALLER 862.684-034
welcome-wagon host/hostess 293.357-018
writer's representative 191.117-034

button & notion—BUTTON AND MISCELLANEOUS NOTIONS INDUSTRY: This designation includes occupations concerned with manufacturing buttons, parts of buttons, button blanks and molds, buckles, parts of buckles, and buckle blanks and molds, regardless of material; artificial trees and flowers; articles made from feathers and plumes; and needles, pins, hooks and eyes, and similar notions.

ACETONE-BUTTON PASTER 734.687-010
ARTIFICIAL-FLOWER MAKER 739.684-014
ASSEMBLER 734.687-018
assembler, slide fastener stringers 734.687-074
automatic-fancy-machine operator 690.685-062
belt back operator 690.685-194
Bottom-Stop Attacher 692.685-206
Box Attacher 692.685-206
Brancher 734.684-010
Bridge Attacher 692.685-206
buckle assembler 734.687-050
buckle coverer 734.687-050
BUCKLE-FRAME SHAPER 692.685-034
buckle gluer 734.687-050
BUCKLE INSPECTOR 734.687-026
BUCKLE SORTER 734.687-030
BUCKLE-WIRE INSERTER 734.687-034
button broacher 690.682-090
button cutter 734.384-010
BUTTON-CUTTING-MACHINE OPERATOR 734.384-010
BUTTON-DECORATING-MACHINE OPERATOR 690.685-062
BUTTON-FACING-MACHINE OPERATOR 690.685-066
BUTTON GRADER 734.687-038
BUTTON SPINDLER 740.687-010
CENTRIFUGAL-CASTING-MACHINE TENDER 556.385-010
chain-machine operator 692.685-270
chop-and-frame operator 692.685-034
classifying-machine operator 692.685-182
CONVEX-GRINDER OPERATOR 673.685-042
COVERED-BUCKLE ASSEMBLER 734.687-050
Curler 734.684-010
Cutter 734.684-010
DEBURRER 603.685-050
DEFINER 599.685-022
DRILLER, HAND 754.684-026
DYER 582.687-014
Feather Boner 734.684-010
FEATHER SHAPER 734.684-010
Feather Trimmer 734.684-010
Felt-Pad Cutter 781.687-030
flower arranger 739.684-014
foliage arranger 739.684-014
FORMING-MACHINE OPERATOR 559.665-022
GRINDER, HAND 734.687-054
GRINDING-MACHINE OPERATOR, AUTOMATIC 690.685-194
HOT-STONE SETTER 734.687-058
INSPECTOR-REPAIRER 734.684-018
INSPECTOR, SLIDE FASTENERS 734.687-062
IRONER 590.685-042
KICK PRESS SETTER 617.380-010
LACQUER-DIPPING-MACHINE OPERATOR 509.685-034
Lacquerer 599.686-014
leaf sticker 734.687-090
MACHINE SETTER 690.380-010
NEEDLE GRINDER 734.584-010
NEEDLE LEADER 502.684-022
NEEDLEMAKER 619.280-010
needle molder 502.684-022
NEEDLE POLISHER 705.684-046
PAINTER 740.381-018
Petal Cutter 781.687-030
Petal Shaper, Hand 739.684-014
Pin Attacher 692.685-206
PINKING-MACHINE OPERATOR 692.685-130
pinmaker 609.482-014
POLISHER 599.685-078
PREFORM-MACHINE OPERATOR 556.380-014
puller 734.687-074
Roping Machine Tender 739.685-058
SAFETY-PIN-ASSEMBLING-MACHINE OPERATOR 616.482-010
scoop-machine operator 692.685-270
SEPARATOR OPERATOR 692.685-166
Sewing-Machine Operator, Plastic Zipper 787.685-034
SEWING-MACHINE OPERATOR, ZIPPER 787.685-034
shaper 734.684-010
SHELL-GRADER 734.687-070
shell sorter 734.687-070
sizer 739.687-178
SLICING-MACHINE OPERATOR 692.685-174
SLIDE-FASTENER-CHAIN ASSEMBLER 734.687-074
SLIDE-FASTENER REPAIRER 734.684-022
SLIDER ASSEMBLER 734.687-078
slider attacher 734.687-078
SORTER 734.687-082
SORTER, MACHINE 692.685-182
spindler 740.687-010
SPLITTER, HAND 734.687-086
STAMPER 734.685-010
STARCHER 739.687-178
STICKER 734.687-090
STOP ATTACHER 692.685-206
STRAIGHT-PIN-MAKING-MACHINE OPERATOR 609.482-014
SUPERVISOR I 692.130-018
SUPERVISOR II 734.131-010
SUPERVISOR III 690.130-010
tool setter 617.380-010
Top-Stop Attacher 692.685-206
TRIMMING-MACHINE OPERATOR 690.682-090
TURNING-AND-BEADING-MACHINE OPERATOR 679.685-026
wire-brushing-machine operator 603.685-050
WIRE COINER 616.685-086
WIRE-FRAME DIPPER 734.684-026

WIRE-FRAME MAKER	734.481-010
Wreath And Garland Maker, Hand	739.684-014
WREATH MACHINE TENDER	739.685-058
Wreath Wrapper, Machine	739.685-058
ZIPPER CUTTER	616.685-090
zipper ironer	590.685-042
zipper joiner	734.687-074
ZIPPER-MACHINE OPERATOR	692.685-270
zipper measurer	734.687-094
zipper repairer	734.684-022
zipper-slide attacher	734.687-078
ZIPPER TRIMMER, HAND	734.687-094
ZIPPER TRIMMER, MACHINE	692.685-266

can. & preserv.—CANNING AND PRESERVING INDUSTRY: This designation includes occupations concerned with cleaning, shelling, processing, canning or quick-freezing, and preserving condiments, fruits, jellies, nuts, pickles, preserves, soups, vegetables, frozen dinners, and related products; and processing and preserving seafood, such as clams, crabs, fish, oysters, and shrimp.

crab picker	525.687-126
ALMOND BLANCHER, HAND	521.687-010
ALMOND-BLANCHER OPERATOR	521.685-014
ALMOND-CUTTING-MACHINE TENDER	521.685-018
Almond Grinder	521.685-234
ALMOND HULLER	521.685-010
Almond Roaster	529.685-174
Almond Sorter	521.687-086
Apple Sorter	529.687-186
Apple Washer	529.685-258
Asparagus Sorter	529.687-186
bait packer	529.687-086
Barrel Filler	529.687-022
BASKET FILLER	529.687-016
blanching-machine operator	521.685-246
BLANCHING-MACHINE OPERATOR	523.685-014
blender	520.685-030
blending-kettle tender	520.685-030
BLENDING-TANK TENDER	520.685-030
BLENDING-TANK TENDER HELPER	520.687-066
Blower	525.687-126
BONE PICKER	521.687-022
Box Icer	922.687-046
box turner	522.687-038
BREADING MACHINE TENDER	524.685-010
BRINE MAKER I	522.685-018
BRINE MAKER II	522.685-022
BRINE-MIXER OPERATOR, AUTOMATIC	520.685-034
BRINER	522.687-014
Briner, Machine	529.685-190
BRINE-TANK-SEPARATOR OPERATOR	521.685-038
BULK FILLER	529.687-022
BUTCHER, FISH	525.684-014
Cabbage Salter	529.687-022
CAGER OPERATOR	921.685-018
CAN-FILLING-AND-CLOSING-MACHINE TENDER	529.685-282
CAN INSPECTOR	920.687-050
CANNERY WORKER	529.686-014
CAN PATCHER	920.687-054
CAN RECONDITIONER	920.687-058
cap inspector	920.687-194
Carrot Washer	529.685-258
CHERRY CUTTER	524.687-010
Cherry Sorter	529.687-186
Clam Grader	529.687-098
Clam Shucker	521.687-122
Clam-Shucking-Machine Tender	529.685-214
Clam Steamer	529.685-214
coil cleaner	529.687-054
cook	526.381-026
cooker	526.381-026
cooker	529.685-174
COOKER CLEANER	529.687-054
cooker helper	529.486-010
Cook, Fish Eggs	526.381-026
Cook, Fruit	526.381-026
COOK, FRY, DEEP FAT	526.685-014
COOK HELPER	529.687-050
Cook Helper, Fruit	529.687-050
Cook Helper, Juice	529.687-050
Cook Helper, Meat	529.687-050
Cook Helper, Preserves	529.687-050
Cook, Jelly	526.381-026
Cook, Juice	526.381-026

COOK, KETTLE	526.381-026
Cook, Mayonnaise	526.381-026
Cook, Pickled Meat	526.381-026
Cook, Preserve	526.381-026
cook, pressure	526.381-026
Cook, Sauce	526.381-026
Cook, Seafood	526.381-026
Cook, Spaghetti	526.381-026
Cook, Starch	526.381-026
COOK, VACUUM KETTLE	526.685-018
Cook, Vegetable	526.381-026
COOLING-PAN TENDER	523.685-046
crab backer	525.684-022
CRAB BUTCHER	525.684-022
CRAB MEAT PROCESSOR	525.687-126
Crab Steamer	529.685-214
Crate Icer	922.687-046
CUTTER, FROZEN MEAT	521.685-098
DEBONER, PET FOOD	521.685-378
dehydrator	523.685-058
DEHYDRATOR TENDER	523.685-054
DETHISTLER OPERATOR	521.685-106
Dicer-Machine Operator	521.685-018
dipper, fish	522.687-014
dock worker	922.687-062
dress-gang worker	525.684-030
DRIER ATTENDANT	523.685-058
DRIER OPERATOR	523.685-062
DRIER OPERATOR	523.682-022
DRIER TENDER	523.685-066
Dry Roaster	529.685-174
Dumper	529.686-014
DUMPING-MACHINE OPERATOR	529.685-102
EGG-BREAKING-MACHINE OPERATOR	521.685-114
egg room supervisor	529.137-042
electric-sorting-machine operator	521.685-238
EVAPORATOR OPERATOR	521.382-010
Evaporator Operator, Molasses	521.382-010
extract operator	521.685-262
EXTRACTOR-MACHINE OPERATOR	521.665-014
Fig Sorter	529.687-186
Filling-Machine Feeder	521.686-034
FILTER TENDER, JELLY	529.685-114
FINISHER OPERATOR	521.685-142
FISH-BIN TENDER	529.687-082
Fish-Boning-Machine Feeder	521.686-034
Fish Checker	221.587-030
FISH CHOPPER, GANG KNIFE	521.687-058
FISH CLEANER	525.684-030
FISH CLEANER MACHINE TENDER	529.685-118
fish cutter	525.684-030
Fish-Cutting-Machine Operator	521.686-034
fish dresser	525.684-030
FISH DRIER	523.687-014
FISH-EGG PACKER	529.687-086
Fish Filleter	525.684-030
fish flaker	523.687-014
Fish Flipper	521.686-034
Fish Grader	529.687-098
fish-house worker	920.687-086
Fish Icer	922.687-046
FISH-LIVER SORTER	521.687-062
FISH-MACHINE FEEDER	521.686-034
FISH PACKER	920.687-086
Fish Pickler	522.684-010
fish pitcher	922.687-062
FISH ROE PROCESSOR	522.687-046
FISH ROE TECHNICIAN	522.384-010
Fish-Skinning-Machine Feeder	521.686-034
FISH SMOKER	522.685-066
Fish Straightener	521.686-034
flaker	523.687-014
flaker operator	523.685-062
flaker tender	523.687-014
fluoroscope operator	529.685-274
FREEZER TUNNEL OPERATOR	523.685-082
FREEZING-ROOM WORKER	523.687-022
FROZEN PIE MAKER	529.684-010
FRUIT-BUYING GRADER	529.387-018
FRUIT COORDINATOR	529.167-010
fruit inspector	529.387-018
FRUIT-PRESS OPERATOR	521.685-146
Fruit Sorter	529.687-186
general production worker	529.686-070
Gherkin Pickler	522.684-010

GRADER	529.687-098
grading-machine feeder	521.685-318
Halver-Machine Operator	521.685-018
horseradish grinder	529.685-142
HORSERADISH MAKER	529.685-142
huller operator	521.687-118
hull sorter	521.687-086
INSPECTOR, CANNED FOOD RECONDITIONING	529.687-118
LABORER, SHELLFISH PROCESSING	529.687-230
LABORER, WHARF	922.687-062
lumper	922.687-062
LYE-PEEL OPERATOR	521.685-206
MANAGER, FOOD PROCESSING PLANT	183.167-026
MATURITY CHECKER	529.485-022
MEAT BLENDER	529.685-166
MEAT-GRADING-MACHINE OPERATOR	521.685-218
metal mover	529.167-010
MINCEMEAT MAKER	520.485-018
MIXING-MACHINE OPERATOR	520.685-166
Mushroom Sorter-Grader	529.687-186
NUT CHOPPER	521.686-046
nut-dehydrator operator	523.685-066
NUT GRINDER	521.685-234
nut picker	521.687-086
NUT-PROCESS HELPER	529.486-010
NUT ROASTER	529.685-174
Nut-Roaster Helper	529.486-010
nut sifter	521.687-086
NUT SORTER	521.687-086
NUT-SORTER OPERATOR	521.685-238
NUT STEAMER	521.687-090
Oil Dispenser	529.685-190
OLIVE BRINE TESTER	522.584-010
Orange Washer	529.685-258
oven roaster	529.685-174
Oyster Shucker	521.687-122
Oyster Washer	529.685-214
parboiler	526.382-026
PASTEURIZER	523.685-110
Peach Sorter	529.687-186
PEANUT BLANCHER	521.685-246
PEANUT-BUTTER MAKER	529.685-178
Peanut Roaster	529.685-174
Peanut Sorter	521.687-086
Peeler	529.686-014
Pepper Pickler	522.684-010
picking-belt operator	521.687-086
pickle maker	522.684-010
pickle processor	522.684-010
PICKLER	522.684-010
pickling-solution maker	522.685-018
platform inspector	529.387-018
powder operator	523.682-022
PREPARATION SUPERVISOR	529.137-010
Preparation Supervisor, Canning	529.137-010
Preparation Supervisor, Freezing	529.137-010
PRESERVATIVE FILLER, MACHINE	529.685-190
PRODUCTION HELPER	529.686-070
PULPER TENDER	521.685-262
QUALITY-CONTROL TECHNICIAN	529.387-030
Raspberry Checker	529.687-186
RELISH BLENDER	520.685-194
relish maker	520.685-194
RETORT OPERATOR	526.682-034
roaster	529.685-174
SALVAGE INSPECTOR	529.687-174
Sawyer	525.687-126
Scalder	521.685-206
SCALING MACHINE OPERATOR	521.685-386
Scallop Shucker	521.687-122
seam checker	920.687-050
SEPARATOR OPERATOR, SHELLFISH MEATS	521.685-286
SETTER, JUICE PACKAGING MACHINES	920.380-010
SHELLER I	521.687-118
SHELLER II	521.685-294
Shellfish Checker	529.687-230
Shellfish Packer	529.687-230
SHELLFISH-PROCESSING-MACHINE TENDER	529.685-214
SHELLFISH SHUCKER	521.687-122
Shellfish Sorter	529.687-230
Shellfish Weigher	529.687-230
Shrimp Blancher	529.685-214
SHRIMP-PEELING-MACHINE OPERATOR	521.682-038
Shrimp-Peeling-Machine Tender	529.685-214
shucker	521.687-122

SIEVE-GRADER TENDER	521.665-026
sizing-machine operator	521.685-318
Slicer-Machine Operator	521.685-018
Slimer	525.684-030
Sliver-Machine Operator	521.685-018
smeller	529.687-118
Sorter	529.686-014
SORTER, AGRICULTURAL PRODUCE	529.687-186
sorter, food products	529.687-186
Sorter-Grader	529.687-186
sorting-machine attendant	521.685-318
SORTING-MACHINE OPERATOR	521.685-318
SPICE MIXER	520.687-062
STEAK SAUCE MAKER	529.484-010
steam drier	523.685-058
steamer operator	521.687-090
steamer operator	526.382-026
STEAM-OVEN OPERATOR	526.382-026
STILL OPERATOR	522.685-098
storage brine worker	522.584-010
storage laborer	522.584-010
SUPERINTENDENT	180.167-054
SUPERVISOR, BRINEYARD	522.134-010
SUPERVISOR, CLEANING	699.137-010
SUPERVISOR, COOK ROOM	529.132-038
SUPERVISOR, EGG PROCESSING	529.137-042
SUPERVISOR, FISH PROCESSING	525.134-010
SUPERVISOR, NUT PROCESSING	529.130-026
Supervisor, Roe Processing	529.137-062
SUPERVISOR, SPECIALTY FOOD PRODUCTS	529.137-062
Sweet-Pickled-Fruit Maker	522.684-010
Sweet-Pickle Maker	522.684-010
SWEET-POTATO DISINTEGRATOR	521.685-358
syruper	529.685-190
Syruper, Machine	529.685-190
TESTING & ANALYSIS DEPARTMENT SUPERVISOR	523.131-010
THERMOSCREW OPERATOR	526.685-058
Tomato-Paste Maker	521.382-010
Tomato-Pulper Operator	521.685-262
TRAINING TECHNICIAN	522.264-010
Trimmer	529.686-014
Trimmer-Sorter	529.687-186
Tube-Filling-Machine Operator	920.685-078
TURNER	522.687-038
UNSCRAMBLER	921.685-070
VACUUM DRIER OPERATOR	523.685-122
VACUUM TESTER, CANS	920.687-194
Vegetable Sorter	529.687-186
Walnut-Dehydrator Operator	523.685-066
WASHER, AGRICULTURAL PRODUCE	529.685-258
Wet Roaster	529.685-174
wharf hand	922.687-062
Wrapper, Hand	920.587-018
X-RAY INSPECTOR	529.685-274
Yolk Spray Drier	523.682-022

carpet & rug—CARPET AND RUG INDUSTRY: This designation includes occupations concerned with manufacturing and repairing carpets, rugs, and mats in which wool, cotton, synthetic, or other fibrous yarns are the principal materials used.

Base-Cloth Inspector	689.685-038
braided-rug maker	782.685-042
brusher and shearer	585.685-102
BURLER	689.684-010
CARPET CUTTER I	781.684-010
CARPET CUTTER II	585.687-014
Carpet-Finishing Supervisor	589.130-010
CARPET INSPECTOR, FINISHED	689.564-010
CARPET-LOOM FIXER	683.260-014
CARPET SEWER	787.682-014
CARPET WEAVER	683.682-010
CARPET WEAVER, JACQUARD LOOM	683.682-014
Carpet Winder	689.685-046
carver	781.684-046
CHAIN REPAIRER	683.684-010
changeover operator	683.687-030
chenille-machine operator	687.682-014
chenille-machine operator	687.685-018
clipper	781.684-046
CLOTH FINISHER	589.130-010
cloth inspector	683.684-034
cloth picker	689.684-010
cloth shearer	585.685-102

cement

COATING-MACHINE OPERATOR	584.562-010
color-setting-machine operator	681.682-018
cut order hand	781.684-010
DIAGRAMMER AND SEAMER	789.484-010
finishing supervisor	589.130-010
fringe-binder operator	787.682-014
FRINGER	789.687-062
knot picker, cloth	689.684-010
LATEXER	584.684-010
leno sewer	787.682-014
LOOM CHANGEOVER OPERATOR	683.687-030
loom fixer	628.281-010
loom inspector	683.684-034
MACHINE FIXER	628.281-010
MENDER	782.684-042
NEEDLE-BAR MOLDER	556.684-022
needle-punch operator	687.682-014
overlay operator	687.682-014
RAKER	789.687-138
roll-coating-machine operator	584.562-010
RUG-BACKING STENCILER	781.687-054
RUG BRAIDER, HAND	782.684-042
RUG CLEANER	689.687-066
RUG CLIPPER	781.684-046
RUG CUTTER	686.662-010
rug cutter	781.684-046
rug cutter	781.684-010
RUG-CUTTER HELPER	686.686-014
Rug Designer	142.061-014
RUG-DRYING-MACHINE OPERATOR	581.685-050
RUG-FRAME MOUNTER	687.464-010
RUG HOOKER	687.684-010
Rug Hooker, Hand	687.684-010
RUG-INSPECTOR HELPER	789.687-158
RUG INSPECTOR I	689.667-010
RUG INSPECTOR II	789.587-022
Rug Mender	782.684-042
RUG-SAMPLE BEVELER	781.684-050
rug scratcher	789.687-138
RUG SETTER, AXMINSTER	681.682-018
Rug Setter, Six-Quarter Machine	681.682-018
Rug Setter, Three-Quarter Machine	681.682-018
Rug Setter, Velvet	681.682-018
SAMPLE CHECKER	229.687-010
sample finisher	781.684-050
Sample Maker	687.684-010
Sample Processor	787.682-010
scouring-machine operator	589.662-010
SCOURING-TRAIN OPERATOR	589.662-010
Scouring-Train Operator, Chief	589.662-010
sewing-machine operator, carpet and rugs	787.682-014
SHEARING-MACHINE OPERATOR	585.685-102
shear operator	585.685-102
slub picker	689.684-010
STEAM-DRIER TENDER	581.685-058
Stenciler	741.684-026
STENCIL MAKER	979.381-038
string picker	689.684-010
Supervisor, Broadloom	687.132-010
Supervisor, Finishing	687.132-010
SUPERVISOR, SEWING DEPARTMENT	689.137-010
SUPERVISOR, TUFTING	687.132-010
SUPERVISOR, WEAVING	689.130-030
THREADING-MACHINE TENDER	683.685-030
Tufting-Machine Fixer	689.260-010
TUFTING-MACHINE OPERATOR	687.685-018
TUFTING-MACHINE OPERATOR, SINGLE-NEEDLE	687.685-022
TUFT-MACHINE OPERATOR	687.682-014
Velvet Weaver	683.682-010
WEAVER	683.682-034
WEAVER, AXMINSTER	683.685-038
WEAVER, HAND LOOM	683.684-030
WEAVE-ROOM SUPERVISOR	683.130-010
WEAVING INSPECTOR	683.684-034
Wilton Weaver	683.682-014
WIRE REPAIRER	628.684-038
YARDAGE-CONTROL CLERK	221.587-050
yardage-tufting-machine operator	687.685-018

cement—CEMENT INDUSTRY: This designation includes occupations concerned with manufacturing cement from rock. The principal product is portland cement.

AUXILIARY-EQUIPMENT TENDER	570.685-010

Ball-Mill Operator	570.685-046
bulk cement loader	921.565-010
bulk loader	921.565-010
calciner	573.382-010
Car-Shakeout Operator	921.685-038
CEMENT-BOAT-AND-BARGE LOADER	921.665-010
CEMENT LOADER	921.565-010
cement mixer	570.685-010
Cement-Railroad-Car Loader	921.565-010
cement-storage worker	579.685-050
Cement-Truck Loader	921.565-010
Clay Hoister	850.683-018
drier operator	573.382-010
Finish-Mill Operator	570.685-046
grinder operator	570.685-046
Hammer-Mill Operator	570.685-046
Kiln Feeder	570.685-010
MILLER	570.685-046
Miller, Rod-Mill	570.685-046
Mixer Tender	570.685-010
NODULIZER	579.685-034
pelletizer	579.685-034
Pug-Mill Operator	570.685-046
Raw-Finish-Mill Operator	570.685-046
regrind mill operator	519.685-030
roaster	573.382-010
ROD-MILL TENDER	519.685-030
ROTARY-KILN OPERATOR	573.382-010
Screen Operator	921.662-018
SILO TENDER	579.685-050
slip mixer	570.685-010
slurry blender	570.685-010
slurry-tank tender	570.685-010
SUPERVISOR	579.137-010
Tube-Mill Operator	570.685-046
Vertical-Mill Operator	570.685-046

chemical—CHEMICAL INDUSTRY: This designation includes occupations concerned with producing heavy or fine chemicals. Among the products are purified elements; alkalies and chlorine; industrial gases; inorganic pigments, industrial organic, and inorganic chemicals; gum and wood chemicals; cyclic (coal tar) crudes, and cyclic intermediates, dyes, and organic pigments (lakes and toners); nitrogenous fertilizers; phosphatic fertilizers; mixing fertilizers; pesticides and agricultural chemicals; adhesives and sealants; explosives; printing ink; carbon black; and other chemicals and chemical preparations, not elsewhere classified.

ABSORPTION OPERATOR	551.382-010
Acetaldehyde-Converter Operator	558.362-010
ACETYLENE-CYLINDER-PACKING MIXER	549.665-010
ACETYLENE-PLANT OPERATOR	549.585-010
acid blower	550.585-030
Acid Loader	914.667-010
ACID-PLANT HELPER	558.565-010
ACID-POLYMERIZATION OPERATOR	558.685-010
Acid Pumper	914.682-010
ACID PURIFIER	559.685-010
ACID SUPERVISOR	559.132-010
acid-wash operator	551.682-010
agitator operator	551.682-010
Alcohol-Still Operator	552.362-022
Alkylation Operator	559.382-018
ALUMINUM-HYDROXIDE-PROCESS OPERATOR	559.685-014
alum mixer	559.362-010
ALUM-PLANT OPERATOR	559.362-010
ammonia operator	558.382-014
Ammonia-Still Operator	552.685-014
Ammonium-Hydroxide Operator	551.382-010
AMMONIUM-NITRATE CRYSTALLIZER	553.685-010
Ammonium-Nitrate Neutralizer	550.585-030
ammonium-sulfate operator	558.362-010
ammunition storekeeper	222.137-018
ammunition supervisor	222.137-018
anode adjuster	558.584-010
ANODE BUILDER	826.684-010
Anthracene Operator	551.685-122
Aqua-Ammonia Operator	551.382-010
atmospheric-drier tender	553.665-026
ATOMIC-FUEL ASSEMBLER	709.381-010
AUTOCLAVE OPERATOR I	553.382-010
AUTOCLAVE OPERATOR II	709.682-010
Bag Printer	920.685-078
BALL-MILL OPERATOR	558.685-014
BATCH-STILL OPERATOR I	552.685-014

Batch-Still Operator II	552.362-022
Batch Weigher	929.687-062
beader tender	550.685-058
BEATER OPERATOR	555.685-010
beeswax bleacher	551.685-158
benzene operator	551.682-010
Benzene-Still Utility Operator	559.682-066
BENZENE-WASHER OPERATOR	551.682-010
benzol operator	551.682-010
Biazzi-Nitrator Operator	558.382-046
BILLET ASSEMBLER	614.684-010
Binitrotoluene Operator	558.382-046
biological-plant operator	558.682-018
BLACK-MILL OPERATOR	553.665-014
Bleach Chlorinator	558.382-030
BLEACHER OPERATOR	558.685-018
BLEACH PACKER	558.687-010
blender	550.685-082
blender	555.685-046
BLENDER I	550.685-014
BLENDER II	550.665-010
blender operator	550.665-010
blender operator	550.382-018
BLOCK-BREAKER OPERATOR	555.686-010
block-press operator	559.685-038
BLOCK-PRESS OPERATOR	556.685-014
Blow-Off Worker	549.587-010
BOILING-TUB OPERATOR	551.685-014
BONE-CHAR KILN TENDER	553.685-018
BONE-CHAR OPERATOR	553.686-010
BONE-COOKING OPERATOR	551.685-018
BONE CRUSHER	555.685-014
bone drier	553.685-022
BONE-DRIER OPERATOR	553.685-022
BONE PICKER	551.687-010
BONE-PROCESS OPERATOR	559.665-010
Bottom-Liquor Attendant	558.682-014
BRINE MAKER I	550.685-018
BRINE MAKER II	551.687-014
brine-process operator	550.685-018
Brine Purifier	550.685-018
BRINE-WELL OPERATOR	559.685-026
BRIQUETTER OPERATOR	559.685-030
Bromination Equipment Operator	559.682-018
BURNER OPERATOR	558.382-014
Butadiene-Compressor Operator	950.382-014
Butadiene-Converter Helper	558.585-010
Butadiene-Converter Operator	558.362-010
Butadiene-Converter Utility Operator	559.682-066
Butadiene Operator, Chief	559.132-078
CADMIUM BURNER	553.685-114
calciner	573.382-010
calciner feeder	553.686-038
calciner operator	553.685-050
carbon-dioxide operator	559.665-030
Carboy Filler	559.687-050
CASTING-AND-CURING OPERATOR	559.682-014
catalyst impregnator	559.685-106
catalyst-manufacturing operator	558.382-034
catalyst operator	553.682-022
CATALYST OPERATOR	term
CATALYST OPERATOR, CHIEF	559.132-018
CATALYST OPERATOR, GASOLINE	559.382-014
catalyst plant supervisor	559.132-018
CATALYST-RECOVERY OPERATOR	551.685-022
catalyst supervisor	559.132-078
catalytic-case operator	558.362-010
CATALYTIC-CONVERTER OPERATOR	558.362-010
CATALYTIC-CONVERTER-OPERATOR HELPER	558.585-010
cathode builder	826.684-022
CATHODE MAKER	554.585-010
Cathode Washer	559.687-022
CAUSTICISER	558.382-022
Caustic Loader	914.667-010
Caustic-Purification Operator	559.382-018
cd-manufacturing supervisor	559.132-010
CD-REACTOR OPERATOR	558.385-010
CD-REACTOR OPERATOR, HEAD	558.362-014
CD-STORAGE-AND-MATERIALS MAKE-UP HELPER	559.685-034
CD-STORAGE-AND-MATERIALS-MAKE-UP OPERATOR, HEAD	559.167-010
cell attendant	558.382-026
cell-attendant helper	558.685-022
CELL CHANGER	826.684-014
CELL CLEANER	559.687-022

CELL INSTALLER	826.684-018
CELL MAKER	844.681-010
CELL REPAIRER	826.384-010
CELL TENDER	558.382-026
CELL-TENDER HELPER	558.685-022
CELL TESTER	558.584-010
CENTRIFUGAL-DRIER OPERATOR	551.685-026
centrifuge operator	551.685-026
CENTRIFUGE-SEPARATOR OPERATOR	551.685-038
CHAIN SAW OPERATOR	454.687-010
CHARCOAL BURNER, BEEHIVE KILN	563.682-010
charcoal unloader	569.686-034
CHARGE-MACHINE OPERATOR	921.662-014
charger	558.687-010
charging operator	559.565-010
CHECKER	559.165-010
CHEMICAL COMPOUNDER	559.682-018
CHEMICAL-COMPOUNDER HELPER	550.687-010
chemical operator	590.464-010
CHEMICAL OPERATOR I	term
CHEMICAL OPERATOR II	558.685-062
CHEMICAL OPERATOR III	559.382-018
CHEMICAL PREPARER	550.685-030
CHIEF OPERATOR	558.260-010
Chief Operator, Ammonium Sulfate	558.260-010
Chief Operator, Purification And Reaction	558.260-010
Chief Operator, Reformer	558.260-010
Chief Operator, Synthesis	558.260-010
CHILLER OPERATOR	551.685-042
CHIP-BIN CONVEYOR TENDER	921.685-022
chip deliverer	921.685-022
CHIPPER	564.685-014
chip-silo tender	921.685-022
CHLORINATOR OPERATOR	558.382-030
Chlorine-Cell Tender	558.382-026
chlorine operator	559.362-018
chlorine-plant operator	559.362-018
Chlorobutadiene-Scrubber Operator	559.382-034
CHLOROPRENE OPERATOR	term
CHOPPER	564.687-010
Clarification Operator	551.685-122
COATING OPERATOR	550.685-022
collier	563.682-010
Color Control Supervisor	559.132-122
COLOR MAKER	550.382-010
Color-Making Supervisor	559.132-122
Composition Mixer	550.382-018
COMPOUNDER	550.685-050
compounder	550.685-090
COMPOUND FILLER	550.686-014
COMPOUND FINISHER	550.685-042
COMPRESSED-GAS-PLANT WORKER	549.587-010
compressed-gas tester	549.364-010
Compressor Operator I	559.362-018
COMPRESSOR OPERATOR II	559.685-038
CONTACT-ACID-PLANT OPERATOR	558.585-014
CONTACT-ACID-PLANT-OPERATOR HELPER	559.687-026
Continuous-Conveyor-Screen Drier	553.582-010
CONTINUOUS-LINTER-DRIER OPERATOR	553.685-034
Continuous-Still Operator	552.362-022
conveyor-weigher operator	559.687-070
COOK	553.665-018
Cotton-Picker Operator	553.685-034
cotton-weigher operator	559.687-070
Cover Maker	844.681-010
cp bleacher operator	558.685-018
Creative Perfumer	022.161-018
crusher operator	555.685-034
CRYSTALLIZER OPERATOR I	559.685-042
Crystallizer Operator II	552.685-014
CUPROUS-CHLORIDE HELPER	558.585-022
CUPROUS-CHLORIDE OPERATOR	558.382-034
CURING-OVEN TENDER	553.685-038
Cylinder Checker	549.587-010
Cylinder Devalver	549.587-010
CYLINDER FILLER	559.565-010
Cylinder Handler	549.587-010
CYLINDER INSPECTOR-AND-TESTER	953.387-010
cylinder loader	559.565-010
Cylinder Steamer	549.587-010
cylinder tester	953.387-010
Cylinder Valver	549.587-010
cylinder-valve repairer	630.381-030
DECKHAND	553.686-022

Degreasing-Solution Mixer	550.685-106
Degreasing-Solution Reclaimer	552.685-014
DEHYDRATING-PRESS OPERATOR	551.685-046
Dehydrogenation-Converter Helper	558.585-010
Dehydrogenation-Converter Operator	558.362-010
Dehydrogenation-Converter Utility Operator	559.682-066
dehydrogenation operator, head	559.132-078
DE-IONIZER OPERATOR	558.685-026
denitrator operator	558.682-022
DEODORIZER	522.685-046
diaphragm builder	826.684-022
digester operator	552.682-018
digester operator	555.686-010
Dimethylaniline-Sulfator Operator	550.585-030
DISPATCHER, RADIOACTIVE-WASTE-DISPOSAL	955.167-010
dissolver operator	550.685-018
dissolver operator	550.685-114
DISSOLVER OPERATOR	558.685-014
DISTILLATION OPERATOR	552.462-010
DISTILLATION-OPERATOR HELPER	552.687-010
distiller	552.685-014
DISTILLER I	552.682-010
DISTILLER II	552.682-014
DOPE-DRY-HOUSE OPERATOR	559.685-046
dope-house operator helper	559.685-046
dope mixer	550.685-106
Dope Mixer	550.382-018
drier-and-evaporator operator	559.685-074
DRIER-AND-PULVERIZER TENDER	559.685-050
DRIER HELPER	553.687-010
drier operator	573.382-010
DRIER OPERATOR	553.685-042
DRIER-OPERATOR HELPER	553.685-058
DRIER OPERATOR I	553.665-026
DRIER OPERATOR II	553.582-010
DRIER OPERATOR III	553.685-050
DRIER OPERATOR IV	553.685-054
DRIER OPERATOR V	553.686-026
DRIER OPERATOR VI	553.685-118
drum carrier	559.687-050
DRUM-DRIER OPERATOR	553.665-030
drum-drier operator	553.685-042
Drum Filler	559.687-050
drum filler	559.565-010
dry-box operator	553.685-022
DRY-HOUSE ATTENDANT	553.585-014
dry-house operator	559.685-046
drying-machine operator	529.382-030
Drying-Room Supervisor	559.132-122
dry mixer	550.665-018
dry-room operator	553.665-026
DUMPER	922.686-010
DUSTLESS OPERATOR	550.685-058
dye blender	550.685-014
DYER	554.384-010
DYNAMITE-CARTRIDGE CRIMPER	692.685-078
DYNAMITE-PACKING-MACHINE FEEDER	692.686-038
DYNAMITE-PACKING-MACHINE OPERATOR	692.662-010
DYNAMITE RECLAIMER	551.687-018
ELECTRIC-CELL TENDER	558.565-014
Emulsion Operator	559.382-034
Ethylbenzene-Compressor Utility Operator	559.682-066
Ethylbenzene-Converter Helper	558.585-010
Ethylbenzene-Converter Operator	558.362-010
Ethylbenzene-Cracking Supervisor	559.132-078
Ethylbenzene Hydrogenator	558.362-010
Ethylbenzene Oxidizer	558.362-010
Ethylene-Compressor Operator	950.382-014
Ethylene-Oxide Panelboard Operator	559.382-018
Ethylene-Plant Helper	558.585-010
Ethylene-Plant Operator	558.362-010
EVAPORATOR OPERATOR I	553.382-014
EVAPORATOR OPERATOR II	553.682-018
Evaporator Repairer	891.687-030
EXPLOSIVE HANDLER	term
explosives operator	694.685-038
extractor	553.665-018
EXTRACTOR-AND-WRINGER OPERATOR	551.685-066
EXTRACTOR LOADER AND UNLOADER	551.685-046
EXTRACTOR OPERATOR	552.682-018
EXTRACTOR OPERATOR	551.685-054
EXTRACTOR-OPERATOR HELPER	552.686-010
EXTRACTOR OPERATOR, SOLVENT PROCESS	551.685-062
EXTRACTOR-PLANT OPERATOR	559.665-018
FERMENTATION OPERATOR	558.682-018
FERTILIZER MIXER	550.665-018
filler	559.565-010
FILTER HELPER	551.685-074
filter operator	550.685-018
Filter-Press Supervisor	559.132-122
FILTER-PRESS TENDER	599.685-042
filter-pulp washer	599.685-038
FILTER-TANK OPERATOR	551.585-010
FILTER WASHER	559.687-042
FILTER WASHER AND PRESSER	599.685-038
FILTRATION OPER., POLYETHYLENE CATALYST	551.562-010
Filtrose Crusher	555.685-034
Final-Block-Press Operator	556.685-014
fine-chemicals operator	559.382-046
Finishing-Compound Mixer	550.685-106
finishing-pan operator	559.685-074
finishing-powder-press operator	557.682-010
FIRER, RETORT	553.685-066
FIREWORKS ASSEMBLER	737.587-014
FIREWORKS DISPLAY SPECIALIST	969.664-010
FIREWORKS MAKER	737.684-018
Firing-Pin Gauger	737.687-062
Flaker Operator	553.685-098
FLAKER OPERATOR	559.685-074
flaking-machine operator	559.685-074
FLASH-DRIER OPERATOR	553.462-010
Floatlight-Loading Supervisor	737.131-010
Floatlight-Powder Mixer	737.687-090
FLUSHER	559.682-026
FLUX MIXER	550.584-010
FOOT WORKER	934.687-010
formulator	559.665-026
FRAME FEEDER	553.686-034
FRAME STRIPPER	559.687-046
fuel assembler	709.381-010
FURNACE HELPER	558.686-010
FURNACE HELPER	553.687-014
FURNACE OPERATOR	558.482-010
FUSE MAKER	559.685-094
gas-cylinder inspector	953.387-010
Gas-Generator Operator	559.382-018
gas-scrubber operator	551.362-010
gas tester	549.364-010
GAS-TRANSFER OPERATOR	914.585-010
gas worker	559.565-010
GELATIN-DYNAMITE-PACKING OPERATOR	692.662-014
GELATIN MAKER, UTILITY	529.382-022
GLAZING OPERATOR, BLACK POWDER	550.686-022
glue-bone crusher	555.685-014
glue-bone drier	553.685-022
glue-drier operator	553.685-118
GLUE MAKER, BONE	559.382-022
GLUE-MILL OPERATOR	559.685-098
glue mixer	550.564-010
Graining Operator	555.685-066
GRAINING-PRESS OPERATOR	557.682-010
Granular Operator	553.685-090
granulator operator	555.685-042
GRINDER OPERATOR	555.685-034
Grinding-Room Supervisor	559.132-122
GROUND MIXER	550.685-066
Guncotton Packer	920.587-018
HARVESTER OPERATOR	930.683-022
HEAD OPERATOR, SULFIDE	559.132-026
HEATING-AND-BLENDING SUPERVISOR	559.132-030
hide-cooking operator	553.665-018
High-Pressure-Kettle Operator	558.382-038
Hoist-Cylinder Loader	549.587-010
HOTHOUSE WORKER	549.687-014
hydraulic-press operator	555.685-042
Hydrochloric-Acid Operator	551.382-010
hydrochloric-manufacturing supervisor	558.134-022
Hydrogen-Cell Tender	558.382-026
hydrostatic tester	953.387-010
Ice Handler	549.587-010
IMPREGNATOR OPERATOR	559.685-106
Incendiaries Supervisor	737.131-010
Incendiary-Powder Mixer	737.687-090
INSECTICIDE MIXER	550.685-070
INSPECTION SUPERVISOR	709.137-010
INSPECTOR	709.687-022
INSPECTOR, FIREWORKS	737.687-062
ION-EXCHANGE OPERATOR	558.685-034
IRISH-MOSS OPERATOR	529.382-030
IRRADIATED-FUEL HANDLER	921.663-034

Isobutylene Operator, Chief	559.132-078
kettle chipper	559.687-062
KETTLE OPERATOR I	558.382-038
Kettle Operator II	559.682-018
Kettle-Room Helper	559.687-050
kiln burner	563.682-010
kiln unloader	569.686-034
laboratory technician	559.382-046
LABORER, CHEMICAL PROCESSING	559.687-050
LABORER, COOK HOUSE	551.687-022
laborer, glue drying	553.685-058
LABORER, VAT HOUSE	559.686-030
labor supervisor	382.137-010
LEAD-NITRATE PROCESSOR	558.585-030
lead-shop operator	558.585-030
Limer	582.482-014
Linter-Drier Operator	553.685-034
LIQUEFACTION-PLANT OPERATOR	559.362-018
liquefier	559.362-018
liquid-chlorine operator	559.362-018
Liquid-Hydrogen-Plant Operator	552.362-014
Low-Chloride Soda Operator	558.685-062
Low-Pressure-Kettle Operator	558.382-038
LYE TREATER	551.685-094
macaroni-press operator	557.682-010
Macerator Operator	550.665-010
MAGAZINE SUPERVISOR	222.137-018
MAINTENANCE MECHANIC, COMPRESSED-GAS PLANT	630.261-010
MAKE-UP OPERATOR	559.382-034
MAKE-UP OPERATOR HELPER	550.587-010
manifold operator	559.565-010
materials-make-up operator	559.382-034
mechanical-press operator	555.685-042
Mercury-Cell Cleaner	826.684-014
MERCURY PURIFIER	551.585-014
mercury recoverer	551.685-098
MERCURY WASHER	551.685-098
METAL-BONDING CRIB ATTENDANT	550.564-010
MILL ATTENDANT I	555.565-010
MILL ATTENDANT II	555.685-038
MILLER I	570.685-042
MILLER II	555.682-010
Miller, Kiln-Dried Salt	555.682-010
mill operator	555.685-034
mixer	550.685-090
MIXER I	559.665-026
MIXER II	737.687-090
MIXER OPERATOR	550.685-082
MIXER OPERATOR I	550.382-018
MIXER OPERATOR II	520.685-142
Mixer Operator, Raw Salt	520.685-142
Mixer Operator, Tablets	520.685-142
Mixer Operator, Vacuum-Pan Salt	520.685-142
mixing-and-dispensing supervisor	559.132-030
mixing-house operator	550.382-018
MIXING-MACHINE FEEDER	550.686-030
MIXING-MACHINE TENDER	550.685-090
mixing-plant operator	550.585-030
Mold-Release Worker	590.464-010
MONOMER-PURIFICATION OPERATOR	552.362-010
Mononitrotoluene Operator	558.382-046
Motor-Generator-Set Operator	952.362-038
multiple-effect evaporator operator	553.382-018
MVA-REACTOR OPERATOR	558.685-046
MVA-REACTOR OPERATOR, HEAD	559.362-022
Naphthalene-Still Operator	552.462-010
neutralizer	558.685-050
NITRATING-ACID MIXER	550.585-030
NITRATOR OPERATOR	558.382-046
nitric-acid-concentrator operator	559.682-062
NITROCELLULOSE OPERATOR	553.684-014
NITROGLYCERIN DISTRIBUTOR	559.664-010
NITROGLYCERIN NEUTRALIZER	558.685-050
Nitroglycerin-Nitrator Operator, Batch	558.382-046
NITROGLYCERIN-SEPARATOR OPERATOR	551.685-102
NITROGLYCERIN SUPERVISOR	559.132-038
NOODLE-CATALYST MAKER	559.685-126
Optical-Brightener Maker	559.682-018
Optical-Brightener-Maker Helper	550.687-010
ORDNANCE ENGINEER	019.061-022
OXYGEN-PLANT OPERATOR	552.362-014
PACKER-FUSER	737.687-094
PANELBOARD OPERATOR	950.562-010
PAN HELPER	551.585-018
pan operator	559.685-074
Paradichlorobenzene-Machine Operator	555.685-034
PARADICHLOROBENZENE TENDER	556.685-054
paradi tender	556.685-054
para operator	556.685-054
paste-mill operator	559.685-098
PASTE MIXER	550.585-034
pearl-glue drier	553.685-118
PEARL-GLUE OPERATOR	550.685-094
Pebble-Mill Operator	599.685-058
pelletizer tender	550.685-058
Pellet-Post Inspector	737.687-062
PELLET-PRESS OPERATOR	555.685-042
PERFUMER	022.161-018
Persulfate Make-Up Operator	559.382-034
PHOSPHORIC-ACID OPERATOR	558.582-010
Photoflash-Powder Mixer	737.687-090
Phthalic-Acid Purifier	559.685-010
Pigment And Lacquer Mixer	550.685-106
pigment blender	550.685-014
PIGMENT FURNACE TENDER	553.685-086
Pigment Presser	551.685-082
PIGMENT PROCESSOR	559.685-130
PILOT-CONTROL OPERATOR	559.382-046
PILOT-CONTROL-OPERATOR HELPER	559.664-014
pilot-plant-operator helper	559.664-014
pilot-plant technician	559.382-046
Pitch Flaker	559.685-074
PLANT OPERATOR, CHANNEL PROCESS	542.685-010
PLANT OPERATOR, FURNACE PROCESS	559.362-026
plant-operator helper	542.685-018
POACHER OPERATOR	551.685-106
Poacher-Wringer Operator	551.685-162
POLYMERIZATION OPERATOR	term
POND TENDER	939.685-010
Potash Flaker	559.685-074
POT BUILDER	826.684-022
POT FIRER	553.582-014
POWDER BLENDER AND POURER	550.485-022
POWDER-CUTTING OPERATOR	559.685-134
POWDER-LINE REPAIRER	629.261-018
Powder Mixer	550.685-090
powder-press operator	556.685-014
powder-press operator	557.682-010
powder shoveler	692.686-038
Powder Trucker	929.687-030
powerhouse attendant	952.362-038
POWERHOUSE HELPER	550.685-098
PRECIPITATE WASHER	551.685-110
Precipitation Equipment Tender	558.685-062
Precipitator Operator	558.682-014
Preliminary-Block-Press Operator	556.685-014
press operator	556.685-078
PRESS OPERATOR I	559.665-030
PRESS OPERATOR II	551.685-118
Press Tender, Incendiary Grenade	694.685-038
PRESS TENDER, PYROTECHNICS	694.685-038
Press Tender, Smoke Signal	694.685-038
Press Tender, Star Signal	694.685-038
PRESSURE-TANK OPERATOR	523.385-010
PRIMER EXPEDITOR AND DRIER	553.385-014
PRIMER-POWDER BLENDER, WET	550.582-010
PRIMING-POWDER-PREMIX BLENDER	550.684-022
process operator	590.464-010
process operator	550.685-090
process operator	559.382-046
process operator, atomic energy	709.381-010
PROCESSOR, SOLID PROPELLANT	590.464-010
PRODUCTION ASSISTANT	221.387-050
PRODUCTION SUPERVISOR, ANHYDROUS AMMONIA	559.132-046
PRODUCTION SUPERVISOR, DEFLUORINATED PHOSPHATE	559.132-050
PROTECTIVE-CLOTHING ISSUER	222.687-046
pulping-machine operator	555.685-010
pulp-screen operator	551.685-106
PULVERIZER	555.685-046
pulverizer tender	555.685-034
PULVERIZING-AND-SIFTING OPERATOR	550.485-026
pumper	559.565-010
PUMPER-GAUGER	914.382-014
PUMPER-GAUGER APPRENTICE	914.382-018
pumphouse operator, chief	559.132-138
pump operator, brine well	559.685-026
purification operator	552.362-022
purification operator	552.462-010

PURIFICATION-OPERATOR HELPER	551.465-010
PURIFICATION OPERATOR I	551.685-122
PURIFICATION OPERATOR II	551.362-010
pyrotechnic assembler	737.587-014
Pyrotechnic-Loading Supervisor	737.131-010
Pyrotechnic Mixer	737.687-090
RABBLE-FURNACE TENDER	553.685-090
reactor operator	558.685-062
reactor operator	559.382-018
reactor operator	558.382-022
RECOVERY OPERATOR	558.682-022
Rectifier Operator	952.362-038
rectifying operator	552.362-022
REDUCTION-FURNACE OPERATOR	553.682-022
REDUCTION-FURNACE-OPERATOR HELPER	559.686-038
refining-still operator	552.682-010
Refrigeration Operator	559.362-030
regeneration operator	558.585-018
Repairer, Evaporator	630.261-018
REPAIRER I	630.261-018
REPAIRER II	630.684-026
Repairer, Pump	630.261-018
Repairer, Still	630.261-018
research-manufacturing operator	559.382-046
RETORT-CONDENSER ATTENDANT	552.685-022
Retort Feeder, Ground Bone	553.686-010
retort forker	569.686-034
Retort Loader	929.687-030
RETORT UNLOADER	569.686-034
Ring Maker	844.681-010
roaster	573.382-010
Rocket-Assembly Operator	590.464-010
ROLL TENDER	559.362-030
ROSIN-BARREL FILLER	920.687-150
ROTARY-DRIER FEEDER	553.686-038
rotary-drier operator	553.685-050
ROTARY-FURNACE TENDER	553.685-094
ROTARY-KILN OPERATOR	573.382-010
salicylic-acid blender	555.685-046
Salt Cutter	551.685-026
Salt-Plant Operator	558.685-062
SALT WASHER	551.685-126
Salt Washer, Harvesting Station	551.685-126
Salt Washer, Processing Station	551.685-126
SAMPLE COLLECTOR	550.587-014
Sampler, Radioactive Waste	922.687-054
SAMPLE TESTER	553.364-010
saturator	551.382-010
SATURATOR OPERATOR	558.362-018
SCALE OPERATOR	555.687-010
SCREEN OPERATOR	551.685-130
SEASONING MIXER	550.685-106
Second Operator	552.685-030
SECOND OPERATOR, MILL TENDER	555.685-054
separator	551.685-102
SEPARATOR OPERATOR	559.685-166
SERVICE MECHANIC, COMPRESSED-GAS EQUIPMENT	630.281-034
SERVICE-MECHANIC HELPER, COMPRESSED-GAS EQUIPMENT	630.664-018
setter-off	969.664-010
setter-up	969.664-010
shaker-screen operator	551.685-130
shelf-drier operator	553.685-106
shell-house operator	649.682-030
SHELL-MACHINE OPERATOR	649.682-030
SHIFT SUPERINTENDENT, CAUSTIC CRESYLATE	552.132-010
Shipping Hand	559.687-050
Shoe-Dressing Maker	559.665-026
SHREDDER TENDER	555.665-010
Side-Shearing-Machine Operator	930.683-014
Silicator	741.687-018
SILVER-SOLUTION MIXER	550.684-026
SODA-COLUMN OPERATOR	558.382-054
Soda-Drier Feeder	553.686-038
Soda-Dry-House Operator	559.685-046
Soda Flaker	559.685-074
Sodium-Chlorite Operator	559.382-018
Sodium-Methylate Operator	558.685-062
solution-make-up operator	559.382-034
solvent-plant operator	551.685-062
SPECIALTIES OPERATOR	559.582-014
SPOUT TENDER I	932.664-014
SPOUT TENDER I	921.685-058
spray drier	553.685-054
Spray-Drier-Operator Helper	553.687-010
SPREADING-MACHINE OPERATOR	559.685-170
STAMPER	556.685-078
stamp-press operator	556.685-078
Starter-Cup-Powder Mixer	737.687-090
Steam-Bone-Press Tender	555.685-014
STILL OPERATOR, BATCH OR CONTINUOUS	552.362-022
STILL-OPERATOR HELPER	552.685-030
still tender	552.682-010
strainer cleaner	559.687-042
stripper	559.687-046
STRONG-NITRIC OPERATOR	559.682-062
Styrene-Continuous-Still Utility Operator	559.682-066
Styrene-Dehydration-Reactor Operator	558.685-062
STYRENE OPERATOR	term
Styrene Operator, Chief	559.132-078
SUBLIMER	542.685-014
sulfate operator	558.362-018
Sulfonation Equipment Operator	559.682-018
Sulfonator Operator	559.382-018
Sulfur Burner	553.685-094
Sulfur-Chloride Operator	558.382-030
Sulfur Feeder	553.686-038
sulfuric-acid-plant operator	558.585-018
SUPERVISOR, ALUM PLANT	559.132-062
SUPERVISOR, BEEHIVE KILN	563.137-010
SUPERVISOR, BLEACH	559.137-018
SUPERVISOR, BONE PLANT	559.132-066
SUPERVISOR, BRINE	558.134-010
SUPERVISOR, CD-AREA	559.132-070
SUPERVISOR, CELL-EFFICIENCY	558.134-018
SUPERVISOR, CELL ROOM	558.134-014
SUPERVISOR, CHANNEL PROCESS	559.137-022
supervisor, chipping	564.132-010
Supervisor, Chlorine-Liquefaction	559.132-106
Supervisor, Color Making	559.132-054
supervisor, color making	559.132-122
SUPERVISOR, COMPOUNDING-AND-FINISHING	550.137-010
SUPERVISOR, COOK HOUSE	559.132-074
SUPERVISOR, DEHYDROGENATION	559.132-078
SUPERVISOR, DRY PASTE	559.132-082
SUPERVISOR, ESTERS-AND-EMULSIFIERS	559.132-086
SUPERVISOR, EVAPORATOR	559.137-026
SUPERVISOR, FERTILIZER	559.132-090
SUPERVISOR, FERTILIZER PROCESSING	559.130-014
SUPERVISOR, FIREWORKS ASSEMBLY	737.131-010
Supervisor, Flushing	559.132-054
SUPERVISOR, FURNACE PROCESS	559.132-094
SUPERVISOR, GELATIN PLANT	559.137-030
SUPERVISOR, GLUE SPECIALTY	559.137-034
SUPERVISOR, HARVESTING	939.137-022
SUPERVISOR, HYDROCHLORIC AREA	558.134-022
SUPERVISOR I	559.132-054
SUPERVISOR II	550.132-010
SUPERVISOR, INSECTICIDE	559.132-102
Supervisor, Intermediates	559.132-054
SUPERVISOR, LIQUEFACTION	559.132-106
SUPERVISOR, MAINTENANCE	382.137-010
SUPERVISOR, PASTE MIXING	550.137-014
SUPERVISOR, PHOSPHATIC FERTILIZER	558.130-010
SUPERVISOR, PHOSPHORIC ACID	558.132-014
SUPERVISOR, PHOSPHORUS PROCESSING	559.132-118
SUPERVISOR, PIGMENT MAKING	559.132-122
SUPERVISOR, POND	939.130-010
SUPERVISOR, POWER-REACTOR	509.130-014
SUPERVISOR, PROCESSING	551.130-010
SUPERVISOR, REACTOR FUELING	929.132-010
SUPERVISOR, REFINING	559.132-126
SUPERVISOR, SHIPPING	550.137-018
SUPERVISOR, SULFURIC-ACID PLANT	558.132-018
SUPERVISOR, TAR DISTILLATION	542.130-014
SUPERVISOR, VAT HOUSE	582.132-022
SWEEPING-COMPOUND BLENDER	550.685-110
SWITCHBOARD OPERATOR	952.362-038
TANK-CAR INSPECTOR	622.684-022
TANK CLEANER	559.687-062
TANK-FARM ATTENDANT	559.665-038
TANNING-SOLUTION MAKER	550.682-014
Tar-Heater Operator	552.462-010
tc operator	559.682-062
Technical Operator, Grain Preparation	590.464-010
terminal supervisor	559.132-138
TESTER, COMPRESSED GASES	549.364-010
Tetryl-Blender Operator	550.665-010
Tetryl-Boiling-Tub Operator	551.685-014
TETRYL-DISSOLVER OPERATOR	550.685-114

Tetryl-Nitrator Operator	558.382-046
TETRYL-SCREEN OPERATOR	551.685-146
tetryl-wringer operator	551.685-162
TNT-LINE SUPERVISOR	559.131-018
Ton-Container Filler	559.565-010
Ton-Container Shipper	549.587-010
Ton-Cylinder Inspector	953.387-010
TOWER HELPER	558.385-014
TOWER OPERATOR I	term
Tower Operator II	558.685-062
TOXIC OPERATOR	term
TRACER-POWDER BLENDER	550.585-042
transfer-and-pumphouse operator	559.665-038
TRANSFER-AND-PUMPHOUSE OPERATOR, CHIEF	559.132-138
TRAY-DRIER OPERATOR	553.665-054
Tube-Filling-Machine Operator	920.685-078
Tube-Trailer Filler	559.565-010
Tub Operator	559.682-018
TUMBLER OPERATOR	550.685-118
tunnel-drier operator	553.582-010
TWITCHELL OPERATOR	558.585-042
ULTRASONIC TESTER	709.687-054
UNIT OPERATOR	542.685-018
unit tender	558.382-026
UTILITY OPERATOR I	559.682-066
UTILITY OPERATOR II	709.684-094
UTILITY OPERATOR III	549.685-042
VACUUM-DRIER TENDER	553.685-106
vacuum-drum-drier operator	553.685-042
vacuum-pan operator	553.382-018
VACUUM-PAN OPERATOR I	551.685-150
VACUUM-PAN OPERATOR II	551.685-154
VACUUM-PAN OPERATOR III	559.585-022
valve inspector-and-assembler	630.381-030
valve inspector	630.381-030
VALVE REPAIRER	630.381-030
Valve Steamer	549.587-010
Vat Tender	582.482-014
vessel ventilation system operator	950.562-010
vibrating-screen operator	551.685-130
WASH HELPER	559.665-042
washing-tub operator	551.685-014
WASH-MILL OPERATOR	559.485-010
WASH OPERATOR	559.662-014
WASH-TANK TENDER	559.685-182
waste-house operator	551.687-018
WASTE-TREATMENT OPERATOR	955.382-014
WATER-TREATMENT-PLANT OPERATOR	551.485-010
WAX BLEACHER	551.685-158
WAX POURER	737.685-018
weed-cooking operator	529.382-030
WEIGHER AND GRADER	559.567-014
WEIGHER AND MIXER	550.685-122
WEIGHER-BULKER	550.582-014
WEIGHER OPERATOR	559.687-070
wet mixer	550.582-010
WET MIXER	550.685-126
WET-MIX OPERATOR	558.382-058
Wheeler	559.687-050
WHEEL-MILL OPERATOR	555.685-066
WOOD-CREW SUPERVISOR	564.132-010
WRINGER OPERATOR	551.685-162

clerical—CLERICAL AND KINDRED OCCUPATIONS: This designation includes the following types of occupations that are common to a number of industries: (1) those occupations whose clerical duties take up a majority of the worker's time; (2) those occupations whose clerical duties take up a minority of the worker's time, but for which the major requirement is the ability to perform the clerical duties; (3) those occupations whose duties, although nonclerical, are dependent on and intimately connected with definite clerical jobs, and for which the promotional sequence usually is to positions of a strictly clerical character; and (4) white collar occupations that are not strictly clerical in character but that are more closely associated with truly clerical workers than with occupations in other occupational groups. Clerical duties in this classification are considered to be: (1) duties related to general office work, such as bookkeeping, taking and transcribing dictation, typing, auditing, and keeping records (often referred to as pencil work or paper work); and (2) duties pertaining to the operation of various office machines, such as adding machines, calculating machines, and duplicating machines. Occupations of a clerical nature that are peculiar to individual industries are not covered by this designation, but are included with the specific industry.

Accident-Report Clerk	209.362-026
Account-Classification Clerk	210.382-030

ACCOUNTING CLERK	216.482-010
Accounts-Payable Bookkeeper	210.382-014
Accounts-Payable Clerk	216.482-010
Accounts-Receivable Bookkeeper	210.382-014
Accounts-Receivable Clerk	216.482-010
ADDRESSER	209.587-010
addressing clerk	209.587-010
ADDRESSING-MACHINE OPERATOR	208.582-010
adjustment clerk	241.367-014
ADMINISTRATIVE CLERK	219.362-010
amortization-schedule clerk	216.362-026
APPOINTMENT CLERK	237.367-010
area coordinator	205.137-014
Asset-Card Clerk	209.687-010
ASSIGNMENT CLERK	249.367-090
Auction Clerk	219.362-010
Audio-Tape Librarian	222.367-026
AUDIT CLERK	210.382-010
AUDIT-MACHINE OPERATOR	216.482-018
authorizer	249.367-022
Automobile Repossessor	241.367-022
award clerk	249.367-066
Benefits Clerk I	209.362-026
BENEFITS CLERK II	205.567-010
bid clerk	249.367-066
Bill Adjuster	241.367-014
bill clerk	214.482-010
bill collector	241.367-010
biller	214.482-010
Billing Checker	209.687-010
billing clerk	214.382-010
billing clerk	214.482-010
BILLING CLERK	214.362-042
BILLING-MACHINE OPERATOR	214.482-010
BILLING TYPIST	214.382-014
Bill-of-Lading Clerk	214.382-014
Bill Sorter	209.687-022
BOOKKEEPER	210.382-014
BUDGET CLERK	216.382-022
budget-record clerk	216.382-022
budget-report clerk	216.382-022
buyer, assistant	249.367-066
CALCULATING-MACHINE OPERATOR	216.482-022
calculator operator	216.482-022
caller	209.667-014
call-out clerk	209.667-014
canceling-and-metering-machine operator	208.685-026
Canceling-Machine Operator	208.685-026
cash-accounting clerk	211.362-010
cash clerk	211.462-010
Cashier, Credit	211.462-010
cashier, general	211.462-010
CASHIER I	211.362-010
CASHIER II	211.462-010
cashier, office	211.462-010
Cashier, Payments Received	211.462-010
cashier, ticket selling	211.467-030
cash-on-delivery clerk	214.382-018
Cash-Sales-Audit Clerk	210.382-010
Casualty-Insurance-Claim Adjuster	241.217-010
Change-of-Address Clerk	206.387-034
charge-account authorizer	249.367-022
CHARGE-ACCOUNT CLERK	205.367-014
Charge-Accounts-Audit Clerk	210.382-010
CHART CHANGER	221.584-010
CHART CLERK	221.382-010
Chart Clerk, Chief	221.132-010
chart collector	221.584-010
check clerk	209.687-010
checker	221.587-030
CHECKER I	222.687-010
CHECKER II	209.687-010
checking clerk	222.687-018
CHIEF CLERK, PRINT SHOP	207.137-010
chief console operator	213.132-010
Claim Clerk	209.362-034
Claims Collector	241.367-010
CLASSIFICATION CLERK	206.387-010
CLASSIFICATION-CONTROL CLERK	210.382-030
CLERK, GENERAL	209.562-010
clerk, general office	219.362-010
clerk-stenographer	202.362-014
clerk, travel reservations	238.362-014
CLERK-TYPIST	203.362-010
C.o.d. Audit Clerk	210.382-010

clerical

SUGGESTION CLERK	209.387-034
SUPERVISOR	master
SUPERVISOR, ACCOUNTING CLERKS	216.132-010
SUPERVISOR, ASSEMBLY STOCK	222.137-042
SUPERVISOR, AUDIT CLERKS	210.132-010
SUPERVISOR, COMPUTER OPERATIONS	213.132-010
SUPERVISOR, CREDIT AND LOAN COLLECTIONS	241.137-010
SUPERVISOR, CUSTOMER-COMPLAINT SERVICE	241.137-014
supervisor, data processing	213.132-010
SUPERVISOR, FILES	206.137-010
SUPERVISOR, ORDER TAKERS	249.137-026
SUPERVISOR, PAYROLL	215.137-014
SUPERVISOR, PERSONNEL CLERKS	209.132-010
SUPERVISOR, PRODUCTION CLERKS	221.137-014
SUPERVISOR, PRODUCTION CONTROL	221.137-018
SUPERVISOR, STENO POOL	202.132-010
SUPERVISOR, SURVEY WORKERS	205.137-014
SUPERVISOR, TELEGRAPHIC-TYPEWRITER OPERATORS	203.132-010
SUPERVISOR, TRANSCRIBING OPERATORS	203.132-014
SUPERVISOR, WORD PROCESSING	203.137-010
supply clerk	222.387-058
supply-room clerk	222.387-058
Survey Compiler	209.387-014
SURVEY WORKER	205.367-054
switchboard operator	235.662-022
Tabular Typist	203.582-066
tabulating clerk	216.382-062
TALLIER	221.587-030
TAPE LIBRARIAN	206.367-018
TAX CLERK	219.487-010
Technical Stenographer	202.362-014
TELEGRAPHIC-TYPEWRITER OPERATOR	203.582-050
telegraphic-typewriter operator, chief	203.132-010
telegraph operator, automatic	203.582-050
TELEPHONE OPERATOR	235.662-022
TELEPHONE OPERATOR, CHIEF	235.137-010
Telephone-Order Clerk	249.362-026
Telephone-Order Dispatcher	249.362-026
telephone-switchboard operator	235.662-022
Template-Storage Clerk	222.387-058
test examiner	249.367-078
TEST TECHNICIAN	249.367-078
ticket clerk	211.462-010
ticketer	221.387-046
TICKET SELLER	211.467-030
Time-Analysis Clerk	216.382-062
Time Checker	215.362-022
TIMEKEEPER	215.362-022
timekeeper supervisor	215.137-014
Title Clerk, Automobile	203.582-066
Tobacco Weigher	222.387-074
tool clerk	222.367-062
TOOL-CRIB ATTENDANT	222.367-062
TOOL-CRIB SUPERVISOR	222.137-046
tracer	241.367-026
Tracer Clerk	241.367-014
TRAFFIC CLERK	214.587-014
Traffic Enumerator	216.382-062
TRAFFIC-RATE CLERK	214.362-038
TRANSCRIBING-MACHINE OPERATOR	203.582-058
transcribing operator, head	203.132-014
travel clerk	238.362-014
tube clerk	239.687-014
tube dispatcher	239.687-014
TUBE OPERATOR	239.687-014
tube-station attendant	239.687-014
Typewriter Operator, Automatic	203.582-038
Typing Checker	209.687-010
TYPING SECTION CHIEF	203.137-014
TYPIST	203.582-066
unloading checker	222.687-018
Utility-Bill Collector	241.367-010
VARITYPE OPERATOR	203.382-026
Warehouse Checker	222.687-010
Warehouse-Record Clerk	222.387-034
warehouse supervisor	222.137-034
weigher	221.587-030
Weight Caller	209.667-014
weight clerk	221.587-030
weight recorder	222.387-074
WORD-PROCESSING-MACHINE OPERATOR	203.382-030
Work Checker	215.362-022
work-order clerk	221.382-022
work-order detailer	221.387-046
yield clerk	221.382-010

clock & watch—CLOCKS, WATCHES, AND ALLIED PRODUCTS INDUSTRY: This designation includes occupations concerned with manufacturing and repairing clocks, watches, chronometers, and other horological instruments, regardless of type of driving power; clockwork-operated devices, such as time fuses and time-recording instruments; clock and watch cases; and clock and watch parts. Occupations concerned with casing purchased movements are also included in this industry. Occupations concerned with manufacturing clock and watch crystals are included in the GLASS PRODUCTS INDUSTRY (glass products). Occupations concerned with manufacturing wrist bands are found in the JEWELRY, SILVERWARE, AND PLATED WARE INDUSTRY (jewelry-silver.); LEATHER PRODUCTS INDUSTRY (leather prod.); or other DOT industry depending on the material from which the band is made.

ADJUSTER, ALARM MECHANISM	715.684-010
adjuster and inspector	715.381-050
Arbor Inspector	715.384-022
ASSEMBLER	715.381-010
ASSEMBLER, MOVEMENT	715.684-014
ASSEMBLER, WATCH TRAIN	715.381-014
automatic-screw-machine setter, swiss-type	604.260-010
BALANCE ASSEMBLER	715.384-010
BALANCE-BRIDGE ASSEMBLER	715.684-022
BALANCE RECESSER	604.685-010
Balance-Staff Inspector	715.384-022
Balance-Staff Staker	715.684-182
BALANCE TRUER	715.684-018
Balance-Wheel-Screw-Hole Driller	606.685-030
BAND ATTACHER	715.687-010
BANKING PIN ADJUSTER	715.381-018
BARREL ASSEMBLER	715.381-022
BARREL-BRIDGE ASSEMBLER	715.381-026
BARREL-CAP SETTER	715.687-014
BARREL-ENDSHAKE ADJUSTER	715.381-030
BARREL FINISHER	715.682-010
Barrel Inspector	715.384-022
BENCH HAND	715.684-026
BEVELER	715.684-030
BEVEL POLISHER	603.685-022
Block Cleaner	715.687-126
BLOCKER	715.684-034
BLOCKER AND POLISHER, GOLD WHEEL	715.381-034
blocker, polishing	715.684-034
Boring-Machine Operator	606.685-030
broacher	770.682-010
BRUSH POLISHER	603.685-038
BURNISHER	603.685-042
BURNISHER, BALANCE WHEEL ARM	715.684-038
BURRER	715.684-042
burrer, hand	715.684-042
BURRER, MACHINE	603.685-046
burring-machine operator	603.685-046
CANNON-PINION ADJUSTER	715.684-046
CAP-JEWEL PLATE ASSEMBLER	715.684-050
Carbide-Tool Maker	601.280-042
Case Inspector	715.384-022
CASER	715.684-054
Chamfering-Machine Operator	606.685-030
CHRONOMETER ASSEMBLER AND ADJUSTER	715.381-038
CHRONOMETER-BALANCE-AND-HAIRSPRING ASSEMBLER	715.381-042
CLEARANCE CUTTER	615.685-014
CLOCK ASSEMBLER	715.684-058
clockmaker	715.281-010
clockmaker apprentice	715.281-014
COLLET DRILLER	715.684-062
COLLETER	715.684-066
COLLET GLUER	715.685-010
COLLET MAKER	609.682-014
CONTROL CLERK	221.387-018
CONTROL CLERK, HEAD	221.137-010
Control Clerk, Repairs	221.387-018
Control Clerk, Subassembly	221.387-018
Control Clerk, Training And Mechanism	221.387-018
COUNTERSINKER	715.682-014
Countersinker, Balance Screw Hole	715.682-014
CROWN ATTACHER	715.684-070
CROWN-WHEEL ASSEMBLER	715.684-074
CRYSTAL ATTACHER	715.687-018
CRYSTAL CUTTER	715.684-078
CRYSTALLOGRAPHER	024.061-010
CUTTER, V-GROOVE	715.685-014
DEBURRER, MACHINE	715.685-018

DEBURRER, STRIP	603.482-010
DESTATICIZER FEEDER	715.686-010
DIAL BRUSHER	715.687-022
DIALER	715.684-086
DIAL MAKER	715.381-046
DIAL REFINISHER	715.584-010
DIAL-SCREW ASSEMBLER	715.684-082
DIAMOND SIZER AND SORTER	770.687-014
Diamond-Tool Maker	601.280-042
DIPPER, CLOCK AND WATCH HANDS	715.687-026
DISASSEMBLER	715.684-090
DRILLER AND BROACHER	715.685-022
DRILLING-MACHINE OPERATOR, AUTOMATIC	606.685-030
END POLISHER	715.685-026
ENGRAVER, AUTOMATIC	609.685-014
escapement matcher	715.381-018
FACER	770.582-010
FACING-MACHINE OPERATOR	604.685-014
FINAL INSPECTOR	715.381-050
Final Inspector, Balance Wheel	715.684-094
FINAL INSPECTOR, MOVEMENT ASSEMBLY	715.684-094
FINER	715.684-098
finishing inspector	715.381-050
FINISH OPENER, JEWEL HOLE	673.682-022
flat-grinder operator	770.682-018
FLAT POLISHER	603.685-054
FLAT SURFACER, JEWEL	770.685-010
Foam Molder	754.684-022
FOOT STRAIGHTENER	715.687-030
Gauge Controller	601.281-022
GAUGER	715.687-034
GRINDER I	603.482-030
GRINDER II	715.685-030
GRINDER, LAP	603.685-066
grinder, outside diameter	770.684-010
grinder, watch parts	603.482-030
groove turner	715.685-014
HAIRSPRING ADJUSTER	715.684-102
HAIRSPRING ASSEMBLER	715.381-054
HAIRSPRING CUTTER I	715.687-038
HAIRSPRING CUTTER II	715.687-042
Hairspring Staker	715.684-182
HAIRSPRING TRUER	715.381-058
HAIRSPRING VIBRATOR	715.381-062
HAMMER ADJUSTER	715.687-046
HAND FILER, BALANCE WHEEL	715.684-106
hands-and-dial inspector	715.687-066
HANDS ASSEMBLER	715.684-110
Hands Inspector	715.384-022
HARDENER	504.382-010
HARDENER HELPER	504.686-018
HOOKING-MACHINE OPERATOR	605.685-018
INSPECTOR, BALANCE-BRIDGE	715.687-058
INSPECTOR, BALANCE TRUING	715.687-050
INSPECTOR, BALANCE WHEEL MOTION	715.687-054
INSPECTOR, BARREL ASSEMBLY	715.684-114
INSPECTOR, CASING	715.687-062
INSPECTOR, DIALS	715.687-066
INSPECTOR, HAIRSPRING I	715.381-066
INSPECTOR, HAIRSPRING II	715.684-122
INSPECTOR, HAIRSPRING TRUING	715.684-118
inspector, jewels	770.687-022
INSPECTOR, MECHANISM	715.384-014
INSPECTOR, POISING	715.384-018
INSPECTOR, SOLDERING	715.687-070
INSPECTOR, TIMERS	715.687-074
INSPECTOR, TIMING	715.685-034
INSPECTOR, WATCH ASSEMBLY	715.381-070
INSPECTOR, WATCH PARTS	715.384-022
INSPECTOR, WATCH TRAIN	715.381-074
INSPECTOR, WHEEL AND PINION	715.684-126
Instructor, Hairspring	715.221-010
INSTRUCTOR, WATCH ASSEMBLY	715.221-010
JEWEL-BEARING BROACHER	770.682-010
JEWEL-BEARING DRILLER	770.682-014
JEWEL-BEARING FACER	770.682-018
JEWEL-BEARING GRINDER	770.685-018
JEWEL-BEARING MAKER	770.381-030
JEWEL-BEARING POLISHER	770.685-022
JEWEL-BEARING TURNER	770.682-022
JEWEL BLOCKER AND SAWYER	770.381-026
JEWEL-CORNER-BRUSHING-MACHINE OPERATOR	770.685-026
JEWEL-CUPPING-MACHINE OPERATOR	770.685-030
Jewel-Diameter Gauger	770.687-018
JEWEL GAUGER	770.687-018
JEWEL GRINDER I	770.685-014
JEWEL GRINDER II	770.684-010
JEWEL-HOLE CORNERER	770.684-014
JEWEL-HOLE DRILLER	770.682-026
jewel-hole finish opener	673.682-022
Jewel-Hole Gauger	770.687-018
jewel-hole rough opener	770.684-018
JEWEL INSERTER	715.684-130
JEWEL INSPECTOR	770.687-022
jewel-oliving-machine operator	770.381-034
jewel polisher	770.685-010
jewel sawyer	770.381-026
Jewel Sorter	770.687-014
JEWEL STAKER	715.684-134
JEWEL STRINGER	770.687-026
JEWEL STRIPPER	605.685-022
JEWEL SUPERVISOR	770.131-010
LACQUERER	715.684-138
lap polisher	603.685-054
LEVER MILLER	605.685-026
LOCATION-AND-MEASUREMENT TECHNICIAN	715.381-078
Location-And-Measurement Technician, Tool Room	715.381-078
MACHINE FEEDER	715.686-014
MACHINE SETTER	600.380-022
Machine Setter, Automatic	600.380-022
Machine Setter, Hand	600.380-022
Machine Setter, Semiautomatic	600.380-022
Mainspring-Barrel-Assembly Cleaner	715.687-126
MAINSPRING FORMER, ARBOR END	715.687-078
MAINSPRING FORMER, BRACE END	715.687-082
Mainspring-Reverse Winder	715.685-038
Mainspring-Strip Gauger	715.384-022
Mainspring-Strip Inspector	715.384-022
mainspring-torque tester	715.685-066
MAINSPRING WINDER AND OILER	715.685-038
mainspring-winding-machine operator	715.685-038
MASKER	715.687-086
MECHANICAL TECHNICIAN, LABORATORY	715.261-010
MECHANISM ASSEMBLER	715.684-142
MODEL MAKER	693.380-010
Motor Checker	715.684-094
MOTOR POLARIZER	715.687-090
MOUNTER, CLOCK AND WATCH HANDS	715.687-094
OILER	715.684-146
OLIVING-MACHINE OPERATOR	770.381-034
OVERCOILER	715.685-150
PAINTER, CLOCK AND WATCH HANDS	715.687-098
PALLET ASSEMBLER	715.684-154
PALLET RECTIFIER	715.684-158
PALLET-STONE INSERTER	715.381-082
PALLET-STONE POSITIONER	715.381-086
Parts Counter-Weigher	221.587-030
PARTS REMOVER	715.687-102
PEARLER	715.684-162
Pin Inserter	715.684-182
PIN INSERTER, REGULATOR	715.684-166
Pinion Inspector	715.384-022
PINION POLISHER	715.685-042
Pinion Staker	715.684-182
pinner, jewel bearing	770.682-010
pivot-end polisher	715.685-026
Pivot Polisher	715.685-042
PLANING-MACHINE OPERATOR	605.685-034
Plate Inspector	715.384-022
poiser, balance	715.681-010
POLISHER	715.682-018
POLISHER, BALANCE SCREWHEAD	715.685-046
POLISHER, DIAL	715.684-170
Polisher, Numeral	715.684-170
PRESS OPERATOR, PIERCE AND SHAVE	715.685-050
production-control clerk	221.387-018
PROFILE-GRINDER TECHNICIAN	601.482-010
PROFILER, HAND	715.685-054
PROFILING-MACHINE OPERATOR	605.685-038
PUT-IN-BEAT ADJUSTER	715.684-174
RACKER	715.687-106
Reamer	606.685-030
REAMER, CENTER HOLE	715.687-110
recessing-machine operator	605.685-038
reliability inspector	715.685-034
REPAIRER, AUTO CLOCKS	715.584-014
Repairer, Hairspring	715.281-010
Repairer, Watchcases	715.281-010
RIM-TURNING FINISHER	604.685-030
Roller Staker	715.684-182

comm. equip.

comm. equip.—RADIO, TELEVISION, AND COMMUNICATION EQUIP-MENT INDUSTRY: This designation includes occupations concerned with manufacturing and repairing radio, television, telephone, and telegraph broadcasting and receiving equipment. This equipment also includes home recorders; loudspeakers; phonographs; PBX equipment; all types of telephone sets; teletypewriters; telephone station equipment; electric communication equipment; electronic field detection apparatus; light and heat emission operating devices; high energy particle accelerator systems and accessories; and electron beam metal cutting, forming, and welding machines.

concrete prod.—CONCRETE PRODUCTS INDUSTRY: This designation includes occupations concerned with manufacturing and repairing concrete products, such as brick, building block and tile, cast stone, pipe and conduit, poles and piling, vaults, and miscellaneous articles made of sand and gravel, crushed rock, or cinders bound together with cement. This designation also includes occupations concerned with manufacturing quicklime, hydrated lime, and dead-burned dolomite from limestone, dolomite shells, or other substances, and occupations concerned with manufacturing plaster, plasterboard, and other products composed wholly or chiefly of gypsum. Occupations concerned with concrete construction work on buildings, bridges, and similar structures are included in the CONSTRUCTION INDUSTRY (construction).

cement patcher 844.684-010
cement rubber 844.684-010
CEMENT SPRAYER HELPER, NOZZLE 844.687-010
Cement Sprayer, Nozzle 869.664-014
Cement-Tile Maker 579.685-042
CENTRIFUGAL SPINNER 575.664-010
Concrete-Batch-Plant Operator 570.682-014
CONCRETE-FLOAT MAKER 869.687-022
CONCRETE-PIPE MAKER 779.684-014
CONCRETE-PIPE-MAKING-MACHINE OPERATOR 575.665-010
concrete pointer 844.684-010
concrete polisher 844.684-010
CONCRETE RUBBER 844.684-010
CONCRETE SCULPTOR 777.281-010
CONCRETE-STONE FABRICATOR 575.461-010
CONCRETE-STONE FINISHER 844.461-010
CONCRETE-VAULT MAKER 579.684-010
CRUSHER OPERATOR 570.685-018
Crusher Operator 570.682-014
CUBING-MACHINE TENDER 920.685-106
CUPOLA CHARGER, INSULATION 572.686-010
CUPOLA OPERATOR, INSULATION 579.382-014
DISPATCHER, CONCRETE PRODUCTS 579.137-030
Dispatcher, Ready-Mix Plant 579.137-030
Drain-Tile-Machine Operator 575.665-010
feeder operator 575.664-010
Flue-Lining Dipper 579.687-042
Form Stripper 869.687-026
INSPECTOR I 779.387-014
INSPECTOR II 579.664-014
KILN CLEANER 573.687-018
kiln firer 573.462-010
kiln-firer helper 573.685-022
KILN-OPERATOR HELPER 573.685-022
KNIFE OPERATOR 579.382-014
LABORER, CONCRETE PLANT 579.687-042
LABORER, PRESTRESSED CONCRETE 575.687-018
LAUNDRY-TUB MAKER 575.684-034
lime burner 573.462-010
LIME-KILN OPERATOR 573.462-010
lime mixer 570.685-034
lime-plant operator 570.685-034
LIME SLAKER 570.685-034
LINING-MACHINE OPERATOR 575.565-010
MAT INSPECTOR 575.687-022
MAT-MACHINE OPERATOR 579.662-010
MAT PACKER 579.686-014
MAT TESTER 579.387-010
milk-of-lime slaker 570.685-034
MIXER HELPER 530.384-010
MIXER OPERATOR 570.685-058
mixer operator 579.682-010
MIXER TENDER, BOARD 570.685-062
MIXER, WET POUR 579.682-010
MODEL-AND-MOLD MAKER, PLASTER 777.381-018
MODEL MAKER, FIBERGLASS 777.381-010
Model Maker, Plaster 777.381-018
MOLDER 518.361-010
MOLDER APPRENTICE 518.361-014
Molder, Bench 518.361-010
mold-forms builder 860.381-034
MOLD LAMINATOR 806.684-086
Mold Maker, Plaster 777.381-018
Mortar Mixer 869.687-026
Packerhead-Machine Operator 575.665-010
PACKER, INSULATION 579.685-038
PAINT SPRAYER, SANDBLASTER 845.381-018
PAPERHANGER 574.585-010
patternmaker 860.381-034
PIPE STRIPPER 575.687-026
PLANT OPERATOR 570.682-014
PLASTERER, MOLDING 842.361-026
plasterer, ornamental 842.361-026
PLASTER MIXER, MACHINE 570.382-014
plug-and-mold finisher 806.684-086
Portable Grout-Mixer Operator 869.687-026
poured-pipe maker 779.684-014
PRECAST MOLDER 579.685-042
precast worker 579.685-042
puddler 530.384-010
PUMP TENDER, CEMENT BASED MATERIALS 849.665-010
QUALITY CONTROL TECHNICIAN 579.364-010
Rotary-Kiln Operator 573.462-010
Rough Patcher 579.687-042
ROUND-UP-RING HAND 579.587-010

sand molder 518.361-010
sand-molder apprentice 518.361-014
SAND PLANT ATTENDANT 934.685-014
SHAKER TENDER 934.685-018
SHOT-COAT TENDER 575.665-018
spinner, concrete pipe 575.664-010
splitter 677.685-050
STONE SPLITTER 677.685-050
STULL INSTALLER 869.684-062
SUPERVISOR, BOARD MILL 579.130-010
SUPERVISOR, CONCRETE BLOCK PLANT 579.130-014
SUPERVISOR, CONCRETE PIPE PLANT 579.130-018
SUPERVISOR, CONCRETE-STONE FABRICATING 575.131-010
SUPERVISOR, CONCRETE-STONE FINISHING 775.131-010
SUPERVISOR, LIME 579.132-014
SUPERVISOR, MOLD CONSTRUCTION 860.131-026
SUPERVISOR, PRECAST AND PRESTRESSED
    CONCRETE 575.131-014
SUPERVISOR, WET POUR 575.137-014
SUPPLY CONTROLLER 570.382-018
TENSIONING-MACHINE OPERATOR 616.665-010
TIP-OUT WORKER 575.687-038
Vertical-Kiln Operator 573.462-010
WINDING-MACHINE OPERATOR 619.665-010
Yarder 579.687-042

construction—CONSTRUCTION INDUSTRY: This designation includes occupations concerned with various types of construction projects (new work, additions, alterations, and repairs), such as bridges, viaducts, and piers; buildings; highways, streets, and related functions as site preparation and landscaping; pipelines; railroads; river and harbor projects; and sewers, tunnels, and waterworks; and with wrecking buildings and other structures. Occupations concerned with remodeling, repairing, and unusual maintenance functions, other than those normally carried on by the various industrial establishments, are included in this industry.

Acidizer, Water Well 939.462-010
ACID-TANK LINER 861.381-010
ACOUSTICAL CARPENTER 860.381-010
acoustical-material worker 860.381-010
Aggregate-Conveyor Operator 579.665-014
AIR-CONDITIONING INSTALLER-SERVICER HELPER,
    WINDOW UNIT 637.687-010
AIR-CONDITIONING INSTALLER-SERVICER, WINDOW
    UNIT 637.261-010
air-conditioning mechanic 637.261-014
air-conditioning-mechanic apprentice 862.281-026
Air-Hammer Operator 869.687-026
AIR-TOOL OPERATOR .... term
Alberene-Stone Setter 861.381-038
ALUMINUM-POOL INSTALLER 809.664-010
Aluminum-Shingle Roofer 866.381-010
Aluminum-Siding Installer 863.684-014
artificial-marble worker 861.381-046
Artificial-Stone Setter 861.381-038
ASBESTOS REMOVAL WORKER 869.684-082
Asbestos-Shingle Roofer 866.381-010
Asbestos-Siding Installer 863.684-010
ASPHALT-DISTRIBUTOR TENDER 853.665-010
ASPHALT-HEATER TENDER 853.685-010
ASPHALT-PAVING-MACHINE OPERATOR 853.663-010
Asphalt-Plant Operator 570.682-014
Asphalt-Plant Worker 869.687-026
Asphalt Raker 869.687-026
asphalt-spreader operator 853.663-010
asphalt-surface-heater operator 853.683-014
asphalt-tamping-machine operator 869.683-018
Asphalt, Tar, And Gravel Roofer 866.381-010
Asphalt-Tile-Floor Layer 864.481-010
ASSEMBLER, METAL BUILDING 801.381-010
ASSISTANT CONSTRUCTION SUPERINTENDENT 869.367-010
AUTOMATIC-DOOR MECHANIC 829.281-010
AUXILIARY-EQUIPMENT TENDER 869.665-010
awning erector 869.484-010
AWNING HANGER 869.484-010
AWNING-HANGER HELPER 869.687-010
awning installer 869.484-010
Backer-Up 869.687-026
backfiller, hand   see DITCH DIGGER
Bag Shaker 579.665-014
BANK BOSS 851.137-010
batch-mixing-truck driver 900.683-010
batch-plant supervisor 570.132-010
Batterboard Setter 869.664-014

construction

Bell-Hole Digger	869.687-026
BELTER	term
Billboard-Erector Helper	869.664-014
bituminous-distributor operator	853.663-018
bituminous-paving-machine operator	853.663-010
blacktop-paver operator	853.663-010
blacktop spreader	853.663-010
blade-grader operator	850.663-022
Block Setter, Gypsum	861.381-018
boring-machine operator	850.662-010
boring-machine-operator helper	850.684-014
Bowling-Alley-Installation Supervisor	860.131-018
bracer	860.381-042
Breast Worker	850.381-010
Brick Cleaner	869.687-026
BRICKLAYER	861.381-018
BRICKLAYER APPRENTICE	861.381-022
BRICKLAYER, FIREBRICK AND REFRACTORY TILE	861.381-026
Bricklayer Helper	869.687-026
BRICKLAYER HELPER, FIREBRICK AND REFRACTORY TILE	861.687-010
Bricklayer, Paving Brick	869.664-014
Bricklayer, Sewer	861.381-018
BRICKLAYER SUPERVISOR	861.131-010
brickmason	861.381-026
brickmason helper	861.687-026
Brick-Paving Checker	869.687-026
Bridge-Maintenance Worker	801.361-014
bridge worker	801.361-014
bridge worker apprentice	801.361-018
BRUSHER	term
buggy pusher see WHEELER	
Building-Construction Inspector	182.267-010
Building-Insulating Carpenter	860.381-022
BUILDING-INSULATION SUPERVISOR	863.134-010
BUILDING SUPERVISOR	term
BULL-GANG WORKER	term
burner	869.685-010
cable placer	829.684-018
CABLE PULLER	829.684-018
cable rigger	829.684-018
CABLE SPLICER	829.361-010
CABLE-SPLICER APPRENTICE	829.361-014
CABLE-SPLICER HELPER	829.667-010
cable-splicing supervisor	829.131-010
CABLE SUPERVISOR	829.131-010
cable-tower operator	850.683-042
Cage Tender	869.687-026
CAISSON WORKER	term
Calciminer	840.381-010
car changer	921.663-014
CARPENTER	860.381-022
CARPENTER APPRENTICE	860.381-026
carpenter, form	860.381-046
Carpenter Helper, Hardwood Flooring	869.687-026
Carpenter Helper, Maintenance	869.664-014
CARPENTER-LABOR SUPERVISOR	860.137-010
CARPENTER, ROUGH	860.381-042
carpenter, wooden-tank erecting	860.381-070
cartridge-actuated-tool operator see STUD-DRIVER OPERATOR	
CAULKER	term
Caulker	869.664-014
Cement-Car Dumper	579.665-014
Cement-Conveyor Operator	579.665-014
cement finisher	844.364-010
cement-finisher apprentice	844.364-014
Cement-Finishing Supervisor	869.131-014
Cement-Gun Operator	849.665-010
Cement Handler	579.665-014
CEMENT MASON	844.364-010
CEMENT-MASON APPRENTICE	844.364-014
Cement-Mason Helper	869.687-026
Cement Mason, Highways And Streets	869.664-014
cement paver	844.364-010
Cement-Sack Breaker	579.665-014
CEMENT SPRAYER HELPER, NOZZLE	844.687-010
Cement Sprayer, Nozzle	869.664-014
Center-Line-Cutter Operator	853.663-014
CHERRY-PICKER OPERATOR	921.663-014
Chimney Builder, Brick	861.381-018
Chimney Builder, Reinforced Concrete	801.361-014
CHIMNEY ERECTOR	term
Chimney Repairer	869.381-030
CHIMNEY SUPERVISOR, BRICK	861.131-014
chute worker see WHEELER	
Cinder-Block Mason	861.381-018
CIRCULAR SAW OPERATOR	869.682-010
Clamper	869.687-026
clean-up supervisor	869.133-010
CLEARING SUPERVISOR	869.133-010
Cofferdam-Construction Supervisor	860.131-018
Cold Patcher	869.687-026
Combination-Window Installer	860.381-022
Composition Roofer	866.381-010
composition-siding worker	863.684-010
COMPOSITION-STONE APPLICATOR	861.361-010
COMPOSITION-WEATHERBOARD APPLIER	863.684-010
Compressed-Air-Pile-Driver Operator	859.682-018
Compressor Operator	869.665-010
CONCRETE-BATCHING AND MIXING-PLANT SUPERVISOR	570.132-010
Concrete-Batch-Plant Operator	570.682-014
Concrete-Block Mason	861.381-018
Concrete-Bucket Hooker	921.667-022
Concrete-Bucket Loader	579.665-014
Concrete Bucket Unloader	579.665-014
CONCRETE CHIPPER	term
Concrete-Conveyor Operator	579.665-014
CONCRETE CURER	term
CONCRETE-FENCE BUILDER	869.681-010
concrete finisher	844.364-010
concrete-finisher apprentice	844.364-014
Concrete-Finishing-Machine Operator	853.663-014
concrete floater	844.364-010
Concrete-Gun Operator	849.665-010
Concrete-Hopper Operator	579.665-014
Concrete-Mixer Loader, Truck Mounted	579.665-014
concrete-mixer-operator helper	579.665-014
CONCRETE-MIXING-TRUCK DRIVER	900.683-010
Concrete-Panel Installer	863.684-014
concrete-paving-form grader	850.683-022
CONCRETE-PAVING-MACHINE OPERATOR	853.663-014
Concrete-Paving Supervisor	869.131-014
Concrete-Pile-Driver Operator	859.682-018
Concrete-Pouring Supervisor	869.131-014
CONCRETE PUDDLER	term
Concrete-Pump Operator	849.665-010
Concrete-Pump-Operator Helper	869.687-026
CONCRETE SCREEDER	term
concrete shoveler see CONCRETE PUDDLER	
concrete spader see CONCRETE PUDDLER	
concrete spreader see CONCRETE PUDDLER	
concrete tamper see CONCRETE PUDDLER	
Concrete-Vibrator Operator	869.687-026
Concrete-Wall-Grinder Operator	869.664-014
CONCRETING SUPERVISOR	869.131-014
CONDUIT MECHANIC	869.361-010
Connector Hand	869.687-026
CONSTRUCTION-EQUIPMENT MECHANIC	620.261-022
CONSTRUCTION-EQUIPMENT-MECHANIC HELPER	620.664-010
CONSTRUCTION INSPECTOR	182.267-010
Construction-Records Clerk	219.362-010
CONSTRUCTION WORKER I	869.664-014
CONSTRUCTION WORKER II	869.687-026
CONTRACTOR	182.167-010
Contractor, General Building	182.167-010
Contractor, General Engineering	182.167-010
Conveyor Tender, Concrete-Mixing Plant	579.665-014
COOLING-PIPE INSPECTOR	862.687-010
CORE-DRILL OPERATOR	869.682-014
CORK INSULATOR, REFRIGERATION PLANT	863.381-010
Cork-Tile-Floor Layer	864.481-010
Corrugated-Sheet-Material Sheeter	869.664-014
Cradle Placer	869.664-014
Crank Hand	869.687-026
Crushed-Stone Grader	869.687-026
Crusher Operator	570.682-014
CURB-MACHINE OPERATOR	853.683-010
Curb Setter	861.381-038
Curb-Setter Helper	869.687-026
Curb Supervisor	869.131-014
Curing-Machine Operator	853.663-014
Dampproofer	869.664-014
decorator	779.381-022
Diesel-Mechanic, Construction	625.281-010
Diesel-Pile-Driver Operator	859.682-018
Diesel-Roller Operator	859.683-030
DISPATCHER	849.137-010
DISPATCHER, CONCRETE PRODUCTS	579.137-030

construction

HOUSE-MOVER SUPERVISOR 869.131-022
HOUSE REPAIRER 869.381-010
housesmith 801.361-014
housesmith 809.381-022
Hydrant-And-Valve Setter 869.664-014
hydraulic-hammer operator 869.683-018
HYDRAULIC-JACK ADJUSTER 869.361-014
hydraulic-jack operator 910.663-010
hydraulic operator 850.682-010
HYDRAULIC PRESS OPERATOR 616.662-010
Inserter 869.687-026
installation helper 869.687-010
INSTALLATION SUPERINTENDENT, PIN-SETTING
    MACHINE 829.131-018
Instrument Fitter 862.281-022
Insulation Installer 869.664-014
INSULATION-POWER-UNIT TENDER 863.685-010
insulation supervisor 863.134-010
INSULATION WORKER 863.364-014
INSULATION-WORKER APPRENTICE 863.364-010
insulation worker, interior surface 863.381-010
insulator apprentice 863.364-010
iron-and-steel-work supervisor 809.131-018
iron erector 801.361-014
ironworker 801.361-014
ironworker apprentice 801.361-018
ironworker, wire-fence erector 869.684-022
IRRIGATION SYSTEM INSTALLER 851.383-010
Jack-Tamp Operator 910.683-018
Jalousie Installer 860.381-022
jeeper operator 862.687-014
jet channeler 930.684-010
jet-piercer operator 930.684-010
JOINT-CLEANING-AND-GROOVING-MACHINE
    OPERATOR 853.683-018
joint-cleaning-machine operator 853.683-018
Joint Filler 869.687-026
Joint-Machine Operator 853.663-014
joint supervisor 843.134-010
Joist Setter, Adjustable Steel 869.664-014
KETTLE TENDER 869.685-010
LABORATORY-EQUIPMENT INSTALLER 869.381-014
LABOR-CREW SUPERVISOR 899.131-010
Laborer, Adjustable Steel Joist 869.664-014
Laborer, Batching Plant 869.687-026
Laborer, Bituminous Paving 869.687-026
Laborer, Carpentry 869.664-014
Laborer, Carpentry, Dock 869.664-014
Laborer, Cement-Gun Placing 869.687-026
LABORER, CONCRETE-MIXING PLANT 579.665-014
Laborer, Concrete Paving 869.687-026
Laborer, Corrugated-Iron-Culvert Placing 869.687-026
Laborer, Electric Power And Transmission Line 869.687-026
laborer, excavation   see DITCH DIGGER ....
Laborer, Heading 869.687-026
laborer, mixing plant 579.665-014
Laborer, Pile Driving, Ground Work 869.687-026
Laborer, Pipe-Line 869.687-026
Laborer, Plumbing 869.687-026
Laborer, Road 869.687-026
Laborer, Shaft Sinking 869.687-026
Laborer, Shore Dredging 869.687-026
Laborer, Steel Handling 869.687-026
Laborer, Stone Block Ramming 869.687-026
Laborer, Wrecking And Salvaging 869.687-026
LABOR EXPEDITER 249.167-018
LANDSCAPE CONTRACTOR 182.167-014
LANE-MARKER INSTALLER 859.684-010
LATHER 842.361-010
LATHER APPRENTICE 842.361-014
LAWN-SPRINKLER INSTALLER 869.684-030
Layer-Out, Plate Glass 869.664-014
Lay-Out Carpenter 860.381-022
Leadite Heater 869.685-010
levee superintendent 851.137-010
LIFT-SLAB OPERATOR 869.662-010
Lightning-Rod Erector 869.664-014
LINE ERECTOR 821.361-018
LINE-ERECTOR APPRENTICE 821.361-030
Linoleum-Floor Layer 864.481-010
Linoleum Layer 864.481-010
Linoleum-Tile-Floor Layer 864.481-010
loader   see WHEELER ....
LOCK MAINTENANCE SUPERVISOR 899.131-014
Lock Tender I 869.665-010

LOCK TENDER II 850.663-018
Loft Worker, Concrete-Mixing Plant 579.665-014
Loft Worker, Pile Driving 869.687-026
Longitudinal-Float Operator 853.663-014
Lower-in Supervisor 899.131-010
machine helper 579.665-014
Machine Mover 921.260-010
Maintainer, Sewer-And-Waterworks 862.281-022
MAINTENANCE MECHANIC 620.281-046
MAINTENANCE MECHANIC HELPER 620.664-014
MANAGER, CAMP 187.167-066
MARBLE FINISHER 861.664-010
marble helper 861.664-010
marble mason helper 861.664-010
marble mechanic helper 861.664-010
MARBLE SETTER 861.381-030
marble setter helper 861.664-010
Marine Driller 899.261-010
Marsh-Buggy Operator 929.683-014
MASON .... term
MASON HELPER .... term
Masonry Inspector 182.267-010
MATERIAL-CREW SUPERVISOR 921.137-014
Material Hauler 869.687-026
MATERIAL LISTER 229.387-010
mechanical-spreader operator 853.663-010
mechanic helper 620.664-014
Metal-Fence Erector 869.684-022
Metal Furrer 842.361-010
Metal Lather 842.361-010
Metal-Sash Setter 809.381-022
metal-tile lather 860.381-010
Metal-Tile Setter 861.381-034
metal-trim erector 809.381-022
MINER 850.381-010
Mineral-Wool-Insulation Supervisor 863.134-010
Miner Helper 869.687-026
MIRROR INSTALLER 865.361-010
Mixer, Hand, Cement Gun 869.687-026
mixer helper 579.665-014
mixer tender 579.665-014
mixing-plant dumper 579.665-014
Mold Maker 869.687-026
MONUMENT SETTER 861.361-014
Mortar Mixer 869.687-026
moto-mix operator 900.683-010
Motor Grader, Fine Grade 850.663-022
MOTOR-GRADER OPERATOR 850.663-022
Motor Grader, Rough Grade 850.663-022
motor-patrol operator 850.663-022
Mucker 869.687-026
Mucker, Cofferdam 869.687-026
mucker operator 850.683-026
MUCKING-MACHINE OPERATOR 850.683-026
Mud-Jack Nozzle Worker 869.687-026
oil-distributor tender 853.665-010
Oil Sprayer 869.687-026
oil sprayer 853.663-018
oil-spreader operator 853.663-018
oil-spreader-truck operator 853.663-018
OPERATING ENGINEER 859.683-010
OPERATING-ENGINEER APPRENTICE 859.683-014
Ornamental-Brick Installer 863.684-014
Ornamental-Bronze Worker 809.381-022
ornamental-iron erector 809.381-022
ORNAMENTAL-IRON WORKER 809.381-022
ORNAMENTAL-IRON-WORKER APPRENTICE 809.381-026
Ornamental-Iron-Worker Helper 869.664-014
ornamental-metal-erector apprentice 809.381-026
Ornamental-Plaster Sticker 842.361-018
Ornamental-Rail Installer 809.381-022
PAINTER 840.381-010
Painter Helper 869.687-026
Painter, Interior Finish 840.381-010
Painter, Rough 869.664-014
Painter, Structural Steel 869.664-014
Paint-Stripping-Machine Operator 869.664-014
PAPERHANGER 841.381-010
Paperhanger, Pipe 869.687-026
Paper Latcher 869.687-026
Paper Spooler 869.687-026
pavement curer   see CONCRETE CURER ....
pavement-joint-cleaning-machine operator 853.683-018
Paving-Bed Maker 869.687-026
paving-form mover   see FORM STRIPPER ....
paving-machine operator, asphalt or bituminous 853.663-010

Paving Rammer	869.687-026
Permastone Dresser	869.664-014
PILE DRIVER	term
PILE-DRIVER OPERATOR	859.682-018
Pile-Driver Operator, Barge Mounted	859.682-018
Pile-Driving Setter	869.664-014
Pipe-And-Test Supervisor	899.131-010
Pipe-Bending-Machine Operator	617.482-010
PIPE BUFFER	705.684-054
Pipe Caulker	869.664-014
PIPE-CLEANING-AND-PRIMING-MACHINE OPERATOR	862.662-010
Pipe-Cleaning-Machine Operator	862.662-010
PIPE CUTTER	term
PIPE FITTER	862.281-022
Pipe Fitter, Ammonia	862.281-022
PIPE-FITTER APPRENTICE	862.281-026
Pipe Fitter, Fire-Sprinkler Systems	862.281-022
Pipe Fitter, Gas Pipe	862.281-022
PIPE-FITTER HELPER	862.684-022
Pipe Fitter, Plastic Pipe	862.281-022
Pipe Fitter, Soft Copper	862.281-022
PIPE-FITTER SUPERVISOR	862.131-010
Pipe Fitter, Welding	862.281-022
pipe inspector	862.687-010
PIPE INSTALLER	869.381-018
pipe jeeper	862.687-014
Pipe Layer	869.664-014
Pipe-Layer Helper	869.687-026
Pipe-Laying Supervisor	899.131-010
PIPE-LINE-CONSTRUCTION INSPECTOR	869.367-018
Pipe-Line Inspector	182.267-010
PIPE-LINE SUPERVISOR	term
Pipe-Line Worker	869.664-014
Pipe-Machine Operator	869.687-026
PIPE THREADER, HAND	term
PIPE-WRAPPING-MACHINE OPERATOR	862.682-014
PLANT OPERATOR	570.682-014
Plaster-Block Layer	861.381-018
PLASTERER	842.361-018
PLASTERER APPRENTICE	842.361-022
Plasterer, Finish	842.361-018
Plasterer Helper	869.687-026
Plasterer, Maintenance	842.361-018
PLASTERER, MOLDING	842.361-026
plasterer, ornamental	842.361-026
Plasterer, Rough	842.361-018
Plasterer, Spray Gun	842.361-018
plasterer, stucco	842.381-014
PLASTER-MACHINE TENDER	842.665-010
Plastic-Panel Installer	863.684-014
Plastic-Tile Layer	861.381-034
Plate-Glass Installer	865.381-010
plow holder	850.663-014
plow shaker	850.663-014
PLUMBER	862.381-030
PLUMBER APPRENTICE	862.381-034
Plumber Helper	869.664-014
plumber, pipe fitting	862.281-022
PLUMBER SUPERVISOR	862.131-018
Plumber Supervisor, Maintenance	862.131-010
PNEUMATIC-HOIST OPERATOR	921.663-046
pneumatic-tool operator see AIR-TOOL OPERATOR	
Pneumatic-Tube Fitter	862.281-022
Pointer, Caulker, And Cleaner	869.664-014
Pole-Truck Driver	904.383-010
Porcelain-Enamel Installer	863.684-014
Portable Grout-Mixer Operator	869.687-026
post-hole digger	859.682-010
POURED-CONCRETE-WALL TECHNICIAN	869.261-018
powder-actuated-tool operator see STUD-DRIVER OPERATOR	
Powder Guard	372.667-034
power-grader operator	850.663-022
PROGRESS CLERK	221.362-022
Puddler, Pile Driving	869.687-026
Pulvi-Mixer Operator	859.683-026
PUMP ERECTOR	637.281-010
Pump-Erector Helper	869.664-014
pump installation and servicer	637.281-010
Pump Tender	869.665-010
PUMP TENDER, CEMENT BASED MATERIALS	849.665-010
rail gang supervisor	869.134-022
RAILROAD SUPERVISOR	term
ready-mix-truck driver	900.683-010
REAMER	term

Receiver Setter	869.664-014
refrigeration-mechanic apprentice	862.281-026
Reinforced-Concrete Inspector	182.267-010
reinforcing-bar setter	801.684-026
reinforcing-iron worker	801.684-026
Reinforcing-Iron-Worker Helper	869.687-026
REINFORCING-METAL WORKER	801.684-026
reinforcing-steel erector	801.684-026
REINFORCING-STEEL-MACHINE OPERATOR	859.683-022
reinforcing-steel placer	801.684-026
reinforcing-steel setter	801.684-026
reinforcing-steel worker	801.684-026
Reinforcing-Steel Worker, Wire Mesh	869.687-026
RIGGER	869.683-014
RIGGING SUPERVISOR	921.130-010
right-of-way supervisor	869.133-010
Riprap Placer	869.687-026
RIVER-AND-HARBOR SUPERVISOR	term
River-Crossing Supervisor	899.131-010
road grader	850.663-022
road-hogger operator	850.663-022
ROAD-MIXER OPERATOR	859.683-026
road-oil distributor	853.663-018
ROAD-OILING-TRUCK DRIVER	853.663-018
ROAD-ROLLER OPERATOR	859.683-030
Road-Roller Operator, Hot Mix	859.683-030
Rockboard Lather	842.361-010
ROCK-DRILL OPERATOR I	850.683-034
ROCK-DRILL OPERATOR II	850.662-014
Rod Inspector	182.267-010
roller operator	859.683-030
roller, pneumatic	859.683-030
roll operator	859.683-030
ROOFER	866.381-010
ROOFER APPLICATOR	866.684-010
ROOFER APPRENTICE	866.381-014
Roofer, Gypsum	866.381-010
Roofer Helper	869.687-026
Roofer Helper, Vinyl Coating	869.687-026
Roofer, Metal	804.281-010
Roofer, Vinyl Coating	869.664-014
ROOFING SUPERVISOR	866.131-010
Roof-Promenade-Tile Setter	861.381-054
Rotary-Drill Operator	930.382-010
rotary-drill-rig operator	859.362-010
rotary-soil-stabilizer operator	859.683-026
roto-mixer operator	859.683-026
Rubber-Tile-Floor Layer	864.481-010
safety-grooving-machine operator	853.683-018
sales representative	250.157-010
Sand-And-Gravel-Plant Operator	570.682-014
SAND HOG	term
Scaffold Builder	860.381-042
Scaffold Builder, Metal	801.361-014
SCRAPER OPERATOR	850.683-038
Screed Operator	853.663-014
Seat Installer	869.664-014
SEPTIC-TANK INSTALLER	851.663-010
Septic-Tank Servicer	869.664-014
service engineer	620.281-046
setter	861.361-014
SEWER-AND-WATERWORKS SUPERVISOR	term
Sewer Tapper	869.664-014
Sheather	860.381-042
Sheeting Puller	869.687-026
Sheet-Pile-Driver Operator	859.682-018
Sheet-Pile-Hammer Operator	869.687-026
sheetrock installer	842.684-014
sheetrock taper	842.664-010
shield operator	850.682-010
SHIELD RUNNER	850.682-010
shifter	859.137-018
Shooter, Water Well	859.261-010
shop mechanic	620.281-046
shop-mechanic helper	620.664-014
SHORE HAND, DREDGE OR BARGE	939.667-018
Shorer	869.664-014
shore-working supervisor	862.134-010
Shower-Enclosure Installer	865.381-010
SIDER	863.684-014
siding applicator	863.684-014
SIGNALER	869.667-014
Silo Erector	861.381-018
Single-Pass-Soil-Stabilizer Operator	859.683-026
Skip Tender, Concrete Mixing Or Batch Plant	869.687-026

construction

Trim Setter	860.381-022
TRUCKLOAD CHECKER	222.367-066
Tuck Pointer	869.664-014
Tunnel-Form-Placing Supervisor	869.131-014
Tunnel-Heading Inspector	182.267-010
tunneling-machine operator	850.662-010
TUNNEL WORKER	term
UTILITY-TRACTOR OPERATOR	850.683-046
Varnisher	840.381-010
Vibrating-Screed Operator	853.663-014
Wagon-Drill Operator	930.382-010
Wallpaper Remover, Steam	869.687-026
Wall Washer	869.687-026
WASHING-AND-SCREENING PLANT SUPERVISOR	570.132-018
Waterproofer	869.664-014
Waterproofer Helper	869.687-026
Water-Truck Driver I	904.383-010
WATER-TRUCK DRIVER II	905.683-010
water-well driller	859.362-010
Weather Stripper	860.381-022
Well Digger	869.687-026
WELL-DRILL OPERATOR	859.362-010
Well-Drill Operator, Cable Tool	859.362-010
Well-Drill-Operator Helper, Cable Tool	869.664-014
Well-Drill-Operator Helper, Rotary Drill	869.664-014
Well-Drill Operator, Rotary Drill	859.362-010
WELL-POINT PUMPING SUPERVISOR	862.132-010
WELL-POINT SETTER	term
Well-Reactivator Operator	859.362-010
wheelbarrow pusher see WHEELER	
WHEELER	term
White Washer	869.687-026
WIND-GENERATING-ELECTRIC-POWER INSTALLER	821.381-018
wire-fence builder	869.684-022
Wire-Fence Erector	869.684-022
wirer	824.261-010
Wooden-Fence Erector	869.684-022
wood-form builder	860.381-046
Wood Lather	842.361-010
Wood-Pile-Driver Operator	859.682-018
Wood-Sash-And-Frame Carpenter	860.381-022
Wood-Shingle Roofer	866.381-010
Wood-Strip-Block Floor Installer	860.381-022
Wrecker	869.664-014
WRECKING SUPERVISOR	869.137-014
YARD SUPERVISOR	229.137-014

cutlery-hrdwr.—CUTLERY, HANDTOOLS, AND HARDWARE INDUSTRY: This designation includes occupations concerned with manufacturing and repairing various kinds of cutlery and handtools. The principal products include: table and kitchen cutlery; all edge tools such as augers, axes, gimlets, hatchets, knives, meat choppers, planes, razors, scissors, and shears; handtools, except power-driven handtools used by farmers, iron-workers, masons, mechanics, and plumbers; files and rasps including recutting these implements; complete handsaws and saw blades for hand- and power-driven saws. This industry also includes occupations engaged in manufacturing miscellaneous metal products, not elsewhere classified, which are usually termed hardware. These include clamps, door bolts and locks, hinges, pulleys, and vacuum bottles. Occupations concerned with the manufacture of plated stainless steel and silver flatware are included in the JEWELRY, SILVERWARE, AND PLATED WARE INDUSTRY (jewelry-silver.).

ASSEMBLER	701.687-010
Assembler, Knife	701.687-010
BLADE GROOVER	705.582-010
blank driller	709.684-082
CALIBRATOR	701.684-010
capper	779.684-034
COLD-PRESS LOADER	701.687-018
DIAMOND BLENDER	590.685-018
Electric-Razor Assembler	701.687-010
etcher	500.685-010
ETCHER, ELECTROLYTIC	500.685-010
ETCHER, HAND	704.687-014
ETCHER, MACHINE	619.685-042
featherer	701.687-030
FILE CUTTER	605.685-014
Final Inspector	701.687-026
glass bender	573.686-018
glass curvature gauger	701.687-022
glass grinder	673.685-066
glass marker	775.684-046
glass setter	701.684-018
GLASS-VIAL-BENDING-CONVEYOR FEEDER	573.686-018

grinder-and-honer operator, automatic	603.685-058
GRINDER OPERATOR, AUTOMATIC	603.685-058
Hacksaw Inspector	709.587-010
inspector	701.687-026
INSPECTOR	709.587-010
INSPECTOR, OPEN DIE	701.684-014
laborer, cutting tool	701.687-018
LEVEL-GLASS-FORMING-MACHINE OPERATOR	679.665-010
LEVEL-GLASS-VIAL FILLER	692.685-114
LEVEL-VIAL CURVATURE GAUGER	701.687-022
LEVEL-VIAL INSIDE GRINDER	673.685-066
LEVEL-VIAL INSPECTOR-AND-TESTER	701.687-026
LEVEL-VIAL MARKER	775.684-046
LEVEL-VIAL SEALER	779.684-034
LEVEL-VIAL SETTER	701.684-018
LOCK ASSEMBLER	706.684-074
NICKING-MACHINE OPERATOR	609.682-026
nick setter	609.682-026
Notched-Blade Loader	701.687-018
Operator, Coating Furnace	554.685-014
PATTERNMAKER, SAMPLE	693.281-022
pinner	701.687-010
POWER-CHISEL OPERATOR	701.687-030
PRINTING-MACHINE OPERATOR, FOLDING RULES	652.685-074
PRINTING-MACHINE OPERATOR, TAPE RULES	652.662-010
PROTECTOR-PLATE ATTACHER	692.685-138
QUALITY-CONTROL INSPECTOR	701.261-010
REPAIRER, HANDTOOLS	701.381-010
SAW-EDGE FUSER, CIRCULAR	701.684-026
SAW MAKER	601.381-034
saw mechanic	601.381-034
Sawsmith	601.381-034
SCRIBING-MACHINE OPERATOR	605.685-042
Shear Assembler	701.687-010
STAB SETTER AND DRILLER	709.684-082
Steel-Rule Inspector	709.587-010
strike-plate attacher	692.685-138
SUPERVISOR	615.130-014
SUPERVISOR, ASSEMBLY-AND-PACKING	701.137-010
TEMPLATE CUTTER	703.684-018
Tester	701.687-026
TRIM ATTACHER	692.685-230
Vial Gauger	701.687-026
WEDGER, MACHINE	701.687-034

dairy products—DAIRY PRODUCTS INDUSTRY: This designation includes occupations concerned with separating, heating, cooling, mixing, curdling, forming, cutting, grinding, freezing, and drying milk and cream preparations and combining milk, cream, flavoring, syrup, and chemical or organic ingredients to make butter, sherbet, and related products. Included are occupations concerned with the collection of milk and cream from farms.

BATCH FREEZER	523.685-010
BLENDER-CONVEYOR OPERATOR	529.685-022
BLENDING-MACHINE OPERATOR	522.685-010
Brine-Room Laborer	529.686-050
BRINE-TANK TENDER	529.685-030
bulk intake worker	222.485-010
Butter-Chilling Equipment Operator	529.362-010
Butter Churner	529.362-010
BUTTERMAKER	529.362-010
BUTTERMAKER, CONTINUOUS CHURN	529.382-010
Buttermaker Helper	529.686-026
Buttermilk-Drier Operator	523.682-022
Butter Production Supervisor	529.131-014
Byproducts Maker	529.382-018
can intake worker	222.585-010
CASTING-MACHINE OPERATOR	520.685-058
Cellar Laborer	529.686-050
CENTRIFUGE OPERATOR	521.685-042
CHEESE BLENDER	520.487-010
cheese cooker	529.361-018
CHEESE CUTTER	529.585-010
CHEESE GRADER	529.387-010
CHEESEMAKER	529.361-018
CHEESEMAKER HELPER	529.682-014
Cheese Production Supervisor	529.131-014
Clarifier Operator	529.382-018
cone chocolate dipper	524.686-014
cone racker	524.686-014
cook blender	526.665-010
COOKER, PROCESS CHEESE	526.665-010
Cooler Operator	529.382-018
Cooler Supervisor	929.137-022

domestic ser.

Cooler Worker	922.687-058
COTTAGE-CHEESE MAKER	522.382-010
Cream-Cheese Maker	526.665-010
DAIRY-EQUIPMENT REPAIRER	629.281-018
DAIRY HELPER	529.686-026
DAIRY-PROCESSING-EQUIPMENT OPERATOR	529.382-018
DECORATOR	524.381-014
DRIER OPERATOR	523.682-022
Equipment Sterilizer	599.684-010
EVAPORATOR OPERATOR	521.382-010
FIELD-CONTACT TECHNICIAN	162.117-026
FLAVOR ROOM WORKER	529.685-130
Flavor-Tank Tender	529.685-146
Formula Bottler	520.487-014
Formula Maker	520.487-014
FORMULA-ROOM WORKER	520.487-014
freezer	529.482-010
freezer assistant	529.685-146
FREEZER OPERATOR	529.482-010
GRATED-CHEESE MAKER	521.685-162
grating-machine operator	521.685-162
Homogenizer Operator	529.382-018
ice-cream freezer	529.482-010
ICE CREAM FREEZER ASSISTANT	529.685-146
ICICLE-MACHINE OPERATOR	920.482-010
ingredient mixer	529.684-014
INGREDIENT SCALER	529.684-014
INSTANTIZER OPERATOR	523.685-106
Instant-Powder Supervisor	529.131-014
KOSHER INSPECTOR	529.687-126
LABORER, CHEESEMAKING	529.686-050
Line Cleaner	599.684-010
malted-milk masher	526.485-010
malted-milk mixer	521.685-222
MASH GRINDER	520.685-130
MILK DRIVER	905.483-010
milk hauler	905.483-010
MILK-POWDER GRINDER	521.685-222
MILK RECEIVER	222.585-010
MILK-RECEIVER, TANK TRUCK	222.485-010
Mix Maker	529.382-018
Mold Filler	529.685-030
Mold Remover	529.685-030
novelty dipper	529.482-014
NOVELTY MAKER I	529.482-014
NOVELTY MAKER II	529.482-014
NOVELTY WORKER	524.686-014
Pasteurizer Helper	529.686-026
Pasteurizer Operator	529.382-018
Pasteurizing Supervisor	529.131-014
Pipe Washer	599.684-010
powder operator	523.682-022
pusher	529.685-030
putter-in	529.685-030
RAW-CHEESE WORKER	529.686-078
SANDWICH-MACHINE OPERATOR	529.685-210
Separator Operator	529.382-018
SLICING-MACHINE OPERATOR	521.685-306
STERILIZER OPERATOR	523.685-114
sticker	524.686-014
Stick Inserter	529.685-030
SUPERVISOR, CLEANING	699.137-010
SUPERVISOR, DAIRY PROCESSING	529.131-014
Supervisor, Dairy Sanitation	529.137-014
SUPERVISOR, MALTED MILK	529.132-070
SUPERVISOR, WHIPPED TOPPING	529.137-066
TABLET-MACHINE OPERATOR	529.685-238
TRAY-CASTING-MACHINE OPERATOR	520.685-218
Truck Washer	919.687-014
WORT EXTRACTOR	526.485-010

domestic ser.—DOMESTIC SERVICE: This designation includes occupations concerned with rendering services for members of households or their guests in or about private homes. Workers in these occupations are usually employees of the household. Workers who are employed by another establishment, but who perform their work in a private home, are included in other industries.

Baby Sitter	301.677-010
BUTLER	309.137-010
BUTLER, SECOND	309.674-010
CARETAKER	301.687-010
CHAUFFEUR	359.673-010
CHILD MONITOR	301.677-010
CHILDREN'S TUTOR	099.227-010

Children's Tutor, Nursery	099.227-010
COMPANION	309.677-010
COOK	305.281-010
DAY WORKER	301.687-014
driver	359.673-010
Family-Dinner Service Specialist	305.281-010
FOSTER PARENT	309.677-014
Gardener	301.687-018
HOUSEKEEPER, HOME	301.137-010
housekeeper, home	301.474-010
HOUSE SITTER	309.367-010
House Worker	301.687-010
HOUSE WORKER, GENERAL	301.474-010
IRONER	302.687-010
LAUNDRY WORKER, DOMESTIC	302.685-010
manager, household	301.137-010
nurse, children's	301.677-010
Nurse, Infants'	301.677-010
odd-job worker	301.687-010
PERSONAL ATTENDANT	309.674-014
YARD WORKER	301.687-018

education—EDUCATION AND INSTRUCTION: This designation includes occupations concerned with imparting knowledge of the arts, sciences, or other fields of learning; or with teaching, advising, or instructing others in any of these fields or in vocations. Occupations occurring in libraries are included in LIBRARY (library); and those occurring in museums, art galleries, and botanical and zoological gardens are included in MUSEUMS, ART GALLERIES, AND BOTANICAL AND ZOOLOGICAL GARDENS (museums).

Academic Counselor	045.107-010
ACADEMIC DEAN	090.117-010
academic vice president	090.117-010
Acting Professor	090.227-010
administrative analyst	090.167-018
administrative assistant	205.367-010
administrative assistant, special education	094.167-014
ADMISSIONS EVALUATOR	205.367-010
ALUMNI SECRETARY	090.117-014
art instructor	149.021-010
ASSISTANT PRINCIPAL	091.107-010
Assistant Professor	090.227-010
assistant superintendent, special education	094.167-014
Associate Professor	090.227-010
athletic coach	153.227-018
ATHLETIC TRAINER	153.224-010
ATTENDANCE CLERK	219.362-014
ATTENDANCE OFFICER	168.367-010
audiovisual specialist	099.167-018
Ballet Master/Mistress	151.027-014
braille coder	203.582-014
braille coder	209.584-010
braille transcriber	203.582-014
BRAILLE TRANSCRIBER, HAND	209.584-010
BRAILLE TYPIST	203.582-014
bridge expert	159.227-010
BURSAR	160.167-042
BUSINESS MANAGER, COLLEGE OR UNIVERSITY	186.117-010
CAREER-GUIDANCE TECHNICIAN	249.367-014
career-information specialist	249.367-014
Career Placement Services Counselor	045.107-010
career resource technician	249.367-014
CERTIFICATION AND SELECTION SPECIALIST	099.167-010
Chairperson, Scholarship And Loan Committee	090.117-030
chancellor	090.117-034
Clinical Instructor	090.227-010
COMMUNICATIONS TECHNICIAN	962.362-010
CONSULTANT, EDUCATION	099.167-014
coordinator of placement	166.167-014
counselor, dormitory	045.107-038
counselor, orientation and mobility	076.224-014
dean of admissions	090.167-014
dean of chapel	129.107-018
dean of instruction	090.117-010
Dean of Men	090.117-018
dean of student affairs	090.117-018
DEAN OF STUDENTS	090.117-018
Dean of Women	090.117-018
degree clerk	205.367-010
department chairperson, college or university	090.167-010
DEPARTMENT HEAD, COLLEGE OR UNIVERSITY	090.167-010
Department Head, Junior College	090.167-010
director, alumni relations	090.117-014

DIRECTOR, ATHLETIC	090.117-022
Director, Child Development Center	092.167-010
DIRECTOR, DAY CARE CENTER	092.167-010
DIRECTOR, EDUCATIONAL PROGRAM	099.117-010
director, evaluation and research	099.167-022
DIRECTOR, EXTENSION WORK	090.117-026
DIRECTOR, FIELD SERVICES	090.167-034
DIRECTOR, INSTRUCTIONAL MATERIAL	099.167-018
Director, Nursery School	092.167-010
director of admissions	090.167-030
DIRECTOR OF ADMISSIONS	090.167-014
director of career planning and placement	166.167-014
director of career resources	166.167-014
director of financial aid and placements	090.117-030
DIRECTOR OF GUIDANCE IN PUBLIC SCHOOLS	045.117-010
DIRECTOR OF INSTITUTIONAL RESEARCH	090.167-018
director of institutional studies	090.167-018
DIRECTOR OF PLACEMENT	166.167-010
DIRECTOR OF PUPIL PERSONNEL PROGRAM	099.167-034
director of recruitment	090.167-034
DIRECTOR OF RELIGIOUS ACTIVITIES	129.107-018
director of religious life	129.107-018
DIRECTOR OF STUDENT AFFAIRS	090.167-022
director of student aid	090.117-030
director of student services	090.117-018
Director, School For Blind	187.117-018
DIRECTOR, SPECIAL EDUCATION	094.167-014
director, student union	090.167-022
DIRECTOR, SUMMER SESSIONS	090.167-026
DIRECTOR, VOCATIONAL TRAINING	097.167-010
dormitory supervisor	045.107-038
EDUCATIONAL SPECIALIST	099.167-022
EDUCATION SUPERVISOR, CORRECTIONAL INSTITUTION	099.117-014
Education Supervisor, Penal Institution	099.117-014
Education Supervisor, Youth Authority	099.117-014
ENERGY-CONTROL OFFICER	199.167-018
EVALUATOR	094.267-010
Evaluator, Transfer Students	205.367-010
faculty dean	090.117-010
FACULTY MEMBER, COLLEGE OR UNIVERSITY	090.227-010
Faculty Member, Technical Institute	090.227-010
FINANCIAL-AID COUNSELOR	169.267-018
FINANCIAL-AIDS OFFICER	090.117-030
FOREIGN-STUDENT ADVISER	090.107-010
FOUR-H CLUB AGENT	096.127-022
Fraternity Adviser	090.167-022
grade recorder	219.467-010
GRADING CLERK	219.467-010
GRADUATE ASSISTANT	090.227-014
Ground Instructor, Advanced	097.227-010
Ground Instructor, Basic	097.227-010
Ground Instructor, Instrument	097.227-010
Guidance Counselor	045.107-010
head resident, dormitory	045.107-038
high school teacher	091.227-010
Instructor	090.227-010
Instructor, Ballroom Dancing	151.027-014
Instructor, Braille	094.224-018
INSTRUCTOR, BRIDGE	159.227-010
INSTRUCTOR, BUSINESS EDUCATION	090.222-010
INSTRUCTOR, CORRESPONDENCE SCHOOL	099.227-014
INSTRUCTOR, DANCING	151.027-014
instructor, dramatic arts	150.027-014
INSTRUCTOR, DRIVING	099.223-010
INSTRUCTOR, EXTENSION WORK	090.227-018
INSTRUCTOR, FLYING I	196.223-010
INSTRUCTOR, FLYING II	097.227-010
Instructor, Illustration	149.021-010
Instructor, Industrial Design	149.021-010
instructor, kindergarten	092.227-014
INSTRUCTOR, MILITARY SCIENCE	099.227-022
INSTRUCTOR, MODELING	099.227-026
instructor of blind	076.224-014
INSTRUCTOR, PHYSICAL	153.227-014
INSTRUCTOR, PHYSICAL EDUCATION	099.224-010
instructor, private	099.227-034
Instructor, Programmable Controllers	166.221-010
INSTRUCTOR, PSYCHIATRIC AIDE	075.127-010
Instructor, Robotics	166.221-010
instructor, self-improvement	099.227-026
INSTRUCTOR, SPORTS	153.227-018
Instructor, Tap Dancing	151.027-014
INSTRUCTOR, TECHNICAL TRAINING	166.221-010
INSTRUCTOR, VOCATIONAL TRAINING	097.221-010
LABORATORY MANAGER	090.164-010
Lecturer	090.227-010
Loan Counselor	169.267-018
Mainstreaming Facilitator	094.267-010
MANAGER, DANCE STUDIO	187.167-086
MANAGER, EDUCATION AND TRAINING	166.167-026
manager of student placement service	166.167-014
manager, student union	090.167-022
mathematics improvement teacher	099.227-042
music instructor	152.021-010
MUSIC SUPERVISOR	099.167-026
ORIENTATION AND MOBILITY THERAPIST FOR THE BLIND	076.224-014
Orientation And Mobility Instructor	076.224-014
orientation therapist for blind	076.224-014
orientor	076.224-014
PHYSICAL THERAPIST	076.121-014
physiotherapist	076.121-014
President, Business School	090.117-034
President, College Or University	090.117-034
PRESIDENT, EDUCATIONAL INSTITUTION	090.117-034
PRINCIPAL	099.117-018
Professor	090.227-010
professor, dance	151.027-014
provost	090.117-010
reading improvement teacher	099.227-042
REGISTRAR, COLLEGE OR UNIVERSITY	090.167-030
Research Assistant	090.227-010
RESIDENCE COUNSELOR	045.107-038
Sales Representative, Business Courses	259.257-010
Sales Representative, Correspondence Courses	259.257-010
SALES REPRESENTATIVE, DANCING INSTRUCTIONS	259.357-014
SALES REPRESENTATIVE, EDUCATION COURSES	259.257-010
SATELLITE-INSTRUCTION FACILITATOR	249.367-086
satellite-project site monitor	249.367-086
Scholarship Counselor	169.267-018
school examiner	099.167-010
SCHOOL-PLANT CONSULTANT	001.167-010
SCHOOL SECRETARY	201.362-022
SECRETARY, BOARD-OF-EDUCATION	169.267-022
shop teacher	091.221-010
student-activities adviser	090.167-022
student-union consultant	090.167-022
SUPERINTENDENT, SCHOOLS	099.117-022
Supervisor, Adult Education	099.117-026
Supervisor, Agricultural Education	099.117-026
supervisor, counseling and guidance	045.117-010
SUPERVISOR, EDUCATION	099.117-026
Supervisor, Elementary Education	099.117-026
Supervisor, Home Economics	099.117-026
Supervisor, Industrial Arts Education	099.117-026
Supervisor, Maintenance And Custodians	381.137-010
Supervisor, Modern Languages	099.117-026
supervisor of guidance and testing	045.117-010
supervisor of research	045.117-010
SUPERVISOR, SPECIAL EDUCATION	094.167-010
SUPERVISOR, SPECIAL SERVICES	169.267-026
Supervisor, Trade And Industrial Education	099.117-026
TEACHER, ADULT EDUCATION	099.227-030
TEACHER, ADVENTURE EDUCATION	099.224-014
teacher aide, clerical	249.367-074
TEACHER AIDE I	099.327-010
TEACHER AIDE II	249.367-074
TEACHER, ART	149.021-010
teacher assistant	099.327-010
Teacher, Ballet	151.027-014
Teacher, Child Development Center	092.227-018
Teacher, Citizenship	099.227-030
teacher, dancing	151.027-014
Teacher, Day Care Center	092.227-018
TEACHER, DRAMA	150.027-014
teacher, dramatics	150.027-014
teacher, driver education	099.223-010
Teacher, Early Childhood Development	092.227-018
TEACHER, ELEMENTARY SCHOOL	092.227-010
TEACHER, EMOTIONALLY IMPAIRED	094.227-010
TEACHER, HEARING IMPAIRED	094.224-010
TEACHER, HOME	term
TEACHER, INDUSTRIAL ARTS	091.221-010
Teacher, Instrumental	152.021-010
Teacher, Junior College	090.227-010
TEACHER, KINDERGARTEN	092.227-014
TEACHER, LEARNING DISABLED	094.227-030
Teacher, Lip Reading	094.224-010
TEACHER, MENTALLY IMPAIRED	094.227-022

TEACHER, MUSIC	152.021-010
Teacher, Nursery School	092.227-018
teacher, physical education	099.224-010
TEACHER, PHYSICALLY IMPAIRED	094.224-014
TEACHER, PRESCHOOL	092.227-018
teacher, private	099.227-034
TEACHER, RESOURCE	099.227-042
TEACHER, SECONDARY SCHOOL	091.227-010
teacher selection specialist	099.167-010
teacher, theater arts	150.027-014
TEACHER, VISUALLY IMPAIRED	094.224-018
Teacher, Vocal	152.021-010
teacher, vocational training	097.221-010
TEACHER, VOCATIONAL TRAINING	094.227-026
Teaching Assistant	090.227-010
TECHNICAL TRAINING COORDINATOR	166.167-054
test clerk	219.467-010
therapist for blind	076.224-014
training administrator	166.167-026
training instructor	166.227-010
TRAINING REPRESENTATIVE	166.227-010
training specialist	166.221-010
truant officer	168.367-010
TUTOR	099.227-034
university dean	090.117-010
veterans' coordinator	169.267-026
vice president for institutional research	090.167-018
vice president for instruction	090.117-010
vice president of student affairs	090.117-018
Visiting Professor	090.227-010
visiting-student counselor	090.107-010
Vocational Adviser	045.107-010
Women's-Activities Adviser	090.167-022
WORK-STUDY COORDINATOR, SPECIAL EDUCATION	094.107-010
Youth Agent	096.127-022

elec. equip.—ELECTRICAL EQUIPMENT INDUSTRY: This designation includes occupations concerned with manufacturing and repairing machinery, apparatus, and supplies that are used in the generation, transmission, distribution, storage, and utilization of electrical energy. The principal products include: (1) electric transmission and distribution equipment, such as transformers, ballasts, and voltage regulators; (2) electrical industrial apparatus, such as motors, generators, coils, armatures, controls, electric welding apparatus, and carbon and graphite products; and (3) miscellaneous electrical machinery, equipment, and supplies, such as storage and primary batteries, x-ray apparatus, electrotherapeutic apparatus, alternators, chimes, and electric fireplace logs. Excluded are occupations concerned with the manufacture of lighting fixtures, LIGHTING FIXTURES INDUSTRY (light. fix.); radios, RADIO, TELEVISION, AND COMMUNICATION EQUIPMENT INDUSTRY (comm. equip.); household appliances, HOUSEHOLD APPLIANCES INDUSTRY (house. appl.); phonograph records and prerecorded magnetic tapes, RECORDING INDUSTRY (recording); and electronic components, ELECTRONIC COMPONENTS AND ACCESSORIES INDUSTRY (electron. comp.).

ACID ADJUSTER	727.484-010
acid changer	727.687-010
ACID DUMPER	727.687-010
ACID FILLER	727.687-014
Acid Leveler	727.687-014
ADJUSTER, ELECTRICAL CONTACTS	724.381-010
ALUMINUM-CONTAINER TESTER	727.687-018
armature-and-field-assembly supervisor	724.131-010
armature-and-rotor winder	721.484-010
Armature Balancer	724.384-014
Armature Connector I	721.684-018
ARMATURE CONNECTOR II	724.684-014
Armature Straightener	721.281-018
ARMATURE TESTER I	724.384-010
Armature Tester II	729.684-058
Armature Tester III	724.364-010
Armature Winder	721.484-010
Asphalt Coater	599.685-026
assembler	729.687-010
assembler	721.684-022
ASSEMBLER AND WIRER, INDUSTRIAL EQUIPMENT	826.361-010
ASSEMBLER, CARBON BRUSHES	721.684-014
assembler, caterpillar spider	721.684-026
Assembler, Communications Equipment	729.684-026
assembler dc field ring	721.484-014
assembler dc field yoke	721.484-014
Assembler, Dielectric Heater	826.361-010
ASSEMBLER, DRY CELL AND BATTERY	727.687-022
ASSEMBLER, ELECTRICAL ACCESSORIES I	729.687-010
ASSEMBLER, ELECTRICAL ACCESSORIES II	729.384-010
assembler-erector	820.361-014
assembler, flexible leads	691.685-018
Assembler, Instrument Motors	721.684-022
assembler-insulator	729.684-030
assembly hand	721.684-022
ASSEMBLY-MACHINE-SET-UP MECHANIC	692.360-010
baked-and-graphite inspector	559.364-010
balancer	727.484-010
battery analyst	727.381-022
BATTERY ASSEMBLER	727.684-010
BATTERY ASSEMBLER, DRY CELL	727.664-010
BATTERY ASSEMBLER, PLASTIC	727.684-014
BATTERY CHARGER	727.587-010
BATTERY CHARGER, CONVEYOR LINE	727.687-026
BATTERY-CHARGER TESTER	729.684-010
BATTERY-CONTAINER-FINISHING HAND	727.687-034
battery-container inspector	727.687-066
battery-container tester, aluminum	727.687-018
battery loader	727.687-030
BATTERY-PARTS ASSEMBLER	727.687-038
Battery Plate Remover	727.687-058
BATTERY RECHARGER	727.381-010
BATTERY STACKER	727.687-030
BATTERY TESTER	727.384-010
battery tester and repairer	727.684-018
Battery Tester, Field	727.384-010
Battery-Vent-Plug Inserter	727.687-038
Bead Stringer	691.685-018
bench assembler, battery	727.684-026
Bender, Armature Coil	724.684-026
binder	724.687-010
blade aligner	706.687-018
BOTTOM POLISHER	603.685-034
Brush-Holder Assembler	721.684-022
brush maker	721.684-014
cable-machine operator	616.682-034
cable maker	728.684-010
cabling-machine operator	616.682-034
CAPACITOR ASSEMBLER	729.684-014
CAPACITOR-PACK-PRESS OPERATOR	726.684-010
Capacitor Repairer	729.684-014
CAPPING-MACHINE OPERATOR	692.685-042
CARBON-AND-GRAPHITE-BRUSH-MACHINE OPERATOR	692.482-010
Carbon Brushes Tester	729.684-058
carbon-brush maker	721.684-014
CARBON CUTTER	677.685-018
Carbon-Paste-Mixer Operator, Panelboard	540.585-010
CARBON ROD INSERTER	692.686-026
CARTRIDGE LOADER	779.687-014
Casting Inspector	502.687-018
casting-machine adjuster	502.684-018
CASTING-MACHINE OPERATOR, AUTOMATIC	502.482-014
CASTING-MACHINE-OPERATOR HELPER	502.686-010
cell assembly, booker	727.687-038
cell assembly, pinner	727.687-038
CELL COVERER	727.687-042
CELL REPAIRER	727.684-018
CELL TUBER, HAND	727.687-046
CELL TUBER, MACHINE	692.685-046
Charging-Plug Placer	727.687-026
Circuit Breaker Assembler	729.687-010
CIRCULATING PROCESS INSPECTOR	829.361-018
Clay-Products Glazer	599.685-026
CLEANER AND PREPARER	721.687-010
CLINCHING-MACHINE OPERATOR	616.685-014
coil assembler	721.484-010
COIL CONNECTOR	721.684-018
Coil-Connector Repairer	721.281-018
Coil Finisher	724.684-026
Coil Former, Template	724.684-026
Coil Taper	724.684-026
Coil Tester	729.684-058
COIL WINDER	724.684-026
Coil Winder, Open Slot	724.684-026
Coil Winder, Strap	724.684-026
COMMUTATOR ASSEMBLER	724.684-030
commutator presser	724.684-030
Commutator Tester	729.684-058
Commutator Undercutter	724.684-030
Commutator V-Ring Assembler	724.684-030
Compound Mixer	726.687-022
COMPRESSION-MOLDING-MACHINE OPERATOR	556.682-014
COMPRESSOR	556.682-022
Concaving-Machine Operator	692.482-010

electron. comp.—ELECTRONIC COMPONENTS AND ACCESSORIES INDUSTRY: This designation includes occupations concerned with manufacturing, assembling, and repairing electronic components. Electronic components are parts of electronic equipment that affect the current characteristics within its circuit. Inclded as electronic components are resistors, capacitors, coils, chokes, inductors, printed circuit boards, semiconductors, tubes, transistors, diodes, television antennas, headphones, piezoelectric crystals and crystal devices, computer logic modules filters, flipflops, gates, inverters, voltage dividers, delay lines, and wave guides. Occupations concerned with the manufacture of electrical machinery, equipment, and appliances or wire telephone or telegraph equipment are included in the ELECTRICAL EQUIPMENT INDUSTRY (elec. equip.) and occupations concerned with the manufacture of radio and tv receiving and broadcasting equipment and accessories are included in the RADIO, TELEVISION, AND COMMUNICATION EQUIPMENT INDUSTRY (comm. equip.). Occupations concerned with manufacturing blank and prerecorded magnetic tapes and phonograph records are included in the RECORDING INDUSTRY (recording).

Armature Coil Winder 724.684-026
ASSEMBLER, ELECTROMECHANICAL 828.381-018
ASSEMBLER, SEMICONDUCTOR 726.684-034
Audio-Coil Winder 724.684-026
automatic component insertion operator 726.685-014
Auto-Test Equipment Operator 726.684-026
Baker, Beads 590.684-014
BEVELER, PRINTED CIRCUIT BOARDS 699.682-034
BLACK OXIDE COATING EQUIPMENT TENDER 501.685-018
black oxide operator 501.685-018
blender 550.685-082
blue print control clerk 206.367-010
Bobbin-Coil Winder 724.684-026
Bonder 726.687-022
BONDER, SEMICONDUCTOR 726.685-066
BREAK-AND-LOAD OPERATOR 726.685-018
Bulb Assembler 725.684-022
cable maker 728.684-010
CALIBRATION LABORATORY TECHNICIAN 019.281-010
Capacitor Inspector 726.684-022
Capacitor Tester 726.684-078
CATHODE RAY TUBE SALVAGE PROCESSOR 725.684-026
CERAMIC CAPACITOR PROCESSOR 590.684-010
CHARGE PREPARATION TECHNICIAN 590.384-010
checker 726.684-022
Check Inspector 726.381-010
CHEMICAL PREPARER 550.685-030
CHEMICAL RECLAMATION EQUIPMENT OPERATOR 558.685-058
circuit board inspector 726.684-062
CLEANING MACHINE TENDER, SEMICONDUCTOR WAFERS 590.685-062
COATING EQUIPMENT OPERATOR, PRINTED CIRCUIT BOARDS 590.685-066
Coil Finisher 724.684-026
Coil Sprayer 741.687-018
COIL WINDER 724.684-026
Coil Winder, Hand 724.684-026
component insertion operator 726.685-014
Component Lead Former 728.684-022
Compound Mixer 726.687-022
COMPUTERIZED ENVIRONMENTAL CONTROL INSTALLER 828.281-026
contact-frame operator 971.382-014
Contact Printer, Dry Film 976.684-030
CONTACT PRINTER, PRINTED CIRCUIT BOARDS 976.684-030
COORDINATE MEASURING EQUIPMENT OPERATOR 726.682-018
Copper Deposition Operator 501.685-022
crystal cutter 677.382-018
crystal evaluator 726.684-054
Crystal Flat Grinder 673.382-026
CRYSTAL GRINDER 673.382-026
CRYSTAL GROWER 590.382-014
crystal growing furnace operator 590.382-014
CRYSTAL GROWING TECHNICIAN 590.262-010
CRYSTAL MACHINING COORDINATOR 679.362-010
CRYSTAL MOUNTER 677.687-014
CRYSTAL SLICER 677.382-018
CUTTER-MACHINE TENDER 615.685-046
Dag Coater 725.684-022
Dag Sprayer 741.687-018
DEBURRER, PRINTED CIRCUIT BOARD PANELS 603.686-014
DEFLASH AND WASH OPERATOR 726.685-022
deposition operator 501.685-022
DESIGN TECHNICIAN, COMPUTER-AIDED 003.362-010
DEVELOPER, PRINTED CIRCUIT BOARD PANELS 976.685-034
Diazo Technician 976.384-010
DIE ATTACHER 726.684-042
DIE ATTACHING MACHINE TENDER 726.685-026
die equipment operator 726.685-062
DIE SET-UP OPERATOR, PRINTED CIRCUIT BOARDS 699.380-010
DIE TESTER 726.685-030
DIFFUSION FURNACE OPERATOR, SEMICONDUCTOR WAFERS 590.685-070
digitizer 003.362-010
Dipper 726.687-022
DISPLAY-SCREEN FABRICATOR 725.685-010
drawing-release clerk 206.367-010
DRILL-BIT SHARPENER 603.682-030
DRILL-PRESS OPERATOR, PRINTED CIRCUIT BOARDS 676.382-010
drill sharpener 603.682-030
Edge-Round Tender 673.685-094
ELECTROLESS PLATER, PRINTED CIRCUIT BOARD PANELS 501.685-022
electron-beam operator 972.382-018
Electron Gun Assembler 725.384-010
Electron Gun Inspector 726.684-022
ELECTRONIC-COMPONENT PROCESSOR 590.684-014
ELECTRONIC EQUIPMENT REPAIRER 726.381-014
ELECTRONIC EQUIPMENT SET-UP OPERATOR 726.380-010
ELECTRONIC-PRODUCTION-LINE-MAINTENANCE MECHANIC 629.261-022
ELECTRONICS ASSEMBLER 726.684-018
ELECTRONICS INSPECTOR 726.381-010
ELECTRONICS INSPECTOR 726.684-022
ELECTRONICS TESTER 726.684-026
ELECTRONICS UTILITY WORKER 726.364-018
ELECTRONICS WORKER 726.687-010
ENCAPSULATOR 726.687-022
ENGINEERING-DOCUMENT-CONTROL CLERK 206.367-010
engineering-release clerk 206.367-010
engraving photographer 971.382-014
EPITAXIAL REACTOR OPERATOR 590.382-018
EPITAXIAL REACTOR TECHNICIAN 590.282-010
ETCHED-CIRCUIT PROCESSOR 590.684-018
ETCHER 590.685-078
Etcher, Printed Circuit Boards 590.685-082
ETCHER-STRIPPER, SEMICONDUCTOR WAFERS 590.684-026
ETCH OPERATOR, SEMICONDUCTOR WAFERS 590.685-074
EXHAUST EQUIPMENT OPERATOR 599.382-014
exhaust operator 599.382-014
exposure machine operator 976.684-030
Filament-Coil Winder 724.684-026
Filler 726.687-022
film inspector 726.384-014
FILM TOUCH-UP INSPECTOR 726.684-050
Filter Inspector 726.684-022
Final Cleaner 599.685-134
finisher 699.682-034
Firer 590.684-014
FIRESETTER 692.360-018
flow-solder machine operator 726.362-014
Foil Cutter 699.682-018
Frit Coater 725.684-022
Funnel Coater 725.684-022
Glass Deposition Tender 590.685-086
GLASS-LATHE OPERATOR 674.382-010
Gold Plater 500.684-026
grinding machine operator 673.382-026
GROUP LEADER, PRINTED CIRCUIT BOARD ASSEMBLY 726.361-014
GROUP LEADER, PRINTED CIRCUIT BOARD QUALITY CONTROL 726.361-018
GROUP LEADER, SEMICONDUCTOR PROCESSING 590.362-018
GROUP LEADER, SEMICONDUCTOR TESTING 726.362-010
group leader, wafer polishing 673.364-010
Gun-Sealing-Machine Operator 725.684-022
harness maker 728.684-010
HEAT TREATER 504.686-022
Helix-Coil Winder 724.684-026
hot roll laminator 554.685-034
Hybrid Tester 726.684-078
imager 976.684-030
IMPREGNATOR AND DRIER 599.682-014
Impregnator, Carbon Products 599.682-014
Impregnator, Electrolytic Capacitors 599.682-014
Inductor Tester 726.684-078
Inner-Layer Scrubber Tender 599.685-134
In-Process Inspector 726.381-010
INSERTION MACHINE TENDER, ELECTRONIC COMPONENTS 726.685-014
INSPECTOR, CIRCUITRY NEGATIVE 726.384-014
inspector, component parts 726.684-022
INSPECTOR, CRYSTAL 726.684-054
INSPECTOR, INTEGRATED CIRCUITS 726.684-058
INSPECTOR, PRINTED CIRCUIT BOARDS 726.684-062
Inspector, Raw Quartz 726.381-010
INSPECTOR, RECEIVING 222.384-010
INSPECTOR, SEMICONDUCTOR WAFER 726.684-066
INSPECTOR, SEMICONDUCTOR WAFER PROCESSING 726.384-018
Inspector, Subassemblies 726.381-010
Inspector, Tubes 726.381-010
INTEGRATED CIRCUIT FABRICATOR 590.684-042
ION IMPLANT MACHINE OPERATOR 590.382-022
JOB SETTER 616.380-014
Lacquer Sprayer 725.684-022
laminating machine tender 554.685-034
LAMINATION ASSEMBLER 729.684-066
LAMINATION ASSEMBLER, PRINTED CIRCUIT BOARDS 726.687-026
Lamination Stacker, Hand 729.684-066

electron. comp.

Television-Receiver Analyzer 726.261-018
Tester, Printed Circuit Boards 726.684-026
TESTER, SEMICONDUCTOR PACKAGES 726.685-054
TESTER, SEMICONDUCTOR WAFERS 726.684-102
TESTER, WAFER SUBSTRATE 726.684-106
TEST FIXTURE ASSEMBLER 726.684-098
TEST FIXTURE DESIGNER 726.364-014
TEST TECHNICIAN, SEMICONDUCTOR PROCESSING
   EQUIPMENT 590.262-014
TOOL PROGRAMMER, NUMERICAL CONTROL 609.262-010
touch-up inspector, printed circuit boards 726.684-062
TOUCH-UP SCREENER, PRINTED CIRCUIT BOARD
   ASSEMBLY 726.684-110
Transformer-Coil Winder 724.684-026
Transformer Tester 726.684-078
Transmitter Tester 726.261-018
TRIMMER, PRINTED CIRCUIT BOARD PANELS 699.685-054
TUBE ASSEMBLER, CATHODE RAY 725.684-022
TUBE ASSEMBLER, ELECTRON 725.384-010
Tube-Component Assembler 725.384-010
Tube Fitter 725.384-010
Tube Inspector 726.684-022
TUBE REBUILDER 725.381-010
Tube Tester 726.684-026
Tube-Test Technician 726.261-018
Vacuum-Evaporation Operator 590.684-014
V-Block Saw Operator 677.382-018
WAFER ABRADING MACHINE TENDER 673.685-102
WAFER BREAKER, SEMICONDUCTORS 726.687-046
WAFER CLEANER 590.685-102
wafer etcher 590.685-078
wafer fab operator 590.684-042
WAFER MOUNTER 726.685-058
wafer polisher 673.685-094
wafer slicer 677.382-018
WAVE-SOLDERING MACHINE OPERATOR 726.362-014
WAVE-SOLDER OFFBEARER 726.686-010
Wax Impregnator 599.682-014
Weight-Count Operator 590.684-014
WIRE HARNESS ASSEMBLER 728.684-010
wire-preparation worker 728.684-022
wirer 728.684-010
Wire Saw Operator 677.382-018
WIREWORKER 728.684-022
WIRE-WRAPPING-MACHINE OPERATOR 726.682-014
X-ray Technician, Printed Circuit Boards 726.684-062

electroplating—ELECTROPLATING INDUSTRY: This designation includes occupations concerned with plating metal objects with chromium, gold, nickel, silver, and other metals by means of electrolysis.

barrel-line operator 500.362-014
Brass Plater 500.380-010
Bronze Plater 500.380-010
Cadmium Plater 500.380-010
Chromium Plater 500.380-010
Cleaner 500.686-010
Copper Plater 500.380-010
drum plater 500.362-014
ELECTROFORMER 500.684-010
ELECTROGALVANIZING-MACHINE OPERATOR 500.362-010
electroplater 500.380-010
electroplater apprentice 500.380-014
electroplater, automatic 500.685-014
electroplater helper 500.686-010
Gold Plater 500.380-010
INSPECTOR, PLATING 500.287-010
LABORER, ELECTROPLATING 500.686-010
Nickel Plater 500.380-010
PLATER 500.380-010
PLATER APPRENTICE 500.380-014
PLATER, BARREL 500.362-014
plater helper 500.686-010
plater, machine 500.362-014
plater production 500.685-014
plater supervisor 500.131-010
plating-department helper 500.686-010
PLATING EQUIPMENT TENDER 500.685-014
Plating Stripper 500.380-010
plating-tank-operator apprentice 500.380-014
plating-tank operator 500.380-010
Rack Cleaner 500.686-010
Racker 500.686-010
sample tester 500.287-010

Sawdust Drier 500.686-010
Silver Plater 500.380-010
SUPERVISOR 500.131-010
Supervisor, Anodizing 500.131-010
Tin Plater 500.380-010
tumbler plater 500.362-014
ZINC-PLATING-MACHINE OPERATOR 500.485-010

engine-turbine—ENGINE AND TURBINE INDUSTRY: This designation includes occupations concerned with manufacturing, repairing, and assembling parts for steam engines (other than locomotives), internal combustion engines, diesel or semidiesel oil engines, water wheels, and all types of steam or hydraulic engines and turbines. Occupations concerned with the manufacture of automobile engines are included in the AUTOMOBILE MANUFACTURING INDUSTRY (auto. mfg.). Occupations concerned with the manufacture of aircraft engines are included in the AIRCRAFT-AEROSPACE MANUFACTURING INDUSTRY (aircraft mfg.).

ASSEMBLER HELPER, INTERNAL COMBUSTION
   ENGINE 801.687-010
ASSEMBLER, INTERNAL COMBUSTION ENGINE 806.481-014
Assembler, Show Motor 806.481-014
ASSEMBLER, STEAM-AND-GAS TURBINE 600.261-010
bench assembler 706.481-010
boat mechanic 623.281-038
Carburetor Assembler 706.481-010
Cylinder-Head Assembler 706.481-010
Diesel-Engine Assembler 806.481-014
DIESEL-ENGINE ERECTOR 625.361-010
diesel-engine fitter 625.361-010
Diesel-Engine Inspector 806.261-010
DIESEL-ENGINE TESTER 625.261-010
Electrical Repairer, Internal Combustion Engines 825.281-022
engine assembler 806.481-014
Engine-Generator Assembler 820.361-010
ENGINE REPAIRER, PRODUCTION 625.381-010
ENGINE REPAIRER, SERVICE 625.281-018
ENGINE-TESTING SUPERVISOR 625.131-010
erector 638.261-014
EXPERIMENTAL MECHANIC, OUTBOARD MOTORS 623.261-010
Gasoline-Engine Assembler 806.481-014
Gasoline-Engine Inspector 806.261-010
Gearcase Assembler 706.481-010
Governor Assembler 706.481-010
group assembler 706.481-010
heavy-machinery assembler 638.261-014
INJECTOR ASSEMBLER 706.684-062
inspector 806.261-010
inspector and tester 806.261-010
INTERNAL-COMBUSTION-ENGINE INSPECTOR 806.261-010
INTERNAL-COMBUSTION-ENGINE SUBASSEMBLER 706.481-010
leadman, turbine assembly 600.261-010
Life Tester, Outboard Motors 623.261-014
MACHINERY ERECTOR 638.261-014
MOTORBOAT MECHANIC 623.281-038
MOTORBOAT-MECHANIC HELPER 623.684-010
Motorcycle-Engine Assembler 806.481-014
Outboard-Motor Assembler 806.481-014
OUTBOARD-MOTOR INSPECTOR 806.687-042
OUTBOARD-MOTOR MECHANIC 623.281-042
OUTBOARD-MOTOR TESTER 623.261-014
PIPE FITTER, DIESEL ENGINE I 862.361-018
PIPE FITTER, DIESEL ENGINE II 862.381-022
piper 862.361-018
Remote-Control Assembler 706.481-010
river tester 623.261-010
ROTARY-ENGINE ASSEMBLER 801.261-018
SUPERVISOR, ELECTRONIC CONTROLS REPAIRER 828.131-010
SUPERVISOR, ENGINE ASSEMBLY 806.130-010
SUPERVISOR, ENGINE-REPAIR 625.131-014
TURBINE-BLADE ASSEMBLER 600.380-026
Turbine Inspector 609.361-010
TURBINE SUBASSEMBLER 706.381-042
Water-Pump Assembler 706.481-010

engraving—ENGRAVING, CHASING, AND ETCHING INDUSTRY: This designation includes occupations concerned with engraving, chasing, and etching on jewelry and silverware, notarial seals, nameplates, metal novelties, and other metal products for purposes other than printing. Occupations concerned with the engraving and etching of plates for printing are included in the PRINTING AND PUBLISHING INDUSTRY (print. & pub.).

carver 704.381-030
CLEANER 704.687-010

fabrication, nec

decorator	704.381-030
Die-Engraving Supervisor	704.131-010
ENGRAVER APPRENTICE, DECORATIVE	704.381-022
Engraver, Flatware	704.381-030
ENGRAVER, HAND, HARD METALS	704.381-026
ENGRAVER, HAND, SOFT METALS	704.381-030
Engraver, Jewelry	704.381-030
Engraver, Lettering	704.381-030
ENGRAVER, MACHINE I	704.682-010
ENGRAVER, MACHINE II	704.582-010
Engraver, Optical Frames	704.381-030
Engraver, Ornamental Design	704.381-030
ENGRAVER, PANTOGRAPH I	704.382-010
ENGRAVER, PANTOGRAPH II	704.682-014
ENGRAVING SUPERVISOR	704.131-010
ETCHER	704.684-010
etcher, hand	704.684-014
Jewelry-Engraving Supervisor	704.131-010
PATTERNMAKER	751.381-010
prototype-machine operator	704.382-010
SILK-SCREEN ETCHER	704.684-014
Stencil Maker	704.381-026
white-work cleaner	704.687-010

fabrication, nec—MISCELLANEOUS FABRICATED PRODUCTS, NOT ELSEWHERE CLASSIFIED: This designation includes occupations concerned with manufacturing and repairing miscellaneous items not included under another specific designation. These include brooms and brushes of all types; signs and advertising displays; burial caskets and related materials, except those made from concrete; floor coverings, not elsewhere classified; fuel briquettes; candles; articles, such as wigs, from human, animal, and artificial hair; matches; models, patterns, mannequins, and wax figures; smoking pipes; and umbrellas and canes.

AIR-HOLE DRILLER	692.685-018
arranger-assembler	739.687-010
ARTIFICIAL-CANDY MAKER	739.684-010
ARTIFICIAL-LOG-MACHINE OPERATOR	569.685-010
ARTIST, MANNEQUIN COLORING	741.684-010
ASSEMBLER-ARRANGER	739.687-010
ASSEMBLER, CORNCOB PIPES	739.687-014
ASSEMBLER, GARMENT FORM	739.687-022
ATOMIZER ASSEMBLER	706.684-030
Awning-Frame Maker	809.381-010
BACKING-IN-MACHINE TENDER	590.685-010
balancer	739.684-118
BAND-SAWING-MACHINE OPERATOR	690.485-010
Barbecue-Briquette-Machine Operator	549.662-010
base-and-wick assembler	739.687-202
BEADING SAWYER	667.685-018
BEADWORKER	789.381-010
beeswax blender	550.585-046
Bight Maker	590.662-022
BIT BENDER	752.684-018
Bit Sander	761.684-030
bit setter	739.687-014
BIT SHAVER	754.684-018
Bit Tripoler	739.684-026
blending-machine operator	680.685-066
block chopper, hand	569.687-026
blocker and sewer	739.384-014
BLOCK FEEDER	663.686-010
block hacker	569.687-026
BLOCK INSPECTOR	739.687-038
Body Coverer	780.684-026
Body Maker	739.684-190
borer, stem	739.687-014
BORING-AND-FILLING-MACHINE OPERATOR	692.682-018
Bottom Sander	761.684-030
Bowl Sander	662.685-038
Bowl Topper	761.684-030
BOWL TURNER	664.684-010
BOX MAKER	762.684-026
BRIAR CUTTER	664.685-010
BRIAR-WOOD SORTER	769.687-058
BRIQUETTE-MACHINE OPERATOR	549.662-010
BRIQUETTE-MACHINE-OPERATOR HELPER	549.686-010
briquette molder	549.662-010
BROOM BUNDLER	692.685-030
BROOMCORN GRADER	739.687-042
broomcorn scraper	692.686-018
BROOMCORN SEEDER	692.686-018
broomcorn sorter	739.687-042
Broom-Handle Dipper	599.685-026
broom-machine operator	692.682-066
BROOMMAKER	739.684-018
BROOM STITCHER	692.682-022
Brush-Fabricating-Machine Setter	692.360-014
BRUSH-FABRICATION SUPERVISOR	692.130-010
BRUSH FILLER, HAND	739.687-046
BRUSH-HEAD MAKER	739.685-018
BRUSH LOADER AND HANDLE ATTACHER	739.687-206
BRUSH-MACHINE SETTER	692.360-014
brush maker	733.684-010
BRUSH MAKER, MACHINE	739.685-014
BRUSH MATERIAL PREPARER	739.684-022
Brush-Trimming-Machine Setter	692.360-014
BUFFER	739.684-026
CALENDER OPERATOR	590.682-010
CANDLE CUTTER	739.687-050
CANDLE-EXTRUSION-MACHINE OPERATOR	692.682-026
CANDLEMAKER	739.664-010
CANDLE MOLDER, HAND	739.687-054
CANDLE MOLDER, MACHINE	692.685-038
candle pourer	739.687-158
Candle Wrapper	920.587-018
CANDLE WRAPPING-MACHINE OPERATOR	920.685-030
Cap Coverer	780.684-026
Cap Maker	739.684-190
Carriage Feeder	590.662-022
Carrier Guider	590.686-014
CASKET ASSEMBLER	739.684-190
CASKET ASSEMBLER, METAL	809.684-014
CASKET COVERER	780.684-026
CASKET INSPECTOR	739.387-010
CASKET LINER	780.684-030
casket trimmer	780.684-026
casket upholsterer	780.684-030
Charcoal-Briquette-Machine Operator	549.662-010
CLEANER	739.687-058
CLEANER, SIGNS	739.687-062
CLIPPER	739.685-022
Coal-Briquette-Machine Operator	549.662-010
coater	590.685-014
COATER, SMOKING PIPE	562.685-022
COATING-MACHINE OPERATOR	590.685-014
COATING-MACHINE-OPERATOR HELPER	590.686-010
Coating-Machine Operator, Metal Tags And Signs	554.685-014
Cob Borer	669.685-094
COB SAWYER	667.685-030
color-depositing-machine tender	652.665-014
Color Receiver	555.685-050
COLOR WEIGHER	590.487-010
COMB-MACHINE OPERATOR	640.685-022
COMPOSITION MIXER	550.665-014
CONTROLS OPERATOR, MOLDED GOODS	590.662-010
CRUSHER	780.684-042
CRUSHER TENDER	555.685-022
cutter	690.485-010
CUTTER I	690.485-118
CUTTER II	692.686-030
decorator	741.684-010
DECORATOR, MANNEQUIN	970.381-014
DESIGN ASSEMBLER	692.685-034
DIGGER	739.687-070
Diorama Model-Maker	739.361-010
Dip Guider, Stoves	590.684-014
DIPPER	590.685-022
DISPLAY FABRICATOR	860.684-022
DISPLAY MAKER	739.361-010
doll-wig maker, rooted hair	731.685-010
draw hand	739.687-046
drier attendant	543.685-014
DRIER TENDER	543.685-014
dry-felt splicer	692.687-010
DYER	599.685-034
ELECTRIC-SIGN ASSEMBLER	729.684-022
EMBOSSING-PRESS OPERATOR, MOLDED GOODS	690.682-034
END FRAZER	665.685-014
EXAMINER	739.687-082
experimental-display builder	739.361-010
ferruler	739.687-014
FILLER	739.687-090
FILLING-AND-STAPLING-MACHINE OPERATOR	692.682-038
Fine Patcher	739.687-146
Fine Sander	761.684-030
FINISHER	731.687-014
FINISHER, BRUSH	739.684-062
First Front Ventilator	739.384-022

fitter	739.684-190
Flusher	761.684-030
FORM COVERER	739.684-070
FOUNDATION MAKER	739.384-014
frame-and-scrap crusher	555.685-022
frame crusher	555.685-022
framer	739.684-162
FRAZER	664.685-022
FRICTION-PAINT-MACHINE TENDER	534.685-014
GARLAND-MACHINE OPERATOR	692.685-090
GAUGE OPERATOR	692.682-042
gauger	590.685-022
GLASS BENDER	772.381-010
glass blower	772.381-010
glass-tube bender	772.381-010
GUIDER	590.686-014
hackler	739.684-086
hair blender	739.387-014
hair blender	739.384-018
Hair-Brush-Boring-And-Filling-Machine Operator	692.682-018
hairdresser	332.361-010
hair mixer	739.387-014
Hairpiece Stylist	332.271-018
HAIR PREPARER	739.384-018
hair-rooting-machine operator	731.685-010
HAIR-SAMPLE MATCHER	739.387-014
HAIR WORKER	739.684-086
hand sander	761.684-030
hand turner	664.684-010
head facer	754.684-018
hurl shaker	692.686-062
INSET CUTTER	739.381-038
INSPECTION CLERK	739.587-010
inspector	739.687-146
INSPECTOR I	739.687-106
INSPECTOR II	590.367-010
INSPECTOR, WREATH	739.687-118
LABORER	590.687-010
Lacquer Polisher	739.684-026
LAMP-SHADE ASSEMBLER	739.684-094
LAMP-SHADE JOINER	692.685-110
LAMP-SHADE SEWER	787.381-010
LEGEND MAKER	979.684-018
loop tender	590.686-010
LOWERATOR OPERATOR	922.686-014
MANNEQUIN-MOLD MAKER	739.381-046
MANNEQUIN MOUNTER	739.684-118
MANNEQUIN SANDER AND FINISHER	739.684-122
MANNEQUIN WIG MAKER	739.381-042
MANUGRAPHER	970.681-022
marbleizing-machine tender	559.665-034
MATCHBOOK ASSEMBLER	649.685-074
material cutter	690.485-010
MECHANICAL OXIDIZER	590.662-014
mixer operator	550.665-014
MIXING-MACHINE OPERATOR	680.685-066
MIXING-ROLL OPERATOR	590.662-018
model maker	739.361-010
Molding Fitter	739.684-190
molding-machine operator	549.662-010
mold maker	739.381-046
mottle line operator	559.665-034
MOTTLER-MACHINE FEEDER	550.684-034
MOTTLER OPERATOR	550.665-022
mounter	739.684-170
MOUNTER, SMOKING PIPE	739.684-130
NAIL-POLISH-BRUSH-MACHINE FEEDER, AUTOMATIC	692.686-054
NEON-SIGN SERVICER	824.281-018
NEON-TUBE PUMPER	824.684-010
NIGHT-PATROL INSPECTOR	824.683-010
novelty-candy maker	739.684-010
OFFBEARER, PIPE SMOKING MACHINE	563.686-018
ORNAMENT MAKER, HAND	739.687-130
OVEN OPERATOR	590.665-014
PAINT-BRUSH MAKER	733.684-010
Painter, Mannequin	740.684-022
PAINT POURER	652.687-022
PAINT-ROLLER ASSEMBLER	739.687-134
PAINT-ROLLER-COVER-MACHINE SETTER	692.682-046
PAINT-ROLLER COVERMAKER	739.684-142
PAINT-ROLLER WINDER	739.685-030
PAINT TRIMMER, PIPE BOWLS	749.684-050
Panel Coverer	780.684-026
Panel Fitter	739.684-190

Panel Maker	762.687-034
paper finisher	739.684-122
paper layer	794.684-026
PAPIER MACHE MOLDER	794.684-026
Part Maker	739.384-022
paster	692.685-110
PATCH DRILLER	739.687-142
PATCHER	739.687-146
PATTERNMAKER	772.381-014
pigment weigher	590.487-010
PIPE RACKER	749.687-034
PIPE-SMOKER-MACHINE OPERATOR	739.687-150
pipe smoking machine operator	563.686-018
PIPE STEM ALIGNER	739.687-210
PIPE STEM REPAIRER	739.684-186
PLASTIC MOLDER	779.684-050
polisher	739.684-026
POURER	739.687-158
POWER-DRIVEN-BRUSH MAKER	692.682-050
PRESS-MACHINE OPERATOR	590.665-014
PRINTER, FLOOR COVERING	652.685-066
PRINTER, FLOOR COVERING, ASSISTANT	652.687-038
PULL-OUT OPERATOR	739.687-162
PUNCH-PRESS OPERATOR	692.685-014
Putty Remover	761.684-030
QUALITY-CONTROL TESTER	543.684-010
RACK LOADER	590.687-018
reamer	739.687-014
repairer	739.687-146
Roll Guider, Mold Goods	590.686-014
ROLL-UP-GUIDER OPERATOR	590.685-050
roll-up helper	739.587-010
roll-up operator	590.665-018
ROOTER OPERATOR	731.685-010
Rough Patcher	739.687-146
Rough Sander	761.684-030
RUBBER MOLDER	556.684-026
RUG CUTTER	590.687-022
Rug Inspector	590.367-010
SALES REPRESENTATIVE, SIGNS	254.357-022
SALES REPRESENTATIVE, SIGNS AND DISPLAYS	254.257-010
SANDER	761.684-030
SATURATION-EQUIPMENT OPERATOR	582.665-022
scrap crusher	555.685-022
SCRATCHER TENDER	555.685-050
SELECTOR	739.687-166
Shank Sander	761.684-030
SHANK THREADER	739.685-034
shank turner	664.685-022
Shellac Polisher	739.684-026
Side Guider	590.686-014
SIGN ERECTOR-AND-REPAIRER	869.361-018
SIGN ERECTOR I	869.381-026
SIGN ERECTOR II	869.684-054
sign hanger	869.381-026
Sign Maker	869.381-026
SLIDE-MACHINE TENDER	641.685-078
smocker	780.684-042
SMOKING-PIPE DRILLER AND THREADER	669.685-078
SMOKING-PIPE LINER	739.687-170
SMOKING-PIPE MAKER	761.381-030
spiral winder	739.685-030
SPLASH-LINE OPERATOR	559.665-034
SPLICER	692.687-010
spot picker	739.667-010
SPOT PICKER, MOLDED GOODS	739.667-010
spotter	739.687-182
spudder	569.687-026
STAINER	739.687-174
stem assembler	739.687-014
stem frazer	665.685-014
STEMHOLE BORER	666.685-010
Stemhole-Borer-And-Topper	666.685-010
STEM-PROCESSING-MACHINE OPERATOR	739.685-042
stem setter	739.687-014
STEM SIZER	692.686-062
STOVE-BOTTOM WORKER	590.667-010
STOVE-CARRIAGE OPERATOR	590.662-022
STRICKLER ATTENDANT	652.665-014
Strip-Machine Tender	590.685-022
stummel selector	739.687-166
SUPERVISOR, ASSEMBLY ROOM	739.134-010
SUPERVISOR, BIT AND SHANK DEPARTMENT	739.130-010
SUPERVISOR, BRIAR SHOP	761.130-010
SUPERVISOR, BROOMMAKING	692.130-026

financial

financial—FINANCIAL INSTITUTIONS: This designation includes occupations occurring in financial organizations, including commercial and savings banks, trust companies, mortgage companies, savings and loan associations, credit unions, personal credit institutions, foreign exchange establishments, security and commodity-contract dealerships, brokerages, exchanges, and holding and other investment offices.

money position officer 186.167-054
MORTGAGE CLERK 249.362-014
MORTGAGE LOAN CLOSER 249.362-018
Mortgage-Loan Officer 186.267-018
Mortgage Loan Originator 186.267-018
MORTGAGE LOAN PROCESSOR 249.362-022
office manager 186.117-034
operations clerk 216.362-046
operations clerk 216.482-034
OPERATIONS OFFICER 186.137-014
Operations Officer, Branch Office 186.137-014
Operations Officer, Trust Department 186.137-014
Out-Of-Town Collection Clerk 216.362-014
Personal Trust Officer 186.117-074
portfolio administrator 186.167-054
position clerk 210.367-014
President, Commercial Bank 186.117-054
President, Credit Union 186.117-054
President, Finance Company 186.117-054
PRESIDENT, FINANCIAL INSTITUTION 186.117-054
President, Mortgage Company 186.117-054
President, Savings Bank 186.117-054
President, Trust Company 186.117-054
proof clerk 217.382-010
PROOF-MACHINE OPERATOR 217.382-010
PROOF-MACHINE-OPERATOR SUPERVISOR 217.132-010
quote clerk 237.367-046
REGISTERED REPRESENTATIVE 250.257-018
rejected-items clerk 216.382-058
RESERVE OFFICER 186.167-054
RESERVES CLERK 216.362-034
RETURNED-ITEM CLERK 216.382-058
Runner 239.567-010
SAFE-DEPOSIT-BOX RENTAL CLERK 295.367-022
safe deposit manager 295.137-010
SALES REPRESENTATIVE, FINANCIAL SERVICES 250.257-022
securities analyst 160.267-026
securities auditor 216.367-014
securities broker 250.257-018
SECURITIES CLERK 219.362-054
securities-research analyst 160.267-026
Securities Supervisor 219.132-014
SECURITIES TRADER 162.167-038
Specialist 162.167-034
special loan officer 186.167-078
STATEMENT CLERK 214.362-046
stock-broker 250.257-018
stock-transfer clerk 216.362-046
STOCK-TRANSFER CLERK, HEAD 216.137-014
stock-transfer technician 216.362-046
SUPERVISOR, LENDING ACTIVITIES 249.137-034
SUPERVISOR, SAFETY DEPOSIT 295.137-010
SUPERVISOR, SECURITIES VAULT 216.132-014
SUPERVISOR, STATEMENT CLERKS 214.137-014
SUPERVISOR, TRUST ACCOUNTS 219.132-014
Tax Clerk 249.362-014
telephone-information clerk 237.367-046
TELEPHONE-QUOTATION CLERK 237.367-046
TELLER 211.362-018
TELLER, HEAD 211.132-010
TELLER, VAULT 211.382-010
trader 162.167-034
trader 162.167-038
TRANSFER CLERK 216.362-046
transit clerk 217.382-010
TREASURER, FINANCIAL INSTITUTION 186.117-070
Treasurer, Savings Bank 186.117-070
trust administrator 186.117-074
TRUST OFFICER 186.117-074
TRUST OPERATIONS ASSISTANT 219.362-074
TRUST-VAULT CLERK 216.367-014
Underwriter, Direct Endorsement 186.267-026
UNDERWRITER, MORTGAGE LOAN 186.267-026
vault custodian 216.367-014
Vice President, Commercial Bank 186.117-078
VICE PRESIDENT, FINANCIAL INSTITUTION 186.117-078
Vice President, Lending 186.117-078
WIRE-TRANSFER CLERK 203.562-010

fishing & hunt.—FISHING, HUNTING, AND TRAPPING: This designation includes occupations concerned with the following types of activity: (1) catching and harvesting of fin fish, shell fish, and aquatic plant and animal life; (2) breeding, seeding, propagating, raising, caring for, and harvesting aquatic plant and animal life; (3) managing aquatic plant and animal life resources; (4) performing functions as services related to the above; (5) hunting and trapping; and (6) operating game preserves. Occupations related to this industry but of a professional and scientific nature are included under PROFESSIONAL AND KINDRED OCCUPATIONS (profess. & kin.). Occupations concerned with canning and preserving aquatic life are included in the CANNING AND PRESERVING INDUSTRY (can. & preserv.).

Abalone Diver 443.664-010
Beaver Trapper 461.684-014
bed worker 446.684-014
BOATSWAIN, OTTER TRAWLER 441.132-010
bounty hunter 461.661-010
Buy-Boat Operator 197.133-010
Captain, Cannery Tender 197.133-010
CAPTAIN, FISHING VESSEL 197.133-010
Clam-Bed Laborer 446.687-014
Clam-Bed Worker 446.684-014
Clam Digger 446.684-014
Clam Dredge Operator 446.663-010
Clam Grower 446.161-014
CLAM SORTER 446.687-010
Clam Tonger 446.684-014
Clam Treader 446.684-014
COOK 315.381-010
cook, fishing vessel 315.381-010
Cougar Hunter 461.661-010
Coyote Hunter 461.661-010
Deck Guard 372.667-034
Deckhand, Clam Dredge 449.667-010
Deckhand, Crab Boat 449.667-010
DECKHAND, FISHING VESSEL 449.667-010
Deckhand, Oyster Dredge 449.667-010
Deckhand, Shrimp Boat 449.667-010
Deckhand, Sponge Boat 449.667-010
Deckhand, Tuna Boat 449.667-010
DIVER PUMPER 899.682-010
dress-gang worker 525.684-030
DULSER 447.687-010
EXPEDITION SUPERVISOR 461.134-010
FISH BAILER 914.685-010
FISH CLEANER 525.684-030
fish culturist 180.167-030
fish cutter 525.684-030
fish dresser 525.684-030
FISHER term
fisher 442.684-010
Fisher, Clam 446.684-014
Fisher, Crab 441.684-014
Fisher, Dip Net 441.684-010
Fisher, Diver Net 441.684-010
FISHER, DIVING 443.664-010
Fisher, Eel 441.684-014
Fisher, Eel Spear 443.684-010
Fisher, Gill Net 441.684-010
Fisher, Hand Line 442.684-010
Fisher, Haul, Drag, Or Beach Seine 441.684-010
Fisher, Hoop Net 441.684-010
Fisher, Lampara Net 441.684-010
FISHER, LINE 442.684-010
Fisher, Lobster 441.684-014
Fisher, Mussel 446.684-014
FISHER, NET 441.684-010
Fisher, Oyster 446.684-014
FISHER, POT 441.684-014
Fisher, Pound Net Or Trap 441.684-010
Fisher, Purse Seine 441.684-010
Fisher, Quahog 446.684-014
Fisher, Reef Net 441.684-010
Fisher, Scallop 446.684-014
fisher, seal 461.684-010
FISHER, SPEAR 443.684-010
FISHER, SPONGE term
fisher, sponge hooking 447.684-010
Fisher, Swordfish 443.684-010
FISHER, TERRAPIN 441.684-018
Fisher, Trammel Net 441.684-010
fisher, trap 441.684-022
Fisher, Trawl Line 442.684-010
Fisher, Trawl Net 441.684-010
Fisher, Troll Line 442.684-010
Fisher, Trot Line 442.684-010
FISHER, WEIR 441.684-022
FISH FARMER 446.161-010
Fish Filleter 525.684-030

food prep., nec

fish hatchery assistant	446.684-010
fish hatchery attendant	446.684-010
Fish Hatchery Laborer	446.687-014
FISH HATCHERY WORKER	446.684-010
fishing captain	197.133-018
FISH-LIVER SORTER	521.687-062
forestry hunter	461.661-010
fur trapper	461.684-014
Gaffer	443.684-010
Geoduck Diver	443.664-010
Harpooner	443.684-010
harpooner, fish	443.684-010
hooker	447.684-010
hunter, skin diver	461.664-010
Hydraulic Dredge Operator	446.663-010
IRISH-MOSS BLEACHER	447.687-014
IRISH-MOSS GATHERER	447.687-018
KELP CUTTER	447.687-022
LABORER, AQUATIC LIFE	446.687-014
MANAGER, FISH HATCHERY	180.167-030
Manager, Marine Life Hatchery	180.167-030
Manager, Shellfish Hatchery	180.167-030
MATE, FISHING VESSEL	197.133-018
Muskrat Trapper	461.684-014
NET REPAIRER	449.664-010
Oyster-Bed Laborer	446.687-014
Oyster-Bed Worker	446.684-014
oyster culturist	446.161-014
Oyster Dredge Operator	446.663-010
Oyster Dredger	446.684-014
OYSTER FLOATER	449.687-014
Oyster Grower	446.161-014
Oyster Picker	446.684-014
Oyster Tonger	446.684-014
Oyster Unloader	446.684-014
Oyster Worker	446.684-014
Pearl Diver	443.664-010
PREDATORY-ANIMAL HUNTER	461.661-010
rigger	449.664-010
Scallop Dredger	446.684-014
Scallop Raker	446.684-014
Seal Driver	461.684-010
SEALER	461.684-010
Seal Killer	461.684-010
Seal Skinner	461.684-010
Self-Propelled Dredge Operator	446.663-010
SHELLFISH-BED WORKER	446.684-014
SHELLFISH DREDGE OPERATOR	446.663-010
SHELLFISH GROWER	446.161-014
shellfish harvester	446.663-010
Shrimp Pond Laborer	446.687-014
SKIFF OPERATOR	441.683-010
skipper	197.133-010
Slimer	525.684-030
SOFT CRAB SHEDDER	446.684-018
spearer	443.684-010
SPONGE CLIPPER	447.687-026
Sponge Diver	443.664-010
SPONGE HOOKER	447.684-010
superintendent, fish hatchery	180.167-030
Supervisor, Clam-Bed	446.133-010
Supervisor, Commercial Fish Hatchery	446.134-010
SUPERVISOR, FISH HATCHERY	446.134-010
Supervisor, Oyster Farm	446.133-010
SUPERVISOR, SHELLFISH FARMING	446.133-010
Supervisor, Shrimp Pond	446.133-010
TRAPPER, ANIMAL	461.684-014
TRAPPER, BIRD	461.684-018
Trout Farmer	446.161-010
UNDERWATER HUNTER-TRAPPER	461.664-010
web worker	449.664-010
Wolf Hunter	461.661-010

food prep., nec—FOOD PREPARATIONS AND FOOD SPECIALTIES IN-DUSTRY, NOT ELSEWHERE CLASSIFIED: This designation includes occupations concerned with manufacturing and processing food preparations and miscellaneous food specialties, not elsewhere classified. Included are occupations concerned with (1) blending, roasting, and grinding coffee and tea, and blending and grinding spices; (2) preparing powdered and granular products and prepared foods, such as gelatin desserts, potato chips, peanut butter, coleslaw, shredded coconut, and strained honey; (3) producing baking powder, yeast, and other leavening compounds; (4) producing vinegar and cider; (5) manufacturing ice for sale; and (6) manufacturing macaroni, spaghetti, vermicelli, noodles, and related products. Occupations concerned with cooking, canning, freezing, or preparing fresh fish and other seafoods are included in the CANNING AND PRESERVING INDUSTRY (can. & preserv.).

Apricot Washer	521.685-110
Baking-Powder Mixer	520.685-162
batch mixer	520.685-014
BATTER MIXER	520.685-014
BLINTZE ROLLER	520.687-014
bulk-system operator	921.382-010
Burrito Maker	520.687-046
CAN-CONVEYOR FEEDER	529.685-046
Can Filler	523.685-102
car ice-bunker filler	910.687-018
CAR ICER	910.687-018
cheese-pancake roller	520.687-014
Chili-Pepper Grinder	521.685-326
Cinnamon Grinder	521.685-326
coffee blender	520.685-110
COFFEE GRINDER	521.685-078
COFFEE ROASTER	523.682-014
COFFEE ROASTER, CONTINUOUS PROCESS	523.685-026
COFFEE-ROASTER HELPER	523.687-010
Coffee Taster	529.281-010
COFFEE WEIGHER	529.687-046
comb capper	521.687-070
CONVEYOR OPERATOR, PNEUMATIC SYSTEM	921.382-010
Cook, Chili	526.134-010
Cook, Enchilada	526.134-010
cooker, chip	526.685-046
COOK, MEXICAN FOOD	526.134-010
COOK, SOYBEAN SPECIALTIES	529.685-290
Cook, Taco	526.134-010
Cook, Tamale	526.134-010
Cook, Tortilla	526.134-010
Corn-Chip Maker	529.685-078
CORN COOKER	522.685-034
CORN GRINDER	521.685-082
CORN-PRESS OPERATOR	529.685-078
Cube Cutter	529.685-150
CUTTER	529.685-082
DIE CLEANER	529.687-062
DRIED FRUIT WASHER	521.685-110
DRIER, BELT CONVEYOR	529.485-018
DRIER, LONG GOODS	523.585-022
DRIER OPERATOR	523.362-014
DRIER OPERATOR, DRUM	529.685-098
DRIER, SHORT GOODS	523.587-010
Dumper	523.685-102
Egg-And-Spice Mixer	520.685-154
Enchilada Maker	520.687-046
fermenter helper	522.686-014
Fig Washer	521.685-110
FILLING-MACHINE SET-UP MECHANIC	920.680-010
FISH-CAKE MAKER	529.685-122
flour distributor	921.382-010
GENERAL HELPER	522.686-014
general production worker	529.686-070
granulizing-machine operator	521.685-078
GREEN-COFFEE BLENDER	520.685-110
HONEYCOMB DECAPPER	521.687-070
HONEY EXTRACTOR	521.685-174
HONEY GRADER-AND-BLENDER	520.361-010
honey liquefier	520.361-010
HONEY PROCESSOR	522.685-070
ICE CUTTER	529.685-150
ICE MAKER	523.685-102
ice platform supervisor	299.137-022
Ice Puller	523.685-102
icer, air conditioning	910.687-018
ice seller	299.377-010
long-goods drier	523.585-022
LONG-GOODS HELPER, MACHINE	529.686-062
LUMPIA WRAPPER MAKER	526.684-014
Maple-Products Maker	523.382-014
MAPLE-SYRUP MAKER	523.382-014
mash-floor operator	522.685-078
Mayonnaise Mixer	520.685-154
MEXICAN-FOOD-MACHINE TENDER	524.685-038
MEXICAN FOOD MAKER, HAND	520.687-046
MIXER	520.685-138
MIXER-AND-BLENDER	520.685-154
MIXER, CHILI POWDER	520.685-158
MIXER, DRY-FOOD PRODUCTS	520.685-162
MIXER OPERATOR, SNACK FOODS	520.685-230

MIXER, WHIPPED TOPPING	520.385-010
MIXING-MACHINE OPERATOR	520.665-014
MOLASSES PREPARER	522.685-078
Mustard Mixer	520.685-154
NOODLE MAKER	529.385-010
NOODLE-PRESS OPERATOR	520.662-010
NUT CHOPPER	521.686-046
pasteurizer	522.685-070
PEANUT-BUTTER MAKER	529.685-178
PEELED-POTATO INSPECTOR	521.687-094
PLATFORM ATTENDANT	299.377-010
pneumatic-systems operator	921.382-010
potato-chip cooker machine	526.685-046
POTATO-CHIP FRIER	526.685-046
POTATO-CHIP-PROCESSING SUPERVISOR	526.137-010
POTATO-CHIP SORTER	526.687-010
POTATO-PANCAKE FRIER	526.685-050
POTATO-PEELING-MACHINE OPERATOR	521.685-250
potato spotter	521.687-094
PRESS TENDER	520.685-186
Press Tender, Long Goods	520.685-186
Press Tender, Short Goods	520.685-186
PROCESSOR, INSTANT POTATO	523.382-022
PRODUCTION HELPER	529.686-070
production helper	921.685-050
PRODUCTION-SUPPLY-EQUIPMENT TENDER	921.685-050
Prune Washer	521.685-110
pure-culture operator	522.685-090
QUALITY-CONTROL TECHNICIAN	529.387-030
Raisin Washer	521.685-110
refrigerator-car icer	910.687-018
sawyer	521.685-342
SCRAP SEPARATOR	529.587-018
SEED-YEAST OPERATOR	522.685-090
Soyfreeze Operator	529.685-290
spaghetti press helper	529.686-062
spice blender	520.585-026
SPICE CLEANER	521.685-322
SPICE FUMIGATOR	529.685-218
spice grinder	521.685-326
spice-grinding-mill operator	521.685-326
SPICE MILLER	521.685-326
Spice Miller, Hammer Mill	521.685-326
Spice Miller, Rolling Mill	521.685-326
SPICE MIXER	520.585-026
STRIPPER-CUTTER, MACHINE	521.685-342
SUPERVISOR	529.132-110
SUPERVISOR, CLEANING	699.137-010
SUPERVISOR, COFFEE	529.130-018
SUPERVISOR, COMPRESSED YEAST	520.132-014
SUPERVISOR, DRIED YEAST	529.132-042
SUPERVISOR, ICE HOUSE	523.137-010
SUPERVISOR, ICE STORAGE, SALE, AND DELIVERY	299.137-022
SUPERVISOR, INSTANT POTATO PROCESSING	529.137-078
SUPERVISOR, LIQUID YEAST	529.132-066
Supervisor, Long Goods	529.132-110
SUPERVISOR, MAPLE PRODUCTS	529.137-050
SUPERVISOR, NUTRITIONAL YEAST	529.132-078
SUPERVISOR, READY-MIXED FOOD PREPARATION	529.137-054
Supervisor, Short Goods	529.132-110
SUPERVISOR, TEA AND SPICE	529.132-102
Taco Maker	520.687-046
TAMALE-MACHINE FEEDER	520.686-038
Tamale Maker	520.687-046
TASTER	529.281-010
Tea-Bag-Machine Tender	920.685-078
Tea Blender	520.585-026
Tea Taster	529.281-010
Tempeh Maker	529.685-290
Tofu Maker	529.685-290
Tortilla Maker	529.685-078
TUMBLER TENDER	520.685-222
VINEGAR MAKER	522.382-038
yeast-cake cutter	529.665-022
yeast-culture operator	522.685-090
YEAST-CUTTING-AND-WRAPPING-MACHINE OPERATOR	529.665-022
Yeast-Drier Operator, Drum	529.685-098
YEAST-FERMENTATION ATTENDANT	522.685-110
yeast stacker	522.686-014
YEAST WASHER	529.685-278

forestry—FORESTRY INDUSTRY: This designation includes occupations concerned with propagating, protecting, and managing forest tracts; gathering plants, barks, greens, saps, gums, and related products from the forest; operating forest nurseries; and growing, harvesting, and preparing Christmas trees for shipment. Occupations concerned with timber harvesting are included in the LOGGING INDUSTRY (logging); occupations concerned with growing ornamental trees are included in AGRICULTURE AND AGRICULTURAL SERVICE (agriculture).

Baler	920.687-046
Buncher	920.687-046
BUNDLER, SEASONAL GREENERY	920.687-046
Cascara-Bark Cutter	453.687-010
Chief Cruiser	459.387-010
CHRISTMAS-TREE FARM WORKER	451.687-010
CHRISTMAS-TREE GRADER	451.687-014
crew boss	451.137-014
CRUISER	459.387-010
Decorative Greens Cutter	453.687-010
fire crew worker	452.687-014
FIRE LOOKOUT	452.367-010
FIRE RANGER	452.367-014
FIRE WARDEN	452.167-010
FOREST ENGINEER	005.167-018
FORESTER AIDE	452.364-010
FOREST-FIRE FIGHTER	452.687-014
FOREST NURSERY SUPERVISOR	451.137-010
FOREST-PRODUCTS GATHERER	453.687-010
forest technician	452.364-010
FOREST WORKER	452.687-014
LABORER, TREE TAPPING	453.687-014
LOGGING-OPERATIONS INSPECTOR	168.267-070
LOGGING-TRACTOR OPERATOR	929.663-010
MANAGER, CHRISTMAS-TREE FARM	180.117-010
Seed-Cone Picker	453.687-010
SEEDLING PULLER	451.687-018
SEEDLING SORTER	451.687-022
Skidder Operator	929.663-010
smoke eater	452.687-014
SMOKE JUMPER	452.364-014
SMOKE JUMPER SUPERVISOR	452.134-010
SUPERVISOR, CHRISTMAS-TREE FARM	451.137-014
Suppression-Crew Leader	452.687-014
Tagger	920.687-046
timber cruiser	459.387-010
TREE PLANTER	452.687-018
tree puller	451.687-018
tree sorter	451.687-022
Trimmer	920.687-046
watcher, lookout tower	452.367-010
YARD SUPERVISOR	922.137-030

forging—FORGING: This designation includes occupations concerned with forging or metal stamping processes, whether performed on a job-lot or production basis. The primary processes include shaping metal by heating and hammering or pressing, or by cold hammering or pressing. Forging is carried on in establishments that specialize in that type of work, and also as part of the manufacturing processes of various industries. This designation includes all occupations concerned with forging, wherever they occur.

anvil smith	610.381-010
AUTOMATIC CASTING-FORGING MACHINE OPERATOR	611.682-014
BLACKSMITH	610.381-010
BLACKSMITH APPRENTICE	610.381-014
blacksmith, hammer operator	610.362-010
BLACKSMITH HELPER	610.684-010
blacksmith supervisor	612.131-010
Board Drophammer Operator	610.362-010
Chain-Forming-Machine Operator	612.462-010
CHAIN-TESTING-MACHINE OPERATOR	616.685-010
charging manipulator	612.683-010
Coining-Press Operator	611.685-010
Cold-Header Operator	612.462-010
die-machine operator	611.482-010
DIE SETTER	612.360-010
DROPHAMMER OPERATOR	610.362-010
Drop-Hammer-Operator Helper	619.686-034
Drophammer Setter-Up	612.360-010
EXTRUDER OPERATOR	614.482-014
Extruder-Operator Helper	619.686-034
extrusion-press operator	614.482-014
extrusion press supervisor	614.132-014
FORGE HELPER	619.686-034
FORGE-SHOP-MACHINE REPAIRER	626.261-010
FORGE-SHOP SUPERVISOR	612.131-010

foundry

forging-machine operator	611.482-010
Forging-Press Lever Tender	612.685-010
FORGING-PRESS OPERATOR I	611.482-010
FORGING-PRESS OPERATOR II	611.685-010
Forging Press Setter-Up	612.360-010
FORGING-ROLL OPERATOR	612.682-014
furnace operator	619.682-022
furnace tender	619.682-022
Hammer Driver	612.685-010
hammer heater	619.682-022
hammer repairer	626.261-010
Hammer-Shop Supervisor	612.131-010
Hammersmith	612.361-010
Hammersmith Helper	612.687-014
HEATER	619.682-022
heater, furnace	619.682-022
Heater Helper, Forge	619.686-034
HEAT READER	612.687-010
HEAVY FORGER	612.361-010
HEAVY-FORGER HELPER	612.687-014
Hot-Header Operator	612.462-010
Impact Hammer Operator	610.362-010
Inspection Supervisor	612.131-010
INSPECTOR	612.261-010
Inspector, Hot Forgings	612.261-010
LEVER TENDER	612.685-010
Load-Chain Welding-Machine Repairer	626.261-010
Machine Rebuilder	626.261-010
MANIPULATOR OPERATOR	612.683-010
metal extrusion supervisor	614.132-014
power hammer repairer	626.261-010
press hand	611.685-010
press helper	619.686-034
press operator	611.685-010
Press Smith	612.361-010
Press-Smith Helper	612.687-014
Restrike Hammer Operator	610.362-010
roll forger	612.682-014
rolling-machine operator	612.682-014
Rotary-Swaging-Machine Operator	612.682-014
Scale Shooter	619.686-034
slug-furnace operator	619.682-022
Steam-Clean-Machine Operator	915.687-026
Steam Hammer Operator	610.362-010
striker	610.684-010
SUPERVISOR, EXTRUSION	614.132-014
Tool-Dresser	610.381-010
Trimming-Press Operator	615.685-030
trim-setter helper	619.686-034
Twisting-Press Operator	611.685-010
UPSETTER	611.662-010
Upsetter Helper	619.686-034
Upsetter Setter-Up	612.360-010
UTILITY WORKER, FORGE	612.684-010

foundry—FOUNDRY: This designation includes occupations occurring in foundries engaged in manufacturing metal castings on a job-lot or production basis. All foundry occupations are included under this designation, whether they occur in independently operated foundries or in foundries operated in conjunction with establishments in various industries.

air-furnace operator	512.362-018
BOILER RELINER, PLASTIC BLOCK	849.484-010
BONDACTOR-MACHINE OPERATOR	899.684-010
bonder	518.685-030
bonding-machine operator	518.685-030
caster, investment casting	512.362-018
Casting Carrier	519.687-022
casting finisher	705.684-074
CASTING INSPECTOR	514.687-010
Casting-Machine-Control-Board Operator	514.562-010
Casting Sorter	519.687-022
Casting Supervisor	519.131-010
casting tester	514.687-010
Casting Trucker	921.683-050
cast-shell grinder	705.684-074
CENTRIFUGAL-CASTING-MACHINE OPERATOR I	514.685-010
CENTRIFUGAL-CASTING-MACHINE OPERATOR II	514.685-014
CENTRIFUGAL-CASTING-MACHINE OPERATOR III	514.562-010
Centrifugal-Wax Molder	549.685-038
Charging-Crane Operator I	921.663-010
Charging-Crane Operator II	921.663-042
Cinder-Crane Operator I	921.663-010
Cinder-Crane Operator II	921.663-042

core-blower operator	518.685-022
CORE CHECKER	518.687-010
core fitter	518.687-014
core inspector	518.687-010
COREMAKER	518.381-014
COREMAKER APPRENTICE	518.381-018
Coremaker, Bench	518.381-014
coremaker, experimental	518.381-014
Coremaker, Floor	518.381-014
coremaker helper	518.687-014
COREMAKER, MACHINE I	518.685-014
COREMAKER, MACHINE II	518.685-018
COREMAKER, MACHINE III	518.685-022
COREMAKER, PIPE	518.684-014
Coremaking Supervisor	519.131-010
core mounter	518.684-018
CORE-OVEN TENDER	518.685-010
core paster	518.687-014
CORE SETTER	518.684-010
core setter	518.684-018
core stripper	518.685-014
CUPOLA CHARGER	512.686-010
CUPOLA HOIST OPERATOR	921.683-030
cupola liner	861.684-010
Cupola-Melting Supervisor	519.131-010
CUPOLA PATCHER	861.684-010
cupola stocker	512.686-010
CUPOLA TAPPER	514.664-010
CUPOLA TENDER	512.662-010
Cupola-Tender Helper	519.687-022
Die-Casting-Machine Maintainer	514.360-010
DIE-CASTING-MACHINE OPERATOR I	514.382-010
DIE-CASTING-MACHINE OPERATOR II	514.685-018
DIE-CASTING-MACHINE SETTER	514.360-010
Die-Cast Patternmaker	661.281-022
Die-Lay-Out Worker	661.281-022
dipper	518.687-022
Dumper, Mold Cleaner	514.685-014
Electric-Arc-Furnace Operator	512.362-018
filer, metal patterns	693.281-018
final inspector	514.687-010
Finishing Supervisor	519.131-010
finish molder	518.684-018
fire regulator	512.667-010
Flask Carrier	519.687-022
flask fitter	518.684-018
floor molder, sweep method	518.361-018
FOUNDRY LABORER, COREROOM	518.687-014
FOUNDRY METALLURGIST	011.061-010
FOUNDRY SUPERVISOR	519.131-010
foundry technician	011.061-010
FOUNDRY WORKER, GENERAL	519.687-022
FURNACE OPERATOR	512.362-018
Furnace Operator, Oil Or Gas	512.362-018
FURNACE TENDER	512.685-010
furnace tender	512.662-010
Hot-Metal Crane Operator I	921.663-010
Hot-Metal-Crane Operator II	921.663-042
Induction-Furnace Operator	512.362-018
Injection-Wax Molder	549.685-038
inspector	518.684-026
INSPECTOR, CHIEF	514.131-010
Jacket Changer	519.687-022
ladle cleaner	519.684-010
ladle handler	514.684-022
LADLE LINER	519.684-010
Ladle-Liner Helper	519.687-022
ladle patcher	519.684-010
Ladle Pusher	519.687-022
MACHINE-CASTINGS PLASTERER	519.687-030
machine line molder	518.682-010
MACHINE MOLDER	518.682-010
Machine Molder, Roll-Over	518.682-010
Machine Molder, Squeeze	518.682-010
melter	553.685-110
MELTER CLERK	221.387-042
METAL CONTROL WORKER	512.487-010
Mold Checker	518.687-010
Mold Clamper	519.687-022
MOLD CLOSER	518.684-018
Mold-Closer Helper	519.687-022
MOLDER	518.361-010
MOLDER APPRENTICE	518.361-014
Molder, Bench	518.361-010
Molder, Fitting	518.682-010

Molder, Floor	518.361-010
Molder Helper	519.687-022
Molder Helper, Machine	519.687-022
MOLDER, PATTERN	693.381-022
MOLDER, SWEEP	518.361-018
mold finisher	518.684-018
Mold-Making Supervisor	519.131-010
Mold Stacker	519.687-022
Pattern Carrier	519.687-022
Pattern Cleaner	519.687-022
PATTERN GATER	801.684-014
PATTERNMAKER, ALL-AROUND	693.280-014
PATTERNMAKER APPRENTICE, METAL	600.280-046
PATTERNMAKER APPRENTICE, WOOD	661.281-018
patternmaker, bench	693.281-018
patternmaker, hand	693.281-018
PATTERNMAKER, METAL	600.280-050
PATTERNMAKER, METAL, BENCH	693.281-018
patternmaker, pressure cast	777.381-034
PATTERNMAKER, WOOD	661.281-022
Pattern-Room Attendant	222.387-058
pattern setter	518.380-010
Pattern Setter	661.281-022
PATTERN-SHOP SUPERVISOR	693.131-010
PERMANENT-MOLD SUPERVISOR	514.130-010
pit-furnace melter	512.362-018
PLASTER MOLDER I	777.381-034
PLASTER MOLDER II	518.484-010
plastic installer	849.484-010
Pourer, Buggy Ladle	514.684-022
Pourer, Bull Ladle	514.684-022
Pourer, Crane Ladle	514.684-022
Pourer, Crucible	514.684-022
POURER, METAL	514.684-022
Puller	514.685-014
remelt operator	512.685-010
rotary-furnace operator	512.362-018
sand conditioner, machine	570.682-018
SAND-CUTTER OPERATOR	570.683-014
sand-cutting-machine operator	570.683-014
sand mill operator	570.682-018
Sand-Mill Operator, Core-Sand	570.682-018
Sand-Mill Operator, Facing-Sand	570.682-018
Sand-Mill Operator, Molding-Sand	570.682-018
SAND MIXER, MACHINE	570.682-018
sand-mixer operator	570.683-014
sand molder	518.361-010
sand-molder apprentice	518.361-014
Sand-Screener Operator	519.687-022
Sand Shoveler	519.687-022
SAND-SLINGER OPERATOR	518.683-010
sand-system operator	570.682-018
sand technologist	777.381-046
SAND TESTER	777.381-046
Sand Wheeler	519.687-022
scratcher, metal patterns	693.281-018
SETTER, MOLDING-AND-COREMAKING MACHINES	518.380-010
Shake-Out Worker	519.687-022
Shell-Core-And-Molding Supervisor	519.131-010
Shell Coremaker	518.685-026
shell mold bonder	518.685-030
SHELL-MOLD-BONDING-MACHINE OPERATOR	518.685-030
SHELL MOLDER	518.685-026
SHOTBLAST-EQUIPMENT OPERATOR	503.362-014
Skimmer	519.687-022
Slag Worker	519.687-022
snagger	705.684-074
SNAG GRINDER	705.684-074
soft-iron inspector	514.687-010
Sprayer	514.685-014
Sprue-Cutting-Press Operator	615.685-030
Sprue Knocker	519.687-022
Stand Grinder	705.684-074
SUPERVISOR, DIE CASTING	514.130-014
swing-frame-grinder operator	705.684-074
swing grinder	705.684-074
TEMPERATURE REGULATOR, PYROMETER	512.667-010
TEST WORKER	519.687-042
Tilting-Furnace Operator, Oil Or Gas	512.362-018
TUBE-CLEANING OPERATOR	514.685-026
tube coremaker	518.685-018
VACUUM CASTER	514.582-010
Wall-Crane Operator	921.663-010
WAX MOLDER	549.685-038
WAX-PATTERN ASSEMBLER	518.684-022

WAX-PATTERN COATER	518.687-022
WAX-PATTERN REPAIRER	518.684-026
WAX-POT TENDER	553.685-110
Wax-Room Supervisor	519.131-010
weight-and-test-bar clerk	221.387-042

fur goods—FUR GOODS INDUSTRY: This designation includes occupations concerned with manufacturing, restyling, and repairing fur and fur-lined goods, such as coats, neckpieces, hats, stoles, and capes, wherever such work is performed, whether in factories, stores, or repair shops. Occupations concerned with preparing furs are included in the LEATHER MANUFACTURING INDUSTRY (leather mfg.). Occupations concerned with manufacturing sheepskin-lined clothing are included in the GARMENT INDUSTRY (garment).

fur beater	369.685-014
FUR CLEANER, MACHINE	369.685-014
FUR CUTTER	783.381-010
FUR DESIGNER	142.081-014
fur drummer	369.685-014
fur dry-cleaner	369.685-014
FUR FINISHER	783.381-014
Fur Finisher, Head	783.131-010
FUR GLAZER	369.684-010
fur glosser	369.684-010
fur grader	783.384-010
fur joiner	783.682-010
Fur Liner	783.381-014
FUR-MACHINE OPERATOR	783.682-010
fur matcher	783.384-010
FUR NAILER	783.684-014
fur operator	783.682-010
fur repairer	783.261-010
FURRIER	783.261-010
fur sewer	783.682-010
fur sewer	783.381-014
FUR SORTER	783.384-010
fur tailor	783.261-010
fur tailor	783.381-014
FUR TRIMMER	783.687-014
saw-dust machine operator	369.685-014
SUPERVISOR, FURRIER SHOP	783.131-010

furniture—FURNITURE AND FIXTURES INDUSTRY: This designation includes occupations concerned with manufacturing and repairing household furniture and fixtures, including kitchen cabinets and furniture and fixtures for barber and beauty parlors, hospitals, laboratories, offices and stores, professional offices, and public buildings from wood, metal, and other materials, such as reed and rattan. Included here are occupations concerned with manufacturing and repairing related products, such as mattresses and bedsprings; curtain and drapery rods, poles, venetian blinds, and other window blinds and shades, regardless of the materials used.

ADJUSTER	709.684-010
Antiquer	763.381-010
Arm Maker	780.684-134
Art Metal-Chair Assembler	709.684-014
ASSEMBLER, METAL FURNITURE	709.684-014
ASSEMBLY INSPECTOR	763.684-010
ASSEMBLY-LINE INSPECTOR	709.684-018
AUTOMATIC BANDSAW TENDER	667.685-070
automatic-coil-machine operator	616.685-018
AWNING MAKER-AND-INSTALLER	869.481-010
Back Maker	780.684-134
BACK PADDER	780.684-010
Back-Panel Padder	780.684-082
Backrest Assembler	709.684-014
BACK TUFTER	780.687-062
bander	619.685-014
BANDING-MACHINE OPERATOR	619.685-014
band-top assembler	780.684-014
BAND-TOP MAKER	780.684-014
BAR AND FILLER ASSEMBLER	706.684-034
BEADER	739.687-034
Bedspring Assembler	780.684-098
bed washer	709.687-014
BENCH HAND	706.381-014
BENCH-SHEAR OPERATOR	703.684-010
BLOW-OFF WORKER	763.687-010
border-machine operator	787.685-022
BORDER MEASURER AND CUTTER	780.687-010
border measurer	780.687-010
BORING-MACHINE OPERATOR	666.685-014
Boxing-Machine Operator	780.682-018
Box-Spring-Frame Builder	762.684-066

furniture

BOX-SPRING MAKER I	780.684-018
BOX-SPRING MAKER II	780.684-022
BRUSHER	term
Brush Shade-Hand	742.684-010
Brush Stainer	742.684-014
bundler	780.587-010
bunk assembler	709.667-010
burnisher	742.684-010
button tufter	687.684-014
button tufter	780.687-050
button-tufting-machine operator	687.685-014
CABINET ASSEMBLER	763.684-014
cabinet finisher	703.684-014
CANE CUTTER	763.687-030
CANER I	763.684-018
CANER II	763.684-022
CASE FITTER	763.684-026
Chair Inspector	763.687-026
CHAIR INSPECTOR AND LEVELER	763.687-014
chair-post-machine operator	669.682-022
Chair-Spring Assembler	780.684-098
chair trimmer	780.684-034
CHAIR UPHOLSTERER	780.684-034
checker	739.687-110
CHUCKING-AND-BORING-MACHINE OPERATOR	669.682-022
CLEANER, FURNITURE	709.687-014
CLIPPER AND TURNER	780.687-014
COIL ASSEMBLER, MACHINE	616.685-018
Coil-Machine Supervisor	616.130-022
coil placer	780.684-098
coil-spring assembler	780.684-098
coil tier	616.685-018
COLOR MIXER	589.464-010
corner-block cutter	669.682-030
CORNER-BRACE-BLOCK-MACHINE OPERATOR	669.682-030
cot assembler	709.667-010
COTTON DISPATCHER	780.684-038
Cotton Picker	680.685-078
cover assembler	780.684-114
Cover Assembler	780.682-010
Cover Cutter, Machine	781.684-014
COVER INSPECTOR	789.687-038
Cover Maker	780.682-018
Cradle-Slide Maker	616.685-058
CRATE LINER	920.687-078
CRATE OPENER	929.685-010
Crib-Pad Maker	780.685-010
CUPBOARD BUILDER	703.684-014
CURTAIN-ROLLER ASSEMBLER	739.684-042
cushion assembler	780.684-054
CUSHION BUILDER	780.684-046
Cushion Closer	780.682-018
Cushion-Cover Inspector	789.687-038
cushion filler	780.684-054
CUSHION MAKER I	780.684-054
Cushion Maker II	780.682-018
cushion-mat maker	780.684-054
Cushion-Spring Assembler	780.684-098
cushion stuffer	780.684-054
DECORATOR	749.684-014
Dental-Chair Assembler	706.684-058
DISTRESSER	763.687-018
Door Fitter	763.684-026
DOUBLE-END-TRIMMER-AND-BORING-MACHINE OPERATOR	669.682-038
Drawer Fitter	763.684-026
drawer-hardware worker	706.684-050
DRAWER LINER	763.684-030
DRAWER UPFITTER	706.684-050
DRAWER WAXER	763.687-022
Duller	742.684-010
EDGE BANDER, HAND	762.684-038
EDGE BANDER, MACHINE	762.685-010
EDGE-BANDING-MACHINE OFFBEARER	762.686-010
EDGE ROLLER	780.684-058
Examining-Chair Assembler	706.381-026
Excelsior Picker	680.685-078
EXPEDITER, SERVICE ORDER	222.367-070
EYELET-PUNCH OPERATOR	699.685-022
fabric assembler	709.667-010
FABRIC-MACHINE OPERATOR I	616.362-010
FABRIC-MACHINE OPERATOR II	616.685-022
FABRIC STRETCHER	709.667-010
felter	680.685-054
felting-machine operator	680.685-054
Fiber Picker	680.685-078
file-drawer finisher	706.684-050
FILLER-BLOCK INSERTER-REMOVER	652.687-018
Filler Wiper	742.687-010
final inspector	763.687-026
finish cleaner	763.684-034
FINISHED-STOCK INSPECTOR	763.687-026
finisher	742.684-010
finisher	616.685-018
finisher, hand	780.684-070
Finish Inspector	763.687-026
FINISH PATCHER	763.684-034
finish remover	749.687-030
finish repairer	763.684-034
Fixture Designer	142.061-022
flat-spring assembler	709.667-010
Foot-Piece Assembler	706.684-082
FRAME REPAIRER	763.681-010
FUMIGATOR AND STERILIZER	582.685-074
FURNITURE ASSEMBLER	763.684-038
furniture cleaner	709.687-014
FURNITURE DESIGNER	142.061-022
FURNITURE REPRODUCER	149.281-010
GARNETTER	680.685-054
gimp tacker	780.684-126
gin feeder	680.685-078
Glaze Wiper	742.687-010
GLAZIER, METAL FURNITURE	865.684-018
GLUE-SIZE-MACHINE OPERATOR	562.685-010
Glue Spreader	795.687-014
Hair-Picking-Machine Operator	680.685-082
HANDLE-AND-VENT-MACHINE OPERATOR	686.685-034
hand-tier	780.684-106
hardboard panel printer	652.662-018
HARDWARE ASSEMBLER	763.684-042
Head-Piece Assembler	706.684-082
HEMMING-AND-TACKING-MACHINE OPERATOR	787.685-022
High-Lighter	742.684-010
HYDRAULIC-CHAIR ASSEMBLER	706.684-058
Inside-Panel Padder	780.684-082
inspector	763.684-010
inspector and patch worker	763.684-070
INSPECTOR, ASSEMBLY	669.364-010
INSPECTOR, FURNITURE DECALS	979.687-030
INSPECTOR I	780.687-066
INSPECTOR II	780.687-022
INSPECTOR III	739.687-110
KERFER-MACHINE OPERATOR	667.685-042
LAG SCREWER	763.684-046
LAMINATED-PLASTIC-TABLETOP-MOLDING WRAPPER	692.686-046
LAMINATING-MACHINE OPERATOR	692.685-106
LAMINATOR, HAND	763.684-050
LEATHER TOOLER	763.684-054
link-fabric-machine operator	616.685-022
link-wire-fabric-machine operator	616.362-010
link-wire-fabric-machine tender	616.685-022
LOADER-DEMOLDER	556.684-030
LOCK ASSEMBLER	706.684-070
LOCK INSTALLER	706.684-078
loom operator	692.685-262
machine riveter	616.685-058
machine stuffer, automatic	780.684-054
MARQUETRY WORKER	761.281-018
MATERIAL ASSEMBLER	781.684-066
MAT-MAKING MACHINE TENDER	692.685-122
MATTRESS-FILLING-MACHINE TENDER	780.685-010
MATTRESS FINISHER	780.684-070
MATTRESS MAKER	780.684-074
Mattress Packer	920.587-018
MATTRESS-SPRING ENCASER	780.687-030
MATTRESS STRIPPER	780.687-026
METAL-BED ASSEMBLER	706.684-082
metal cleaner	709.687-014
METAL-FINISH INSPECTOR	703.687-018
metal-furniture assembler	709.684-014
METAL SANDER AND FINISHER	705.687-018
MODEL BUILDER	709.381-014
mounter	763.684-042
MULTI-PURPOSE MACHINE OPERATOR	669.382-022
Office-Chair Assembler	709.684-014
OPERATING-TABLE ASSEMBLER	706.381-026
padded-box sewer	787.685-022
PADDER, CUSHION	780.684-078
PADDING GLUER	780.687-034

pad maker	780.685-014
pad tufter	780.687-050
pad tufter	687.684-014
paint and table edger	740.687-022
PAINTER, PANEL EDGE	740.687-022
Painter, Spring	599.685-026
panel assembler	706.684-082
panel coverer	780.684-086
PANEL COVERER, METAL FURNITURE	780.684-082
PANEL CUTTER	761.684-050
PANEL MAKER	780.684-086
parts assembler	763.684-038
parts inspector	763.684-070
PATTERNMAKER	709.381-034
PATTERNMAKER	781.361-014
PATTERNMAKER	661.280-010
PICKER-MACHINE OPERATOR	680.685-078
pin-machine operator	763.684-046
PLASTERER	749.687-026
plasterer, spot	749.687-026
PLASTIC-TOP ASSEMBLER	763.684-062
Plastic-Top Installer	763.684-050
POCKETED-SPRING ASSEMBLER	780.684-090
pocketed-spring-machine operator	616.685-050
POCKET-MACHINE OPERATOR	616.685-050
prefitter	763.684-026
PRINT-LINE FEEDER	652.686-026
PRINT-LINE INSPECTOR	652.687-034
PRINT-LINE OPERATOR	652.662-018
print-line supervisor	652.662-018
PRINT-LINE TAILER	652.686-030
putty-and-patch worker	763.684-070
QUALITY CONTROL INSPECTOR	569.687-030
racker	780.684-090
Radio-And-Television-Cabinet Inspector	763.687-026
Rattan Worker	763.684-078
Reed Worker	763.684-078
refinisher	763.684-034
REPAIRER	709.684-062
REPAIRER, VENEER SHEET	769.684-058
Repairer, Wood Furniture	769.684-038
retoucher	763.684-034
RIP-AND-GROOVE-MACHINE OPERATOR	667.682-062
RIPPER	617.685-030
rivet-hammer-machine operator	616.685-058
RIVETING-MACHINE OPERATOR	616.685-058
RODDING MACHINE TENDER	665.685-038
Roll-Edge Stitcher, Hand	780.684-070
ROLL-OR-TAPE-EDGE-MACHINE OPERATOR	787.682-038
ROUTER TENDER	665.685-042
rubber	742.687-010
RUBBER	742.684-010
salvage worker	709.684-062
SAMPLE CLERK	221.382-026
SAMPLE CUTTER	781.684-070
Satin Finisher	742.684-010
SCOOPING-MACHINE TENDER	665.685-026
scraper, hand	761.684-038
scraper tender	665.685-026
Seat Assembler	709.684-014
Seat Maker	780.684-134
seat padder	780.684-078
seat scooper, machine	665.685-026
SEWING-MACHINE OPERATOR	780.682-010
SEWING-MACHINE OPERATOR, SPECIAL EQUIPMENT	689.685-118
SHADE-CLOTH FINISHER	585.687-026
SHAPER, HAND	761.684-038
SHAPING MACHINE TENDER	665.685-046
Side-Panel Padder	780.684-082
side-piece coverer	780.684-082
Side-Stitcher	780.684-070
sisal operator	780.687-042
Sisal Picker	680.685-078
Sizing Sprayer	741.687-018
Skin Carver	761.281-010
skirt clipper	780.687-070
SKIRT PANEL ASSEMBLER	780.687-070
SLAT TWISTER	616.685-066
SLICING-MACHINE TENDER	663.685-034
SLIP-SEAT COVERER	780.684-094
SLOT ROUTER	763.684-066
Sofa-Cover Inspector	789.687-038
Sofa Inspector	763.687-026
SORTER, UPHOLSTERY PARTS	780.587-010
SPRING ASSEMBLER	780.684-098
Spring-Assembler Supervisor	616.130-022
SPRING CLIPPER	780.684-102
SPRING COVERER	780.687-038
Spring Crater	920.685-078
spring encaser	780.687-030
SPRINGER	780.684-106
spring setter	780.684-106
spring tacker	780.684-106
spring tier	780.684-106
spring upholsterer	780.684-106
Stacker	569.685-066
Stain Dipper	599.685-026
STAINER	742.684-014
Stain Wiper	742.687-010
Stapler, Coil Unit	780.687-042
STAPLER, HAND	780.687-042
STAPLER, MACHINE	692.685-198
Steam Cleaner	780.687-058
Stenciler	749.684-014
sterilizer operator	582.685-074
stitcher, hand	780.684-070
STOCK-PARTS INSPECTOR	763.684-070
Striper	749.684-014
STRIPPER	749.687-030
Studio-Couch-Frame Builder	762.684-066
STUFFING-MACHINE OPERATOR	780.685-014
SUPERVISOR, ASSEMBLY ROOM	669.130-010
Supervisor, Border Department	780.137-010
SUPERVISOR, CUTTING-AND-SEWING DEPARTMENT	780.131-010
Supervisor, Cutting-And-Sewing Room	780.137-010
Supervisor, Cutting Department	780.131-010
SUPERVISOR, DIMENSION WAREHOUSE	769.134-010
supervisor, engraving	652.132-010
Supervisor, Finish-End	669.130-022
SUPERVISOR, FINISHING	742.134-010
Supervisor, Finishing Department	780.137-010
SUPERVISOR, FRAME SAMPLE AND PATTERN	661.137-010
SUPERVISOR, FURNITURE ASSEMBLY	763.134-014
Supervisor, Inspect, Clean-Up, And Wrap	920.137-026
SUPERVISOR, MATTRESS AND BOXSPRINGS	780.137-010
SUPERVISOR, METAL FURNITURE ASSEMBLY	709.134-010
Supervisor, Metal Furniture Fabrication	619.130-030
SUPERVISOR, PRINT LINE	652.132-010
SUPERVISOR, QUALITY CONTROL	763.134-010
Supervisor, Rough-End	669.130-022
SUPERVISOR, SAWING AND ASSEMBLY	669.132-010
Supervisor, Sewing Department	780.131-010
SUPERVISOR, SPRING-UP	780.134-014
SUPERVISOR, STEEL DIVISION	616.130-022
Table-And-Desk Finisher	709.687-014
Table Assembler, Metal	709.684-014
TESTER, CONVERTIBLE SOFA BEDSPRING	780.684-110
TICKET-CHOPPER ASSEMBLER	739.684-154
tick sewer	780.682-010
topper	780.685-018
Tow Picker	680.685-078
Tow-Picker Operator	680.685-082
TRAVERSE-ROD ASSEMBLER	739.687-186
TRIMMING ASSEMBLER	780.684-114
TUFTER	687.684-014
TUFTER, HAND	780.687-050
tufter operator	687.684-014
TUFTING-MACHINE OPERATOR	687.685-014
TURNING LATHE TENDER	664.685-034
upfitter	763.684-042
upholsterer	780.684-046
UPHOLSTERER, ASSEMBLY LINE	780.684-134
upholsterer helper	780.684-010
UPHOLSTERER, INSIDE	780.381-038
UPHOLSTERER, OUTSIDE	780.684-118
upholstery bundler	780.587-010
UPHOLSTERY CLEANER	780.687-058
Upholstery Cutter, Machine	781.684-014
upholstery handler	780.587-010
UPHOLSTERY REPAIRER	780.684-122
UPHOLSTERY TRIMMER	780.684-126
Vacuum-Spindle Sander	761.682-010
Varnish Dipper	599.685-026
veneer-edge bander	762.684-038
Veneer Matcher	769.687-046
VENETIAN-BLIND ASSEMBLER	739.684-166
VENETIAN-BLIND INSTALLER	869.484-018
Venetian-Blind-Tape Cutter	781.687-026
Vertical-Shade Assembler	739.684-166
Washcoat Wiper	742.687-010

galvanizing

weaver	763.684-018
weaver	692.685-262
WEBBING TACKER	780.684-130
Welt Sewer	780.684-018
WICKER WORKER	763.684-078
Willow Worker	763.684-078
Window-Shade-Cloth Sewer	787.682-026
WINDOW-SHADE CUTTER AND MOUNTER	692.685-250
window-shade-ring coverer	692.685-254
WINDOW-SHADE-RING SEWER	692.685-254
WIPER	742.687-010
wiper-blender	742.687-010
WIRE BENDER	709.687-058
WIRE-BORDER ASSEMBLER	780.685-018
wire stitcher, hand	780.687-042
wire-stitcher, machine	692.685-198
WOODEN-FRAME BUILDER	762.684-066
WOODEN-SHADE HARDWARE INSTALLER	739.684-174
WOOD-WEB-WEAVING-MACHINE OPERATOR	692.685-262
wooling-machine operator	680.685-078
Woven-Blind-Loom Tender	692.685-262
WOVEN-WOOD SHADE ASSEMBLER	739.684-178

galvanizing—GALVANIZING AND OTHER COATING INDUSTRY: This designation includes occupations concerned with galvanizing or coating steel and iron sheets or formed products with zinc; coating steel and iron sheets or formed products with aluminum and lead; or retinning cans and utensils.

BRANNER-MACHINE TENDER	509.685-014
COATING-MACHINE OPERATOR	501.362-010
Galvanizer, Zinc	501.685-010
galvanizing dipper	501.685-010
Lead Coater	501.485-010
PLATER, HOT DIP	501.685-010
pot runner	501.685-010
strand galvanizer	501.485-010
SUPERVISOR, HOT-DIP PLATING	501.137-010
Tin Dipper	501.685-010
Tinner, Automatic	501.362-010
WIRE-COATING OPERATOR, METAL	501.485-010
wire galvanizer	501.485-010
Wire Tinner	501.485-010

garment—GARMENT INDUSTRY: This designation includes occupations concerned with manufacturing and repairing various types of garments from purchased fabrics (including simulated fur) and leather (including simulated leather), the principal products being men's and boys' outer garments and furnishings, such as overcoats, suits, jackets, trousers, raincoats, shirts, pajamas, underwear, and belts, except leather belts which are included in the LEATHER PRODUCTS INDUSTRY (leather prod.); women's and girls' outer garments and furnishings, such as suits, dresses, blouses, skirts, lingerie, and aprons; men's and women's handkerchiefs; work clothing, such as overalls, jackets, trousers, and shirts; blanket-lined and sheepskin-lined clothing; vestments and regalia for academic, ceremonial, clerical, fraternal, and similar purposes; brassieres, corsets, and allied garments, except surgical and orthopedic garments which are included in the PERSONAL PROTECTIVE AND MEDICAL DEVICES AND SUPPLIES INDUSTRY (protective dev.); and garments of rubberized material, except those of vulcanized rubber which are included in the RUBBER GOODS INDUSTRY (rubber goods). Occupations concerned with the manufacture of fur garments are included in the FUR GOODS INDUSTRY (fur goods); occupations concerned with the manufacture of gloves and mittens are included in the GLOVE AND MITTEN INDUSTRY (glove & mit.); those concerned with the manufacture of hats and caps are included in the HAT AND CAP INDUSTRY (hat & cap); and those concerned with the manufacture of hosiery and fully knitted garments are included in the KNITTING INDUSTRY (knitting).

ALTERATION TAILOR	785.261-010
alterer	785.261-010
alterer apprentice	785.261-018
APPLIQUER, ZIGZAG	786.682-010
Armhole-And-Shoulder Off-Presser	363.682-018
Armhole Baster, Hand	782.684-058
ARMHOLE BASTER, JUMPBASTING	786.682-014
ARMHOLE FELLER, HANDSTITCHING MACHINE	786.682-018
Armhole Raiser, Lockstitch	786.682-238
ARMHOLE-SEW-AND-TRIM OPERATOR, LOCKSTITCH	786.682-022
ASSEMBLER	781.687-010
ASSISTANT DESIGNER	781.361-010
assorter	781.687-010
BACK MAKER, LOCKSTITCH	786.682-026
BAGGER	920.687-190
Band Cutter	699.685-014
Band-Cutting-Machine Operator	686.685-066

bander	920.687-190
Band Presser	363.682-018
Baster, Hand	782.684-058
BASTING-MACHINE OPERATOR	786.682-030
basting marker	782.687-058
BASTING PULLER	782.687-010
Belt Cutter	699.685-014
Belt-Loop Cutter	699.685-014
Belt-Loop Maker	787.685-014
Belt Turner	789.687-182
BINDER, CHAINSTITCH	786.682-034
BINDER, COVERSTITCH	786.682-038
BINDER, LOCKSTITCH	786.682-042
Binding Cutter	686.685-066
BLINDSTITCH-MACHINE OPERATOR	786.682-046
BONER	789.687-018
Bookseamer, Blindstitch	786.682-126
Bow Attacher	782.684-058
BOW MAKER	784.684-010
BOXING INSPECTOR	789.587-010
box marker	652.685-018
box stamper, machine	652.685-018
Brassiere-Cup-Mold Cutter	781.682-010
BRASSIERE-SLIDE-MAKING-MACHINE TENDER, AUTOMATIC	692.685-026
bundler	920.687-190
bundler	781.687-010
bundle tier	781.687-010
busheler	785.261-014
BUTTON-ATTACHING-MACHINE OPERATOR	699.685-010
button bradder	699.685-010
Button-Buttonhole Marker	781.687-042
button clamper	699.685-010
BUTTONER	782.687-014
BUTTONHOLE-AND-BUTTON-SEWING-MACHINE OPERATOR	786.685-042
BUTTONHOLE-MACHINE OPERATOR	786.685-014
Buttonhole Maker, Hand	782.684-058
Buttonhole Tacker	782.684-058
button riveter	699.685-010
Button Sewer, Hand	782.684-058
BUTTON-SEWING-MACHINE OPERATOR	786.685-010
button tacker	699.685-010
CANVAS BASTER, JUMPBASTING	786.682-050
CARTON MARKER, MACHINE	652.685-018
carton stamper	652.685-018
CHAINSTITCH SEWING MACHINE OPERATOR	786.682-054
CLOTHING MAKER	term
clothing operator see CLOTHING MAKER	
CLOTHING-PATTERN PREPARER	781.287-010
CLOTH MEASURER, MACHINE	589.685-022
CLOTH SHADER	582.685-026
CLOTH TEARER	781.687-018
CLOTH TESTER	029.381-010
Coat Baster	785.361-022
Coat Draper	781.684-026
Coat Fitter	785.261-014
Coat Ironer, Hand	363.684-018
COAT JOINER, LOCKSTITCH	786.682-058
Coat Padder	785.361-022
Coat Tailor	785.261-014
Collar-Band Creaser	583.685-042
COLLAR BASTER, JUMPBASTING	786.682-062
Collar Closer, Lockstitch	786.682-070
Collar Feller	782.684-058
COLLAR FELLER, HANDSTITCHING MACHINE	786.682-066
collar-folder operator	580.685-018
Collar Fuser	363.682-018
Collar Padder, Blindstitch	786.682-150
collar pointer	583.685-102
Collar Setter	785.361-022
COLLAR SETTER, LOCKSTITCH	786.682-070
COLLAR SETTER, OVERLOCK	786.682-074
collar-shaper operator	580.685-018
Collar-Stay-Fuser Tender	583.685-046
Collar Tacker	782.684-058
collar-top turner	583.685-102
Collar Trimmer	699.685-014
Collar Trimmer	781.687-010
Collar Turner	789.687-182
COLLAR-TURNER OPERATOR	580.685-018
contour stitcher	786.685-026
COPYIST	142.281-010
Corder	787.682-022
Corset Repairer	782.684-038

Cotton Presser	363.684-018
COVERSTITCH-MACHINE OPERATOR	786.682-078
creaser	583.685-042
creasing-machine operator	583.685-042
crimper	583.685-042
Cuff Creaser	583.685-042
Cuff Setter, Lockstitch	786.682-070
Cuff Setter, Overlock	786.682-074
cuff-turner-machine operator	583.685-102
CUP SETTER, LOCKSTITCH	786.682-082
Curtain Feller, Blindstitch	786.682-046
CUSTOM TAILOR	785.261-014
Cutting Inspector	789.687-070
damage cutter	782.684-038
dopster	781.287-010
Double-Needle Operator, Lockstitch	786.682-170
DRAPER	781.684-026
Dress Draper	781.684-026
Dressmaker	782.684-058
Dress Marker	781.384-014
DRIER	581.685-014
DRIER ATTENDANT	581.686-018
Duplicate Maker	785.361-018
Edge Baster	786.682-030
Edge Maker	782.684-058
Edge Stitcher, Lockstitch	786.682-238
ELASTIC ATTACHER, CHAINSTITCH	786.682-086
ELASTIC ATTACHER, COVERSTITCH	786.682-090
ELASTIC ATTACHER, OVERLOCK	786.682-094
ELASTIC ATTACHER, ZIGZAG	786.682-098
Elastic Cutter	699.685-014
ELASTIC-TAPE INSERTER	782.687-022
Emblem-Fuser Tender	583.685-046
EMBROIDERY-MACHINE OPERATOR	786.685-018
FABRIC-AND-ACCESSORIES ESTIMATOR	221.482-010
FACING BASTER, JUMPBASTING	786.682-102
Facing-Cutting-Machine Operator	686.685-066
Facing-Slitter	699.682-030
Fagoting-Machine Operator	786.682-278
fashion model	297.667-014
fastener-sewing-machine operator	786.685-010
feed-cup-sewing-machine operator	786.682-122
feeder	781.687-010
FELLED-SEAM OPERATOR, CHAINSTITCH	786.682-106
feller	786.682-126
Feller, Hand	782.684-058
felling-machine operator	786.682-106
FINAL ASSEMBLER	789.687-046
Finished-Garment Inspector	789.687-070
Finisher, Hand	782.684-058
finisher-tailor apprentice	785.361-026
finishing tunnel operator	582.685-150
fitter, factory	781.687-010
FLATLOCK-SEWING-MACHINE OPERATOR	786.682-110
Fly Raiser, Lockstitch	786.682-238
Fly Setter	786.682-286
folder	781.687-010
folder	583.685-042
FOLDING-MACHINE OPERATOR	583.685-042
FRONT-EDGE-TAPE SEWER, LOCKSTITCH	786.682-118
FRONT MAKER, LOCKSTITCH	786.682-114
FUR-MACHINE OPERATOR	786.682-122
FUSING-MACHINE FEEDER	583.686-014
FUSING-MACHINE TENDER	583.685-046
GARMENT FOLDER	789.687-066
garment maker see CLOTHING MAKER	
Garment-Parts Cutter, Hand	781.684-074
Garment-Parts Cutter, Machine	781.684-014
Garment Ripper, Alterations	782.687-038
GARMENT SORTER	222.687-014
GARMENT TURNER	789.687-074
Gimp-Buttonhole-Machine Operator	786.685-014
GRADER MARKER	781.381-034
HANDKERCHIEF FOLDER	920.687-098
Hem Marker	781.687-042
HEMMER, BLINDSTITCH	786.682-126
HEMMER, CHAINSTITCH	786.682-130
HEMMER, LOCKSTITCH	786.682-134
HEMMER, OVERLOCK	786.682-138
HEMSTITCHING-MACHINE OPERATOR	786.682-142
Hook-And-Eye Attacher	782.684-058
Hook-And-Eye Attacher, Machine	699.685-018
Hose-Suspender Cutter	699.685-014
house model	297.667-014
Initial Maker	782.684-018

JUMPBASTING-MACHINE OPERATOR	786.682-146
Jump-Iron-Machine Presser	363.682-018
Label Cutter	699.685-014
Label Cutter	699.685-022
Label-Fuser Tender	583.685-046
Lace Pinner	782.687-026
Lapel Baster	782.684-058
Lapel Padder	785.361-022
Lapel Padder	782.684-058
LAPEL PADDER, BLINDSTITCH	786.682-150
LEATHER ETCHER	583.685-066
Letterer	787.682-022
LINING BASTER, JUMPBASTING	786.682-154
LINING FELLER, BLINDSTITCH	786.682-158
Lining Finisher	782.684-058
LINING MAKER, LOCKSTITCH	786.682-162
Lining Presser	363.684-018
LINING SETTER, LOCKSTITCH	786.682-166
LOCKSTITCH-MACHINE OPERATOR	786.682-170
LOCKSTITCH-SEWING-MACHINE OPERATOR, COMPLETE GARMENT	786.682-174
longseam-machine operator	786.685-026
made-to-measure tailor	785.261-014
made-to-measure-tailor apprentice	785.261-022
MARKER	781.687-042
MARKING STITCHER	781.687-046
master-tailor apprentice	785.261-022
Matcher	781.687-042
matcher	781.687-010
MATCH-UP WORKER	782.684-038
measurer, machine	589.685-022
measuring percher-and-inspector	589.685-022
MENDER, KNIT GOODS	782.684-046
MODEL	297.667-014
MOLDER, SHOULDER PAD	789.684-026
MULTINEEDLE-CHAINSTITCH-MACHINE OPERATOR	786.682-178
multineedle shirrer	786.682-178
nailhead puncher	789.685-010
Nailhead Setter	789.685-010
Neck Feller	782.684-058
NECKTIE-CENTRALIZING-MACHINE OPERATOR I	786.682-186
NECKTIE-CENTRALIZING-MACHINE OPERATOR II	786.682-190
NECKTIE OPERATOR, POCKETS AND PIECES	786.682-182
necktie stitcher	786.682-186
Necktie Turner	789.687-182
NEEDLE-TRADE WORKER	term
ORNAMENT SETTER	789.685-010
outsewer	786.682-166
OVERLOCK-MACHINE OPERATOR, COMPLETE GARMENT	786.682-198
OVERLOCK SEWING MACHINE OPERATOR	786.682-194
pants closer	786.682-202
PANTS OUTSEAMER, CHAINSTITCH	786.682-202
patent-button machine operator, automatic	699.685-010
PATTERN GRADER-CUTTER	781.381-022
PATTERNMAKER	781.361-014
PICKED-EDGE SEWING-MACHINE OPERATOR	786.682-206
Piece Presser	363.684-018
piecer-up	781.687-010
pinker	686.685-042
PINKING-MACHINE OPERATOR	686.685-042
PINNER	782.687-026
Piped-Buttonhole-Machine Operator	786.685-022
PIPED-POCKET-MACHINE OPERATOR	786.685-022
pipe steamer	789.687-166
Piping-Cutting-Machine Operator	686.685-066
PLEAT PATTERNMAKER	781.484-010
Pocket Creaser	583.685-042
Pocket-Flap-Creasing-Machine Operator	583.685-042
pocket-maker	786.682-210
Pocket Marker	781.687-042
Pocket Presser	363.684-018
POCKET SETTER, LOCKSTITCH	786.682-210
Production-Control Pegboard Clerk	221.382-018
PROFILE-STITCHING-MACHINE OPERATOR	786.685-026
QUALITY-CONTROL CHECKER	789.387-010
REPAIR OPERATOR	786.682-214
reserve operator	786.682-262
Rhinestone Setter	789.685-010
Ribbon Cutter	699.685-014
RIPPER	782.687-038
RIVETER, HAND	789.687-154
rivet-hole-machine operator	686.685-054
RIVET-HOLE PUNCHER	686.685-054
runstitching-machine operator	786.685-026

Safety-Stitch-Machine Operator 786.682-194
SAMPLE CLERK, HANDKERCHIEF 920.587-022
Sample Cutter 699.685-014
sample maker 785.361-018
sample maker, original 785.361-018
sample sewer 785.361-018
SAMPLE STITCHER 785.361-018
sample tailor 785.361-018
Seam Presser 363.684-018
SEAM STEAMER 789.687-166
SEAT JOINER, CHAINSTITCH 786.682-218
Second Facing Baster 786.682-102
Seconds Inspector 789.687-070
SEWING-MACHINE OPERATOR, SEMIAUTOMATIC 786.685-030
sew-out operator 786.682-166
SHAPER AND PRESSER 583.685-102
Shell Maker, Lockstitch 786.682-174
Shirt Creaser 583.685-042
Shirt Finisher 363.682-018
Shirt Folder 789.687-066
SHIRT-FOLDING-MACHINE OPERATOR 369.685-030
Shirt Marker 781.384-014
Shirt Sorter 222.687-014
Shirt Turner 789.687-074
SHOP TAILOR 785.361-022
SHOP TAILOR APPRENTICE 785.361-026
SHOULDER JOINER, LOCKSTITCH 786.682-222
Silk Presser I 363.684-018
Silk Presser II 363.682-018
single-needle operator 786.682-170
Sleeve Baster 782.684-058
Sleeve-Bottom Feller 782.684-058
SLEEVE MAKER, LOCKSTITCH 786.682-226
SLEEVE SETTER, LOCKSTITCH 786.682-230
SLEEVE SETTER, OVERLOCK 786.682-234
Sleeve Setter, Safety-Stitch 786.682-234
Sleeve Tailor 785.361-022
Sleeve Turner 789.687-074
SLIDER ASSEMBLER 734.687-078
slider attacher 734.687-078
slipstitch-machine operator 786.682-190
small-piece cutter 781.684-062
Smocking-Machine Operator 786.682-178
SPOT CLEANER 582.684-014
stayer 789.687-018
STEAMING-CABINET TENDER 582.685-150
STENCILER 781.687-066
STRAP BUCKLER, MACHINE 689.665-010
Strap Cutter 699.685-014
Strap-Machine Operator, Automatic 787.685-014
stripper 789.687-018
stud setter 789.685-010
Suit Finisher 785.361-022
Supervisor, Finishing Department 786.132-010
SUPERVISOR, GARMENT MANUFACTURING 786.132-010
Supervisor, Inspection Department 786.132-010
SUPERVISOR, PATTERN MARKING 781.131-010
SUPERVISOR, PRESSING DEPARTMENT 583.132-010
Supervisor, Sewing Room 786.132-010
Suspender Cutter 686.685-066
SWATCH CLERK 222.587-050
table draper 782.687-026
Tacker 782.684-058
TACKING-MACHINE OPERATOR 786.685-034
tailor 785.261-014
TAILOR APPRENTICE, ALTERATION 785.261-018
TAILOR APPRENTICE, CUSTOM 785.261-022
Tape Cutter 699.682-030
Tape Cutter 699.685-014
Tape-Cutting-Machine Operator 686.685-066
TAPE STRINGER 782.687-054
tearer 781.687-018
thread cutter 782.684-038
THREAD MARKER 782.687-058
THREAD-PULLING-MACHINE ATTENDANT 689.686-046
TICKET PRINTER AND TAGGER 652.685-094
TIE BINDER 920.687-190
tier 781.687-010
top-bottom-attaching-machine operator 699.685-010
Top-Collar Baster 782.684-058
Top-Collar Maker 785.361-022
TOPSTITCHER, LOCKSTITCH 786.682-238
TOPSTITCHER, ZIGZAG 786.682-242
TRIMMER, MACHINE 781.682-010
Trimming Cutter 699.682-022
Trimming Finisher 782.684-058
TRIMMING-MACHINE OPERATOR 583.685-122
TRIMMING SEWER, AUTOMATIC 787.685-050
Try-on Baster 785.261-014
TUNNEL-ELASTIC OPERATOR, CHAINSTITCH 786.682-246
TUNNEL-ELASTIC OPERATOR, LOCKSTITCH 786.682-250
TUNNEL-ELASTIC OPERATOR, ZIGZAG 786.682-254
ULTRASONIC-SEAMING-MACHINE OPERATOR 786.682-258
ULTRASONIC-SEAMING-MACHINE OPERATOR, SEMIAUTOMATIC 786.685-038
Underbaster 786.682-102
Undercollar Baster 785.361-022
Undercollar Maker 785.361-022
Underpresser, Hand 363.684-018
UTILITY OPERATOR 786.682-262
Vest-Front Presser 363.682-018
Vest Presser 363.684-018
Vest Tailor 785.361-022
WAISTBAND SETTER, LOCKSTITCH 786.682-266
WAISTLINE JOINER, LOCKSTITCH 786.682-270
WAISTLINE JOINER, OVERLOCK 786.682-274
Waist Presser 363.684-018
washer 582.684-014
WASTE SALVAGER 781.684-062
welt-pocket-machine operator 786.685-022
winder 583.685-122
YARDAGE ESTIMATOR 221.484-010
ZIGZAG-MACHINE OPERATOR 786.682-278
ZIPPER SETTER, CHAINSTITCH 786.682-282
ZIPPER SETTER, LOCKSTITCH 786.682-286
zipper-slide attacher 734.687-078

glass mfg.—GLASS MANUFACTURING INDUSTRY: This designation includes occupations concerned with manufacturing and repairing glass and glass products from raw materials of which the principal kinds are window and plate glass; pressed ware, such as plates, cups, and tumblers; blown ware, such as bottles; glass fibers; fiber optics strands; glass blocks; and pressed or blown scientific, technical, and industrial glassware. Excluded are occupations concerned with producing glass products from purchased glass, such as cut-glass tableware and leaded, stained, and art-glass windows, which are included in the GLASS PRODUCTS INDUSTRY (glass products). Certain occupations concerned with manufacturing fiberglass insulation are included in the ABRASIVE, ASBESTOS, AND MISCELLANEOUS NONMETALLIC MINERAL PRODUCTS INDUSTRY (nonmet. min.). Occupations concerned with the manufacture of insulated fiber optic cable are included in the NONFERROUS METAL ALLOYS AND PRIMARY PRODUCTS INDUSTRY (nonfer. metal).

automatic forming machine operator 575.382-014
automatic lehr operator 573.685-026
BALCONY WORKER 575.687-010
ball maker 575.684-026
Bander, Hand 740.681-010
BATCH-AND-FURNACE OPERATOR 572.382-010
batch mixer 570.685-054
batch-plant operator 570.685-054
Batch Unloader 570.685-026
BEVELER 775.684-010
beveler 673.682-014
beveler 573.685-018
BEVELING-AND-EDGING-MACHINE OPERATOR 673.682-014
BEVELING-AND-EDGING-MACHINE-OPERATOR HELPER 673.686-010
beveling-machine operator 673.682-014
Beveling-Machine-Operator Helper 673.686-010
BINDER TECHNICIAN 550.585-010
BLANKMAKER 579.382-022
BLOCKER 673.685-026
BLOCKER, AUTOMATIC 673.685-030
blower 772.381-022
BOBBIN DISKER 734.687-022
bobbin salvager 922.687-018
BOBBIN SORTER 922.687-018
BOBBIN-WINDER TENDER 619.685-022
bonded-strand operator 574.665-010
Bottle Blower 772.381-022
bottle-blowing-machine tender 575.685-038
Bottle Inspector 579.384-018
Bottle-Machine Operator 575.382-014
Caser, Rolled Glass 920.587-018
clay-house worker 579.664-010
CLAY-STRUCTURE BUILDER AND SERVICER 579.664-010
cleaning-machine operator 673.685-030
combustion analyst 572.360-010
cone inspector 681.687-030

creel selector	689.687-038
CROSSCUTTER, ROLLED GLASS	575.684-022
crusher operator	570.685-026
CULLET CRUSHER-AND-WASHER	570.685-026
cut-off-machine helper	677.665-010
cut-off-machine unloader	677.665-010
cut-off tender, glass	677.685-030
CUTTING-MACHINE TENDER, DECORATIVE	775.685-010
DECORATING-EQUIPMENT SETTER	652.380-010
DECORATING INSPECTOR	579.687-014
Decorating-Machine Tender	979.685-010
DECORATOR	740.381-010
DEFECT REPAIRER, GLASSWARE	772.684-010
disk setter	734.687-022
DRAWING-KILN OPERATOR	575.362-010
DRAWING-KILN SUPERVISOR	575.137-010
drawing-machine operator	575.362-010
EDGER, HAND	775.684-014
EDGING-MACHINE FEEDER	673.686-022
END FINDER, ROVING DEPARTMENT	689.687-038
FIBERGLASS-BONDING-MACHINE TENDER	574.665-010
FIBER-MACHINE TENDER	575.685-030
filling inspector	681.687-030
finished-yarn examiner	681.687-030
finisher	573.685-018
finishing-machine operator, automatic	677.562-010
FLOOR ATTENDANT	579.687-018
Floor Inspector	579.384-018
flow floor attendant	579.687-018
flow machine operator	575.382-014
Foot Caster	772.381-018
forming fixer	629.281-026
FORMING-MACHINE ADJUSTER	629.281-026
FORMING-MACHINE OPERATOR	575.382-014
FORMING-MACHINE TENDER	575.685-038
FORMING-MACHINE UPKEEP MECHANIC	575.380-010
FORMING-MACHINE UPKEEP-MECHANIC HELPER	575.687-014
forming operator	575.685-030
frickertron checker	575.685-082
furnace attendant	572.382-010
FURNACE-COMBUSTION ANALYST	572.360-010
furnace operator	573.685-026
gaffer	772.381-022
GATHERER	575.684-026
glass artist	740.381-010
glass bender	575.685-054
GLASS BLOWER	772.381-022
glass blower, machine forming	575.382-014
glass breaker	779.684-054
glass buffer	775.684-038
GLASS-BULB-MACHINE ADJUSTER	575.360-010
GLASS-BULB-MACHINE FORMER, TUBULAR STOCK	575.382-018
glass crusher	570.685-026
GLASS-CUT-OFF SUPERVISOR	677.131-010
GLASS CUT-OFF TENDER	677.685-030
glass cutter, hand	779.684-054
GLASS CUTTER, OVAL OR CIRCULAR	779.684-022
GLASS-CUTTING-MACHINE OPERATOR, AUTOMATIC	677.562-010
GLASS DECORATOR	775.381-014
GLASS DRILLER	775.687-014
Glass Etcher	775.381-014
GLASS GRINDER	775.684-034
Glass-Loading-Equipment Tender	677.665-010
Glass-Mold Repairer	519.684-018
GLASS POLISHER	775.684-038
glass-products inspector	579.687-030
glass pulverizer equipment operator	570.685-026
GLASS-RIBBON-MACHINE OPERATOR	575.362-010
GLASS-RIBBON-MACHINE-OPERATOR ASSISTANT	575.365-010
GLASS-ROLLING-MACHINE OPERATOR	575.382-022
glass sagger	575.685-054
glass smoother	775.684-038
glass technologist	772.687-010
GLASS-UNLOADING-EQUIPMENT TENDER	677.665-010
glassware finisher	772.381-018
GLASS-WORKER, PRESSED OR BLOWN	772.687-010
GLAZING-MACHINE OPERATOR	573.685-018
groove-machine operator	673.682-026
hand blocker	673.685-026
hand decorator	740.381-014
heat treat worker	573.685-026
inspector, machine-cut glass	579.687-030
inspector-packer, glass container	579.687-030
JOINER	673.687-010
kiln operator	575.362-010
laboratory technician	579.384-014
LAYER	673.686-026
lehr attendant	573.685-026
Lehr Cutter	779.684-054
lehr operator	573.685-026
lehr stripper	573.685-026
LEHR TENDER	573.685-026
lens molder	575.685-054
LENS-MOLDING-EQUIPMENT OPERATOR	575.685-054
Lip-And-Gate Builder	861.381-026
load blocker	673.685-030
LUSTER APPLICATOR	740.381-014
MARBLE-MACHINE TENDER	575.685-058
MARKER MACHINE ATTENDANT	579.685-070
MARK-UP DESIGNER	775.684-050
mat selector	689.687-038
MITER GRINDER OPERATOR	673.682-026
MIXER	570.685-054
mix-house operator	570.685-054
mold changer	575.687-014
mold cleaner	579.685-030
MOLD POLISHER	579.685-030
Mold-Press Operator	575.382-014
multicut-line operator	677.562-010
OVEN TENDER	573.685-010
PAPER INSERTER	920.687-138
platform worker	575.687-010
POLISHER	775.684-058
press-and-blow-machine tender	575.685-038
PRESSER	575.685-074
PRODUCTION-MACHINE TENDER, GLASS CUTTING-OR-GRINDING	679.685-014
punch press operator	575.685-054
pyroglazer	740.381-010
QUALITY-CONTROL INSPECTOR	579.367-010
QUALITY-CONTROL TECHNICIAN	579.367-014
QUALITY TECHNICIAN, FIBERGLASS	579.384-014
quill inspector	681.687-030
refractory specialist	579.664-010
roving selector	689.687-038
Sandblaster, Glass	775.381-014
scrubber	673.685-026
SECOND CUTTER	779.684-054
SELECTOR	579.687-030
shift supervisor, melting	579.137-026
sliver former	575.685-030
sliver handler	575.685-030
spool salvager	922.687-018
SPOTTER	772.687-014
Squeegee-Machine Tender	979.685-010
Staple-Fiber-Machine Tender	575.685-030
Stenciling-Machine Tender	979.685-010
Stopper Grinder	775.684-034
Straightedge-Machine-Operator Helper	673.686-010
straight edger	673.685-078
STRAIGHT-LINE EDGER	673.685-078
STRIPPER	673.666-014
supervisor, automatic cutting machines	677.131-010
Supervisor, Bottle Machines	575.130-018
Supervisor, Crack-Off	775.130-010
SUPERVISOR, DECORATING	652.130-010
SUPERVISOR, FINISHING	775.130-010
SUPERVISOR, FORMING DEPARTMENT I	575.130-018
SUPERVISOR, FORMING DEPARTMENT II	579.130-022
supervisor, furnace	579.137-026
supervisor, furnace room	579.137-026
Supervisor, Grinding	775.130-010
SUPERVISOR, INSPECTION	579.134-010
SUPERVISOR, MOLD CLEANING AND STORAGE	579.137-018
SUPERVISOR, MOLD MAKING	609.131-014
SUPERVISOR, MOLD SHOP	609.131-018
Supervisor, Polishing	775.130-010
SUPERVISOR, RECEIVING AND PROCESSING	579.137-026
tank-and-batch operator	572.382-010
Tank-Furnace Operator	572.382-010
technician	579.367-014
Television-Tube Inspector	579.384-018
TEST-SKEIN WINDER	575.685-082
tube closing machine operator	573.685-018
tube finishing machine operator	573.685-018
turn-out worker	579.687-018
TWISTER TENDER	681.685-130
upkeep mechanic	575.380-010
WARE FINISHER	772.381-018
Warehouse Cutter	779.684-054

glass products

WARE SERVER	652.686-046
WARE TESTER	579.384-018
WARM-IN WORKER	772.684-018
window-glass cutter off	677.685-030
WIRE SETTER	579.665-018
YARDAGE-CONTROL OPERATOR, FORMING	575.662-014
YARN EXAMINER	681.687-030
yarn inspector	681.687-030

glass products—GLASS PRODUCTS INDUSTRY: This designation includes occupations concerned with producing and repairing glass products from purchased glass, such as cut-glass tableware; leaded, stained, and art-glass windows; scientific glass apparatus; mosaic glass; ground glass; glass watch crystals; framed and unframed mirrors; and glass novelties, such as glass fruit, trees, or flowers.

ANNEALER	573.685-010
ASSEMBLER, FILTERS	739.687-018
AUTOMATIC PATTERN EDGER	673.682-010
Bander, Hand	740.681-010
belt seamer	775.684-042
BEVELER	775.684-010
beveler	673.682-014
BEVELER	673.685-018
BEVELING-AND-EDGING-MACHINE OPERATOR	673.682-014
BEVELING-AND-EDGING-MACHINE-OPERATOR HELPER	673.686-010
beveling-machine operator	673.682-014
Beveling-Machine-Operator Helper	673.686-010
BLOCKER	673.685-026
BLOCKER, AUTOMATIC	673.685-030
BREAKER	779.687-010
CIRCLE BEVELER	673.685-034
CIRCLE EDGER	673.685-038
cleaning-machine operator	673.685-030
CLIP-AND-HANGER ATTACHER	739.684-038
colored-liquid-plastic applier	840.684-010
conveyor loader	579.686-022
CUTTING SUPERVISOR	775.134-010
DECORATING-EQUIPMENT SETTER	652.380-010
DECORATING-MACHINE OPERATOR	652.685-026
DECORATOR	740.381-010
Diamond-Wheel Edger	775.684-014
DRILLER, MACHINE	676.685-014
driller, multiple spindle	676.682-010
DRILL OPERATOR, AUTOMATIC	676.682-010
edge grinder, machine	775.684-062
Edge Polisher	775.684-058
EDGER, HAND	775.684-014
EDGER, TOUCH-UP	775.684-018
EDGING-MACHINE SETTER	673.380-010
ENGRAVER	775.381-010
engraver	775.584-010
ENGRAVER TENDER	673.685-050
Engravings Polisher	775.684-058
EYE-DROPPER ASSEMBLER	739.687-086
face cleaner	779.687-022
FIBERGLASS-CONTAINER-WINDING OPERATOR	579.584-010
FIBERGLASS-MACHINE OPERATOR	574.682-010
FINAL INSPECTOR	779.387-010
FINGER-GRIP-MACHINE OPERATOR	673.685-054
firer	573.685-010
flower cutter	775.381-010
FRAMER	739.684-078
FRAME REPAIRER	739.684-074
glass artist	740.381-010
GLASS BLOWER, LABORATORY APPARATUS	772.281-010
GLASS-BLOWING-LATHE OPERATOR	772.482-010
glass breaker	779.687-010
GLASS-BULB SILVERER	779.687-018
GLASS CALIBRATOR	775.584-010
GLASS-CLEANING-MACHINE TENDER	579.685-018
GLASS-CUTTING-MACHINE FEEDER	677.686-014
GLASS DECORATOR	775.381-014
Glass Etcher	775.381-014
glass-etcher helper	779.687-038
GLASS FINISHER	775.684-026
GLASS GRINDER	775.684-030
GLASS GRINDER, LABORATORY APPARATUS	775.382-010
glass inspector	779.687-022
Glass-Novelty Maker	770.381-010
GLASS SANDER, BELT	775.684-042
glass technician	006.261-010
glass technologist	772.281-010

glass technologist	006.261-010
GLASS TINTER	840.684-010
glassware engraver	775.381-010
GLASS-WOOL-BLANKET-MACHINE FEEDER	579.685-022
glazier artist	779.381-010
GLAZIER, STAINED GLASS	779.381-010
groove-machine operator	673.682-026
hand blocker	673.685-026
hand decorator	740.381-014
HOT-WIRE GLASS-TUBE CUTTER	772.684-014
INSPECTOR, GLASS OR MIRROR	779.687-022
Joiner	779.381-010
load blocker	673.685-030
LUSTER APPLICATOR	740.381-014
mirror inspector	779.687-022
MIRROR-MACHINE FEEDER	579.686-022
mirror silverer	574.684-014
MIRROR SPECIALIST	779.684-038
miter cutter	775.381-010
MITER GRINDER OPERATOR	673.682-026
MOSAIC WORKER	779.381-014
notcher	673.685-070
NOTCH GRINDER	673.685-070
PAINTER, MIRROR	741.684-022
paint sprayer	741.684-022
PAINT-SPRAY TENDER	574.685-014
PATTERNMAKER	779.584-010
POLISHER	775.684-058
PRINTER	979.681-014
pyroglazer	740.381-010
RADIUS CORNER MACHINE OPERATOR	673.685-098
Rougher	775.684-010
Sandblaster, Glass	775.381-014
sander	775.684-042
SCIENTIFIC GLASS BLOWER	006.261-010
Scratch Polisher	775.684-058
scrubber	673.685-026
SILVERER	574.684-014
SILVERING APPLICATOR	574.582-010
SILVER STRIPPER, MACHINE	579.685-054
Smoother	775.684-010
statler operator	677.686-014
Steel-Wheel Engraver	775.381-010
Stenciling-Machine Tender	979.685-010
STOCK SHEETS CLEANER-INSPECTOR	779.687-034
Straightedge-Machine-Operator Helper	673.686-010
straight edger	673.685-078
STRAIGHT-LINE EDGER	673.685-078
SUPERVISOR, EDGING	673.130-010
SUPERVISOR, HAND SILVERING	574.134-010
SUPERVISOR, MIRROR FABRICATION	679.137-014
SUPERVISOR, MIRROR MANUFACTURING DEPARTMENT	579.131-010
Supervisor, Packing	920.137-026
SUPERVISOR, SILVERING DEPARTMENT	574.132-014
SUPERVISOR, WALL MIRROR DEPARTMENT	739.137-022
VACUUM-BOTTLE ASSEMBLER	739.687-194
WATCH-CRYSTAL EDGE GRINDER	775.684-062
WATCH-CRYSTAL MOLDER	772.684-022
WAXER	779.687-038
wheel engraver	775.381-010

glove & mit.—GLOVE AND MITTEN INDUSTRY: This designation includes occupations concerned with producing cloth, cloth-and-leather, leather, or coated-fabric gloves and mittens for dress, work, sport, or novelty wear. Occupations concerned with manufacturing knitted gloves are found in the KNITTING INDUSTRY (knitting).

ASSEMBLER	781.687-010
ASSEMBLER	781.667-010
assorter	781.687-010
BAND-AND-CUFF CUTTER	784.685-010
bundler	781.687-010
bundle tier	781.687-010
CLICKING-MACHINE OPERATOR	789.382-010
Closer	784.682-010
CUFF CUTTER	686.685-018
Cuff Slitter	699.682-030
CUTTER	699.682-014
EXAMINER	789.687-042
feeder	781.687-010
Fingerer	784.682-010
fitter, factory	781.687-010
folder	781.687-010

Fourchette Sewer	784.682-010
gauntlet pairer	784.687-034
Glove Cutter	781.687-030
glove finisher	363.687-010
GLOVE FORMER	363.687-010
GLOVE PAIRER	784.687-034
Glove-Parts Cutter	699.682-022
GLOVE-PARTS INSPECTOR	781.687-034
glove presser	363.687-010
GLOVE PRINTER	652.685-034
GLOVE SEWER	784.682-010
Glove Tagger	652.685-094
GLOVE TURNER	784.687-038
Glove Turner-And-Former	784.687-038
glove turner and former	363.687-010
GLOVE TURNER AND FORMER, AUTOMATIC	583.686-018
inspector trimmer	789.687-042
ironer	363.687-010
knit-wrist cutter	686.685-018
Knuckle-Strap Sewer	784.682-010
layer-off	363.687-010
Leather Cutter	789.382-010
LEATHER GRADER	784.387-014
leather-piece inspector	781.687-034
leather sorter	784.387-014
LINER	784.687-046
matcher	781.687-010
Mender	784.682-010
Mitten Stitcher	784.682-010
Palm-And-Back Forger	784.682-010
piecer-up	781.687-010
PULLER-THROUGH	782.687-030
QUILTING-MACHINE OPERATOR	689.685-106
	689.685-106
stitcher	784.682-010
Strapper	784.682-010
SUPERVISOR	784.132-010
Thumb Sewer	784.682-010
tier	781.687-010
Tipper	784.682-010
Tip Sewer	787.685-042
turner and former, automatic	583.686-018
Wrist Closer	784.682-010
Wrister	784.682-010
Wrist Hemmer	787.682-026
Wrist Liner	784.682-010

government ser.—GOVERNMENT SERVICES: This designation includes occupations concerned with local, state, federal, and international government activities that are confined to government and are not covered by other designations. Typical of the activities included are police and fire protection, judicial services, food and drug inspection, street maintenance, and tax collection. Excluded are such occupations as those occurring in municipal transit operation, the military services, primary construction of highways and related structures, public education services, and public utilities services. Certain administrative specialization and technical occupations occurring in government as well as other industries are found under PROFESSIONAL AND KINDRED OCCUPATIONS (profess. & kin.).

ACCIDENT-PREVENTION-SQUAD POLICE OFFICER	375.263-010
ADJUDICATOR	119.167-010
ADMEASURER	169.284-010
Administrative Officer	188.117-106
Administrator, Pesticide	188.117-134
Administrator, Structural Pest Control	188.117-134
AERIAL-PHOTOGRAPH INTERPRETER	029.167-010
Agri-Business Agent	096.127-010
agricultural agent	096.127-010
AGRICULTURAL-CHEMICALS INSPECTOR	168.267-082
Agricultural Commodity Grading Supervisor	188.117-134
Agricultural-Extension Specialist	096.127-014
Air-Carrier Electronics Inspector	168.264-010
Air-Carrier Maintenance Inspector	168.264-010
air-carrier operations inspector	196.163-010
AIRCRAFT-ARMAMENT MECHANIC	632.261-010
aircraft armorer	632.261-010
airport-control operator	193.162-018
Airport Safety And Security Duty Officer	375.133-010
Airport Safety And Security Officer	375.263-014
Air-Traffic-Control Specialist, Center	193.162-014
AIR-TRAFFIC-CONTROL SPECIALIST, STATION	193.162-014
AIR-TRAFFIC-CONTROL SPECIALIST, TOWER	193.162-018
air-traffic-control supervisor	193.167-010
AIR-TRAFFIC COORDINATOR	193.162-010
ALARM OPERATOR	379.162-010

ALCOHOL-AND-DRUG-ABUSE-ASSISTANCE PROGRAM ADMINISTRATOR	195.167-042
Ambulance Driver	375.263-014
appeals board referee	119.107-010
APPEALS REFEREE	119.267-014
APPEALS REVIEWER, VETERAN	119.117-010
Appellate Conferee	160.167-050
Appellate-Court Judge	111.107-010
appointment clerk	205.362-010
APPRAISER	188.167-010
Appraiser, Aircraft	188.167-010
Appraiser, Auditor	188.167-010
Appraiser, Boats And Marine	188.167-010
Appraiser, Buildings	188.167-010
appraiser, irrigation tax	188.167-014
Appraiser, Land	188.167-010
Appraiser, Oil And Water	188.167-010
Appraiser, Personal Property	188.167-010
Appraiser, Real Estate	188.167-010
Appraiser, Timber	188.167-010
APPRENTICESHIP CONSULTANT	188.117-010
area representative	188.117-010
area specialist	188.117-014
Armorer	632.261-018
ARTIST, SUSPECT	970.361-018
ASSESSOR-COLLECTOR, IRRIGATION TAX	188.167-014
assignment officer	188.167-026
AUDITOR, COUNTY OR CITY	160.167-030
automobile inspector	168.267-058
AUTOMOBILE TESTER	379.364-010
AUTOMOTIVE TECHNICIAN, EXHAUST EMISSIONS	620.281-014
aviation-safety officer	168.264-010
Baggage Inspector	168.267-022
BAILIFF	377.667-010
BALLISTICS EXPERT, FORENSIC	199.267-010
Bank Examiner	160.167-054
BANK-NOTE DESIGNER	142.061-010
BATTALION CHIEF	373.167-010
Bomb-Disposal Specialist	632.261-018
Bombsight Specialist	632.261-010
BORDER GUARD	375.363-010
Border Inspector	168.267-022
border patrol agent	375.363-010
BRAND RECORDER	206.587-010
BUDGET ANALYST	161.267-030
BUSINESS-ENTERPRISE OFFICER	188.117-014
Business Regulation Investigator	168.167-090
business-service officer	188.117-122
Campground Caretaker	406.687-010
captain	375.167-034
CAPTAIN, FIRE-PREVENTION BUREAU	373.167-010
Cargo Inspector	168.267-022
CASEWORKER	169.262-010
Census Clerk	216.382-062
Census Enumerator	205.367-054
CHEMICAL-RADIATION TECHNICIAN	015.261-010
Chief, Airport Safety And Security	375.167-034
CHIEF BANK EXAMINER	160.167-046
chief clerk	375.137-022
CHIEF CONTROLLER	193.167-010
Chief Controller, Center	193.167-010
Chief Controller, Station	193.167-010
Chief Controller, Tower	193.167-010
chief engineer	373.117-010
CHIEF, FISHERY DIVISION	188.117-018
Chief of Field Operations	373.117-010
chief of vital statistics	188.167-022
CHIEF WARDEN	188.167-018
Child Day Care Program Supervisor	168.167-090
CHILD SUPPORT OFFICER	195.267-022
cipher expert	199.267-014
City Auditor	160.167-030
city carrier	230.367-010
Civil Preparedness Coordinator	188.117-022
CIVIL PREPAREDNESS OFFICER	188.117-022
Civil Preparedness Operations Officer	188.117-022
Civil Preparedness Public Information Officer	169.127-010
Civil Preparedness Radiological Officer	188.117-022
Civil Preparedness Supply Specialist	188.117-022
CIVIL PREPAREDNESS TRAINING OFFICER	169.127-010
CIVIL-SERVICE CLERK	205.362-010
CLAIMS ADJUDICATOR	169.267-010
CODE INSPECTOR	168.367-018
COMMANDER, IDENTIFICATION AND RECORDS	375.137-010
COMMANDER, INTERNAL AFFAIRS	375.167-050

COMMANDER, POLICE RESERVES 375.137-030
Commanding Officer, Automobile Section 375.167-022
commanding officer, detectives 375.167-022
commanding officer, garage 375.167-018
commanding officer, highway district 375.163-010
COMMANDING OFFICER, HOMICIDE SQUAD 375.167-010
COMMANDING OFFICER, INVESTIGATION DIVISION .. 375.167-014
COMMANDING OFFICER, MOTOR EQUIPMENT 375.167-018
COMMANDING OFFICER, MOTORIZED SQUAD 375.163-010
commanding officer, motor transport division 375.167-018
COMMANDING OFFICER, POLICE 375.137-034
commanding officer, precinct 375.167-034
commanding officer, radio division communications officer ... 193.167-018
Commanding Officer, Traffic Division 375.163-010
commanding officer, vehicle maintenance unit 375.167-018
commanding officer, vice squad 375.167-014
Commercial Officer 188.117-106
COMMISSIONER, CONSERVATION OF RESOURCES 188.117-026
Commissioner, Iron Range Resources And Rehabilitation 188.117-026
COMMISSIONER OF CONCILIATION 188.217-010
commissioner of relocation services 188.167-070
COMMISSIONER, PUBLIC WORKS 188.117-030
COMMUNITY SERVICE OFFICER, PATROL 372.367-010
COMMUNITY-SERVICES-AND-HEALTH-EDUCATION OFFICER 079.167-010
COMMUNITY WORKER 195.367-018
COMPLAINT EVALUATION OFFICER 375.367-014
COMPLAINT EVALUATION SUPERVISOR 375.137-038
Conciliation-Court Judge 111.107-010
CONGRESSIONAL-DISTRICT AIDE 209.362-030
conservation officer 379.167-010
Consular Officer 188.117-106
CONSULTANT, EDUCATIONAL, STATE BOARD OF NURSING 075.117-010
CONTACT REPRESENTATIVE 169.167-018
control-tower-radio operator 193.162-018
cooperative extension advisor specialist 096.127-014
COORDINATOR, SKILL-TRAINING PROGRAM 169.167-062
CORONER 168.161-010
Corporate Trust Officer 186.117-074
correctional officer 188.167-026
CORRECTION OFFICER 372.667-018
correction officer 372.677-010
correction officer 375.367-010
Correction Officer, City Or County Jail 372.667-018
CORRECTION OFFICER, HEAD 372.137-010
Correction Officer, Penitentiary 372.667-018
Correction Officer, Reformatory 372.667-018
counselor, vocational rehabilitation 045.107-042
county adviser 096.127-010
county agent 096.127-010
COUNTY-AGRICULTURAL AGENT 096.127-010
County Auditor 160.167-030
County Director, Welfare 188.117-126
COUNTY HOME-DEMONSTRATION AGENT 096.121-010
COURT ADMINISTRATOR 188.117-130
COURT CLERK 243.362-010
court officer 377.667-010
crash-squad accident investigator 375.263-010
CREEL CLERK 205.367-026
Criminal-Court Judge 111.107-010
criminal investigator 375.167-042
criminal investigator, customs 188.167-090
CRYPTANALYST 199.267-014
cryptographer 199.267-014
Cultural Affairs Officer 188.117-106
customs examiner 168.267-018
CUSTOMS IMPORT SPECIALIST 168.267-018
CUSTOMS INSPECTOR 168.267-022
CUSTOMS PATROL OFFICER 168.167-010
Dance-Hall Inspector 375.263-014
deputy assessor 188.167-010
deputy assessor 191.367-010
deputy, building guard 377.667-014
DEPUTY, COURT 377.137-018
deputy, grand jury 377.363-010
DEPUTY INSURANCE COMMISSIONER 186.117-022
DEPUTY SHERIFF, BUILDING GUARD 377.667-014
DEPUTY SHERIFF, CHIEF 377.167-010
DEPUTY SHERIFF, CIVIL DIVISION 377.667-018
DEPUTY SHERIFF, COMMANDER, CIVIL DIVISION 377.137-010
DEPUTY SHERIFF, COMMANDER, CRIMINAL AND PATROL DIVISION 377.137-014
DEPUTY SHERIFF, GRAND JURY 377.363-010
DEPUTY UNITED STATES MARSHALL 377.267-010
Desk Captain 375.137-014
Desk Lieutenant 375.137-014
DESK OFFICER 375.137-014
Desk Sergeant 375.137-014
detail sergeant 375.133-010
DETECTIVE 375.267-010
Detective, Automobile Section 375.267-010
detective-bureau chief 375.167-022
Detective Captain 375.167-022
DETECTIVE CHIEF 375.167-022
detective, criminal investigation 375.267-010
Detective, Homicide Squad 375.267-010
Detective Lieutenant 375.167-022
DETECTIVE, NARCOTICS AND VICE 375.267-014
Detective, Precinct 375.267-010
Detective Sergeant I 375.167-022
Detective Sergeant II 375.267-010
Detective, Youth Bureau 375.267-010
Diplomatic Officer 188.117-106
DIRECTOR, AERONAUTICS COMMISSION 188.117-034
DIRECTOR, AGRICULTURAL SERVICES 188.117-038
DIRECTOR, ARTS-AND-HUMANITIES COUNCIL 188.117-042
Director, Civil Preparedness 188.117-022
Director, Civil Preparedness Warden 188.117-022
DIRECTOR, CLASSIFICATION AND TREATMENT 188.167-026
DIRECTOR, COMMISSION FOR THE BLIND 094.117-010
DIRECTOR, COMPLIANCE 188.117-046
DIRECTOR, CONSUMER AFFAIRS 188.117-050
DIRECTOR, CORRECTIONAL AGENCY 188.117-054
DIRECTOR, COUNCIL ON AGING 188.117-058
director, educational board of nurse examiners 075.117-010
DIRECTOR, EMPLOYMENT RESEARCH AND PLANNING 050.117-010
DIRECTOR, EMPLOYMENT SERVICES 188.117-078
DIRECTOR, FIELD REPRESENTATIVES 188.117-062
DIRECTOR, FINANCIAL RESPONSIBILITY DIVISION 188.167-030
DIRECTOR, LABOR STANDARDS 188.117-066
DIRECTOR, LAW ENFORCEMENT 188.117-070
director, recreation 187.117-054
DIRECTOR, LICENSING AND REGISTRATION 188.117-074
DIRECTOR, MEDICAL FACILITIES SECTION 188.117-082
DIRECTOR, MERIT SYSTEM 188.117-086
director of social services 188.117-126
DIRECTOR OF VITAL STATISTICS 188.167-022
Director, Reactor Projects 188.117-134
DIRECTOR, REGULATORY AGENCY 188.117-134
DIRECTOR, REVENUE 188.117-090
DIRECTOR, SAFETY COUNCIL 188.167-034
director, sanitation bureau 188.167-098
DIRECTOR, SECURITIES AND REAL ESTATE 188.167-038
DIRECTOR, STATE-ASSESSED PROPERTIES 188.167-042
director, traffic and planning 005.167-022
Director, Transportation Utilities Regulation 188.117-134
DIRECTOR, UNEMPLOYMENT INSURANCE 188.117-094
DIRECTOR, UTILITY ACCOUNTS 160.267-014
Director, Weights And Measures 188.117-134
Director, Youth Correctional Facility 187.117-018
Disability-Insurance-Hearing Officer 119.107-010
dispatcher 379.362-018
dispatcher 379.362-010
DISPATCHER 193.262-014
DISPATCHER, RADIO 379.362-010
DISPATCHER, STREET DEPARTMENT 239.367-030
distribution clerk 209.687-014
Distribution Clerk, Railway Or Highway Post Office 209.687-014
District Agricultural Agent 096.167-010
DISTRICT ATTORNEY 110.117-010
district captain 375.167-034
District-Court Judge 111.107-010
DISTRICT CUSTOMS DIRECTOR 188.117-098
DISTRICT CUSTOMS DIRECTOR, DEPUTY 188.167-046
DISTRICT EXTENSION SERVICE AGENT 096.167-010
District Fire Chief 373.117-010
District Home Economics Agent 096.167-010
District Lieutenant 375.167-014
District Manager, Postal Service 188.167-086
division commander 375.267-026
division sergeant 375.133-010
DOG CATCHER 379.673-010
Dog-Pound Attendant 410.674-010
dog warden 379.673-010
DRIVER'S LICENSE EXAMINER 168.267-034
ECONOMIC DEVELOPMENT COORDINATOR 188.117-102
Economic Officer 188.117-106
ELECTION ASSISTANT 188.167-050

ELECTION CLERK	205.367-030
election supervisor	188.167-050
ELIGIBILITY-AND-OCCUPANCY INTERVIEWER	168.267-038
ELIGIBILITY WORKER	195.267-010
Emergency-Detail Driver	375.263-014
EMPLOYMENT-AND-CLAIMS AIDE	169.367-010
Employment Counselor	045.107-010
engineering technician, parking	199.261-014
entrance guard	205.367-038
ENVIRONMENTAL ANALYST	199.167-022
ENVIRONMENTAL EPIDEMIOLOGIST	041.167-010
EQUAL-OPPORTUNITY REPRESENTATIVE	168.267-014
equipment processer, storage	929.367-010
EXAMINATION PROCTOR	199.267-018
EXAMINER	169.267-014
EXAMINER, QUESTIONED DOCUMENTS	199.267-022
EXECUTIVE SECRETARY, STATE BOARD OF NURSING	169.117-010
extension agent	096.127-010
extension-service agent	096.127-010
EXTENSION SERVICE SPECIALIST	096.127-014
extension supervisor	096.167-010
extension worker	096.127-010
FACILITIES-FLIGHT-CHECK PILOT	196.263-034
farm adviser	096.127-010
farm agent	096.127-010
Farm-Management Agent	096.127-010
FEDERAL AID COORDINATOR	188.167-054
Feed Inspection Supervisor	168.167-090
Field Auditor	160.167-038
field control inspector	375.267-026
field inspector	373.267-010
FINGERPRINT CLASSIFIER	375.387-010
FINGERPRINT CLERK I	209.367-026
FINGERPRINT CLERK II	206.387-014
fingerprint expert	375.387-010
fire-alarm dispatcher	379.162-010
firearms expert	199.267-010
FIRE ASSISTANT	169.167-022
FIRE CAPTAIN	373.134-010
Fire Captain, Marine	373.134-010
FIRE CHIEF	373.117-010
Fire Chief, Deputy	373.117-010
FIRE CHIEF'S AIDE	373.363-010
fire-control assistant	169.167-022
FIRE-CONTROL MECHANIC	632.261-014
fire-control technician	632.261-014
fire deputy	169.167-022
FIRE-FIGHTING-EQUIPMENT SPECIALIST	638.281-010
FIRE INSPECTOR	373.267-010
FIRE-INVESTIGATION LIEUTENANT	373.267-018
Fire Lieutenant	373.134-010
Fire Lieutenant, Marine	373.134-010
FIRE MARSHAL	373.267-014
FISH AND GAME WARDEN	379.167-010
Fish-And-Game Warden, Marine Patrol	379.167-010
Fish Protector	379.167-010
flight-control-tower operator	193.162-010
FLIGHT-OPERATIONS INSPECTOR	196.163-010
FOOD AND DRUG INSPECTOR	168.267-042
FOOD-MANAGEMENT AIDE	195.367-022
FOREIGN-SERVICE OFFICER	188.117-106
forensic artist	141.061-034
Forest Fire Equipment Operator	850.683-010
game and fish protector	379.167-010
Game Protector	379.167-010
game warden	379.167-010
Gas Inspector, Liquefied	168.264-018
Groundskeeper, Parks And Grounds	406.687-010
guard	372.667-018
Guard, Deputy	372.667-018
GUARD, IMMIGRATION	372.567-014
guard, range	379.167-010
GUARD, SCHOOL-CROSSING	371.567-010
hand-spray operator	379.687-014
handwriting expert	199.267-022
HARBOR MASTER	375.167-026
Harbor-Police Captain	375.167-030
Harbor-Police Lieutenant	375.167-030
HAZARDOUS-WASTE MANAGEMENT SPECIALIST	168.267-086
HEALTH OFFICER, FIELD	168.167-018
HEARING OFFICER	119.107-010
HIGHWAY-ADMINISTRATIVE ENGINEER	005.167-022
Highway Engineer	005.061-038
HIGHWAY-MAINTENANCE SUPERVISOR	899.134-010

HIGHWAY-MAINTENANCE WORKER	899.684-014
highway worker	899.684-014
home agent	096.121-010
home-demonstration agent	096.121-010
Home Economics Specialist	096.127-014
home-extension agent	096.121-010
Homicide-Squad Captain	375.167-010
Homicide-Squad Lieutenant	375.167-010
Homicide-Squad Sergeant	375.167-010
Horticultural Agent	096.127-010
HOUSING-MANAGEMENT OFFICER	188.117-110
Humane Officer	379.673-010
IDENTIFICATION CLERK	209.362-022
IDENTIFICATION OFFICER	377.264-010
IMMIGRATION INSPECTOR	168.167-022
Immigration Patrol Inspector	168.167-022
Industrial Relations Representative	166.167-034
Information Officer	188.117-106
Insect Sprayer, Mobile Unit	906.683-022
INSPECTOR, AGRICULTURAL COMMODITIES	168.287-010
INSPECTOR, AIR-CARRIER	168.264-010
INSPECTOR, AIRCRAFT LAUNCHING AND ARRESTING SYSTEMS	806.264-014
INSPECTOR, BUILDING	168.167-030
INSPECTOR, ELECTRICAL	168.167-034
INSPECTOR, ELEVATORS	168.167-038
INSPECTOR, FURNITURE AND BEDDING	168.267-046
INSPECTOR, GOVERNMENT PROPERTY	168.267-050
INSPECTOR, HEALTH CARE FACILITIES	168.167-042
INSPECTOR, HEATING AND REFRIGERATION	168.167-046
INSPECTOR, INDUSTRIAL WASTE	168.267-054
INSPECTOR, MOTOR VEHICLES	168.267-058
Inspector, Pawnshop Detail	375.267-030
INSPECTOR, PLUMBING	168.167-050
INSPECTOR, QUALITY ASSURANCE	168.287-014
INSPECTOR, RAILROAD	168.287-018
INSPECTOR, WATER-POLLUTION CONTROL	168.267-090
Inspector, Weights And Measures	168.267-062
INSTRUCTOR-TRAINER, CANINE SERVICE	379.227-010
Insurance Licensing Supervisor	168.167-090
INTELLIGENCE SPECIALIST	059.267-010
Investigation Division Captain	375.167-014
Investigation Division Lieutenant	375.167-014
Investigation Division Sergeant	375.167-014
INVESTIGATOR	168.267-062
Investigator, Claims	168.267-062
investigator, communicable disease	168.167-018
INVESTIGATOR, INTERNAL AFFAIRS	375.267-034
Investigator, Internal Revenue	168.267-062
INVESTIGATOR, NARCOTICS	375.267-018
INVESTIGATOR, VICE	375.267-022
Investigator, Welfare	168.267-062
JAILER	372.367-014
JAILER, CHIEF	372.167-018
jail keeper	372.367-014
JUDGE	111.107-010
justice	111.107-010
justice-court judge	111.107-014
justice of the peace	111.107-014
Juvenile-Court Judge	111.107-010
land-lease-information clerk	237.367-026
LAND-LEASING EXAMINER	237.367-026
LANDSCAPE SPECIALIST	406.687-010
LAUNCH COMMANDER, HARBOR POLICE	375.167-030
Leaf-Sucker Operator	919.683-022
Legislative Aide	199.267-034
LEGISLATIVE ASSISTANT	169.167-066
letter carrier	230.367-010
LICENSE CLERK	205.367-034
LICENSE INSPECTOR	168.267-066
Lieutenant, Ballistics	199.267-010
Livestock Agent	096.127-010
Loan-Approval Agent	205.367-022
MAGISTRATE	111.107-014
MAIL CARRIER	230.367-010
MAIL CENSOR	243.367-010
MAIL-DISTRIBUTION-SCHEME EXAMINER	239.367-018
MAIL HANDLER	209.687-014
MAIL-PROCESSING-EQUIPMENT MECHANIC	633.261-014
MAINTENANCE SUPERVISOR, FIRE-FIGHTING-EQUIPMENT	638.131-018
MAINTENANCE WORKER, MUNICIPAL	899.684-046
MANAGER, CITY	188.117-114
manager, county	188.117-114
Manager For Health, Safety, And Environment	188.117-134

Manager, Governmental Program	189.167-030
MANAGER, OFFICE	188.167-058
MANAGER, REGULATED PROGRAM	168.167-090
MANAGER, SOLID-WASTE-DISPOSAL	184.167-078
manager, surplus property	188.117-122
manager, town	188.117-114
Meat And Poultry Specialist Supervisor	168.167-090
MEDICAL COORDINATOR, PESTICIDE USE	041.067-010
medical examiner	168.161-010
Medical Officer	070.101-046
Meter Attendant	375.587-010
Mine Inspector, Federal	168.267-074
Mine Inspector, State	168.267-074
morals-squad police officer	375.267-022
MORTICIAN INVESTIGATOR	168.267-078
MOSQUITO SPRAYER	379.687-014
Motorcycle Police Officer	375.263-014
Motor-Equipment Captain	375.167-018
Motor-Equipment Lieutenant	375.167-018
Motor-Equipment Sergeant	375.167-018
Motorized-Squad Captain	375.163-010
Motorized-Squad Lieutenant	375.163-010
Motorized-Squad Sergeant	375.163-010
motor-transport inspector	168.267-058
motor-vehicle inspector	379.364-010
Mounted Police Officer	375.263-014
Municipal-Court Judge	111.107-010
MUNICIPAL-SERVICES SUPERVISOR	term
Munitions Worker	632.261-018
narcotics investigator	375.267-018
Night-Court Magistrate	111.107-014
Nuclear Weapons Mechanical Specialist	632.261-018
nutrition aide	195.367-022
Nutritionist, Public Health	077.127-010
occupational-safety-and-health-compliance officer	168.167-062
OCCUPATIONAL-SAFETY-AND-HEALTH INSPECTOR	168.167-062
Office Auditor	160.167-038
OPENER-VERIFIER-PACKER, CUSTOMS	168.387-010
operations inspector	168.264-010
operations officer	375.137-014
operations supervisor	185.167-066
ORDNANCE ARTIFICER	632.261-018
ORDNANCE-ARTIFICER HELPER	632.684-010
Paint-Crew Supervisor	869.137-010
Parcel-Post Carrier	230.367-010
PARK AIDE	249.367-082
PARKING ANALYST	199.261-014
parking enforcement agent	375.587-010
PARKING ENFORCEMENT OFFICER	375.587-010
PARKING-METER SERVICER	710.384-026
PARK NATURALIST	049.127-010
PARK RANGER	169.167-042
PARK SUPERINTENDENT	188.167-062
park technician	249.367-082
park worker	406.687-010
PASSPORT-APPLICATION EXAMINER	169.267-030
Patent Clerk	119.267-026
PATIENT-RESOURCES-AND-REIMBURSEMENT AGENT	195.267-018
patrol commander	375.167-034
PATROL CONDUCTOR	372.677-010
Patrol Driver	375.263-014
patrol officer	375.263-014
patrol sergeant	375.133-010
PERSONAL PROPERTY ASSESSOR	191.367-010
PESTICIDE-CONTROL INSPECTOR	168.267-098
Petroleum Products District Supervisor	168.167-090
Petroleum Products Inspection Supervisor	188.117-134
PILOT, HIGHWAY PATROL	375.163-014
plain-clothes officer	375.267-010
PLAN CHECKER	168.267-102
PLANIMETER OPERATOR	219.387-022
PLANNER, PROGRAM SERVICES	188.167-110
POLICE-ACADEMY INSTRUCTOR	375.227-010
POLICE ACADEMY PROGRAM COORDINATOR	375.167-054
POLICE AIDE	243.362-014
POLICE ARTIST	141.061-034
POLICE CAPTAIN, PRECINCT	375.167-034
police captain, senior	375.267-026
POLICE CHIEF	375.117-010
Police Chief, Deputy	375.267-026
POLICE CLERK	375.362-010
POLICE COMMISSIONER I	188.117-118
Police Commissioner II	375.117-010
police-department secretary	375.137-022
police inspector, chief	375.117-010
POLICE INSPECTOR I	375.267-026
POLICE INSPECTOR II	375.267-030
police judge	111.107-014
police justice	111.107-014
POLICE LIEUTENANT, COMMUNITY RELATIONS	375.137-018
POLICE LIEUTENANT, PATROL	375.167-038
Police Lieutenant, Precinct	375.167-034
police magistrate	111.107-014
POLICE OFFICER, BOOKING	375.367-018
POLICE OFFICER, CRIME PREVENTION	375.264-010
POLICE OFFICER, IDENTIFICATION AND RECORDS	375.384-010
POLICE OFFICER I	375.263-014
POLICE OFFICER II	375.367-010
POLICE OFFICER III	375.267-038
POLICE OFFICER, SAFETY INSTRUCTION	375.267-042
police radio dispatcher	379.362-010
POLICE SERGEANT, PRECINCT I	375.133-010
Police Sergeant, Precinct II	375.167-034
Police Sergeant, Radio Patrol	375.133-010
Police Stenographer	202.362-014
POLICE SURGEON	070.101-082
Political Officer	188.117-106
poll clerk	205.367-030
Pool-Hall Inspector	375.263-014
port warden	375.167-026
Position Classifier	166.267-018
postal clerk	243.367-014
Postal Inspector	168.267-062
POSTMASTER	188.167-066
POST-OFFICE CLERK	243.367-014
post-office supervisor	243.137-010
Poultry Specialist Supervisor	168.167-090
power equipment mechanic	620.281-014
precinct captain	375.167-034
PREPAROLE-COUNSELING AIDE	195.367-026
PRESERVATION INSPECTOR, MARINE EQUIPMENT	929.367-010
Probate Judge	111.107-010
procurement inspector	168.287-014
Program Analyst	160.162-022
PROOF-COIN COLLECTOR	709.667-010
PROPERTY-ASSESSMENT MONITOR	241.367-042
PROPERTY CLERK	222.367-054
property custodian	222.367-054
Property Manager	186.117-042
PROPERTY-UTILIZATION OFFICER	188.117-122
prosecuting attorney	110.117-010
prosecutor	110.117-010
PROTECTIVE OFFICER	372.363-010
Public Affairs Officer	188.117-106
Public Finance Specialist	160.162-022
PUBLIC-HEALTH MICROBIOLOGIST	041.261-010
PUBLIC HEALTH PHYSICIAN	070.101-046
PUBLIC HEALTH REGISTRAR	169.167-046
PUBLIC HEALTH SERVICE OFFICER	187.117-050
PUBLIC-SAFETY OFFICER	379.263-014
Public Utilities Complaint Analyst Supervisor	168.167-090
public-works commissioner	188.117-030
RADIATION-PROTECTION SPECIALIST	168.261-010
Radio-Division Captain	193.167-018
Radio-Division Lieutenant	193.167-018
RADIO-INTELLIGENCE OPERATOR	193.362-014
Radio Police Officer	375.263-014
ranger	169.167-042
ranger aide	249.367-082
Rate Analyst	160.267-014
Real-Estate-Utilization Officer	188.117-122
recruitment clerk	205.362-010
referee	119.107-010
REFERRAL-AND-INFORMATION AIDE	237.367-042
regional coordinator for aging	188.117-058
regional extension-service specialist	096.167-010
REGISTRAR	205.367-038
REGISTRATION CLERK	205.367-042
REGISTRATION SPECIALIST, AGRICULTURAL CHEMICALS	168.267-106
REHABILITATION CENTER MANAGER	195.167-038
RELOCATION COMMISSIONER	188.167-070
RESEARCH-CONTRACTS SUPERVISOR	162.117-030
Residential Building Inspector	168.167-030
Resource Agent	096.127-010
RESOURCE-RECOVERY ENGINEER	019.167-018
RETIREMENT OFFICER	166.267-030
returning officer	205.367-030
REVENUE AGENT	160.167-050
REVENUE OFFICER	188.167-074

REVIEWING OFFICER, DRIVER'S LICENSE 168.167-074
ROADS SUPERVISOR 188.167-078
Rooming-House Inspector 168.267-066
RURAL MAIL CARRIER 230.363-010
safety engineer, elevators 168.167-038
sanitarian 379.687-014
Sanitary Inspector 168.267-042
SANITATION INSPECTOR 168.267-110
scheme examiner 239.367-018
SCHOOL BUS MONITOR 372.667-042
SECRETARY OF POLICE 375.137-022
SECRETARY OF STATE 188.167-082
secretary to board of commissioners 375.137-022
secret-code expert 199.267-014
SECTIONAL CENTER MANAGER, POSTAL SERVICE 188.167-086
security inspector 372.363-010
security technician 372.363-010
sergeant 375.133-010
Shelter Management Officer 188.117-022
SHERIFF, DEPUTY 377.263-010
Show Inspector 375.263-014
Snow-Plow Operator, Truck 899.684-014
Snow-Plow Tractor Operator 899.684-014
Snow Ranger 169.167-042
snow remover 955.687-014
SNOW-REMOVING SUPERVISOR 955.137-010
SNOW SHOVELER 955.687-014
solicitor, city or state 110.117-010
SPECIAL AGENT 375.167-042
SPECIAL AGENT, CUSTOMS 188.167-090
Special Agent, FBI 375.167-042
Special Agent, IRS 375.167-042
Special Agent, Secret Service 375.167-042
Special-Delivery Carrier 230.367-010
Special-Distribution Clerk 209.687-014
SPECIALIST-IN-CHARGE, EXTENSION SERVICE 096.167-014
sprayer, insecticide 379.687-014
squad leader 377.137-014
squad sergeant 375.133-010
STAFF TOXICOLOGIST 041.061-094
STATE-HIGHWAY POLICE OFFICER 375.263-018
state's attorney 110.117-010
State-Surplus-Commodity-And-Property Representative 188.117-122
state trooper 375.263-018
station operator 379.362-010
STREET CLEANER 955.687-018
street sweeper 955.687-018
STREET-SWEEPER OPERATOR 919.683-022
SUPERINTENDENT, INDUSTRIES, CORRECTIONAL FACILITY 188.167-094
superintendent, landfill operations 184.167-078
superintendent, police 375.117-010
SUPERINTENDENT, RADIO COMMUNICATIONS 193.167-018
SUPERINTENDENT, RECREATION 187.117-054
Superintendent, Refuse Disposal 188.167-098
SUPERINTENDENT, SANITATION 188.167-098
Superintendent, Sewage-Treatment 188.167-098
Superior-Court Judge 111.107-010
SUPERVISING AIRPLANE PILOT 196.163-014
SUPERVISOR 188.137-010
SUPERVISOR, ARTIST, SUSPECT 970.131-014
supervisor, education and custody 375.367-010
SUPERVISOR, HISTORIC SITES 102.117-010
SUPERVISOR, IDENTIFICATION AND COMMUNICATIONS 377.134-010
SUPERVISOR, LIQUOR STORES AND AGENCIES 185.167-062
SUPERVISOR, MAIL CARRIERS 230.137-018
SUPERVISOR, MAILS 243.137-010
Supervisor, Self-Service Store 185.167-062
SUPERVISOR, SEWER MAINTENANCE 851.137-014
SUPERVISOR, TELECOMMUNICATOR 379.132-010
SUPERVISOR, TRAVEL-INFORMATION CENTER 237.137-014
Supervisor, Weights and Measures, Gas And Oil Inspection 168.167-090
supervisory park ranger 188.167-062
Supreme-Court Justice 111.107-010
surgeon, chief 070.101-082
SURVEILLANCE-SYSTEM MONITOR 379.367-010
SURVIVAL-EQUIPMENT REPAIRER 739.381-054
SWITCHBOARD OPERATOR, POLICE DISTRICT 235.562-014
Tavern Inspector 168.267-066
Tax Analyst 160.167-038
Tax Examiner 160.167-038
TECHNICAL COORDINATOR 209.132-014
TELECOMMUNICATOR 379.362-018
Toll-Bridge Attendant 211.462-038
TOLL COLLECTOR 211.462-038
Torpedo Specialist 632.261-018
TOURIST-INFORMATION ASSISTANT 237.367-050
TOWN CLERK 243.367-018
tractor-sweeper driver 919.683-022
TRAFFIC CHECKER 205.367-058
Traffic-Court Magistrate 111.107-014
Traffic Engineer 005.061-038
TRAFFIC LIEUTENANT 375.167-046
Traffic-Maintenance Officer 869.137-010
TRAFFIC-MAINTENANCE SUPERVISOR 869.137-010
traffic officer 375.263-014
Traffic Police Officer 375.263-014
TRAFFIC-SAFETY ADMINISTRATOR 188.167-102
TRAFFIC SERGEANT 375.137-026
Traffic-Signal Supervisor, Maintenance 869.137-010
Traffic-Sign Erection Supervisor 869.137-010
TRAFFIC TECHNICIAN 199.267-030
Transportation Planning Engineer 005.061-038
TRAVEL CLERK 238.167-010
turnkey 372.367-014
UNCLAIMED PROPERTY OFFICER 188.167-106
Unemployment-Insurance-Hearing Officer 119.107-010
uniform-force captain 375.167-034
united states attorney 110.117-010
VECTOR CONTROL ASSISTANT 049.364-014
vehicle-safety inspector 379.364-010
vending-enterprises supervisor 185.167-066
VENDING-STAND SUPERVISOR 185.167-066
Veterinarian, Public Health 073.101-010
VETERINARY LIVESTOCK INSPECTOR 073.161-010
VETERINARY MEAT-INSPECTOR 073.264-010
veterinary medical officer 073.264-010
Veterinary Milk-Specialist 073.264-010
Veterinary-Poultry Inspector 073.264-010
VETERINARY VIRUS-SERUM INSPECTOR 073.261-010
vice-squad police officer 375.267-022
VOCATIONAL REHABILITATION CONSULTANT 094.117-018
VOCATIONAL-REHABILITATION COUNSELOR 045.107-042
Voting-Machine Repairer 828.261-022
Warden 187.117-018
watch commander 377.137-014
weigh-station inspector 168.267-058
WELFARE DIRECTOR 188.117-126
WILDLIFE AGENT, REGIONAL 379.137-018
WILDLIFE CONTROL AGENT 379.267-010

grain-feed mills—GRAIN AND FEED MILLING INDUSTRY: This designation includes occupations concerned with manufacturing flour and meal from wheat, corn, rice, and other grains; prepared feeds for animals and fowls from grain and other ingredients, such as ground oyster shells, alfalfa, and bonemeal; cleaned and polished rice; cereal breakfast foods; and cornstarch, syrup, oil, sugar, and byproducts.

baker, laboratory 526.381-018
BAKER, TEST 526.381-018
BARREL FILLER 529.485-010
batch-mixer operator 520.685-098
BATCH-TANK CONTROLLER 521.685-022
BIN CLEANER 529.687-014
blender 520.685-106
blender helper 520.686-022
BLENDING SUPERVISOR 520.132-010
BOLTER 521.685-030
BOLTER HELPER 521.686-010
bolter helper 520.686-022
BONE-CHAR KILN OPERATOR 523.662-010
Bottom Steep Tender 522.465-010
BRAN MIXER 599.685-014
bump-grader operator 529.685-262
Burr-Mill Operator 521.682-026
BUYER, GRAIN 162.167-010
CAKE TESTER 526.381-022
CENTRIFUGAL OPERATOR 521.682-010
CENTRIFUGE OPERATOR 521.685-046
cereal miller 521.682-022
cereal popper 523.382-010
CHAR-FILTER-TANK TENDER, HEAD 521.665-010
CHAR PULLER 521.687-030
chocolate maker 523.685-022
chocolate-mixer operator 523.685-022
CHOCOLATE TEMPERER 523.685-022
CLARIFIER 521.685-054
CLEAN-RICE BROKER 162.167-018

CLEAN-RICE GRADER AND REEL TENDER	521.685-062
COATING OPERATOR	524.685-018
control board operator, sugar refining	521.362-018
CONVERTER OPERATOR	526.382-018
cook	526.381-026
cooker	526.381-026
COOKER	526.685-022
COOK, KETTLE	526.381-026
cook, pressure	526.381-026
COOLER TENDER	523.685-038
Corn-Cutter Operator	521.685-122
CORN-GRINDER OPERATOR, AUTOMATIC	521.685-086
Corn-Husk Baler	920.685-010
Corn Miller	521.682-026
corn-oil extractor	529.685-106
Corn-Sheller Operator	521.685-122
Crimper Operator	521.685-122
Crusher-Machine Operator	521.685-122
CRYSTALLIZER OPERATOR	523.685-050
CURING-BIN OPERATOR	522.685-038
CUSTOM-FEED-MILL OPERATOR	529.132-010
CUSTOM-FEED-MILL-OPERATOR HELPER	521.686-026
CUT-IN WORKER	521.686-030
Dairy-Feed-Mixing Operator	520.685-098
dehydrator	523.685-058
DEXTRINE MIXER	523.682-018
Door Slinger	529.685-154
DRIER ATTENDANT	523.685-058
DRIER TENDER	523.685-070
DRIP-BOX TENDER	521.687-038
DRUM DRIER	523.682-026
DRY-STARCH OPERATOR	520.362-014
DRY-STARCH OPERATOR, AUTOMATIC	529.362-014
elevator tender	921.365-010
EXPELLER OPERATOR	529.685-106
EXTRUDER OPERATOR	520.682-018
feed-and-pellet operator	520.685-178
FEED BLENDER	520.685-094
Feed-Drier Tender	523.685-058
feed elevator worker	920.685-058
feeder loader	520.686-018
feeder operator	520.685-098
Feeder Operator, Automatic	520.685-098
FEED GRINDER	521.685-122
FEED-IN WORKER	929.685-034
feed miller	521.682-026
FEED MIXER	520.685-098
FEED-MIXER HELPER	520.686-018
FEED WEIGHER	920.685-058
FILTERING-MACHINE TENDER	521.685-138
FILTER OPERATOR	521.682-018
FILTER-PRESS TENDER, HEAD	521.665-018
FILTER-TANK-TENDER HELPER, HEAD	521.685-134
FILTER TENDER	522.665-010
Fire Drier	523.685-058
flake-miller helper	526.585-010
FLAKE MILLER, WHEAT AND OATS	521.682-022
flake-or-shred-roll operator	520.685-102
FLAKING-ROLL OPERATOR	520.685-102
FLASH-DRIER OPERATOR	529.582-014
FLAVOR EXTRACTOR	529.685-126
FLOUR BLENDER	520.685-106
FLOUR-BLENDER HELPER	520.686-022
FLOUR MIXER	520.485-010
flour-mixer helper	520.686-022
flour tester	526.381-018
FLUMER	521.686-038
flusher	529.687-210
FOOD MIXER	520.687-034
GENERAL SUPERINTENDENT, MILLING	183.167-014
Germ Drier	523.685-058
GLUTEN-SETTLING TENDER	521.685-150
grain blender	520.485-014
grain cleaner	521.685-254
Grain Distributor	921.662-018
GRAIN-DRIER OPERATOR	523.685-090
grain-elevator agent	162.167-010
GRAIN ELEVATOR CLERK	222.567-010
Grain-Elevator-Motor Starter	921.685-026
Grain-Elevator Operator	921.662-018
GRAIN MIXER	520.485-014
GRAIN PICKER	529.687-110
GRAIN RECEIVER	921.365-010
Grain Unloader	921.667-018
Grain Unloader, Machine	921.685-038
grain weigher	222.567-010
GRINDER OPERATOR	521.682-026
GRINDER OPERATOR	521.685-166
gristmiller	521.682-026
GUNNER	523.382-010
Hammer-Mill Operator	521.685-122
head kiln operator	523.662-010
hopper loader	520.686-018
HULLER OPERATOR	521.682-030
INSPECTOR, GRAIN MILL PRODUCTS	529.387-026
inspector technician	529.387-026
LABORATORY MILLER	521.685-194
LABORER, STARCH FACTORY	529.685-154
LABORER, SYRUP MACHINE	521.687-074
Limer	520.685-098
machine repairer	629.281-030
MAINTENANCE MECHANIC	629.281-030
manager, grain elevator	162.167-010
mash-feed-mixer operator	520.685-098
MEAL-GRINDER TENDER	521.685-210
milled-rice broker	162.167-018
miller, first	521.130-010
miller, head	521.130-010
MILLER, HEAD, ASSISTANT, WET PROCESS	629.684-014
MILLER, HEAD, WET PROCESS	629.261-014
MILLER SUPERVISOR	521.130-010
MILLER, WET PROCESS	521.662-010
MILL FEEDER	520.685-134
MILL HAND	term
milling superintendent	183.167-014
mill operator	521.130-010
mill operator	521.682-026
MILL OPERATOR	521.685-226
mixer-and-scaler	520.485-010
mixer-machine feeder	520.686-018
mixer operator	520.485-010
MOLASSES AND CARAMEL OPERATOR	526.382-022
Molasses-Feed Mixer	520.685-098
MONITOR-AND-STORAGE-BIN TENDER	521.685-230
NEUTRALIZER	522.685-082
Oil-Expeller	529.685-106
OVEN OPERATOR	526.585-010
PELLET-MILL OPERATOR	520.685-178
Pellet Operator	520.682-018
PERCOLATOR OPERATOR	523.682-034
PLANT SUPERVISOR	529.132-014
Poultry-Feed-Mixer Operator	520.685-098
Poultry Feed Supervisor	529.132-054
Premix Operator, Concentrate	523.685-022
PRESS PULLER	529.687-170
Press Tender, Head, Feed House	521.665-018
PROCESSOR, GRAIN	521.685-254
PROCESSOR HELPER	521.686-050
Purifier	521.685-030
REFINERY OPERATOR	521.362-018
REFINERY OPERATOR, ASSISTANT	521.462-010
RICE CLEANING MACHINE TENDER	521.665-022
Rice-Drier Operator	523.685-090
ROASTER, GRAIN	523.585-034
Rolled-Oats-Mill Operator	521.685-122
roller-mill operator	521.682-026
roller tender	521.685-210
roll operator	520.685-102
roll operator	529.685-106
ROUGH-RICE GRADER	529.367-026
ROUGH-RICE TENDER	521.685-274
ROUTING-EQUIPMENT TENDER	521.685-278
SACK-DEPARTMENT SUPERVISOR	229.137-010
Self-Rising-Flour Mixer	520.485-010
SEPARATOR OPERATOR	521.382-014
Separator Tender I	521.685-254
SEPARATOR TENDER II	521.685-290
SHAKER REPAIRER	769.664-010
SHAKER WASHER	521.687-114
shooter	523.382-010
SIEVE MAKER	529.684-018
Sieve Repairer	529.684-018
sifter operator	521.685-030
smutter	521.685-254
STARCHMAKER	520.485-030
Starch Presser	521.687-038
STARCH-TREATING ASSISTANT	520.665-018
steam drier	523.685-058
STEEP TENDER	522.465-010
stonecutter	629.261-014

stonecutter, assistant	629.684-014
storage-bin adjuster	521.685-230
SUGAR-CHIPPER-MACHINE OPERATOR	521.685-354
SUGAR DRIER	523.665-010
sugar grinder	521.685-354
SUGAR PRESSER	521.685-350
Sugar Trucker	929.687-030
SUPERINTENDENT, GRAIN ELEVATOR	529.137-022
SUPERVISOR, CEREAL	529.132-030
SUPERVISOR, DRY-STARCH	529.132-046
SUPERVISOR, FEED HOUSE	529.132-050
SUPERVISOR, FEED MILL	529.132-054
SUPERVISOR, MILL HOUSE	529.132-074
SUPERVISOR, RICE MILLING	521.131-010
SUPERVISOR, SUGAR HOUSE	529.132-090
SUPERVISOR, SUGAR REFINERY	529.132-094
SYRUP-MIXER ASSISTANT	520.687-058
SYRUP MIXER	529.462-010
TIPPLE TENDER	521.685-366
Top Steep Tender	522.465-010
TRACK SUPERVISOR	921.132-010
WASHER	529.687-210
WHEAT CLEANER	529.685-262
YIELD-LOSS INSPECTOR	529.367-030

hat & cap—HAT AND CAP INDUSTRY: This designation includes occupations concerned with converting materials, such as textiles, fur, straw braid, paper, and leather, into men's and women's hats, helmets, and caps. Occupations concerned with the production of hatter's fur for making fur-felt hats are included in this designation.

Band-Lining Bander	787.682-010
Band-Plating-Machine Operator	580.685-038
BEAD-MACHINE OPERATOR	583.686-010
BEVELING-MACHINE OPERATOR	690.686-010
Binding Cutter	699.682-030
blender	680.685-062
BLOCKER, HAND I	580.684-010
BLOCKER, HAND II	580.684-014
blocker, heated metal-forms	580.684-010
blocking-machine operator	580.685-026
Blocking-Machine Operator, Second	580.685-038
blower	680.685-046
body finisher	589.685-062
BOW MAKER	784.684-010
Bow Tacker I	782.684-058
Bow Tacker II	787.685-042
Braided-Band Assembler	784.684-022
breaker-up	589.685-014
BREAKER-UP-MACHINE OPERATOR	589.685-014
BRIM-AND-CROWN PRESSER	583.685-022
Brim Buffer	585.685-014
brim buster	583.685-018
brim buster	583.685-022
BRIM CURLER	583.685-014
brim cutter	585.685-086
Brim Cutter	699.682-022
brim-edge trimmer	686.685-074
brim flanger	784.684-026
brim flexer	585.685-066
Brim-Greaser Operator	582.685-082
BRIM IRONER, HAND	784.684-014
brimmer	583.685-018
BRIMMER	term
brimmer blocker	580.685-010
brimming-machine operator	580.685-010
brim molder	580.685-042
brim plater	583.685-018
brim pouncer	585.685-010
BRIM-POUNCING-MACHINE OPERATOR	585.685-010
BRIM PRESSER I	583.685-018
Brim Presser II	580.685-038
BRIM RAISER	784.687-010
brim rounder	784.684-050
brim setter	784.684-014
brim setter	583.685-022
brim shaper	784.684-026
Brim Slotter	686.685-038
Brim Stiffener	589.687-038
BRIM STITCHER I	784.685-014
Brim Stitcher II	784.682-014
brim stretcher	580.685-010
BRIM-STRETCHING-MACHINE OPERATOR	580.685-010
Brim-Welt-Sewing-Machine Operator	784.682-014

brusher	784.387-010
brusher, hand	784.687-014
BRUSHER, MACHINE	587.685-014
Buckle-Attaching-Machine Operator	699.685-018
Buckram Cutter	699.682-022
BUFFER	585.685-014
buffing-machine operator	585.685-014
bumper-machine operator	586.685-034
burring-machine operator	583.686-010
BUTTON-ATTACHING-MACHINE OPERATOR	699.685-010
button bradder	699.685-010
button clamper	699.685-010
button riveter	699.685-010
button tacker	699.685-010
cap blocker	580.684-014
cap-machine operator	784.684-018
CAP MAKER	784.684-018
cap operator	784.684-018
Cap-Parts Cutter	699.682-022
Cap Sizer	784.682-014
CARROTER	784.687-014
CARROTING-MACHINE OFFBEARER	586.686-010
CARROTING-MACHINE OPERATOR	586.685-010
caster	784.361-010
CHIN-STRAP CUTTER	686.685-010
Chin-Strap Maker	699.685-018
Chin-Strap Sewer	784.682-014
chopper	585.685-046
clicker-machine operator	686.685-038
clipper	585.685-046
cloth-covered-helmet puller	689.685-074
cloth coverer	689.685-074
COLORING-MACHINE OPERATOR	582.685-034
combiner	584.685-026
cone former	586.685-030
cone-machine feeder	586.686-018
coner	586.685-030
Conical Mixer	680.685-062
crimping machine operator	689.685-074
Crown Buffer	585.685-014
Crown Finisher	589.685-062
crown-finishing-machine operator	585.685-058
Crown-Greaser Operator	582.685-082
crown ironer	583.685-022
crown-perforator operator	686.685-038
crown pouncer	585.685-058
crown pouncer	585.685-074
CROWN POUNCER, HAND	784.687-018
Crown Presser	580.685-038
cutter	585.685-046
cutting-machine operator	585.685-086
Cylindrical Mixer	680.685-062
DECORATOR	784.684-022
devil tender	680.685-062
dipper	589.687-038
Dress-Cap Maker	784.684-018
DRUMMER	589.685-034
dryer feeder	581.686-022
DRYING-OVEN ATTENDANT	581.686-022
DRYING-ROOM ATTENDANT	581.687-014
DUSTER	587.685-026
dyer	582.685-034
DYER HELPER	589.685-042
Ear-Flap Binder	787.682-010
EAR-MUFF ASSEMBLER	784.687-022
Eight-Section Blower	680.685-046
ENDBAND CUTTER, HAND	784.687-026
endbander	784.687-026
endband sizer	784.687-026
end-lathe operator	585.685-074
extractor	581.685-046
eyelet cutter	686.685-038
fast-brim pouncer	585.685-010
feeder	586.686-018
Felt-Hat-Flanging Operator	784.684-026
Felt-Hat Inspector And Packer	784.687-042
Felt-Hat-Mellowing-Machine Operator	585.685-066
felt-hat-pouncing operator, hand	784.687-018
FELT-HAT STEAMER	582.687-018
felt puller	580.684-010
flange cutter	585.685-086
FLANGER	784.684-026
flanging-machine operator	690.686-058
flanging operator	784.684-026
Flap-Lining Binder	787.682-010

FLOORWORKER-DISTRIBUTOR	784.687-030
FOLDING-MACHINE OPERATOR	690.686-034
forming-machine operator	586.685-030
FOUNDATION MAKER	784.684-030
fur blower	680.685-046
FUR-BLOWER OPERATOR	680.685-046
fur-blowing-machine attendant	680.685-046
fur-blowing-machine operator	680.685-046
FUR-CUTTING-MACHINE OPERATOR	585.685-046
fur feeder	586.686-018
fur mixer	680.685-046
fur-mixer operator	680.685-062
fur-trimming machine operator	585.685-046
fur weigher	586.686-018
GREASER OPERATOR	582.685-082
Half-Section Ironer	583.685-098
hand hardener	784.684-034
hand pouncer	784.687-018
hand trimmer	784.684-050
hardener	586.685-026
HARDENER	784.684-034
HARDENING-MACHINE OPERATOR	586.685-026
Hat-And-Cap-Parts Cutter, Hand	781.684-074
HAT-AND-CAP SEWER	784.682-014
hat-band attacher	784.684-078
hat blocker	580.684-010
HAT-BLOCKING-MACHINE OPERATOR I	580.685-026
HAT-BLOCKING-MACHINE OPERATOR II	580.685-030
hat-blocking operator	580.684-014
Hat-Body Inspector	784.387-010
HAT-BODY SORTER	784.587-010
HAT BRAIDER	784.684-038
hat-brim-and-crown-laminating operator	584.685-026
hat-brim curler	784.684-014
hat-brim curler	784.684-014
Hat Brusher, Machine	587.685-026
Hat Buffer, Automatic	585.685-014
HAT CONDITIONER	784.687-086
Hat-Cone Inspector	784.387-010
Hat Designer	142.061-018
Hat-Designer Helper	784.684-042
HAT FINISHER	589.685-062
HAT-FINISHING-MATERIALS PREPARER	559.684-030
HAT-FORMING-MACHINE FEEDER	586.686-018
HAT-FORMING-MACHINE OPERATOR	586.685-030
Hat Lacer	784.684-022
HAT-LINING BLOCKER	583.685-050
HAT MAKER	784.684-042
Hat Marker	781.384-014
hat measurer	784.387-010
Hat-Parts Cutter, Machine	781.684-014
Hat Sprayer	741.684-026
HAT-STOCK-LAMINATING-MACHINE OPERATOR	584.685-026
HATTER	term
hat trimmer	784.684-022
Helmet Binder	787.682-010
Helmet-Brim Coverer	689.685-074
HELMET COVERER	689.685-074
Helmet-Crown Coverer	689.685-074
Helmet-Hat-Brim Cutter	699.685-022
Helmet-Hat Puncher	686.685-038
Helmet-Hat-Sweatband Puncher	686.685-038
HYDRAULIC BLOCKER	580.685-038
Hydraulic-Brim-Flanging-Machine Operator	580.685-038
hydraulic-press operator	580.685-038
Hydraulic Press Operator, First Pressing	580.685-038
INSPECTOR	784.387-010
INSPECTOR-PACKER	784.687-042
ironer	584.685-026
ironer	583.685-022
Jigger-Brim-Pouncing-Machine Operator	585.685-010
JIGGER-CROWN-POUNCING-MACHINE OPERATOR	585.685-058
Label Sewer	784.682-014
Lacquer Sizer	589.687-038
Ladies'-Hat Trimmer	784.684-022
Leather Fitter	784.682-014
Leather Flanger	690.686-058
LINING CEMENTER	795.687-022
Lining Maker	784.682-014
lining printer	651.682-022
lurer	784.684-062
machine sizer	589.687-038
manual hardener	784.684-034
MATERIAL ASSEMBLER	784.687-050
MELLOWING-MACHINE OPERATOR	585.685-066

MENDER	784.684-046
MIXER	680.685-062
mixing-machine operator	680.685-062
MOLDER	580.685-042
mold maker	784.361-010
muller	784.687-086
OPENER I	784.687-054
OPENER II	589.686-030
Panama-Hat Blocker	580.684-014
Panama-Hat Flanger	784.684-026
Panama-Hat-Hydraulic-Press Operator	580.685-038
Panama-Hat Smearer	589.687-038
passer	784.387-010
PASTER, HAT LINING	692.686-070
patent-button machine operator, automatic	699.685-010
PATTERNMAKER	784.361-010
pelt shearer	585.685-046
PERFORATING-MACHINE OPERATOR	686.685-038
perforator	686.685-038
perforator operator	686.685-038
plaster whittler	784.361-010
pouncer	784.687-018
pouncer	585.685-074
pouncer, machine	585.685-074
POUNCING-LATHE OPERATOR	585.685-074
pouncing-machine operator	585.685-074
pouncing-machine operator	585.685-058
POWDERER	784.687-058
presser	580.685-038
presser	584.685-026
Presser, First	583.685-110
Presser, Second	583.685-110
PRINTER, MACHINE	652.685-070
pugg maker	690.686-034
punching-machine operator	686.685-038
Quarter-Section Ironer	583.685-098
racker	784.387-010
Reeding-Machine Operator	784.682-014
repairer	784.387-010
Retouching Operator	589.687-038
Ribbon Cutter	784.687-050
Ribbon-Sweatband Operator	784.682-014
ROLLER OPERATOR	580.685-046
roper	580.684-010
round-cutter operator	585.685-086
rounder	585.685-086
ROUNDER, HAND	784.684-050
Rounding-Machine Operator	699.682-022
ROUNDING-MACHINE OPERATOR	585.685-086
sander	585.685-014
scratcher	585.685-014
Screen-Vent Binder	787.682-010
SEAM PRESSER	583.685-098
selector	784.387-010
Set-Off Blocker	580.684-014
Set-Off-Press Operator	583.685-018
SHAKER	589.685-094
shaver	585.685-046
shearer	585.685-046
SHRINKING-MACHINE OPERATOR	586.685-034
Silk-Lining Cutter, Machine	699.682-022
silk-top-hat-body maker	784.684-074
SINGER	784.687-062
Single-Beam Clicker	699.682-022
Six-Section Blower	680.685-046
size cutter	585.685-122
sizer	784.684-054
sizer	586.685-034
sizer	589.687-038
SIZER, HAND	784.684-054
SIZER, MACHINE	784.684-058
sizing brusher	589.687-038
sizing end-bander	784.687-026
sizing sponger	589.687-038
skin-drying-room attendant	581.686-022
skiver-machine operator	690.686-010
SLICKER	784.684-062
smearer	589.687-038
SMOKE-ROOM OPERATOR	784.687-066
SMOOTHER	784.684-066
softener	589.685-034
Soft-Hat Binder	787.682-010
specialty trimmer	784.684-078
spray-gun sizer	589.687-038
SPREADER	581.687-022

stamper 580.685-042
stamper blocker 580.685-026
starter 784.684-058
starter 586.685-034
steam blocker 580.685-026
Steamer 784.687-078
STEAMER-BLOCKER 784.684-070
steam finisher 784.687-010
STICKER 784.687-070
sticker-on 784.687-070
STIFFENER 589.687-038
stiff-straw-hat washer 784.687-078
Strawhat Blocker 580.684-014
strawhat-blocking operator 580.684-014
Straw-Hat-Brim-Cutter Operator 585.685-086
straw-hat-brim-raiser operator 784.687-010
STRAW-HAT BRUSHER 784.687-074
straw-hat finishing operator 784.687-010
Straw-Hat-Hydraulic-Press Operator 580.685-038
Strawhat Inspector And Packer 784.687-042
Straw-Hat-Machine Operator 784.682-014
STRAW-HAT-PLUNGER OPERATOR 583.685-114
straw-hat presser 583.685-114
STRAW HAT PRESSER, MACHINE 583.685-110
Strawhat Sizer 589.687-038
STRAW-HAT-WASHER OPERATOR 784.687-078
STRETCHER 580.685-054
stretcher and drier 581.687-022
stumper 784.684-058
stumper 586.685-034
Supervisor, Back Shop 784.130-010
Supervisor, Body Department 784.130-010
Supervisor, Braid Department 784.130-010
SUPERVISOR, CAP-AND-HAT PRODUCTION ... 784.130-010
Supervisor, Finishing Department 784.130-010
Supervisor, Harvest-Hat Department 784.130-010
Supervisor, Sewing Department 784.130-010
SWEATBAND-CUTTING-MACHINE OPERATOR ... 690.686-062
Sweatband-Decorating-Machine Operator 583.685-030
sweatband drummer 583.686-010
SWEATBAND FLANGER 690.686-058
Sweatband Maker 699.685-018
sweatband perforator 686.685-038
Sweatband Printer 652.682-030
SWEATBAND SEPARATOR 585.685-122
SWEATBAND SHAPER 784.687-090
Tip Maker 784.682-014
tipper 580.685-062
tipper 580.685-026
tipping-machine operator 580.685-062
TIP PRINTER 651.682-022
TIP STRETCHER 580.685-062
top-bottom-attaching-machine operator 699.685-010
TOP-HAT-BODY MAKER 784.684-074
Top Stitcher 784.682-014
TRIMMER 784.684-078
trimmer 784.387-010
Trimming-Department Blocker 580.684-014
Trimming Inspector 784.387-010
trim preparer 784.687-050
tube roller 690.686-034
turning-machine operator 690.686-034
turn-machine operator 585.685-074
Twin-Beam Clicker 699.682-022
Uniform-Cap Operator 784.684-018
Varnisher 589.687-038
waxer 582.685-082
welt cutter 686.685-074
welt-edge rounder 784.684-050
WELT-TRIMMING-MACHINE OPERATOR 686.685-074
western-felt-hat blocker 580.685-026
wet-crown-blocking operator 580.685-026
whittling-room operator 784.361-010
WHIZZER 581.685-070
whizzer operator 581.685-070
wired-sweatband cutter 585.685-122
WIRE INSERTER 784.687-082
Wire-Machine Operator 784.682-014
Wire-Shape Maker 784.684-030
Wool-Hat Blocker 580.685-026
Wool-Hat Finisher 589.685-062
Wool-Hat Flanger 784.684-070
Wool-Hat-Forming-Machine Tender 586.685-030
Wool-Hat Hydraulicker 580.685-038
wool-hat-sanding-machine operator 585.685-014

Woven-Paper-Hat-Hydraulic-Press Operator Finisher 580.685-038
Woven-Paper-Hat Mender 784.684-046

heat treating—HEAT TREATING: This designation includes occupations concerned with heattreating metals in the solid state to remove strains and stresses; alter hardness, tensile strength, ductility, grain structure, and electrical and magnetic properties; and improve machinability, cutting properties, and wear resistant characteristics. Such occupations involve heating and quenching (cooling) the metal to alter its physical and chemical properties, during which temperatures, time cycles, and surrounding media are essential factors. The various heat-treating processes include: annealing, baking (heating to remove gases absorbed during pickling), carburizing, cyaniding, hardening, nitriding, normalizing, patenting, siliconizing, spheroidizing, and tempering. Excluded from this designation are those occupations concerned with smelting ores, refining metals, or merely heating metals to working temperatures (for rolling, extrusion, and like operations) in forges, foundries, steel mills, and other plants.

ANNEALER 504.682-010
bluing-oven tender 504.685-018
carbonizer 504.685-026
carbonizer 504.682-014
carburizer 504.682-014
case hardener 504.685-026
CASE HARDENER 504.682-010
Continuous-Annealing Furnace Operator 504.682-010
Cyanide Furnace Operator 504.682-014
Die Case Hardener 504.682-014
draw-furnace tender 504.685-018
dulite-machine bluer 504.682-022
electronic induction hardener 504.685-022
Flame-Annealing-Machine Operator 504.685-014
FLAME-ANNEALING-MACHINE SETTER 504.360-010
FLAME-HARDENING-MACHINE OPERATOR ... 504.685-014
FLAME-HARDENING-MACHINE SETTER 504.380-014
furnace feeder 504.685-018
FURNACE HELPER 504.686-014
furnace loader 504.685-018
gas-anneal feeder 504.685-014
HARDNESS INSPECTOR 504.387-010
HEAT-TREATER APPRENTICE 504.382-018
heat treater, head 504.131-010
HEAT-TREATER HELPER 504.685-018
HEAT TREATER I 504.382-014
HEAT TREATER II 504.682-018
HEAT-TREATING BLUER 504.682-022
HEAT-TREAT INSPECTOR 504.281-010
heat-treat puller 504.685-018
HEAT-TREAT SUPERVISOR 504.131-010
INDUCTION-MACHINE OPERATOR 504.685-022
INDUCTION-MACHINE SETTER 504.380-014
normalizer 504.682-010
Pot Annealer 504.682-010
PRODUCTION HARDENER 504.685-026
RIVET HEATER 504.485-010
Rivet Heater, Electric 504.485-010
Rivet Heater, Gas 504.485-010
supervisor, hardening 504.131-010
supervisor, heat treating 504.131-010
TEMPERER 504.682-026
tempering-kiln tender 504.685-018

hotel & rest.—HOTEL AND RESTAURANT INDUSTRY: This designation includes occupations concerned with providing and maintaining lodging, dining, and beverage services. Occupations are typically found in establishments such as commercial, residential, tourist, and club hotels; motels; apartment houses; trailer courts, tourist camps, and homes; rooming houses; restaurants, cafeterias, and lunch counters; industrial, institutional, and private catering services; taverns, cocktail lounges, night clubs, and tea rooms; boarding houses; and fraternity and sorority houses. Occupations concerned with preparing foods for relatively immediate consumption on the premises or for take-out are included here, while occupations concerned with preparing and preserving foods for consumption at a later time are included in the CANNING AND PRESERVING INDUSTRY (can. & preserv.). Occupations concerned with the entertainment of patrons in such establishments are included under AMUSEMENT AND RECREATION (amuse. & rec.).

ANALYST, FOOD AND BEVERAGE 310.267-010
Appetizer Packer 319.484-010
ATTENDANT, LODGING FACILITIES 329.467-010
auto-camp attendant 329.467-010
BAGGAGE PORTER, HEAD 324.137-010
BAKER 313.381-010
baker apprentice, pastry 313.381-018
Baker, Biscuit 313.381-010

Hot-Bread Baker	313.381-010
HOTEL CLERK	238.367-038
Hot-Food Packer	319.484-010
HOUSECLEANER	323.687-018
Housecleaner, Floor	323.687-018
house detective	376.367-018
HOUSEKEEPER	321.137-010
HOUSE OFFICER	376.367-018
house steward/stewardess	310.137-018
ICE-CREAM CHEF	313.381-034
ice cream dispenser	319.474-010
inside steward/stewardess	318.137-010
INSPECTOR	321.137-014
Key Clerk	238.367-038
kitchen chef	313.131-014
KITCHEN CLERK	222.587-022
kitchen hand	318.687-010
KITCHEN HELPER	318.687-010
kitchen porter	318.687-010
kitchen runner	318.687-010
KITCHEN STEWARD/STEWARDESS	318.137-010
KITCHEN SUPERVISOR	319.137-030
linen checker	222.387-030
linen clerk	222.387-030
linen-exchange attendant	222.387-030
LINEN-ROOM ATTENDANT	222.387-030
linen-room houseperson	222.387-030
Linen-Room Worker	323.687-018
LUNCH-TRUCK DRIVER	292.463-010
lunch-truck operator	292.463-010
Lunch-Wagon Operator	292.463-010
Manager, Apartment House	320.137-014
Manager, Banquet	187.167-106
MANAGER, BAR	term
Manager, Beer Parlor	187.167-126
MANAGER, BOARDING HOUSE	320.137-010
MANAGER, BRANCH OPERATION EVALUATION	187.167-062
manager, business promotion	163.117-018
Manager, Cafeteria Or Lunchroom	187.167-106
Manager, Catering	187.167-106
manager, club	187.167-126
Manager, Cocktail Lounge	187.167-126
MANAGER, CONVENTION	187.167-078
MANAGER, FLIGHT KITCHEN	319.137-014
Manager, Food And Beverage	187.167-106
MANAGER, FOOD CONCESSION	185.167-022
manager, food production	187.161-010
MANAGER, FOOD SERVICE	187.167-106
MANAGER, FRONT OFFICE	187.137-018
manager, general	187.117-038
manager, guest house	320.137-010
Manager, Hotel	320.137-014
MANAGER, HOTEL OR MOTEL	187.117-038
MANAGER, INDUSTRIAL CAFETERIA	319.137-018
manager, kitchen	319.137-030
MANAGER, LIQUOR ESTABLISHMENT	187.167-126
MANAGER, LODGING FACILITIES	320.137-014
Manager, Marina	320.137-014
Manager, Motel	320.137-014
manager, motor hotel	187.117-038
manager, motor inn	187.117-038
Manager, Night Club	187.167-126
MANAGER, PROMOTION	163.117-018
MANAGER, RESERVATIONS	238.137-010
manager, resident	187.117-038
Manager, Restaurant Or Coffee Shop	187.167-106
Manager, Rooming House	320.137-010
manager, sales	163.117-018
manager, school lunch program	187.167-026
manager, service	329.137-010
Manager, Tavern	187.167-126
Manager, Tourist Camp	320.137-014
Manager, Trailer Park	320.137-014
meat carver	316.661-010
meat cutter	316.681-010
moshgiach	319.137-026
Motel Cleaner	323.687-014
motel clerk	238.367-038
motor-lodge clerk	238.367-038
mover	323.687-018
NIGHT AUDITOR	210.382-054
Night Baker	313.381-010
night cleaner	323.687-018
night-clerk auditor	210.382-054
ORDER CLERK, FOOD AND BEVERAGE	209.567-014
oven tender	313.381-010
overseer, kosher kitchen	319.137-026
Oyster Preparer	311.674-014
package clerk	324.577-010
Page	324.677-010
page	352.667-018
PANTRY GOODS MAKER	317.684-014
Pantry Goods Maker Helper	317.687-010
Pantry Steward/Stewardess	318.137-010
PARLOR CHAPERONE	352.667-014
PASTRY CHEF	313.131-022
pastry helper	313.687-010
pie chef	313.361-038
PIE MAKER	313.361-038
PORTER, BAGGAGE	324.477-010
Porter, Lobby	323.687-018
porter, luggage	324.477-010
poultry-and-fish butcher	316.684-010
preparation center coordinator	313.131-018
RAW SHELLFISH PREPARER	311.674-014
receiving-room clerk	324.577-010
Record Clerk	203.582-066
research worker, kitchen	310.267-010
Reservation Clerk	238.367-038
Rolls Baker	313.381-010
Room Clerk	238.367-038
Room Service Assistant	311.677-018
ROOM-SERVICE CLERK	324.577-010
Runner	311.677-018
runner	324.577-010
Salad Counter Attendant	311.677-014
Salad Maker	317.684-014
SALES REPRESENTATIVE, HOTEL SERVICES	259.157-014
sandwich-counter attendant	317.664-010
SANDWICH MAKER	317.664-010
security officer	376.367-018
server	311.477-026
server	311.477-030
server	311.677-014
service attendant, cafeteria	311.677-010
Service-Bar Cashier	211.462-010
Service Bartender	312.474-010
service supervisor	329.137-010
Sewer, Linen Room	787.682-030
SILVER WRAPPER	318.687-018
Sleeping Room Cleaner	323.687-014
soda clerk	319.474-010
soda dispenser	319.474-010
soda jerker	319.474-010
sommelier	310.357-010
SOUS CHEF	313.131-026
special officer	376.367-018
Special Officer, Automat	376.667-014
SPECIALTY CHEF	term
steamtable attendant	311.677-014
Steamtable Worker	311.677-018
STEWARD/STEWARDESS	310.137-018
STEWARD/STEWARDESS, BANQUET	310.137-022
storeroom food-checker	222.587-022
superintendent, house	329.137-010
SUPERINTENDENT, SERVICE	329.137-010
Supervising Chef	313.131-026
supervising-chef assistant	313.131-026
SUPERVISOR, CASHIERS	211.137-010
SUPERVISOR, COMMISSARY PRODUCTION	319.137-022
SUPERVISOR, FOOD CHECKERS AND CASHIERS	211.137-014
SUPERVISOR, HOUSECLEANER	323.137-010
supervisor, kashruth	319.137-026
SUPERVISOR, KOSHER DIETARY SERVICE	319.137-026
supply service worker	319.484-010
table attendant, cafeteria	311.677-010
Table Setter	311.677-018
Telephone-Order Clerk, Drive-in	209.567-014
Telephone-Order Clerk, Room Service	209.567-014
tourist-camp attendant	329.467-010
transportation clerk	238.367-030
TRAVEL CLERK	238.367-030
tray setter	319.484-010
uniform attendant	222.387-030
Vacuum Worker	323.687-018
Valet Manager	369.167-010
VENDING-MACHINE ATTENDANT	319.464-014
WAITER/WAITRESS, BANQUET, HEAD	311.137-014
Waiter/Waitress, Banquet	311.477-026
WAITER/WAITRESS, BAR	311.477-018

WAITER/WAITRESS, BUFFET 311.674-018
waiter/waitress, cafeteria 311.677-010
WAITER/WAITRESS, CAPTAIN 311.137-018
WAITER/WAITRESS, CLUB 352.677-018
waiter/waitress, cocktail lounge 311.477-018
waiter/waitress, counter 311.477-014
WAITER/WAITRESS, FORMAL 311.477-026
WAITER/WAITRESS, HEAD 311.137-022
waiter/waitress, head 310.137-010
WAITER/WAITRESS, INFORMAL 311.477-030
WAITER/WAITRESS, ROOM SERVICE 311.477-034
WAITER/WAITRESS, TAKE OUT 311.477-038
Waiter/Waitress, Tavern 311.477-018
Water Server 311.677-018
Wine-Cellar Stock Clerk 222.387-058
WINE STEWARD/STEWARDESS 310.357-010

house. appl.—HOUSEHOLD APPLIANCES INDUSTRY: This designation includes occupations concerned with manufacturing and repairing household appliances, such as cooking equipment, refrigerators, freezers, laundry equipment, electric housewares, fans, vacuum cleaners, sewing machines, dishwashers, and trash compactors.

APPLIANCE ASSEMBLER, LINE 827.684-010
Appliance Inspector 729.387-022
APPLIANCE REPAIRER 723.584-010
Appliance Tester 729.387-022
ASSEMBLER 723.684-010
assembler, latches and springs 706.687-030
Brush-Holder Inspector 729.384-022
Clothes-Drier Assembler 827.684-010
Commutator Inspector 729.384-022
Deep-Fryer Assembler 723.684-010
DUST-BRUSH ASSEMBLER 739.687-074
Electric-Fan Assembler 723.684-010
Electric-Frying-Pan Repairer 723.584-010
Electric-Heater Assembler 723.684-010
Food-Mixer Assembler 723.684-010
Food-Mixer Repairer 723.584-010
Heating-Element Repairer 723.584-010
HEATING-ELEMENT WINDER 723.685-010
INSPECTOR 729.387-022
model maker 600.280-054
PATCHER 723.687-010
Power-Tool Assembler 723.684-010
PUSH-CONNECTOR ASSEMBLER 706.687-030
repairer 723.584-010
SAMPLE MAKER, APPLIANCES 600.280-054
Shaft Inspector 729.384-022
Steam-Iron Assembler 723.684-010
supervisor, assembly line 723.131-010
SUPERVISOR, MAJOR APPLIANCE ASSEMBLY 827.131-014
SUPERVISOR, SMALL APPLIANCE ASSEMBLY 723.131-010
TESTER, ELECTRICAL CONTINUITY 729.684-058
TESTER, WASTE DISPOSAL LEAKAGE 723.687-018
Toaster-Element Repairer 723.584-010
Vacuum-Cleaner Repairer 723.584-010
Washing-Machine Assembler 827.684-010
WINDING INSPECTOR 729.384-022
WIRE COILER 724.362-010&Q10

inst. & app.—INSTRUMENTS AND APPARATUS INDUSTRY: This designation includes occupations concerned with manufacturing and repairing instruments and apparatus for professional, scientific, commercial, and industrial purposes. The following classes of products are typical of those produced in the industry: surgical, dental, and veterinary instruments; physicians' diagnostic apparatus; surveying, nautical, aeronautical, automotive, and similar precision and measuring instruments; sighting and fire-control equipment, such as bomb sights, gun data computers, percentage correctors, wind correctors, directors, and sound locators; indicating and recording instruments; hypodermic syringes; speedometers; barometers and thermometers; compasses; micrometers; and spectroscopes. Occupations concerned with the manufacture of lenses, prisms, field glasses, microscopes, telescopes, and other optical goods are found in the OPTICAL GOODS INDUSTRY (optical goods).

ASSEMBLER, ELECTROMECHANICAL 828.381-018
ASSEMBLER, PLASTIC HOSPITAL PRODUCTS 712.687-010
ASSEMBLY LOADER 711.684-010
BELLOWS ASSEMBLER 710.684-042
BELLOWS FILLER 710.684-014
BELLOWS TESTER 710.687-014
calibration technician 710.381-034
CALIBRATOR 710.381-034
CALIBRATOR, BAROMETERS 710.381-042
CONTACT PRINTER, PHOTORESIST 976.684-034
Development Technician 710.281-018
die setter 556.380-010
electroformer 500.684-034
electromechanical instrument mechanic 710.381-054
ELECTROMECHANICAL TECHNICIAN 710.281-018
ELECTRONICS INSPECTOR 726.381-010
ELEMENT WINDING MACHINE TENDER 724.685-010
ENGINEERING MODEL MAKER 693.260-018
field return repairer 710.381-050
FIRESETTER 692.360-018
FLANGER 712.684-018
Flowmeter Test And Certification Technician 710.281-022
flow-solder machine operator 726.362-014
GLASS BLOWER, LABORATORY APPARATUS 772.281-010
glass-cylinder flanger 712.684-018
GLASS GRINDER, LABORATORY APPARATUS 775.382-010
glass technologist 772.281-010
GLAZIER 712.684-026
HEARING-AID REPAIRER 719.381-014
HYDROMETER CALIBRATOR 710.381-030
hydrometer finisher 710.381-030
INSPECTOR, ELECTROMECHANICAL 729.361-010
INSPECTOR, SURGICAL INSTRUMENTS 712.684-050
INSTRUMENT ASSEMBLER 710.684-046
instrument calibrator 710.381-042
INSTRUMENT INSPECTOR 710.684-050
INSTRUMENT MECHANIC, WEAPONS SYSTEM 711.281-014
LASER TECHNICIAN 019.261-034
MECHANICAL-TEST TECHNICIAN 869.261-014
Medical-Apparatus Model Maker 693.260-018
METALLIZATION EQUIPMENT TENDER, SEMICONDUCTORS 590.685-086
MOLD SETTER 556.380-010
PLATER 500.684-034
production repairer 710.381-050
quality control inspector 726.381-010
Receiving Inspector 729.361-010
Regulator Assembler 710.684-046
REPAIRER, GYROSCOPE 710.381-054
reticle printer 976.684-034
setter, plastics-molding machine 556.380-010
Supervisor, Assembly Line 710.131-042
Supervisor, Calibration 710.131-042
Supervisor, Inspection 710.131-042
SUPERVISOR, INSTRUMENT ASSEMBLY 710.131-038
SUPERVISOR, OPTICAL INSTRUMENTS 711.137-010
SUPERVISOR, PLASTICS PRODUCTION 556.130-010
Supervisor, Rework 710.131-042
SUPERVISOR, THERMOSTAT CONTROLS 710.131-042
SURGICAL-FORCEPS FABRICATOR 712.684-054
systems inspector 726.381-010
THERMOMETER MAKER 710.681-026
THERMOMETER PRODUCTION WORKER 710.685-014
THERMOMETER TESTER 710.384-030
Thermostat Assembler 710.684-046
THERMOSTAT-ASSEMBLY-MACHINE TENDER, AUTOMATIC 692.685-218
THERMOSTAT REPAIRER 710.381-050
TRACK LAMINATING MACHINE TENDER 692.685-290
Valve Assembler 710.684-046
WAVE-SOLDERING MACHINE OPERATOR 726.362-014
WIRE DRAWING MACHINE OPERATOR 614.382-018

insurance—INSURANCE INDUSTRY: This designation includes occupations concerned with operating insurance carriers, including both home and branch offices. The primary functions covered include the sale and preparation of insurance contracts, the administration of insurance organizations, and keeping necessary records. The principal types of insurance written are accident and health, casualty, fidelity and surety bonding, fire, liability, life, marine, and theft.

Abstract Checker 219.482-014
Accident-And-Health-Insurance-Claim Examiner 241.267-018
Actuarial Clerk 216.382-062
Address-Change Clerk 203.582-066
Agency Cashier 211.362-010
Agency Clerk 219.362-010
AGENT-CONTRACT CLERK 241.267-010
AGENT-LICENSING CLERK 209.367-010
agents'-records clerk 209.367-010
Application-Register Clerk 203.582-066
APPRAISER, AUTOMOBILE DAMAGE 241.267-014

automobile-damage appraiser	241.267-014
Automobile-Insurance-Claim Adjuster	241.217-010
Automobile-Insurance-Claim Examiner	241.267-018
Brokerage Manager	166.167-046
BUILDING INSPECTOR	168.267-010
Calculation Clerk	216.382-050
Calculation Reviewer	216.382-050
CANCELLATION CLERK	203.382-014
Cash-Surrender Calculator	216.382-050
CLAIM ADJUSTER	241.217-010
claim attorney	110.117-014
CLAIM EXAMINER	241.267-018
CLAIM EXAMINER	168.267-014
claims administrator	241.137-018
CLAIMS CLERK I	241.362-010
CLAIMS CLERK II	205.367-018
collateral placement officer	186.167-054
Commission Auditor	210.382-010
contract administrator	241.267-010
CONTROL CLERK, AUDITING	209.362-014
correspondent	249.262-010
customer-service clerk	249.262-010
Death-Claim Clerk	219.362-010
Death-Claim Examiner	241.267-018
Disability-Insurance-Claim Examiner	241.267-018
district agent	186.167-034
District Branch Manager	186.167-034
District Claims Manager	186.167-034
District Sales Manager	186.167-034
dividend-deposit-entry clerk	216.482-026
DIVIDEND-DEPOSIT-VOUCHER CLERK	216.482-026
Endorsement Clerk	203.582-066
ESTATE PLANNER	186.167-010
estimator, automobile damage	241.267-014
examiner-rating clerk	214.482-018
Extended-Insurance Clerk	216.382-050
Federal-Housing-Administration-Loan Auditor	210.382-010
Fidelity-And-Surety-Bonds-Claim Adjuster	241.217-010
Filing Writer	203.582-066
final-application reviewer	209.687-018
Fire-Insurance-Claim Adjuster	241.217-010
Fire-Insurance-Claim Examiner	241.267-018
General Agent	250.257-010
Group-Contract Analyst	169.267-034
HOSPITAL-INSURANCE REPRESENTATIVE	166.267-014
insurance adjustor	241.217-010
insurance agent	250.257-010
Insurance Application Investigator	241.267-030
INSURANCE ATTORNEY	110.117-014
Insurance Broker	250.257-010
INSURANCE CHECKER	219.482-014
insurance-claim approver	241.267-018
insurance-claim auditor	241.267-018
insurance-claim representative	241.217-010
INSURANCE CLERK	219.367-014
Insurance Collector	241.367-010
insurance counsel	110.117-014
insurance investigator	241.217-010
INVESTMENT ANALYST	160.267-026
LOAN OFFICER	186.267-018
loss-claim clerk	205.367-018
loss-control technician	168.167-078
Manager, Farm Underwriters	186.167-034
Manager, Field Underwriters	186.167-034
Manager, Insurance Agency	186.167-034
MANAGER, INSURANCE OFFICE	186.167-034
MAP CLERK	209.587-030
Marine-Insurance-Claim Adjuster	241.217-010
Marine-Insurance-Claim Examiner	241.267-018
Master-Sheet Clerk	203.582-066
medical-fee clerk	214.482-018
MEDICAL-VOUCHER CLERK	214.482-018
memorandum-statement clerk	203.382-014
money position officer	186.167-054
MORTGAGE-LOAN-COMPUTATION CLERK	210.382-050
Mortgage-Loan Officer	186.267-018
Mortgage-Papers-Assignment-And-Assembly Clerk	203.582-066
new-business clerk	209.687-018
Payroll Auditor	160.167-054
Pensionholder-Information Clerk	249.262-010
PLACER	239.267-010
policy-cancellation clerk	203.382-014
POLICY-CHANGE CLERK	219.362-042
Policy Checker	219.482-014
POLICYHOLDER-INFORMATION CLERK	249.262-010
Policy-Issue Clerk	203.362-010
policy-issue supervisor	219.132-022
Policy-Loan Calculator	216.382-050
policy rater	214.482-022
POLICY-VALUE CALCULATOR	216.382-050
Policy Writer	203.582-066
portfolio administrator	186.167-054
premium-cancellation clerk	203.382-014
premium-card-cancellation clerk	203.382-014
Premium-Note Interest-Calculator Clerk	216.482-022
rate inserter	214.482-022
RATER	214.482-022
rating clerk	214.482-022
reinstatement clerk	219.362-050
REINSURANCE CLERK	219.482-018
Remittance-On-Farm-Rental-And-Soil-Conservation Auditor	210.382-010
Rent And Miscellaneous Remittance Clerk	216.482-010
RESEARCH ANALYST	169.267-034
RESERVE OFFICER	186.167-054
REVIEWER	209.687-018
REVIVAL CLERK	219.362-050
safety engineer	168.167-078
SAFETY INSPECTOR	168.167-078
Sales Agent, Casualty Insurance	250.257-010
Sales Agent, Fire Insurance	250.257-010
SALES AGENT, INSURANCE	250.257-010
Sales Agent, Life Insurance	250.257-010
Sales Agent, Marine Insurance	250.257-010
sales representative	166.167-046
sales-review clerk	209.687-018
securities analyst	160.267-026
securities-research analyst	160.267-026
settlement technician	209.382-014
SPECIAL AGENT	166.167-046
SPECIAL AGENT, GROUP INSURANCE	169.167-050
SPECIAL-CERTIFICATE DICTATOR	209.382-014
SUPERVISOR, AGENCY APPOINTMENTS	209.137-018
SUPERVISOR, CLAIMS	241.137-018
SUPERVISOR, CORRESPONDENCE SECTION	249.137-018
SUPERVISOR, POLICY-CHANGE CLERKS	219.132-010
supervisor, records change	219.132-010
SUPERVISOR, UNDERWRITING CLERKS	219.132-022
termination clerk	203.382-014
UNDERWRITER	169.267-046
underwriting analyst	219.367-038
UNDERWRITING CLERK	219.367-038

jewelry-silver.—JEWELRY, SILVERWARE, AND PLATED WARE INDUSTRY: This designation includes occupations concerned with making and repairing precious metal and costume jewelry and jewelry cases; cutting, grinding, and setting precious stones; and flatware, hollow ware, toilet ware, ecclesiastical ware, and related products made of pewter, stainless steel, nickel silver, sterling silver, metal-plated silver, gold, or other metal. Occupations concerned with the manufacture of clocks and watches are included in the CLOCKS, WATCHES, AND ALLIED PRODUCTS INDUSTRY (clock & watch). Occupations concerned with the manufacture of leather jewelry cases are included in the LEATHER PRODUCTS INDUSTRY (leather prod.).

ANNEALER	504.687-010
ARBORER	700.684-010
ARTIFICIAL-PEARL MAKER	770.687-010
ASSEMBLER	700.684-014
baker	590.685-034
BEAD MAKER	770.381-010
BEAD STRINGER	735.684-010
bench hand	700.687-026
bench hand	700.687-062
BENCH HAND	735.381-010
BENCH-MOLDER APPRENTICE	518.381-010
bench worker	735.381-010
bench-worker apprentice	700.281-014
BENCH WORKER, HOLLOW HANDLE	700.687-010
bench worker	700.281-010
bender	700.684-010
Bezel Cutter	770.261-010
Blocker	770.261-010
BOILER-OUT	700.687-014
BRACELET AND BROOCH MAKER	735.681-010
Bracelet-Form Coverer	739.687-138
Bracelet Former	739.687-138
Bracelet Maker, Novelty	700.684-014
Breaker-Off	700.687-062
BRIGHT CUTTER	700.684-018
BRILLIANDEER-LOPPER	770.261-010

jewelry-silver.

brooch-and-bracelet maker	735.681-010
Brooch Maker, Novelty	700.684-014
buffing-machine operator, semiautomatic	603.682-022
BUFFING-MACHINE OPERATOR, SILVERWARE	603.682-010
caster	502.682-018
CASTER	502.381-010
CASTER HELPER	700.687-022
CENTRIFUGAL-CASTING-MACHINE OPERATOR	502.682-018
Centrifugal-Wax Molder	549.685-038
CHAIN MAKER, HAND	700.381-010
CHAIN MAKER, MACHINE	700.684-022
Chain Mender	735.687-014
CHARGER I	740.684-010
CHARGER II	700.687-026
CHASER	704.381-010
chaser	700.381-034
chaser apprentice	700.381-038
chaser helper	700.687-050
cleaver	770.381-014
COLORING CHECKER	735.587-010
COMPACT ASSEMBLER	739.687-066
cracker	770.687-030
crafter	700.381-046
craft worker	700.381-014
Cushion Maker, Hand	739.687-138
cutter	770.281-014
cutter and edge trimmer	700.687-066
diamond assorter	770.281-010
DIAMOND CLEAVER	770.381-014
DIAMOND CUTTER	term
DIAMOND EXPERT	770.267-010
diamond grader	770.281-010
DIAMOND SELECTOR	770.281-010
Diamond Setter	700.381-054
DIAMOND SIZER AND SORTER	770.687-014
die cutter	601.381-014
die-cutter apprentice	601.381-022
DIE MAKER	601.381-014
DIE-MAKER APPRENTICE	601.381-022
DIPPER	735.687-010
DRILLER	700.684-026
drill-press operator	700.684-026
EARRING MAKER	700.684-030
Ecclesiastical-Art-Metal Worker	619.260-014
enamel cracker	770.687-030
ENAMELER	740.684-018
enamel pulverizer	770.687-030
ENGINE TURNER	704.381-018
ESTIMATOR, JEWELRY	221.387-022
etcher, enameling	735.687-010
facer	705.682-014
FANCY-WIRE DRAWER	700.381-014
FILER	700.684-034
finding fastener	735.687-022
Finisher	705.684-022
FIRER	590.685-034
fitter	700.684-034
flat hammerer	700.381-022
FLATWARE MAKER	700.682-010
Forcer Maker	601.381-014
GEM CUTTER	770.281-014
gem expert	199.281-010
GEMOLOGIST	199.281-010
GIRDLER	770.261-014
glass-bead maker	770.381-010
glass blower	770.381-010
Goldsmith	700.281-010
Grainer	700.687-066
GREASE BUFFER	705.684-022
HAMMERSMITH	700.381-022
heat treater	504.687-010
HOLLOW-HANDLE-KNIFE ASSEMBLER	700.684-042
hub cutter	601.381-014
hub-cutter apprentice	601.381-022
Industrial-Diamond Polisher	770.281-014
Injection-Wax Molder	549.685-038
INK PRINTER	652.685-038
INSPECTOR	700.687-034
JEWELER	700.281-010
JEWELER APPRENTICE	700.281-014
jewelry-casting-model maker	709.381-018
jewelry-casting-model-maker apprentice	709.381-022
JEWELRY COATER	590.685-046
jewelry jobber	700.281-010
jewelry repairer	700.281-010
jewelry-repairer apprentice	700.281-014
jewelry setter	700.381-054
JIGGER	705.687-010
jigsaw operator	700.684-046
JIGSAWYER	700.684-046
kiln operator	590.685-034
Knife Glazer	603.685-062
LACQUERER	749.684-034
lapidary	770.281-014
Lapper	700.687-058
LATHE HAND	700.682-014
LATHE OPERATOR	770.382-014
LAY-OUT WORKER	700.381-026
Lining Maker, Hand	739.687-138
Link Assembler	735.687-014
LINKER	735.687-014
linker-up	735.687-014
LOCKET MAKER	700.381-030
MELTER	700.687-042
MESH CUTTER	700.684-050
MIRROR-FINISHING-MACHINE OPERATOR	603.682-022
MODEL-MAKER APPRENTICE	709.381-022
MODEL MAKER I	700.281-018
MODEL MAKER II	709.381-018
molder	502.381-010
MOLDER, BENCH	518.381-022
mold maker	559.684-018
MOLD-MAKER APPRENTICE	700.381-038
MOLD-MAKER HELPER	700.687-050
MOLD MAKER I	700.381-034
MOLD MAKER II	777.381-022
NECKER	692.686-058
Novelty-Chain Maker	700.684-022
OXIDIZER	700.684-054
Pad Assembler	739.687-138
PAINTER	735.687-018
PART MAKER	739.687-138
Pavilion Cutter	770.261-010
pearl dipper	770.687-010
Pearl Hand	735.687-034
pearl maker	770.687-010
pearl peeler	735.381-014
PEARL RESTORER	735.381-014
Pearl Stringer	735.684-010
PEWTER CASTER	502.384-010
PEWTERER	700.261-010
PEWTER FINISHER	700.281-026
PIN-OR-CLIP FASTENER	735.687-022
PLANISHER	700.687-054
Platinumsmith	700.281-010
plier worker	735.687-014
POLISHER	700.687-058
POLISHER, SAND	705.684-070
polishing-machine operator, semiautomatic	603.682-022
power-press supervisor	615.130-010
PREPARER	700.687-062
PREPARER, MAKING DEPARTMENT	700.684-058
PREPARER, SAMPLES AND REPAIRS	700.684-062
PRESS-HAND SUPERVISOR	615.130-010
PROFILE-SAW OPERATOR	700.682-018
PROFILE TRIMMER	607.682-014
Pronger	735.687-034
PULVERIZER	770.687-030
RACKER	735.687-026
Rhinestone Setter	735.687-034
ring maker	700.684-010
RING MAKER	700.381-042
RING STAMPER	700.684-066
ring striker	700.684-066
Rolled-Gold Plater	813.482-010
ROLLER	613.682-018
roller	735.687-042
RUBBER-MOLD MAKER	559.684-018
rubber-off	700.687-058
SAMPLE MAKER I	700.381-046
SAMPLE MAKER II	735.381-018
sand caster	518.381-022
sand-caster apprentice	518.381-010
sawyer	770.382-010
sawyer	700.682-014
SCRAPER	700.687-066
Scratch Brusher	700.687-058
set-up and charger	700.687-026
shaper	700.684-034
Silversmith I	700.281-010

1118

SILVERSMITH II 700.281-022
SILVERWARE ASSEMBLER 700.684-070
sizer 700.684-010
slush caster 502.381-010
SOLDERER 700.381-050
SORTER 735.687-030
SPINNER 700.684-074
splitter 770.381-014
stonecutter 770.281-014
Stone Gluer 735.687-034
STONER 735.684-014
STONE SETTER 735.687-034
STONE SETTER 700.381-054
STONE-SETTER APPRENTICE 700.381-058
straight edger 705.682-014
STRETCHER 700.684-078
STRINGER 509.687-018
Stringer-Up, Soldering Machine 509.687-018
SUPERVISOR 700.130-010
SUPERVISOR 700.131-010
SUPERVISOR, DIAMOND FINISHING 770.131-014
Supervisor, Hand Workers 700.131-010
SUPERVISOR, JEWELRY DEPARTMENT 700.131-018
Supervisor, Machine Workers 700.131-010
SUPERVISOR, PRINTING AND STAMPING 652.130-010
SWEDGER 735.687-038
SYNTHETIC-GEM-PRESS OPERATOR 575.685-078
tipper 705.682-014
tool setter 615.130-010
TRIMMER 705.682-014
TROPHY ASSEMBLER 735.684-018
TUBBER 599.685-098
washer-off 735.687-010
WATCH-BAND ASSEMBLER 700.684-082
WAX MOLDER 549.685-038
WIRE DRAWER 735.687-042
WIRE DRAWING MACHINE OPERATOR 614.382-018

knitting—KNITTING INDUSTRY: This designation includes occupations concerned with knitting tubular or flat fabrics and shaped garments, including hosiery. Occupations concerned with preparing knitting yarns and the finishing of knitted fabrics are found in the TEXTILE INDUSTRY (textile). Occupations concerned with manufacturing garments cut and sewn from knitted fabrics are found in the GARMENT INDUSTRY (garment). Occupations concerned with the weaving of lace are found in the TEXTILE PRODUCTS INDUSTRY, NOT ELSEWHERE CLASSIFIED (tex. prod., nec).

assembler 685.687-010
AUTOCLAVE OPERATOR 587.585-010
automatic clipper and stripper 684.686-010
BAGGER 582.687-010
Band Cutter 781.687-026
Band-Cutting-Machine Operator 686.685-066
batcher tender 689.685-114
beam warper 681.685-018
BEAM-WARPER TENDER, AUTOMATIC 681.685-018
boarder 589.685-010
boarder 589.686-042
boarder 583.687-010
boarder, hand 589.686-042
boarder, machine 589.685-010
boarder, steam 589.686-042
boarder tender 589.686-042
BOARDING-MACHINE OPERATOR 589.685-010
BOXING-AND-PRESSING SUPERVISOR 789.137-010
BUTTONER 782.687-014
BUTTON RECLAIMER 734.687-042
calenderer 580.485-010
CALENDERING-MACHINE OPERATOR 580.485-010
CARDBOARD INSERTER 920.687-062
Circular Knitter 685.665-014
Circular-Knitter Helper 685.686-014
clipper, automatic 684.686-010
CLIPPER, MACHINE 684.686-010
CLOTH DRIER 580.685-014
CLOTH INSPECTOR 685.687-010
cloth spreader 580.685-014
Cloth Weigher 222.387-074
Collarette Separator 789.687-030
Collar Knitter 685.665-014
Collar Separator 789.687-030
Collar Trimmer 781.682-010
COLLECTOR 684.687-022
COLOR MATCHER 582.261-010

combining-machine operator 584.682-014
crocheter 685.682-010
CROCHETER, HAND 782.684-014
CROCHET-MACHINE OPERATOR 685.682-010
CUFF FOLDER 685.687-014
Cuff Knitter 685.665-014
Cuff Presser 583.685-070
Cuff Separator 789.687-030
Cuff Turner 789.687-182
cuff turner 685.687-014
darner 782.684-030
DETACKER 589.685-030
DIPPER 589.687-018
DRAPER 781.684-026
DRIER 581.686-014
drier tender 580.685-014
drum-dyeing-machine operator 582.685-170
DRY CLEANER 589.685-038
dry folder, cloth 589.685-058
Drying-Machine Back-Tender 589.686-010
drying-machine operator 580.685-014
drying-machine operator 581.686-038
drying-machine tender 581.686-014
Dye-Boarding-Machine Operator 589.685-010
dye-house supervisor 582.131-014
DYEING-MACHINE OPERATOR .... term
DYE-LAB TECHNICIAN 582.384-010
dyer 582.685-170
dyer assistant 582.261-010
DYER, SUPERVISOR 582.131-014
DYE-TUB OPERATOR 582.685-170
Emblem-Fuser Tender 583.685-046
examiner 684.687-010
extractor 589.485-010
Facing-End Trimmer 781.687-070
Facing-Slitter 699.682-030
Finished-Garment Inspector 789.687-070
finisher 580.485-010
Finish Mender 782.684-030
FIXER, BOARDING ROOM 580.380-010
Flat Knitter 685.665-014
Flat-Knitter Helper 685.686-014
fleecer 585.665-010
folder operator 589.685-058
FOLDING-MACHINE OPERATOR 589.685-058
folding-machine operator 580.485-010
FRINGING-MACHINE OPERATOR 685.686-010
FUSING-MACHINE TENDER 583.685-046
GARMENT FOLDER 789.687-066
Garment Looper 689.682-010
GARMENT STEAMER 582.685-078
GARMENT TURNER 789.687-074
Garment Weigher 222.387-074
Greige-Goods Inspector 789.687-070
Greige Mender 782.684-030
grey inspector 684.684-010
Hose Turner 789.687-182
Hosiery Looper 689.682-010
HOSIERY MENDER 782.684-030
HYDRAULIC-PRESS OPERATOR 583.685-054
inspector and clipper 684.684-010
ironer 583.685-070
JACQUARD-PLATE MAKER 685.381-010
Jersey Knitter 685.665-014
Knit-Goods Cutter, Hand 781.684-074
KNIT-GOODS WASHER 582.685-094
Knitted-Cloth Examiner 689.685-038
knitter 685.665-014
knitter 685.665-018
knitter 684.685-010
KNITTER, FULL-FASHIONED GARMENT 685.665-010
knitter helper 685.686-014
knitter, machine 685.665-014
knitter, machine 685.380-010
KNITTER MECHANIC 685.360-010
Knitting Inspector 684.684-010
KNITTING-MACHINE FIXER 689.260-026
KNITTING-MACHINE FIXER, HEAD 689.130-018
KNITTING-MACHINE OPERATOR 685.665-014
knitting-machine operator, automatic 685.380-010
knitting-machine operator, automatic 684.685-010
KNITTING-MACHINE OPERATOR, FULL-FASHIONED
    HOSIERY, AUTOMATIC 684.682-010
KNITTING-MACHINE OPERATOR HELPER 685.686-014
knitting-machine operator, seamless hosiery 684.685-010

laundry & rel.

knitting-order distributor	221.667-010
Label Cutter	699.685-014
Lace Inspector	689.685-038
LAMINATING-MACHINE OPERATOR	584.682-014
layer-up	589.685-058
length control tester	684.684-014
LINK-AND-LINK-KNITTING-MACHINE OPERATOR	685.380-010
LOOPER	689.682-010
Looping Inspector	684.684-010
LOOSE-END FINDER, BOBBIN	681.687-014
mangle operator, garments	583.685-070
MANGLER	583.685-070
mangle tender, cloth	580.485-010
MARKING-MACHINE OPERATOR	652.685-050
mender, hand	782.684-030
MENDER, KNIT GOODS	782.684-046
mender, machine	782.684-030
Milanese-Knitting-Machine Operator	685.665-018
muffler fringer	685.686-010
NAPPER TENDER	585.665-010
NEEDLE STRAIGHTENER	628.684-018
ODD-PIECE CHECKER	221.587-018
Paddle-Dyeing-Machine Operator	582.685-170
PAD-EXTRACTOR TENDER	589.485-010
PAIRER	684.687-010
pairer-inspector	684.687-010
Pairer, Odds	684.687-010
Pairer, Substandard	684.687-010
Pantyhose-Crotch-Closing-Machine Operator	787.682-074
PATROLLER	685.687-022
pattern-and-chain maker	685.360-010
PATTERN ASSEMBLER	685.685-014
Pattern-Drum Maker	685.684-010
patternmaker	685.381-010
pattern puncher	685.684-010
PATTERN WHEEL MAKER	685.684-010
Pile-Fabric Knitter	685.665-014
pleating-machine operator	589.685-086
Pocket Creaser	583.685-042
POMPOM MAKER	789.687-126
Preboarder	589.685-010
PRESS FEEDER	583.686-030
PRESS HAND	583.687-010
pressing machine operator	583.685-070
processor	589.485-010
QUALITY-CONTROL TESTER	684.384-010
Raschel-Knitting-Machine Operator	685.665-018
RAVELER	782.687-034
RECORDER	221.587-026
REDYE HAND	789.687-142
reexaminer	684.687-014
REINSPECTOR	684.687-014
Rib-Cloth Knitter	685.665-014
Rib-Trim Separator	789.687-030
roller-presser operator	583.686-030
ROLLING-DOWN-MACHINE OPERATOR	589.685-086
ROLLING-MACHINE TENDER	689.685-114
rolling-up-machine operator	580.485-010
ROLL TURNER	689.685-110
Rotary-Drum Dyer	582.685-170
SAMPLE DISPLAY PREPARER	222.687-026
Seamer	787.682-074
Seamer, Elastic Band	787.682-074
Seamer, Pantyhose	787.682-074
Seaming Inspector	684.684-010
SEAMLESS-HOSIERY KNITTER	684.685-010
seamless sizer	684.684-014
SECONDS HANDLER	782.684-050
Seconds Inspector	789.687-070
section beamer	681.685-018
section warper	681.685-018
SEWER AND INSPECTOR	684.682-014
SEWING-MACHINE OPERATOR	787.682-074
SEWING-MACHINE OPERATOR	787.682-050
SHAKER	589.687-058
Shirt Folder	789.687-066
Shirt Turner	789.687-074
shortage worker	221.587-018
SIZER	684.684-014
size tester	684.684-014
Sleeve Separator	789.687-030
Sleeve Turner	789.687-074
SLITTER	781.684-054
SOCK BOARDER	589.686-042
Sock Examiner	684.684-010
Sock Knitter	684.685-010
sock-knitting-machine operator	684.685-010
SPOT CLEANER	582.684-014
STEAMER-BLOCKER	784.684-070
steam hand	582.685-078
steaming-machine operator	580.685-014
STOCKING INSPECTOR	684.684-010
straightener	628.684-018
STRIPE MATCHER	689.662-014
superintendent, dyeing	582.131-014
SUPERVISOR	684.137-010
Supervisor, Boarding	684.137-010
Supervisor, Inspecting	685.130-010
Supervisor, Knitting I	684.137-010
SUPERVISOR, KNITTING II	685.130-010
Supervisor, Looping I	684.137-010
Supervisor, Looping II	685.130-010
Supervisor, Mending I	684.137-010
Supervisor, Mending II	685.130-010
Supervisor, Pairing And Inspecting	684.137-010
Supervisor, Seaming	684.137-010
Supervisor, Transferring And Boxing	684.137-010
swing-folding-machine operator	589.685-086
Tacker, Elastic Band	787.682-074
Tape Cutter	699.682-030
TAPE STRINGER	782.687-054
THREADER	685.680-010
Tie-Knitter Helper	685.686-014
TIE PRESSER	789.687-178
Tissue Inserter	920.687-062
TOE-CLOSING-MACHINE TENDER	787.685-046
TOE PUNCHER	689.685-162
Toe Sewer	787.682-074
TOPPER	685.687-026
transfer-iron operator	659.685-022
transfer knitter	685.685-010
TRANSFER-MACHINE OPERATOR	659.685-022
TRAY DRIER	581.686-038
Tricot-Knitting-Machine Operator	685.665-018
tricot-warper tender	681.685-018
TRIMMER, MACHINE	781.682-010
TRIMMING-MACHINE OPERATOR	583.685-122
tube turner	689.685-110
TUBULAR-SPLITTING-MACHINE TENDER	686.685-070
tumbler-dyeing-machine operator	582.685-170
TUMBLER TENDER	581.685-062
turner	689.685-110
turning-machine operator	689.685-110
warper tender	681.685-018
Warp-Knitter Helper	685.686-014
WARP-KNITTING-MACHINE OPERATOR	685.665-018
washer	582.684-014
wheel blocker	685.684-010
winder	583.685-122
WORK-TICKET DISTRIBUTOR	221.667-010

laundry & rel.—LAUNDRY, CLEANING, DYEING, AND PRESSING IN-DUSTRY: This designation includes occupations concerned with washing, dye-ing, cleaning, drying, ironing, blocking, and mending of wearing apparel and of household articles, such as blankets, curtains, and rugs, as carried on in com-mercial laundries and in other establishments and institutions, such as hospitals and hotels. Occupations found in establishments such as rug and upholstery cleaners which work on the customers' premises are classified in this industry. Occupations concerned with laundering wearing apparel and houshold articles in private homes are included in DOMESTIC SERVICE (domestic ser.).

ASSEMBLER	369.687-010
ASSEMBLER, WET WASH	361.687-010
assorter, laundry	361.687-014
attendant, coin-operated laundry	369.677-010
attendant, laundry-and-dry-cleaning service	369.677-010
BAGGER	920.687-018
baller	363.687-018
BLOCKER	363.684-010
Body Presser	363.685-026
Bosom Presser	363.685-026
boucle finisher	363.684-010
Brim Blocker	363.684-014
brusher-down	362.687-014
bundle clerk	361.687-018
Bundle Weigher	361.687-018
carder, blankets	363.687-022
carpet cleaner	369.384-014
CHECKER	369.687-014

Chute Worker	361.687-018
CLASSIFIER	361.687-014
cleaner assistant	362.686-010
cleaner helper	362.686-010
Clipper	361.687-018
clothes marker	369.687-026
combination presser	363.682-014
CONDITIONER-TUMBLER OPERATOR	361.685-010
CONTINUOUS-TOWEL ROLLER	361.685-014
counter attendant	369.477-014
Crown Blocker	363.684-014
Crown-Ironer Operator	363.684-014
CURB ATTENDANT	369.477-010
curtain drier	363.687-022
curtain framer	363.687-022
curtain stretcher	363.687-022
distributor	369.687-010
drier operator	369.685-034
DRY CLEANER	362.382-014
DRY-CLEANER APPRENTICE	362.382-010
dry cleaner, furniture, hand	362.684-022
DRY-CLEANER, HAND	362.684-010
DRY-CLEANER HELPER	362.686-010
dry-cleaning-machine operator	362.382-014
dry-cleaning-machine-operator apprentice	362.382-010
dry-cleaning-machine-operator helper	362.686-010
drying-machine operator	369.685-034
drying-tumbler operator	369.685-034
DYER	364.361-010
dyer assistant	364.687-010
DYER HELPER	364.687-010
dye-room helper	364.687-010
entry clerk	369.687-026
FEATHER RENOVATOR	362.685-010
Finisher, Hand	363.681-010
Flatwork Assembler	369.687-010
Flatwork Catcher	363.686-010
Flatwork Feeder	363.686-010
FLATWORK FINISHER	363.686-010
Flatwork Finisher, Hand	363.684-018
Flatwork Folder	363.686-010
Flatwork Supervisor	361.137-010
FLATWORK TIER	361.587-010
Flatwork Washer	361.665-010
FOLDER	369.687-018
FOLDING-MACHINE OPERATOR	369.686-010
Form-Finishing-Machine Operator	363.681-010
Form-Press Operator	363.682-018
fur beater	369.685-014
FUR CLEANER	362.684-014
FUR CLEANER, HAND	362.684-018
FUR CLEANER, MACHINE	369.685-014
fur drummer	369.685-014
fur dry-cleaner	369.685-014
fur dry-cleaner	362.684-014
fur dry-cleaner, hand	362.684-018
FUR-GLAZING-&-POLISHING-MACHINE OPERATOR	369.685-022
fur ironer	369.685-022
FUR IRONER	369.685-018
FURNITURE CLEANER	362.684-022
furniture shampooer	362.684-022
Fur-Polishing-Machine Operator	369.685-022
furrier	362.684-014
garment examiner	369.687-022
garment marker	369.687-026
GLOVE CLEANER, HAND	362.687-010
glove finisher	363.687-010
GLOVE FORMER	363.687-010
glove presser	363.687-010
glove turner and former	363.687-010
handkerchief ironer	363.685-022
HAT BLOCKER	363.684-014
hat finisher	363.684-014
HATTER	369.384-010
HAT TRIMMER	782.381-010
Hot-Head-Machine Operator	363.681-010
INSPECTOR	369.687-022
ironer	363.687-010
IRONER, SOCK	363.687-014
Isolation-Washer	361.665-010
knitted-garment finisher	363.684-010
knitted-goods shaper	363.684-010
LAUNDERER, HAND	361.684-010
LAUNDRY HAND	term
LAUNDRY LABORER	361.687-018
LAUNDRY-MACHINE MECHANIC	629.261-010
Laundry-Marker Supervisor	361.137-010
LAUNDRY OPERATOR	369.684-014
Laundry Operator, Finishing	369.684-014
Laundry Operator, Wash Room	369.684-014
LAUNDRY PRICING CLERK	216.482-030
layer-off	363.687-010
LEATHER CLEANER	362.684-026
LEATHER FINISHER	363.682-010
Legger-Press Operator	363.682-018
LINEN CONTROLLER	299.357-010
LINEN GRADER	361.687-022
LINEN-ROOM SUPERVISOR	222.137-014
LINEN-SUPPLY LOAD-BUILDER	920.687-118
Linen-Supply-Room Worker	361.687-018
lining brusher	362.687-014
lining cleaner	362.687-014
Lining Finisher	783.381-014
Lining Presser	363.684-018
Lining Presser	363.682-018
LINING SCRUBBER	362.687-014
MANAGER, BRANCH STORE	369.467-010
MANAGER, LAUNDROMAT	369.167-010
MANAGER, SALES	187.167-138
MARKER	369.687-026
matcher	369.687-010
Mushroom-Press Operator	363.682-018
net checker-hanger	361.687-010
Net Sorter	361.687-018
Overall Washer	361.665-010
PAINTER, RUG TOUCH-UP	364.381-010
Pants Presser, Automatic	363.685-014
PATCHING-MACHINE OPERATOR	361.685-022
pillow cleaner	362.685-010
Pin Sorter And Bagger	361.687-018
Pin Worker	361.687-018
Pleat Presser	363.681-010
PRESSER, ALL-AROUND	363.682-014
presser-and-blocker, knitted goods	363.684-010
presser-and-shaper, knitted goods	363.684-010
PRESSER, AUTOMATIC	363.685-014
PRESSER, HANDKERCHIEF	363.685-022
presser, leather garments	363.682-010
PRESS OPERATOR	363.685-010
press operator, automatic	363.685-014
pricer	216.482-030
puffer	363.687-018
PUFF IRONER	363.687-018
Puff-Iron Operator I	363.681-010
Puff-Iron Operator II	363.682-018
Puller	361.686-010
Rag Baler	920.685-010
Rag Washer	361.665-010
receiving checker	369.687-026
Receiving, Marking, And Washing Supervisor	'61.137-010
Return Checker	369.687-014
RUG CLEANER, HAND	369.384-014
RUG-CLEANER HELPER	362.686-014
RUG CLEANER, MACHINE	361.682-010
RUG-DRY-ROOM ATTENDANT	369.685-026
RUG-DYER HELPER	364.687-014
RUG DYER I	364.361-014
RUG DYER II	364.684-010
RUG INSPECTOR	369.687-030
RUG MEASURER	369.367-014
rug-receiving clerk	369.367-014
rug renovator	369.384-014
RUG REPAIRER	782.381-018
rug scrubber	369.384-014
rug shampooer	369.384-014
rug washer	369.384-014
sample dyer	364.361-010
saw-dust machine operator	369.685-014
sawdust-machine operator	362.684-014
SELF-SERVICE-LAUNDRY-AND-DRY-CLEANING ATTENDANT	369.677-010
separator	361.687-014
SERVICE-ESTABLISHMENT ATTENDANT	369.477-014
Sewing Inspector	369.687-022
Shaker, Flatwork	363.686-010
SHAKER, WEARING APPAREL	361.687-026
SHAVER	362.687-018
Shirt-Collar-And-Cuff Presser	363.685-026
Shirt Folder I	369.687-018
Shirt Folder II	363.685-026

leather mfg.

SHIRT-FOLDING-MACHINE OPERATOR	369.685-030
Shirt-Ironer Supervisor	361.137-010
SHIRT PRESSER	363.685-026
Shirt Presser, Automatic	363.685-014
SILK FINISHER	363.681-010
Silk Spotter	362.381-010
sock-and-stocking ironer	363.687-014
sock drier	363.687-014
sock folder	363.687-014
soiled linen distributor	361.687-014
sorter, laundry articles	361.687-014
Sorting-And-Folding Supervisor	361.137-010
SPOTTER I	361.684-018
SPOTTER II	362.381-010
spray dyer	364.684-018
SPRAYER, LEATHER	364.684-018
steam cleaner, machine	361.665-010
STRETCHER-DRIER OPERATOR	363.687-022
stretcher operator	363.687-022
subsorter	369.687-010
SUPERINTENDENT, LAUNDRY	187.167-194
SUPERVISOR, DRY CLEANING	369.137-010
supervisor, industrial garment	222.137-014
SUPERVISOR, LAUNDRY	361.137-010
SUPERVISOR, RUG CLEANING	369.137-010
tagger	369.687-026
Tie Presser	363.681-010
Topper-Press Operator	363.682-018
Topper-Press Operator, Automatic	363.682-018
towel-rolling-machine operator	361.685-014
tumbler-drier operator	369.685-034
TUMBLER OPERATOR	369.685-034
tumbler operator	361.685-010
VAULT CUSTODIAN	369.587-010
Velvet Steamer	363.681-010
washateria attendant	369.677-010
Wash-Clothes Presser	363.682-018
Washer, Blanket	361.665-010
WASHER, HAND	361.687-030
Washer Helper, Machine	361.686-010
WASHER, MACHINE	361.665-010
WASHING-MACHINE LOADER-AND-PULLER	361.686-010
Washing-Machine Loader I	361.686-010
Washing-Machine Loader II	361.687-018
Washroom Supervisor	361.137-010
Wearing-Apparel Assembler	369.687-010
Wearing-Apparel Finisher, Hand	363.684-018
Wearing-Apparel Folder	369.687-018
wearing-apparel presser	363.685-010
wet cleaner, machine	361.665-010
wet washer, machine	361.665-010
Wool Presser	363.682-018
Wool Spotter	362.381-010
Yoke Presser	363.685-026

leather mfg.—LEATHER MANUFACTURING INDUSTRY: This designation includes occupations concerned with cleaning, tanning, currying, finishing, and dressing hides, skins, furs, and pelts to convert them into leather for subsequent use in manufacturing products, such as belts, boots, shoes, gloves, saddles, and dyed furs.

assorter	589.387-010
Back Roller	583.685-094
Bark Tanner	582.482-018
beam-house inspector	585.687-010
BEAMING INSPECTOR	585.687-010
Beating-Machine Operator	589.686-022
Belly Roller	583.685-094
Belly Wringer	589.685-098
bend sorter	589.387-010
bend trimmer	585.684-010
blackener	599.685-094
blacking-machine operator	599.685-094
Blacking-Wheel Tender	582.685-050
Black-Leather Buffer	585.685-018
Black-Leather Trimmer	585.684-010
Bleaching Supervisor	582.131-010
block trimmer	585.684-010
Blue-Leather Setter	589.685-098
Blue-Leather Sorter	589.387-010
blue-line hanger	589.686-026
blue-line trimmer	585.684-010
Blue-Split Trimmer	585.684-010
breaker-wheel operator	582.685-050

BUFFER, MACHINE	585.685-018
buffing-wheel operator	585.685-018
burnisher	585.685-018
buzzle buffer	585.685-018
cellar hand	589.686-026
cementer	585.687-022
Chestnut Tanner	582.482-018
Chrome-Tanning-Drum Operator	582.482-018
Colored-Leather Setter	589.685-098
COLORER, HIDES AND SKINS	582.482-010
colorer, machine	582.482-010
COLOR MATCHER	550.381-010
color mixer	550.381-010
Comber	589.686-022
counter-pocket trimmer	585.684-010
Crop Roller	583.685-094
Crop-Setting-Out-Machine Operator	589.685-098
Cutter	589.686-022
Degreasing-Wheel Operator	582.685-050
Delimer	582.482-014
department helper	589.686-026
doper	584.687-010
Dope Sprayer	584.687-014
DRUM ATTENDANT	582.685-050
Drummer	589.686-022
drum tender	582.482-018
Dry-Mill Worker	582.685-050
Dry Roller	583.685-094
DYE-HOUSE SUPERVISOR	582.131-010
DYE-HOUSE WORKER	582.686-010
Dyeing Supervisor	582.131-010
dye mixer	582.482-010
dyer and washer	582.482-010
dye weigher	582.482-010
edge trimmer	585.684-010
EMBOSSER	690.682-030
embossing-machine operator	690.682-030
embossing-press operator	690.682-030
enameler	584.687-010
extractor operator	589.685-098
extract wringer	589.685-098
Final-Coat Sprayer	584.687-014
finished-leather presser	690.682-030
fitter-up	629.280-010
FLESHER	585.681-010
Fleshing-Machine Operator	585.685-094
floorworker	589.686-022
Frame Maker	860.281-010
FUR BLENDER	783.681-010
Fur Clipper	589.686-022
FUR DRESSER	589.361-010
fur dyer	783.681-010
FUR-FLOOR WORKER	589.686-022
FUR PLUCKER	585.681-014
Fur Puller	589.686-022
fur scraper	585.681-010
Fur Stretcher	589.686-022
fur tinter	783.681-010
Glazing-Machine Operator	583.685-094
grader	585.684-010
grader	589.387-010
Graining-Machine Operator	583.685-094
Greaser	589.686-022
Gum Sprayer	584.687-014
Hair Baler	920.685-010
HAIR-BOILER OPERATOR	582.685-086
HAIR CLIPPER, POWER	789.684-022
HAIR-SPINNING-MACHINE OPERATOR	689.686-030
hand finisher	584.687-010
hefter	589.387-010
hide cleaner	585.681-010
hide examiner	783.687-018
HIDE INSPECTOR	783.687-018
hide-measuring-machine operator	589.686-070
hide sorter	589.387-010
HIDE SPLITTER	690.580-010
HIDE STRETCHER, HAND	580.687-014
INSPECTOR AND SORTER	589.387-010
japanner	584.687-010
Laborer, Beam House	589.686-026
Laborer, Drying Department	589.686-026
laborer, drying department	580.687-014
LABORER, GENERAL	589.686-026
Laborer, Hide House	589.686-026
Laborer, Tan House	589.686-026

Lambskin Trimmer	585.684-010
Leather Baler	920.685-010
LEATHER COATER	584.687-010
leather colorer	582.482-010
leather dresser	584.687-010
leather leveler	690.686-054
leather patcher	585.687-022
leather polisher	583.685-094
leather pourer	584.687-014
leather repairer	585.687-022
leather sander	585.685-018
Leather Softener, Drum	582.482-010
leather sorter	589.387-010
leather sprayer	584.687-014
lime hide inspector	585.687-010
Limer	582.482-014
Lime Trimmer	585.684-010
load mixer	584.687-010
MAINTENANCE MECHANIC	629.280-010
measurer	589.685-070
MEASURING-MACHINE OPERATOR	589.685-070
mill attendant	582.685-050
mixer, pigment	550.381-010
Oak Tanner	582.482-018
Offal Baler	920.685-010
Oiling-Machine Operator	582.685-050
Oil Sprayer	584.687-014
passer	589.387-010
PATCHER	585.687-022
Patent-Leather Sorter	589.387-010
pelt scraper	585.681-010
Pickler	582.482-014
pit tanner	582.482-018
plating-press operator	690.682-030
pourer	584.687-010
pourer	584.687-014
preparer	585.684-010
printer	690.682-030
PULLER, MACHINE	589.685-078
putter-out, machine	589.685-098
Quebracho Tanner	582.482-018
Rabbit Flesher	585.681-010
Raw-Hide Trimmer	585.684-010
Retanned-Leather Roller	583.685-094
retanner	582.482-018
ripper	585.684-010
ROLLER-MACHINE OPERATOR	583.685-094
Roll Filler	629.280-010
roll-press operator	589.685-098
roustabout	589.686-026
Russet-Leather Sorter	589.387-010
scudding inspector	585.687-010
seasoner, hand	584.687-010
Seasoning Sprayer	584.687-014
setter, machine	589.685-098
SHAVING-MACHINE OPERATOR	585.685-094
shearer	585.685-098
shearer	585.685-126
SHEARING-MACHINE FEEDER	585.685-098
Shearing-Machine Operator	585.685-094
smooth plater	690.682-030
snipper	585.684-010
softener	582.685-050
split-leather mosser	584.687-010
SPLITTING-MACHINE FEEDER	690.686-054
Sponger	589.685-098
SPRAYER, HAND	584.687-014
SPRAYER, MACHINE	599.685-094
spray-machine operator	599.685-094
STAKER, MACHINE	580.685-050
stencil sprayer	584.687-014
streaker-off, hand	584.687-010
Stretching-Machine Tender, Frame	580.685-050
striker-out, machine	589.685-098
stuffer, machine	582.685-050
Sueding-Wheel Operator	585.685-018
Sumac Tanner	582.482-018
SUPERVISOR, BEAM DEPARTMENT	589.134-010
Supervisor, Buffing-And-Pasting	589.130-030
Supervisor, Drying-And-Softening	589.130-030
SUPERVISOR, FINISHING ROOM	589.130-018
Supervisor, Fleshing	589.130-022
SUPERVISOR, FUR DRESSING	589.130-022
Supervisor, Fur-Floor Worker	589.130-022
Supervisor, Hanging-And-Trimming	589.130-030

SUPERVISOR, HIDE HOUSE	922.137-014
SUPERVISOR, PACKING ROOM	589.137-010
Supervisor, Shaving-And-Splitting	589.130-030
Supervisor, Shearing	589.130-022
SUPERVISOR, SPLIT AND DRUM ROOM	589.132-014
SUPERVISOR, SPLIT LEATHER DEPARTMENT	589.130-030
SUPERVISOR, TAN ROOM	582.132-018
SUPERVISOR, VAT HOUSE	582.132-022
swabber	584.687-010
tanner	582.482-018
tanner	589.361-010
TANNER, ROTARY DRUM, CONTINUOUS PROCESS	582.482-014
tannery gummer	584.687-010
TANNING-DRUM OPERATOR	582.482-018
Tanning Supervisor	582.131-010
Tanning-Wheel Filler	582.685-050
tawer	582.482-018
temperer	582.685-050
toggler	589.686-026
trimmer and sorter	585.684-010
TRIMMER, HAND	585.684-010
TRIMMER, MACHINE	585.685-126
unbundler	585.684-010
unhairing inspector	585.687-010
Unhairing-Machine Operator	585.685-094
Washing-Machine Operator	582.685-050
wet-milling-wheel operator	582.685-050
Wet Roller	583.685-094
Wet Trimmer	585.684-010
White-Kid Buffer	585.685-018
WOOL PULLER	589.687-050
wringer and setter	589.685-098
WRINGER-MACHINE OPERATOR	589.685-098

leather prod.—LEATHER PRODUCTS INDUSTRY: This designation includes occupations concerned with producing and repairing leather articles, such as belts, harnesses, pocketbooks, power belting, purses, saddles, wallets, jewelry cases, instrument cases, and suitcases and related cases and luggage made of leather and other materials. Occupations concerned with manufacturing boots and shoes are included in the BOOT AND SHOE INDUSTRY (boot & shoe); occupations concerned with the manufacture and repair of garments are included in the GARMENT INDUSTRY (garment); occupations concerned with producing gloves and mittens are included in the GLOVE AND MITTEN INDUSTRY (glove. & mit.).

applier	589.687-034
Applique Sewer	783.682-014
Assembler, Handbags	783.684-010
ASSEMBLER, LEATHER GOODS I	783.684-010
ASSEMBLER, LEATHER GOODS II	783.687-010
Assembly-Department Supervisor	783.132-010
Belting Cutter	585.685-038
belt puncher	690.685-266
belt roller	920.685-070
Boot-Lace Cutter, Machine	585.685-038
Briefcase Sewer	783.682-014
Buckram Cutter	699.682-022
bundler	222.587-046
cartridge belt puncher	690.685-266
case assembler	739.684-034
CASE FINISHER	739.684-034
Case Repairer	739.684-034
cementer, machine	690.686-022
CLICKING-MACHINE OPERATOR	789.382-010
Cloth-And-Leather-Department Supervisor	783.132-010
COATING-MACHINE FEEDER	690.686-022
Coin-Purse Assembler	783.684-010
Coin-Purse Framer	739.684-090
color finisher	589.687-034
Color Sprayer	584.687-014
COVERING-MACHINE TENDER	783.685-010
CREASER	783.685-014
CUSTOM-LEATHER-PRODUCTS MAKER	783.361-010
CUT-LACE-MACHINE OPERATOR	585.685-038
cutter, machine	585.685-038
Cutting-Department Supervisor	783.132-010
DECORATOR	739.684-046
decorator	781.381-018
DISK-AND-TAPE-MACHINE TENDER	783.685-018
EDGE STAINER I	589.685-046
EDGE STAINER II	749.684-022
EMBOSSER	690.682-030
embossing-machine operator	690.682-030
embossing-press operator	690.682-030

library

Fancy Sewer	783.682-014
Filler And Trimmer	783.687-010
finished-leather presser	690.682-030
FOLDING-MACHINE OPERATOR	690.685-178
Frame Coverer	783.687-010
frame opener	222.687-042
framer	739.684-090
Glove Cutter	781.687-030
glue-machine feeder	690.686-022
GLUE-SPREADING-MACHINE OPERATOR	584.665-014
gusset folder	690.685-178
Handbag Designer	142.061-018
Handbag Finisher	783.682-014
HANDBAG FRAMER	739.684-090
Handbag-Parts Cutter	699.682-022
Handle Attacher	783.687-010
Handle Maker	783.687-010
Handle Sewer	783.682-014
hardware assembler	739.684-046
HARNESS MAKER	783.381-018
Harness Repairer	783.381-018
Hat-Parts Cutter	699.682-022
Holster Maker	783.684-026
INK PRINTER	652.685-038
INSPECTOR, HANDBAG FRAMES	222.687-042
INSPECTOR-REPAIRER	783.684-018
instrument-case finisher	739.684-034
Inverter-And-Clipper	789.687-182
Keycase Assembler	783.684-010
LACE-ROLLER OPERATOR	920.685-070
LAMINATOR I	690.685-258
LAMINATOR II	783.685-022
Leather-Belt-Loop Cutter	690.685-266
LEATHER-BELT MAKER	690.685-266
Leather-Belt Puncher	690.685-266
Leather-Belt Shaper	690.685-266
Leather-Cartridge-Belt Maker	690.685-266
leather-case finisher	739.684-034
Leather Crafter	142.061-018
Leather Cutter	789.382-010
LEATHER CUTTER	783.684-022
Leather-Novelty-Parts Cutter	699.682-022
LEATHER STAMPER	781.381-018
leather-stripping-machine operator	585.685-038
leather tooler	781.381-018
LEATHER WORKER	783.684-026
Lining-Parts Sewer	783.682-014
LUGGAGE MAKER	783.381-022
MARKING-MACHINE TENDER	783.685-026
MATCHER, LEATHER PARTS	783.687-022
Men's Leather-Dress-Belt Maker	690.685-266
MOLDER, FIBERGLASS LUGGAGE	575.685-066
OIL-SEAL ASSEMBLER	739.684-138
pad cutter and assembler	780.381-030
PAD HAND	780.381-030
PASTER, HAND OR MACHINE	783.687-026
plating-press operator	690.682-030
Pocketbook Framer	739.684-090
Pocket-Secretary Assembler	783.684-010
printer	690.682-030
puncher	690.685-266
Purse Framer	739.684-090
RAWHIDE-BONE ROLLER	789.684-042
Rifle-Case Repairer	783.684-026
Roller Stainer	749.684-022
SADDLE MAKER	783.381-026
Saddler	783.381-026
Sewing-Department Supervisor	783.132-010
SEWING MACHINE OPERATOR	783.682-014
shaver	585.685-114
Silk-Lining Cutter, Machine	699.682-022
Single-Beam Clicker	699.682-022
SKIVER	690.685-374
Skiver, Hand	690.685-374
smearer	589.687-034
smooth plater	690.682-030
Sole-Stock Cutter	585.685-038
Spanisher	781.381-018
splitter	585.685-114
SPLITTER, MACHINE	585.685-114
Spray Cementer	741.687-018
Spray Stainer	749.684-022
STACKER	222.587-046
STAINER	589.687-034
stripper	585.685-114

SUPERVISOR	783.132-010
SUPERVISOR, PRINTING AND STAMPING	652.130-014
TABLE WORKER	783.687-030
tanned-hide-cutter, machine	585.685-038
tooler	781.381-018
Twin-Beam Clicker	699.682-022
UTILITY BAG ASSEMBLER	783.684-030
Wallet Assembler	783.684-010
Western-Saddle Maker	783.381-026
width stripper	585.685-038
Women's Leather-Belt Maker	690.685-266
zipper-lining folder	690.685-178

library—LIBRARY: This designation includes occupations in all types of libraries, such as circulating, lending (fee), and public libraries, and the libraries of institutions and other organizations, such as universities and schools.

ACQUISITIONS LIBRARIAN	100.267-010
Art Librarian	100.167-026
AUDIOVISUAL LIBRARIAN	100.167-010
book-loan clerk	249.367-046
Bookmobile Clerk	249.367-046
BOOKMOBILE DRIVER	249.363-010
BOOKMOBILE LIBRARIAN	100.167-014
BRAILLE-AND-TALKING BOOKS CLERK	222.587-010
Branch-Library Clerk	249.367-046
Business Librarian	100.167-026
cataloger	100.387-010
CATALOG LIBRARIAN	100.387-010
Chief Librarian, Branch	100.127-010
CHIEF LIBRARIAN, BRANCH OR DEPARTMENT	100.127-010
Chief Librarian, Circulation Department	100.127-010
Chief Librarian, Extension Department	100.127-010
Chief Librarian, General Reference Department	100.127-010
Chief Librarian, Music Department	100.127-010
Chief Librarian, Periodical Reading Room	100.127-010
Chief Librarian, Readers' Advisory Service	100.127-010
Chief Librarian, Work With Blind	100.127-010
CHILDREN'S LIBRARIAN	100.167-018
circulation clerk	249.367-046
Circulation Librarian	100.127-014
City-Library Director	100.117-010
CLASSIFIER	100.367-014
County-Library Director	100.117-010
descriptive catalog librarian	100.387-010
desk attendant	249.367-046
Engineering Librarian	100.167-026
film librarian	100.167-010
hospital librarian	100.167-022
INSTITUTION LIBRARIAN	100.167-022
Law Librarian	100.167-026
LIBRARIAN	100.127-014
librarian, head	100.117-010
librarian, school	100.167-030
LIBRARIAN, SPECIAL COLLECTIONS	100.267-014
LIBRARIAN, SPECIAL LIBRARY	100.167-026
LIBRARY ASSISTANT	249.367-046
library assistant	100.367-018
library attendant	249.367-046
library clerk	249.367-046
Library Clerk, Art Department	249.367-046
LIBRARY CLERK, TALKING BOOKS	209.387-026
LIBRARY CONSULTANT	100.117-014
LIBRARY DIRECTOR	100.117-010
library helper	249.367-046
LIBRARY TECHNICAL ASSISTANT	100.367-018
library technician	100.367-018
Map Librarian	100.167-026
media center director, school	100.167-030
MEDIA SPECIALIST, SCHOOL LIBRARY	100.167-030
Medical Librarian	100.167-026
news information resource manager	100.167-038
NEWS LIBRARIAN	100.167-038
news library director	100.167-038
newspaper library manager	100.167-038
Outreach Librarian	100.127-014
PAGE	249.687-014
patient's librarian	100.167-022
Photo-Graphics Librarian	100.167-038
principal librarian	100.127-010
prison librarian	100.167-022
Readers'-Advisory-Service Librarian	100.127-014
recordings librarian	100.167-010
Reference Librarian	100.127-014

REGISTRATION CLERK	249.365-010
RESTORER, PAPER-AND-PRINTS	109.361-010
runner	249.687-014
senior librarian	100.127-010
shelver	249.687-014
shelving clerk	249.687-014
SHELVING SUPERVISOR	109.137-010
stack clerk	249.687-014
supervising librarian	100.127-010
YOUNG-ADULT LIBRARIAN	100.167-034

light. fix.—LIGHTING FIXTURES INDUSTRY: This designation includes occupations concerned with manufacturing and repairing electric, gas, gasoline, carbide, and kerosene lighting equipment and related products. The principal products of the industry are chandeliers, lighting fixtures, motor vehicle lamps, shades, reflectors, and incandescent electric bulbs. The designation does not include occupations concerned with the production of glass products from raw materials, which are included in the GLASS MANUFACTURING INDUSTRY (glass mfg.).

assembler	729.687-010
ASSEMBLER, ELECTRICAL ACCESSORIES I	729.687-010
Assembler, Fluorescent Lights	723.684-014
ASSEMBLER I	723.684-014
ASSEMBLER II	723.684-018
Assembler, Incandescent Lights	723.684-014
Automobile-Headlight Assembler	729.684-034
automobile-light assembler	729.684-034
Automobile-Taillight Assembler	729.684-034
BASE REMOVER	692.686-014
Baser	692.685-118
BEAD INSPECTOR	725.687-010
BULB FILLER	692.686-022
cable-machine operator	616.682-034
cabling-machine operator	616.682-034
Chandelier Maker	600.380-010
COILED-COIL INSPECTOR	725.684-010
COILER	725.687-014
contact assembler	729.687-010
DECORATOR, LIGHTING FIXTURES	749.684-018
DRILLER AND DEBURRER, REFLECTOR	676.686-014
FIXTURE MAKER	600.380-010
FLASHER ADJUSTER	723.684-022
FOCUSER	725.687-018
GETTERER	725.687-022
getterer	509.685-026
GETTERING-FILAMENT-MACHINE OPERATOR	509.685-026
getter operator	509.685-026
impregnating helper	599.685-050
IMPREGNATOR-AND-DRIER HELPER	599.685-050
lamp decorator	749.684-018
lamp wirer	723.684-014
LIGHT-BULB ASSEMBLER	692.685-118
Light-Bulb Tester	729.684-058
model maker	600.280-054
MODEL MAKER, FLUORESCENT LIGHTING	723.361-010
MOTOR-VEHICLE-LIGHT ASSEMBLER	729.684-034
MOUNTER, HAND	725.684-014
MOUNTER I	692.686-050
MOUNTER II	692.685-126
Neck Cutter	692.685-118
Pull-Socket Assembler	729.687-010
QUALITY-CONTROL INSPECTOR	725.687-026
RIVETER	616.685-054
SAMPLE MAKER, APPLIANCES	600.280-054
Sealer	692.685-118
SEALING-MACHINE OPERATOR	692.685-162
Sprayer, Light Bulbs	599.686-014
Starter Adjuster	724.381-010
STEM MOUNTER	725.684-018
stem-mounting-machine operator	692.686-050
Strand Buncher, Fine Wire	616.682-034
strander operator	616.682-034
STRANDING-MACHINE OPERATOR	616.682-034
SUPERVISOR, FABRICATION DEPARTMENT	723.132-010
switchboard contact assembler	729.687-010
TESTER AND INSPECTOR, LAMPS	723.687-014
TESTER, ELECTRICAL CONTINUITY	729.684-058
Truck-Headlight Assembler	729.684-034
WIPER	723.687-022

logging—LOGGING INDUSTRY: This designation includes occupations concerned with felling trees and cutting trees into logs or products, such as cordwood, shakes, and posts in the forest; yarding and trucking logs from the forest; and grading, sorting, rafting, and reloading logs for transportation to processing plants or shipping terminals. Occupations concerned with the harvesting of Christmas trees and gathering of tree bark, sap, boughs, and seed cones in the forest are included in the FORESTRY INDUSTRY (forestry). Occupations concerned with the transporting of logs by rail are included in the RAILROAD TRANSPORTATION INDUSTRY (r.r. trans.).

Boat Tender	911.663-010
Boomboat Operator	911.663-010
Boom Supervisor	455.134-010
BUCKER	454.684-010
Busheler	454.384-010
Cat Chaser	921.667-014
Cat Hooker	921.687-014
CHAIN SAW OPERATOR	454.687-010
CHASER	921.667-014
chipper	564.662-010
CHOKE SETTER	921.687-014
chopper	454.384-010
CRUISER	459.387-010
cutting supervisor	183.167-038
FALLER I	454.384-010
FALLER II	454.684-014
Feller-Buncher Operator	454.683-010
feller operator	454.683-010
Fire Patroller	372.667-034
Firewood Cutter	454.684-026
FOREST ENGINEER	005.167-018
grapple operator	921.683-058
Grapple Operator Helper	921.687-022
Grapple-Yarder Operator	921.663-066
Head Rigger	921.664-014
heel-boom operator	921.683-058
High-Lead Yarder	921.663-066
hooker	921.131-010
HOOK TENDER	921.131-010
JAMMER OPERATOR	921.683-054
Jammer Operator Helper	921.687-022
LABORER, TANBARK	454.687-014
Landing Scaler	455.487-010
Limber	454.687-010
Loader Helper, Sorting Yard	921.687-022
LOG-CHIPPER OPERATOR	564.662-010
LOGGER	term
LOGGER, ALL-ROUND	454.684-018
Logging-Arch Operator	929.663-010
Logging Contractor	183.167-038
LOGGING-EQUIPMENT MECHANIC	620.281-042
LOGGING-OPERATIONS INSPECTOR	168.267-070
LOGGING-TRACTOR OPERATOR	929.663-010
Logging-Tractor Operator, Swamp	929.663-010
LOG GRADER	455.367-010
log hauler	904.683-010
LOG LOADER	921.683-058
LOG LOADER HELPER	921.687-022
LOG MARKER	455.687-010
LOG MARKER	454.687-018
LOG SCALER	455.487-010
LOG SORTER	455.684-010
Log-Stacker Operator	929.663-010
LOG-TRUCK DRIVER	904.683-010
MANAGER, CAMP	187.167-066
marker	455.687-010
powersaw supervisor	454.134-010
Pullboat Engineer	921.663-066
PULP PILER	922.687-082
pulp roller	922.687-082
Pulpwood Cutter	454.684-026
RAFTER	455.664-010
Rail-Car Operator	919.663-014
Rail Splitter	454.684-022
RIGGER	921.664-014
RIGGER, THIRD	921.687-030
RIGGING SLINGER	921.364-010
RIVER	454.684-022
saw boss	454.134-010
second loader	921.687-022
second rigger	921.664-014
Shake Splitter	454.684-022
Shingle-Bolt Cutter	454.684-022
Shovel-Loader Operator	921.683-058
Side Boss	459.133-010
Skidder Operator	929.663-010
Skid-Grapple Operator	929.663-010

machinery mfg.

Sky-Line Yarder	921.663-066
Slack-Line Yarder	921.663-066
Snaker	919.664-010
SORTING-GRAPPLE OPERATOR	921.683-066
Stave-Block Splitter	454.684-022
Steel-Spar Operator	921.663-066
stiff-neck loader	921.683-054
stumper-feller	454.684-014
SUPERINTENDENT, LOGGING	183.167-038
SUPERVISOR, FELLING-BUCKING	454.134-010
SUPERVISOR, LOGGING	459.133-010
SUPERVISOR, LOG SORTING	455.134-010
tanbark peeler	454.687-014
timber cruiser	459.387-010
timber supervisor	454.134-010
Trailer Steerer	904.683-010
Transfer Engineer	921.663-030
TREE CUTTER	454.684-026
TREE-SHEAR OPERATOR	454.683-010
Triple-Drum Operator	921.663-066
Truck Driver, Flatbed	905.663-014
Water Chaser	921.667-014
Water Hauler	905.663-014
WOODS BOSS	459.137-010
woods overseer	459.137-010
yarder operator	921.663-066
YARDING ENGINEER	921.663-066
yarding supervisor	459.133-010
yarding supervisor	183.167-038

machinery mfg.—MACHINERY MANUFACTURING INDUSTRY: This designation includes occupations concerned with manufacturing and repairing all types of machinery not elsewhere classified. Typical of the products of the industry are construction, mining, and related machinery; oil-field machinery and tools; food-products machinery; textile machinery; woodworking machinery; paper mill, pulp mill, and paper-products machinery; printing-trades machinery; smelting and refining equipment; foundry machinery and equipment; and household and service-industry machines; elevators, escalators, conveyors, and hoists; industrial trucks; pumps and pumping equipment; ball and roller bearings; air and gas compressors; blowers, exhaust, and ventilation fans; speed changers, gears, and industrial high speed drives; industrial process furnaces and ovens; mechanical power transmission equipment, not elsewhere classified, general industrial machinery and equipment, not elsewhere classified; non-electrical machinery, not elsewhere classified; and metal type printers' leads and slugs. Occupations concerned with the manufacture of metalworking machinery and accessories are included in the MACHINE TOOLS AND ACCESSORIES INDUSTRY (machine tools).

ASSEMBLER	706.361-010
ASSEMBLER AND WIRER, INDUSTRIAL EQUIPMENT	826.361-010
assembler, hydraulic backhoe	801.261-010
ASSEMBLER, MINING MACHINERY	801.261-010
assembler, portable oil-well drilling rig	801.261-010
assembler, special machine	600.281-022
AUTOMATED EQUIPMENT ENGINEER-TECHNICIAN	638.261-010
BALL SORTER	609.685-010
bearing inspector	706.382-014
BEARING-RING ASSEMBLER	706.684-038
bench hand	600.281-022
BLOWER AND COMPRESSOR ASSEMBLER	801.361-010
CALENDER-ROLL PRESS OPERATOR	692.462-010
caster operator	654.382-010
CASTING-MACHINE OPERATOR	654.382-010
composing-machine operator	650.582-014
Compressor Assembler	801.361-010
Crusher Assembler	706.361-010
engineer, automated equipment	638.261-010
erector	638.261-014
FABRICATOR, INDUSTRIAL FURNACE	826.381-010
field engineer	638.261-018
field servicer	638.261-018
FIELD SERVICE TECHNICIAN	638.261-026
fitter	600.281-022
Fixture Builder	600.281-022
Gasket Attacher	795.687-014
heavy-machinery assembler	638.261-014
HEDDLE-MACHINE OPERATOR	616.685-026
hydraulic and mechanical assembler	801.261-010
JIG FITTER	801.684-010
LETTERER	979.681-010
liner	759.684-050
MACHINE ASSEMBLER	638.361-010
MACHINE-ASSEMBLER SUPERVISOR	638.131-014
MACHINE BUILDER	600.281-022

Machinery Crater	920.684-010
MACHINERY ERECTOR	638.261-014
MACHINE TESTER	629.382-010
machinist, bench	600.281-022
MANUFACTURER'S SERVICE REPRESENTATIVE	638.261-018
MATRIX INSPECTOR	654.687-010
monotype caster	654.382-010
MONOTYPE-KEYBOARD OPERATOR	650.582-014
monotype operator	650.582-014
PAGER	654.687-010
panel assembler and wirer	826.361-010
Pump Assembler	801.361-010
raiser	979.681-010
REED MAKER	709.381-038
REMELTER	502.685-014
robot technician	638.261-026
roller-bearing assembler	706.687-034
ROLLER-BEARING INSPECTOR	706.687-034
rubber insulator	759.684-050
RUBBER LINER	759.684-050
SALVAGE ENGINEER	600.131-014
service engineer	638.261-018
service representative	638.261-018
SEWING-MACHINE ASSEMBLER	706.381-034
Sewing-Machine Attachment Tester	709.382-010
SEWING-MACHINE TESTER	709.382-010
sketcher	979.681-010
SUBASSEMBLER	706.381-038
SUPERVISOR, ELECTRICAL ASSEMBLIES	826.131-014
SUPERVISOR, TYPE-DISK QUALITY CONTROL	979.137-026
SUPERVISOR, TYPE PHOTOGRAPHY	976.131-026
Tank Insulator, Rubber	759.684-050
technician, automated equipment	638.261-010
TESTER, SOUND	706.382-014
tester, vibrator equipment	825.361-014
type caster	654.382-010
TYPE-COPY EXAMINER	979.687-026
TYPE COPYIST	970.381-042
TYPE-PROOF REPRODUCER	652.685-106
unit assembler	706.684-038
Valve Liner, Rubber	759.684-050
Vibrator Assembler	706.361-010
VIBRATOR-EQUIPMENT TESTER	825.361-014
vise hand	600.281-022
WELDER-ASSEMBLER	819.381-010

machine shop—MACHINE SHOP: This designation includes occupations occurring in job, repair, and production machine shops except those that are peculiar to individual industries and those occurring in mass production industries in which the work is highly repetitive and of limited scope, not requiring more than superficial knowledge of immediate processes involved. Aside from these exceptions, the classification covers all machine shop occupations, whether they occur in independently operated machine shops or in machine shops that are operated in conjunction with establishments in various industries.

all-around-gear-machine operator	602.380-010
assembler	706.684-018
ASSEMBLER, PRODUCT	706.684-018
automatic-lathe tender	604.685-026
automatic-screw-machine operator	604.380-022
automatic-screw-machine operator	604.280-014
automatic-screw-machine operator	604.280-018
AUTOMATIC-WHEEL-LINE OPERATOR	609.682-010
BABBITTER	709.684-022
band-saw operator	607.682-010
bar-machine operator, multiple spindle	604.280-014
bar-machine operator, multiple spindle	604.382-010
bar-machine operator, production	604.685-034
bar-machine operator, single spindle	604.280-018
bar-machine operator, single spindle	604.382-014
bench die maker	601.281-010
bench-lathe operator	604.380-018
bevel-gear-generator operator	602.382-018
body-die maker	601.280-010
Bolt-Threading-Machine Operator	604.682-014
BORING-MACHINE OPERATOR	606.382-022
BORING-MACHINE OPERATOR, PRODUCTION	606.685-010
BORING-MACHINE SET-UP OPERATOR, JIG	606.280-010
BORING-MILL SET-UP OPERATOR, HORIZONTAL	606.280-014
Boring-Mill Set-Up Operator, Vertical	606.280-014
Brass Reclaimer	609.684-014
Broach Grinder	603.280-038
BROACHING-MACHINE OPERATOR, PRODUCTION	605.682-014
BROACHING-MACHINE SET-UP OPERATOR	605.382-010

1127

machine shop

TOOL MAKER	601.280-042
TOOL-MAKER APPRENTICE	601.280-058
TOOL MAKER, BENCH	601.281-026
Tool Marker	609.684-014
Tool Repairer	601.280-042
Tool Repairer, Bench	601.281-026
tool-room gear-machine operator	602.280-010
tool-room-lathe operator	604.280-010
tool sharpener	603.280-038
tracer-controlled-milling-machine operator	605.280-018
tracer-lathe set-up operator	604.280-010
Tracing-Lathe Set-Up Operator	604.380-018
TRANSFER-MACHINE OPERATOR	609.685-022
trim die maker	601.280-014
trimmer maker	601.280-014
Turret Lathe Operator, Numerical Control	604.362-010
TURRET-LATHE SET-UP OPERATOR	604.380-026
TURRET-LATHE SET-UP OPERATOR, TOOL	604.280-022
Turret-Lathe Set-Up Operator, Tool, Vertical	604.280-022
turret-lathe tender	604.685-026
universal grinder, tool	603.280-030
VALVE GRINDER	706.684-098
valve lapper	706.684-098

machine tools—MACHINE TOOLS AND ACCESSORIES INDUSTRY: This designation includes occupations concerned with manufacturing and repairing power-driven machines, such as lathes, milling machines, and planers; the manufacture of accessories for such metalworking machines as milling cutters, reamers, taps, twist drills, and dies for the direct machining of metal; and the manufcture of power-driven handtools.

assembler, special machine	600.281-022
bench hand	600.281-022
Broaching-Machine Repairer	638.261-030
detail maker and fitter	600.360-010
DIAMOND-DIE POLISHER	770.381-022
DIAMOND DRILLER	770.381-018
DIAMOND MOUNTER	739.384-010
die cutter, diamond	770.381-022
Die Filer	705.484-010
die polisher	770.381-022
driller, fine-diamond dies	770.381-018
field engineer	638.261-018
field servicer	638.261-018
Finisher, Fine-Diamond Dies	770.381-018
fitter	600.281-022
Honing-Machine Try-Out Setter	600.360-010
loft patternmaker	777.381-038
MACHINE BUILDER	600.281-022
MACHINE TRY-OUT SETTER	600.360-010
machinist, bench	600.281-022
MANUFACTURER'S SERVICE REPRESENTATIVE	638.261-018
PLASTER-PATTERN CASTER	777.381-038
PLASTIC DUPLICATOR	754.684-038
service engineer	638.261-018
service representative	638.261-018
SPOTTER	770.381-042
vise hand	600.281-022

meat products—MEAT PRODUCTS INDUSTRY: This designation includes occupations concerned with slaughtering cattle, hogs, sheep, and other animals; preparing and packing meat products, including lard; dressing and packing poultry, rabbits, and other small game; and drying and freezing eggs. Occupations concerned with the production of oleomargarine, tallow, and certain lubricants are included in the ANIMAL AND VEGETABLE OILS, FATS, AND GREASE INDUSTRY (oils & grease). Occupations concerned with the production of soap are included in the SOAP, CLEANING, AND TOILET PREPARATION INDUSTRY (soap & rel.). Occupations concerned with the preparation of glue are included in the CHEMICAL INDUSTRY (chemical).

Aitchbone Breaker	525.684-018
ANIMAL EVISCERATOR	525.687-010
Backer	525.684-046
bagger	525.587-010
Bagger, Meat	525.587-014
BAND-SAW OPERATOR	525.685-010
beamer	525.687-046
Beef Boner	525.684-010
Beef Grader	525.387-010
Beef-Pluck Trimmer	525.684-038
Beef Ribber	525.684-018
beef trimmer	521.687-106
Belly Opener	525.687-010
Belly Packer	525.687-026
Belly Trimmer	525.684-054
Bladder Trimmer	525.684-038
Blade Boner	525.684-010
BLEACHER, LARD	521.685-026
Bologna Lacer	529.687-034
BONER, MEAT	525.684-010
Bone Sawyer	525.684-018
BOX-TRUCK WASHER	529.687-018
Brain Picker	525.684-034
Breast Sawyer	525.684-018
Bruise Trimmer	525.687-010
Bulk-Sausage-Casing Tier-Off	529.687-034
Bulk-Sausage-Stuffing-Machine Operator	520.685-210
Bung Dropper	525.687-010
Bung Grader	525.684-038
Bung-Gut Tier	525.687-010
bung sewer	529.687-030
BUTCHER, ALL-ROUND	525.381-014
BUTCHER APPRENTICE	525.381-010
Butt Presser	520.685-182
Butt Trimmer	525.684-054
Calf Skinner	525.684-046
Calfskin Trimmer	525.687-046
Calf Sticker	525.684-050
Canadian-Bacon Tier	529.687-034
CARCASS SPLITTER	525.684-018
car ice-bunker filler	910.687-018
CAR ICER	910.687-018
CASING CLEANER	525.686-010
CASING GRADER	529.687-026
casing inspector	529.687-026
Casing-Machine Operator	525.686-010
Casing Packer	525.686-010
Casing Puller	525.684-038
casing runner	525.685-014
CASING-RUNNING-MACHINE TENDER	525.685-014
Casing Salter	525.687-026
CASING SEWER	529.687-030
Casing Soaker	525.686-010
casing sorter	529.687-026
CASING SPLITTER	525.687-014
casing tester	529.687-026
CASING TIER	529.687-034
Cattle Dropper And Pritcher	525.684-046
Cattle Header	525.684-046
Cattle Sticker	525.684-050
Caul-Fat Puller	525.687-010
Chicken Cleaner	525.687-074
Chicken Dresser	525.687-070
CHILLER TENDER	523.585-014
CHILLING-HOOD OPERATOR	523.685-018
Chiseler, Head	525.684-034
CHOPPING-MACHINE OPERATOR	520.685-066
Chuck Boner	525.684-010
Comber	525.587-014
CONVEYOR LOADER I	525.687-018
CONVEYOR LOADER II	525.686-014
COOK	526.685-010
COOK-BOX FILLER	523.685-030
COOK, DOG-AND-CAT FOOD	526.682-014
Cooker And Presser	529.685-202
Cooler-Conveyor Loader	525.686-014
COOLER ROOM WORKER	525.687-022
Cow Trimmer	525.687-046
Crackling-Press Operator	529.685-202
curing packer	522.687-034
CUTLET MAKER, PORK	529.686-022
DEHAIRING-MACHINE TENDER	525.685-018
Dropper, Dehairing Machine	525.685-018
DRY CURER	525.687-026
Fatback Trimmer	525.684-054
Feed-in Tender, Dehairing Machine	525.685-018
FINAL-DRESSING CUTTER	525.684-026
Final-Rail Cutter	525.684-026
Foot Cutter	525.687-074
frankfurter inspector	529.587-014
fresh-meat grader	529.687-106
GAMBRELER	525.687-030
GAMBRELER HELPER	525.687-034
Gizzard-Skin Remover	525.687-074
GRADER, DRESSED POULTRY	529.687-102
GRADER, GREEN MEAT	529.687-106
GRADER, MEAT	525.387-010
Grader, Sausage And Wiener	920.587-018
green-hide inspector	525.687-042

meat products

green-meat packer	522.687-034
Gut Puller	525.687-010
Gut Sorter	525.687-010
gutter	525.687-010
Halal Butcher	525.361-010
Ham Boner	525.684-010
Ham-Hock Mopper	525.687-026
Ham Molder	520.685-182
HAM-ROLLING-MACHINE OPERATOR	529.685-138
Ham Sawyer	525.684-018
Hand Molder, Meat	520.685-174
hanger	525.687-086
Hanger, Meat	525.587-014
hanger-off	525.687-030
HASHER OPERATOR	521.685-170
head-bone grinder	521.687-130
head boner	525.684-034
HEAD-MACHINE FEEDER	525.686-018
HEAD TRIMMER	525.684-034
hide grader	525.687-042
HIDE HANDLER	525.687-038
HIDE INSPECTOR	525.687-042
HIDE PULLER	525.685-022
Hide Salter	525.687-038
hide selector	525.687-038
Hide Shaker	525.687-038
Hide Spreader	525.687-038
HIDE TRIMMER	525.687-046
hide washer	582.685-134
Hog Grader	525.387-010
Hog-Head Singer	525.687-098
Hog Ribber	525.684-010
Hog Sawyer	525.684-018
Hog Sticker	525.684-050
Hog Stomach Preparer	529.687-034
icer, air conditioning	910.687-018
injection-machine operator	522.685-086
Islamic Butcher	525.361-010
Jawbone Breaker	525.684-034
Jowl Trimmer	525.684-034
Kosher Cutter And Searcher	525.361-010
LABORER	529.687-130
lard maker	521.685-026
LARD REFINER	529.685-158
lard trimmer	521.687-106
Lard-Tub Washer	599.684-010
Leaf-Fat Scraper	525.687-010
Leak Patcher	525.687-010
Leg Skinner	525.684-046
Lime-Vat Tender	582.685-126
LINKER	529.687-150
LINKING-MACHINE OPERATOR	529.685-162
Liver Trimmer	525.684-038
Loin Boner	525.684-010
Loin Trimmer	525.684-054
Lung Splitter	525.684-038
MEAT GRINDER	521.685-214
meat smoker	525.682-010
Melter Loader	921.685-030
mincing-machine operator	521.685-170
MOLDER, MEAT	520.685-174
neck pinner	525.687-050
NECK SKEWER	525.687-050
OFFAL ICER, POULTRY	525.687-054
OFFAL SEPARATOR	525.684-038
Oil-Expeller	529.685-202
ORDER RUNNER	525.587-058
Packager, Meat	920.587-018
Packer, Dried Beef	920.587-018
Packer, Sausage And Wiener	920.587-018
PAINTER, DEPILATORY	525.687-062
pelt inspector	525.687-042
pelt salter	525.687-038
PICKLE PUMPER	522.685-086
PICKLER	522.687-034
pickle-water-pump operator	522.685-086
Pickling-Drum Operator	582.685-126
pickling grader	529.687-106
PICKLING SOLUTION MAKER	522.485-010
piece-meat trimmer	521.687-106
piece trimmer	521.687-106
Pigskin Trimmer	525.687-046
Plate Boner	525.684-010
POULTRY BONER	525.687-066
POULTRY DRESSER	525.687-070

POULTRY-DRESSING WORKER	525.687-082
POULTRY EVISCERATOR	525.687-074
POULTRY HANGER	525.687-078
POULTRY KILLER	525.684-042
Poultry Picker	525.687-070
POULTRY-PICKING MACHINE TENDER	525.685-026
Poultry Scalder	525.687-070
Press Operator	529.685-202
PRESS OPERATOR, MEAT	520.685-182
Pull-Through Hooker	525.685-018
PULVERIZER	521.685-266
Pumper, Hand	522.685-086
Rabbit Dresser	525.687-010
refrigerator-car icer	910.687-018
RENDERING-EQUIPMENT TENDER	529.685-202
Resin Worker	525.687-094
Retaining-Room Cutter	525.684-026
retrimmer	521.687-106
ribber	525.684-010
Rib Boner	525.684-010
roast tier	525.687-118
Rolled-Ham Lacer	529.687-034
roper	529.687-150
Round Boner	525.684-010
Rump Sawyer	525.684-018
Salt-Bellies Overhauler	525.687-026
salter	525.687-026
salt spreader	525.687-038
SAUSAGE INSPECTOR	529.587-014
sausage linker	529.687-150
SAUSAGE MAKER	520.685-202
SAUSAGE-MEAT TRIMMER	521.687-106
SAUSAGE MIXER	520.685-206
sausage stuffer	520.685-210
Scalder	525.685-018
SCALER-PACKER	929.687-046
Scaler, Sliced Bacon	920.587-018
Scraper, Meat	525.587-014
SEASONING MIXER	520.687-054
selector	525.687-046
SHACKLER	525.687-086
Shactor	525.361-010
SHACTOR HELPER	525.687-090
Shank Boner	525.684-010
SHAVER	525.687-094
Sheep Boner	525.684-010
Sheep Or Calf Grader	525.387-010
SHEEPSKIN PICKLER	582.685-126
Sheep Sticker	525.684-050
shirring tender	525.685-014
Shochet	525.361-010
Shoulder Boner	525.684-010
Shoulder Puncher	525.684-046
Shoulder Sawyer	525.684-018
SHROUDER	525.587-010
Side Splitter	525.684-018
SINGER	525.687-098
skin bundler	525.687-102
SKIN GRADER	525.687-102
SKIN LIFTER, BACON	521.687-126
SKINNER	525.684-046
SKINNING-MACHINE FEEDER	525.686-022
SKIN-PEELING-MACHINE OPERATOR	525.685-030
SKULL GRINDER	521.687-130
slat grader	589.387-018
slat pickler	582.685-126
slaughter-and-butcher apprentice	525.381-010
SLAUGHTERER, RELIGIOUS RITUAL	525.361-010
SLICING-MACHINE OPERATOR	521.685-306
SLUNK-SKIN CURER	525.687-106
Slunk Skinner	525.684-046
Small-Stock Facer	525.684-046
SMOKED MEAT PREPARER	525.587-014
smokehouse attendant	525.682-010
SMOKER	525.682-010
Snout Puller	525.684-034
SOAKER, HIDES	582.685-134
Soaker, Meat	525.587-014
Spareribs Trimmer	525.684-054
spice mixer	520.687-054
Splitter, Head	525.684-034
STEAK TENDERIZER, MACHINE	529.686-082
STEAMER	525.687-110
sticker	525.684-042
STICKER, ANIMAL	525.684-050

stuffed-casing tier 529.687-034
STUFFER 520.685-210
STUNNER, ANIMAL 525.687-114
SUPERVISOR, ABATTOIR 525.131-010
SUPERVISOR, CURED-MEAT PACKING 529.135-014
SUPERVISOR, CURED MEATS 525.132-010
SUPERVISOR, CUTTING AND BONING 525.131-014
SUPERVISOR, POULTRY PROCESSING 525.134-014
SUPERVISOR, SPECIALTY FOOD PRODUCTS 529.137-062
SUPERVISOR, TANK HOUSE 525.132-014
Tallow Pumper 529.685-202
Tankage-Grinder Operator 529.685-202
Tank Charger 529.685-202
TARE WEIGHER 221.587-034
TEMPERATURE INSPECTOR 529.687-202
Temple-Meat Cutter 525.684-034
templer, head 525.684-034
TIER 525.687-118
Tier, Meat 525.587-014
tipper 525.687-070
Toe Puller 525.687-094
Tongue Cutter 525.684-034
Tree Loader, Meat 525.587-014
TRIMMER, MEAT 525.684-054
TRIPE COOKER 526.685-062
TROLLEY CLEANER 529.687-206
turbinated-bone grinder 521.687-130
Turkey Cleaner 525.687-074
Turkey Dresser 525.687-070
TURKEY-ROLL MAKER 525.684-058
vat overhauler 522.687-034
vat packer 522.687-034
vein pumper 522.685-086
Viscera Washer 525.684-038
VOTATOR-MACHINE OPERATOR 529.685-250
WASHER, CARCASS 525.687-122
Washer, Meat 525.587-014
Weasand Rodder 525.687-010
WOOL-AND-PELT GRADER 589.387-018
WOOL PULLER 589.687-050

medical ser.—MEDICAL SERVICES: This designation includes professional occupations concerned with treating and caring for sick and injured persons and animals, wherever such jobs exist. Also included are nonprofessional occupations occurring typically in establishments operated primarily for the care of the sick and injured, such as hospitals, sanitariums, and clinics, or establishments that provide related health services, such as medical laboratories. Occupations of a public health nature, which are generally performed by governmental officials, are included under GOVERNMENT SERVICES (government ser.). Occupations concerned with fabrication of dentures and related dental appliances are included under PERSONAL PROTECTIVE AND MEDICAL DEVICES AND SUPPLIES INDUSTRY (protective dev.).

ACUPRESSURIST 079.271-014
ACUPUNCTURIST 079.271-010
ADMINISTRATOR, HEALTH CARE FACILITY 187.117-010
admissions clerk 205.362-018
ADMITTING OFFICER 205.162-010
allergist 070.101-102
ALLERGIST-IMMUNOLOGIST 070.101-102
allergy specialist 070.101-102
AMBULANCE ATTENDANT 355.374-010
AMBULANCE DRIVER 913.683-010
ANESTHESIOLOGIST 070.101-010
Anesthesiologist Assistant 079.364-018
angiographer 078.362-046
animal health technician 079.361-014
ANIMAL-HOSPITAL CLERK 245.367-010
animal technician 079.361-014
ART THERAPIST 076.127-010
assistant therapy aide 355.377-014
asylum attendant 355.377-014
AUDIOLOGIST 076.101-010
autoclave operator 599.585-010
BIOCHEMISTRY TECHNOLOGIST 078.261-010
BIRTH ATTENDANT 354.377-010
blood-bank-booking clerk 245.367-018
BLOOD-DONOR RECRUITER 293.357-010
BLOOD-DONOR-UNIT ASSISTANT 245.367-014
CALENDAR-CONTROL CLERK, BLOOD BANK 245.367-018
CARDIAC MONITOR TECHNICIAN 078.367-010
CARDIOLOGIST 070.101-014
CARDIOPULMONARY TECHNOLOGIST 078.362-030
CARDIOPULMONARY TECHNOLOGIST, CHIEF 078.161-014
cardiovascular technologist 078.362-030
central-service technician 381.687-010
CENTRAL-SUPPLY WORKER 381.687-010
CENTRIFUGE OPERATOR, PLASMA PROCESSING 599.685-018
CEPHALOMETRIC ANALYST 078.384-010
cephalometric technician 078.384-010
cephalometric tracer 078.384-010
CERTIFIED MEDICATION TECHNICIAN 355.374-014
charge attendant 355.377-014
Charting Clerk 245.362-010
chemical dependency attendant 355.377-014
Chief Electroencephalographic Technologist 078.362-022
chief, nuclear medicine technologist 078.131-010
CHIEF OF NUCLEAR MEDICINE 070.117-010
Chief Ophthalmic Technician 078.361-038
Chief Polysomnographic Technician 078.362-042
chief, radiology 078.162-010
CHIEF TECHNOLOGIST, NUCLEAR MEDICINE 078.131-010
chiropodist 079.101-022
chiropractic 079.101-010
CHIROPRACTOR 079.101-010
CHIROPRACTOR ASSISTANT 079.364-010
CLEANER, HOSPITAL 323.687-010
Clinical Pathologist 070.061-010
Clinical Transplant Coordinator 079.151-010
clinical veterinarian 073.061-030
clinic clerk 205.362-018
COMMUNICATIONS COORDINATOR 239.167-010
company doctor 070.101-078
coordinator, auxiliary personnel 079.127-010
COORDINATOR OF REHABILITATION SERVICES 076.117-010
CORRECTIVE THERAPIST 076.361-010
COUNSELOR, NURSES' ASSOCIATION 045.107-014
counselor, orientation and mobility 076.224-014
CREDIT CLERK, BLOOD BANK 245.367-022
ct technologist 078.362-054
Custodian, Blood Bank 222.387-058
CYTOGENETIC TECHNOLOGIST 078.261-026
CYTOTECHNOLOGIST 078.281-010
DANCE THERAPIST 076.127-018
dean, school of nursing 075.117-030
DENTAL ASSISTANT 079.361-018
DENTAL HYGIENIST 078.361-010
dental surgeon 072.101-010
DENTIST 072.101-010
DERMATOLOGIST 070.101-018
diagnostic cardiac sonographer 078.364-014
diagnostic medical sonographer 078.364-010
DIALYSIS TECHNICIAN 078.362-014
dietary aide 319.677-014
DIET CLERK 245.587-010
Director, Bio-Communications Laboratory 076.104-010
DIRECTOR, COMMUNITY-HEALTH NURSING 075.117-014
DIRECTOR, DENTAL SERVICES 072.117-010
DIRECTOR, DIAGNOSTIC-AND-EVALUATION CLINIC 070.107-018
DIRECTOR, EDUCATIONAL, COMMUNITY-HEALTH NURSING 075.117-018
director, educational, public-health nursing 075.117-018
director, industrial nursing 075.117-026
Director, Medical Records 079.167-014
DIRECTOR, NURSES' REGISTRY 187.167-034
DIRECTOR, NURSING SERVICE 075.117-022
DIRECTOR, OCCUPATIONAL HEALTH NURSING 075.117-026
Director, Occupational Therapy 076.121-010
director of rehabilitative services 076.117-010
DIRECTOR, OUTPATIENT SERVICES 187.117-058
DIRECTOR, PHARMACY SERVICES 074.167-010
Director, Physical Therapy 076.121-014
director, public-health nursing 075.117-014
DIRECTOR, SCHOOL OF NURSING 075.117-030
DIRECTOR, SPEECH-AND-HEARING 079.131-010
Dispensary Clerk 203.362-010
doctor, chiropractic 079.101-010
DOCTOR, NATUROPATHIC 079.101-014
doctor, osteopathic 071.101-010
dosimetrist 078.261-034
druggist 074.161-010
ecg technician 078.362-018
ECHOCARDIOGRAPH TECHNICIAN 078.364-014
educational/development assistant 076.364-010
eeg technologist 078.362-022
ekg technician 078.362-018
ELECTROCARDIOGRAPH TECHNICIAN 078.362-018
ELECTROENCEPHALOGRAPHIC TECHNOLOGIST 078.362-022
ELECTROMYOGRAPHIC TECHNICIAN 078.362-038

medical ser.

EMERGENCY MEDICAL SERVICES COORDINATOR	079.117-010
EMERGENCY MEDICAL TECHNICIAN	079.374-010
emg technician	078.362-038
emt-paramedic	079.364-026
ENDODONTIST	072.101-014
escort, patients	355.677-014
EXECUTIVE DIRECTOR, NURSES' ASSOCIATION	075.117-034
executive secretary, nurses' association	075.117-034
EXERCISE PHYSIOLOGIST	076.121-018
eye specialist	070.101-058
family physician	070.101-026
FAMILY PRACTITIONER	070.101-026
flight physiologist	070.101-030
FLIGHT SURGEON	070.101-030
floor housekeeper	321.137-010
FOOD-SERVICE WORKER, HOSPITAL	319.677-014
foot specialist	079.101-022
Forensic Pathologist	070.061-010
GENERAL PRACTITIONER	070.101-022
Geriatric Nurse Assistant	355.674-014
GYNECOLOGIST	070.101-034
HEALER	term
HEALTH-EQUIPMENT SERVICER	359.363-010
health unit clerk	245.362-014
heart specialist	070.101-014
hemodialysis technician	078.362-014
hemotherapist	078.261-042
histologic technologist	078.261-030
histologist	041.061-054
HISTOPATHOLOGIST	041.061-054
HISTOTECHNOLOGIST	078.261-030
HOLTER SCANNING TECHNICIAN	078.264-010
holter technician	078.264-010
Home Health Aide	355.674-014
Home Health Nurse, Licensed Practical	079.374-014
HORTICULTURAL THERAPIST	076.124-018
Hospital Administrator	187.117-010
HOSPITAL-ADMITTING CLERK	205.362-018
Hospital Collection Clerk	241.357-010
hospital-insurance clerk	214.362-022
hospital-receiving clerk	205.362-018
HOUSEKEEPER	321.137-010
housekeeper, hospital	323.687-010
IMMUNOHEMATOLOGIST	078.221-010
INDUSTRIAL THERAPIST	076.167-010
INSERVICE COORDINATOR, AUXILIARY PERSONNEL	079.127-010
instructor of blind	076.224-014
INSURANCE CLERK	214.362-022
internal medicine specialist	070.101-042
INTERNIST	070.101-042
laboratory assistant	078.381-014
laboratory assistant	599.687-026
LABORATORY ASSISTANT, BLOOD AND PLASMA	078.687-010
Laryngologist	070.101-062
linen checker	222.387-030
linen clerk	222.387-030
linen-exchange attendant	222.387-030
LINEN-ROOM ATTENDANT	222.387-030
linen-room houseperson	222.387-030
magnetic resonance imaging technologist	078.362-058
Manager, Tumor Registry	079.362-018
MANUAL-ARTS THERAPIST	076.124-010
MEDICAL ASSISTANT	079.362-010
medical clerk	205.362-018
medical laboratory manager	078.161-010
MEDICAL-LABORATORY TECHNICIAN	078.381-014
medical pathologist	070.061-010
Medical Photographer	143.362-010
Medical Physiologist	041.061-078
MEDICAL RADIATION DOSIMETRIST	078.261-034
MEDICAL-RECORD ADMINISTRATOR	079.167-014
MEDICAL-RECORD CLERK	245.362-010
Medical-Records Auditor	210.382-010
MEDICAL RECORD TECHNICIAN	079.362-014
MEDICAL SECRETARY	201.362-014
medical technician	078.381-014
MEDICAL TECHNOLOGIST	078.261-038
medical technologist, bacteriology	078.261-014
medical technologist, chemistry	078.261-010
MEDICAL TECHNOLOGIST, CHIEF	078.161-010
MEDICAL TECHNOLOGIST, TEACHING SUPERVISOR	078.121-010
MENTAL-RETARDATION AIDE	355.377-018
MICROBIOLOGY TECHNOLOGIST	078.261-014
MORGUE ATTENDANT	355.667-010
MUSIC THERAPIST	076.127-014
naturopathic physician	079.101-014
nerve specialist	070.101-050
NEUROLOGIST	070.101-050
Neuropathologist	070.061-010
Neurosurgeon	070.101-094
NUCLEAR MEDICAL TECHNOLOGIST	078.361-018
nurse see NURSE, PROFESSIONAL	
nurse aide	355.674-014
NURSE ANESTHETIST	075.371-010
NURSE ASSISTANT	355.674-014
nurse, certified see NURSE, PROFESSIONAL	
Nurse, College	075.124-010
NURSE, CONSULTANT	075.127-014
NURSE, GENERAL DUTY	075.364-010
NURSE, HEAD	075.137-014
NURSE, INFECTION CONTROL	075.127-034
NURSE, INSTRUCTOR	075.124-018
nurse, licensed see NURSE, PROFESSIONAL	
NURSE, LICENSED PRACTICAL	079.374-014
NURSE-MIDWIFE	075.264-014
NURSE, OFFICE	075.374-014
NURSE, PRACTICAL	354.374-010
NURSE PRACTITIONER	075.264-010
NURSE, PRIVATE DUTY	075.374-018
NURSE, PROFESSIONAL	term
nurse, registered see NURSE, PROFESSIONAL	
NURSE, SCHOOL	075.124-010
nurse, special	075.374-018
nurse, staff	075.364-010
NURSE, STAFF, COMMUNITY HEALTH	075.124-014
nurse, staff, industrial	075.374-022
NURSE, STAFF, OCCUPATIONAL HEALTH NURSING	075.374-022
NURSE, SUPERVISOR	075.167-010
NURSE, SUPERVISOR, COMMUNITY-HEALTH NURSING	075.127-026
NURSE, SUPERVISOR, EVENING-OR-NIGHT	075.127-030
nurse supervisor, industrial nursing	075.137-010
NURSE, SUPERVISOR, OCCUPATIONAL HEALTH NURSING	075.137-010
Nursing Home Administrator	187.117-010
OBSTETRICIAN	070.101-054
OCCUPATIONAL THERAPIST	076.121-010
OCCUPATIONAL THERAPY AIDE	355.377-010
OCCUPATIONAL THERAPY ASSISTANT	076.364-010
oculist	070.101-058
operating-room technician	079.374-022
OPHTHALMIC PHOTOGRAPHER	143.362-014
OPHTHALMIC TECHNICIAN	078.361-038
OPHTHALMOLOGIST	070.101-058
OPTOMETRIST	079.101-018
ORAL AND MAXILLOFACIAL SURGEON	072.101-018
ORAL PATHOLOGIST	072.061-010
oral surgeon	072.101-018
ORDER-CONTROL CLERK, BLOOD BANK	245.367-026
ORDERLY	355.674-018
organ transplant coordinator	079.151-010
ORIENTATION AND MOBILITY THERAPIST FOR THE BLIND	076.224-014
orientation therapist for blind	076.224-014
orientor	076.224-014
ORTHODONTIST	072.101-022
ORTHOPEDIC ASSISTANT	078.664-010
orthopedic cast specialist	078.664-010
Orthopedic Surgeon	070.101-094
ORTHOPTIST	079.371-014
ORTHOTICS ASSISTANT	078.361-022
Orthotics-Prosthetics Assistant	078.361-022
ORTHOTIST	078.261-018
Orthotist-Prosthetist	078.261-018
osteopath	071.101-010
OSTEOPATHIC PHYSICIAN	071.101-010
OTOLARYNGOLOGIST	070.101-062
Otologist	070.101-062
otorhinolaryngologist	070.101-062
OUTPATIENT-ADMITTING CLERK	205.362-030
Outpatient Receptionist	237.367-038
PARAMEDIC	079.364-026
PATHOLOGIST	070.061-010
patient-insurance clerk	214.362-022
PEDIATRIC DENTIST	072.101-026
PEDIATRICIAN	070.101-066
Pediatric Nurse Practitioner	075.264-010
perodontist	072.101-026
PERFUSIONIST	078.362-034
PERIODONTIST	072.101-030

PHARMACIST	074.161-010
Pharmacist, Hospital	074.161-010
pharmacy clerk	074.382-010
PHARMACY TECHNICIAN	074.382-010
PHERESIS SPECIALIST	078.261-042
PHLEBOTOMIST	079.364-022
PHYSIATRIST	070.101-070
PHYSICAL-INTEGRATION PRACTITIONER	076.264-010
physical medicine specialist	070.101-070
PHYSICAL THERAPIST	076.121-014
PHYSICAL THERAPIST ASSISTANT	076.224-010
PHYSICAL THERAPY AIDE	355.354-010
Physical Therapy Aide, Hydrotherapy	355.354-010
Physical Therapy Aide, Transport	355.354-010
physical therapy assistant	076.224-010
physical therapy technician	076.224-010
PHYSICIAN ASSISTANT	079.364-018
physician, general practice	070.101-022
PHYSICIAN, HEAD	070.101-074
physician, industrial	070.101-070
PHYSICIAN, OCCUPATIONAL	070.101-078
PHYSICIAN, RESEARCH	term
physiotherapist	076.121-014
pinner	712.687-014
Plastic Surgeon	070.101-094
PODIATRIC ASSISTANT	079.374-018
Podiatric Surgeon	079.101-022
PODIATRIST	079.101-022
Podiatrist, Orthopedic	079.101-022
Podopediatrician	079.101-022
POLYSOMNOGRAPHIC TECHNICIAN	078.362-042
polysomnographic technologist	078.362-042
pooling operator	599.687-026
primary care nurse practitioner	075.264-010
PROCTOLOGIST	070.101-086
Procurement Transplant Coordinator	079.151-010
prosthetic dentist	072.101-034
PROSTHETICS ASSISTANT	078.361-026
PROSTHETIST	078.261-022
PROSTHODONTIST	072.101-034
PSYCHIATRIC AIDE	355.377-014
psychiatric attendant	355.377-014
PSYCHIATRIC TECHNICIAN	079.374-026
PSYCHIATRIST	070.107-014
PUBLIC-HEALTH DENTIST	072.101-038
public-health nurse	075.124-014
PULMONARY-FUNCTION TECHNICIAN	078.262-010
pulmonary-function technologist	078.262-010
QUALITY ASSURANCE COORDINATOR	075.167-014
RADIATION-THERAPY TECHNOLOGIST	078.361-034
radiographer	078.362-026
radiographer, angiogram	078.362-046
radiographer, cardiac catheterization	078.362-050
RADIOLOGICAL-EQUIPMENT SPECIALIST	719.261-014
radiologic electronic specialist	719.261-014
RADIOLOGIC TECHNOLOGIST	078.362-026
RADIOLOGIC TECHNOLOGIST, CHIEF	078.162-010
Radiologic Technologist, Mammogram	078.362-026
RADIOLOGIST	070.101-090
RADIOLOGY ADMINISTRATOR	187.117-062
RADIOPHARMACIST	074.161-014
Receptionist, Doctor's Office	237.367-038
RECREATIONAL THERAPIST	076.124-014
registrar, nurses' registry	187.167-034
resident care aide	355.377-018
RESPIRATORY THERAPIST	076.361-014
RESPIRATORY-THERAPY AIDE	355.674-022
Rhinologist	070.101-062
SAFETY MANAGER	168.167-086
Ship's Doctor	070.101-022
SIPHON OPERATOR	599.687-026
skin specialist	070.101-018
SPECIAL PROCEDURES TECHNOLOGIST, ANGIOGRAM	078.362-046
SPECIAL PROCEDURES TECHNOLOGIST, CARDIAC CATHETERIZATION	078.362-050
SPECIAL PROCEDURES TECHNOLOGIST, CT SCAN	078.362-054
SPECIAL PROCEDURES TECHNOLOGIST, MAGNETIC RESONANCE IMAGING (MRI)	078.362-058
special vascular imaging technologist	078.362-050
STERILIZER	599.585-010
stress technician	078.362-062
STRESS TEST TECHNICIAN	078.362-062
SUPERVISOR, BLOOD-DONOR RECRUITERS	293.137-010
SUPERVISOR, CENTRAL SUPPLY	381.137-014

Supervisor, Cytogenetic Laboratory	078.261-026
Supervisor, Cytology	078.281-010
Supervisor, Histology	078.261-030
Supervisor, Microbiology Technologists	078.261-014
supervisor, public-health nursing	075.127-026
SURGEON	070.101-094
Surgeon Assistant	079.364-018
surgical orderly	079.374-022
Surgical Pathologist	070.061-010
SURGICAL TECHNICIAN	079.374-022
technologist, biochemistry	078.261-010
telemetry technician	078.367-010
therapeutic recreation worker	076.124-014
therapist for blind	076.224-014
tissue technologist	078.261-030
tracer	078.384-010
TRANSPLANT COORDINATOR	079.151-010
TRANSPORTER, PATIENTS	355.677-014
trauma coordinator	079.117-010
Tray-Line Supervisor	319.137-010
tray worker	319.677-014
TUMOR REGISTRAR	079.362-018
ULTRASOUND TECHNOLOGIST	078.364-010
uniform attendant	222.387-030
UNIT CLERK	245.362-014
UROLOGIST	070.101-098
UTILIZATION-REVIEW COORDINATOR	079.267-010
VETERINARIAN, LABORATORY ANIMAL CARE	073.061-010
VETERINARIAN	073.101-010
veterinary assistant	079.361-014
Veterinary-Hospital Attendant	410.674-010
VETERINARY PATHOLOGIST	073.061-030
Veterinary Radiologist	073.101-010
VETERINARY TECHNICIAN	079.361-014
ward attendant	355.377-014
ward clerk	245.362-014
Ward Supervisor	355.377-014
X-Ray-Developing-Machine Operator	976.685-014
x-ray technologist	078.362-026
ZOO VETERINARIAN	073.101-018

metal prod., nec—FABRICATED METAL PRODUCTS, NOT ELSEWHERE CLASSIFIED: This designation includes occupations concerned with manufacturing and repairing metal novelties and specialties, and other metal products not elsewhere classified. Typical products include leaf, hot, wound, coiled, flat, and wire springs; fabricated wire products, such as fencing, screening, and paper clips; metal foil and leaf; and safes and safe deposit boxes.

art-metal worker	619.260-014
art-metal-worker apprentice	619.260-010
art-metal-worker helper	619.484-010
asphalt-machine operator	590.362-014
ASSEMBLER, WIRE-MESH GATE	801.384-010
Automatic-Coil-Winding-Machine Operator	616.485-010
BALE-TIE-MACHINE OPERATOR	616.682-014
BARBED-WIRE-MACHINE OPERATOR	616.382-010
BENCH WORKER	616.485-010
BIRD-CAGE ASSEMBLER	709.684-026
bobbin winder	691.685-026
Bolt-Up Worker	706.684-090
BRIMER	700.687-018
Bushing-And-Broach Operator	706.684-090
cable-machine operator	616.682-034
cabling-machine operator	616.682-034
Catcher	706.684-090
CLIP-BOLTER AND WRAPPER	709.684-038
Clip Riveter	706.684-090
clip wrapper	709.684-038
Closer	616.682-034
Closing Supervisor	691.130-014
coiler	619.482-010
coil-machine operator	616.485-014
CUTCH CLEANER	700.687-030
Double-End-Production Grinder	616.485-010
Double-Spindle-Disk Grinder Tender	603.685-062
Ecclesiastical-Art-Metal Worker	619.260-014
Experimental Fabricator-And-Installer	709.381-046
FENCE-MAKING MACHINE OPERATOR	616.582-010
finished-wire inspector	691.367-010
finish roller	613.682-022
fitter, hand	709.381-042
Flexible-Shaft Winder	619.482-010
GOLDBEATER	700.381-018
GOLD CUTTER	700.684-038

mfd. bldgs.

mfd. bldgs.—MANUFACTURED BUILDINGS INDUSTRY: This designation includes occupations concerned with fabricating, assembling, and erecting manufactured buildings, such as mobile, modular, and prefabricated homes, sections, and panels in the plant and on the construction site. Occupations normally performed under general contractors or subcontractors in the on-site construction of manufactured as well as other types of buildings are included in the CONSTRUCTION INDUSTRY (construction).

Side-Panel Hanger 809.684-030
SIDER 863.684-014
SIDER 860.684-014
siding applicator 863.684-014
Subassembly Supervisor 869.131-030
SUPERVISOR, COMPONENT ASSEMBLER 762.134-010
supervisor, loading 921.137-014
SUPERVISOR, MANUFACTURED BUILDINGS 869.131-030
SUPERVISOR, METAL HANGING 809.134-014
TAPER 842.664-010
taper and bedder 842.664-010
taper and floater 842.664-010
Tile Installer 869.684-026
TILE SETTER 861.684-018
Trim-Crew Supervisor 869.131-018
TRIMMER 869.684-066
UTILITY WORKER 869.684-074
WHEEL ASSEMBLER 809.684-038
Wheel Installer 869.684-010
Window Installer 809.684-030

military ser.—MILITARY SERVICES: This designation includes occupations in the uniformed military services that are unique to military requirements and for which there are no identifiable counterparts covered by other industry designations. Specific occupations found in the military services that have identifiable civilian job counterparts are classified according to the industrial designations of the appropriate civilian equivalent.

AEROSPACE PHYSIOLOGICAL TECHNICIAN 199.682-010
AIRBORNE SENSOR SPECIALIST 378.382-010
AIRCRAFT LAUNCH AND RECOVERY TECHNICIAN 912.682-010
AMPHIBIAN CREWMEMBER 378.683-010
ANTITANK ASSAULT GUNNER 378.464-010
ARMOR RECONNAISSANCE SPECIALIST 378.363-010
ARTILLERY OR NAVAL GUNFIRE OBSERVER 378.367-010
AVIATION SUPPORT EQUIPMENT REPAIRER 639.281-010
CAMOUFLAGE SPECIALIST 378.684-010
career counselor 166.267-026
COMBAT RIFLE CREWMEMBER 378.684-014
COMBAT SURVEILLANCE AND TARGET
   ACQUISITION CREWMEMBER 378.687-010
COMBAT SURVEILLANCE AND TARGET
   ACQUISITION NONCOMMISSIONED OFFICER 378.161-010
COMMAND AND CONTROL SPECIALIST 235.662-010
COUNTERINTELLIGENCE AGENT 378.267-010
DEEP SUBMERGENCE VEHICLE CREWMEMBER 623.281-014
DEEP SUBMERGENCE VEHICLE OPERATOR 911.263-010
DEFENSIVE FIRE CONTROL SYSTEMS OPERATOR 378.382-014
DISASTER OR DAMAGE CONTROL SPECIALIST 378.267-014
drill sergeant 378.227-014
ELECTRONIC INTELLIGENCE OPERATIONS
   SPECIALIST 193.382-010
FIELD ARTILLERY CREWMEMBER 378.684-018
FIELD ARTILLERY OPERATIONS SPECIALIST 378.367-014
FIELD ARTILLERY SENIOR SERGEANT 378.132-010
FLASH RANGING CREWMEMBER 378.367-018
FLIGHT OPERATIONS SPECIALIST 248.387-010
GRAVES REGISTRATION SPECIALIST 355.687-014
INFANTRY INDIRECT FIRE CREWMEMBER 378.684-022
INFANTRY OPERATIONS SPECIALIST 378.367-022
INFANTRY UNIT LEADER 378.137-010
INFANTRY WEAPONS CREWMEMBER 378.684-026
IN-FLIGHT REFUELING OPERATOR 912.662-010
IN-FLIGHT REFUELING SYSTEM REPAIRER 829.281-018
INTELLIGENCE CLERK 249.387-014
INTELLIGENCE SPECIALIST 059.267-014
LIGHT AIR DEFENSE ARTILLERY CREWMEMBER 378.684-030
MAINTENANCE DATA ANALYST 221.367-038
MARKSMANSHIP INSTRUCTOR 378.227-010
MEDICAL-SERVICE TECHNICIAN 079.367-018
MISSILE FACILITIES REPAIRER 828.281-018
OCEANOGRAPHER, ASSISTANT 025.267-010
OPERATIONS AND INTELLIGENCE ASSISTANT 378.367-026
PHARMACIST ASSISTANT 074.381-010
POWERED BRIDGE SPECIALIST 378.683-014
RECONNAISSANCE CREWMEMBER 378.367-030
RECRUITER 166.267-026
RECRUIT INSTRUCTOR 378.227-014
REDEYE GUNNER 378.682-010
RUBBER AND PLASTICS WORKER 891.684-014
SENIOR ENLISTED ADVISOR 166.167-042
SMOKE AND FLAME SPECIALIST 378.682-014
SOUND RANGING CREWMEMBER 378.362-010
SURVIVAL SPECIALIST 378.227-018

TANK AND AMPHIBIAN TRACTOR OPERATIONS
   CHIEF 620.137-010
TANK CREWMEMBER 378.683-018
TARGET AIRCRAFT TECHNICIAN 378.281-010
UNATTENDED-GROUND-SENSOR SPECIALIST 378.382-018
VULCAN CREWMEMBER 378.663-010

millwork-plywood—MILLWORK, VENEER, PLYWOOD, AND STRUCTURAL WOOD MEMBERS INDUSTRY: This designation includes occupations concerned with slicing and peeling wood blocks and logs to form veneer sheets, gluing sheets to form plywood or other products, and laminating and fabricating trusses, arches, and other structural members. Occupations concerned with manufacturing nonlaminated roof trusses are included in the MANUFACTURED BUILDINGS INDUSTRY (mfd. bldgs.).

BACK FEEDER, PLYWOOD LAYUP LINE 569.686-010
BARKER OPERATOR 663.682-010
BREAK-OFF WORKER 663.686-014
CHAIN SAW OPERATOR 454.687-010
chute feeder 921.686-022
CLAMP REMOVER 569.687-010
CLIPPER, AUTOMATIC 663.585-010
clipper offbearer 663.686-018
cold-press operator 569.685-058
CORE-COMPOSER FEEDER 669.685-038
CORE-COMPOSER-MACHINE TENDER 569.685-022
core feeder 569.685-042
CORE FEEDER, PLYWOOD LAYUP LINE 569.685-018
core layer, plywood 762.684-026
CORE LAYER, PLYWOOD LAYUP LINE 569.686-014
CORE-LAYING-MACHINE OPERATOR 569.685-026
CREW LEADER, GLUING 569.565-010
CROSSBAND LAYER 762.685-026
defect cutter 663.585-010
drop clipper 663.685-050
dry-clipper tender 663.685-050
EDGE BANDER, MACHINE 762.685-010
EDGE-BANDING-MACHINE OFFBEARER 762.686-010
EDGE-GLUE-MACHINE TENDER 569.685-034
Edge Gluer 569.685-062
edge plugger 769.685-010
face layer 762.687-066
Flitch Hanger 663.686-022
glue spreader helper 762.687-026
glue-spreader operator 569.685-042
GLUE SPREADER, VENEER 569.685-042
GREEN-CHAIN OFFBEARER 663.686-018
Hot-Plate Plywood-Press Feeder 569.686-026
Hot-Plate Plywood-Press Offbearer 569.686-026
HOT-PLATE-PLYWOOD-PRESS OPERATOR 569.685-054
hot-plate-press operator 569.685-054
HYDRAULIC-PRESS OPERATOR 569.685-058
jacker feeder 921.686-022
LABORER, HOT-PLATE PLYWOOD PRESS 569.686-026
LATHE SPOTTER 663.686-022
log-chain feeder 921.686-022
Log Hooker 921.667-022
LOG MARKER 454.687-018
LOG SCALER 455.487-010
Multiple-Cut-Off-Saw Operator 667.682-022
OPERATOR, PREFINISH 562.685-018
PANEL EDGE SEALER 769.685-010
platen-drier operator 563.685-026
Plywood Builder 762.687-026
Plywood Patcher 769.684-030
PLYWOOD-SCARFER TENDER 665.685-022
Plywood-Stock Grader 569.687-034
poler 921.686-022
POND WORKER 921.686-022
QUALITY CONTROL INSPECTOR 569.687-030
Raimann-Machine Operator 669.685-098
rotary-slicing-machine operator 664.662-010
rotary-veneer-machine operator 664.662-010
SAMPLE MAKER, VENEER 769.684-042
scarfer operator 665.685-022
SCARF GLUER 762.684-054
SHEET TURNER 762.687-062
SIDING STAPLER 762.684-058
sinker puller 921.686-022
Skoog-Machine Operator 669.685-098
slip feeder 921.686-022
splicer matcher 769.687-046
SPLICER OPERATOR 569.685-062
STACKER TENDER 921.685-062

mine & quarry

straight-slicing-machine operator	663.682-018
SUPERVISOR, DRYING	563.135-010
SUPERVISOR, GREEN END DEPARTMENT	663.132-010
SUPERVISOR, LOG SORTING	455.134-010
SUPERVISOR, VENEER	569.135-010
tape machine tailer	569.686-054
tenderizer tender	669.685-038
TIPPLE TENDER	669.685-090
VENEER CLIPPER	663.685-050
VENEER-CLIPPER HELPER	663.686-030
veneer cutter	663.685-050
VENEER DRIER	563.685-022
VENEER-DRIER FEEDER	563.686-014
veneer-drier tailer	563.685-022
veneer-glue-jointer feedback	665.686-018
veneer gluer	569.685-042
VENEER GRADER	569.687-034
veneer joiner	569.685-074
VENEER JOINTER	665.682-038
VENEER-JOINTER HELPER	665.686-018
VENEER-JOINTER OFFBEARER	665.686-022
veneer-jointer returner	665.686-018
VENEER-LATHE OPERATOR	664.662-010
VENEER MATCHER	769.687-046
veneer-press operator	569.685-054
VENEER REDRIER	563.685-026
VENEER REPAIRER, MACHINE	669.685-098
VENEER-SLICING-MACHINE OPERATOR	663.682-018
Veneer Sorter	921.685-054
veneer splicer	569.685-062
Veneer Stacker	569.687-010
VENEER-STOCK LAYER	762.687-066
VENEER TAPER	569.685-074
VENEER-TAPING-MACHINE OFFBEARER	569.686-054
veneer-taping-machine operator	569.685-074
veneer trimmer	663.685-
WOOD SCRAP HANDLER	564.686-010

mine & quarry—COAL, METAL, AND NONMETAL MINING AND QUARRYING INDUSTRY: This designation includes occupations concerned with extracting coal; metal and nonmetal ores; and rocks, stone, gravel, salt, and sand from underground and surface excavations, such as mines, pits, and quarries. It includes exploraion, prospecting, and development operations, as well as excavation operations such as: undercutting, drilling, and blasting; loading, hauling, and hoisting; and timbering, ventilating, draining, and reclaiming. Also included are the preparation of coal, which includes operations, such as crushing, cleaning, and sizing; the primary (mine-site type) crushing, reduction, and processing of metal and nonmetal ores, rocks, stones, and minerals; and the dressing of ferrous ores. Occupations concerned with the dressing of nonferrous metal ores are included in the SMELTING AND REFINING INDUSTRY (smelt. & refin.).

additive-plant operator	939.362-014
AERIAL-TRAM OPERATOR	932.685-010
Airdox Fitter	862.281-022
air-drill operator	930.684-018
air-hammer operator	930.684-018
AIR-TABLE OPERATOR	549.685-010
Auger Supervisor	939.137-018
BANK BOSS	932.132-010
battery charger	729.684-042
Battery Starter	932.687-010
BELT PICKER	939.687-010
bit grinder	603.685-030
BIT-SHARPENER OPERATOR	603.685-030
BLASTER	931.261-010
bolting-machine operator	930.683-026
BOTTOMER I	932.667-010
Bottomer II	939.667-010
braddisher	869.684-058
breaker boss	549.137-014
Breaker Repairer	630.281-022
bucker	579.484-010
BURNER TENDER	571.685-010
CAGER	939.667-010
calciner	573.382-010
CALCINER OPERATOR	513.362-010
CALCINER-OPERATOR HELPER	513.667-010
Car Cleaner	939.687-014
car distributor	932.167-010
CAR DROPPER	932.683-010
Car Inspector	622.381-030
Carpenter, Mine	860.281-010
car pincher	932.683-010

car runner	932.683-010
Car Salter	939.687-014
Car-Shakeout Operator	921.685-038
Chain-Hoist Operator	921.663-026
channeling-machine operator	930.383-010
CHANNELING-MACHINE RUNNER	930.383-010
check viewer	168.267-074
chute blaster	933.687-010
CHUTE LOADER	932.687-010
chute tapper	933.687-010
cleaner	939.687-014
coal-cutting-machine operator	930.683-014
coal-drier operator	543.682-014
coal inspector	579.687-014
Coal-Mine Inspector	168.267-074
COAL WASHER	541.382-010
coal-washer tender	541.382-010
Colliery Clerk	219.362-010
COMPANY LABORER	939.687-014
CONE OPERATOR	934.685-010
CONTINUOUS-MINING-MACHINE OPERATOR	930.683-010
CONTROLLER, COAL OR ORE	939.167-010
conveyor attendant	939.362-014
CRAYON GRADER	579.684-014
CRAYON SAWYER	677.685-022
crusher, dry-ground mica	579.685-010
crusher operator	939.362-014
CRUSHER SETTER	933.664-010
crusher, wet-ground mica	570.685-038
CUTTER OPERATOR	930.683-014
CUTTER-OPERATOR HELPER	930.687-018
cutting-machine operator	930.683-014
digger	939.687-014
dimension-quarry supervisor	939.137-014
Dinkey Operator, Mine	919.663-014
Dinkey Operator, Slate	919.663-014
director, safety	010.061-026
DISPATCHER	932.167-010
dragger	921.663-050
Dragline Oiler	850.684-018
DREDGE OPERATOR	850.663-010
DREDGE OPERATOR SUPERVISOR	939.132-010
dredge pumper	850.663-010
DRIER-AND-GRINDER TENDER	579.685-010
drier operator	573.382-010
DRIER OPERATOR	543.682-014
Drift Miner	939.281-010
DRILLER HELPER	930.666-010
DRILLER, MACHINE	930.382-010
driller operator	930.382-010
DRILLING-MACHINE OPERATOR	930.482-010
DRY-PLACER-MACHINE OPERATOR	939.382-010
Duck-Bill Operator	850.683-030
DUST-COLLECTOR ATTENDANT	511.685-022
DUST SAMPLER	939.585-010
dynamiter	931.261-010
Electric-Hoist Operator	921.663-026
Entry-Driver Operator	930.683-014
Entry Miner	939.281-010
Feed-Preparation Operator	511.685-050
firer	931.261-010
FLAME CHANNELER	930.684-010
Flume Maker	860.381-010
Foot Cager	939.667-010
foot tender	932.667-010
furnace operator	543.682-014
Gas Inspector	168.267-074
Gravity-Meter Observer	010.261-018
grinding-mill operator	939.362-014
GRINDING-MILL OPERATOR	515.382-010
GRIZZLY WORKER	933.687-010
HARDNESS TESTER	519.585-010
hardness tester	579.484-010
haulage boss	932.167-010
Head Cager	939.667-010
heavy-equipment operator	859.683-010
heavy-equipment-operator apprentice	859.683-014
HEAVY-MEDIA OPERATOR	541.685-010
HOIST OPERATOR	921.663-026
horizontal-drill operator	930.482-010
hydraulic-jack operator	910.663-010
inspector	779.687-026
JACKHAMMER OPERATOR	930.684-018
JACK SETTER	939.684-010
jet channeler	930.684-010

lander	939.667-010
LATRINE CLEANER	939.687-022
LEASE BUYER	191.117-030
leaser	191.117-030
LINER REPLACER	801.664-010
loader	932.687-010
Loader, machine	939.687-014
loader, machine	932.683-014
loader operator	932.683-018
LOADING-MACHINE OPERATOR	932.683-014
LOADING-MACHINE-OPERATOR HELPER	939.686-010
LOADING-SHOVEL OILER	932.667-014
LOAD-OUT SUPERVISOR	921.133-014
long-wall-mining-machine helper	930.666-014
LONG-WALL-MINING-MACHINE TENDER	930.665-010
LONG-WALL SHEAR OPERATOR	930.662-010
machine boss	939.137-018
MACHINE RUNNER	term
Magnetometer Operator	010.261-018
MAINTENANCE SUPERVISOR, MOBILE BATTERY EQUIPMENT	638.131-034
materials inspector	579.484-010
measurer	679.567-010
mechanic	630.281-022
MECHANICAL-SHOVEL OPERATOR	932.683-018
Metal-Mine Inspector	168.267-074
MICA INSPECTOR	779.687-026
MICA-LAMINATING-MACHINE FEEDER	579.686-018
MICA PATCHER	579.687-026
MICA-PLATE LAYER	579.685-026
MICA-PLATE LAYER, HAND	579.684-022
MICA SIZER	779.687-030
MICA SPLITTER	779.681-010
MICA-WASHER GLUER	729.687-022
mill attendant	939.362-014
MILLER	570.685-038
mine captain	939.137-018
MINE-CAR REPAIRER	622.381-030
Mine Electrician	824.261-010
MINE INSPECTOR	168.267-074
Mine-Machinery Mechanic	620.261-022
MINER I	939.281-010
MINER II	term
Miner, Pick	939.281-010
MINER, PLACER	939.684-014
MINE SUPERINTENDENT	181.117-014
MINING ENGINEER	010.061-014
mining-machine operator see MACHINE RUNNER	
MONITOR CAR OPERATOR	939.682-010
motor boss	932.167-010
muck boss	939.137-018
Mucker	939.687-014
mucking-machine operator	932.683-018
Nozzle Worker	939.684-014
oiler	850.684-018
OPERATING ENGINEER	859.683-010
OPERATING-ENGINEER APPRENTICE	859.683-014
ore grader	939.167-010
ore sampler	579.484-010
PANELBOARD OPERATOR	939.362-014
passing boss	932.167-010
PIPE CHANGER	891.564-010
pit car repairer	622.381-030
PIT SUPERVISOR	939.137-014
Placer Miner, Hydraulic	939.684-014
plug-drill operator	930.684-018
POWDER LOADER	931.667-010
Preparation-Plant Repairer	630.281-022
PRESS OPERATOR	575.685-070
PULLEY MAINTAINER	630.687-010
QUARRY PLUG-AND-FEATHER DRILLER	930.684-022
QUARRY SUPERVISOR, DIMENSION STONE	930.134-014
QUARRY SUPERVISOR, OPEN PIT	939.131-010
QUARRY WORKER	939.667-014
railroad-car loader	932.687-010
raise driller	930.683-026
Raise Miner	939.281-010
REPAIRER	630.281-022
RESEARCH ENGINEER, MINING-AND-OIL-WELL EQUIPMENT	010.061-022
roaster	573.382-010
Rock Contractor	939.281-010
ROCK-DUST SPRAYER	939.687-026
rock splitter	930.684-022
ROOF BOLTER	930.683-026

room boss	939.137-018
Rotary-Drill Operator	930.382-010
Rotary-Dump Operator	921.685-038
ROTARY-KILN OPERATOR	573.382-010
SAFETY ENGINEER, MINES	010.061-026
safety inspector	168.267-074
SAFETY-LAMP KEEPER	729.684-042
SALES ENGINEER, MINING-AND-OIL-WELL EQUIPMENT AND SERVICES	010.151-010
SAMPLER	579.484-010
SAMPLE TESTER-GRINDER	519.585-018
SAND FILLER	939.687-034
SANDFILL OPERATOR	939.485-010
Sandfill Operator, Surface	939.485-010
Sandfill Operator, Underground	939.485-010
SAND PLANT ATTENDANT	934.685-014
Sandstone Splitter	930.684-022
scraper	939.687-014
SCRAPER-LOADER OPERATOR	921.663-050
Scraper Operator	850.683-010
SCREEN-AND-CYCLONE REPAIRER	630.664-014
SCREEN REPAIRER, CRUSHER	630.684-030
SECTION SUPERVISOR	939.137-018
SHAFT MECHANIC	899.684-034
shaft repairer	899.684-034
Shaft Sinker	939.281-010
shaft tender	899.684-034
SHAKER TENDER	934.685-018
SHALE PLANER OPERATOR	930.663-010
SHALE PLANER OPERATOR HELPER	930.667-010
shift boss	939.137-018
shooter	931.261-010
shop blacksmith	622.381-030
SHORE HAND, DREDGE OR BARGE	939.667-018
shot firer	931.261-010
shot lighter	931.261-010
Shoveler	939.687-014
shovel operator	932.683-018
SHUTTLE-CAR OPERATOR	932.683-022
skip tender	939.667-010
Slope-Hoist Operator	921.663-026
sluice tender	939.684-014
slusher operator	921.663-050
sorter	933.687-010
Specimen Boss	939.137-018
SPIRAL RUNNER	934.685-022
splitter	779.681-010
spragger	932.683-010
Steam-Hoist Operator	921.663-026
STONE GRADER	679.567-010
Stope Miner	939.281-010
STOPPING BUILDER	869.684-058
strip-mine supervisor	939.137-014
Stripper	939.687-014
STRIPPING-SHOVEL OILER	850.684-018
STRIPPING-SHOVEL OPERATOR	850.663-026
superintendent, colliery	181.117-014
superintendent, quarry	181.117-014
SUPERVISOR	570.137-010
Supervisor, Blasting	939.137-014
Supervisor, Drilling And Shooting	939.137-014
supervisor, general	181.167-018
SUPERVISOR, MINE	181.167-018
SUPERVISOR, PREPARATION PLANT	549.137-014
SUPERVISOR, RECLAMATION	850.133-010
SURFACE SUPERVISOR	932.132-014
switch-house operator	939.362-014
TAILER	930.666-010
TEST ENGINEER, MINING-&-OILFIELD EQUIPMENT	010.061-030
tester	579.484-010
TIER-AND-DETONATOR	931.664-010
Timber Cutter	667.682-022
TIMBER FRAMER	869.381-034
TIMBER-FRAMER HELPER	869.687-042
timber repairer	869.381-034
Timber Sprinkler	741.687-018
Tipple Repairer	630.281-022
tipple supervisor	549.137-014
Top Cager	939.667-010
Tower-Hoist Operator	921.663-026
track-laying-machine operator	910.663-010
TRACK-MOVING-MACHINE OPERATOR	910.663-010
Tractor-Drill Operator	930.382-010
Tractor Operator, Battery	929.683-014
Trimmer	939.687-014

Tractor-Drill Operator	930.382-010
Tractor Operator, Battery	929.683-014
Trimmer	939.687-014
Tripod-Drill Operator	930.684-018
TROLLEY-WIRE INSTALLER	821.684-022
Tugger Operator	921.663-026
Tunnel Miner	939.281-010
turn keeper	932.167-010
undercutter	930.683-014
ventilation worker	869.684-058
Wagon-Drill Operator	930.382-010
Walking-Dragline Oiler	850.684-018
wash-box operator	541.382-010
wash-box operator	939.362-014
WASHER-AND-CRUSHER TENDER	939.685-014
washer operator	541.382-010
washery boss	549.137-014

motion picture—MOTION PICTURE INDUSTRY: This designation includes occupations concerned with producing motion pictures. It does not include entertainers or occupations involved in the distribution and projection of films in theaters, which are included in AMUSEMENT AND RECREATION (amuse. & rec.). Occupations involved in the recording of images on electromagnetic tape for transmission by television stations or networks are included in the RADIO AND TELEVISION BROADCASTING INDUSTRY (radio-tv broad.). Occupations concerned with developing, printing, and preparing film are included in the PHOTOFINISHING INDUSTRY (photofinishing).

Ager	840.681-010
animated-cartoon artist	141.081-010
animator	141.081-010
ART DIRECTOR	142.061-062
assistant camera operator	962.361-010
audiovisual equipment operator	960.362-010
board operator	194.262-018
BODY-MAKE-UP ARTIST	333.271-010
boom operator	962.384-010
buyer-renter	162.157-030
CAMERA OPERATOR	143.062-022
CAMERA OPERATOR, ANIMATION	143.382-010
camera operator, first	143.062-010
camera operator, head	143.062-010
Camera Operator, Second	143.062-022
Camera Operator, Sound Effects	143.062-022
CAMERA OPERATOR, TITLE	976.382-010
Camera-Storeroom Clerk	222.387-058
CAPTION WRITER	203.362-026
Cartoon-Background Artist	141.081-010
CARTOONIST, MOTION PICTURES	141.081-010
Cartoonist, Special Effects	141.081-010
CHIEF PROJECTIONIST	960.132-010
cinematographer	143.062-010
cinetechnician	714.281-018
cinetechnician supervisor	714.131-010
Construction Grip	962.687-022
CONTINUITY CLERK	209.382-010
COSTUMER	346.261-010
COSTUMER ASSISTANT	346.374-010
custodian, wardrobe	346.374-010
cutter	962.262-010
daily release and dupe printer	976.682-010
Densitometrist	976.381-010
DENSITY CONTROL PUNCHER	976.684-010
developer operator	976.382-018
Developing-Machine Tender	976.685-018
DIRECTOR, CASTING	159.267-010
DIRECTOR, MOTION PICTURE	159.067-010
DIRECTOR, MUSIC	152.047-018
DIRECTOR OF PHOTOGRAPHY	143.062-010
Director of Photography, Special Effects	143.062-010
DIRECTOR, RESEARCH	052.167-010
Disk Recordist	962.382-010
DOUBLE	961.364-010
DRAPER	962.381-010
Drying-Machine Tender	976.685-018
DUBBING-MACHINE OPERATOR	962.665-010
editing-machine operator	962.382-014
editor, sound	962.382-014
ELECTRICIAN, CHIEF	824.137-010
ENTERTAINER	term
EXTRA	159.647-014
FILM DEVELOPER	976.382-018
Film Inspector	976.684-014
FILM LABORATORY TECHNICIAN	976.684-014

FILM LABORATORY TECHNICIAN I	976.381-010
FILM LABORATORY TECHNICIAN II	976.685-018
Film Librarian	222.367-026
FILM LOADER	962.687-014
Film Numberer	976.685-018
FILM OR VIDEOTAPE EDITOR	962.262-010
FILM PRINTER	976.682-010
Film Recordist	962.382-010
FILM-REPLACEMENT ORDERER	976.567-010
Film Splicer	976.684-014
film technician	976.131-010
FILM-VAULT SUPERVISOR	222.137-010
GARDENER, SPECIAL EFFECTS AND INSTRUCTION MODELS	406.381-010
General Extra	159.647-014
Greens Planter	406.381-010
GRIP	962.687-022
GRIP BOSS	962.137-010
ILLUSTRATOR, SET	141.061-030
INKER AND OPAQUER	970.681-018
laboratory contact supervisor	976.131-014
LIGHT TECHNICIAN	962.362-014
LOCATION MANAGER	191.167-018
MACHINIST, MOTION-PICTURE EQUIPMENT	714.281-018
MAKE-UP ARTIST	333.071-010
Matte Cutter	976.684-010
MICROPHONE-BOOM OPERATOR	962.384-010
miniature-set builder	962.381-018
MINIATURE-SET CONSTRUCTOR	962.381-018
Miniature Set Designer	142.061-046
mixer operator	194.262-018
model-set artist	962.381-018
motion-picture-camera repairer	714.281-018
motion-picture commentator	150.147-010
MOTION-PICTURE PROJECTIONIST	960.362-010
MOTOR-POWER CONNECTOR	962.684-018
musical director	152.047-018
music department head	152.047-018
music mixer	194.262-018
NARRATOR	150.147-010
Negative Developer	976.382-018
Negative Notcher	976.684-010
operative supervisor	962.134-010
operator, lights	962.362-014
OPTICAL-EFFECTS-CAMERA OPERATOR	143.260-010
OPTICAL-EFFECTS LAYOUT PERSON	962.361-010
optical-effects-line-up person	962.361-010
OUTSIDE PROPERTY AGENT	162.157-030
PAINTER, ANIMATED CARTOONS	970.681-026
painter, set	840.681-010
PAINTER, STAGE SETTINGS	840.681-010
performer see ENTERTAINER	
plotter	962.361-010
Positive Developer	976.382-018
positive printer operator	976.682-010
process projectionist	960.362-010
PRODUCER	187.167-174
PRODUCER, ASSISTANT	187.167-182
Production Grip	962.687-022
projectionist	960.362-010
PROPERTY CUSTODIAN	222.387-042
property handler	962.687-022
PROP MAKER	962.281-010
READER	131.087-014
RECORDIST	962.382-010
RECORDIST, CHIEF	962.134-010
RERECORDING MIXER	194.362-014
Rewinder	976.685-018
SALES REPRESENTATIVE, AUDIOVISUAL PROGRAM PRODUCTIONS	259.157-010
scenario writer	131.067-050
Scenic Artist	144.061-010
SCREEN WRITER	131.067-050
script reader	131.087-014
SCRIPT SUPERVISOR	201.362-026
script writer	131.067-050
Sensitometrist	976.381-010
SET DECORATOR	142.061-042
SET DESIGNER	142.061-046
set electrician, assistant chief	962.362-014
set-model builder	962.381-018
Sewing Room Grip	962.687-022
Silent Bit Extra	159.647-014
SINGER	152.047-022
sketch maker	141.061-030

SOUND CUTTER 962.382-014
sound installation worker 194.381-010
SOUND MIXER 194.262-018
Special Ability Extra 159.647-014
SPECIAL EFFECTS SPECIALIST 962.281-018
Stand-By 358.677-010
STAND-IN 961.667-014
Stock Clerk, Makeup 222.387-042
story analyst 131.087-014
STORY EDITOR 132.037-026
studio engineer 194.262-018
studio technician 194.262-018
STUNT PERFORMER 159.341-014
subtitle writer 203.362-026
Supervising Editor, Feature 962.132-010
Supervising Editor, Trailer 962.132-010
SUPERVISING FILM EDITOR 962.132-010
SUPERVISOR, COSTUMING 962.137-018
SUPERVISOR, CUTTING AND SPLICING 976.134-010
Supervisor, Drapery Hanging 962.137-022
SUPERVISOR, FILM PROCESSING 976.131-014
supervisor, grips 962.137-022
SUPERVISOR, MOTION-PICTURE EQUIPMENT 714.131-010
SUPERVISOR, PROPERTIES 962.137-026
SUPERVISOR, PROP-MAKING 962.137-022
SUPERVISOR, SCENIC ARTS 149.031-010
Supervisor, Special Effects 962.137-022
Supervisor, Stage Carpentry 962.137-022
Supervisor, Upholstering 962.137-022
talent director 159.267-010
TECHNICAL TESTING ENGINEER 194.381-010
theater projectionist 960.362-010
theatrical performer   see ENTERTAINER ....
Timer 976.381-010
Title Artist 141.061-022
wardrobe draper 346.374-010
WARDROBE-SPECIALTY WORKER 969.381-010
Waxer Tender 976.685-018

motor-bicycles—MOTORCYCLES, BICYCLES, AND PARTS INDUSTRY: This designation includes occupations concerned with manufacturing complete motorcycles and sidecars; bicycles; and motorcycle and bicycle parts, such as saddles, seat posts, frames, and handlebars. Occupations concerned with the assembly of complete motorcycles and bicycles from purchased parts are included in this designation. Occupations concerned with the sale of motorcycles and bicycles are included in the RETAIL TRADE INDUSTRY (retail trade). Occupations involving repair of motorcycles are included under AUTOMOTIVE SERVICES (automotive ser.).

ASSEMBLER, BICYCLE I 806.684-014
ASSEMBLER, BICYCLE II 806.687-010
BENCH HAND 706.684-046
Bicycle, Subassembler 806.687-010
Brake Assembler 806.684-094
Clutch Assembler 806.684-094
development mechanic 600.260-014
EXPERIMENTAL MECHANIC 600.260-014
EXPERIMENTAL MECHANIC, ELECTRICAL 806.281-014
FINAL INSPECTOR, MOTORCYLES 806.281-018
Fork Assembler 806.684-094
Fork Repairer 620.684-026
frame aligner 807.484-010
Frame Assembler 806.684-094
FRAME REPAIRER 807.381-018
FRAME STRAIGHTENER 807.484-010
Handle-Bar Assembler 806.684-094
INSPECTOR, BICYCLE 806.687-030
MOTORCYCLE ASSEMBLER 806.684-090
MOTORCYCLE SUBASSEMBLER 806.684-094
MOTORCYCLE SUBASSEMBLY REPAIRER 620.684-026
MOTORCYCLE TESTER 620.384-010
Repairer, Assembly Line 620.684-026
roller-bearing assembler 706.684-034
ROLLER-BEARING INSPECTOR 706.687-034
straightener-and-aligner 807.484-010
STRIPER, MACHINE 749.686-010
SUPERVISOR, ASSEMBLY 806.131-014
Supervisor, Frame Assembly 806.131-014
SUPERVISOR, INSPECTION AND TESTING 806.131-026
Supervisor, Motorcycle And Wheel Assembly 806.131-014
Supervisor, Transmission And Fork Assembly 806.131-014
Test Rider 806.281-018
Transmission Assembler 806.684-094
Transmission Repairer 620.684-026

Utility Assembler 806.684-090
wheel assembler 706.684-106
WHEEL LACER AND TRUER 706.684-106
wheel truer 706.684-106
WHEEL-TRUING MACHINE TENDER 706.685-014

motor trans.—MOTOR VEHICLE TRANSPORTATION INDUSTRY: This designation includes occupations concerned with providing all types of public motor vehicle transportation for passengers and freight, including operating public warehousing and storage establishments. The principal types of activities include: (1) bus transportation lines for city, suburban, intercity, and long-distance use, and for such other purposes as sightseeing and charter trips; (2) taxicab services; (3) all types of public warehousing and storage establishments; (4) truck lines engaged in local and long-distance hauling; and (5) collecting and carting garbage and rubbish.

assignment agent 215.367-010
ASSIGNMENT CLERK 215.367-010
BAGGAGE CHECKER 357.477-010
Bulk Driver 905.663-018
bulletin clerk 215.367-010
BUS ATTENDANT 352.577-010
BUS DISPATCHER, INTERSTATE 913.167-010
BUS DRIVER 913.463-010
Bus Driver, Garage 909.663-010
Bus Driver, School 913.463-010
cab driver 913.463-018
cab starter 913.367-010
charter representative 214.362-030
Chauffeur, Airport Limousine 913.463-018
chauffeur, motorbus 913.463-010
CHECKER 919.687-010
city service supervisor 184.117-018
coach operator 913.463-010
CRATING-AND-MOVING ESTIMATOR 252.357-010
DIRECTOR, TRANSPORTATION 184.117-014
dispatcher 913.367-010
dispatcher 913.167-010
dispatcher 184.163-010
DISPATCHER, BUS AND TROLLEY 913.167-014
DISPATCHER, TRAFFIC OR SYSTEM 919.162-010
DISTRICT SUPERVISOR 184.117-018
division superintendent 184.167-158
DOCUMENTATION-BILLING CLERK 214.362-014
DRIVER 913.663-018
DRIVERS'-CASH CLERK 211.462-030
DRIVER SUPERVISOR 909.137-010
EMPLOYEE RELATIONS SPECIALIST 166.267-042
ESCORT-VEHICLE DRIVER 919.663-022
EXPRESS CLERK 222.367-022
FARE-REGISTER REPAIRER 729.384-014
Freight-Traffic Agent 252.257-010
furniture mover 905.687-014
furniture-mover driver 905.663-018
GARBAGE-COLLECTION SUPERVISOR 909.137-014
GARBAGE COLLECTOR 955.687-022
GARBAGE COLLECTOR DRIVER 905.663-010
gas-and-oil checker 915.587-010
GAS-AND-OIL SERVICER 915.587-010
GENERAL AGENT, OPERATIONS 184.167-042
GENERAL CLAIMS AGENT 186.117-030
hook-up driver 909.663-010
HOSTLER 909.663-010
INFORMATION CLERK 237.367-018
INSTRUCTOR, BUS, TROLLEY, AND TAXI 919.223-010
INTERLINE CLERK 214.382-022
LABORER, GENERAL 909.687-014
labor-gang supervisor 929.137-018
luggage checker 357.477-010
MANAGER, BUS TRANSPORTATION 184.167-054
MANAGER, OPERATIONS 184.117-050
manager, rates and schedules 184.117-066
MANAGER, REGIONAL 184.117-054
MANAGER, TRAFFIC 184.117-066
MANAGER, TRAFFIC I 184.167-102
MANAGER, TRAFFIC II 237.367-030
MANAGER, TRUCK TERMINAL 184.167-110
Manifest Clerk 214.362-014
MOBILE-LOUNGE DRIVER 913.663-014
Motor-Coach Driver 913.463-010
Motor-Express Clerk 222.367-022
NEW-CAR INSPECTOR 919.363-010
operations manager 184.117-050
OPERATIONS MANAGER 184.167-118

museums

Passenger Traffic Agent	252.257-010
Pick-Up Driver	906.683-022
PORTER	357.677-010
porter, baggage	357.677-010
RATE ANALYST, FREIGHT	214.267-010
RATE CLERK, PASSENGER	214.362-030
redcap	357.677-010
REVISING CLERK	214.382-026
ROAD SUPERVISOR	913.133-010
rubbish-collection supervisor	909.137-014
SAFETY COORDINATOR	909.127-010
SAFETY INSPECTOR, TRUCK	919.687-018
sales representative	252.257-010
SALES REPRESENTATIVE	250.357-022
SALES REPRESENTATIVE, SHIPPING SERVICES	252.357-014
SCHEDULE MAKER	913.167-018
service center manager	184.167-042
service inspector	168.167-082
shop superintendent	184.167-170
shuttle-bus driver	913.663-018
SUPERINTENDENT, DIVISION	184.167-158
superintendent, drivers	913.133-010
SUPERINTENDENT, MAINTENANCE	184.167-170
SUPERINTENDENT, MAINTENANCE OF EQUIPMENT	184.167-178
SUPERINTENDENT, STATIONS	184.167-206
supervisor	909.127-010
SUPERVISOR, CAB	913.133-014
Supervisor, Car-Loading-And-Unloading	929.137-018
SUPERVISOR, CUSTOMER SERVICES	248.137-018
Supervisor, Lost And Found	241.137-014
SUPERVISOR, TELEPHONE INFORMATION	237.137-010
SUPERVISOR, TERMINAL OPERATIONS	184.167-242
TAXICAB COORDINATOR	215.367-018
TAXICAB STARTER	913.367-010
TAXI DRIVER	913.463-018
TAXI SERVICER	915.687-030
terminal manager	184.167-110
Tour Agent	252.152-010
TRAFFIC AGENT	252.257-010
TRAFFIC INSPECTOR	184.163-010
transit-operations supervisor	913.167-014
transportation inspector	184.163-010
TRANSPORTATION INSPECTOR	168.167-082
Transport Driver	904.383-010
trash-collection supervisor	909.137-014
Trash Collector	955.687-022
TRAVEL AGENT	252.152-010
travel clerk	237.367-018
travel counselor	252.152-010
Traveling-Freight-And-Passenger Agent	252.257-010
Trolley-Coach Driver	913.463-010
TRUCK SUPERVISOR	909.137-018
undercover agent	168.167-082
VAN DRIVER	905.663-018
van driver	913.663-018
VAN-DRIVER HELPER	905.687-014
van helper	905.687-014
Vehicle-Fare Collector	211.462-038
WAREHOUSE SUPERVISOR	929.137-018
Waybill Clerk	214.362-014
yard spotter	909.663-010

museums—MUSEUMS, ART GALLERIES, AND BOTANICAL AND ZOO-LOGICAL GARDENS: This designation includes occupations concerned with operating all types of museums, art galleries, and botanical and zoological gardens, in whatever institutions or organizations they may occur.

ANIMAL-NURSERY WORKER	412.674-014
Antique-Auto-Museum-Maintenance Worker	899.384-010
ARMORER TECHNICIAN	109.281-010
ART CONSERVATOR	102.167-010
art preparator	102.367-010
astro-technician	962.261-010
children's zoo caretaker	412.674-014
COMMISSARY ASSISTANT	412.687-010
commissary helper	412.687-010
CONSERVATION TECHNICIAN	102.261-010
CRAFT DEMONSTRATOR	109.364-010
CURATOR	102.017-010
Curator, Art Gallery	102.017-010
Curator, Herbarium	102.017-010
Curator, Horticultural Museum	102.017-010
Curator, Medical Museum	102.017-010
Curator, Natural History Museum	102.017-010

Curator, Zoological Museum	102.017-010
DIRECTOR, EDUCATION	099.117-030
Director, Industrial Museum	102.017-010
DIRECTOR, MUSEUM-OR-ZOO	102.117-014
EDUCATIONAL RESOURCE COORDINATOR	099.167-030
education department registrar	238.367-034
EXHIBIT ARTIST	149.261-010
EXHIBIT BUILDER	739.261-010
Exhibit Carpenter	739.261-010
Exhibit Cleaner	899.384-010
EXHIBIT DESIGNER	142.061-058
Exhibit Electrician	739.261-010
exhibition specialist	739.261-010
exhibit technician	739.261-010
FINE ARTS PACKER	102.367-010
Finish Specialist	763.380-010
food preparer	412.687-010
furnishings conservator	763.380-010
FURNITURE RESTORER	763.380-010
gardener-florist	406.684-018
GARDENER, SPECIAL EFFECTS AND INSTRUCTION MODELS	406.381-010
GARDEN WORKER	406.684-018
Guard, Museum	372.667-034
HISTORIC-SITE ADMINISTRATOR	102.167-014
INSTALLER	922.687-050
Maintenance Carpenter	899.384-010
maintenance worker	899.384-010
MUSEUM ATTENDANT	109.367-010
museum craft worker	739.261-010
MUSEUM INTERN	term
museum preparator	102.381-010
museum service scheduler	238.367-034
MUSEUM TECHNICIAN	102.381-010
Planetarium Sky Show Technician	739.261-010
PLANETARIUM TECHNICIAN	962.261-010
REGISTRAR, MUSEUM	102.167-018
renovator	899.384-010
RESEARCH ASSOCIATE	109.067-014
RESTORER, CERAMIC	102.361-014
RESTORER, LACE AND TEXTILES	102.361-010
RESTORER, PAPER-AND-PRINTS	109.361-010
SCHEDULER	238.367-034
Science Center, Display Builder	739.261-010
Security Chief, Museum	372.167-014
SUPERINTENDENT, HORTICULTURE	180.161-014
SUPERVISOR, LANDSCAPE	406.134-014
TEACHER	099.227-038
technical specialist	962.261-010
TRANSPORTATION-EQUIPMENT-MAINTENANCE WORKER	899.384-010
transportation-museum helper	899.384-010
Upholstery Restorer	763.380-010

musical inst.—MUSICAL INSTRUMENTS AND PARTS INDUSTRY: This industry includes occupations concerned with making and repairing all musical instruments and parts by cutting, shaping, machining, assembling, polishing, and finishing.

ACCORDION MAKER	730.281-010
adjuster, piano action	730.681-010
assembler	730.381-018
ASSEMBLER, MUSICAL INSTRUMENTS	730.684-010
ASSEMBLER, PIANO	730.384-010
ball-ender	730.685-010
band-instrument maker	730.381-018
Bass-Mechanism Maker	730.281-010
Bass-String Winder	692.682-062
BELL MAKER	730.381-014
Bell Maker, Sousaphones	730.381-014
BELL-NECK HAMMERER	730.684-014
Bellows Maker	730.281-010
BELL SPINNER	619.682-010
Bell Spinner, Sousaphones	619.682-010
BELLY BUILDER	730.684-018
body maker	730.682-010
Bottom Board And Truss Leg Installer	763.684-058
BOW MAKER	730.281-058
Box Maker	730.281-010
BRASS-WIND-INSTRUMENT MAKER	730.381-018
Bridge Fitter	730.684-010
chipper	730.684-026
CHIP TUNER	730.684-026
CONSOLE ASSEMBLER	730.684-030

CROOK OPERATOR 609.682-018
CUTTER, WOODWIND REEDS 730.686-010
DRILLER-AND-REAMER, AUTOMATIC 606.382-010
Drum-Shell Maker 730.381-042
ELECTRIC-ORGAN ASSEMBLER AND CHECKER 730.381-022
ELECTRIC-ORGAN INSPECTOR AND REPAIRER 730.281-018
Final Assembler, Brass-Wind Instruments 730.684-010
FINAL INSPECTOR 730.367-010
Finisher, Accordion 730.281-010
folder-and-notcher 730.684-014
FRETTED-INSTRUMENT INSPECTOR 730.684-034
FRETTED-INSTRUMENT MAKER, HAND 730.281-022
gate tender 690.686-042
Guitar Maker, Hand 730.281-022
Harmonic Tuner 730.381-058
HARP-ACTION ASSEMBLER 730.381-030
HARP MAKER 730.281-030
HARP REGULATOR 730.381-026
HARPSICHORD MAKER 730.281-034
INJECTION-MOLDING-MACHINE OFFBEARER 690.686-042
INSPECTOR, WOODWIND INSTRUMENTS 730.684-038
Key-Bed Installer 763.684-058
KEYBOARD-ACTION ASSEMBLER 730.684-042
Knobber 730.381-058
LOOPER 730.685-010
MANUAL WINDER 730.684-046
Mounter, Brass-Wind Instruments 730.684-010
Mounter, Clarinets 730.684-010
Mounter, Flutes And Piccolos 730.684-010
Mounter, Keyed Instruments 730.684-010
Mounter, Saxophones 730.684-010
Mounter, Sousaphones 730.684-010
Mounter, Trombones 730.684-010
Mounter, Trumpets And Cornets 730.684-010
MOUTHPIECE MAKER 730.685-014
MUSICAL-STRING MAKER 730.684-050
Neck Fitter 730.684-010
Octave Tuner 730.381-058
organ installer 730.381-046
Organ-Pipe Finisher 730.381-038
ORGAN-PIPE MAKER, METAL 709.381-030
ORGAN-PIPE VOICER 730.381-038
pedal assembler 730.684-090
Piano Bench Assembler 763.684-058
PIANO CASE AND BENCH ASSEMBLER 763.684-058
Piano-Case Maker 660.280-010
PIANO REGULATOR-INSPECTOR 730.681-010
Piano-Sounding-Board Matcher 761.684-018
PIANO STRINGER 730.684-054
PIPE-ORGAN BUILDER 730.281-042
PIPE-ORGAN INSTALLER 730.381-046
PISTON MAKER 730.681-014
PLAYER-PIANO TECHNICIAN 730.381-050
PREASSEMBLER AND INSPECTOR 730.684-058
RACKER, OCTAVE BOARD 730.684-062
Rib Bender 569.685-014
SANDER-AND-BUFFER 730.684-066
Saxophone Assembler 730.381-018
SEAM HAMMERER 730.684-070
SHEET-METAL-PATTERN CUTTER 730.684-074
Side Gluer 763.684-058
SLIDING-JOINT MAKER 730.684-078
SOCKET PULLER 730.682-010
STOPBOARD ASSEMBLER 730.684-082
Stringed-Instrument Assembler 730.684-010
STRING-WINDING-MACHINE OPERATOR 692.682-062
SUPERVISOR 730.131-010
TESTER 730.684-086
TONE CABINET ASSEMBLER 730.684-090
TONE REGULATOR 730.684-094
Top Case Assembler 763.684-058
TROMBONE-SLIDE ASSEMBLER 730.381-054
TUBE BENDER, BRASS-WIND INSTRUMENTS 617.382-010
TUNER, PERCUSSION 730.381-058
Valve Maker I 730.381-018
VALVE MAKER II 730.681-018
VIOLIN MAKER, HAND 730.281-046
Violin Restorer 730.281-046
voicer 730.381-038
Wood Buffer 761.684-026

narrow fabrics—NARROW FABRICS INDUSTRY: This designation includes occupations concerned with manufacturing narrow woven and braided articles, such as belts, belting, binding, edgings, shoelaces, tape, weaving tape, webbing,

and wicks. Occupations concerned with the weaving of lace are included in the TEXTILE PRODUCTS INDUSTRY, NOT ELSEWHERE CLASSIFIED (tex. prod., nec).

beam warper 681.685-018
BEAM-WARPER TENDER, AUTOMATIC 681.685-018
BELTING-AND-WEBBING INSPECTOR 683.487-010
BLOCKER 689.685-014
braider tender 683.685-010
BRAIDING-MACHINE OPERATOR 683.685-010
braid maker 683.260-010
BRAID-PATTERN SETTER 683.260-010
CARD CUTTER, JACQUARD 683.582-010
CARD LACER, JACQUARD 683.685-018
CLOTH EXAMINER, HAND 689.687-022
dobby-loom chain-pegger 689.687-054
endless-belt finisher 782.684-062
FINISHING-MACHINE OPERATOR 582.682-010
fixer 683.260-018
fixer supervisor 683.130-014
FLOOR SUPERVISOR, ENDLESS-BELT-WEAVING
    DEPARTMENT 683.130-010
FOLDER 686.685-030
HANDER-IN 683.687-018
HEDDLES TIER, JACQUARD LOOM 683.680-014
HOOK PULLER 683.687-022
inspector 689.687-022
jackspooler 681.685-142
JACQUARD-LOOM WEAVER 683.682-022
knotting-machine operator, portable 683.685-034
knot-tying operator 683.685-034
Label Cutter 585.685-062
LABEL-CUTTING-AND-FOLDING-MACHINE
    OPERATOR, AUTOMATIC 689.685-086
LABEL PINKER 585.685-062
lacing-machine operator, jacquard cards 683.685-018
LOOM FIXER 683.260-018
LOOM-FIXER SUPERVISOR 683.130-014
loom repairer 683.260-018
NARROW-FABRIC CALENDERER 583.685-074
Narrow-Fabric-Loom Fixer 683.260-018
PEGGER, DOBBY LOOMS 689.687-054
piano-machine operator 683.582-010
Quill Changer 689.686-038
Quill Winder 681.685-154
Ribbon Blocker 689.685-014
RIBBON CUTTER 781.687-050
Ribbon Weaver 683.682-046
section beamer 681.685-018
section warper 681.685-018
shoelace tipper 686.685-062
SHOELACE-TIPPING-MACHINE OPERATOR ... 686.685-062
shuttleless-loom weaver 683.665-010
SINGER 585.687-030
SKEINER 681.685-102
skein winder 681.685-102
SMASH HAND 683.684-026
splicer 782.684-062
spooler 681.685-142
Spooler 689.685-014
Tape Weaver 683.682-046
Tape Winder 689.685-014
tipping-machine operator, automatic 686.685-062
tricot-warper tender 681.685-018
tying-in-machine operator 683.685-034
WARPER 681.685-146
warper tender 681.685-018
WARP SPOOLER 681.685-142
Warp-Spool Slasher 582.562-010
warp-tying-machine knotter 683.685-034
WARP-TYING-MACHINE TENDER 683.685-034
WEAVER, HAND 782.684-062
WEAVER, NARROW FABRICS 683.682-046
WEAVER, NEEDLE LOOM 683.665-010
Woven-Label Designer 142.061-014

nonfer. metal—NONFERROUS METAL ALLOYS AND PRIMARY PRODUCTS INDUSTRY: This designation includes occupations concerned with producing nonferrous metal alloys, such as aluminum, brass, bronze, babbitt, solder, and other white metals; rolling, drawing, insulating, extruding, and otherwise forming nonferrous alloys and metals into primary shapes, such as bars, extrusions, pipe, plates, rods, sheets, tubing, and wire; and fabricating primary nonferrous alloy and metal products not elsewhere classified. Also included are occupations concerned with the manufacture of insulated fiber optic

cable. Occupations concerned with the manufacture of glass fiber optic materials are included in the GLASS MANUFACTURING INDUSTRY (glass mfg.).

ALODIZE-MACHINE HELPER	509.685-010
ALODIZE-MACHINE OPERATOR	509.462-010
Aluminum-Foil-Spooling-Machine Operator	699.682-030
Approach-Table Operator	613.682-026
armored-cable-machine operator	691.685-010
ARMORING-MACHINE OPERATOR	691.685-010
ASBESTOS-WIRE FINISHER	691.682-010
BAND-REAMER-MACHINE OPERATOR	603.685-010
BATCH MAKER	515.685-010
BATTERY-WRECKER OPERATOR	515.686-010
billet header	514.584-010
blender	510.685-018
bobbin winder	691.685-026
braider	691.682-014
BRAIDER OPERATOR	691.682-014
braider tender	691.682-014
breaker operator	614.684-014
briquette-press operator	617.685-038
cable armorer	691.685-010
cable-machine operator	616.682-034
cable-mill helper	616.687-010
Cable Spooler	691.685-026
cabling-machine operator	616.682-034
CASTER	502.482-010
casting header	514.584-010
CASTING-HOUSE WORKER	514.587-014
CASTING-MACHINE OPERATOR	502.682-014
CASTING OPERATOR	514.662-010
CASTING-OPERATOR HELPER	514.687-018
CENTRIFUGE-SEPARATOR TENDER	541.585-010
charge-gang weigher	509.687-022
Chip-Crusher Operator	519.686-010
Chip Drier	519.686-010
Coarse-Wire Drawer	614.382-010
coat-insulator operator	691.682-018
coat-operator, insulator	691.682-018
COIL BINDER	619.687-010
COILER	613.685-010
coiler operator	613.685-010
COIL-REWIND-MACHINE OPERATOR	619.685-030
coining-press operator	617.685-038
Cold-Mill Operator	613.462-018
Cold-Mill Supervisor	619.132-014
compact-press operator	617.685-038
Continuous-Vulcanizing-Machine Operator	691.382-010
DEBRIDGING-MACHINE OPERATOR	607.685-014
Delivery-Table Operator	613.682-026
DENTAL-AMALGAM PROCESSOR	509.382-014
DIE POLISHER	601.381-018
Double-Lay-Winder-And-Paraffin-Unit Operator	691.682-018
draw-bench operator	614.685-022
DRAW-BENCH OPERATOR	614.482-010
DRAW-BENCH-OPERATOR HELPER	614.686-010
EMBOSSING-MACHINE OPERATOR	617.685-018
EXTRUDING-MACHINE OPERATOR	691.382-010
extruding-press operator	691.382-014
EXTRUSION-DIE REPAIRER	705.381-014
fettler	512.684-014
FILLING-MACHINE OPERATOR	699.685-038
Fine-Wire Drawer	614.382-010
finished-wire inspector	691.367-010
Floor Worker, Transfer Bay	921.667-022
FLUOROSCOPE OPERATOR	502.382-014
FLUX-TUBE ATTENDANT	519.687-018
FURNACE CHARGER	512.684-014
FURNACE HELPER	512.666-010
FURNACE OPERATOR	613.462-014
FURNACE OPERATOR	512.362-014
FURNACE TENDER	512.685-010
General Scrap Worker	519.686-010
header	514.584-010
Hot-Metal Crane Operator I	921.663-010
Hot-Mill Operator	613.462-018
Hot-Mill Supervisor	619.132-014
hydraulic-corrugating-machine operator	611.685-014
HYDRAULIC OPERATOR	611.685-014
IMPREGNATOR	509.685-030
INGOT HEADER	514.584-010
INSPECTION SUPERVISOR	709.137-010
Inspection Supervisor	691.130-014
Inspection Supervisor	691.130-010
INSPECTOR, BALL POINTS	733.687-046
INSPECTOR I	619.364-010
Inspector II	519.686-010
INSPECTOR, INSULATION	691.387-010
INSPECTOR, WIRE	691.367-010
INSULATING-MACHINE OPERATOR	691.682-018
LABORER, GENERAL	519.686-010
LABORER, SOLDER MAKING	519.667-014
LAGGING-MACHINE OPERATOR	691.685-014
LEAD-PRESS OPERATOR	691.382-014
lead-sheet cutter	502.684-014
LINER ASSEMBLER	613.667-010
LUBRICATOR-GRANULATOR	509.685-042
MAGNESIUM-MILL OPERATOR	607.686-010
materials-handling coordinator	222.167-010
METAL-CONTROL COORDINATOR	222.167-010
Metal Expediter	512.132-018
METALLIC-YARN-SLITTING-MACHINE OPERATOR	619.685-070
METAL-SPONGE-MAKING-MACHINE OPERATOR	616.685-038
Metal-Storage Worker	921.683-050
MILL HELPER	502.684-014
Mill Recorder	221.382-018
MIXER	510.685-018
nicker and breaker	614.684-014
NOZZLE-AND-SLEEVE WORKER	514.684-018
NOZZLE TENDER	512.685-014
PAIRING-MACHINE OPERATOR	691.685-022
PALLETIZER	929.687-054
Paper-Wrapping-Machine Operator	691.682-018
PERMANENT-MOLD SUPERVISOR	514.130-010
picker	509.686-018
piercer operator	613.482-014
PIERCING-MACHINE OPERATOR	613.482-014
Plastic-Extruding-Machine Operator	691.382-010
Plastic-Tubing-Insulation Supervisor	691.130-010
PNEUMATIC JACKETER	691.667-010
press operator	691.382-014
PRESS SETTER	617.480-014
PRODUCTION HELPER	691.687-010
push-bench-operator helper	614.686-010
REAMING-MACHINE TENDER	606.685-034
RECLAMATION SUPERVISOR	512.132-014
Reel Tender	691.685-030
REMELT-FURNACE EXPEDITER	512.132-018
remelt operator	512.685-010
Rod-Drawing Supervisor	614.132-010
ROD-PULLER AND COILER	619.685-078
ROLLING-MILL OPERATOR	613.462-018
ROLLING-MILL-OPERATOR HELPER	613.685-026
Salvager, Inserts	509.686-018
SALVAGE WORKER	619.387-010
sampler	509.584-010
SCALPER OPERATOR	605.682-022
scalp-machine operator	605.682-022
Scrap Baler	920.685-010
SCRAP BALLER	509.685-046
SCRAP SORTER	509.686-018
seamless-tube drawer	614.685-022
SHEET-MILL SUPERVISOR	619.132-014
SINTERING-PRESS OPERATOR	617.685-038
SLAB-CONDITIONER SUPERVISOR	609.132-010
slitting-machine coiler	613.685-010
soaking-pit operator	613.462-014
Soap Worker	519.686-010
Solder Cream Maker	519.667-014
sparker and patcher	728.684-018
SPARK TESTER	728.684-018
special-machine operator	509.382-014
Spooler And Coiler	691.685-030
SPOOLING-MACHINE OPERATOR	691.685-026
SPOOL WINDER	619.485-010
steel sampler	509.584-010
strander operator	616.682-034
STRANDING-MACHINE OPERATOR	616.682-034
STRANDING-MACHINE-OPERATOR HELPER	616.687-010
strand-machine operator	616.682-034
STRETCHER-LEVELER OPERATOR	619.682-010
STRETCHER-LEVELER-OPERATOR HELPER	619.686-030
STRIPING-MACHINE OPERATOR	652.682-026
STRUCTURAL-MILL SUPERVISOR	619.132-022
SUPERVISOR	691.130-010
SUPERVISOR, DRAWING	614.132-010
Supervisor, Electrolytic Tinning	500.131-010

SUPERVISOR, POWDERED METAL	509.130-010
SUPERVISOR, SOLDER MAKING	519.132-022
TABLE OPERATOR	613.682-026
Tandem-Mill Operator	613.462-018
Tandem-Taping-And-Paper-Wrapping-Machine Operator	691.682-018
tape armorer	691.685-010
TAPPER	514.664-014
test assembler	509.584-010
test carrier	509.584-010
TESTER OPERATOR	614.684-014
TESTER-OPERATOR HELPER	614.686-014
TEST PREPARER	509.584-010
TRUCK LOADER, OVERHEAD CRANE	921.663-070
TUBE DRAWER	614.685-022
tube-draw helper	614.686-010
Tube-Drawing Supervisor	614.132-010
tube-machine operator	691.382-010
Tuber Feeder	691.685-030
TUBING-MACHINE OPERATOR	613.685-030
UTILITY WORKER, EXTRUSION	691.685-030
Varnish-Cambric-Covering-Machine Operator	691.682-018
WEIGHER, ALLOY	509.687-022
WIRE DRAWER	614.382-010
WIRE-DRAWING-MACHINE TENDER	614.685-026
Wire-Drawing Supervisor	614.132-010
wire-draw operator	614.382-010
wire-taping-machine operator	691.682-018

nonmet. min.—ABRASIVE, ASBESTOS, AND MISCELLANEOUS NONMETALLIC MINERAL PRODUCTS INDUSTRY: This designation includes occupations concerned with (1) manufacturing and repairing abrasive grinding wheels of natural or synthetic materials and other abrasive products; (2) manufacturing and repairing asbestos textiles, asbestos building materials, and insulating materials for covering boilers and pipes; (3) manufacturing and repairing gaskets, gasketing materials, compression packings, molded packings, oil seals, and mechanical seals, regardless of material; (4) crushing, grinding, pulverizing, or otherwise preparing clay, ceramic and refractory minerals, barite, graphite, and miscellaneous nonmetallic minerals that are not fuels; (5) manufacturing and repairing mineral wool and mineral wool insulation products made of such silicious materials as rock, slag, and glass, or combinations thereof; (6) manufacturing and repairing statuary and art goods made of plaster of paris and papier mache; and (7) manufacturing and repairing sand lime products and other nonmetallic products, not elsewhere classified.

ABRASIVE-BAND WINDER	692.685-010
ABRASIVE-COATING-MACHINE OPERATOR	574.462-010
ABRASIVE GRINDER	673.685-010
ABRASIVE MIXER	570.485-010
ABRASIVE-MIXER HELPER	570.686-014
ABRASIVE SAWYER	677.685-010
ABRASIVE-WHEEL MOLDER	575.685-010
alley tender	680.665-018
alley tender	680.685-018
APRON CLEANER	680.687-010
apron scratcher	680.687-010
Asbestos-Cloth Inspector	689.685-038
ASBESTOS-SHINGLE INSPECTOR	679.687-010
ASBESTOS-SHINGLE SHEARING-MACHINE OPERATOR	679.686-010
BATTING-MACHINE OPERATOR, INSULATION	677.382-010
beam warper	681.685-018
BEAM-WARPER TENDER, AUTOMATIC	681.685-018
beater	570.686-018
BELT MAKER	776.684-010
BELT-MAKER HELPER	776.687-010
BEVELER	673.685-022
Blending-Machine Feeder	570.686-018
BLOCKER	689.685-014
braider tender	683.685-010
BRAIDING-MACHINE OPERATOR	683.685-010
BRAKE-LINING CURER	573.686-010
BRAKE-LINING FINISHER, ASBESTOS	579.665-010
BRAKE-LINING-FINISHER HELPER, ASBESTOS	579.687-010
BUSHER	502.687-014
CALENDER-MACHINE OPERATOR	583.585-010
card-apron cleaner	680.687-010
card fixer	680.380-010
CARD GRINDER	680.380-010
card hand	680.685-018
card operator	680.685-018
Cardroom Supervisor	579.137-014
CARDROOM WORKER	term
card setter	680.380-010
CARD TENDER	680.685-018
CASTER	575.684-018
caster	779.684-046
cloth calender	583.585-010
COATER, BRAKE LININGS	574.685-010
Cop Winder	681.685-154
CUT-OFF-SAW OPERATOR, PIPE BLANKS	677.685-026
Cutter, Brake Lining	579.687-010
CUTTER-INSPECTOR	751.684-010
cutter operator, asbestos shingle	679.686-010
DIAMOND-POWDER TECHNICIAN	673.685-046
Diamond-Wheel Molder	575.685-010
DISC-PAD GRINDER	673.685-086
DISC-PAD GRINDING MACHINE FEEDER	673.686-030
DISC-PAD KNOCKOUT WORKER	579.687-034
DISC-PAD-PLATE FILLER	579.687-038
drier unloader	921.583-010
DRILLER, BRAKE LINING	676.685-010
Emery-Wheel Molder	575.685-010
facing grinder	673.685-010
feeder	570.685-050
FINISHER	775.687-010
FINISHER-CARD TENDER	680.685-042
FINISHING-MACHINE OPERATOR	674.682-010
fixer	683.260-018
Foam Caster	754.684-022
FOLDER-TIER	759.684-034
GASKET INSPECTOR	739.687-102
GRAPHITE PAN-DRIER TENDER	549.685-014
Grinder, Brake Lining	579.687-010
GRINDING-WHEEL INSPECTOR	776.487-010
GROOVER	673.685-062
HAMMER-MILL OPERATOR	570.685-030
HOT-PRESS OPERATOR	575.685-042
imitation-marble mechanic	556.484-010
impregnator operator	579.665-010
INSPECTOR	776.667-010
inspector, brake lining	776.667-010
intermediate-card tender	680.665-018
LACER	774.687-014
LOOM FIXER	683.260-018
loom operator apprentice	683.682-042
loom operator	683.682-038
loom repairer	683.260-018
MACHINE SETTER	692.260-010
MIDDLE-CARD TENDER	680.665-018
MILL SUPERVISOR	559.132-034
MIXER	570.685-050
mixer	550.382-030
MIXER, DIAMOND POWDER	570.484-010
mixer helper	550.686-038
mixer operator	570.485-010
molder	575.685-010
MOLDER-MACHINE TENDER	575.685-062
MOLD MAKER	777.684-014
MOSAIC WORKER	779.381-014
OVEN-PRESS TENDER I	573.685-042
OVEN-PRESS TENDER II	573.685-046
picker	739.687-102
Picker Feeder	570.686-018
Plaque Maker	779.684-046
PLASTER MAKER	779.684-046
PREPARATION-ROOM WORKER	570.686-018
PRODUCTION SUPERVISOR	539.137-014
radius grinder	673.685-010
ROOF-CEMENT-AND-PAINT MAKER	550.382-030
ROOF-CEMENT-AND-PAINT-MAKER HELPER	550.686-038
ROOFING-MACHINE TENDER	590.685-098
ROPE MAKER, MACHINE	681.685-082
SAMPLER-TESTER	579.585-010
SAWYER I	677.686-010
SAWYER II	677.685-038
SCAGLIOLA MECHANIC	556.484-010
section beamer	681.685-018
section warper	681.685-018
SIZING-MACHINE OPERATOR	554.685-026
sleeve maker	776.684-010
sleeve wheel maker	776.684-010
spinner	682.685-010
SPINNER, FRAME	682.685-010
SPINNER, MULE	682.685-014
spinning-frame tender	682.685-010
STEAM-TANK OPERATOR	573.683-010
STEEL-WOOL-MACHINE OPERATOR	605.482-010
STICKER-ON	774.684-034
Stock Mixer	570.686-018

nonprofit org.

STRAND-AND-BINDER CONTROLLER	680.685-106
SUPERVISOR, ASBESTOS-CEMENT SHEET	679.130-018
SUPERVISOR, ASBESTOS PIPE	679.130-014
SUPERVISOR, ASBESTOS TEXTILE	579.137-014
Supervisor, Braiding	692.130-022
Supervisor, Finishing	692.130-022
SUPERVISOR, FINISHING DEPARTMENT	679.137-010
SUPERVISOR I	779.131-010
SUPERVISOR II	579.132-010
SUPERVISOR III	575.130-014
SUPERVISOR, INSULATION	590.130-014
SUPERVISOR IV	692.132-010
Supervisor, Molding	679.130-014
SUPERVISOR, SCOURING PADS	759.135-010
SUPERVISOR V	692.132-014
SUPERVISOR VI	692.130-022
TAB-MACHINE OPERATOR	754.685-010
tape calender	583.585-010
TAPE COATER	692.685-210
Tape Weaver	683.682-046
Tape Winder	689.685-014
TRANSFER-CAR OPERATOR, DRIER	921.583-010
tricot-warper tender	681.685-018
tube maker	692.685-234
TUBE WINDER, HAND	692.685-234
TWISTER TENDER	681.685-130
warper tender	681.685-018
WEAVER	683.682-038
WEAVER APPRENTICE	683.682-042
weaver, broadloom	683.682-038
WEAVER, NARROW FABRICS	683.682-046
WEAVING SUPERVISOR	683.130-022
winder operator	692.685-234

nonprofit org.—NONPROFIT MEMBERSHIP, CHARITABLE, AND RELIGIOUS ORGANIZATIONS: This designation includes occupations concerned with promoting interests of members of organizations functioning on a nonprofit membership basis. Typical organizations are business and professional associations; labor interests; civil, social, and fraternal clubs and societies; nonprofit organizations that promote the interests of a national, state, or local political party or candidate; animal humane societies; automobile owners' clubs; farm granges; historical clubs; and religious and charitable organizations. Occupations found in membership golf clubs are included in AMUSEMENT AND RECREATION (amuse. & rec.). Occupations found in insurance offices maintained by fraternal organizations are included in the INSURANCE INDUSTRY (insurance). Occupations found in group health associations are included in MEDICAL SERVICES (medical ser.). Occupations found in credit unions are included in FINANCIAL INSTITUTIONS (financial). Occupations in organizations providing social and rehabilitative services are included under SOCIAL SERVICES (social ser.).

Activities Director, Scouting	187.117-046
animal control officer	379.263-010
animal humane agent supervisor	379.137-010
ANIMAL-SHELTER CLERK	249.367-010
animal shelter supervisor	410.134-018
ANIMAL TREATMENT INVESTIGATOR	379.263-010
Archivist, Nonprofit Foundation	101.167-010
AUTOMOBILE-CLUB-SAFETY-PROGRAM COORDINATOR	249.167-010
Book Sorter	222.387-054
braille coder	203.582-014
braille coder	209.584-010
BRAILLE PROOFREADER	209.367-014
braille transcriber	203.582-014
BRAILLE TRANSCRIBER, HAND	209.584-010
BRAILLE TYPIST	203.582-014
Chief Clerk, Shelter	249.137-010
chief, dog license inspector	379.137-014
Claims And Insurance Information Clerk, Automobile Club	237.267-010
Clothing Sorter	222.387-054
community planning director, community chest	187.167-234
contribution solicitor	293.357-014
counselor, orientation and mobility	076.224-014
department manager, chamber of commerce	187.167-042
DIRECTOR, COMMUNITY ORGANIZATION	187.167-234
director, council of social agencies	187.167-234
director, federated fund	187.167-234
DIRECTOR, FUNDRAISING	165.117-010
DIRECTOR, RELIGIOUS EDUCATION	129.107-022
DIRECTOR, SERVICE	187.167-214
director, united fund	187.167-234
Disaster Director	187.167-214
DISTRICT ADVISER	187.117-022

district director	187.117-022
District Scout Executive	187.117-022
DIVISION MANAGER, CHAMBER OF COMMERCE	187.167-042
DOG LICENSER	249.367-030
EVALUATOR	249.367-034
executive, community planning	187.167-234
Executive Director, Contract Shop	187.117-026
EXECUTIVE DIRECTOR, RED CROSS	187.117-066
EXECUTIVE DIRECTOR, SHELTERED WORKSHOP	187.117-026
EXECUTIVE VICE PRESIDENT, CHAMBER OF COMMERCE	187.117-030
FUND RAISER I	293.157-010
FUND RAISER II	293.357-014
INFORMATION CLERK, AUTOMOBILE CLUB	237.267-010
inspector	379.137-010
instructor of blind	076.224-014
janitor, church	389.667-010
Jewelry Sorter	222.387-054
liaison officer	187.167-198
MANAGER, ANIMAL SHELTER	187.167-218
Manager, Aviation And Space	187.167-042
manager, chamber of commerce	187.117-030
Manager, Construction Industries	187.167-042
Manager, Domestic Trade	187.167-042
MANAGER, WORLD TRADE AND MARITIME DIVISION	187.167-170
MEMBERSHIP SECRETARY	201.362-018
national insurance officer	187.167-198
OFFICE SUPERVISOR, ANIMAL HOSPITAL	249.137-010
ORDER-CONTROL CLERK, BLOOD BANK	245.367-026
ORIENTATION AND MOBILITY THERAPIST FOR THE BLIND	076.224-014
orientation therapist for blind	076.224-014
orientor	076.224-014
PASTORAL ASSISTANT	129.107-026
Picket, Labor Union	299.687-014
pricer-sorter	222.387-054
Program Director, Scouting	187.117-046
RECEIVER-DISPATCHER	239.367-022
REHABILITATION CLERK	205.367-046
rehabilitation officer	187.167-198
ROUTING CLERK	249.367-070
Safety Director	187.167-214
SALES EXHIBITOR	279.357-010
service aide	239.367-022
service officer	187.167-198
SEXTON	389.667-010
SORTER-PRICER	222.387-054
SUPERVISOR, ANIMAL CRUELTY INVESTIGATION	379.137-010
SUPERVISOR, CONTRACT-SHELTERED WORKSHOP	187.134-010
SUPERVISOR, DOG LICENSE OFFICER	379.137-010
SUPERVISOR, KENNEL	410.134-018
therapist for blind	076.224-014
touring counselor	238.167-014
Transportation Director	187.167-214
TRAVEL COUNSELOR, AUTOMOBILE CLUB	238.167-014
traveling clerk	238.167-014
Travel-Ticketing Reviewer	238.167-014
verger	389.667-010
veterans' claims representative	187.167-198
VETERANS CONTACT REPRESENTATIVE	187.167-198
veterans' counselor	187.167-198
veterans' service officer	187.167-198
Wares Sorter	222.387-054
World-Travel Counselor	238.167-014

nut & bolt—SCREW MACHINE PRODUCTS AND BOLTS, NUTS, SCREWS, RIVETS, AND WASHERS INDUSTRY: This designation includes occupations concerned with manufacturing bolts, nuts, screws, rivets, lock washers, plate washers, turnbuckles, toggle bolts, and similar products.

Bolt-Machine Operator	612.462-010
BURRING-MACHINE OPERATOR	615.685-010
FASTENER TECHNOLOGIST	612.260-010
NUT-AND-BOLT ASSEMBLER	929.587-010
NUT FORMER	612.462-014
nutter-up	929.587-010
PRODUCTION-MACHINE TENDER	619.365-010
Rivet Maker	612.462-010
ROLL-THREADER OPERATOR	619.462-010
SUPERVISOR	616.130-010
TAPPER OPERATOR	606.682-022
Tapping-Machine Operator, Automatic	619.365-010
TRIMMER OPERATOR	619.462-014

office machines—OFFICE, COMPUTING, AND ACCOUNTING MACHINES INDUSTRY: This designation includes occupations concerned with manufacturing and repairing such machines as typewriters, teletypewriters, adding and calculating machines, electronic computers and peripheral equipment, bookkeeping machines, cash registers, coin changers, fare registers and recording fare boxes, ticket-counting machines, nonlaboratory balances and scales, and addressing, check-writing, mailing, duplicating, and other related machines. Occupations concerned with the manufacture of electronic components for computers are included in the ELECTRONIC COMPONENTS AND ACCESSORIES INDUSTRY (electron. comp.). Occupations concerned with the manufacture of photocopy and microfilm equipment are included in the PHOTOGRAPHIC APPARATUS AND MATERIALS INDUSTRY (photo. appar.).

oils & grease—ANIMAL AND VEGETABLE OILS, FATS, AND GREASE INDUSTRY: This designation includes occupations concerned with extracting and refining oils from plant seeds, such as nuts, kernels, and grains, and from animal sources; treating these oils to produce products, such as shortening, salad oils, margarine, industrial oils, and lubricating greases; rendering grease and soap stock from animal fat, bones, meat scraps; and rendering tallow from fat. These operations include extracting and purifying the oils by mechanical or chemical processing, and modifying their physical properties by processes such as hydrogenation (solidifying) or winterizing (removal of fatty stearin). These oils frequently are marketed to other industries before or after refining for use in other products. Occupations concerned with the processing of by-products, such as meal, cake, and lint, are included in this designation. Occupations concerned with processing corn and its derivatives, including corn oil, are included in the GRAIN AND FEED MILLING INDUSTRY (grain-feed mills). Occupations concerned with producing aromatic synthetic oils and perfume bases of coal-tar origin are included in the CHEMICAL INDUSTRY (chemical). Occupations concerned with refining fish and vegetable oils for medicinal purposes are included in the PHARMACEUTICALS AND RELATED PRODUCTS INDUSTRY (pharmaceut.) and occupations concerned with manufacturing lubricating greases in petroleum refineries are included in the PETROLEUM REFINING INDUSTRY (petrol. refin.).

optical goods

Hide Shaker	525.687-038
HIDE TRIMMER	525.687-046
HOPPER FEEDER	551.686-018
HYDROGENATION OPERATOR	529.382-026
knocker	521.686-014
lard maker	521.685-026
LARD REFINER	529.685-158
linseed-oil-mill tender	559.685-122
LINSEED-OIL-PRESS TENDER	559.685-122
LINSEED-OIL REFINER	559.382-030
linter	521.685-198
LINTER-SAW SHARPENER	603.682-018
LINTER TENDER	521.685-198
MAT SEWER	529.687-154
meal cook	523.685-034
meal temperer	523.685-034
MIXING-TANK OPERATOR	520.685-170
Oil-Expeller	529.685-106
OILSEED-MEAT PRESSER	521.685-242
oil winterizer	521.685-374
Oleo-Hasher-And-Renderer	529.685-158
ORDER FILLER, LINSEED OIL	920.686-022
Packaging Supervisor	529.137-030
pan shaker	521.685-242
pan shoveler	521.685-242
pan shover	521.685-242
PASTEURIZER	523.585-026
pelt salter	525.687-038
picker-box operator	520.565-010
PRESS OPERATOR	551.685-114
PRESSROOM WORKER, FAT	559.685-146
REDUCTION-FURNACE-OPERATOR HELPER	559.685-038
refiner bleacher	559.685-146
refinery operator	559.382-030
Refinery Supervisor	529.137-030
REFINING-MACHINE OPERATOR	529.685-198
roll operator	529.685-106
salt spreader	525.687-038
SAMPLER	529.387-034
saw filer	603.682-018
scale-tank operator	529.485-026
seed cleaner	599.665-010
SEED-CLEANER OPERATOR	599.665-010
seed-cleaning-machine operator	599.665-010
selector	525.687-046
sharpener	603.682-018
Sharples-Machine Operator	529.685-198
Shortening Mixer	520.685-070
SUPERVISOR	529.137-030
SUPERVISOR, GREASE REFINING	553.132-010
tank charger	921.685-030
VOTATOR-MACHINE OPERATOR	529.685-250
WEIGH-TANK OPERATOR	529.485-026
WHIPPED-TOPPING FINISHER	529.682-034
WINTERIZER	521.685-374

optical goods—OPTICAL GOODS INDUSTRY: This designation includes occupations concerned with grinding lenses and manufacturing and repairing optical goods. The major products are spectacles, eyeglasses, goggles, eyeglass frames, lenses, prisms, opera and field glasses, microscopes, and telescopes.

ABRASIVE GRADER	570.682-010
ABRASIVE-GRADER HELPER	570.686-010
ARTIFICIAL-GLASS-EYE MAKER	713.261-010
ARTIFICIAL-PLASTIC-EYE MAKER	713.261-014
ASSEMBLER, CLIP-ON SUNGLASSES	713.684-010
ASSEMBLER, GOLD FRAME	713.384-010
ASSEMBLER, MOLDED FRAMES	713.684-014
backside grinder	716.685-018
Bench-Lay-Out Technician	716.381-014
BENCH WORKER	713.684-018
BLOCKER AND CUTTER, CONTACT LENS	716.681-010
BLOCKER, HAND	716.684-010
BLOCKING-MACHINE TENDER	716.685-010
BURR GRINDER	673.686-014
Camera-Lens Inspector	716.381-010
Cataract-Lens Generator	716.682-014
CEMENTER	711.684-014
cleaner	716.687-010
clip baker	713.687-010
CLIP COATER	713.687-010
clocker	716.687-026
Contact-Lens-Curve Grinder	716.685-022
contact-lens cutter	716.382-010

Contact-Lens-Edge Buffer	716.685-022
CONTACT-LENS-FLASHING PUNCHER	713.687-014
Contact-Lens Inspector	716.381-010
CONTACT-LENS MOLDER	690.685-090
Contact-Lens Polisher	716.682-018
CONTACT PRINTER, PHOTORESIST	976.684-034
DEBLOCKER	716.687-010
dipper	713.687-010
DRILLER	716.685-014
edging-machine catcher	673.686-014
edging-machine feeder	673.686-014
EMBOSSER	713.684-022
EXPEDITER CLERK	221.387-026
EYEGLASS-FRAME TRUER	713.684-026
EYEGLASS-LENS CUTTER	716.682-014
Eyeglass-Lens Generator	716.682-014
Eyeglass-Lens Grinder	716.382-018
feeder	575.686-014
FINAL ASSEMBLER	713.687-018
Final Inspector	716.381-010
flat optical element maker	716.280-018
frame assembler	713.684-014
FRAME CARVER, SPINDLE	713.684-030
furnace clerk	573.686-014
FUSING-FURNACE LOADER	573.686-014
Fusing-Line Inspector	716.687-018
Fusion-Juncture Grinder	716.685-022
GLASS CHECKER	716.687-014
GLASS CUTTER, HAND	716.681-014
glass etcher	716.681-022
GRINDER, HAND	716.685-018
Groover	713.684-018
heating-fixture tender	713.687-042
in-Process Inspector	716.381-010
INSPECTOR, CLIP-ON SUNGLASSES	713.667-010
INSPECTOR, EYEGLASS	713.384-014
INSPECTOR, EYEGLASS FRAMES	713.687-022
inspector-in-process	716.687-022
INSPECTOR, MULTIFOCAL LENS	716.687-018
inspector, optical elements	716.381-010
INSPECTOR, OPTICAL INSTRUMENT	711.281-010
INSPECTOR, PRECISION	716.381-010
Instrument-Lens Generator	716.682-014
Instrument-Lens Grinder	716.382-018
instrument-lens-grinder apprentice	716.382-022
Instrument-Lens Inspector	716.381-010
jewelry setter	700.381-054
LAP CUTTER-TRUER OPERATOR	604.685-022
LATHE OPERATOR, CONTACT LENS	716.382-010
LAY-OUT TECHNICIAN	716.381-014
lens assorter	716.687-026
lens assorter	716.687-022
LENS-BLANK GAUGER	716.687-026
LENS-BLOCK GAUGER	716.687-030
lens cutter	716.682-010
Lens-Edge Grinder, Machine	716.685-022
LENS EXAMINER	716.687-022
LENS-FABRICATING-MACHINE TENDER	716.685-022
Lens-Generating-Machine Tender	716.685-022
lens grinder	716.382-018
lens-grinder apprentice	716.382-022
lens grinder, rough	673.685-074
LENS HARDENER	573.685-030
LENS INSERTER	713.687-026
lens inspector	716.687-022
lens inspector	716.381-010
LENS MATCHER	713.687-030
LENS-MOLD SETTER	713.381-010
Lens Mounter I	690.685-014
LENS MOUNTER II	713.681-010
LENS POLISHER, HAND	716.681-018
melter	713.687-042
Metal-Frame Inserter	713.681-010
MOLDER	575.381-010
MOLDER HELPER	575.686-014
Molding-Room Supervisor	716.130-010
mold setter	713.381-010
multifocal-button assembler	713.684-034
Multifocal-Button Countersink Grinder	716.685-022
Multifocal-Button Generator	716.682-014
Multifocal-Button Grinder	716.382-018
Multifocal-Button Inspector	716.687-018
MULTIFOCAL-LENS ASSEMBLER	713.684-034
neutralizer	716.687-026
ocularist	713.261-014

ocularist, glass 713.261-010
Ophthalmic-Lens Inspector 716.381-010
ophthalmic-technician apprentice 716.280-010
OPTICAL-ELEMENT COATER 716.382-014
OPTICAL-GLASS ETCHER 716.681-022
optical-glass inspector 716.687-034
OPTICAL-GLASS SILVERER 574.484-010
OPTICAL-INSTRUMENT ASSEMBLER 711.381-010
optical mechanic 716.280-014
optical-mechanic apprentice 716.280-010
optical model maker and tester 716.280-018
optical technician 716.382-018
OPTICIAN 716.280-014
OPTICIAN 716.280-018
OPTICIAN APPRENTICE 716.280-010
OPTICIAN APPRENTICE, DISPENSING 299.361-014
Optician, Contact-Lens Dispensing 299.361-010
OPTICIAN, DISPENSING II 299.361-010
OPTOMECHANICAL TECHNICIAN 007.161-030
pad maker 739.687-154
picker 573.686-014
PITCH WORKER 551.666-010
plastic-eye technician 713.261-014
Plastic-Frame Inserter 713.681-010
POLISHER, EYEGLASS FRAMES 713.684-038
POLISHER, IMPLANT 713.687-034
POLISHING-PAD MOUNTER 739.687-154
PRECISION-LENS CENTERER AND EDGER ... 716.462-010
PRECISION-LENS GENERATOR 716.682-014
PRECISION-LENS GRINDER 716.382-018
PRECISION-LENS-GRINDER APPRENTICE ... 716.382-022
PRECISION-LENS POLISHER 716.682-018
precision lens technician 716.280-018
PRECISION-OPTICAL WORKER .... term
Prescription Clerk, Frames 222.367-050
PRESCRIPTION CLERK, LENS-AND-FRAMES ... 222.367-050
Prescription Clerk, Lenses 222.367-050
Prism Inspector 716.381-010
puncher 713.687-014
REDUCING-MACHINE OPERATOR 614.685-018
reticle printer 976.684-034
roll-over loader 713.687-026
ROLL-OVER-PRESS OPERATOR 690.685-326
ROUGE MIXER 570.685-082
ROUGE SIFTER AND MILLER 579.685-046
SALVAGER 713.687-038
SAWYER, OPTICAL GLASS 677.382-014
sifter and miller 579.685-046
Silk Screener 920.685-078
silverer 574.484-010
sizer 716.687-026
SIZER, MACHINE 716.360-010
stone operator 673.685-074
STONE ROUGHER 673.685-074
STONE SETTER 700.381-054
STONE-SETTER APPRENTICE 700.381-058
Stone Setter, Metal Optical Frames 700.381-054
SUNGLASS-CLIP ATTACHER 713.687-042
SUPERVISOR 716.130-010
Supervisor, Contact Lens 716.130-010
Supervisor, Fusing Room 716.130-010
Supervisor, Grinding And Polishing 716.130-010
Supervisor, Inspecting 716.130-010
Supervisor, Lens Generating 716.130-010
Supervisor, Multifocal Lens 716.130-010
Supervisor, Precision Optical Elements 716.130-010
Supervisor, Sunglasses 716.130-010
Surface-Lay-Out Technician 716.381-014
Topside Inspector 716.687-026
Trim Mounter I 713.684-022
Trim Mounter II 713.681-010
Truer 716.682-014
WASHER 713.684-042
WET INSPECTOR, OPTICAL GLASS 716.687-034

ordnance—ORDNANCE AND ACCESSORIES (EXCEPT VEHICLES AND GUIDED MISSILES) INDUSTRY: This designation includes occupations concerned with manufacturing and repairing ammunition; small arms having a bore less than 30 mm; and ordnance and related accessories having a bore more than 30 mm, such as field artillery, bazookas, tanks, flame throwers, and torpedo tubes. Occupations concerned with manufacturing guided missiles are included in the AIRCRAFT-AEROSPACE MANUFACTURING INDUSTRY (aircraft mfg.).

adjuster leader 619.137-010
aligner 736.684-042
ALIGNER, BARREL AND RECEIVER 736.684-010
ammunition storekeeper 222.137-018
ammunition supervisor 222.137-018
ANVIL-SEATING-PRESS OPERATOR 694.685-010
ARTILLERY-MAINTENANCE SUPERVISOR ... 632.131-010
ASSEMBLER 737.684-010
ASSEMBLER I 736.381-010
ASSEMBLER, IGNITER 737.381-010
ASSEMBLER II 736.684-014
ASSEMBLER, MECHANICAL ORDNANCE ... 737.684-010
assembly-machine tool setter 616.360-034
assembly-machine tool setter 616.360-030
AUTOMOTIVE-TIRE TESTER 736.367-010
AUTOMOTIVE-TIRE-TESTING SUPERVISOR ... 736.131-010
BAG LOADER 737.687-014
ballistics tester 739.484-010
BANDING-MACHINE OPERATOR 619.685-018
BANDOLEER PACKER 920.687-034
BANDOLEER STRAIGHTENER-STAMPER ... 737.587-010
bar-gauger and lubricator tender 590.685-058
BARREL FINISHER 736.684-018
Barrel Lapper 603.685-070
BARREL LOADER AND CLEANER 736.587-010
BARREL POLISHER, INSIDE 603.685-014
Barrel Reamer 606.682-014
BARREL REPAIRER 736.684-022
BARREL-RIB MATTING-MACHINE OPERATOR ... 605.682-010
BARREL RIFLER 605.685-010
Barrel Rifler, Broach 605.685-010
Barrel Rifler, Button 605.685-010
Barrel Rifler, Hook 605.685-010
barrel-rifler operator 605.685-010
BARREL STRAIGHTENER I 736.684-026
Barrel Straightener II 617.482-026
BASE-DRAW OPERATOR 504.685-010
Base-Wad Operator-Adjuster 535.482-010
BB SHOT PACKER 920.685-018
belt-and-link-shop supervisor 737.137-022
BLASTING-CAP ASSEMBLER 737.687-018
Bluer 599.685-026
BOMB LOADER 737.684-014
BOOSTER ASSEMBLER 737.687-022
Borderer 761.381-034
BROWNING PROCESSOR 505.685-010
BUCKSHOT-SWAGE OPERATOR 612.682-010
BULLET-ASSEMBLY-PRESS OPERATOR 694.685-014
BULLET-ASSEMBLY-PRESS SETTER-OPERATOR ... 694.682-010
BULLET-CASTING OPERATOR 502.682-010
BULLET-GROOVING-SIZING-AND-LUBRICATING-
    MACHINE OPERATOR 619.382-010
BULLET-LUBRICANT MIXER 543.685-010
BULLET-LUBRICATING-MACHINE OPERATOR ... 694.685-018
BULLET-SLUG-CASTING-MACHINE OPERATOR ... 502.382-010
bullet-swaging-machine adjuster 617.360-014
bullet-swaging-machine operator 617.585-010
BURNING-PLANT OPERATOR 509.685-018
CAMOUFLAGE ASSEMBLER 869.687-014
cartridge-assembling-machine adjuster 632.360-014
cartridge gauger 737.684-026
cartridge-loading operator 694.685-026
Carver And Checkerer, Specials 761.381-034
CASE-FINISHING-MACHINE ADJUSTER 626.381-010
CASE PREPARER-AND-LINER 509.384-010
Centerless-Grinding-Machine Adjuster 638.261-030
CHAMFERING-MACHINE OPERATOR I 606.685-014
CHAMFERING-MACHINE OPERATOR II 606.685-018
checkerer, hand 761.381-034
CHECKERING-MACHINE ADJUSTER 669.360-010
checkering-machine operator 665.685-034
CHECK WEIGHER 737.687-026
CHEST-PAINTING AND SEALING SUPERVISOR ... 749.137-010
chest-painting leader 749.137-010
chip separator 694.585-010
CHOKE REAMER 606.685-022
CHRONOGRAPH OPERATOR 739.484-010
CLEANER 503.684-010
cleaner-greaser 736.687-010
CLIP-LOADING-MACHINE ADJUSTER 694.362-010
CLIP-LOADING-MACHINE FEEDER 694.686-010
Cloth Printer 651.685-022
cold-working supervisor 619.130-010
cold-work operator 694.682-014
compressor operator-adjuster 535.482-010

continuous-washer operator	503.685-026
CORE LOADER	737.687-030
cup filler	737.687-102
CUP-TRIMMING-MACHINE OPERATOR	615.685-018
CUT-AND-PRINT-MACHINE OPERATOR	659.682-010
cut-off-machine operator	609.685-026
CUT-OFF-MACHINE OPERATOR	615.685-022
DEMOLITION SPECIALIST	737.687-034
DETONATOR ASSEMBLER	737.687-038
DIP-LUBE OPERATOR	503.685-014
DROP TESTER	737.387-010
DRY-HOUSE TENDER	559.585-010
dry mixer	550.565-010
electric-blasting-cap assembler	737.687-018
EMBOSSING-MACHINE OPERATOR	619.685-038
EMBOSSING TOOLSETTER	616.260-010
enthone solder stripper	503.685-046
Explosive Operator, Bomb	737.687-046
Explosive Operator, Fuse	737.687-046
Explosive Operator, Grenade	737.687-046
EXPLOSIVE OPERATOR I	737.687-042
EXPLOSIVE OPERATOR II	737.687-046
EXPLOSIVE-OPERATOR SUPERVISOR	694.132-010
EXPLOSIVES-TRUCK DRIVER	903.683-010
EXTRUDING-PRESS OPERATOR	614.685-010
FELT CUTTER	686.685-026
FILER, FINISH	705.481-010
Filer Repairer	705.481-010
FILING-AND-POLISHING SUPERVISOR	603.137-010
final assembler	736.381-010
Final Inspector	736.387-010
Finisher, Special Stocks	763.381-010
FIREARMS-ASSEMBLY SUPERVISOR	736.131-014
FITTER, VENTILATED RIB	736.381-014
FOILING-MACHINE ADJUSTER	629.381-010
FOILING-MACHINE OPERATOR	692.685-086
forming-machine operator	617.585-010
FRONT-SIGHT ATTACHER	736.684-030
FURNACE-AND-WASH-EQUIPMENT OPERATOR	503.685-026
FUSE ASSEMBLER	737.684-022
FUSE-CUP EXPANDER	694.685-022
Gaging-Machine Operator	737.685-010
GAS-CHECK-PAD MAKER	736.684-034
GAUGE-AND-WEIGH-MACHINE ADJUSTER	632.360-010
GAUGE-AND-WEIGH-MACHINE OPERATOR	737.685-010
GREASER	736.687-010
grip checkerer, machine	665.685-034
GUN EXAMINER	736.281-010
Gun Examiner And Repairer	736.281-010
gun numberer	652.582-010
GUN-REPAIR CLERK	222.387-022
GUNSMITH, BALLISTICS LABORATORY	609.260-010
gunstock repairer	761.381-038
Gunstock-Spray-Unit Adjuster	599.382-010
Gunstock-Spray-Unit Feeder	599.686-014
GUN SYNCHRONIZER	632.381-010
HEAD-GAUGE-UNIT OPERATOR	619.685-054
heading-and-priming operator	694.685-042
heading-and-priming tool setter	616.360-030
HOPPER FEEDER	619.686-018
HYDRAULIC-PRESS SERVICER	626.381-018
HYDRAULIC-PRESSURE-AUTO-FRETTAGE-MACHINE OPERATOR	694.682-014
HYDRAULIC-PRESSURE-AUTO-FRETTAGE-MACHINE-OPERATOR SUPERVISOR	619.130-010
IGNITER CAPPER	737.687-050
INLETTER	669.682-050
inside polisher	603.685-014
INSPECTING-MACHINE ADJUSTER	632.380-010
INSPECTION SUPERVISOR I	736.131-018
INSPECTION SUPERVISOR II	737.134-010
INSPECTOR, ASSEMBLY	736.387-010
INSPECTOR, BARREL	736.687-014
INSPECTOR, BULLET SLUGS	737.687-058
INSPECTOR, CHIEF	737.137-010
INSPECTOR, COLD WORKING	612.384-010
INSPECTOR, FIREARMS	632.381-014
INSPECTOR I	737.387-014
INSPECTOR II	737.687-054
INSPECTOR III	737.367-010
INSPECTOR IV	559.387-010
INSPECTOR, LIVE AMMUNITION	736.687-018
inspector, materials and processes	737.364-010
INSPECTOR, SALVAGE	737.684-026
INSPECTOR, SHELLS	737.687-066
IRON-PLASTIC BULLET MAKER	590.365-010
KNURLING-MACHINE OPERATOR	604.685-018
laboratory-mechanic helper	736.387-014
LABORER, AMMUNITION ASSEMBLY I	737.687-070
LABORER, AMMUNITION ASSEMBLY II	737.687-074
lacquer-machine feeder	694.685-046
LACQUER-PIN-PRESS OPERATOR	737.687-078
lacquer-press adjuster	632.380-018
LEAD HANDLER	599.687-018
LEAD-SECTION SUPERVISOR	619.132-010
LOADING-MACHINE ADJUSTER	632.360-014
LOADING-MACHINE OPERATOR	694.685-026
loading-machine operator	694.665-010
LOADING-MACHINE TOOL-SETTER	694.260-010
LOADING-UNIT OPERATOR	694.685-030
Loading-Unit Operator, Crimping	694.685-030
Loading-Unit Operator, Powder Charging	694.685-030
Loading-Unit Operator, Seating	694.685-030
loading-unit plate filler	737.685-014
LOADING-UNIT TOOL-SETTER	632.380-014
LUBRICATING-MACHINE TENDER	509.685-038
MACHINE-ADJUSTER LEADER	619.137-010
Machine-Adjuster Leader, Bullet Assembly	619.137-010
Machine-Adjuster Leader, Cannelure And Finish	619.137-010
Machine-Adjuster Leader, Case Trim	619.137-010
Machine-Adjuster Leader, Primer Assembly	619.137-010
machine-casting operator and adjuster	502.382-010
MACHINE-PACK ASSEMBLER	920.687-122
machine pack-shaker lubricator	694.685-046
MAGAZINE SUPERVISOR	222.137-018
MANUAL-PLATE FILLER	737.687-082
MARKER	652.582-010
MERCURY-CRACKING TESTER	737.687-086
MODEL MAKER, FIREARMS	600.260-018
MOLDER, LEAD INGOT	502.685-010
MUNITIONS HANDLER	929.687-034
Munitions-Handler Supervisor	922.137-018
oiler and packer, gun parts	736.687-010
ORDNANCE ENGINEER	019.061-022
ORDNANCE TRUCK INSTALLATION MECHANIC	806.684-098
outside repairer, special	761.381-038
OVEN TENDER	534.565-010
package opener	222.387-022
PACKER	929.684-010
Painter, Ordnance	741.684-026
patcher-wood welder	761.684-042
PELLET-PRESS OPERATOR	694.685-034
piece marker, small arms	652.582-010
plate filler	737.685-014
POWDER-AND-PRIMER-CANNING LEADER	737.137-014
POWDER-TRUCK DRIVER	903.683-014
Powder Trucker	929.687-030
POWDER WORKER, TNT	737.684-030
PRESSURE-TEST OPERATOR	737.387-014
primer-and-powder-canning leader	737.137-014
primer assembler	694.685-010
PRIMER ASSEMBLER	737.687-098
PRIMER BOXER	737.587-018
PRIMER CHARGER	737.687-102
PRIMER-CHARGING TOOL SETTER	694.360-010
PRIMER-INSERTING-MACHINE ADJUSTER	632.360-010
PRIMER-INSERTING-MACHINE OPERATOR	694.685-042
PRIMER INSPECTOR	737.687-106
PRIMER-POWDER BLENDER, DRY	550.565-010
primer-press operator	694.685-010
PRIMER SUPERVISOR	737.132-010
PRIMER-WATERPROOFING-MACHINE ADJUSTER	632.380-018
PRIMER-WATERPROOFING-MACHINE OPERATOR	694.685-046
priming-machine operator	694.685-042
PRIMING-MIXTURE CARRIER	922.587-010
PROCESS CHECKER	737.364-010
PROCESS INSPECTOR	736.381-018
PRODUCTION ASSEMBLER	737.684-034
PROOF INSPECTOR	736.384-010
PROOF TECHNICIAN	199.171-010
PROOF-TECHNICIAN HELPER	736.387-014
proof tester	736.384-010
PROPELLANT-CHARGE LOADER	737.487-010
PROPELLANT-CHARGE-ZONE ASSEMBLER	737.687-110
pyrometer operator	619.662-010
Renovation-Plant Supervisor	694.132-010
Repairer And Checker	761.381-034
RESTRICTIVE-PREPARATION OPERATOR	559.685-154
rib matcher and fitter	736.381-014
rim-fire charger operator	694.685-050

RIM-FIRE-PRIMING OPERATOR	694.685-050
RIM-FIRE-PRIMING TOOL SETTER	632.380-022
ROCKET-TEST-FIRE WORKER	806.384-022
salvage inspector, wood parts	769.387-010
SALVAGE-MACHINE OPERATOR	694.382-010
salvage-machine operator	737.684-026
SALVAGER I	737.687-114
SALVAGER II	737.687-118
sample maker	600.260-018
SANDBLAST OPERATOR	503.685-038
SCREW-EYE ASSEMBLER	737.687-122
Screw-Machine Adjuster, Automatic	638.261-030
SHADOWGRAPH-SCALE OPERATOR	737.687-126
SHAKER-PLATE OPERATOR	737.685-014
shaper	761.381-038
SHELLACKER	737.687-130
SHELL ASSEMBLER	737.684-038
shell-reprint operator	659.685-018
SHELL-SHOP SUPERVISOR	619.132-018
SHELL-SIEVE OPERATOR	694.585-010
shell-trim operator	609.685-026
shell-trim tool setter	609.280-010
shooter	736.384-010
SHOT BAGGER	920.687-170
SHOT DROPPER	502.362-010
SHOT-GRINDER OPERATOR	603.685-074
SHOTGUN-SHELL-ASSEMBLY-MACHINE ADJUSTER	616.360-030
SHOTGUN-SHELL-ASSEMBLY-MACHINE OPERATOR	694.385-010
SHOTGUN-SHELL-LOADING-MACHINE OPERATOR	694.665-010
SHOTGUN-SHELL-REPRINTING-UNIT OPERATOR	659.685-018
shot packer	920.687-170
SHOT POLISHER AND INSPECTOR	509.485-014
shot-tube-machine tender	920.685-018
SHRINK-PIT OPERATOR	619.662-010
SHRINK-PIT SUPERVISOR	619.131-018
sighter	736.684-042
SIGHT MOUNTER	736.481-010
SIZING-MACHINE OPERATOR	649.582-014
SKIVING-MACHINE OPERATOR	664.682-018
SLURRY MIXER	539.362-018
SOLDERER, BARREL RIBS	736.684-038
SPACE-AND-STORAGE CLERK	219.387-026
STEEL-SHOT-HEADER OPERATOR	611.682-010
STOCK CHECKERER I	761.381-034
STOCK CHECKERER II	665.685-034
STOCKING-AND-BOX-SHOP SUPERVISOR	769.137-010
STOCK MAKER, CUSTOM	761.381-038
STOCK PATCHER	761.684-042
stock repairer	761.684-042
STOCK SHAPER	761.684-046
Stock Turner	664.685-018
Straightener, Gun Parts	709.484-014
STRAIGHT-LINE-PRESS SETTER	616.360-034
STRIP-TANK TENDER	503.685-046
subassembler	736.684-034
SUPERINTENDENT, AMMUNITION STORAGE	189.167-038
SUPERVISOR	737.137-018
Supervisor, Ammunition-Loading	737.137-018
SUPERVISOR, BELT-AND-LINK ASSEMBLY	737.137-022
SUPERVISOR, ORDNANCE TRUCK INSTALLATION	806.137-014
Supervisor, Powder-And-Primer-Canning	737.137-018
Supervisor, Propellant-Charge-Loading	737.137-018
Supervisor, Pyrotechnic-Loading	737.137-018
SUPERVISOR, ROCKET PROPELLANT PLANT	559.137-046
SUPERVISOR, TUMBLERS	599.132-010
SWAGE TENDER	617.685-042
swage toolsetter	617.360-014
SWAGING-MACHINE ADJUSTER	617.360-014
SWAGING-MACHINE OPERATOR	617.585-010
TAPPER, HAND	737.687-134
TARGETEER	736.684-042
Thermite-Bomb Loader	737.684-014
THREADING-MACHINE OPERATOR	604.685-038
tracer-bullet assembly-machine tool setter	616.360-034
TRACER-BULLET-CHARGING-MACHINE OPERATOR	694.382-014
TRACER-BULLET-SECTION SUPERVISOR	694.131-010
trim and burr operator	609.685-026
TRIM-MACHINE ADJUSTER	609.280-026
TRIM-MACHINE OPERATOR	609.685-026
TUBE SIZER-AND-CUTTER OPERATOR	640.685-086
VARNISHING-UNIT OPERATOR	737.687-138
VARNISHING-UNIT TOOL SETTER	632.380-026
volumetric weigher	920.687-170
WAD-BLANKING-PRESS ADJUSTER	690.360-010
WAD-COMPRESSOR OPERATOR-ADJUSTER	535.482-010

WAD IMPREGNATOR	590.685-054
WAD LUBRICATOR	590.685-058
WAD-PRINTING-MACHINE OPERATOR	652.685-102
wash-barrel leader	599.132-010
WINDING-LATHE OPERATOR	619.685-086
WOODWORK-SALVAGE INSPECTOR	769.387-010

paint & varnish—PAINT AND VARNISH INDUSTRY: This designation includes occupations concerned with manufacturing paints in paste form, paints mixed ready for use, varnishes, lacquers, calcimines, japans, putty, enamels, fillers, stains, and shellac. Occupations concerned with the manufacture of boneblack, carbon black, and lampblack are included in the CHEMICAL INDUSTRY (chemical).

baker, paint	553.685-082
Barytes Grinder	599.685-058
batch mixer	550.685-078
Black-Ash Worker	559.685-110
blender	550.685-078
blender	550.585-038
Bulk-Pigment Reducer	550.585-038
CADMIUM-LIQUOR MAKER	553.685-026
CALCINE FURNACE LOADER	553.486-010
CALCINE-FURNACE TENDER	553.685-030
CENTRIFUGE OPERATOR	551.685-034
chip applier	641.685-030
CHIP-APPLYING-MACHINE TENDER	641.685-030
chipper	559.684-022
COLOR-CARD MAKER	794.687-014
color matcher	550.381-014
color shader	550.381-014
Cover Marker	920.685-078
dispersion mixer	550.685-078
enamel burner	553.685-082
Enamel Shader	550.381-014
Equipment Cleaner	559.685-110
finish mixer	550.381-014
Formula Figurer	216.482-022
furnace-room supervisor	559.132-110
furnace tender	572.685-010
Glass Enamel Mixer	550.685-078
GLASS-FURNACE TENDER	572.685-010
grinder operator see PAINT GRINDER	553.685-030
kiln operator	553.685-082
kiln tender	559.685-110
LABORER, GENERAL	550.685-078
Lacquer Blender	551.685-034
Lacquer Filterer	559.685-030
LACQUER MAKER	559.682-030
lacquer mixer	550.381-014
Lacquer Shader	550.381-014
Latex-Paint Shader	553.685-026
liquor maker	550.685-078
MIXER	641.685-030
mounting-machine operator	550.381-014
Oil-Paint Shader	553.685-082
OVEN TENDER	558.685-054
oxide-furnace tender	term
PAINT GRINDER	555.682-014
paint grinder, roller mill	555.682-022
paint grinder, stone mill	550.685-078
Paint Maker	550.381-014
paint tinter	741.684-026
Panel Finisher	550.685-078
Paste Mixer	550.585-038
Paste Thinner	599.685-058
Pebble-Mill Operator	550.685-078
Pigment Mixer	559.685-130
PIGMENT PROCESSOR	550.685-078
Putty Maker	559.482-014
PUTTY TINTER-MAKER	558.685-054
RED-LEAD BURNER	550.585-038
reducer	551.685-034
Resin Filterer	555.682-014
ROLLER-MILL OPERATOR	559.137-010
SALVAGE SUPERVISOR	550.584-014
SAMPLE-COLOR MAKER	555.682-018
SAND-MILL GRINDER	550.381-014
shader	550.585-038
Stain Maker	
stock grinder see PAINT GRINDER	555.682-022
stone-grinder operator	555.682-022
STONE-MILL OPERATOR	559.685-110
Strainer	

paper & pulp

paper & pulp—PAPER AND PULP INDUSTRY: This designation includes occupations concerned with manufacturing pulp and producing paper, molded pulp goods, and paperboard of all kinds from either woodpulp or rags. Coating, coloring, glazing, waxing, and impregnating paper are also included in this designation.

PLATING-MACHINE OPERATOR 649.686-026
Pocket-Grinder Operator 530.662-014
poler 921.686-022
pondsaw operator 667.685-034
Pond Scaler 455.487-010
POND WORKER 921.686-022
Pony-Roll Finisher 920.685-090
POWER-BARKER OPERATOR 669.485-010
PULP-AND-PAPER TESTER 539.364-010
PULPER 530.685-010
PULPER, SYNTHETIC SOIL BLOCKS 530.582-010
PULP GRINDER AND BLENDER 530.682-010
pulp-machine operator 539.685-030
pulp-making-plant operator 532.686-010
PULP-PRESS TENDER 532.685-026
PULP-REFINER OPERATOR 530.382-010
Pulp Tester 539.364-010
Pulpwood Scaler 455.487-010
PUMP MECHANIC 629.281-034
PUMP-PRESS OPERATOR 539.685-022
RAG-CUTTING-MACHINE FEEDER 530.666-010
RAG-CUTTING-MACHINE TENDER 530.665-014
RAG INSPECTOR 530.687-010
rag-willow operator 533.685-030
RECOVERY OPERATOR 552.362-018
Riffler Tender 533.685-022
Ring-Grinder Operator 530.662-014
Rod-Machine Operator 533.685-022
ROLL EXAMINER 640.687-010
ROLL FINISHER 920.685-090
roll skinner 539.686-010
Roll Weigher 222.387-074
roll wrapper 920.685-090
ROTARY-CUTTER FEEDER 640.686-010
rotary-filter operator 533.682-010
SAMPLE CLERK, PAPER 209.587-046
SAVE-ALL OPERATOR 533.685-018
SCREEN HANDLER 539.685-026
screen-room operator 533.685-022
SCREEN TENDER 533.685-022
SCREEN TENDER 534.665-010
SCREEN TENDER, CHIPS 533.685-026
SCREEN-TENDER HELPER 533.687-010
screen washer 533.687-010
second hand, paper machine 534.662-010
sheeter helper 649.685-066
Sheeter Operator 649.682-022
sheet taker 539.686-010
Siding-Coreboard Inspector 539.667-010
sinker puller 921.686-022
SIZE MAKER 550.682-010
skinner 539.686-010
SLASHER OPERATOR 667.685-054
slasher sawyer 667.685-054
slip feeder 921.686-022
Slitter-And-Cutter Operator 649.682-038
slusher operator 530.685-014
solid-fiber-paster operator 534.682-026
sorter 649.687-010
spudder 569.687-026
starch and prosize mixer 550.682-010
Stock Pitcher 539.587-010
SUPERCALENDER OPERATOR 534.682-038
Supercalender-Operator Helper 534.686-010
Superintendent, Board Mill 539.132-010
SUPERVISOR, BEATER ROOM 530.132-014
Supervisor, Bleach Plant 539.132-014
SUPERVISOR, CALENDERING 534.132-010
SUPERVISOR, COREMAKER 640.132-010
supervisor, groundwood mill 530.132-022
SUPERVISOR, PAPER COATING 534.132-014
SUPERVISOR, PAPER MACHINE 539.132-010
SUPERVISOR, PAPER TESTING 539.134-010
SUPERVISOR, PULP PLANT 539.132-014
SUPERVISOR, RAG ROOM 539.137-010
SUPERVISOR, REPULPING 539.132-018
SUPERVISOR, WET ROOM 539.130-014
SUPERVISOR, WOOD ROOM 530.132-018
THRASHER FEEDER 533.685-030
timber trimmer 667.685-034
TOWER ATTENDANT 559.666-010
TRANSFER OPERATOR 921.685-066
WASHER ENGINEER 533.685-034
WASHER-ENGINEER HELPER 533.686-014
WASTE-PAPER-HAMMERMILL OPERATOR 530.686-018

WATER-QUALITY TESTER 539.367-014
web-machine tender 539.686-010
WEIGHT TESTER 539.485-010
Wet-End Tester 539.364-010
WET-MACHINE TENDER 539.685-030
wet-press tender 539.686-010
WINDER HELPER 539.687-010
wood barker 569.687-026
WOOD GRINDER, HEAD 530.132-022
WOOD GRINDER OPERATOR 530.662-014
WOOD HACKER 569.687-026
WOOD HANDLER 921.687-034
WOOD INSPECTOR 663.687-010
wood-mill supervisor 530.132-018
wood-preparation supervisor 530.132-018
YARD LABORER 922.687-102

paper goods—PAPER GOODS INDUSTRY: This designation includes occupations concerned with making paper, paperboard, and cardboard products, such as cardboard boxes, cards, containers, envelopes, paper bags, tags, tubes, spools, cones, mailing cases with or without metal ends, paper napkins, towels, straws, and designing and printing wallpaper. Occupations concerned with the making of bags from cellulose, polyethylene, glassine, and similar films from purchased materials are also included in this designation. Occupations concerned with making paper, paperboard, and cardboard from pulp and other materials are included in the PAPER AND PULP INDUSTRY (paper & pulp). Occupations concerned with coating, finishing, and laminating materials with vinyl for covering and decorating walls and ceilings are included in the TEXTILE PRODUCTS INDUSTRY, NOT ELSEWHERE CLASSIFIED (tex. prod., nec).

Adjustable-Die Cutter 699.682-022
air-hammer stripper 794.687-050
Assembly Inspector 649.367-010
AUTOMATIC-MACHINE ATTENDANT 649.685-010
back tender 652.687-050
bag-end sewer 787.686-010
bag inspector 649.367-010
BAG-MACHINE OPERATOR 649.685-014
BAG-MACHINE-OPERATOR HELPER 649.686-010
Bag-Machine Set-Up Operator 649.380-010
bag-making-machine operator 649.685-014
BAG REPAIRER 794.684-010
BAG SEWER 787.686-010
BANDER, HAND 920.687-026
BAND-SAW OPERATOR 640.685-090
BENDER, MACHINE 641.685-010
bending-machine operator 641.685-010
binder operator 641.685-090
BINDERY WORKER 649.685-018
blanker operator 649.685-118
blanker-press operator 649.682-026
BLANKET-WINDER HELPER 641.686-010
BLANKET-WINDER OPERATOR 641.682-010
Board-Lining-Machine Operator 641.562-010
body-rolling-machine tender 641.685-062
BOOK-JACKET-COVER-MACHINE OPERATOR 640.685-014
Book-Pocket-Machine Operator 649.685-042
BOTTOMING-MACHINE OPERATOR 649.685-022
BOX BENDER 641.687-010
Box Coverer, Hand 795.687-014
box-covering-machine operator 641.685-034
BOX-FOLDING-MACHINE OPERATOR 649.682-026
BOX-LINING-MACHINE FEEDER 641.685-018
BOX-SEALING INSPECTOR 641.687-014
BOX-SEALING-MACHINE OPERATOR 641.662-010
breaker 794.687-050
calender operator 649.682-022
CARTON-FORMING-MACHINE TENDER 641.685-026
Carton-Waxing-Machine Operator 534.482-010
Cellophane-Bag-Machine Operator 649.685-014
clasp machine operator 649.685-070
Clay-Coating-Machine Tender 534.685-018
COATING-MACHINE OPERATOR 534.682-018
COATING-MACHINE OPERATOR, HARDBOARD 534.682-022
Coating-Machine-Operator Helper 534.686-010
Combination Valving-And-Sewing-Machine Operator .. 641.685-094
COMBINER OPERATOR 534.682-026
Combiner-Operator Helper 534.686-010
combiner-sheet operator 534.682-026
COMPENSATOR 640.685-026
CONE TREATER 534.687-010
CONVOLUTE-TUBE WINDER 640.682-010
cook 532.362-010

paper goods

REELER	640.685-054
reel operator	640.685-046
rewinder	640.685-058
REWINDER OPERATOR	640.685-058
RIBBON-HANKING-MACHINE OPERATOR	640.385-010
RING-MAKING-MACHINE OPERATOR	649.685-098
roll-embosser operator	649.682-022
ROLLING-MACHINE OPERATOR	640.685-070
ROLL RECLAIMER	640.685-062
Roll Weigher	222.387-074
roll winder	640.685-058
Rotary-Envelope-Machine Operator	649.685-042
ROUND-CORNER-CUTTER OPERATOR	640.685-074
RULING-MACHINE SET-UP OPERATOR	659.682-022
SALVAGE WINDER AND INSPECTOR	649.685-102
SAMPLE-BOOK MAKER	659.685-014
SAMPLE CLERK, PAPER	209.587-046
SAMPLE MAKER, HAND	794.684-030
scheduler	221.162-010
SCORER	641.685-070
Scorer, Double	641.685-070
SCORER HELPER	641.686-030
Scorer, Single	641.685-070
scoring-machine-operator helper	641.686-030
SCRAPPER	794.687-050
SCREEN MAKER	739.684-150
SCREEN-PRINTING-EQUIPMENT SETTER	979.360-010
SEALING-MACHINE OPERATOR	641.685-074
semiautomatic-stitcher operator	649.685-114
semiautomatic-taper operator	649.685-126
SEWING-MACHINE OPERATOR, PAPER BAGS	787.685-054
sheeter	640.685-046
sheeter helper	649.685-066
Sheeter-Machine Operator	659.685-014
sheeter-waxer operator	534.482-010
SHOT-TUBE-MACHINE TENDER	649.685-106
Side-Seam-Envelope-Machine Operator	649.685-042
Single-Corner Cutter	640.685-030
Single-Ending-Machine Operator	641.685-042
Single-End Sewer	787.686-010
Single-Facing-Corrugating-Machine Operator	641.562-010
Single-Fold-Machine Operator	649.685-046
SLEEVER	641.686-034
Slitter-And-Cutter Operator	649.682-038
SLITTER-CREASER-SLOTTER HELPER	649.686-030
SLITTER-CREASER-SLOTTER OPERATOR	649.682-034
SLITTER-SCORER-CUT-OFF OPERATOR	649.682-038
SLOTTER OPERATOR	640.685-078
SLOTTER-OPERATOR HELPER	640.686-014
Solid-Die Cutter	699.682-022
solid-fiber-paster operator	534.682-026
SORTING-MACHINE OPERATOR	649.685-010
SPIRAL BINDER	653.685-030
spiral-bind operator	653.685-030
SPIRAL-MACHINE OPERATOR	692.685-186
SPIRAL-TUBE WINDER	640.682-022
SPIRAL-TUBE-WINDER HELPER	640.687-014
spiral-winding-machine helper	640.687-014
SPOOL MAKER	641.685-082
staying-machine operator	641.685-054
steel-rule die maker	739.381-018
steel-rule-die-maker apprentice	739.381-022
STEEL-TIE ADJUSTER, AUTOMATIC	649.685-110
STITCHER OPERATOR	649.685-114
Stitcher Set-Up Operator, Automatic	649.380-010
straight ruling machine operator	659.682-022
STRAP-MACHINE OPERATOR	534.682-034
strap-making-machine operator	534.682-034
STRINGER	794.687-054
Stringing-Machine Operator	649.685-054
STRING-TOP SEALER	641.685-086
STRIPER	651.682-018
stripping-machine operator	641.685-034
STRIPPING-MACHINE OPERATOR	641.685-090
stuffing-machine operator	649.685-094
SUPERVISOR, INSPECTING	979.137-014
SUPERVISOR, PAPER COATING	534.132-014
SUPERVISOR, PAPER PRODUCTS	649.130-010
SUPERVISOR, PAPER TESTING	539.134-010
SUPERVISOR, PRODUCTION	979.137-018
surface printer	652.662-014
TABBER	794.687-058
TABLET-MAKING-MACHINE OPERATOR	649.682-042
TABLET-MAKING-MACHINE-OPERATOR HELPER	649.685-130
table worker	794.687-022

tagger	794.687-058
TAG-MACHINE OPERATOR	649.685-118
TAG-PRESS OPERATOR	649.682-046
TAPE-FASTENER-MACHINE OPERATOR	649.685-122
TAPER OPERATOR	649.685-126
tension machine operator	649.685-070
tie fastener	649.685-122
tie-tape-machine operator	649.685-122
TIGHTENING-MACHINE OPERATOR	640.685-082
tin-tie machine operator, automatic	649.685-110
Towel Bander	920.687-026
TRIMMER, HAND	794.687-062
trimming-machine operator	640.685-034
tube cutter	640.685-034
Tube Inspector	649.367-010
TUBE-MACHINE OPERATOR	641.662-014
TUBE-MACHINE-OPERATOR HELPER	641.686-038
tube maker	641.662-014
tube-making-machine operator	641.662-014
tuber helper	641.686-038
TYING-MACHINE OPERATOR	929.685-014
VALVING-MACHINE OPERATOR	641.685-094
VULCANIZED-FIBER-UNIT OPERATOR	539.565-010
WALLCOVERING TEXTURER	749.684-054
wallpaper-embosser helper	640.685-070
WALLPAPER INSPECTOR	652.687-042
WALLPAPER INSPECTOR AND SHIPPER	652.687-046
WALLPAPER-PRINTER HELPER	652.687-050
WALLPAPER PRINTER I	652.662-014
Wallpaper Printer II	979.684-034
Waterproof-Coating-Machine Tender	534.682-018
wax-coating-machine tender	534.482-010
Waxed-Bag-Machine Operator	649.685-014
waxer operator	534.482-010
WAXING-MACHINE OPERATOR	534.482-010
Waxing-Machine-Operator Helper	534.686-010
winder	640.682-022
winder helper	640.687-014
window-machine operator	641.685-066
wire-spiral binder	653.685-030
Wiring-Machine Operator	649.685-054
wrapping-machine operator	641.685-034
WRAPPING-MACHINE OPERATOR	641.685-098

pen & pencil—PEN, PENCIL, MARKING DEVICE, AND ARTISTS' MATE-RIALS MANUFACTURING INDUSTRY: This designation includes occupations concerned with manufacturing pens, fountain pens, ballpoint pens, refill ink cartridges, metal pen points, and mechanical pencils; wood-cased lead pencils, holders, and leads; crayons; rubber marking and branding merchandise; artists' materials, such as drawing boards, palettes, colors, waxes, and drafting equipment; carbon paper; inked ribbons for typewriters and other business machines; and related merchandise. Occupations concerned with the manufacture of drafting instruments are included in the INSTRUMENTS AND APPARA-TUS INDUSTRY (inst. & app.); occupations concerned with the manufacture of drawing, writing, and stamp pad inks are included in the CHEMICAL IN-DUSTRY (chemical).

air-hammer operator	733.687-014
ASSEMBLER	733.685-010
ASSEMBLER, MARKING DEVICES	733.687-010
ASSEMBLER, MECHANICAL PENCILS AND BALLPOINT PENS	733.687-014
Assembly-Machine Feeder	692.686-010
Assembly-Machine Offbearer	692.686-010
ASSEMBLY-MACHINE OPERATOR	692.686-010
BALLPOINT-PEN-ASSEMBLY-MACHINE OPERATOR	692.382-010
BALLPOINT PEN CARTRIDGE TESTER	733.281-010
BANDER	733.687-018
bench-assembler operator	733.687-014
bench-assembler operator	733.687-034
bench-boring-machine operator	733.685-018
CARBON-COATER-MACHINE OPERATOR	534.682-014
CARBON-PAPER-COATING-MACHINE SETTER	534.380-010
CARBON-PAPER INTERLEAFER	640.685-018
Cartridge Assembler	733.685-010
Cartridge Feeder	692.686-010
Cementer	733.687-030
CHALK CUTTER	733.687-022
CHALK-EXTRUDING-MACHINE OPERATOR	575.685-018
CHALK-MOLDING-MACHINE OPERATOR	575.685-022
CLAMPER	733.687-026
coater, carbon paper	534.682-014
COATING-MACHINE OPERATOR	692.685-054
Crayon-Molding-Machine Operator	575.685-022

personal ser.

CRAYON-SORTING-MACHINE FEEDER	929.686-018
cut-off-machine operator	690.685-306
DATER ASSEMBLER	733.687-030
DESK-PEN-SET ASSEMBLER	733.687-034
DIPPER	733.687-038
drum sander	662.685-030
end trimmer	669.685-062
end trimmer	662.685-030
ENGRAVER, RUBBER	733.381-010
ENGRAVER, SEALS	704.381-034
engraver, signature	733.381-010
FELT-TIPPING-MACHINE TENDER	686.686-010
FILLING-MACHINE OPERATOR	733.685-014
FORMULA WEIGHER	559.685-082
Fountain-Brush Assembler	733.687-010
FOUNTAIN PEN TURNER	690.685-190
Fountain-Roller Assembler	733.687-010
GLUE-MACHINE OPERATOR	692.685-094
GOLD-NIB GRINDER	705.682-010
GROOVING-MACHINE OPERATOR	733.685-018
Guillotine Operator	699.685-014
HEADING-MACHINE OPERATOR	669.685-062
HYDRAULIC-BILLET MAKER	575.685-046
hydraulic-press operator	733.687-026
IMPREGNATOR	562.685-014
INJECTION-MOLDING-MACHINE OFFBEARER	690.686-038
inking-machine tender	692.685-142
INSPECTOR	733.687-042
INSPECTOR, FINAL ASSEMBLY	733.687-050
INSPECTOR, RUBBER-STAMP DIE	733.687-054
inter-fold roll cutter	640.685-066
Knurling-Machine Tender	604.685-026
LEAD FORMER	575.685-050
lead-laying-and-gluing-machine operator	692.685-094
lead presser	575.685-050
marker assembler	733.687-010
mixing-and-molding-machine operator	570.685-066
MOLDING-MACHINE TENDER	570.685-066
nib adjuster	733.687-042
Nib Assembler	733.685-010
NIB FINISHER	705.684-050
NIB INSPECTOR	733.687-058
painting-machine operator	692.685-054
Pen Assembler	733.687-010
PENCIL INSPECTOR	733.687-062
pencil sorter	733.687-062
pen-point smoother	733.685-026
PLATE MOLDER	556.582-010
PLUG CUTTER	690.685-306
PRINTER	652.685-062
QUALITY-CONTROL TECHNICIAN, INKED RIBBONS	733.364-010
REPAIRER, PENS AND PENCILS	733.384-010
RIBBON INKER	692.685-142
RIBBON WINDER	733.685-022
ROLL-SLICING-MACHINE TENDER	640.685-066
ROUNDING-MACHINE TENDER	663.685-026
RUBBER-ROLLER GRINDER	690.686-050
rubber-stamp assembler	733.684-018
RUBBER-STAMP MAKER	733.381-014
salvage clerk	733.384-010
Sander, Wooden Pencils	662.685-014
SET-UP MECHANIC	692.380-010
SET-UP MECHANIC, AUTOMATIC LINE	692.380-014
Set-Up Mechanic, Coating Machines	692.380-010
Set-Up Mechanic, Heading Machines	692.380-010
Set-Up Mechanic, Stamping Machines	692.380-010
shaping-machine tender	663.685-026
SIZING-MACHINE TENDER	662.685-030
small kick-press operator	733.687-014
small press operator	733.687-014
SMOOTHER	733.685-026
spooler	733.685-022
STAMPING-MACHINE OPERATOR	692.685-194
stamp maker	733.381-014
STAMP MOUNTER	733.684-018
STAMP-PAD FINISHER	733.687-066
STAMP-PAD MAKER	733.687-070
STENCIL INSPECTOR	733.687-074
SUPERVISOR, ASSEMBLY	733.137-010
SUPERVISOR, CARBON-PAPER-COATING	534.137-010
SUPERVISOR, CUTTING DEPARTMENT	669.130-014
SUPERVISOR, ENGRAVING	704.131-014
SUPERVISOR, FINISHING DEPARTMENT	733.137-014
SUPERVISOR, INSPECTION	733.137-018
SUPERVISOR, PAINTING DEPARTMENT	692.137-010
SUPERVISOR, PLATING AND POINT ASSEMBLY	733.130-010
SUPERVISOR, RUBBER STAMPS AND DIES	733.131-010
SWAGER OPERATOR	616.685-078
TIP BANDER	733.685-030
tip-banding-machine operator	733.685-030
tipper	733.685-034
TIPPING-MACHINE OPERATOR	733.685-034
tipping-machine operator	686.686-010
tip tightener	733.687-014
trimmer	662.685-030
typewriter-ribbon winder	733.685-022
Vulcanizer, Rubber Plate	556.582-010
WASHER	733.687-078
winder	640.685-018

personal ser.—PERSONAL SERVICE: This designation includes occupations concerned with rendering services either upon or for persons and animals or upon personal effects. With very few exceptions, the services rendered are personal in the sense that there is fairly close and often physical contact between the providers and recipients of the services; or the services are performed on personal effects, such as wearing apparel. These services characteristically are performed in establishments devoted primarily to the rendering of such services, but they are also performed in establishments operated for other purposes. Typical of the services included are those performed in the following establishments: barber shops; beauty parlors; costume and dress-suit rental agencies; garment alteration and repair shops; glove repair shops; photographic studios; physical culture schools and gymnasiums; public baths, including turkish baths, sulfur baths, and steam baths; shoe repair shops; shoeshine shops; textile weaving (re-weaving) and mending shops; and undertaking establishments.

alcohol rubber	335.677-010
ALTERATION TAILOR	785.261-010
alterer	785.261-010
alterer apprentice	785.261-018
BARBER	330.371-010
BARBER APPRENTICE	330.371-014
barker	353.363-010
bath attendant	334.677-010
bath attendant	334.374-010
bath-house attendant	334.374-010
beautician	332.271-010
beautician apprentice	332.271-014
beauty culturist	332.271-010
beauty-culturist apprentice	332.271-014
beauty operator	332.271-010
beauty-operator apprentice	332.271-014
Beauty Parlor Cleaner	323.687-014
BLIND AIDE	359.573-010
BODYGUARD	372.667-014
bootblack	366.677-010
boot polisher	366.677-010
busheler	785.261-014
cage clerk	358.677-014
Caterer	187.167-106
CATERER HELPER	319.677-010
CHAPERON	359.667-010
CHAUFFEUR, FUNERAL CAR	359.673-014
CHILD-CARE ATTENDANT, SCHOOL	355.674-010
cicerone	353.363-010
clerk guide	359.573-010
cobbler	365.361-014
COOLING-ROOM ATTENDANT	335.677-010
cosmetician	332.271-010
cosmetician apprentice	332.271-014
COSMETOLOGIST	332.271-010
COSMETOLOGIST APPRENTICE	332.271-014
counter attendant	369.477-014
CREMATOR	359.685-010
CUSTOM TAILOR	785.261-014
DIRECTOR, FUNERAL	187.167-030
dispensary attendant	339.687-010
DOG BATHER	418.677-010
dog beautician	418.674-010
DOG GROOMER	418.674-010
dog-hair clipper	418.674-010
dressing-room attendant	358.677-014
Dry-Heat-Cabinet Attendant	335.677-010
Dry-Heat-Room Attendant	335.677-010
electric-bath attendant	335.677-010
electric-needle specialist	339.371-010
ELECTROLOGIST	339.371-010
electrolysis operator	339.371-010
EMBALMER	338.371-014
EMBALMER APPRENTICE	338.371-010

embalmer assistant	339.361-010
ESCORT	359.367-010
escort, blind	359.573-010
Facial Operator	332.271-010
FINGERNAIL FORMER	331.674-014
Finger Waver	332.271-010
Finnish Rubber	334.677-010
french weaver	782.381-022
FUNERAL ATTENDANT	359.677-014
funeral driver	359.673-014
funeral-home attendant	339.361-010
Funeral-Limousine Driver	359.673-014
GUIDE	353.367-010
GUIDE, ALPINE	353.164-010
Guide, Cruise	353.167-010
Guide, Delegate	353.167-010
Guide, Domestic Tour	353.167-010
guide escort	359.367-010
guide, excursion	353.167-010
Guide, Foreign Tour	359.167-010
guide, itinerary	353.167-010
GUIDE, SIGHTSEEING	353.363-010
guide, tour	353.167-010
GUIDE, TRAVEL	353.167-010
guide, visitor	353.367-010
hair-and-scalp specialist	339.371-014
Hair Colorist	332.271-010
haircutter	330.371-010
hairdresser	332.361-010
hairdresser	332.271-018
HAIR STYLIST	332.271-018
Hair Tinter	332.271-010
Hearse Driver	359.673-014
HOME ATTENDANT	354.377-014
home health aide	354.377-014
HOT-ROOM ATTENDANT	335.677-014
hypertrichologist	339.371-010
inweaver	782.381-022
jagger	339.571-010
locker attendant	358.677-014
LOCKER-ROOM ATTENDANT	358.677-014
locker-room clerk	358.677-014
made-to-measure tailor	785.261-014
made-to-measure-tailor apprentice	785.261-022
MANAGER, BARBER OR BEAUTY SHOP	187.167-058
MANAGER, FOOD SERVICE	187.167-106
manager, funeral home	187.167-030
MANAGER, HEALTH CLUB	339.137-010
MANICURIST	331.674-010
Marceller	332.271-010
MASSEUR/MASSEUSE	334.374-010
master-tailor apprentice	785.261-022
mortician	187.167-030
MORTUARY BEAUTICIAN	339.361-010
nutrition educator	359.367-014
overweaver	782.381-022
PALLBEARER	359.687-010
Permanent Waver	332.271-010
personal attendant	358.677-014
porter, bath	335.677-014
public-bath attendant	335.677-014
REDUCING-SALON ATTENDANT	359.567-010
rehabilitation technician	365.131-010
repair weaver	782.381-022
reweaver	782.381-022
RUBBER	334.677-010
rubber	334.374-010
Russian Rubber	334.677-010
SALESPERSON, WIGS	261.351-010
scalp specialist	339.371-014
SCALP-TREATMENT OPERATOR	339.371-014
section weaver	782.381-022
SECURITY CONSULTANT	189.167-054
SERVICE-ESTABLISHMENT ATTENDANT	369.477-014
Shampooer	332.271-010
SHOE DYER	364.684-014
shoemaker	365.361-014
shoe polisher	366.677-010
SHOE REPAIRER	365.361-014
SHOE-REPAIRER HELPER	365.674-010
SHOE-REPAIR SUPERVISOR	365.131-010
SHOE SHINER	366.677-010
shoe tinter	364.684-014
Shower Attendant	335.677-014
slumber-room attendant	335.677-010

spieler	353.363-010
Steam-Room Attendant	335.677-014
storekeeper	339.687-010
suit attendant	358.677-014
SUPPLY CLERK	339.687-010
sweat-box attendant	335.677-014
tailor	785.261-014
TAILOR APPRENTICE, ALTERATION	785.261-018
TAILOR APPRENTICE, CUSTOM	785.261-022
TATTOO ARTIST	339.571-010
tattooer	339.571-010
tattooist	339.571-010
thread weaver	782.381-022
tonsorial artist	330.371-010
trichologist	339.371-014
tub attendant	335.677-014
Turkish Rubber	334.677-010
undertaker	187.167-030
undertaker assistant	359.677-014
usher	359.677-014
WEAVER, HAND	782.381-022
WEIGHT-REDUCTION SPECIALIST	359.367-014
WIG DRESSER	332.361-010
Wig Stylist	261.351-010

petrol. & gas—PETROLEUM AND NATURAL GAS PRODUCTION INDUSTRY: This designation includes occupations concerned with extracting crude petroleum and natural gas from the earth through wells drilled into oil-bearing or gas-bearing strata. Activities include prospecting for gas or oil; drilling wells; controlling the natural flow of the fluids; pumping of the fluids; maintenance and cleaning out of productive wells; and maintenance of oil or gas well storage facilities, treating facilities, flow lines, and other lease facilities and equipment. Occupations primarily concerned with petroleum refining are included in the PETROLEUM REFINING INDUSTRY (petrol. refin.). Occupations primarily concerned with the transportation of petroleum and gas products through pipelines are included in the PIPE LINES INDUSTRY (pipe lines).

Acidizer	939.462-010
Acidizer Helper	939.684-018
Acoustical Logging Engineer	010.261-022
analyst, geochemical prospecting	024.381-010
Back-Up Worker	930.684-026
Bailer	930.363-010
Bottom-Hole-Pressure-Recording Operator	930.167-010
BOTTOM-HOLE-PRESSURE-RECORDING-OPERATOR HELPER	930.687-010
BULK-STATION OPERATOR	570.362-010
cable splicer	728.684-014
CASER	930.664-010
casing puller	930.382-030
Cathead Worker	930.684-026
Cementer Helper	939.684-018
Cementer, Oil Well	939.462-010
CHIEF CLERK, MEASUREMENT DEPARTMENT	221.132-010
CHIEF DISPATCHER	939.137-010
CHIEF ENGINEER	010.167-010
Chief Engineer, Drilling And Recovery	010.167-010
Chief Engineer, Pipe-Line	010.167-010
Chief Engineer, Production	010.167-010
CHIEF ENGINEER, RESEARCH	010.161-010
chief gauger	914.134-010
CHIEF PETROLEUM ENGINEER	010.161-014
Chief, Reservoir Engineering	010.167-010
CLAIM AGENT	191.167-014
CLEAN-OUT DRILLER	930.363-010
CLEAN-OUT-DRILLER HELPER	930.664-014
connection worker	869.684-046
core analyst	024.381-010
core driller	930.382-018
core driller	930.382-026
CRUDE-OIL TREATER	541.382-014
dehydrator operator	541.382-014
DERRICK WORKER, WELL SERVICE	930.683-018
diesel-engine engineer	950.382-022
DIGITIZER OPERATOR	213.582-010
Director, Geothermal Operations	010.161-014
DISPATCHER, CHIEF I	184.167-038
DISPATCHER, CHIEF II	914.167-010
Dispatcher, Chief, Natural Gas	184.167-038
DISPATCHER, OIL	914.167-014
DISPATCHER, OIL WELL SERVICES	939.362-010
district gauger	914.134-010
district superintendent	181.167-014
district superintendent, gas and gasoline	914.167-010

DISTRICT SUPERVISOR, MUD-ANALYSIS WELL
  LOGGING 010.167-014
division superintendent 181.167-014
DRAFTER, DIRECTIONAL SURVEY 010.281-010
DRAFTER, GEOLOGICAL 010.281-014
DRAFTER, GEOPHYSICAL 010.281-018
DRAFTER, OIL AND GAS 017.281-030
Drafter, Seismograph 010.281-018
driller 930.382-018
driller 930.382-026
driller helper 930.684-026
Drilling Engineer 010.061-018
drilling inspector 930.167-010
DUMPER-BAILER OPERATOR 931.684-010
ELECTRICAL-LINE SPLICER 728.684-014
electrical-logging engineer 010.261-014
electrical-prospecting operator 010.261-014
Electrical Prospector 024.061-026
ELECTRICAL SUPERVISOR 826.131-010
electronics supervisor 710.131-034
FIELD ENGINEER, SPECIALIST 010.261-010
field gauger 914.384-010
Field Mechanic 629.381-014
Field Operator 710.381-022
field operator 914.382-022
field-party manager 181.167-010
field seismologist 010.161-018
FIELD SUPERVISOR, OIL-WELL SERVICES 930.131-010
Fire-Truck Driver 905.663-014
FISHING-TOOL TECHNICIAN, OIL WELL 930.261-014
FLOOR WORKER, WELL SERVICE 930.684-014
Formation-Fracturing Operator 939.462-010
Formation-Fracturing-Operator Helper 939.684-018
FORMATION-TESTING OPERATOR 930.261-014
gang supervisor, pipe lines 862.131-022
gang worker 869.684-046
gas-engine engineer 950.382-022
GAUGER 914.384-010
GAUGER, CHIEF 914.134-010
general manager, land department 186.117-046
general-office dispatcher 914.167-010
GEOLOGICAL AIDE 024.267-010
GEOLOGIST, PETROLEUM 024.061-022
geophysical operator 010.161-018
GEOPHYSICAL PROSPECTOR 024.061-026
Gravity-Meter Observer 010.261-018
gravity-prospecting operator 010.261-018
gravity-prospecting-operator helper 939.663-010
Gravity Prospector 024.061-026
gun perforator 931.382-010
GUN-PERFORATOR LOADER 931.384-010
head well-puller 939.131-018
HOIST OPERATOR 932.363-010
Hydraulic Oil-Tool Operator 930.382-030
INSTRUMENT-MAKER AND REPAIRER 600.280-014
LABORATORY ASSISTANT 024.381-010
laboratory tester 024.381-010
LABORER 939.687-018
land-and-leases supervisor 186.117-046
land department head 186.117-046
Lead-Tong Worker 930.684-026
lease agent 186.117-046
LEASE BUYER 191.117-030
leaser 191.117-030
leases-and-land supervisor 186.117-046
lease supervisor 939.131-014
line rider 869.564-010
LINE WALKER 869.564-010
Magnetic Prospector 024.061-026
Magnetometer Operator 010.261-018
MAINTENANCE MECHANIC 620.281-046
MAINTENANCE MECHANIC HELPER 620.664-014
MANAGER, CONTRACTS 163.117-010
Manager, Contracts-And-Titles 186.167-038
Manager, Divisional Leasing 186.117-046
MANAGER, FIELD PARTY, GEOPHYSICAL
  PROSPECTING 181.167-010
manager, land department 186.117-046
MANAGER, LAND LEASES-AND-RENTALS 186.167-038
MANAGER, LEASING 186.117-046
Manager, Natural-Gas Utilization 163.117-010
manager, oil-well services 010.161-018
Manager, Titles-And-Land-Records 186.167-038
Material Stockkeeper, Yard 222.387-058
measurement superintendent 184.167-190

mechanic helper 620.664-014
mud-analysis-well-logging captain 010.131-010
mud-analysis-well-logging operator 010.281-022
mud-analysis-well-logging supervisor, district ... 010.167-014
mud engineer 010.161-018
mud-logging superintendent 010.167-014
MUD-PLANT OPERATOR 930.685-010
NATURAL-GAS-TREATING-UNIT OPERATOR ... 549.382-010
Nuclear Logging Engineer 010.261-022
OBSERVER, ELECTRICAL PROSPECTING 010.261-014
OBSERVER, GRAVITY PROSPECTING 010.261-018
observer helper 939.364-010
OBSERVER HELPER, GRAVITY PROSPECTING ... 939.663-010
OBSERVER HELPER, SEISMIC PROSPECTING ... 939.364-010
OBSERVER, SEISMIC PROSPECTING 010.161-018
oil dispatcher 914.167-014
OIL-FIELD EQUIPMENT MECHANIC 629.381-014
OIL-FIELD EQUIPMENT MECHANIC SUPERVISOR ... 629.131-014
Oil-Field-Pipe-Line Supervisor 862.131-022
OIL-PIPE INSPECTOR 930.267-010
OIL-PIPE-INSPECTOR HELPER 930.364-010
OIL PUMPER 914.382-030
oil-well-electrical-wall-sampling-device operator ... 931.361-010
oil-well-fishing-tool operator 930.261-010
oil-well formation tester 930.261-014
oil-well-gun-perforator operator 931.382-010
oil-well-logging engineer 010.261-022
oil-well pumper 914.382-010
OIL-WELL-SERVICE OPERATOR 939.462-010
OIL-WELL-SERVICE-OPERATOR HELPER 939.684-018
OIL-WELL-SERVICES SUPERVISOR 939.132-014
oil-well shooter 931.361-010
oil-well-sounding-device operator 930.361-010
PERFORATOR OPERATOR, OIL WELL 931.382-010
PERMIT AGENT, GEOPHYSICAL PROSPECTING ... 191.117-042
PETROLEUM ENGINEER 010.061-018
pipe inspector 930.267-010
pipe-line gauger 914.384-010
pipe puller 930.382-030
Pipe Racker 930.684-026
PIPE TESTER 930.382-014
pipe-thread inspector 862.381-038
playback operator 194.382-010
PNEUMATIC-JACK OPERATOR 939.682-014
Production Engineer 010.061-018
production operator 541.382-014
Property-And-Equipment Clerk 222.387-026
PROSPECTING DRILLER 930.382-018
Prospecting-Driller Helper 939.364-010
pulling-machine operator 930.382-030
pumper 541.382-014
pumper 914.382-010
PUMPER, HEAD 914.382-022
RADIOACTIVITY-INSTRUMENT MAINTENANCE
  TECHNICIAN 828.281-022
radioactivity technician 828.281-022
recorder, gravity prospecting 010.261-018
recorder helper, gravity prospecting 939.663-010
recorder helper, seismograph 939.364-010
RESEARCH ENGINEER, MINING-AND-OIL-WELL
  EQUIPMENT 010.061-022
Reservoir Engineer 010.061-018
rig operator 930.382-030
ROTARY DERRICK OPERATOR 930.382-022
ROTARY DRILLER 930.382-026
ROTARY-DRILLER HELPER 930.684-026
Rotary Driller, Marine Operations 930.382-026
rotary driller, prospecting 930.382-018
rotary helper 930.684-026
ROTARY-RIG ENGINE OPERATOR 950.382-022
roughneck 930.684-026
roughneck 869.684-046
roustabout 939.687-018
ROUSTABOUT 869.684-046
roustabout, head 862.131-022
SALES ENGINEER, MINING-AND-OIL-WELL
  EQUIPMENT AND SERVICES 010.151-010
SAMPLE-TAKER OPERATOR 931.361-010
SAMPLE WASHER 939.687-030
SCOUT 010.267-010
SECTION-PLOTTER OPERATOR 194.382-010
section-plotter operator 010.161-018
Seismic Prospector 024.061-026
seismograph-operator helper 939.364-010
service engineer 620.281-046

1156

SERVICE-UNIT OPERATOR, OIL WELL 930.361-010
SHOOTER 931.361-014
Shooter Helper, Seismograph 939.364-010
SHOOTER, SEISMOGRAPH 931.361-018
shop mechanic 620.281-046
shop-mechanic helper 620.664-014
shot-hole driller 930.382-018
shot-hole shooter 931.361-018
superintendent, drilling 930.130-010
SUPERINTENDENT, DRILLING AND PRODUCTION 181.167-014
superintendent, land department 186.117-046
SUPERINTENDENT, MEASUREMENT 184.167-190
Superintendent, Oil-Field Drilling 181.167-014
SUPERINTENDENT, OIL-WELL SERVICES 010.167-018
superintendent, pressure 914.167-010
Superintendent, Production 181.167-014
superintendent, scheduling 184.167-038
SUPERVISOR, MAPPING 018.167-030
SUPERVISOR, NATURAL-GAS-FIELD PROCESSING 549.131-010
SUPERVISOR, PIPE-LINES 862.131-022
SUPERVISOR, PRODUCTION 939.131-014
supervisor, research shop 710.131-034
SUPERVISOR, SHOP 710.131-034
Supply Representative, Dry Gas 163.117-010
supply representative, petroleum products 163.117-010
SURVEYOR, GEOPHYSICAL PROSPECTING 018.167-042
SURVEYOR, OIL-WELL DIRECTIONAL 010.261-022
Swabber 930.363-010
tank builder 801.361-022
tank-builder helper 801.687-018
tank-farm gauger 914.384-010
TANK SETTER 801.361-022
TANK-SETTER HELPER 801.687-018
TECHNICAL OPERATOR 930.167-010
terminal gauger 914.384-010
TEST ENGINEER, MINING-&-OILFIELD EQUIPMENT 010.061-030
testing-tool operator 930.261-014
THREAD INSPECTOR 862.381-038
TITLE CLERK 162.267-010
TOOL PUSHER 930.130-010
Tool Pusher, Shallow-Exploratory Drilling 930.130-010
torpedo shooter 931.361-014
treater 541.382-014
tube puller 930.382-030
Water-Truck Driver I 904.383-010
WATER-TRUCK DRIVER II 905.683-010
well cleaner 930.363-010
well driller 930.382-026
WELL-LOGGING CAPTAIN, MUD ANALYSIS 010.131-010
WELL-LOGGING OPERATOR, MUD ANALYSIS 010.281-022
WELL PULLER 930.382-030
WELL PULLER, HEAD 939.131-018
well shooter 931.361-014
winch operator 932.363-010
work-over rig operator 930.382-030

petrol. refin.—PETROLEUM REFINING INDUSTRY: This designation includes occupations concerned with refining crude petroleum by such methods as distillation, absorption, extraction, adsorption, thermal and catalytic cracking and reforming, polymerization, coking, alkylation, treating, and blending. The principal products are gasoline, kerosene, fuel and lubricating oils, gases, solvents, asphalts (including paving materials), waxes, greases, and petroleum coke.

Absorption-Plant Operator 549.260-010
Absorption-Plant-Operator Helper 542.362-014
Acid-Tank Cleaner 891.687-022
Acid Treater 549.362-014
Alkylation Operator 559.382-018
Asphalt Blender 540.462-010
Batch-Unit Treater 549.362-014
BLENDER 540.462-010
burner operator 573.685-014
Butadiene Operator, Chief 559.132-078
Butane-Compressor Operator 950.382-014
CARGO INSPECTOR 549.387-010
catalyst supervisor 559.132-078
chart clerk 216.685-010
chief gauger 914.134-010
chief operator 549.132-030
chief operator, hydroformer 549.132-030
clay burner 573.685-014
Clay-Plant Treater 549.362-014
CLAY ROASTER 573.685-014
COMPOUNDER 540.382-010
COMPOUNDER HELPER 540.686-010
CONSTRUCTION-AND-MAINTENANCE INSPECTOR 914.362-014
CONTROL-PANEL OPERATOR 546.382-010
Control-Panel Operator, Cracking Unit 546.382-010
Control-Panel Operator, Crude Unit 546.382-010
Control-Panel Operator, Polymerization Unit 546.382-010
Control-Panel Operator, Solvent-Treating Unit 546.382-010
Cooling-Tower Operator 549.362-010
Crude-Oil Treater 549.362-014
crude tester 029.261-022
dehydrogenation operator, head 559.132-078
DISPATCHER, CHIEF I 184.167-038
DISPATCHER, CHIEF II 914.167-010
Dispatcher, Chief, Petroleum Products 184.167-038
DISPATCHER, OIL 914.167-014
district gauger 914.134-010
district superintendent, gas and gasoline 914.167-010
DRAFTER, OIL AND GAS 017.281-030
drum chainer 599.687-034
DRUM CLEANER 599.687-034
DRUM TESTER 599.687-038
earth burner 573.685-014
Electrician, Refinery 829.261-018
Ethylbenzene-Cracking Supervisor 559.132-078
Ethyl Blender 540.462-010
extraction supervisor 549.132-030
field gauger 914.384-010
FIELD-MECHANICAL-METER TESTER 953.281-010
field operating superintendent 181.117-010
Fire Marshal, Refinery 373.167-018
fractionation operator, head 549.132-030
fractionation supervisor 549.132-030
Fuel-Oil-Delivery Driver 903.683-018
FURNACE OPERATOR 542.562-010
gang boss 899.137-018
gang pusher 899.137-018
gas analyst 029.261-022
Gas-Delivery Driver 903.683-018
gasoline finisher 540.462-010
GAS-REGULATOR REPAIRER 710.381-026
GAS-REGULATOR-REPAIRER HELPER 710.384-010
GAS USAGE METER CLERK 216.685-010
GAUGER 914.384-010
GAUGER, CHIEF 914.134-010
general-office dispatcher 914.167-010
GREASE MAKER 549.682-010
GREASE MAKER, HEAD 549.132-010
Hydrogen Treater 549.362-014
inspector 549.261-010
laboratory inspector 029.261-022
laboratory sampler 549.587-014
laboratory technician 029.261-022
laboratory tester 029.261-022
Laborer, Filter Plant 549.687-018
LABORER, PETROLEUM REFINERY 549.687-018
lead blender 540.462-010
LEAD RECOVERER, CONTINUOUS-NAPHTHA-TREATING PLANT 541.685-014
Leak Operator, Paraffin Plant 541.682-010
line rider 869.564-010
LINE WALKER 869.564-010
LOADING-RACK SUPERVISOR 914.137-014
loading supervisor 549.137-018
MANAGER, BULK PLANT 181.117-010
MANAGER, CONTRACTS 163.117-010
MECHANICAL INSPECTOR 549.261-010
mechanical-meter tester 953.281-010
meter inspector 953.281-010
MOLDER, WAX 549.685-018
Naphtha-Plant Treater 549.362-014
oil dispatcher 914.167-014
OIL-RECOVERY-UNIT OPERATOR 549.382-014
oil tester 029.261-022
operator, control room 546.382-010
Painter, Barrel 741.687-018
PAINT STRIPPER 599.685-130
PARAFFIN-PLANT OPERATOR 541.682-010
PARAFFIN-PLANT-SWEATER OPERATOR 543.682-022
Pilot-Plant Research-Technician 008.261-010
pipe-line gauger 914.384-010
plant supervisor 542.130-010
Press Operator, Paraffin Plant 541.682-010
process helper 549.687-018

pharmaceut.

process pumper	549.362-010
PUMPER	549.360-010
PUMPER-GAUGER	914.382-014
PUMPER-GAUGER APPRENTICE	914.382-018
PUMPER HELPER	549.684-010
pump operator	549.362-010
Purification Operator	549.260-010
Purification-Operator Helper	542.362-014
reclamation supervisor	929.131-010
REFINERY OPERATOR	549.260-010
Refinery Operator, Alkylation	549.260-010
Refinery Operator, Coking	549.260-010
Refinery Operator, Cracking Unit	549.260-010
Refinery Operator, Crude Unit	549.260-010
Refinery Operator, Gas Plant	549.260-010
REFINERY OPERATOR HELPER	542.362-014
Refinery Operator Helper, Cracking Unit	542.362-014
Refinery Operator Helper, Crude Unit	542.362-014
Refinery Operator, Light-Ends Recovery	549.260-010
Refinery Operator, Polymerization Plant	549.260-010
Refinery Operator, Reforming Unit	549.260-010
Refinery Operator, Vapor Recovery Unit	549.260-010
Refinery Operator, Visbreaking	549.260-010
research-test-engine evaluator	010.261-026
research-test-engine operator	029.261-018
SALVAGER	709.684-070
salvage repairer	709.684-070
SALVAGER HELPER	709.687-034
SAMPLER	549.587-014
Solvent-Plant Treater	549.362-014
Still And Tank Inspector	549.261-010
Still Cleaner, Tube	891.687-030
STILL-PUMP OPERATOR	549.362-010
Styrene Operator, Chief	559.132-078
superintendent, pressure	914.167-010
superintendent, scheduling	184.167-038
Supervisor, Benzene-Refining	549.132-030
SUPERVISOR, DEHYDROGENATION	559.132-078
SUPERVISOR, DOCK	914.137-018
supervisor, grease making	549.132-030
SUPERVISOR, MAINTENANCE	899.137-018
SUPERVISOR, METER-AND-REGULATOR SHOP	710.137-014
SUPERVISOR, NATURAL-GAS PLANT	542.130-010
SUPERVISOR, PURIFICATION	549.132-030
SUPERVISOR, SALVAGE	929.131-010
SUPERVISOR, SPECIALTY PLANT	549.137-018
Supervisor, Tank Cleaning	899.137-018
SUPERVISOR, TOWER	549.130-010
SUPERVISOR, TREATING AND PUMPING	549.132-034
Supply Representative, Dry Gas	163.117-010
supply representative, petroleum products	163.117-010
sweater operator	543.682-022
Tank-Car Cleaner	891.687-022
TANK-CAR INSPECTOR	910.384-014
tank-farm gauger	914.384-010
TANK-TRUCK DRIVER	903.683-018
Tar Heat-Exchanger Cleaner	891.687-030
terminal gauger	914.384-010
terminal superintendent	181.117-010
terminal supervisor	914.137-018
TEST-ENGINE EVALUATOR	010.261-026
TEST-ENGINE OPERATOR	029.261-018
TESTER	029.261-022
TITLE CLERK	162.267-010
Trailer-Tank-Truck Driver	903.683-018
TREATER	549.362-014
TREATER HELPER	549.685-030
treating and pumping supervisor	549.132-034
treating-plant operator	549.362-014
valve repairer, reclamation	709.684-070
wax pumper	541.682-010
Wax Treater	549.362-014
wharf tender, head	914.137-018

pharmaceut.—PHARMACEUTICALS AND RELATED PRODUCTS INDUSTRY: This designation includes occupations concerned with producing medicinal chemicals and ethical and proprietary pharmaceuticals, such as capsules, ointments, pills, serums, vaccines, and powdered, liquid, and emulsified compounds. Also inccluded are occupations concerned with grading, grinding, and milling botanicals. Occupations concerned with producing cosmetics, perfumes and colognes, and related products are included in the SOAP, CLEANING, AND TOILET PREPARATION INDUSTRY (soap & rel.).

ALUMINUM-HYDROXIDE-PROCESS OPERATOR	559.685-014

AMPOULE EXAMINER	559.687-010
AMPOULE FILLER	559.685-018
ampoule filler and sealer	559.685-018
AMPOULE SEALER	559.687-014
AMPOULE-WASHING-MACHINE OPERATOR	559.685-022
autoclave operator	599.585-010
batcher	559.686-022
CAPSULE-FILLING-MACHINE OPERATOR	559.682-010
CENTRIFUGE OPERATOR, PLASMA PROCESSING	599.685-018
Chemical Mixer	550.685-090
CHEMICAL-PROCESSING SUPERVISOR	559.130-010
COATER	554.382-010
compounder	550.685-090
COMPOUNDER	550.685-046
compounder, sterile products	559.682-054
COMPRESSOR	556.682-022
COSMETICS PRESSER	556.685-026
COSMETICS SUPERVISOR	550.131-010
Cream Maker	550.685-090
Dental-Cream Maker	550.685-090
DRIER OPERATOR	553.685-042
drum-drier operator	553.685-042
EFFERVESCENT-SALTS COMPOUNDER	559.685-058
EGG PROCESSOR	559.687-034
EXTRACTOR OPERATOR	551.685-058
FERMENTER OPERATOR	559.685-070
FREEZING-MACHINE OPERATOR	559.685-090
granulator	559.382-026
GRANULATOR-MACHINE OPERATOR	559.382-026
harvester	559.687-034
Helper, Animal Laboratory	410.674-010
INSPECTOR	559.387-014
INSPECTOR, PACKAGING MATERIALS	920.387-010
ION-EXCHANGE OPERATOR	558.685-038
laboratory aide	559.384-010
laboratory assistant	599.687-026
LABORATORY ASSISTANT, BLOOD AND PLASMA	078.687-010
LABORATORY ASSISTANT, CULTURE MEDIA	559.384-010
laboratory technician	559.382-042
LABORATORY TECHNICIAN PHARMACEUTICAL	559.685-170
LABORER	559.686-022
Lanolin-Plant Operator	559.382-018
Lipstick Molder	556.687-022
Liquid Compounder I	559.382-042
Liquid Compounder II	550.685-090
medical technologist, bacteriology	078.261-014
MICROBIOLOGY TECHNOLOGIST	078.261-014
mixer	550.685-090
MIXING-MACHINE TENDER	550.685-090
molder	556.685-026
MOLDER, MACHINE	556.685-050
MOLDER, TOILET PRODUCTS	556.687-022
Ointment-Mill Tender	550.685-090
packaging inspector	920.387-010
Perfume And Toilet Water Maker	550.685-090
perfume compounder	550.685-046
PHARMACEUTICAL-COMPOUNDING SUPERVISOR	559.131-010
PHARMACEUTICAL OPERATOR	559.382-042
pill coater	554.382-010
pooling operator	599.687-026
POULTICE-MACHINE OPERATOR	692.685-134
Powder Compounder	550.685-090
process operator	559.685-058
process operator	550.685-090
QUALITY-CONTROL CLERK	229.587-014
QUALITY-CONTROL COORDINATOR	168.167-066
Roller-Mill Tender	550.685-090
Rouge Mixer	550.685-090
rouge presser	556.685-026
shell-freezing-machine operator	559.685-090
SIFTER	551.687-030
SIPHON OPERATOR	599.687-026
STERILE-PRODUCTS PROCESSOR	559.682-054
STERILIZER	599.585-010
SUPERVISOR, ANIMAL MAINTENANCE	410.137-018
Suppository Molder	556.687-022
SUPPOSITORY-MOLDING-MACHINE OPERATOR	556.686-022
synthetic department supervisor	559.130-010
tablet coater	554.382-010
TABLET TESTER	559.667-010
technical assistant	559.384-010
TOXICOLOGIST	022.081-010
UTILITY WORKER, PRODUCTION	559.684-034
utility worker, virus	559.684-034
vacuum-drum-drier operator	553.685-042

washing-machine operator 559.685-022
wet-mix operator 559.382-026

photo. appar.—PHOTOGRAPHIC APPARATUS AND MATERIALS INDUSTRY: This designation includes occupations concerned with manufacturing and repairing photographic apparatus, equipment, parts, attachments, and accessories, such as still and motion cameras and projection apparatus; photocopy and microfilm equipment; blueprinting and diazo-type (white printing) machines; tripods, plate holders, film rewinders and reels, and developing tanks; sensitized film, paper, and cloth; dry plates and films; and lantern and stereopticon slides, and slide viewers. Occupations concerned with the manufacture of lenses are included in the OPTICAL GOODS INDUSTRY (optical goods).

AIRCRAFT-PHOTOGRAPHIC-EQUIPMENT MECHANIC . 714.281-010
ASSEMBLER, PHOTOGRAPHIC EQUIPMENT 714.381-010
assembler, precision-mechanical 714.381-010
ASSEMBLER, PRODUCTION LINE 714.684-010
bellows assembler 714.684-014
BELLOWS MAKER 714.684-014
Blueprint-Paper-Coating-Machine Operator 534.582-010
Camera Assembler 714.684-010
CAMERA REPAIRER 714.281-014
CHECKER, FILM TESTS 714.687-010
cinetechnician 714.281-018
cinetechnician supervisor 714.131-010
coater 534.582-010
Dye Mixer 550.685-090
FIELD-SERVICE ENGINEER 826.261-010
FILM SPOOLER 692.685-082
INSPECTOR, PHOTOGRAPHIC EQUIPMENT 714.381-014
inspector, precision 714.381-014
MACHINIST, MOTION-PICTURE EQUIPMENT 714.281-018
Meter Assembler 714.684-010
motion-picture-camera repairer 714.281-018
OPTOMECHANICAL TECHNICIAN 007.161-030
PAPER-COATING-MACHINE OPERATOR 534.582-010
PHOTOGRAPHIC-EQUIPMENT-MAINTENANCE TECHNICIAN 714.281-026
PHOTOGRAPHIC EQUIPMENT TECHNICIAN 714.281-022
Photographic-Paper-Coating-Machine Operator 534.582-010
Projector Assembler 714.684-010
research assembler 714.281-010
research mechanic 714.281-010
SENSITIZED-PAPER TESTER 714.667-010
sensitizer 534.582-010
SUPERVISOR, COATING 534.130-010
SUPERVISOR, MOTION-PICTURE EQUIPMENT 714.131-010
Synchro Assembler 714.684-010
technical-maintenance technician 714.281-026

photofinishing—PHOTOFINISHING INDUSTRY: This designation includes occupations concerned with developing exposed still and movie film of various types and sizes and making photographic prints and enlargements for the trade and general public. Occupations concerned with the processing of motion picture film for use in theaters and television are included in this designation.

checker 976.687-014
checking department supervisor 976.137-014
CHEMICAL MIXER 550.485-010
COLORIST, PHOTOGRAPHY 970.381-010
Color-Laboratory Technician 976.681-010
COLOR-PRINTER OPERATOR 976.382-014
Color-Print Inspector 976.687-014
COMPUTER-CONTROLLED-COLOR-PHOTOGRAPH-PRINTER OPERATOR 976.380-010
continuous process machine operator 976.685-014
COUNTER CLERK 249.366-010
CUTTER 976.685-010
darkroom worker 976.681-010
DETAILER, SCHOOL PHOTOGRAPHS 976.564-010
DEVELOPER 976.681-010
DEVELOPER, AUTOMATIC 976.685-014
developer operator 976.382-018
doper 976.681-010
EDITOR, SCHOOL PHOTOGRAPH 976.687-010
film cutter 976.685-010
FILM DEVELOPER 976.382-018
FILM INSPECTOR 976.362-010
FILM LABORATORY TECHNICIAN 976.684-014
film machine operator 976.685-014
film numberer 976.687-018
film sorter 976.687-018
film technician 976.131-014
finishing department supervisor 976.137-014
Full-Roll Inspector 976.687-014
hand developer 976.681-010
inspector 976.687-014
LABORATORY CHIEF 976.131-010
laboratory contact supervisor 976.131-014
laboratory manager 976.131-010
MOUNTER, AUTOMATIC 976.685-022
MOUNTER, HAND 976.684-018
Mounting Inspector 976.687-014
Negative Developer 976.382-018
Negative Spotter 970.381-034
PHOTO CHECKER AND ASSEMBLER 976.687-014
PHOTOFINISHING LABORATORY WORKER 976.687-018
photograph enlarger 976.381-018
PHOTOGRAPH FINISHER 976.487-010
photographic-laboratory supervisor 976.131-010
photograph printer 976.682-014
PHOTOGRAPH RETOUCHER 970.281-018
Positive Developer 976.382-018
pricer-bagger 976.687-018
PRINT CONTROLLER 976.360-010
print cutter 976.685-010
PRINT DEVELOPER, AUTOMATIC 976.685-026
PRINTER OPERATOR, BLACK-AND-WHITE 976.682-014
print finisher 976.487-010
PRINT INSPECTOR 976.687-022
PRINT WASHER 976.684-022
projection-camera operator 976.381-018
PROJECTION PRINTER 976.381-018
proof sorter 976.687-018
quality-control projectionist 976.362-010
QUALITY-CONTROL TECHNICIAN 976.267-010
racker 976.687-018
reel-film inspector 976.362-010
reprint sorter 976.687-018
retoucher 970.281-018
Reversal-Print Inspector 976.687-014
SERVICE TECHNICIAN, COMPUTERIZED-PHOTOFINISHING EQUIPMENT 714.281-030
Slitter, Processed Film 976.684-026
solution mixer 550.485-010
sorter-packer 976.687-018
SPLICER 976.684-026
SPOTTER, PHOTOGRAPHIC 970.381-034
SUPERVISOR, CUTTING AND SPLICING 976.134-010
SUPERVISOR, FILM PROCESSING 976.131-014
SUPERVISOR, FILM PROCESSING 976.132-010
SUPERVISOR, FINISHING DEPARTMENT 976.137-014
SUPERVISOR, QUALITY CONTROL 976.131-022
Take-Down Inspector 976.687-014
TAKE-DOWN SORTER 976.665-010
tinter, photograph 970.381-010
Trailer Chief 976.131-010
UTILITY WORKER, FILM PROCESSING 976.685-030

pipe lines—PIPE LINES INDUSTRY: This designation includes occupations concerned with transporting crude petroleum or refined petroleum products, such as gasoline and fuel oil, through pipelines. Also included are occupations concerned with the transportation of such materials as coal slurry and mixed, natural, and manufactured gases; the operation of pumping or compressor stations; and the maintenance of pipelines. Occupations pertaining to pipeline construction are included in the CONSTRUCTION INDUSTRY (construction).

CARGO INSPECTOR 549.387-010
chart clerk 216.685-010
CHIEF CLERK, MEASUREMENT DEPARTMENT 221.132-010
CHIEF ENGINEER 010.167-010
chief gauger 914.134-010
CLAIM AGENT 191.167-014
COAL-PIPE-LINE OPERATOR 914.362-010
Compressor-Station Engineer 950.382-014
COMPRESSOR-STATION ENGINEER, CHIEF 914.132-010
CORROSION-CONTROL FITTER 820.361-010
crew supervisor 869.134-018
Dispatcher, Chief, Coal Slurry 184.167-038
DISPATCHER, CHIEF I 184.167-038
DISPATCHER, CHIEF II 914.167-010
Dispatcher, Chief, Natural Gas 184.167-038
Dispatcher, Chief, Oil 184.167-038
Dispatcher, Chief, Petroleum Products 184.167-038
DISPATCHER, OIL 914.167-014
Dispatcher, Refinery 914.167-014
DISPATCHER, RELAY 221.362-014
DISTRIBUTION SUPERVISOR 914.137-010

district gauger 914.134-010
district superintendent, gas and gasoline 914.167-010
district supervisor 914.132-022
DRIP PUMPER 953.583-010
field gauger 914.384-010
FIELD-MECHANICAL-METER TESTER 953.281-010
Fitter 869.664-014
GAS DISPATCHER 953.167-010
GAS-LEAK INSPECTOR 953.367-010
GAS-LEAK INSPECTOR HELPER 953.667-010
GAS-REGULATOR REPAIRER 710.381-026
GAS-REGULATOR-REPAIRER HELPER 710.384-010
GAS USAGE METER CLERK 216.685-010
GAUGER 914.384-010
GAUGER, CHIEF 914.134-010
gauger, chief delivery 914.132-022
Gauger, Delivery 914.384-010
general-office dispatcher 914.167-010
LABORER, PIPE-LINES 914.687-010
leak locator 953.367-010
line rider 869.564-010
LINE WALKER 869.564-010
maintenance-crew supervisor 869.134-018
maintenance inspector 953.367-010
MAINTENANCE MECHANIC 620.281-046
MAINTENANCE MECHANIC HELPER 620.664-014
MANAGER, CONTRACTS 163.117-010
measurement superintendent 184.167-190
mechanical-meter tester 953.281-010
mechanic helper 620.664-014
meter inspector 953.281-010
oil dispatcher 914.167-014
oil-pump-station operator, chief 914.132-014
pipe-line gauger 914.384-010
pipe-line maintenance supervisor 869.134-018
PIPELINER 899.684-026
Pipe-Line Superintendent, District 184.167-198
Pipe-Line Superintendent, Division 184.167-198
PIPE-WRAPPING-MACHINE OPERATOR 862.682-014
plant superintendent 914.132-010
PUMPER-GAUGER 914.382-014
PUMPER-GAUGER APPRENTICE 914.382-018
pump-station operator 914.362-018
SENIOR TECHNICIAN, CONTROLS 828.261-018
service engineer 620.281-046
shop mechanic 620.281-046
shop-mechanic helper 620.664-014
station chief 914.132-014
STATION ENGINEER, CHIEF 914.132-014
STATION ENGINEER, MAIN LINE 914.362-018
Station Engineer, Operating Chief 914.132-014
station operator 914.362-018
SUPERINTENDENT, COMPRESSOR STATIONS 184.167-146
SUPERINTENDENT, MEASUREMENT 184.167-190
SUPERINTENDENT, PIPE-LINES 184.167-198
superintendent, pressure 914.167-010
superintendent, scheduling 184.167-038
SUPERVISOR, DOCK 914.137-018
SUPERVISOR, FIELD-PIPE-LINES 914.132-022
SUPERVISOR, MAPPING 018.167-030
SUPERVISOR, NATURAL-GAS-FIELD PROCESSING 549.131-010
SUPERVISOR, PIPE-LINE MAINTENANCE 869.134-018
Supply Representative, Dry Gas 163.117-010
supply representative, petroleum products 163.117-010
tank-farm gauger 914.384-010
terminal gauger 914.384-010
terminal-gauger supervisor 914.132-022
terminal supervisor 914.137-018
TITLE CLERK 162.267-010
wharf tender, head 914.137-018

plastic prod.—FABRICATED PLASTIC PRODUCTS INDUSTRY: This designation includes occupations concerned with fabricating, including molding and casting, plastics materials (which are usually known by trade names, such as Celluloid, Lucite, and Bakelite) into products or articles. Occupations concerned with manufacturing plastics materials, such as pyroxylin plastics and phenolic plastics used in fabricating plastics products, are included in the PLASTIC AND SYNTHETIC MATERIALS INDUSTRY (plastic-synth.). Occupations concerned with manufacturing cellophane bags (from purchased cellophane) are included in the PAPER GOODS INDUSTRY (paper goods).

ASSEMBLER 754.684-010
ASSEMBLER-AND-GLUER, LAMINATED PLASTICS 754.684-014
ASSEMBLER, SKYLIGHTS 869.684-014
ASSEMBLY-MACHINE TENDER 754.685-014
BAGGER 553.685-014
BATCH-RECORDS CLERK 221.387-054
biscuit-machine operator 556.685-058
Blender 550.685-134
BLENDER HELPER 550.586-010
BLOW-MOLDING-MACHINE OPERATOR 556.682-010
briquetting-machine operator 556.685-058
BUFFER 752.684-022
CALENDER OPERATOR, FOUR-ROLL 554.662-010
CASTER 754.684-022
CELLOPHANE-CASTING-MACHINE REPAIRER 629.281-014
CENTRIFUGAL-CASTING-MACHINE TENDER 556.685-090
Cold-Molding-Press Operator 556.682-014
Color Mixer 550.685-134
compounder helper 550.586-010
COMPRESSION-MOLDING-MACHINE OPERATOR 556.682-014
Compression-Molding-Machine Setter 556.380-010
COMPRESSION-MOLDING-MACHINE TENDER 556.685-022
customer-return inspector 559.381-010
cutter operator 555.685-026
Cutter, Plastics Sheets 690.685-122
DECORATING-AND-ASSEMBLY SUPERVISOR 754.130-010
DESIGN INSERTER 692.685-070
die setter 556.380-010
dip-tube assembler, machine 690.682-074
EAR-MOLD LABORATORY TECHNICIAN 777.361-010
EDGE GRINDER 690.685-142
EXTRUDER-OPERATOR HELPER 557.564-010
EXTRUDER OPERATOR 557.382-010
fabricator 754.684-010
FIBERGLASS-DOWEL-DRAWING-MACHINE OPERATOR 575.682-010
FINISHER, HAND 754.684-030
FINISHER, MACHINE 690.685-170
flexigraphic printer 651.382-026
FOAM-GUN OPERATOR 741.684-014
FOAM-MACHINE OPERATOR 559.685-078
FORM MAKER, PLASTER 777.684-010
GLUER, WET SUIT 795.687-018
GRINDER 555.685-026
GROOVING-LATHE TENDER 690.685-202
HEAT WELDER, PLASTICS 553.684-010
injection molder 556.382-014
INJECTION-MOLDING-MACHINE OPERATOR 556.382-014
Injection-Molding-Machine Setter 556.380-010
INJECTION-MOLDING-MACHINE TENDER 556.685-038
INK PRINTER 652.685-038
Inlayer, Silver 692.685-070
INSPECTOR 559.381-010
INSPECTOR AND HAND PACKAGER 559.687-074
INTERNAL CARVER 754.381-010
jig and form maker 754.381-014
KNOCK-OUT HAND 754.684-034
LABORER, GENERAL 754.687-010
Lacquer Coater 599.685-074
LACQUERER 599.685-054
Laminating-Press Operator 690.682-062
LAMINATOR, PREFORMS 754.684-050
MACHINE SETTER-AND-REPAIRER 690.380-014
Mandrel Cleaner 690.685-438
Mandrel Puller 690.685-438
MATERIAL MIXER 550.685-130
MIXING-MACHINE OPERATOR 550.685-134
MIXING SUPERVISOR 550.135-014
molder 556.685-022
molder 556.382-014
molder 777.684-010
molder operator 556.685-090
MOLDER, PIPE COVERING 556.665-018
molder, vacuum 556.685-082
MOLDING SUPERVISOR 556.130-018
MOLD SETTER 556.380-010
mold stripper 556.686-018
PAD CUTTER 690.685-302
PATTERNMAKER, ALL-AROUND 693.280-014
PATTERNMAKER, PLASTICS 754.381-014
pelletizer 556.685-058
pellet-machine operator 556.685-058
PILLING-MACHINE OPERATOR 556.685-058
plastic-press molder 556.685-022
PLASTIC ROLLER 690.685-498
plastics bench mechanic 754.381-018
PLASTICS FABRICATOR 754.381-018
plastics fabricator and assembler 754.381-018

Plastic-Sheeting Cutter	699.682-026
Plastic-Sign Fabricator	754.381-018
Plastics Plater	500.380-010
PLASTICS REPAIRER	754.684-046
plate worker	690.682-062
plug maker	754.381-014
POINTING-MACHINE OPERATOR	690.685-310
POLYSTYRENE-BEAD MOLDER	556.382-018
POLYSTYRENE-MOLDING-MACHINE TENDER	556.685-062
pourer	754.684-022
preformer, impregnated fabrics	754.684-050
preform-machine operator	556.685-058
PRESS HELPER	651.586-010
PRESS OPERATOR	690.682-062
PRINTER, PLASTIC	651.382-026
process inspector	559.381-010
pulverizer	555.685-026
QUALITY-CONTROL SUPERVISOR	559.134-010
Regrinder Operator	555.685-026
Rework Machine Operator	605.685-054
Rotary Preformer	556.685-058
ROUTER MACHINE OPERATOR	605.685-054
SAMPLE CLERK	222.387-066
SAWYER	690.482-010
SEQUINS STRINGER	754.687-014
sequins winder	920.686-046
setter, plastics-molding machine	556.380-010
SHAPING-MACHINE OPERATOR	690.685-354
Single-Stroke Preformer	556.685-058
SKI-TOP TRIMMER	690.685-370
SLINGER, SEQUINS	692.685-178
slusher	777.684-010
solid-glass-rod-dowel-machine operator	575.682-010
SPAGHETTI-MACHINE OPERATOR	690.682-074
Specialty Molder	556.665-018
SPONGE BUFFER	690.685-390
SPOOLER, SEQUINS	920.685-046
squeegeer and former	754.684-050
STOCK PREPARER	751.387-010
Straightening-Press Operator	690.682-062
STRETCH-MACHINE OPERATOR	559.682-058
STRIPPER	556.686-018
Stripper, Soft Plastic	556.686-018
stuffer, vertical hydraulic	557.382-010
SUPERVISOR	690.130-018
SUPERVISOR	700.131-010
SUPERVISOR, EXTRUDING DEPARTMENT	557.130-010
Supervisor, Hand Workers	700.131-010
Supervisor, Machine Workers	700.131-010
SUPERVISOR, PLASTIC SHEETS	557.130-014
SUPERVISOR, PLASTICS PRODUCTION	556.130-010
tablet-machine operator	556.685-058
Tacker	690.685-438
TRIMMER	690.482-014
TUBE MOLDER, FIBERGLASS	690.685-438
Tube Roller	690.685-438
tuber operator	557.382-010
UTILITY WORKER, MOLDING	559.684-026
vacuum-forming-machine operator	553.685-014
VACUUM PLASTIC-FORMING-MACHINE OPERATOR	556.685-082
welder, plastic	553.684-010
Wrapper	690.685-438

plastic-synth.—PLASTIC AND SYNTHETIC MATERIALS INDUSTRY: This designation includes occupations concerned with manufacturing synthetic resins and plastic materials, synthetic rubbers, and cellulosic and man-made organic fibers. Occupations concerned with the preliminary synthesizing or processing of the chemical components used in producing plastic materials are included in the CHEMICAL INDUSTRY (chemical); occupations concerned with the fabrication of plastic articles are included in the FABRICATED PLASTIC PRODUCTS INDUSTRY (plastic prod.). Occupations concerned with throwing, spinning, or weaving synthetic fibers are included in the TEXTILE INDUSTRY (textile); occupations concerned with knitting synthetic fibers are included in the KNITTING INDUSTRY (knitting).

ACETONE-RECOVERY WORKER	552.685-010
Acid-Bath Tender	557.685-030
Acid-Correction Hand	550.684-010
AGER OPERATOR	553.482-010
aging room operator	559.585-018
BALER	690.685-022
bath mixer	550.684-010
BATH-MIX OPERATOR	552.685-018
bath-solution maker	550.684-010

biscuit-machine operator	556.685-058
bleacher	582.685-162
Blender	550.685-134
BLENDER HELPER	550.586-010
Bobbin Drier	581.685-018
bobbin salvager	922.687-018
BOBBIN SORTER	922.687-018
Bobbin Washer	582.685-162
BOX TENDER	689.280-010
briquetting-machine operator	556.685-058
BULK-SEALER OPERATOR	554.685-010
Cake Inspector	681.687-018
CAKE-PRESS OPERATOR	556.665-010
CAKE-PRESS-OPERATOR HELPER	556.686-010
Cake Washer	582.685-162
CAKE WRAPPER	589.687-010
Cake Wringer	581.685-038
calender-roll operator	554.682-018
CALENDER SUPERVISOR	559.132-014
caster	559.682-022
Casting-And-Locker-Room Servicer	381.687-018
CASTING-MACHINE-SERVICE OPERATOR	559.687-018
CASTING-ROOM OPERATOR	556.585-010
CAUSTIC OPERATOR	554.684-010
caustic-room attendant	551.685-138
CELL INSPECTOR	556.684-010
cell-making supervisor, plastics sheets	579.137-022
CELLOPHANE-BATH MIXER	550.585-014
cell pourer	556.684-018
CELL PREPARER	556.687-014
CELL STRIPPER	556.686-014
cell stripper, final	556.587-010
chemical-building worker see CHEMICAL-DEPARTMENT WORKER	
CHEMICAL-DEPARTMENT WORKER	term
chemical operator see CHEMICAL-DEPARTMENT WORKER	
CHURN TENDER	550.685-034
clarifier	559.687-038
COAGULATING-BATH MIXER	550.684-010
coagulating-bath operator	550.585-014
Coagulating-Drying Supervisor	559.132-022
COAGULATION OPERATOR	559.582-010
coagulator	559.685-190
COATER OPERATOR	554.585-014
COLD-ROLL INSPECTOR	751.584-010
COLOR MATCHER	550.381-010
color mixer	550.381-010
Color Mixer	550.685-134
COMBINING-MACHINE OPERATOR	554.685-018
compounder helper	550.586-010
cone inspector	681.687-030
CORRUGATOR OPERATOR	556.665-014
cotton cleaner	559.687-030
COTTON WASHER	559.687-030
Cotton Wringer	559.687-030
CRACKING-UNIT OPERATOR	558.682-010
crimping-machine operator	589.685-102
customer-return inspector	559.381-010
cutter operator	555.685-026
CUTTER OPERATOR	555.585-010
cutter, plastics rolls	690.665-010
Cutter, Plastics Sheets	690.685-122
DEBUBBLIZER	553.585-010
DEHYDRATING-PRESS OPERATOR	551.685-046
Desulfurizer, Hand	582.685-162
Desulfurizer, Machine	582.685-162
DICER OPERATOR	690.685-130
Dipper	582.685-162
dipping-machine operator	554.585-014
Disulfurizer Tender	550.685-034
doffer	582.685-162
DRAW-MACHINE OPERATOR	680.665-014
Drier Operator, Head	559.132-042
DRIER OPERATOR I	559.562-010
DRIER OPERATOR II	553.685-046
DRIER OPERATOR III	581.685-018
DRUM-DRIER OPERATOR	581.685-082
DRY-END OPERATOR	559.665-014
drying-machine operator	581.685-018
drying-room operator	581.685-018
EMBOSSING-MACHINE-OPERATOR HELPER	583.685-038
EXTRUDER-OPERATOR HELPER	557.564-010
EXTRUDER OPERATOR	557.382-010
filling inspector	681.687-030

plastic-synth.

plumbing-heat.—PLUMBING AND HEATING SUPPLIES INDUSTRY: This designation includes occupations concerned with manufacturing and repairing porcelain-enameled (enameled-iron) sanitary ware, such as bathtubs, laundry tubs, lavatories, and sinks; plumbers' brass goods, plumbers' woodwork, galvanized-iron and copper range boilers, and miscellaneous bathroom and other fixtures closely related to plumbing work; and heating equipment (nonelectric or warm air), such as gas, oil, and stoker coal fired equipment, for the automatic utilization of gaseous, liquid, and solid fuels. The designation does not include occupations concerned with the manufacture of vitreous-china sanitary ware, which are included in the POTTERY AND PORCELAIN WARE INDUSTRY (pottery & porc.).

assembler	706.684-086
enamel drier	509.684-010
ENAMELER	509.684-010
FITTINGS FINISHER	619.382-014
fittings tightener	706.684-086
lead fabricator	619.382-014
PLUMBING-HARDWARE ASSEMBLER	706.684-086
SUPERVISOR	609.130-018

pottery & porc.—POTTERY AND PORCELAIN WARE INDUSTRY: This designation includes occupations concerned with producing and repairing such clay products as chinaware, earthenware, porcelain ware, stoneware, vitreous-china plumbing fixtures, and porcelain electrical insulation materials.

back grinder	774.684-042
back polisher	774.684-042
bander	740.681-010
BANDING-MACHINE OPERATOR	679.682-010
batter	575.684-010
BATTER-OUT	575.684-010
BEDDER	573.687-010
BISQUE CLEANER	774.684-010
bisque finisher	774.684-010
bisque grader	774.684-010
BISQUE GRADER	774.687-010
Bisque-Kiln Drawer	573.667-010
Bisque-Kiln Placer	573.686-026
block and case maker	777.684-018
blocker	777.684-018
blunger-machine operator	570.482-010
caser	777.684-018
CASTER	575.684-014
Ceramic Sprayer	741.684-026
claying-up worker	573.687-010
CLAY MAKER	570.482-010
clay mixer	570.482-010
clay temperer	570.382-010
clay thrower	774.381-010
clay washer	570.482-010
Decorating-Kiln Operator	573.662-010
DECORATOR	740.684-014
decorator, hand	740.681-010
decorator inspector	774.687-018
DIE PRESSER	575.685-026
DIPPER	774.684-014
duster	574.684-010
Dye Tester	774.687-026
Enameler	741.684-026
fettler	774.684-018
FINISHER	774.684-018
finisher	774.687-022
FINISH-MACHINE TENDER	673.685-058
Firer, Bisque Kiln	573.662-010
Firer, Glost Kiln	573.662-010
FIRER, KILN	573.662-010
Firer, Round Kiln	573.662-010
Firer, Tunnel Kiln	573.662-010
Flatwork Finisher	774.684-018
FLOWER-POT-PRESS OPERATOR	575.685-034
Flush Tester	774.687-026
former	575.685-026
frit burner	579.685-014
frit maker	570.685-098
FRIT-MIXER-AND-BURNER	579.685-014
gilder	740.681-010
GLAZE MAKER	570.685-098
GLAZE SUPERVISOR	574.132-010
Glost-Kiln Drawer	573.667-010
Glost-Kiln Placer	573.686-026
gold bander, striper	679.682-010
GOLD BURNISHER	775.687-022
grinder	774.684-010

GROUND LAYER	574.684-010
Handle Finisher	774.684-018
HANDLE MAKER	575.684-030
HANDLER	774.684-022
handle sticker	774.684-022
INSPECTOR I	575.687-034
INSPECTOR II	774.384-010
INSTRUCTOR, DECORATING	740.221-010
jigger operator	774.382-010
Jollier	774.382-010
kiln burner	573.662-010
KILN DRAWER	573.667-010
KILN-FURNITURE CASTER	579.684-018
kiln maintenance laborer	573.687-022
kiln operator	573.662-010
KILN PLACER	573.686-026
kiln setter	573.686-026
KILN WORKER	573.687-022
line decorator	740.681-010
LINER	740.681-010
MACHINE OPERATOR, CERAMICS	679.685-010
MILL OPERATOR	570.382-010
mixer	570.685-086
modeler	777.281-014
MODEL MAKER	777.281-014
MOLD MAKER	777.684-018
PATCHER	774.684-046
patternmaker	777.281-014
PIN MAKER	575.686-018
PLASTER-DIE MAKER	774.684-026
pot maker	774.381-010
pot maker	774.382-010
pot-press operator	575.685-034
Potter	774.382-010
POTTERY-MACHINE OPERATOR	774.382-010
Pottery Striper	741.687-022
pourer	575.684-014
press operator	575.685-026
Print Decorator	749.684-010
PRINT INSPECTOR	774.687-018
pugger helper	570.685-074
Pug Mill Operator	575.382-010
PUG-MILL-OPERATOR HELPER	570.685-074
pulverizer	570.685-098
ram-die maker	774.684-026
RAM-PRESS OPERATOR	575.682-022
round-kiln drawer	573.667-010
sagger filler	573.686-026
Sagger Former	774.381-010
SAGGER MAKER	774.684-030
SAGGER PREPARER	570.685-086
sagger soak	570.685-086
sander-up	573.687-010
scourer	774.684-010
scraper	774.684-010
setter-in	573.686-026
shaper	774.684-018
Sketch Liner	970.381-022
slip maker	570.482-010
slip mixer	570.482-010
sponger	774.684-018
sprayer, automatic spray machine	574.682-014
SPRAY-MACHINE LOADER	574.686-010
SPRAY-MACHINE OPERATOR	574.682-014
STAMPER, MACHINE	652.682-022
sticker	774.684-022
SUPERVISOR, CLAY PREPARATION	570.130-010
SUPERVISOR, CLAY SHOP	774.130-010
Supervisor, Decaling	749.131-010
SUPERVISOR, DECORATING	749.131-010
SUPERVISOR, MOLD SHOP	777.131-010
TESTER	774.687-026
THROWER	774.381-010
TOOL FILER	701.684-030
tube-machine operator	575.685-026
Tunnel-Kiln Drawer	573.667-010
Tunnel-Kiln Repairer	861.381-014
TURNER	774.684-038
WARE CLEANER	774.687-022
WARE DRESSER	774.684-042
WARE FORMER	term
Ware Washer	599.687-030
wet mixer	570.482-010

print. & pub.—PRINTING AND PUBLISHING INDUSTRY: This designation includes occupations concerned with printing and publishing newspapers, peri-

print. & pub.

odicals, books, music, banknotes, bonds, blankbooks, maps, greeting cards, and other material, including designing, coloring, and related processes. In addition to including the usual functions carried on by printing and publishing establishments, this designation also includes allied processes that are frequently performed by separate establishments. Typical functions are: (1) preparing steel and copper engraving plates, preparing photoengraved, electrotype, and stereotype plates, and preparing wood cuts; and (2) printing from such plates and wood cuts. Occupations concerned with printing signs in small quantities, as performed in retail stores and other establishments that print signs for their own use, are not included as are printing occupations found in photocopying service establishments.

profess. & kin.—PROFESSIONAL AND KINDRED OCCUPATIONS: This designation includes occupations requiring extensive study or experience in pro-fessions, technical services, sciences, art, and related types of work. The prepa-ration for these occupations (with certain exceptions, such as occur in art and literature) is typically acquired through university, college, and technical insti-tute training; experience providing institute training; experience providing equivalent backgrounds; or some combination of these. The functions of these occupations are predominantly mental rather than manual. This designation in-cludes only occupations which cross industrial designation lines or which by the nature of the jobs cannot be identified as belonging to any one industry. Occupations which are found in only one DOT industry are classified in that industry rather than here.

Archivist, Political History	101.167-010
AREA ENGINEER	term
area supervisor	187.167-238
ARRANGER	152.067-010
ART DIRECTOR	141.031-010
artist	141.061-022
artist	144.061-010
artist, scientific	141.061-026
ASSAYER	022.281-010
ASSOCIATION EXECUTIVE	189.117-010
ASTRONOMER	021.067-010
attorney	110.107-010
audiometric technician	078.362-010
AUDIOMETRIST	078.362-010
AUDIOVISUAL PRODUCTION SPECIALIST	149.061-010
AUDITOR	160.167-054
AUDITOR, INTERNAL	160.167-034
AUDITOR, TAX	160.167-038
AUTHOR	term
bacteriologist	041.061-058
Bacteriologist, Dairy	041.061-058
Bacteriologist, Fishery	041.061-058
Bacteriologist, Food	041.061-058
Bacteriologist, Industrial	041.061-058
Bacteriologist, Medical	041.061-058
Bacteriologist, Pharmaceutical	041.061-058
Bacteriologist, Soil	041.061-058
band leader	152.047-014
BAR EXAMINER	110.167-010
BIBLIOGRAPHER	100.367-010
BIOCHEMIST	041.061-026
BIOGRAPHER	052.067-010
BIOLOGICAL PHOTOGRAPHER	143.362-010
BIOLOGIST	041.061-030
BIOLOGY SPECIMEN TECHNICIAN	041.381-010
biomedical electronics technician	019.261-010
biomedical engineering technician	019.261-010
BIOMEDICAL ENGINEER	019.061-010
BIOMEDICAL EQUIPMENT TECHNICIAN	019.261-010
BIOPHYSICIST	041.061-034
BOTANIST	041.061-038
broker	162.157-018
Budget Consultant	160.207-010
BUDGET OFFICER	161.117-010
Building-Illuminating Engineer	003.061-046
business and financial counsel	110.117-022
BUSINESS REPRESENTATIVE, LABOR UNION	187.167-018
buyer	162.157-038
BUYER	162.157-018
calligrapher	970.661-014
CANTOR	129.027-010
CARTOGRAPHIC TECHNICIAN	term
cartographic technician	018.261-026
CERAMIC DESIGN ENGINEER	006.061-010
CERAMIC ENGINEER	006.061-014
CERAMIC RESEARCH ENGINEER	006.061-018
CERAMICS TEST ENGINEER	006.061-022
Certified Financial Planner	250.257-014
certified public accountant see ACCOUNTANT, CERTIFIED PUBLIC	
Chaplain	120.107-010
CHEMICAL DESIGN ENGINEER, PROCESSES	008.061-014
CHEMICAL ENGINEER	008.061-018
CHEMICAL-ENGINEERING TECHNICIAN	008.261-010
Chemical-Engineering Technician, Prototype-Development	008.261-010
CHEMICAL-EQUIPMENT SALES ENGINEER	008.151-010
CHEMICAL-LABORATORY CHIEF	022.161-010
CHEMICAL-LABORATORY TECHNICIAN	022.261-010
CHEMICAL RESEARCH ENGINEER	008.061-022
CHEMICAL-TEST ENGINEER	008.061-026
CHEMIST	022.061-010
Chemist, Analytical	022.061-010
chemist, biological	041.061-026
Chemist, Clinical	041.061-026
Chemist, Enzymes	041.061-026
CHEMIST, FOOD	022.061-014
Chemist, Inorganic	022.061-010
CHEMIST, INSTRUMENTATION	022.261-018
Chemist, Organic	022.061-010
Chemist, Pharmaceutical	041.061-026
Chemist, Physical	022.061-010
Chemist, Proteins	041.061-026
Chemist, Steroids	041.061-026
CHEMIST, WASTEWATER-TREATMENT PLANT	022.261-022
chief chemist	022.161-010
CHIEF COMPUTER PROGRAMMER	030.167-010
CHIEF DRAFTER	007.261-010
chief engineer	019.167-014
chief information officer	109.067-010
CHIEF OF PARTY	018.167-010
Chief Planner	199.167-014
Child Psychologist	045.061-010
choir leader	152.047-010
CHORAL DIRECTOR	152.047-010
CHRISTIAN SCIENCE NURSE	129.107-010
CHRISTIAN SCIENCE PRACTITIONER	129.107-010
city planner	199.167-014
CITY PLANNING AIDE	199.364-010
city-planning engineer	199.167-014
CIVIL ENGINEER	005.061-014
CIVIL ENGINEERING TECHNICIAN	005.261-014
CLERGY MEMBER	120.107-010
CLERICAL-METHODS ANALYST	161.267-010
clinical counselor	045.107-050
Clinical Engineer	019.061-010
CLINICAL PSYCHOLOGIST	045.107-022
CLINICAL SOCIOLOGIST	054.107-010
CLINICAL THERAPIST	045.107-050
CLOTH DESIGNER	142.061-014
clothes designer	142.061-018
cloth pattern maker	142.061-014
color consultant	141.051-010
COLOR EXPERT	141.051-010
COLORIST	022.161-014
colorist	141.051-010
color maker	022.161-014
color matcher	022.161-014
color specialist	141.051-010
Combat Operations Research Specialist	059.167-010
Comedy Writer	131.067-026
commercial artist	141.061-022
commercial artist, lettering	970.661-014
COMMERCIAL DESIGNER	141.061-038
commercial photographer	143.062-030
commercial photographer apprentice	143.062-018
Commodity-Industry Analyst	050.067-010
COMMUNITY DIETITIAN	077.127-010
community health educator	079.117-014
community planner	001.061-018
COMPOSER	152.067-014
comptroller	160.167-058
Computer-Laboratory Technician	003.161-014
COMPUTER PROGRAMMER	030.162-010
COMPUTER SECURITY COORDINATOR	033.162-010
COMPUTER SECURITY SPECIALIST	033.362-010
computer systems engineer	033.167-010
COMPUTER SYSTEMS HARDWARE ANALYST	033.167-010
CONCILIATOR	169.207-010
Conductor, Dance Band	152.047-014
CONDUCTOR, ORCHESTRA	152.047-014
Conductor, Symphonic-Orchestra	152.047-014
CONFIGURATION MANAGEMENT ANALYST	012.167-010
CONSERVATOR, ARTIFACTS	055.381-010
CONSULTANT	189.167-010
CONSULTING ENGINEER	term
consumer services consultant	096.121-014
CONTRACT CLERK	119.267-018
contract consultant	119.267-018
contract coordinator	162.117-010
CONTRACT SPECIALIST	162.117-018
contract technician	119.267-018
CONTROLLER	160.167-058
CONTROLS DESIGNER	003.261-014
Controls Designer, Computer-Assisted	003.261-014
controls project engineer	003.261-014
coordinator, computer programming	030.167-010
COPY WRITER	131.067-014
corporate counsel	110.117-022
corrosion-control specialist	003.167-022
corrosion engineer	003.167-022
cost estimator	169.267-038
Costume Designer	142.061-018
counseling-center manager	045.107-018
counselor	110.107-010
COUNSELOR	045.107-010
counselor-at law	110.107-010
COUNSELOR, MARRIAGE AND FAMILY	045.107-054
court abstractor	119.267-010
cpa see ACCOUNTANT, CERTIFIED PUBLIC	
CREATIVE DIRECTOR	141.067-010

profess. & kin.

ENVIRONMENTAL ENGINEER	term
ENVIRONMENTALIST	term
environmental planner	001.061-018
Environmental-Research Test Technician	003.261-010
environmental scientist	029.081-010
environmental technician	029.261-014
Equipment Specialist	096.121-014
ESCROW OFFICER	119.367-010
ESTIMATOR	169.267-038
Ethnographer	055.067-022
ETHNOLOGIST	055.067-022
Etymologist	059.067-014
Executive Secretary	189.117-010
executive secretary, social welfare	195.117-010
experimental technician	007.161-026
factory engineer	007.167-014
FACTORY LAY-OUT ENGINEER	012.167-018
farm-seed specialist	040.361-014
Fashion Consultant	096.121-014
FASHION DESIGNER	142.061-018
FIBER TECHNOLOGIST	040.061-026
FIELD-MAP EDITOR	018.262-010
FIELD REPRESENTATIVE	189.267-010
FIELD SERVICE ENGINEER	828.261-014
field service representative	828.261-014
field technical assistant	828.261-014
Financial Economist	050.067-010
FINANCIAL PLANNER	250.257-014
fire-loss-prevention engineer	012.167-022
FIRE-PREVENTION RESEARCH ENGINEER	012.167-022
FIRE-PROTECTION ENGINEER	012.167-026
FIRE-PROTECTION ENGINEERING TECHNICIAN	019.261-014
flag decorator and designer	142.051-010
food scientist	041.081-010
FOOD TECHNOLOGIST	041.081-010
FOREST ECOLOGIST	040.061-030
FORESTER	040.167-010
Forestry Supervisor	040.167-010
FORMS ANALYST	161.267-018
Gag Writer	131.067-026
GAMMA-FACILITIES OPERATOR	015.362-014
GENEALOGIST	052.067-018
general secretary, social welfare	195.117-010
GENETICIST	041.061-050
GEODESIST	024.061-014
GEODETIC COMPUTATOR	018.167-014
GEOGRAPHER	029.067-010
GEOGRAPHER, PHYSICAL	029.067-014
Geological Engineer	024.061-018
GEOLOGIST	024.061-018
Geomagnetician	024.061-030
Geomorphologist	024.061-018
GEOPHYSICAL-LABORATORY CHIEF	024.167-010
GEOPHYSICIST	024.061-030
Glaciologist	024.061-030
Gold-And-Silver Assayer	022.281-010
GRANT COORDINATOR	169.117-014
graphic artist	141.061-022
GRAPHIC DESIGNER	141.061-018
GRAPHOLOGIST	199.267-038
head counselor	045.107-018
HEALTH PHYSICIST	015.021-010
health-physics technician	199.167-010
hearing-test technician	078.362-010
Heating Technician	007.181-010
HEAT-TRANSFER TECHNICIAN	007.181-010
Helminthologist	041.061-070
help desk representative	032.262-010
help desk supervisor	032.132-010
HERBARIUM WORKER	041.384-010
Herpetologist	041.061-090
Highway-Landscape Architect	001.061-018
HISTORIAN	052.067-022
HISTORIAN, DRAMATIC ARTS	052.067-026
Historical Archeologist	055.067-018
home and school visitor	195.107-038
HOME ECONOMIST	096.121-014
Home Economist, Consumer Service	096.121-014
HOME-SERVICE DIRECTOR	096.161-010
HORTICULTURIST	040.061-038
HOT-CELL TECHNICIAN	015.362-018
human factors specialist	045.061-014
HUMAN RESOURCE ADVISOR	166.267-046
HUMORIST	131.067-026
HYDRAULIC ENGINEER	005.061-018
hydrologic engineer	005.061-018
HYDROLOGIST	024.061-034
HYPNOTHERAPIST	079.157-010
hypnotist	079.157-010
Ic Designer, Custom	003.261-018
Ic Designer, Gate Arrays	003.261-018
Ic Designer, Standard Cells	003.261-018
Ichthyologist	041.061-090
ILLUMINATING ENGINEER	003.061-046
Illuminator	970.661-010
ILLUSTRATOR	141.061-022
ILLUSTRATOR, MEDICAL AND SCIENTIFIC	141.061-026
INDUSTRIAL DESIGNER	142.061-026
Industrial Economist	050.067-010
INDUSTRIAL ENGINEER	012.167-030
INDUSTRIAL ENGINEERING TECHNICIAN	012.267-010
INDUSTRIAL-HEALTH ENGINEER	012.167-034
industrial hygiene engineer	012.167-034
INDUSTRIAL HYGIENIST	079.161-010
Industrial-Illuminating Engineer	003.061-046
Industrial Occupational Analyst	166.067-010
Industrial Renderer	970.281-014
Industrial Sociologist	054.067-014
information broker	109.067-010
information center specialist	032.262-010
information manager	109.067-010
information processing engineer	033.167-010
information resources director	109.067-010
information resources manager	109.067-010
INFORMATION SCIENTIST	109.067-010
information security	033.162-010
INSPECTOR, BOILER	168.167-026
INSTALLATION ENGINEER	term
institutional-nutrition consultant	077.127-018
instructional technology specialist	149.061-010
INSTRUMENTATION ENGINEER	term
INSTRUMENTATION TECHNICIAN	003.261-010
INTEGRATED CIRCUIT LAYOUT DESIGNER	003.261-018
INTELLIGENCE RESEARCH SPECIALIST	059.167-010
Interior Decorator	142.051-014
INTERIOR DESIGNER	142.051-014
International-Trade Economist	050.067-010
INTERPRETER	137.267-010
INTERPRETER, DEAF	137.267-014
Invertebrate Zoologist	041.061-090
irradiation technician	015.362-018
IRRIGATION ENGINEER	005.061-022
isotope-production technician	015.362-022
JOB ANALYST	166.267-018
JOB DEVELOPMENT SPECIALIST	166.267-034
laboratory assistant	199.364-014
LABORATORY CHIEF	term
laboratory-development technician	007.161-026
LABORATORY SUPERVISOR	022.137-010
Labor Economist	050.067-010
Labor Relations Consultant	166.167-034
labor relations representative	166.167-034
Labor Relations Supervisor	166.167-034
land agent	186.117-058
land planner	001.061-018
land planner	199.167-014
LANDSCAPE ARCHITECT	001.061-018
LAND SURVEYOR	018.167-018
law clerk	119.267-026
law examiner	110.167-010
LAWYER	110.107-010
LAWYER, ADMIRALTY	110.117-018
LAWYER, CORPORATION	110.117-022
LAWYER, CRIMINAL	110.107-014
LAWYER, PATENT	110.117-026
LAWYER, PROBATE	110.117-030
LAWYER, REAL ESTATE	110.117-034
layer-out	007.261-010
layout artist	141.061-018
lay-out drafter	007.261-010
legal aid	119.267-026
legal assistant	119.267-026
legal assistant	119.267-022
LEGAL INVESTIGATOR	119.267-022
legislative advocate	165.017-010
LETTERER	970.661-014
lexicographer	132.067-018
LIBRETTIST	131.067-030
lie-detection examiner	199.267-026
Limnologist	041.061-022

linguist 059.067-014
LINGUIST .... term
LOBBYIST 165.017-010
LOGISTICS ENGINEER 019.167-010
logistics specialist 019.167-010
loss-prevention research engineer 012.167-022
LYRICIST 131.067-034
lyric writer 131.067-034
MAINTAINABILITY ENGINEER 019.081-010
Mammalogist 041.061-090
MANAGEMENT ANALYST 161.167-010
MANAGER, AGRICULTURAL-LABOR CAMP 187.167-050
MANAGER, BENEFITS 166.167-018
MANAGER, COMPENSATION 166.167-022
MANAGER, COMPUTER OPERATIONS 169.167-082
MANAGER, CUSTOMER TECHNICAL SERVICES 189.117-018
MANAGER, DATA PROCESSING 169.167-030
manager, employee benefits 166.167-018
manager, employee services 166.167-018
MANAGER, EMPLOYEE WELFARE 166.117-014
MANAGER, EMPLOYMENT 166.167-030
MANAGER, EMPLOYMENT AGENCY 187.167-098
MANAGER, FORMS ANALYSIS 161.167-014
MANAGER, HOUSING PROJECT 186.167-030
manager, human resources 166.117-018
MANAGER, LABOR RELATIONS 166.167-034
MANAGER, LAND SURVEYING 018.167-022
manager, material control 162.167-022
MANAGER, PERSONNEL 166.117-018
manager, personnel services 166.167-018
MANAGER, PROCUREMENT SERVICES 162.167-022
manager, production 012.167-070
MANAGER, QUALITY CONTROL 012.167-014
MANAGER, RECORDS ANALYSIS 161.167-018
MANAGER, REPORTS ANALYSIS 161.167-022
manager, technical and scientific publications 132.017-018
manager, welfare 166.117-014
MANUFACTURING ENGINEER 012.167-042
map maker 018.261-018
mapper 018.261-010
Marine Biologist 041.061-022
MARINE ENGINEER 014.061-014
MARINE SURVEYOR 014.167-010
marketing engineer   see SALES ENGINEER ....
MARKET-RESEARCH ANALYST I 050.067-014
Market-Research Analyst II 045.107-030
mask designer 003.261-018
master hypnotist 079.157-010
MATERIALS ENGINEER 019.061-014
MATERIALS SCIENTIST 029.081-014
MATHEMATICAL TECHNICIAN 020.162-010
MATHEMATICIAN 020.067-014
Mathematician, Applied 020.067-014
Mathematician, Research 020.067-014
MECHANICAL-DESIGN ENGINEER, FACILITIES 007.061-018
MECHANICAL-DESIGN ENGINEER, PRODUCTS 007.061-022
mechanical design technician 007.161-018
MECHANICAL ENGINEER 007.061-014
MECHANICAL-ENGINEERING TECHNICIAN 007.161-026
MECHANICAL RESEARCH ENGINEER 007.161-022
mechanical technician 007.161-026
MEDIA DIRECTOR 164.117-018
mediator 169.207-010
Medical Anthropologist 055.067-014
Medical Parasitologist 041.061-070
MEDICAL PHYSICIST 079.021-014
Medical Sociologist 054.067-014
MEMBERSHIP DIRECTOR 189.167-026
Membership Secretary 189.117-010
METALLOGRAPHER 011.061-014
metallurgical-laboratory assistant 011.261-010
METALLURGICAL TECHNICIAN 011.261-010
metallurgical tester 011.261-010
METALLURGIST, EXTRACTIVE 011.061-018
METALLURGIST, PHYSICAL 011.061-022
metallurgist, process 011.061-018
meteorological technician 025.267-014
METEOROLOGIST 025.062-010
methods analyst, data processing 033.167-010
methods-and-procedures analyst 012.167-070
Methods-Study Analyst 012.267-010
METROLOGIST 012.067-010
MICROBIOLOGIST 041.061-058
MICROCOMPUTER SUPPORT SPECIALIST 039.264-010
Micropaleontologist 024.061-042

MINERALOGIST 024.061-038
minister 120.107-010
Missionary 120.107-010
MOHEL 129.271-010
MOSAICIST 018.261-022
Motion-Study Analyst 012.267-010
Mushroom-Spawn Maker 041.061-062
MYCOLOGIST 041.061-062
NATURALIST .... term
naval designer 001.061-014
NEMATOLOGIST 041.061-066
Noise-Abatement Engineer 019.081-018
NONDESTRUCTIVE TESTER 011.261-018
NUCLEAR-CRITICALITY SAFETY ENGINEER 015.067-010
Nuclear-Decontamination Research Specialist 015.021-010
NUCLEAR ENGINEER 015.061-014
NUCLEAR-FUELS RECLAMATION ENGINEER 015.061-026
NUCLEAR-FUELS RESEARCH ENGINEER 015.061-030
NUCLEAR-TEST-REACTOR PROGRAM COORDINATOR 015.167-014
NUMISMATIST .... term
Nutritionist 096.121-014
OCCUPATIONAL ANALYST 166.067-010
Oceanographer, Geological 024.061-018
Oceanographer, Physical 024.061-030
office automation analyst 032.262-010
OPERATIONS-RESEARCH ANALYST 020.067-018
optical designer 019.061-018
OPTICAL ENGINEER 019.061-018
OPTOMETRIC ASSISTANT 079.364-014
orchestra leader 152.047-014
ORCHESTRATOR 152.067-022
Ornithologist 041.061-090
Outdoor-Illuminating Engineer 003.061-046
Pace Analyst 012.267-010
PACKAGE DESIGNER 142.081-018
PACKAGING ENGINEER 019.187-010
PAINTER 144.061-010
paintings conservator 102.261-014
PAINTINGS RESTORER 102.261-014
Paleobotanist 024.061-042
PALEONTOLOGICAL HELPER 024.364-010
PALEONTOLOGIST 024.061-042
PARALEGAL 119.267-026
PARASITOLOGIST 041.061-070
Park-Landscape Architect 001.061-018
Parole Officer 195.107-046
Pastor 120.107-010
PATENT AGENT 119.167-014
patent attorney 110.117-026
pattern designer 142.061-014
Penologist 054.067-014
personnel administrator 166.167-018
personnel analyst 166.267-018
personnel interviewer 166.267-010
personnel monitor 199.167-010
PERSONNEL RECRUITER 166.267-038
PETROLOGIST 024.061-046
PHARMACOLOGIST 041.061-074
PHILATELIST .... term
PHILOLOGIST 059.067-010
Photogeologist 024.061-018
PHOTOGRAMMETRIC ENGINEER 018.167-026
PHOTOGRAMMETRIST 018.261-018
PHOTOGRAPHER, AERIAL 143.062-014
PHOTOGRAPHER, APPRENTICE 143.062-018
Photographer, Motion Picture 143.062-022
PHOTOGRAPHER, SCIENTIFIC 143.062-026
PHOTOGRAPHER, STILL 143.062-030
PHOTOGRAPHIC ENGINEER 019.081-014
photograph restorer 970.261-010
photo-optical instrumentation engineer 019.081-014
PHOTO-OPTICS TECHNICIAN 029.280-010
physical-laboratory assistant 011.261-010
physical tester 011.361-010
physical-testing supervisor 011.161-010
PHYSICIST 023.061-014
Physicist, Acoustics 023.061-014
Physicist, Astrophysics 023.061-014
Physicist, Atomic, Electronic And Molecular 023.061-014
Physicist, Cryogenics 023.061-014
Physicist, Electricity And Magnetism 023.061-014
Physicist, Fluids 023.061-014
Physicist, Light And Optics 023.061-014
Physicist, Nuclear 023.061-014
Physicist, Plasma 023.061-014

profess. & kin.

protective dev.—PERSONAL PROTECTIVE AND MEDICAL DEVICES AND SUPPLIES INDUSTRY: This designation includes occupations concerned with manufacturing medical (surgical, orthopedic, and prosthetic dental) devices and supplies and personal safety devices. It includes the manufacture of such products as artificial teeth, limbs, braces, splints, abdominal supporters and trusses, adhesive tape and plasters, cotton swabs, elastic hosiery, arch supporters, bandages, gauze dressings, sutures, dental floss, industrial and gas masks, bullet-proof vests, ear and nose protectors, and safety gloves and belts. Occupations concerned with the manufacture of medical instruments are included in the INSTRUMENTS AND APPARATUS INDUSTRY (inst. & app.). Occupations concerned with fabricating personal protective devices used in athletic and sporting activities are included in the TOYS, GAMES, AND SPORTS EQUIPMENT INDUSTRY (toy-sport equip.). Also excluded from this designation are occupations concerned with fabricating safety glasses, which are included in the OPTICAL GOODS INDUSTRY (optical goods); and safety shoes, which are included in the BOOT AND SHOE INDUSTRY (boot & shoe).

ADHESIVE-BANDAGE-MACHINE OPERATOR 692.685-014
ARCH-SUPPORT TECHNICIAN 712.381-010
Assembler, Patient Lifting Device 706.684-018
ASSEMBLER, SURGICAL GARMENT 712.684-010
autoclave operator 599.585-010
BITE-BLOCK MAKER 712.684-014
BLOCK MAKER 719.381-018
BONER 789.687-018
CARRIER PACKER 920.687-066
ceramics technician 712.381-042
COILER 712.687-014
CONTOUR WIRE SPECIALIST, DENTURE 712.381-014
COTTON-BALL BAGGER 920.686-014
COTTON-BALL-MACHINE TENDER 580.685-022
COTTON-ROLL PACKER 920.685-054
DENTAL CERAMIST 712.381-042
DENTAL CERAMIST ASSISTANT 712.664-010
DENTAL FLOSS PACKER 920.687-082
DENTAL-LABORATORY TECHNICIAN 712.381-018
DENTAL-LABORATORY-TECHNICIAN APPRENTICE 712.381-022
dental technician 712.381-018
dental-technician apprentice 712.381-022
Dental Technician, Crown And Bridge 712.381-018
Dental Technician, Metal 712.381-018
denture finisher 712.381-050
DENTURE-MODEL MAKER 712.684-046
DENTURE WAXER 712.381-046
DESIGNER 712.281-014
DIAPER MACHINE TENDER 692.685-278
durable medical equipment repairer 639.281-022
Elastic Assembler 712.684-010
FABRICATOR, ARTIFICIAL BREAST 712.684-042
finisher 712.381-050
FINISHER, DENTURE 712.381-050
finisher-polisher 712.381-050
GAS-MASK ASSEMBLER 712.684-022
GAS-MASK INSPECTOR 712.687-022
GAUGER 712.687-018
gut winder 712.687-034
Inspector 789.687-070
INSPECTOR, SURGICAL GARMENT 712.487-010
KICK-PRESS OPERATOR 692.685-102
LACER 789.687-094
LATEXER I 584.685-038
Latexer II 712.684-010
Leather Worker 712.684-010
MANAGER, DENTAL LABORATORY 187.167-090
MEDICAL-EQUIPMENT REPAIRER 639.281-022
molder 712.684-034
OPAQUER 712.684-030
ORTHODONTIC BAND MAKER 712.381-026
ORTHODONTIC TECHNICIAN 712.381-030
ORTHOPEDIC-BOOT-AND-SHOE DESIGNER AND MAKER 788.261-010
Orthotics-Prosthetics Technician 712.381-034
ORTHOTICS TECHNICIAN 712.381-034
PACKER, DENTURE 712.684-034
packing-and-final-assembly supervisor 712.137-014
pad maker 689.685-130
POLY-PACKER AND HEAT-SEALER 920.686-038
porcelain-buildup assistant 712.684-030
porcelain finisher 712.664-010
porcelain waxer 712.664-010
PRESS OPERATOR 686.685-050
PROSTHETICS TECHNICIAN 712.381-038
REFINER 712.684-038
restoration technician 712.381-038
SANITARY-NAPKIN-MACHINE TENDER 692.685-150
SEWING-MACHINE OPERATOR 787.682-050
SPLICER 759.684-070
Spring Bender 712.684-010
stayer 789.687-018
STERILIZER 599.585-010
STRINGER-MACHINE TENDER 692.485-010
stripper 789.687-018
SUPERVISOR, ARTIFICIAL BREAST FABRICATION 712.134-010
SUPERVISOR, DENTAL LABORATORY 712.131-010
Supervisor, Denture Department 712.131-010
SUPERVISOR, FACEPIECE LINE 712.137-010
SUPERVISOR, FINAL ASSEMBLY AND PACKING 712.137-014
Supervisor, Gold Department 712.131-010
SUPERVISOR, HEARING-AID ASSEMBLY 726.131-014
SUPERVISOR I 692.137-014
SUPERVISOR II 789.134-014
Supervisor, Partial Denture Department 712.131-010
Supervisor, Porcelain Department 712.131-010
SUPERVISOR, SURGICAL GARMENT ASSEMBLY 712.132-010
SURGICAL-DRESSING MAKER 689.685-130
SURGICAL-ELASTIC KNITTER, HAND FRAME 685.382-010
suture gauger 712.687-018
suture measurer 712.687-018
SUTURE POLISHER 712.687-030
SUTURE WINDER, HAND 712.687-034
TESTER, REGULATOR 710.387-010
TOOTH CLERK 222.687-038
TOOTH INSPECTOR 712.687-038
Truss Assembler 712.684-010
waxer 712.381-046
wheelchair repairer 639.281-022

radio-tv broad.—RADIO AND TELEVISION BROADCASTING INDUSTRY: This designation includes occupations concerned with creating and broadcasting local, national, and international aural and visual programs, including the following phases of work: preparing and directing musical programs, plays, and skits; making electrical recordings; operating and maintaining broadcasting, audio, and video equipment; selling programs to sponsors; and transmitting such special events as public rallies and sporting engagements. Program participants, such as actors, comedians, musicians, and speakers, are included under AMUSEMENT AND RECREATION (amuse. & rec.). Occupations concerned with recording and manufacturing records and tapes are included in the RECORDING INDUSTRY (recording).

ACCESS COORDINATOR, CABLE TELEVISION 194.122-010
account executive 259.357-018
adjustment clerk 239.362-014
Anchorperson 131.262-010
animated-cartoon artist 141.081-010
animator 141.081-010
ANNOUNCER 159.147-010
Announcer, International Broadcast 159.147-010
application clerk 239.362-014
Art Critic 131.067-018
ART DIRECTOR 142.061-062
ASSIGNMENT EDITOR 132.132-010
assistant camera operator 962.687-010
associate director 962.167-014
associate producer 159.117-010
audio engineer 194.262-010
AUDIO OPERATOR 194.262-010
audio technician 194.262-010
board operator 194.262-018
Book Critic 131.067-018
boom operator 962.384-010
BROADCAST CHECKER 249.387-010
CABLE TELEVISION INSTALLER 821.281-010
CABLE TELEVISION LINE TECHNICIAN 821.261-010
camera control operator 194.282-010
CAMERA OPERATOR 143.062-022
camera operator, first 143.062-010
camera operator, head 143.062-010
Camera Operator, Second 143.062-022
Camera Operator, Sound Effects 143.062-022
Camera Operator, Television 143.062-022
CAPTION WRITER 203.362-026
Cartoon-Background Artist 141.081-010
CARTOONIST, MOTION PICTURES 141.081-010
Cartoonist, Special Effects 141.081-010
chief engineer, broadcasting operations 003.167-030
cinematographer 143.062-010
CLERK, TELEVISION PRODUCTION 221.367-086
color-television console monitor 194.282-010
COLUMNIST/COMMENTATOR 131.067-010
Combination Operator 159.147-014
Commentator 131.067-010
COMMERCIAL ENGINEER 003.187-014
CONTESTANT COORDINATOR 166.167-010
CONTINUITY DIRECTOR 132.037-010
Continuity Reader 131.267-022
CONTINUITY WRITER 131.087-010
coordinator, program planning 132.067-030
copy reader 131.267-022
copyright clerk 249.267-010
COPYRIGHT EXPERT 249.267-010
Correspondent 131.262-018

railroad equip.

Statistician	216.382-062
STENOCAPTIONER	202.382-010
story analyst	131.087-014
STORY EDITOR	132.037-026
studio engineer	194.262-018
studio technician	194.262-018
studio technician-video operator	194.382-018
STUNT PERFORMER	159.341-014
subtitle writer	203.362-026
Supervising Editor, Feature	962.132-010
Supervising Editor, News Reel	962.132-010
Supervising Editor, Trailer	962.132-010
SUPERVISING FILM EDITOR	962.132-010
SUPERVISOR, COSTUMING	962.137-018
SUPERVISOR, FILM PROCESSING	976.131-014
SUPERVISOR, MICROWAVE	003.167-058
SUPERVISOR, SCENIC ARTS	149.031-010
switching operator	962.162-010
talent	159.147-018
talent director	159.267-010
talk show host/hostess	159.147-018
tape duplicator	194.382-014
Tape-Recording-Machine Operator	194.362-010
TAPE TRANSFERRER	194.382-014
TECHNICIAN, NEWS GATHERING	194.362-022
technician-photographer/editor	194.362-022
TECHNICIAN, PLANT AND MAINTENANCE	822.281-030
TELECINE OPERATOR	194.362-018
Television Announcer	159.147-010
Television Producer	159.117-010
TELEVISION-SCHEDULE COORDINATOR	199.382-010
TELEVISION TECHNICIAN	194.062-010
theatrical performer see ENTERTAINER	
Title Artist	141.061-022
TRAFFIC CLERK	209.382-022
traffic engineer	003.187-014
traffic manager	209.382-022
transmission engineer	003.167-030
transmitter engineer	003.167-034
transmitter engineer	193.262-038
TRANSMITTER OPERATOR	193.262-038
UTILIZATION COORDINATOR	169.167-078
video engineer	194.282-010
VIDEO OPERATOR	194.282-010
videotape engineer	194.382-018
VIDEOTAPE OPERATOR	194.382-018
Videotape-Recording Engineer	194.362-010
wardrobe draper	346.374-010
WARDROBE-SPECIALTY WORKER	969.381-010

railroad equip.—RAILROAD EQUIPMENT BUILDING AND REPAIRING INDUSTRY: This designation includes occupations concerned with building, rebuilding, and repairing railroad cars and locomotives in steam railroad, electric railroad, diesel-electric railroad, and street railway shops; car- and locomotive-building companies; and other establishments, such as petroleum refineries and mines.

Accessories Repairer	825.281-026
AIR-COMPRESSOR MECHANIC	622.684-010
AIR-VALVE REPAIRER	622.381-010
BATTERY INSPECTOR	829.684-010
Bearing-Press-Machine Operator	616.682-010
BLOWER INSULATOR	863.664-010
Boxcar Weigher	221.587-030
car-body inspector	807.381-026
car-body-inspector helper	807.687-014
car cleaner	845.684-010
CAR INSPECTOR	910.667-010
Car Letterer	970.381-038
CARPENTER, RAILCAR	860.381-038
Carpenter, Streetcar	860.381-038
CAR REPAIRER	622.381-014
car repairer	721.381-010
CAR-REPAIRER APPRENTICE	622.381-022
CAR-REPAIRER HELPER	622.684-014
Car-Roof Repairer	807.381-026
CAR SCRUBBER	845.684-010
Car Straightener	622.381-014
Car Tester	622.684-014
Car-Top Bolter	622.684-014
CAR TRIMMER	806.684-046
Car Varnisher	740.684-022
compressor repairer	622.684-010
control inspector	825.381-018

CONTROLLER REPAIRER-AND-TESTER	825.381-018
Destination-Sign Repairer	807.381-026
Door-Engine Repairer	620.381-018
drop-pit worker	622.381-014
Electrical Inspector	807.381-026
Electrician, Control Equipment	825.281-026
ELECTRICIAN, LOCOMOTIVE	825.281-026
Electrician Supervisor, Locomotive	829.131-014
ELECTRIC-MOTOR FITTER	721.381-010
FLOOR-COVERING LAYER	622.381-026
Freight-Air-Brake Fitter	862.281-022
hose handler	863.664-010
INSTALLER, DOOR FURRING	806.687-034
INSTALLER, METAL FLOORING	806.684-070
INSTALLER, MOVABLE BULKHEAD	806.684-074
LINE MOVER	921.664-010
LOCOMOTIVE INSPECTOR	622.281-010
Locomotive Repairer, Diesel	625.281-010
machinist	622.381-014
machinist apprentice	622.381-022
machinist helper	622.684-014
MECHANICAL-UNIT REPAIRER	620.381-018
motor assembler	721.381-010
motor overhauler	721.381-010
passenger-car scrubber	845.684-010
pit inspector	622.281-010
PORTABLE SAWYER	899.684-030
railroad-car inspector	910.667-010
RAILROAD-CAR-TRUCK BUILDER	806.684-114
RAILROAD WHEELS AND AXLE INSPECTOR	622.381-034
RIVETER	800.684-010
ROOF FITTER	806.684-126
ROUTER OPERATOR, HAND	806.684-150
SALVAGE INSPECTOR	622.381-038
Sash Repairer	807.381-026
STENCIL CUTTER	970.381-038
STREETCAR REPAIRER	807.381-026
STREETCAR-REPAIRER HELPER	807.684-014
Streetcar Sandbox And Lifeguard-Unit Repairer	807.381-026
SUPERINTENDENT, CAR CONSTRUCTION	183.167-034
SUPERVISOR, CAR INSTALLATIONS	806.137-010
SUPERVISOR, ERECTION SHOP	806.131-022
SUPERVISOR, RAILROAD CAR REPAIR	622.131-010
SUPERVISOR, ROUNDHOUSE	622.131-014
SUPERVISOR, SHIPPING TRACK	806.137-018
SUPERVISOR, WHEEL SHOP	622.131-018
Tank-Car Repairer	622.381-014
test rack operator	622.382-010
TRANSFER-TABLE OPERATOR	910.683-022
TRANSFER-TABLE OPERATOR HELPER	910.667-030
TRIPLE-AIR-VALVE TESTER	622.382-010
wheel and axle inspector	622.381-034
Wheel Fitter	622.381-014
WHEEL-PRESS CLERK	221.587-046
Wheel-Press Operator	616.682-010
Windshield-Wiper Repairer	620.381-018
Wirer, Passenger Car	825.281-026

real estate—REAL ESTATE INDUSTRY: This designation includes occupations concerned with the operation of various types of real estate offices and the functions of real estate agents, brokers, and dealers. The principal functions include real estate development (not including construction); real estate management, operation, ownership, and rental of property, such as auditoriums, concert halls, houses, and office buildings; and buying and selling buildings and land.

abstract manager	186.167-090
abstractor	209.367-046
APPRAISER, REAL ESTATE	191.267-010
business investor	189.157-010
BUSINESS-OPPORTUNITY-AND-PROPERTY-	
INVESTMENT BROKER	189.157-010
CEMETERY WORKER	406.684-010
chief of production	186.167-090
CLOSER	186.167-074
CONDOMINIUM MANAGER	186.167-062
floor housekeeper	321.137-010
gravedigger	406.684-010
HOUSEKEEPER	321.137-010
LEASING AGENT, RESIDENCE	250.357-014
MANAGER, APARTMENT HOUSE	186.167-018
MANAGER, CEMETERY	187.167-074
MANAGER, LAND DEVELOPMENT	186.117-042
MANAGER, PROPERTY	186.167-046

MANAGER, REAL-ESTATE FIRM 186.167-066
MANAGER, TITLE SEARCH 186.167-090
property investor 189.157-010
real-estate agent 250.357-018
Real-Estate Broker 250.357-018
rental agent 250.357-014
SALES AGENT, REAL ESTATE 250.357-018
superintendent, cemetery 187.167-074
SUPERVISOR, CEMETERY WORKERS 406.134-010
SUPERVISOR, REAL-ESTATE OFFICE 249.137-030
Tax Searcher 209.367-046
TITLE SEARCHER 209.367-046

recording—RECORDING INDUSTRY: This designation includes occupations concerned with manufacturing and repairing blank and prerecorded phonograph records, magnetic tapes, and similar devices. Included here are occupations concerned with making master recordings for duplication onto records and tapes.

board operator 194.262-018
Breaker Table Worker 559.686-010
cartridge loader 726.685-010
CENTER-PUNCH OPERATOR 690.685-078
COMPOUND WORKER 559.686-010
die setter 556.380-010
Disk-Recording-Machine Operator 194.362-010
Dubbing-Machine Operator 194.362-010
finisher 500.684-014
Grinder 559.686-010
INJECTION-MOLDING-MACHINE TENDER 556.685-038
LABEL DRIER 532.687-010
LABELING-MACHINE OPERATOR 920.685-066
MAGNETIC-TAPE WINDER 726.685-010
Maintenance Mechanic, Record Processing Equipment 638.281-014
MATRIX-BATH ATTENDANT 500.384-014
matrix inspector 194.387-010
MATRIX PLATER 500.384-010
MATRIX WORKER 500.684-014
mixer operator 194.262-018
MOLD SETTER 556.380-010
MOTHER REPAIRER 705.684-042
mother tester 194.387-010
music mixer 194.262-018
QUALITY-CONTROL INSPECTOR 194.387-010
RECORDING ENGINEER 194.362-010
RECORDING STUDIO SET-UP WORKER 962.664-014
RECORD-PRESS TENDER 556.685-070
RECORD TESTER 194.387-014
Roller Hand 559.686-010
setter, plastics-molding machine 556.380-010
SILVER SPRAY WORKER 500.684-022
SONG PLUGGER 165.157-010
SOUND MIXER 194.262-018
sound recording technician 194.362-010
studio engineer 194.262-018
studio technician 194.262-018
SUPERVISOR, MATRIX 500.134-010
SUPERVISOR, RECORD PRESS 559.130-018
tape duplicator 194.382-014
Tape-Recording-Machine Operator 194.362-010
TAPE TRANSFERRER 194.382-014
Weigher 559.686-010

retail trade—RETAIL TRADE INDUSTRY: This designation includes occupations concerned with the sale of goods to ultimate consumers for consumption or utilization, and with services incidental to the sale of goods. Most retailing is carried on in places of business that are open to the general public.

Adjustment Clerk 219.362-010
advertising clerk 216.382-066
alteration inspector 789.687-078
ALTERATIONS WORKROOM CLERK 221.367-010
ALTERATION TAILOR 785.261-010
alterer 785.261-010
alterer apprentice 785.261-018
Aluminum-Siding Installer 863.684-014
APPAREL-RENTAL CLERK 295.357-010
AREA SUPERVISOR, RETAIL CHAIN STORE 185.117-014
ARTIFICIAL-FOLIAGE ARRANGER 899.364-014
Asbestos-Siding Installer 863.684-014
Asphalt-Tile-Floor Layer 864.481-010
attendant, self-service store 299.677-010
AUCTION ASSISTANT 294.667-010
AUCTION CLERK 294.567-010
AUCTIONEER 294.257-010
Auctioneer, Art 294.257-010
Auctioneer, Furniture 294.257-010
Auctioneer, Livestock 294.257-010
Auctioneer, Real Estate 294.257-010
audio-visual-equipment-rental clerk 295.367-018
AUTOMOBILE LOCATOR 296.367-010
awning erector 869.484-010
AWNING HANGER 869.484-010
AWNING-HANGER HELPER 869.687-010
awning installer 869.484-010
AWNING MAKER-AND-INSTALLER 869.481-010
BABY-STROLLER & WHEELCHAIR RENTAL CLERK 295.367-014
BAGGER 920.687-014
Baked-Goods Stock Clerk 299.367-014
Bakery Demonstrator 297.354-010
BICYCLE-RENTAL CLERK 295.467-010
Billiard-Table Repairer 732.384-010
blower 369.685-010
BLOWER INSULATOR 863.664-010
boat accessories installer 806.464-010
BOAT-HOIST OPERATOR 921.683-010
BOAT-HOIST-OPERATOR HELPER 921.667-010
BOAT RIGGER 806.464-010
Building-Insulating Carpenter 860.381-022
busheler 785.261-010
butcher 316.684-018
butcher apprentice 316.684-022
BUYER, ASSISTANT 162.157-022
CALL-OUT OPERATOR 237.367-014
Candy-Department Manager 299.137-010
canvasser 291.357-010
car checker 806.361-026
car cleaner 915.687-022
CARPET CUTTER 929.381-010
CARPET LAYER 864.381-010
CARPET-LAYER HELPER 864.687-010
CARPET SEWER 787.682-014
car porter 915.687-022
carrier 292.457-010
CASHIER-CHECKER 211.462-014
CASHIER, COURTESY BOOTH 211.467-010
CASHIER, TUBE ROOM 211.482-010
CASHIER-WRAPPER 211.462-018
Ceramic-Maker Demonstrator 297.354-010
charge-account identification clerk 241.367-030
CHECK WRITER 219.382-010
coach see SPONSOR ....
Coat Baster 785.361-022
Coat Padder 785.361-022
Coat-Repair Inspector 783.387-010
Collar Setter 785.361-022
COMPARISON SHOPPER 296.367-014
Concrete-Panel Installer 863.684-014
CONTRACT CLERK, AUTOMOBILE 219.362-026
Contract-Post-Office Clerk 243.367-014
Conveyor Belt Package Sorter 222.687-022
Cork-Tile-Floor Layer 864.481-010
CORSET FITTER 782.361-010
corsetier 261.354-010
Cosmetics Demonstrator 297.354-010
Costume-Rental Clerk 295.357-010
counter clerk 279.357-062
Counter Clerk, Appliance Parts 279.357-062
Counter Clerk, Automotive Parts 279.357-062
Counter Clerk, Farm Equipment Parts 279.357-062
Counter Clerk, Industrial Machinery And Equipment Parts 279.357-062
Counter Clerk, Radio, Television, And Electronics Parts 279.357-062
Counter Clerk, Tractor Parts 279.357-062
Counter Clerk, Truck Parts 279.357-062
COUPON-REDEMPTION CLERK 290.477-010
CREDIT-CARD CLERK 209.587-014
CREDIT REFERENCE CLERK 209.362-018
CUSTOMER-SERVICE CLERK 299.367-010
Customer Service Manager 299.137-010
customer-service specialist, post exchange 299.367-010
Custom Garment Designer 142.061-018
CUSTOM TAILOR 785.261-014
DEALER-COMPLIANCE REPRESENTATIVE 168.267-026
decorator consultant 295.357-018
decorator, store 298.081-010
Delicatessen-Goods Stock Clerk 299.367-014
DELI CUTTER-SLICER 316.684-014
DELIVERER, CAR RENTAL 919.663-010
Deliverer, Food 299.477-010
DELIVERER, MERCHANDISE 299.477-010

retail trade

Deliverer, Pharmacy	299.477-010	huckster	291.457-018
delivery-route truck driver	292.353-010	Ice-Cream Vendor	291.457-018
DEMONSTRATOR	297.354-010	Importer	185.157-018
DEMONSTRATOR, KNITTING	297.354-014	installation helper	869.687-010
DEMONSTRATOR, SEWING TECHNIQUES	297.454-010	installation worker, draperies	869.484-014
Department-Store-Collection Clerk	241.357-010	installer	869.484-014
department supervisor	299.137-010	INSTRUCTOR, PAINTING	297.451-010
director, merchandise	185.167-034	instructor, training see SPONSOR	
DIRECTOR, SERVICE	189.167-014	INSULATION-POWER-UNIT TENDER	863.685-010
Discount-Variety-Store Stock Clerk	299.367-014	INVESTIGATOR, CASH SHORTAGE	376.267-010
dispatcher, route sales-delivery drivers	292.137-014	INVESTIGATOR, FRAUD	376.267-014
DISPLAYER, MERCHANDISE	298.081-010	Lapel Padder	785.361-022
display trimmer	298.081-010	LAYAWAY CLERK	299.467-010
DRAPERY AND UPHOLSTERY ESTIMATOR	299.387-014	lei maker	291.454-010
DRAPERY AND UPHOLSTERY MEASURER	299.364-010	LEI SELLER	291.454-010
Drapery Estimator	299.387-010	leno sewer	787.682-014
DRAPERY HANGER	869.484-014	Linoleum Cutter	929.381-010
DRAPERY-HEAD FORMER	781.684-030	Linoleum-Floor Layer	864.481-010
DRAPERY OPERATOR	787.682-018	Linoleum Layer	864.481-010
DRAPERY-ROD ASSEMBLER	706.484-010	Linoleum-Tile-Floor Layer	864.481-010
Drapery Room Supervisor	789.132-010	Liquor-Store Stock Clerk	299.367-014
drapery worker	787.682-018	LOCKER-PLANT ATTENDANT	922.684-010
DRIVER HELPER, SALES ROUTE	292.667-010	LOT ATTENDANT	915.583-010
DRIVER, SALES ROUTE	292.353-010	lot caller	294.667-010
durable medical equipment repairer	639.281-022	made-to-measure tailor	785.261-014
electric-motor-repair clerk	271.354-010	made-to-measure-tailor apprentice	785.261-022
EMBROIDERY PATTERNMAKER	782.361-014	Mail-Order Biller	214.382-014
Fancy Packer	920.587-018	Mail-Order Sorter	222.387-038
FASHION ARTIST	141.061-014	maintenance worker, house trailer	899.484-010
FASHION COORDINATOR	185.157-010	make-ready mechanic	806.361-026
fashion model	297.667-014	MANAGER, AUTOMOBILE SERVICE STATION	185.167-014
fashion stylist	185.157-010	MANAGER, BULK PLANT	181.117-010
FEED AND FARM MANAGEMENT ADVISER	096.127-018	MANAGER, CUSTOMER SERVICES	187.167-082
feeder worker power-unit operator	863.685-010	MANAGER, DEPARTMENT	299.137-010
field operating superintendent	181.117-010	MANAGER, DEPARTMENT STORE	185.117-010
field representative	168.267-026	MANAGER, DISPLAY	142.031-014
FIGURE REFINISHER AND REPAIRER	739.381-034	MANAGER, FAST FOOD SERVICES	185.137-010
film booker	295.367-018	manager, floor	299.137-010
FILM-RENTAL CLERK	295.367-018	MANAGER, MARKET	186.167-042
finisher-tailor apprentice	785.361-026	MANAGER, MEAT SALES AND STORAGE	185.167-030
fitter	739.684-146	MANAGER, MERCHANDISE	185.167-034
fitter	276.257-022	MANAGER, NURSERY	180.167-042
floor coverer	864.481-010	manager, operating and occupancy	189.167-014
floor-coverer apprentice	864.481-014	MANAGER, PARTS	185.167-038
Floor-Coverings Estimator	270.357-026	Manager, Retail Nursery	180.167-042
floor-covering-tile layer	864.481-010	MANAGER, RETAIL STORE	185.167-046
FLOOR LAYER	864.481-010	Manager, Self-Service Gasoline Station	185.167-014
FLOOR-LAYER APPRENTICE	864.481-014	manager, stockroom	185.167-038
Floor-Layer Helper	869.687-026	MANAGER, TRAVEL AGENCY	187.167-158
Floral Arranger	142.081-010	MARKER	781.687-042
FLORAL DESIGNER	142.081-010	MARKER	209.587-034
florist	142.081-010	marking clerk	209.587-034
Food Demonstrator	297.354-010	master-tailor apprentice	785.261-022
Formal-Wear-Rental Clerk	295.357-010	MEASURER	869.367-014
fringe-binder operator	787.682-014	MEAT CLERK	222.684-010
Fuel-Oil-Delivery Driver	903.683-018	Meat Counter Clerk	290.477-018
fur beater	369.685-014	MEAT CUTTER	316.684-018
FUR BLOWER	369.685-010	MEAT-CUTTER APPRENTICE	316.684-022
FUR CLEANER, MACHINE	369.685-010	Meat Inspector	316.684-018
fur drummer	369.685-014	Meat Stock Clerk	299.367-014
fur dry-cleaner	369.685-014	Meat Wrapper	920.587-018
FURNITURE ASSEMBLER-AND-INSTALLER	739.684-082	MEDICAL-EQUIPMENT REPAIRER	639.281-022
Furniture Packer	920.587-018	Men's Garment Fitter	785.361-014
FURNITURE-RENTAL CONSULTANT	295.357-018	Merchandise-Adjustment Clerk	241.367-014
FUR-REPAIR INSPECTOR	783.387-010	MERCHANDISE DISTRIBUTOR	219.367-018
FUR-STORAGE CLERK	369.367-010	merchandise marker	209.587-034
fur-vault attendant	369.367-010	Metal-Tile Setter	861.381-034
GARMENT-ALTERATION EXAMINER	789.687-078	MILKING-SYSTEM INSTALLER	809.381-018
GARMENT FITTER	785.361-014	MILLINER	784.261-010
Gas-Delivery Driver	903.683-018	MOBILE-HOME-LOT UTILITY WORKER	899.484-010
GIFT WRAPPER	299.364-014	Model Dresser	298.081-010
Glassware-Maker Demonstrator	297.354-010	MODEL	297.667-014
Grocery Checker	211.462-014	NEW-CAR GET-READY MECHANIC	806.361-026
Grocery Clerk	290.477-018	NEWSPAPER CARRIER	292.457-010
grocery packer	920.687-014	newspaper deliverer	292.457-010
haberdasher	261.357-054	operations manager	185.117-014
HARNESS MAKER	783.381-018	ophthalmic-technician apprentice	716.280-010
hawker	291.457-018	optical mechanic	716.280-014
Head of Stock	222.137-034	optical-mechanic apprentice	716.280-010
HEARING AID SPECIALIST	276.354-010	OPTICIAN	716.280-014
hearing instrument specialist	276.354-010	OPTICIAN APPRENTICE	716.280-010
Hem Marker	781.687-042	OPTICIAN APPRENTICE, DISPENSING	299.361-014
hose handler	863.664-010	Optician, Contact-Lens Dispensing	299.361-010
house model	297.667-014	ORDER FILLER	222.487-014
Housewares Demonstrator	297.354-010	Ornamental-Brick Installer	863.684-014

orthopedic-shoe fitter	276.257-018
outboard-motorboat rigger	806.464-010
outgoing inspector	789.687-078
Pants Busheler	785.261-010
parts clerk	279.357-062
PAWNBROKER	191.157-010
peddler	291.357-010
PEDDLER	291.457-018
PERSONAL SHOPPER	296.357-010
Pet Shop Attendant	410.674-010
Pharmacy Stock Clerk	299.367-014
philatelic consultant	299.387-014
PICTURE FRAMER	739.684-146
Plastic-Panel Installer	863.684-014
Plastic-Tile Layer	861.381-034
PLAYGROUND-EQUIPMENT ERECTOR	801.684-018
Porcelain-Enamel Installer	863.684-014
PORTER, USED-CAR LOT	915.687-022
price marker	209.587-034
Produce Clerk I	290.477-018
Produce Clerk II	922.687-058
Produce-Department Manager	299.137-010
Produce Stock Clerk	299.367-014
PRODUCE WEIGHER	299.587-010
PRODUCTION PROOFREADER	247.667-010
professional shopper	296.357-010
Proprietor-Manager, Retail Automotive Service	185.167-014
relief clerk see SALESPERSON. CONTINGENT	
rental clerk, furniture	295.357-018
rental clerk, tool-and-equipment	295.357-014
RIPPER	782.687-038
ROCK BREAKER	770.687-034
route driver	292.353-010
route driver helper	292.667-010
route supervisor	292.137-014
Rubber-Tile-Floor Layer	864.481-010
RUG MEASURER	369.367-014
rug-receiving clerk	369.367-014
Saddler	783.381-026
sales agent see SALES REPRESENTATIVE	
sales associate see SALES REPRESENTATIVE	
SALES ATTENDANT	299.677-010
SALES ATTENDANT, BUILDING MATERIALS	299.677-014
SALES CLERK	290.477-014
Sales Clerk, Fish	290.477-018
SALES CLERK, FOOD	290.477-018
Sales Clerk, Fresh Poultry	316.684-010
SALESPERSON	master
salesperson apprentice, meats	316.684-022
SALESPERSON, ART OBJECTS	277.457-010
SALESPERSON, AUTOMOBILE ACCESSORIES	273.357-030
SALESPERSON, AUTOMOBILES	273.353-010
SALESPERSON, BOOKS	277.357-034
SALESPERSON, BURIAL NEEDS	279.357-042
Salesperson, Burial Plots	279.357-042
salesperson, cemetery	279.357-042
Salesperson, Children's Shoes	261.357-062
Salesperson, China And Glassware	270.357-018
SALESPERSON, CHINA AND SILVERWARE	270.357-018
SALESPERSON, CONTINGENT	term
SALESPERSON, CORSETS	261.354-010
SALESPERSON, COSMETICS AND TOILETRIES	262.357-018
SALESPERSON, CURTAINS AND DRAPERIES	270.357-022
Salesperson, Custom Draperies	270.357-022
SALESPERSON-DEMONSTRATOR, PARTY PLAN	279.357-038
SALESPERSON, ELECTRIC MOTORS	271.354-010
Salesperson, Fashion Accessories	261.357-066
SALESPERSON, FLOOR COVERINGS	270.357-026
SALESPERSON, FLOWERS	260.357-026
SALESPERSON, FLYING SQUAD	279.357-046
SALESPERSON, FURNITURE	270.357-030
SALESPERSON, FURS	261.357-042
SALESPERSON, GENERAL HARDWARE	279.357-050
SALESPERSON, GENERAL MERCHANDISE	279.357-054
Salesperson, Grave Coverings And Markers	279.357-042
Salesperson, Handbags	261.357-066
salesperson, hearing aids	276.354-010
SALESPERSON, HORTICULTURAL AND NURSERY PRODUCTS	272.357-022
Salesperson, Hosiery	261.357-066
SALESPERSON, HOUSEHOLD APPLIANCES	270.357-034
SALESPERSON, INFANTS' AND CHILDREN'S WEAR	261.357-046
SALESPERSON, JEWELRY	279.357-058
salesperson, ladies' wear	261.357-066
SALESPERSON, LEATHER-AND-SUEDE APPAREL-AND-ACCESSORIES	261.357-074
Salesperson, Lingerie	261.357-066
salesperson, meats	316.684-018
SALESPERSON, MEN'S AND BOYS' CLOTHING	261.357-050
SALESPERSON, MEN'S FURNISHINGS	261.357-054
Salesperson, Men's Hats	261.357-054
Salesperson, Men's Shoes	261.357-062
SALESPERSON, MILLINERY	261.357-058
SALESPERSON, MUSICAL INSTRUMENTS AND ACCESSORIES	277.357-038
Salesperson, Neckties	261.357-054
Salesperson, New Cars	273.353-010
SALESPERSON, ORTHOPEDIC SHOES	276.257-018
Salesperson, Paint	279.357-050
SALESPERSON, PARTS	279.357-062
salesperson, part time see SALESPERSON, CONTINGENT	
SALESPERSON, PETS AND PET SUPPLIES	277.357-042
SALESPERSON, PHONOGRAPH RECORDS AND TAPE RECORDINGS	277.357-046
SALESPERSON, PHOTOGRAPHIC SUPPLIES AND EQUIPMENT	277.357-050
SALESPERSON, PIANOS AND ORGANS	277.354-010
salesperson, recreational vehicles	273.357-034
salesperson, relief see SALESPERSON, CONTINGENT	
SALESPERSON, SEWING MACHINES	270.352-010
SALESPERSON, SHEET MUSIC	277.357-054
SALESPERSON, SHOES	261.357-062
Salesperson, Silverware	270.357-018
SALESPERSON, SPORTING GOODS	277.357-058
SALESPERSON, STAMPS OR COINS	277.357-062
SALESPERSON, STEREO EQUIPMENT	270.357-038
SALESPERSON, SURGICAL APPLIANCES	276.257-022
Salesperson, Terrazzo Tiles	270.357-026
SALESPERSON, TOY TRAINS AND ACCESSORIES	277.357-066
SALESPERSON, TRAILERS AND MOTOR HOMES	273.357-034
Salesperson, Used Cars	273.353-010
salesperson, utility staff	279.357-046
Salesperson, Wall Coverings	279.357-050
SALESPERSON, WIGS	261.351-010
SALESPERSON, WOMEN'S APPAREL AND ACCESSORIES	261.357-066
Salesperson, Women's Dresses	261.357-066
salesperson, women's hats	261.357-058
Salesperson, Women's Shoes	261.357-062
Salesperson, Women's Sportswear	261.357-066
SALESPERSON, YARD GOODS	261.357-070
SALES REPRESENTATIVE	master
SALES REPRESENTATIVE, AIRCRAFT	273.253-010
SALES REPRESENTATIVE, BOATS AND MARINE SUPPLIES	273.357-018
SALES REPRESENTATIVE, DOOR-TO-DOOR	291.357-010
SALES REPRESENTATIVE, FUELS	269.357-010
SALES REPRESENTATIVE, HOBBIES AND CRAFTS	277.357-010
Sales Representative, Marine Supplies	273.357-018
SALES REPRESENTATIVE, OFFICE MACHINES	275.357-034
SALES REPRESENTATIVE, POULTRY EQUIPMENT AND SUPPLIES	272.357-018
SALES REPRESENTATIVE, TOBACCO PRODUCTS AND SMOKING SUPPLIES	260.357-022
Sales Representative, Toys And Games	277.357-026
SALES REPRESENTATIVE, UNIFORMS	261.357-034
SALES REPRESENTATIVE, UPHOLSTERY AND FURNITURE REPAIR	259.357-026
SALES REPRESENTATIVE, WATER-SOFTENING EQUIPMENT	279.357-034
SALES-SERVICE REPRESENTATIVE, MILKING MACHINES	299.251-010
saw-dust machine operator	369.685-014
SERVICE MANAGER	185.164-010
sewing-machine operator, carpet and rugs	787.682-014
shopper's aid	296.357-010
SHOP TAILOR	785.361-022
SHOP TAILOR APPRENTICE	785.361-026
Showcase Trimmer	298.081-010
SIDER	863.684-014
siding applicator	863.684-014
Sleeve Tailor	785.361-022
SLIPCOVER CUTTER	780.381-034
Slip-Cover Estimator	299.364-010
SOFT-TILE SETTER	861.381-034
solicitor	291.357-010
special shopper	296.357-010
SPONSOR	term
STAMP ANALYST	299.387-014
STAMP CLASSIFIER	299.387-018

r.r. trans.

STATISTICAL CLERK, ADVERTISING	216.382-066
STOCK CHECKER, APPAREL	299.667-014
STOCK CLERK	299.367-014
stock clerk, self-service store	299.367-014
STORAGE-FACILITY RENTAL CLERK	295.367-026
Store Detective	376.367-014
store manager	185.167-046
stroller rental clerk	295.367-014
STUBBER	222.687-034
SUBSCRIPTION CREW LEADER	291.157-010
Suit Finisher	785.361-022
superintendent, nonselling	189.167-014
superintendent, operating	189.167-014
Supermarket Stock Clerk	299.367-014
SUPERVISOR, ALTERATION WORKROOM	785.131-010
SUPERVISOR, CASHIERS	211.137-010
SUPERVISOR, CONTINGENTS	205.367-050
SUPERVISOR, MARINA SALES AND SERVICE	299.137-026
SUPERVISOR, MARKING ROOM	209.137-026
SUPERVISOR, ROUTE SALES-DELIVERY DRIVERS	292.137-014
surgical-appliance fitter	276.257-022
tailor	785.261-014
TAILOR APPRENTICE, ALTERATION	785.261-018
TAILOR APPRENTICE, CUSTOM	785.261-022
Tailor, Men's Ready-To-Wear Garment	785.261-010
Tailor, Women's-Garment Alteration	785.261-010
TANK-TRUCK DRIVER	903.683-018
terminal superintendent	181.117-010
THROW-OUT CLERK	241.367-030
ticket maker	209.587-034
tile setter	861.381-034
TIRE ADJUSTER	241.367-034
TOBACCO BLENDER	790.381-010
TOOL-AND-EQUIPMENT-RENTAL CLERK	295.357-014
Top-Collar Maker	785.361-022
TOY ASSEMBLER	731.684-014
Toy-Department Manager	299.137-010
TOY-ELECTRIC-TRAIN REPAIRER	731.684-022
Trailer-Tank-Truck Driver	903.683-018
TRAVEL AGENT	252.152-010
travel counselor	252.152-010
truck driver, sales route	292.353-010
Undercollar Baster	785.361-022
Undercollar Maker	785.361-022
undercover agent	376.367-026
UNDERCOVER OPERATOR	376.367-026
upholstery and drapery measurer	299.364-010
Upholstery Estimator	299.387-010
used-car conditioner	620.684-034
used-car-lot attendant	915.687-022
USED-CAR RENOVATOR	620.684-034
Vegetable Vendor	291.457-018
vendor	291.457-018
VENETIAN-BLIND ASSEMBLER	739.684-166
VENETIAN-BLIND INSTALLER	869.484-018
Vest Busheler	785.261-010
Vest Tailor	785.361-022
washer driver	919.663-010
WATCH-AND-CLOCK-REPAIR CLERK	299.367-018
WEDDING CONSULTANT	299.357-018
wheelchair and baby-stroller rental clerk	295.367-014
wheelchair repairer	639.281-022
will-call clerk	299.467-010
Window Dresser	298.081-010
Window-Shade Estimator	299.364-010
Women's Garment Fitter	785.361-014
wrapper	299.364-014
WRONG-ADDRESS CLERK	209.587-050
yard salesperson	299.677-014
YARD SUPERVISOR, BUILDING MATERIALS OR LUMBER	929.137-030
YARD WORKER, USED BUILDING MATERIALS	922.667-010

r.r. trans.—RAILROAD TRANSPORTATION INDUSTRY: This designation includes occupations concerned with operating, maintaining, and repairing company railroads, railroad equipment, and allied services, such as sleeping and dining car service. Occupations concerned with major repairs as carried on in repair shops are included in the RAILROAD EQUIPMENT BUILDING AND REPAIRING INDUSTRY (railroad equip.). Occupations concerned with major railroad construction projects are included in the CONSTRUCTION INDUSTRY (construction). This industry also includes interurban railway and street and suburban railway occupations.

ACCOUNTS-ADJUSTABLE CLERK	214.462-010

agent-telegrapher	910.137-038
Armed Guard	372.667-034
assistant engineer	910.363-010
assistant signal maintainer	822.684-018
assistant superintendent, transportation	184.167-254
AUTOMAT-CAR ATTENDANT	319.464-010
BAGGAGE-AND-MAIL AGENT	910.137-010
BAGGAGE HANDLER	910.687-010
Ballast-Cleaning-Machine Operator	859.683-018
Ballast-Regulator Operator	859.683-018
Bar Attendant	311.477-022
BATTERY INSPECTOR	829.684-010
BRAKE COUPLER, ROAD FREIGHT	910.367-010
brake inspector	910.387-014
BRAKE REPAIRER, RAILROAD	622.261-010
BRAKER, PASSENGER TRAIN	910.364-010
BRIDGE INSPECTOR	869.287-010
BRIDGE OPERATOR, SLIP	919.682-010
bridge repairer	860.381-030
bridge tender	919.682-010
bridge tender	371.362-010
CALLER	215.563-010
car checker	910.387-014
CAR CHECKER	222.387-014
Car Cleaner	919.687-014
CAR-CLEANING SUPERVISOR	910.137-014
CAR CLERK, PULLMAN	215.167-010
CAR DISTRIBUTOR	910.367-014
CARPENTER, BRIDGE	860.381-030
car-record clerk	214.362-010
CAR REPAIRER, PULLMAN	622.381-018
CAR-RETARDER OPERATOR	910.382-010
Car Rider	910.664-010
car supplier	910.367-014
check clerk	209.367-054
chef	315.381-018
chief clerk, yard office	910.367-014
claims clerk	219.362-066
classification inspector	910.387-014
Coach Cleaner	919.687-014
CONDUCTOR	910.667-014
CONDUCTOR, PASSENGER CAR	198.167-010
CONDUCTOR, PULLMAN	198.167-014
CONDUCTOR, ROAD FREIGHT	198.167-018
conductor, sleeping car	198.167-014
CONDUCTOR, YARD	910.137-022
Conduit Installer	825.381-038
Cook, Fry	315.381-018
COOK, RAILROAD	315.381-018
CRATING-AND-MOVING ESTIMATOR	252.357-010
ctc operator	184.167-262
DEMURRAGE CLERK	214.362-010
Derrick-Car Operator	919.663-014
DINING-SERVICE INSPECTOR	168.267-030
dispatcher	184.163-010
dispatcher	184.167-262
DISPATCHER CLERK	215.362-014
DISPATCHER, TRAFFIC OR SYSTEM	919.162-010
DITCHER OPERATOR	850.683-014
DIVISION OFFICER	term
DIVISION ROAD SUPERVISOR	184.167-282
division superintendent	184.167-158
DOCUMENTATION-BILLING CLERK	214.362-014
DRAWBRIDGE OPERATOR	371.362-010
Electric-Freight-Car Operator	921.683-050
ELECTRIC-TRACK-SWITCH MAINTAINER	825.261-010
ENGINE DISPATCHER	910.367-018
Engineer, Remote Control, Diesel	910.363-018
engine supervisor	910.137-022
equipment inspector	910.387-014
EXPRESS CLERK	222.367-022
farebox repairer	710.681-018
Firer, Diesel Locomotive	910.363-010
Firer, Electric Locomotive	910.363-010
FIRER, LOCOMOTIVE	910.363-010
freight and passenger agent	910.137-038
FREIGHT-CAR CLEANER, DELTA SYSTEM	910.687-022
FREIGHT-LOADING SUPERVISOR	910.137-026
Freight-Traffic Agent	252.257-010
Gate Guard	376.667-018
GENERAL AGENT, OPERATIONS	184.167-042
GENERAL CAR SUPERVISOR, YARD	184.167-286
GENERAL CLAIMS AGENT	186.117-030
GRINDING-MACHINE OPERATOR, PORTABLE	910.684-010
Ground Helper, Street Railway	821.684-014

head switcher	910.137-022
host/hostess, railway	352.677-010
HOSTLER	910.683-010
industrial clerk	910.667-018
INFORMATION CLERK	237.367-018
INSTRUCTOR, BUS, TROLLEY, AND TAXI	919.223-010
INTERLINE CLERK	214.382-022
Interlocking Tower Operator	910.362-010
journal-box inspector	910.387-014
LABORER, CAR BARN	910.583-010
LINE INSTALLER, STREET RAILWAY	821.361-022
line installer, trolley	821.361-022
LOADING INSPECTOR	910.667-018
locomotive engineer	910.363-018
LOCOMOTIVE ENGINEER	910.363-014
Locomotive Engineer, Diesel	910.363-014
Locomotive Engineer, Electric	910.363-014
LOCOMOTIVE LUBRICATING-SYSTEMS CLERK	221.367-030
LOCOMOTIVE OPERATOR HELPER	910.367-022
LOUNGE-CAR ATTENDANT	291.457-014
Mail Sorter	222.687-022
maintenance inspector	910.367-030
maintenance-of-way supervisor	184.167-234
MANAGER, CAR INSPECTION AND REPAIR	184.117-086
Manager, Industrial Development	186.117-042
MANAGER, OPERATIONS	184.117-050
Manifest Clerk	214.362-014
Mileage Clerk	216.382-062
MOTOR OPERATOR	910.683-014
News Agent	291.457-014
operations manager	184.117-050
painter, railroad car	845.681-010
Painter, Sign, Maintenance	970.381-026
Pantry Attendant	311.477-022
Passenger-Car-Cleaning Supervisor	910.137-014
Passenger-Car Inspector	910.387-014
PASSENGER REPRESENTATIVE	910.367-026
PASSENGER SERVICE REPRESENTATIVE I	352.677-010
PASSENGER SERVICE REPRESENTATIVE II	910.677-010
Passenger Traffic Agent	252.257-010
PATROLLER	376.667-018
Per Diem Clerk	214.382-022
PERISHABLE-FREIGHT INSPECTOR	910.667-022
PORTER	357.677-010
porter, baggage	357.677-010
porter, pullman	351.677-010
PRODUCTION ENGINEER, TRACK	005.167-026
Pullman Attendant	315.381-018
pullman clerk	215.167-010
Rail-Express Clerk	222.367-022
Rail-Flaw-Detector-Car Operator	910.363-014
RAIL-FLAW-DETECTOR OPERATOR	910.263-010
railroad-car-cleaning supervisor	910.137-014
RAILROAD-CAR INSPECTOR	910.387-014
RAILROAD-CAR LETTERER	845.681-010
railroad-car retarder operator	910.382-010
RAILROAD-CONSTRUCTION DIRECTOR	182.167-018
RAILROAD-MAINTENANCE CLERK	221.362-026
railroad supervisor of engines	910.137-034
RAILWAY-EQUIPMENT OPERATOR	859.683-018
RATE ANALYST, FREIGHT	214.267-010
redcap	357.677-010
REGIONAL SUPERINTENDENT, RAILROAD CAR INSPECTION AND REPAIR	184.117-090
REGISTER REPAIRER	710.681-018
RESERVATION CLERK	238.367-014
retarder operator	910.382-010
REVISING CLERK	214.382-026
Right-of-Way Inspector	376.667-018
Road Clerk	221.362-026
Road Engineer, Freight	910.363-014
Road Engineer, Passenger	910.363-014
Road-Freight Firer	910.363-010
Road-Passenger Firer	910.363-010
ROAD SUPERVISOR OF ENGINES	910.137-034
sales representative	252.257-010
sandwich seller	291.457-014
Scaler	222.387-074
schedule clerk	219.462-014
Section-Crews-Activities Clerk	221.362-026
section-gang worker	910.684-014
SERVICE ATTENDANT, SLEEPING CAR	351.677-010
service center manager	184.167-042
service inspector	168.167-082
service inspector	168.267-030

SERVICE RESTORER, EMERGENCY	821.261-022
signal inspector	822.281-026
SIGNAL MAINTAINER	822.281-026
SIGNAL MAINTAINER HELPER	822.684-018
signal repairer	822.281-026
SIGNAL SUPERVISOR	822.131-026
signal-tower operator	910.362-010
slip tender	919.682-010
SPECIAL AGENT	372.267-010
SPECIAL AGENT-IN-CHARGE	376.167-010
Special-Trackwork Blacksmith	610.381-010
Sprayer, Railroad Car	741.684-026
STATION AGENT I	910.137-038
Station Agent II	211.467-030
STATION MANAGER	184.167-130
Station Patroller	376.667-018
station telegrapher	236.562-014
Steamtable Attendant, Railroad	311.677-014
Steward/Stewardess, Club Car	310.137-026
STEWARD/STEWARDESS, RAILROAD DINING CAR	310.137-026
STREETCAR OPERATOR	913.463-014
Substation Operator, Distribution	952.362-026
SUPERINTENDENT, DIVISION	184.167-158
superintendent, electrical department	184.167-202
SUPERINTENDENT, MAINTENANCE OF EQUIPMENT	184.167-178
SUPERINTENDENT, MAINTENANCE OF WAY	182.167-030
SUPERINTENDENT, POWER	184.167-202
SUPERINTENDENT, STATIONS	184.167-206
SUPERVISOR, BRAKE REPAIR	622.137-010
SUPERVISOR, BRIDGES AND BUILDINGS	182.167-034
SUPERVISOR, CAR AND YARD	622.137-014
SUPERVISOR, COMMUNICATIONS-AND-SIGNALS	184.167-290
SUPERVISOR, LINE DEPARTMENT	825.137-010
SUPERVISOR, LOCOMOTIVE	625.137-010
SUPERVISOR OF WAY	184.167-234
SUPERVISOR, TRAIN OPERATIONS	184.167-294
Switching Clerk	222.387-014
SWITCH REPAIRER	622.684-018
SWITCH TENDER	910.667-026
SWITCHYARD WORKER	term
Tamping-Machine Operator	859.683-018
TARIFF INSPECTOR	214.362-034
TELEGRAPHER	236.562-010
TELEGRAPHER AGENT	236.562-014
telephoner	236.562-010
teletype-telegrapher	236.562-010
TERMINAL SUPERINTENDENT	184.167-254
THIRD-RAIL INSTALLER	825.381-038
TOWER OPERATOR	910.362-010
track-grinder operator	910.684-010
track inspector	910.367-030
track laborer	910.684-014
TRACK OILER	910.687-026
TRACK REPAIRER	910.684-014
track supervisor	910.367-030
TRAFFIC AGENT	252.257-010
traffic-control operator	184.167-262
TRAFFIC INSPECTOR	184.163-010
TRAIN CLERK	219.462-014
TRAIN DISPATCHER	184.167-262
TRAIN DISPATCHER, ASSISTANT CHIEF	910.167-014
TRANSFER-TABLE OPERATOR	910.683-022
TRANSFER-TABLE OPERATOR HELPER	910.667-030
transportation inspector	184.163-010
TRANSPORTATION INSPECTOR	168.167-082
travel clerk	237.367-018
Traveling-Freight-And-Passenger Agent	252.257-010
trolley-car operator	913.463-014
undercover agent	168.167-082
Upholsterer	780.381-018
vendor	291.457-014
VOUCHER CLERK	219.362-066
WAITER/WAITRESS, DINING CAR	311.477-022
Waybill Clerk	214.362-014
WAY INSPECTOR	910.367-030
WHEEL INSPECTOR	806.387-014
YARD CLERK	209.367-054
YARD COUPLER	910.664-010
YARD ENGINEER	910.363-018
YARD MANAGER	184.167-278
Yard Patroller	376.667-018
yard supervisor	910.137-022

rubber goods—RUBBER GOODS INDUSTRY: This designation includes occupations concerned with manufacturing and repairing rubber articles, such as

rubber goods

belting, clothing, erasers, footwear, garden hose, hard-rubber goods, rubber bands, molded rubber tire sundries and repair materials, and rubberized fabrics. Occupations concerned with manufacturing rubber tires and tubes are included in the RUBBER TIRE AND TUBE INDUSTRY (rubber tire).

rubber reclaim.

rubber reclaim.—RUBBER RECLAIMING INDUSTRY: This designation includes occupations concerned with reclaiming rubber stock from used tires, scrap, and miscellaneous waste rubber.

rubber tire

Devulcanizer Inspector	559.132-058
devulcanizer operator	558.585-026
DEVULCANIZER TENDER	558.585-026
digester charger	558.585-026
DRIER FEEDER	559.686-014
Drier Operator	553.665-038
DRIER-OPERATOR HELPER	553.686-030
drum filler	914.665-010
dry-room helper	553.686-030
fabric-separator operator	551.365-010
Final-Inspection Supervisor	559.132-058
Fine Grinder	555.685-030
GRINDER	555.685-030
Grinding-Room Inspector	559.132-058
HEATER TENDER	553.665-038
High-Pressure Devulcanizer Operator	558.585-026
hog operator	555.685-030
hog-room supervisor	559.132-058
LABORER, GENERAL	559.686-026
Millroom Supervisor	559.132-058
pan devulcanizer	550.685-022
pan-devulcanizer helper	553.686-014
pan reclaim processor	550.685-022
PIGMENT PUMPER	914.665-010
pigment supplier	914.665-010
PRESS OPERATOR	559.685-138
PULVERIZER-MILL OPERATOR	555.382-010
roll-contour grinder	629.682-010
ROLL GRINDER	629.682-010
Rubber-Compounder Supervisor	559.132-058
rubber curer	553.665-038
Rubber-Goods Inspector-Trimmer	759.684-074
RUBBER-MILL TENDER	550.685-102
Scrap-Tire Shearer	690.685-386
shipping-room supervisor	559.132-058
skiver	690.685-386
Slab Inspector	759.684-074
slitting-machine operator	690.685-386
solvent-station attendant	914.665-010
SPLITTING-MACHINE OPERATOR	690.685-386
strainer-mill operator	551.365-010
STRAINER TENDER	551.365-010
SUPERVISOR	559.132-058
Tire Debeader	690.685-386
trimming-machine operator	690.685-386
tube depatcher	559.687-066
tuber operator	551.365-010
TUBE SORTER	559.687-066
turner-splitter-machine operator	690.685-386
vulcanizer operator	553.665-038
washing-machine operator	559.685-138
weigh and charge worker	558.666-010

rubber tire—RUBBER TIRE AND TUBE INDUSTRY: This designation includes occupations concerned with manufacturing and repairing pneumatic tires, solid and cushion rubber tires, and inner tubes; and the retreading of special-purpose tires that cannot be accommodated by tire-retreading establishments. Tire-retreading occupations found in tire-retreading establishments and automotive equipment dealers are included here.

AIR-BAG CURER	556.685-010
Band-Bias-Machine Operator	690.682-022
BAND BUILDER	750.684-010
Batch Trucker	929.687-030
BEAD BUILDER	750.684-014
Bead Filler	750.684-014
Bead Flipper	750.684-014
BEAD-FORMING-MACHINE OPERATOR	692.682-014
Bead Supervisor	750.130-010
Bead Wrapper	750.684-014
bias-cutting-machine operator	690.682-022
Bias-Cutting-Machine Operator, Vertical	690.682-022
BIAS-MACHINE OPERATOR	690.682-022
BIAS-MACHINE-OPERATOR HELPER	690.686-014
Bladder Changer	629.684-010
BOOKER	599.687-014
BUFFER	759.684-022
calender helper	554.665-010
CALENDER-LET-OFF HELPER	554.686-014
CALENDER-LET-OFF OPERATOR	554.682-010
CALENDER OPERATOR	554.362-010
Calender Operator, Fabric	554.382-010
CALENDER OPERATOR, FOUR-ROLL	554.662-010
Calender Operator, Gum Stock	554.362-010

CALENDER-OPERATOR HELPER	554.686-018
CALENDER-WIND-UP HELPER	554.686-022
CALENDER-WIND-UP TENDER	554.665-010
CEMENT MIXER	550.685-026
cord splicer	759.684-058
curer	553.665-038
curing finisher	553.685-102
CURING-PRESS MAINTAINER	629.684-010
CURING-PRESS OPERATOR	553.686-018
Curing Supervisor	750.130-010
Dip-Unit Operator	554.682-010
extruder operator	690.662-014
final inspector	750.684-030
FORCE-VARIATION EQUIPMENT TENDER	690.685-182
forming-press operator	556.685-066
GREEN-TIRE INSPECTOR	750.684-018
HEATER TENDER	553.665-038
hydraulic-steam-press operator	556.685-066
Inner-Tube Cutter	690.685-446
INNER-TUBE INSERTER	750.687-010
Inner-Tube Tester	759.684-074
Inner-Tube Tuber-Machine Operator	690.662-014
LABORER, GENERAL	559.686-026
LINER REROLL TENDER	554.685-022
liner-roll changer	554.686-018
MILLED-RUBBER TENDER	553.685-078
Millroom Supervisor	750.130-010
Mill Tender, Break-Down	550.685-102
Mill Tender, Warm-Up	550.685-102
Mill Tender, Washing	550.685-102
Mix-Mill Tender	550.685-102
Mold Changer	629.684-010
mold dresser	709.381-026
molding-press operator	556.685-066
MOLD STAMPER AND REPAIRER	709.381-026
Painter, Blackwall Tire	741.687-018
Passenger-Tire Inspector	750.684-030
ply cutter	690.682-022
ply splicer	759.684-058
pocket builder	750.684-010
PRESS TENDER	556.685-066
QUALITY-CONTROL INSPECTOR	750.367-010
reroll tender	554.685-022
retread-mold operator	553.685-102
RETREAD SUPERVISOR	750.132-010
Rim-Strip Tuber-Machine Operator	690.662-014
roll changer	554.665-010
rubber-calender helper	554.686-018
Rubber Compounder	929.687-062
Rubber-Compounder Supervisor	750.130-010
rubber curer	553.665-038
RUBBER CUTTER	559.685-158
Rubber-Flap Cutter	690.685-446
Rubber-Flap Tuber-Machine Operator	690.662-014
Rubber-Goods Inspector-Trimmer	759.684-074
Rubber-Goods Tester, Water	759.684-074
RUBBER-MILL TENDER	550.685-102
RUBBER TESTER	559.381-014
Slab-Off Mill Tender	550.685-102
Solid-Tire Finisher	750.684-034
Solid-Tire Tuber-Machine Operator	690.662-014
SPLICER	759.684-058
spreader machine tender	554.362-010
SQUEEGEE TENDER	750.685-010
Stock-Preparation Supervisor	750.130-010
stock roller	759.684-058
SUPERVISOR	750.130-010
TIRE BALANCER	750.687-014
TIRE-BLADDER MAKER	750.684-042
Tire Buffer	759.684-022
TIRE BUILDER	term
TIRE BUILDER, AUTOMOBILE	750.384-010
Tire Builder, Heavy Service	750.384-010
Tire-Building Supervisor	750.130-010
TIRE CLASSIFIER	750.387-010
Tire-Finishing Supervisor	750.130-010
TIRE INSPECTOR	750.684-030
TIRE MOLDER	553.685-102
TIRE REPAIRER	750.681-010
Tire-Room Supervisor	750.130-010
TIRE SORTER	750.687-022
tire spotter	750.687-014
TIRE TECHNICIAN	750.382-010
TIRE TRIMMER, HAND	750.684-034
Tire Trucker	929.687-030

Tire Wrapper 920.685-078
Tread-Tuber-Machine Operator 690.662-014
Truck-Tire Inspector 750.684-030
TUBE BALANCER 750.684-046
TUBE BUILDER, AIRPLANE 750.384-014
Tube Packer 920.587-018
tuber 750.687-010
TUBE REPAIRER 750.684-050
TUBER-MACHINE CUTTER 690.685-446
TUBER-MACHINE OPERATOR 690.662-014
TUBER-MACHINE-OPERATOR HELPER 690.686-070
Tube-Room Supervisor 750.130-010
TUBE SPLICER 690.685-442
vulcanizer operator 553.665-038
White-Sidewall-Tire Buffer 759.684-022
wind-up operator 554.686-018
wrapper rewinder 554.685-022

sanitary ser.—SANITARY SERVICES: This designation includes occupations concerned with the disposal of garbage, ashes, rubbish, and sewage, including the operation and maintenance of establishments that destroy or process such wastes. Occupations concerned with collecting and carting such wastes are included in the MOTOR VEHICLE TRANSPORTATION INDUSTRY (motor trans.). Occupations concerned with the purifying and distribution of water for domestic and industrial use are included in the WATERWORKS INDUSTRY (waterworks).

Activated-Sludge Attendant 955.585-010
Activated-Sludge Operator 955.362-010
Catch-Basin Cleaner 955.687-010
disposal-plant operator 955.362-010
Grit-Removal Operator 955.362-010
Grit Station Attendant 955.585-010
HYDRAULIC-RUBBISH-COMPACTOR MECHANIC 638.281-030
INCINERATOR OPERATOR I 955.685-010
INCINERATOR OPERATOR II 955.362-014
INCINERATOR-PLANT-GENERAL SUPERVISOR 184.167-046
INCINERATOR PLANT LABORER 955.687-010
INSTRUCTOR, WASTEWATER-TREATMENT PLANT 955.222-010
Pump-And-Blower Attendant 955.585-010
Pump-And-Blower Operator 955.362-010
SANITARY LANDFILL OPERATOR 955.463-010
SANITARY-LANDFILL SUPERVISOR 955.133-010
SEWAGE-DISPOSAL WORKER 955.687-010
sewage-plant attendant 955.585-010
sewage-plant operator 955.362-010
sewage plant supervisor 955.130-010
SEWER-LINE PHOTO-INSPECTOR 851.362-010
SEWER-LINE REPAIRER 869.664-018
SEWER-LINE REPAIRER, TELE-GROUT 851.262-010
Sludge-Control Attendant 955.585-010
Sludge-Control Operator 955.362-010
Sludge-Filtration Attendant 955.585-010
Sludge-Filtration Operator 955.362-010
solid waste facility operator 955.463-010
solid waste facility supervisor 955.133-010
SUPERVISOR, INCINERATOR PLANT 955.131-010
SUPERVISORY WASTEWATER-TREATMENT-PLANT
    OPERATOR 955.130-010
utilities operator 955.362-010
WASTEWATER-TREATMENT-PLANT ATTENDANT 955.585-010
WASTEWATER-TREATMENT-PLANT OPERATOR 955.362-010

saw. & plan.—SAWMILL AND PLANING MILL INDUSTRY: This designation includes occupations concerned with milling wood to produce products and byproducts, such as cooperage stock, laths, rough lumber, and shingles. The industry also includes occupations concerned with surfacing and sizing lumber and manufacturing wood excelsior and wood excelsior products. Occupations concerned with plywood production are included in the MILLWORK, VENEER, PLYWOOD, AND STRUCTURAL WOOD MEMBERS INDUSTRY (millwork-plywood).

ARTIFICIAL-LOG-MACHINE OPERATOR 569.685-010
AUTOMATIC-NAILING-MACHINE FEEDER 669.686-010
backer board 663.685-030
Band-Head-Saw Operator 667.662-010
band-log-mill-and-carriage operator 667.662-010
Band-Resaw Operator 667.682-058
band-sawmill operator 667.662-010
bill cutter 667.482-018
BLIND-SLAT-STAPLING-MACHINE OPERATOR 669.685-018
Boat Worker 921.686-022
BOLTER 667.685-022
BOLT LOADER 922.687-022

bolt sawyer 667.685-022
BOTTOM-SAW OPERATOR 667.682-014
BREAKER-MACHINE OPERATOR 564.685-010
BULL-CHAIN OPERATOR 921.685-014
BUNDLE TIER AND LABELER 920.685-110
butt sawyer 667.685-034
car loader 922.687-022
CHAIN OFFBEARER 669.686-018
CHIPPER 564.685-014
chute feeder 921.686-022
Circular-Gang-Saw Operator 667.682-030
Circular-Head-Saw Operator 667.662-010
Circular-Resaw Operator 667.682-058
Construction Millwright 860.381-042
cut-off-saw operator 667.682-078
CUT-OFF SAWYER, LOG 667.685-034
Cut-Off Sawyer, Shingle Mill 667.685-022
deck sawyer 667.685-034
Deck Scaler 455.487-010
deck worker 921.685-014
Door-Clamp Operator 669.685-030
Door-Glass Installer 865.684-014
Door Maker 669.380-014
double-cut sawyer 667.682-034
DOWEL-INSERTING-MACHINE OPERATOR 669.682-042
Drum-Saw Operator 667.682-022
Dry-Chain Offbearer 669.686-018
EDGER, AUTOMATIC 667.682-026
equalizer 667.682-074
equalizer operator 667.682-074
excelsior-machine feeder 663.685-014
EXCELSIOR-MACHINE TENDER 663.685-014
Fire Chief 373.167-018
FLATCAR WHACKER 807.667-010
Flooring Grader 669.687-030
Flooring-Machine Feeder 669.686-030
frame-gate-mortiser operator 667.482-014
Frame Maker 669.380-014
frame-pulley-mortising-machine operator 666.482-010
FUEL-HOUSE ATTENDANT 951.686-010
GANG SAWYER 667.682-030
gate cutter 667.482-014
gate-mortiser operator 667.482-014
Green-Chain Marker 669.687-030
Green-Chain Offbearer 669.686-018
HEADING-SAW OPERATOR 667.682-038
HEAD SAWYER 667.662-010
HEAD SAWYER, AUTOMATIC 667.682-034
Horizontal-Resaw Operator 667.682-058
Hydraulic-Barker Operator 669.485-010
jacker feeder 921.686-022
jump-roll operator 921.682-022
knee bolter 667.685-022
Knife And Spur Grinder 603.664-010
KNIFE SETTER 663.380-010
laborer, sawmill 669.687-018
log-chain feeder 921.686-022
log culler 667.687-014
LOG-CUT-OFF SAWYER, AUTOMATIC 667.682-090
log-deck tender 921.685-014
LOGGING-TRACTOR OPERATOR 929.663-010
LOG GRADER 455.367-010
log handler 677.687-010
LOG-HAUL CHAIN FEEDER 921.686-018
Log Hooker 921.667-022
LOG INSPECTOR 667.687-014
LOG PEELER 569.684-010
Log Rider 921.686-022
LOG ROLLER 677.687-010
LOG SCALER 455.487-010
Log-Stacker Operator 929.663-010
LOG WASHER 569.687-014
LOG-YARD CRANE OPERATOR .... term
Log-Yard Derrick Operator 921.663-022
Louver-Mortiser Operator 665.482-014
Lumber-Carrier Driver 921.683-070
lumber guider 669.687-018
lumber sorter, machine 921.685-054
LUMBER STRAIGHTENER 669.687-018
PACKAGER, HEAD 667.682-046
PAD-MACHINE FEEDER 920.686-034
PAD-MACHINE OFFBEARER 569.686-030
Panel-Raiser Operator 665.482-034
PICKER 669.687-022
Planer-Chain Offbearer 669.686-018

ship-boat mfg.

planer feeder	665.686-014
Planer-Mill Grader	669.687-030
planer operator	665.482-018
PLOW-AND-BORING-MACHINE TENDER	665.685-018
Pocket-And-Pulley-Machine Operator	667.482-014
POCKET CUTTER	667.482-014
pole peeler	663.682-014
POLE-PEELING-MACHINE OPERATOR	663.682-014
poler	921.686-022
pole shaver	663.682-014
pondsaw operator	667.685-034
Pond Scaler	455.487-010
POND WORKER	921.686-022
PONY EDGER	667.682-050
POWER-BARKER OPERATOR	669.485-010
PULLEY-MORTISER OPERATOR	666.482-010
Puncher	669.687-030
Racker	922.687-074
rail-doweling-machine operator	669.682-042
rebut-machine tail offbearer	667.686-018
Ring-Barker Operator	669.485-010
Sash-Clamp Operator	669.685-030
Sash-Gang-Saw Operator	667.682-030
Sash Maker	669.380-014
Sawmill-Relief Worker	667.687-018
SAWMILL WORKER	667.687-018
Scrap Sawyer	667.685-022
SCREEN TACKER	762.687-058
separator	921.682-022
SHAKE BACKBOARD NOTCHER	663.685-030
Shake Feeder	669.686-030
Shake Packer	920.687-158
SHAKE SAWYER	667.682-070
SHINGLE PACKER	920.687-158
SHINGLE SAWYER	667.485-010
SHINGLE TRIMMER	667.685-050
shingle weaver	920.687-158
short-log-bolter operator	667.685-022
shredding-machine tender	663.685-014
sinker puller	921.686-022
Slab Picker	929.687-030
SLASHER OPERATOR	667.685-054
slasher sawyer	667.685-054
slip feeder	921.686-022
Sorter-Lumber Straightener	669.687-018
SORTER OPERATOR	921.685-054
SPLITTER TENDER	663.685-038
STACKER-AND-SORTER OPERATOR	921.682-018
Stacker-Straightener	669.687-018
STAVE-BOLT EQUALIZER	667.682-074
STAVE-LOG-CUT-OFF SAW OPERATOR	667.682-078
STAVE-LOG-RIPSAW OPERATOR	667.685-058
STAVE-PLANER TENDER	665.686-014
STEAM-TUNNEL FEEDER	562.686-010
STICKER	563.686-010
STOCK CUTTER	667.482-018
stock-saw operator	667.482-018
supervisor, chipping	564.132-010
SUPERVISOR, SAWMILL	669.130-026
SUPERVISOR, WOOD-CREW	669.137-010
swamper	667.687-018
TIE INSPECTOR	669.687-026
TIMBER PACKER	922.687-094
TIMBER-SIZER OPERATOR	665.482-018
timber trimmer	667.685-034
TIPPLE OPERATOR	921.662-026
TRANSFER CONTROLLER	921.682-022
TRIMMER HELPER	667.686-050
Trimmer Loader	669.687-018
TRIMMER SAWYER	667.682-094
Trimmer Tailer	669.687-018
trim sawyer	667.482-018
TRUSS ASSEMBLER	762.684-062
UTILITY OPERATOR	669.682-070
Window Assembler	865.684-014
WOOD-CREW SUPERVISOR	564.132-010

ship-boat mfg.—SHIP AND BOAT MANUFACTURING AND REPAIRING INDUSTRY: This designation includes occupations concerned with constructing and repairing all types of ships, boats (except rubber boats), barges, and lighters, whether propelled by sail, motor, or manual power, or towed by other craft. This designation includes occupations concerned with the manufacture of plastic or fiberglass pleasure craft. Occupations concerned with the manufacture of rubber boats are included in the RUBBER GOODS INDUSTRY (rubber goods).

ASSEMBLER, ALUMINUM BOATS	806.481-010
ASSEMBLER, DECK AND HULL	806.684-022
ASSEMBLER, INSULATION AND FLOORING	806.684-026
assembler, plastic boat	806.684-146
assembly detailer	807.684-014
ballaster	809.684-022
boat accessories installer	806.464-010
boat bottomer	806.684-106
BOAT BUFFER, PLASTIC	849.684-010
BOATBUILDER APPRENTICE, WOOD	860.381-014
BOATBUILDER, WOOD	860.361-010
boat garnisher	806.684-146
boat joiner	860.381-050
boat mechanic	623.281-038
BOAT OUTFITTER	806.684-146
BOAT PATCHER, PLASTIC	807.684-014
boat puller	809.667-010
BOAT REPAIRER	807.361-014
BOAT RIGGER	806.464-010
boat wrapper	869.684-078
Bulkhead Carpenter	860.361-010
Bulwark Carpenter	860.361-010
CANOE INSPECTOR, FINAL	769.687-018
CANVAS WORKER	739.381-010
CANVAS-WORKER APPRENTICE	739.381-014
carpenter apprentice, ship	860.381-062
Carpenter, Cradle And Dolly	860.381-042
carpenter helper	860.664-018
CARPENTER, PROTOTYPE	806.281-058
CARPENTER, SHIP	860.281-014
carpenter, ship	860.381-058
carpenter supervisor, wooden ship	860.131-014
CAULKER	term
Cementer	844.364-010
COPPERSMITH	862.281-010
COPPERSMITH APPRENTICE	862.281-014
CUTTER, ALUMINUM SHEET	804.684-010
deck and hull assembler	806.684-022
Deck Molder	806.684-054
Diesel-Engine Mechanic, Marine	625.281-010
DOCK HAND	891.684-010
DOCK SUPERVISOR	891.131-010
ELECTRICIAN	825.381-030
ELECTRICIAN APPRENTICE	825.381-034
ELECTRICIAN HELPER	829.684-026
electrician, marine	825.381-030
electrician, outside	825.381-030
Electrician, Ship	825.381-030
Electrician, Shop	825.381-030
ELECTRICIAN SUPERVISOR	825.131-010
Electrician, Yard	825.381-030
engineer, steam	623.281-030
erector	806.261-014
erector appentice	806.261-018
EXTRUSION BENDER	804.684-014
FIBERGLASS LAMINATOR	806.684-054
final assembler, boat	806.684-146
FINISHER, FIBERGLASS BOAT PARTS	809.684-022
fitter	806.381-046
Gel-Coat Sprayer	741.684-026
grinder	809.684-022
HULL AND DECK REMOVER	809.667-010
Hull Builder	860.361-010
HULL INSPECTOR	806.264-010
Hull Molder	806.684-054
INSPECTOR, ALUMINUM BOAT	806.687-026
INSTALLER, ELECTRICAL, PLUMBING, MECHANICAL	806.381-062
JOINER	860.381-050
JOINER APPRENTICE	860.381-054
JOINER HELPER	860.664-014
Keel Assembler	860.361-010
LABORER, SHIPYARD	809.687-022
laminator	806.684-054
loft rigger	806.261-014
LOFT WORKER	661.281-010
LOFT WORKER APPRENTICE	661.281-014
LOFT WORKER, HEAD	661.131-010
Machinery Erector	921.260-010
MACHINIST APPRENTICE, MARINE ENGINE	623.281-018
MACHINIST APPRENTICE, OUTSIDE	623.281-022
machinist helper, marine	623.687-010
MACHINIST HELPER, OUTSIDE	623.687-010
machinist, installation	623.281-030
MACHINIST, MARINE ENGINE	623.281-026
MACHINIST, OUTSIDE	623.281-030

smelt. & refin.—SMELTING AND REFINING INDUSTRY: This designation includes occupations concerned with the dressing, smelting, and refining of nonferrous metal ores, including the entire treatment of materials from crude ore to finished metals or minerals. It includes (1) crushing to reduce ore to workable size; (2) fine grinding to further reduce ore to a size amenable to the extraction of gold and silver or to the concentration of minerals containing valuable metals or ore; (3) concentration to separate valuable metal or metal-bearing minerals from waste minerals; (4) roasting to drive off sulfur and other volatile constituents of ore; (5) reduction of ore to its metallic and nonmetallic constituents by melting in a furnace; and (6) refining of recovered metal by further heat treatment, electrolytic methods, or both. This industry also includes occupations concerned with the recovery of nonferrous metals from scrap and dross.

smelt. & refin.

finishing-pan operator	559.685-074
FLAKER OPERATOR	559.685-074
flaking-machine operator	559.685-074
Flotation Supervisor	511.135-010
FLOTATION TENDER	511.685-026
FLOTATION-TENDER HELPER	511.687-018
flue-dust laborer	519.687-014
FLUX-TUBE ATTENDANT	519.687-018
FURNACE CHARGER	512.684-014
FURNACE HELPER	512.666-010
FURNACE OPERATOR	512.362-014
FURNACE OPERATOR	513.462-010
GENERAL-HANDLING SUPERVISOR	929.137-010
Grease-Machine Worker	519.565-014
GRINDER, CARBON PLANT	544.565-010
GRINDER-MILL OPERATOR	519.485-010
grinding-mill operator	939.362-014
GRINDING-MILL OPERATOR	515.382-010
GRIZZLY WORKER	933.687-010
GROUT-MACHINE TENDER	519.685-014
HAMMER-MILL OPERATOR	515.687-010
header	514.584-010
Hot-Billet-Shear Operator	615.685-034
Hot-Metal-Crane Operator II	921.663-042
HYDRATE-CONTROL TENDER	511.585-010
hydrate-thickener operator	511.562-010
HYDRAULIC-BOOM OPERATOR	921.683-046
INGOT HEADER	514.584-010
ION-EXCHANGE OPERATOR	558.685-030
IRON-LAUNDER OPERATOR	511.565-018
KETTLE OPERATOR	519.685-018
KETTLE TENDER I	519.685-022
KETTLE TENDER II	511.685-030
KETTLE TENDER, PLATINUM AND PALLADIUM	511.685-034
kiln-head house operator	511.565-010
KILN OPERATOR	513.565-010
KILN-OPERATOR HELPER	513.587-010
LABORER, GENERAL	519.687-026
ladle cleaner	519.684-010
LADLE LINER	519.684-010
ladle patcher	519.684-010
LADLE POURER	514.684-014
LEACHER	511.582-010
Lead Loader	921.683-050
LEAD OPERATOR	630.381-018
LEAF COVERER	519.684-014
LINER REPLACER	801.664-010
line supervisor	511.130-010
Looper	519.565-014
MANOMETER TECHNICIAN	519.387-010
metal pourer	514.684-010
mill attendant	939.362-014
MILL-LABOR SUPERVISOR	519.131-014
MILL SUPERVISOR	515.130-010
mixer operator	570.685-070
MIXER OPERATOR, CARBON PASTE	540.585-010
mixer tender	510.685-022
MIX-HOUSE TENDER	510.685-014
Mixing-Pan Tender	510.685-014
MOLD MAKER	518.664-010
MOLD-MAKER HELPER	518.687-018
Molybdenum-Flotation Operator	511.685-026
Molybdenum-Leaching-Plant Operator	511.582-010
MOLYBDENUM-STEAMER OPERATOR	511.485-010
MUD BOSS	519.585-014
mud grinder	570.685-070
mud-mill operator	570.685-070
MUD-MILL TENDER	519.685-026
MUD-MIXER OPERATOR	570.685-070
NICKEL-PLANT OPERATOR	519.362-010
ore crusher	515.685-014
PANELBOARD OPERATOR	939.362-014
pan operator	559.685-074
pellet-press operator	519.685-010
Pin Puller	630.684-010
POTLINE MONITOR	512.467-010
POT LINER	519.664-014
POT-LINING SUPERVISOR	519.134-010
pot puncher	512.685-018
POT-ROOM SUPERVISOR	512.135-010
POT TENDER	512.685-018
pourer	514.682-010
PRECIPITATOR I	511.685-038
PRECIPITATOR II	511.685-042
PRECIPITATOR OPERATOR	term
PRECIPITATOR SUPERVISOR	511.132-010
PRESS OPERATOR, CARBON BLOCKS	514.682-014
PUG-MILL OPERATOR	510.685-022
Quantometer Operator	519.387-010
rapper	511.687-014
RAW SAMPLER	519.484-014
Reactor Operator	513.362-010
REAGENT TENDER	511.685-046
REAGENT TENDER HELPER	511.686-010
RECLAMATION KETTLE TENDER, METAL	512.685-022
RECOVERY OPERATOR	519.582-010
RECOVERY-OPERATOR HELPER	519.485-014
Red-Mud Thickener Operator	511.485-014
REDUCTION-PLANT SUPERVISOR	512.130-010
regrind mill operator	519.685-030
REPAIRER	630.281-026
REPAIRER HELPER	630.664-010
Roaster Supervisor	513.132-010
RODDING-ANODE WORKER	519.687-034
ROD-MILL TENDER	519.685-030
Roll Repairer	630.281-026
rotary-drier operator	511.565-014
ROTARY-KILN OPERATOR	513.682-010
sample carrier	519.484-014
SAMPLER, FIRST	619.682-038
SAMPLER, HEAD	519.130-014
SCALE-RECLAMATION TENDER	515.585-010
SCREEN OPERATOR	511.685-050
Screen Supervisor	511.135-010
Selenium-Plant Operator	511.685-054
service-crew supervisor	630.134-010
SETTLEMENT CLERK	214.382-030
Sheet Hanger	519.565-014
shift adjuster	511.130-010
shredder operator	515.687-010
SILICA-SPRAY MIXER	570.685-090
SINTER-MACHINE OPERATOR	510.685-026
SKIMMER, REVERBERATORY	511.687-022
SLIME-PLANT-OPERATOR HELPER	511.685-058
SLIME-PLANT OPERATOR I	510.685-030
SLIME-PLANT OPERATOR II	511.685-054
SLURRY-CONTROL TENDER	510.465-014
slurry-plant operator	570.685-090
SMELTERY WORKER	term
SMOKE TESTER	012.281-010
sorter	933.687-010
SPOUT WORKER	514.667-018
SPRAYER OPERATOR	505.682-010
Stack Supervisor	511.132-010
STAMPING-MILL TENDER	515.685-018
Starting-Sheet-Tank Operator	519.362-014
Strap Setter	630.684-010
Stripper	519.565-014
Stripper Truck Operator	921.683-050
Stud Driver	630.684-010
SUPERVISOR, BLAST FURNACE	512.132-022
Supervisor, Calcining	519.130-026
Supervisor, Cell Maintenance	630.134-010
SUPERVISOR, CELL OPERATION	519.132-018
SUPERVISOR, DIE CASTING	514.130-014
supervisor, grinding	515.130-010
SUPERVISOR, LEAD REFINERY	519.130-018
supervisor, ore dressing	515.130-010
SUPERVISOR, PUMPING	914.131-010
SUPERVISOR, REVERBERATORY FURNACE	519.130-022
SUPERVISOR, SHEET MANUFACTURING	500.132-010
SUPERVISOR, SINTERING PLANT	519.130-026
SUPERVISOR, URANIUM PROCESSING	519.130-030
switch-house operator	939.362-014
TABLE TENDER	511.685-062
Table Tender, Sludge	511.685-062
TAILINGS-DAM LABORER	511.687-026
Tailings-Dam Pumper	914.682-010
TAILINGS MACHINERY TENDER	term
Tailing-Thickener Operator	511.485-014
TANK-HOUSE OPERATOR	519.362-014
TANK-HOUSE-OPERATOR HELPER	519.565-014
TANK TENDER	509.685-054
TAPPER	514.664-014
TAPPER SUPERVISOR	514.134-010
THICKENER OPERATOR	511.485-014
Thimble-Press Operator	519.664-010
TIN RECOVERY WORKER	512.382-018
TOOL REPAIRER	519.684-026
TOP-PRECIPITATOR OPERATOR	511.465-010

TOP-PRECIPITATOR-OPERATOR HELPER 511.586-010
tray thickener operator 511.562-010
TROMMEL TENDER 511.685-066
TUNGSTEN REFINER 511.382-010
wash-box operator 939.362-014
WEIGHER-AND-CRUSHER 515.567-010
Wet-Pan Mixer 570.685-070
WET-PLANT OPERATOR 519.665-010
YARD SUPERVISOR 929.137-026
ZINC-CHLORIDE OPERATOR 511.385-010

soap & rel.—SOAP, CLEANING, AND TOILET PREPARATION INDUS-
TRY: This designation includes occupations concerned with manufacturing
soap, soap base products, and glycerin. The principal soap products are bar, liquid, powdered, and paste soaps, soap chips, and soaps blended with perfume,
cold cream, lanolin, and other cosmetic ingredients for use as toilet products.
Occupations concerned with the manufacture of such toilet articles as shaving
cream, lotions, and toothpaste are included here.

BATCH MIXER 550.685-010
BLEACHER OPERATOR 558.685-018
blender 550.685-010
BOILER 553.382-014
CENTRIFUGE OPERATOR 551.685-030
COMPOUNDER 550.685-046
COPRA PROCESSOR 555.685-018
cp bleacher operator 558.685-018
CRUTCHER 550.685-054
CRUTCHER HELPER 550.686-018
cutter and presser 559.685-142
cutter, first 559.686-042
cutting-table operator, first 559.686-042
drier-machine hand 553.685-098
drier tender 553.585-018
DRYING-ROOM ATTENDANT 553.585-018
DUST-COLLECTOR OPERATOR 551.685-050
Fats And Oils Loader 914.667-010
flake drier 553.685-098
FRAME STRIPPER 559.685-086
frame stripper and crusher 555.685-062
Glycerin Operator 552.685-014
KETTLE WORKER 553.685-070
LYE TREATER 551.685-094
NEUTRALIZER 558.585-034
perfume compounder 550.685-046
PLODDER OPERATOR 556.682-018
plodding-machine operator 556.682-018
PRESSER 559.685-142
roll-machine attendant 553.685-098
salt operator 551.685-030
SCREENER-PERFUMER 559.685-162
SLABBER 559.686-042
Slabber, Light 559.686-042
slabbing-machine operator 559.686-042
soap boiler 559.382-054
SOAP CHIPPER 555.686-014
SOAP-DRIER OPERATOR 553.685-098
SOAP GRINDER 555.685-062
SOAP INSPECTOR 559.687-058
SOAP MAKER 559.382-054
soap-press feeder 559.685-142
soap slabber 559.686-042
SUPERVISOR, GLYCERIN 559.132-098
SUPERVISOR, TOILET-AND-LAUNDRY SOAP 559.132-130
TOWER OPERATOR 559.362-034

social ser.—SOCIAL SERVICES: This designation includes occupations concerned with providing social and rehabilitative services to those persons with
social or personal problems requiring special services and to the handicapped
and the disadvantaged. Also included are occupations concerned with soliciting
funds to be used directly for these and related services. Occupations concerned
with providing instruction or vocational training are included under EDU-
CATION AND INSTRUCTION (education). Occupations which provide health
care are included under MEDICAL SERVICES (medical ser.).

CASE AIDE 195.367-010
case supervisor 195.137-010
CASEWORKER 195.107-010
Caseworker, Child Placement 195.107-014
CASEWORKER, CHILD WELFARE 195.107-014
CASEWORKER, FAMILY 195.107-018
Caseworker, Intake 195.107-014
Caseworker, Protective Services 195.107-014
CASEWORK SUPERVISOR 195.137-010

child development specialist 195.227-018
COMMUNITY ORGANIZATION WORKER 195.167-010
community placement worker 195.107-010
COMMUNITY-RELATIONS-AND-SERVICES ADVISOR,
    PUBLIC HOUSING 195.167-014
community service consultant 195.167-010
COORDINATOR, VOLUNTEER SERVICES 187.167-022
CORRECTIONAL-TREATMENT SPECIALIST 195.107-042
development disability specialist 195.227-018
DIRECTOR, CAMP 195.167-018
DIRECTOR, FIELD 195.167-022
DIRECTOR, RECREATION CENTER 195.167-026
DIRECTOR, VOLUNTEER SERVICES 187.167-038
family counselor 195.107-018
field director 195.167-022
group leader 195.227-018
GROUP WORKER 195.164-010
HOMEMAKER 309.354-010
infant educator 195.227-018
information and referral director 195.167-010
intake worker 195.107-010
MANAGEMENT AIDE 195.367-014
parent trainer 195.227-018
PROGRAM AIDE, GROUP WORK 195.227-010
program consultant 195.167-010
RECREATION AIDE 195.367-030
RECREATION LEADER 195.227-014
Senior Service Aide 195.367-010
SOCIAL GROUP WORKER 195.107-022
SOCIAL-SERVICES AIDE 195.367-034
social service worker 195.107-010
Social-Work Consultant, Casework 195.107-010
SOCIAL WORKER, DELINQUENCY PREVENTION 195.107-026
social work unit supervisor 195.137-010
TEACHER, HOME THERAPY 195.227-018
tenant relations coordinator 195.167-014
volunteer coordinator 187.167-022
Youth Nutritional Monitor 195.367-010

steel & rel.—BLAST FURNACE, STEEL WORK, AND ROLLING AND FIN-
ISHING MILL INDUSTRY: This designation includes occupations concerned
with manufacturing hot metal, pig iron, silvery pig iron, and ferro alloys from
iron ore and iron and steel scrap; converting pig iron, scrap iron, and scrap steel
into steel; rolling iron and steel into basic shapes, such as plates, sheets, strips,
rods, bars, and tubing; and manufacturing coke. Also included are occupations
concerned with manufacturing ferro and nonferrous additive alloys by
electrometallurgical or metallothermic processes; drawing wire from such products as nails, spikes, and staples; cold rolling steel sheets and strip, cold drawing steel bars and steel shapes, and producing other cold finished steel; and producing welded or seamless steel pipe and tubes and heavy riveted steel pipe.

Acid-Crane Operator 921.663-042
ACID EXTRACTOR 558.382-010
acid-wash operator 551.682-010
agitator operator 551.682-010
air-furnace operator 512.362-018
AMMONIA-STILL OPERATOR 559.382-010
ammonium-sulfate operator 558.362-018
Approach-Table Operator 613.682-026
ASSORTER 703.687-010
Axle Inspector 619.381-010
BATCH MAKER 515.685-010
BED OPERATOR 613.685-034
belling machine operator 617.685-022
Belt Cleaner 911.687-014
benzene operator 551.682-010
BENZENE-WASHER OPERATOR 551.682-010
benzol operator 551.682-010
Bessemer-Bottom Maker 861.381-026
Billet Inspector 619.381-010
BIN TRIPPER OPERATOR 922.665-014
BLAST-FURNACE KEEPER 502.664-014
BLAST-FURNACE-KEEPER HELPER 502.687-010
blender 510.685-018
blower, blast furnace 519.132-010
Boat Cleaner 911.687-014
BOTTOM MAKER 509.687-010
BREAKER TENDER 544.685-010
briquette-press operator 617.685-038
bulldogger 613.362-018
CAR PINCHER 922.687-034
car shifter 922.687-034
caster 502.664-014
caster, investment casting 512.362-018

steel & rel.

CATCHER 613.686-010
charger 504.665-014
charger 512.683-010
charger-car operator 519.683-014
CHARGER-OPERATOR HELPER 504.686-010
CHARGER OPERATOR 504.665-014
charging-car operator 519.683-014
Charging-Crane Operator I 921.663-010
Charging-Crane Operator II 921.663-042
CHARGING-MACHINE OPERATOR 512.683-010
CHASER, TAR 549.687-010
Cinder-Crane Operator I 921.663-010
Cinder-Crane Operator II 921.663-042
Clay Mixer 570.685-070
COILER 613.685-010
coiler operator 613.685-010
COILER OPERATOR 613.382-010
Coil Strapper 920.587-018
coining-press operator 617.685-038
COKE BURNER 543.682-010
COKE-CRUSHER OPERATOR 544.662-010
COKE DRAWER, HAND 543.687-010
COKE INSPECTOR 542.567-010
COKE LOADER 921.563-010
Coke-Oven Mason 861.381-026
Cold-Mill Inspector 619.381-010
COLD-MILL OPERATOR 613.662-018
Cold-Roll Packer, Sheet Iron 921.663-042
compact-press operator 617.685-038
Conveyor Feeder 509.687-026
COUPLING-MACHINE OPERATOR 619.682-014
Crane Operator-Hooker 921.663-010
CRUSHER-AND-BLENDER OPERATOR 544.582-010
Crusher Feeder 509.687-026
CUT-OFF-MACHINE OPERATOR 619.685-094
dauber 543.687-014
Delivery-Table Operator 613.682-026
DESULFURIZER OPERATOR 541.362-010
Dock Cleaner 911.687-014
DOOR-MACHINE OPERATOR 519.663-010
Door Repairer 861.381-026
draw-bench operator 614.685-022
DRAW-BENCH OPERATOR 614.482-010
DRAW-BENCH-OPERATOR HELPER 614.686-010
Drier Tender, Naphthalene 551.665-010
DRIFTER 503.685-018
drifting-machine operator 503.685-018
EDDY-CURRENT INSPECTOR 619.381-014
Electric-Arc-Furnace Operator 512.362-018
engineer, byproduct 950.362-010
ENGINEER, EXHAUSTER 950.362-010
EXPANDING MACHINE OPERATOR 617.685-022
fettler 512.684-014
FINISHER 613.382-014
Finisher, Cold Rolling 613.382-014
Finisher, Hot Strip 613.382-014
Finisher, Merchant Products 613.382-014
Finisher, Plate 613.382-014
finisher, screwdown 613.382-018
Finishing Inspector 619.381-010
finishing supervisor, weld-pipe continuous ... 619.130-038
FIRST HELPER 512.362-010
FLYING-SHEAR OPERATOR 615.682-010
FURNACE CHARGER 512.684-014
furnace-charging-machine operator 512.683-010
FURNACE OPERATOR 512.362-018
Gag-Press Straightener 617.482-026
gas desulfurizer 541.362-010
gas tender 519.683-014
GRANULATOR TENDER 519.665-010
graphite-mill operator 549.685-026
GUIDE SETTER 613.361-010
HEATER HELPER 613.685-014
heater helper 542.665-010
HEATER I 613.361-010
HEATER II 542.362-010
helper, patcher 861.687-014
HELPER, SHEAR OPERATOR 615.687-010
hotbed operator 613.685-034
hotbed transfer operator 613.685-034
Hot-Billet-Shear Operator 615.685-034
hot blaster 512.382-014
HOT-CAR OPERATOR 519.663-014
Hot-Metal Charger 512.683-010
Hot-Metal Crane Operator I 921.663-010

Hot-Metal-Crane Operator II 921.663-042
Hot-Roll Inspector 619.381-010
Hot-Strip-Mill Inspector 619.381-010
HOT-TOP LINER 709.684-046
HOT-TOP-LINER HELPER 709.687-018
IMPREGNATOR 509.685-030
ingot buggy operator 919.683-018
Ingot Stripper I 921.663-010
Ingot Stripper II 921.663-042
Ingot Weigher 221.587-030
INSPECTOR 619.381-010
KILN OPERATOR 509.565-010
LABORATORY ASSISTANT, LIAISON INSPECTION 169.167-026
LABORATORY ASSISTANT, METALLURGICAL 011.261-022
laboratory coordinator 169.167-026
LABORER, GENERAL 509.687-026
LARRY OPERATOR 519.683-014
light-oil operator 549.382-010
LIME MIXER TENDER 514.685-022
Loading Checker 509.687-026
LUBRICATOR-GRANULATOR 509.685-042
luter 543.687-014
Magnet Placer 921.667-022
MANIPULATOR 613.682-010
Marker 509.687-026
melter assistant 512.362-010
MELTER SUPERVISOR 512.132-010
Melter Supervisor, Electric-Arc Furnace 512.132-010
Melter Supervisor, Open-Hearth Furnace 512.132-010
Melter Supervisor, Oxygen Furnace 512.132-010
metallurgical analyst 011.261-022
metallurgical inspector 011.261-022
MILL HAND, PLATE MILL 613.667-014
MILL RECORDER, COMPUTERIZED MILL 221.367-046
MILL STENCILER 659.685-026
MIXER 510.685-018
mixer operator 570.685-070
MIXER OPERATOR HELPER, HOT METAL 509.566-010
MIXER OPERATOR, HOT METAL 509.362-010
mold-car operator 514.362-010
MOLD WORKER 514.567-010
mud grinder 570.685-070
mud-mill operator 570.685-070
MUD-MIXER HELPER 549.687-022
MUD-MIXER OPERATOR 570.685-070
Mud Trucker 902.683-010
NAIL-ASSEMBLY-MACHINE OPERATOR 616.682-030
nail-machine operator 616.460-010
NAIL-MAKING-MACHINE SETTER 616.460-010
NAIL-MAKING-MACHINE TENDER 617.665-010
NAPHTHALENE OPERATOR 551.665-010
NAPHTHALENE-OPERATOR HELPER 551.687-026
Oiling-Machine Operator 599.685-074
Open-Hearth Door-Liner 861.381-026
open-hearth-furnace laborer 512.687-014
open-hearth-furnace operator 512.362-010
open-hearth-furnace-operator helper 512.684-010
OVEN DAUBER 543.687-014
OVEN-EQUIPMENT REPAIRER 630.261-014
OVEN-HEATER HELPER 542.665-010
OXYGEN-FURNACE OPERATOR 512.382-010
paster 543.687-014
PATCHER 861.684-014
PATCHER HELPER 861.684-014
PIERCING-MILL OPERATOR 613.685-018
PIG-MACHINE OPERATOR 514.362-010
PIG-MACHINE-OPERATOR HELPER 514.667-014
Pipe Coater 740.684-022
pipe processor 619.662-014
pit-furnace melter 512.362-018
PLATE CONDITIONER 819.664-010
Plate Inspector 619.381-010
PLUGGER 613.687-010
poker-in 512.683-010
PRECIPITATOR SUPERVISOR 511.132-010
PRESS SETTER 617.480-014
product inspector 619.381-010
Provider 221.387-046
pulverizer operator 544.582-010
pump-and-still operator 559.382-010
PUMP OPERATOR, BYPRODUCTS 541.362-014
pump tender 541.362-010
push-bench-operator helper 614.686-010
pusher 504.665-014
PUSHER OPERATOR 519.663-018

pusher runner 512.683-010
PYRIDINE OPERATOR 552.382-010
pyridine-recovery operator 552.382-010
Racker 509.687-026
Rail Inspector 619.381-010
RAIL-TRACTOR OPERATOR 919.683-018
RECORDER 221.367-050
reeler operator 613.682-014
REELING-MACHINE OPERATOR 613.682-014
REFRACTORY MIXER 570.685-078
Reversing-Mill Roller 613.662-018
Rod-Drawing Supervisor 614.132-010
ROLL BUILDER 801.664-018
Roller, Billet Mill 613.362-014
Roller, Blooming Mill 613.362-014
ROLLER-LEVELER OPERATOR 613.685-022
roller, merchant mill 613.130-014
Roller, Plate Mill 613.130-018
ROLLER, PRIMARY MILL 613.362-014
Roller, Slabbing Mill 613.362-014
roller, structural mill 613.130-018
ROLLING ATTENDANT 613.662-010
rolling-mill plugger 613.687-010
rolling supervisor, continuous-pipe mill 619.130-022
roll setter 613.360-014
roll setter, pipe mill 613.360-014
ROLL-TUBE SETTER 613.360-014
rotary-bar operator 619.682-042
Rotary-Dump Operator 921.685-038
rotary-furnace operator 512.362-018
ROUGHER 613.362-018
Rougher, Bar Mill 613.362-018
Rougher, Hot-Strip Mill 613.362-018
Rougher, Merchant Mill 613.362-018
ROUGHER OPERATOR 613.662-014
sampler 509.584-010
SAMPLER 599.684-014
Sampler, Ovens 599.684-014
SATURATOR OPERATOR 558.362-018
scale-and-skip-car operator 921.683-062
SCARFING MACHINE OPERATOR 816.682-010
Scrap Baler 920.685-010
SCRAP BALLER 509.685-046
Scrap Breaker 509.687-026
Scrap-Crane Operator I 921.663-010
Scrap-Crane Operator II 921.663-042
SCREENER-AND-BLENDER OPERATOR 549.685-026
SCREWDOWN OPERATOR 613.382-018
seamless-tube drawer 614.685-022
seamless-tube-mill operator 619.682-042
SEAMLESS-TUBE ROLLER 619.682-042
SECOND HELPER 512.684-010
shaker operator 541.665-010
SHAKER TENDER 541.665-010
Sheet Tester 011.361-010
sidehand 615.687-010
SINTER FEEDER 513.685-010
SINTERING-PRESS OPERATOR 617.685-038
SINTER-MACHINE OPERATOR 510.685-026
SKELP PROCESSOR 619.662-014
SKIP OPERATOR 921.683-062
SLAB-DEPILER OPERATOR 504.665-010
slag expander 519.665-010
slitting-machine coiler 613.685-010
SPEED OPERATOR 613.362-022
SPIKE-MACHINE FEEDER 612.666-010
SPIKE-MACHINE HEATER 619.686-026
SPIKE-MACHINE OPERATOR 612.662-010
SPIKEMAKING SUPERVISOR 612.130-010
STANDPIPE TENDER 519.665-014
Staple-Shear Operator 615.682-018
steel inspector 619.381-010
STEEL POURER 502.664-014
STEEL-POURER HELPER 502.664-018
steel sampler 509.584-010
Stock-Crane Operator 921.663-042
STOPPER MAKER 519.684-022
STOPPER-MAKER HELPER 519.687-038
stopper-rod maker 519.684-022
STOVE TENDER 512.382-014
strander 613.686-010
SULFATE DRIER-MACHINE OPERATOR 551.685-142
sulfate operator 558.362-018
Supervisor, Baking 549.137-010
SUPERVISOR, BLAST FURNACE 519.132-010
SUPERVISOR, BLAST-FURNACE-AUXILIARIES 519.132-014
SUPERVISOR, BLOOMING MILL 613.130-010
SUPERVISOR, BYPRODUCTS 542.132-010
SUPERVISOR, CARBON ELECTRODES 549.137-010
Supervisor, Cleaning And Annealing 619.130-018
SUPERVISOR, COAL HANDLING 549.132-018
SUPERVISOR, COKE HANDLING 549.132-022
SUPERVISOR, COLD ROLLING 619.130-018
SUPERVISOR, CONDITIONING YARD 619.134-010
SUPERVISOR, CONTINUOUS-WELD-PIPE MILL 619.130-022
Supervisor, Dock 921.137-010
SUPERVISOR, DRAWING 614.132-010
Supervisor, Extrusion 549.137-010
SUPERVISOR, FINISHING-AND-SHIPPING 619.132-026
SUPERVISOR, FLAME CUTTING 819.132-010
Supervisor, Graphite 549.137-010
SUPERVISOR, HOT-DIP-TINNING 501.130-010
SUPERVISOR, HOT-STRIP MILL 613.132-010
SUPERVISOR, MERCHANT-MILL ROLLING AND FINISHING 613.130-014
SUPERVISOR, MOLD YARD 519.137-010
SUPERVISOR, OPEN-HEARTH STOCKYARD 922.137-022
SUPERVISOR, OVENS 542.132-014
SUPERVISOR, PASTE PLANT 549.132-026
SUPERVISOR, PIG-MACHINE 514.137-010
SUPERVISOR, PIPE FINISHING 619.130-038
SUPERVISOR, PIT-AND-AUXILIARIES 514.137-014
SUPERVISOR, PLATE HEATING, ROLLING, AND FINISHING 619.132-030
SUPERVISOR, POWDERED METAL 509.130-010
SUPERVISOR, ROLL SHOP 604.130-010
SUPERVISOR, SCRAP PREPARATION 519.137-014
SUPERVISOR, SMOKE CONTROL 861.134-010
SUPERVISOR, SOAKING PITS 509.132-010
SUPERVISOR, SPECIALTY MANUFACTURING 616.130-014
SUPERVISOR, STRUCTURAL ROLLING-AND-FINISHING 613.130-018
table and slab depiler 504.665-010
TABLE OPERATOR 613.682-026
Table Operator 919.683-018
Tandem-Mill Roller 613.662-018
tar-and-ammonia pump operator 541.362-014
tar chaser 549.687-010
tar runner 549.687-010
Temper-Mill Roller 613.662-018
test assembler 509.584-010
test carrier 509.584-010
TEST PREPARER 509.584-010
THAW-SHED HEATER TENDER 543.685-022
THIRD HELPER 512.687-014
Tilting-Table Operator 613.682-026
TIN ROLLER, HOT MILL 613.360-018
Transfer-Table Operator 613.682-026
TUBE DRAWER 614.685-022
tube-draw helper 614.686-010
Tube-Drawing Supervisor 614.132-010
tube roller 619.682-042
Tubing Inspector 619.381-010
TUBING-MACHINE OPERATOR 613.685-030
Tuyere Fitter 862.281-022
UTILITY WORKER, MERCHANT MILL 801.664-014
Vessel Liner 861.381-026
wash-oil-cooler operator 549.382-018
WASH-OIL-PUMP OPERATOR 549.382-018
WASH-OIL-PUMP OPERATOR HELPER 549.685-034
Welder, Pipe Making 616.360-026
Wet-Pan Mixer 570.685-070
WHARF TENDER 542.667-010
Wheel Inspector 619.381-010
Wire-Drawing Supervisor 614.132-010

stonework—STONEWORK INDUSTRY: This designation includes occupations concerned with cutting, finishing, and shaping granite, limestone, marble, sandstone, slate, and other stones for building, monumental, ornamental, and miscellaneous purposes. Occupations concerned with processing grindstones, pulpstones, hones, and whetstones for abrasive uses are included in the ABRASIVE, ASBESTOS, AND MISCELLANEOUS NONMETALLIC MINERAL PRODUCTS INDUSTRY (nonmet. min.). Occupations concerned with quarrying stone are included in the COAL, METAL, AND NONMETAL MINING AND QUARRYING INDUSTRY (mine & quarry).

banker 679.664-010
BED RUBBER 673.685-014
BED SETTER 679.664-010

struct. metal

BELT SANDER, STONE	673.666-010
BEVELER	771.484-010
blaster	771.281-010
block maker	771.684-010
buffer	775.664-010
buffer	673.382-018
Building Stonecutter	771.381-014
checker	670.384-010
chisel worker	771.381-014
CIRCULAR-SAWYER HELPER	677.486-010
CIRCULAR SAWYER, STONE	677.462-010
CONTOUR GRINDER	675.682-010
Contour Wire Sawyer	677.462-014
COPER, HAND	771.384-010
CULTURED-MARBLE-PRODUCTS MAKER	575.684-050
Curbing Stonecutter	771.381-014
cut-off-saw operator	677.462-010
cutter	771.384-010
decorator	779.381-022
Diamond Sander	673.682-030
Diamond-Saw Operator	677.462-010
driller	771.684-010
driller	676.682-014
Drill Operator, Pneumatic	676.682-014
dry sander	673.666-010
EDGER-MACHINE HELPER	673.686-010
EDGER-MACHINE OPERATOR	673.682-018
finisher	673.382-018
finishing wire sawyer	677.462-014
gang-saw operator	670.362-010
GANG SAWYER, STONE	670.362-010
Granite Carver	771.281-014
granite cutter apprentice	771.381-010
granite polisher apprentice	673.382-022
Granite Polisher, Hand	775.664-010
Granite Polisher, Machine	673.382-018
granite sandblaster apprentice	673.382-014
guillotine cutter	677.685-046
hand carver	771.281-014
inspector	670.384-010
INSPECTOR-REPAIRER, SANDSTONE	779.684-030
jackhammer-splitter operator	677.685-042
lathe operator	674.662-010
lumper	679.664-010
Marble Carver	771.281-014
marble coper	771.384-010
Marble-Cutter Operator	677.462-010
Marble Polisher, Hand	775.664-010
Marble Polisher, Machine	673.382-018
MEMORIAL DESIGNER	142.061-030
Monument Carver	771.281-014
Monument Stonecutter	771.381-014
Multiple-Wire Sawyer	677.462-014
PATCH SANDER	775.684-054
PATTERNMAKER	703.381-010
Paving-Block Cutter I	677.685-046
Paving-Block Cutter II	771.684-010
PLANER, STONE	675.682-018
planing-machine operator	675.682-018
polisher, hand	775.664-010
polishing-machine operator	673.382-018
profile grinder	675.682-010
Radial-Drill Operator	676.682-014
ROCK BREAKER	770.687-034
ROCK SPLITTER	771.684-010
rotary-saw operator	677.462-010
ROUTER OPERATOR	676.462-010
rubber cutter	771.281-010
rubber cutter and shape carver	673.382-010
rubbing-bed operator	673.685-014
SANDBLASTER, STONE	673.382-010
SANDBLASTER, STONE APPRENTICE	673.382-014
sandblast operator	673.382-010
saw maker	701.684-022
SAW SETTER	701.684-022
SAWYER	term
sculptor	771.281-014
setter	679.664-010
shape carver	771.281-014
shaper	673.382-010
single-wire-saw operator	677.462-014
SINK CUTTER	677.682-018
SLAB GRINDER	673.682-030
Slab Polisher	673.682-030
Slate Cutter	676.682-014

Slate-Cutter Operator	677.462-010
Slate Splitter	771.684-010
slate trimmer	670.685-010
SPLITTER OPERATOR	677.685-042
SPLITTING-MACHINE OPERATOR	677.685-046
SPLITTING-MACHINE-OPERATOR HELPER	677.666-010
STENCIL CUTTER	771.281-010
sticker	779.684-058
stone banker	679.664-010
STONE CARVER	771.281-014
STONECUTTER APPRENTICE, HAND	771.381-010
STONECUTTER, HAND	771.381-014
STONECUTTER, MACHINE	677.682-022
stone dresser	771.381-014
STONE DRILLER	676.682-014
STONE-DRILLER HELPER	676.686-010
stone finisher	775.664-010
stone finisher	673.382-018
stone finisher see STONE MECHANIC	
STONE GRADER	670.384-010
STONE-LATHE OPERATOR	674.662-010
Stone-Lathe Polisher	674.662-010
STONE LAYOUT MARKER	670.587-010
STONE MECHANIC	term
STONE POLISHER, HAND	775.664-010
STONE POLISHER, MACHINE	673.382-018
STONE POLISHER, MACHINE APPRENTICE	673.382-022
STONE REPAIRER	779.684-058
stone rubber	775.664-010
stone sawyer	670.362-010
stone splitter	677.685-042
STONE TRIMMER	670.685-010
stoneworker	771.381-014
STRIP POLISHER	673.685-082
SUPERVISOR	679.130-010
SUPERVISOR, SLATE SPLITTING	771.137-010
SURFACE-PLATE FINISHER	775.281-010
surfacer operator	677.682-022
surfacing-machine operator	677.682-022
THERMAL-SURFACING-MACHINE OPERATOR	679.685-018
TOP POLISHER	673.662-010
TRACER	779.381-022
turner	674.662-010
wire-saw operator	677.462-014
WIRE SAWYER	677.462-014

struct. metal—STRUCTURAL AND ORNAMENTAL METAL PRODUCTS INDUSTRY: This designation includes occupations concerned with fabricating and repairing architectural, structural, and ornamental metalwork. The primary products are structural steel for buildings and bridges; solid-metal, hollow-metal, and metal-covered doors, window sashes, window and door frames, store fronts, and molding and trim; storm and screen doors and windows, and weather strip; structural and ornamental metal for balconies, bank fixtures, elevator enclosures, fire escapes, gratings, portable buildings, and stairs and staircases; power and marine boilers, pressure and nonpressure tanks, and processing and storage vessels; sheet metalwork; and metal bars used to reinforce concrete products. Occupations concerned with the manufacture of wire screening are included under FABRICATED METAL PRODUCTS, NOT ELSEWHERE CLASSIFIED (metal prod., nec).

art-metal designer	142.061-034
assembler-fitter	809.684-010
ASSEMBLER, PRODUCTION LINE	809.684-010
ASSEMBLER, UNIT	809.681-010
BOILERMAKER APPRENTICE	805.261-010
boilermaker, assembly and erection	805.261-014
Boilermaker, Central Steam Plant	805.381-010
BOILERMAKER FITTER	805.361-014
BOILERMAKER HELPER I	805.687-010
BOILERMAKER HELPER II	805.664-010
BOILERMAKER I	805.261-014
BOILERMAKER II	805.381-010
Boilermaker, Industrial Boilers	805.381-010
boilermaker mechanic	805.381-010
Boilermaker, Ship	805.381-010
Channel Installer	809.684-010
crimper-assembler	809.684-010
Door-Lock Installer	809.684-010
FABRICATOR, SHOWER DOORS AND PANELS	739.381-030
Fireproof-Door Assembler	809.681-010
Frame Assembler	809.684-010
Hardware Installer	809.684-010
INSPECTOR AND TESTER	809.687-018
Kick-Plate Installer	809.684-010

MEASURER 869.487-010
Metal-Door Assembler 809.681-010
Metal Screen, Storm Door, And Window Builder 809.381-010
Metal-Window-Screen Assembler 809.681-010
ORNAMENTAL-METALWORK DESIGNER 142.061-034
PANEL LAMINATOR 809.684-042
Screen-Frame Enameler 599.685-026
Screen Installer 809.684-010
SCROLL-MACHINE OPERATOR 616.685-062
SHOP SUPERVISOR 619.131-014
Spliner 809.684-010
SUPERVISOR 617.130-010
SUPERVISOR, ASSEMBLY DEPARTMENT 809.130-010
SUPERVISOR, BOILERMAKING 805.131-010
Supervisor, Boilermaking Shop 805.131-010
Supervisor, Field Assembly-And-Erection 805.131-010
SUPERVISOR, GRINDING AND SPRAYING 809.134-010
Supervisor Mechanic, Boilermaking 805.131-010
Welder, Boilermaker 810.384-014

sugar & conf.—SUGAR AND CONFECTIONERY PRODUCTS INDUSTRY: This designation includes occupations concerned with (1) manufacturing and refining sugar and molasses from sugar beets and sugarcane; (2) manufacturing candy and confectionery products; (3) shelling, roasting, and grinding cocoa beans for chocolate liquor, cocoa powder and butter, and chocolate bars and coatings; (4) manufacturing chewing gum. Occupations concerned with manufacturing principal sugar byproducts, such as monosodium glutamate, beet pulp for cattle feed, and soil conditioners, are included here. Occupations concerned with manufacturing and selling confectionery products in the same establishment are included here. However, sales occupations found in establishments with no manufacturing are included in the RETAIL TRADE INDUSTRY (retail trade).

Almond-Pan Finisher 524.382-010
ALMOND-PASTE MIXER 529.361-010
ALMOND-PASTE MOLDER 520.684-010
BALL-MACHINE OPERATOR 520.686-010
ball-rolling-machine operator 520.686-010
batch maker 529.361-014
batch-roller operator 520.682-030
bean dumper 521.685-066
beet flumer 521.686-042
beet flumer 922.665-010
BLOW-UP OPERATOR 529.485-014
boiler 529.361-014
BOILER-OPERATOR HELPER 950.585-014
Bonbon-Cream Warmer 526.382-014
Bonbon Dipper 524.684-010
breaker operator 521.685-034
BREAKING-MACHINE OPERATOR 521.685-034
BULK-PLANT OPERATOR 520.362-010
Candy-Bar-Core Inspector 529.686-034
Candy Catcher 529.686-034
candy-cooker helper 520.685-050
CANDY CUTTER, HAND 790.687-010
candy cutter, machine 521.685-102
Candy Decorator 524.684-014
CANDY DIPPER, HAND 524.684-010
candy feeder 524.686-010
CANDY MAKER 529.361-014
Candy Maker, Bar 520.687-022
candy-maker helper 520.687-022
CANDY-MAKER HELPER 520.685-050
candy mixer 520.684-014
CANDY MOLDER, HAND 520.687-018
Candy Packer 920.587-018
candy polisher 524.382-010
CANDY PULLER 520.685-046
candy roller 520.686-010
candy roller 520.684-014
candy-rolling-machine operator 520.685-198
candy separator, enrobing 524.686-010
Candy Separator, Hard 529.686-034
CANDY SPREADER 520.687-022
Candy-Spreader Helper 529.686-034
candy-starch-mold printer 526.687-014
Candy-Waffle Assembler 529.686-034
Candy-Wrapping-Machine Operator 920.685-078
Caramel-Candy Maker 529.361-014
Caramel-Candy-Maker Helper 520.685-050
Caramel Cutter, Hand 790.687-010
Caramel-Cutter Helper 529.686-034
Caramel Cutter, Machine 521.685-102
CARBONATION EQUIPMENT OPERATOR 529.582-010

carrier operator 521.685-090
casting-machine operator 520.682-014
CASTING-MACHINE OPERATOR 520.685-062
CENTER-MACHINE OPERATOR 520.682-014
center maker, hand 520.684-014
CENTRIFUGAL OPERATOR 521.682-010
Centrifugal Separator 521.685-070
CENTRIFUGAL-STATION OPERATOR, AUTOMATIC 521.585-010
centrifugal supervisor 529.130-042
CENTRIFUGE OPERATOR 529.682-010
CHAR-CONVEYOR TENDER 529.685-050
Char Conveyor Tender, Cellar 529.685-050
CHAR-DUST CLEANER AND SALVAGER 529.687-038
CHAR-FILTER OPERATOR 521.365-010
CHAR-FILTER-OPERATOR HELPER 521.687-034
CHAR PULLER 521.687-030
CHEESE SPRAYER 524.685-014
Cherry Dipper 524.684-010
CHICLE-GRINDER FEEDER 521.686-018
Chocolate Coater 524.684-010
Chocolate-Drops-Machine Operator 520.685-078
chocolate finisher 521.682-034
chocolate-finisher operator 521.682-034
Chocolate-Machine Operator 524.382-014
Chocolate Molder 520.687-018
CHOCOLATE MOLDER, MACHINE 529.685-054
Chocolate-Peanut Coating-Machine Operator 524.382-010
CHOCOLATE-PRODUCTION-MACHINE OPERATOR 529.382-014
chocolate refiner 521.682-034
chocolate-refining roller 521.682-034
CHOCOLATE TEMPERER 523.682-010
coater 524.382-010
Coating-Machine Helper 529.686-034
COATING-MACHINE OPERATOR 524.382-010
COCOA-BEAN CLEANER 521.685-066
COCOA-BEAN-ROASTER HELPER 523.666-010
COCOA-BEAN ROASTER I 523.362-010
COCOA-BEAN ROASTER II 523.380-010
COCOA-BUTTER-FILTER OPERATOR 521.685-070
cocoa-milling-machine operator 521.685-202
cocoa-mill operator 521.685-074
COCOA-POWDER-MIXER OPERATOR 520.685-074
COCOA-PRESS OPERATOR 521.682-014
COCOA-ROOM OPERATOR 521.685-074
Coconut-Candy Maker 529.361-014
Coconut Cooker 526.382-014
Coconut-Jelly Roller 520.682-030
conche loader and unloader 526.382-010
CONCHE OPERATOR 526.382-010
confectioner 529.361-014
CONFECTIONERY COOKER 526.382-014
CONFECTIONERY-DROPS-MACHINE OPERATOR 520.685-078
CONTINUOUS-ABSORPTION-PROCESS OPERATOR 521.362-010
cook, candy 529.361-014
COOLER TENDER 520.585-018
CORN POPPER 526.685-026
cracker-fanner operator 521.385-010
CRACKING-AND-FANNING-MACHINE OPERATOR 521.385-010
Cream Dipper 524.684-010
CRUSHER OPERATOR 521.685-090
CRYSTALLIZER OPERATOR 523.585-018
Crystal-Syrup Maker 526.382-014
Cubelet-Centrifugal Operator 521.682-010
Cut-Roll-Machine Offbearer 529.686-034
cut-roll-machine operator 520.685-198
cutter, machine 521.685-102
CUTTING-MACHINE OPERATOR 521.685-102
cutting-machine operator 521.685-034
Cutting-Machine-Operator Helper 529.686-034
Dairy-Powder-Mixer Operator 520.685-074
Date Puller 521.687-066
DECORATOR 524.684-014
decorator, hand 524.684-014
decorator, hand 524.684-018
DEPOSITING-MACHINE OPERATOR 529.682-018
DIFFUSER OPERATOR 523.562-010
DORR OPERATOR 522.685-050
drier operator 529.682-010
DRIER OPERATOR 529.682-022
enrober tender 524.686-010
ENROBING-MACHINE CORDER 524.684-018
ENROBING-MACHINE FEEDER 524.686-010
ENROBING-MACHINE OPERATOR 524.382-014
EVAPORATOR OPERATOR 521.382-010
extruding-machine operator 520.682-014

sugar & conf.

FACTORY HELPER	529.686-034
FILTER OPERATOR	521.685-126
finisher	524.382-010
FIRER, KILN	523.685-078
first helper	529.682-018
five-roll-refiner batch mixer	520.685-150
FLOOR WORKER	920.687-090
FLUMER I	922.665-010
FLUMER II	521.686-042
Fondant Cooker	526.382-014
Fondant-Machine Operator	521.585-018
Fondant-Puff Maker	520.682-014
FRUIT-BAR MAKER	529.685-134
FRUIT CUTTER	521.687-066
Fruit Stuffer	524.687-014
Fudge-Candy Maker	529.361-014
GARNISHER	524.687-014
GENERAL HELPER	529.686-046
general utility helper	529.686-034
general utility machine operator	529.382-014
glazer	524.382-010
glosser	524.382-010
GLUCOSE-AND-SYRUP WEIGHER	520.686-026
GRANULATOR OPERATOR	523.685-098
Gum Coater	524.382-010
Gum Maker	526.382-014
GUM PULLER	520.687-038
gum-rolling-machine tender	520.682-022
GUM-SCORING-MACHINE OPERATOR	520.682-022
hard-candy batch-mixer	520.685-046
Hard-Candy Maker	529.361-014
hard-candy spinner	520.682-030
High-Raw-Sugar Boiler	522.382-034
HOPPER ATTENDANT	521.685-182
Icing Coater	524.684-010
Icing Maker	526.382-014
INSPECTOR	529.687-114
INSPECTOR, PROCESSING	529.687-226
KETTLE TENDER	520.685-118
Kieselguhr-Regenerator Operator	573.685-034
King Maker	526.382-014
Kiss Mixer	520.685-122
KISS SETTER, HAND	529.687-122
KNIFE SETTER	638.684-014
LIQUID-SUGAR FORTIFIER	520.585-022
LIQUID-SUGAR MELTER	520.382-014
LIQUOR-BRIDGE OPERATOR	521.565-010
LIQUOR-BRIDGE-OPERATOR HELPER	521.687-078
liquor-gallery operator	521.565-010
LIQUOR-GRINDING-MILL OPERATOR	521.685-202
liquor runner	521.565-010
lollypop-machine operator	529.685-234
lollypop maker	529.685-234
Low-Raw-Sugar Cutter	521.682-010
LOZENGE-DOUGH MIXER	520.685-122
LOZENGE MAKER	529.682-026
Lozenge-Maker Helper	529.686-034
Marshmallow Maker	526.382-014
Marshmallow Packer	529.686-034
Marshmallow Runner	520.682-014
marzipan maker	529.361-010
marzipan molder	520.684-010
Melangeur Operator	520.685-150
MELTER OPERATOR	523.382-018
Melt-House Centrifugal Operator	521.682-010
MELT-HOUSE DRAG OPERATOR	529.687-158
MILL PLATFORM SUPERVISOR	521.132-010
MINGLER OPERATOR	520.665-010
Mint-Lozenge Mixer	520.685-122
Mint-Machine Operator	521.685-102
Mint-Wafer Depositor	529.682-018
MIXER OPERATOR	520.685-150
mogul feeder	520.686-030
mogul operator	520.682-026
molder, hand	520.687-018
MOLDING-MACHINE OPERATOR	520.682-026
MOLDING-MACHINE-OPERATOR HELPER	520.686-030
Nougat-Candy Maker	529.361-014
Nougat-Candy-Maker Helper	520.685-050
Nougat Cutter, Machine	521.685-102
novelty-candy maker	520.687-018
NUT CHOPPER	521.686-046
ornamenter	524.684-014
pan operator	524.382-010
PANTRY WORKER	520.487-018
Pan Washer, Hand	529.686-034
paste worker	520.687-018
Pecan-Mallow Dipper	524.684-010
PICKING-TABLE WORKER	521.687-102
polisher	524.382-010
POPCORN-CANDY MAKER	526.685-042
popcorn maker	526.685-026
popped-corn oven attendant	526.685-026
Powdered-Sugar-Pulverizer Operator	521.585-018
POWDER-MILL OPERATOR	521.585-018
printer	526.687-014
PULP-DRIER FIRER	523.585-030
PULP-PRESS TENDER	521.685-258
QUALITY CONTROL INSPECTOR	529.367-034
Quick-Mixer Operator	520.685-074
Raisin-Separator Operator	529.686-034
RAW-JUICE WEIGHER	529.685-194
Receiving-Tank Operator	529.585-014
REFINED-SYRUP OPERATOR	520.485-022
REFINING-MACHINE OPERATOR	521.682-034
REGENERATOR OPERATOR	573.685-034
Remelt-Centrifugal Operator	521.682-010
Remelt-Pan-Tank Operator	529.585-014
Remelt-Sugar Boiler	522.382-034
Remelt-Sugar Cutter	521.682-010
roaster helper	523.666-010
ROLLER I	520.684-014
Roller II	524.687-014
roller operator	520.685-198
ROLLING-MACHINE OPERATOR	520.685-198
Salvage Grinder	521.686-018
SANDING-MACHINE OPERATOR	524.665-010
Sanding-Machine Operator Helper	529.686-034
Scrapper	529.686-034
SCREEN-ROOM OPERATOR	521.685-282
sea-foam-kiss maker	529.687-122
slab worker	520.684-014
slicing-machine feeder	521.685-102
Soft-Sugar Boiler	522.382-034
Soft-Sugar Cutter	521.682-010
SOFT-SUGAR OPERATOR, HEAD	521.565-018
SPINNER	520.682-030
Spinner Helper	529.686-034
stack puller	520.686-030
starch crab	529.682-018
Starch Dumper	520.686-030
STARCHMAKER	526.687-014
Steamer, Gum Candy	529.686-034
stick-candy puller	520.682-030
stick roller	520.684-014
stick spinner	520.682-030
streaker	524.684-018
stringer	524.684-018
stripper-machine operator	521.685-102
stroker	524.684-018
SUCKER-MACHINE OPERATOR	529.685-234
SUGAR BOILER	522.382-034
Sugar-Coating Hand	529.686-034
SUGAR CONTROLLER	529.565-010
sugar drier	523.685-098
sugar-end supervisor	529.130-034
SUGAR GRINDER	521.685-346
SUGAR-REPROCESS OPERATOR, HEAD	529.137-018
SUPERVISOR	920.130-010
SUPERVISOR, BEET END	529.132-018
SUPERVISOR, CANDY	529.130-010
SUPERVISOR, CHAR HOUSE	523.132-010
SUPERVISOR, CHOCOLATE-AND-COCOA PROCESSING	529.130-014
Supervisor, Enrobing	529.130-010
SUPERVISOR, FILTRATION	529.130-022
Supervisor, Hard Candy	529.130-010
SUPERVISOR, INSPECTION	529.137-074
Supervisor, Inspection Room	920.137-018
SUPERVISOR, MELT HOUSE	522.130-010
SUPERVISOR, PACKING	920.130-010
SUPERVISOR, POWDERED SUGAR	521.130-014
SUPERVISOR, PROCESSING	529.137-082
SUPERVISOR, PULP HOUSE	529.130-030
SUPERVISOR, REFINING	529.130-034
Supervisor, Remelt	522.130-010
SUPERVISOR, SOFT SUGAR	529.130-038
SUPERVISOR, STEFFEN HOUSE	529.132-086
SUPERVISOR, SYRUP SHED	529.137-058
Supervisor, Unwrapping Room	920.137-018

SUPERVISOR, WHITE SUGAR	529.130-042
Supervisor, Wrapping Room	920.137-018
Syrup Crystallizer	529.686-034
SYRUP MAKER	529.482-022
Table Filler	529.686-034
Taffy-Candy Maker	529.361-014
Taffy Puller	520.685-046
TANK TENDER	529.585-014
TARE WEIGHER	221.587-034
tempering-machine operator	523.682-010
Toy Sorter	529.686-034
UTILITY WORKER	529.686-086
Vacuum-Cooker Operator	526.382-014
Vanilla-Chocolate-Coin Counter	529.686-034
Vortex Operator	520.585-018
WASHER, AGRICULTURAL PRODUCE	529.685-258
WASHROOM CLEANER	529.687-214
WASHROOM OPERATOR	529.665-014
WET-AND-DRY-SUGAR-BIN OPERATOR	529.665-018
Wet-Char Conveyor Tender	529.685-050
whipper-beater	520.685-050
White-Sugar Boiler	522.382-034
White-Sugar Centrifugal Operator	521.682-010
White-Sugar-Pan-Tank Operator	529.585-014
White-Sugar-Syrup Operator	529.585-014

svc. ind. mach.—REFRIGERATION AND SERVICE INDUSTRY MACHINERY INDUSTRY: This designation includes occupations concerned with manufacturing and repairing automatic (vending and coin-operated) merchandising equipment; industrial and commercial laundry, dry cleaning, and pressing machines; commercial, industrial, and residential air-conditioning, warm-air heating equipment, and refrigeration equipment; soda fountains; beer dispensing equipment; gasoline and oil measuring and dispensing pumps; and service industry machines, not elsewhere classified. Occupations concerned with manufacturing electric warm-air furnaces and comfort heating equipment are included in the ELECTRICAL EQUIPMENT INDUSTRY (elec. equip.). Occupations concerned with manufacturing household refrigerators and freezers are included in the HOUSEHOLD APPLIANCES INDUSTRY (house. appl.).

AIR-CONDITIONING-COIL ASSEMBLER	706.684-010
Air-Conditioning-Unit Assembler	827.684-010
AIR-CONDITIONING-UNIT TESTER	827.361-010
APPLIANCE ASSEMBLER, LINE	827.684-010
ASSEMBLER	731.687-010
Assembler, Coolers	827.684-010
Automobile Air-Conditioner Assembler	827.684-010
Carpenter, Refrigerator	860.381-022
charging-board operator	827.485-010
coil fin assembler	706.684-010
COIN-MACHINE ASSEMBLER	731.684-010
COIN-MACHINE-SERVICE REPAIRER	639.281-014
FOAM CHARGER	827.585-010
GAS CHARGER	827.485-010
GAS-LEAK TESTER	827.584-014
manager, vending department	637.131-010
METAL-WASHING-MACHINE OPERATOR	503.685-034
PIN-GAME-MACHINE INSPECTOR	729.381-014
plate fin assembler	706.684-010
QUALITY-CONTROL TECHNICIAN	637.684-014
REFRIGERATION MECHANIC	827.361-014
REFRIGERATION UNIT REPAIRER	637.381-014
Refrigerator Cabinetmaker	660.280-010
Refrigerator Crater	920.684-010
REFRIGERATOR GLAZIER	865.684-022
REFRIGERATOR TESTER	827.384-010
SUPERVISOR, COIN-MACHINE	706.130-010
SUPERVISOR, COOLER SERVICE	637.131-010
switchpanel mounter	731.684-010
VENDING-MACHINE ASSEMBLER	706.684-102
vending-machine repairer	639.281-014
WIRE CUTTER	731.687-038

tel. & tel.—TELEPHONE AND TELEGRAPH INDUSTRY: This designation includes occupations concerned with the maintenance and operation of communications systems for wire and radio transmission of messages, including local and long-distance telephone and telegraph systems, stock ticker, time-signal, teletype, television cable, and other special communications services. Excluded are occupations concerned with creating and broadcasting radio and television programs, which are included in the RADIO AND TELEVISION BROADCASTING INDUSTRY (radio-tv broad.).

Adjustment Clerk	219.362-010
adjustment clerk	239.362-014
application clerk	239.362-014

ASSEMBLER	722.381-010
assembler, equipment	722.381-010
ASSIGNMENT CLERK	219.387-010
AUTOMATIC-EQUIPMENT TECHNICIAN	822.281-010
automatic maintainer	822.261-026
cable dispatcher	239.167-014
CABLE ENGINEER, OUTSIDE PLANT	003.167-010
CABLESHIP WORKER	term
CABLE SPLICER	829.361-010
CABLE-SPLICER APPRENTICE	829.361-014
CABLE-SPLICER HELPER	829.667-010
cable-splicing supervisor	829.131-010
CABLE SUPERVISOR	829.131-010
CABLE SUPERVISOR	184.161-010
CABLE TESTER	822.361-010
Call-Box Wirer	822.381-010
CENTRAL-OFFICE EQUIPMENT ENGINEER	003.187-010
CENTRAL-OFFICE INSTALLER	822.361-014
central-office maintainer	822.281-014
CENTRAL-OFFICE OPERATOR	235.462-010
CENTRAL-OFFICE-OPERATOR SUPERVISOR	235.132-010
CENTRAL-OFFICE REPAIRER	822.281-014
CENTRAL-OFFICE-REPAIRER SUPERVISOR	822.131-010
Central-Office Supervisor	822.131-010
City-Plant Supervisor	822.131-010
clerk, cable transfer	219.387-010
clerk-operator	239.362-010
clerk, personal service bureau	219.362-022
clerk, private wire-billing and control	219.362-022
clerk, rating	214.587-010
CLERK, ROUTE	235.562-010
CLERK, TELEGRAPH SERVICE	219.362-022
coin-box collector	292.687-010
COIN-MACHINE COLLECTOR	292.687-010
COMMERCIAL-INSTRUCTOR SUPERVISOR	239.137-010
commercial representative	253.257-010
commercial service representative	253.357-010
COMMUNICATIONS CONSULTANT	253.157-010
Communications Consultant, Commercial Services	253.157-010
Communications Consultant, Industrial Services	253.157-010
Communications Consultant, Residential Services	253.157-010
Communications-Equipment Supervisor	722.131-010
COUNTER CLERK	249.362-010
CUSTOMER-EQUIPMENT ENGINEER	003.187-018
CUSTOMER-FACILITIES SUPERVISOR	822.131-014
CUSTOMER-SERVICE REPRESENTATIVE	239.362-014
CUSTOMER-SERVICE-REPRESENTATIVE INSTR.	239.227-010
CUSTOMER-SERVICE REPRESENTATIVE SUPERVISOR	239.137-014
cw operator	193.262-030
DIRECTORY-ASSISTANCE OPERATOR	235.662-018
DISPATCHER	239.167-014
dispatcher	822.361-030
District-Plant Supervisor	822.131-010
electrician, cable-splicing	829.361-010
ELECTRICIAN, OFFICE	822.261-010
electrician, station, assistant	822.261-010
EQUIPMENT INSPECTOR	822.261-014
equipment installer	822.361-010
EQUIPMENT INSTALLER	822.381-010
equipment installer	822.381-022
EQUIPMENT MECHANIC	term
FACILITY EXAMINER	959.367-014
facsimile operator	193.362-010
force dispatcher	215.137-018
FRAME WIRER	822.684-010
Ground Helper	821.684-014
Hole-Digger-Truck Driver	905.663-014
Inside-Plant Supervisor	822.131-010
inspector, line	822.267-010
Installation Supervisor	822.131-014
installation supervisor	822.131-014
INSTRUMENT REPAIRER	722.281-010
INSTRUMENT-SHOP SUPERVISOR	722.131-010
Jointer, Submarine Cable	829.361-010
LINE INSPECTOR	822.267-010
LINE INSTALLER-REPAIRER	822.381-014
Line Installer-Repairer, City	822.381-014
Line Maintainer, Section	822.381-014
LINE SUPERVISOR	822.131-018
Long-Distance Operator	235.462-010
maintainer, central office	822.381-022
maintainer, equipment	822.381-022
maintainer, plant	822.381-022
maintenance chief	822.131-010
MAINTENANCE INSPECTOR	822.261-018

maintenance supervisor 822.131-014
MANAGER, COMMUNICATIONS STATION 184.167-062
MANAGER, CUSTOMER SERVICE 168.167-058
Manager, Prorate 822.131-014
manager, service 822.131-014
MANAGER, TELEGRAPH OFFICE 184.167-086
MANAGER, TRAFFIC I 184.167-098
MANAGER, TRAFFIC II 184.167-106
Money-Order Clerk 249.362-010
monitor 239.367-026
monitor chief 239.137-022
Multiplex-Machine Operator 203.582-050
observer 239.367-026
operations chief 822.131-010
OPERATIONS MANAGER 184.117-070
Operations Technician 822.281-010
order clerk 239.362-014
outside contact clerk 239.362-014
OUTSIDE-PLANT ENGINEER 003.167-042
Outside-Plant Supervisor 822.131-010
PAY-STATION ATTENDANT 237.367-034
pay-station collector 292.687-010
pbx installer 822.381-018
pbx repairer 822.281-022
PHOTORADIO OPERATOR 193.362-010
PLANNING ENGINEER, CENTRAL OFFICE FACILITIES 003.061-050
plant chief 184.117-082
Pole-Truck Driver 904.383-010
POWER OPERATOR 952.382-014
Printer Maintainer 822.281-010
PRIVATE-BRANCH-EXCHANGE INSTALLER 822.381-018
Private-Branch-Exchange Installer, Mobile Radio 822.381-018
PRIVATE-BRANCH-EXCHANGE REPAIRER 822.281-022
PRIVATE-BRANCH-EXCHANGE SERVICE ADVISER 235.222-010
Private-Branch-Exchange Teletypewriter 822.381-018
Radio Installer 822.381-018
RADIO-MESSAGE ROUTER 235.387-010
radio-photo technician 193.362-010
radiotelegraphist 193.262-030
RADIOTELEGRAPH OPERATOR 193.262-030
rate marker 214.587-010
REGULATORY ADMINISTRATOR 168.167-070
repeater attendant 822.261-026
REPRESENTATIVE, PERSONAL SERVICE 236.252-010
REVENUE-SETTLEMENTS ADMINISTRATOR 184.117-074
rigger, chief 823.131-014
RIGGER SUPERVISOR 823.131-014
ROUTE AIDE 239.687-010
ROUTE SUPERVISOR 239.137-018
SALES REPRESENTATIVE, PUBLIC UTILITIES 253.357-010
Sales Representative, Telephone And Telegraph Services 253.357-010
SALES REPRESENTATIVE, TELEPHONE SERVICES 253.257-010
Section Maintainer 822.261-022
service-center supervisor 822.131-014
Service Investigator 241.367-014
SERVICE OBSERVER 239.367-026
SERVICE OBSERVER, CHIEF 239.137-022
service representative 239.362-014
services engineer 003.187-018
shop repairer 722.281-010
special-service representative 253.157-010
splicer 829.361-010
splicer apprentice 829.361-014
Station Installer 822.261-022
STATION INSTALLER-AND-REPAIRER 822.261-022
Station Repairer 822.261-022
SUPERINTENDENT, COMMUNICATIONS 184.117-082
SUPERVISOR, DELIVERY DEPARTMENT 230.137-014
SUPERVISOR, FORCE ADJUSTMENT 215.137-018
SUPERVISOR, PUBLIC MESSAGE SERVICE 239.137-026
SUPERVISOR, TELEPHONE CLERKS 239.132-010
switchboard operator 235.462-010
technician, automatic 822.281-010
TECHNICIAN, SUBMARINE CABLE EQUIPMENT 822.281-034
technician, terminal and repeater 822.261-026
Telegram Messenger 230.663-010
telegraph-equipment maintainer 822.281-010
Telegraphic-Instrument Supervisor 722.131-010
Telegraphic-Service Dispatcher 959.167-010
Telegraphic-Typewriter Installer 822.381-010
Telegraphic-Typewriter Repairer 822.281-010
TELEGRAPH-PLANT MAINTAINER 822.381-022
Telegraph-Repeater Installer 822.381-010
Telegraph-Repeater Technician 822.261-026
TELEGRAPH-SERVICE RATER 214.587-010
TELEPHONE CLERK, TELEGRAPH OFFICE 239.362-010
Telephone Coin-Box Collector 292.687-010
Telephone-Instrument Supervisor 722.131-010
telephone operator 235.462-010
telephone-plant power operator 952.382-014
telephone repairer 822.281-022
telephone supervisor 239.132-010
telephoto engineer 193.362-010
Telephoto Installer 822.381-018
Teleprinter Installer 822.381-018
Teletype Installer 822.381-010
TEST-DESK SUPERVISOR 822.131-030
tester, equipment 822.261-026
TESTING-AND-REGULATING CHIEF 184.167-258
TESTING-AND-REGULATING TECHNICIAN 822.261-026
Ticker Installer 822.381-010
Time-Signal Wirer 822.381-010
Toll-Line Repairer 822.381-014
Toll Repairer, Central Office 822.281-014
Tower-Truck Driver 905.663-014
traffic chief 184.167-106
traffic controller, cable 239.137-026
traffic superintendent 184.167-106
TRANSMISSION-AND-PROTECTION ENGINEER 003.167-066
transmission engineer 003.167-066
Transmission-Maintenance Supervisor 822.131-014
TRANSMISSION TESTER 822.361-026
TREE TRIMMER 408.664-010
tree trimmer, line clearance 408.664-010
tree-trimming-line technician 408.664-010
TROUBLE LOCATOR, TEST DESK 822.361-030
Video Installer 822.381-018
Watch Electrician 829.261-018
wire-and-repeater technician 822.261-026
wire chief 822.131-010
wirer 722.381-010

tex. prod., nec—TEXTILE PRODUCTS INDUSTRY, NOT ELSEWHERE CLASSIFIED: This designation includes occupations concerned with manufacturing textile products not elswhere classified, such as lace, banners, flags, pennants, parachutes, automobile seat covers, felt, processed waste, recovered fibers, flock, padding, batting, upholstery filling, coated (non-rubberized) fabrics, cordage, twine, rope, tire cord, canvas, pleating, automotive trimmings, apparel findings, embroidery, and textile bags. Included are occupations concerned with manufacturing household furnishings, such as bedspreads, pillowcases, sheets, towels, curtains, draperies, pillows, and quilts. Also included are occupations concerned with hand-knitting and hand-weaving textile products. Occupations concerned with assembling and installing awnings are included here. Occupations that are concerned with manufacturing felt used in hats are included in the HAT AND CAP INDUSTRY (hat & cap). Occupations concerned with impregnating fabrics with rubber are included in the RUBBER GOODS INDUSTRY (rubber goods).

Air Tucker 787.682-082
Air-Turning-Machine Feeder 689.685-146
Applique Cutter, Hand 781.684-074
ASSEMBLER 734.687-014
ASSEMBLER, FINGER BUFFS 739.685-010
automatic embroidery machine tender 689.685-150
AUTOMATIC-PAD-MAKING-MACHINE OPERATOR 689.382-010
AUTOMATIC-PAD-MAKING-MACHINE OPERATOR HELPER 689.686-010
automatic-splicing-machine operator 689.685-122
Awning Assembler 787.682-058
awning erector 869.484-010
Awning Finisher 789.484-014
AWNING-FRAME MAKER 809.484-010
AWNING HANGER 869.484-010
AWNING-HANGER HELPER 869.687-010
awning installer 869.484-010
Awning Maker 739.381-010
Awning Spreader 789.687-090
Back-Pad Inspector 789.687-086
back winder 681.685-154
Bag-And-Sack Sewer 787.682-058
BAG CUTTER 789.687-010
Bag Inspector 789.587-014
BAG LINER 789.687-014
Bag-Making-Machine Tender 787.685-014
BALL-FRINGE-MACHINE OPERATOR 689.685-010
Ball-Mill Mixer 550.382-014
band cutter 689.687-018
BAND-SAW OPERATOR 686.682-010
Bat Carrier 586.686-022

BATTING-MACHINE OPERATOR 680.585-010
BEATER-AND-PULPER FEEDER 530.686-010
BEATER ENGINEER 530.662-010
BEATER-ENGINEER HELPER 530.665-010
Beater, Lead 530.662-010
beater operator 530.662-010
beater-operator helper 530.665-010
Bedspread Cutter, Hand 781.684-074
Bedspread Folder 589.687-014
Bedspread Inspector 789.587-014
Bedspread Seamer 787.682-066
Bias-Binding Cutter 686.685-066
bias-binding folder 689.685-134
BIAS-CUTTING-MACHINE OPERATOR 686.682-014
BINDING CUTTER, SYNTHETIC CLOTH 699.682-010
Blanket Binder 787.682-010
Blanket Cutter, Hand 781.684-074
BLANKET-CUTTING-MACHINE OPERATOR 689.585-010
Blanket Folder 589.687-014
Blanket Inspector 789.587-014
BLOCKER 920.685-022
BOAT-CANVAS MAKER-INSTALLER 789.261-010
bobbin fixer 681.687-026
BOBBIN PRESSER 689.685-018
BOBBIN STRIPPER 689.685-022
BOBBIN WINDER, MACHINE 681.585-014
book folder 589.687-014
border-machine operator 689.382-010
BOUFFANT-CURTAIN-MACHINE TENDER 689.685-026
BOW-MAKER-MACHINE TENDER, AUTOMATIC 689.685-030
Box Feeder 586.686-022
Brass-Bobbin Winder 681.685-154
breaker-wheel operator 582.685-050
brim cutter 585.685-086
brushing operator 585.685-070
Buckram Sewer 787.682-066
BUFFING TURNER-AND-COUNTER 789.687-022
BUFFING-WHEEL FORMER, AUTOMATIC 689.685-034
BUFFING-WHEEL FORMER, HAND 789.684-014
BUFFING-WHEEL INSPECTOR 789.687-026
BUNDLE BREAKER 689.687-018
bundle cutter 689.687-018
Burlap-Bag Sewer 787.682-058
Burlap-Sizing-Machine Operator 582.665-026
BURLAP SPREADER 581.687-010
BURN-OUT TENDER, LACE 589.685-018
BUTTON MAKER AND INSTALLER 734.685-014
CALENDER OPERATOR 583.685-026
CALENDER OPERATOR, ARTIFICIAL LEATHER 584.685-010
Calender-Operator Helper 589.687-026
Calender Supervisor 589.130-014
calender tender 583.685-026
Canopy Inspector 789.687-114
CANOPY STRINGER 789.684-018
Canvas-Bag Maker 787.682-058
Canvas Cutter, Hand 781.684-074
Canvas Cutter, Machine 781.684-014
Canvas Marker 781.384-014
CANVAS WORKER 739.381-010
CANVAS-WORKER APPRENTICE 739.381-014
CARDING-MACHINE OPERATOR 681.685-030
Charge-Bag Sewer 787.682-058
CARTOON DESIGNER 781.381-010
chenille-machine operator 687.682-014
clipping, stringing, and turning machine tender 689.585-018
CLOTH FOLDER, HAND 589.687-014
Cloth Joiner, Tents 787.682-058
Cloth Numberer 787.682-022
Cloth-Printer Helper 586.686-022
Cloth-Printing-Machine-Operator Helper 589.687-026
CLOTH-STOCK SORTER 789.687-034
Coated Fabric Cutter 699.682-026
Coater Helper 586.686-022
COATING-AND-EMBOSSING-UNIT OPERATOR 583.682-010
COATING-MACHINE OPERATOR 584.562-010
Coating-Machine-Operator Helper 589.687-026
COATING-MACHINE OPERATOR I 584.382-010
COATING-MACHINE OPERATOR II 584.685-018
Coating Supervisor 589.130-014
COILER 681.685-034
COLOR MAKER 550.382-014
COLOR MATCHER 550.381-010
color mixer 550.381-010
combing-machine tender 680.685-034
continuous-drier helper 581.687-018
continuous-drier operator 581.685-034
CONTINUOUS PILLOWCASE CUTTER 686.685-014
Corder 787.682-022
Core-Covering Sewer 787.682-058
Core Inserter 739.685-010
Cotton-Bag Clipper 789.687-030
Cotton-Bag-Cutting-Machine Offbearer 689.686-018
Cotton-Bag-Cutting-Machine Operator 686.585-010
Cotton-Bag Sewer 787.682-058
Cover Assembler 787.682-066
Cover Cutter, Machine 781.684-014
CRUSHER-AND-BINDER OPERATOR 689.685-054
crushing-mill operator 589.686-018
Curtain Cutter, Hand 781.684-074
Curtain Hemmer, Automatic 787.685-018
Curtain Inspector 789.587-014
Curtain Supervisor 787.132-010
Cushion Closer 780.682-018
Cushion-Cover Inspector 789.687-038
Cushion Filler 780.684-066
cushion sweeper 789.687-122
CUTTER 699.682-014
cutter 789.687-134
CUTTER 686.685-022
CUTTER, BARREL DRUM 690.682-026
cutter operator 530.666-010
CUTTER, ROTARY SHEAR 781.684-018
CUTTING-AND-PRINTING-MACHINE OPERATOR 652.685-022
Cutting-And-Sewing Supervisor 789.132-010
Cutting-Department Supervisor 789.132-014
CUTTING INSPECTOR 781.684-022
CUTTING-MACHINE OFFBEARER 689.686-018
cutting-machine operator 585.685-086
CUTTING-MACHINE OPERATOR 686.585-010
Daub-Color Matcher 550.382-014
Daub-Color Mixer 550.382-014
decorator, hand 782.684-018
Depth-Stretching-Machine Operator 580.685-058
die cutter 686.462-010
DIE-CUTTING-MACHINE OPERATOR, AUTOMATIC 686.462-010
Die-Cutting-Machine-Operator Helper, Automatic 586.686-022
Dishcloth Folder 589.687-014
Dish-Cloth Inspector 789.587-014
Down Filler 780.684-066
Drapery Cutter, Hand 781.684-074
Drapery Cutter, Machine 781.684-014
Drapery Hemmer, Automatic 787.685-018
Drapery Inspector 789.587-014
Drapery Room Supervisor 789.132-010
Drapery Sewer, Hand 782.684-058
Drapery Supervisor 787.132-010
DRAW-FRAME TENDER 680.685-034
DRAWSTRING KNOTTER 689.685-058
drier 581.685-034
DRUM ATTENDANT 582.685-050
drum-reel cutter 690.682-026
DRYING-UNIT-FELTING-MACHINE OPERATOR 581.685-034
DRYING-UNIT-FELTING-MACHINE-OPERATOR HELPER 581.687-018
dry-mop maker 739.687-078
Dull-Coat-Mill Operator 584.382-010
DUST-MILL OPERATOR 581.686-030
DUST-MOP MAKER 739.687-078
dye-house supervisor 582.131-014
dye-machine-tender helper 582.686-030
DYER, SUPERVISOR 582.131-014
DYE-TANK TENDER 582.685-054
Elastic Sewer 787.682-066
ELECTRIC BLANKET WIRER 789.684-054
EMBLEM DRAWER-IN 689.380-010
EMBOSSING-MACHINE OPERATOR 583.685-034
Embossing-Machine-Operator Helper 589.687-026
EMBROIDERER, HAND 782.684-018
Embroidery Supervisor 787.132-010
EMBROIDERY SUPERVISOR 689.130-010
examiner 789.687-050
Examiner-Mender 787.682-030
extractor operator 589.685-098
EXTRACTOR OPERATOR 582.685-062
extract wringer 589.685-098
EXTRUDING-MACHINE OPERATOR 557.565-010
FABRIC-COATING SUPERVISOR 589.130-014
Facer, Buffing Wheel 585.685-086
Feather Baler 920.685-010
feather-crushing-machine operator 589.686-018

FEATHER-CURLING-MACHINE OPERATOR	589.686-018
FEATHER-CUTTING-MACHINE FEEDER	585.686-010
FEATHER-DRYING-MACHINE OPERATOR	581.686-034
FEATHER-DUSTER WINDER	734.684-014
Feather Grader	929.687-062
FEATHER MIXER	589.685-050
feather renovator	589.685-082
FEATHER SEPARATOR	589.685-054
FEATHER WASHER	582.685-066
feeder tender	680.686-018
FELT CARBONIZER	586.687-010
felt-coating-and-mixing supervisor	589.130-014
FELT-CUTTING-MACHINE OPERATOR	686.682-018
Felt-Dyeing-Machine Tender	582.685-070
felter	680.685-054
felt finisher	586.685-038
Felt-Finishing Supervisor	589.130-014
FELT-GOODS SUPERVISOR, NEEDLE PROCESS	689.130-014
felting-machine operator	680.685-054
FELTING-MACHINE OPERATOR	586.662-010
FELTING-MACHINE-OPERATOR HELPER	586.686-014
FELTMAKER AND WEIGHER	586.685-022
Felt-Pad Cutter	585.687-014
FELT-STRIP FINISHER	586.685-018
FELT-WASHING-MACHINE TENDER	582.685-070
FILLER	780.684-066
filler	789.687-130
filling inspector	681.687-026
Filter-Cloth Maker	787.682-058
Finger-Buff Sewer	787.682-058
Finish-Coat-Mill Operator	584.382-010
FINISHER	789.687-050
FINISHER, HAND	789.484-014
FIRST-BREAKER FEEDER	680.686-014
First-Coat Operator	584.382-010
FISHING-LINE-WINDING-MACHINE OPERATOR	689.685-066
FISH-NET STRINGER	782.684-026
Fitted-Sheet Binder	787.682-010
flange cutter	585.685-086
FLAT DRIER	581.685-078
flexigraphic printer	651.382-026
FLOCKER	789.687-054
flower cheniller	687.682-010
FLOWER-MACHINE OPERATOR	687.682-010
FOLDER	789.687-058
folder, hand	589.687-014
FOLDING-MACHINE FEEDER	920.686-018
Formula Checker	221.387-046
frame bender	809.484-014
FRAME HAND	689.687-046
FRINGER	789.687-062
Fringer	787.682-066
fringer, hand	782.684-050
FULLING-MACHINE OPERATOR	586.382-010
Gang-Hemstitching-Machine Operator	787.685-018
GARNETTER	680.685-054
Garnett Feeder	680.686-018
Garnett Fixer	689.260-010
Garnett-Machine-Operator Helper	586.686-022
general worker	586.686-022
Gill-Net Stringer	782.684-026
Gray Mixing Operator	680.850-010
Grinding Operator	550.382-014
guillotine operator	680.686-018
Hair-Picking-Machine Operator	680.685-082
hand-booked folder and stitcher	589.687-014
handle maker	739.687-122
hands parter	689.687-018
hardening-machine operator	586.662-010
hardening-machine-operator helper	586.686-014
HARNESS-AND-BAG INSPECTOR	789.687-086
Harness Inspector	789.687-086
HARNESS RIGGER	789.687-082
HASSOCK MAKER	780.685-018
Header	787.682-026
Hem Inspector	789.687-114
Hem Marker	781.687-042
HEMMER, AUTOMATIC	787.685-018
Hemstitching-Machine Operator	787.682-058
HOOD MAKER	804.481-010
hopper feeder	680.686-018
Horizontal-Stick-Turning-Machine Operator	689.685-146
House-Furnishings Cutter, Machine	781.684-014
HYDRAULIC-PRESS OPERATOR	583.685-058
inspector and mender	782.487-010

Inspector, Canvas Products	789.587-014
Inspector, Coated Fabrics	689.685-038
INSPECTOR, FINISHING	589.387-022
installation helper	869.687-010
jacquard-lace weaver	683.682-026
JACQUARD-TWINE-POLISHER OPERATOR	583.685-062
joiner	787.682-066
Jute-Bag Clipper	789.687-030
Jute-Bag-Cutting-Machine Operator	686.585-010
Jute-Bag Sewer	787.682-058
KAPOK-AND-COTTON-MACHINE OPERATOR	689.685-082
kersey-department supervisor	689.130-014
kettle-tender helper	582.686-030
KNITTER, HAND	782.684-034
KNITTING-MACHINE OPERATOR	685.685-010
knotter	789.684-030
knotter, hand	789.684-030
Label Tacker	787.685-042
LABORER, CANVAS SHOP	789.687-090
LABORER, GENERAL	589.687-026
Lace Breaker	689.665-014
lace-machine operator	683.682-026
Lace Pinner	782.687-026
Lace Separator	689.665-014
Lace Stripper	689.665-014
LACE WINDER	685.687-018
Lacing Presser	739.685-010
LAMINATOR	584.685-034
LAUNDRY-MACHINE TENDER	589.685-066
LAY-OUT-MACHINE OPERATOR	781.684-034
lay-up presser	586.662-010
LEVERS-LACE MACHINE OPERATOR	683.682-026
Lining Sewer	787.682-066
loom operator	685.685-010
l-tacker	787.685-026
MACHINE FEEDER, RAW STOCK	680.686-018
MACHINE HELPER	586.686-022
maker-up, folding	589.687-014
MARKER	781.687-042
MARKING-MACHINE OPERATOR	652.685-050
Mender	787.682-058
mender	782.487-010
mender	789.684-038
microgrinder operator	586.685-018
mill attendant	582.685-050
MIXER I	550.685-074
MIXER II	789.687-098
mixer, pigment	550.381-010
Mixing Supervisor	589.130-014
molder	692.685-286
MOLDER, AUTOMOBILE CARPETS	692.685-286
molder-trimmer	692.685-286
MONOGRAM-AND-LETTER PASTER	789.687-102
MOP-HANDLE ASSEMBLER	739.687-122
Mophead Sewer	787.682-066
MOPHEAD TRIMMER-AND-WRAPPER	789.687-106
mop-machine operator	739.685-026
MOP MAKER	739.685-026
nailhead puncher	789.685-010
Nailhead Setter	789.685-010
napper	585.685-070
napper operator	585.685-070
NAPPER TENDER	585.685-070
NEEDLE-BOARD REPAIRER	739.684-134
NEEDLE-CONTROL CHENILLER	687.685-010
NEEDLE-FELT-MAKING-MACHINE OPERATOR	689.362-010
NEEDLE-LOOM OPERATOR	689.662-010
Needle-Loom-Operator Helper	586.686-022
NEEDLE-LOOM SETTER	689.360-010
NEEDLE-LOOM TENDER	689.685-090
needle-punch operator	687.682-014
needle setter	739.684-134
net finisher	582.685-054
net hanger	782.684-026
NET MAKER	789.684-030
NETTING INSPECTOR	782.487-010
netting machine operator	685.685-010
NYLON-HOT-WIRE CUTTER	781.684-038
OIL BOILER	543.362-010
Oiling-Machine Operator	582.685-050
OIL-SPOT WASHER	689.687-050
ORNAMENT SETTER	789.685-010
overlay operator	687.682-014
package winder	681.685-154
Padding-Machine Operator	584.685-018

PAIRER	789.687-110
Panel Sewer	787.682-066
paper twister	681.685-134
Parachute-Accessories Attacher	787.682-058
Parachute-Crown Sewer	787.682-058
Parachute-Cushion Installer	787.682-058
PARACHUTE FOLDER	789.684-034
parachute-harness rigger	789.687-082
PARACHUTE INSPECTOR	789.687-114
PARACHUTE-LINE TIER	789.687-118
PARACHUTE MARKER	789.587-018
PARACHUTE MENDER	789.684-038
Parachute-Panel Joiner	787.682-058
Parachute Taper	787.682-010
PASSEMENTERIE WORKER	782.684-050
paster	789.687-102
PATTERNMAKER	781.361-014
pattern-perforating-machine operator	781.684-042
PATTERN RULER	794.687-038
PERFORATOR	781.684-042
Picker Feeder	680.686-018
Picking-Machine-Operator Helper	586.686-022
Pillow-And-Cushion-Department Supervisor	789.132-010
Pillowcase Cleaner	689.687-050
pillowcase cutter	686.685-014
Pillowcase Folder	589.687-014
Pillowcase Sewer	787.682-026
Pillowcase Sewer, Automatic	787.685-014
PILLOWCASE TURNER	583.685-078
PILLOW CLEANER	789.687-122
Pillow Filler	780.684-066
Pin-Feather-Machine Operator	589.685-054
PINNER	782.687-026
PINNER	782.684-054
PLEATER	787.685-026
PLEATER, HAND	583.684-010
PLEAT PATTERNMAKER	781.484-010
PLEAT TAPER	789.487-010
Pot-Holder Binder	787.682-010
power-cutting-machine operator	686.682-018
prehemmer	781.684-034
PREPLEATER	686.685-046
PRESSER, BUFFING WHEEL	583.685-090
Print-Color Matcher	550.382-014
Print-Color Mixer	550.382-014
print-color operator	550.382-014
printer	652.685-022
PRINTER, PLASTIC	651.382-026
Printing Supervisor	589.130-014
Production Clerk, Lace Tearing	221.382-018
PUNCHER	689.582-010
putter-out, machine	589.685-098
QUILL-BUNCHER-AND-SORTER	734.687-066
Quill-Picking-Machine Operator	589.685-054
QUILTER FIXER	689.260-014
quilting-machine helper	689.686-010
QUILTING-MACHINE OPERATOR	689.685-106
QUILTING-MACHINE OPERATOR	584.382-014
Quilt Sewer	787.682-066
Quilt Sewer, Hand	782.684-018
QUILT STUFFER	789.687-130
QUILT STUFFER, MACHINE	689.685-102
RAG-CUTTING-MACHINE FEEDER	530.666-010
RAG-CUTTING-MACHINE TENDER	530.665-014
RAG SORTER AND CUTTER	789.687-134
RAKER, BUFFING WHEEL	589.684-010
Raw-Calender Operator	584.685-010
reeler	681.685-034
reel slitter	690.682-026
RENOVATOR-MACHINE OPERATOR	589.685-082
repairer	681.687-026
Returned-Goods Inspector	789.587-014
Reverser	789.687-182
rewinder	681.685-154
Rhinestone Setter	789.685-010
RIGGER	789.684-046
Ring Attacher	787.685-026
Ring Sewer	789.687-090
RIPPER	782.687-038
roll-calender tender	583.685-026
roll-coating-machine operator	584.562-010
roll-press operator	589.685-098
ROLL-SHEETING CUTTER	699.682-026
rope-coiling-machine operator	681.685-086
ROPE-LAYING-MACHINE OPERATOR	681.685-086

ROPE-MACHINE SETTER	681.380-010
ROPE-MAKER, ROPEWALK	681.682-014
rope-twisting-machine operator	681.685-086
round-cutter operator	585.685-086
rounder	585.685-086
ROUNDING-MACHINE OPERATOR	585.685-086
ruffler	787.685-038
Ruffling Hemmer, Automatic	787.685-018
RUG INSPECTOR	585.685-090
RUG-INSPECTOR HELPER	589.686-038
Safety-Net Maker	789.684-030
SAIL CUTTER	781.384-018
Sail Finisher, Hand	789.484-014
Sail Finisher, Machine	787.682-058
SAIL-LAY-OUT WORKER	781.381-030
Sailmaker	739.381-010
sail, tent, and awning-maker apprentice	739.381-014
SAMPLE SELECTOR	789.387-014
saturator	584.382-010
SCALLOP CUTTER, MACHINE	686.685-058
SCREEN-MACHINE OPERATOR	559.682-070
SCRUBBING-MACHINE OPERATOR	582.685-122
seamer	787.682-066
Seat-Pack Inspector	789.687-086
Second-Calender Operator	584.685-010
setter, machine	589.685-098
Sewer-And-Cutter, Finger-Buff Material	787.685-014
sewer, hand	782.684-050
SEWING MACHINE OPERATOR I	787.682-066
SEWING-MACHINE OPERATOR II	787.682-058
Sheet Cleaner	689.687-050
Sheet Cutter I	699.685-014
Sheet Cutter II	787.685-014
sheet-cutting operator	686.585-010
Sheet Folder	589.687-014
Sheet Inspector	789.587-014
Sheet Sewer	787.682-026
SHIRRING-MACHINE OPERATOR, AUTOMATIC	787.685-038
shredder picker	680.686-018
Shroud-Line Tier	789.687-118
Shroud-Web Inspector	789.687-114
SHUTTLER	689.687-070
shuttler	789.684-054
side hemmer	787.685-018
SIZING-MACHINE-AND-DRIER OPERATOR	582.665-026
Sizing-Machine-And-Drier-Operator Helper	586.686-022
Sleeping-Bag Filler	780.684-066
SLIPCOVER CUTTER	780.381-034
SLIP-COVER SEWER	780.682-014
slugger	782.684-026
softener	582.685-050
Sorter	789.685-146
SPANNER	689.687-074
SPINNING-MACHINE TENDER	681.685-110
splicer	689.682-018
SPLICING-MACHINE OPERATOR	689.682-018
SPLICING-MACHINE OPERATOR, AUTOMATIC	689.685-122
spooler	681.685-154
Spooler	689.685-014
spooler	681.685-114
SPOOLING-MACHINE OPERATOR	681.685-114
spot washer	689.687-050
STAINING-MACHINE OPERATOR	582.685-142
STAMPER I	781.687-062
STAMPER II	652.685-082
STEAMER	789.687-170
STENCILER	781.687-066
sterilizer	589.685-082
stitcher	689.685-106
STITCHER	689.682-022
Straight Cutter, Machine	699.682-030
STRAND-FORMING-MACHINE OPERATOR	681.685-118
STRETCHING-MACHINE OPERATOR	580.685-058
striker-out, machine	589.685-098
string-glue-and-printing-machine operator	689.685-138
STRINGING-MACHINE TENDER	689.585-018
stud setter	789.685-010
STUFFER	780.687-046
stuffer	780.684-066
stuffer, machine	582.685-050
superintendent, dyeing	582.131-014
Supervisor, Camp Department	787.132-010
Supervisor, Canvas Products	789.132-018
SUPERVISOR, CLOTH WINDING	689.130-022
Supervisor, Felting	586.130-010

SUPERVISOR, FOAM CUTTING 690.130-022
Supervisor, Fulling 586.130-010
SUPERVISOR I 789.132-014
SUPERVISOR II 789.134-010
SUPERVISOR III 789.132-018
SUPERVISOR IV 789.132-010
SUPERVISOR, LACE TEARING 689.134-014
SUPERVISOR, MILL 589.130-026
SUPERVISOR, MIXING 680.135-010
SUPERVISOR, PARACHUTE MANUFACTURING 789.132-026
SUPERVISOR, PLEATING 583.137-010
SUPERVISOR, PRODUCTION 589.135-010
supervisor, production 689.130-010
Supervisor, Sleeping-Bag Department 787.132-010
SUPERVISOR, STITCHING DEPARTMENT 787.132-018
SUPERVISOR V 586.130-010
SUPERVISOR VI 589.132-010
SUPERVISOR, WEBBING 789.137-014
Suspension-Cord Tier 789.687-118
TABLE-COVER FOLDER 920.687-186
table draper 782.687-026
tabler 781.684-034
table worker 734.687-014
taker-off 589.686-046
Taker-Off, Braker Machine 589.686-046
Taker-Off, Drying Kiln 589.686-046
TAKER-OFF, HEMP FIBER 589.686-046
Taker-Off, Scutcher Machine 589.686-046
tangled-yarn-spool straightener 681.687-026
Tape-Cutting-Machine Operator 686.685-066
TAPE-FOLDING-MACHINE OPERATOR 689.685-134
TAPE-MAKING-MACHINE OPERATOR 689.685-138
Taping Machine Operator 787.682-066
TARRING-MACHINE OPERATOR 584.685-046
TASSEL-MAKING-MACHINE OPERATOR 689.685-142
temperer 582.685-050
Tennis-Net Maker 789.684-030
Tent Assembler 787.682-058
Tent Finisher 789.484-014
Tentmaker 739.381-010
Terry-Cloth Cutter, Hand 781.684-074
Terry Cloth Cutter, Machine 781.684-014
TESTING-MACHINE OPERATOR 586.685-038
textile-scrap salvager 789.687-010
Thermoelectric-Heat-Sealing-Machine Operator 754.684-010
Third-Calender Operator 584.685-010
THREAD-CUTTER TENDER 689.665-014
thread drawer 789.687-174
THREADER 689.687-078
THREAD SEPARATOR 789.687-174
Tie-Back Sewer, Automatic 787.685-014
Tire-Fabric-Impregnating-Range Back-Tender 589.686-010
TIRE-FABRIC-IMPREGNATING-RANGE OPERATOR, CHIEF 589.662-014
Tire-Fabric-Impregnating-Range Tender 589.685-026
Tire-Fabric Inspector 689.685-038
TOBACCO-CLOTH RECLAIMER 589.686-050
TOP-DYEING-MACHINE LOADER 582.686-030
Towel Folder 589.687-014
Towel Inspector 789.587-014
Towel Sewer 787.682-026
Tow Feeder 680.686-014
transfer-iron operator 659.685-022
TRANSFER-MACHINE OPERATOR 659.685-022
TRAWL NET MAKER 789.381-018
trimmer 789.687-050
Trimmer, Buffing Wheel 585.685-086
TRIMMING SEWER, AUTOMATIC 787.685-050
Trimming Supervisor 589.130-014
trim operator 699.682-026
TUFT-MACHINE OPERATOR 687.682-014
tumbler-machine operator 582.685-066
turner 689.685-146
TURNING-MACHINE OPERATOR 689.685-146
twine operator 689.685-138
Twine-Reeling-Machine Operator 681.685-078
Twine Winder 681.685-154
TWISTER 681.685-126
TWISTER TENDER, PAPER 681.685-134
twisthand 683.682-026
TYING-MACHINE OPERATOR 929.685-014
VACUUM-DRIER OPERATOR 581.685-066
Valance Shirrer 787.685-038
Vertical-Stretching-Machine Operator 580.685-058
WAIST PLEATER 583.684-014
Washcloth Folder 589.687-014
WASTE CHOPPER 689.686-054
waste-cotton cleaner 680.685-114
waste duster 680.685-114
WASTE-MACHINE OFFBEARER 680.686-022
WASTE-MACHINE TENDER 680.685-114
WATCHER, AUTOMAT 689.685-150
Watcher, Automat, Frame Goods 689.685-150
Watcher, Automat, Long Goods 689.685-150
WATCHER, PANTOGRAPH 689.685-154
Waterproof-Bag-Cutting-Machine Operator 686.585-010
Waterproof-Bag Sewer 787.682-058
waterproof-material folder 789.687-058
WEAVER, TIRE CORD 683.682-050
Webbing Seamer, Pound Net 782.684-026
wet-milling-wheel operator 582.685-050
White Mixing Operator 680.685-010
willow-machine operator 680.685-114
willow-machine tender 680.685-114
winder 681.685-154
winder 681.685-114
winding-machine operator 681.685-154
winding-machine operator 681.685-114
WINDING-RACK OPERATOR 581.685-074
Winding-Rack-Operator Helper 589.687-026
Wiping-Rag Washer 361.685-018
wool-batting worker 789.687-130
wrapper 689.380-010
wringer and setter 589.685-098
WRINGER-MACHINE OPERATOR 589.685-098
YARN CLEANER 681.687-026
yarn salvager 681.687-026
YARN WINDER 681.685-154

textile—TEXTILE INDUSTRY: This designation includes occupations concerned with preparing natural fibers for processing into thread and yarn; spinning, throwing, twisting, dyeing, and finishing thread and yarn from synthetic or natural fibers; weaving natural, synthetic, or mixed yarn into fabrics; and dyeing and finishing such fabrics. Included also are all other functions performed preparatory to and incidental to such processes. The finishing processes include bleaching, drying, dyeing, mercerizing, printing, shrinking, starching, texturizing, and waterproofing. This designation covers these processes wherever they occur. Occupations concerned with the manufacture of glass fibers are included in the GLASS MANUFACTURING INDUSTRY (glass mfg.); occupations concerned with the manufacture of rubber fibers are included in the RUBBER GOODS INDUSTRY (rubber goods); and occupations concerned with the manufacture of other synthetic fibers are included in the PLASTIC AND SYNTHETIC MATERIALS INDUSTRY (plastic-synth.). Occupations concerned with processes that are considered peculiar to the manufacture of narrow fabrics are included in the NARROW FABRICS INDUSTRY (narrow fabrics).

Acid-Bath Mixer 550.585-018
Acid-Strength Inspector 582.587-010
Acid-Washer Operator 582.685-030
AGER OPERATOR 582.585-010
AGING-DEPARTMENT SUPERVISOR 582.132-010
Alley Cleaner 381.687-018
alley tender 680.665-018
alley tender 680.685-018
Ammonia-Solution Preparer 550.585-018
attenuator 680.585-014
AUTOCLAVE OPERATOR 587.682-010
automatic-silk-screen printer 652.682-018
backer and bander, cloth 920.587-010
backfiller 589.665-014
Back-Gray-Cloth Washer 582.685-030
Back Sizer 589.665-014
BACK TENDER 589.686-010
BACK TENDER, CLOTH PRINTING 652.685-010
BACK WASHER 582.685-010
back winder 681.685-154
BAGGING SALVAGER 689.687-010
bale-breaker operator 680.685-070
bale coverer 782.687-018
Bale Piler 929.687-030
baller tender 681.685-010
BALLING-MACHINE OPERATOR 681.685-014
ball-thread-machine tender 681.685-010
BALL-WARPER TENDER 681.685-010
ball winder 681.685-014
ball winder 681.685-010
battery filler 683.686-010
battery hand 683.686-010

BATTERY LOADER	683.686-010
BATTING-MACHINE OPERATOR	680.585-010
beam doffer	681.686-010
beam dyer	582.685-102
BEAM-DYER OPERATOR	582.685-014
Beam Dyer, Recessed Vat	582.685-014
BEAMER	681.585-010
beamer hand	681.685-058
BEAMER HELPER	681.686-014
beaming-machine operator	681.685-058
BEAM RACKER	681.686-010
beam warper	681.685-018
BEAM-WARPER TENDER, AUTOMATIC	681.685-018
beck tender	582.665-014
BINDER AND BOX BUILDER	628.684-010
binder fixer	628.684-010
Binding Cutter	686.685-066
BINDING PRINTER	652.685-014
bin piler	589.685-074
bleacher	582.685-102
BLEACH-RANGE OPERATOR	582.685-018
BLENDING-MACHINE OPERATOR	680.685-010
BLOWER FEEDER, DYED RAW STOCK	581.686-010
Blow-Machine Tender, Starch Spraying	582.685-138
Blunger Loader	929.687-030
BOBBIN CLEANER, HAND	689.687-014
BOBBIN-CLEANING-MACHINE OPERATOR	689.686-014
bobbin fixer	681.687-026
Bobbin Handler	929.687-030
bobbin salvager	922.687-018
BOBBIN SORTER	922.687-018
bobbin-stripper	689.686-014
Bobbin Winder	681.685-154
BOBBIN WINDER, MACHINE	681.585-014
BOBBIN WINDER, SEWING MACHINE	681.685-026
Boiling-Off Winder	689.685-046
BOIL-OFF-MACHINE OPERATOR, CLOTH	582.685-022
BONDING-MACHINE SETTER	589.360-010
BONDING-MACHINE TENDER	589.665-010
book folder	589.687-014
BREAKER-MACHINE TENDER	583.685-010
breaker operator	680.685-070
brusher and shearer	585.685-102
brushing operator	585.685-070
BRUSH OPERATOR	587.685-010
Brush Washer	599.687-030
bulking-machine operator	689.685-158
burlapper	929.687-042
burlapper	782.687-018
BURLER	689.684-010
button-breaker operator	583.685-010
Cake Winder	681.685-154
CALENDER OPERATOR	583.685-026
calender tender	583.685-026
CAN DOFFER	680.686-010
can-drier operator	581.685-022
can pusher	680.686-010
cans operator	581.685-022
can tender	581.685-022
CANVAS SHRINKER	587.687-010
CARBONIZER	581.585-010
CARD CHANGER, JACQUARD LOOM	683.685-014
Card Cleaner	699.687-014
CARD CLOTHIER	628.381-010
card-cutter helper	689.587-010
CARD CUTTER, JACQUARD	683.582-010
Card Doffer	680.686-010
carder	680.685-050
card fixer	680.380-010
Card Fixer	689.260-010
card-gill tender	680.685-058
CARD GRINDER	680.380-010
CARD GRINDER HELPER	680.684-010
card hand	680.685-018
card hanger	683.685-014
carding doubler	680.685-086
carding doubler	680.685-094
Carding-Machine Feeder	680.686-018
CARD LACER, JACQUARD	683.685-018
card operator	680.685-018
CARDROOM WORKER	term
card setter	680.380-010
CARD STRIPPER	680.685-014
CARD TENDER	680.685-018
carrier loader	589.687-062
Caustic Mixer	550.585-018
Caustic-Strength Inspector	582.587-010
CHAIN BUILDER, LOOM CONTROL	683.381-010
chainer	683.381-010
chain maker, loom control	683.381-010
chain pegger	683.381-010
chain splitter	683.381-010
CHECKER	221.587-010
chemical checker	582.587-010
CHEMICAL MIXER	550.585-018
CHEMICAL-STRENGTH TESTER	582.587-010
chenille-machine operator	687.685-018
CHINCHILLA-MACHINE OPERATOR	585.685-022
CHOPPED-STRAND OPERATOR	680.685-022
chopper feeder	680.685-102
CLARIFYING-PLANT OPERATOR	955.382-010
CLOTH-BALE HEADER	782.687-018
Cloth Baler	920.685-010
cloth beamer	689.685-046
Cloth-Bin Packer	922.687-058
Cloth-Bleaching-Range Back-Tender	589.686-010
Cloth-Bleaching-Range Operator, Chief	589.562-010
Cloth-Bleaching-Range Tender	589.685-026
Cloth-Bleaching Supervisor	589.130-010
CLOTH-BOLT BANDER	920.587-010
Cloth-Brushing-And-Sueding Supervisor	589.130-010
cloth classer	689.387-010
Cloth-Colors Examiner	781.687-014
Cloth-Cutting Inspector	781.687-014
Cloth-Desizing-Range Operator, Chief	589.562-010
Cloth-Desizing-Range Tender	589.685-026
CLOTH DOFFER	689.686-058
CLOTH-DOUBLING-AND-WINDING-MACHINE OPERATOR	689.685-050
cloth drier	589.686-010
cloth-dry-can operator	581.685-022
Cloth-Dyeing-Range Operator, Chief	589.562-010
Cloth-Dyeing-Range Tender	589.685-026
cloth dyer	582.665-014
cloth dyer	582.582-010
CLOTH-EDGE SINGER	585.687-018
CLOTH EXAMINER, HAND	781.687-014
CLOTH EXAMINER, MACHINE	689.685-038
CLOTH FEEDER	589.686-014
CLOTH FINISHER	589.130-010
Cloth-Finishing-Range Back-Tender	589.686-010
CLOTH-FINISHING-RANGE OPERATOR	589.665-014
CLOTH-FINISHING-RANGE OPERATOR, CHIEF	589.562-010
CLOTH-FINISHING-RANGE TENDER	589.685-026
CLOTH FOLDER	term
CLOTH FOLDER, HAND	589.687-014
cloth folder, machine	689.585-014
cloth folder, machine	689.685-078
CLOTH FRAMER	689.687-026
CLOTH GRADER	689.387-010
CLOTH-GRADER SUPERVISOR	689.134-010
cloth handler	689.686-058
Cloth Hauler	929.687-030
cloth inspector	683.684-034
cloth inspector	689.685-038
Cloth-Laminating Supervisor	589.130-010
cloth layer-out	781.687-038
CLOTH MEASURER, MACHINE	589.685-022
Cloth-Mercerizer Back-Tender	589.686-010
CLOTH-MERCERIZER OPERATOR	584.685-014
Cloth-Mercerizing Supervisor	589.130-010
Cloth-Napping Supervisor	589.130-010
Cloth Neutralizer	582.685-030
cloth opener, hand	589.685-090
cloth picker	689.684-010
cloth presser	584.685-042
CLOTH-PRINTING INSPECTOR	652.567-010
CLOTH REELER	689.685-042
cloth-roll winder	689.685-046
CLOTH SANDER	581.685-010
Cloth-Seconds Sorter	789.687-146
CLOTH SHADER	582.685-026
cloth shearer	585.685-102
Cloth-Shearing Supervisor	589.130-010
cloth shrinker	587.685-018
CLOTH-SHRINKING-MACHINE OPERATOR	587.685-018
CLOTH-SHRINKING-MACHINE-OPERATOR HELPER	587.686-010
Cloth-Shrinking Supervisor	589.130-010
CLOTH-SHRINKING TESTER	587.384-010
cloth sponger	587.685-018

CLOTH SPREADER, SCREEN PRINTING 652.687-010
CLOTH-STOCK SORTER 789.687-034
cloth stretcher 580.685-066
CLOTH TESTER 029.381-010
CLOTH TESTER, QUALITY 689.384-010
Cloth Trimmer, Hand 781.687-070
CLOTH TRIMMER, MACHINE 585.685-026
Cloth-Washer Back-Tender 589.686-010
CLOTH-WASHER OPERATOR 582.685-030
CLOTH WINDER 689.685-046
COATER 584.682-010
COATER HELPER 584.665-010
COATING-AND-EMBOSSING-UNIT OPERATOR 583.682-010
cold-water machine operator 587.685-018
COLOR CHECKER, ROVING OR YARN 582.387-010
COLOR DIPPER 652.687-014
COLOR MIXER .... term
color-mixer assistant 550.687-014
COLOR-PASTE MIXER 550.685-038
COLOR STRAINER 550.687-014
Color-Straining-Bag Washer 361.685-018
Comber Fixer 689.260-010
COMBER TENDER 680.685-118
combining-machine operator 584.682-014
compounder 550.585-018
CONDITIONER TENDER 587.685-022
conditioning-room worker 587.685-022
cone inspector 681.687-030
coner 681.685-098
Cone Winder 681.685-154
CONTINUOUS-CRUSHER OPERATOR 586.685-014
continuous-yarn dyeing-machine operator 582.685-158
cop breaker 689.686-014
copper-roller handler, printing 652.385-010
Cop Winder 681.685-154
CORDUROY-BRUSHER OPERATOR 585.685-034
CORDUROY-CUTTER OPERATOR 585.565-010
COTTON CLASSER 429.387-010
cotton grader 429.387-010
COTTON SAMPLER 922.687-042
COVERING-MACHINE OPERATOR 681.685-038
COVERING-MACHINE-OPERATOR HELPER 681.685-042
CRABBER 582.685-038
Creel Cleaner 699.687-014
crimping-machine operator 589.686-034
CRIMPING-MACHINE OPERATOR 680.685-030
CRIMP SETTER 680.685-026
curing oven tender 581.685-030
curling-machine operator 585.685-022
CUTTING-MACHINE FIXER 585.380-010
cutting-machine operator 585.565-010
CYLINDER BATCHER 582.665-010
cylinder dyer 582.685-014
DECATING-MACHINE OPERATOR 582.685-042
Desizing-Machine Back-Tender 589.686-010
desizing-machine offbearer 589.686-010
DESIZING-MACHINE OPERATOR, HEAD-END 582.685-046
desizing-pad operator 582.685-046
DETACKER 589.685-030
devil tender 680.685-050
die cutter 686.462-010
DIE-CUTTING-MACHINE OPERATOR, AUTOMATIC 686.462-010
DIPPER 589.687-018
dobby-loom chain-pegger 689.687-054
Dobby-Loom Fixer 683.260-018
DOFFER 689.686-022
doubler 681.685-046
doubling-and-rolling-machine operator 689.685-050
doubling-machine operator 689.685-050
DOUBLING-MACHINE OPERATOR 681.685-046
draft-roller picker 680.687-014
drawer 683.684-014
drawer 680.685-038
Drawer-In, Dobby Loom 683.684-014
DRAWER-IN, HAND 683.684-014
DRAWER-IN HELPER, HAND 683.687-010
Drawer-In, Jacquard Loom 683.684-014
Drawer-In, Plain Loom 683.684-014
DRAWER-IN, STITCH-BONDING MACHINE 689.684-014
DRAWING-FRAME TENDER 680.685-038
drawing-in hand 683.684-014
DRAWING-IN-MACHINE TENDER 683.682-018
DRAWING-IN-MACHINE-TENDER HELPER 683.685-022
drawing tender 680.685-038
draw-in hand 683.684-014
DRESSER TENDER 681.682-010
drier operator 581.685-026
drier tender 581.685-022
drier tender 580.685-066
DROP-WIRE ALIGNER 689.685-062
DROP-WIRE BUILDER 689.687-034
DROP-WIRE HANGER 683.687-014
drop-wire stringer 689.687-034
Dry-Cans Back-Tender 589.686-010
DRY-CANS OPERATOR 581.685-022
dry folder, cloth 589.685-058
Drying-Machine Back-Tender 589.686-010
drying-machine operator 581.685-054
DRYING-MACHINE OPERATOR, PACKAGE YARNS 581.685-026
drying-machine receiver 589.686-010
drying machine tender 581.685-022
drying-machine tender 589.686-010
drying-machine tender 580.685-066
DRYING-MACHINE TENDER 581.685-030
dry-slasher tender 681.585-010
DYE AUTOMATION OPERATOR 582.362-014
dye-beck-reel operator 582.665-014
DYED-YARN OPERATOR 582.685-058
dye feeder 582.582-010
dye-house supervisor 582.131-014
Dyeing-Machine Back-Tender 589.686-010
dyeing-machine feeder 582.582-010
dyeing-machine tender 582.685-102
dye-machine tender 582.685-130
dye-machine-tender helper 582.686-030
dye-padder operator 582.685-106
dye-range feeder 582.582-010
DYE-RANGE OPERATOR, CLOTH 582.582-010
DYE-REEL OPERATOR 582.665-014
DYE-REEL-OPERATOR HELPER 582.686-014
dye-room helper 582.686-014
DYER, SUPERVISOR 582.131-014
DYE-STAND LOADER 589.687-062
dye-tub operator 582.665-014
dye-winch operator 582.665-014
elastic-yarn twister 681.685-038
elastic-yarn-twister helper 681.685-042
ELECTRIFIER OPERATOR 585.685-042
END FINDER, FORMING DEPARTMENT 681.687-010
END FINDER, TWISTING DEPARTMENT 689.687-042
endless-belt finisher 782.684-062
Endless-Steamer Tender 582.585-010
Ends-Down Checker 221.367-034
engraved-roller inspector 979.381-026
EXTRACTOR OPERATOR 581.685-042
Extractor Tender, Raw Stock 581.685-038
fabric inspector 781.687-014
FABRIC-LAY-OUT WORKER 589.687-022
feeder tender 680.686-018
fiber-drier operator 581.685-046
Filling Hauler, Weaving 929.687-030
filling inspector 681.687-026
filling inspector 681.687-030
filling separator 689.687-086
filling sorter and hauler 689.687-086
filling winder 681.685-074
final inspector 689.685-038
finished-cloth checker 781.687-014
Finished-Cloth Examiner 689.685-038
finished-yarn examiner 681.687-030
finished-yarn examiner 689.687-082
FINISHER-CARD TENDER 680.685-042
Finishing-Range Feeder 589.686-014
finishing-range operator 589.665-014
finishing range supervisor 589.562-010
finishing supervisor 589.130-010
fixer 683.260-018
fixer 689.260-010
FLAT CLOTHIER 628.382-010
flat-folding-machine operator 689.585-014
float remover 689.685-094
FLOOR WINDER 681.685-050
flyer builder 628.687-010
FLYER REPAIRER 628.687-010
foaming machine operator 584.685-030
folded-cloth taper 920.587-010
folder, hand 589.687-014
folder, machine 689.585-014
folder operator 589.685-058
FOLDING-MACHINE OPERATOR 589.685-058

napper operator	585.685-070
NAPPER TENDER	585.685-070
NEEDLE-PUNCH-MACHINE OPERATOR	689.682-014
NEEDLE-PUNCH-MACHINE-OPERATOR HELPER	689.686-034
Novelty-Printing-Machine Operator	652.382-010
Novelty-Twister Tender	681.685-130
Nub-Card Tender	680.686-018
NUMBERER AND WIRER	689.587-010
OIL-SPOT WASHER	689.687-050
OPEN-DEVELOPER OPERATOR	582.685-098
OPENER TENDER	680.685-070
Opening-Machine Cleaner	699.687-014
opening-machine tender	680.685-070
open-tenter operator	580.685-066
oven-drier tender	581.685-026
OVERHAULER	628.261-010
OVERHAULER HELPER	628.664-010
OVERHEAD CLEANER MAINTAINER	628.684-022
overseer	789.222-010
PACKAGE CRIMPER	589.686-034
package drier	581.685-026
PACKAGE-DYEING-MACHINE OPERATOR	582.685-102
package dyer	582.685-102
package-dye-stand loader	589.687-062
package winder	681.685-154
padder	589.687-030
padding-machine operator	587.685-018
PADDING-MACHINE OPERATOR	582.685-106
PAD MAKER	589.687-030
PANELBOARD OPERATOR	582.362-010
PASTER, SCREEN PRINTING	652.687-026
patch developer	582.685-110
PATCH FINISHER	582.684-010
PATCH WASHER	582.685-110
PATTERN-CHAIN MAKER SUPERVISOR	683.132-010
pattern changer and repairer	683.685-014
PATTERN DUPLICATOR	683.685-026
pattern hanger	683.685-014
PATTERN-LEASE INSPECTOR	683.384-010
PEGGER, DOBBY LOOMS	689.687-054
percher	689.685-038
perch-machine inspector	689.685-038
piano-machine operator	683.582-010
picker	680.685-074
Picker Feeder	680.686-018
PICKER TENDER	680.685-074
PICK-PULLING-MACHINE OPERATOR	689.685-094
PICK REMOVER	689.687-058
PICK-UP OPERATOR	689.685-098
piece-dyeing-machine tender	582.665-014
piece-dye worker	582.665-014
Piece-Goods Packer	920.587-018
Piece Hand	681.685-154
pilot	582.685-130
Pin Cleaner	699.687-014
pin-drafting-machine operator	680.685-058
pin-machine tender	680.685-058
pin-tenter operator	580.685-066
Pirn Winder	681.685-154
plaiter	589.685-074
PLEATER	589.685-074
pleating-machine operator	589.685-086
Plisse-Machine Operator	652.382-010
Plisse-Machine Operator Helper	652.686-010
PLUSH WEAVER	683.682-030
port drier	581.685-026
PRECISE WINDER	681.685-066
presetter operator	587.685-018
PRESS FEEDER	583.686-030
PRESS OPERATOR	583.685-086
PRINTING-ROLLER HANDLER	652.385-010
PROCESS CONTROLLER	689.364-014
PRODUCT TESTER, FIBERGLASS	589.384-010
QUALITY CONT. CHECKER, TEXTURING PROCESS	681.387-010
quill cleaner	689.686-014
quill cleaner, hand	689.687-014
quill-cleaning-machine operator	689.686-014
quiller	681.685-074
quiller hand	681.685-074
Quiller-Machine Fixer	689.260-010
QUILLER OPERATOR	681.685-070
quiller tender	681.685-074
QUILLING-MACHINE OPERATOR, AUTOMATIC	681.685-074
quill inspector	681.687-030
quill-machine tender	681.685-070

quill skinner	689.686-014
quill stripper	689.686-014
Rack Cleaner	699.687-014
range feeder	589.686-014
range operator	589.562-010
Rapier-Insertion Loom Fixer	683.260-018
RAW-SILK GRADER	689.687-062
RAW-STOCK-DRIER TENDER	581.685-046
Raw-Stock-Dyeing-Machine Tender	582.685-102
RAW-STOCK-MACHINE LOADER	582.686-018
rebeamer	681.585-010
Rechecker	689.685-038
RECORD CLERK	206.387-022
Redraw Operator	681.685-154
reed cleaner	699.687-010
reed cleaner	628.484-010
reed maker	628.484-010
reed polisher	628.484-010
REED REPAIRER	628.484-010
reeler	681.685-078
Reeling-And-Tubing-Machine Operator	689.685-046
reeling-machine operator	689.685-042
REELING-MACHINE OPERATOR	681.685-078
reel tender	681.685-078
REMNANTS CUTTER	789.687-150
REMNANT SORTER	789.687-146
repairer	681.687-026
repeater operator	683.685-026
RETURNED-GOODS SORTER	922.687-086
rewinder	681.685-154
RIBBON-LAP-MACHINE TENDER	680.685-086
roll-calender tender	583.685-026
ROLL COVERER, BURLAP	929.687-042
roller	689.685-046
ROLLER CHECKER	682.684-010
ROLLER CLEANER	680.687-014
ROLLER COVERER	628.682-010
Roller Inspector	979.381-026
roller inspector and mender	979.381-026
roller maker	628.682-010
roller-presser operator	583.686-030
roller printer	652.582-014
ROLLER REPAIRER	979.381-026
roller-shop worker	628.682-010
ROLLING-DOWN-MACHINE OPERATOR	589.685-086
rolling-machine operator	689.685-046
ROLLING-MACHINE OPERATOR	585.685-078
roll picker	680.687-014
roll tester	652.685-090
ROPE CLEANER	699.687-022
ROPE-SILICA-MACHINE OPERATOR	582.685-114
ROTARY-SCREEN-PRINTING-MACHINE OPERATOR	652.582-014
roving changer	689.686-026
roving-frame tender	681.685-106
ROVING SIZER	680.367-010
Roving Stock Handler	929.687-030
roving technician	589.384-010
roving tender	680.685-098
roving tester, laboratory	689.384-014
ROVING-WEIGHT GAUGER	680.687-018
ROVING WINDER, FIBERGLASS	681.485-010
rubber coverer	681.685-038
rubber-covering-machine operator	681.685-038
sack-cleaning hand	689.687-010
Salvage Winder	681.685-154
SAMPLE CHECKER	229.687-010
SAMPLE CLERK	789.587-026
Sample Cutter	699.685-014
sampler	922.687-042
SAMPLE-ROOM SUPERVISOR	299.137-018
sample steamer	582.685-110
sample supervisor	299.137-018
Sample Weaver	683.682-038
sander	581.685-010
sanding machine operator	581.685-010
scouring-machine operator	589.662-010
SCOURING-TRAIN OPERATOR	589.662-010
Scouring-Train Operator, Chief	589.662-010
SCREEN MAKER, TEXTILE	971.381-046
SCREEN PRINTER	979.684-030
SCREEN-PRINTING-MACHINE OPERATOR	652.682-018
SCREEN-PRINTING-MACHINE-OPERATOR HELPER	652.686-038
SCUTCHER TENDER	589.685-090
SECOND HAND	term
seconds grader	689.387-010

tinware

tinware—TINWARE AND OTHER METAL CANS AND CONTAINERS INDUSTRY: This designation includes occupations concerned with manufacturing and repairing metal cans, such as tin cans and aluminum cans; and metal shipping containers, such as barrels, drums, kegs, and pails, except pressed tinware.

AUTOMATIC STACKER 619.686-010
Bag Sealer 709.686-010
bail attacher 703.685-010
Body Maker 616.685-042
BODY-MAKER-MACHINE SETTER 616.360-010
can-line examiner 709.367-010
Can-Reforming-Machine Operator 709.686-010
can-repairer 709.587-014
Can Stacker 709.686-010
can technician 709.367-010
can tester 703.685-014
Cleaner 709.686-010
coating mixer 509.485-010
COMPOUND-COATING-MACHINE OFFBEARER 509.666-010
COMPOUND MIXER 509.485-010
Doper Operator 741.687-018
end packer 509.666-010
INSPECTOR, METAL CAN 709.367-010
kinker 703.685-010
LABORER, TIN CAN 709.686-010
LITHOGRAPHED-PLATE INSPECTOR 651.687-010
LITHOGRAPH-PRESS OPERATOR, TINWARE 651.382-014
NAILER 739.687-126
PAIL BAILER 703.685-010
pail tester 703.685-014
PRESS FEEDER 652.685-058
Production Mechanic, Tin Cans 616.260-014
Seaming-Machine Operator 619.685-046
SLITTER SERVICE AND SETTER 615.280-010
snapper-on 703.685-010
SPOILAGE WORKER 709.587-014
SPRAY-MACHINE TENDER 599.685-090
SUPERVISOR, METAL CANS 703.132-010
TESTING-MACHINE OPERATOR 703.685-014
TIN STACKER 922.687-098

tobacco—TOBACCO INDUSTRY: This designation includes occupations concerned with stemming tobacco and manufacturing cigarettes, cigars, chewing tobacco, smoking tobacco, and snuff. Occupations concerned with the manufacture of cigarettes from vegetable substances are also included in this designation.

AUTOMATIC LUMP MAKING MACHINE TENDER 529.685-014
AUTO ROLLER 529.685-010
Bag-Filler-Machine Operator 920.685-098
BANDER-AND-CELLOPHANER HELPER, MACHINE 920.686-010
BANDER-AND-CELLOPHANER, MACHINE 920.685-014
BANDER, HAND 920.685-030
banding-and-cellophane-wrapping-machine-operator helper 920.686-010
binder 790.684-010
BINDER-AND-WRAPPER PACKER 922.687-014
Binder Caser 522.687-026
BINDER CUTTER, HAND 521.687-014
BINDER LAYER 529.685-018
binder roller 790.684-010
BINDER SELECTOR 521.687-018
binder sorter 521.687-018
Binder Stripper, Hand 521.687-134
Binder Stripper, Machine 521.687-334
BIN FILLER 922.687-010
bin packer 922.687-010
BLENDER 520.387-010
BLENDER LABORER 520.687-010
BLENDER, SNUFF 520.685-022
BLENDING-LINE ATTENDANT 520.685-026
BLENDING SUPERVISOR 520.136-010
BOOKING PRIZER 216.462-010
BULKER 522.687-018
BULKER, CUT TOBACCO 529.685-034
Bull-Gang Supervisor 922.137-018
BULL-GANG WORKER 922.687-026
bunch breaker 790.684-010
bunch-breaker-machine operator 529.685-038
buncher, hand 790.684-010
buncher, machine 529.685-038
BUNCH MAKER, HAND 790.684-010
BUNCH MAKER, MACHINE 529.685-038
BUNCH TRIMMER, MOLD 521.687-026
bundle shaker 521.687-110
BUNDLES HANGER 529.686-010
BUTT MAKER 529.685-042
can feeder 920.686-030
CAN FILLER 922.687-030

Can-Filling-Machine Operator 920.685-098
carrier blower 529.687-194
carrier washer 529.687-194
CARTON-COUNTER FEEDER 921.686-010
carton filler 920.687-130
CARTON INSPECTOR 920.687-070
CARTON-PACKAGING-MACHINE OPERATOR 920.665-010
carton searcher 920.687-070
case packer 920.687-130
CASE PACKER AND SEALER 920.685-038
caser helper 522.687-030
case sealer 920.687-130
CASING-FLUID TENDER 520.685-054
CASING-MACHINE OPERATOR 522.685-030
CASING-MATERIAL WEIGHER 520.687-026
casing mixer 520.687-026
casing wetter 522.687-026
casing-wringer operator 522.685-106
CATCHER, FILTER TIP 529.666-010
catcher, plug 529.666-010
catching inspector 529.567-010
cellophane-wrapping examiner 920.667-010
cheese cutter 521.685-298
chute feeder 529.686-038
cigar bander, hand 920.687-030
CIGAR BRANDER 920.685-046
cigarette and assembly-machine inspector ... 529.666-014
cigarette and assembly machine operator ... 529.685-066
CIGARETTE-AND-FILTER CHIEF INSPECTOR 529.367-010
Cigarette-Boxing-Machine Operator 920.665-010
Cigarette-Carton Sealer 920.685-074
cigarette examiner 529.567-010
CIGARETTE-FILTER-MAKING-MACHINE OPERATOR ... 529.685-062
CIGARETTE INSPECTOR 529.567-010
cigarette-making examiner 529.567-010
CIGARETTE-MAKING-MACHINE CATCHER 529.666-014
CIGARETTE-MAKING-MACHINE-HOPPER FEEDER 529.686-018
CIGARETTE-MAKING-MACHINE OPERATOR 529.685-066
CIGARETTE-PACKAGE EXAMINER 920.667-010
CIGARETTE-PACKING-MACHINE OPERATOR 920.685-050
CIGARETTE TESTER 529.387-014
cigar-head holer 529.685-058
cigar-head pegger 529.685-058
cigar-head perforator 529.685-058
CIGAR-HEAD PIERCER 529.685-058
cigar-head puncher 529.685-058
cigar-head stringer 529.685-058
CIGAR INSPECTOR 529.687-042
CIGAR MAKER 790.684-014
CIGAR MAKER, LONG-FILLER MACHINE ...... term
CIGAR PACKER 790.687-014
cigar packer and grader 790.687-014
cigar packer and picker 790.687-014
cigar packer and shader 790.687-014
cigar packer and sorter 790.687-014
cigar-packing examiner 529.687-042
cigar patcher 790.684-018
cigar roller 790.684-022
cigar sorter 790.687-014
Cigar-Tobacco Rehandler 522.687-026
CIGAR-WRAPPER TENDER, AUTOMATIC 529.685-286
conditioning-machine operator 522.682-010
container-packer operator 920.685-038
conveyor feeder 529.686-038
COOKER, CASING 520.685-082
COOKING, CASING, AND DRYING SUPERVISOR 529.135-010
crusher operator 521.685-330
Cut-Plug Packer 920.687-130
DEFECTIVE-CIGARETTE SLITTER 529.685-090
DISTRIBUTOR-CLEANER 529.687-070
drying-oven tender 523.685-118
DRYING-ROOM ATTENDANT 523.587-014
embossing clerk 529.567-014
FEEDER-CATCHER, TOBACCO 529.686-038
filler blender 520.687-030
FILLER FEEDER 529.686-042
filler-leaf cutter, long 521.687-014
FILLER MIXER 520.687-030
filler opener 521.687-110
Filler Picker 521.687-098
FILLER ROOM ATTENDANT 522.687-022
filler shaker 521.687-110
FILLER-SHREDDER HELPER 529.687-078
FILLER SHREDDER, MACHINE 529.685-110
filler-shredding-machine loader 529.687-078

tobacco

filler-sifter helper	529.687-078
filler sifter, machine	529.685-110
FILLER SPREADER	521.687-046
filler stemmer, hand	521.687-134
Filter-Cigarette-Making-Machine Operator	529.685-066
final cigar and box examiner	529.687-042
finished-cigar maker	790.684-014
flavoring-machine operator	522.685-030
flavoring maker	520.685-054
flavor maker	520.685-082
floor hand	529.687-070
FLOOR-SPACE ALLOCATOR	222.367-030
fluoroscope operator	529.685-274
FRESH-WORK INSPECTOR	529.687-090
fresh-work wrapper-layer	529.685-266
Frog Shaker	521.687-110
Granulated-Tobacco Screener	521.685-270
granulating blender	520.387-010
GRANULATING-MACHINE OPERATOR	521.685-158
granulator operator	521.685-158
Green-Prize Packer	920.687-142
hand roller	790.687-030
hand shaker	521.687-110
hands hanger	529.686-010
hands-size sorter	920.687-142
head-out worker	920.687-110
Hogshead Dumper	929.687-030
hogshead filler	920.687-142
hogshead hand	920.687-102
HOGSHEAD INSPECTOR	529.367-014
hogshead liner	920.687-110
HOGSHEAD OPENER	920.687-102
hogshead packer	920.687-142
hogshead-press operator	920.685-062
hogshead roller	922.687-026
Hogshead-Stock Clerk	222.387-058
hogshead stripper	920.687-102
hogshead unpacker	920.687-102
hogshead wrecker	920.687-102
hopper feeder	529.686-038
HUMIDIFIER ATTENDANT	950.485-010
humidifier-maintenance worker	950.485-010
humid-system operator	950.485-010
HYDRAULIC-PRESS OPERATOR	920.685-062
INSPECTOR, FILTER TIP	529.667-010
inspector, plug seam	529.667-010
KNIFE CHANGER	638.684-010
knife setter	638.684-010
lamina searcher	521.687-098
leaf binner	922.687-010
leaf blender	520.387-010
LEAF CONDITIONER	522.687-026
LEAF-CONDITIONER HELPER	522.687-026
LEAF-SIZE PICKER	529.687-142
LEAF SORTER	529.687-134
leaf stemmer, hand	521.687-134
LEAF TIER	529.687-138
leaf tinner	922.687-010
LINE-OUT WORKER I	920.687-110
LINE-OUT WORKER II	920.687-114
LINER INSERTER	929.687-026
load-out worker	922.687-026
long-filler-cigar roller, machine	529.685-266
loose-hand packer	920.687-142
LUMP INSPECTOR	790.687-018
lump receiver	790.687-018
Machine Adjuster	638.281-014
making-machine catcher	529.666-014
making-machine operator, filter	529.685-066
MARKER, COMPANY	529.567-014
MOISTURE-MACHINE TENDER	529.685-170
MOISTURE-METER OPERATOR	529.687-162
moisture-test puller	529.587-022
mold carrier	790.687-022
MOLD PRESSER	790.687-022
ODD BUNDLE WORKER	529.687-166
ordering-box operator	522.682-014
ORDERING-MACHINE OPERATOR	522.682-014
out-and-out cigar maker, hand	790.684-014
overshot operator	522.685-030
package reinspector	920.667-010
Packaging-Machine-Supplies Distributor	929.687-010
packaging operator	920.685-050
PACKER	920.687-130
packer	920.687-142

PACKER OPERATOR, AUTOMATIC	920.685-082
packing-and-stamping machine operator	920.685-098
PACKING-FLOOR WORKER	920.686-026
PACKING-MACHINE CAN FEEDER	920.686-030
Packing-Machine Feeder	529.686-038
packing-machine inspector	920.665-010
packing-machine inspector	920.667-010
PACKING-MACHINE-PILOT CAN ROUTER	920.685-086
packing-machine relief-operator-and-salvager see RELIEF WORKER	
packing presser	920.686-050
patcher	790.684-018
PATCH WORKER	790.684-018
PICKER	521.687-098
pilot-can router	920.685-086
plug-cutter	529.685-182
plug-cutting-and-wrapping-machine operator	529.685-182
PLUG-CUTTING-MACHINE OPERATOR	529.685-182
plug-making operator	529.685-062
PLUG-OVERWRAP-MACHINE TENDER	529.685-186
PLUG SHAPER, HAND	520.687-050
PLUG SHAPER, MACHINE	520.686-034
Pouch-Making-Machine Operator	920.685-098
PRESS MACHINE FEEDER	529.686-066
press operator, automatic	920.685-082
prize jacker	920.685-062
PRIZER	920.687-142
racker	529.687-090
RACK LOADER I	529.686-074
Rack Loader II	529.686-038
REDRYING-MACHINE OPERATOR	522.662-014
REJECT OPENER	790.687-026
reject opener and filler	790.687-026
RELIEF WORKER	term
reroller, hand	790.684-018
RESERVE OPERATOR	529.685-206
RIDDLER OPERATOR	521.685-270
ripper operator	529.685-090
roller	922.687-010
ROLLER, HAND	790.684-022
roller operator	521.685-330
Sample Driller	529.587-022
sample puller	529.587-022
Scrap-Bunch Maker	529.685-038
scrap cutter, machine	529.685-110
scrap-filler-cigar roller, machine	529.685-270
scrap picker	521.687-098
scrap preparer	520.687-030
Scrap Sorter	521.687-098
Scrap Stripper, Hand	521.687-134
searcher	521.687-098
Seed And Havana-Scrap Preparer	520.687-030
selector	529.687-134
selector	529.687-090
SHAKER	521.687-110
shape hand	520.687-050
short-filler-bunch-machine operator	529.685-038
Shorts Sifter	521.685-270
shredded-filler cigar-maker, machine	529.685-270
shredded-filler-cutter operator	529.685-110
SHREDDED-FILLER HOPPER-FEEDER	529.687-182
shredded-filler-machine wrapper-layer	529.685-270
shredding-machine-knife changer	638.684-010
shredding-machine operator	521.685-338
SILO OPERATOR	529.682-030
slice-cutting-machine operator	521.685-298
slice-cutting-machine-operator helper	521.686-054
SLICE-PLUG-CUTTER OPERATOR	521.685-298
SLICE-PLUG-CUTTER-OPERATOR HELPER	521.686-054
slitting-machine feeder	529.685-090
SMOKING-TOBACCO-CUTTER OPERATOR	521.685-310
Smoking-Tobacco Packer, Hand	920.687-130
Smoking-Tobacco-Packing-Machine Hand	920.685-098
SNUFF-BOX FINISHER	920.687-174
SNUFF-CONTAINER INSPECTOR	920.667-014
Snuff Drier	523.685-118
SNUFF GRINDER AND SCREENER	521.685-314
SNUFF-PACKING-MACHINE OPERATOR	920.685-094
soft-work-cigar-machine operator	529.685-270
SPECIAL TESTER	529.487-010
SPREADER OPERATOR, AUTOMATIC	529.685-222
sprigger	521.687-134
steam-box tender	522.682-014
STEAM-CONDITIONER OPERATOR	522.685-094
steamer	522.682-014

steam-pressure-chamber operator 522.685-102
stem-cleaning-machine feeder 521.685-362
STEM-DRYER MAINTAINER 529.685-230
STEMMER, HAND 521.687-134
STEMMER, MACHINE 521.685-334
STEM-ROLLER-OR-CRUSHER OPERATOR 521.685-330
stem-threshing-machine operator 521.685-362
stick feeder 529.686-074
stogie maker, hand 790.684-014
Stogie Packer 790.687-014
STRIP-CUTTING-MACHINE OPERATOR 521.685-338
strip feeder 529.685-222
stripping-and-booking-machine operator 521.685-334
SUCTION-PLATE-CARRIER CLEANER 529.687-194
suction-plate roller, hand 790.684-022
suction roller 790.684-022
SUMATRA OPENER 529.687-198
SUPERVISOR 529.137-026
Supervisor, Cigarette-Filter Making Department 529.137-026
Supervisor, Cigarette-Making Department 529.137-026
Supervisor, Cigarette-Packing Department 529.137-026
SUPERVISOR, CIGAR MAKING, HAND 790.134-010
SUPERVISOR, CIGAR-MAKING MACHINE 529.132-034
Supervisor, Cigar Processing 529.137-026
SUPERVISOR, CIGAR TOBACCO PROCESSING 529.137-034
SUPERVISOR, CURING ROOM 529.137-038
SUPERVISOR, LUMP ROOM 520.137-010
SUPERVISOR, PICKING 521.137-010
supervisor, rolling room 520.137-010
SUPERVISOR, THRESHING DEPARTMENT 521.132-014
TABLE HAND 521.687-138
table inspector 529.687-090
tag-meter operator 529.687-162
TARE WEIGHER 221.587-034
tester operator 529.387-014
test puller 529.587-022
THRESHING-MACHINE OPERATOR 521.685-362
TICKET PULLER 221.687-014
TICKET WORKER 221.482-018
tin-can feeder 920.686-030
TIN-CONTAINER STRIAGHTENER 709.687-046
TIP-LENGTH CHECKER 529.467-010
tip tester 529.467-010
Toaster Operator 523.685-118
Tobacco Baler 920.685-010
tobacco cleaner 521.685-270
tobacco conditioner 522.687-026
tobacco curer 522.687-026
tobacco cutter 521.685-338
tobacco cutter 521.685-310
tobacco cutter 521.685-298
tobacco dipper 522.687-026
TOBACCO-DRIER OPERATOR 523.685-118
tobacco drying-machine operator 522.662-014
tobacco flavorer 522.685-030
TOBACCO-PACKING-MACHINE OPERATOR 920.685-098
tobacco roller 790.687-030
TOBACCO-SAMPLE PULLER 529.587-022
Tobacco-Scrap Sifter 521.685-270
tobacco shaker 521.687-110
tobacco-sieve operator 521.685-270
tobacco sprayer 522.687-042
Tobacco-Stem-Drier Operator 523.685-118
tobacco stemmer, machine 521.685-334
tobacco stripper, hand 521.687-134
tobacco-stripping-machine operator 521.685-334
top flavor attendant 520.687-026
TRAY FILLER 920.686-050
tray packer 920.686-050
Turkish-Line Attendant 520.685-026
TWISTER, HAND 790.687-030
twist maker 790.687-030
Twist Packer 920.687-130
utility hand see RELIEF WORKER
VACUUM-CONDITIONER OPERATOR 522.685-102
Virginia-Line Attendant 520.685-026
Wrapper Caser 522.687-026
WRAPPER COUNTER 929.687-050
wrapper dipper 522.685-106
wrapper, hand 790.684-022
WRAPPER-HANDS SPRAYER 522.687-042
WRAPPER LAYER 529.685-266
WRAPPER-LAYER-AND-EXAMINER, SOFT WORK 529.685-270
wrapper-leaf inspector 529.687-134
Wrapper Opener 521.687-110
WRAPPER SELECTOR 529.687-218
wrapper sizer 529.687-218
wrapper sorter 529.687-218
wrapper stemmer, hand 521.687-134
wrapper-stemmer operator 521.685-334
Wrapper Stripper 521.685-334
Wrapper Stripper, Hand 521.687-134
WRAPPING MACHINE HELPER 529.687-222
WRINGER OPERATOR 522.685-106
X-RAY INSPECTOR 529.685-274

toy-sport equip.—TOYS, GAMES, AND SPORTS EQUIPMENT INDUSTRY: This designation includes occupations concerned with manufacturing and repairing apparatus for games, toys of all kinds, children's vehicles, baby carriages, related products, and sporting and athletic goods, not elsewhere classified. Other typical products include dolls, golf and tennis goods, baseball, football, basketball, and boxing equipment, roller and ice skates, gymnasium and playground equipment, billiard and pool tables, and fishing equipment. Occupations concerned with manufacturing rubber dolls are included in the RUBBER GOODS INDUSTRY (rubber goods). Occupations concerned with manufacturing sports apparel are included in the GARMENT INDUSTRY (garment).

ADHESIVE PRIMER 732.687-010
Air-Tank Assembler 732.684-014
Arrow-Point Attacher 795.687-014
ARROWSMITH 732.684-010
artificial-fly tier 732.684-074
ASSEMBLER 732.684-014
ASSEMBLER, BILLIARD-TABLE 732.384-010
ASSEMBLER, FISHING FLOATS 732.687-014
Assembler, Golf-Wood Head 732.381-022
ASSEMBLER, LAY-UPS 677.685-014
ASSEMBLER, LIQUID CENTER 732.684-018
ASSEMBLER, PING-PONG TABLE 732.684-022
Assembler, Toy Voices 731.687-034
Assembly Supervisor 732.130-010
Bait Painter 741.684-018
bait tier 732.684-074
balancer 732.687-086
BALL ASSEMBLER 732.684-026
BALL-TRUING-MACHINE OPERATOR 690.682-014
baseball-glove stuffer 732.687-042
BASEBALL INSPECTOR AND REPAIRER 732.684-030
BASEBALL SEWER, HAND 732.684-034
Baseball Winder 692.685-246
BASE FILLER 732.687-018
BASE-FILLER OPERATOR 732.685-010
Basketball Assembler 732.684-026
Bender 569.685-014
Billiard-Table Repairer 732.384-010
blower 731.685-014
BLOW-MOLDING-MACHINE TENDER 556.685-086
Bottom Stitcher 732.684-050
BOWLING-BALL ENGRAVER 732.584-010
BOWLING-BALL FINISHER 690.685-038
BOWLING-BALL GRADER AND MARKER 732.381-014
BOWLING-BALL-MOLD ASSEMBLER 556.687-010
BOWLING-BALL MOLDER 556.685-018
BOWLING-BALL WEIGHER AND PACKER 732.487-010
BOW MAKER, CUSTOM 732.381-010
BOW MAKER, PRODUCTION 732.684-038
Bow Repairer, Custom 732.381-010
BOW-STRING MAKER 732.684-042
breaker 732.687-050
Carcass Assembler 732.684-026
CASTING-PLUG ASSEMBLER 732.687-022
CELLULOID TRIMMER 732.684-046
Closer 787.682-054
club former 732.381-018
CORE SHAPER 692.685-058
Core Shaper, Sides 692.685-058
Core Shaper, Top 692.685-058
CORK GRINDER 662.685-010
cover treater 559.685-102
Crester 732.684-010
Crossbow Maker 732.684-038
Cushion Former 732.384-010
Cushion Installer 732.384-010
CUSTOM SKI MAKER 732.281-010
cutter 732.685-014
DECORATOR 749.684-014
DICE MAKER 731.381-010
Dice Spotter 740.687-018
Diving-Board Assembler 732.684-014

toy-sport equip.

winder, gammeter 692.685-246
Wood-Club-Neck Whipper 732.684-082

utilities—UTILITIES (LIGHT, HEAT, AND POWER) INDUSTRY: This designation includes occupations concerned with generating electricity in steam and hydroelectric power plants; transmitting and distributing electricity; distributing manufactured and natural heating and illuminating gas; producing and distributing steam heat and power; and the activities related to such functions. Occupations concerned with transporting petroleum and gas products are included in the PIPE LINES INDUSTRY (pipe lines).

ACCOUNT-INFORMATION CLERK 210.367-010
adjustment clerk 239.362-014
APPLIANCE-SERVICE SUPERVISOR 187.167-010
application clerk 239.362-014
arc trimmer 952.667-010
area-development consultant 184.117-030
AUXILIARY-EQUIPMENT OPERATOR 952.362-010
BATTERY MAINTAINER, LARGE EMERGENCY STORAGE 820.381-010
BILLING-CONTROL CLERK 214.387-010
billing supervisor 214.137-022
Bill Recapitulation Clerk 216.482-010
boulevard-glassware cleaner 952.667-010
boulevard-glassware replacer 952.667-010
BUILDING-EQUIPMENT INSPECTOR 956.387-010
CABLE INSTALLER-REPAIRER 821.361-010
Cable Installer-Repairer Helper 821.667-010
CABLE MAINTAINER 952.464-010
cable placer 829.684-018
CABLE PULLER 829.684-018
cable rigger 829.684-018
CABLE SPLICER 829.361-010
CABLE-SPLICER APPRENTICE 829.361-014
CABLE-SPLICER HELPER 829.667-010
cable-splicing supervisor 829.131-010
CABLE SUPERVISOR 829.131-010
carbon-lamp cleaner 952.667-010
Central-Control-Room Operator 952.362-042
CHART CALCULATOR 214.487-010
chart clerk 216.685-010
chief dispatcher 952.137-010
CHIEF LOAD DISPATCHER 952.137-010
chief-maintenance supervisor 862.137-014
chief operating engineer 184.167-166
chief power dispatcher 184.167-150
chief, relay tester 729.131-014
Circuit-Breaker Mechanic 829.261-018
Circuit-Breaker Supervisor 829.131-014
COAL-EQUIPMENT OPERATOR 921.683-022
COAL SAMPLER 922.687-038
coal-transport-and-mill operator 544.665-010
COMMERCIAL-INSTRUCTOR SUPERVISOR 239.137-010
commercial service representative 253.357-010
COMPLAINT INSPECTOR 829.261-010
complaint supervisor 953.137-018
compressor-house operator 953.382-010
CONDUIT MECHANIC 869.361-010
CONSTRUCTION CHECKER 821.367-010
Construction-Records Clerk 219.362-010
CONTACT CLERK 209.387-018
CORROSION-CONTROL FITTER 820.361-010
COST-AND-SALES-RECORD SUPERVISOR 216.137-010
Cost-Estimating Clerk 216.382-034
CUSTOMER-SERVICE REPRESENTATIVE 239.362-014
CUSTOMER SERVICE REPRESENTATIVE 959.361-010
customer-service representative 241.267-034
CUSTOMER-SERVICE-REPRESENTATIVE INSTR. 239.227-010
CUSTOMER-SERVICE REPRESENTATIVE SUPERVISOR 239.137-014
Demand Equipment Repairer 715.281-010
demand inspector 952.367-010
DEMONSTRATOR, ELECTRIC-GAS APPLIANCES 297.357-010
DEPOSIT CLERK 241.267-026
DEPOSIT-REFUND CLERK 214.482-014
detail and lay-out drafter 019.261-014
development-and-planning engineer 003.167-026
DIESEL-PLANT OPERATOR 952.382-010
Diesel-Powerplant Mechanic 631.261-014
Diesel-Powerplant-Mechanic Helper 631.684-010
Diesel-Powerplant Supervisor 631.131-010
DISPATCHER, CHIEF, SERVICE OR WORK 959.137-010
dispatcher, electric power 952.167-014
DISPATCHER, SERVICE 959.167-010
DISPATCHER, SERVICE, CHIEF 959.137-014
DISPATCHER, SERVICE OR WORK 952.167-010
DISTRIBUTION-ACCOUNTING CLERK 210.362-010
distribution district supervisor 952.137-018
distribution estimator 019.261-014
DISTRIBUTION-FIELD ENGINEER 003.167-014
district manager 184.167-150
Division Field Inspector 168.264-018
DRAFTER, CHIEF, DESIGN 017.161-010
DRIER OPERATOR 543.382-010
DRIP PUMPER 953.583-010
duct layer 869.361-010
Duct-Layer Helper 821.667-010
Duct-Layer Supervisor 899.131-010
dynamo operator see GENERATOR OPERATOR
earth-auger operator 859.682-010
EARTH-BORING-MACHINE OPERATOR 859.682-010
electrical-appliance service supervisor 187.167-010
ELECTRICAL ENGINEER, POWER SYSTEM 003.167-018
ELECTRICAL-INSTALLATION SUPERVISOR 821.131-010
ELECTRICAL TESTER term
Electrical-Tests Supervisor 184.167-218
electrical-transmission engineer 003.167-050
ELECTRIC-DISTRIBUTION CHECKER 824.281-014
electric-distribution engineer 003.167-046
ELECTRICIAN APPRENTICE, POWERHOUSE 820.261-010
electrician, cable-splicing 829.361-010
electrician-constructor supervisor 821.131-026
electrician helper 821.667-010
Electrician Helper, Powerhouse 821.667-010
ELECTRICIAN, POWERHOUSE 820.261-014
Electrician, Rectifier Maintenance 829.261-018
ELECTRICIAN, SUBSTATION 820.261-018
ELECTRICIAN SUPERVISOR, SUBSTATION 820.131-010
electrician, underground 821.361-010
electric-meter inspector 821.364-010
Electric-Meter-Installer Helper 821.667-010
ELECTRIC-METER INSTALLER I 821.361-014
ELECTRIC-METER INSTALLER II 821.684-010
Electric-Meter Reader 209.567-010
ELECTRIC-METER REPAIRER 729.281-014
ELECTRIC-METER-REPAIRER APPRENTICE 729.281-018
Electric-Meter-Repairer Helper 821.564-010
ELECTRIC-METER TESTER 821.381-010
Electric-Meter-Tester Helper 821.564-010
electric-meter tester, shop 729.281-034
ELECTRIC POWERLINE EXAMINER 959.367-010
electric-repair supervisor 820.131-010
Emergency-Crew Supervisor 821.131-014
ENERGY-CONSERVATION REPRESENTATIVE 959.367-018
engineer, booster and exhauster 953.382-010
Engineer, Design-And-Construction 003.167-018
engineer, gas-pumping station 953.382-010
ENGINEER OF SYSTEM DEVELOPMENT 003.167-026
Engineer, Operations-And-Maintenance 003.167-018
ESTIMATOR AND DRAFTER 019.261-014
Expenditure-Requisition Clerk 216.382-022
EXTENSION CLERK 219.362-030
FEEDER-SWITCHBOARD OPERATOR 952.362-014
field clerk 229.367-010
field inspector 869.387-010
field inspector 959.361-010
FIELD-MECHANICAL-METER TESTER 953.281-010
FIELD RECORDER 229.367-010
FIXED-CAPITAL CLERK 210.382-042
FURNACE INSTALLER 862.361-010
Furnace Installer Helper 862.684-022
GAS DISPATCHER 953.167-010
GAS-DISTRIBUTION-AND-EMERGENCY CLERK 249.367-042
gas-distribution supervisor 862.137-010
gas fitter 953.364-010
GAS INSPECTOR 168.264-018
GAS-LEAK INSPECTOR 953.367-010
GAS-LEAK INSPECTOR HELPER 953.667-010
GAS-MAIN FITTER 862.361-014
gas-meter adjuster 710.281-022
GAS-METER CHECKER 953.367-014
GAS-METER INSTALLER 953.364-010
GAS-METER-INSTALLER HELPER 953.687-010
GAS-METER MECHANIC I 710.381-022
GAS-METER MECHANIC II 710.684-026
GAS-METER PROVER 710.281-022
Gas-Meter Reader 209.567-010
gas-meter repairer 710.684-026
GAS-METER TESTER term
GAS-PUMPING-STATION HELPER 953.684-010

GAS-PUMPING-STATION OPERATOR	953.382-010
GAS-PUMPING-STATION SUPERVISOR	953.137-010
GAS-REGULATOR REPAIRER	710.381-026
GAS-REGULATOR-REPAIRER HELPER	710.384-010
gas-substation operator	953.382-010
Gas-Turbine-Powerplant Mechanic	631.261-014
Gas-Turbine-Powerplant-Mechanic Helper	631.684-010
GAS USAGE METER CLERK	216.685-010
general superintendent, power sales and service	163.167-022
general utility worker	952.687-010
generating-substation-operator assistant	952.367-014
generation-mechanic helper	631.684-010
GENERATOR OPERATOR	term
generator-switchboard operator	952.362-034
Geothermal-Powerplant Mechanic	631.261-014
Geothermal-Powerplant-Mechanic Helper	631.684-010
Geothermal-Powerplant Supervisor	631.131-010
Ground Helper	821.684-014
Grounding Engineer	003.167-054
HELPER, ELECTRICAL	821.667-010
HELPER, LIQUEFACTION-AND-REGASIFICATION	953.584-010
hiker	821.361-026
HISTORY-CARD CLERK	209.587-022
hole-digger operator	859.682-010
Hole-Digger-Truck Driver	905.663-014
HOUSE-PIPING INSPECTOR	953.367-018
HYDROELECTRIC-MACHINERY MECHANIC	631.261-010
HYDROELECTRIC-MACHINERY-MECHANIC HELPER	631.364-010
HYDROELECTRIC-PLANT MAINTAINER	952.687-010
Hydroelectric-Powerplant Supervisor	631.131-010
HYDROELECTRIC-STATION OPERATOR	952.362-018
HYDROELECTRIC-STATION OPERATOR, CHIEF	952.137-014
INDUCTION-COORDINATION POWER ENGINEER	003.167-038
INDUSTRIAL-GAS FITTER	862.381-014
INDUSTRIAL-GAS SERVICER	637.261-022
INDUSTRIAL-GAS-SERVICER HELPER	637.384-010
Industrial-Gas-Servicer Supervisor	953.137-018
industrial servicer	862.381-014
INSIDE-METER TESTER	729.281-034
inside tester	729.281-034
inspector and clerk	821.367-010
INSPECTOR, CHIEF	956.267-010
inspector, outside steam-distribution	862.361-022
Instrument Repairer, Steam Plant	710.281-030
INSTRUMENT TECHNICIAN	710.281-030
INSTRUMENT-TECHNICIAN APPRENTICE	710.281-042
INSTRUMENT-TECHNICIAN HELPER	710.684-030
INSULATOR TESTER	729.387-026
INVESTIGATOR	376.267-022
INVESTIGATOR, UTILITY-BILL COMPLAINTS	241.267-034
Jointer, Submarine Cable	829.361-010
LABORATORY ASSISTANT	029.361-018
LABORATORY HELPER	821.564-010
laboratory technician	579.384-014
LABOR-CREW SUPERVISOR	899.131-010
LABORER, CONSTRUCTION OR LEAK GANG	862.684-014
Laborer, Electric Power And Transmission Line	869.687-026
laborer, pole crew	821.687-010
LABORER, POWERHOUSE	952.665-010
lamp cleaner, street-light	952.667-010
lay-out and detail drafter	019.261-014
lead-relay tester	729.131-014
Leak-Gang Supervisor	862.137-010
leak locator	953.367-010
line-and-frame poler	959.684-010
Line-Construction Supervisor	821.131-014
LINE ERECTOR	821.361-018
LINE-ERECTOR APPRENTICE	821.361-030
line inspector	003.167-014
LINE REPAIRER	821.361-026
Line Repairer, Tower	821.361-026
line servicer	821.361-026
LINE SUPERVISOR	821.131-014
Line Supervisor, Tower	821.131-014
LIQUEFACTION-AND-REGASIFICATION-PLANT OPERATOR	953.362-014
LOAD CHECKER	952.367-010
LOAD DISPATCHER	952.167-014
Load Dispatcher, Local	952.167-014
machinist apprentice	631.261-018
MAINS-AND-SERVICE SUPERVISOR	862.137-010
maintenance inspector	953.367-010
MAINTENANCE SUPERVISOR	184.167-050
Maintenance Supervisor, Electrical	184.167-050
Maintenance Supervisor, Mechanical	184.167-050
MANAGER, AREA DEVELOPMENT	184.117-030
Manager, Commerical Sales	163.167-022
manager, electric distribution department	184.167-150
Manager, Industrial Sales	163.167-022
manager, public utility, rural	184.167-162
Manager, Residential Sales	163.167-022
MANAGER, UTILITY SALES AND SERVICE	163.167-022
manhole-and-underground-steam-line inspector	862.361-022
mechanical-meter tester	953.281-010
merchandise supervisor	187.167-010
meter-and-service-line inspector	953.367-014
meter-changes records clerk	209.587-022
meter inspector	953.281-010
METER INSPECTOR	710.384-022
meter installer	953.364-010
Meter Installer-And-Remover	821.361-014
METER READER	209.567-010
METER READER, CHIEF	209.137-014
meter-record clerk	209.587-022
meter repairer	729.281-014
meter-repairer apprentice	729.281-018
meter shop superintendent	184.167-194
meter tester	710.381-022
meter tester	821.381-010
Meter Tester, Demand Meters	821.381-010
Meter Tester, Polyphase	821.381-010
Meter Tester, Primary	821.381-010
Meter Tester, Single Phase	821.381-010
MILL-AND-COAL-TRANSPORT OPERATOR	544.665-010
mill operator	544.665-010
MOTOR-ROOM CONTROLLER	820.662-010
network-relay tester	729.281-038
nuclear plant control operator	952.362-022
Nuclear-Plant-Instrument Technician	710.281-030
NUCLEAR-PLANT TECHNICAL ADVISOR	015.167-010
Nuclear-Powerplant Mechanic	631.261-014
Nuclear-Powerplant-Mechanic Helper	631.684-010
Nuclear-Powerplant Supervisor	631.131-010
OPERATIONS SUPERVISOR, NUCLEAR POWER PLANT	952.132-010
order clerk	239.362-014
Order Clerk	203.362-010
ORDER DISPATCHER, CHIEF	959.137-018
oscillograph technician	710.281-030
outside contact clerk	239.362-014
Overhead-Distribution Engineer	003.167-046
pipe fitter	862.361-014
Pipe Fitter, Street Service	862.361-014
PIPE INSTALLER	869.381-018
planning-division superintendent	184.167-210
planning engineer	003.167-026
plant machinist	631.261-010
POLE FRAMER	959.684-010
POLE INSPECTOR	869.387-010
pole setter	821.687-010
pole tester	869.387-010
Pole-Truck Driver	904.383-010
POLEYARD SUPERVISOR	929.137-014
post-hole digger	859.682-010
power dispatcher	952.167-014
POWER-DISTRIBUTION ENGINEER	003.167-046
power engineer	952.382-018
power engineer	003.167-018
powerhouse engineer	952.382-018
POWERHOUSE MECHANIC	631.261-014
POWERHOUSE-MECHANIC APPRENTICE	631.261-018
POWERHOUSE-MECHANIC HELPER	631.684-010
POWERHOUSE-MECHANIC SUPERVISOR	631.131-010
power-line inspector	821.367-014
power-plant assistant	952.367-014
power-plant engineer	952.382-018
POWER-PLANT OPERATOR	952.382-018
POWER-REACTOR OPERATOR	952.362-022
power-switchboard operator	952.362-026
POWER-TRANSFORMER REPAIRER	821.361-034
Power-Transformer-Repair Supervisor	829.131-014
POWER-TRANSMISSION ENGINEER	003.167-050
PRESSURE CONTROLLER	953.362-018
pressure-control supervisor	953.137-014
PRESSURE SUPERVISOR	953.137-014
production superintendent, hydro	952.137-014
PROTECTION ENGINEER	003.167-054
public improvement inspector	859.267-010
pump-room operator	952.362-010
rate-and-cost analyst	216.137-010
RATE REVIEWER	214.387-014

reactor operator 952.362-022
receiving-distribution-station operator 952.362-026
regulation supervisor 953.137-014
REGULATOR INSPECTOR 820.361-018
Relay Engineer 003.167-054
RELAY-RECORD CLERK 221.367-054
RELAY-SHOP SUPERVISOR 729.131-014
relay-shop tester 729.281-038
RELAY TECHNICIAN 821.261-018
RELAY TESTER 729.281-038
Relay-Tester Helper 821.564-010
remittance clerk 211.462-034
RUBBER-GOODS TESTER 759.381-010
Rural-Service Engineer 003.167-046
safety-equipment tester 759.381-010
SAFETY INSPECTOR 821.367-014
SALES ENGINEER, MECHANICAL EQUIPMENT 007.151-010
Sales Representative, Electric Service 253.357-010
Sales Representative, Gas Service 253.357-010
SALES REPRESENTATIVE, PUBLIC UTILITIES 253.357-010
Sales Representative, Rural Power 253.357-010
SALVAGER 729.687-030
Salvage Repairer I 829.261-018
SALVAGE REPAIRER II 729.384-018
schedule clerk 959.167-010
Service-Crew Supervisor 862.137-010
service inspector 821.131-010
Service Investigator 241.367-014
service-order dispatcher, chief 959.137-014
service representative 239.362-014
SERVICE REPRESENTATIVE 959.574-010
SERVICE SUPERVISOR I 953.137-018
SERVICE SUPERVISOR II 821.131-018
SERVICE SUPERVISOR III 184.167-126
service tester 821.381-014
Service-Transformer-Repair Supervisor 829.131-014
special-gas-and-electric service investigator 959.361-010
special inspecting-and-testing supervisor 820.131-010
splicer 829.361-010
splicer apprentice 829.361-014
station mechanic 631.261-014
station-mechanic apprentice 631.261-018
station mechanic helper 631.684-010
statistician 216.137-010
STEAM-DISTRIBUTION SUPERVISOR 862.137-014
Steam-Generating-Powerplant Mechanic 631.261-014
Steam-Generating-Powerplant-Mechanic Helper 631.684-010
Steam-Meter Reader 209.567-010
Steam-Plant Records Clerk 216.382-062
Steam-Powerplant Supervisor 631.131-010
STEAM SERVICE INSPECTOR 862.361-022
STEEL-POST INSTALLER 821.687-010
STEEL-POST-INSTALLER SUPERVISOR 821.131-022
street-light changer-and-renewer 952.667-010
STREET-LIGHT CLEANER 952.667-010
street-light inspector 952.667-010
street-light repairer 824.381-010
STREET-LIGHT REPAIRER 729.381-018
STREET-LIGHT-REPAIRER HELPER 729.684-050
STREET-LIGHT SERVICER 824.381-010
STREET-LIGHT-SERVICER HELPER 824.664-010
STREET-LIGHT-SERVICER SUPERVISOR 824.137-014
STREET-OPENINGS INSPECTOR 859.267-010
Substation Engineer 003.167-046
SUBSTATION INSPECTOR 952.261-010
Substation Inspector, Automatic 952.261-010
SUBSTATION OPERATOR 952.362-026
SUBSTATION OPERATOR APPRENTICE 952.362-030
Substation Operator, Automatic 952.362-026
SUBSTATION OPERATOR, CHIEF 952.131-010
Substation Operator, Conversion 952.362-026
Substation Operator, Distribution 952.362-026
Substation Operator, Generation 952.362-026
SUBSTATION-OPERATOR HELPER 952.687-014
Substation Operator Helper, Generator 952.367-014
Substation Operator, Transforming 952.362-026
superintendent, city plant 184.167-154
SUPERINTENDENT, DISTRIBUTION I 184.167-150
SUPERINTENDENT, DISTRIBUTION II 184.167-154
SUPERINTENDENT, ELECTRIC POWER 184.167-162
superintendent, gas distribution 184.167-154
SUPERINTENDENT, GENERATING PLANT 184.167-166
SUPERINTENDENT, LOCAL 952.137-018
Superintendent, Materials-And-Apparatus Tests 184.167-218
SUPERINTENDENT, METERS 184.167-194
Superintendent, Meter Tests 184.167-218
SUPERINTENDENT OF GENERATION 184.167-138
superintendent, operations 184.167-138
superintendent, operations division 184.167-154
Superintendent, Overhead Distribution 184.167-150
Superintendent, Research-And-Fault-Analysis Tests 184.167-218
superintendent, service 953.137-018
Superintendent, Station-And-Protection-System Tests 184.167-218
SUPERINTENDENT, SYSTEM OPERATION 184.167-210
SUPERINTENDENT, TESTS 184.167-218
SUPERINTENDENT, TRANSMISSION 184.167-222
Superintendent, Underground Distribution 184.167-150
SUPERVISOR, ACCOUNTS RECEIVABLE 214.137-022
SUPERVISOR, CONTACT AND SERVICE CLERKS 249.137-014
SUPERVISOR, CUSTOMER RECORDS DIVISION 249.137-022
SUPERVISOR, ELECTRICAL REPAIR AND TELEPHONE LINE MAINTENANCE 829.131-022
supervisor, energy conservation representative 959.137-022
SUPERVISOR, ESTIMATOR AND DRAFTER 019.161-010
SUPERVISOR, GAS METER REPAIR 710.131-010
SUPERVISOR, HOME-ENERGY CONSULTANT 959.137-022
SUPERVISOR, INSTRUMENT MECHANICS 710.131-018
SUPERVISOR, LIQUEFACTION-AND-REGASIFICATION 953.132-010
SUPERVISOR, METER-AND-REGULATOR SHOP 710.137-014
SUPERVISOR, METER REPAIR SHOP 710.131-026
SUPERVISOR, OPERATIONS 952.137-026
SUPERVISOR, RIGHT-OF-WAY MAINTENANCE 859.133-010
SUPERVISOR, TELLERS 211.137-022
SUPERVISOR, TREE-TRIMMING 408.137-014
SWITCHBOARD OPERATOR 952.362-034
SWITCHBOARD OPERATOR ASSISTANT 952.367-014
switchboard-operator helper 952.367-014
SWITCH INSPECTOR 952.381-010
system dispatcher 952.167-014
system operator, chief 952.137-010
system operator 952.167-014
system-planning engineer 003.167-026
Tax-Record Clerk 216.482-010
TELLER 211.462-034
TOWER ERECTOR 821.361-038
TOWER ERECTOR HELPER 821.684-014
Tower-Truck Driver 905.663-014
Traffic-Signal Repairer 824.381-010
transformer assembler 821.361-034
Transformer-Coil Winder 829.261-018
TRANSFORMER-STOCK CLERK 222.587-054
TRANSFORMER TESTER 724.281-010
transmission-and-coordination engineer 003.167-050
transmission-line engineer 003.167-050
TREE TRIMMER 408.664-010
TREE-TRIMMER HELPER 408.667-010
tree trimmer helper, line clearance 408.667-010
tree trimmer, line clearance 408.664-010
tree-trimming-line technician 408.664-010
trouble dispatcher 959.167-010
trouble dispatcher 952.167-010
TROUBLE SHOOTER I 952.364-010
TROUBLE SHOOTER II 821.261-026
TURBINE ATTENDANT 952.567-010
TURBINE OPERATOR 952.362-042
TURBINE OPERATOR, HEAD 952.137-022
turbogenerator operator 952.362-042
Underground-Distribution Engineer 003.167-046
Underground Repairer 829.261-018
Underground Supervisor 829.131-010
UTILITIES SERVICE INVESTIGATOR 821.364-010
Utility-Bill-Collection Clerk 241.357-010
UTILITY CLERK 239.367-034
Utility Inspector 953.367-018
UTILIZATION ENGINEER 007.061-034
utilization supervisor 187.167-010
VOLTAGE TESTER 821.381-014
WIND-GENERATING-ELECTRIC-POWER INSTALLER 821.381-018
Wirer Helper 821.667-010
Wirer, Maintenance 829.261-018
WIRER, STREET LIGHT 821.684-018
WIREWORKER SUPERVISOR 821.131-026
WORK-ORDER-SORTING CLERK 221.367-082

vehicles, nec—MISCELLANEOUS VEHICLES AND TRANSPORTATION EQUIPMENT INDUSTRY, NOT ELSEWHERE CLASSIFIED: This designation includes occupations concerned with manufacturing transportation equipment not elsewhere classified, such as motorized travel trailers, travel trailers for attachment to passenger cars, horse-drawn vehicles (carriages,

water trans.

sleighs, and sleds), all-terrain vehicles (golf carts and snowmobiles), wheelbarrows, handcarts, and pushcarts. Occupations concerned with the manufacture of parts for these vehicles are included here unless the occupation is peculiar to another industry, such as AUTOMOBILE MANUFACTURING INDUSTRY (auto. mfg.); RUBBER TIRE AND TUBE INDUSTRY (rubber tire); ELECTRICAL EQUIPMENT INDUSTRY (elec. equip.); LIGHTING FIXTURES INDUSTRY (light. fix.); or INSTRUMENTS AND APPARATUS INDUSTRY (inst. & app.). Occupations concerned exclusively with the manufacture of mobile homes are included in the MANUFACTURED BUILDINGS INDUSTRY (mfd. bldgs.). Occupations concerned with the manufacture of military tanks are included in the ORDNANCE AND ACCESSORIES (EXCEPT VEHICLES AND GUIDED MISSILES) INDUSTRY (ordnance).

Appliance Installer	869.684-026
Appliance Installer	806.684-018
ASSEMBLER	869.684-010
ASSEMBLER, CAMPER	806.684-018
ASSEMBLER, COMPONENT	762.684-014
ASSEMBLER, SUBASSEMBLY	869.684-018
Assembly Supervisor	869.131-030
BODY WIRER	829.684-014
Cabinet-And-Trim Installer	869.684-026
Cabinet-And-Trim Installer	806.684-018
Cabinet Assembler	762.684-014
coach wirer	829.684-014
Counter Top Assembler	762.684-014
DOOR ASSEMBLER	806.684-050
Door Installer I	809.684-030
Door Installer II	869.684-026
electrician, wiring	829.684-014
FIBERGLASS LAMINATOR	806.684-054
final finisher	869.684-026
Final-Finish Supervisor	869.131-030
Floor Finisher	869.684-010
Floor Finisher	806.684-018
Floor Framer	869.684-010
Floor Framer	806.684-018
framer	869.684-010
Hardware Installer	869.684-026
INSTALLER	869.684-026
INSTALLER-INSPECTOR, FINAL	806.684-066
laminator	806.684-054
METAL HANGER	809.684-030
Millroom Supervisor	869.131-030
mock-up assembler	693.381-018
MOCK-UP BUILDER	693.381-018
Partition Assembler	762.684-014
REPAIRER, MANUFACTURED BUILDINGS	869.384-010
REPAIRER, RECREATIONAL VEHICLE	869.261-022
Roof Framer	869.684-010
Roof-Panel Hanger	809.684-030
Servicer, Travel Trailers	869.384-010
Sheller	869.684-010
Side Framer	869.684-010
Side Framer	806.684-018
Side-Panel Hanger	809.684-030
Subassembly Supervisor	869.131-030
SUPERVISOR, MANUFACTURED BUILDINGS	869.131-030
Supervisor, Travel Trailer	869.131-030
Tile Installer	869.684-026
UTILITY WORKER	869.684-074
WHEEL ASSEMBLER	809.684-038
Wheel Installer	869.684-010
Window Installer	809.684-030
wirer	829.684-014

water trans.—WATER TRANSPORTATION INDUSTRY: This designation includes occupations concerned with operating ships, barges, ferries, tugboats, and other vessels engaged in transporting freight and passengers, and such supporting services as loading and unloading cargo and booking steamship passage. Occupations concerned with the regulation of port traffic, collection of customs and duties, and inspection and certification of vessels by public authorities are included under GOVERNMENT SERVICES (government ser.).

able-bodied seaman	911.364-010
ABLE SEAMAN	911.364-010
Baker Scullion	318.687-014
barge captain	197.163-014
BARGE CAPTAIN	911.137-010
barge-crane operator	921.683-034
Barge Engineer	197.130-010
Barge Hand	911.687-022
Barge Loader	911.364-014
Barge-Loader Helper	911.687-010

BOAT DISPATCHER	184.167-010
BOAT-LOADER HELPER	911.687-010
BOAT LOADER I	911.364-014
BOAT LOADER II	921.685-010
boat puller	911.687-018
BOATSWAIN	911.131-010
BOOKING CLERK	248.367-014
BOOKING SUPERVISOR	248.137-010
Bulk-Loader Operator	921.662-018
Butcher Scullion	318.687-014
CADET, DECK	911.133-010
Cadet Engineer	197.130-010
canal-lock tender, chief operator	911.131-014
canal-structure operator	911.362-010
Cannery-Tender Engineer	197.130-010
CANTILEVER-CRANE OPERATOR	921.683-018
captain see MASTER	
CARGO CHECKER	222.367-010
cargo-gear mechanic	222.387-062
CHEF, PASSENGER VESSEL	315.137-010
chief lock-operator	911.131-014
coal-tower operator	921.683-074
COAL TRIMMER	911.687-018
Container-Cargo Clerk	248.367-014
CONTAINER COORDINATOR	248.367-022
container crane operator	921.683-018
cook, boat	315.371-010
COOK, CHIEF	315.131-010
COOK, LARDER	315.381-014
COOK, MESS	315.371-010
Cook, Ship	315.361-010
cook, ship	315.371-010
COOK, STATION	315.361-022
Cook, Station, Breakfast	315.361-022
Cook, Station, Grill	315.361-022
Cook, Station, Roast	315.361-022
Cook, Station, Soup And Fish	315.361-022
COOK, THIRD	315.381-014
cost-report clerk	216.382-054
Cotton Header	911.137-018
DECK ENGINEER	623.281-014
deck-engine operator	921.683-034
Deck Guard	372.667-034
DECKHAND	911.687-022
Deckhand, Maintenance	911.364-010
derrick-barge operator	921.683-034
DERRICK-BOAT CAPTAIN	911.137-014
DERRICK-BOAT OPERATOR	921.683-034
derrick-boat runner	911.137-014
director, recreation	352.167-010
DIRECTOR, SOCIAL	352.167-010
DISPATCHER, SHIP PILOT	248.367-026
DISPATCHER, TUGBOAT	911.167-010
dock boss	911.137-018
dock hand	911.364-010
dock helper	911.687-010
DOCUMENTATION-BILLING CLERK	214.362-014
DOCUMENTATION SUPERVISOR	214.137-010
DREDGE CAPTAIN	197.161-010
Dredge Deckhand	911.687-022
DREDGE MATE	197.137-010
dredge operator	197.161-010
dredge runner	197.161-010
ELECTRICIAN	825.281-014
Electrician, Chief	825.281-014
Electrician, Deck	825.281-014
Electrician, Second	825.281-014
Electrician, Sound	825.281-014
Electrician, Third	825.281-014
ENGINEER	197.130-010
Engineer, Chief	197.130-010
Engineer, First Assistant	197.130-010
Engineer, Fishing Vessel	197.130-010
Engineer, Second Assistant	197.130-010
Engineer, Third Assistant	197.130-010
FERRYBOAT CAPTAIN	197.163-010
Ferryboat Deckhand	911.687-022
ferryboat helper	911.667-010
FERRYBOAT OPERATOR	911.363-010
FERRYBOAT OPERATOR, CABLE	911.664-010
FERRYBOAT-OPERATOR HELPER	911.667-010
ferry operator	911.664-010
ferry operator	911.363-010
ferry-terminal agent	911.137-026
FIRER, MARINE	951.685-018

Firer-Watertender 951.685-018
floating-derrick operator 921.683-034
floor runner 222.567-014
freight checker 222.367-010
freight clerk 248.167-010
Freight-Traffic Agent 252.257-010
gang boss 911.137-018
garde manger 315.381-014
GEAR REPAIRER 623.381-010
General-Cargo Clerk 248.367-014
GENERAL CLAIMS AGENT 186.117-030
Glass Scullion 318.687-014
hatch supervisor 911.137-018
HATCH TENDER 911.667-014
HEADER 911.137-018
Header, Dock 911.137-018
Header, Ship 911.137-018
HEADWAITER/HEADWAITRESS 350.137-010
INCOMING-FREIGHT CLERK 248.362-010
INFORMATION CLERK 237.367-018
INSPECTOR OF DREDGING 850.387-010
laborer, marine terminal 911.687-026
Lift-Truck Operator 911.663-014
LINES TENDER 911.687-026
Lock-And-Dam Equipment Repairer 899.281-010
LOCK OPERATOR 911.362-010
LOCK TENDER, CHIEF OPERATOR 911.131-014
Main-Galley Scullion 318.687-014
MAINTENANCE MECHANIC, ENGINE 623.281-034
MANAGER, HARBOR DEPARTMENT 184.117-042
MANAGER, MARINA DRY DOCK 187.167-226
MANAGER, OPERATIONS 184.117-050
manager, rates and schedules 184.117-066
MANAGER, TRAFFIC 184.117-066
Manifest Clerk 214.362-014
marine clerk 222.367-010
marine engineer 197.130-010
MARINE OILER 911.584-010
Marine-Service-Station Attendant 915.477-010
MASTER term
Master, Bays, Sounds, And Lakes 197.167-010
Master, Coastal Waters 197.167-010
Master, Coastwise Yacht 197.133-014
Master, Great Lakes 197.167-010
Master, Ocean 197.167-010
Master, Ocean Yacht 197.133-014
MASTER, PASSENGER BARGE 197.163-014
MASTER, RIVERBOAT 197.163-018
MASTER, SHIP 197.167-010
Master, Steam Yacht 197.133-014
MASTER, YACHT 197.133-014
Mate, Chief 197.133-022
Mate, First 197.133-022
Mate, Fourth 197.133-022
Mate, Relief 197.133-022
Mate, Second 197.133-022
MATE, SHIP 197.133-022
Mate, Third 197.133-022
mechanic, marine engine 197.130-010
MESS ATTENDANT 350.677-010
Mess Attendant, Crew 350.677-010
Mess Attendant, Officers' Room 350.677-010
Mess Attendant, Officers' Salon 350.677-010
oiler 911.584-010
operations manager 184.117-050
ORDINARY SEAMAN 911.687-030
PAPER-CONTROL CLERK 219.367-022
PASSENGER ATTENDANT 350.677-014
Passenger Traffic Agent 252.257-010
PASTRY CHEF 315.131-014
pier hand 911.364-014
pier hand helper 911.687-010
Pilot-Boat Deckhand 911.687-022
PILOT, SHIP 197.133-026
Pilot, Steam Yacht 197.133-026
Pilot, Tank Vessel 197.133-026
Port Captain 184.167-182
PORT ENGINEER 014.167-014
PORTER, MARINA 329.677-010
PORT PURSER 166.167-038
PORT-TRAFFIC MANAGER 184.167-122
PURCHASING-AND-CLAIMS SUPERVISOR 248.137-014
PURSER 197.167-014
QUARTERMASTER 911.363-014
RADIO OFFICER 193.262-022
radio operator 193.262-022
RATE ANALYST, FREIGHT 214.267-010
RECEIPT-AND-REPORT CLERK 216.382-054
Reefer Engineer 950.362-014
Refrigerated-Cargo Clerk 248.367-014
riverboat captain 197.163-018
Run-Boat Operator 911.663-010
runner 222.567-014
SAILOR term
sailor-merchant mariner see SAILOR
SAILOR, PLEASURE CRAFT 911.664-014
SALAD MAKER 317.384-010
sales representative 252.257-010
scow captain 911.137-010
Scow Deckhand 911.687-022
scow-derrick operator 921.683-034
SCULLION 318.687-014
Scullion Chief 318.687-014
second assistant engineer 623.281-034
SECOND COOK AND BAKER 315.381-026
Second Steward/Stewardess, Night 350.137-022
SERVICES CLERK 214.387-018
ship boss 911.137-018
ship officer 197.133-022
ship purser 197.167-014
SHIP RUNNER 222.567-014
ship's captain 197.167-010
Sightseeing-Boat Operator 911.663-010
Silverware Washer 318.687-014
skipper see MASTER
SOUS CHEF 315.137-014
Stevedore, Dock 922.687-090
Stevedore, Front 922.687-090
Stevedore, Hold 922.687-090
STEVEDORE I 911.663-014
STEVEDORE II 922.687-090
Stevedoring Superintendent, Container Handling 911.137-022
stevedoring supervisor 911.137-018
STEWARD/STEWARDESS 350.677-022
STEWARD/STEWARDESS, BATH 350.677-018
STEWARD/STEWARDESS, CHIEF, CARGO VESSEL 350.137-014
STEWARD/STEWARDESS, CHIEF, PASSENGER SHIP 350.137-018
Steward/Stewardess, Deck 350.677-022
steward/stewardess, dining room 350.677-030
Steward/Stewardess, Economy Class 350.137-022
Steward/Stewardess, Lounge 350.677-022
Steward/Stewardess, Night 350.677-022
Steward/Stewardess, Room 350.677-022
STEWARD/STEWARDESS, SECOND 350.137-022
Steward/Stewardess, Second Class 350.137-022
Steward/Stewardess, Smoke Room 350.677-022
STEWARD/STEWARDESS, THIRD 350.137-026
Steward/Stewardess, Third Class 350.137-022
Steward/Stewardess, Tourist Class 350.137-022
STEWARD/STEWARDESS, WINE 350.677-026
storage-wharfage clerk 248.362-010
STOREKEEPER 222.387-062
Storekeeper, Deck 222.387-062
Storekeeper, Engineering 222.387-062
Storekeeper, Steward 222.387-062
striker 911.584-010
SUPERCARGO 248.167-010
SUPERINTENDENT, COMMISSARY 184.117-078
Superintendent, Container Terminal 184.167-214
SUPERINTENDENT, MARINE 184.167-182
SUPERINTENDENT, MARINE OIL TERMINAL 184.167-186
Superintendent, Pier 184.167-214
SUPERINTENDENT, STEVEDORING 911.137-022
SUPERINTENDENT, TERMINAL 184.167-214
SUPERVISOR, FERRY TERMINAL 911.137-026
SUPERVISOR, GEAR REPAIR 623.131-014
SUPERVISOR, TANK CLEANING 891.137-018
third assistant engineer 623.281-034
TICKET TAKER, FERRYBOAT 911.677-010
TONNAGE-COMPILATION CLERK 248.387-014
TOWER-LOADER OPERATOR 921.683-074
Tractor Operator 911.663-014
TRAFFIC AGENT 252.257-010
travel clerk 237.367-018
Traveling-Freight-And-Passenger Agent 252.257-010
TUGBOAT CAPTAIN 197.133-030
Tugboat Deckhand 911.687-022
Tugboat Engineer 197.130-010
TUGBOAT MATE 197.133-034
Turnstile Collector 211.462-038

waterworks

Utility Hand	318.687-014
Vegetable Scullion	318.687-014
Vehicle-Fare Collector	211.462-038
WAITER/WAITRESS	350.677-030
Waiter/Waitress, Cabin Class	350.677-030
Waiter/Waitress, Economy Class	350.677-030
Waiter/Waitress, First Class	350.677-030
Waiter/Waitress, Second Class	350.677-030
Waiter/Waitress, Third Class	350.677-030
Waiter/Waitress, Tourist Class	350.677-030
Watchstander	911.364-010
Water-Taxi Driver	911.663-010
WATERWAY TRAFFIC CHECKER	248.367-030
Waybill Clerk	214.362-014
wharf hand	911.364-010
wharf helper	911.687-010
WHARFINGER	184.387-010
WHARFINGER, CHIEF	184.167-274
wharf operator	911.364-014
wharf tender	911.364-014
wharf-tender helper	911.687-010
WHARF WORKER	921.667-026
WINCH DRIVER	921.683-082
Winch Operator	911.663-014
YEOMAN	term

waterworks—WATERWORKS INDUSTRY: This designation includes occupations concerned with storing, filtering, purifying, and distributing water for domestic and industrial use; and operating water-supply systems for the purpose of irrigation. Occupations concerned with treating waste water are included under SANITARY SERVICES (sanitary ser.).

adjustment clerk	239.362-014
application clerk	239.362-014
aqueduct-and-reservoir keeper	954.382-018
BASIN OPERATOR	954.385-010
billing supervisor	214.137-022
CANAL-EQUIPMENT MECHANIC	899.281-010
canal tender	954.362-010
CHEMIST, WATER PURIFICATION	022.281-014
CHIEF ENGINEER, WATERWORKS	005.167-010
COMMERCIAL-INSTRUCTOR SUPERVISOR	239.137-010
CUSTOMER-SERVICE REPRESENTATIVE	239.362-014
CUSTOMER-SERVICE-REPRESENTATIVE INSTR.	239.227-010
CUSTOMER-SERVICE REPRESENTATIVE SUPERVISOR	239.137-014
dam tender	954.382-018
DITCH RIDER	954.362-010
ditch tender	954.362-010
DRAINAGE-DESIGN COORDINATOR	005.167-014
filter operator	954.382-014
filtration-plant mechanic	630.281-038
HYDROGRAPHER	025.264-010
laborer, filter plant	954.587-010
maintenance supervisor	899.130-010
MANAGER, IRRIGATION DISTRICT	184.117-046
manager, water department	184.117-046
METER READER	209.567-010
METER READER, CHIEF	209.137-014
needle-valve operator	954.382-018
order clerk	239.362-014
outside contact clerk	239.362-014
pumping-plant operator	954.382-010
PUMP-STATION OPERATOR, WATERWORKS	954.382-010
purifying-plant operator	954.382-014
reservoir caretaker	954.382-018
sand-cleaning-machine operator	954.587-010
service representative	239.362-014
SERVICE REPRESENTATIVE	959.574-010
SUPERINTENDENT, WATER-AND-SEWER SYSTEMS	184.161-014
SUPERVISOR, ACCOUNTS RECEIVABLE	214.137-022
SUPERVISOR, CANAL-EQUIPMENT MAINTENANCE	899.130-010
SUPERVISOR, LANDSCAPE	406.134-014
SUPERVISOR, METER SHOP	710.131-030
SUPERVISOR, PUMPING STATION	954.130-010
SUPERVISOR, SEWER SYSTEM	184.167-238
SUPERVISOR, WATER TREATMENT PLANT	954.132-010
SUPERVISOR, WATERWORKS	184.167-246
TREATMENT-PLANT MECHANIC	630.281-038
WATER-AND-SEWER-SYSTEMS SUPERVISOR	862.137-018
water-control-station engineer	954.382-014
WATER CONTROL SUPERVISOR	184.167-270
WATER-FILTER CLEANER	954.587-010
water filterer	954.382-014
water-filterer helper	954.587-010

water-maintenance supervisor	862.137-018
WATER-METER INSTALLER	954.564-010
Water-Meter Reader	209.567-010
water-plant-pump operator	954.382-010
water-plant-pump-operator supervisor	954.130-010
water purifier	954.382-014
WATER REGULATOR AND VALVE REPAIRER	862.684-030
WATER-SERVICE DISPATCHER	954.367-010
water-service supervisor	862.137-018
WATERSHED TENDER	954.382-018
water supervisor	862.137-018
water tender	954.362-010
water-treatment-plant mechanic	630.281-038
WATER-TREATMENT-PLANT OPERATOR	954.382-014
zanjero	954.362-010

welding—WELDING AND RELATED PROCESSES: This designation includes occupations concerned with fusing and bonding parts by welding, brazing, and soldering to join, assemble, and repair metal articles, and all occupations concerned with cutting metal by oxidation or melting, using gas flame or electric arc. The designation covers all welding processes wherever they occur, except assembly or repair occupations in which welding, brazing, soldering, and flame or arc cutting are only incidental tasks. Such occupations are included under the industries covering those assembly or repair processes.

arc-air operator	816.364-010
ARC CUTTER	816.364-010
Arc Cutter, Gas-Tungsten Arc	816.364-010
Arc Cutter, Plasma Arc	816.364-010
brazer	813.684-010
BRAZER, ASSEMBLER	813.684-010
BRAZER, CONTROLLED ATMOSPHERIC FURNACE	813.685-010
Brazer, Crawler Torch	813.684-010
brazer, electronic	813.382-010
BRAZER, FURNACE	813.482-010
Brazer Helper, Furnace	819.666-010
Brazer Helper, Induction	819.666-010
BRAZER, INDUCTION	813.382-010
Brazer, Production Line	819.684-010
Brazer, Repair And Salvage	813.684-010
BRAZER, RESISTANCE	813.682-010
Brazing-Furnace Feeder	819.686-010
Brazing-Machine Feeder	819.686-010
BRAZING-MACHINE OPERATOR	813.382-014
brazing-machine operator, automatic	813.382-014
Brazing-Machine-Operator Helper	819.666-010
BRAZING-MACHINE SETTER	813.360-010
burner, hand	816.464-010
burning-machine operator	816.482-010
burn-out-scarfing operator	816.364-010
certified welder see WELDER- CERTIFIED	
cutter, gas	816.464-010
Electronic-Eye-Thermal-Cutting-Machine Operator	816.482-010
flame-brazing-machine operator	813.382-014
flame-cutting-machine operator	816.482-010
Flame-Cutting-Machine-Operator Helper	819.666-010
flame gouger	816.464-010
flame planer	816.482-010
Flame Scarfer	816.464-010
Flash-Welding-Machine Operator	812.682-010
Flux Brusher	819.666-010
gas-cutting-machine operator	816.482-010
hydrogen braze-furnace operator	813.685-010
Laser-Beam Cutter	815.682-010
LASER-BEAM-MACHINE OPERATOR	815.682-010
LEAD BURNER	819.281-010
LEAD-BURNER APPRENTICE	819.281-014
LEAD-BURNER SUPERVISOR	819.131-010
lead welder	819.281-010
MACHINE FEEDER	819.686-010
MACHINE HELPER	819.666-010
machine helper	819.686-010
Magnetic-Thermal-Cutting-Machine Operator	816.482-010
Percussion-Welding-Machine Operator	812.682-010
Performance-Test Inspector	819.281-018
Plasma-Cutting-Machine Operator	816.482-010
production solderer	813.684-014
Projection-Welding-Machine Operator	812.682-010
radiograph operator	816.482-010
Repairer, Cylinder Heads	819.384-010
Repairer, Resistance-Welding Machines	626.361-010
REPAIRER, WELDING, BRAZING, AND BURNING MACHINES	626.361-010
REPAIRER, WELDING EQUIPMENT	626.384-010

REPAIRER, WELDING SYSTEMS AND EQUIPMENT	626.261-014
returned-goods repairer	813.684-014
salvage cutter	816.684-010
scrap burner	816.684-010
scrap cutter	816.684-010
SETTER, INDUCTION-HEATING EQUIPMENT	813.360-014
Side-Seam Tender	819.685-010
Slag Scraper	819.666-010
SOLDERER-ASSEMBLER	813.684-014
Solderer, Assembly Repair	813.684-014
SOLDERER-DIPPER	813.684-018
solderer, electronic	813.382-010
solderer, furnace	813.482-010
Solderer, Induction	813.382-010
SOLDERER, PRODUCTION LINE	813.684-022
SOLDERER, SILVER	term
SOLDERER, TORCH I	813.684-026
Solderer, Torch II	813.684-010
SOLDERER, ULTRASONIC, HAND	813.684-030
Soldering-Machine Feeder	819.686-010
Soldering-Machine Operator	813.382-014
soldering-machine operator, automatic	813.382-014
Soldering-Machine-Operator Helper	819.666-010
Spot Welder	819.685-010
spot welder, body assembly	810.664-010
spot welder, line	810.664-010
SUPERVISOR, WELDING EQUIPMENT REPAIRER	626.137-010
tacker	810.684-010
THERMAL CUTTER, HAND I	816.464-010
THERMAL CUTTER, HAND II	816.684-010
Thermal-Cutter Helper	819.687-014
THERMAL-CUTTING-MACHINE OPERATOR	816.482-010
Thermal-Cutting-Tracer-Machine Operator	816.482-010
torch brazer	813.684-010
torch cutter	816.464-010
Track-Template-Thermal-Cutting-Machine Operator	816.482-010
Upset-Welding-Machine Operator	812.682-010
Welder, Acetylene	811.684-014
WELDER APPRENTICE, ARC	810.384-010
WELDER APPRENTICE, COMBINATION	819.384-008
WELDER APPRENTICE, GAS	811.684-010
WELDER, ARC	810.384-014
Welder, Carbon Arc	810.384-014
WELDER, CERTIFIED	term
WELDER, COMBINATION	819.384-010
WELDER, EXPERIMENTAL	819.281-022
WELDER, EXPLOSION	814.684-010
WELDER-FITTER	819.361-010
WELDER-FITTER APPRENTICE	819.361-014
Welder-Fitter, Arc	819.361-010
Welder-Fitter, Gas	819.361-010
Welder, Flux-Cored Arc	810.384-014
WELDER, GAS	811.684-014
welder, gas, automatic	811.482-010
Welder, Gas-Metal Arc	810.384-014
Welder, Gas-Tungsten Arc	810.384-014
WELDER, GUN	810.664-010
Welder, Hand, Submerged Arc	810.384-014
WELDER HELPER	819.687-014
Welder, Oxyacetylene	811.684-014
Welder, Oxyhydrogen	811.684-014
Welder, Plasma Arc	810.384-014
WELDER, PRODUCTION LINE	819.684-010
Welder, Production Line, Arc	819.684-010
Welder, Production Line, Combination	819.684-010
Welder, Production Line, Gas	819.684-010
Welder, Repair	819.384-010
WELDER SETTER, ELECTRON-BEAM MACHINE	815.380-010
WELDER SETTER, RESISTANCE MACHINE	812.360-010
Welder, Shielded-Metal Arc	810.384-014
Welder, Structural Repair	819.361-010
WELDER, TACK	810.684-010
Welder, Tool And Die	819.361-010
Welding-Machine Feeder	819.686-010
WELDING-MACHINE OPERATOR, ARC	810.382-010
Welding-Machine Operator, Electro-Gas	810.382-010
WELDING-MACHINE OPERATOR, ELECTRON BEAM	815.382-010
WELDING-MACHINE OPERATOR, ELECTROSLAG	815.382-014
WELDING-MACHINE OPERATOR, FRICTION	814.382-010
WELDING-MACHINE OPERATOR, GAS	811.482-010
Welding-Machine Operator, Gas-Metal Arc	810.382-010
Welding-Machine Operator, Gas-Tungsten Arc	810.382-010
Welding-Machine-Operator Helper, Arc	819.666-010
Welding-Machine-Operator Helper, Gas	819.666-010
Welding-Machine Operator, Plasma Arc	810.382-010
WELDING-MACHINE OPERATOR, RESISTANCE	812.682-010
Welding-Machine Operator, Submerged Arc	810.382-010
WELDING-MACHINE OPERATOR, THERMIT	815.682-014
WELDING-MACHINE OPERATOR, ULTRASONIC	814.682-010
WELDING-MACHINE TENDER	819.685-010
WELDING SUPERVISOR	819.131-014
Welding Supervisor, Electric-Weld Pipe Mill	819.131-014
welding tester	819.281-018
WELD INSPECTOR I	819.281-018
WELD INSPECTOR II	819.687-010
Wire-Drawing-Machine Tender	819.685-010

wholesale tr.—WHOLESALE TRADE INDUSTRY: This designation includes occupations concerned with selling to retailers, institutions, industrial consumers, and other wholesale organizations for resale or other processing rather than for personal or home consumption. The designation covers sales activities, whether by wholesale organizations or by manufacturing concerns. In addition to the sale of commodities at wholesale, the designation includes occupations concerned with the related processes normally carried on by wholesale establishments, and also the functions of agents and brokers who operate in the wholesale market in effecting purchases and sales between other parties. The principal types of wholesale activities are full-service and limited-function wholesales, manufacturers' sales branches and offices, functional middlemen, such as agents and brokers, and assemblers of agricultural commodities.

Apple Packer	920.687-134
Apple Sorter	529.687-186
Apple Washer	529.685-258
Apricot Packer	920.687-134
Asparagus Sorter	529.687-186
AUCTION ASSISTANT	294.667-010
AUCTION CLERK	294.567-010
AUCTIONEER	294.257-010
Auctioneer, Art	294.257-010
Auctioneer, Automobile	294.257-010
Auctioneer, Furniture	294.257-010
Auctioneer, Livestock	294.257-010
Auctioneer, Real Estate	294.257-010
Auctioneer, Tobacco	294.257-010
AUTOMOBILE WRECKER	620.684-010
Avocado Packer	920.687-134
Banana Grader	529.687-186
Banana-Ripening-Room Supervisor	920.137-010
BLOWER INSULATOR	863.664-010
BOOKING CLERK	216.587-010
broker, agricultural produce	260.357-010
BROKER-AND-MARKET OPERATOR, GRAIN	162.157-010
BUILDING CONSULTANT	250.357-010
butcher	316.684-018
butcher apprentice	316.684-022
BUYER, GRAIN	162.167-010
Buyer, Grain	162.157-010
buyer, head	162.167-014
BUYER, TOBACCO, HEAD	162.167-014
Capper Picker	529.687-186
car cleaner	915.687-022
car porter	915.687-022
Carrot Washer	529.685-258
Cherry Packer	920.687-134
Cherry Sorter	529.687-186
circuit rider	162.167-014
circuit walker	162.167-014
Citrus-Fruit Packer	920.687-134
Citrus-Fruit-Packing Grader	529.687-186
COLORER, CITRUS FRUIT	529.685-070
COMMISSION AGENT, AGRICULTURAL PRODUCE	260.357-010
COMMISSION AGENT, LIVESTOCK	162.157-026
COMPARISON SHOPPER	296.367-014
counter clerk	279.357-062
Counter Clerk, Appliance Parts	279.357-062
Counter Clerk, Automotive Parts	279.357-062
Counter Clerk, Farm Equipment Parts	279.357-062
Counter Clerk, Industrial Machinery And Equipment Parts	279.357-062
Counter Clerk, Radio, Television, And Electronics Parts	279.357-062
Counter Clerk, Tractor Parts	279.357-062
Counter Clerk, Truck Parts	279.357-062
Cranberry Sorter	529.687-186
Crate Tier	920.687-134
Cull Grader	529.687-186
CUTTER, BANANA ROOM	929.687-010
DEALER-COMPLIANCE REPRESENTATIVE	168.267-026
DECAY-CONTROL OPERATOR	529.685-086
delivery-route truck driver	292.353-010
DEMONSTRATOR	297.354-010

Demonstrator, Construction Equipment 859.683-010
DENTAL-EQUIPMENT INSTALLER AND SERVICER 829.261-014
detailer, pharmaceuticals 262.157-010
director, merchandise 185.167-034
dispatcher, route sales-delivery drivers 292.137-014
distribution manager 163.267-010
DISTRIBUTION SUPERVISOR 914.137-010
distributor, motor vehicles and supplies 273.357-022
distributor, publications 277.357-022
DRIVER HELPER, SALES ROUTE 292.667-010
DRIVER, SALES ROUTE 292.353-010
DUMPING-MACHINE OPERATOR 529.685-102
Egg Packer 920.687-134
egg room supervisor 529.137-042
EGG WASHER, MACHINE 529.686-030
electric-motor-repair clerk 271.354-010
EMBROIDERY PATTERNMAKER 782.361-014
Exporter 185.157-018
Fancy Packer 920.587-014
fashion model 297.667-014
feeder worker power-unit operator 863.685-010
FIELD REPRESENTATIVE 163.267-010
field representative 168.267-026
Fig Sorter 529.687-186
Fish Icer 922.687-046
Floor-Coverings Estimator 270.357-026
FLOOR-SPACE ALLOCATOR 222.367-030
Food Demonstrator 297.354-010
FRUIT-BUYING GRADER 529.387-018
FRUIT-GRADER OPERATOR 529.665-010
fruit inspector 529.387-018
Fruit Packer, Face-And-Fill 920.687-134
Fruit Packer, Wrap-And-Place 920.687-134
Fruit Sorter 529.687-186
Fuel-Oil-Delivery Driver 903.683-018
fur beater 369.685-014
FUR CLEANER, MACHINE 369.685-014
fur drummer 369.685-014
fur dry-cleaner 369.685-014
Gas-Delivery Driver 903.683-018
GENERAL MANAGER, FARM 180.167-018
grain-elevator agent 162.167-010
grain trader 162.157-010
GREENS TIER 920.687-094
Header 920.687-134
hose handler 863.664-010
house model 297.667-014
house supervisor 920.137-010
Housewares Demonstrator 297.354-010
ICER 922.687-046
Importer 185.157-018
INSULATION-POWER-UNIT TENDER 863.685-010
Lidder 920.687-134
LOCKER-PLANT ATTENDANT 922.684-010
lot caller 294.667-010
Magazine-Delivery Driver 292.363-010
Mail-Order Biller 214.382-014
MANAGER, DISTRIBUTION WAREHOUSE 185.167-018
MANAGER, FAST FOOD SERVICES 185.137-010
manager, grain elevator 162.167-010
MANAGER, MARKET 186.167-042
MANAGER, MEAT SALES AND STORAGE 185.167-030
MANAGER, MERCHANDISE 185.167-034
MANAGER, NURSERY 180.167-042
MANAGER, PARTS 185.167-038
manager, service 187.167-142
MANAGER, SERVICE DEPARTMENT 187.167-142
manager, stockroom 185.167-038
MANAGER, TEXTILE CONVERSION 185.167-050
MANAGER, TOBACCO WAREHOUSE 185.167-054
manufacturers' agent 279.157-010
MANUFACTURERS' REPRESENTATIVE 279.157-010
MARKER 209.587-034
marking clerk 209.587-034
MEAT CUTTER 316.684-018
MEAT-CUTTER APPRENTICE 316.684-022
Meat Inspector 316.684-018
merchandise marker 209.587-034
MODEL 297.667-014
NEWSPAPER-DELIVERY DRIVER 292.363-010
Orange Washer 529.685-258
ORDER FILLER 222.487-014
PACKING-HOUSE SUPERVISOR 920.137-010
packing-shed supervisor 920.137-010
parts clerk 279.357-062

Peach Sorter 529.687-186
Pear Packer 920.687-134
PERISHABLE-FRUIT INSPECTOR 910.387-010
PHARMACEUTICAL DETAILER 262.157-010
platform inspector 529.387-018
Plum Packer 920.687-134
PORTER, SAMPLE CASE 299.687-010
PORTER, USED-CAR LOT 915.687-022
Potato Grader 529.687-186
Potato Sorter 529.687-186
price marker 209.587-034
ranch manager 180.167-018
RECLAMATION WORKER 621.684-014
Ring Packer 920.687-134
route driver 292.353-010
route driver helper 292.667-010
route supervisor 292.137-014
SAFE-AND-VAULT SERVICE MECHANIC 869.381-022
safe repairer 869.381-022
sales agent   see SALES REPRESENTATIVE ....
Sales Agent, Food-Vending Service 251.357-010
sales associate   see SALES REPRESENTATIVE ....
SALESPERSON .... master
salesperson apprentice, meats 316.684-022
SALESPERSON, AUTOMOBILE ACCESSORIES 273.357-030
Salesperson, China And Glassware 270.357-018
SALESPERSON, CHINA AND SILVERWARE 270.357-018
SALESPERSON, ELECTRIC MOTORS 271.354-010
SALESPERSON, FLOOR COVERINGS 270.357-026
SALESPERSON, FLORIST SUPPLIES 275.357-054
SALESPERSON, GENERAL HARDWARE 279.357-050
SALESPERSON, GENERAL MERCHANDISE 279.357-054
SALESPERSON, HORTICULTURAL AND NURSERY
    PRODUCTS 272.357-022
salesperson, meats 316.684-018
Salesperson, Paint 279.357-050
SALESPERSON, PARTS 279.357-062
SALESPERSON, PHOTOGRAPHIC SUPPLIES AND
    EQUIPMENT 277.357-050
SALESPERSON, STAMPS OR COINS 277.357-062
Salesperson, Terrazzo Tiles 270.357-026
Salesperson, Wall Coverings 279.357-050
SALES-PROMOTION REPRESENTATIVE 269.357-018
SALES REPRESENTATIVE .... master
SALES REPRESENTATIVE, ABRASIVES 274.357-010
Sales Representative, Adding Machines 275.357-034
Sales Representative, Addressing Machines 275.357-034
SALES REPRESENTATIVE, AIRCRAFT 273.253-010
SALES REPRESENTATIVE, AIRCRAFT EQUIPMENT
    AND PARTS 273.357-010
SALES REPRESENTATIVE, ANIMAL-FEED PRODUCTS 272.357-010
SALES REPRESENTATIVE, APPAREL TRIMMINGS 261.357-010
SALES REPRESENTATIVE, ARCHITECTURAL AND
    ENGINEERING SUPPLIES 276.357-010
Sales Representative, Automobile Parts And Supplies 273.357-022
SALES REPRESENTATIVE, BARBER AND BEAUTY
    EQUIPMENT AND SUPPLIES 275.357-010
SALES REPRESENTATIVE, BOATS AND MARINE
    SUPPLIES 273.357-018
Sales Representative, Bookkeeping-And-Accounting
    Machines 275.357-034
SALES REPRESENTATIVE, BOTTLES AND BOTTLING
    EQUIPMENT 274.357-014
Sales Representative, Bottles And Jars 274.357-014
Sales Representative, Bottling Equipment 274.357-014
SALES REPRESENTATIVE, BUILDING EQUIPMENT
    AND SUPPLIES 274.357-018
Sales Representative, Calculating Machines 275.357-034
SALES REPRESENTATIVE, CANVAS PRODUCTS 261.357-014
Sales Representative, Cash Registers 275.357-034
Sales Representative, Cattle-And-Poultry Feed Supplements .. 272.357-010
Sales Representative, Check-Endorsing-And-Signing
    Machines 275.357-034
SALES REPRESENTATIVE, CHEMICALS AND DRUGS .. 262.357-010
Sales Representative, Church Furniture 275.357-014
SALES REPRESENTATIVE, CHURCH FURNITURE AND
    RELIGIOUS SUPPLIES 275.357-014
SALES REPRESENTATIVE, COMMERCIAL EQUIPMENT
    AND SUPPLIES 275.357-018
SALES REPRESENTATIVE, COMMUNICATION
    EQUIPMENT 271.257-010
SALES REPRESENTATIVE, COMPUTERS AND EDP
    SYSTEMS 275.257-010
SALES REPRESENTATIVE, CONSTRUCTION
    MACHINERY 274.357-022

wood. container—WOODEN CONTAINER INDUSTRY: This designation includes occupations concerned with manufacturing and repairing box shooks; cases for eggs and canned goods; carrier trays; crates for berries, butter, fruits, and vegetables; and wooden boxes. Occupations concerned with manufacturing and repairing baskets and nonfurniture articles from rattan, reed, and willow are included here. Also included are occupations concerned with manufacturing and repairing tight and slack barrels, buckets, casks, hogsheads, kegs, tanks, and tubs made of staves.

wood. container

ASSEMBLER, FAUCETS	764.687-014
assembling inspector	762.687-014
Back-Roll-Lathe Operator	664.662-010
BANDER	762.687-010
Band-Resaw Operator	667.682-058
BAND-SAW OPERATOR	667.685-010
BARREL ASSEMBLER	669.685-014
BARREL-ASSEMBLER HELPER	669.685-010
BARREL BRANDER	764.684-010
barrel-bung-remover and dumper	764.687-018
barrel burner	764.684-014
BARREL CHARRER	764.684-014
BARREL-CHARRER HELPER	764.687-034
barrel coater	764.687-026
BARREL DRAINER	764.687-018
BARREL INSPECTOR, TIGHT	764.687-022
BARREL-LATHE OPERATOR, INSIDE	664.682-010
BARREL-LATHE OPERATOR, OUTSIDE	664.682-014
barrel leveler	764.687-094
BARREL LINER	764.687-026
barrel maker	764.684-018
BARREL MARKER	764.687-030
barrel planer	664.682-014
BARREL RAISER	764.684-018
BARREL-RAISER HELPER	764.687-038
barrel repairer	764.684-022
barrel-repairer helper	764.687-050
barrel roller	764.687-030
barrel-stave inspector	764.687-054
barrel tester and drainer	764.687-022
Barrel Waterer	764.687-010
BASKET ASSEMBLER I	669.685-014
BASKET ASSEMBLER II	769.684-010
Basket-Bottom-Machine Operator	669.685-014
Basket-Bottom-Rounding-Machine Operator	667.685-066
basket-factory machine hand	669.685-074
BASKET GRADER	769.687-010
basket-machine operator	669.685-074
basket maker	769.684-054
basket maker	669.685-014
BASKET MENDER	762.684-022
BASKET PATCHER	769.684-014
Board Layer	669.686-014
BOARD-LINER OPERATOR	641.685-014
bolt sawyer	667.685-062
BOTTOM-HOOP DRIVER	669.685-022
Bottom Maker	669.685-014
Bottom Nailer	669.682-058
bottom turner	669.685-026
BOTTOM-TURNING-LATHE TENDER	665.685-010
BOX-BLANK-MACHINE OPERATOR	669.662-010
BOX-BLANK-MACHINE-OPERATOR HELPER	669.686-014
Box Gluer	762.687-034
box-hinge and lock attacher	762.687-046
BOX INSPECTOR	762.687-014
BOX MAKER, WOOD	760.684-014
Box Nailer	762.687-046
Box Repairer I	760.684-014
BOX REPAIRER II	762.687-018
box-shook patcher	762.687-018
box strapper	692.682-058
Box-Top-Stitching-Machine Operator	669.685-042
Braider	669.685-014
BUCKET CHUCKER	664.685-014
BUCKET TURNER	669.682-018
bumper operator	669.685-046
BUNG DRIVER	764.687-042
Bunghole Borer	666.382-010
carpenter, box	760.684-014
case maker	760.684-014
cask maker	764.684-026
CHANNEL INSTALLER	764.687-046
charrer	764.684-014
charrer helper	764.687-034
charring-room worker, barrel	764.684-014
charring-room-worker helper, barrel	764.687-034
CIRCLE-CUTTING-SAW OPERATOR	669.685-026
Circular-Resaw Operator	667.682-058
Circular-Tank Cooper	764.684-030
CLEAT FEEDER	669.687-010
Cleat Layer	669.686-014
Cleat Nailer	669.682-058
Cleat Notcher	669.382-010
cleat thrower	669.687-010
coiler	619.682-034

COOPER	764.684-022
COOPER HELPER	764.687-050
CORNER FORMER	617.685-014
CORNER-TRIMMER OPERATOR	667.682-018
Cover-Machine Operator	669.685-014
Cover-Mat-Machine Operator	669.685-014
crate builder	760.684-014
Croze Cutter	669.682-014
Croze-Cutter Helper	669.685-010
CROZE-MACHINE OPERATOR	669.682-034
crozer	669.682-034
CULLER	764.687-054
DOVETAIL-MACHINE OPERATOR	669.685-046
doweler	764.687-062
edger	795.684-014
EDGE STRIPPER	795.684-014
end operator	669.685-054
END STAPLER	669.685-054
estimator, lumber	221.482-014
EXPERIMENTAL-BOX TESTER	761.281-014
final inspector	764.687-022
final tester	764.687-022
FINISHER	749.684-026
flarer	619.682-034
forming operator	669.685-046
Frame Nailer	669.682-058
Hamper Maker	769.684-054
Hamper Maker, Machine	669.685-014
hand-cooper helper	764.687-050
Handhole-Machine Operator	665.682-030
Handle Bender	669.685-014
Handle-Machine Operator	669.685-014
HARDWARE ASSEMBLER	762.687-046
Hardware Press Operator	762.687-046
Head Charrer	764.684-014
HEADER	764.687-058
header-up	764.687-058
HEADING MATCHER AND ASSEMBLER	764.687-062
heading pinner	764.687-062
HEADING REPAIRER	764.687-066
HEAD INSPECTOR	764.387-010
Head-Inspector-And-Center Marker	764.387-010
head setter	764.687-058
Head-Turning-Machine Operator	667.685-066
Head-Up Operator	669.682-014
Head-Up-Operator Helper	669.685-010
Heater Operator	669.682-014
Heater Operator Helper	669.685-010
hogshead builder	764.687-074
HOGSHEAD COOPER I	764.684-026
HOGSHEAD COOPER II	764.687-070
HOGSHEAD COOPER III	764.687-074
hogshead head-matcher	667.685-010
HOGSHEAD HOOPER	764.687-078
HOGSHEAD MAT ASSEMBLER	764.687-082
HOGSHEAD MAT INSPECTOR	764.687-086
HOOP BENDER, TANK	619.682-026
hoop-bending-machine operator	619.682-026
HOOP COILER	617.686-010
Hoop-Coiling-Machine Operator	669.685-014
Hoop-Driving-Machine Operator	669.682-014
Hoop-Driving-Machine-Operator Helper	669.685-010
hooper	764.687-078
HOOP-FLARING-AND-COILING-MACHINE OPERATOR	619.682-034
Hoop-Flaring-Machine Operator	619.682-030
Hoop-Flaring-Machine-Operator Helper	619.686-014
HOOP-MAKER HELPER, MACHINE	619.686-014
HOOP MAKER, MACHINE	619.682-030
Hoop-Punch-And-Coiler Operator	619.682-030
Hoop-Punch-And-Coiler-Operator Helper	619.686-014
Hoop-Punch-Operator Helper	619.687-014
Hoop-Riveting-Machine Operator	619.682-030
Hoop-Riveting-Machine-Operator Helper	619.686-014
hoop-rolls operator	617.686-010
JIG BUILDER	761.381-014
keg inspector	764.687-022
keg-lathe operator, inside	664.682-010
keg raiser	764.684-018
KEG VARNISHER	749.687-014
lathe operator	664.682-014
Leveler Helper	669.685-010
LEVELER I	764.687-094
Leveler II	669.682-014
LOG COOKER	562.665-010
looper	692.685-258

Loop-Machine Operator	669.685-014
LUMBER ESTIMATOR	221.482-014
MACHINE-TANK OPERATOR	667.662-014
Market-Basket Maker I	669.685-014
Market-Basket Maker II	769.684-054
MATERIAL INSPECTOR	764.387-014
Mat-Machine Tender	669.685-014
Multiple-Cut-Off-Saw Operator	667.682-022
Multiple-Resaw Operator	667.682-058
PARTITION ASSEMBLER	762.687-054
Partition Notcher	669.382-010
patented-hogshead assembler	764.687-070
PIPE-AND-TANK FABRICATOR	669.380-018
PLUGGER	764.687-098
power-saw operator	667.662-014
PUTTY MIXER AND APPLIER	769.687-038
quality-control-inspector, heading	764.387-010
raiser	764.684-014
raiser helper	764.687-038
Rattan Worker	769.684-054
Rectangular-Tank Cooper	764.684-030
rounding-machine operator	667.685-066
Sander	669.682-014
Sander Helper	669.685-010
setter	761.381-014
setter-up	764.684-018
setting-up-and-windlass-machine operator	764.684-018
setting-up-and-windlass-machine-operator helper	764.687-038
shop cooper	764.684-022
Slack Cooper	764.684-022
SLAT-BASKET MAKER HELPER, MACHINE	669.686-026
SLAT-BASKET MAKER, MACHINE	669.685-074
Slat-Basket-Top Maker	669.685-014
SQUEEZER OPERATOR	669.685-082
stave grader	764.387-014
stave inspector	764.387-014
stave inspector and culler	764.687-054
STAVE JOINTER	665.685-030
STAVE-MACHINE TENDER	663.685-046
stave matcher	764.687-054
STAVE-SAW OPERATOR	667.685-062
steam-vat tender	562.665-010
STEEL-BARREL REAMER	703.687-022
Stitcher Feeder	669.686-030
Stitcher Operator	669.685-014
stitching-machine operator	669.662-010
STITCHING-MACHINE OPERATOR	669.685-086
Strap Nailer	669.682-058
strapper	692.682-058
STRAPPING-MACHINE OPERATOR	692.682-058
Strap Recesser	669.382-010
STRIP-METAL-PUNCH-AND-STRAIGHTENER OPERATOR	615.685-038
Supervisor, Barrel Assembly	764.134-010
SUPERVISOR, COOPERAGE SHOP	764.134-010
Supervisor, Heading	764.134-010
SUPERVISOR, STAVE CUTTING	667.137-010
Supervisor, Stave Finishing	764.134-010
TANK ASSEMBLER	764.684-030
Tank-Bottom Assembler	764.684-030
tank cooper	764.684-030
Tank-Stave Assembler	764.684-030
Tap-Out Operator	669.682-014
Tight Cooper	764.684-022
Truss Driver	669.682-014
Truss-Driver Helper	669.685-010
Truss Puller	669.682-014
Truss-Puller Helper	669.685-010
tub chucker	664.685-014
tub turner	669.682-018
turner-machine operator	667.685-066
TURNING-MACHINE OPERATOR	667.685-066
TURNING-MACHINE-OPERATOR HELPER	667.686-022
VENEER-STOCK GRADER	769.687-050
WEAVER	769.684-054
Webb Layer	669.685-014
wicker worker	769.684-054
Willow Worker	769.684-054
Wire Bender	669.686-014
Wire-Bound-Box-Machine Helper	669.686-014
Wire-Bound-Box-Machine Operator	669.662-010
WIRE-TURNING-MACHINE OPERATOR	692.685-258
WIRE-WINDING-MACHINE OPERATOR	619.685-090
wood cooker	562.665-010

wood prod., nec—WOOD PRODUCTS INDUSTRY, NOT ELSEWHERE CLASSIFIED: This designation includes occupations which are not included in other industries concerned with manufacturing, repairing, and preserving wood products. Typical occupations include those concerned with (1) treating wood with creosote or other preservatives to prevent decay and to protect against fire and insects; (2) manufacturing wood panel products from small wood particles; and (3) manufacturing and repairing cork products, hardboard, lasts and related products, and wood and metal mirror and picture frames.

Adzing-And-Boring-Machine Feeder	669.686-030
Adzing-And-Boring-Machine Helper	561.686-010
ADZING-AND-BORING-MACHINE OPERATOR	669.682-010
ANTICHECKING-IRON WORKER	563.687-010
BACK TENDER, INSULATION BOARD	532.685-010
Beegle-Iron Worker	563.687-010
board handler	569.686-042
BREAKER-MACHINE OPERATOR	564.685-010
Broke-Beater Tender	530.685-014
burnisher	742.684-010
CALENDER OPERATOR, INSULATION BOARD	539.482-010
chip mixer	560.465-010
CHIP-MIXING-MACHINE OPERATOR	560.465-010
CHIPPING-MACHINE OPERATOR	564.682-010
C-Iron Worker	563.687-010
coater, hand	562.687-014
COATER OPERATOR, INSULATION BOARD	539.685-010
Coating-Line Checker	539.667-010
COATING-MACHINE OPERATOR, HARDBOARD	534.682-022
COMPO CASTER	769.381-010
COMPOUNDER, CORK	560.587-010
CONTROL INSPECTOR	539.667-010
core feeder	569.685-042
cork coater	562.687-014
cork mixer	560.585-010
cork mixer	560.587-010
CORK MOLDER	569.685-030
CORK-PRESSING-MACHINE OPERATOR	569.686-018
cork sorter	769.687-042
Cross-Tie-Tram Loader	561.686-010
Cross-Tie Turner	669.687-018
CYLINDER-MACHINE OPERATOR	539.362-010
dip tanker	561.665-010
DRIER TENDER	563.585-010
DRILL-PRESS OPERATOR, ACOUSTICAL TILE	649.682-018
EMBOSSING-MACHINE OPERATOR	669.682-046
END-TOUCHING-MACHINE OPERATOR	662.686-010
EXTRUDER OPERATOR	569.685-038
Extruder Operator, Horizontal	569.685-038
Extruder Operator, Multiple	569.685-038
Extruder Operator, Vertical	569.685-038
filler and sander	769.687-022
finisher	742.684-010
fitter	739.684-146
FLAKE-CUTTER OPERATOR	564.682-014
FLOOR WORKER	739.687-098
FOOT-MITER OPERATOR	739.684-066
FRAMER	739.684-078
framer	669.662-014
FRAMER	666.684-010
FRAME-TABLE OPERATOR	669.662-014
FRAME-TABLE-OPERATOR HELPER	669.685-058
FRAME TRIMMER I	749.684-030
FRAME TRIMMER II	769.687-022
framing-mill operator	669.662-014
framing-mill-operator helper	669.685-058
GASKET SUPERVISOR	569.130-010
glue-mixer operator	560.465-010
glue-plant operator	560.465-010
glue-spreader operator	569.685-042
GLUE SPREADER, VENEER	569.685-042
GRINDER, HARDBOARD	569.682-010
grinding operator	662.685-026
GROOVER-AND-STRIPER OPERATOR	669.685-102
hand-miter operator	739.684-066
hardboard panel printer	652.662-018
HEADER	665.682-014
HEAD-SAW OPERATOR, INSULATION BOARD	677.682-010
Heel Grinder	669.682-054
HIGH-DENSITY FINISHING OPERATOR	539.562-010
High-Density-Talc-Coater Operator	534.682-022
Hollow-Core Door-Frame Assembler	762.687-022
HUMIDIFIER OPERATOR	562.682-010
Hydropulper	530.685-014
INCISING-MACHINE OPERATOR	569.662-010

woodworking

INSPECTOR, FIBROUS WALLBOARD	539.487-010
INSPECTOR, PICTURE FRAMES	769.687-030
ironer	739.684-098
LABORER, WOOD-PRESERVING PLANT	561.686-010
LAMINATING-MACHINE FEEDER	569.686-042
LAMINATING-MACHINE OFFBEARER	569.686-046
LAMINATOR	554.685-030
laminator grader	569.686-046
Last-Code Striper	740.684-022
last grinder	662.685-018
LAST IRONER	739.684-098
LAST MARKER	739.684-102
LAST-MODEL MAKER	761.381-018
LAST-PATTERN GRADER	693.382-010
Last Polisher	761.684-026
LAST REMODELER-REPAIRER	739.684-106
LAST REPAIRER	739.684-110
LAST SAWYER	690.685-262
LAST SCOURER	662.685-018
LAST TRIMMER	669.682-054
Last Turner	664.685-018
line-and-frame poler	959.684-010
LINE TENDER, FLAKEBOARD	569.382-010
load tallier	221.167-022
Louver-Door Assembler	762.687-022
MAT CUTTER	739.684-126
MIRROR SPECIALIST	779.684-038
MIXING-MACHINE TENDER	560.585-010
Mixing-Machine Tender, Cork Gasket	560.585-010
Mixing-Machine Tender, Cork Rod	560.585-010
model maker	761.381-018
Mold Filler	569.685-030
Mold Hoister	569.685-030
Mold Sprayer	569.685-030
ORNAMENTAL-MACHINE OPERATOR	690.682-054
ornamenter, hand	769.381-010
paint-coating-machine operator	534.682-022
PATTERN-GRADER SUPERVISOR	693.132-010
PATTERNMAKER, ACOUSTICAL TILE	649.685-086
perforating-machine operator	569.662-010
PICTURE FRAMER	739.684-146
platform worker	561.665-010
pole classifier	561.587-010
POLE FRAMER	959.684-010
Pole Framer, Machine	669.662-014
Pole-Incisor Operator	569.662-010
POLE INSPECTOR	561.587-010
pole peeler	663.682-014
pole-peeler helper	665.686-010
POLE-PEELING-MACHINE OPERATOR	663.682-014
POLE-PEELING-MACHINE-OPERATOR HELPER	665.686-010
pole shaver	663.682-014
pole-shaver helper	665.686-010
polisher and sander	662.685-026
Powder Gilder	763.381-010
PRESS BREAKER	569.686-050
PRESS OPERATOR, HARDBOARD	569.682-014
PRINT-LINE OPERATOR	652.662-018
print-line supervisor	652.662-018
pulp drier	532.685-010
PULPER	530.685-014
PULP GRINDER AND BLENDER	530.682-010
PUNCH PRESS OPERATOR	669.685-106
QUALITY-CONTROL TESTER	569.384-010
REED-PRESS FEEDER	669.686-022
remodeler	739.684-106
Repairer, Mirror And Picture Frame	769.684-038
Repairer, Sash And Door	769.684-038
RESIN COATER	562.687-014
retort engineer	561.362-010
RETORT-LOAD EXPEDITER	221.167-022
RUBBER	742.684-010
SANDING-MACHINE BUFFER	662.685-022
SANDING-MACHINE TENDER	662.685-026
Satin Finisher	742.684-010
SAWYER, CORK SLABS	667.685-046
scaffold worker	561.665-010
SCREEN CLEANER	569.687-018
SCREEN TENDER	534.665-010
shader and toner	749.684-030
Siding-Coreboard Inspector	539.687-010
S-Iron Worker	563.687-010
SLICING-MACHINE TENDER	663.686-026
slusher operator	530.685-014
SORTER I	569.687-022

SORTER II	769.687-042
SPAR-MACHINE OPERATOR	664.682-022
SPAR-MACHINE-OPERATOR HELPER	664.685-030
SPLITTING-MACHINE TENDER	663.685-042
Spray-Painter, Machine	599.685-074
STAIN APPLICATOR	561.585-010
STAINER	742.684-014
Stiff-Leg Derrick Operator	921.663-022
SUPERVISOR, FABRICATION	769.130-010
SUPERVISOR, FRAMING MILL	669.130-018
SUPERVISOR, HARDBOARD	539.130-010
Supervisor, Incising	561.131-010
SUPERVISOR, LAST-MODEL DEPARTMENT	761.131-010
SUPERVISOR, PARTICLEBOARD	569.132-010
Supervisor, Pole Yard	669.130-018
Supervisor, Tie Yard	669.130-018
SUPERVISOR, WET END	539.131-010
TANKER	561.665-010
TENONER OPERATOR	677.682-026
Tie Handler	561.686-010
tie-mill operator	669.682-010
Tile-Machine Operator	539.562-010
Timber-Incisor Operator	569.662-010
timber-treating-tank operator	561.362-010
Toe Stripper	669.682-054
TREATING ENGINEER	561.362-010
TREATING-ENGINEER HELPER	561.685-010
TREATING INSPECTOR	569.367-010
TREATING-PLANT OPERATOR	563.662-010
treating-plant operator	561.362-010
TREATING-PLANT SUPERVISOR	561.131-010
veneer gluer	569.685-042
WET-END HELPER	534.685-034
Whitener	763.381-010
WHITING-MACHINE OPERATOR	562.485-010
Wincher	561.686-010
WOOD-POLE TREATER	561.687-010

woodworking—WOODWORKING: This designation includes occupations concerned with various phases of woodworking and related processes wherever found. Typical of the processes included are fabricating, grading, planing, sawing, and shaping lumber and wooden articles. Occupations concerned with the manufacture of metal doors and screens are included in the STRUCTURAL AND ORNAMENTAL METAL PRODUCTS INDUSTRY (struct. metal).

ASSEMBLY OPERATOR	762.684-018
automatic-lathe operator	664.382-010
Automatic-Lathe Setter	669.280-010
automatic-mold sander	662.682-010
Band-Ripsaw Operator	667.682-066
band-saw marker	761.684-022
BAND-SAW OPERATOR	667.685-014
BAND-SCROLL-SAW OPERATOR	667.682-010
Bat-Lathe Operator	664.382-010
Belt Sander	761.682-014
BENCH CARPENTER	760.684-010
BENDER, HAND	769.684-018
BENDER, MACHINE	569.685-014
bending-press operator	569.685-014
binder	929.685-018
BOAT-OAR MAKER	761.381-010
BOBBIN INSPECTOR	769.687-014
Boring-Machine Feeder	669.686-030
BORING-MACHINE OPERATOR	666.382-010
Boring-Machine Operator, Double End	666.382-010
Boring-Machine Operator, Horizontal	666.382-010
Boring-Machine Operator, Vertical	666.382-010
Box-Blank-Machine Feeder	669.686-030
Brush Sander	761.682-014
bundler	929.685-018
CABINETMAKER	660.280-010
CABINETMAKER APPRENTICE	660.280-014
Cabinetmaker, Maintenance	660.280-010
CABINETMAKER, SUPERVISOR	660.130-010
CARVER, HAND	761.281-010
carver, machine	761.682-018
carving-machine operator	761.682-018
Chain-Mortiser Operator	665.482-014
Check Grader	669.687-030
Chisel-Mortiser Operator	665.482-014
CHUCKING-AND-SAWING-MACHINE OPERATOR	669.682-026
CHUCKING-MACHINE OPERATOR	665.382-010
Circular-Ripsaw Operator	667.682-066
Clamp-Carrier Operator	762.687-034

woodworking

retort operator	562.665-014
Ripsaw Grader	667.382-010
Ripsaw Matcher	667.682-066
RIPSAW OPERATOR	667.682-066
ripsawyer	667.682-066
rotary profile-shaper operator, automatic	665.682-026
Rough-Lumber Grader	669.687-030
ROUGH PLANER TENDER	665.665-010
ROUTER OPERATOR	665.682-030
Router Setter	669.280-010
routing-machine operator	665.682-030
sander and filer	705.684-018
SANDER, HAND	761.687-010
SANDER, MACHINE	761.682-014
SANDER, PORTABLE MACHINE	761.684-034
Sander Setter	669.280-010
sanding-machine tender, automatic	662.685-038
Sash Assembler	762.687-050
Saw-Handle Assembler	762.687-042
Saw Offbearer	669.686-034
Screen Roller	762.687-058
scroll-saw operator	667.682-010
scroll-saw operator	667.682-042
separator	922.687-074
SHAPER OPERATOR	665.682-034
Shaper Setter	669.280-010
shook splicer	669.685-042
Shovel-Handle Assembler	762.687-042
SHUTTLE INSPECTOR	769.684-046
SHUTTLE SPOTTER	664.685-026
Single-End-Trimming-And-Boring-Machine Operator	669.682-038
sizer grader	669.687-030
Small-Parts-Shaper Operator	665.682-034
Snath-Handle Assembler	762.687-042
SPEED-BELT-SANDER TENDER	662.685-034
SPINDLE CARVER	761.682-018
Spindle Sander	761.682-014
splicer-machine operator	669.685-042
splitter	667.682-058
Spool Sander	761.682-014
stacker	569.685-066
STACKER, MACHINE	569.685-066
stave steamer	562.665-014
STEAM-BOX OPERATOR	562.665-014
steam-tunnel feeder	562.665-014
stitcher operator	669.685-042
STOCK GRADER	667.382-010
STOCK-PATCH SAWYER	667.682-082
Strapper And Buffer	705.684-014
STROKE-BELT-SANDER OPERATOR	662.682-018
SUPERVISOR, ASSEMBLY	769.137-014
Supervisor, Gluing	769.137-014
SUPERVISOR, MACHINING	669.130-022
SUPERVISOR, SANDING	662.132-010
SUPERVISOR, SHUTTLE FITTING	669.130-030
SUPERVISOR, SHUTTLE PREPARATION	669.130-034
SUPERVISOR, SHUTTLE VENEERING	669.130-038
Swinging-Cut-Off-Saw Operator	667.682-022
SWING-TYPE-LATHE OPERATOR	664.382-010
Table-Cut-Off-Saw Operator	667.682-022
tailer	669.686-034
Television-Cabinet Finisher	763.381-010
Tenoner Offbearer	669.686-034
TENONER OPERATOR	669.382-018
tester	762.384-010
tilting-head band-sawyer	667.682-010
Tilting-Saw Operator	667.682-022
TIP INSERTER	669.682-066
Tongue-And-Groove-Machine Feeder	669.686-030
TONGUE-AND-GROOVE-MACHINE OPERATOR	669.662-018
Tongue-And-Groove-Machine Setter	669.280-010
Towel-Rack Assembler	762.687-070
transfer operator	569.683-010
Treadle-Cut-Off-Saw Operator	667.682-022
trimmer operator	667.682-022
Turner	669.686-030
TURNING-SANDER TENDER	662.685-038
TYING-MACHINE OPERATOR, LUMBER	929.685-018
universal-saw operator	667.682-086
Unstacker	569.685-066
variety-lathe operator	664.382-010
VARIETY-SAW OPERATOR	667.682-086
Veneer Marker	761.684-022
Veneer Sander	662.682-014
Warble-Saw Operator	669.382-010
wedger-and-gluer	762.687-038
wood carver, hand	761.281-010
WOOD-CARVING-MACHINE OPERATOR	665.382-018
WOODENWARE ASSEMBLER	762.687-070
wood finisher	763.381-010
wood-finisher apprentice	763.381-014
wood-lathe operator	664.382-014
wood piler	569.685-066
wood-stock-blank handler	563.685-018
WOOD-TURNING-LATHE OPERATOR	664.382-014
WOODWORKING-MACHINE FEEDER	669.686-030
WOODWORKING-MACHINE OFFBEARER	669.686-034
woodworking-machine operator	669.380-014
WOODWORKING-SHOP HAND	769.687-054
woodworking-shop laborer	769.687-054
YARD SUPERVISOR	929.133-010

ALPHABETICAL INDEX OF OCCUPATIONAL TITLES

A

Abalone Diver (fishing & hunt.) 443.664-010
able-bodied seaman (water trans.) 911.364-010
ABLE SEAMAN (water trans.) 911.364-010
abrading machine tender (electron. comp.) 673.685-102
ABRASIVE-BAND WINDER (nonmet. min.) 692.685-010
abrasive-blasting equipment operator (any industry) 503.687-010
ABRASIVE-COATING-MACHINE OPERATOR (nonmet. min.) 574.462-010
ABRASIVE GRADER (optical goods) 570.682-010
ABRASIVE-GRADER HELPER (optical goods) 570.686-010
ABRASIVE GRINDER (nonmet. min.) 673.685-010
ABRASIVE MIXER (nonmet. min.) 570.485-010
ABRASIVE-MIXER HELPER (nonmet. min.) 570.686-014
ABRASIVE SAWYER (nonmet. min.) 677.685-010
Abrasive Water Jet Cutter Operator (aircraft mfg.) 699.382-010
ABRASIVE-WHEEL MOLDER (nonmet. min.) 575.685-010
ABSORPTION-AND-ADSORPTION ENGINEER (profess. & kin.) 008.061-010
ABSORPTION OPERATOR (chemical) 551.382-010
Absorption-Plant Operator (petrol. refin.) 549.260-010
Absorption-Plant-Operator Helper (petrol. refin.) 542.362-014
Abstract Checker (insurance) 219.482-014
abstract clerk (profess. & kin.) 119.267-010
abstract maker (profess. & kin.) 119.267-010
abstract manager (real estate) 186.167-090
abstractor (real estate) 209.367-046
ABSTRACTOR (profess. & kin.) 119.267-010
abstract searcher (profess. & kin.) 119.267-010
abstract writer (profess. & kin.) 119.267-010
Academic Counselor (education) 045.107-010
ACADEMIC DEAN (education) 090.117-010
academic vice president (education) 090.117-010
ACCELERATOR OPERATOR (profess. & kin.) 015.362-010
ACCESS COORDINATOR, CABLE TELEVISION (radio-tv broad.) 194.122-010
Accessories Repairer (railroad equip.) 825.281-026
Accident-And-Health-Insurance-Claim Examiner (insurance) 241.267-018
ACCIDENT-PREVENTION-SQUAD POLICE OFFICER (government ser.) 375.263-010
Accident-Report Clerk (clerical) 209.362-026
Accompanist (amuse. & rec.) 152.041-010
ACCORDION MAKER (musical inst.) 730.281-010
ACCORDION REPAIRER (any industry) 730.281-014
ACCORDION TUNER (any industry) 730.381-010
ACCOUNTANT (profess. & kin.) 160.162-018
ACCOUNTANT, BUDGET (profess. & kin.) 160.162-022
ACCOUNTANT, CERTIFIED PUBLIC (profess. & kin.) term
ACCOUNTANT, COST (profess. & kin.) 160.162-026
Accountant, Machine Processing (profess. & kin.) 160.167-026
ACCOUNTANT, PROPERTY (profess. & kin.) 160.167-022
ACCOUNTANT, SYSTEMS (profess. & kin.) 160.167-026
ACCOUNTANT, TAX (profess. & kin.) 160.162-010
Account-Classification Clerk (clerical) 210.382-030
ACCOUNT EXECUTIVE (business ser.) 164.167-010
account executive (financial) 250.257-018
account executive (radio-tv broad.) 259.357-018
ACCOUNT-INFORMATION CLERK (utilities) 210.367-010
ACCOUNTING CLERK (clerical) 216.482-010
Accounting-Machine Servicer (any industry) 633.281-018
accounting-system expert (profess. & kin.) 160.167-026
ACCOUNTS-ADJUSTABLE CLERK (r.r. trans.) 214.462-010
Accounts-Payable Bookkeeper (clerical) 210.382-014
Accounts-Payable Clerk (clerical) 216.482-010
Accounts-Receivable Bookkeeper (clerical) 210.382-014
Accounts-Receivable Clerk (clerical) 216.482-010
Acetaldehyde-Converter Operator (chemical) 558.362-010
ACETONE-BUTTON PASTER (button & notion) 734.687-010
ACETONE-RECOVERY WORKER (plastic-synth.) 552.685-010
ACETYLENE-CYLINDER-PACKING MIXER (chemical) 549.665-010
ACETYLENE-PLANT OPERATOR (chemical) 549.585-010
ACID ADJUSTER (elec. equip.) 727.484-010
Acid-Bath Mixer (textile) 550.585-018
Acid-Bath Tender (plastic-synth.) 557.685-030
acid blower (chemical) 550.585-030
acid changer (elec. equip.) 727.687-010
Acid-Concentration-Plant-Equipment Engineer (any industry) 950.382-026
Acid Conditioner (smelt. & refin.) 511.687-014
Acid-Correction Hand (plastic-synth.) 550.684-010
Acid-Crane Operator (steel & rel.) 921.663-042

Acid Cutter (concrete prod.) 579.687-042
acid dipper (any industry) 503.685-030
ACID DUMPER (elec. equip.) 727.687-010
ACID EXTRACTOR (steel & rel.) 558.382-010
ACID FILLER (elec. equip.) 727.687-014
Acidizer (petrol. & gas) 939.462-010
Acidizer Helper (petrol. & gas) 939.684-018
Acidizer, Water Well (construction) 939.462-010
Acid Leveler (elec. equip.) 727.687-014
Acid Loader (chemical) 914.667-010
ACID MAKER (paper & pulp) 559.662-010
ACID-PLANT HELPER (chemical) 558.565-010
ACID-POLYMERIZATION OPERATOR (chemical) 558.685-010
Acid Pumper (chemical) 914.682-010
ACID PURIFIER (chemical) 559.685-010
Acid-Strength Inspector (textile) 582.587-010
ACID SUPERVISOR (chemical) 559.132-010
Acid-Tank Cleaner (petrol. refin.) 891.687-022
ACID-TANK LINER (construction) 861.381-010
Acid Treater (petrol. refin.) 549.362-014
acidulator (oils & grease) 551.685-070
Acid-Washer Operator (textile) 582.685-030
acid-wash operator (chemical; steel & rel.) 551.682-010
ACOUSTICAL CARPENTER (construction) 860.381-010
Acoustical Logging Engineer (petrol. & gas) 010.261-022
acoustical-material worker (construction) 860.381-010
ACQUISITIONS LIBRARIAN (library) 100.267-010
ACROBAT (amuse. & rec.) 159.247-010
Acrobatic Dancer (amuse. & rec.) 151.047-010
ACROBATIC RIGGER (amuse. & rec.) 962.684-010
Acting Professor (education) 090.227-010
Activated-Sludge Attendant (sanitary ser.) 955.585-010
Activated-Sludge Operator (sanitary ser.) 955.362-010
Activities Director, Scouting (nonprofit org.) 187.117-046
ACTOR (amuse. & rec.) 150.047-010
Actress (amuse. & rec.) 150.047-010
Actuarial Clerk (insurance) 216.382-062
ACTUARY (profess. & kin.) 020.167-010
Actuary, Casualty (profess. & kin.) 020.167-010
Actuary, Life (profess. & kin.) 020.167-010
ACUPRESSURIST (medical ser.) 079.271-014
ACUPUNCTURIST (medical ser.) 079.271-010
adapter (profess. & kin.) 152.067-010
ad clerk (print. & pub.) 247.367-010
Ad Compositor (print. & pub.) 973.381-010
Adding-Machine Servicer (any industry) 633.281-018
additive-plant operator (mine & quarry; smelt. & refin.) 939.362-014
Address-Change Clerk (insurance) 203.582-066
ADDRESSER (clerical) 209.587-010
addressing clerk (clerical) 209.587-010
ADDRESSING-MACHINE OPERATOR (clerical) 208.582-010
Adhesion Tester (rubber goods) 759.684-074
ADHESIVE-BANDAGE-MACHINE OPERATOR (protective dev.) 692.685-014
ADHESIVE PRIMER (toy-sport equip.) 732.687-010
Adhesive Sprayer (any industry) 795.687-014
Ad Hoc Arbitrator (profess. & kin.) 169.107-010
ADJUDICATOR (government ser.) 119.167-010
adjuster (any industry) see MACHINE ADJUSTER
ADJUSTER (furniture) 709.684-010
Adjuster (office machines) 706.381-030
ADJUSTER, ALARM MECHANISM (clock & watch) 715.684-010
adjuster and inspector (clock & watch) 715.381-050
ADJUSTER, ELECTRICAL CONTACTS (elec. equip.) 724.381-010
adjuster leader (ordnance) 619.137-010
adjuster, piano action (musical inst.) 730.681-010
adjustment clerk (clerical) 241.367-014
adjustment clerk (radio-tv broad.; tel. & tel.; utilities; waterworks) 239.362-014
Adjustment Clerk (retail trade; tel. & tel.) 219.362-010
ADMEASURER (government ser.) 169.284-010
administrative analyst (any industry) 169.167-010
administrative analyst (education) 090.167-018
ADMINISTRATIVE ASSISTANT (any industry) 169.167-010
administrative assistant (education) 205.367-010
administrative assistant, special education (education) 094.167-014
ADMINISTRATIVE CLERK (clerical) 219.362-010
administrative officer (any industry) 169.167-010
Administrative Officer (government ser.) 188.117-106
ADMINISTRATIVE SECRETARY (any industry) 169.167-014

ADMINISTRATOR, HEALTH CARE FACILITY (medical ser.) 187.117-010
Administrator, Pesticide (government ser.) 188.117-134
ADMINISTRATOR, SOCIAL WELFARE (profess. & kin.) 195.117-010
Administrator, Structural Pest Control (government ser.) 188.117-134
admissions clerk (medical ser.) 205.362-018
ADMISSIONS EVALUATOR (education) 205.367-010
ADMITTING OFFICER (medical ser.) 205.162-010
Adobe-Ball Mixer (smelt. & refin.) 570.685-070
Adobe Maker (brick & tile) 575.684-042
adsorption-and-absorption engineer (profess. & kin.) 008.061-010
ad-terminal-makeup operator (print. & pub.) 208.382-010
ADVANCE AGENT (amuse. & rec.) 191.167-010
ADVERTISING CLERK (business ser.) 247.387-010
advertising clerk (retail trade) 216.382-066
ADVERTISING-DISPATCH CLERK (print. & pub.) 247.387-014
Advertising-Display Rotator (business ser.) 869.684-054
ADVERTISING-MATERIAL DISTRIBUTOR (any industry) 230.687-010
advertising-sales representative (print. & pub.) 254.357-014
advertising solicitor (print. & pub.) 254.357-014
ADVERTISING-SPACE CLERK (print. & pub.) 247.387-018
adviser (any industry) 187.167-186
advisor (auto. mfg.) 806.134-010
advocate (profess. & kin.) 110.107-010
Adzing-And-Boring-Machine Feeder (wood prod., nec) 669.686-030
Adzing-And-Boring-Machine Helper (wood prod., nec) 561.686-010
ADZING-AND-BORING-MACHINE OPERATOR (wood prod., nec) 669.682-010
aerial-applicator pilot (agriculture) 196.263-010
AERIALIST (amuse. & rec.) 159.247-014
aerial navigator (air trans.) 196.167-014
AERIAL-PHOTOGRAPH INTERPRETER (government ser.) 029.167-010
AERIAL-TRAM OPERATOR (mine & quarry) 932.685-010
AERODYNAMICIST (aircraft mfg.) 002.061-010
aerodynamics engineer (aircraft mfg.) 002.061-010
AERONAUTICAL-DESIGN ENGINEER (aircraft mfg.) 002.061-022
AERONAUTICAL ENGINEER (aircraft mfg.) 002.061-014
AERONAUTICAL PROJECT ENGINEER (aircraft mfg.) 002.167-018
AERONAUTICAL-RESEARCH ENGINEER (aircraft mfg.) 002.061-026
AERONAUTICAL TEST ENGINEER (aircraft mfg.) 002.061-018
aerophysics engineer (aircraft mfg.) 002.061-010
Aerosol-Line Operator (any industry) 920.685-078
AEROSPACE ENGINEER (profess. & kin.) term
AEROSPACE PHYSIOLOGICAL TECHNICIAN (military ser.) 199.682-010
aerospace project engineer (aircraft mfg.) 002.167-018
AGATE SETTER (office machines) 710.684-010
Agency Cashier (insurance) 211.362-010
Agency Clerk (insurance) 219.362-010
agent (any industry) 183.117-010
AGENT-CONTRACT CLERK (insurance) 241.267-010
AGENT-LICENSING CLERK (insurance) 209.367-010
agents'-records clerk (insurance) 209.367-010
agent-telegrapher (r.r. trans.) 910.137-038
Ager (motion picture) 840.681-010
AGER OPERATOR (plastic-synth.) 553.482-010
AGER OPERATOR (textile) 582.585-010
Aggregate-Conveyor Operator (construction) 579.665-014
AGING-DEPARTMENT SUPERVISOR (textile) 582.132-010
aging room operator (plastic-synth.) 559.585-018
agitator operator (chemical; steel & rel.) 551.682-010
Agri-Business Agent (government ser.) 096.127-010
agricultural agent (government ser.) 096.127-010
AGRICULTURAL AIDE (agriculture) term
agricultural-aircraft pilot (agriculture) 196.263-010
AGRICULTURAL-CHEMICALS INSPECTOR (government ser.) 168.267-082
Agricultural Commodity Grading Supervisor (government ser.) 188.117-134
Agricultural Economist (profess. & kin.) 050.067-010
AGRICULTURAL ENGINEER (profess. & kin.) 013.061-010
AGRICULTURAL-ENGINEERING TECHNICIAN (profess. & kin.) 013.161-010
Agricultural-Extension Specialist (government ser.) 096.127-014
AGRICULTURAL-RESEARCH ENGINEER (profess. & kin.) 013.061-014
AGRICULTURIST (profess. & kin.) term
AGRONOMIST (profess. & kin.) 040.061-010
AIR ANALYST (profess. & kin.) 012.261-010
AIR AND HYDRONIC BALANCING TECHNICIAN (any industry) 637.261-034
AIR-AND-WATER FILLER (wood. container) 764.687-010
air-and-water-tester (wood. container) 764.687-010
AIR-BAG CURER (rubber tire) 556.685-010
AIRBORNE SENSOR SPECIALIST (military ser.) 378.382-010
AIRBRUSH ARTIST (profess. & kin.) 970.281-010
Airbrush Artist, Photography (profess. & kin.) 970.281-010
Airbrush Artist, Technical (profess. & kin.) 970.281-010
Air-Carrier Electronics Inspector (government ser.) 168.264-010
Air-Carrier Maintenance Inspector (government ser.) 168.264-010

air-carrier operations inspector (government ser.) 196.163-010
AIR-COMPRESSOR MECHANIC (railroad equip.) 622.684-010
AIR-COMPRESSOR OPERATOR (any industry) 950.685-010
Air-Compressor Operator, Stationary (any industry) 950.685-010
Air-Compressor-Station Engineer (any industry) 950.382-026
AIR-CONDITIONING-COIL ASSEMBLER (svc. ind. mach.) 706.684-010
AIR-CONDITIONING INSTALLER-SERVICER HELPER, WINDOW UNIT (construction) 637.687-010
AIR-CONDITIONING INSTALLER-SERVICER, WINDOW UNIT (construction) 637.261-010
air-conditioning mechanic (construction) 637.261-014
AIR-CONDITIONING MECHANIC (automotive ser.) 620.281-010
air-conditioning-mechanic apprentice (construction) 862.281-026
Air-Conditioning-Mechanic Helper, Industrial (any industry) 637.664-010
Air-Conditioning Mechanic, Industrial (any industry) 637.261-014
Air-Conditioning Technician (profess. & kin.) 007.181-010
Air-Conditioning-Unit Assembler (svc. ind. mach.) 827.684-010
AIR-CONDITIONING-UNIT TESTER (svc. ind. mach.) 827.361-010
air-control tender (any industry) 950.585-010
aircraft and engine electrician, field and hangar (aircraft mfg.; air trans.) 825.261-018
Aircraft-And-Engine Mechanic, Field-And-Hangar (aircraft mfg.) 621.281-014
AIRCRAFT-ARMAMENT MECHANIC (government ser.) 632.261-010
aircraft armorer (government ser.) 632.261-010
AIRCRAFT BODY REPAIRER (air trans.) 807.261-010
aircraft charter dispatcher (air trans.) 295.367-010
aircraft-delivery checker (aircraft mfg.) 222.387-010
Aircraft-Engine Assembler (air trans.) 621.281-014
Aircraft-Engine-Cylinder Mechanic (air trans.) 621.281-014
Aircraft-Engine Dismantler (air trans.) 621.281-014
Aircraft-Engine Installer (air trans.) 621.281-014
Aircraft-Engine Mechanic (air trans.) 621.281-014
Aircraft-Engine Mechanic, Overhaul (air trans.) 621.281-014
aircraft-inspection-record clerk (air trans.) 221.362-010
Aircraft Instrument Repairer (air trans.) 710.281-026
AIRCRAFT LAUNCH AND RECOVERY TECHNICIAN (military ser.) 912.682-010
AIRCRAFT-LOG CLERK (air trans.) 221.362-010
aircraft mechanic (aircraft mfg.; air trans.) 621.281-014
AIRCRAFT MECHANIC, ARMAMENT (aircraft mfg.) 806.361-030
aircraft mechanic, electrical (aircraft mfg.; air trans.) 825.261-018
AIRCRAFT MECHANIC, ELECTRICAL AND RADIO (aircraft mfg.) 825.381-010
AIRCRAFT MECHANIC, ENVIRONMENTAL CONTROL SYSTEM (aircraft mfg.) 806.381-014
AIRCRAFT MECHANIC, PLUMBING AND HYDRAULICS (aircraft mfg.) 806.381-066
aircraft mechanic, rigger (aircraft mfg.) 806.381-018
AIRCRAFT MECHANIC, RIGGING AND CONTROLS (aircraft mfg.) 806.381-018
aircraft mechanic, structures (aircraft mfg.) 806.381-026
AIRCRAFT-PHOTOGRAPHIC-EQUIPMENT MECHANIC (photo. appar.) 714.281-010
aircraft pilot (agriculture) 196.263-010
AIRCRAFT-SHIPPING CHECKER (aircraft mfg.) 222.387-010
AIRCRAFT SKIN BURNISHER (aircraft mfg.) 807.684-018
aircraft-time clerk (air trans.) 221.362-010
air deodorizer servicer (business ser.) 389.687-010
Airdox Fitter (mine & quarry) 862.281-022
AIR-DRIER-MACHINE OPERATOR (paper & pulp) 534.682-010
air-drill operator (mine & quarry) 930.684-018
Air Filler (wood. container) 764.687-010
AIRFRAME-AND-POWER-PLANT MECHANIC (aircraft mfg.; air trans.) 621.281-014
AIRFRAME-AND-POWER-PLANT-MECHANIC APPRENTICE (air trans.) 621.281-018
AIRFRAME-AND-POWER-PLANT-MECHANIC HELPER (aircraft mfg.; air trans.) 621.684-010
Airframe-And-Power-Plant Mechanic, Line Service (air trans.) 621.281-014
air-freight agent (air trans.) 248.367-018
air-furnace operator (foundry; steel & rel.) 512.362-018
Air-Hammer Operator (construction) 869.687-026
air-hammer operator (mine & quarry) 930.684-018
air-hammer operator (pen & pencil) 733.687-014
air-hammer stripper (paper goods) 794.687-050
AIR-HOLE DRILLER (fabrication, nec) 692.685-018
Air Intelligence Specialist (profess. & kin.) 059.167-010
AIRLINE-RADIO OPERATOR (air trans.; business ser.) 193.262-010
AIRLINE-RADIO OPERATOR, CHIEF (air trans.; business ser.) 193.162-022
AIRLINE SECURITY REPRESENTATIVE (air trans.) 372.667-010
air-motor repairer (any industry) 630.281-010
airplane-and-engine inspector (air trans.) 621.261-010
airplane-cabin attendant (air trans.) 352.367-010
Airplane Captain (air trans.) 196.263-014
AIRPLANE-CHARTER CLERK (air trans.) 295.367-010

Airplane Cleaner (air trans.) 919.687-014
AIRPLANE COVERER (aircraft mfg.; air trans.) 849.381-010
AIRPLANE-DISPATCH CLERK (air trans.) 248.367-010
airplane dispatcher (air trans.) 912.167-010
Airplane First-Officer (air trans.) 196.263-014
AIRPLANE-FLIGHT ATTENDANT (air trans.) 352.367-010
AIRPLANE-GAS-TANK-LINER ASSEMBLER (rubber goods) 759.684-010
AIRPLANE INSPECTOR (air trans.) 621.261-010
airplane mechanic (aircraft mfg.; air trans.) 621.281-014
airplane-mechanic apprentice (air trans.) 621.281-018
airplane-mechanic helper (aircraft mfg.; air trans.) 621.684-010
airplane navigator (air trans.) 196.167-014
Airplane-Patrol Pilot (business ser.) 196.263-014
AIRPLANE PILOT (agriculture) 196.263-010
Airplane Pilot (air trans.) 196.263-014
airplane pilot, chief (air trans.) 196.167-010
AIRPLANE PILOT, COMMERCIAL (air trans.) 196.263-014
airplane pilot, crop dusting (agriculture) 196.263-010
AIRPLANE-PILOT HELPER (agriculture) 409.667-010
AIRPLANE PILOT, PHOTOGRAMMETRY (business ser.) 196.263-018
airplane-rental clerk (air trans.) 295.367-010
Air Pollution Analyst (profess. & kin.) 029.081-010
Air-Pollution Engineer (profess. & kin.) 019.081-018
AIRPORT ATTENDANT (air trans.) 912.364-010
Airport Clerk (air trans.) 219.362-010
airport-control operator (government ser.) 193.162-018
AIRPORT ELECTRICIAN (air trans.) 824.281-010
AIRPORT ENGINEER (profess. & kin.) 005.061-010
Airport Guide (air trans.) 353.367-014
AIRPORT-MAINTENANCE CHIEF (air trans.) 899.137-010
Airport Safety And Security Duty Officer (government ser.) 375.133-010
Airport Safety And Security Officer (government ser.) 375.263-014
AIRPORT UTILITY WORKER (air trans.) 912.663-010
AIR-PRESS OPERATOR (any industry) term
AIR PURIFIER SERVICER (business ser.) 389.687-010
AIR-TABLE OPERATOR (mine & quarry) 549.685-010
Air-Tank Assembler (toy-sport equip.) 732.684-014
air tester (profess. & kin.) 012.261-010
air tester (wood. container) 764.687-022
AIR-TOOL OPERATOR (construction) term
Air-Traffic-Control Specialist, Center (government ser.) 193.162-018
AIR-TRAFFIC-CONTROL SPECIALIST, STATION (government ser.) 193.162-014
AIR-TRAFFIC-CONTROL SPECIALIST, TOWER (government ser.) 193.162-018
air-traffic-control supervisor (government ser.) 193.167-010
AIR-TRAFFIC COORDINATOR (government ser.) 193.162-010
Air Tucker (tex. prod., nec) 787.682-082
Air-Turning-Machine Feeder (tex. prod., nec) 689.685-146
AIR-VALVE REPAIRER (railroad equip.) 622.381-010
Aitchbone Breaker (meat products) 525.684-018
ALARM INVESTIGATOR (business ser.) 376.367-010
ALARM OPERATOR (government ser.) 379.162-010
alarm-signal operator (any industry) 379.362-014
Alberene-Stone Setter (construction) 861.381-038
ALCOHOL-AND-DRUG-ABUSE-ASSISTANCE PROGRAM ADMINIS-
    TRATOR (government ser.) 195.167-042
alcohol rubber (personal ser.) 335.677-010
Alcohol-Still Operator (chemical) 552.362-022
aligner (electron. comp.) 976.382-030
aligner (ordnance) 736.684-042
ALIGNER, BARREL AND RECEIVER (ordnance) 736.684-010
ALIGNER, TYPEWRITER (office machines) 706.381-010
alignment mechanic (automotive ser.) 620.281-038
alining checker (office machines) 706.687-022
Alkylation Operator (chemical; petrol. refin.) 559.382-018
all-around-gear-machine operator (machine shop) 602.380-010
allergist (medical ser.) 070.101-102
ALLERGIST-IMMUNOLOGIST (medical ser.) 070.101-102
allergy specialist (medical ser.) 070.101-102
Alley Cleaner (textile) 381.687-018
alley tender (nonmet. min.; textile) 680.665-018
alley tender (nonmet. min.; textile) 680.685-018
Alligator-Shear Operator (any industry) 615.685-034
Allocations Clerk (electron. comp.) 221.387-046
ALMOND BLANCHER, HAND (can. & preserv.) 521.687-010
ALMOND-BLANCHER OPERATOR (can. & preserv.) 521.685-014
ALMOND-CUTTING-MACHINE TENDER (can. & preserv.) 521.685-018
Almond Grinder (can. & preserv.) 521.685-234
ALMOND HULLER (can. & preserv.) 521.685-010
Almond-Pan Finisher (sugar & conf.) 524.382-010
ALMOND-PASTE MIXER (sugar & conf.) 529.361-010
ALMOND-PASTE MOLDER (sugar & conf.) 520.684-010
Almond Roaster (can. & preserv.) 529.685-174
Almond Sorter (can. & preserv.) 521.687-086

ALODIZE-MACHINE HELPER (nonfer. metal) 509.685-010
ALODIZE-MACHINE OPERATOR (nonfer. metal) 509.462-010
alteration inspector (retail trade) 789.687-078
ALTERATIONS WORKROOM CLERK (retail trade) 221.367-010
ALTERATION TAILOR (garment; personal ser.; retail trade) 785.261-010
alterer (garment; personal ser.; retail trade) 785.261-010
alterer apprentice (garment; personal ser.; retail trade) 785.261-018
ALUMINA-PLANT SUPERVISOR (smelt. & refin.) 511.130-010
Aluminizer (electron. comp.) 725.684-022
ALUMINUM-CONTAINER TESTER (elec. equip.) 727.687-018
Aluminum-Foil-Spooling-Machine Operator (nonfer. metal) 699.682-030
ALUMINUM-HYDROXIDE-PROCESS OPERATOR (chemical; pharmaceut.)
    559.685-010
ALUMINUM-POOL INSTALLER (construction) 809.664-010
Aluminum-Shingle Roofer (construction) 866.381-010
Aluminum-Siding Installer (construction; retail trade) 863.684-014
alum mixer (chemical) 559.362-010
ALUMNI SECRETARY (education) 090.117-014
ALUM-PLANT OPERATOR (chemical) 559.362-010
AMALGAMATOR (smelt. & refin.) 511.685-010
AMBULANCE ATTENDANT (medical ser.) 355.374-010
Ambulance Driver (government ser.) 375.263-014
AMBULANCE DRIVER (medical ser.) 913.683-010
ammonia operator (chemical) 558.382-014
ammonia-print operator (any industry) 979.682-014
Ammonia-Solution Preparer (textile) 550.585-018
Ammonia-Still Operator (chemical) 552.685-014
AMMONIA-STILL OPERATOR (steel & rel.) 559.382-010
Ammonium-Hydroxide Operator (chemical) 551.382-010
AMMONIUM-NITRATE CRYSTALLIZER (chemical) 553.685-010
Ammonium-Nitrate Neutralizer (chemical) 550.585-030
ammonium-sulfate operator (chemical; steel & rel.) 558.362-018
ammunition storekeeper (chemical; ordnance) 222.137-018
ammunition supervisor (chemical; ordnance) 222.137-018
amortization-schedule clerk (clerical) 216.362-026
AMPHIBIAN CREWMEMBER (military ser.) 378.683-010
AMPOULE EXAMINER (pharmaceut.) 559.687-010
AMPOULE FILLER (pharmaceut.) 559.685-018
ampoule filler and sealer (pharmaceut.) 559.685-018
AMPOULE SEALER (pharmaceut.) 559.687-014
AMPOULE-WASHING-MACHINE OPERATOR (pharmaceut.) 559.685-022
amusement-equipment operator (amuse. & rec.) 342.663-010
Amusement-Game Machine Coin Collector (business ser.) 292.483-010
AMUSEMENT PARK ENTERTAINER (amuse. & rec.) 159.647-010
AMUSEMENT PARK WORKER (amuse. & rec.) 349.664-010
ANALYST, FOOD AND BEVERAGE (hotel & rest.) 310.267-010
analyst, geochemical prospecting (petrol. & gas) 024.381-010
ANATOMIST (profess. & kin.) 041.061-010
Anchorperson (radio-tv broad.) 131.262-010
anchor tacker (boot & shoe) 690.685-162
anchor-tack puller (boot & shoe) 788.687-146
ANESTHESIOLOGIST (medical ser.) 070.101-010
Anesthesiologist Assistant (medical ser.) 079.364-018
angiographer (medical ser.) 078.362-046
Angledozer Operator (any industry) 850.683-010
Angle-Roll Operator (any industry) 619.362-014
ANGLE SHEAR OPERATOR (any industry) 615.482-010
animal attendant (any industry) 410.674-010
ANIMAL BREEDER (agriculture) 410.161-010
ANIMAL BREEDER (profess. & kin.) 041.061-014
animal caretaker (amuse. & rec.) 412.674-010
ANIMAL CARETAKER (any industry) 410.674-010
animal control officer (nonprofit org.) 379.263-010
Animal Cytologist (profess. & kin.) 041.061-042
Animal Ecologist (profess. & kin.) 041.061-090
ANIMAL EVISCERATOR (meat products) 525.687-010
animal health technician (medical ser.) 079.361-014
ANIMAL-HOSPITAL CLERK (medical ser.) 245.367-010
animal humane agent supervisor (nonprofit org.) 379.137-010
Animal Impersonator (amuse. & rec.) 159.047-018
ANIMAL KEEPER (amuse. & rec.) 412.674-010
ANIMAL KEEPER, HEAD (amuse. & rec.) 412.137-010
ANIMAL-NURSERY WORKER (amuse. & rec.; museums) 412.674-014
Animal Nutritionist (profess. & kin.) 040.061-014
Animal Physiologist (profess. & kin.) 041.061-078
ANIMAL-RIDE ATTENDANT (amuse. & rec.) 349.674-010
ANIMAL-RIDE MANAGER (amuse. & rec.) 349.224-010
ANIMAL SCIENTIST (profess. & kin.) 040.061-014
ANIMAL-SHELTER CLERK (nonprofit org.) 249.367-010
animal shelter supervisor (nonprofit org.) 410.134-018
Animal Taxonomist (profess. & kin.) 041.061-090
animal technician (medical ser.) 079.361-014
ANIMAL TRAINER (amuse. & rec.) 159.224-010
ANIMAL TREATMENT INVESTIGATOR (nonprofit org.) 379.263-010
animated-cartoon artist (motion picture; radio-tv broad.) 141.081-010

animator

animator (motion picture; radio-tv broad.) 141.081-010
ANKLE-PATCH MOLDER (boot & shoe) 692.682-010
ANNEALER (glass products) 573.685-010
ANNEALER (heat treating) 504.682-010
ANNEALER (jewelry-silver.) 504.687-010
ANNOUNCER (amuse. & rec.) 159.347-010
ANNOUNCER (radio-tv broad.) 159.147-010
Announcer, International Broadcast (radio-tv broad.) 159.147-010
anode adjuster (chemical) 558.584-010
Anode-Assembly Cleaner I (smelt. & refin.) 515.685-014
Anode-Assembly Cleaner II (smelt. & refin.) 519.664-010
ANODE BUILDER (chemical) 826.684-010
ANODE-CREW SUPERVISOR (smelt. & refin.) 630.134-010
ANODE REBUILDER (smelt. & refin.) 630.684-010
ANODIZER (any industry) 500.682-010
ANTENNA INSTALLER (any industry) 823.684-010
ANTENNA INSTALLER, SATELLITE COMMUNICATIONS (any industry) 823.261-022
Anthracene Operator (chemical) 551.685-122
Anthropological Linguist (profess. & kin.) 055.067-010
ANTHROPOLOGIST (profess. & kin.) 055.067-010
ANTHROPOLOGIST, PHYSICAL (profess. & kin.) 055.067-014
Anthropometrist (profess. & kin.) 055.067-014
ANTICHECKING-IRON WORKER (wood prod., nec) 563.687-010
Antique-Auto-Museum-Maintenance Worker (museums) 899.384-010
Antiquer (boot & shoe) 788.684-066
Antiquer (furniture) 763.381-010
antisqueak applier (boot & shoe) 788.687-010
antisqueak chalker (boot & shoe) 788.687-010
ANTISQUEAK FILLER (boot & shoe) 788.687-010
ANTITANK ASSAULT GUNNER (military ser.) 378.464-010
ANVIL-SEATING-PRESS OPERATOR (ordnance) 694.685-010
anvil smith (forging) 610.381-010
Aperture-Mask Etcher (electron. comp.) 725.685-010
apex trimmer (boot & shoe) 690.685-150
apiarist (agriculture) 413.161-010
APICULTURIST (profess. & kin.) 041.061-018
apparatus-repair mechanic (any industry) 626.381-014
APPAREL-RENTAL CLERK (retail trade) 295.357-010
appeals board referee (government ser.) 119.107-010
APPEALS REFEREE (government ser.) 119.267-014
APPEALS REVIEWER, VETERAN (government ser.) 119.117-010
Appellate Conferee (government ser.) 160.167-050
Appellate-Court Judge (government ser.) 111.107-010
Appetizer Packer (hotel & rest.) 319.684-010
Apple Checker (agriculture) 221.587-030
Apple Grower (agriculture) 403.161-010
Apple Packer (agriculture; wholesale tr.) 920.687-134
APPLE-PACKING HEADER (agriculture) 920.687-010
Apple-Picking Supervisor (agriculture) 409.131-010
Apple Sorter (agriculture; can. & preserv.; wholesale tr.) 529.687-186
Apple Washer (agriculture; can. & preserv.; wholesale tr.) 529.685-258
APPLIANCE ASSEMBLER, LINE (house. appl.; svc. ind. mach.) 827.684-010
Appliance Inspector (house. appl.) 729.387-022
Appliance Installer (mfd. bldgs.; vehicles, nec) 869.684-026
Appliance Installer (vehicles, nec) 806.684-018
appliance painter-and-refinisher (any industry) 741.684-030
APPLIANCE REPAIRER (any industry) term
APPLIANCE REPAIRER (house. appl.) 723.584-010
appliance servicer (any industry) 637.261-018
appliance-service representative (any industry) 827.261-010
appliance-service representative (any industry) 723.381-010
APPLIANCE-SERVICE SUPERVISOR (utilities) 187.167-010
Appliance Tester (house. appl.) 729.387-022
application clerk (radio-tv broad.; tel. & tel.; utilities; waterworks) 239.362-014
Application-Register Clerk (insurance) 203.582-066
APPLICATIONS ENGINEER (profess. & kin.) term
APPLICATIONS ENGINEER, MANUFACTURING (profess. & kin.) 007.061-038
applications programmer (profess. & kin.) 030.162-010
applications programmer-analyst (profess. & kin.) 030.162-014
applicator (any industry) 582.687-030
Applied Anthropologist (profess. & kin.) 055.067-010
applier (any industry) 582.687-030
applier (leather prod.) 589.687-034
Applique Cutter, Hand (tex. prod., nec) 781.684-074
APPLIQUER, ZIGZAG (garment) 786.682-010
Applique Sewer (leather prod.) 783.682-014
APPOINTMENT CLERK (clerical) 237.367-010
appointment clerk (government ser.) 205.362-010
APPRAISER (any industry) 191.287-010
APPRAISER (government ser.) 188.167-010
Appraiser, Aircraft (government ser.) 188.167-010
APPRAISER, ART (profess. & kin.) 191.287-014
Appraiser, Auditor (government ser.) 188.167-010

APPRAISER, AUTOMOBILE DAMAGE (business ser.; insurance) 241.267-014
Appraiser, Boats And Marine (government ser.) 188.167-010
Appraiser, Buildings (government ser.) 188.167-010
appraiser, irrigation tax (government ser.) 188.167-014
Appraiser, Land (government ser.) 188.167-010
Appraiser, Oil And Water (government ser.) 188.167-010
Appraiser, Personal Property (government ser.) 188.167-010
Appraiser, Real Estate (government ser.) 188.167-010
APPRAISER, REAL ESTATE (real estate) 191.267-010
Appraiser, Timber (government ser.) 188.167-010
APPRENTICE (any industry) master
APPRENTICESHIP CONSULTANT (government ser.) 188.117-010
Approach-Table Operator (nonfer. metal; steel & rel.) 613.682-026
Apricot Packer (agriculture; wholesale tr.) 920.687-134
Apricot Washer (food prep., nec) 521.685-110
APRON CLEANER (nonmet. min.) 680.687-010
apron operator (paper & pulp) 539.587-010
apron scratcher (nonmet. min.) 680.687-010
Apron Trimmer (boot & shoe) 690.685-434
Aqua-Ammonia Operator (chemical) 551.382-010
Aquaculturist (profess. & kin.) 041.061-022
AQUARIST (amuse. & rec.) 449.674-010
aquarium tank attendant (amuse. & rec.) 449.674-010
AQUATIC BIOLOGIST (profess. & kin.) 041.061-022
aquatic ecologist (profess. & kin.) 041.061-022
AQUATIC PERFORMER (amuse. & rec.) 159.347-014
aqueduct-and-reservoir keeper (waterworks) 954.382-018
ARBITRATOR (profess. & kin.) 169.107-010
ARBORER (jewelry-silver.) 700.684-010
Arbor Inspector (clock & watch) 715.384-022
ARBOR-PRESS OPERATOR I (any industry) 616.682-010
Arbor-Press Operator II (any industry) 690.685-014
arc-air operator (welding) 816.364-010
ARC CUTTER (welding) 816.364-010
Arc Cutter, Gas-Tungsten Arc (welding) 816.364-010
Arc Cutter, Plasma Arc (welding) 816.364-010
ARCH-CUSHION-PRESS OPERATOR (rubber goods) 556.362-010
ARCH-CUSHION-SKIVING-MACHINE OPERATOR (rubber goods) 690.682-010
ARCHEOLOGIST (profess. & kin.) 055.067-018
Archeologist, Classical (profess. & kin.) 055.067-018
archer (boot & shoe) 690.682-070
Archery-Equipment Repairer (any industry) 732.684-122
ARCHITECT (profess. & kin.) 001.061-010
ARCHITECT, MARINE (profess. & kin.) 001.061-014
architect, naval (profess. & kin.) 001.061-014
Architectural Renderer (profess. & kin.) 970.281-014
ARCHIVIST (profess. & kin.) 101.167-010
Archivist, Economic History (profess. & kin.) 101.167-010
Archivist, Military History (profess. & kin.) 101.167-010
Archivist, Nonprofit Foundation (nonprofit org.) 101.167-010
Archivist, Political History (profess. & kin.) 101.167-010
Arch-Pad Cementer (boot & shoe) 788.687-030
ARCH-SUPPORT TECHNICIAN (protective dev.) 712.381-010
arc trimmer (utilities) 952.667-010
area coordinator (clerical) 205.137-014
area-development consultant (utilities) 184.117-030
AREA ENGINEER (profess. & kin.) term
area representative (government ser.) 188.117-010
area specialist (government ser.) 188.117-014
area supervisor (profess. & kin.) 187.167-238
AREA SUPERVISOR, RETAIL CHAIN STORE (retail trade) 185.117-014
armament assembler (aircraft mfg.) 806.361-030
armament installer (aircraft mfg.) 806.361-030
armature-and-field-assembly supervisor (elec. equip.) 724.131-010
armature-and-rotor winder (elec. equip.) 721.484-010
Armature Balancer (elec. equip.) 724.384-014
ARMATURE BANDER (any industry) 724.684-010
Armature Coil Winder (electron. comp.) 724.684-026
Armature Connector I (elec. equip.) 721.684-018
ARMATURE CONNECTOR II (elec. equip.) 724.684-014
armature repairer (any industry) 724.684-018
Armature Straightener (elec. equip.) 721.281-018
ARMATURE TESTER I (elec. equip.) 724.384-010
Armature Tester II (elec. equip.) 729.684-058
Armature Tester III (elec. equip.) 724.364-010
Armature Varnisher (any industry) 599.685-030
Armature Winder (elec. equip.) 721.484-010
Armature Winder, Automotive (automotive ser.) 724.684-018
ARMATURE-WINDER HELPER, REPAIR (any industry) 721.684-010
ARMATURE WINDER, REPAIR (any industry) 724.684-018
armed guard (business ser.) 376.367-010
Armed Guard (r.r. trans.) 372.667-034
Armhole-And-Shoulder Off-Presser (garment) 363.682-018

Armhole Baster, Hand (garment) 782.684-058
ARMHOLE BASTER, JUMPBASTING (garment) 786.682-014
ARMHOLE FELLER, HANDSTITCHING MACHINE (garment) 786.682-018
Armhole Raiser, Lockstitch (garment) 786.682-238
ARMHOLE-SEW-AND-TRIM OPERATOR, LOCKSTITCH (garment) 786.682-022
Arm Maker (furniture) 780.684-134
armored-cable-machine operator (nonfer. metal) 691.685-010
ARMORED-CAR GUARD (business ser.) 372.567-010
ARMORED-CAR GUARD AND DRIVER (business ser.) 372.563-010
armored-car messenger (business ser.) 372.567-010
armored-car messenger (business ser.) 372.563-010
Armorer (government ser.) 632.261-018
ARMORER TECHNICIAN (museums) 109.281-010
ARMORING-MACHINE OPERATOR (nonfer. metal) 691.685-010
ARMOR RECONNAISSANCE SPECIALIST (military ser.) 378.363-010
ARRANGER (profess. & kin.) 152.067-010
arranger-assembler (fabrication, nec) 739.687-010
Arrow-Point Attacher (toy-sport equip.) 795.687-014
ARROWSMITH (toy-sport equip.) 732.684-010
ART CONSERVATOR (museums) 102.167-010
Art Critic (print. & pub.; radio-tv broad.) 131.067-018
ART DIRECTOR (motion picture; radio-tv broad.) 142.061-062
ART DIRECTOR (profess. & kin.) 141.031-010
ARTIFICIAL-BREEDING DISTRIBUTOR (agriculture) 180.167-010
ARTIFICIAL-BREEDING TECHNICIAN (agriculture) 418.384-014
ARTIFICIAL-CANDY MAKER (fabrication, nec) 739.684-010
ARTIFICIAL-FLOWER MAKER (button & notion) 739.684-014
artificial-fly tier (toy-sport equip.) 732.684-074
ARTIFICIAL-FOLIAGE ARRANGER (retail trade) 899.364-014
ARTIFICIAL-GLASS-EYE MAKER (optical goods) 713.261-010
artificial-insemination technician (agriculture) 411.384-010
ARTIFICIAL INSEMINATOR (agriculture) 418.384-010
ARTIFICIAL-LOG-MACHINE OPERATOR (fabrication, nec; saw. & plan.) 569.685-010
artificial-marble worker (construction) 861.381-046
ARTIFICIAL-PEARL MAKER (jewelry-silver.) 770.687-010
ARTIFICIAL-PLASTIC-EYE MAKER (optical goods) 713.261-014
Artificial-Stone Setter (construction) 861.381-038
ARTILLERY-MAINTENANCE SUPERVISOR (ordnance) 632.131-010
ARTILLERY OR NAVAL GUNFIRE OBSERVER (military ser.) 378.367-010
art instructor (education) 149.021-010
artist (any industry) 970.381-022
artist (profess. & kin.) 141.061-022
artist (profess. & kin.) 144.061-010
ARTIST AND REPERTOIRE MANAGER (amuse. & rec.) 159.167-010
artist, color separation (print. & pub.) 970.281-026
artist consultant (amuse. & rec.) 191.117-010
ARTIST, MANNEQUIN COLORING (fabrication, nec) 741.684-010
Artists' Booking Representative (amuse. & rec.) 191.117-014
artist, scientific (profess. & kin.) 141.061-026
ARTIST'S MANAGER (amuse. & rec.) 191.117-010
artist's representative (amuse. & rec.) 191.117-010
ARTIST, SUSPECT (government ser.) 970.361-018
artist, woodblock (print. & pub.) 979.281-014
Art Librarian (library) 100.167-026
Art Metal-Chair Assembler (furniture) 709.684-014
art-metal designer (struct. metal) 142.061-034
art-metal worker (metal prod., nec) 619.260-014
art-metal-worker apprentice (metal prod., nec) 619.260-010
art-metal-worker helper (metal prod., nec) 619.484-010
art preparator (museums) 102.367-010
ART THERAPIST (medical ser.) 076.127-010
Asbestos-Cloth Inspector (nonmet. min.) 689.685-038
ASBESTOS REMOVAL WORKER (construction) 869.684-082
ASBESTOS-SHINGLE INSPECTOR (nonmet. min.) 679.687-010
Asbestos-Shingle Roofer (construction) 866.381-010
ASBESTOS-SHINGLE SHEARING-MACHINE OPERATOR (nonmet. min.) 679.686-010
Asbestos-Siding Installer (construction; retail trade) 863.684-014
ASBESTOS-WIRE FINISHER (nonfer. metal) 691.682-010
Asparagus Grader And Buncher (agriculture) 529.687-186
Asparagus Sorter (agriculture; can. & preserv.; wholesale tr.) 529.687-186
Asphalt Blender (petrol. refin.) 540.462-010
Asphalt Coater (elec. equip.) 599.685-026
ASPHALT-DISTRIBUTOR TENDER (construction) 853.665-010
ASPHALT-HEATER TENDER (construction) 853.685-010
asphalt-machine operator (metal prod., nec) 590.362-014
ASPHALT-PAVING-MACHINE OPERATOR (construction) 853.663-010
Asphalt-Plant Operator (construction) 570.682-014
Asphalt-Plant Worker (construction) 869.687-026
Asphalt Raker (construction) 869.687-026
asphalt-spreader operator (construction) 853.663-014
asphalt-surface-heater operator (construction) 853.683-014
asphalt-tamping-machine operator (construction) 869.683-018

Asphalt, Tar, And Gravel Roofer (construction) 866.381-010
Asphalt-Tile-Floor Layer (construction; retail trade) 864.481-010
ASSAYER (profess. & kin.) 022.281-010
assembler (any industry) 782.684-058
assembler (any industry) 780.684-062
ASSEMBLER (clock & watch) 715.381-010
ASSEMBLER (cutlery-hrdwr.) 701.687-010
assembler (elec. equip.; light. fix.) 729.687-010
assembler (elec. equip.) 721.684-022
ASSEMBLER (garment; glove & mit.) 781.687-010
ASSEMBLER (glove & mit.) 781.667-010
ASSEMBLER (house. appl.) 723.684-010
ASSEMBLER (jewelry-silver.) 700.684-014
assembler (knitting) 685.687-010
ASSEMBLER (laundry & rel.) 369.687-010
assembler (machine shop) 706.684-018
ASSEMBLER (machinery mfg.) 706.361-010
ASSEMBLER (mfd. bldgs.; vehicles, nec) 869.684-010
assembler (musical inst.) 730.381-018
ASSEMBLER (ordnance) 737.687-010
ASSEMBLER (pen & pencil) 733.685-010
ASSEMBLER (plastic prod.) 754.684-010
ASSEMBLER (svc. ind. mach.) 731.687-010
ASSEMBLER (tel. & tel.) 722.381-010
ASSEMBLER (tex. prod., nec) 734.687-014
ASSEMBLER (toy-sport equip.) 732.684-014
ASSEMBLER (wood. container) 762.684-010
assembler-adjuster (office machines) 706.684-014
assembler, aircraft, plumbing and hydraulics (aircraft mfg.) 806.381-066
ASSEMBLER, AIRCRAFT POWER PLANT (aircraft mfg.) 806.381-022
ASSEMBLER, AIRCRAFT, STRUCTURES AND SURFACES (aircraft mfg.) 806.381-026
ASSEMBLER, ALUMINUM BOATS (ship-boat mfg.) 806.481-010
ASSEMBLER-AND-GLUER, LAMINATED PLASTICS (plastic prod.) 754.684-014
ASSEMBLER AND TESTER, ELECTRONICS (office machines) 710.281-010
ASSEMBLER AND WIRER, INDUSTRIAL EQUIPMENT (elec. equip.; machinery mfg.) 826.361-010
ASSEMBLER-ARRANGER (fabrication, nec) 739.687-010
ASSEMBLER, AUTOMOBILE (auto. mfg.) 806.684-010
ASSEMBLER, BICYCLE I (motor-bicycles) 806.684-014
ASSEMBLER, BICYCLE II (motor-bicycles) 806.687-010
ASSEMBLER, BILLIARD-TABLE (toy-sport equip.) 732.384-010
Assembler, Body (auto. mfg.) 806.684-010
assembler, bonding (aircraft mfg.) 806.384-030
ASSEMBLER (button & notion) 734.687-018
ASSEMBLER, CAMPER (vehicles, nec) 806.684-018
ASSEMBLER, CARBON BRUSHES (elec. equip.) 721.684-014
Assembler, Cards And Announcements (print. & pub.) 794.687-010
assembler, caterpillar spider (elec. equip.) 721.684-026
Assembler, Chassis (auto. mfg.) 806.684-010
ASSEMBLER, CLIP-ON SUNGLASSES (optical goods) 713.684-010
Assembler, Communications Equipment (comm. equip.; elec. equip.) 729.684-026
ASSEMBLER, COMPONENT (mfd. bldgs.; vehicles, nec) 762.684-014
assembler, convertible top (automotive ser.) 807.684-026
Assembler, Coolers (svc. ind. mach.) 827.684-010
ASSEMBLER, CORNCOB PIPES (fabrication, nec) 739.687-014
assembler-crimper (rubber goods) 759.687-014
assembler dc field ring (elec. equip.) 721.484-014
assembler dc field yoke (elec. equip.) 721.484-014
ASSEMBLER, DECK AND HULL (ship-boat mfg.) 806.684-022
Assembler, Dielectric Heater (elec. equip.) 826.361-010
ASSEMBLER, DRY CELL AND BATTERY (elec. equip.) 727.687-022
ASSEMBLER, ELECTRICAL ACCESSORIES I (elec. equip.; light. fix.) 729.687-010
ASSEMBLER, ELECTRICAL ACCESSORIES II (elec. equip.) 729.384-010
ASSEMBLER, ELECTROMECHANICAL (aircraft mfg.; electron. comp.; inst. & app.) 828.381-018
Assembler, Engine (auto. mfg.) 806.684-010
assembler, equipment (tel. & tel.) 722.381-010
assembler-erector (elec. equip.) 820.361-014
ASSEMBLER, FAUCETS (wood. container) 764.687-014
ASSEMBLER, FILTERS (auto. mfg.) 739.687-026
ASSEMBLER, FILTERS (glass products) 739.687-018
Assembler, Final (auto. mfg.) 806.684-010
ASSEMBLER, FINGER BUFFS (tex. prod., nec) 739.685-010
ASSEMBLER, FISHING FLOATS (toy-sport equip.) 732.687-014
assembler-fitter (struct. metal) 809.684-010
assembler, flexible leads (elec. equip.) 691.685-018
Assembler, Fluorescent Lights (light. fix.) 723.684-014
ASSEMBLER FOR PULLER-OVER, HAND (boot & shoe) 788.684-010
ASSEMBLER FOR PULLER-OVER, MACHINE (boot & shoe) 690.685-010
ASSEMBLER, GARMENT FORM (fabrication, nec) 739.687-022
ASSEMBLER, GOLD FRAME (optical goods) 713.384-010

Assembler, Golf-Wood Head (toy-sport equip.) 732.381-022
ASSEMBLER, GROUND SUPPORT EQUIPMENT (aircraft mfg.) 809.261-010
Assembler, Handbags (leather prod.) 783.684-010
ASSEMBLER HELPER, INTERNAL COMBUSTION ENGINE (engine-turbine) 801.687-010
assembler, hydraulic backhoe (machinery mfg.) 801.261-010
ASSEMBLER I (light. fix.) 723.684-014
ASSEMBLER I (office machines) 706.684-014
ASSEMBLER I (ordnance) 736.381-010
ASSEMBLER, IGNITER (ordnance) 737.381-010
ASSEMBLER II (light. fix.) 723.684-018
ASSEMBLER II (office machines) 710.381-010
ASSEMBLER II (ordnance) 736.684-014
Assembler, Incandescent Lights (light. fix.) 723.684-014
assembler-installer, cable controlled systems (aircraft mfg.) 806.381-018
ASSEMBLER-INSTALLER, GENERAL (aircraft mfg.) 806.361-014
assembler-installer, structures (aircraft mfg.) 806.381-026
Assembler-Installer, Wing Structures (aircraft mfg.) 806.381-026
Assembler, Instrument Motors (elec. equip.) 721.684-022
ASSEMBLER, INSULATION AND FLOORING (ship-boat mfg.) 806.684-026
assembler-insulator (elec. equip.) 729.684-030
ASSEMBLER, INTERNAL COMBUSTION ENGINE (engine-turbine) 806.481-014
Assembler, Knife (cutlery-hrdwr.) 701.687-010
assembler, latches and springs (house. appl.) 706.687-030
assembler, lawn-and-garden machinery (agric. equip.) 801.684-022
ASSEMBLER, LAY-UPS (toy-sport equip.) 677.685-014
ASSEMBLER, LEATHER GOODS I (leather prod.) 783.684-010
ASSEMBLER, LEATHER GOODS II (leather prod.) 783.687-010
ASSEMBLER, LIQUID CENTER (toy-sport equip.) 732.684-018
ASSEMBLER, MARKING DEVICES (pen & pencil) 733.687-010
ASSEMBLER, MECHANICAL ORDNANCE (ordnance) 737.684-010
ASSEMBLER, MECHANICAL PENCILS AND BALLPOINT PENS (pen & pencil) 733.687-014
ASSEMBLER, METAL BONDING (aircraft mfg.) 806.384-030
ASSEMBLER, METAL BUILDING (construction) 801.381-010
ASSEMBLER, METAL FURNITURE (furniture) 709.684-014
ASSEMBLER, MINING MACHINERY (machinery mfg.) 801.261-010
ASSEMBLER, MOLDED FRAMES (optical goods) 713.684-014
ASSEMBLER, MOVEMENT (clock & watch) 715.684-014
ASSEMBLER, MUSICAL INSTRUMENTS (musical inst.) 730.684-010
Assembler, Patient Lifting Device (protective dev.) 706.684-018
ASSEMBLER, PHOTOGRAPHIC EQUIPMENT (photo. appar.) 714.381-010
ASSEMBLER, PIANO (musical inst.) 730.384-010
ASSEMBLER, PING-PONG TABLE (toy-sport equip.) 732.684-022
assembler, plastic boat (ship-boat mfg.) 806.684-146
ASSEMBLER, PLASTIC HOSPITAL PRODUCTS (inst. & app.) 712.687-010
assembler (plumbing-heat.) 706.684-086
assembler, portable oil-well drilling rig (machinery mfg.) 801.261-010
assembler, precision-mechanical (photo. appar.) 714.381-010
assembler, press operator (any industry) 616.682-026
ASSEMBLER, PRINTED PRODUCTS (print. & pub.) 794.687-010
ASSEMBLER, PRODUCT (machine shop) 706.684-018
ASSEMBLER, PRODUCTION (any industry) 706.687-010
ASSEMBLER, PRODUCTION LINE (photo. appar.) 714.684-010
ASSEMBLER, PRODUCTION LINE (struct. metal) 809.684-010
assembler, radio and electrical (aircraft mfg.) 729.384-026
assembler, rubber footwear (boot & shoe) 753.687-026
ASSEMBLER, SANDAL PARTS (boot & shoe) 788.684-014
Assembler, Seat (auto. mfg.) 806.684-010
ASSEMBLER, SEMICONDUCTOR (electron. comp.) 726.684-034
Assembler, Show Motor (engine-turbine) 806.481-014
ASSEMBLER, SKYLIGHTS (plastic prod.) 869.684-014
assembler, slide fastener stringers (button & notion) 734.687-074
ASSEMBLER, SMALL PRODUCTS I (any industry) 706.684-022
ASSEMBLER, SMALL PRODUCTS II (any industry) 739.687-030
assembler, special machine (machinery mfg.; machine tools) 600.281-022
ASSEMBLER, STEAM-AND-GAS TURBINE (engine-turbine) 600.261-010
ASSEMBLER, SUBASSEMBLY (aircraft mfg.) 806.384-034
ASSEMBLER, SUBASSEMBLY (mfd. bldgs.; vehicles, nec) 869.684-018
ASSEMBLER, SURGICAL GARMENT (protective dev.) 712.684-010
Assembler, Toy Voices (toy-sport equip.) 731.687-034
assembler, tractor (agric. equip.) 801.684-022
Assembler, Trim (auto. mfg.) 806.684-010
assembler, truck-trailer (auto. mfg.) 806.381-058
ASSEMBLER, TUBING (aircraft mfg.) 806.381-034
ASSEMBLER, TYPE-BAR-AND-SEGMENT (office machines) 706.684-026
ASSEMBLER, UNIT (struct. metal) 809.681-010
Assembler, Utility Buildings (mfd. bldgs.) 869.684-010
ASSEMBLER, WATCH TRAIN (clock & watch) 715.381-014
ASSEMBLER, WET WASH (laundry & rel.) 361.687-010
assembler, wire group (aircraft mfg.) 729.384-026
ASSEMBLER, WIRE-MESH GATE (metal prod., nec) 801.384-010
assembling inspector (wood. container) 762.687-014

ASSEMBLY ADJUSTER (comm. equip.) 720.684-010
ASSEMBLY CLEANER (smelt. & refin.) 519.664-010
Assembly-Department Supervisor (leather prod.) 783.132-010
assembly detailer (ship-boat mfg.) 807.684-014
assembly hand (elec. equip.) 721.684-022
assembly inspector (agric. equip.) 801.381-018
ASSEMBLY INSPECTOR (agric. equip.) 706.361-014
ASSEMBLY INSPECTOR (furniture) 763.684-010
Assembly Inspector (paper goods) 649.367-010
ASSEMBLY-INSPECTOR HELPER (agric. equip.) 801.663-010
ASSEMBLY-LINE INSPECTOR (furniture) 709.684-018
Assembly Line Robot Operator (aircraft mfg.) 606.382-026
ASSEMBLY LOADER (inst. & app.) 711.684-010
Assembly-Machine Feeder (pen & pencil) 692.686-010
Assembly-Machine Offbearer (pen & pencil) 692.686-010
ASSEMBLY-MACHINE OPERATOR (pen & pencil) 692.686-010
ASSEMBLY-MACHINE-SET-UP MECHANIC (elec. equip.) 692.360-010
ASSEMBLY-MACHINE TENDER (plastic prod.) 754.685-014
assembly-machine tool setter (ordnance) 616.360-034
assembly-machine tool setter (ordnance) 616.360-030
ASSEMBLY OPERATOR (woodworking) 762.684-018
ASSEMBLY-PRESS OPERATOR (any industry) 690.685-014
ASSEMBLY REPAIRER (agric. equip.) 624.381-010
ASSEMBLY SUPERVISOR (any industry) 739.137-010
Assembly Supervisor (mfd. bldgs.; vehicles, nec) 869.131-030
Assembly Supervisor (toy-sport equip.) 732.130-010
ASSEMBLY TECHNICIAN (office machines) 633.261-010
ASSESSOR-COLLECTOR, IRRIGATION TAX (government ser.) 188.167-014
Asset-Card Clerk (clerical) 209.687-010
assignment agent (motor trans.) 215.367-010
ASSIGNMENT CLERK (clerical) 249.367-090
ASSIGNMENT CLERK (motor trans.) 215.367-010
ASSIGNMENT CLERK (tel. & tel.) 219.387-010
ASSIGNMENT EDITOR (radio-tv broad.) 132.132-010
assignment officer (government ser.) 188.167-026
ASSISTANT (any industry) term
ASSISTANT BRANCH MANAGER, FINANCIAL INSTITUTION (financial) 186.167-070
assistant camera operator (motion picture) 962.361-010
assistant camera operator (radio-tv broad.) 962.687-010
ASSISTANT CONSTRUCTION SUPERINTENDENT (construction) 869.367-010
ASSISTANT DESIGNER (garment) 781.361-010
assistant editor (print. & pub.) 132.267-014
assistant engineer (r.r. trans.) 910.363-010
ASSISTANT-PRESS OPERATOR (print. & pub.) 651.585-010
ASSISTANT PRESS OPERATOR, OFFSET (print. & pub.) 651.685-026
ASSISTANT PRINCIPAL (education) 091.107-010
Assistant Professor (education) 090.227-010
assistant signal maintainer (r.r. trans.) 822.684-018
assistant superintendent (any industry)   see ASSISTANT
assistant superintendent, special education (education) 094.167-014
assistant superintendent, transportation (r.r. trans.) 184.167-254
assistant supervisor (any industry)   see ASSISTANT
assistant therapy aide (medical ser.) 355.377-014
associate director (radio-tv broad.) 962.167-014
associate editor (print. & pub.) 132.267-014
associate producer (radio-tv broad.) 159.117-010
Associate Professor (education) 090.227-010
ASSOCIATION EXECUTIVE (profess. & kin.) 189.117-010
assorter (garment; glove & mit.) 781.687-010
assorter (leather mfg.) 589.387-014
ASSORTER (steel & rel.) 703.687-010
assorter, laundry (laundry & rel.) 361.687-014
ASTROLOGER (amuse. & rec.) 159.207-010
ASTRONOMER (profess. & kin.) 021.067-010
astro-technician (museums) 962.261-010
asylum attendant (medical ser.) 355.377-014
athletic coach (amuse. & rec.; education) 153.227-018
ATHLETIC TRAINER (amuse. & rec.; education) 153.224-010
Athletic Turf Worker (amuse. & rec.) 408.684-010
atmospheric-drier tender (chemical) 553.665-026
ATOMIC-FUEL ASSEMBLER (chemical) 709.381-010
ATOMIZER ASSEMBLER (fabrication, nec) 706.684-030
attacher (boot & shoe) 690.685-074
ATTENDANCE CLERK (education) 219.362-014
ATTENDANCE OFFICER (education) 168.367-010
ATTENDANT, ARCADE (amuse. & rec.) 342.667-014
ATTENDANT, CAMPGROUND (amuse. & rec.) 329.683-010
ATTENDANT, CHILDREN'S INSTITUTION (any industry) 359.677-010
attendant, coin-operated laundry (laundry & rel.) 369.677-010
attendant, laundry-and-dry-cleaning service (laundry & rel.) 369.677-010
ATTENDANT, LODGING FACILITIES (hotel & rest.) 329.467-010
attendant, self-service store (retail trade) 299.677-010
attenuator (textile) 680.585-014

attorney (profess. & kin.) 110.107-010
AUCTION ASSISTANT (retail trade; wholesale tr.) 294.667-010
Auction Clerk (clerical) 219.362-010
AUCTION CLERK (retail trade; wholesale tr.) 294.567-010
AUCTIONEER (retail trade; wholesale tr.) 294.257-010
Auctioneer, Art (retail trade; wholesale tr.) 294.257-010
Auctioneer, Automobile (wholesale tr.) 294.257-010
Auctioneer, Furniture (retail trade; wholesale tr.) 294.257-010
Auctioneer, Livestock (retail trade; wholesale tr.) 294.257-010
Auctioneer, Real Estate (retail trade; wholesale tr.) 294.257-010
Auctioneer, Tobacco (wholesale tr.) 294.257-010
Audio-Coil Winder (electron. comp.) 724.684-026
audio engineer (radio-tv broad.) 194.262-010
AUDIOLOGIST (medical ser.) 076.101-010
audiometric technician (profess. & kin.) 078.362-010
AUDIOMETRIST (profess. & kin.) 078.362-010
AUDIO OPERATOR (radio-tv broad.) 194.262-010
Audio-Tape Librarian (clerical) 222.367-026
audio technician (radio-tv broad.) 194.262-010
AUDIO-VIDEO REPAIRER (any industry) 729.281-010
audiovisual-aids technician (any industry) 729.281-010
audiovisual equipment operator (amuse. & rec.; motion picture) 960.362-010
audiovisual-equipment operator (any industry) 960.382-010
audio-visual-equipment-rental clerk (business ser.; retail trade) 295.367-018
AUDIOVISUAL LIBRARIAN (library) 100.167-010
AUDIOVISUAL PRODUCTION SPECIALIST (profess. & kin.) 149.061-010
audiovisual specialist (education) 099.167-018
AUDIOVISUAL TECHNICIAN (any industry) 960.382-010
AUDIT CLERK (clerical) 210.382-010
AUDIT-MACHINE OPERATOR (clerical) 216.482-018
AUDITOR (profess. & kin.) 160.167-054
AUDITOR, COUNTY OR CITY (government ser.) 160.167-030
AUDITOR, DATA PROCESSING (financial) 160.162-030
auditor, information systems (financial) 160.162-030
AUDITOR, INTERNAL (profess. & kin.) 160.167-034
AUDITOR, TAX (profess. & kin.) 160.167-038
auger-machine offbearer (brick & tile) 579.686-026
Auger-Press Operator (brick & tile) 575.382-010
AUGER PRESS OPERATOR, MANUAL CONTROL (brick & tile) 575.462-010
Auger Supervisor (mine & quarry) 939.137-018
AUTHOR (profess. & kin.) term
authorizer (clerical) 249.367-022
author's agent (business ser.) 191.117-034
Auto-Body Painter (automotive ser.) 845.381-014
AUTO-BODY REPAIRER, FIBERGLASS (automotive ser.) 807.381-030
auto-camp attendant (hotel & rest.) 329.467-010
AUTOCLAVE OPERATOR (aircraft mfg.) 553.362-014
AUTOCLAVE OPERATOR (knitting) 587.585-010
autoclave operator (medical ser.; pharmaceut.; protective dev.) 599.585-010
AUTOCLAVE OPERATOR I (chemical) 553.382-010
AUTOCLAVE OPERATOR II (chemical) 709.682-010
AUTOCLAVE OPERATOR (textile) 587.682-010
AUTO-DESIGN CHECKER (auto. mfg.) 017.261-010
AUTO-DESIGN DETAILER (auto. mfg.) 017.281-010
auto-glass worker (automotive ser.) 865.684-010
AUTOMAT-CAR ATTENDANT (r.r. trans.) 319.464-010
AUTOMATED CUTTING MACHINE OPERATOR (aircraft mfg.) 699.362-010
AUTOMATED EQUIPMENT ENGINEER-TECHNICIAN (machinery mfg.) 638.261-010
AUTOMATIC BANDSAW TENDER (furniture) 667.685-070
Automatic-Beading-Lathe Operator (any industry) 619.685-082
AUTOMATIC CASTING-FORGING MACHINE OPERATOR (forging) 611.682-014
automatic clipper and stripper (knitting) 684.686-010
automatic-coil-machine operator (furniture) 616.685-018
Automatic-Coil-Winding-Machine Operator (metal prod., nec) 616.485-010
automatic component insertion operator (comm. equip.; electron. comp.; office machines) 726.685-014
AUTOMATIC-DOOR MECHANIC (construction) 829.281-010
automatic embroidery machine tender (tex. prod., nec) 689.685-150
AUTOMATIC-EQUIPMENT TECHNICIAN (tel. & tel.) 822.281-010
automatic-fancy-machine operator (button & notion) 690.685-062
automatic forming machine operator (glass mfg.) 575.382-014
automatic-lathe operator (woodworking) 664.382-010
Automatic-Lathe Setter (woodworking) 669.280-010
automatic-lathe tender (machine shop) 604.685-026
automatic lehr operator (glass mfg.) 573.685-026
AUTOMATIC LUMP MAKING MACHINE TENDER (tobacco) 529.685-014
AUTOMATIC-MACHINE ATTENDANT (paper goods) 649.685-010
automatic maintainer (tel. & tel.) 822.261-026
automatic-mold sander (woodworking) 662.682-010
AUTOMATIC-NAILING-MACHINE FEEDER (saw. & plan.) 669.686-010

AUTOMATIC-PAD-MAKING-MACHINE OPERATOR (tex. prod., nec) 689.382-010
AUTOMATIC-PAD-MAKING-MACHINE OPERATOR HELPER (tex. prod., nec) 689.686-010
AUTOMATIC PATTERN EDGER (glass products) 673.682-010
automatic-screw-machine operator (machine shop) 604.380-022
automatic-screw-machine operator (machine shop) 604.280-014
automatic-screw-machine operator (machine shop) 604.280-018
automatic-screw-machine setter, swiss-type (clock & watch) 604.260-010
automatic-silk-screen printer (textile) 652.682-018
automatic-splicing-machine operator (tex. prod., nec) 689.685-122
automatic-spray-machine operator (any industry) 741.685-010
AUTOMATIC STACKER (tinware) 619.686-010
Automatic-Transmission Mechanic (automotive ser.) 620.281-062
AUTOMATIC-WHEEL-LINE OPERATOR (machine shop) 609.682-010
AUTOMATIC-WINDOW-SEAT-AND-TOP-LIFT REPAIRER (automotive ser.) 825.381-014
AUTOMOBILE-ACCESSORIES INSTALLER (automotive ser.) 806.684-038
Automobile Air-Conditioner Assembler (svc. ind. mach.) 827.684-010
automobile-and-truck-mechanic apprentice (automotive ser.) 620.261-012
AUTOMOBILE-BODY CUSTOMIZER (automotive ser.) 807.361-010
automobile-body repair chief (automotive ser.) 807.137-010
AUTOMOBILE-BODY REPAIRER (automotive ser.) 807.381-010
Automobile-Body Repairer, Combination (automotive ser.) 807.381-010
AUTOMOBILE-BODY-REPAIRER HELPER (automotive ser.) 807.687-010
automobile-body worker (automotive ser.) 807.381-010
AUTOMOBILE-BUMPER STRAIGHTENER (automotive ser.) 807.684-010
AUTOMOBILE-CLUB-SAFETY-PROGRAM COORDINATOR (nonprofit org.) 249.167-010
automobile-damage appraiser (business ser.; insurance) 241.267-014
AUTOMOBILE DETAILER (automotive ser.) 915.687-034
Automobile-Headlight Assembler (light. fix.) 729.684-034
automobile inspector (automotive ser.) 620.261-018
automobile inspector (government ser.) 168.267-058
Automobile-Insurance-Claim Adjuster (business ser.; insurance) 241.217-010
Automobile-Insurance-Claim Examiner (business ser.; insurance) 241.267-018
automobile-light assembler (light. fix.) 729.684-034
AUTOMOBILE LOCATOR (retail trade) 296.367-010
AUTOMOBILE MECHANIC (automotive ser.) 620.261-010
AUTOMOBILE-MECHANIC APPRENTICE (automotive ser.) 620.261-012
automobile-mechanic assistant (automotive ser.) 620.684-014
AUTOMOBILE-MECHANIC HELPER (automotive ser.) 620.684-014
Automobile Mechanic, Motor (automotive ser.) 620.261-010
automobile mechanic, radiator (automotive ser.) 620.381-010
automobile-mechanic supervisor (automotive ser.) 620.131-014
automobile parker (automotive ser.) 915.473-010
AUTOMOBILE RACER (amuse. & rec.) 153.243-010
AUTOMOBILE-RADIATOR MECHANIC (automotive ser.) 620.381-010
Automobile Radio Repairer (any industry) 720.281-010
automobile-refrigeration mechanic (automotive ser.) 620.281-010
automobile rental agent (automotive ser.) 295.467-026
AUTOMOBILE RENTAL CLERK (automotive ser.) 295.467-026
automobile rental representative (automotive ser.) 295.467-026
AUTOMOBILE-REPAIR-SERVICE ESTIMATOR (automotive ser.) 620.261-018
Automobile Repossessor (clerical) 241.367-022
AUTOMOBILE-SEAT-COVER-AND-CONVERTIBLE-TOP INSTALLER (automotive ser.) 780.384-010
AUTOMOBILE-SEAT-COVER INSTALLER (automotive ser.) 915.687-010
AUTOMOBILE-SELF-SERVE-SERVICE-STATION ATTENDANT (automotive ser.) 915.477-010
AUTOMOBILE-SERVICE-STATION ATTENDANT (automotive ser.) 915.467-010
AUTOMOBILE-SERVICE-STATION MECHANIC (automotive ser.) 620.261-030
automobile-spring repairer (automotive ser.) 619.380-018
Automobile-Taillight Assembler (light. fix.) 729.684-034
AUTOMOBILE TESTER (automotive ser.) 620.261-014
AUTOMOBILE TESTER (government ser.) 379.364-010
AUTOMOBILE UPHOLSTERER (automotive ser.) 780.381-010
AUTOMOBILE-UPHOLSTERER APPRENTICE (automotive ser.) 780.381-014
automobile-upholstery-trim installer (automotive ser.) 780.384-010
Automobile Washer (automotive ser.) 919.687-014
automobile washer, steam (automotive ser.) 915.687-026
AUTOMOBILE WRECKER (wholesale tr.) 620.684-010
Automotive Air-Conditioner Installer (automotive ser.) 620.281-010
AUTOMOTIVE-COOLING-SYSTEM DIAGNOSTIC TECHNICIAN (automotive ser.) 620.261-034
AUTOMOTIVE ENGINEER (auto. mfg.) 007.061-010
AUTOMOTIVE-GENERATOR-AND-STARTER REPAIRER (automotive ser.) 721.281-010
Automotive-Generator Repairer (automotive ser.) 721.281-010
automotive-maintenance-equipment repairer (any industry) 620.281-018

Bakery Worker (bakery products) 920.587-018
BAKERY WORKER, CONVEYOR LINE (bakery products) 524.687-022
bakeshop cleaner (hotel & rest.) 313.687-010
Baking-Powder Mixer (food prep., nec) 520.685-162
BALANCE ASSEMBLER (clock & watch) 715.384-010
BALANCE-BRIDGE ASSEMBLER (clock & watch) 715.684-022
balancer (elec. equip.) 727.484-010
balancer (fabrication, nec) 739.684-118
balancer (toy-sport equip.) 732.687-086
BALANCE RECESSER (clock & watch) 604.685-010
BALANCER, SCALE (office machines) 710.381-014
Balance-Staff Inspector (clock & watch) 715.384-022
Balance-Staff Staker (clock & watch) 715.684-182
BALANCE TRUER (clock & watch) 715.684-018
Balance-Wheel-Screw-Hole Driller (clock & watch) 606.685-030
BALANCING-MACHINE OPERATOR (any industry) 609.462-010
BALANCING-MACHINE SET-UP WORKER (any industry) 809.382-010
BALCONY WORKER (glass mfg.) 575.687-010
bale-breaker operator (textile) 680.685-070
bale coverer (textile) 782.687-018
Bale Piler (textile) 929.687-030
baler (any industry) 929.687-058
Baler (forestry) 920.687-046
BALER (plastic-synth.) 690.685-022
baler operator (any industry) 920.685-010
BALE SEWER (agriculture) 920.687-022
BALE-TIE-MACHINE OPERATOR (metal prod., nec) 616.682-014
BALING-MACHINE TENDER (any industry) 920.685-010
baling-press operator (any industry) 920.685-010
BALL ASSEMBLER (toy-sport equip.) 732.684-026
Ballast-Cleaning-Machine Operator (r.r. trans.) 859.683-018
ballaster (ship-boat mfg.) 809.684-022
Ballast-Regulator Operator (r.r. trans.) 859.683-018
ball-ender (musical inst.) 730.685-010
baller (laundry & rel.) 363.687-018
baller tender (textile) 681.685-010
Ballet Dancer (amuse. & rec.) 151.047-010
Ballet Master/Mistress (education) 151.027-014
BALL-FRINGE-MACHINE OPERATOR (tex. prod., nec) 689.685-010
BALLING-MACHINE OPERATOR (textile) 681.685-014
BALLISTICS EXPERT, FORENSIC (government ser.) 199.267-010
ballistics tester (ordnance) 739.484-010
ball laster (boot & shoe) 690.685-186
BALL-MACHINE OPERATOR (sugar & conf.) 520.686-010
ball maker (glass mfg.) 575.684-026
Ball-Mill Mixer (tex. prod., nec) 550.382-014
Ball-Mill Operator (any industry) 599.685-058
Ball-Mill Operator (cement) 570.685-046
BALL-MILL OPERATOR (chemical) 558.685-014
BALLOON DIPPER (rubber goods) 599.687-010
BALLOON MAKER (rubber goods) 752.684-010
Balloon Tester (rubber goods) 759.684-074
BALLPOINT-PEN-ASSEMBLY-MACHINE OPERATOR (pen & pencil) 692.382-010
BALLPOINT PEN CARTRIDGE TESTER (pen & pencil) 733.281-010
Ball-Point Splitter (boot & shoe) 585.685-114
ball racker (amuse. & rec.) 340.477-010
ball-rolling-machine operator (sugar & conf.) 520.686-010
Ballroom Dancer (amuse. & rec.) 151.047-010
BALL SORTER (machinery mfg.) 609.685-010
ball-thread-machine tender (textile) 681.685-010
BALL-TRUING-MACHINE OPERATOR (toy-sport equip.) 690.682-014
BALL-WARPER TENDER (textile) 681.685-010
ball winder (textile) 681.685-014
ball winder (textile) 681.685-010
Banana Grader (agriculture; wholesale tr.) 529.687-186
Banana-Ripening-Room Supervisor (wholesale tr.) 920.137-010
BAND-AND-CUFF CUTTER (glove & mit.) 784.685-010
BAND ATTACHER (clock & watch) 715.687-010
Band-Bias-Machine Operator (rubber tire) 690.682-022
Band Booker (amuse. & rec.) 191.117-014
BAND BUILDER (rubber tire) 750.684-010
Band, Cutter (garment) 699.685-014
Band Cutter (knitting) 781.687-010
BAND CUTTER (rubber goods) 690.685-026
band cutter (tex. prod., nec) 689.687-018
Band-Cutting-Machine Operator (garment; knitting) 686.685-066
bander (any industry) 782.684-058
bander (furniture) 619.685-014
bander (garment) 920.687-190
BANDER (pen & pencil) 733.687-018
bander (pottery & porc.) 740.681-010
BANDER (wood. container) 762.687-010
BANDER-AND-CELLOPHANER HELPER, MACHINE (tobacco) 920.686-010
BANDER-AND-CELLOPHANER, MACHINE (tobacco) 920.685-014

BANDER, HAND (any industry) 929.687-058
Bander, Hand (glass mfg.; glass products) 740.681-010
BANDER, HAND (paper goods) 920.687-026
BANDER, HAND (tobacco) 920.687-030
Band-Head-Saw Operator (saw. & plan.) 667.662-010
banding-and-cellophane-wrapping-machine-operator helper (tobacco) 920.686-010
BANDING-MACHINE OPERATOR (furniture) 619.685-014
BANDING-MACHINE OPERATOR (ordnance) 619.685-018
BANDING-MACHINE OPERATOR (pottery & porc.) 679.682-010
band-instrument maker (musical inst.) 730.381-018
band leader (profess. & kin.) 152.047-014
Band-Lining Bander (hat & cap) 787.682-010
band-log-mill-and-carriage operator (saw. & plan.) 667.662-010
BAND-MACHINE OPERATOR (rubber goods) 690.685-030
BAND MAKER (agriculture) 619.685-010
BANDOLEER PACKER (ordnance) 920.687-034
BANDOLEER STRAIGHTENER-STAMPER (ordnance) 737.587-010
Band-Plating-Machine Operator (hat & cap) 580.685-038
Band Presser (garment) 363.682-018
BAND-REAMER-MACHINE OPERATOR (nonfer. metal) 603.685-010
Band-Resaw Operator (saw. & plan.; wood. container) 667.682-058
Band-Ripsaw Operator (woodworking) 667.682-066
BAND SALVAGER (agriculture) 929.686-014
Band-Saw Filer (any industry) 701.381-014
BAND-SAWING-MACHINE OPERATOR (fabrication, nec) 690.485-010
band-saw marker (woodworking) 761.684-022
band-sawmill operator (saw. & plan.) 667.662-010
band-saw operator (machine shop) 607.682-010
BAND-SAW OPERATOR (meat products) 525.685-010
BAND-SAW OPERATOR (paper goods) 640.685-090
BAND-SAW OPERATOR (tex. prod., nec) 686.682-014
BAND-SAW OPERATOR (wood. container) 667.685-010
BAND-SAW OPERATOR (woodworking) 667.685-014
Band-Saw Operator, Cake Cutting (bakery products) 521.685-302
BAND-SCROLL-SAW OPERATOR (woodworking) 667.682-010
band sewer (any industry) 782.684-058
Band Shover, Press (agriculture) 920.686-042
band splicer (agriculture) 619.685-010
Band Splitter (boot & shoe) 585.685-114
band straightener (agriculture) 929.686-014
Band Tacker (any industry) 787.685-042
band-top assembler (furniture) 780.684-014
BAND-TOP MAKER (furniture) 780.684-014
BAND TUMBLER (rubber goods) 551.685-010
BANK BOSS (construction) 851.137-010
BANK BOSS (mine & quarry) 932.132-010
Bank-Credit-Card-Collection Clerk (financial) 241.357-010
banker (stonework) 679.664-010
Bank Examiner (government ser.) 160.167-054
BANKING PIN ADJUSTER (clock & watch) 715.381-018
BANK-NOTE DESIGNER (government ser.) 142.061-010
Banquet Captain (hotel & rest.) 311.137-018
Banquet Chef (hotel & rest.) 313.131-014
BAR AND FILLER ASSEMBLER (furniture) 706.684-034
bar attendant (hotel & rest.) 312.474-010
BAR ATTENDANT (hotel & rest.) 312.477-010
Bar Attendant (r.r. trans.) 311.477-022
BARBED-WIRE-MACHINE OPERATOR (metal prod., nec) 616.382-010
Barbecue-Briquette-Machine Operator (fabrication, nec) 549.662-010
BARBER (personal ser.) 330.371-010
BARBER APPRENTICE (personal ser.) 330.371-014
Barber-Tool Sharpener (any industry) 701.381-018
Bareback Rider (amuse. & rec.) 159.344-010
BAR EXAMINER (profess. & kin.) 110.167-010
bar-gauger and lubricator tender (ordnance) 590.685-058
barge captain (water trans.) 197.163-014
BARGE CAPTAIN (water trans.) 911.137-010
barge-crane operator (water trans.) 921.683-034
Barge Engineer (water trans.) 197.130-010
Barge Hand (water trans.) 911.687-022
Barge Loader (water trans.) 911.364-014
Barge-Loader Helper (water trans.) 911.687-010
barkeeper (hotel & rest.) 312.474-010
BARKER (amuse. & rec.) 342.657-010
barker (amuse. & rec.; personal ser.) 353.363-010
BARKER OPERATOR (millwork-plywood) 663.682-010
BARK-PRESS OPERATOR (paper & pulp) 563.685-010
Bark Tanner (leather mfg.) 582.482-018
BARLEY STEEPER (beverage) 522.685-114
Bar-Machine Operator (bakery products) 520.682-034
bar-machine operator, multiple spindle (machine shop) 604.280-014
bar-machine operator, multiple spindle (machine shop) 604.382-010
bar-machine operator, production (machine shop) 604.685-034
bar-machine operator, single spindle (machine shop) 604.280-018

bar-machine operator, single spindle

bar-machine operator, single spindle (machine shop) 604.382-014
BARN BOSS (any industry) 410.131-010
barnworker, groom (any industry) 410.674-022
bar porter (hotel & rest.) 312.687-010
BARREL ASSEMBLER (clock & watch) 715.381-022
BARREL ASSEMBLER (wood. container) 669.682-014
BARREL-ASSEMBLER HELPER (wood. container) 669.685-010
BARREL BRANDER (wood. container) 764.684-010
BARREL-BRIDGE ASSEMBLER (clock & watch) 715.381-026
barrel-bung-remover and dumper (wood. container) 764.687-018
barrel burner (wood. container) 764.684-014
BARREL-CAP SETTER (clock & watch) 715.687-014
BARREL CHARRER (wood. container) 764.684-014
BARREL-CHARRER HELPER (wood. container) 764.687-034
barrel coater (wood. container) 764.687-026
Barrel Cutter (beverage) 529.687-066
BARREL-DEDENTING-MACHINE OPERATOR (beverage) 617.682-010
BARREL DRAINER (wood. container) 764.687-018
BARREL-ENDSHAKE ADJUSTER (clock & watch) 715.381-030
Barrel Filler (can. & preserv.) 529.687-022
BARREL FILLER (grain-feed mills) 529.485-010
Barrel Filler, Head (any industry) 920.132-010
BARREL FILLER I (beverage) 522.687-010
BARREL FILLER II (beverage) 914.485-010
BARREL FINISHER (clock & watch) 715.682-010
BARREL FINISHER (ordnance) 736.684-018
Barrel Inspector (clock & watch) 715.384-022
BARREL INSPECTOR, TIGHT (wood. container) 764.687-022
Barrel Lapper (ordnance) 603.685-070
BARREL-LATHE OPERATOR, INSIDE (wood. container) 664.682-010
BARREL-LATHE OPERATOR, OUTSIDE (wood. container) 664.682-014
barrel leveler (wood. container) 764.687-094
barrel-line operator (electroplating) 500.362-014
BARREL LINER (wood. container) 764.687-026
BARREL LOADER AND CLEANER (ordnance) 736.587-010
barrel maker (wood. container) 764.684-018
BARREL MARKER (wood. container) 764.687-030
barrel painter (any industry) 599.685-070
barrel planer (wood. container) 664.682-014
BARREL POLISHER, INSIDE (ordnance) 603.685-014
BARREL RAISER (wood. container) 764.684-018
BARREL-RAISER HELPER (wood. container) 764.687-038
Barrel Reamer (ordnance) 606.682-014
BARREL REPAIRER (ordnance) 736.684-022
barrel repairer (wood. container) 764.684-022
barrel-repairer helper (wood. container) 764.687-050
BARREL-RIB MATTING-MACHINE OPERATOR (ordnance) 605.682-010
BARREL RIFLER (ordnance) 605.685-010
Barrel Rifler, Broach (ordnance) 605.685-010
Barrel Rifler, Button (ordnance) 605.685-010
Barrel Rifler, Hook (ordnance) 605.685-010
barrel-rifler operator (ordnance) 605.685-010
Barrel Roller (beverage) 529.687-066
barrel roller (wood. container) 764.687-030
Barrel Scraper (beverage) 529.687-066
barrel-stave inspector (wood. container) 764.687-054
BARREL STRAIGHTENER I (ordnance) 736.684-026
Barrel Straightener II (ordnance) 617.482-026
barrel tester and drainer (wood. container) 764.687-022
Barrel Washer, Machine (any industry) 529.685-074
Barrel Waterer (wood. container) 764.687-010
Barrer And Tacker (boot & shoe) 690.682-082
bar runner (hotel & rest.) 312.687-010
Bar-Straightening-Machine Operator (any industry) 613.662-022
Bar Tacker (any industry) 787.685-042
BARTENDER (hotel & rest.) 312.474-010
BARTENDER HELPER (hotel & rest.) 312.687-010
Barytes Grinder (paint & varnish) 599.685-058
base-and-wick assembler (fabrication, nec) 739.687-202
baseball-glove stuffer (toy-sport equip.) 732.687-042
BASEBALL INSPECTOR AND REPAIRER (toy-sport equip.) 732.684-030
Baseball Scout (amuse. & rec.) 153.117-018
BASEBALL SEWER, HAND (toy-sport equip.) 732.684-034
Baseball Winder (toy-sport equip.) 692.685-246
Base-Cloth Inspector (carpet & rug) 689.685-038
BASE-DRAW OPERATOR (ordnance) 504.685-010
BASE FILLER (toy-sport equip.) 732.687-018
BASE-FILLER OPERATOR (toy-sport equip.) 732.685-010
BASE-PLY HAND (rubber goods) 759.684-014
BASE REMOVER (light. fix.) 692.686-014
Baser (light. fix.) 692.685-118
Base-Wad Operator-Adjuster (ordnance) 535.482-010
BASIN OPERATOR (waterworks) 954.385-010
BASKET ASSEMBLER I (wood. container) 669.685-014
BASKET ASSEMBLER II (wood. container) 769.684-010

Basketball Assembler (toy-sport equip.) 732.684-026
Basketball Coach (amuse. & rec.) 153.227-010
Basketball Scout (amuse. & rec.) 153.117-018
Basket-Bottom-Machine Operator (wood. container) 669.685-014
Basket-Bottom-Rounding-Machine Operator (wood. container) 667.685-066
basket-factory machine hand (wood. container) 669.685-074
BASKET FILLER (can. & preserv.) 529.687-010
BASKET GRADER (wood. container) 769.687-010
basket-machine operator (wood. container) 669.685-074
basket maker (wood. container) 769.684-054
basket maker (wood. container) 669.685-014
BASKET MENDER (wood. container) 762.684-022
BASKET PATCHER (wood. container) 769.684-014
Basket Turner (agriculture) 920.687-134
Bass-Mechanism Maker (musical inst.) 730.281-010
Bass-String Winder (musical inst.) 692.682-062
Bass-Viol Repairer (any industry) 730.281-050
Baster, Hand (garment) 782.684-058
BASTING-MACHINE OPERATOR (garment) 786.682-030
basting marker (garment) 782.687-058
BASTING PULLER (garment) 782.687-010
Bat Boy/Girl (amuse. & rec.) 358.677-014
Bat Carrier (tex. prod., nec) 586.686-022
BATCH-AND-FURNACE OPERATOR (glass mfg.) 572.382-010
batcher (pharmaceut.) 559.686-022
batcher tender (knitting) 689.685-114
BATCH FREEZER (dairy products) 523.685-010
BATCH MAKER (nonfer. metal; steel & rel.) 515.685-010
batch maker (sugar & conf.) 529.361-014
BATCH MIXER (brick & tile) 570.687-010
batch mixer (food prep., nec) 520.685-014
batch mixer (glass mfg.) 570.685-054
batch mixer (paint & varnish) 550.685-078
BATCH MIXER (soap & rel.) 550.685-010
batch-mixer operator (grain-feed mills) 520.685-098
batch-mixing-truck driver (construction) 900.683-010
batch-plant operator (glass mfg.) 570.685-054
batch-plant supervisor (construction) 570.132-010
BATCH-RECORDS CLERK (plastic prod.) 221.387-054
batch-roller operator (sugar & conf.) 520.682-030
BATCH-STILL OPERATOR I (chemical) 552.685-014
Batch-Still Operator II (chemical) 552.362-022
BATCH-TANK CONTROLLER (grain-feed mills) 521.685-022
BATCH TRUCKER (rubber reclaim.) 550.686-010
Batch Trucker (rubber tire) 929.687-030
Batch-Unit Treater (petrol. refin.) 549.362-014
Batch Unloader (glass mfg.) 570.685-026
Batch Weigher (chemical) 929.687-062
batch weigher and mixer (rubber reclaim.) 550.686-010
bath attendant (personal ser.) 334.677-010
bath attendant (personal ser.) 334.374-010
bath-house attendant (personal ser.) 334.374-010
bath mixer (plastic-synth.) 550.684-010
BATH-MIX OPERATOR (plastic-synth.) 552.685-018
bath-solution maker (plastic-synth.) 550.684-010
Bat-Lathe Operator (woodworking) 664.382-010
BATTALION CHIEF (government ser.) 373.167-010
batter (pottery & porc.) 575.684-010
Batterboard Setter (construction) 869.664-014
batter depositor (bakery products) 526.682-010
BATTER MIXER (bakery products) 520.685-010
BATTER MIXER (food prep., nec) 520.685-014
Batter-Mixer Helper (bakery products) 526.686-010
BATTER-OUT (pottery & porc.) 575.684-010
BATTER SCALER (bakery products) 526.682-010
battery analyst (elec. equip.) 727.381-022
BATTERY ASSEMBLER (elec. equip.) 727.684-010
BATTERY ASSEMBLER, DRY CELL (elec. equip.) 727.664-010
BATTERY ASSEMBLER, PLASTIC (elec. equip.) 727.684-014
BATTERY CHARGER (any industry) 825.684-018
BATTERY CHARGER (elec. equip.) 727.587-010
battery charger (mine & quarry) 729.684-042
BATTERY CHARGER, CONVEYOR LINE (elec. equip.) 727.687-026
BATTERY-CHARGER TESTER (elec. equip.) 729.684-010
BATTERY-CONTAINER-FINISHING HAND (elec. equip.) 727.687-034
battery-container inspector (elec. equip.) 727.687-066
battery-container tester, aluminum (elec. equip.) 727.687-018
battery filler (textile) 683.686-010
battery hand (textile) 683.686-010
BATTERY INSPECTOR (railroad equip.; r.r. trans.) 829.684-010
battery loader (elec. equip.) 727.687-030
BATTERY LOADER (textile) 683.686-010
BATTERY MAINTAINER, LARGE EMERGENCY STORAGE (utilities) 820.381-010
BATTERY-PARTS ASSEMBLER (elec. equip.) 727.687-038

Battery Plate Remover (elec. equip.) 727.687-058
BATTERY RECHARGER (elec. equip.) 727.381-010
BATTERY REPAIRER (any industry) 727.381-014
BATTERY STACKER (elec. equip.) 727.687-030
Battery Starter (mine & quarry) 932.687-010
battery tester (any industry) 727.381-014
BATTERY TESTER (elec. equip.) 727.384-010
battery tester and repairer (elec. equip.) 727.684-018
Battery Tester, Field (elec. equip.) 727.384-010
Battery-Vent-Plug Inserter (elec. equip.) 727.687-038
BATTERY-WRECKER OPERATOR (nonfer. metal) 515.686-010
BATTING-MACHINE OPERATOR (tex. prod., nec; textile) 680.585-010
BATTING-MACHINE OPERATOR, INSULATION (nonmet. min.) 677.382-010
BB SHOT PACKER (ordnance) 920.685-018
BEACH LIFEGUARD (amuse. & rec.) 379.364-014
bead blasting machine tender (any industry) 503.685-042
BEAD BUILDER (rubber tire) 750.684-014
BEADER (furniture) 739.687-034
beader tender (chemical) 550.685-058
Bead Filler (rubber tire) 750.684-014
Bead Flipper (rubber tire) 750.684-014
BEAD-FORMING-MACHINE OPERATOR (rubber tire) 692.682-014
Beading-Machine Operator I (any industry) 617.482-014
Beading-Machine Operator II (any industry) 619.685-046
BEADING SAWYER (fabrication, nec) 667.685-018
BEAD INSPECTOR (light. fix.) 725.687-010
BEAD-MACHINE OPERATOR (hat & cap) 583.686-010
BEAD MAKER (jewelry-silver.) 770.381-010
BEAD PICKER (rubber reclaim.) 551.686-010
BEAD PREPARER (rubber goods) 692.685-022
beadsaw operator (rubber goods; rubber reclaim.) 690.685-386
Bead Stringer (elec. equip.) 691.685-018
BEAD STRINGER (jewelry-silver.) 735.684-010
Bead Supervisor (rubber tire) 750.130-010
BEADWORKER (fabrication, nec) 789.381-010
Bead Wrapper (rubber tire) 750.684-014
beam doffer (textile) 681.686-010
beam dyer (textile) 582.685-102
BEAM-DYER OPERATOR (textile) 582.685-014
Beam Dyer, Recessed Vat (textile) 582.685-014
beamer (meat products; oils & grease) 525.687-046
BEAMER (textile) 681.585-010
beamer hand (textile) 681.685-058
BEAMER HELPER (textile) 681.686-014
beam-house inspector (leather mfg.) 585.687-010
BEAMING INSPECTOR (leather mfg.) 585.687-010
beaming-machine operator (textile) 681.685-058
beam-machine operator (any industry) 699.682-022
Beam-Press Operator (rubber goods) 699.682-022
BEAM RACKER (textile) 681.686-010
beam warper (knitting; narrow fabrics; nonmet. min.; textile) 681.685-018
BEAM-WARPER TENDER, AUTOMATIC (knitting; narrow fabrics; nonmet. min.; textile) 681.685-018
bean dumper (sugar & conf.) 521.685-066
Bean-Sprout Grower (agriculture) 405.161-018
Bean-Sprout Laborer (agriculture) 405.687-014
bearing inspector (machinery mfg.) 706.382-014
Bearing-Press-Machine Operator (railroad equip.) 616.682-010
BEARING-RING ASSEMBLER (machinery mfg.) 706.684-038
Bear Keeper (amuse. & rec.) 412.674-010
beater (boot & shoe) 690.685-074
beater (nonmet. min.) 570.686-018
BEATER-AND-PULPER FEEDER (paper & pulp; tex. prod., nec) 530.686-010
BEATER ENGINEER (paper & pulp; tex. prod., nec) 530.662-010
BEATER-ENGINEER HELPER (paper & pulp; tex. prod., nec) 530.665-010
beater, head (paper & pulp) 530.132-014
Beater, Lead (paper & pulp; tex. prod., nec) 530.662-010
BEATER OPERATOR (chemical) 555.685-010
beater operator (paper & pulp; tex. prod., nec) 530.662-010
beater-operator helper (paper & pulp; tex. prod., nec) 530.665-010
beater-out, leveling machine (boot & shoe) 690.685-382
Beating-Machine Operator (leather mfg.) 589.686-022
beautician (personal ser.) 332.271-010
beautician apprentice (personal ser.) 332.271-014
beauty culturist (personal ser.) 332.271-010
beauty-culturist apprentice (personal ser.) 332.271-014
beauty operator (personal ser.) 332.271-010
beauty-operator apprentice (personal ser.) 332.271-014
Beauty Parlor Cleaner (personal ser.) 323.687-014
Beaver Trapper (fishing & hunt.) 461.684-014
beck tender (textile) 582.665-014
BEDDER (pottery & porc.) 573.687-010
BED LASTER (boot & shoe) 690.682-018
BED OPERATOR (steel & rel.) 613.685-034

BED RUBBER (stonework) 673.685-014
BED SETTER (stonework) 679.664-010
Bedspread Cutter, Hand (tex. prod., nec) 781.684-074
Bedspread Folder (tex. prod., nec) 589.687-014
Bedspread Inspector (tex. prod., nec) 789.587-014
Bedspread Seamer (tex. prod., nec) 787.682-066
Bedspring Assembler (furniture) 780.684-098
bed washer (furniture) 709.687-014
bed worker (fishing & hunt.) 446.684-014
bee farmer (agriculture) 413.161-010
Beef Boner (meat products) 525.684-010
Beef Grader (meat products) 525.387-010
Beef-Pluck Trimmer (meat products) 525.684-038
Beef Ribber (meat products) 525.684-018
beef trimmer (meat products) 521.687-106
Beegle-Iron Worker (wood prod., nec) 563.687-010
BEEKEEPER (agriculture) 413.161-010
Bee Producer (agriculture) 413.161-010
bee raiser (agriculture) 413.161-010
bee rancher (agriculture) 413.161-010
Beer-Coil Cleaner (any industry) 599.684-010
beer-still runner compounder (beverage) 522.382-026
beeswax bleacher (chemical) 551.685-158
beeswax blender (fabrication, nec) 550.585-046
beet flumer (sugar & conf.) 521.686-042
beet flumer (sugar & conf.) 922.665-010
BEE WORKER (agriculture) 413.687-018
BELL CAPTAIN (hotel & rest.) 324.137-014
Bell-Hole Digger (construction) 869.687-026
BELLHOP (hotel & rest.) 324.677-010
belling machine operator (steel & rel.) 617.685-022
BELL MAKER (musical inst.) 730.381-014
Bell Maker, Sousaphones (musical inst.) 730.381-014
BELL-NECK HAMMERER (musical inst.) 730.684-014
BELLOWS ASSEMBLER (inst. & app.) 710.684-042
bellows assembler (photo. appar.) 714.684-014
BELLOWS FILLER (inst. & app.) 710.684-014
Bellows Maker (musical inst.) 730.281-010
BELLOWS MAKER (photo. appar.) 714.684-014
BELLOWS TESTER (inst. & app.) 710.687-014
BELL SPINNER (musical inst.) 619.682-010
Bell Spinner, Sousaphones (musical inst.) 619.682-010
Bell Tier (concrete prod.) 579.687-042
BELLY BUILDER (musical inst.) 730.684-018
Belly Dancer (amuse. & rec.) 151.047-010
Belly Opener (meat products) 525.687-010
Belly Packer (meat products) 525.687-026
Belly Roller (leather mfg.) 583.685-094
Belly Trimmer (meat products) 525.684-054
Belly Wringer (leather mfg.) 589.685-098
belt-and-link-shop supervisor (ordnance) 737.137-022
belt back operator (button & notion) 690.685-194
Belt Brander (rubber goods) 690.685-454
BELT BUILDER (rubber goods) 752.684-014
BELT-BUILDER HELPER (rubber goods) 759.684-018
Belt Cleaner (steel & rel.) 911.687-014
Belt Cutter (garment) 699.685-014
BELTER (construction) term
BELTING-AND-WEBBING INSPECTOR (narrow fabrics) 683.487-010
Belting Cutter (leather prod.) 585.685-038
Belt-Loop Cutter (garment) 699.685-014
Belt-Loop Maker (garment) 787.685-014
BELT MAKER (nonmet. min.) 776.684-010
BELT-MAKER HELPER (nonmet. min.) 776.687-010
Belt Measurer (rubber goods) 690.685-454
Belt Notcher (rubber goods) 690.685-454
BELT PICKER (mine & quarry) 939.687-010
BELT-PRESS OPERATOR I (rubber goods) 553.362-010
BELT-PRESS OPERATOR II (rubber goods) 553.665-010
belt puncher (leather prod.) 690.685-266
BELT REPAIRER (any industry) 630.684-014
belt roller (leather prod.) 920.685-070
Belt Sander (woodworking) 761.682-014
BELT SANDER, STONE (stonework) 673.666-010
belt seamer (glass products) 775.684-042
belt tender (any industry) 921.685-026
Belt Turner (garment) 789.687-182
BENCH ASSEMBLER (agric. equip.) 706.684-042
bench assembler (any industry) 706.684-022
bench assembler (engine-turbine) 706.481-010
bench assembler, battery (elec. equip.) 727.684-026
bench assembler, electrical (aircraft mfg.) 729.384-026
bench-assembler operator (pen & pencil) 733.687-014
bench-assembler operator (pen & pencil) 733.687-034
bench-boring-machine operator (pen & pencil) 733.685-018

BENCH CARPENTER (woodworking) 760.684-010
bench die maker (machine shop) 601.281-010
BENCH GRINDER (any industry) 705.684-010
BENCH HAND (bakery products) 520.384-010
BENCH HAND (clock & watch) 715.684-026
BENCH HAND (furniture) 706.381-014
bench hand (jewelry-silver.) 700.687-026
bench hand (jewelry-silver.) 700.687-062
BENCH HAND (jewelry-silver.) 735.381-010
bench hand (machinery mfg.; machine tools) 600.281-022
BENCH HAND (motor-bicycles) 706.684-046
Bench-Hand Helper (bakery products) 526.686-010
bench hand, machine (bakery products) 520.685-214
bench inspector (any industry) 609.684-010
bench-lathe operator (machine shop) 604.380-018
Bench-Lay-Out Technician (optical goods) 716.381-014
BENCH-MOLDER APPRENTICE (jewelry-silver.) 518.381-010
bench-press operator (any industry) 616.682-026
bench-press operator (any industry) 690.685-014
BENCH-SHEAR OPERATOR (furniture) 703.684-010
bench worker (jewelry-silver.) 735.381-010
BENCH WORKER (metal prod., nec) 616.485-010
BENCH WORKER (optical goods) 713.684-018
bench-worker apprentice (jewelry-silver.) 700.281-014
BENCH WORKER, BINDING (print. & pub.) 977.684-026
BENCH WORKER, HOLLOW HANDLE (jewelry-silver.) 700.687-010
bench worker (jewelry-silver.) 700.281-010
BEN-DAY ARTIST (print. & pub.) 970.681-010
bender (jewelry-silver.) 700.684-010
Bender (toy-sport equip.) 569.685-014
Bender, Armature Coil (elec. equip.) 724.684-026
bender, hand (any industry) 709.684-090
BENDER, HAND (woodworking) 769.684-018
BENDER, MACHINE (paper goods) 641.685-010
BENDER, MACHINE (woodworking) 569.685-014
bending-machine operator (paper goods) 641.685-010
Bending-Machine-Operator Helper (any industry) 619.687-014
BENDING-MACHINE OPERATOR I (any industry) 617.482-010
BENDING-MACHINE OPERATOR II (any industry) 617.685-010
bending-press operator (any industry) 617.260-010
bending-press operator (woodworking) 569.685-014
bending-roll operator (any industry) 619.362-014
bend sorter (leather mfg.) 589.387-010
bend trimmer (leather mfg.) 585.684-010
Benefits Clerk I (clerical) 209.362-026
BENEFITS CLERK II (clerical) 205.567-010
benzene operator (chemical; steel & rel.) 551.682-010
Benzene-Still Utility Operator (chemical) 559.682-066
BENZENE-WASHER OPERATOR (chemical; steel & rel.) 551.682-010
benzol operator (chemical; steel & rel.) 551.682-010
berry grower (agriculture) 403.161-014
Bessemer-Bottom Maker (steel & rel.) 861.381-026
Bet Taker (amuse. & rec.) 211.462-022
beveler (boot & shoe; rubber goods) 690.685-378
BEVELER (clock & watch) 715.684-030
BEVELER (glass mfg.; glass products) 775.684-010
beveler (glass mfg.; glass products) 673.682-014
beveler (glass mfg.) 573.685-018
BEVELER (glass products) 673.685-018
BEVELER (nonmet. min.) 673.685-022
BEVELER (stonework) 771.484-010
BEVELER, PRINTED CIRCUIT BOARDS (electron. comp.) 699.682-034
bevel-gear-generator operator (machine shop) 602.382-018
BEVELING-AND-EDGING-MACHINE OPERATOR (glass mfg.; glass products) 673.682-014
BEVELING-AND-EDGING-MACHINE-OPERATOR HELPER (glass mfg.; glass products) 673.686-010
beveling-machine operator (glass mfg.; glass products) 673.682-014
BEVELING-MACHINE OPERATOR (hat & cap) 690.686-010
Beveling-Machine-Operator Helper (glass mfg.; glass products) 673.686-010
BEVEL POLISHER (clock & watch) 603.685-022
beverage-inspection-machine tender (beverage) 529.685-026
Bezel Cutter (jewelry-silver.) 770.261-010
Bias-Binding Cutter (tex. prod., nec) 686.685-066
bias-binding folder (rubber goods; tex. prod., nec) 689.685-134
bias-cutting-machine operator (rubber tire) 690.682-022
BIAS-CUTTING-MACHINE OPERATOR (tex. prod., nec) 686.682-014
Bias-Cutting-Machine Operator, Vertical (rubber tire) 690.682-022
BIAS-MACHINE OPERATOR (rubber tire) 690.682-022
BIAS-MACHINE-OPERATOR HELPER (rubber tire) 690.686-014
Biazzi-Nitrator Operator (chemical) 558.382-046
BIBLIOGRAPHER (profess. & kin.) 100.367-010
bicycle mechanic (any industry) 639.681-010
BICYCLE-RENTAL CLERK (retail trade) 295.467-010
BICYCLE REPAIRER (any industry) 639.681-010

Bicycle, Subassembler (motor-bicycles) 806.687-010
bid clerk (clerical) 249.367-066
Bight Maker (fabrication, nec) 590.662-022
Bill Adjuster (clerical) 241.367-014
Billboard-Erector Helper (construction) 869.664-014
bill clerk (clerical) 214.482-010
bill collector (clerical) 241.367-010
bill cutter (saw. & plan.) 667.482-018
biller (clerical) 214.482-010
BILLET ASSEMBLER (chemical) 614.684-010
billet header (nonfer. metal; smelt. & refin.) 514.584-010
Billet Inspector (steel & rel.) 619.381-010
Billiard-Table Repairer (retail trade; toy-sport equip.) 732.384-010
Billing Checker (clerical) 209.687-010
billing clerk (clerical) 214.382-014
billing clerk (clerical) 214.482-010
BILLING CLERK (clerical) 214.362-042
BILLING-CONTROL CLERK (utilities) 214.387-010
BILLING-MACHINE OPERATOR (clerical) 214.482-010
billing supervisor (utilities; waterworks) 214.137-022
BILLING TYPIST (clerical) 214.382-014
Bill-of-Lading Clerk (clerical) 214.382-014
BILLPOSTER (any industry) 299.667-010
BILLPOSTER (business ser.) 841.684-010
Bill Recapitulation Clerk (utilities) 216.482-010
Bill Sorter (clerical) 209.687-022
BIN CLEANER (beverage; grain-feed mills) 529.687-014
BINDER (any industry) 787.682-010
binder (elec. equip.) 724.687-010
binder (rubber goods) 690.686-026
binder (tobacco) 790.684-010
binder (woodworking) 929.685-018
BINDER AND BOX BUILDER (textile) 628.684-010
BINDER-AND-WRAPPER PACKER (tobacco) 922.687-014
Binder Caser (tobacco) 522.687-026
BINDER, CHAINSTITCH (garment) 786.682-034
BINDER, COVERSTITCH (garment) 786.682-038
BINDER CUTTER, HAND (tobacco) 521.687-014
binder fixer (textile) 628.684-010
BINDER LAYER (tobacco) 529.685-018
BINDER, LOCKSTITCH (garment) 786.682-042
binder operator (paper goods) 641.685-090
binder roller (tobacco) 790.684-010
BINDER SELECTOR (tobacco) 521.687-018
binder sorter (tobacco) 521.687-018
Binder Stripper, Hand (tobacco) 521.687-134
Binder Stripper, Machine (tobacco) 521.685-334
BINDER TECHNICIAN (glass mfg.) 550.585-010
bindery chief (print. & pub.) 653.131-010
bindery leadperson (print. & pub.) 653.360-018
BINDERY-MACHINE FEEDER-OFFBEARER (print. & pub.) 653.686-026
BINDERY-MACHINE SETTER (print. & pub.) 653.360-018
bindery operator (print. & pub.) 640.685-010
bindery operator (print. & pub.) 653.685-010
BINDERY WORKER (paper goods) 649.685-018
BINDERY WORKER (print. & pub.) 653.685-010
Binding Cementer, French Cord (boot & shoe) 690.686-018
Binding Cutter (garment; textile) 686.685-066
Binding Cutter (hat & cap) 699.682-030
BINDING CUTTER, SYNTHETIC CLOTH (tex. prod., nec) 699.682-010
binding-end stitcher (any industry) 787.682-010
BINDING FOLDER, MACHINE (boot & shoe) 788.684-018
binding-machine operator (any industry) 787.682-010
Binding Nicker (boot & shoe) 690.685-298
BINDING PRINTER (textile) 652.685-014
Binding Stitcher (boot & shoe) 690.682-082
BIN FILLER (tobacco) 922.687-010
Binitrotoluene Operator (chemical) 558.382-046
bin packer (tobacco) 922.687-010
bin piler (textile) 589.685-074
BIN TRIPPER OPERATOR (steel & rel.) 922.665-014
BIOCHEMIST (profess. & kin.) 041.061-026
BIOCHEMISTRY TECHNOLOGIST (medical ser.) 078.261-010
BIOGRAPHER (profess. & kin.) 052.067-010
BIOLOGICAL AIDE (agriculture) 049.364-018
BIOLOGICAL PHOTOGRAPHER (profess. & kin.) 143.362-010
biological-plant operator (chemical) 558.682-018
BIOLOGIST (profess. & kin.) 041.061-030
BIOLOGY SPECIMEN TECHNICIAN (profess. & kin.) 041.381-010
biomedical electronics technician (profess. & kin.) 019.261-010
biomedical engineering technician (profess. & kin.) 019.261-010
BIOMEDICAL ENGINEER (profess. & kin.) 019.061-010
BIOMEDICAL EQUIPMENT TECHNICIAN (profess. & kin.) 019.261-010
BIOPHYSICIST (profess. & kin.) 041.061-034
BIRD-CAGE ASSEMBLER (metal prod., nec) 709.684-026

Bird Keeper (amuse. & rec.) 412.674-010
BIRTH ATTENDANT (medical ser.) 354.377-010
biscuit-machine operator (plastic prod.; plastic-synth.) 556.685-058
BISQUE CLEANER (pottery & porc.) 774.684-010
bisque finisher (pottery & porc.) 774.684-010
bisque grader (pottery & porc.) 774.684-010
BISQUE GRADER (pottery & porc.) 774.687-010
Bisque-Kiln Drawer (pottery & porc.) 573.667-010
Bisque-Kiln Placer (pottery & porc.) 573.686-026
Bisque-Tile Burner (brick & tile) 573.382-018
BIT BENDER (fabrication, nec) 752.684-018
BITE-BLOCK MAKER (protective dev.) 712.684-014
bit grinder (any industry) 603.685-026
bit grinder (mine & quarry) 603.685-030
Bit Sander (fabrication, nec) 761.684-030
bit setter (fabrication, nec) 739.687-014
BIT SHARPENER (any industry) 603.685-026
BIT-SHARPENER OPERATOR (mine & quarry) 603.685-030
BIT SHAVER (fabrication, nec) 754.684-018
Bit Tripoler (fabrication, nec) 739.684-026
bituminous-distributor operator (construction) 853.663-018
bituminous-paving-machine operator (construction) 853.663-010
BLACK-ASH-BURNER OPERATOR (paper & pulp) 553.682-010
Black-Ash Worker (paint & varnish) 559.685-110
blackener (leather mfg.) 599.685-094
blacking-machine operator (leather mfg.) 599.685-094
Blacking-Wheel Tender (leather mfg.) 582.685-050
Black-Leather Buffer (leather mfg.) 585.685-018
Black-Leather Trimmer (leather mfg.) 585.684-010
BLACK-MILL OPERATOR (chemical) 553.665-014
BLACK OXIDE COATING EQUIPMENT TENDER (electron. comp.) 501.685-018
black oxide operator (electron. comp.) 501.685-018
BLACKSMITH (forging) 610.381-010
BLACKSMITH APPRENTICE (forging) 610.381-014
Blacksmith, Farm (agriculture) 610.381-010
blacksmith, hammer operator (aircraft mfg.; forging) 610.362-010
BLACKSMITH HELPER (forging) 610.684-010
blacksmith supervisor (forging) 612.131-010
blacktop-paver operator (construction) 853.663-010
blacktop spreader (construction) 853.663-010
Bladder Changer (rubber tire) 629.684-010
Bladder Trimmer (meat products) 525.684-038
blade aligner (elec. equip.) 706.687-018
BLADE BALANCER (agric. equip.) 701.687-014
Blade Boner (meat products) 525.684-010
blade-grader operator (construction) 850.663-022
BLADE GROOVER (cutlery-hrdwr.) 705.582-010
blanching-machine operator (can. & preserv.) 521.685-246
BLANCHING-MACHINE OPERATOR (can. & preserv.) 523.685-014
Blankbook Forwarder (print. & pub.) 794.687-026
Blankbook-Stitching-Machine Operator I (print. & pub.) 653.685-014
Blankbook-Stitching-Machine Operator II (print. & pub.) 653.682-010
blank driller (cutlery-hrdwr.) 709.684-082
blanker operator (paper goods) 649.685-118
blanker-press operator (paper goods) 649.682-026
Blanket Binder (tex. prod., nec) 787.682-010
Blanket Cutter, Hand (tex. prod., nec) 781.684-074
BLANKET-CUTTING-MACHINE OPERATOR (tex. prod., nec) 689.585-010
Blanket Folder (tex. prod., nec) 589.687-014
Blanket Inspector (tex. prod., nec) 789.587-014
BLANKET WASHER (smelt. & refin.) 511.687-010
BLANKET-WINDER HELPER (paper goods) 641.686-010
BLANKET-WINDER OPERATOR (paper goods) 641.682-010
Blanking-Machine Operator (any industry) 617.685-026
BLANKMAKER (glass mfg.) 579.382-022
BLASTER (any industry) 859.261-010
BLASTER (mine & quarry) 931.261-010
blaster (stonework) 771.281-010
BLASTER HELPER (any industry) 859.687-010
BLAST-FURNACE KEEPER (steel & rel.) 502.664-010
BLAST-FURNACE-KEEPER HELPER (steel & rel.) 502.687-010
BLASTING-CAP ASSEMBLER (ordnance) 737.687-018
BLEACH-BOILER FILLER (paper & pulp) 533.685-010
bleach-boiler packer (paper & pulp) 533.685-010
Bleach-Boiler Puller (paper & pulp) 539.587-010
Bleach Chlorinator (chemical) 558.382-030
bleacher (boot & shoe) 788.687-014
bleacher (plastic-synth.) 582.685-162
bleacher (textile) 582.685-102
Bleacher, Groundwood Pulp (paper & pulp) 533.362-010
Bleacher, Kraft Pulp (paper & pulp) 533.362-010
BLEACHER, LARD (meat products; oils & grease) 521.685-026
BLEACHER OPERATOR (chemical; soap & rel.) 558.685-018
BLEACHER, PULP (paper & pulp) 533.362-010

Bleacher, Sulfite Pulp (paper & pulp) 533.362-010
Bleaching Supervisor (leather mfg.) 582.131-010
BLEACH-LIQUOR MAKER (paper & pulp) 550.662-010
BLEACH PACKER (chemical) 558.687-010
BLEACH-RANGE OPERATOR (textile) 582.685-018
BLEMISH REMOVER (boot & shoe) 788.684-022
BLENDER (bakery products) 520.585-010
blender (beverage; can. & preserv.) 520.685-030
blender (build. mat., nec) 570.685-094
blender (chemical; electron. comp.) 550.685-082
blender (chemical) 555.685-046
blender (grain-feed mills) 520.685-106
blender (hat & cap) 680.685-062
blender (nonfer. metal; steel & rel.) 510.685-018
Blender (oils & grease) 529.382-026
blender (paint & varnish) 550.685-078
blender (paint & varnish) 550.585-038
BLENDER (petrol. refin.) 540.462-010
Blender (plastic prod.; plastic-synth.) 550.685-134
blender (soap & rel.) 550.685-010
BLENDER (tobacco) 520.387-010
BLENDER-CONVEYOR OPERATOR (dairy products) 529.685-022
blender helper (grain-feed mills) 520.686-022
BLENDER HELPER (plastic prod.; plastic-synth.) 550.586-010
BLENDER I (chemical) 550.685-014
BLENDER II (chemical) 550.665-010
BLENDER LABORER (tobacco) 520.687-010
BLENDER-MACHINE OPERATOR (oils & grease) 520.685-018
blender operator (any industry) 680.685-082
Blender Operator (brick & tile) 570.382-010
blender operator (chemical) 550.665-010
blender operator (chemical) 550.382-018
BLENDER, SNUFF (tobacco) 520.685-022
blending-kettle tender (beverage; can. & preserv.) 520.685-030
BLENDING-LINE ATTENDANT (tobacco) 520.685-026
Blending-Machine Feeder (nonmet. min.) 570.686-018
BLENDING-MACHINE OPERATOR (dairy products) 522.685-010
blending-machine operator (fabrication, nec) 680.685-066
BLENDING-MACHINE OPERATOR (textile) 680.685-010
BLENDING-PLANT OPERATOR (oils & grease) 520.682-010
BLENDING SUPERVISOR (grain-feed mills) 520.132-010
BLENDING SUPERVISOR (tobacco) 520.136-010
BLENDING-TANK TENDER (beverage; can. & preserv.) 520.685-030
BLENDING-TANK TENDER HELPER (can. & preserv.) 520.687-066
BLIND AIDE (personal ser.) 359.573-010
Blind Eyeletter (boot & shoe) 699.685-018
Blind Hooker (boot & shoe) 699.685-018
BLIND-SLAT-STAPLING-MACHINE OPERATOR (saw. & plan.) 669.685-018
BLINDSTITCH-MACHINE OPERATOR (garment) 786.682-046
BLINTZE ROLLER (food prep., nec) 520.687-014
Blister-Packing-Machine Tender (any industry) 920.685-078
block and case maker (pottery & porc.) 777.684-018
Block Breaker (concrete prod.) 579.687-042
BLOCK-BREAKER OPERATOR (chemical) 555.686-010
block chopper, hand (fabrication, nec; paper & pulp) 569.687-026
Block Cleaner (clock & watch) 715.687-126
Block Cuber (concrete prod.) 579.687-042
block cutter (print. & pub.) 979.281-014
blocker (any industry) 363.685-018
BLOCKER (clock & watch) 715.684-034
BLOCKER (glass mfg.; glass products) 673.685-026
Blocker (jewelry-silver.) 770.261-010
BLOCKER (laundry & rel.) 363.684-010
BLOCKER (narrow fabrics; nonmet. min.) 689.685-014
blocker (pottery & porc.) 777.684-018
BLOCKER (tex. prod., nec) 920.685-022
BLOCKER AND CUTTER, CONTACT LENS (optical goods) 716.681-010
BLOCKER AND POLISHER, GOLD WHEEL (clock & watch) 715.381-034
blocker and sewer (fabrication, nec) 739.384-014
BLOCKER, AUTOMATIC (glass mfg.; glass products) 673.685-030
BLOCKER, HAND (optical goods) 716.684-010
BLOCKER, HAND I (hat & cap) 580.684-010
BLOCKER, HAND II (hat & cap) 580.684-014
blocker, heated metal-forms (hat & cap) 580.684-010
BLOCKER I (print. & pub.) 979.682-010
BLOCKER II (print. & pub.) 971.684-010
BLOCKER, METAL BASE (print. & pub.) 974.682-010
blocker, polishing (clock & watch) 715.684-034
BLOCK FEEDER (fabrication, nec) 663.686-010
block hacker (fabrication, nec; paper & pulp) 569.687-026
blocking-machine operator (hat & cap) 580.685-026
Blocking-Machine Operator, Second (hat & cap) 580.685-038
BLOCKING-MACHINE TENDER (optical goods) 716.685-010
BLOCK INSPECTOR (fabrication, nec) 739.687-038

BLOCK MAKER (protective dev.) 719.381-018
block maker (concrete prod.) 575.685-014
block maker (stonework) 771.684-010
BLOCK-MAKING-MACHINE OPERATOR (concrete prod.) 575.685-014
block-press operator (chemical) 559.685-038
BLOCK-PRESS OPERATOR (chemical) 556.685-014
Block Setter, Gypsum (construction) 861.381-018
BLOCK-SPLITTER OPERATOR (paper & pulp) 663.685-010
block trimmer (leather mfg.) 585.684-010
blood-bank-booking clerk (medical ser.) 245.367-018
BLOOD-DONOR RECRUITER (medical ser.) 293.357-010
BLOOD-DONOR-UNIT ASSISTANT (medical ser.) 245.367-014
BLOOD TESTER, FOWL (agriculture) 411.364-010
Blower (can. & preserv.) 525.687-126
blower (glass mfg.) 772.381-022
blower (hat & cap) 680.685-046
blower (retail trade) 369.685-010
blower (toy-sport equip.) 731.685-014
BLOWER AND COMPRESSOR ASSEMBLER (machinery mfg.) 801.361-010
blower, blast furnace (steel & rel.) 519.132-010
BLOWER FEEDER, DYED RAW STOCK (textile) 581.686-010
BLOWER INSULATOR (railroad equip.; retail trade; wholesale tr.) 863.664-010
blower-room attendant (any industry) 950.585-010
Blow-Machine Tender, Starch Spraying (textile) 582.685-138
BLOW-MOLDING-MACHINE OPERATOR (plastic prod.) 556.682-010
BLOW-MOLDING-MACHINE TENDER (toy-sport equip.) 556.685-086
Blow-Off Worker (chemical) 549.587-010
BLOW-OFF WORKER (furniture) 763.687-010
BLOW-PIT HELPER (paper & pulp) 533.686-010
BLOW-PIT OPERATOR (paper & pulp) 533.665-010
BLOW-UP OPERATOR (sugar & conf.) 529.485-014
Blueberry Grower (agriculture) 403.161-014
Blue-Leather Setter (leather mfg.) 589.685-098
Blue-Leather Sorter (leather mfg.) 589.387-010
blue-line hanger (leather mfg.) 589.686-026
blue-line operator (any industry) 979.682-014
blue-line trimmer (leather mfg.) 585.684-010
blueprint assembler (any industry) 920.687-038
blue print control clerk (aircraft mfg.; electron. comp.) 206.367-010
BLUEPRINTING-MACHINE OPERATOR (any industry) 979.682-014
blueprint maker (any industry) 979.682-014
Blueprint-Paper-Coating-Machine Operator (photo. appar.) 534.582-010
BLUEPRINT TRIMMER (any industry) 920.687-038
Bluer (ordnance) 599.685-026
Blue-Split Trimmer (leather mfg.) 585.684-010
bluing-oven tender (heat treating) 504.685-018
Blunger Loader (textile) 929.687-030
blunger-machine operator (brick & tile; pottery & porc.) 570.482-010
BOARD ATTENDANT (amuse. & rec.) 249.587-010
Board Drophammer Operator (forging) 610.362-010
boarder (knitting) 589.685-010
boarder (knitting) 589.686-042
boarder (knitting) 583.687-010
boarder, hand (knitting) 589.686-042
boarder, machine (knitting) 589.685-010
boarder, steam (knitting) 589.686-042
boarder tender (knitting) 589.686-042
board handler (wood prod., nec) 569.686-042
BOARDING-MACHINE OPERATOR (knitting) 589.685-010
Board Layer (wood. container) 669.686-014
BOARD-LINER OPERATOR (wood. container) 641.685-014
Board-Lining-Machine Operator (paper goods) 641.562-010
BOARD-MACHINE SET-UP OPERATOR (concrete prod.) 579.380-010
board operator (motion picture; radio-tv broad.; recording) 194.262-018
boat accessories installer (retail trade; ship-boat mfg.) 806.464-010
boat bottomer (ship-boat mfg.) 806.684-106
BOAT BUFFER, PLASTIC (ship-boat mfg.) 849.684-010
BOATBUILDER APPRENTICE, WOOD (ship-boat mfg.) 860.381-014
BOATBUILDER, WOOD (ship-boat mfg.) 860.361-010
BOAT-CANVAS MAKER-INSTALLER (tex. prod., nec) 789.261-010
Boat Cleaner (steel & rel.) 911.687-014
BOAT DISPATCHER (water trans.) 184.167-010
boat garnisher (ship-boat mfg.) 806.684-146
BOAT-HOIST OPERATOR (retail trade) 921.683-010
BOAT-HOIST-OPERATOR HELPER (retail trade) 921.667-010
boat joiner (ship-boat mfg.) 860.381-050
BOAT-LOADER HELPER (water trans.) 911.687-010
BOAT LOADER I (water trans.) 911.364-014
BOAT LOADER II (water trans.) 921.685-010
boat mechanic (engine-turbine; ship-boat mfg.) 623.281-038
BOAT-OAR MAKER (woodworking) 761.381-010
BOAT OUTFITTER (ship-boat mfg.) 806.684-146
BOAT PATCHER, PLASTIC (ship-boat mfg.) 807.684-014
boat puller (ship-boat mfg.) 809.667-010

boat puller (water trans.) 911.687-018
BOAT-RENTAL CLERK (amuse. & rec.) 295.467-014
BOAT REPAIRER (ship-boat mfg.) 807.361-014
boat-ride operator (amuse. & rec.) 342.667-010
BOAT RIGGER (retail trade; ship-boat mfg.) 806.464-010
BOATSWAIN (water trans.) 911.131-010
BOATSWAIN, OTTER TRAWLER (fishing & hunt.) 441.132-010
Boat-Tank Attendant (amuse. & rec.) 342.667-010
Boat Tender (logging) 911.663-010
Boat Worker (saw. & plan.) 921.686-022
boat wrapper (ship-boat mfg.) 869.684-078
BOBBIN CLEANER, HAND (textile) 689.687-014
BOBBIN-CLEANING-MACHINE OPERATOR (textile) 689.686-014
Bobbin-Coil Winder (electron. comp.) 724.684-026
BOBBIN DISKER (glass mfg.) 734.687-022
Bobbin Drier (plastic-synth.) 581.685-010
bobbin fixer (tex. prod., nec; textile) 681.687-026
Bobbin Handler (textile) 929.687-030
BOBBIN INSPECTOR (woodworking) 769.687-014
BOBBIN PRESSER (tex. prod., nec) 689.685-018
bobbin salvager (glass mfg.; plastic-synth.; textile) 922.687-018
BOBBIN SORTER (glass mfg.; plastic-synth.; textile) 922.687-018
BOBBIN STRIPPER (tex. prod., nec) 689.685-022
bobbin-stripper (textile) 689.686-014
Bobbin Washer (plastic-synth.) 582.685-162
bobbin winder (metal prod., nec; nonfer. metal) 691.685-026
Bobbin Winder (textile) 681.685-154
BOBBIN WINDER, MACHINE (boot & shoe) 681.685-022
BOBBIN WINDER, MACHINE (tex. prod., nec; textile) 681.585-014
BOBBIN WINDER, SEWING MACHINE (textile) 681.685-026
BOBBIN-WINDER TENDER (glass mfg.) 619.685-022
body builder (auto. mfg.; automotive ser.) 807.281-010
Body Coverer (fabrication, nec) 780.684-026
body-die maker (machine shop) 601.280-010
body finisher (hat & cap) 589.685-062
BODYGUARD (personal ser.) 372.667-014
body-line finisher (automotive ser.) 807.381-010
Body Maker (fabrication, nec) 739.684-190
body maker (musical inst.) 730.682-010
Body Maker (tinware) 616.685-042
BODY-MAKER-MACHINE SETTER (tinware) 616.360-010
BODY-MAKE-UP ARTIST (amuse. & rec.; motion picture) 333.271-010
body masker (any industry) 749.687-018
Body Presser (laundry & rel.) 363.685-026
body repairer, bus (automotive ser.) 807.381-010
body-rolling-machine tender (paper goods) 641.685-062
Body Trimmer (automotive ser.) 780.381-010
BODY WIRER (auto. mfg.; vehicles, nec) 829.684-014
BOILER (soap & rel.) 553.382-014
boiler (sugar & conf.) 529.361-014
Boiler Cleaner (any industry) 891.687-022
boiler cleaner, chief (any industry) 805.667-010
BOILER HOUSE INSPECTOR (any industry) 805.667-010
BOILER HOUSE MECHANIC (any industry) 805.361-010
boiler house operator (any industry) 950.382-010
boiler house supervisor (any industry) 950.131-014
BOILERMAKER APPRENTICE (struct. metal) 805.261-010
boilermaker, assembly and erection (struct. metal) 805.261-014
Boilermaker, Central Steam Plant (struct. metal) 805.381-010
BOILERMAKER FITTER (struct. metal) 805.361-014
BOILERMAKER HELPER I (struct. metal) 805.687-010
BOILERMAKER HELPER II (struct. metal) 805.664-010
BOILERMAKER I (struct. metal) 805.261-014
BOILERMAKER II (struct. metal) 805.381-010
Boilermaker, Industrial Boilers (struct. metal) 805.381-010
boilermaker mechanic (struct. metal) 805.381-010
Boilermaker, Ship (struct. metal) 805.381-010
boiler mechanic (any industry) 805.361-010
BOILER OPERATOR (any industry) 950.382-010
boiler operator (any industry) 951.685-014
boiler-operator helper (any industry) 950.685-014
BOILER-OPERATOR HELPER (sugar & conf.) 950.585-014
BOILER-OUT (jewelry-silver.) 700.687-014
BOILER RELINER, PLASTIC BLOCK (foundry) 849.484-010
boiler-room helper (any industry) 699.687-018
BOILER-ROOM HELPER (any industry) 950.685-014
Boiler-Shop Supervisor (any industry) 809.130-014
boiler tender (any industry) 951.685-010
Boiler-Tube Blower (any industry) 891.687-030
Boiler-Tube Reamer (any industry) 891.687-030
Boiling-Off Winder (textile) 689.685-046
BOILING-TUB OPERATOR (chemical) 551.685-014
BOIL-OFF-MACHINE OPERATOR, CLOTH (textile) 582.685-022
Bologna Lacer (meat products) 529.687-034
bolter (bakery products) 520.585-010

BOLTER (grain-feed mills) 521.685-030
BOLTER (saw. & plan.) 667.685-022
BOLTER HELPER (grain-feed mills) 521.686-010
bolter helper (grain-feed mills) 520.686-022
bolting-machine operator (mine & quarry) 930.683-026
BOLT LOADER (saw. & plan.) 922.687-022
Bolt-Machine Operator (nut & bolt) 612.462-010
bolt sawyer (saw. & plan.) 667.685-022
bolt sawyer (wood. container) 667.685-062
Bolt-Threading-Machine Operator (machine shop) 604.682-014
Bolt-Up Worker (metal prod., nec) 706.684-090
Bomb-Disposal Specialist (government ser.) 632.261-018
BOMB LOADER (ordnance) 737.684-014
Bombsight Specialist (government ser.) 632.261-010
Bonbon-Cream Warmer (sugar & conf.) 526.382-014
Bonbon Dipper (sugar & conf.) 524.684-010
BONDACTOR-MACHINE OPERATOR (foundry) 899.684-010
bonded-strand operator (glass mfg.) 574.665-010
BONDED STRUCTURES REPAIRER (aircraft mfg.) 807.381-014
Bonder (electron. comp.) 726.687-022
bonder (foundry) 518.685-030
BONDER, AUTOMOBILE BRAKES (automotive ser.) 620.685-010
Bonderite Operator (any industry) 599.382-010
Bonderizer (auto. mfg.) 599.685-026
bonder, rework and repair (aircraft mfg.) 807.381-014
BONDER, SEMICONDUCTOR (electron. comp.) 726.685-066
BONDING AGENT (business ser.) 186.267-010
Bonding And Composite Fabricator (aircraft mfg.) 754.381-018
bonding equipment operator (aircraft mfg.) 553.362-014
bonding-machine operator (any industry) 690.685-154
bonding-machine operator (foundry) 518.685-030
BONDING-MACHINE SETTER (textile) 589.360-010
BONDING-MACHINE TENDER (textile) 589.665-010
BONE-CHAR KILN OPERATOR (grain-feed mills) 523.662-010
BONE-CHAR KILN TENDER (chemical) 553.685-018
BONE-CHAR OPERATOR (chemical) 553.686-010
BONE-COOKING OPERATOR (chemical) 551.685-018
BONE CRUSHER (chemical) 555.685-014
bone drier (chemical) 553.685-022
BONE-DRIER OPERATOR (chemical) 553.685-022
BONE PICKER (can. & preserv.) 521.687-022
BONE PICKER (chemical) 551.687-010
BONE-PROCESS OPERATOR (chemical) 559.665-010
BONER (garment; protective dev.) 789.687-018
BONER, MEAT (meat products) 525.684-010
Bone Sawyer (meat products) 525.684-018
BONSAI CULTURIST (agriculture) 405.161-010
BOOKBINDER (print. & pub.) 977.381-010
BOOKBINDER APPRENTICE (print. & pub.) 977.381-014
bookbinder, chief (print. & pub.) 653.131-010
Book Critic (print. & pub.; radio-tv broad.) 131.067-018
booker (amuse. & rec.) 191.117-014
BOOKER (rubber goods; rubber tire) 599.687-014
book folder (tex. prod., nec; textile) 589.687-014
bookie (amuse. & rec.) 187.167-014
booking agent (amuse. & rec.) 191.117-014
BOOKING CLERK (water trans.) 248.367-014
BOOKING CLERK (wholesale tr.) 216.587-010
BOOKING MANAGER (amuse. & rec.) 191.117-014
BOOKING PRIZER (tobacco) 216.462-010
BOOKING SUPERVISOR (water trans.) 248.137-010
BOOK-JACKET-COVER-MACHINE OPERATOR (paper goods) 640.685-014
BOOKKEEPER (clerical) 210.382-014
book-loan clerk (library) 249.367-046
BOOKMAKER (amuse. & rec.) 187.167-014
bookmaker (print. & pub.) 977.381-010
bookmaker, map (print. & pub.) 979.684-022
book mender (any industry) 977.684-010
Bookmobile Clerk (library) 249.367-046
BOOKMOBILE DRIVER (library) 249.363-010
BOOKMOBILE LIBRARIAN (library) 100.167-014
book paster (print. & pub.) 977.684-018
Book-Pocket-Machine Operator (paper goods) 649.685-042
BOOK REPAIRER (any industry) 977.684-010
Bookseamer, Blindstitch (garment) 786.682-126
book sewer (print. & pub.) 653.685-014
BOOK-SEWING-MACHINE OPERATOR I (print. & pub.) 653.685-014
BOOK-SEWING-MACHINE OPERATOR II (print. & pub.) 653.682-010
Book Sorter (nonprofit org.) 222.387-054
book stripper (print. & pub.) 972.381-022
BOOK TRIMMER (print. & pub.) 640.685-010
Boomboat Operator (logging) 911.663-010
BOOM-CONVEYOR OPERATOR (any industry) 921.683-014
boom operator (motion picture; radio-tv broad.) 962.384-010
Boom Supervisor (logging) 455.134-010

BOOSTER ASSEMBLER (ordnance) 737.687-022
bootblack (personal ser.) 366.677-010
Boot-Lace Cutter, Machine (leather prod.) 585.685-038
boot-liner maker (rubber goods) 795.684-026
BOOTMAKER, HAND (rubber goods) 753.381-010
boot polisher (personal ser.) 366.677-010
Boot Tester (rubber goods) 759.684-074
Boot Trimmer (boot & shoe) 690.685-434
Boot Turner (boot & shoe) 788.687-130
Borderer (ordnance) 761.381-034
BORDER GUARD (government ser.) 375.363-010
Border Inspector (government ser.) 168.267-022
border-machine operator (furniture) 787.685-022
border-machine operator (tex. prod., nec) 689.382-010
BORDER MEASURER AND CUTTER (furniture) 780.687-010
border measurer (furniture) 780.687-010
border patrol agent (government ser.) 375.363-010
borer, stem (fabrication, nec) 739.687-014
BORING-AND-FILLING-MACHINE OPERATOR (fabrication, nec) 692.682-018
Boring-Machine Feeder (woodworking) 669.686-030
Boring-Machine Operator (clock & watch) 606.685-030
boring-machine operator (construction) 850.662-010
BORING-MACHINE OPERATOR (furniture) 666.685-014
BORING-MACHINE OPERATOR (machine shop) 606.382-022
Boring-Machine Operator (rubber goods) 690.680-010
BORING-MACHINE OPERATOR (woodworking) 666.382-010
Boring-Machine Operator, Double End (woodworking) 666.382-010
boring-machine-operator helper (construction) 850.684-014
Boring-Machine Operator, Horizontal (woodworking) 666.382-010
BORING-MACHINE OPERATOR, PRODUCTION (machine shop) 606.685-010
Boring-Machine Operator, Vertical (woodworking) 666.382-010
BORING-MACHINE SET-UP OPERATOR, JIG (machine shop) 606.280-010
BORING-MILL SET-UP OPERATOR, HORIZONTAL (machine shop) 606.280-014
Boring-Mill Set-Up Operator, Vertical (machine shop) 606.280-014
Bosom Presser (laundry & rel.) 363.685-026
boss (any industry) 899.133-010
boss (any industry)   see SUPERVISOR
BOTANIST (profess. & kin.) 041.061-038
Bottle Assembler (rubber goods) 752.684-038
Bottle Blower (glass mfg.) 772.381-022
bottle-blowing-machine tender (glass mfg.) 575.685-038
BOTTLED-BEVERAGE INSPECTOR (beverage) 529.685-026
BOTTLE GAUGER (beverage) 529.587-010
Bottle-House Pumper (beverage) 914.665-014
BOTTLE-HOUSE QUALITY-CONTROL TECHNICIAN (beverage) 029.361-010
bottle inspector (beverage) 529.685-026
Bottle Inspector (glass mfg.) 579.384-018
Bottle-Label Inspector (beverage) 920.687-042
Bottle-Machine Operator (glass mfg.) 575.382-014
BOTTLE PACKER (beverage) 920.685-026
Bottle-Packing-Machine Cleaner (any industry) 699.687-014
Bottle Washer, Machine I (any industry) 529.685-074
Bottle Washer, Machine II (any industry) 920.685-078
BOTTLING-LINE ATTENDANT (beverage) 920.687-042
Bottling Supervisor (any industry) 920.132-010
BOTTOM BLEACHER (boot & shoe) 788.687-014
Bottom Board And Truss Leg Installer (musical inst.) 763.684-058
Bottom Brusher (boot & shoe) 788.687-018
Bottom Buffer (boot & shoe) 690.685-046
Bottom Burnisher (boot & shoe) 690.685-058
Bottom Cementer I (boot & shoe) 690.686-018
Bottom Cementer II (boot & shoe) 788.687-030
BOTTOMER I (mine & quarry) 932.667-010
Bottomer II (mine & quarry) 939.667-010
BOTTOM FILLER (boot & shoe) 788.684-026
Bottom-Hole-Pressure-Recording Operator (petrol. & gas) 930.167-010
BOTTOM-HOLE-PRESSURE-RECORDING-OPERATOR HELPER (petrol. & gas) 930.687-010
BOTTOM-HOOP DRIVER (wood. container) 669.685-022
BOTTOMING-MACHINE OPERATOR (paper goods) 649.685-022
Bottoming-Room Inspector (boot & shoe) 788.384-018
Bottoming-Room Supervisor (boot & shoe) 788.131-010
bottom ironer (boot & shoe) 690.685-034
Bottom-Liquor Attendant (chemical) 558.682-014
BOTTOM MAKER (steel & rel.) 509.687-010
Bottom Maker (wood. container) 669.685-014
Bottom Nailer (wood. container) 669.682-058
BOTTOM POLISHER (elec. equip.) 603.685-034
Bottom Pounder, Cement Shoes (boot & shoe) 690.685-314
BOTTOM-PRECIPITATOR OPERATOR (smelt. & refin.) 511.664-010
BOTTOM PRESSER (boot & shoe) 690.685-034

Bottom Sander (fabrication, nec) 761.684-030
BOTTOM-SAW OPERATOR (saw. & plan.) 667.682-014
bottom scrubber (boot & shoe) 788.687-014
bottom stainer (boot & shoe) 788.687-098
Bottom Stamper (boot & shoe) 690.685-158
Bottom Steep Tender (grain-feed mills) 522.465-010
Bottom Stitcher (toy-sport equip.) 732.684-050
Bottom-Stop Attacher (button & notion) 692.685-206
bottom turner (wood. container) 669.685-026
BOTTOM-TURNING-LATHE TENDER (wood. container) 665.685-010
BOTTOM WHEELER (boot & shoe) 788.684-030
boucle finisher (laundry & rel.) 363.684-010
BOUFFANT-CURTAIN-MACHINE TENDER (tex. prod., nec) 689.685-026
boulevard-glassware cleaner (utilities) 952.667-010
boulevard-glassware replacer (utilities) 952.667-010
BOUNCER (amuse. & rec.) 376.667-010
bounty hunter (fishing & hunt.) 461.661-010
Bow Attacher (garment) 782.684-058
Bowling-Alley-Installation Supervisor (construction) 860.131-018
BOWLING-BALL ENGRAVER (toy-sport equip.) 732.584-010
BOWLING-BALL FINISHER (toy-sport equip.) 690.685-038
BOWLING-BALL GRADER AND MARKER (toy-sport equip.) 732.381-014
BOWLING-BALL-MOLD ASSEMBLER (toy-sport equip.) 556.687-010
BOWLING-BALL MOLDER (toy-sport equip.) 556.685-018
BOWLING-BALL WEIGHER AND PACKER (toy-sport equip.) 732.487-010
bowling-pin-machine mechanic (any industry) 638.261-022
Bowl Sander (fabrication, nec) 662.685-038
Bowl Topper (fabrication, nec) 761.684-030
BOWL TURNER (fabrication, nec) 664.684-010
BOW MAKER (any industry) 789.684-010
BOW MAKER (boot & shoe) 788.684-034
BOW MAKER (garment; hat & cap) 784.684-010
BOW MAKER (musical inst.) 730.281-058
BOW MAKER, CUSTOM (toy-sport equip.) 732.381-010
Bow Maker, Gift Wrapping (any industry) 920.587-018
BOW-MAKER-MACHINE TENDER, AUTOMATIC (tex. prod., nec) 689.685-030
BOW MAKER, PRODUCTION (toy-sport equip.) 732.684-038
BOW REHAIRER (any industry) 730.684-022
Bow Repairer (any industry) 730.281-050
Bow Repairer, Custom (toy-sport equip.) 732.381-010
Bow Stapler (boot & shoe) 690.685-162
BOW-STRING MAKER (toy-sport equip.) 732.684-042
Bow Tacker I (hat & cap) 782.684-058
Bow Tacker II (hat & cap) 787.685-042
Box Attacher (button & notion) 692.685-206
BOX BENDER (paper goods) 641.687-010
Box-Blank-Machine Feeder (woodworking) 669.686-030
BOX-BLANK-MACHINE OPERATOR (wood. container) 669.662-010
BOX-BLANK-MACHINE-OPERATOR HELPER (wood. container) 669.686-014
Boxcar Weigher (railroad equip.) 221.587-030
Box Coverer, Hand (paper goods) 795.687-014
box-covering-machine operator (paper goods) 641.685-034
boxer (any industry) 920.684-010
Boxer (agriculture) 920.687-134
Box Feeder (tex. prod., nec) 586.686-022
BOX-FOLDING-MACHINE OPERATOR (paper goods) 649.682-010
Box Gluer (wood. container) 762.687-034
box-hinge and lock attacher (wood. container) 762.687-046
Box Icer (can. & preserv.) 922.687-046
BOXING-AND-PRESSING SUPERVISOR (knitting) 789.137-010
BOXING INSPECTOR (garment) 789.587-010
Boxing-Machine Operator (furniture) 780.682-018
BOX INSPECTOR (wood. container) 762.687-014
box labeler (any industry) 652.682-010
BOX-LINING-MACHINE FEEDER (paper goods) 641.685-018
box maker (any industry) 669.682-058
BOX MAKER (fabrication, nec) 762.684-026
Box Maker (musical inst.) 730.281-010
Box Maker, Cardboard (any industry) 920.587-018
BOX MAKER, PAPERBOARD (any industry) 794.684-014
Box Maker, Wood (any industry) 762.684-050
BOX MAKER, WOOD (wood. container) 760.684-014
box marker (boot & shoe; garment) 652.685-018
Box Nailer (wood. container) 762.687-046
BOX PRINTER (any industry) 652.682-010
box-printing-machine operator (any industry) 652.682-010
Box Repairer (any industry) 762.684-050
Box Repairer I (wood. container) 760.684-014
BOX REPAIRER II (wood. container) 762.687-018
BOX-SEALING INSPECTOR (paper goods) 641.687-014
Box-Sealing-Machine Catcher (any industry) 920.685-074
Box-Sealing-Machine Feeder (any industry) 920.685-074
BOX-SEALING-MACHINE OPERATOR (paper goods) 641.662-010

box-shook patcher (wood. container) 762.687-018
Box-Spring-Frame Builder (furniture) 762.684-066
BOX-SPRING MAKER I (furniture) 780.684-018
BOX-SPRING MAKER II (furniture) 780.684-022
box stamper, machine (boot & shoe; garment) 652.685-018
box strapper (wood. container) 692.682-058
BOX TENDER (plastic-synth.) 689.280-010
Box-Toe Buffer (boot & shoe) 690.685-046
Box-Toe Cementer (boot & shoe) 788.687-030
Box-Toe Cutter (boot & shoe) 699.682-022
box-toe flanger, stitchdowns (boot & shoe) 690.685-426
Box-Toe Stitcher (boot & shoe) 690.682-082
Box-Top-Stitching-Machine Operator (wood. container) 669.685-042
BOX-TRUCK WASHER (meat products) 529.687-018
box turner (can. & preserv.) 522.687-038
Box Wrapper (any industry) 920.587-018
BRACELET AND BROOCH MAKER (jewelry-silver.) 735.681-010
Bracelet-Form Coverer (jewelry-silver.) 739.687-138
Bracelet Former (jewelry-silver.) 739.687-138
Bracelet Maker, Novelty (jewelry-silver.) 700.684-014
bracer (construction) 860.381-042
braddisher (mine & quarry) 869.684-058
Braid Cutter (rubber goods) 699.685-014
Braided-Band Assembler (hat & cap) 784.684-022
braided-rug maker (carpet & rug) 782.687-042
braider (nonfer. metal) 691.682-014
Braider (wood. container) 669.685-014
BRAIDER OPERATOR (nonfer. metal) 691.682-014
BRAIDER SETTER (rubber goods) 759.664-010
braider tender (narrow fabrics; nonmet. min.) 683.685-010
braider tender (nonfer. metal) 691.682-014
braid folder (boot & shoe) 788.684-018
BRAIDING-MACHINE OPERATOR (narrow fabrics; nonmet. min.) 683.685-010
BRAIDING-MACHINE TENDER (rubber goods) 692.665-010
braid maker (narrow fabrics) 683.260-010
BRAID-PATTERN SETTER (narrow fabrics) 683.260-010
BRAILLE-AND-TALKING BOOKS CLERK (library) 222.587-014
braille coder (education; nonprofit org.; print. & pub.) 203.582-014
braille coder (education; nonprofit org.; print. & pub.) 209.584-010
BRAILLE-DUPLICATING-MACHINE OPERATOR (print. & pub.) 207.685-010
BRAILLE OPERATOR (print. & pub.) 203.582-010
BRAILLE PROOFREADER (nonprofit org.; print. & pub.) 209.367-014
braille-thermoform operator (print. & pub.) 207.685-010
braille transcriber (education; nonprofit org.; print. & pub.) 203.582-014
BRAILLE TRANSCRIBER, HAND (education; nonprofit org.; print. & pub.) 209.584-010
BRAILLE TYPIST (education; nonprofit org.; print. & pub.) 203.582-014
Brain Picker (meat products) 525.684-034
BRAKE ADJUSTER (automotive ser.) 620.684-018
Brake Assembler (motor-bicycles) 806.684-094
Brake Coupler, Dinkey (any industry) 910.664-010
BRAKE COUPLER, ROAD FREIGHT (r.r. trans.) 910.367-010
BRAKE-DRUM-LATHE OPERATOR (automotive ser.) 620.682-010
BRAKE HOLDER (any industry) 932.664-010
brake inspector (r.r. trans.) 910.387-014
BRAKE-LINING CURER (nonmet. min.) 573.686-010
BRAKE-LINING FINISHER, ASBESTOS (nonmet. min.) 579.665-010
BRAKE-LINING-FINISHER HELPER, ASBESTOS (nonmet. min.) 579.687-010
Brake Machine Setter (any industry) 616.360-022
brake mechanic (automotive ser.) 620.281-026
Brake Operator, Heavy Duty (any industry) 617.360-010
Brake-Operator Helper (any industry) 619.687-014
BRAKE OPERATOR I (any industry) 617.360-010
BRAKE OPERATOR II (any industry) 619.685-026
Brake Operator, Sheet Metal I (any industry) 617.360-010
Brake Operator, Sheet Metal II (any industry) 619.685-026
BRAKE REPAIRER (automotive ser.) 620.281-026
Brake Repairer, Air (automotive ser.) 620.281-026
Brake Repairer, Bus (automotive ser.) 620.281-026
Brake Repairer, Hydraulic (automotive ser.) 620.281-026
BRAKE REPAIRER, RAILROAD (r.r. trans.) 622.261-010
brake-repair mechanic (automotive ser.) 620.281-026
BRAKER, PASSENGER TRAIN (r.r. trans.) 910.364-010
brakeshoe repairer (automotive ser.) 620.281-026
Brancher (button & notion) 734.684-010
Branch-Library Clerk (library) 249.367-046
branch maker (brick & tile) 862.684-010
branch manager (financial) 186.117-034
brander (boot & shoe) 753.687-014
BRANDING-MACHINE TENDER (rubber goods) 690.685-042
BRAND RECORDER (government ser.) 206.587-010
BRAN MIXER (grain-feed mills) 599.685-014

BRANNER-MACHINE TENDER (galvanizing) 509.685-014
Brass-Bobbin Winder (tex. prod., nec) 681.685-154
Brassiere-Cup-Mold Cutter (garment) 781.682-010
BRASSIERE-SLIDE-MAKING-MACHINE TENDER, AUTOMATIC (garment) 692.685-026
Brass Plater (electroplating) 500.380-010
Brass Reclaimer (machine shop) 609.684-014
BRASS-WIND-INSTRUMENT MAKER (musical inst.) 730.381-018
Brasswind-Instrument Repairer (any industry) 730.281-054
brazer (welding) 813.684-010
BRAZER, ASSEMBLER (welding) 813.684-010
BRAZER, CONTROLLED ATMOSPHERIC FURNACE (welding) 813.685-010
Brazer, Crawler Torch (welding) 813.684-010
brazer, electronic (welding) 813.382-010
BRAZER, FURNACE (welding) 813.482-010
Brazer Helper, Furnace (welding) 819.666-010
Brazer Helper, Induction (welding) 819.666-010
BRAZER, INDUCTION (welding) 813.382-010
Brazer, Production Line (welding) 819.684-010
Brazer, Repair And Salvage (welding) 813.684-010
BRAZER, RESISTANCE (welding) 813.682-010
Brazing-Furnace Feeder (welding) 819.686-010
Brazing-Machine Feeder (welding) 819.686-010
BRAZING-MACHINE OPERATOR (welding) 813.382-014
brazing-machine operator, automatic (welding) 813.382-014
Brazing-Machine-Operator Helper (welding) 819.666-010
BRAZING-MACHINE SETTER (welding) 813.360-010
Bread-Dough Mixer (bakery products) 520.685-234
Bread Icer (bakery products) 524.684-022
Bread Icer, Machine (bakery products) 524.685-034
BREADING MACHINE TENDER (can. & preserv.) 524.685-010
bread maker (hotel & rest.) 313.381-010
Bread-Pan Greaser (bakery products) 526.685-034
Bread Slicer, Machine (bakery products) 521.685-302
Bread Supervisor (bakery products) 526.131-010
Bread-Wrapping-Machine Feeder (bakery products) 920.685-078
BREAK-AND-LOAD OPERATOR (electron. comp.) 726.685-018
BREAKER (glass products) 779.687-010
breaker (paper goods) 794.687-050
breaker (toy-sport equip.) 732.687-050
breaker boss (mine & quarry) 549.137-014
BREAKER-MACHINE OPERATOR (saw. & plan.; wood prod., nec) 564.685-010
BREAKER-MACHINE TENDER (textile) 583.685-010
Breaker-Off (jewelry-silver.) 700.687-062
breaker operator (nonfer. metal) 614.684-014
breaker operator (sugar & conf.) 521.685-034
breaker operator (textile) 680.685-070
Breaker Repairer (mine & quarry) 630.281-022
Breaker Table Worker (recording) 559.686-010
BREAKER TENDER (steel & rel.) 544.685-010
breaker-up (hat & cap) 589.685-014
BREAKER-UP-MACHINE OPERATOR (hat & cap) 589.685-014
breaker-wheel operator (leather mfg.; tex. prod., nec) 582.685-050
BREAKING-MACHINE OPERATOR (sugar & conf.) 521.685-034
BREAK-OFF WORKER (millwork-plywood) 663.686-014
Breast Buffer (boot & shoe) 690.685-046
breast finisher (boot & shoe) 788.684-126
Breast Sawyer (meat products) 525.684-018
Breast Worker (construction) 850.381-010
breeding technician (agriculture) 418.384-014
BREWERY CELLAR WORKER (beverage) 522.685-014
BREWING DIRECTOR (beverage) 183.167-010
brewing superintendent (beverage) 183.167-010
BRIAR CUTTER (fabrication, nec) 664.685-010
BRIAR-WOOD SORTER (fabrication, nec) 769.687-058
BRICK-AND-TILE-MAKING-MACHINE OPERATOR (brick & tile) 575.382-010
brick burner, head (brick & tile) 573.132-010
Brick Cleaner (construction) 869.687-026
Brick-Kiln Burner (brick & tile) 573.682-010
BRICKLAYER (brick & tile) 861.381-014
BRICKLAYER (construction) 861.381-018
BRICKLAYER APPRENTICE (construction) 861.381-022
BRICKLAYER, FIREBRICK AND REFRACTORY TILE (construction) 861.381-026
Bricklayer Helper (construction) 869.687-026
BRICKLAYER HELPER, FIREBRICK AND REFRACTORY TILE (construction) 861.687-010
Bricklayer, Maintenance (any industry) 861.381-018
Bricklayer, Paving Brick (construction) 869.664-014
Bricklayer, Sewer (construction) 861.381-018
BRICKLAYER SUPERVISOR (construction) 861.131-010
brickmason (construction) 861.381-026

brickmason helper (construction) 861.687-010
Brick-Molder, Hand (brick & tile) 575.684-042
Brick-Paving Checker (construction) 869.687-026
BRICK SETTER OPERATOR (brick & tile) 579.685-058
Brick Sorter (brick & tile) 573.687-034
BRICK TESTER (brick & tile) 579.384-010
BRICK UNLOADER TENDER (brick & tile) 579.685-062
Brick Veneer Maker (concrete prod.) 579.685-042
Bridge Attacher (button & notion) 692.685-206
Bridge Crane Operator (any industry) 921.663-010
bridge expert (education) 159.227-010
Bridge Fitter (musical inst.) 730.684-010
BRIDGE INSPECTOR (r.r. trans.) 869.287-010
Bridge-Maintenance Worker (construction) 801.361-014
BRIDGE OPERATOR, SLIP (r.r. trans.) 919.682-010
bridge repairer (r.r. trans.) 860.381-030
bridge tender (r.r. trans.) 919.682-010
bridge tender (r.r. trans.) 371.362-010
bridge worker (construction) 801.361-014
bridge worker apprentice (construction) 801.361-018
Briefcase Sewer (leather prod.) 783.682-014
BRIGHT CUTTER (jewelry-silver.) 700.684-018
BRILLIANDEER-LOPPER (jewelry-silver.) 770.261-010
BRIM-AND-CROWN PRESSER (hat & cap) 583.685-022
Brim Blocker (laundry & rel.) 363.684-014
Brim Buffer (hat & cap) 585.685-014
brim buster (hat & cap) 583.685-018
brim buster (hat & cap) 583.685-022
BRIM CURLER (hat & cap) 583.685-014
brim cutter (hat & cap; tex. prod., nec) 585.685-086
Brim Cutter (hat & cap) 699.682-022
brim-edge trimmer (hat & cap) 686.685-074
BRIMER (metal prod., nec) 700.687-018
brim flanger (hat & cap) 784.684-026
brim flexer (hat & cap) 585.685-066
Brim-Greaser Operator (hat & cap) 582.685-082
BRIM IRONER, HAND (hat & cap) 784.684-014
brimmer (hat & cap) 583.685-018
BRIMMER (hat & cap) term
brimmer blocker (hat & cap) 580.685-010
brimming-machine operator (hat & cap) 580.685-010
brim molder (hat & cap) 580.685-042
brim plater (hat & cap) 583.685-018
brim pouncer (hat & cap) 585.685-010
BRIM-POUNCING-MACHINE OPERATOR (hat & cap) 585.685-010
BRIM PRESSER I (hat & cap) 583.685-018
Brim Presser II (hat & cap) 580.685-038
BRIM RAISER (hat & cap) 784.687-010
brim rounder (hat & cap) 784.684-050
brim setter (hat & cap) 784.684-014
brim setter (hat & cap) 583.685-022
brim shaper (hat & cap) 784.684-026
Brim Slotter (hat & cap) 686.685-038
Brim Stiffener (hat & cap) 589.687-038
BRIM STITCHER I (hat & cap) 784.685-014
Brim Stitcher II (hat & cap) 784.682-014
brim stretcher (hat & cap) 580.685-010
BRIM-STRETCHING-MACHINE OPERATOR (hat & cap) 580.685-010
Brim-Welt-Sewing-Machine Operator (hat & cap) 784.682-014
BRINE MAKER I (chemical) 550.685-018
BRINE MAKER I (can. & preserv.) 522.685-018
BRINE MAKER II (chemical) 551.687-014
BRINE MAKER II (can. & preserv.) 522.685-022
BRINE-MIXER OPERATOR, AUTOMATIC (can. & preserv.) 520.685-034
brine-process operator (chemical) 550.685-018
Brine Purifier (chemical) 550.685-018
BRINER (can. & preserv.) 522.687-014
Briner, Machine (can. & preserv.) 529.685-190
Brine-Room Laborer (dairy products) 529.686-050
BRINE-TANK-SEPARATOR OPERATOR (can. & preserv.) 521.685-038
BRINE-TANK TENDER (dairy products) 529.685-030
BRINE-WELL OPERATOR (chemical) 559.685-026
BRIQUETTE-MACHINE OPERATOR (fabrication, nec) 549.662-010
BRIQUETTE-MACHINE-OPERATOR HELPER (fabrication, nec) 549.686-010
briquette molder (fabrication, nec) 549.662-010
BRIQUETTE OPERATOR (brick & tile) 579.685-066
briquette-press operator (nonfer. metal; steel & rel.) 617.685-038
BRIQUETTER OPERATOR (chemical) 559.685-030
briquetting-machine operator (plastic prod.; plastic-synth.) 556.685-058
BRIQUETTING-MACHINE OPERATOR (smelt. & refin.) 519.685-010
broacher (clock & watch) 770.682-010
Broach Grinder (machine shop) 603.280-038
BROACHING-MACHINE OPERATOR, PRODUCTION (machine shop) 605.682-014
Broaching-Machine Repairer (machine tools) 638.261-030

BROACHING-MACHINE SET-UP OPERATOR (machine shop) 605.382-010
broach operator (machine shop) 605.682-014
BROADCAST CHECKER (radio-tv broad.) 249.387-010
Broke-Beater Tender (paper & pulp; wood prod., nec) 530.685-014
Broke Handler (paper & pulp) 929.687-022
broker (financial) 162.167-038
broker (financial) 250.257-018
broker (financial) 162.167-034
broker (profess. & kin.) 162.157-018
BROKERAGE CLERK I (financial) 219.482-010
BROKERAGE CLERK II (financial) 219.362-018
Brokerage Manager (insurance) 166.167-046
broker, agricultural produce (wholesale tr.) 260.357-010
BROKER-AND-MARKET OPERATOR, GRAIN (financial; wholesale tr.) 162.157-010
Bromination Equipment Operator (chemical) 559.682-018
Bronze Plater (electroplating) 500.380-010
Bronzer (print. & pub.) 970.681-014
brooch-and-bracelet maker (jewelry-silver.) 735.681-010
Brooch Maker, Novelty (jewelry-silver.) 700.684-014
BROOM BUNDLER (fabrication, nec) 692.685-030
BROOMCORN GRADER (fabrication, nec) 739.687-042
broomcorn scraper (fabrication, nec) 692.686-018
BROOMCORN SEEDER (fabrication, nec) 692.686-018
broomcorn sorter (fabrication, nec) 739.687-042
Broom-Handle Dipper (fabrication, nec) 599.685-026
broom-machine operator (fabrication, nec) 692.682-066
BROOMMAKER (fabrication, nec) 739.684-018
BROOM STITCHER (fabrication, nec) 692.682-022
BROTH MIXER (bakery products) 520.585-014
broth setter (bakery products) 520.585-014
BROWNING PROCESSOR (ordnance) 505.685-010
BROWN-STOCK WASHER (paper & pulp) 533.685-014
Bruise Trimmer (meat products) 525.687-010
Brush Clearer, Surveying (any industry) 869.567-010
BRUSHER (any industry) term
brusher (any industry) 459.687-010
BRUSHER (boot & shoe) 788.687-018
brusher (boot & shoe) 690.685-046
brusher (boot & shoe) 690.685-058
BRUSHER (construction; furniture) term
brusher (hat & cap) 784.387-010
brusher and shearer (carpet & rug; textile) 585.685-102
brusher-down (laundry & rel.) 362.687-014
brusher, hand (hat & cap) 784.687-014
BRUSHER, MACHINE (hat & cap) 587.685-014
Brush-Fabricating-Machine Setter (fabrication, nec) 692.360-014
BRUSH-FABRICATION SUPERVISOR (fabrication, nec) 692.130-010
BRUSH FILLER, HAND (fabrication, nec) 739.687-046
BRUSH-HEAD MAKER (fabrication, nec) 739.685-018
Brush-Holder Assembler (elec. equip.) 721.684-022
Brush-Holder Inspector (house. appl.) 729.384-022
brushing operator (tex. prod., nec; textile) 585.685-070
BRUSH LOADER AND HANDLE ATTACHER (fabrication, nec) 739.687-206
BRUSH-MACHINE SETTER (fabrication, nec) 692.360-014
brush maker (elec. equip.) 721.684-014
brush maker (fabrication, nec) 733.684-010
BRUSH MAKER, MACHINE (fabrication, nec) 739.685-014
BRUSH MATERIAL PREPARER (fabrication, nec) 739.684-022
BRUSH OPERATOR (textile) 587.685-010
BRUSH POLISHER (clock & watch) 603.685-038
Brush Sander (woodworking) 761.682-014
Brush Shade-Hand (furniture) 742.684-010
Brush Stainer (furniture) 742.684-014
Brush-Trimming-Machine Setter (fabrication, nec) 692.360-014
Brush Washer (textile) 599.687-030
BUCKER (logging) 454.684-010
bucker (mine & quarry) 579.484-010
BUCKET CHUCKER (wood. container) 664.685-014
BUCKET OPERATOR (concrete prod.) 575.683-010
BUCKET TURNER (wood. container) 669.682-018
buckle-and-button maker (any industry) 734.687-046
buckle assembler (button & notion) 734.687-050
Buckle-Attaching-Machine Operator (hat & cap) 699.685-018
buckle coverer (button & notion) 734.687-050
BUCKLE-FRAME SHAPER (button & notion) 692.685-034
buckle gluer (button & notion) 734.687-050
BUCKLE INSPECTOR (button & notion) 734.687-026
BUCKLER AND LACER (boot & shoe) 788.687-022
Buckle-Sewer, Machine (boot & shoe) 690.682-082
BUCKLE SORTER (button & notion) 734.687-030
Buckle Stapler (boot & shoe) 690.685-162
BUCKLE-STRAP-DRUM OPERATOR (rubber goods) 554.485-010
Buckle-Strap Puncher (boot & shoe) 690.685-114

BUCKLE-WIRE INSERTER (button & notion) 734.687-034
buck presser (any industry) 363.682-018
Buckram Cutter (boot & shoe; hat & cap; leather prod.) 699.682-022
Buckram Sewer (tex. prod., nec) 787.682-066
BUCKSHOT-SWAGE OPERATOR (ordnance) 612.682-010
BUDDER (agriculture) 405.684-010
BUDGET ANALYST (government ser.) 161.267-030
BUDGET CLERK (clerical) 216.382-022
Budget Consultant (profess. & kin.) 160.207-010
BUDGET OFFICER (profess. & kin.) 161.117-010
budget-record clerk (clerical) 216.382-022
budget-report clerk (clerical) 216.382-022
buffer (automotive ser.) 690.685-422
BUFFER (boot & shoe) 690.685-046
BUFFER (fabrication, nec) 739.684-026
BUFFER (hat & cap) 585.685-014
BUFFER (plastic prod.) 752.684-022
BUFFER (rubber goods; rubber tire) 759.684-022
buffer (stonework) 775.664-010
buffer (stonework) 673.382-018
BUFFER, AUTOMATIC (boot & shoe) 690.685-050
Buffer, Chrome (any industry) 705.684-014
Buffer, Copper (any industry) 705.684-014
BUFFER I (any industry) 705.684-014
Buffer II (any industry) 705.687-014
BUFFER, INFLATED-PAD (boot & shoe) 690.685-054
BUFFER, MACHINE (leather mfg.) 585.685-018
Buffer, Nickel (any industry) 705.684-014
BUFFING-AND-POLISHING-WHEEL REPAIRER (any industry) 739.684-030
BUFFING-AND-SUEDING-MACHINE OPERATOR (boot & shoe) 753.684-010
BUFFING-LINE SET-UP WORKER (any industry) 603.360-010
BUFFING-MACHINE OPERATOR (any industry) 603.382-010
buffing-machine operator (boot & shoe) 690.685-046
buffing-machine operator (hat & cap) 585.685-014
buffing-machine operator, semiautomatic (jewelry-silver.) 603.682-022
BUFFING-MACHINE OPERATOR, SILVERWARE (jewelry-silver.) 603.682-010
BUFFING-MACHINE TENDER (any industry) 603.665-010
BUFFING TURNER-AND-COUNTER (tex. prod., nec) 789.687-022
BUFFING-WHEEL FORMER, AUTOMATIC (tex. prod., nec) 689.685-034
BUFFING-WHEEL FORMER, HAND (tex. prod., nec) 789.684-014
BUFFING-WHEEL INSPECTOR (tex. prod., nec) 789.687-026
buffing-wheel operator (leather mfg.) 585.685-018
buff-wheel fabricator (any industry) 739.684-030
buggy pusher (construction)   see WHEELER
BUILDER, BEAM (mfd. bldgs.) 860.684-010
building-and-grounds supervisor (any industry) 891.137-010
BUILDING CLEANER (any industry) 891.684-022
Building-Construction Inspector (construction) 182.267-010
BUILDING CONSULTANT (wholesale tr.) 250.357-010
BUILDING-EQUIPMENT INSPECTOR (utilities) 956.387-010
Building-Illuminating Engineer (profess. & kin.) 003.061-046
BUILDING INSPECTOR (insurance) 168.267-010
Building-Insulating Carpenter (construction; retail trade) 860.381-022
BUILDING-INSULATION SUPERVISOR (construction) 863.134-010
Building-Maintenance Supervisor, Electrical (any industry) 829.131-014
building-maintenance supervisor, mechanical (any industry) 891.137-010
building repairer (any industry) 899.381-010
building-service supervisor (any industry) 187.167-190
Building Stonecutter (stonework) 771.381-014
building supervisor (any industry) 891.137-010
BUILDING SUPERVISOR (construction) term
Bulb Assembler (electron. comp.) 725.684-022
BULB FILLER (light. fix.) 692.686-022
Bulb Grower (agriculture) 405.161-014
Bulb Sorter (agriculture) 529.687-186
bulk cement loader (cement) 921.565-010
Bulk Driver (motor trans.) 905.663-018
BULKER (tobacco) 522.687-018
BULKER, CUT TOBACCO (tobacco) 529.685-034
BULK FILLER (can. & preserv.) 529.687-022
Bulkhead Carpenter (ship-boat mfg.) 860.361-010
bulking-machine operator (textile) 689.685-158
bulk intake worker (dairy products) 222.485-010
bulk loader (any industry) 921.667-018
bulk loader (cement) 921.565-010
Bulk-Loader Operator (water trans.) 921.662-018
Bulk-Pigment Reducer (paint & varnish) 550.585-038
BULK-PLANT OPERATOR (sugar & conf.) 520.362-010
Bulk-Sausage-Casing Tier-Off (meat products) 529.687-034
Bulk-Sausage-Stuffing-Machine Operator (meat products) 520.685-210
BULK-SEALER OPERATOR (plastic-synth.) 554.685-010
BULK-STATION OPERATOR (petrol. & gas) 570.362-010
bulk-system operator (food prep., nec) 921.382-010

BULL-CHAIN OPERATOR (saw. & plan.) 921.685-014
bulldogger (steel & rel.) 613.362-018
BULLDOZER OPERATOR I (any industry) 850.683-010
Bulldozer Operator II (any industry) 617.260-010
BULLET-ASSEMBLY-PRESS OPERATOR (ordnance) 694.685-014
BULLET-ASSEMBLY-PRESS SETTER-OPERATOR (ordnance) 694.682-010
BULLET-CASTING OPERATOR (ordnance) 502.682-010
BULLET-GROOVING-SIZING-AND-LUBRICATING-MACHINE OPERA-TOR (ordnance) 619.382-010
bulletin clerk (motor trans.) 215.367-010
BULLET-LUBRICANT MIXER (ordnance) 543.685-010
BULLET-LUBRICATING-MACHINE OPERATOR (ordnance) 694.685-018
BULLET-SLUG-CASTING-MACHINE OPERATOR (ordnance) 502.382-010
bullet-swaging-machine adjuster (ordnance) 617.360-014
bullet-swaging-machine operator (ordnance) 617.585-010
bull-gang supervisor (any industry) 899.133-010
Bull-Gang Supervisor (tobacco) 922.137-018
BULL-GANG WORKER (construction) term
BULL-GANG WORKER (tobacco) 922.687-026
bull riveter (any industry) 800.662-010
Bulwark Carpenter (ship-boat mfg.) 860.361-010
bumper-machine operator (hat & cap) 586.685-034
bumper operator (wood. container) 669.685-046
bumper straightener (automotive ser.) 807.684-010
bump-grader operator (grain-feed mills) 529.685-262
bunch breaker (tobacco) 790.684-010
bunch-breaker-machine operator (tobacco) 529.685-038
Buncher (forestry) 920.687-046
buncher, hand (tobacco) 790.684-010
buncher, machine (tobacco) 529.685-038
BUNCH MAKER, HAND (tobacco) 790.684-010
BUNCH MAKER, MACHINE (tobacco) 529.685-038
BUNCH TRIMMER, MOLD (tobacco) 521.687-026
BUNDLE BREAKER (tex. prod., nec) 689.687-018
bundle clerk (laundry & rel.) 361.687-018
bundle cutter (tex. prod., nec) 689.687-018
Bundler (any industry) 920.587-018
bundler (furniture) 780.587-010
bundler (garment) 920.687-190
bundler (garment; glove & mit.) 781.687-010
bundler (leather prod.) 222.587-046
bundler (woodworking) 929.685-018
BUNDLER, SEASONAL GREENERY (forestry) 920.687-046
bundle shaker (tobacco) 521.687-110
BUNDLES HANGER (tobacco) 529.686-010
BUNDLE TIER AND LABELER (saw. & plan.) 920.685-110
bundle tier (garment; glove & mit.) 781.687-010
Bundle Weigher (laundry & rel.) 361.687-018
BUNG DRIVER (wood. container) 764.687-042
Bung Dropper (meat products) 525.687-010
Bung Grader (meat products) 525.684-038
Bung-Gut Tier (meat products) 525.687-010
Bunghole Borer (wood. container) 666.382-010
Bung Remover (beverage) 529.687-066
bung sewer (meat products) 529.687-030
bunk assembler (furniture) 709.667-010
BUREAU CHIEF (print. & pub.) 132.067-010
burglar-alarm installer (business ser.) 822.361-018
burglar-alarm installer and servicer (business ser.) 822.361-022
burglar-alarm-repairer helper (business ser.) 822.684-014
burglar-alarm superintendent (business ser.) 822.131-022
Burlap-Bag Sewer (tex. prod., nec) 787.682-058
burlapper (textile) 929.687-042
burlapper (textile) 782.687-018
Burlap-Sizing-Machine Operator (tex. prod., nec) 582.665-026
BURLAP SPREADER (tex. prod., nec) 581.687-010
BURLER (carpet & rug; textile) 689.684-014
burner (brick & tile) 573.682-010
BURNER (brick & tile) 573.685-038
burner (construction) 869.685-010
burner, hand (welding) 816.464-010
Burner, Hearth (brick & tile) 573.685-038
BURNER OPERATOR (chemical) 558.382-014
burner operator (petrol. refin.) 573.685-014
Burner, Shaft (brick & tile) 573.685-038
BURNER TENDER (mine & quarry) 571.685-010
burning-machine operator (welding) 816.482-010
BURNING-PLANT OPERATOR (ordnance) 509.685-018
BURNING SUPERVISOR (brick & tile) 573.132-010
burnisher (boot & shoe) 690.685-034
BURNISHER (boot & shoe) 690.685-058
BURNISHER (clock & watch) 603.685-042
burnisher (furniture; wood prod., nec) 742.684-010
burnisher (leather mfg.) 585.685-018
BURNISHER, BALANCE WHEEL ARM (clock & watch) 715.684-038

burn-out-scarfing operator (welding) 816.364-010
BURN-OUT TENDER, LACE (tex. prod., nec) 589.685-018
Burnt-Lime Drawer (concrete prod.) 921.683-050
BURRER (clock & watch) 715.684-042
Burrer (machine shop) 705.687-014
burrer, hand (clock & watch) 715.684-042
BURRER, MACHINE (clock & watch) 603.685-046
Burrer-Marker, Axle (machine shop) 705.687-014
BURR GRINDER (optical goods) 673.686-014
burring-machine operator (clock & watch) 603.685-046
burring-machine operator (hat & cap) 583.686-010
BURRING-MACHINE OPERATOR (nut & bolt) 615.685-010
Burrito Maker (food prep., nec) 520.687-046
Burr-Mill Operator (grain-feed mills) 521.682-026
BURSAR (education) 160.167-042
BUS ATTENDANT (motor trans.) 352.577-010
Bus Cleaner (automotive ser.) 919.687-014
BUS DISPATCHER, INTERSTATE (motor trans.) 913.167-010
BUS DRIVER (motor trans.) 913.463-010
BUS DRIVER, DAY-HAUL OR FARM CHARTER (agriculture) 913.363-010
Bus Driver, Garage (motor trans.) 909.663-010
Bus Driver, School (motor trans.) 913.463-010
busheler (garment; personal ser.; retail trade) 785.261-010
Busheler (logging) 454.384-010
BUSHER (nonmet. min.) 502.687-014
Bushing-And-Broach Operator (metal prod., nec) 706.684-090
business agent (amuse. & rec.) 191.117-018
business and financial counsel (profess. & kin.) 110.117-022
BUSINESS-ENTERPRISE OFFICER (government ser.) 188.117-014
business investor (business ser.; real estate) 189.157-010
Business Librarian (library) 100.167-026
business-machine mechanic (any industry) 633.281-018
business-machine-mechanic apprentice (any industry) 633.281-022
BUSINESS MANAGER (amuse. & rec.) 191.117-018
BUSINESS MANAGER, COLLEGE OR UNIVERSITY (education) 186.117-010
BUSINESS-OPPORTUNITY-AND-PROPERTY-INVESTMENT BROKER (business ser.; real estate) 189.157-010
Business Regulation Investigator (government ser.) 168.167-090
BUSINESS REPRESENTATIVE, LABOR UNION (profess. & kin.) 187.167-018
business-service officer (government ser.) 188.117-122
BUS INSPECTOR (automotive ser.) 620.281-030
Bus Mechanic (automotive ser.) 620.261-010
bus person (hotel & rest.) 311.677-018
Bus Upholsterer (automotive ser.) 780.381-010
Butadiene-Compressor Operator (chemical) 950.382-014
Butadiene-Converter Helper (chemical) 558.585-010
Butadiene-Converter Operator (chemical) 558.362-010
Butadiene-Converter Utility Operator (chemical) 559.682-066
Butadiene Operator, Chief (chemical; petrol. refin.) 559.132-078
Butane-Compressor Operator (petrol. refin.) 950.382-014
butcher (hotel & rest.) 316.681-010
butcher (retail trade; wholesale tr.) 316.684-018
BUTCHER, ALL-ROUND (meat products) 525.381-014
BUTCHER APPRENTICE (meat products) 525.381-010
butcher apprentice (retail trade; wholesale tr.) 316.684-022
BUTCHER, CHICKEN AND FISH (hotel & rest.) 316.684-010
BUTCHER, FISH (can. & preserv.) 525.684-014
Butcher, Head (hotel & rest.) 316.681-010
BUTCHER, MEAT (hotel & rest.) 316.681-010
Butcher Scullion (water trans.) 318.687-014
BUTLER (domestic ser.) 309.137-010
BUTLER, SECOND (domestic ser.) 309.674-010
Butter-Chilling Equipment Operator (dairy products) 529.362-010
Butter Churner (dairy products) 529.362-010
BUTTER LIQUEFIER (oils & grease) 523.585-010
BUTTERMAKER (dairy products) 529.362-010
BUTTERMAKER, CONTINUOUS CHURN (dairy products) 529.382-010
Buttermaker Helper (dairy products) 529.686-026
butter melter (oils & grease) 523.585-010
Buttermilk-Drier Operator (dairy products) 523.682-022
Butter Production Supervisor (dairy products) 529.131-014
BUTT MAKER (tobacco) 529.685-042
BUTTON-AND-BUCKLE MAKER (any industry) 734.687-046
Button-Attaching-Machine Operator (any industry) 699.685-018
BUTTON-ATTACHING-MACHINE OPERATOR (garment; hat & cap) 699.685-010
button bradder (any industry) 699.685-018
button bradder (garment; hat & cap) 699.685-010
button-breaker operator (textile) 583.685-010
button broacher (button & notion) 690.682-090
Button-Buttonhole Marker (garment) 781.687-042
button clamper (any industry) 699.685-018
button clamper (garment; hat & cap) 699.685-010

button cutter (button & notion) 734.384-010
BUTTON-CUTTING-MACHINE OPERATOR (button & notion) 734.384-010
BUTTON-DECORATING-MACHINE OPERATOR (button & notion) 690.685-062
BUTTONER (garment; knitting) 782.687-014
BUTTON-FACING-MACHINE OPERATOR (button & notion) 690.685-066
BUTTON GRADER (button & notion) 734.687-038
BUTTONHOLE-AND-BUTTON-SEWING-MACHINE OPERATOR (garment) 786.685-042
BUTTONHOLE-MACHINE OPERATOR (garment) 786.685-014
BUTTONHOLE MAKER (boot & shoe) 788.684-038
Buttonhole Maker, Hand (garment) 782.684-058
Buttonhole Tacker (garment) 782.684-058
BUTTON MAKER AND INSTALLER (tex. prod., nec) 734.685-014
BUTTON RECLAIMER (knitting) 734.687-042
button riveter (any industry) 699.685-018
button riveter (garment; hat & cap) 699.685-010
Button Sewer, Hand (garment) 782.684-058
BUTTON-SEWING-MACHINE OPERATOR (garment) 786.685-010
BUTTON SPINDLER (button & notion) 740.687-010
button tacker (garment; hat & cap) 699.685-010
button tufter (furniture) 687.684-014
button tufter (furniture) 780.687-050
button-tufting-machine operator (furniture) 687.685-014
Butt Presser (meat products) 520.685-182
butt sawyer (paper & pulp; saw. & plan.) 667.685-034
Butt Trimmer (meat products) 525.684-054
Buy-Boat Operator (fishing & hunt.) 197.133-010
buyer (profess. & kin.) 162.157-038
BUYER (profess. & kin.) 162.157-018
buyer, assistant (clerical) 249.367-066
BUYER, ASSISTANT (retail trade) 162.157-022
BUYER, GRAIN (grain-feed mills; wholesale tr.) 162.167-010
Buyer, Grain (wholesale tr.) 162.157-010
buyer, head (wholesale tr.) 162.167-014
buyer-renter (motion picture) 162.157-030
BUYER, TOBACCO, HEAD (wholesale tr.) 162.167-014
buzzle buffer (leather mfg.) 585.685-018
BUZZSAW OPERATOR (any industry) 667.685-026
BUZZSAW-OPERATOR HELPER (any industry) 667.687-010
Byproducts Maker (dairy products) 529.382-018

C

CABANA ATTENDANT (amuse. & rec.) 349.677-010
Cabbage Salter (can. & preserv.) 529.687-022
cab driver (motor trans.) 913.463-018
CABIN-EQUIPMENT SUPERVISOR (air trans.) 869.131-010
Cabinet-Abrasive Sandblaster (any industry) 503.687-010
Cabinet-And-Trim Installer (mfd. bldgs.; vehicles, nec) 869.684-026
Cabinet-And-Trim Installer (vehicles, nec) 806.684-018
CABINET ASSEMBLER (furniture) 763.684-014
Cabinet Assembler (mfd. bldgs.; vehicles, nec) 762.684-014
Cabinet Assembler (mfd. bldgs.) 763.684-050
cabinet finisher (furniture) 703.684-014
CABINETMAKER (woodworking) 660.280-010
CABINETMAKER APPRENTICE (woodworking) 660.280-014
Cabinetmaker, Maintenance (woodworking) 660.280-010
CABINETMAKER, SUPERVISOR (woodworking) 660.130-010
cabin furnishings installer (aircraft mfg.) 806.381-078
Cabin-Service Agent (air trans.) 919.687-014
cable armorer (nonfer. metal) 691.685-010
cable assembler (aircraft mfg.) 806.381-042
CABLE ASSEMBLER AND SWAGER (aircraft mfg.) 806.381-042
cable cutter and swager (aircraft mfg.) 806.381-042
cable dispatcher (tel. & tel.) 239.167-014
CABLE ENGINEER, OUTSIDE PLANT (tel. & tel.) 003.167-010
CABLE INSTALLER-REPAIRER (utilities) 821.361-010
Cable Installer-Repairer Helper (utilities) 821.667-010
cable-machine operator (elec. equip.; light. fix.; metal prod., nec; nonfer. metal) 616.682-034
CABLE MAINTAINER (utilities) 952.464-010
cable maker (elec. equip.; electron. comp.; office machines) 728.684-010
cable-mill helper (nonfer. metal) 616.687-010
cable placer (construction; utilities) 829.684-018
CABLE PULLER (construction; utilities) 829.684-018
cable rigger (construction; utilities) 829.684-018
CABLESHIP WORKER (tel. & tel.) term
CABLE SPLICER (construction; tel. & tel.; utilities) 829.361-010
cable splicer (petrol. & gas) 728.684-014
CABLE-SPLICER APPRENTICE (construction; tel. & tel.; utilities) 829.361-014
CABLE-SPLICER HELPER (construction; tel. & tel.; utilities) 829.667-010
cable-splicing supervisor (construction; tel. & tel.; utilities) 829.131-010

Cable Spooler (nonfer. metal) 691.685-026
CABLE SUPERVISOR (construction; tel. & tel.; utilities) 829.131-010
CABLE SUPERVISOR (tel. & tel.) 184.161-010
CABLE TELEVISION INSTALLER (radio-tv broad.) 821.281-010
CABLE TELEVISION LINE TECHNICIAN (radio-tv broad.) 821.261-010
CABLE TESTER (tel. & tel.) 822.361-010
cable-tower operator (construction) 850.683-042
Cableway Operator (any industry) 921.663-030
cabling-machine operator (elec. equip.; light. fix.; metal prod., nec; nonfer. metal) 616.682-034
cab starter (motor trans.) 913.367-010
CADDIE (amuse. & rec.) 341.677-010
CADDIE SUPERVISOR (amuse. & rec.) 341.137-010
CADET, DECK (water trans.) 911.133-010
Cadet Engineer (water trans.) 197.130-010
CADMIUM BURNER (chemical) 553.685-114
CADMIUM-LIQUOR MAKER (paint & varnish) 553.685-026
Cadmium Plater (electroplating) 500.380-010
CAFETERIA ATTENDANT (hotel & rest.) 311.677-010
Cafeteria Cashier (hotel & rest.) 211.462-010
cage clerk (personal ser.) 358.677-014
CAGE MAKER (concrete prod.) 709.684-030
CAGE MAKER, MACHINE (concrete prod.) 616.682-018
Cage Operator (any industry) 921.663-030
CAGER (mine & quarry) 939.667-010
CAGER OPERATOR (can. & preserv.) 921.685-018
Cage Tender (construction) 869.687-026
CAISSON WORKER (construction) term
Cake-Batter Mixer (bakery products) 520.685-010
Cake-Batter Scaler (bakery products) 526.682-010
Cake Cutter, Machine (bakery products) 521.685-302
CAKE DECORATOR (bakery products) 524.381-010
CAKE FORMER (oils & grease) 520.685-038
Cake Icer (bakery products) 524.684-022
Cake Icer, Machine (bakery products) 524.685-034
Cake Inspector (plastic-synth.) 681.687-018
cake maker (hotel & rest.) 313.381-026
Cake-Pan Greaser (bakery products) 526.685-034
CAKE-PRESS OPERATOR (plastic-synth.) 556.665-010
CAKE-PRESS-OPERATOR HELPER (plastic-synth.) 556.686-010
CAKE PULLER (oils & grease) 521.686-014
CAKE STRIPPER (oils & grease) 520.685-042
Cake Supervisor (bakery products) 526.131-010
CAKE TESTER (grain-feed mills) 526.381-022
Cake Washer (plastic-synth.) 582.685-162
Cake Winder (textile) 681.685-154
CAKE WRAPPER (plastic-synth.) 589.687-010
Cake Wringer (plastic-synth.) 581.685-038
Calciminer (construction) 840.381-010
calcination helper (smelt. & refin.) 513.587-010
CALCINE FURNACE LOADER (paint & varnish) 553.486-010
CALCINE-FURNACE TENDER (paint & varnish) 553.685-030
calciner (cement; chemical; mine & quarry) 573.382-010
calciner feeder (chemical) 553.686-038
CALCINER, GYPSUM (concrete prod.) 579.382-010
calciner operator (chemical) 553.685-050
CALCINER OPERATOR (mine & quarry; smelt. & refin.) 513.362-010
CALCINER-OPERATOR HELPER (mine & quarry; smelt. & refin.) 513.667-010
CALCULATING-MACHINE OPERATOR (clerical) 216.482-022
Calculating-Machine Servicer (any industry) 633.281-018
Calculation Clerk (insurance) 216.382-050
Calculation Reviewer (insurance) 216.382-050
calculator operator (clerical) 216.482-022
CALENDAR-CONTROL CLERK, BLOOD BANK (medical ser.) 245.367-018
calenderer (knitting) 580.485-010
CALENDER FEEDER (rubber goods) 554.686-010
calender helper (rubber goods; rubber tire) 554.665-010
CALENDERING-MACHINE OPERATOR (knitting) 580.485-010
Calender Inspector (rubber goods) 759.684-074
CALENDER-LET-OFF HELPER (rubber goods; rubber tire) 554.686-014
CALENDER-LET-OFF OPERATOR (rubber goods; rubber tire) 554.682-010
CALENDER-MACHINE OPERATOR (nonmet. min.) 583.585-010
CALENDER OPERATOR (fabrication, nec) 590.682-010
calender operator (paper goods) 649.682-022
CALENDER OPERATOR (rubber goods; rubber tire) 554.362-010
CALENDER OPERATOR (tex. prod., nec; textile) 583.685-026
CALENDER OPERATOR, ARTIFICIAL LEATHER (tex. prod., nec) 584.685-010
Calender Operator, Fabric (rubber goods; rubber tire) 554.362-010
CALENDER OPERATOR, FOUR-ROLL (plastic prod.; rubber goods; rubber tire) 554.662-010
Calender Operator, Gum Stock (rubber goods; rubber tire) 554.362-010
CALENDER-OPERATOR HELPER (rubber goods; rubber tire) 554.686-018
Calender-Operator Helper (tex. prod., nec) 589.687-026

CALENDER OPERATOR, INSULATION BOARD (wood prod., nec) 539.482-010
calender-roll operator (plastic-synth.) 554.682-018
CALENDER-ROLL PRESS OPERATOR (machinery mfg.) 692.462-010
CALENDER SUPERVISOR (plastic-synth.) 559.132-014
Calender Supervisor (tex. prod., nec) 589.130-014
calender tender (tex. prod., nec; textile) 583.685-026
CALENDER-WIND-UP HELPER (rubber goods; rubber tire) 554.686-022
CALENDER-WIND-UP TENDER (rubber goods; rubber tire) 554.665-010
Calf Skinner (meat products) 525.684-046
Calfskin Trimmer (meat products) 525.687-046
Calf Sticker (meat products) 525.684-050
CALIBRATION LABORATORY TECHNICIAN (aircraft mfg.; electron. comp.) 019.281-010
calibration technician (inst. & app.) 710.381-034
CALIBRATOR (cutlery-hrdwr.) 701.684-010
CALIBRATOR (inst. & app.) 710.381-034
CALIBRATOR, BAROMETERS (inst. & app.) 710.381-042
California Seamer (boot & shoe) 690.682-082
Call-Box Wirer (tel. & tel.) 822.381-010
caller (clerical) 209.667-014
CALLER (r.r. trans.) 215.563-010
calligrapher (profess. & kin.) 970.661-010
Calliope Player (amuse. & rec.) 152.041-010
call-out clerk (clerical) 209.667-014
CALL-OUT OPERATOR (business ser.; retail trade) 237.367-014
Camera Assembler (photo. appar.) 714.684-010
camera control operator (radio-tv broad.) 194.282-010
Camera-Lens Inspector (optical goods) 716.381-010
CAMERA OPERATOR (motion picture; radio-tv broad.) 143.062-022
CAMERA OPERATOR, ANIMATION (motion picture) 143.382-010
camera operator, first (motion picture; radio-tv broad.) 143.062-010
camera operator, head (motion picture; radio-tv broad.) 143.062-010
Camera Operator, Second (motion picture; radio-tv broad.) 143.062-022
Camera Operator, Sound Effects (motion picture; radio-tv broad.) 143.062-022
Camera Operator, Television (radio-tv broad.) 143.062-022
CAMERA OPERATOR, TITLE (motion picture) 976.382-010
CAMERA REPAIRER (photo. appar.) 714.281-014
Camera-Storeroom Clerk (motion picture) 222.387-058
Camera Supervisor (print. & pub.) 972.137-010
cam-milling-machine operator (machine shop) 605.382-026
cam-milling-machine operator (machine shop) 605.280-014
CAMOUFLAGE ASSEMBLER (ordnance) 869.687-014
CAMOUFLAGE SPECIALIST (military ser.) 378.684-010
Campground Caretaker (government ser.) 406.687-010
campground hand (amuse. & rec.) 329.683-010
Camp Guard (any industry) 372.667-034
camp-laundry operator (any industry) 361.684-014
CAMP TENDER (agriculture) 410.137-010
Canadian-Bacon Tier (meat products) 529.687-034
CANAL-EQUIPMENT MECHANIC (waterworks) 899.281-010
canal-lock tender, chief operator (water trans.) 911.131-014
canal-structure operator (water trans.) 911.362-010
canal tender (waterworks) 954.362-010
CANARY BREEDER (agriculture) 411.161-010
can-bander operator (beverage) 920.685-042
CANCELING-AND-CUTTING CONTROL CLERK (financial) 219.367-042
canceling-and-metering-machine operator (clerical) 208.685-026
Canceling-Machine Operator (clerical) 208.685-026
CANCELLATION CLERK (insurance) 203.382-014
CAN-CONVEYOR FEEDER (food prep., nec) 529.685-046
CANDLE CUTTER (fabrication, nec) 739.687-050
CANDLE-EXTRUSION-MACHINE OPERATOR (fabrication, nec) 692.682-026
CANDLEMAKER (fabrication, nec) 739.664-010
CANDLE MOLDER, HAND (fabrication, nec) 739.687-054
CANDLE MOLDER, MACHINE (fabrication, nec) 692.685-038
candle pourer (fabrication, nec) 739.687-158
Candle Wrapper (fabrication, nec) 920.587-018
CANDLE WRAPPING-MACHINE OPERATOR (fabrication, nec) 920.685-030
CAN DOFFER (textile) 680.686-010
can-drier operator (textile) 581.685-022
Candy-Bar-Core Inspector (sugar & conf.) 529.686-034
Candy Catcher (sugar & conf.) 529.686-034
candy-cooker helper (sugar & conf.) 520.685-050
CANDY CUTTER, HAND (sugar & conf.) 790.687-010
candy cutter, machine (sugar & conf.) 521.685-102
Candy Decorator (sugar & conf.) 524.684-014
Candy-Department Manager (retail trade) 299.137-010
CANDY DIPPER, HAND (sugar & conf.) 524.684-010
candy feeder (sugar & conf.) 524.686-010
CANDY MAKER (sugar & conf.) 529.361-014
Candy Maker, Bar (sugar & conf.) 520.687-022
candy-maker helper (sugar & conf.) 520.687-022
CANDY-MAKER HELPER (sugar & conf.) 520.685-050

candy mixer (sugar & conf.) 520.684-014
CANDY MOLDER, HAND (sugar & conf.) 520.687-018
Candy Packer (sugar & conf.) 920.587-018
candy polisher (sugar & conf.) 524.382-010
CANDY PULLER (sugar & conf.) 520.685-046
candy roller (sugar & conf.) 520.686-010
candy roller (sugar & conf.) 520.684-014
candy-rolling-machine operator (sugar & conf.) 520.685-198
candy separator, enrobing (sugar & conf.) 524.686-010
Candy Separator, Hard (sugar & conf.) 529.686-034
CANDY SPREADER (sugar & conf.) 520.687-022
Candy-Spreader Helper (sugar & conf.) 529.686-034
candy-starch-mold printer (sugar & conf.) 526.687-014
Candy-Waffle Assembler (sugar & conf.) 529.686-034
Candy-Wrapping-Machine Operator (sugar & conf.) 920.685-078
CANE CUTTER (furniture) 763.687-030
CANER I (furniture) 763.684-018
CANER II (furniture) 763.684-022
can feeder (tobacco) 920.686-030
Can Filler (food prep., nec) 523.685-102
CAN FILLER (tobacco) 922.687-030
CAN-FILLING-AND-CLOSING-MACHINE TENDER (can. & preserv.) 529.685-282
Can-Filling-Machine Operator (tobacco) 920.685-098
Can-Filling-Room Sweeper (beverage) 381.687-018
CAN INSPECTOR (beverage; can. & preserv.) 920.687-050
can intake worker (dairy products) 222.585-010
can-line examiner (tinware) 709.367-010
Cannery-Tender Engineer (water trans.) 197.130-010
CANNERY WORKER (can. & preserv.) 529.686-014
CANNON-PINION ADJUSTER (clock & watch) 715.684-046
CANOE INSPECTOR, FINAL (ship-boat mfg.) 769.687-018
Canopy Inspector (tex. prod., nec) 789.687-114
CANOPY STRINGER (tex. prod., nec) 789.684-018
CAN PATCHER (can. & preserv.) 920.687-054
can pusher (textile) 680.686-010
CAN RECONDITIONER (can. & preserv.) 920.687-058
Can-Reforming-Machine Operator (tinware) 709.686-010
can-repairer (tinware) 709.587-014
cans operator (textile) 581.685-022
Can Stacker (tinware) 709.686-010
Can Supervisor (any industry) 920.132-010
can technician (tinware) 709.367-010
CANTEEN OPERATOR (any industry) 311.674-010
can tender (textile) 581.685-022
can tester (tinware) 703.685-014
CANTILEVER-CRANE OPERATOR (water trans.) 921.683-018
CANTOR (profess. & kin.) 129.027-010
Canvas-Bag Maker (tex. prod., nec) 787.682-058
CANVAS BASTER, JUMPBASTING (garment) 786.682-050
Canvas Cutter, Hand (tex. prod., nec) 781.684-074
Canvas Cutter, Machine (tex. prod., nec) 781.684-014
Canvas Marker (tex. prod., nec) 781.384-014
CANVAS REPAIRER (any industry) 782.684-010
canvasser (retail trade) 291.357-010
CANVAS SHRINKER (textile) 587.687-010
CANVAS WORKER (ship-boat mfg.; tex. prod., nec) 739.381-010
CANVAS-WORKER APPRENTICE (ship-boat mfg.; tex. prod., nec) 739.381-014
Can Washer, Machine (any industry) 529.685-074
CAPACITOR ASSEMBLER (elec. equip.) 729.684-014
Capacitor Inspector (electron. comp.) 726.684-022
CAPACITOR-PACK-PRESS OPERATOR (elec. equip.) 726.684-010
Capacitor Repairer (elec. equip.) 729.684-014
Capacitor Tester (electron. comp.) 726.684-078
Cap-And-Stud-Machine Operator (rubber goods) 699.685-018
cap blocker (hat & cap) 580.684-014
Cap Coverer (hat & cap) 780.684-026
cap inspector (can. & preserv.) 920.687-194
CAP-JEWEL PLATE ASSEMBLER (clock & watch) 715.684-050
cap-lining-machine operator (any industry) 692.685-062
cap-machine operator (hat & cap) 784.684-018
Cap Maker (fabrication, nec) 739.684-190
CAP MAKER (hat & cap) 784.684-018
CAPONIZER (agriculture) 411.684-010
cap operator (hat & cap) 784.684-018
Cap-Parts Cutter (hat & cap) 699.682-022
Capper (agriculture) 920.687-134
capper (cutlery-hrdwr.) 779.684-034
Capper Picker (agriculture; wholesale tr.) 529.687-186
Capping-Machine Operator (any industry) 920.685-078
CAPPING-MACHINE OPERATOR (elec. equip.) 692.685-042
Cap Sizer (hat & cap) 784.682-014
CAPSULE-FILLING-MACHINE OPERATOR (pharmaceut.) 559.682-010
captain (government ser.) 375.167-034

captain

captain (hotel & rest.) 311.137-018
captain (water trans.)   see MASTER
Captain, Cannery Tender (fishing & hunt.) 197.133-010
CAPTAIN, FIRE-PREVENTION BUREAU (government ser.) 373.167-014
CAPTAIN, FISHING VESSEL (fishing & hunt.) 197.133-010
Captain, Room Service (hotel & rest.) 311.137-022
CAPTION WRITER (motion picture; radio-tv broad.) 203.362-026
Caramel-Candy Maker (sugar & conf.) 529.361-014
Caramel-Candy-Maker Helper (sugar & conf.) 520.685-050
Caramel Cutter, Hand (sugar & conf.) 790.687-010
Caramel-Cutter Helper (sugar & conf.) 529.686-034
Caramel Cutter, Machine (sugar & conf.) 521.685-102
Carbide-Die Maker (machine shop) 601.280-018
carbide grinder (machine shop) 601.380-010
CARBIDE OPERATOR (machine shop) 601.380-010
CARBIDE-POWDER PROCESSOR (machine shop) 510.465-010
Carbide-Tool Maker (clock & watch) 601.280-042
CAR BLOCKER (any industry) 860.684-018
car-body inspector (railroad equip.) 807.381-026
car-body-inspector helper (railroad equip.) 807.687-014
CARBON-AND-GRAPHITE-BRUSH-MACHINE OPERATOR (elec. equip.) 692.482-010
carbonating-stone cleaner (beverage) 529.687-190
CARBONATION EQUIPMENT OPERATOR (sugar & conf.) 529.582-010
CARBONATION EQUIPMENT TENDER (beverage) 522.685-026
CARBONATION TESTER (beverage) 522.587-010
Carbon Brushes Tester (elec. equip.) 729.684-058
carbon-brush maker (elec. equip.) 721.684-014
CARBON-COATER-MACHINE OPERATOR (pen & pencil) 534.682-014
CARBON CUTTER (elec. equip.) 677.685-018
carbon-dioxide operator (chemical) 559.665-030
CARBON-FURNACE OPERATOR (smelt. & refin.) 543.562-010
CARBON-FURNACE-OPERATOR HELPER (smelt. & refin.) 543.664-010
carbonizer (heat treating) 504.685-026
carbonizer (heat treating) 504.682-014
CARBONIZER (textile) 581.585-010
carbon-lamp cleaner (utilities) 952.667-010
CARBON-PAPER-COATING-MACHINE SETTER (pen & pencil) 534.380-010
CARBON-PAPER INTERLEAFER (pen & pencil) 640.685-018
Carbon-Paste-Mixer Operator, Panelboard (elec. equip.; smelt. & refin.) 540.585-010
CARBON PRINTER (print. & pub.) 979.684-010
CARBON ROD INSERTER (elec. equip.) 692.686-026
CARBON SETTER (smelt. & refin.) 519.667-010
Carboy Filler (chemical) 559.687-050
Carburetor Assembler (engine-turbine) 706.481-010
Carburetor Mechanic (air trans.) 621.281-014
CARBURETOR MECHANIC (automotive ser.) 620.281-034
carburetor repairer (automotive ser.) 620.281-034
carburizer (heat treating) 504.682-014
Carcass Assembler (toy-sport equip.) 732.684-026
CARCASS SPLITTER (meat products) 525.684-018
Carcass Trimmer (rubber reclaim.) 690.685-386
car changer (construction) 921.663-014
CAR CHASER (beverage) 910.167-010
car checker (automotive ser.; retail trade) 806.361-026
car checker (r.r. trans.) 910.367-014
CAR CHECKER (r.r. trans.) 222.387-014
Car Cleaner (mine & quarry) 939.687-014
car cleaner (retail trade; wholesale tr.) 915.687-022
car cleaner (railroad equip.) 845.684-010
Car Cleaner (r.r. trans.) 919.687-014
CAR-CLEANING SUPERVISOR (r.r. trans.) 910.137-014
CAR CLERK, PULLMAN (r.r. trans.) 215.167-010
CAR COOPER (any industry) 910.687-014
card-apron cleaner (nonmet. min.) 680.687-010
card assembler (any industry) 920.685-034
Cardboard Cutter (any industry) 690.685-122
CARDBOARD INSERTER (knitting) 920.687-062
CARD CHANGER, JACQUARD LOOM (textile) 683.685-014
Card Cleaner (textile) 699.687-014
CARD CLOTHIER (textile) 628.381-010
card-cutter helper (textile) 689.587-010
CARD CUTTER, JACQUARD (narrow fabrics; textile) 683.582-010
CARD DECORATOR (print. & pub.) 649.686-014
Card Doffer (textile) 680.686-010
CARDER (any industry) 920.685-034
carder (textile) 680.685-050
carder, blankets (laundry & rel.) 363.687-022
card fixer (nonmet. min.; textile) 680.380-010
Card Fixer (textile) 689.260-010
card-gill tender (textile) 680.685-058
card grader (amuse. & rec.) 343.687-010
CARD GRINDER (nonmet. min.; textile) 680.380-010

CARD GRINDER HELPER (textile) 680.684-010
card hand (nonmet. min.; textile) 680.685-018
card hanger (textile) 683.685-014
CARDIAC MONITOR TECHNICIAN (medical ser.) 078.367-010
carding doubler (textile) 680.685-086
carding doubler (textile) 680.685-094
Carding-Machine Feeder (textile) 680.686-018
carding-machine operator (any industry) 920.685-034
CARDING-MACHINE OPERATOR (tex. prod., nec) 681.685-030
CARDIOLOGIST (medical ser.) 070.101-014
CARDIOPULMONARY TECHNOLOGIST (medical ser.) 078.362-030
CARDIOPULMONARY TECHNOLOGIST, CHIEF (medical ser.) 078.161-014
cardiovascular technologist (medical ser.) 078.362-030
car distributor (mine & quarry) 932.167-010
CAR DISTRIBUTOR (r.r. trans.) 910.367-014
CARD LACER, JACQUARD (narrow fabrics; textile) 683.685-018
card operator (nonmet. min.; textile) 680.685-018
CARD PLAYER (amuse. & rec.) 343.367-010
card processing clerk (financial) 249.367-026
Card Reader (amuse. & rec.) 159.647-018
car driver (auto. mfg.; automotive ser.) 919.683-014
CARDROOM ATTENDANT I (amuse. & rec.) 343.467-010
CARDROOM ATTENDANT II (amuse. & rec.) 343.577-010
Cardroom Supervisor (nonmet. min.) 579.137-014
CARDROOM WORKER (nonmet. min.; textile) term
CAR DROPPER (mine & quarry) 932.683-010
card setter (nonmet. min.; textile) 680.380-010
CARD STRIPPER (textile) 680.685-014
CARD TENDER (nonmet. min.; textile) 680.685-018
Car Dumper (any industry) 921.667-018
car-dumper operator (any industry) 921.685-038
CAR-DUMPER OPERATOR (beverage) 921.662-010
CAR-DUMPER-OPERATOR HELPER (beverage) 921.687-010
card writer, hand (any industry) 970.281-022
career counselor (military ser.) 166.267-026
CAREER-GUIDANCE TECHNICIAN (education) 249.367-014
career-information specialist (education) 249.367-014
Career Placement Services Counselor (education) 045.107-010
career resource technician (education) 249.367-014
CARETAKER (domestic ser.) 301.687-010
CARETAKER, FARM (agriculture) term
caretaker, grounds (any industry) 406.684-014
caretaker, resort (hotel & rest.) 329.467-010
car filler (any industry) 914.667-010
Charge-Bag Sewer (tex. prod., nec) 787.682-058
CARGO AGENT (air trans.) 248.367-018
CARGO CHECKER (water trans.) 222.367-010
cargo-gear mechanic (water trans.) 222.387-062
Cargo Inspector (government ser.) 168.267-022
CARGO INSPECTOR (petrol. refin.; pipe lines) 549.387-010
CAR HOP (hotel & rest.) 311.477-010
Caricaturist (amuse. & rec.) 149.041-010
car ice-bunker filler (food prep., nec; meat products) 910.687-018
CAR ICER (food prep., nec; meat products) 910.687-018
Car Inspector (mine & quarry) 622.381-030
CAR INSPECTOR (railroad equip.) 910.667-010
Car Jockey (automotive ser.) 919.683-014
Car Letterer (railroad equip.) 970.381-038
Car Loader (any industry) 929.687-030
car loader (saw. & plan.) 922.687-022
CARNALLITE-PLANT OPERATOR (smelt. & refin.) 519.484-010
carney (amuse. & rec.) 342.657-010
CARPENTER (construction) 860.381-022
CARPENTER APPRENTICE (construction) 860.381-026
carpenter apprentice, ship (ship-boat mfg.) 860.381-062
carpenter, box (wood. container) 760.684-014
CARPENTER, BRIDGE (r.r. trans.) 860.381-030
Carpenter, Cradle And Dolly (ship-boat mfg.) 860.381-042
carpenter, form (construction) 860.381-046
carpenter helper (ship-boat mfg.) 860.664-018
Carpenter Helper, Hardwood Flooring (construction) 869.687-026
Carpenter Helper, Maintenance (construction) 869.664-014
CARPENTER I (mfd. bldgs.) 860.664-010
CARPENTER II (mfd. bldgs.) 860.681-010
CARPENTER INSPECTOR (any industry) 860.261-010
CARPENTER-LABOR SUPERVISOR (construction) 860.137-010
CARPENTER, MAINTENANCE (any industry) 860.281-010
Carpenter, Mine (mine & quarry) 860.281-010
CARPENTER, MOLD (brick & tile; concrete prod.) 860.381-034
carpenter, packing (any industry) 920.684-010
CARPENTER, PROTOTYPE (ship-boat mfg.) 806.281-058
CARPENTER, RAILCAR (railroad equip.) 860.381-038
Carpenter, Refrigerator (svc. ind. mach.) 860.381-022
carpenter, repair (any industry) 860.281-010
CARPENTER, ROUGH (construction) 860.381-042

CARPENTER, SHIP (ship-boat mfg.) 860.281-014
carpenter, ship (ship-boat mfg.) 860.381-058
Carpenter, Streetcar (railroad equip.) 860.381-038
carpenter supervisor, wooden ship (ship-boat mfg.) 860.131-014
carpenter, wooden-tank erecting (construction) 860.381-070
carpet cleaner (laundry & rel.) 369.384-014
CARPET CUTTER (retail trade) 929.381-010
CARPET CUTTER I (carpet & rug) 781.684-010
CARPET CUTTER II (carpet & rug) 585.687-014
Carpet-Finishing Supervisor (carpet & rug) 589.130-010
CARPET INSPECTOR, FINISHED (carpet & rug) 689.564-010
CARPET LAYER (retail trade) 864.381-010
CARPET-LAYER HELPER (retail trade) 864.687-010
CARPET-LOOM FIXER (carpet & rug) 683.260-014
CARPET SEWER (carpet & rug; retail trade) 787.682-014
CARPET WEAVER (carpet & rug) 683.682-014
CARPET WEAVER, JACQUARD LOOM (carpet & rug) 683.682-014
Carpet Winder (carpet & rug) 689.685-046
car pincher (mine & quarry) 932.683-010
CAR PINCHER (steel & rel.) 922.687-034
car porter (retail trade; wholesale tr.) 915.687-022
car-record clerk (r.r. trans.) 214.362-010
car rental clerk (automotive ser.) 295.467-026
CAR REPAIRER (railroad equip.) 622.381-014
car repairer (railroad equip.) 721.381-010
CAR-REPAIRER APPRENTICE (railroad equip.) 622.381-022
CAR-REPAIRER HELPER (railroad equip.) 622.684-014
CAR REPAIRER, PULLMAN (r.r. trans.) 622.381-018
CAR-RETARDER OPERATOR (r.r. trans.) 910.382-010
Carriage Feeder (fabrication, nec) 590.662-022
car rider (any industry) 932.664-010
Car Rider (r.r. trans.) 910.664-010
carrier (retail trade) 292.457-010
carrier blower (tobacco) 529.687-194
Carrier Guider (fabrication, nec) 590.686-014
carrier loader (textile) 589.687-062
carrier operator (sugar & conf.) 521.685-090
CARRIER PACKER (protective dev.) 920.687-066
carrier washer (tobacco) 529.687-194
Car-Roof Repairer (railroad equip.) 807.381-026
CARROTER (hat & cap) 784.687-014
Carrot Grader-Inspector (agriculture) 409.687-010
CARROTING-MACHINE OFFBEARER (hat & cap) 586.686-010
CARROTING-MACHINE OPERATOR (hat & cap) 586.685-010
Carrot Washer (agriculture; can. & preserv.; wholesale tr.) 529.685-258
car runner (mine & quarry) 932.683-010
Car Salter (mine & quarry) 939.687-014
CAR SCRUBBER (railroad equip.) 845.684-010
Car-Shakeout Operator (cement; mine & quarry) 921.685-038
car shifter (steel & rel.) 922.687-034
car spotter (beverage) 910.167-010
Car Straightener (railroad equip.) 622.381-014
car supplier (r.r. trans.) 910.367-014
Cart Driver (any industry) 919.664-010
car tester (auto. mfg.) 806.283-014
Car Tester (railroad equip.) 622.684-014
CARTOGRAPHIC TECHNICIAN (profess. & kin.) term
cartographic technician (profess. & kin.) 018.261-026
carton catcher (any industry) 921.686-014
CARTON-COUNTER FEEDER (tobacco) 921.686-010
carton filler (tobacco) 920.687-130
Carton-Forming-Machine Adjuster (any industry) 638.281-014
CARTON-FORMING-MACHINE HELPER (any industry) 641.686-014
CARTON-FORMING-MACHINE OPERATOR (any industry) 641.685-022
CARTON-FORMING-MACHINE TENDER (paper goods) 641.685-026
Carton-Gluing-Machine Operator (any industry) 920.685-078
CARTON INSPECTOR (tobacco) 920.687-070
carton-lettering-machine operator (any industry) 652.682-010
CARTON MARKER, MACHINE (boot & shoe; garment) 652.685-018
CARTON-PACKAGING-MACHINE OPERATOR (tobacco) 920.665-010
Carton Repairer (beverage) 529.687-066
carton searcher (tobacco) 920.687-070
carton stamper (boot & shoe; garment) 652.685-018
Carton Stapler (any industry) 920.587-018
Carton Stenciler (any industry) 920.687-178
Carton-Waxing-Machine Operator (paper goods) 534.482-010
Cartoon-Background Artist (motion picture; radio-tv broad.) 141.081-010
CARTOON DESIGNER (tex. prod., nec) 781.381-010
CARTOONIST (print. & pub.) 141.061-010
CARTOONIST, MOTION PICTURES (motion picture; radio-tv broad.) 141.081-010
Cartoonist, Special Effects (motion picture; radio-tv broad.) 141.081-010
Car-Top Bolter (railroad equip.) 622.684-014
cartridge-actuated-tool operator (construction)   see STUD-DRIVER OPERA-
TOR

cartridge assembler (comm. equip.) 720.684-014
Cartridge Assembler (pen & pencil) 733.685-010
cartridge-assembling-machine adjuster (ordnance) 632.360-014
cartridge belt puncher (leather prod.) 690.685-266
Cartridge Feeder (pen & pencil) 692.686-010
cartridge gauger (ordnance) 737.684-026
CARTRIDGE LOADER (elec. equip.) 779.687-014
cartridge loader (recording) 726.685-010
cartridge-loading operator (ordnance) 694.685-026
CAR TRIMMER (railroad equip.) 806.684-046
car unloader (beverage) 921.662-010
car-unloader helper (beverage) 921.687-010
Car Varnisher (railroad equip.) 740.684-022
carver (boot & shoe) 788.684-082
carver (carpet & rug) 781.684-046
carver (engraving) 704.381-030
CARVER (hotel & rest.) 316.661-010
Carver And Checkerer, Specials (ordnance) 761.381-034
CARVER, HAND (woodworking) 761.281-010
carver, machine (woodworking) 761.682-018
carving-machine operator (woodworking) 761.682-018
CAR-WASH ATTENDANT, AUTOMATIC (automotive ser.) 915.667-010
CAR-WASH SUPERVISOR (automotive ser.) 915.137-010
car whacker (any industry) 910.687-014
Cascara-Bark Cutter (forestry) 453.687-010
CASE AIDE (social ser.) 195.367-010
case assembler (leather prod.) 739.684-034
case assembler (agric. equip.) 801.684-022
CASE FINISHER (leather prod.) 739.684-034
CASE-FINISHING-MACHINE ADJUSTER (ordnance) 626.381-010
CASE FITTER (furniture) 763.684-026
case hardener (heat treating) 504.685-026
CASE HARDENER (heat treating) 504.682-014
Case Inspector (clock & watch) 715.384-022
CASE-LOADER OPERATOR (beverage) 920.685-042
case maker (any industry) 920.684-010
case maker (wood. container) 760.684-014
CASE-MAKING-MACHINE OPERATOR (print. & pub.) 653.685-018
case packer (tobacco) 920.687-130
CASE PACKER AND SEALER (tobacco) 920.685-038
CASE PREPARER-AND-LINER (ordnance) 509.384-010
caser (beverage) 920.685-026
caser (boot & shoe) 788.687-026
CASER (clock & watch) 715.684-054
CASER (petrol. & gas) 930.664-010
caser (pottery & porc.) 777.684-018
Caser (print. & pub.) 977.684-018
Case Repairer (leather prod.) 739.684-034
caser helper (tobacco) 522.687-030
caser-in (print. & pub.) 653.686-010
caser-in (print. & pub.) 977.684-018
caser operator (print. & pub.) 653.685-018
Caser, Rolled Glass (glass mfg.) 920.587-018
CASER, SHOE PARTS (boot & shoe) 788.687-026
case sealer (tobacco) 920.687-130
case supervisor (social ser.) 195.137-010
CASEWORKER (government ser.) 169.262-010
CASEWORKER (social ser.) 195.107-010
Caseworker, Child Placement (social ser.) 195.107-014
CASEWORKER, CHILD WELFARE (social ser.) 195.107-014
CASEWORKER, FAMILY (social ser.) 195.107-018
Caseworker, Intake (social ser.) 195.107-014
Caseworker, Protective Services (social ser.) 195.107-014
CASEWORK SUPERVISOR (social ser.) 195.137-010
cash-accounting clerk (clerical) 211.362-010
cash clerk (clerical) 211.462-010
cash grain grower (agriculture) 401.161-010
cashier (financial) 186.117-070
cashier, automobile services (automotive ser.) 915.477-010
Cashier, Box Office (amuse. & rec.) 211.467-030
cashier, check-cashing agency (business ser.) 211.462-026
CASHIER-CHECKER (retail trade) 211.462-014
CASHIER, COURTESY BOOTH (retail trade) 211.467-010
Cashier, Credit (clerical) 211.462-010
cashier, fast foods restaurant (hotel & rest.) 311.472-010
Cashier, Front Office (hotel & rest.) 211.362-010
CASHIER, GAMBLING (amuse. & rec.) 211.462-022
cashier, general (clerical) 211.462-010
CASHIER I (clerical) 211.362-010
CASHIER II (clerical) 211.462-010
cashier, office (clerical) 211.462-010
Cashier, Parking Lot (automotive ser.) 211.462-010
Cashier, Payments Received (clerical) 211.462-010
Cashier, Self-Service Gasoline (automotive ser.) 211.462-010
cashier, ticket selling (clerical) 211.467-030

CASHIER, TUBE ROOM (retail trade) 211.482-010
CASHIER-WRAPPER (retail trade) 211.462-018
cash-on-delivery clerk (clerical) 214.382-018
cash-register repairer (any industry) 633.281-010
CASH-REGISTER SERVICER (any industry) 633.281-010
Cash-Sales-Audit Clerk (clerical) 210.382-010
Cash-Surrender Calculator (insurance) 216.382-050
CASING CLEANER (meat products) 525.686-010
CASING-FLUID TENDER (tobacco) 520.685-054
CASING GRADER (meat products) 529.687-026
CASING-IN-LINE FEEDER (print. & pub.) 653.686-010
CASING-IN-LINE SETTER (print. & pub.) 653.360-010
casing inspector (meat products) 529.687-026
Casing-Machine Operator (meat products) 525.686-010
CASING-MACHINE OPERATOR (tobacco) 522.685-030
CASING-MATERIAL WEIGHER (tobacco) 520.687-026
casing mixer (tobacco) 520.687-026
Casing Packer (meat products) 525.686-010
Casing Puller (meat products) 525.684-038
casing puller (petrol. & gas) 930.382-030
casing runner (meat products) 525.685-014
CASING-RUNNING-MACHINE TENDER (meat products) 525.685-014
Casing Salter (meat products) 525.687-026
CASING SEWER (meat products) 529.687-030
Casing Soaker (meat products) 525.686-010
casing sorter (meat products) 529.687-026
CASING SPLITTER (meat products) 525.687-014
casing tester (meat products) 529.687-026
CASING TIER (meat products) 529.687-034
casing wetter (tobacco) 522.687-026
casing-wringer operator (tobacco) 522.685-106
CASKET ASSEMBLER (fabrication, nec) 739.684-190
CASKET ASSEMBLER, METAL (fabrication, nec) 809.684-014
CASKET COVERER (fabrication, nec) 780.684-026
CASKET INSPECTOR (fabrication, nec) 739.387-010
CASKET LINER (fabrication, nec) 780.684-030
casket trimmer (fabrication, nec) 780.684-026
casket upholsterer (fabrication, nec) 780.684-030
cask maker (wood. container) 764.684-026
Casserole Preparer (hotel & rest.) 319.484-010
castables worker (brick & tile) 579.684-026
CASTER (brick & tile) 579.684-026
caster (hat & cap) 784.361-010
caster (jewelry-silver.) 502.682-018
CASTER (jewelry-silver.) 502.381-010
CASTER (nonfer. metal) 502.482-010
CASTER (nonmet. min.) 575.684-018
caster (nonmet. min.) 779.684-046
CASTER (plastic prod.) 754.684-022
caster (plastic-synth.) 559.682-022
CASTER (pottery & porc.) 575.684-014
CASTER (smelt. & refin.) 514.684-010
caster (steel & rel.) 502.664-014
CASTER HELPER (jewelry-silver.) 700.687-022
caster, investment casting (foundry; steel & rel.) 512.362-018
caster operator (machinery mfg.; print. & pub.) 654.382-010
CASTING-AND-CURING OPERATOR (chemical) 559.682-014
Casting-And-Locker-Room Servicer (plastic-synth.) 381.687-018
Casting Carrier (foundry) 519.687-022
casting finisher (foundry) 705.684-074
casting header (nonfer. metal; smelt. & refin.) 514.584-010
CASTING-HOUSE WORKER (nonfer. metal) 514.687-014
Casting Inspector (elec. equip.) 502.687-018
CASTING INSPECTOR (foundry) 514.687-010
casting-machine adjuster (elec. equip.) 502.684-018
Casting-Machine-Control-Board Operator (foundry) 514.562-010
CASTING-MACHINE OPERATOR (dairy products) 520.685-058
CASTING-MACHINE OPERATOR (machinery mfg.; print. & pub.) 654.382-010
CASTING-MACHINE OPERATOR (nonfer. metal) 502.682-014
casting-machine operator (sugar & conf.) 520.682-014
CASTING-MACHINE OPERATOR (sugar & conf.) 520.685-062
CASTING-MACHINE OPERATOR, AUTOMATIC (elec. equip.) 502.482-014
CASTING-MACHINE-OPERATOR HELPER (elec. equip.) 502.686-010
CASTING-MACHINE-SERVICE OPERATOR (plastic-synth.) 559.687-018
CASTING OPERATOR (nonfer. metal) 514.662-010
CASTING-OPERATOR HELPER (nonfer. metal) 514.687-018
CASTING-PLUG ASSEMBLER (toy-sport equip.) 732.687-022
CASTING REPAIRER (any industry) 619.281-010
CASTING-ROOM OPERATOR (plastic-synth.) 556.585-010
Casting Sorter (foundry) 519.687-022
casting supervisor (concrete prod.) 575.131-010
Casting Supervisor (foundry) 519.131-010
casting tester (foundry) 514.687-010
Casting Trucker (foundry) 921.683-050

CASTING-WHEEL OPERATOR (smelt. & refin.) 514.682-010
CASTING-WHEEL-OPERATOR HELPER (smelt. & refin.) 514.667-010
cast-shell grinder (foundry) 705.684-074
Casual-Shoe Inspector (boot & shoe) 788.384-010
Casualty-Insurance-Claim Adjuster (clerical) 241.217-010
cataloger (library) 100.387-010
CATALOG LIBRARIAN (library) 100.387-010
catalyst impregnator (chemical) 559.685-106
catalyst-manufacturing operator (chemical) 558.382-034
catalyst operator (chemical) 553.682-022
CATALYST OPERATOR (chemical) term
CATALYST OPERATOR, CHIEF (chemical) 559.132-018
CATALYST OPERATOR, GASOLINE (chemical) 559.382-014
catalyst plant supervisor (chemical) 559.132-018
CATALYST-RECOVERY OPERATOR (chemical) 551.685-022
catalyst supervisor (chemical; petrol. refin.) 559.132-078
catalytic-case operator (chemical) 558.362-010
CATALYTIC-CONVERTER OPERATOR (chemical) 558.362-010
CATALYTIC-CONVERTER-OPERATOR HELPER (chemical) 558.585-010
Cataract-Lens Generator (optical goods) 716.682-014
Cat Breeder (agriculture) 410.161-010
Cat Chaser (logging) 921.667-014
Catch-Basin Cleaner (sanitary ser.) 955.687-010
Catcher (metal prod., nec) 706.684-090
CATCHER (steel & rel.) 613.686-010
CATCHER, FILTER TIP (tobacco) 529.666-010
catcher, plug (tobacco) 529.666-010
catching inspector (tobacco) 529.567-010
Caterer (personal ser.) 187.167-106
CATERER HELPER (personal ser.) 319.677-010
catering-truck operator (hotel & rest.) 292.463-010
Cathead Worker (petrol. & gas) 930.684-026
CATHETER BUILDER (rubber goods) 752.684-026
Catheter Finisher-And-Inspector (rubber goods) 759.684-074
cathode builder (chemical) 826.684-022
CATHODE MAKER (chemical) 554.585-010
CATHODE RAY TUBE SALVAGE PROCESSOR (electron. comp.) 725.684-026
Cathode Washer (chemical) 559.687-022
Cat Hooker (logging) 921.687-014
Cattle Dropper And Pritcher (meat products) 525.684-046
Cattle Header (meat products) 525.684-046
Cattle Rancher (agriculture) 410.161-010
Cattle Sticker (meat products) 525.684-050
Caul-Fat Puller (meat products) 525.687-010
Cauliflower-Harvesting-And-Packing Supervisor (agriculture) 409.131-010
caulker (any industry) 843.684-010
CAULKER (construction; ship-boat mfg.) term
Caulker (construction) 869.664-014
CAUSTICISER (chemical) 558.382-022
CAUSTICISER (paper & pulp) 558.382-018
caustic-liquor maker (paper & pulp) 558.382-018
Caustic Loader (chemical) 914.667-010
Caustic Mixer (textile) 550.585-018
CAUSTIC OPERATOR (paper & pulp) 558.485-010
CAUSTIC OPERATOR (plastic-synth.) 554.684-010
Caustic-Purification Operator (chemical) 559.382-018
caustic-room attendant (plastic-synth.) 551.685-138
Caustic-Strength Inspector (textile) 582.587-010
cd-manufacturing supervisor (chemical) 559.132-070
CD-MIXER (rubber reclaim.) 550.685-022
CD-MIXER HELPER (rubber reclaim.) 553.686-014
CD-REACTOR OPERATOR (chemical) 558.385-010
CD-REACTOR OPERATOR, HEAD (chemical) 558.362-014
CD-STORAGE-AND-MATERIALS MAKE-UP HELPER (chemical) 559.685-034
CD-STORAGE-AND-MATERIALS-MAKE-UP OPERATOR, HEAD (chemical) 559.167-010
Ceiling Cleaner (any industry) 381.687-018
ceiling installer (mfd. bldgs.) 869.684-038
cellar hand (leather mfg.) 589.686-026
Cellar Laborer (dairy products) 529.686-050
Cellar Pumper (beverage) 914.665-014
CELLAR SUPERVISOR (beverage) 529.131-010
cellar worker (beverage) 914.665-014
cell assembly, booker (elec. equip.) 727.687-038
cell assembly, pinner (elec. equip.) 727.687-038
cell attendant (chemical) 558.382-026
cell-attendant helper (chemical) 558.685-022
CELL CHANGER (chemical) 826.684-014
CELL CLEANER (chemical) 559.687-022
CELL COVERER (elec. equip.) 727.687-042
CELL-FEED-DEPARTMENT SUPERVISOR (smelt. & refin.) 519.130-010
CELL INSPECTOR (plastic-synth.) 556.684-010
CELL INSTALLER (chemical) 826.684-018

CELL MAKER (chemical) 844.681-010
cell-making supervisor, plastics sheets (plastic-synth.) 579.137-022
Cellophane-Bag-Machine Operator (paper goods) 649.685-014
CELLOPHANE-BATH MIXER (plastic-synth.) 550.585-014
CELLOPHANE-CASTING-MACHINE REPAIRER (plastic prod.) 629.281-014
Cellophane Sheeter (any industry) 699.682-018
Cellophane Wrapper, Machine (any industry) 920.685-078
cellophane-wrapping examiner (tobacco) 920.667-010
CELL PLASTERER (smelt. & refin.) 519.687-010
cell pourer (plastic-synth.) 556.684-018
CELL PREPARER (plastic-synth.) 556.687-014
CELL REPAIRER (chemical) 826.384-010
CELL REPAIRER (elec. equip.) 727.684-018
CELL STRIPPER (plastic-synth.) 556.686-014
cell stripper, final (plastic-synth.) 556.587-010
CELL TENDER (chemical) 558.382-026
CELL-TENDER HELPER (chemical) 558.685-022
CELL TESTER (chemical) 558.584-010
CELL TUBER, HAND (elec. equip.) 727.687-046
CELL TUBER, MACHINE (elec. equip.) 692.685-046
CELLULOID TRIMMER (toy-sport equip.) 732.684-046
CEMENT-BOAT-AND-BARGE LOADER (cement) 921.665-010
Cement-Car Dumper (construction) 579.665-014
Cement-Conveyor Operator (construction) 579.665-014
cementer (any industry) 795.687-014
cementer (any industry) 780.684-062
cementer (automotive ser.) 750.684-038
cementer (leather mfg.) 585.687-022
CEMENTER (optical goods) 711.684-014
Cementer (pen & pencil) 733.687-030
Cementer (ship-boat mfg.) 844.364-010
CEMENTER AND FOLDER, MACHINE (boot & shoe) 690.685-070
Cementer For Folding, Machine (boot & shoe) 690.686-018
CEMENTER, HAND (boot & shoe) 788.687-030
Cementer Helper (petrol. & gas) 939.684-018
CEMENTER, MACHINE (boot & shoe) 692.685-050
cementer, machine (leather prod.) 690.686-022
CEMENTER, MACHINE APPLICATOR (boot & shoe) 690.686-018
CEMENTER, MACHINE JOINER (boot & shoe) 690.685-074
Cementer, Oil Well (petrol. & gas) 939.462-010
cement finisher (construction) 844.364-010
cement-finisher apprentice (construction) 844.364-014
Cement-Finishing Supervisor (construction) 869.131-014
CEMENT FITTINGS MAKER (concrete prod.) 779.684-010
Cement-Gun Operator (concrete prod.; construction) 849.665-010
Cement Handler (construction) 579.665-014
CEMENT LOADER (cement) 921.565-010
CEMENT MASON (construction) 844.364-010
CEMENT-MASON APPRENTICE (construction) 844.364-014
Cement-Mason Helper (construction) 869.687-026
Cement Mason, Highways And Streets (construction) 869.664-014
Cement Mason, Maintenance (any industry) 844.364-010
cement mixer (cement) 570.685-010
CEMENT MIXER (rubber goods; rubber tire) 550.685-026
cement patcher (concrete prod.) 844.684-010
cement paver (construction) 844.364-010
Cement-Railroad-Car Loader (cement) 921.565-010
cement rubber (concrete prod.) 844.684-010
Cement-Sack Breaker (construction) 579.665-014
CEMENT SPRAYER HELPER, NOZZLE (concrete prod.; construction) 844.687-010
Cement Sprayer, Nozzle (concrete prod.; construction) 869.664-014
cement-storage worker (cement) 579.685-050
Cement-Tile Maker (concrete prod.) 579.685-042
Cement-Truck Loader (cement) 921.565-010
CEMETERY WORKER (real estate) 406.684-010
Census Clerk (government ser.) 216.382-062
Census Enumerator (government ser.) 205.367-054
Centerless-Grinder Tender (machine shop) 603.685-062
Centerless-Grinding-Machine Adjuster (ordnance) 638.261-030
centerless-grinding-machine operator (machine shop) 603.382-014
Center-Line-Cutter Operator (construction) 853.663-014
CENTER-MACHINE OPERATOR (sugar & conf.) 520.682-014
center maker, hand (sugar & conf.) 520.684-014
CENTER-PUNCH OPERATOR (recording) 690.685-078
Central-Control-Room Operator (utilities) 952.362-042
CENTRAL-OFFICE EQUIPMENT ENGINEER (tel. & tel.) 003.187-010
CENTRAL-OFFICE INSTALLER (tel. & tel.) 822.361-014
central-office maintainer (tel. & tel.) 822.281-014
CENTRAL-OFFICE OPERATOR (tel. & tel.) 235.462-010
CENTRAL-OFFICE-OPERATOR SUPERVISOR (tel. & tel.) 235.132-010
CENTRAL-OFFICE REPAIRER (tel. & tel.) 822.281-014
CENTRAL-OFFICE-REPAIRER SUPERVISOR (tel. & tel.) 822.131-010
Central-Office Supervisor (tel. & tel.) 822.131-010
central-service technician (medical ser.) 381.687-010

CENTRAL-SUPPLY WORKER (medical ser.) 381.687-010
CENTRIFUGAL-CASTING-MACHINE OPERATOR (jewelry-silver.) 502.682-018
CENTRIFUGAL-CASTING-MACHINE OPERATOR I (foundry) 514.685-010
CENTRIFUGAL-CASTING-MACHINE OPERATOR II (foundry) 514.685-014
CENTRIFUGAL-CASTING-MACHINE OPERATOR III (foundry) 514.562-010
CENTRIFUGAL-CASTING-MACHINE TENDER (button & notion) 556.385-010
CENTRIFUGAL-CASTING-MACHINE TENDER (plastic prod.) 556.685-090
CENTRIFUGAL-DRIER OPERATOR (chemical) 551.685-026
centrifugal-extractor operator (any industry) 581.685-018
CENTRIFUGAL OPERATOR (grain-feed mills; sugar & conf.) 521.682-010
Centrifugal-Screen Tender (paper & pulp) 533.685-022
Centrifugal Separator (sugar & conf.) 521.685-070
CENTRIFUGAL SPINNER (concrete prod.) 575.664-010
CENTRIFUGAL-STATION OPERATOR, AUTOMATIC (sugar & conf.) 521.585-010
centrifugal supervisor (sugar & conf.) 529.130-042
Centrifugal-Wax Molder (foundry; jewelry-silver.) 549.685-038
CENTRIFUGE OPERATOR (dairy products) 521.685-042
CENTRIFUGE OPERATOR (grain-feed mills) 521.685-046
CENTRIFUGE OPERATOR (oils & grease) 521.685-050
CENTRIFUGE OPERATOR (paint & varnish) 551.685-034
CENTRIFUGE OPERATOR (soap & rel.) 551.685-030
CENTRIFUGE OPERATOR (sugar & conf.) 529.682-010
Centrifuge Operator (beverage) 521.685-118
centrifuge operator (chemical) 551.685-026
CENTRIFUGE OPERATOR, PLASMA PROCESSING (medical ser.; pharmaceut.) 599.685-018
CENTRIFUGE-SEPARATOR OPERATOR (chemical) 551.685-038
CENTRIFUGE-SEPARATOR TENDER (nonfer. metal) 541.585-010
CEPHALOMETRIC ANALYST (medical ser.) 078.384-010
cephalometric technician (medical ser.) 078.384-010
cephalometric tracer (medical ser.) 078.384-010
CERAMIC CAPACITOR PROCESSOR (electron. comp.) 590.684-010
CERAMIC COATER, MACHINE (any industry) 509.685-022
CERAMIC DESIGN ENGINEER (profess. & kin.) 006.061-010
CERAMIC ENGINEER (profess. & kin.) 006.061-014
Ceramic-Maker Demonstrator (retail trade) 297.354-010
ceramic plater (any industry) 509.685-022
CERAMIC RESEARCH ENGINEER (profess. & kin.) 006.061-018
Ceramic Saw, Tender (brick & tile) 677.685-034
Ceramic Sprayer (brick & tile; pottery & porc.) 741.684-026
ceramics technician (protective dev.) 712.381-042
CERAMICS TEST ENGINEER (profess. & kin.) 006.061-022
cereal miller (grain-feed mills) 521.682-022
cereal popper (grain-feed mills) 523.382-010
CERTIFICATION AND SELECTION SPECIALIST (education) 099.167-010
Certified Financial Planner (profess. & kin.) 250.257-014
CERTIFIED MEDICATION TECHNICIAN (medical ser.) 355.374-014
certified public accountant (profess. & kin.)   see ACCOUNTANT, CERTIFIED PUBLIC
certified welder (welding)   see WELDER, CERTIFIED
CHAIN BUILDER, LOOM CONTROL (textile) 683.381-010
chainer (textile) 683.381-010
Chain-Forming-Machine Operator (forging) 612.462-010
Chain-Hoist Operator (mine & quarry) 921.663-026
chain-machine operator (button & notion) 692.685-270
CHAIN MAKER, HAND (jewelry-silver.) 700.381-010
chain maker, loom control (textile) 683.381-010
CHAIN MAKER, MACHINE (jewelry-silver.) 700.684-022
Chain Mender (jewelry-silver.) 735.687-014
Chain-Mortiser Operator (woodworking) 665.482-014
CHAIN OFFBEARER (saw. & plan.) 669.686-018
chain pegger (textile) 683.381-010
CHAIN REPAIRER (carpet & rug) 683.684-010
chain-saw mechanic (any industry) 625.281-030
CHAIN SAW OPERATOR (chemical; logging; millwork-plywood) 454.687-010
chain splitter (textile) 683.381-010
CHAINSTITCH SEWING MACHINE OPERATOR (garment) 786.682-054
CHAIN-TESTING-MACHINE OPERATOR (forging) 616.685-010
Chair Inspector (furniture) 763.687-026
CHAIR INSPECTOR AND LEVELER (furniture) 763.687-014
Chairperson, Scholarship And Loan Committee (education) 090.117-030
chair-post-machine operator (furniture) 669.682-022
Chair-Spring Assembler (furniture) 780.684-098
chair trimmer (furniture) 780.684-034
CHAIR UPHOLSTERER (furniture) 780.684-034
CHALK CUTTER (pen & pencil) 733.687-022
chalker, soles (boot & shoe) 788.687-010
CHALK-EXTRUDING-MACHINE OPERATOR (pen & pencil) 575.685-018
CHALK-MOLDING-MACHINE OPERATOR (pen & pencil) 575.685-022
Chamfering-Machine Operator (clock & watch) 606.685-030

CHAMFERING-MACHINE OPERATOR I

CHAMFERING-MACHINE OPERATOR I (ordnance) 606.685-014
CHAMFERING-MACHINE OPERATOR II (ordnance) 606.685-018
Champagne Maker (beverage) 183.161-014
chancellor (education) 090.117-034
Chandelier Maker (light. fix.) 600.380-010
Change-Booth Cashier (amuse. & rec.) 211.462-010
CHANGE-HOUSE ATTENDANT (any industry) 358.687-010
Change-of-Address Clerk (clerical) 206.387-034
changeover operator (carpet & rug) 683.687-030
CHANGE PERSON (amuse. & rec.) 211.467-034
Channel Cementer, Insole, Machine (boot & shoe) 690.686-018
Channel Cementer, Outsole, Machine (boot & shoe) 690.686-018
CHANNELER, INSOLE (boot & shoe) 690.685-086
Channeler, Outsole (boot & shoe) 690.685-086
channeling-machine operator (mine & quarry) 930.383-010
CHANNELING-MACHINE RUNNER (mine & quarry) 930.383-010
Channel Installer (struct. metal) 809.684-010
CHANNEL INSTALLER (wood. container) 764.687-046
channel-lip stiffener, insoles (boot & shoe) 788.687-062
CHANNEL OPENER, OUTSOLES (boot & shoe) 690.685-082
Channel Rebuilder (smelt. & refin.) 630.684-010
Channel Rougher (boot & shoe) 690.685-046
channel turner (boot & shoe) 690.685-082
chaperon (any industry) 187.167-186
CHAPERON (personal ser.) 359.667-010
Chaplain (profess. & kin.) 120.107-010
Character Actor (amuse. & rec.) 150.047-010
Character Actress (amuse. & rec.) 150.047-010
Charcoal-Briquette-Machine Operator (fabrication, nec) 549.662-010
CHARCOAL BURNER, BEEHIVE KILN (chemical) 563.682-010
charcoal unloader (chemical) 569.686-034
CHAR-CONVEYOR TENDER (sugar & conf.) 529.685-050
Char Conveyor Tender, Cellar (sugar & conf.) 529.685-050
CHAR-DUST CLEANER AND SALVAGER (sugar & conf.) 529.687-038
CHAR-FILTER OPERATOR (sugar & conf.) 521.365-010
CHAR-FILTER-OPERATOR HELPER (sugar & conf.) 521.687-034
CHAR-FILTER-TANK TENDER, HEAD (grain-feed mills) 521.665-010
charge-account authorizer (clerical) 249.367-022
CHARGE-ACCOUNT CLERK (clerical) 205.367-014
charge-account identification clerk (retail trade) 241.367-030
Charge-Accounts-Audit Clerk (clerical) 210.382-010
charge attendant (medical ser.) 355.377-014
charge-gang weigher (nonfer. metal) 509.687-022
charge loader (oils & grease) 921.685-030
CHARGE-MACHINE OPERATOR (chemical) 921.662-014
CHARGE PREPARATION TECHNICIAN (electron. comp.) 590.384-010
charger (chemical) 558.687-010
charger (oils & grease) 521.685-242
charger (steel & rel.) 504.665-014
charger (steel & rel.) 512.683-010
charger-car operator (steel & rel.) 519.683-014
CHARGER I (jewelry-silver.) 740.684-010
CHARGER II (jewelry-silver.) 700.687-026
CHARGER-OPERATOR HELPER (steel & rel.) 504.686-010
CHARGER-OPERATOR (steel & rel.) 504.665-014
charging-board operator (svc. ind. mach.) 827.485-010
charging-car operator (steel & rel.) 519.683-014
Charging-Crane Operator I (foundry; steel & rel.) 921.663-010
Charging-Crane Operator II (foundry; steel & rel.) 921.663-042
CHARGING-MACHINE OPERATOR (steel & rel.) 512.683-010
charging manipulator (forging) 612.683-010
charging operator (chemical) 559.565-010
Charging-Plug Placer (elec. equip.) 727.687-026
CHAR PULLER (grain-feed mills; sugar & conf.) 521.687-030
charrer (wood. container) 764.684-014
charrer helper (wood. container) 764.687-034
charring-room worker, barrel (wood. container) 764.684-014
charring-room-worker helper, barrel (wood. container) 764.687-034
CHART CALCULATOR (utilities) 214.487-010
CHART CHANGER (clerical) 221.584-010
CHART CLERK (clerical) 221.382-010
chart clerk (petrol. refin.; pipe lines; utilities) 216.685-010
Chart Clerk, Chief (clerical) 221.132-010
chart collector (clerical) 221.584-010
CHARTER (amuse. & rec.) 249.367-018
Charter-Boat Operator (amuse. & rec.) 911.663-010
charter representative (motor trans.) 214.362-030
Charting Clerk (medical ser.) 245.362-010
CHASER (jewelry-silver.) 704.381-010
chaser (jewelry-silver.) 700.381-034
CHASER (logging) 921.667-014
chaser apprentice (jewelry-silver.) 700.381-038
chaser helper (jewelry-silver.) 700.687-050
CHASER, TAR (steel & rel.) 549.687-010
chassis driver (auto. mfg.) 806.283-014

Chassis Inspector (auto. mfg.) 806.687-018
Chassis Inspector (automotive ser.) 620.281-030
chassis mechanic (automotive ser.) 620.281-038
CHAUFFEUR (any industry) 913.663-010
CHAUFFEUR (domestic ser.) 359.673-010
Chauffeur, Airport Limousine (motor trans.) 913.463-018
CHAUFFEUR, FUNERAL CAR (personal ser.) 359.673-014
chauffeur, motorbus (motor trans.) 913.463-010
check-and-transfer beader (any industry) 509.687-014
CHECK CASHIER (business ser.) 211.462-026
check clerk (clerical) 209.687-010
check clerk (r.r. trans.) 209.367-054
checker (auto. mfg.) 806.687-018
checker (beverage) 522.687-010
CHECKER (chemical) 559.165-010
checker (clerical) 221.587-030
checker (electron. comp.) 726.684-022
checker (furniture) 739.687-110
CHECKER (laundry & rel.) 369.687-014
CHECKER (motor trans.) 919.687-010
checker (photofinishing) 976.687-014
checker (rubber reclaim.) 914.665-010
checker (stonework) 670.384-010
CHECKER (textile) 221.587-010
CHECKER, BAKERY PRODUCTS (bakery products) 222.487-010
CHECKER, DUMP GROUNDS (business ser.) 219.367-010
checkerer, hand (ordnance) 761.381-034
CHECKER, FILM TESTS (photo. appar.) 714.687-010
CHECKER I (clerical) 222.687-010
CHECKER II (clerical) 209.687-010
CHECKER-IN (boot & shoe) 221.587-014
CHECKERING-MACHINE ADJUSTER (ordnance) 669.360-010
checkering-machine operator (ordnance) 665.685-034
checker, product design (auto. mfg.) 017.261-010
Check Grader (woodworking) 669.687-030
Check Imprinter (print. & pub.) 651.362-010
checking clerk (clerical) 222.687-018
checking department supervisor (photofinishing) 976.137-014
Check Inspector (electron. comp.) 726.381-010
Checkout Mechanic, Hydraulic And Rigging (aircraft mfg.) 806.261-050
CHECK PILOT (air trans.) 196.263-022
CHECKROOM ATTENDANT (any industry) 358.677-010
CHECKROOM CHIEF (any industry) 358.137-010
check viewer (mine & quarry) 168.267-074
CHECK WEIGHER (ordnance) 737.687-026
CHECK WRITER (retail trade) 219.382-010
CHEESE BLENDER (dairy products) 520.487-010
cheese cooker (dairy products) 529.361-018
CHEESE CUTTER (dairy products) 529.585-010
cheese cutter (tobacco) 521.685-298
CHEESE GRADER (dairy products) 529.387-010
CHEESEMAKER (dairy products) 529.361-018
CHEESEMAKER HELPER (dairy products) 529.682-014
cheese-pancake roller (food prep., nec) 520.687-014
Cheese Production Supervisor (dairy products) 529.131-014
CHEESE SPRAYER (sugar & conf.) 524.685-014
CHEF (hotel & rest.) 313.131-014
chef (r.r. trans.) 315.381-018
chef assistant (hotel & rest.) 313.131-026
Chef, Broiler Or Fry (hotel & rest.) 313.131-014
chef de cuisine (hotel & rest.) 187.161-010
CHEF DE FROID (hotel & rest.) 313.281-010
chef, department (hotel & rest.)　　　see SPECIALTY CHEF
Chef, French (hotel & rest.) 313.131-014
Chef, German (hotel & rest.) 313.131-014
chef, head (hotel & rest.) 187.161-010
Chef, Italian (hotel & rest.) 313.131-014
Chef, PASSENGER VESSEL (water trans.) 315.137-010
Chef, Saucier (hotel & rest.) 313.131-014
chef, station (hotel & rest.)　　　see SPECIALTY CHEF
chef, under (hotel & rest.) 313.131-026
chemical-building worker (plastic-synth.)　　　see CHEMICAL DEPARTMENT WORKER
chemical checker (textile) 582.587-010
CHEMICAL COMPOUNDER (chemical) 559.682-018
CHEMICAL-COMPOUNDER HELPER (chemical) 550.687-010
CHEMICAL-DEPARTMENT WORKER (plastic-synth.) term
chemical dependency attendant (medical ser.) 355.377-014
CHEMICAL DESIGN ENGINEER, PROCESSES (profess. & kin.) 008.061-014
CHEMICAL ENGINEER (profess. & kin.) 008.061-018
CHEMICAL-ENGINEERING TECHNICIAN (profess. & kin.) 008.261-010
Chemical-Engineering Technician, Prototype-Development (profess. & kin.) 008.261-010
CHEMICAL-EQUIPMENT SALES ENGINEER (profess. & kin.) 008.151-010

CHEMICAL-ETCHING PROCESSOR (aircraft mfg.) 704.381-014
CHEMICAL-LABORATORY CHIEF (profess. & kin.) 022.161-010
CHEMICAL-LABORATORY TECHNICIAN (profess. & kin.) 022.261-010
chemical-milling processor (aircraft mfg.) 704.381-014
Chemical Mixer (pharmaceut.) 550.685-090
CHEMICAL MIXER (photofinishing) 550.485-010
CHEMICAL MIXER (textile) 550.585-018
chemical operator (chemical) 590.464-010
chemical operator (plastic-synth.) see CHEMICAL DEPARTMENT WORKER
chemical operator (smelt. & refin.) 511.382-010
CHEMICAL OPERATOR I (chemical) term
CHEMICAL OPERATOR II (chemical) 558.685-062
CHEMICAL OPERATOR III (chemical) 559.382-018
CHEMICAL PREPARER (chemical; electron. comp.) 550.685-030
CHEMICAL-PROCESSING SUPERVISOR (pharmaceut.) 559.130-010
CHEMICAL-RADIATION TECHNICIAN (government ser.) 015.261-010
CHEMICAL RECLAMATION EQUIPMENT OPERATOR (electron. comp.) 558.685-058
CHEMICAL RESEARCH ENGINEER (profess. & kin.) 008.061-022
CHEMICAL-STRENGTH TESTER (textile) 582.587-010
CHEMICAL-TEST ENGINEER (profess. & kin.) 008.061-026
chemical weigher (any industry) 550.684-014
CHEMIST (profess. & kin.) 022.061-010
Chemist, Analytical (profess. & kin.) 022.061-010
chemist, biological (profess. & kin.) 041.061-026
Chemist, Clinical (profess. & kin.) 041.061-026
Chemist, Enzymes (profess. & kin.) 041.061-026
CHEMIST, FOOD (profess. & kin.) 022.061-014
Chemist, Inorganic (profess. & kin.) 022.061-010
CHEMIST, INSTRUMENTATION (profess. & kin.) 022.261-018
Chemist, Organic (profess. & kin.) 022.061-010
Chemist, Pharmaceutical (profess. & kin.) 041.061-026
Chemist, Physical (profess. & kin.) 022.061-010
Chemist, Proteins (profess. & kin.) 041.061-026
Chemist, Steroids (profess. & kin.) 041.061-026
CHEMIST, WASTEWATER-TREATMENT PLANT (profess. & kin.) 022.261-022
CHEMIST, WATER PURIFICATION (waterworks) 022.281-014
chenille-machine operator (carpet & rug; tex. prod., nec) 687.682-014
chenille-machine operator (carpet & rug; textile) 687.685-018
CHERRY CUTTER (can. & preserv.) 524.687-010
Cherry Dipper (sugar & conf.) 524.684-010
Cherry Grower (agriculture) 403.161-010
Cherry Packer (agriculture; wholesale tr.) 920.687-134
CHERRY-PICKER OPERATOR (construction) 921.663-014
Cherry Sorter (agriculture; can. & preserv.; wholesale tr.) 529.687-186
Chestnut Tanner (leather mfg.) 582.482-018
CHEST-PAINTING AND SEALING SUPERVISOR (ordnance) 749.137-010
chest-painting leader (ordnance) 749.137-010
chicken-and-fish cleaner (hotel & rest.) 316.684-010
Chicken Cleaner (meat products) 525.687-074
Chicken Dresser (meat products) 525.687-070
chicken fancier (agriculture) 411.161-014
Chicken Vaccinator (agriculture) 411.684-014
CHICK GRADER (agriculture) 411.687-010
CHICK SEXER (agriculture) 411.687-014
CHICLE-GRINDER FEEDER (sugar & conf.) 521.686-018
chief (any industry) see SUPERVISOR
Chief, Airport Safety And Security (government ser.) 375.167-034
CHIEF BANK EXAMINER (government ser.) 160.167-046
chief chemist (profess. & kin.) 022.161-010
chief clerk (any industry) 169.167-034
chief clerk (government ser.) 375.137-022
CHIEF CLERK, MEASUREMENT DEPARTMENT (petrol. & gas; pipe lines) 221.132-010
CHIEF CLERK, PRINT SHOP (clerical) 207.137-010
Chief Clerk, Shelter (nonprofit org.) 249.137-010
chief clerk, yard office (r.r. trans.) 910.367-014
CHIEF COMPUTER PROGRAMMER (profess. & kin.) 030.167-010
chief console operator (clerical) 213.132-010
CHIEF CONTROLLER (government ser.) 193.167-010
Chief Controller, Center (government ser.) 193.167-010
Chief Controller, Station (government ser.) 193.167-010
Chief Controller, Tower (government ser.) 193.167-010
Chief Cruiser (forestry) 459.387-010
CHIEF DISPATCHER (petrol. & gas) 939.137-010
chief dispatcher (utilities) 952.137-010
chief, dog license inspector (nonprofit org.) 379.137-014
CHIEF DRAFTER (profess. & kin.) 007.261-010
Chief Electroencephalographic Technologist (medical ser.) 078.362-022
chief engineer (any industry) 959.131-010
chief engineer (government ser.) 373.117-010
CHIEF ENGINEER (petrol. & gas; pipe lines) 010.167-010
chief engineer (profess. & kin.) 019.167-014

chief engineer, broadcasting operations (radio-tv broad.) 003.167-030
Chief Engineer, Drilling And Recovery (petrol. & gas) 010.167-010
Chief Engineer, Pipe-Line (petrol. & gas) 010.167-010
Chief Engineer, Production (petrol. & gas) 010.167-010
CHIEF ENGINEER, RESEARCH (petrol. & gas) 010.161-010
CHIEF ENGINEER, WATERWORKS (waterworks) 005.167-010
CHIEF, FISHERY DIVISION (government ser.) 188.117-018
chief gauger (petrol. & gas; petrol. refin.; pipe lines) 914.134-010
chief information officer (profess. & kin.) 109.067-010
CHIEF INSPECTOR (office machines) 706.131-018
Chief Librarian, Branch (library) 100.127-010
CHIEF LIBRARIAN, BRANCH OR DEPARTMENT (library) 100.127-010
Chief Librarian, Circulation Department (library) 100.127-010
Chief Librarian, Extension Department (library) 100.127-010
Chief Librarian, General Reference Department (library) 100.127-010
Chief Librarian, Music Department (library) 100.127-010
Chief Librarian, Periodical Reading Room (library) 100.127-010
Chief Librarian, Readers' Advisory Service (library) 100.127-010
Chief Librarian, Work With Blind (library) 100.127-010
CHIEF LOAD DISPATCHER (utilities) 952.137-010
chief lock-operator (water trans.) 911.131-014
chief-maintenance supervisor (utilities) 862.137-014
chief, nuclear medicine technologist (medical ser.) 078.131-010
Chief of Field Operations (government ser.) 373.117-010
CHIEF OF NUCLEAR MEDICINE (medical ser.) 070.117-010
CHIEF OF PARTY (profess. & kin.) 018.167-010
chief of production (real estate) 186.167-090
chief of vital statistics (government ser.) 188.167-022
chief operating engineer (utilities) 184.167-166
CHIEF OPERATOR (chemical) 558.260-010
chief operator (petrol. refin.) 549.132-030
Chief Operator, Ammonium Sulfate (chemical) 558.260-010
chief operator, hydroformer (petrol. refin.) 549.132-030
Chief Operator, Purification And Reaction (chemical) 558.260-010
Chief Operator, Reformer (chemical) 558.260-010
Chief Operator, Synthesis (chemical) 558.260-010
Chief Ophthalmic Technician (medical ser.) 078.361-038
CHIEF PETROLEUM ENGINEER (petrol. & gas) 010.161-014
CHIEF PILOT (air trans.) 196.167-010
Chief Planner (profess. & kin.) 199.167-014
Chief Polysomnographic Technician (medical ser.) 078.362-042
chief power dispatcher (utilities) 184.167-150
CHIEF PROJECTIONIST (motion picture) 960.132-010
chief, radiology (medical ser.) 078.162-010
chief, relay tester (utilities) 729.131-014
Chief, Reservoir Engineering (petrol. & gas) 010.167-010
chief steward/stewardess (hotel & rest.) 310.137-018
chief technician (any industry) 823.131-010
CHIEF TECHNOLOGIST, NUCLEAR MEDICINE (medical ser.) 078.131-010
chief, vendor quality (any industry) 012.167-062
CHIEF WARDEN (government ser.) 188.167-018
child-care attendant (any industry) 359.677-010
CHILD-CARE ATTENDANT, SCHOOL (personal ser.) 355.674-010
child-care leader (any industry) 359.677-018
child-day-care center worker (any industry) 359.677-018
Child Day Care Program Supervisor (government ser.) 168.167-090
child development specialist (social ser.) 195.227-018
CHILD MONITOR (domestic ser.) 301.677-010
Child Psychologist (profess. & kin.) 045.061-010
CHILDREN'S ATTENDANT (amuse. & rec.) 349.677-018
CHILDREN'S LIBRARIAN (library) 100.167-018
CHILDREN'S TUTOR (domestic ser.) 099.227-010
Children's Tutor, Nursery (domestic ser.) 099.227-010
children's zoo caretaker (amuse. & rec.; museums) 412.674-014
CHILD SUPPORT OFFICER (government ser.) 195.267-022
Chili-Pepper Grinder (food prep., nec) 521.685-326
CHILLER OPERATOR (chemical) 551.685-042
CHILLER TENDER (meat products) 523.585-014
CHILLING-HOOD OPERATOR (meat products) 523.685-018
Chimney Builder, Brick (construction) 861.381-018
Chimney Builder, Reinforced Concrete (construction) 801.361-014
chimney cleaner (any industry) 891.687-010
CHIMNEY ERECTOR (construction) term
CHIMNEY REPAIRER (business ser.) 899.364-010
Chimney Repairer (construction) 869.381-030
CHIMNEY SUPERVISOR, BRICK (construction) 861.131-014
CHIMNEY SWEEP (any industry) 891.687-010
Chinchilla Farmer (agriculture) 410.161-014
CHINCHILLA-MACHINE OPERATOR (textile) 585.685-022
CHIN-STRAP CUTTER (hat & cap) 686.685-010
Chin-Strap Maker (hat & cap) 699.685-018
Chin-Strap Sewer (hat & cap) 784.682-014
chip (amuse. & rec.) 343.467-010
chip applier (paint & varnish; print. & pub.) 641.685-030
CHIP-APPLYING-MACHINE TENDER (paint & varnish; print. & pub.) 641.685-030

CHIP-BIN CONVEYOR TENDER (chemical; paper & pulp) 921.685-022
Chip-Crusher Operator (nonfer. metal) 519.686-010
chip deliverer (chemical; paper & pulp) 921.685-022
Chip Drier (nonfer. metal) 519.686-010
chip mixer (wood prod., nec) 560.465-010
CHIP-MIXING-MACHINE OPERATOR (wood prod., nec) 560.465-010
CHIPPER (chemical; paper & pulp; saw. & plan.) 564.685-014
chipper (logging) 564.662-010
chipper (musical inst.) 730.684-026
chipper (paint & varnish) 559.684-022
Chipper I (any industry) 705.684-030
Chipper II (any industry) 809.684-026
CHIPPING-MACHINE OPERATOR (wood prod., nec) 564.682-010
chip separator (ordnance) 694.585-010
chip-silo tender (chemical; paper & pulp) 921.685-022
CHIP TESTER (paper & pulp) 539.387-010
CHIP TUNER (musical inst.) 730.684-026
CHIP UNLOADER (paper & pulp) 921.663-018
CHIP WASHER (beverage) 522.686-010
chiropodist (medical ser.) 079.101-022
chiropractic (medical ser.) 079.101-010
CHIROPRACTOR (medical ser.) 079.101-010
CHIROPRACTOR ASSISTANT (medical ser.) 079.364-010
Chiseler, Head (meat products) 525.684-034
Chisel Grinder (any industry) 603.664-010
Chisel-Mortiser Operator (woodworking) 665.482-014
chisel worker (stonework) 771.381-014
CHLORINATOR OPERATOR (chemical) 558.382-030
Chlorine-Cell Tender (chemical) 558.382-026
chlorine operator (chemical) 559.362-018
chlorine-plant operator (chemical) 559.362-018
Chlorobutadiene-Scrubber Operator (chemical) 559.382-034
CHLOROPRENE OPERATOR (chemical) term
Chocolate Coater (sugar & conf.) 524.684-010
chocolate-coating-machine operator (bakery products) 524.685-026
Chocolate-Drops-Machine Operator (sugar & conf.) 520.685-078
chocolate finisher (sugar & conf.) 521.682-034
chocolate-finisher operator (sugar & conf.) 521.682-034
Chocolate-Machine Operator (bakery products; sugar & conf.) 524.382-014
chocolate maker (bakery products; grain-feed mills) 523.685-022
chocolate-mixer operator (bakery products; grain-feed mills) 523.685-022
Chocolate Molder (sugar & conf.) 520.687-018
CHOCOLATE MOLDER, MACHINE (sugar & conf.) 529.685-054
Chocolate-Peanut Coating-Machine Operator (sugar & conf.) 524.382-010
CHOCOLATE-PRODUCTION-MACHINE OPERATOR (sugar & conf.) 529.382-014
chocolate refiner (sugar & conf.) 521.682-034
chocolate-refining roller (sugar & conf.) 521.682-034
CHOCOLATE TEMPERER (bakery products; grain-feed mills) 523.685-022
CHOCOLATE TEMPERER (sugar & conf.) 523.682-010
choir leader (profess. & kin.) 152.047-010
CHOKE REAMER (ordnance) 606.685-022
CHOKE SETTER (logging) 921.687-014
chop-and-frame operator (button & notion) 692.685-034
CHOPPED-STRAND OPERATOR (textile) 680.685-022
CHOPPER (chemical) 564.687-010
chopper (hat & cap) 585.685-046
chopper (logging) 454.384-010
chopper and cracker feeder (rubber goods; rubber reclaim.) 555.685-030
chopper feeder (textile) 680.685-102
CHOPPING-MACHINE OPERATOR (meat products) 520.685-066
CHORAL DIRECTOR (profess. & kin.) 152.047-010
CHOREOGRAPHER (amuse. & rec.) 151.027-010
chore tender (agriculture) 421.687-010
Chorus Dancer (amuse. & rec.) 151.047-010
CHRISTIAN SCIENCE NURSE (profess. & kin.) 129.107-010
CHRISTIAN SCIENCE PRACTITIONER (profess. & kin.) 129.107-014
CHRISTMAS-TREE CONTRACTOR (any industry) 162.117-010
CHRISTMAS-TREE FARM WORKER (forestry) 451.687-010
CHRISTMAS-TREE GRADER (forestry) 451.687-014
Chrome Cleaner (any industry) 709.687-010
Chrome-Tanning-Drum Operator (leather mfg.) 582.482-018
Chromium Plater (electroplating) 500.380-010
CHRONOGRAPH OPERATOR (ordnance) 739.484-010
CHRONOMETER ASSEMBLER AND ADJUSTER (clock & watch) 715.381-038
CHRONOMETER-BALANCE-AND-HAIRSPRING ASSEMBLER (clock & watch) 715.381-042
Chuck Boner (meat products) 525.684-010
CHUCKING-AND-BORING-MACHINE OPERATOR (furniture) 669.682-022
CHUCKING-AND-SAWING-MACHINE OPERATOR (woodworking) 669.682-026
chucking-lathe operator (machine shop) 604.380-010
CHUCKING-MACHINE OPERATOR (woodworking) 665.382-010

Chucking-Machine Setter, Multiple Spindle, Vertical (machine shop) 604.380-014
CHUCKING-MACHINE SET-UP OPERATOR (machine shop) 604.380-010
CHUCKING-MACHINE SET-UP OPERATOR, MULTIPLE SPINDLE, VERTICAL (machine shop) 604.380-014
Chucking-Machine Set-Up Operator, Tool (machine shop) 604.280-022
CHURNER (oils & grease) 520.565-010
CHURN OPERATOR, MARGARINE (oils & grease) 520.685-070
CHURN TENDER (plastic-synth.) 550.685-034
chute blaster (mine & quarry; smelt. & refin.) 933.687-010
chute feeder (millwork-plywood; paper & pulp; saw. & plan.) 921.686-022
chute feeder (tobacco) 529.686-038
CHUTE LOADER (mine & quarry) 932.687-010
chute tapper (mine & quarry; smelt. & refin.) 933.687-010
chute worker (construction)   see WHEELER
Chute Worker (laundry & rel.) 361.687-018
Ciaio-Counter Molder (boot & shoe) 690.685-102
Ciaio-Lumite Injector (boot & shoe) 690.685-278
cicerone (amuse. & rec.; personal ser.) 353.363-010
cigar bander, hand (tobacco) 920.687-030
CIGAR BRANDER (tobacco) 920.685-046
cigarette and assembly-machine inspector (tobacco) 529.666-014
cigarette and assembly machine operator (tobacco) 529.685-066
CIGARETTE-AND-FILTER CHIEF INSPECTOR (tobacco) 529.367-010
Cigarette-Boxing-Machine Operator (tobacco) 920.665-010
Cigarette-Carton Sealer (tobacco) 920.685-074
cigarette examiner (tobacco) 529.567-010
CIGARETTE-FILTER-MAKING-MACHINE OPERATOR (tobacco) 529.685-062
CIGARETTE INSPECTOR (tobacco) 529.567-010
CIGARETTE-LIGHTER REPAIRER (any industry) 709.684-034
cigarette-making examiner (tobacco) 529.567-010
CIGARETTE-MAKING-MACHINE CATCHER (tobacco) 529.666-014
CIGARETTE-MAKING-MACHINE-HOPPER FEEDER (tobacco) 529.686-018
CIGARETTE-MAKING-MACHINE OPERATOR (tobacco) 529.685-066
CIGARETTE-PACKAGE EXAMINER (tobacco) 920.667-010
CIGARETTE-PACKING-MACHINE OPERATOR (tobacco) 920.685-050
CIGARETTE TESTER (tobacco) 529.387-014
CIGARETTE VENDOR (hotel & rest.) 291.457-010
cigar-head holer (tobacco) 529.685-058
cigar-head pegger (tobacco) 529.685-058
cigar-head perforator (tobacco) 529.685-058
CIGAR-HEAD PIERCER (tobacco) 529.685-058
cigar-head puncher (tobacco) 529.685-058
cigar-head stringer (tobacco) 529.685-058
CIGAR INSPECTOR (tobacco) 529.687-042
CIGAR MAKER (tobacco) 790.684-014
CIGAR MAKER, LONG-FILLER MACHINE (tobacco) term
CIGAR PACKER (tobacco) 790.687-014
cigar packer and grader (tobacco) 790.687-014
cigar packer and picker (tobacco) 790.687-014
cigar packer and shader (tobacco) 790.687-014
cigar packer and sorter (tobacco) 790.687-014
cigar-packing examiner (tobacco) 529.687-042
cigar patcher (tobacco) 790.684-018
cigar roller (tobacco) 790.684-022
cigar sorter (tobacco) 790.687-014
Cigar-Tobacco Rehandler (tobacco) 522.687-026
CIGAR-WRAPPER TENDER, AUTOMATIC (tobacco) 529.685-286
Cinder-Block Mason (construction) 861.381-018
Cinder-Crane Operator I (foundry; steel & rel.) 921.663-010
Cinder-Crane Operator II (foundry; steel & rel.) 921.663-042
cinematographer (motion picture; radio-tv broad.) 143.062-010
cinetechnician (motion picture; photo. appar.) 714.281-018
cinetechnician supervisor (motion picture; photo. appar.) 714.131-010
Cinnamon Grinder (food prep., nec) 521.685-326
cipher expert (government ser.) 199.267-014
CIRCLE BEVELER (glass products) 673.685-034
CIRCLE-CUTTING-SAW OPERATOR (wood. container) 669.685-026
CIRCLE EDGER (glass products) 673.685-038
circuit board inspector (electron. comp.) 726.684-062
Circuit Breaker Assembler (elec. equip.) 729.687-010
Circuit-Breaker Mechanic (utilities) 829.261-018
Circuit-Breaker Supervisor (utilities) 829.131-014
circuit rider (wholesale tr.) 162.167-014
circuit walker (wholesale tr.) 162.167-014
Circular-Gang-Saw Operator (saw. & plan.) 667.682-030
Circular-Head-Saw Operator (saw. & plan.) 667.662-010
Circular-Knife Cutter, Machine (any industry) 781.684-014
Circular Knitter (knitting) 685.665-014
Circular-Knitter Helper (knitting) 685.686-014
Circular-Resaw Operator (saw. & plan.; wood. container) 667.682-058
Circular-Ripsaw Operator (woodworking) 667.682-066
Circular-Saw Filer (any industry) 701.381-014
CIRCULAR SAW OPERATOR (construction) 869.682-010

CLEARING-HOUSE CLERK (financial) 216.382-026
Clearing Inspector (office machines) 706.387-014
CLEARING SUPERVISOR (construction) 869.133-010
CLEAT FEEDER (wood. container) 669.687-010
Cleat Layer (wood. container) 669.686-014
Cleat Nailer (wood. container) 669.682-058
Cleat Notcher (wood. container) 669.382-010
cleat thrower (wood. container) 669.687-010
cleaver (jewelry-silver.) 770.381-014
CLERGY MEMBER (profess. & kin.) 120.107-010
CLERICAL-METHODS ANALYST (profess. & kin.) 161.267-010
clerk, cable transfer (tel. & tel.) 219.387-010
CLERK, GENERAL (clerical) 209.562-010
clerk, general office (clerical) 219.362-010
clerk guide (personal ser.) 359.573-010
CLERK-OF-SCALES (amuse. & rec.) 153.467-010
clerk-operator (tel. & tel.) 239.362-010
clerk, personal service bureau (tel. & tel.) 219.362-022
clerk, private wire-billing and control (tel. & tel.) 219.362-022
clerk, rating (tel. & tel.) 214.587-010
CLERK, ROUTE (tel. & tel.) 235.562-010
clerk-stenographer (clerical) 202.362-014
CLERK, TELEGRAPH SERVICE (tel. & tel.) 219.362-022
CLERK, TELEVISION PRODUCTION (radio-tv broad.) 221.367-086
clerk, travel reservations (clerical) 238.362-014
CLERK-TYPIST (clerical) 203.362-010
clicker (any industry) 699.682-022
clicker-machine operator (hat & cap) 686.685-038
clicker operator (any industry) 699.682-022
clicking-machine operator (any industry) 699.682-022
CLICKING-MACHINE OPERATOR (boot & shoe; glove & mit.; leather prod.) 789.382-010
CLINCHING-MACHINE OPERATOR (elec. equip.) 616.685-014
clinical counselor (profess. & kin.) 045.107-050
Clinical Engineer (profess. & kin.) 019.061-010
Clinical Instructor (education) 090.227-010
Clinical Pathologist (medical ser.) 070.061-010
CLINICAL PSYCHOLOGIST (profess. & kin.) 045.107-022
CLINICAL SOCIOLOGIST (profess. & kin.) 054.107-010
CLINICAL THERAPIST (profess. & kin.) 045.107-050
Clinical Transplant Coordinator (medical ser.) 079.151-010
clinical veterinarian (medical ser.) 073.061-030
clinic clerk (medical ser.) 205.362-018
CLIP-AND-HANGER ATTACHER (glass products) 739.684-038
clip baker (optical goods) 713.687-010
CLIP-BOLTER AND WRAPPER (metal prod., nec) 709.684-038
CLIP COATER (optical goods) 713.687-010
CLIP-LOADING-MACHINE ADJUSTER (ordnance) 694.362-010
CLIP-LOADING-MACHINE FEEDER (ordnance) 694.686-010
CLIPPER (any industry) 789.687-030
CLIPPER (boot & shoe) 753.687-010
clipper (carpet & rug) 781.684-046
CLIPPER (fabrication, nec) 739.685-022
clipper (hat & cap) 585.685-046
Clipper (laundry & rel.) 361.687-018
clipper and turner (any industry) 789.687-182
CLIPPER AND TURNER (furniture) 780.687-014
clipper, automatic (knitting) 684.686-010
CLIPPER, AUTOMATIC (millwork-plywood) 663.585-010
Clipper, Counters (rubber goods) 753.687-010
CLIPPER, MACHINE (knitting) 684.686-010
clipper offbearer (millwork-plywood) 663.686-018
Clipper, Outside Back Stay (rubber goods) 753.687-010
Clipper, Tongues (rubber goods) 753.687-010
clipping marker (business ser.) 249.387-022
clipping, stringing, and turning machine tender (tex. prod., nec) 689.585-018
Clip Riveter (metal prod., nec) 706.684-090
clip wrapper (metal prod., nec) 709.684-038
CLOCK ASSEMBLER (clock & watch) 715.684-058
CLOCKER (amuse. & rec.) 153.367-010
clocker (optical goods) 716.687-026
clockmaker (clock & watch) 715.281-010
clockmaker apprentice (clock & watch) 715.281-014
closer (boot & shoe) 690.682-082
Closer (glove & mit.) 784.682-010
Closer (metal prod., nec) 616.682-034
CLOSER (real estate) 186.167-074
Closer (toy-sport equip.) 787.682-054
closet builder (mfd. bldgs.) 869.684-038
Closing Supervisor (metal prod., nec) 691.130-014
Cloth-And-Leather-Department Supervisor (leather prod.) 783.132-010
CLOTH-BALE HEADER (textile) 782.687-018
Cloth Baler (textile) 920.685-010
cloth beamer (textile) 689.685-046
Cloth-Bin Packer (textile) 922.687-058

Cloth-Bleaching-Range Back-Tender (textile) 589.686-010
Cloth-Bleaching-Range Operator, Chief (textile) 589.562-010
Cloth-Bleaching-Range Tender (textile) 589.685-026
Cloth-Bleaching Supervisor (textile) 589.130-010
CLOTH-BOLT BANDER (textile) 920.587-010
Cloth-Brushing-And-Sueding Supervisor (textile) 589.130-010
cloth calender (nonmet. min.) 583.585-010
cloth changer (beverage) 529.667-014
cloth classer (textile) 689.387-010
Cloth-Colors Examiner (textile) 781.687-014
cloth-covered-helmet puller (hat & cap) 689.685-074
cloth coverer (hat & cap) 689.685-074
Cloth-Cutting Inspector (textile) 781.687-014
cloth-cutting-machine operator (any industry) 781.684-014
CLOTH DESIGNER (profess. & kin.) 142.061-014
Cloth-Desizing-Range Operator, Chief (textile) 589.562-010
Cloth-Desizing-Range Tender (textile) 589.685-026
CLOTH DOFFER (textile) 689.686-058
CLOTH-DOUBLING-AND-WINDING-MACHINE OPERATOR (textile) 689.685-050
CLOTH DRIER (knitting) 580.685-014
cloth drier (textile) 589.686-010
cloth-dry-can operator (textile) 581.685-022
Cloth-Dyeing-Range Operator, Chief (textile) 589.562-010
Cloth-Dyeing-Range Tender (textile) 589.685-026
cloth dyer (textile) 582.665-014
cloth dyer (textile) 582.582-010
CLOTH-EDGE SINGER (textile) 585.687-018
clothes designer (profess. & kin.) 142.061-018
Clothes-Drier Assembler (house. appl.) 827.684-010
Clothes-Drier Repairer (any industry) 827.261-010
clothes marker (laundry & rel.) 369.687-026
CLOTHESPIN-DRIER OPERATOR (woodworking) 563.685-014
CLOTHESPIN-MACHINE OPERATOR (woodworking) 667.686-010
clothes wringer (any industry) 581.685-038
CLOTH EXAMINER, HAND (narrow fabrics) 689.687-022
CLOTH EXAMINER, HAND (textile) 781.687-014
CLOTH EXAMINER, MACHINE (textile) 689.685-038
CLOTH FEEDER (textile) 589.686-014
CLOTH FINISHER (carpet & rug; textile) 589.130-010
Cloth-Finishing-Range Back-Tender (textile) 589.686-010
CLOTH-FINISHING-RANGE OPERATOR (textile) 589.665-014
CLOTH-FINISHING-RANGE OPERATOR, CHIEF (textile) 589.562-010
CLOTH-FINISHING-RANGE TENDER (textile) 589.685-026
CLOTH FOLDER (textile) term
CLOTH FOLDER, HAND (tex. prod., nec; textile) 589.687-014
cloth folder, machine (textile) 689.585-014
cloth folder, machine (textile) 689.685-078
CLOTH FRAMER (textile) 689.687-026
CLOTH GRADER (textile) 689.387-010
CLOTH-GRADER SUPERVISOR (textile) 689.134-010
cloth handler (textile) 689.686-058
Cloth Hauler (textile) 929.687-030
CLOTHING MAKER (garment) term
clothing operator (garment)   see CLOTHING MAKER
CLOTHING-PATTERN PREPARER (garment) 781.287-010
Clothing Sorter (nonprofit org.) 222.387-054
cloth inspector (carpet & rug; textile) 683.684-034
CLOTH INSPECTOR (knitting) 685.687-010
cloth inspector (textile) 689.685-038
Cloth Joiner, Tents (tex. prod., nec) 787.682-058
Cloth-Laminating Supervisor (textile) 589.130-010
cloth layer (any industry) 781.687-058
cloth layer-out (textile) 781.687-038
CLOTH MEASURER, MACHINE (garment; textile) 589.685-022
Cloth-Mercerizer Back-Tender (textile) 589.686-010
CLOTH-MERCERIZER OPERATOR (textile) 584.685-014
Cloth-Mercerizing Supervisor (textile) 589.130-010
Cloth-Napping Supervisor (textile) 589.130-010
Cloth Neutralizer (textile) 582.685-030
Cloth Numberer (tex. prod., nec) 787.682-022
cloth opener, hand (textile) 589.685-090
cloth pattern maker (profess. & kin.) 142.061-014
cloth picker (carpet & rug; textile) 689.684-010
cloth presser (textile) 584.685-042
CLOTH PRINTER (any industry) 652.382-010
Cloth Printer (ordnance) 651.685-022
CLOTH-PRINTER HELPER (any industry) 652.686-010
Cloth-Printer Helper (tex. prod., nec) 586.686-022
CLOTH-PRINTING INSPECTOR (textile) 652.567-010
Cloth-Printing-Machine-Operator Helper (tex. prod., nec) 589.687-026
CLOTH REELER (textile) 689.685-042
cloth-roll winder (textile) 689.685-046
CLOTH SANDER (textile) 581.685-010
Cloth-Seconds Sorter (textile) 789.687-146

CLOTH SHADER (garment; textile) 582.685-026
cloth shearer (carpet & rug; textile) 585.685-102
Cloth-Shearing Supervisor (textile) 589.130-010
cloth shrinker (textile) 587.685-018
CLOTH-SHRINKING-MACHINE OPERATOR (textile) 587.685-018
CLOTH-SHRINKING-MACHINE-OPERATOR HELPER (textile) 587.686-010
Cloth-Shrinking Supervisor (textile) 589.130-010
CLOTH-SHRINKING TESTER (textile) 587.384-010
cloth sponger (textile) 587.685-018
cloth spreader (any industry) 781.687-058
cloth spreader (knitting) 580.685-014
CLOTH SPREADER, SCREEN PRINTING (textile) 652.687-010
CLOTH-STOCK SORTER (tex. prod., nec; textile) 789.687-034
cloth stretcher (textile) 580.685-066
CLOTH TEARER (garment) 781.687-018
CLOTH TESTER (garment; textile) 029.381-010
CLOTH TESTER, QUALITY (textile) 689.384-010
Cloth Trimmer, Hand (textile) 781.687-070
CLOTH TRIMMER, MACHINE (textile) 585.685-026
Cloth Washer (any industry) 361.685-018
Cloth-Washer Back-Tender (textile) 589.686-010
CLOTH-WASHER OPERATOR (textile) 582.685-030
Cloth Weigher (knitting) 222.387-074
CLOTH WINDER (textile) 689.685-046
CLOWN (amuse. & rec.) 159.047-010
club former (toy-sport equip.) 732.381-018
Clubhouse Attendant (amuse. & rec.) 358.677-014
Cluster-Bore Operator (woodworking) 666.382-010
Clutch Assembler (motor-bicycles) 806.684-094
CLUTCH REBUILDER (automotive ser.) 620.684-022
coach (amuse. & rec.) 153.227-010
coach (retail trade)   see SPONSOR
Coach Cleaner (r.r. trans.) 919.687-014
COACH DRIVER (business ser.) 349.677-014
coach operator (motor trans.) 913.463-010
Coach-Player (amuse. & rec.) 153.117-010
COACH, PROFESSIONAL ATHLETES (amuse. & rec.) 153.227-010
coach wirer (auto. mfg.; vehicles, nec) 829.684-014
Coagulant Dipper (rubber goods) 556.685-030
COAGULATING-BATH MIXER (plastic-synth.) 550.684-010
coagulating-bath operator (plastic-synth.) 550.585-014
Coagulating-Drying Supervisor (plastic-synth.) 559.132-022
COAGULATION OPERATOR (plastic-synth.) 559.582-010
coagulator (plastic-synth.) 559.685-190
coal-and-ash supervisor (any industry) 921.137-010
Coal-Briquette-Machine Operator (fabrication, nec) 549.662-010
Coal-Conveyor Operator (any industry) 921.662-018
coal-cutting-machine operator (mine & quarry) 930.683-014
coal-drier operator (mine & quarry) 543.682-014
COAL-EQUIPMENT OPERATOR (utilities) 921.683-022
Coal Hauler (any industry) 902.683-010
coal inspector (mine & quarry) 579.484-010
Coal-Mine Inspector (mine & quarry) 168.267-074
Coal Passer (any industry) 929.687-030
COAL-PIPE-LINE OPERATOR (pipe lines) 914.362-010
Coal-Pulverizer Operator (any industry) 544.582-010
COAL SAMPLER (utilities) 922.687-038
coal-tower operator (water trans.) 921.683-074
coal-transport-and-mill operator (utilities) 544.665-010
COAL TRIMMER (water trans.) 911.687-010
COAL WASHER (mine & quarry) 541.382-010
coal-washer tender (mine & quarry) 541.382-010
COAL-YARD SUPERVISOR (any industry) 921.137-010
Coarse-Wire Drawer (nonfer. metal) 614.382-010
Coat Baster (garment; retail trade) 785.361-022
Coat Checker (any industry) 358.677-010
Coat Draper (garment) 781.684-026
Coated Fabric Cutter (tex. prod., nec) 699.682-026
COATER (business ser.) 503.685-010
coater (fabrication, nec) 590.685-014
COATER (pharmaceut.) 554.382-010
coater (photo. appar.) 534.582-010
coater (sugar & conf.) 524.382-010
COATER (textile) 584.682-010
coater (woodworking) 763.381-010
Coater, Asphalt (build. mat., nec) 554.682-022
COATER, BRAKE LININGS (nonmet. min.) 574.685-010
coater, carbon paper (pen & pencil) 534.682-014
coater, hand (wood prod., nec) 562.687-014
Coater Helper (tex. prod., nec) 586.686-022
COATER HELPER (textile) 584.665-010
COATER OPERATOR (any industry) 509.382-010
COATER OPERATOR (plastic-synth.) 554.585-014
COATER OPERATOR, INSULATION BOARD (wood prod., nec) 539.685-010
Coater, Slate (build. mat., nec) 554.682-022

COATER, SMOKING PIPE (fabrication, nec) 562.685-022
Coat Fitter (garment) 785.261-014
COAT-HANGER-SHAPER-MACHINE OPERATOR (woodworking) 669.685-034
COATING-AND-BAKING OPERATOR (any industry) 554.685-014
COATING-AND-EMBOSSING-UNIT OPERATOR (tex. prod., nec; textile) 583.682-010
COATING EQUIPMENT OPERATOR, PRINTED CIRCUIT BOARDS (electron. comp.) 590.685-066
Coating-Line Checker (paper & pulp; wood prod., nec) 539.667-010
COATING-MACHINE FEEDER (leather prod.) 690.686-022
Coating-Machine Helper (sugar & conf.) 529.686-034
coating-machine operator (any industry) 599.685-046
COATING-MACHINE OPERATOR (carpet & rug; tex. prod., nec) 584.562-010
COATING-MACHINE OPERATOR (fabrication, nec) 590.685-014
COATING-MACHINE OPERATOR (galvanizing) 501.362-010
COATING-MACHINE OPERATOR (paper & pulp; paper goods) 534.682-018
COATING-MACHINE OPERATOR (pen & pencil) 692.685-054
COATING-MACHINE OPERATOR (sugar & conf.) 524.382-010
COATING-MACHINE OPERATOR, HARDBOARD (paper goods; wood prod., nec) 534.682-022
COATING-MACHINE-OPERATOR HELPER (fabrication, nec) 590.686-010
Coating-Machine-Operator Helper (paper & pulp; paper goods) 534.686-010
Coating-Machine-Operator Helper (tex. prod., nec) 589.687-026
COATING-MACHINE OPERATOR I (tex. prod., nec) 584.382-010
COATING-MACHINE OPERATOR II (tex. prod., nec) 584.685-018
Coating-Machine Operator, Metal Tags And Signs (fabrication, nec) 554.685-014
coating mixer (tinware) 509.485-010
COATING-MIXER SUPERVISOR (paper & pulp) 530.132-010
COATING-MIXER TENDER (paper & pulp) 530.685-010
COATING OPERATOR (chemical) 550.585-022
COATING OPERATOR (grain-feed mills) 524.685-018
Coating Supervisor (tex. prod., nec) 589.130-014
coat-insulator operator (nonfer. metal) 691.682-018
Coat Ironer, Hand (garment) 363.684-018
COAT JOINER, LOCKSTITCH (garment) 786.682-058
coat-operator, insulator (nonfer. metal) 691.682-018
Coat Padder (garment; retail trade) 785.361-022
Coat Presser (any industry) 363.682-018
Coat-Repair Inspector (retail trade) 783.387-010
Coat Tailor (garment) 785.261-014
COBBLER (boot & shoe) 788.381-010
cobbler (personal ser.) 365.361-014
Cobbler, Mckay (boot & shoe) 788.381-010
Cobbler, Sole (boot & shoe) 788.381-010
Cobbler, Upper (boot & shoe) 788.381-010
Cob Borer (fabrication, nec) 669.685-094
COB SAWYER (fabrication, nec) 667.685-030
COCOA-BEAN CLEANER (sugar & conf.) 521.685-066
COCOA-BEAN-ROASTER HELPER (sugar & conf.) 523.666-010
COCOA-BEAN ROASTER I (sugar & conf.) 523.362-010
COCOA-BEAN ROASTER II (sugar & conf.) 523.380-010
COCOA-BUTTER-FILTER OPERATOR (sugar & conf.) 521.685-070
cocoa-milling-machine operator (sugar & conf.) 521.685-202
cocoa-mill operator (sugar & conf.) 521.685-074
COCOA-POWDER-MIXER OPERATOR (sugar & conf.) 520.685-074
COCOA-PRESS OPERATOR (sugar & conf.) 521.682-014
COCOA-ROOM OPERATOR (sugar & conf.) 521.685-074
Coconut-Candy Maker (sugar & conf.) 529.361-014
Coconut Cooker (sugar & conf.) 526.382-014
Coconut-Jelly Roller (sugar & conf.) 520.682-030
C.o.d. Audit Clerk (clerical) 210.382-010
C.O.D. Biller (clerical) 214.382-014
C.O.D. CLERK (clerical) 214.382-018
CODE AND TEST CLERK (financial) 209.667-018
code clerk (clerical) 203.582-018
CODE INSPECTOR (government ser.) 168.367-018
coding file clerk (clerical) 206.387-010
coffee blender (food prep., nec) 520.685-110
COFFEE GRINDER (food prep., nec) 521.685-078
COFFEE MAKER (hotel & rest.) 317.684-010
Coffee-Maker Servicer (any industry) 827.261-010
COFFEE ROASTER (food prep., nec) 523.682-014
COFFEE ROASTER, CONTINUOUS PROCESS (food prep., nec) 523.685-026
COFFEE-ROASTER HELPER (food prep., nec) 523.687-010
Coffee Server, Cafeteria Or Restaurant (hotel & rest.) 311.677-010
Coffee Taster (food prep., nec) 529.281-010
coffee-urn attendant (hotel & rest.) 317.684-010
COFFEE WEIGHER (food prep., nec) 529.687-046
Cofferdam-Construction Supervisor (construction) 860.131-018
coil assembler (elec. equip.) 721.484-010
COIL ASSEMBLER, MACHINE (furniture) 616.685-018
COIL BINDER (nonfer. metal) 619.687-010

coil cleaner (can. & preserv.) 529.687-054
COIL CONNECTOR (elec. equip.) 721.684-018
Coil-Connector Repairer (elec. equip.) 721.281-018
COILED-COIL INSPECTOR (light. fix.) 725.684-010
COILER (light. fix.) 725.687-014
coiler (metal prod., nec) 619.482-010
COILER (nonfer. metal; steel & rel.) 613.685-010
COILER (protective dev.) 712.687-014
COILER (tex. prod., nec) 681.685-034
coiler (wood. container) 619.682-034
coiler operator (nonfer. metal; steel & rel.) 613.685-010
COILER OPERATOR (steel & rel.) 613.382-010
coil fin assembler (svc. ind. mach.) 706.684-010
Coil Finisher (elec. equip.; electron. comp.) 724.684-026
Coil Former, Template (elec. equip.) 724.684-026
coil-machine operator (metal prod., nec) 616.485-014
Coil-Machine Supervisor (furniture) 616.130-022
coil placer (furniture) 780.684-098
COIL-REWIND-MACHINE OPERATOR (nonfer. metal) 619.685-030
COIL SHAPER (any industry) 724.684-022
Coil Sprayer (electron. comp.) 741.687-018
coil spreader (any industry) 724.684-022
coil-spring assembler (furniture) 780.684-098
Coil Strapper (steel & rel.) 920.587-018
Coil Taper (elec. equip.) 724.684-026
Coil Tester (elec. equip.) 729.684-058
coil tier (furniture) 616.685-018
COIL WINDER (elec. equip.; electron. comp.) 724.684-026
Coil Winder, Hand (electron. comp.) 724.684-026
Coil Winder, Open Slot (elec. equip.) 724.684-026
COIL WINDER, REPAIR (any industry) 724.381-014
Coil Winder, Strap (elec. equip.) 724.684-026
coin-box collector (business ser.; tel. & tel.) 292.687-010
COIN COLLECTOR (business ser.) 292.483-010
COIN-COUNTER-AND-WRAPPER (financial) 217.585-010
Coining-Press Operator (forging) 611.685-010
coining-press operator (nonfer. metal; steel & rel.) 617.685-038
COIN-MACHINE ASSEMBLER (svc. ind. mach.) 731.684-010
COIN-MACHINE COLLECTOR (business ser.; tel. & tel.) 292.687-010
COIN-MACHINE-COLLECTOR SUPERVISOR (clerical) 292.137-010
coin-machine operator (financial) 217.585-010
COIN-MACHINE-SERVICE REPAIRER (svc. ind. mach.) 639.281-014
Coin-Purse Assembler (leather prod.) 783.684-010
Coin-Purse Framer (leather prod.) 739.684-090
coin teller (financial) 217.585-010
Coin-Vault Guard (any industry) 372.667-034
COKE BURNER (steel & rel.) 543.682-010
COKE-CRUSHER OPERATOR (steel & rel.) 544.662-010
COKE DRAWER, HAND (steel & rel.) 543.687-010
COKE INSPECTOR (steel & rel.) 542.567-010
COKE LOADER (steel & rel.) 921.563-010
Coke-Oven Mason (steel & rel.) 861.381-026
Cold-Food Packer (hotel & rest.) 319.484-010
Cold-Header Operator (forging) 612.462-010
cold-meat chef (hotel & rest.) 313.361-034
Cold-Mill Inspector (steel & rel.) 619.381-010
Cold-Mill Operator (nonfer. metal) 613.462-018
COLD-MILL OPERATOR (steel & rel.) 613.662-018
Cold-Mill Supervisor (nonfer. metal) 619.132-014
Cold-Molding-Press Operator (plastic prod.) 556.682-014
Cold Patcher (construction) 869.687-026
COLD-PRESS LOADER (cutlery-hrdwr.) 701.687-018
cold-press operator (millwork-plywood) 569.685-058
COLD-ROLL INSPECTOR (plastic-synth.) 751.584-010
Cold-Roll Packer, Sheet Iron (steel & rel.) 921.663-042
cold-water machine operator (textile) 587.685-018
cold-working supervisor (ordnance) 619.130-010
cold-work operator (ordnance) 694.682-014
Collar-Band Creaser (garment) 583.685-042
COLLAR BASTER, JUMPBASTING (garment) 786.682-062
Collar Closer, Lockstitch (garment) 786.682-070
Collarette Separator (knitting) 789.687-030
Collar Feller (garment) 782.684-058
COLLAR FELLER, HANDSTITCHING MACHINE (garment) 786.682-066
collar-folder operator (garment) 580.685-018
Collar Fuser (garment) 363.682-018
Collar Knitter (knitting) 685.665-014
Collar Padder, Blindstitch (garment) 786.682-150
collar pointer (garment) 583.685-102
Collar Separator (knitting) 789.687-030
Collar Setter (garment; retail trade) 785.361-022
COLLAR SETTER, LOCKSTITCH (garment) 786.682-070
COLLAR SETTER, OVERLOCK (garment) 786.682-074
collar-shaper operator (garment) 580.685-018
Collar-Stay-Fuser Tender (garment) 583.685-046

Collar Tacker (garment) 782.684-058
collar-top turner (garment) 583.685-102
Collar Trimmer (garment) 699.685-014
Collar Trimmer (garment; knitting) 781.682-010
Collar Turner (garment) 789.687-182
COLLAR-TURNER OPERATOR (garment) 580.685-018
collateral placement officer (financial; insurance) 186.167-054
COLLATING-MACHINE OPERATOR (print. & pub.) 653.382-014
COLLATOR (print. & pub.) 653.687-010
COLLATOR, HAND (print. & pub.) 977.687-010
COLLATOR OPERATOR (clerical) 208.685-010
collection agent (clerical) 241.367-010
Collection-Card Clerk (clerical) 203.362-010
COLLECTION CLERK (clerical) 241.357-010
COLLECTION CLERK (financial) 216.362-014
collect-on-delivery clerk (clerical) 214.382-018
COLLECTOR (clerical) 241.367-010
COLLECTOR (knitting) 684.687-022
COLLET DRILLER (clock & watch) 715.684-062
COLLETER (clock & watch) 715.684-066
COLLET GLUER (clock & watch) 715.685-010
COLLET MAKER (clock & watch) 609.682-014
collier (chemical) 563.682-010
Colliery Clerk (mine & quarry) 219.362-010
collision estimator (automotive ser.) 620.261-018
color buffer (any industry) 705.684-014
COLOR-CARD MAKER (paint & varnish) 794.687-014
COLOR CHECKER, ROVING OR YARN (textile) 582.387-010
color consultant (profess. & kin.) 141.051-010
Color-Control Operator (print. & pub.) 651.362-030
Color Control Supervisor (chemical) 559.132-122
color corrector (print. & pub.) 972.281-010
color-depositing-machine tender (fabrication, nec) 652.665-014
COLOR DEVELOPER (paper & pulp) 530.261-010
COLOR DIPPER (textile) 652.687-014
Colored-Leather Setter (leather mfg.) 589.685-098
colored-liquid-plastic applier (glass products) 840.684-010
COLORER (brick & tile) 773.684-010
COLORER (print. & pub.) 970.681-014
COLORER, CITRUS FRUIT (wholesale tr.) 529.685-070
COLORER, HIDES AND SKINS (leather mfg.) 582.482-010
colorer, machine (leather mfg.) 582.482-010
COLOR EXPERT (profess. & kin.) 141.051-010
color finisher (leather prod.) 589.687-034
COLORING CHECKER (jewelry-silver.) 735.587-010
COLORING-MACHINE OPERATOR (hat & cap) 582.685-034
COLORIST (profess. & kin.) 022.161-014
colorist (profess. & kin.) 141.051-010
COLORIST, PHOTOGRAPHY (photofinishing) 970.381-010
Color-Laboratory Technician (photofinishing) 976.681-010
COLOR MAKER (chemical) 550.382-010
color maker (profess. & kin.) 022.161-014
COLOR MAKER (tex. prod., nec) 550.382-014
Color-Making Supervisor (chemical) 559.132-122
COLOR MATCHER (boot & shoe) 788.687-034
COLOR MATCHER (knitting) 582.261-010
COLOR MATCHER (leather mfg.; plastic-synth.; tex. prod., nec) 550.381-010
color matcher (paint & varnish) 550.381-014
color matcher (profess. & kin.) 022.161-014
COLOR MIXER (furniture) 589.464-010
color mixer (leather mfg.; plastic-synth.; tex. prod., nec) 550.381-010
Color Mixer (plastic prod.; plastic-synth.) 550.685-134
COLOR MIXER (textile) term
color-mixer assistant (textile) 550.687-014
color-mixer helper (any industry) 550.687-018
COLOR-PASTE MIXER (textile) 550.685-038
COLOR-PRINTER OPERATOR (photofinishing) 976.382-014
Color-Print Inspector (photofinishing) 976.687-014
Color Receiver (fabrication, nec) 555.685-050
color repairer (boot & shoe) 788.684-022
colors custodian (amuse. & rec.) 346.677-014
color-setting-machine operator (carpet & rug) 681.682-018
color shader (paint & varnish) 550.381-014
color-shop helper (any industry) 550.687-018
color specialist (profess. & kin.) 141.051-010
Color Sprayer (leather prod.) 584.687-014
COLOR STRAINER (textile) 550.687-014
Color-Straining-Bag Washer (textile) 361.685-018
color stripper (print. & pub.) 972.281-022
color-television console monitor (radio-tv broad.) 194.282-010
COLOR TESTER (smelt. & refin.) 511.667-014
color weigher (any industry) 550.684-014
COLOR WEIGHER (fabrication, nec) 590.487-010
Columnist (print. & pub.) 131.067-010
COLUMNIST/COMMENTATOR (print. & pub.; radio-tv broad.) 131.067-010

COLUMN PRECASTER (mfd. bldgs.) 869.667-010
Combat Operations Research Specialist (profess. & kin.) 059.167-010
COMBAT RIFLE CREWMEMBER (military ser.) 378.684-014
COMBAT SURVEILLANCE AND TARGET ACQUISITION CREW-MEMBER (military ser.) 378.687-010
COMBAT SURVEILLANCE AND TARGET ACQUISITION NON-COMMISSIONED OFFICER (military ser.) 378.161-010
comb capper (food prep., nec) 521.687-070
Comber (leather mfg.) 589.686-022
Comber (meat products) 525.587-014
Comber Fixer (textile) 689.260-010
COMBER TENDER (textile) 680.685-118
Combination Operator (radio-tv broad.) 159.147-014
combination presser (laundry & rel.) 363.682-014
combination-saw operator (woodworking) 667.682-086
Combination Valving-And-Sewing-Machine Operator (paper goods) 641.685-094
Combination-Window Installer (construction) 860.381-022
Combine Inspector (agric. equip.) 624.361-010
combiner (hat & cap) 584.685-026
COMBINER OPERATOR (paper & pulp; paper goods) 534.682-026
Combiner-Operator Helper (paper & pulp; paper goods) 534.686-010
combiner-sheet operator (paper & pulp; paper goods) 534.682-026
combing-machine tender (tex. prod., nec) 680.685-034
combining-machine operator (knitting; textile) 584.682-014
COMBINING-MACHINE OPERATOR (plastic-synth.) 554.685-018
COMB-MACHINE OPERATOR (fabrication, nec) 640.685-022
combustion analyst (glass mfg.) 572.360-010
COMEDIAN (amuse. & rec.) 159.047-014
Comedy Diver (amuse. & rec.) 159.347-018
Comedy Writer (profess. & kin.) 131.067-026
comic (amuse. & rec.) 159.047-014
COMMAND AND CONTROL SPECIALIST (military ser.) 235.662-010
COMMANDER, IDENTIFICATION AND RECORDS (government ser.) 375.137-010
COMMANDER, INTERNAL AFFAIRS (government ser.) 375.167-050
COMMANDER, POLICE RESERVES (government ser.) 375.137-030
Commanding Officer, Automobile Section (government ser.) 375.167-022
commanding officer, detectives (government ser.) 375.167-022
commanding officer, garage (government ser.) 375.167-018
commanding officer, highway district (government ser.) 375.163-010
COMMANDING OFFICER, HOMICIDE SQUAD (government ser.) 375.167-010
COMMANDING OFFICER, INVESTIGATION DIVISION (government ser.) 375.167-014
COMMANDING OFFICER, MOTOR EQUIPMENT (government ser.) 375.167-018
COMMANDING OFFICER, MOTORIZED SQUAD (government ser.) 375.163-010
commanding officer, motor transport division (government ser.) 375.167-018
COMMANDING OFFICER, POLICE (government ser.) 375.137-034
commanding officer, precinct (government ser.) 375.167-034
commanding officer, radio division communications officer (government ser.) 193.167-018
Commanding Officer, Traffic Division (government ser.) 375.163-010
commanding officer, vehicle maintenance unit (government ser.) 375.167-018
commanding officer, vice squad (government ser.) 375.167-014
Commentator (radio-tv broad.) 131.067-010
Commercial Account Officer (financial) 186.267-018
commercial artist (profess. & kin.) 141.061-022
commercial artist, lettering (profess. & kin.) 970.661-014
COMMERCIAL DECORATOR (any industry) term
commercial decorator (any industry) 298.381-010
COMMERCIAL DESIGNER (profess. & kin.) 141.061-038
COMMERCIAL ENGINEER (radio-tv broad.) 003.187-014
COMMERCIAL-INSTRUCTOR SUPERVISOR (tel. & tel.; utilities; waterworks) 239.137-010
COMMERCIAL LOAN COLLECTION OFFICER (financial) 186.167-078
Commercial Officer (government ser.) 188.117-106
commercial photographer (profess. & kin.) 143.062-030
commercial photographer apprentice (profess. & kin.) 143.062-018
commercial pilot (air trans.) 196.263-014
commercial representative (tel. & tel.) 253.257-010
commercial service representative (tel. & tel.; utilities) 253.357-010
commercial stripper (print. & pub.) 972.281-022
Commissary Agent (air trans.) 922.687-058
COMMISSARY ASSISTANT (amuse. & rec.; museums) 412.687-010
commissary helper (amuse. & rec.; museums) 412.687-010
COMMISSARY MANAGER (any industry) 185.167-010
COMMISSION AGENT, AGRICULTURAL PRODUCE (wholesale tr.) 260.357-010
COMMISSION AGENT, LIVESTOCK (wholesale tr.) 162.157-026
Commission Auditor (insurance) 210.382-010

COMMISSIONER, CONSERVATION OF RESOURCES (government ser.) 188.117-026
Commissioner, Iron Range Resources And Rehabilitation (government ser.) 188.117-026
COMMISSIONER OF CONCILIATION (government ser.) 188.217-010
commissioner of relocation services (government ser.) 188.167-070
COMMISSIONER, PUBLIC WORKS (government ser.) 188.117-030
commodities requirements analyst (aircraft mfg.) 012.167-082
Commodity-Industry Analyst (profess. & kin.) 050.067-010
COMMUNICATION-CENTER COORDINATOR (air trans.) 235.132-014
COMMUNICATION-CENTER OPERATOR (air trans.) 235.662-014
COMMUNICATIONS CONSULTANT (tel. & tel.) 253.157-010
Communications Consultant, Commercial Services (tel. & tel.) 253.157-010
Communications Consultant, Industrial Services (tel. & tel.) 253.157-010
Communications Consultant, Residential Services (tel. & tel.) 253.157-010
COMMUNICATIONS COORDINATOR (medical ser.) 239.167-010
COMMUNICATIONS ELECTRICIAN SUPERVISOR (any industry) 823.131-010
Communications-Equipment Supervisor (tel. & tel.) 722.131-010
Communications Manager (print. & pub.) 132.037-022
COMMUNICATIONS TECHNICIAN (education) 962.362-010
communication technician (any industry) 828.261-022
COMMUNITY DIETITIAN (profess. & kin.) 077.127-010
community health educator (profess. & kin.) 079.117-014
COMMUNITY ORGANIZATION WORKER (social ser.) 195.167-010
community placement worker (social ser.) 195.107-010
community planner (profess. & kin.) 001.061-018
community planning director, community chest (nonprofit org.) 187.167-234
COMMUNITY-RELATIONS-AND-SERVICES ADVISOR, PUBLIC HOUSING (social ser.) 195.167-014
community service consultant (social ser.) 195.167-010
COMMUNITY SERVICE OFFICER, PATROL (government ser.) 372.367-010
COMMUNITY-SERVICES-AND-HEALTH-EDUCATION OFFICER (government ser.) 079.167-010
COMMUNITY WORKER (government ser.) 195.367-018
COMMUTATOR ASSEMBLER (elec. equip.) 724.684-030
Commutator Inspector (house. appl.) 729.384-022
commutator presser (elec. equip.) 724.684-030
Commutator Repairer (any industry) 721.281-018
Commutator Tester (elec. equip.) 729.684-058
Commutator Undercutter (elec. equip.) 724.684-030
Commutator V-Ring Assembler (elec. equip.) 724.684-030
COMPACT ASSEMBLER (jewelry-silver.) 739.687-066
compact-press operator (nonfer. metal; steel & rel.) 617.685-038
COMPANION (domestic ser.) 309.677-010
company doctor (medical ser.) 070.101-078
COMPANY LABORER (mine & quarry) 939.687-014
company laundry worker (any industry) 361.684-014
Company Manager (amuse. & rec.) 191.117-038
company pilot (any industry) 196.263-030
COMPARATOR OPERATOR (any industry) 699.384-010
COMPARISON SHOPPER (retail trade; wholesale tr.) 296.367-014
COMPENSATOR (paper goods) 640.685-026
COMPILER (clerical) 209.387-014
COMPLAINT CLERK (boot & shoe) 221.387-014
COMPLAINT EVALUATION OFFICER (government ser.) 375.367-014
COMPLAINT EVALUATION SUPERVISOR (government ser.) 375.137-038
COMPLAINT INSPECTOR (utilities) 239.261-010
complaint supervisor (utilities) 953.137-018
COMPO CASTER (wood prod., nec) 769.381-010
Compo-Conveyor Operator (boot & shoe) 690.685-074
component insertion operator (comm. equip.; electron. comp.; office machines) 726.685-014
Component Lead Former (electron. comp.) 728.684-022
composer (print. & pub.) 971.382-018
COMPOSER (profess. & kin.) 152.067-014
composing-machine operator (machinery mfg.; print. & pub.) 650.582-014
composing-machine operator (print. & pub.) 650.582-010
composing-machine operator (print. & pub.) 203.382-018
COMPOSING-ROOM MACHINIST (print. & pub.) 627.261-010
Composite Assembler (aircraft mfg.) 754.684-042
Composite Bond Worker (aircraft mfg.) 754.684-042
Composite Laminator (aircraft mfg.) 754.684-042
Composite Layup Worker (aircraft mfg.) 754.684-042
Composites Fabricator And Assembler (aircraft mfg.) 754.381-018
Composite Trim And Drill Worker (aircraft mfg.) 754.684-042
composite worker (aircraft mfg.) 754.684-042
composition-board-press operator (paper & pulp) 535.685-010
Composition Mixer (chemical) 550.382-018
COMPOSITION MIXER (fabrication, nec) 550.665-014
COMPOSITION-ROLL MAKER AND CUTTER (rubber goods) 559.482-010
Composition Roofer (construction) 866.381-010
composition-siding worker (construction) 863.684-010
COMPOSITION-STONE APPLICATOR (construction) 861.361-010
COMPOSITION-WEATHERBOARD APPLIER (construction) 863.684-010

COMPOSITOR (print. & pub.) 973.381-010
COMPOSITOR APPRENTICE (print. & pub.) 973.381-014
COMPOUND-COATING-MACHINE OFFBEARER (tinware) 509.666-010
COMPOUNDER (chemical) 550.685-050
compounder (chemical; pharmaceut.) 550.685-090
COMPOUNDER (petrol. refin.) 540.382-010
COMPOUNDER (pharmaceut.; soap & rel.) 550.685-046
Compounder (rubber reclaim.) 929.687-062
compounder (textile) 550.585-018
COMPOUNDER, CORK (wood prod., nec) 560.587-010
COMPOUNDER, FLAVORINGS (beverage) 529.381-010
COMPOUNDER HELPER (petrol. refin.) 540.686-010
compounder helper (plastic prod.; plastic-synth.) 550.586-010
compounder, sterile products (pharmaceut.) 559.682-054
COMPOUND FILLER (chemical) 550.686-014
COMPOUND FINISHER (chemical) 550.685-042
compound-machine operator (boot & shoe) 690.685-278
Compound Mixer (elec. equip.; electron. comp.) 726.687-022
COMPOUND MIXER (tinware) 509.485-010
COMPOUND WORKER (recording) 559.686-010
Compressed-Air-Pile-Driver Operator (construction) 859.682-018
COMPRESSED-GAS-PLANT WORKER (chemical) 549.587-010
compressed-gas tester (chemical) 549.364-010
COMPRESSION-MOLDING-MACHINE OPERATOR (elec. equip.; plastic prod.) 556.682-014
Compression-Molding-Machine Setter (plastic prod.) 556.380-010
COMPRESSION-MOLDING-MACHINE TENDER (plastic prod.) 556.685-022
COMPRESSOR (elec. equip.; pharmaceut.) 556.682-022
Compressor Assembler (machinery mfg.) 801.361-010
compressor engineer (any industry) 950.685-010
compressor-house operator (utilities) 953.382-010
Compressor Mechanic, Bus (automotive ser.) 620.261-010
compressor operator (any industry) 950.685-010
Compressor Operator (construction) 869.665-010
compressor operator-adjuster (ordnance) 535.482-010
Compressor Operator I (chemical) 559.362-018
COMPRESSOR OPERATOR II (chemical) 559.685-038
Compressor Operator, Portable (any industry) 950.685-010
compressor repairer (railroad equip.) 622.684-010
Compressor-Station Engineer (pipe lines) 950.382-014
COMPRESSOR-STATION ENGINEER, CHIEF (pipe lines) 914.132-010
Compress Trucker (agriculture) 929.687-030
comptroller (profess. & kin.) 160.167-058
Computer-Assisted Retoucher, Photoengraving (print. & pub.) 970.381-030
COMPUTER-CONTROLLED-COLOR-PHOTOGRAPH-PRINTER OPERA-TOR (photofinishing) 976.380-010
COMPUTERIZED ENVIRONMENTAL CONTROL INSTALLER (electron. comp.) 828.281-026
Computer-Laboratory Technician (profess. & kin.) 003.161-014
computer-numerical-control nesting operator (aircraft mfg.) 007.362-010
COMPUTER OPERATOR (clerical) 213.362-010
COMPUTER-PERIPHERAL-EQUIPMENT OPERATOR (clerical) 213.382-010
COMPUTER PROCESSING SCHEDULER (clerical) 221.362-030
COMPUTER PROGRAMMER (profess. & kin.) 030.162-010
computer-programmer, numerical control (any industry) 007.167-018
COMPUTER SECURITY COORDINATOR (profess. & kin.) 033.162-010
COMPUTER SECURITY SPECIALIST (profess. & kin.) 033.362-010
computer systems engineer (profess. & kin.) 033.167-010
COMPUTER SYSTEMS HARDWARE ANALYST (profess. & kin.) 033.167-010
COMPUTER TYPESETTER-KEYLINER (print. & pub.) 979.382-026
CONCAVING-MACHINE OPERATOR (boot & shoe) 585.685-030
Concaving-Machine Operator (elec. equip.) 692.482-010
CONCENTRATOR OPERATOR (smelt. & refin.) 511.462-010
Concert Or Lecture Hall Manager (amuse. & rec.) 191.117-014
conche loader and unloader (sugar & conf.) 526.382-010
CONCHE OPERATOR (sugar & conf.) 526.382-010
Conciliation-Court Judge (government ser.) 111.107-010
CONCILIATOR (profess. & kin.) 169.207-010
CONCRETE-BATCHING AND MIXING-PLANT SUPERVISOR (construction) 570.132-010
Concrete-Batch-Plant Operator (concrete prod.; construction) 570.682-014
Concrete-Block Mason (construction) 861.381-018
Concrete-Bucket Hooker (construction) 921.667-022
Concrete-Bucket Loader (construction) 579.665-014
Concrete Bucket Unloader (construction) 579.665-014
CONCRETE-BUILDING ASSEMBLER (mfd. bldgs.) 869.664-010
CONCRETE CHIPPER (construction) term
Concrete-Conveyor Operator (construction) 579.665-014
CONCRETE CURER (construction) term
CONCRETE-FENCE BUILDER (construction) 869.681-010
concrete finisher (construction) 844.364-010
concrete-finisher apprentice (construction) 844.364-014
Concrete-Finishing-Machine Operator (construction) 853.663-014
concrete floater (construction) 844.364-010

CONCRETE-FLOAT MAKER (concrete prod.) 869.687-022
Concrete-Gun Operator (construction) 849.665-010
Concrete-Hopper Operator (construction) 579.665-014
Concrete-Mixer Loader, Truck Mounted (construction) 579.665-014
concrete-mixer-operator helper (construction) 579.665-014
CONCRETE-MIXING-TRUCK DRIVER (construction) 900.683-010
Concrete-Panel Installer (construction; retail trade) 863.684-014
concrete-paving-form grader (construction) 850.683-022
CONCRETE-PAVING-MACHINE OPERATOR (construction) 853.663-014
Concrete-Paving Supervisor (construction) 869.131-014
Concrete-Pile-Driver Operator (construction) 859.682-018
CONCRETE-PIPE MAKER (concrete prod.) 779.684-014
CONCRETE-PIPE-MAKING-MACHINE OPERATOR (concrete prod.) 575.665-010
concrete pointer (concrete prod.) 844.684-010
concrete polisher (concrete prod.) 844.684-010
Concrete-Pouring Supervisor (construction) 869.131-014
CONCRETE PUDDLER (construction) term
Concrete-Pump Operator (construction) 849.665-010
Concrete-Pump-Operator Helper (construction) 869.687-026
CONCRETE RUBBER (concrete prod.) 844.684-010
CONCRETE SCREEDER (construction) term
CONCRETE SCULPTOR (concrete prod.) 777.281-010
concrete shoveler (construction)   see CONCRETE PUDDLER
concrete spader (construction)   see CONCRETE PUDDLER
concrete spreader (construction)   see CONCRETE PUDDLER
CONCRETE-STONE FABRICATOR (concrete prod.) 575.461-010
CONCRETE-STONE FINISHER (concrete prod.) 844.461-010
concrete tamper (construction)   see CONCRETE PUDDLER
CONCRETE-VAULT MAKER (concrete prod.) 579.684-010
Concrete-Vibrator Operator (construction) 869.687-026
Concrete-Wall-Grinder Operator (construction) 869.664-014
CONCRETING SUPERVISOR (construction) 869.131-014
CONDENSER SETTER (smelt. & refin.) 512.687-010
CONDENSER-TUBE TENDER (smelt. & refin.) 511.685-018
CONDITIONER TENDER (textile) 587.685-022
CONDITIONER-TUMBLER OPERATOR (laundry & rel.) 361.685-010
conditioning-machine operator (tobacco) 522.682-014
conditioning-room worker (textile) 587.685-022
CONDOMINIUM MANAGER (real estate) 186.167-062
CONDUCTOR (r.r. trans.) 910.667-014
Conductor, Dance Band (profess. & kin.) 152.047-014
CONDUCTOR, ORCHESTRA (profess. & kin.) 152.047-014
CONDUCTOR, PASSENGER CAR (r.r. trans.) 198.167-010
CONDUCTOR, PULLMAN (r.r. trans.) 198.167-014
CONDUCTOR, ROAD FREIGHT (r.r. trans.) 198.167-018
conductor, sleeping car (r.r. trans.) 198.167-014
Conductor, Symphonic-Orchestra (profess. & kin.) 152.047-014
CONDUCTOR, YARD (r.r. trans.) 910.137-022
Conduit Installer (r.r. trans.) 825.381-038
CONDUIT MECHANIC (construction; utilities) 869.361-010
Cone Baker, Machine (bakery products) 526.685-066
cone chocolate dipper (dairy products) 524.686-014
Cone-Classifier Tender (smelt. & refin.) 511.685-014
cone former (hat & cap) 586.685-030
cone inspector (glass mfg.; plastic-synth.; textile) 681.687-030
cone-machine feeder (hat & cap) 586.686-018
CONE OPERATOR (mine & quarry) 934.685-010
cone racker (dairy products) 524.686-014
coner (hat & cap) 586.685-030
coner (textile) 681.685-098
Cone Spooler (any industry) 681.685-154
CONE TREATER (paper goods) 534.687-010
Cone Winder (textile) 681.685-154
confectioner (sugar & conf.) 529.361-014
CONFECTIONERY COOKER (sugar & conf.) 526.382-014
CONFECTIONERY-DROPS-MACHINE OPERATOR (sugar & conf.) 520.685-078
conference service coordinator (clerical) 238.367-022
CONFIGURATION MANAGEMENT ANALYST (profess. & kin.) 012.167-010
conformal pad former (boot & shoe) 788.687-094
CONGRESSIONAL-DISTRICT AIDE (government ser.) 209.362-030
Conical Mixer (hat & cap) 680.685-062
connection worker (petrol. & gas) 869.684-046
connector (elec. equip.) 721.684-018
Connector Hand (construction) 869.687-026
conservation officer (government ser.) 379.167-010
CONSERVATION TECHNICIAN (museums) 102.261-010
CONSERVATOR, ARTIFACTS (profess. & kin.) 055.381-010
CONSOLE ASSEMBLER (musical inst.) 730.684-030
console operator (print. & pub.) 979.282-010
CONSTRUCTION-AND-MAINTENANCE INSPECTOR (petrol. refin.) 914.362-014
CONSTRUCTION CHECKER (utilities) 821.367-010

CONSTRUCTION-EQUIPMENT MECHANIC (construction) 620.261-022
CONSTRUCTION-EQUIPMENT-MECHANIC HELPER (construction) 620.664-010
Construction Grip (motion picture) 962.687-022
CONSTRUCTION INSPECTOR (construction) 182.267-010
Construction-Machinery-And-Equipment-Rental Clerk (business ser.) 295.467-022
Construction Millwright (saw. & plan.) 860.381-042
Construction-Records Clerk (construction; utilities) 219.362-010
CONSTRUCTION WORKER I (construction) 869.664-014
CONSTRUCTION WORKER II (construction) 869.687-026
Consular Officer (government ser.) 188.117-106
consultant (any industry) 199.251-010
CONSULTANT (profess. & kin.) 189.167-010
CONSULTANT, EDUCATION (education) 099.167-014
CONSULTANT, EDUCATIONAL, STATE BOARD OF NURSING (government ser.) 075.117-010
CONSULTING ENGINEER (profess. & kin.) term
consumer-relations-complaint clerk (clerical) 241.367-014
consumer services consultant (profess. & kin.) 096.121-014
CONTACT-ACID-PLANT OPERATOR (chemical) 558.585-018
CONTACT-ACID-PLANT-OPERATOR HELPER (chemical) 559.687-026
contact assembler (elec. equip.; light. fix.) 729.687-010
CONTACT CLERK (utilities) 209.387-018
Contact-Finger Assembler (elec. equip.) 729.687-010
contact-frame operator (electron. comp.; print. & pub.) 971.382-014
Contact-Lens-Curve Grinder (optical goods) 716.685-022
contact-lens cutter (optical goods) 716.382-010
Contact-Lens-Edge Buffer (optical goods) 716.685-022
CONTACT-LENS-FLASHING PUNCHER (optical goods) 713.687-014
Contact-Lens Inspector (optical goods) 716.381-010
CONTACT-LENS MOLDER (optical goods) 690.685-090
Contact-Lens Polisher (optical goods) 716.682-018
Contact Printer, Dry Film (electron. comp.) 976.684-030
CONTACT PRINTER, PHOTORESIST (inst. & app.; optical goods) 976.684-034
CONTACT PRINTER, PRINTED CIRCUIT BOARDS (electron. comp.) 976.684-030
CONTACT REPRESENTATIVE (government ser.) 169.167-018
CONTACT WORKER, LITHOGRAPHY (print. & pub.) 976.684-038
Container-Cargo Clerk (water trans.) 248.367-014
CONTAINER COORDINATOR (water trans.) 248.367-022
container crane operator (water trans.) 921.683-018
Container Filler (any industry) 920.587-018
container finisher (elec. equip.) 727.687-034
Container-Maker-Filler-Packer Operator (any industry) 920.685-078
container-packer operator (tobacco) 920.685-038
container repairer (any industry) 619.685-034
CONTAINER WASHER, MACHINE (any industry) 529.685-074
content checker (beverage) 522.667-010
CONTESTANT COORDINATOR (radio-tv broad.) 166.167-010
CONTINUITY CLERK (motion picture) 209.382-010
CONTINUITY DIRECTOR (radio-tv broad.) 132.037-010
Continuity Reader (radio-tv broad.) 131.267-022
CONTINUITY WRITER (radio-tv broad.) 131.087-010
CONTINUOUS-ABSORPTION-PROCESS OPERATOR (sugar & conf.) 521.362-010
Continuous-Annealing Furnace Operator (heat treating) 504.682-010
Continuous-Conveyor-Screen Drier (chemical) 553.582-010
CONTINUOUS-CRUSHER OPERATOR (textile) 586.685-014
continuous-drier helper (tex. prod., nec) 581.687-018
continuous-drier operator (tex. prod., nec) 581.685-034
continuous-dryout operator (any industry) 503.362-010
continuous-dryout-operator helper (any industry) 503.686-010
CONTINUOUS-LINTER-DRIER OPERATOR (chemical) 553.685-034
continuous-loft operator (paper & pulp) 534.682-010
CONTINUOUS-MINING-MACHINE OPERATOR (mine & quarry) 930.683-010
CONTINUOUS PILLOWCASE CUTTER (tex. prod., nec) 686.685-014
continuous process machine operator (photofinishing) 976.685-014
Continuous-Still Operator (chemical) 552.362-022
CONTINUOUS-TOWEL ROLLER (laundry & rel.) 361.685-014
Continuous-Vulcanizing-Machine Operator (nonfer. metal) 691.382-010
continuous-washer operator (ordnance) 503.685-026
continuous-yarn dyeing-machine operator (textile) 582.685-158
Contortionist (amuse. & rec.) 159.247-010
CONTOUR-BAND-SAW OPERATOR, VERTICAL (machine shop) 607.382-010
CONTOUR GRINDER (stonework) 675.682-010
Contour-Path Tape-Mill Operator (machine shop) 605.380-010
contour sander (woodworking) 662.682-010
contour stitcher (garment) 786.685-026
Contour Wire Sawyer (stonework) 677.462-014
CONTOUR WIRE SPECIALIST, DENTURE (protective dev.) 712.381-014
CONTRACT ADMINISTRATOR (any industry) 162.117-014

contract administrator (insurance) 241.267-010
CONTRACT CLERK (profess. & kin.) 119.267-018
CONTRACT CLERK, AUTOMOBILE (retail trade) 219.362-026
contract consultant (profess. & kin.) 119.267-018
contract coordinator (profess. & kin.) 162.117-018
CONTRACTOR (construction) 182.167-010
Contractor, Broomcorn Threshing (agriculture) 409.117-010
Contractor, Field Hauling (agriculture) 409.117-010
Contractor, General Building (construction) 182.167-010
Contractor, General Engineering (construction) 182.167-010
Contract-Post-Office Clerk (retail trade) 243.367-014
CONTRACT SPECIALIST (profess. & kin.) 162.117-018
contract technician (profess. & kin.) 119.267-018
contribution solicitor (nonprofit org.) 293.357-014
control-board operator (clerical) 235.662-022
control board operator, sugar refining (grain-feed mills) 521.362-018
Control-Cabinet Assembler (elec. equip.) 826.361-010
CONTROL CLERK (clock & watch) 221.387-018
CONTROL CLERK, AUDITING (insurance) 209.362-014
control clerk, food-and-beverage (hotel & rest.) 216.362-022
CONTROL CLERK, HEAD (clock & watch) 221.137-010
Control Clerk, Repairs (clock & watch) 221.387-018
Control Clerk, Subassembly (clock & watch) 221.387-018
Control Clerk, Training And Mechanism (clock & watch) 221.387-018
CONTROL INSPECTOR (paper & pulp; wood prod., nec) 539.667-010
control inspector (railroad equip.) 825.381-018
Controlled-Area Checker (any industry) 372.667-030
CONTROLLER (profess. & kin.) 160.167-058
CONTROLLER, COAL OR ORE (mine & quarry) 939.167-010
CONTROLLER, REMOTELY-PILOTED VEHICLE (RPV) (aircraft mfg.) 196.263-026
CONTROLLER REPAIRER-AND-TESTER (railroad equip.) 825.381-018
CONTROL OPERATOR (smelt. & refin.) 511.482-010
Control Operator, Flow Coat (elec. equip.) 599.382-010
control-panel assembler (elec. equip.) 721.381-014
control-panel operator (bakery products) 520.462-010
CONTROL-PANEL OPERATOR (petrol. refin.) 546.382-010
Control-Panel Operator, Cracking Unit (petrol. refin.) 546.382-010
Control-Panel Operator, Crude Unit (petrol. refin.) 546.382-010
Control-Panel Operator, Polymerization Unit (petrol. refin.) 546.382-010
Control-Panel Operator, Solvent-Treating Unit (petrol. refin.) 546.382-010
CONTROL-PANEL TESTER (elec. equip.) 827.381-010
control-room operator (any industry) 950.382-010
CONTROLS DESIGNER (profess. & kin.) 003.261-014
Controls Designer, Computer-Assisted (profess. & kin.) 003.261-014
Controls Development Mechanic (aircraft mfg.) 693.261-014
CONTROLS OPERATOR, MOLDED GOODS (fabrication, nec) 590.662-010
controls project engineer (profess. & kin.) 003.261-014
control-tower-radio operator (government ser.) 193.162-018
CONVERTER OPERATOR (grain-feed mills) 526.382-018
CONVERTER SUPERVISOR (smelt. & refin.) 513.132-010
Convertible-Power-Shovel Operator (any industry) 850.683-030
CONVEX-GRINDER OPERATOR (button & notion) 673.685-042
conveyor attendant (mine & quarry; smelt. & refin.) 939.362-014
Conveyor Belt Package Sorter (retail trade) 222.687-022
Conveyor-Belt Repairer (any industry) 630.684-014
conveyor console operator (any industry) 921.662-018
Conveyor Feeder (steel & rel.) 509.687-026
conveyor feeder (tobacco) 529.686-038
CONVEYOR FEEDER-OFFBEARER (any industry) 921.686-014
Conveyorized Oven Tender (bakery products) 526.685-070
conveyor loader (glass products) 579.686-022
CONVEYOR LOADER I (meat products) 525.687-018
CONVEYOR LOADER II (meat products) 525.686-014
CONVEYOR-MAINTENANCE MECHANIC (any industry) 630.381-010
conveyor monitor (any industry) 921.685-026
CONVEYOR OPERATOR, PNEUMATIC SYSTEM (food prep., nec) 921.382-010
CONVEYOR-SYSTEM OPERATOR (any industry) 921.662-018
CONVEYOR TENDER (any industry) 921.685-026
Conveyor Tender, Concrete-Mixing Plant (construction) 579.665-014
conveyor-weigher operator (chemical) 559.687-070
CONVOLUTE-TUBE WINDER (paper goods) 640.682-010
COOK (any industry) 315.361-010
cook (beverage; can. & preserv.; grain-feed mills) 526.381-026
COOK (chemical) 553.665-018
COOK (domestic ser.) 305.281-010
COOK (fishing & hunt.) 315.381-010
COOK (hotel & rest.) 313.361-014
COOK (meat products) 526.685-010
cook (paper & pulp; paper goods) 532.362-010
COOK APPRENTICE (hotel & rest.) 313.361-018
COOK APPRENTICE, PASTRY (hotel & rest.) 313.381-018
COOK, BARBECUE (hotel & rest.) 313.381-022
cook blender (dairy products) 526.665-010

cook, boat (water trans.) 315.371-010
COOK-BOX FILLER (meat products) 523.685-030
COOK, BREAKFAST (hotel & rest.) term
Cook, Broiler (hotel & rest.) 313.361-014
Cook, Camp (any industry) 315.361-010
cook, candy (sugar & conf.) 529.361-014
cook, chief (hotel & rest.) 313.131-014
COOK, CHIEF (water trans.) 315.131-010
Cook, Chili (food prep., nec) 526.134-010
Cook, Chinese-Style Food (hotel & rest.) 313.361-030
cook, cold meat (hotel & rest.) 313.361-034
Cook, Dessert (hotel & rest.) 313.361-014
Cook, Dinner (hotel & rest.) 313.361-014
COOK, DOG-AND-CAT FOOD (meat products) 526.682-014
cooked foods supervisor (hotel & rest.) 319.137-022
cookee (hotel & rest.) 318.687-010
Cook, Enchilada (food prep., nec) 526.134-010
cooker (beverage) 522.382-022
cooker (beverage; can. & preserv.; grain-feed mills) 526.381-026
cooker (can. & preserv.) 529.685-174
COOKER (grain-feed mills) 526.685-022
cooker (oils & grease) 523.685-034
Cooker And Presser (meat products) 529.685-202
COOKER, CASING (tobacco) 520.685-082
cooker, chip (food prep., nec) 526.685-046
COOKER CLEANER (can. & preserv.) 529.687-054
cooker helper (can. & preserv.) 529.486-010
COOKER LOADER (oils & grease) 921.685-030
COOKER, MEAL (oils & grease) 523.685-034
Cooker, Pie Filling (bakery products) 520.685-114
COOKER, PROCESS CHEESE (dairy products) 526.665-010
Cooker, Soda (paper & pulp; paper goods) 532.362-010
Cooker, Sulfate (paper & pulp; paper goods) 532.362-010
Cooker, Sulfite (paper & pulp; paper goods) 532.362-010
cooker, syrup (beverage) 520.485-026
COOKER TENDER (oils & grease) 553.665-022
COOKER TENDER (paper & pulp) 532.685-014
COOK, FAST FOOD (hotel & rest.) 313.374-010
Cook, Fish And Chips (hotel & rest.) 313.361-026
Cook, Fish Eggs (can. & preserv.) 526.381-026
cook, fishing vessel (fishing & hunt.) 315.381-010
cook, frozen dessert (hotel & rest.) 313.381-034
Cook, Fruit (can. & preserv.) 526.381-026
Cook, Fry (hotel & rest.) 313.361-014
Cook, Fry (r.r. trans.) 315.381-018
COOK, FRY, DEEP FAT (can. & preserv.; hotel & rest.) 526.685-014
COOK, HEAD, SCHOOL CAFETERIA (hotel & rest.) 313.131-018
COOK HELPER (can. & preserv.) 529.687-050
cook helper (hotel & rest.) 318.687-010
COOK HELPER (hotel & rest.) 317.687-010
cook helper (paper & pulp; paper goods) 532.686-010
Cook Helper, Broiler Or Fry (hotel & rest.) 317.687-010
Cook Helper, Dessert (hotel & rest.) 317.687-010
Cook Helper, Fruit (can. & preserv.) 529.687-050
Cook Helper, Juice (can. & preserv.) 529.687-050
Cook Helper, Meat (can. & preserv.) 529.687-050
COOK HELPER, PASTRY (hotel & rest.) 313.687-010
Cook Helper, Preserves (can. & preserv.) 529.687-050
Cook Helper, Vegetable (hotel & rest.) 317.687-010
cook, ice cream (hotel & rest.) 313.381-034
cookie breaker (boot & shoe) 788.685-010
Cookie Mixer (bakery products) 520.685-234
Cookie-Mixer Helper (bakery products) 526.686-010
COOKING, CASING, AND DRYING SUPERVISOR (tobacco) 529.135-010
Cook, Institution (any industry) 315.361-010
Cook, Italian-Style Food (hotel & rest.) 313.361-030
Cook, Jelly (can. & preserv.) 526.381-026
Cook, Juice (can. & preserv.) 526.381-026
COOK, KETTLE (beverage; can. & preserv.; grain-feed mills) 526.381-026
Cook, Kosher-Style Food (hotel & rest.) 313.361-030
COOK, LARDER (water trans.) 315.381-014
cook, mess (any industry) 315.361-010
COOK, MESS (water trans.) 315.371-010
COOK, MEXICAN FOOD (food prep., nec) 526.134-010
Cook, Morning (hotel & rest.) 313.361-014
Cook, Night (hotel & rest.) 313.361-014
COOK, PASTRY (hotel & rest.) 313.381-026
cook, pastry (hotel & rest.) 313.361-038
Cook, Pickled Meat (can. & preserv.) 526.381-026
cook, pie (hotel & rest.) 313.361-038
Cook, Preserve (can. & preserv.) 526.381-026
cook, pressure (beverage; can. & preserv.; grain-feed mills) 526.381-026
COOK, RAILROAD (r.r. trans.) 315.381-018
Cook, Ranch (agriculture) 315.361-010

Cook, Relief (hotel & rest.) 313.361-014
cook, restaurant (hotel & rest.) 313.361-014
Cook, Roast (hotel & rest.) 313.361-014
Cook, Roast Pig (hotel & rest.) 313.381-022
Cook, Sauce (can. & preserv.) 526.381-026
Cook, Sauce (hotel & rest.) 313.361-014
COOK, SCHOOL CAFETERIA (hotel & rest.) 313.381-030
Cook, Seafood (can. & preserv.) 526.381-026
COOK, SECOND (hotel & rest.) term
Cook, Ship (water trans.) 315.361-010
cook, ship (water trans.) 315.371-010
COOK, SHORT ORDER (hotel & rest.) 313.374-014
Cook, Soup (hotel & rest.) 313.361-014
COOK, SOYBEAN SPECIALTIES (food prep., nec) 529.685-290
Cook, Spaghetti (can. & preserv.) 526.381-026
Cook, Spanish-Style Food (hotel & rest.) 313.361-030
Cook, Special Diet (hotel & rest.) 313.361-014
COOK, SPECIALTY (hotel & rest.) 313.361-026
COOK, SPECIALTY, FOREIGN FOOD (hotel & rest.) 313.361-030
Cook, Starch (can. & preserv.) 526.381-026
COOK, STATION (water trans.) 315.361-022
Cook, Station, Breakfast (water trans.) 315.361-022
Cook, Station, Grill (water trans.) 315.361-022
Cook, Station, Roast (water trans.) 315.361-022
Cook, Station, Soup And Fish (water trans.) 315.361-022
COOK, SYRUP MAKER (beverage) 526.682-018
Cook, Taco (food prep., nec) 526.134-010
Cook, Tamale (food prep., nec) 526.134-010
COOK, THIRD (water trans.) 315.381-022
Cook, Tortilla (food prep., nec) 526.134-010
COOK, VACUUM KETTLE (can. & preserv.) 526.685-018
Cook, Vegetable (can. & preserv.) 526.381-026
Cook, Vegetable (hotel & rest.) 313.361-014
Cooler-Conveyor Loader (meat products) 525.686-014
cooler operator (beverage) 523.685-042
Cooler Operator (dairy products) 529.382-018
COOLER ROOM WORKER (meat products) 525.687-022
cooler servicer (any industry) 637.381-010
Cooler Supervisor (dairy products) 929.137-022
COOLER TENDER (grain-feed mills) 523.685-038
COOLER TENDER (sugar & conf.) 520.585-018
Cooler Worker (dairy products) 922.687-058
COOLING-MACHINE OPERATOR (beverage) 523.685-042
COOLING-PAN TENDER (can. & preserv.) 523.685-046
COOLING-PIPE INSPECTOR (construction) 862.687-010
COOLING-ROOM ATTENDANT (personal ser.) 335.677-010
cooling-system operator (any industry) 950.362-014
Cooling-Tower Operator (petrol. refin.) 549.362-010
COOPER (wood. container) 764.684-022
cooperative extension advisor specialist (government ser.) 096.127-014
COOPER HELPER (wood. container) 764.687-050
COORDINATE MEASURING EQUIPMENT OPERATOR (electron. comp.) 726.682-018
coordinator, auxiliary personnel (medical ser.) 079.127-010
coordinator, computer programming (profess. & kin.) 030.167-010
coordinator of placement (education) 166.167-014
COORDINATOR OF REHABILITATION SERVICES (medical ser.) 076.117-010
coordinator, program planning (radio-tv broad.) 132.067-030
COORDINATOR, SKILL-TRAINING PROGRAM (government ser.) 169.167-062
COORDINATOR, VOLUNTEER SERVICES (social ser.) 187.167-022
cop breaker (textile) 689.686-014
COPER, HAND (stonework) 771.384-010
Copilot (air trans.) 196.263-014
Copper Deposition Operator (electron. comp.) 501.685-022
Copper Etcher (print. & pub.) 971.381-014
Copper-Flotation Operator (smelt. & refin.) 511.685-026
Copper Plater (electroplating) 500.380-010
copper-roller handler, printing (textile) 652.385-010
Coppersmith (any industry) 804.281-010
COPPERSMITH (ship-boat mfg.) 862.281-010
COPPERSMITH APPRENTICE (ship-boat mfg.) 862.281-014
COPRA PROCESSOR (soap & rel.) 555.685-018
Cop Winder (nonmet. min.; textile) 681.685-154
copy-camera operator (any industry) 976.361-010
copy-camera-operator apprentice (print. & pub.) 972.382-010
COPY CUTTER (print. & pub.) 221.167-010
COPY HOLDER (print. & pub.) 209.667-010
COPYIST (any industry) 152.267-010
COPYIST (garment) 142.281-010
copyist (paper goods) 794.684-022
COPY-LATHE TENDER (woodworking) 664.685-018
Copy Reader (print. & pub.) 132.267-014
copy reader (radio-tv broad.) 131.267-022

Copy Reader, Book (print. & pub.) 132.267-014
copyright clerk (radio-tv broad.) 249.267-010
COPYRIGHT EXPERT (radio-tv broad.) 249.267-010
COPY WRITER (profess. & kin.) 131.067-014
corder (any industry) 787.682-082
Corder (garment; tex. prod., nec) 787.682-022
cording-machine operator (any industry) 787.682-082
cord-reel operator (paper goods) 640.685-046
cord splicer (rubber tire) 759.684-058
CORDUROY-BRUSHER OPERATOR (textile) 585.685-034
CORDUROY-CUTTER OPERATOR (textile) 585.565-010
cordwood-cutter helper (any industry) 667.687-010
core analyst (petrol. & gas) 024.381-010
core-assembly supervisor (elec. equip.) 619.130-042
core-blower operator (foundry) 518.685-022
CORE CHECKER (foundry) 518.687-010
CORE-COMPOSER FEEDER (millwork-plywood) 669.685-038
CORE-COMPOSER-MACHINE TENDER (millwork-plywood) 569.685-022
Core-Covering Sewer (tex. prod., nec) 787.682-058
Core Cutter (paper & pulp) 649.685-026
CORE-CUTTER AND REAMER (paper goods) 649.685-026
core driller (petrol. & gas) 930.382-018
core driller (petrol. & gas) 930.382-026
CORE-DRILL OPERATOR (any industry) 930.682-010
CORE-DRILL OPERATOR (construction) 869.682-014
CORE-DRILL-OPERATOR HELPER (any industry) 930.687-014
Core Dropper (elec. equip.) 727.687-022
CORE EXTRUDER (elec. equip.) 557.685-010
core feeder (millwork-plywood; wood prod., nec) 569.685-042
CORE FEEDER, PLYWOOD LAYUP LINE (millwork-plywood) 569.685-018
core fitter (foundry) 518.687-014
Core Inserter (tex. prod., nec) 739.685-010
core inspector (foundry) 518.687-010
core layer, plywood (millwork-plywood) 762.687-026
CORE LAYER, PLYWOOD LAYUP LINE (millwork-plywood) 569.686-014
CORE-LAYING-MACHINE OPERATOR (millwork-plywood) 569.685-026
CORE LOADER (ordnance) 737.687-030
COREMAKER (foundry) 518.381-014
Coremaker (paper goods) 640.682-022
COREMAKER APPRENTICE (foundry) 518.381-018
Coremaker, Bench (foundry) 518.381-014
coremaker, experimental (foundry) 518.381-014
Coremaker, Floor (foundry) 518.381-014
coremaker helper (foundry) 518.687-014
COREMAKER, MACHINE I (foundry) 518.685-014
COREMAKER, MACHINE II (foundry) 518.685-018
COREMAKER, MACHINE III (foundry) 518.685-022
COREMAKER, PIPE (foundry) 518.684-014
COREMAKING-MACHINE OPERATOR (elec. equip.) 692.682-030
Coremaking Supervisor (foundry) 519.131-010
core mounter (foundry) 518.684-018
CORE-OVEN TENDER (foundry) 518.685-010
core paster (foundry) 518.687-014
CORE SETTER (foundry) 518.684-010
core setter (foundry) 518.684-018
CORE SHAPER (toy-sport equip.) 692.685-058
Core Shaper, Sides (toy-sport equip.) 692.685-058
Core Shaper, Top (toy-sport equip.) 692.685-058
core stripper (foundry) 518.685-014
CORE WINDING OPERATOR (paper & pulp) 640.682-014
cork coater (wood prod., nec) 562.687-014
corker (beverage) 920.665-014
CORK GRINDER (toy-sport equip.) 662.685-010
CORK INSULATOR, REFRIGERATION PLANT (construction) 863.381-010
cork mixer (wood prod., nec) 560.585-010
cork mixer (wood prod., nec) 560.587-010
CORK MOLDER (wood prod., nec) 569.685-030
CORK-PRESSING-MACHINE OPERATOR (wood prod., nec) 569.686-018
cork sorter (wood prod., nec) 769.687-042
Cork-Tile-Floor Layer (construction; retail trade) 864.481-010
Corn-Chip Maker (food prep., nec) 529.685-078
CORN COOKER (food prep., nec) 522.685-034
Corn-Cutter Operator (grain-feed mills) 521.685-122
corner-block cutter (furniture) 669.682-030
CORNER-BRACE-BLOCK-MACHINE OPERATOR (furniture) 669.682-030
CORNER CUTTER (paper goods) 640.685-030
corner-cutter-machine operator (paper goods) 640.685-030
CORNER FORMER (wood. container) 617.685-014
CORNER-TRIMMER OPERATOR (wood. container) 667.682-018
CORN GRINDER (food prep., nec) 521.685-082
CORN-GRINDER OPERATOR, AUTOMATIC (grain-feed mills) 521.685-086
Corn Grower (agriculture) 401.161-010
Corn-Husk Baler (grain-feed mills) 920.685-010
Cornice Upholsterer (any industry) 780.381-018
Corn Miller (grain-feed mills) 521.682-026

corn-oil extractor (grain-feed mills; oils & grease) 529.685-106
CORN POPPER (sugar & conf.) 526.685-026
CORN-PRESS OPERATOR (food prep., nec) 529.685-078
Corn-Sheller Operator (grain-feed mills) 521.685-122
CORONER (government ser.) 168.161-010
corporate counsel (profess. & kin.) 110.117-022
Corporate Pilot (air trans.) 196.263-014
Corporate Trust Officer (government ser.) 186.117-074
corporation pilot (any industry) 196.263-030
corral boss (any industry) 410.131-010
correctional officer (government ser.) 188.167-026
CORRECTIONAL-TREATMENT SPECIALIST (social ser.) 195.107-042
CORRECTION OFFICER (government ser.) 372.667-018
correction officer (government ser.) 372.677-010
correction officer (government ser.) 375.367-010
Correction Officer, City Or County Jail (government ser.) 372.667-018
CORRECTION OFFICER, HEAD (government ser.) 372.137-010
Correction Officer, Penitentiary (government ser.) 372.667-018
Correction Officer, Reformatory (government ser.) 372.667-018
CORRECTIVE THERAPIST (medical ser.) 076.361-010
CORRESPONDENCE CLERK (clerical) 209.362-034
CORRESPONDENCE-REVIEW CLERK (clerical) 209.367-018
Correspondent (print. & pub.; radio-tv broad.) 131.262-018
correspondent (insurance) 249.262-010
CORROSION-CONTROL FITTER (pipe lines; utilities) 820.361-010
corrosion-control specialist (profess. & kin.) 003.167-022
corrosion engineer (profess. & kin.) 003.167-022
corrugated-combining-machine operator (paper goods) 641.562-010
CORRUGATED-FASTENER DRIVER (woodworking) 669.685-042
Corrugated-Sheet-Material Sheeter (construction) 869.664-014
corrugator (brick & tile) 779.684-042
CORRUGATOR OPERATOR (paper goods) 641.562-010
CORRUGATOR OPERATOR (plastic-synth.) 556.665-014
corrugator operator (woodworking) 669.685-042
CORRUGATOR-OPERATOR HELPER (paper goods) 641.686-018
CORSET FITTER (retail trade) 782.361-010
corsetier (retail trade) 261.354-010
Corset Repairer (garment) 782.684-038
cosmetician (personal ser.) 332.271-010
cosmetician apprentice (personal ser.) 332.271-014
Cosmetics Demonstrator (retail trade) 297.354-010
COSMETICS PRESSER (pharmaceut.) 556.685-026
COSMETICS SUPERVISOR (pharmaceut.) 550.131-010
COSMETOLOGIST (personal ser.) 332.271-010
COSMETOLOGIST APPRENTICE (personal ser.) 332.271-014
cost-accounting clerk (clerical) 216.382-034
COST-AND-SALES-RECORD SUPERVISOR (utilities) 216.137-010
COST CLERK (clerical) 216.382-034
cost development engineer (aircraft mfg.) 002.167-010
Cost-Estimating Clerk (utilities) 216.382-034
cost estimator (profess. & kin.) 169.267-038
cost-report clerk (water trans.) 216.382-054
Costume Designer (profess. & kin.) 142.061-018
COSTUMER (motion picture; radio-tv broad.) 346.261-010
COSTUMER ASSISTANT (motion picture; radio-tv broad.) 346.374-010
Costume-Rental Clerk (retail trade) 295.357-010
cot assembler (furniture) 709.667-010
COTTAGE-CHEESE MAKER (dairy products) 522.382-010
cottage parent (any industry) 187.167-186
Cotton-Bag Clipper (tex. prod., nec) 789.687-030
Cotton-Bag-Cutting-Machine Offbearer (tex. prod., nec) 689.686-018
Cotton-Bag-Cutting-Machine Operator (tex. prod., nec) 686.585-010
Cotton-Bag Sewer (tex. prod., nec) 787.682-058
COTTON BALER (agriculture) 920.685-114
COTTON-BALL BAGGER (protective dev.) 920.686-014
COTTON-BALL-MACHINE TENDER (protective dev.) 580.685-022
COTTON CLASSER (agriculture; textile) 429.387-010
COTTON CLASSER AIDE (agriculture) 429.587-010
cotton cleaner (plastic-synth.) 559.687-030
COTTON DISPATCHER (furniture) 780.684-038
Cotton Farmworker (agriculture) 404.687-010
cotton grader (agriculture; textile) 429.387-010
Cotton Grower (agriculture) 404.161-010
Cotton Header (water trans.) 911.137-018
Cotton Picker (furniture) 680.685-078
Cotton-Picker Operator (chemical) 553.685-034
Cotton Presser (garment) 363.684-018
COTTON PULLER (oils & grease) 521.686-022
COTTON-ROLL PACKER (protective dev.) 920.685-054
COTTON SAMPLER (agriculture; textile) 922.687-042
cottonseed-meat presser (oils & grease) 521.685-242
COTTON TIER (agriculture) 920.687-074
COTTON WASHER (plastic-synth.) 559.687-030
Cotton Weigher (agriculture) 221.587-030
cotton-weigher operator (chemical) 559.687-070

Cotton Wringer (plastic-synth.) 559.687-030
Cottrell Blower (smelt. & refin.) 511.687-014
Cougar Hunter (fishing & hunt.) 461.661-010
counseling-center manager (profess. & kin.) 045.107-018
counselor (hotel & rest.) 352.667-014
counselor (profess. & kin.) 110.107-010
COUNSELOR (profess. & kin.) 045.107-010
counselor-at law (profess. & kin.) 110.107-010
COUNSELOR, CAMP (amuse. & rec.) 159.124-010
counselor, dormitory (education) 045.107-038
COUNSELOR, MARRIAGE AND FAMILY (profess. & kin.) 045.107-054
COUNSELOR, NURSES' ASSOCIATION (medical ser.) 045.107-014
counselor, orientation and mobility (education; medical ser.; nonprofit org.) 076.224-014
counselor, vocational rehabilitation (government ser.) 045.107-042
counter (clerical) 221.587-030
counter and upper tacker (boot & shoe) 690.685-010
counter attendant (laundry & rel.; personal ser.) 369.477-014
COUNTER ATTENDANT, CAFETERIA (hotel & rest.) 311.677-014
COUNTER ATTENDANT, LUNCHROOM OR COFFEE SHOP (hotel & rest.) 311.477-014
Counter Buffer (boot & shoe) 690.685-046
counter caser (boot & shoe) 788.687-026
COUNTER CLERK (photofinishing) 249.366-010
counter clerk (retail trade; wholesale tr.) 279.357-062
COUNTER CLERK (tel. & tel.) 249.362-010
Counter Clerk, Appliance Parts (retail trade; wholesale tr.) 279.357-062
Counter Clerk, Automotive Parts (retail trade; wholesale tr.) 279.357-062
Counter Clerk, Farm Equipment Parts (retail trade; wholesale tr.) 279.357-062
Counter Clerk, Industrial Machinery And Equipment Parts (retail trade; wholesale tr.) 279.357-062
Counter Clerk, Radio, Television, And Electronics Parts (retail trade; wholesale tr.) 279.357-062
Counter Clerk, Tractor Parts (retail trade; wholesale tr.) 279.357-062
Counter Clerk, Truck Parts (retail trade; wholesale tr.) 279.357-062
COUNTER CUTTER (boot & shoe) 690.685-094
Counter Dish Carrier (hotel & rest.) 311.677-018
COUNTER FORMER (boot & shoe) 690.685-098
COUNTER, HAND (paper goods) 794.687-018
COUNTERINTELLIGENCE AGENT (military ser.) 378.267-010
counter maker (boot & shoe) 690.685-094
counter molder (boot & shoe) 690.685-350
COUNTER MOLDER (boot & shoe) 690.685-102
Counter-Pocket Sewer (boot & shoe) 690.682-082
counter-pocket trimmer (leather mfg.) 585.684-010
COUNTER ROLLER (boot & shoe) 690.685-106
COUNTERSINKER (clock & watch) 715.682-014
Countersinker, Balance Screw Hole (clock & watch) 715.682-014
COUNTER SUPERVISOR (hotel & rest.) 311.137-010
COUNTER-SUPPLY WORKER (hotel & rest.) 319.687-010
counter tacker (boot & shoe) 788.684-078
Counter Top Assembler (mfd. bldgs.; vehicles, nec) 762.684-014
counter-weigher (clerical) 221.587-030
COUNTING-MACHINE OPERATOR (paper goods) 649.685-030
country printer (print. & pub.) 973.381-018
country-printer apprentice (print. & pub.) 973.381-022
county adviser (government ser.) 096.127-010
county agent (government ser.) 096.127-010
COUNTY-AGRICULTURAL AGENT (government ser.) 096.127-010
County Auditor (government ser.) 160.167-030
County Director, Welfare (government ser.) 188.117-126
COUNTY HOME-DEMONSTRATION AGENT (government ser.) 096.121-010
County-Library Director (library) 100.117-010
couper (beverage) 764.687-090
COUPLE (any industry) term
coupler (any industry) 932.664-010
coupler (rubber goods) 759.687-014
COUPLING-MACHINE OPERATOR (steel & rel.) 619.682-014
Coupon-And-Bond-Collection Clerk (financial) 216.362-014
COUPON CLERK (financial) 219.462-010
Coupon-Collection Clerk (financial) 216.362-014
Coupon-Manifest Clerk (clerical) 209.687-010
COUPON-REDEMPTION CLERK (retail trade) 290.477-010
courier (clerical) 230.663-010
court abstractor (profess. & kin.) 119.267-010
COURT ADMINISTRATOR (government ser.) 188.117-130
COURT CLERK (government ser.) 243.362-010
court officer (government ser.) 377.667-010
court reporter (clerical) 202.362-010
cover assembler (furniture) 780.684-114
Cover Assembler (furniture) 780.682-010
Cover Assembler (tex. prod., nec) 787.682-066
cover creaser (boot & shoe) 690.685-174
cover cutter (boot & shoe) 788.687-042

Cover Cutter, Machine (furniture; tex. prod., nec) 781.684-014
COVERED-BUCKLE ASSEMBLER (button & notion) 734.687-050
covered button maker (any industry) 734.687-046
COVERER, LOOSELEAF BINDER (print. & pub.) 795.687-010
covering-machine operator (paper goods) 641.685-098
COVERING-MACHINE OPERATOR (print. & pub.) 653.682-014
Covering-Machine Operator (rubber goods) 690.662-014
COVERING-MACHINE OPERATOR (textile) 681.685-038
Covering-Machine-Operator Helper (rubber goods) 690.686-070
COVERING-MACHINE-OPERATOR HELPER (textile) 681.685-042
COVERING-MACHINE TENDER (leather prod.) 783.685-010
COVER INSPECTOR (furniture) 789.687-038
Cover-Machine Operator (wood. container) 669.685-014
Cover Maker (boot & shoe) 690.682-082
Cover Maker (chemical) 844.681-010
Cover Maker (furniture) 780.682-018
cover-making-machine operator (print. & pub.) 653.685-018
Cover Marker (paint & varnish) 920.685-078
Cover-Mat-Machine Operator (wood. container) 669.685-014
cover remover (boot & shoe) 788.687-042
COVERSTITCH-MACHINE OPERATOR (garment) 786.682-078
COVER STRIPPER (paper goods) 641.685-034
cover treater (toy-sport equip.) 559.685-102
COWPUNCHER (agriculture) 410.674-014
Cow Trimmer (meat products) 525.687-046
Coyote Hunter (fishing & hunt.) 461.661-010
cpa (profess. & kin.)   see ACCOUNTANT, CERTIFIED PUBLIC
cp bleacher operator (chemical; soap & rel.) 558.685-018
crab backer (can. & preserv.) 525.684-022
CRABBER (textile) 582.685-038
CRAB BUTCHER (can. & preserv.) 525.684-022
CRAB MEAT PROCESSOR (can. & preserv.) 525.687-126
Crab Steamer (can. & preserv.) 529.685-214
cracker (jewelry-silver.) 770.687-030
cracker (rubber goods; rubber reclaim.) 555.685-030
CRACKER-AND-COOKIE-MACHINE OPERATOR (bakery products) 520.682-034
Cracker-And-Cookie-Machine-Operator Helper (bakery products) 526.686-010
Cracker-Dough Mixer (bakery products) 520.685-234
cracker-fanner operator (sugar & conf.) 521.385-010
CRACKER SPRAYER (bakery products) 524.685-022
CRACKING-AND-FANNING-MACHINE OPERATOR (sugar & conf.) 521.385-010
CRACKING-UNIT OPERATOR (plastic-synth.) 558.682-010
Crackling-Press Operator (meat products) 529.685-202
Cradle Placer (construction) 869.664-014
Cradle-Slide Maker (furniture) 616.685-058
CRAFT DEMONSTRATOR (museums) 109.364-010
crafter (jewelry-silver.) 700.381-014
craft supervisor (any industry) 638.131-022
craft worker (jewelry-silver.) 700.381-014
Cranberry-Farm Supervisor (agriculture) 403.131-014
Cranberry Grower (agriculture) 403.161-014
Cranberry Sorter (agriculture; wholesale tr.) 529.687-186
CRANE-CREW SUPERVISOR (any industry) 921.133-010
crane engineer (any industry)   see CRANE OPERATOR
crane follower (any industry) 921.667-022
crane hooker (any industry) 921.667-022
crane operator (any industry) 921.663-022
CRANE OPERATOR (any industry) term
crane operator, cab (any industry) 921.663-010
crane operator, ground control (any industry) 921.663-010
Crane Operator-Hooker (steel & rel.) 921.663-010
Crane Operator-Hooktender (aircraft mfg.) 921.663-010
crane rigger (any industry) 921.260-010
Crank Hand (construction) 869.687-026
Crankshaft Straightener (auto. mfg.) 617.482-026
crash-squad accident investigator (government ser.) 375.263-010
crate builder (wood. container) 760.684-014
Crate Icer (can. & preserv.) 922.687-046
CRATE LINER (furniture) 920.687-078
CRATE OPENER (furniture) 929.685-010
CRATER (any industry) 920.684-010
Crater (agriculture) 920.687-134
Crate Repairer (any industry) 920.684-010
Crate Tier (agriculture; wholesale tr.) 920.687-134
CRATING-AND-MOVING ESTIMATOR (motor trans.; r.r. trans.) 252.357-010
crawler-crane operator (any industry) 921.663-058
Crawler-Dragline Operator (any industry) 850.683-018
Crawler-Tractor Operator (any industry) 850.683-010
CRAYON GRADER (mine & quarry) 579.684-014
Crayon-Molding-Machine Operator (pen & pencil) 575.685-022
CRAYON SAWYER (mine & quarry) 677.685-022
CRAYON-SORTING-MACHINE FEEDER (pen & pencil) 929.686-018

CUFF FOLDER (knitting) 685.687-014
Cuff Knitter (knitting) 685.665-014
Cuff Presser (knitting) 583.685-070
Cuff Separator (knitting) 789.687-030
Cuff Setter, Lockstitch (garment) 786.682-070
Cuff Setter, Overlock (garment) 786.682-074
Cuff Slitter (glove & mit.) 699.682-030
Cuff Turner (knitting) 789.687-182
cuff turner (knitting) 685.687-014
cuff-turner-machine operator (garment) 583.685-102
Culled-Fruit Packer (agriculture) 920.687-134
CULLER (wood. container) 764.687-054
CULLET CRUSHER-AND-WASHER (glass mfg.) 570.685-026
Cull Grader (agriculture; wholesale tr.) 529.687-186
Cultural Affairs Officer (government ser.) 188.117-106
CULTURED-MARBLE-PRODUCTS MAKER (stonework) 575.684-050
Culture-Room Worker (beverage) 522.662-010
CUPBOARD BUILDER (furniture) 703.684-014
cup filler (ordnance) 737.687-102
CUPOLA CHARGER (foundry) 512.686-010
CUPOLA CHARGER, INSULATION (concrete prod.) 572.686-010
CUPOLA HOIST OPERATOR (foundry) 921.683-030
cupola liner (foundry) 861.684-010
Cupola-Melting Supervisor (foundry) 519.131-010
CUPOLA OPERATOR, INSULATION (concrete prod.) 579.382-014
CUPOLA PATCHER (foundry) 861.684-010
cupola stocker (foundry) 512.686-010
CUPOLA TAPPER (foundry) 514.664-010
CUPOLA TENDER (foundry) 512.662-010
Cupola-Tender Helper (foundry) 519.687-022
CUPROUS-CHLORIDE HELPER (chemical) 558.585-022
CUPROUS-CHLORIDE OPERATOR (chemical) 558.382-034
CUP SETTER, LOCKSTITCH (garment) 786.682-082
CUP-TRIMMING-MACHINE OPERATOR (ordnance) 615.685-018
CURATOR (museums) 102.017-010
Curator, Art Gallery (museums) 102.017-010
Curator, Herbarium (museums) 102.017-010
Curator, Horticultural Museum (museums) 102.017-010
Curator, Medical Museum (museums) 102.017-010
Curator, Natural History Museum (museums) 102.017-010
Curator, Zoological Museum (museums) 102.017-010
CURB ATTENDANT (laundry & rel.) 369.477-010
Curbing Stonecutter (stonework) 771.381-014
CURB-MACHINE OPERATOR (construction) 853.683-010
Curb Setter (construction) 861.381-038
Curb-Setter Helper (construction) 869.687-026
Curb Supervisor (construction) 869.131-014
curer (rubber goods; rubber reclaim.; rubber tire) 553.665-038
Curer, Acid Drum (rubber goods) 556.685-066
CURER, FOAM RUBBER (rubber goods) 553.682-014
CURING-BIN OPERATOR (grain-feed mills) 522.685-038
curing finisher (rubber tire) 553.685-102
Curing-Machine Operator (construction) 853.663-014
CURING-OVEN TENDER (chemical) 553.685-038
curing oven tender (textile) 581.685-030
curing packer (meat products) 522.687-034
CURING-PRESS MAINTAINER (rubber tire) 629.684-010
CURING-PRESS OPERATOR (rubber tire) 553.686-018
Curing Supervisor (rubber goods) 559.137-014
Curing Supervisor (rubber tire) 750.130-010
Curler (button & notion) 734.684-010
curling-machine operator (textile) 585.685-022
CURRENCY COUNTER (financial) 217.485-010
currency-machine operator (financial) 217.485-010
Curtain Cleaner (hotel & rest.) 323.687-018
Curtain Cutter, Hand (tex. prod., nec) 781.684-074
curtain drier (laundry & rel.) 363.687-022
Curtain Feller, Blindstitch (garment) 786.682-046
curtain framer (laundry & rel.) 363.687-022
Curtain Hemmer, Automatic (tex. prod., nec) 787.685-018
Curtain Inspector (tex. prod., nec) 789.587-014
CURTAIN-ROLLER ASSEMBLER (furniture) 739.684-042
curtain stretcher (laundry & rel.) 363.687-022
CURTAIN-STRETCHER ASSEMBLER (woodworking) 762.684-030
Curtain Supervisor (tex. prod., nec) 787.132-010
curved-tooth-gear-generator operator (machine shop) 602.382-014
cushion assembler (furniture) 780.684-054
CUSHION BUILDER (furniture) 780.684-046
cushion cementer (boot & shoe) 788.684-026
Cushion Closer (furniture; tex. prod., nec) 780.682-018
Cushion-Cover Inspector (furniture; tex. prod., nec) 789.687-038
cushion filler (furniture) 780.684-054
Cushion Filler (tex. prod., nec) 780.684-066
Cushion Former (toy-sport equip.) 732.384-010
Cushion Installer (toy-sport equip.) 732.384-010

Cushion Maker, Hand (jewelry-silver.) 739.687-138
CUSHION MAKER I (furniture) 780.684-054
Cushion Maker II (furniture) 780.682-018
cushion-mat maker (furniture) 780.684-054
Cushion-Spring Assembler (furniture) 780.684-098
cushion stuffer (furniture) 780.684-054
cushion sweeper (tex. prod., nec) 789.687-122
Cushion Trimmer (boot & shoe) 690.682-086
custodial services manager (any industry) 187.167-046
CUSTODIAN, ATHLETIC EQUIPMENT (amuse. & rec.) 969.367-010
Custodian, Blood Bank (medical ser.) 222.387-058
custodian, wardrobe (motion picture; radio-tv broad.) 346.374-010
CUSTOMER-COMPLAINT CLERK (clerical) 241.367-014
customer engineer (any industry) 633.281-030
Customer-Engineering Specialist (office machines) 828.261-022
CUSTOMER-EQUIPMENT ENGINEER (tel. & tel.) 003.187-018
CUSTOMER-FACILITIES SUPERVISOR (tel. & tel.) 822.131-014
customer-order clerk (clerical) 249.362-026
customer-return inspector (plastic prod.; plastic-synth.) 559.381-010
customer security clerk (air trans.) 372.667-010
customer service agent (air trans.) 248.367-018
customer-service clerk (insurance) 249.262-010
CUSTOMER-SERVICE CLERK (retail trade) 299.367-010
Customer Service Manager (retail trade) 299.137-010
customer servicer (any industry) 637.261-018
CUSTOMER SERVICE REPRESENTATIVE (financial) 205.362-026
customer service representative (profess. & kin.) 032.262-010
CUSTOMER-SERVICE REPRESENTATIVE (radio-tv broad.; tel. & tel.; utilities; waterworks) 239.362-014
CUSTOMER SERVICE REPRESENTATIVE (utilities) 959.361-010
customer-service representative (utilities) 241.267-034
CUSTOMER-SERVICE-REPRESENTATIVE INSTRUCTOR (tel. & tel.; utilities; waterworks) 239.227-010
CUSTOMER-SERVICE REPRESENTATIVE SUPERVISOR (radio-tv broad.; tel. & tel.; utilities; waterworks) 239.137-014
customer-servicer helper (any industry) 637.684-010
CUSTOMER SERVICES COORDINATOR (print. & pub.) 221.167-026
customer services instructor (air trans.) 099.227-018
customer-service specialist, post exchange (retail trade) 299.367-010
CUSTOM-FEED-MILL OPERATOR (grain-feed mills) 529.132-010
CUSTOM-FEED-MILL-OPERATOR HELPER (grain-feed mills) 521.686-026
Custom-Frame Assembler (auto. mfg.) 806.381-058
Custom Garment Designer (retail trade) 142.061-018
CUSTOM-LEATHER-PRODUCTS MAKER (leather prod.) 783.361-010
CUSTOMS BROKER (financial) 186.117-018
Customs-Entry Clerk (clerical) 214.467-010
customs examiner (government ser.) 168.267-018
Custom-Shoe Designer And Maker (boot & shoe) 788.381-014
customs-house broker (financial) 186.117-018
CUSTOMS IMPORT SPECIALIST (government ser.) 168.267-018
CUSTOMS INSPECTOR (government ser.) 168.267-022
CUSTOM SKI MAKER (toy-sport equip.) 732.281-010
CUSTOMS PATROL OFFICER (government ser.) 168.167-010
CUSTOM TAILOR (garment; personal ser.; retail trade) 785.261-014
CUSTOM VAN CONVERTER (auto. mfg.; automotive ser.) 806.381-070
CUT-AND-COVER LINE WORKER (boot & shoe) 753.684-014
CUT-AND-PRINT-MACHINE OPERATOR (ordnance) 659.682-010
CUTCH CLEANER (metal prod., nec) 700.687-030
CUT-FILE CLERK (print. & pub.) 222.367-014
CUT-IN WORKER (grain-feed mills) 521.686-030
CUT-LACE-MACHINE OPERATOR (leather prod.) 585.685-038
cutlery grinder (any industry) 701.381-018
CUTLET MAKER, PORK (meat products) 529.686-022
cut-off-machine helper (glass mfg.) 677.665-010
cut-off-machine operator (ordnance) 609.685-026
CUT-OFF-MACHINE OPERATOR (ordnance) 615.685-022
CUT-OFF-MACHINE OPERATOR (paper goods) 640.685-034
cut-off-machine operator (pen & pencil) 690.685-306
CUT-OFF-MACHINE OPERATOR (steel & rel.) 619.685-094
cut-off-machine unloader (glass mfg.) 677.665-010
Cut-Off-Saw Grader (woodworking) 667.382-010
cut-off-saw operator (saw. & plan.) 667.682-078
cut-off-saw operator (stonework) 677.462-010
CUT-OFF-SAW OPERATOR I (woodworking) 667.682-022
CUT-OFF-SAW OPERATOR II (woodworking) 667.685-074
CUT-OFF-SAW OPERATOR, METAL (machine shop) 607.682-010
CUT-OFF-SAW OPERATOR, PIPE BLANKS (nonmet. min.) 677.685-026
CUT-OFF SAW TENDER, METAL (machine shop) 607.685-010
CUT-OFF SAWYER, LOG (paper & pulp; saw. & plan.) 667.685-034
Cut-Off Sawyer, Shingle Mill (saw. & plan.) 667.685-022
cut-off tender, glass (glass mfg.) 677.685-030
cut order hand (carpet & rug) 781.684-010
CUT-OUT-AND-MARKING-MACHINE OPERATOR (boot & shoe) 690.685-110
CUT-OUT-MACHINE OPERATOR (boot & shoe) 690.685-114

cut-out marker (boot & shoe) 788.584-014
cut-out-press operator (boot & shoe) 690.685-114
Cut-Out Stitcher (boot & shoe) 690.682-082
Cut-Out Worker (boot & shoe) 690.685-434
Cut-Plug Packer (tobacco) 920.687-130
Cut-Roll-Machine Offbearer (sugar & conf.) 529.686-034
cut-roll-machine operator (sugar & conf.) 520.685-198
cutter (agriculture) 404.686-010
CUTTER (any industry) term
cutter (any industry) 775.684-022
cutter (any industry) 920.687-038
CUTTER (brick & tile) 579.684-030
Cutter (button & notion) 734.684-010
cutter (fabrication, nec) 690.485-010
CUTTER (food prep.) 529.685-082
CUTTER (glove & mit.; tex. prod., nec) 699.682-014
cutter (hat & cap) 585.685-046
cutter (jewelry-silver.) 770.281-014
Cutter (leather mfg.) 589.686-022
cutter (motion picture; radio-tv broad.) 962.262-010
Cutter (paper & pulp) 539.587-010
CUTTER (photofinishing) 976.685-010
cutter (stonework) 771.384-010
cutter (tex. prod., nec) 789.687-134
CUTTER (tex. prod., nec) 686.685-022
cutter (toy-sport equip.) 732.685-014
CUTTER, ALUMINUM SHEET (ship-boat mfg.) 804.684-010
cutter and edge trimmer (jewelry-silver.) 700.687-066
CUTTER-AND-PASTER, PRESS CLIPPINGS (business ser.) 249.587-014
cutter and presser (soap & rel.) 559.685-142
CUTTER APPRENTICE, HAND (any industry) 781.684-078
CUTTER, BANANA ROOM (wholesale tr.) 929.687-010
CUTTER, BARREL DRUM (tex. prod., nec) 690.682-026
Cutter, Brake Lining (nonmet. min.) 579.687-010
cutter, first (soap & rel.) 559.686-042
CUTTER, FROZEN MEAT (can. & preserv.) 521.685-098
cutter, gas (welding) 816.464-010
cutter grinder (machine shop) 603.280-038
cutter-grinder operator (machine shop) 603.280-038
CUTTER, HAND (rubber goods) 751.684-014
CUTTER, HAND I (any industry) 781.684-074
CUTTER, HAND II (any industry) 781.687-026
CUTTER, HAND III (any industry) 781.687-030
cutter-head sharpener (machine shop) 603.382-038
CUTTER HELPER (any industry) 781.687-022
CUTTER, HOT KNIFE (boot & shoe; rubber goods) 751.684-018
CUTTER I (fabrication, nec) 690.685-118
CUTTER II (fabrication, nec) 692.686-030
cutter-in (boot & shoe) 690.682-046
CUTTER-INSPECTOR (nonmet. min.) 751.684-010
cutter, machine (leather prod.) 585.685-038
cutter, machine (sugar & conf.) 521.685-102
CUTTER, MACHINE I (any industry) 781.684-014
CUTTER, MACHINE II (any industry) 699.685-014
CUTTER-MACHINE TENDER (electron. comp.) 615.685-046
CUTTER OPERATOR (any industry) 699.682-018
CUTTER OPERATOR (mine & quarry) 930.683-014
cutter operator (paper & pulp; tex. prod., nec) 530.666-010
cutter operator (plastic prod.; plastic-synth.) 555.685-026
CUTTER OPERATOR (plastic-synth.) 555.585-010
cutter operator (print. & pub.) 640.682-018
cutter operator, asbestos shingle (nonmet. min.) 679.686-010
Cutter Operator, Brick (brick & tile) 575.382-010
CUTTER-OPERATOR HELPER (mine & quarry) 930.687-018
Cutter Operator, Tile (brick & tile) 575.382-010
cutter, plastics rolls (plastic-synth.) 690.665-010
Cutter, Plastics Sheets (plastic prod.; plastic-synth.) 690.685-122
CUTTER, ROTARY SHEAR (tex. prod., nec) 781.684-018
CUTTER, V-GROOVE (clock & watch) 715.685-014
CUTTER, WET MACHINE (paper & pulp) 539.686-010
CUTTER, WOODWIND REEDS (musical inst.) 730.686-010
cutting-and-creasing-machine operator (paper goods) 649.682-014
cutting-and-creasing-press operator (paper goods) 659.662-010
CUTTING-AND-PRINTING-MACHINE OPERATOR (tex. prod., nec) 652.685-022
Cutting-And-Sewing Supervisor (tex. prod., nec) 789.132-010
Cutting-Department Supervisor (leather prod.) 783.132-010
Cutting-Department Supervisor (tex. prod., nec) 789.132-014
Cutting Inspector (garment) 789.687-070
CUTTING INSPECTOR (tex. prod., nec) 781.684-022
CUTTING-MACHINE FIXER (textile) 585.380-010
CUTTING-MACHINE OFFBEARER (tex. prod., nec) 689.686-018
cutting-machine operator (beverage) 640.565-010
cutting-machine operator (hat & cap; tex. prod., nec) 585.685-086
cutting-machine operator (mine & quarry) 930.683-014

CUTTING-MACHINE OPERATOR (print. & pub.) 640.682-018
Cutting-Machine Operator (rubber goods) 690.680-010
CUTTING-MACHINE OPERATOR (sugar & conf.) 521.685-102
cutting-machine operator (sugar & conf.) 521.685-034
CUTTING-MACHINE OPERATOR (tex. prod., nec) 686.585-010
cutting-machine operator (textile) 585.565-010
Cutting-Machine-Operator Helper (sugar & conf.) 529.686-034
CUTTING-MACHINE TENDER (any industry) 690.685-122
CUTTING-MACHINE TENDER, DECORATIVE (glass mfg.) 775.685-010
CUTTING-MACHINE-TENDER HELPER (any industry) 690.686-030
Cutting-Room Supervisor (boot & shoe) 788.131-010
CUTTING SUPERVISOR (glass products) 775.134-010
cutting supervisor (logging) 183.167-038
cutting-table operator (rubber goods) 751.686-010
cutting-table operator, first (soap & rel.) 559.686-042
cw operator (tel. & tel.) 193.262-030
Cyanide Furnace Operator (heat treating) 504.682-014
cycle repairer (any industry) 639.681-010
CYLINDER BATCHER (textile) 582.665-010
Cylinder-Block-Hole Reliner (automotive ser.) 616.682-010
Cylinder Checker (chemical) 549.587-010
Cylinder Devalver (chemical) 549.587-010
CYLINDER-DIE-MACHINE HELPER (paper goods) 649.686-018
CYLINDER-DIE-MACHINE OPERATOR (paper goods) 649.682-014
cylinder dyer (textile) 582.685-014
CYLINDER FILLER (chemical) 559.565-010
CYLINDER GRINDER (print. & pub.) 500.381-010
Cylinder Handler (chemical) 549.587-010
Cylinder-Head Assembler (engine-turbine) 706.481-010
cylinder honer (machine shop) 603.482-034
CYLINDER INSPECTOR-AND-TESTER (chemical) 953.387-010
cylinder loader (chemical) 559.565-010
CYLINDER-MACHINE OPERATOR (paper & pulp; wood prod., nec) 539.362-010
Cylinder-Machine Operator, Pulp Drier (paper & pulp) 539.362-010
CYLINDER-PRESS FEEDER (print. & pub.) 651.686-010
CYLINDER-PRESS OPERATOR (print. & pub.) 651.362-010
CYLINDER-PRESS-OPERATOR APPRENTICE (print. & pub.) 651.362-014
cylinder-press-operator helper (print. & pub.) 651.686-010
CYLINDER-SANDER OPERATOR (woodworking) 662.685-014
Cylinder Steamer (chemical) 549.587-010
cylinder tester (chemical) 953.387-010
Cylinder Valver (chemical) 549.587-010
cylinder-valve repairer (chemical) 630.381-030
Cylindrical Mixer (hat & cap) 680.685-062
Cylindrical grinder, tool (machine shop) 603.280-010
Cylindrical Mixer (hat & cap) 680.685-062
CYTOGENETIC TECHNOLOGIST (medical ser.) 078.261-026
CYTOLOGIST (profess. & kin.) 041.061-042
CYTOTECHNOLOGIST (medical ser.) 078.281-010

D

DADO OPERATOR (woodworking) 669.382-010
Dag Coater (electron. comp.) 725.684-022
Dag Sprayer (electron. comp.) 741.687-018
daily release and dupe printer (motion picture) 976.682-010
DAIRY-EQUIPMENT REPAIRER (dairy products) 629.281-018
Dairy Farmer (agriculture) 410.161-018
Dairy-Feed-Mixing Operator (grain-feed mills) 520.685-098
DAIRY HELPER (dairy products) 529.686-026
Dairy-Management Specialist (profess. & kin.) 040.061-018
dairy-manufacturing technologist (profess. & kin.) 040.061-022
Dairy-Nutrition Specialist (profess. & kin.) 040.061-018
Dairy-Powder-Mixer Operator (sugar & conf.) 520.685-074
DAIRY-PROCESSING-EQUIPMENT OPERATOR (dairy products) 529.382-018
dairy-products technologist (profess. & kin.) 040.061-022
DAIRY SCIENTIST (profess. & kin.) 040.061-018
DAIRY TECHNOLOGIST (profess. & kin.) 040.061-022
damage cutter (garment) 782.684-038
DAMPENER OPERATOR (paper & pulp) 534.685-010
Dampproofer (construction) 869.664-014
dam tender (waterworks) 954.382-018
Dance-Hall Inspector (government ser.) 375.263-014
DANCER (amuse. & rec.) 151.047-010
DANCE THERAPIST (medical ser.) 076.127-018
darkroom worker (photofinishing) 976.681-010
darner (knitting) 782.684-030
Darning-Machine Operator (any industry) 787.682-030
data acquisition laboratory technician (aircraft mfg.) 002.262-010
DATA BASE ADMINISTRATOR (profess. & kin.) 039.162-010
DATA BASE DESIGN ANALYST (profess. & kin.) 039.162-014
data clerk (clerical) 209.687-010
DATA COMMUNICATIONS ANALYST (any industry) 031.262-010

DATA COMMUNICATIONS TECHNICIAN (any industry) 823.261-030
data communications technician supervisor (any industry) 031.132-010
Data Dictionary Administrator (profess. & kin.) 039.162-014
DATA ENTRY CLERK (clerical) 203.582-054
data entry operator (clerical) 203.582-054
DATA-EXAMINATION CLERK (clerical) 209.387-022
DATA RECOVERY PLANNER (profess. & kin.) 033.162-014
data-reduction technician (profess. & kin.) 020.162-010
data security coordinator (profess. & kin.) 033.162-010
Date Puller (sugar & conf.) 521.687-066
DATER ASSEMBLER (pen & pencil) 733.687-030
Daub-Color Matcher (tex. prod., nec) 550.382-014
Daub-Color Mixer (tex. prod., nec) 550.382-014
dauber (steel & rel.) 543.687-014
day care worker (any industry) 359.677-018
Day Guard (any industry) 372.667-034
Day-Haul Youth Supervisor (agriculture) 913.363-010
DAY WORKER (domestic ser.) 301.687-014
dead header (boot & shoe; rubber goods) 922.687-066
DE-ALCOHOLIZER (beverage) 522.685-042
DEALER-COMPLIANCE REPRESENTATIVE (retail trade; wholesale tr.) 168.267-026
dean of admissions (education) 090.167-014
dean of chapel (education) 129.107-018
dean of instruction (education) 090.117-010
Dean of Men (education) 090.117-018
dean of student affairs (education) 090.117-018
DEAN OF STUDENTS (education) 090.117-018
Dean of Women (education) 090.117-018
dean, school of nursing (medical ser.) 075.117-030
Death-Claim Clerk (insurance) 219.362-010
Death-Claim Examiner (insurance) 241.267-018
debeader (rubber goods; rubber reclaim.) 690.685-386
debeaker (agriculture) 411.687-026
DEBLOCKER (optical goods) 716.687-010
DEBONER, PET FOOD (can. & preserv.) 521.685-378
DEBRANDER (boot & shoe) 753.687-014
DEBRIDGING-MACHINE OPERATOR (nonfer. metal) 607.685-014
debtor (clerical) 241.367-026
DEBUBBLIZER (plastic-synth.) 553.585-010
DEBURRER (button & notion) 603.685-050
DEBURRER, MACHINE (clock & watch) 715.685-018
DEBURRER, PRINTED CIRCUIT BOARD PANELS (electron. comp.) 603.686-014
DEBURRER, STRIP (clock & watch) 603.482-010
DEBURRING-AND-TOOLING-MACHINE OPERATOR (office machines) 690.280-010
DECAL APPLIER (any industry) 749.684-010
decal transferrer (any industry) 749.684-010
DECATING-MACHINE OPERATOR (textile) 582.685-042
DECAY-CONTROL OPERATOR (wholesale tr.) 529.685-086
deck and hull assembler (ship-boat mfg.) 806.684-022
DECK ENGINEER (water trans.) 623.281-014
deck-engine operator (water trans.) 921.683-034
DECKER OPERATOR (paper & pulp) 533.682-010
Deck Guard (fishing & hunt.; water trans.) 372.667-034
DECKHAND (chemical) 553.686-022
DECKHAND (water trans.) 911.687-022
Deckhand, Clam Dredge (fishing & hunt.) 449.667-010
Deckhand, Crab Boat (fishing & hunt.) 449.667-010
DECKHAND, FISHING VESSEL (fishing & hunt.) 449.667-010
Deckhand, Maintenance (water trans.) 911.364-010
Deckhand, Oyster Dredge (fishing & hunt.) 449.667-010
Deckhand, Shrimp Boat (fishing & hunt.) 449.667-010
Deckhand, Sponge Boat (fishing & hunt.) 449.667-010
Deckhand, Tuna Boat (fishing & hunt.) 449.667-010
Deck Molder (ship-boat mfg.) 806.684-054
deck sawyer (paper & pulp; saw. & plan.) 667.685-034
Deck Scaler (saw. & plan.) 455.487-010
deck worker (saw. & plan.) 921.685-014
DECONTAMINATOR (any industry) 199.384-010
DECORATING-AND-ASSEMBLY SUPERVISOR (plastic prod.) 754.130-010
DECORATING-EQUIPMENT SETTER (glass mfg.; glass products) 652.380-010
DECORATING INSPECTOR (glass mfg.) 579.687-014
Decorating-Kiln Operator (pottery & porc.) 573.662-010
DECORATING-MACHINE OPERATOR (glass products) 652.685-026
Decorating-Machine Tender (glass mfg.) 979.685-010
Decorative Greens Cutter (forestry) 453.687-014
decorator (any industry) 970.381-022
decorator (any industry) 979.684-034
DECORATOR (any industry) 298.381-010
decorator (bakery products) 524.684-022
DECORATOR (bakery products; sugar & conf.) 524.684-014
decorator (brick & tile) 773.381-010

decorator (construction; stonework) 779.381-022
DECORATOR (dairy products) 524.381-014
decorator (engraving) 704.381-030
decorator (fabrication, nec) 741.684-010
DECORATOR (furniture; toy-sport equip.) 749.684-014
DECORATOR (glass mfg.; glass products) 740.381-010
DECORATOR (hat & cap) 784.684-022
DECORATOR (leather prod.) 739.684-046
decorator (leather prod.) 781.381-018
DECORATOR (pottery & porc.) 740.684-014
decorator consultant (retail trade) 295.357-018
decorator, hand (bakery products; sugar & conf.) 524.684-014
decorator, hand (pottery & porc.) 740.681-010
decorator, hand (sugar & conf.) 524.684-018
decorator, hand (tex. prod., nec) 782.684-018
decorator inspector (pottery & porc.) 774.687-018
DECORATOR, LIGHTING FIXTURES (light. fix.) 749.684-018
DECORATOR, MANNEQUIN (fabrication, nec) 970.381-014
decorator, store (retail trade) 298.081-010
DECORATOR, STREET AND BUILDING (any industry) 899.687-010
dedenter (any industry) 619.685-034
dedenter (beverage) 617.682-010
Deep-Fryer Assembler (house. appl.) 723.684-010
DEEP SUBMERGENCE VEHICLE CREWMEMBER (military ser.) 623.281-014
DEEP SUBMERGENCE VEHICLE OPERATOR (military ser.) 911.263-010
defect cutter (millwork-plywood) 663.585-010
defect cutter (woodworking) 667.682-082
DEFECTIVE-CIGARETTE SLITTER (tobacco) 529.685-090
DEFECT REPAIRER, GLASSWARE (glass mfg.) 772.684-010
DEFENSIVE FIRE CONTROL SYSTEMS OPERATOR (military ser.) 378.382-014
Defensive-Line Coach (amuse. & rec.) 153.227-010
DEFINER (button & notion) 599.685-022
DEFLASH AND WASH OPERATOR (electron. comp.) 726.685-022
DEFLECTOR OPERATOR (beverage) 529.687-058
Degreaser (any industry) 503.685-030
Degreasing-Solution Mixer (chemical) 550.685-106
Degreasing-Solution Reclaimer (chemical) 552.685-014
Degreasing-Wheel Operator (leather mfg.) 582.685-050
degree clerk (education) 205.367-010
DEHAIRING-MACHINE TENDER (meat products) 525.685-018
DEHYDRATING-PRESS OPERATOR (chemical; plastic-synth.) 551.685-046
dehydrator (can. & preserv.; grain-feed mills) 523.685-058
dehydrator operator (petrol. & gas) 541.382-014
DEHYDRATOR TENDER (can. & preserv.) 523.685-054
Dehydrogenation-Converter Helper (chemical) 558.585-010
Dehydrogenation-Converter Operator (chemical) 558.362-010
Dehydrogenation-Converter Utility Operator (chemical) 559.682-066
dehydrogenation operator, head (chemical; petrol. refin.) 559.132-078
DEICER ASSEMBLER, ELECTRIC (rubber goods) 739.684-050
Deicer Assembler, Pneumatic (rubber goods) 739.684-050
DEICER-ELEMENT WINDER, HAND (rubber goods) 739.684-058
DEICER-ELEMENT WINDER, MACHINE (rubber goods) 692.685-066
DEICER FINISHER (rubber goods) 739.684-054
DEICER INSPECTOR, ELECTRIC (rubber goods) 729.387-010
DEICER INSPECTOR, PNEUMATIC (rubber goods) 759.687-010
DEICER-KIT ASSEMBLER (rubber goods) 759.684-030
Deicer Repairer, Electric (rubber goods) 759.684-026
Deicer Repairer, Pneumatic (rubber goods) 759.684-026
DEICER REPAIRER (rubber goods) 759.684-026
DEICER TESTER (rubber goods) 729.387-014
DE-IONIZER OPERATOR (chemical) 558.685-026
Delicatessen-Goods Stock Clerk (retail trade) 299.367-014
DELI CUTTER-SLICER (retail trade) 316.684-014
Delimer (leather mfg.) 582.482-014
DELINEATOR (profess. & kin.) 970.281-014
delinquent-account clerk (clerical) 241.357-010
Delinquent-Notice-Machine Operator (clerical) 214.482-010
DELIVERER, CAR RENTAL (automotive ser.; retail trade) 919.663-010
Deliverer, Food (retail trade) 299.477-010
DELIVERER, MERCHANDISE (retail trade) 299.477-010
DELIVERER, OUTSIDE (clerical) 230.663-010
Deliverer, Pharmacy (retail trade) 299.477-010
delivery-room clerk (hotel & rest.) 324.577-014
delivery-route truck driver (retail trade; wholesale tr.) 292.353-010
Delivery-Table Operator (nonfer. metal; steel & rel.) 613.682-026
Delivery-Truck Driver, Heavy (any industry) 905.663-014
Demand Equipment Repairer (utilities) 715.281-010
demand inspector (utilities) 952.367-010
Demographer I (profess. & kin.) 020.167-026
Demographer II (profess. & kin.) 054.067-014
Demolition-Crane Operator I (any industry) 921.663-058
Demolition-Crane Operator II (any industry) 921.663-062
DEMOLITION SPECIALIST (ordnance) 737.687-034

devulcanizer, head (rubber reclaim.) 559.132-058
Devulcanizer Inspector (rubber reclaim.) 559.132-058
devulcanizer operator (rubber reclaim.) 558.585-026
DEVULCANIZER TENDER (rubber reclaim.) 558.585-026
DEWATERER OPERATOR (smelt. & refin.) 511.565-010
Dewatering-Filtering Supervisor (smelt. & refin.) 511.135-010
DEXTRINE MIXER (grain-feed mills) 523.682-018
diagnostic cardiac sonographer (medical ser.) 078.364-014
diagnostic medical sonographer (medical ser.) 078.364-010
DIAGRAMMER AND SEAMER (carpet & rug) 789.484-010
DIAL BRUSHER (clock & watch) 715.687-022
DIALER (clock & watch) 715.684-086
DIAL MAKER (clock & watch) 715.381-046
DIAL MAKER (office machines) 710.684-018
DIAL MARKER (elec. equip.) 729.684-018
dial printer (print. & pub.) 651.685-018
DIAL REFINISHER (clock & watch) 715.584-010
DIAL-SCREW ASSEMBLER (clock & watch) 715.684-082
DIALYSIS TECHNICIAN (medical ser.) 078.362-014
diamond assorter (jewelry-silver.) 770.281-010
DIAMOND BLENDER (cutlery-hrdwr.) 590.685-018
DIAMOND CLEAVER (jewelry-silver.) 770.381-014
DIAMOND CUTTER (jewelry-silver.) term
Diamond-Die Maker (machine shop) 601.280-018
DIAMOND-DIE POLISHER (machine tools) 770.381-022
Diamond Driller (any industry) 930.682-010
DIAMOND DRILLER (machine tools) 770.381-018
Diamond-Driller Helper (any industry) 930.687-014
DIAMOND EXPERT (jewelry-silver.) 770.267-010
diamond grader (jewelry-silver.) 770.281-010
DIAMOND MOUNTER (machine tools) 739.384-010
DIAMOND-POWDER TECHNICIAN (nonmet. min.) 673.685-046
Diamond Sander (stonework) 673.682-030
Diamond-Saw Operator (stonework) 677.462-010
DIAMOND SELECTOR (jewelry-silver.) 770.281-010
Diamond Setter (jewelry-silver.) 700.381-054
DIAMOND SIZER AND SORTER (clock & watch; jewelry-silver.) 770.687-014
Diamond-Tool Maker (clock & watch) 601.280-042
Diamond-Wheel Edger (glass products) 775.684-014
Diamond-Wheel Molder (nonmet. min.) 575.685-010
DIANETIC COUNSELOR (profess. & kin.) 199.207-010
dianeticist (profess. & kin.) 199.207-010
DIAPER MACHINE TENDER (protective dev.) 692.685-278
diaphragm builder (chemical) 826.684-022
Diathermy-Equipment Repairer (any industry) 729.281-030
Diazo Technician (electron. comp.) 976.384-010
Dice Dealer (amuse. & rec.) 343.464-010
DICE MAKER (toy-sport equip.) 731.381-010
Dicer-Machine Operator (can. & preserv.) 521.685-018
DICER OPERATOR (plastic-synth.) 690.685-130
Dice Spotter (toy-sport equip.) 740.687-018
dictating-machine transcriber (clerical) 203.582-058
dictating-machine typist (clerical) 203.582-058
DICTATING-TRANSCRIBING-MACHINE SERVICER (any industry) 633.281-014
Dictating-Transcribing-Machine Servicer, Grooved Tape (any industry) 633.281-014
Dictating-Transcribing-Machine Servicer, Magnetic Tape (any industry) 633.281-014
DIE ATTACHER (electron. comp.) 726.684-042
DIE ATTACHING MACHINE TENDER (electron. comp.) 726.685-026
DIE BARBER (machine shop) 705.381-010
Die Case Hardener (heat treating) 504.682-014
die-cast-die maker (machine shop) 601.280-030
Die-Casting-Machine Maintainer (foundry) 514.360-010
die-casting machine operator (elec. equip.) 502.482-018
DIE-CASTING-MACHINE OPERATOR I (foundry) 514.382-010
DIE-CASTING-MACHINE OPERATOR II (foundry) 514.685-018
DIE-CASTING-MACHINE SETTER (foundry) 514.360-010
Die-Cast Patternmaker (foundry) 661.281-022
DIE CLEANER (food prep., nec) 529.687-062
DIE CUTTER (any industry) 699.682-022
die cutter (jewelry-silver.) 601.381-014
die cutter (print. & pub.) 979.281-010
die cutter (tex. prod., nec; textile) 686.462-010
die-cutter apprentice (jewelry-silver.) 601.381-022
die cutter, diamond (machine tools) 770.381-022
Die-Cutting-Machine Operator, Automatic (rubber goods) 686.462-010
DIE-CUTTING-MACHINE OPERATOR, AUTOMATIC (tex. prod., nec; textile) 686.462-010
Die-Cutting-Machine-Operator Helper, Automatic (tex. prod., nec) 586.686-022
die design drafter (machine shop) 007.161-010
DIE DESIGNER (machine shop) 007.161-010
DIE-DESIGNER APPRENTICE (machine shop) 007.161-014

die developer (machine shop) 007.161-010
DIE-DRAWING CHECKER (profess. & kin.) 007.167-010
die engraver (print. & pub.) 979.281-010
Die-Engraving Supervisor (engraving) 704.131-010
die equipment operator (electron. comp.) 726.685-062
Die Filer (machine tools) 705.484-010
die-finisher, forging (machine shop) 705.484-014
DIE FINISHER (machine shop) 601.381-010
die fitter (machine shop) 601.381-010
Die-Lay-Out Worker (foundry) 661.281-022
dielectric-heat-sealing-machine operator (any industry) 690.685-154
DIELECTRIC-PRESS OPERATOR (auto. mfg.) 692.685-074
Dielectric Tester (rubber goods) 759.684-074
dielectric-testing-machine operator (elec. equip.) 727.687-050
die-machine operator (forging) 611.482-010
DIE MAKER (jewelry-silver.) 601.381-014
die maker (machine shop) 601.281-010
DIE MAKER (paper goods) 739.381-018
DIE MAKER (print. & pub.) 979.281-010
DIE-MAKER APPRENTICE (jewelry-silver.) 601.381-022
DIE-MAKER APPRENTICE (paper goods) 739.381-022
DIE MAKER, BENCH, STAMPING (machine shop) 601.281-010
DIE MAKER, ELECTRONIC (machine shop) 601.381-042
DIE MAKER, STAMPING (machine shop) 601.280-010
DIE MAKER, TRIM (machine shop) 601.280-014
DIE MAKER, WIRE DRAWING (machine shop) 601.280-018
DIE MOUNTER (paper goods) 659.684-010
die-out-machine operator (boot & shoe) 690.685-114
die polisher (machine tools) 770.381-022
DIE POLISHER (nonfer. metal) 601.381-018
DIE PRESSER (pottery & porc.) 575.685-026
die-press operator (any industry) 699.682-022
die-press operator (rubber goods) 690.685-286
Die Repairer, Forging (machine shop) 601.280-022
Die Repairer, Stamping (machine shop) 601.280-010
Die Repairer, Trimmer Dies (machine shop) 601.280-014
Diesel-Dragline Operator (any industry) 850.683-018
Diesel-Engine Assembler (engine-turbine) 806.481-014
diesel-engine engineer (petrol. & gas) 950.382-022
DIESEL-ENGINE ERECTOR (engine-turbine) 625.361-010
diesel-engine fitter (engine-turbine) 625.361-010
Diesel-Engine Inspector (engine-turbine) 806.261-010
diesel-engine-mechanic apprentice (any industry) 625.281-014
Diesel-Engine Mechanic, Automobile (automotive ser.) 625.281-010
Diesel-Engine Mechanic, Bus (automotive ser.) 625.281-010
Diesel-Engine Mechanic, Marine (ship-boat mfg.) 625.281-010
Diesel-Engine Mechanic, Truck (automotive ser.) 625.281-010
Diesel-Engine Operator, Stationary (any industry) 950.382-026
DIESEL-ENGINE TESTER (engine-turbine) 625.261-010
Diesel-Locomotive-Crane Operator (any industry) 921.663-038
DIESEL MECHANIC (any industry) 625.281-010
DIESEL-MECHANIC APPRENTICE (any industry) 625.281-014
Diesel-Mechanic, Construction (construction) 625.281-010
Diesel-Mechanic, Farm (agric. equip.) 625.281-010
DIESEL-MECHANIC HELPER (any industry) 625.684-010
Diesel-Pile-Driver Operator (construction) 859.682-018
DIESEL-PLANT OPERATOR (utilities) 952.382-010
Diesel-Powerplant Mechanic (utilities) 631.261-014
Diesel-Powerplant-Mechanic Helper (utilities) 631.684-010
Diesel-Powerplant Supervisor (utilities) 631.131-010
Diesel-Power-Shovel Operator (any industry) 850.683-030
Diesel-Roller Operator (construction) 859.683-030
Diesel-Tractor Operator (any industry) 929.683-014
Diesel-Truck-Crane Operator (any industry) 921.663-062
die setter (inst. & app.; office machines; plastic prod.; recording) 556.380-010
DIE SETTER (forging) 612.360-010
DIE SET-UP OPERATOR, PRINTED CIRCUIT BOARDS (electron. comp.) 699.380-010
DIE SINKER (machine shop) 601.280-022
die-sinking-machine operator (machine shop) 605.280-014
die-sinking-machine operator (machine shop) 605.382-026
die-stamping-press operator (print. & pub.) 651.382-010
Die-Storage Clerk (clerical) 222.367-062
dietary aide (medical ser.) 319.677-014
dietary assistant (hotel & rest.) 319.137-030
DIETARY MANAGER (hotel & rest.) 187.167-206
DIET CLERK (medical ser.) 245.587-010
DIE TESTER (electron. comp.) 726.685-030
DIETETIC TECHNICIAN (profess. & kin.) 077.124-010
DIETITIAN (profess. & kin.) term
dietitian, administrative (profess. & kin.) 077.117-010
DIETITIAN, CHIEF (profess. & kin.) 077.117-010
DIETITIAN, CLINICAL (profess. & kin.) 077.127-014
DIETITIAN, CONSULTANT (profess. & kin.) 077.127-018
DIETITIAN, RESEARCH (profess. & kin.) 077.061-010

DIETITIAN, TEACHING (profess. & kin.) 077.127-022
dietitian, therapeutic (profess. & kin.) 077.127-014
DIE TRIPPER (brick & tile) 575.665-014
DIE-TRY-OUT WORKER, STAMPING (machine shop) 601.281-014
Differential Repairer (auto. mfg.) 620.381-022
Differential Repairer (automotive ser.) 620.261-010
DIFFUSER OPERATOR (sugar & conf.) 523.562-010
DIFFUSION FURNACE OPERATOR, SEMICONDUCTOR WAFERS (electron. comp.) 590.685-070
digester charger (rubber reclaim.) 558.585-026
digester cook (paper & pulp; paper goods) 532.362-010
digester-cook helper (paper & pulp; paper goods) 532.686-010
digester operator (chemical) 552.682-018
digester operator (chemical) 555.686-010
DIGESTER OPERATOR (paper & pulp; paper goods) 532.362-010
DIGESTER-OPERATOR HELPER (paper & pulp; paper goods) 532.686-010
DIGESTION OPERATOR (smelt. & refin.) 519.565-010
DIGGER (fabrication, nec) 739.687-070
digger (mine & quarry) 939.687-014
digitizer (electron. comp.) 003.362-010
DIGITIZER OPERATOR (business ser.; petrol. & gas) 213.582-010
dimension-quarry supervisor (mine & quarry) 939.137-014
Dimethylaniline-Sulfator Operator (chemical) 550.585-030
DINING ROOM ATTENDANT (hotel & rest.) 311.677-018
dining-room attendant, cafeteria (hotel & rest.) 311.677-010
Dining-Room Cashier (hotel & rest.) 211.462-010
dining-room manager (hotel & rest.) 310.137-010
DINING-SERVICE INSPECTOR (r.r. trans.) 168.267-030
dining-service supervisor (hotel & rest.) 319.137-018
dining-service worker (hotel & rest.) 319.484-010
dinker (any industry) 781.687-030
DINKEY OPERATOR (any industry) 919.663-014
Dinkey Operator, Compressed Air (any industry) 919.663-014
Dinkey-Operator Helper (any industry) 932.664-010
Dinkey Operator, Mine (mine & quarry) 919.663-014
Dinkey Operator, Slag (smelt. & refin.) 919.663-014
Dinkey Operator, Slate (mine & quarry) 919.663-014
dinking-machine operator (any industry) 699.682-022
Diorama Model-Maker (fabrication, nec) 739.361-010
Dip Guider, Stoves (fabrication, nec) 590.686-014
Diplomatic Officer (government ser.) 188.117-106
DIP-LUBE OPERATOR (ordnance) 503.685-014
dip painter (any industry) 599.685-026
DIPPER (any industry) 599.685-026
Dipper (elec. equip.; electron. comp.) 726.687-022
DIPPER (fabrication, nec) 590.685-022
dipper (foundry) 518.687-022
dipper (hat & cap) 589.687-038
DIPPER (jewelry-silver.) 735.687-010
DIPPER (knitting; textile) 589.687-018
dipper (optical goods) 713.687-010
DIPPER (pen & pencil) 733.687-038
Dipper (plastic-synth.) 582.685-162
DIPPER (pottery & porc.) 774.684-014
DIPPER (rubber goods) 556.685-030
DIPPER AND BAKER (any industry) 599.685-030
DIPPER AND DRIER (woodworking) 749.687-010
DIPPER, CLOCK AND WATCH HANDS (clock & watch) 715.687-026
dipper, fish (can. & preserv.) 522.687-014
dipping-machine operator (plastic-synth.) 554.585-014
DIPPING-MACHINE OPERATOR (rubber goods) 556.685-034
dip tanker (wood prod., nec) 561.665-010
dip-tube assembler, machine (plastic prod.) 690.682-074
Dip-Unit Operator (rubber goods; rubber tire) 554.682-010
DIRECT-MAIL CLERK (clerical) 209.587-018
director, advertising (any industry) 164.117-010
DIRECTOR, AERONAUTICS COMMISSION (government ser.) 188.117-034
DIRECTOR, AGRICULTURAL SERVICES (government ser.) 188.117-038
director, airport (air trans.) 184.117-026
Director, Airport Operations (air trans.) 184.117-026
director, alumni relations (education) 090.117-014
DIRECTOR, ARTS-AND-HUMANITIES COUNCIL (government ser.) 188.117-042
DIRECTOR, ATHLETIC (education) 090.117-022
Director, Bio-Communications Laboratory (medical ser.) 076.104-010
director, broadcast (radio-tv broad.) 159.167-014
DIRECTOR, CAMP (social ser.) 195.167-018
DIRECTOR, CASTING (motion picture; radio-tv broad.) 159.267-010
director, chemical laboratory (profess. & kin.) 022.161-010
Director, Child Development Center (education) 092.167-010
Director, Child Support Enforcement Program (profess. & kin.) 195.117-010
Director, Civil Preparedness (government ser.) 188.117-022
Director, Civil Preparedness Warden (government ser.) 188.117-022
DIRECTOR, CLASSIFICATION AND TREATMENT (government ser.) 188.167-026
DIRECTOR, COMMISSION FOR THE BLIND (government ser.) 094.117-010

Director, Community Center (profess. & kin.) 195.117-010
DIRECTOR, COMMUNITY-HEALTH NURSING (medical ser.) 075.117-014
DIRECTOR, COMMUNITY ORGANIZATION (nonprofit org.) 187.167-234
DIRECTOR, COMPLIANCE (government ser.) 188.117-046
DIRECTOR, CONSUMER AFFAIRS (government ser.) 188.117-050
DIRECTOR, CORRECTIONAL AGENCY (government ser.) 188.117-054
director, council of social agencies (nonprofit org.) 187.167-234
DIRECTOR, COUNCIL ON AGING (government ser.) 188.117-058
director, counseling bureau (profess. & kin.) 045.107-018
DIRECTOR, CRAFT CENTER (profess. & kin.) 187.167-202
director, dance (amuse. & rec.) 151.027-010
director, data processing (profess. & kin.) 169.167-030
DIRECTOR, DAY CARE CENTER (education) 092.167-010
DIRECTOR, DENTAL SERVICES (medical ser.) 072.117-010
DIRECTOR, DIAGNOSTIC-AND-EVALUATION CLINIC (medical ser.) 070.107-018
director, dietetics department (profess. & kin.) 077.117-010
DIRECTOR, EDUCATION (museums) 099.117-030
director, educational board of nurse examiners (government ser.) 075.117-010
DIRECTOR, EDUCATIONAL, COMMUNITY-HEALTH NURSING (medical ser.) 075.117-018
DIRECTOR, EDUCATIONAL PROGRAM (education) 099.117-010
DIRECTOR, EDUCATIONAL PROGRAMMING (radio-tv broad.) 169.167-070
director, educational, public-health nursing (medical ser.) 075.117-018
Director, Educational Radio (radio-tv broad.) 184.117-010
DIRECTOR, EMPLOYMENT RESEARCH AND PLANNING (government ser.) 050.117-010
DIRECTOR, EMPLOYMENT SERVICES (government ser.) 188.117-078
director, evaluation and research (education) 099.167-022
DIRECTOR, EXTENSION WORK (education) 090.117-026
director, federated fund (nonprofit org.) 187.167-234
DIRECTOR, FIELD (social ser.) 195.167-022
DIRECTOR, FIELD REPRESENTATIVES (government ser.) 188.117-062
DIRECTOR, FIELD SERVICES (education) 090.167-034
DIRECTOR, FINANCIAL RESPONSIBILITY DIVISION (government ser.) 188.167-030
DIRECTOR, FOOD AND BEVERAGE (amuse. & rec.) 187.167-210
DIRECTOR, FOOD SERVICES (hotel & rest.) 187.167-026
DIRECTOR, FUNDRAISING (nonprofit org.) 165.117-010
DIRECTOR, FUNDS DEVELOPMENT (profess. & kin.) 165.117-014
DIRECTOR, FUNERAL (personal ser.) 187.167-030
director, geophysical laboratory (profess. & kin.) 024.167-010
Director, Geothermal Operations (petrol. & gas) 010.161-014
director, housekeeping (any industry) 187.167-046
Director, Industrial Museum (museums) 102.017-010
director, industrial nursing (medical ser.) 075.117-026
DIRECTOR, INDUSTRIAL RELATIONS (profess. & kin.) 166.117-010
DIRECTOR, INSTITUTION (any industry) 187.117-018
DIRECTOR, INSTRUCTIONAL MATERIAL (education) 099.167-018
Director, International Broadcasting (radio-tv broad.) 184.117-062
Director, International Programs (radio-tv broad.) 184.167-030
director, laboratory (profess. & kin.)   see LABORATORY CHIEF
DIRECTOR, LABOR STANDARDS (government ser.) 188.117-066
DIRECTOR, LAW ENFORCEMENT (government ser.) 188.117-070
director, recreation (government ser.) 187.117-054
DIRECTOR, LICENSING AND REGISTRATION (government ser.) 188.117-074
director, management information systems (profess. & kin.) 169.167-030
Director, Marketing Research And Analysis (profess. & kin.) 189.117-014
DIRECTOR, MEDIA MARKETING (radio-tv broad.) 163.117-022
DIRECTOR, MEDICAL FACILITIES SECTION (government ser.) 188.117-082
Director, Medical Records (medical ser.) 079.167-014
Director, Mental Health Agency (profess. & kin.) 195.117-010
director, merchandise (retail trade; wholesale tr.) 185.167-034
DIRECTOR, MERIT SYSTEM (government ser.) 188.117-086
DIRECTOR, MOTION PICTURE (motion picture) 159.067-010
DIRECTOR, MUSEUM-OR-ZOO (museums) 102.117-014
DIRECTOR, MUSIC (motion picture; radio-tv broad.) 152.047-018
director, music (profess. & kin.) 152.047-014
DIRECTOR, NEWS (radio-tv broad.) 184.167-014
Director, Nursery School (education) 092.167-010
DIRECTOR, NURSES' REGISTRY (medical ser.) 187.167-034
DIRECTOR, NURSING SERVICE (medical ser.) 075.117-022
DIRECTOR, OCCUPATIONAL HEALTH NURSING (medical ser.) 075.117-026
Director, Occupational Therapy (medical ser.) 076.121-010
director of admissions (education) 090.167-030
DIRECTOR OF ADMISSIONS (education) 090.167-014
director of career planning and placement (education) 166.167-014
director of career resources (education) 166.167-014
director of consumer services (any industry) 199.251-010
DIRECTOR OF COUNSELING (profess. & kin.) 045.107-018
director of engineering (radio-tv broad.) 003.167-034

director of financial aid and placements (education) 090.117-030
director of flight operations (business ser.) 184.167-026
DIRECTOR OF GUIDANCE IN PUBLIC SCHOOLS (education) 045.117-010
director of home economics (profess. & kin.) 096.161-010
DIRECTOR OF INSTITUTIONAL RESEARCH (education) 090.167-018
director of institutional studies (education) 090.167-018
director of major or capital gifts (profess. & kin.) 165.117-014
director of photography (business ser.) 184.167-026
DIRECTOR OF PHOTOGRAPHY (motion picture; radio-tv broad.) 143.062-010
Director of Photography, Special Effects (motion picture; radio-tv broad.) 143.062-010
DIRECTOR OF PLACEMENT (education) 166.167-014
Director of Publications (profess. & kin.) 189.117-010
DIRECTOR OF PUPIL PERSONNEL PROGRAM (education) 099.167-034
director of recruitment (education) 090.167-034
director of rehabilitative services (medical ser.) 076.117-010
DIRECTOR OF RELIGIOUS ACTIVITIES (education) 129.107-018
director of religious life (education) 129.107-018
director of social services (government ser.) 188.117-126
DIRECTOR OF STUDENT AFFAIRS (education) 090.167-022
director of student aid (education) 090.117-030
director of student services (education) 090.117-018
DIRECTOR OF VITAL STATISTICS (government ser.) 188.167-022
DIRECTOR, OPERATIONS (radio-tv broad.) 184.167-018
DIRECTOR, OPERATIONS, BROADCAST (radio-tv broad.) 184.167-022
DIRECTOR, OUTPATIENT SERVICES (medical ser.) 187.117-058
DIRECTOR, PHARMACY SERVICES (medical ser.) 074.167-010
DIRECTOR, PHOTOGRAMMETRY FLIGHT OPERATIONS (business ser.) 184.167-026
Director, Physical Therapy (medical ser.) 076.121-014
Director, Planning (profess. & kin.) 199.167-014
director, procurement services (profess. & kin.) 162.167-022
director, product assurance (profess. & kin.) 189.117-042
Director, Product Research And Development (profess. & kin.) 189.117-014
DIRECTOR, PROGRAM (radio-tv broad.) 184.167-030
director, public-health nursing (medical ser.) 075.117-014
DIRECTOR, PUBLIC SERVICE (radio-tv broad.) 184.117-010
DIRECTOR, QUALITY ASSURANCE (profess. & kin.) 189.117-042
DIRECTOR, RADIO (radio-tv broad.) 159.167-014
Director, Radio News (radio-tv broad.) 184.167-014
Director, Reactor Projects (government ser.) 188.117-134
DIRECTOR, RECORDS MANAGEMENT (profess. & kin.) 161.117-014
director, recreation (hotel & rest.; water trans.) 352.167-010
DIRECTOR, RECREATION CENTER (social ser.) 195.167-026
DIRECTOR, REGULATORY AGENCY (government ser.) 188.117-134
Director, Rehabilitation Program (profess. & kin.) 195.117-010
DIRECTOR, RELIGIOUS EDUCATION (nonprofit org.) 129.107-022
DIRECTOR, RESEARCH (motion picture; radio-tv broad.) 052.167-010
DIRECTOR, RESEARCH AND DEVELOPMENT (any industry) 189.117-014
DIRECTOR, REVENUE (government ser.) 188.117-090
director, safety (mine & quarry) 010.061-026
DIRECTOR, SAFETY COUNCIL (government ser.) 188.167-034
director, sales (hotel & rest.) 163.117-018
director, sanitation bureau (government ser.) 188.167-098
Director, School For Blind (education) 187.117-018
DIRECTOR, SCHOOL OF NURSING (medical ser.) 075.117-030
DIRECTOR, SECURITIES AND REAL ESTATE (government ser.) 188.167-038
DIRECTOR, SERVICE (nonprofit org.) 187.167-214
DIRECTOR, SERVICE (retail trade) 189.167-014
DIRECTOR, SOCIAL (hotel & rest.; water trans.) 352.167-010
Director, Social Service (profess. & kin.) 195.117-010
director, social welfare (profess. & kin.) 195.117-010
DIRECTOR, SPECIAL EDUCATION (education) 094.167-014
DIRECTOR, SPEECH-AND-HEARING (medical ser.) 079.131-010
DIRECTOR, SPORTS (radio-tv broad.) 184.167-034
DIRECTOR, STAGE (amuse. & rec.) 150.067-010
DIRECTOR, STATE-ASSESSED PROPERTIES (government ser.) 188.167-042
DIRECTOR, STATE-HISTORICAL SOCIETY (profess. & kin.) 052.067-014
director, student union (education) 090.167-022
DIRECTOR, SUMMER SESSIONS (education) 090.167-026
DIRECTOR, TECHNICAL (radio-tv broad.) 962.162-010
Director, Teen Post (profess. & kin.) 187.117-046
DIRECTOR, TELEVISION (radio-tv broad.) 159.067-014
Director, Television News (radio-tv broad.) 184.167-014
director, traffic and planning (government ser.) 005.167-022
DIRECTOR, TRANSLATION (profess. & kin.) 137.137-010
DIRECTOR, TRANSPORTATION (motor trans.) 184.117-014
Director, Transportation Utilities Regulation (government ser.) 188.117-134
director, underwriter sales (radio-tv broad.) 163.117-026
DIRECTOR, UNDERWRITER SOLICITATION (radio-tv broad.) 163.117-026
DIRECTOR, UNEMPLOYMENT INSURANCE (government ser.) 188.117-094
director, united fund (nonprofit org.) 187.167-234

DIRECTOR, UTILITY ACCOUNTS (government ser.) 160.267-014
director, vocational counseling (profess. & kin.) 045.107-018
DIRECTOR, VOCATIONAL TRAINING (education) 097.167-010
DIRECTOR, VOLUNTEER SERVICES (social ser.) 187.167-038
Director, Weights And Measures (government ser.) 188.117-134
DIRECTORY-ASSISTANCE OPERATOR (tel. & tel.) 235.662-018
Directory Compiler (clerical) 209.387-014
Director, Youth Correctional Facility (government ser.) 187.117-018
Disability-Insurance-Claim Examiner (insurance) 241.267-018
Disability-Insurance-Hearing Officer (government ser.) 119.107-010
DISASSEMBLER (clock & watch) 715.684-090
Disassembler, Product (machine shop) 706.684-018
Disaster Director (nonprofit org.) 187.167-214
DISASTER OR DAMAGE CONTROL SPECIALIST (military ser.) 378.267-014
disaster recovery coordinator (profess. & kin.) 033.162-014
Disbursement Clerk (clerical) 211.362-010
DISBURSEMENT CLERK (financial) 219.367-046
Discount-Variety-Store Stock Clerk (retail trade) 299.367-014
DISC-PAD GRINDER (nonmet. min.) 673.685-086
DISC-PAD GRINDING MACHINE FEEDER (nonmet. min.) 673.686-030
DISC-PAD KNOCKOUT WORKER (nonmet. min.) 579.687-034
DISC-PAD-PLATE FILLER (nonmet. min.) 579.687-038
disc-ruler operator (paper goods; print. & pub.) 659.682-022
disease-and-insect-control boss (agriculture) 408.137-010
Dish Carrier (hotel & rest.) 311.677-018
Dishcloth Folder (tex. prod., nec) 589.687-014
Dish-Cloth Inspector (tex. prod., nec) 789.587-014
Dishing-Machine Operator (any industry) 617.260-010
Dishwasher Preparer (any industry) 827.584-010
Dishwashing-Machine Repairer (any industry) 827.261-010
DISK-AND-TAPE-MACHINE TENDER (leather prod.) 783.685-018
DISK JOCKEY (radio-tv broad.) 159.147-014
disk recoater (any industry) 739.684-030
Disk-Recording-Machine Operator (radio-tv broad.; recording) 194.362-010
Disk Recordist (motion picture) 962.382-010
Disk Sander (woodworking) 761.682-014
disk setter (glass mfg.) 734.687-022
DISPATCHER (air trans.) 912.167-010
dispatcher (clerical) 239.367-014
dispatcher (clerical) 222.587-038
DISPATCHER (construction) 849.137-010
dispatcher (government ser.) 379.362-018
dispatcher (government ser.) 379.362-010
DISPATCHER (government ser.) 193.262-014
DISPATCHER (mine & quarry) 932.167-010
dispatcher (motor trans.) 913.367-010
dispatcher (motor trans.) 913.167-010
dispatcher (motor trans.; r.r. trans.) 184.163-010
dispatcher (r.r. trans.) 184.167-262
DISPATCHER (tel. & tel.) 239.167-014
dispatcher (tel. & tel.) 822.361-030
Dispatcher, Automobile Rental (automotive ser.) 249.167-014
DISPATCHER, BUS AND TROLLEY (motor trans.) 913.167-014
Dispatcher, Chief, Coal Slurry (pipe lines) 184.167-038
DISPATCHER, CHIEF I (petrol. & gas; petrol. refin.; pipe lines) 184.167-038
DISPATCHER, CHIEF II (petrol. & gas; petrol. refin.; pipe lines) 914.167-010
Dispatcher, Chief, Natural Gas (petrol. & gas; pipe lines) 184.167-038
Dispatcher, Chief, Oil (pipe lines) 184.167-038
Dispatcher, Chief, Petroleum Products (petrol. refin.; pipe lines) 184.167-038
DISPATCHER, CHIEF, SERVICE OR WORK (utilities) 959.137-010
DISPATCHER CLERK (r.r. trans.) 215.362-014
DISPATCHER, CONCRETE PRODUCTS (concrete prod.; construction) 579.137-030
dispatcher, electric power (utilities) 952.167-014
Dispatcher, Industrial Locomotive (any industry) 910.367-018
dispatcher, maintenance (clerical) 221.367-066
DISPATCHER, MAINTENANCE SERVICE (clerical) 239.367-014
DISPATCHER, MOTOR VEHICLE (clerical) 249.167-014
DISPATCHER, OIL (petrol. & gas; petrol. refin.; pipe lines) 914.167-014
DISPATCHER, OIL WELL SERVICES (petrol. & gas) 939.362-010
DISPATCHER, RADIO (government ser.) 379.362-010
DISPATCHER, RADIOACTIVE-WASTE-DISPOSAL (chemical) 955.167-010
Dispatcher, Ready-Mix Plant (concrete prod.; construction) 579.137-030
Dispatcher, Refinery (pipe lines) 914.167-014
DISPATCHER, RELAY (pipe lines) 221.362-014
dispatcher, route sales-delivery drivers (retail trade; wholesale tr.) 292.137-014
DISPATCHER, SECURITY GUARD (business ser.) 372.167-010
DISPATCHER, SERVICE (utilities) 959.167-010
DISPATCHER, SERVICE, CHIEF (utilities) 959.137-014
DISPATCHER, SERVICE OR WORK (utilities) 952.167-010
DISPATCHER, SHIP PILOT (water trans.) 248.367-026
DISPATCHER, STREET DEPARTMENT (government ser.) 239.367-030
Dispatcher, Tow Truck (automotive ser.) 249.167-014
DISPATCHER, TRAFFIC OR SYSTEM (motor trans.; r.r. trans.) 919.162-010

DISPATCHER, TUGBOAT (water trans.) 911.167-010
dispensary attendant (personal ser.) 339.687-010
Dispensary Clerk (medical ser.) 203.362-010
dispersion mixer (paint & varnish) 550.685-078
display and banner designer (profess. & kin.) 142.051-010
Display Artist (profess. & kin.) 142.051-010
display-card writer (any industry) 659.682-026
display carver (hotel & rest.) 316.661-010
DISPLAY DESIGNER (profess. & kin.) 142.051-010
Display Designer, Outside (profess. & kin.) 142.051-010
DISPLAYER, MERCHANDISE (retail trade) 298.081-010
DISPLAY FABRICATOR (fabrication, nec) 860.684-022
DISPLAY MAKER (fabrication, nec) 739.361-010
DISPLAY-SCREEN FABRICATOR (electron. comp.) 725.685-010
display trimmer (retail trade) 298.081-010
disposal-plant operator (sanitary ser.) 955.362-010
disposition clerk (clerical) 209.367-042
dissolver operator (chemical) 550.685-018
dissolver operator (chemical) 550.685-114
DISSOLVER OPERATOR (chemical) 558.682-014
DISTILLATION OPERATOR (chemical) 552.462-010
DISTILLATION-OPERATOR HELPER (chemical) 552.687-010
distiller (chemical) 552.685-014
DISTILLER I (chemical) 552.682-010
DISTILLER II (chemical) 552.682-014
DISTILLERY WORKER, GENERAL (beverage) 529.687-066
DISTILLING-DEPARTMENT SUPERVISOR (beverage) 522.131-010
DISTRESSER (furniture) 763.687-018
DISTRIBUTING CLERK (clerical) 222.587-018
DISTRIBUTION-ACCOUNTING CLERK (utilities) 210.362-010
distribution clerk (government ser.) 209.687-014
Distribution Clerk, Railway Or Highway Post Office (government ser.) 209.687-014
distribution district supervisor (utilities) 952.137-018
distribution estimator (utilities) 019.261-014
DISTRIBUTION-FIELD ENGINEER (utilities) 003.167-014
distribution manager (business ser.; wholesale tr.) 163.267-010
DISTRIBUTION SUPERVISOR (pipe lines; wholesale tr.) 914.137-010
Distribution-Transformer Assembler (elec. equip.) 820.381-014
distributor (any industry) 929.687-030
distributor (laundry & rel.) 369.687-010
distributor, advertising material (any industry) 230.687-010
DISTRIBUTOR-CLEANER (tobacco) 529.687-070
distributor, motor vehicles and supplies (wholesale tr.) 273.357-022
distributor, publications (wholesale tr.) 277.357-022
DISTRICT ADVISER (nonprofit org.) 187.117-022
district agent (insurance) 186.167-034
District Agricultural Agent (government ser.) 096.167-010
DISTRICT ATTORNEY (government ser.) 110.117-010
District Branch Manager (insurance) 186.167-034
district captain (government ser.) 375.167-034
District Claims Manager (insurance) 186.167-034
District-Court Judge (government ser.) 111.107-010
DISTRICT CUSTOMS DIRECTOR (government ser.) 188.117-098
DISTRICT CUSTOMS DIRECTOR, DEPUTY (government ser.) 188.167-046
district director (nonprofit org.) 187.117-022
district director (profess. & kin.) 187.167-238
DISTRICT EXTENSION SERVICE AGENT (government ser.) 096.167-010
District Fire Chief (government ser.) 373.117-010
district gauger (petrol. & gas; petrol. refin.; pipe lines) 914.134-010
District Home Economics Agent (government ser.) 096.167-010
District Lieutenant (government ser.) 375.167-014
district manager (utilities) 184.167-150
District Manager, Postal Service (government ser.) 188.167-086
District-Plant Supervisor (tel. & tel.) 822.131-010
District Sales Manager (insurance) 186.167-034
District Scout Executive (nonprofit org.) 187.117-022
district superintendent (petrol. & gas) 181.167-014
district superintendent, gas and gasoline (petrol. & gas; petrol. refin.; pipe lines) 914.167-010
DISTRICT SUPERVISOR (motor trans.) 184.117-018
district supervisor (pipe lines) 914.132-022
DISTRICT SUPERVISOR, MUD-ANALYSIS WELL LOGGING (petrol. & gas) 010.167-014
Disulfurizer Tender (plastic-synth.) 550.685-034
DITCH DIGGER (construction) term
DITCHER OPERATOR (r.r. trans.) 850.683-014
Ditch Inspector (construction) 182.267-010
DITCH RIDER (waterworks) 954.362-010
ditch tender (waterworks) 954.362-010
DIVER (amuse. & rec.) 349.247-010
DIVER (any industry) 899.261-010
diver assistant (any industry) 899.664-010
DIVER HELPER (any industry) 899.664-010
DIVER PUMPER (construction; fishing & hunt.) 899.682-010

diversion clerk (clerical) 209.367-042
diver tender (any industry) 899.664-010
DIVIDEND CLERK (financial) 216.482-034
dividend-deposit-entry clerk (insurance) 216.482-026
DIVIDEND-DEPOSIT-VOUCHER CLERK (insurance) 216.482-026
divider (bakery products) 526.682-010
DIVIDING-MACHINE OPERATOR (bakery products) 520.685-086
Dividing-Machine-Operator Helper (bakery products) 526.686-010
Diving-Board Assembler (toy-sport equip.) 732.684-014
division commander (government ser.) 375.267-026
Division Field Inspector (utilities) 168.264-018
DIVISION MANAGER, CHAMBER OF COMMERCE (nonprofit org.) 187.167-042
DIVISION OFFICER (r.r. trans.) term
DIVISION ROAD SUPERVISOR (r.r. trans.) 184.167-282
division sergeant (government ser.) 375.133-010
division superintendent (motor trans.; r.r. trans.) 184.167-158
division superintendent (petrol. & gas) 181.167-014
division supervisor (any industry) 183.167-018
dobby-loom chain-pegger (narrow fabrics; textile) 689.687-054
Dobby-Loom Fixer (textile) 683.260-018
dock attendant (amuse. & rec.) 342.667-010
dock boss (water trans.) 911.137-018
Dock Builder (construction) 860.381-042
Dock Cleaner (steel & rel.) 911.687-014
Dock Grader (woodworking) 669.687-030
Dock Guard (any industry) 372.667-034
DOCK HAND (air trans.) 919.683-010
DOCK HAND (ship-boat mfg.) 891.684-010
dock hand (water trans.) 911.364-014
dock helper (water trans.) 911.687-010
DOCK SUPERVISOR (ship-boat mfg.) 891.131-010
dock worker (can. & preserv.) 922.687-062
doctor, chiropractic (medical ser.) 079.101-010
DOCTOR, NATUROPATHIC (medical ser.) 079.101-014
doctor, osteopathic (medical ser.) 071.101-010
DOCUMENTATION-BILLING CLERK (air trans.; motor trans.; r.r. trans.; water trans.) 214.362-014
DOCUMENTATION ENGINEER (profess. & kin.) 012.167-078
DOCUMENTATION SUPERVISOR (water trans.) 214.137-010
DOCUMENT PREPARER, MICROFILMING (business ser.) 249.587-018
DOCUMENT RESTORER (profess. & kin.) 979.361-010
doffer (plastic-synth.) 582.685-162
DOFFER (textile) 689.686-022
DOG BATHER (personal ser.) 418.677-010
dog beautician (personal ser.) 418.674-010
Dog Breeder (agriculture) 410.161-010
DOG CATCHER (government ser.) 379.673-010
Dog-Food Dough Mixer (bakery products) 520.685-234
DOG GROOMER (personal ser.) 418.674-010
dog-hair clipper (personal ser.) 418.674-010
DOG LICENSER (nonprofit org.) 249.367-030
Dog-Pound Attendant (government ser.) 410.674-010
dog warden (government ser.) 379.673-010
Doll-Eye-Setter (toy-sport equip.) 731.687-034
DOLL REPAIRER (any industry) 731.684-010
doll-wig maker, rooted hair (fabrication, nec) 731.685-010
DOLLY PUSHER (radio-tv broad.) 962.687-010
DOMER (paper goods) 641.685-038
DOOR ASSEMBLER (mfd. bldgs.; vehicles, nec) 806.684-050
DOOR ASSEMBLER I (woodworking) 762.684-034
Door Assembler II (woodworking) 762.687-050
Door-Clamp Operator (saw. & plan.) 669.685-030
Door Closer (toy-sport equip.) 732.684-026
DOOR-CLOSER MECHANIC (any industry) 630.381-014
DOOR CORE ASSEMBLER (woodworking) 762.687-030
Door-Engine Repairer (automotive ser.; railroad equip.) 620.381-018
Door Fitter (furniture) 763.684-026
Door-Frame Assembler, Machine (woodworking) 669.685-042
Door-Glass Installer (saw. & plan.) 865.684-014
Door Hanger (construction) 860.381-022
Door Installer I (mfd. bldgs.; vehicles, nec) 809.684-030
Door Installer II (mfd. bldgs.; vehicles, nec) 869.684-026
DOORKEEPER (any industry) 324.677-014
Door-Lock Installer (struct. metal) 809.684-010
DOOR-MACHINE OPERATOR (steel & rel.) 519.663-010
Door Maker (saw. & plan.) 669.380-014
Door Patcher (woodworking) 769.684-030
Door Repairer (steel & rel.) 861.381-026
door repairer, bus (automotive ser.) 807.381-010
doorshaker (business ser.) 372.667-038
Door Slinger (grain-feed mills) 529.685-154
dope-and-fabric worker (aircraft mfg.; air trans.) 849.381-010
DOPE-DRY-HOUSE OPERATOR (chemical) 559.685-046
Dope Edger (boot & shoe) 788.684-066

dope firer (construction) 869.685-010
dope heater (construction) 869.685-010
dope-house operator helper (chemical) 559.685-046
dope mixer (chemical) 550.685-106
Dope Mixer (chemical) 550.382-018
Dope Pourer (construction) 869.687-026
doper (aircraft mfg.; air trans.) 849.381-010
doper (leather mfg.) 584.687-010
doper (photofinishing) 976.681-010
Doper Operator (tinware) 741.687-018
Dope Sprayer (leather mfg.) 584.687-014
dopster (garment) 781.287-010
dormitory supervisor (education) 045.107-038
DORR OPERATOR (sugar & conf.) 522.685-050
dosimetrist (medical ser.) 078.261-034
DOT ETCHER APPRENTICE (print. & pub.) 972.281-018
DOT ETCHER (print. & pub.) 972.281-010
DOUBLE (motion picture; radio-tv broad.) 961.364-010
Double-Bottom Driver (any industry) 904.383-010
Double-Corner Cutter (paper goods) 640.685-030
Double-Cut-Off-Saw Operator (woodworking) 667.682-022
double-cut sawyer (paper & pulp; saw. & plan.) 667.682-034
Double Cutter (boot & shoe) 699.682-022
Double-End-Chucking-Machine Operator (woodworking) 665.382-010
Double-Ending-Machine Operator (paper goods) 641.685-042
Double-End-Production Grinder (metal prod., nec) 616.485-010
Double-End Sewer (paper goods) 787.686-010
Double-End-Tenoner Operator (woodworking) 669.382-018
Double-End-Tenoner Setter (woodworking) 669.280-010
DOUBLE-END-TRIMMER-AND-BORING-MACHINE OPERATOR (furniture) 669.682-038
Double-Facing-Corrugating-Machine Operator (paper goods) 641.562-010
Double-Fold-Machine Operator (paper goods) 649.685-046
Double-Lay-Winder-And-Paraffin-Unit Operator (nonfer. metal) 691.682-018
Double-Needle Operator, Lockstitch (garment) 786.682-170
Double-Needle Stitcher (boot & shoe) 690.682-082
doubler (textile) 681.685-046
Double-Spindle-Disk Grinder Tender (metal prod., nec) 603.685-062
Double-Spindle-Shaper Operator (woodworking) 665.682-034
doubling-and-rolling-machine operator (textile) 689.685-050
doubling-machine operator (rubber goods) 554.665-014
doubling-machine operator (textile) 689.685-050
DOUBLING-MACHINE OPERATOR (textile) 681.685-046
DOUGH-BRAKE-MACHINE OPERATOR (bakery products) 520.685-090
DOUGH MIXER (bakery products) 520.685-234
Dough-Mixer Helper (bakery products) 526.686-010
DOUGH-MIXER OPERATOR (bakery products) 520.462-010
dough molder, hand (bakery products) 520.384-010
Doughnut-Batter Mixer (bakery products) 520.685-010
doughnut-cooking-machine operator (bakery products) 526.682-022
Doughnut-Dough Mixer (bakery products) 520.685-234
Doughnut Icer (bakery products) 524.684-022
Doughnut Icer, Machine (bakery products) 524.685-034
DOUGHNUT-MACHINE OPERATOR (bakery products) 526.682-022
Doughnut-Machine-Operator Helper (bakery products) 526.686-010
DOUGHNUT MAKER (bakery products) 526.684-010
Doughnut-Maker Helper, Hand (bakery products) 526.686-010
dough sheeter (bakery products) 520.685-214
DOVETAIL-MACHINE OPERATOR (wood. container) 669.685-046
Dovetail-Machine Operator (woodworking) 665.382-014
doweler (wood. container) 764.687-062
doweler (woodworking) 669.685-050
DOWELING-MACHINE OPERATOR (woodworking) 669.685-050
DOWEL-INSERTING-MACHINE OPERATOR (saw. & plan.) 669.682-042
DOWEL INSPECTOR (woodworking) 669.687-014
DOWEL-MACHINE OPERATOR (woodworking) 665.682-010
DOWEL POINTER (woodworking) 667.685-038
Dowel-Sander Operator (woodworking) 662.685-014
dowel-setting-machine operator (woodworking) 669.685-050
dowel-sticker operator (woodworking) 665.682-010
Down Filler (tex. prod., nec) 780.684-066
DRAFTER (profess. & kin.) master
Drafter (cad), Electrical (profess. & kin.) 003.281-010
DRAFTER, AERONAUTICAL (aircraft mfg.) 002.261-010
DRAFTER APPRENTICE (profess. & kin.) 017.281-014
DRAFTER, ARCHITECTURAL (profess. & kin.) 001.261-010
DRAFTER, ASSISTANT (profess. & kin.) 017.281-018
DRAFTER, AUTOMOTIVE DESIGN (auto. mfg.) 017.261-042
DRAFTER, AUTOMOTIVE DESIGN LAYOUT (auto. mfg.) 017.281-026
Drafter (CAD), Electronic (profess. & kin.) 003.281-014
DRAFTER, CARTOGRAPHIC (profess. & kin.) 018.261-010
DRAFTER, CASTINGS (profess. & kin.) 007.261-014
DRAFTER, CHIEF, DESIGN (utilities) 017.161-010
DRAFTER, CIVIL (profess. & kin.) 005.281-010
Drafter, Civil (CAD) (profess. & kin.) 005.281-010

drafter, civil engineering (profess. & kin.) 005.281-010
DRAFTER, COMMERCIAL (profess. & kin.) 017.261-026
drafter, construction (profess. & kin.) 005.281-010
DRAFTER, DETAIL (profess. & kin.) 017.261-030
DRAFTER, DIRECTIONAL SURVEY (petrol. & gas) 010.281-010
DRAFTER, ELECTRICAL (profess. & kin.) 003.281-010
drafter, electromechanical (profess. & kin.) 003.281-014
DRAFTER, ELECTRONIC (profess. & kin.) 003.281-014
drafter, engineering (profess. & kin.) 007.281-010
drafter, engineering (profess. & kin.) 005.281-010
DRAFTER, GEOLOGICAL (petrol. & gas) 010.281-014
DRAFTER, GEOPHYSICAL (petrol. & gas) 010.281-018
DRAFTER, HEATING AND VENTILATING (profess. & kin.) 017.261-034
DRAFTER, LANDSCAPE (profess. & kin.) 001.261-014
DRAFTER, MARINE (profess. & kin.) 014.281-010
DRAFTER, MECHANICAL (profess. & kin.) 007.281-010
DRAFTER, OIL AND GAS (petrol. & gas; petrol. refin.) 017.281-030
DRAFTER, PATENT (profess. & kin.) 007.261-010
DRAFTER, PLUMBING (profess. & kin.) 017.261-038
Drafter, Refrigeration (profess. & kin.) 017.261-034
Drafter, Seismograph (petrol. & gas) 010.281-018
DRAFTER, STRUCTURAL (profess. & kin.) 005.281-014
DRAFTER, TOOL DESIGN (profess. & kin.) 007.261-022
Drafter, Topographical (profess. & kin.) 005.281-010
draft-roller picker (textile) 680.687-014
dragger (mine & quarry) 921.663-050
Dragline Oiler (mine & quarry) 850.684-018
DRAGLINE OPERATOR (any industry) 850.683-018
DRAINAGE-DESIGN COORDINATOR (waterworks) 005.167-014
Drain Layer (construction) 869.664-014
Drain-Tile-Machine Operator (concrete prod.) 575.665-010
Drain-Tile-Press Operator (brick & tile) 575.462-010
Drama Critic (print. & pub.; radio-tv broad.) 131.067-018
DRAMATIC COACH (profess. & kin.) 150.027-010
Dramatic Reader (amuse. & rec.) 150.047-010
dramatist (profess. & kin.) 131.067-038
DRAPER (garment; knitting) 781.684-026
DRAPER (motion picture; radio-tv broad.) 962.381-010
DRAPERY AND UPHOLSTERY ESTIMATOR (retail trade) 299.387-010
DRAPERY AND UPHOLSTERY MEASURER (retail trade) 299.364-010
Drapery Cutter, Hand (tex. prod., nec) 781.684-074
Drapery Cutter, Machine (tex. prod., nec) 781.684-014
Drapery Estimator (retail trade) 299.387-010
DRAPERY HANGER (retail trade) 869.484-014
DRAPERY-HEAD FORMER (retail trade) 781.684-030
Drapery Hemmer, Automatic (tex. prod., nec) 787.685-018
Drapery Inspector (tex. prod., nec) 789.587-014
DRAPERY OPERATOR (retail trade) 787.682-018
DRAPERY-ROD ASSEMBLER (retail trade) 706.484-010
Drapery Room Supervisor (retail trade; tex. prod., nec) 789.132-010
Drapery Sewer, Hand (tex. prod., nec) 782.684-058
Drapery Supervisor (tex. prod., nec) 787.132-010
drapery worker (retail trade) 787.682-018
DRAW-BENCH OPERATOR (any industry) 614.682-010
draw-bench operator (nonfer. metal; steel & rel.) 614.685-022
DRAW-BENCH OPERATOR (nonfer. metal; steel & rel.) 614.482-010
DRAW-BENCH-OPERATOR HELPER (nonfer. metal; steel & rel.) 614.686-010
DRAWBRIDGE OPERATOR (r.r. trans.) 371.362-010
drawer (textile) 683.684-014
drawer (textile) 680.685-038
drawer (brick & tile) 929.687-014
Drawer Fitter (furniture) 763.684-026
drawer-hardware worker (furniture) 706.684-050
Drawer-In, Dobby Loom (textile) 683.684-014
DRAWER-IN, HAND (textile) 683.684-014
DRAWER-IN HELPER, HAND (textile) 683.687-010
Drawer-In, Jacquard Loom (textile) 683.684-014
Drawer-In, Plain Loom (textile) 683.684-014
DRAWER-IN, STITCH-BONDING MACHINE (textile) 689.684-014
DRAWER LINER (furniture) 763.684-030
DRAWER UPFITTER (furniture) 706.684-050
DRAWER WAXER (furniture) 763.687-022
DRAW-FRAME TENDER (tex. prod., nec) 680.685-034
draw-furnace tender (heat treating) 504.685-018
draw hand (fabrication, nec) 739.687-046
DRAWING-FRAME TENDER (textile) 680.685-038
drawing-in hand (textile) 683.684-014
DRAWING-IN-MACHINE TENDER (textile) 683.682-018
DRAWING-IN-MACHINE-TENDER HELPER (textile) 683.685-022
DRAWING-KILN OPERATOR (glass mfg.) 575.362-010
DRAWING-KILN SUPERVISOR (glass mfg.) 575.137-010
drawing-machine operator (glass mfg.) 575.362-010
drawing-release clerk (aircraft mfg.; electron. comp.) 206.367-010
DRAWINGS CHECKER, ENGINEERING (profess. & kin.) 007.267-010

drawing tender (textile) 680.685-038
draw-in hand (textile) 683.684-014
DRAW-MACHINE OPERATOR (plastic-synth.) 680.665-014
Draw-Press Operator (any industry) 615.382-010
DRAWSTRING KNOTTER (tex. prod., nec) 689.685-058
Dray Driver (any industry) 919.664-010
DREDGE CAPTAIN (water trans.) 197.161-010
Dredge Deckhand (water trans.) 911.687-022
DREDGE MATE (water trans.) 197.137-010
DREDGE OPERATOR (construction; mine & quarry) 850.663-010
dredge operator (water trans.) 197.161-010
DREDGE OPERATOR SUPERVISOR (mine & quarry) 939.132-010
Dredge Pipe Installer (construction) 869.687-026
dredge pumper (construction; mine & quarry) 850.663-010
dredge runner (water trans.) 197.161-010
Dress-Cap Maker (hat & cap) 784.684-018
Dress Draper (garment) 781.684-026
DRESSER (amuse. & rec.) 346.674-010
DRESSER (boot & shoe) 788.687-038
DRESSER TENDER (textile) 681.682-010
dress-gang worker (can. & preserv.; fishing & hunt.) 525.684-030
dressing-room attendant (personal ser.) 358.677-014
DRESSMAKER (any industry) 785.361-010
Dressmaker (garment) 782.684-058
Dress Marker (garment) 781.384-014
Dress-Shoe Inspector (boot & shoe) 788.384-010
DRIED FRUIT WASHER (food prep., nec) 521.685-110
DRIER (garment) 581.685-014
DRIER (knitting) 581.686-014
Drier (rubber goods) 553.665-038
drier (tex. prod., nec) 581.685-034
drier-and-evaporator operator (chemical; smelt. & refin.) 559.685-074
DRIER-AND-GRINDER TENDER (mine & quarry) 579.685-010
DRIER-AND-PULVERIZER TENDER (chemical) 559.685-050
drier attendant (fabrication, nec) 543.685-014
DRIER ATTENDANT (can. & preserv.; grain-feed mills) 523.685-058
DRIER ATTENDANT (garment) 581.686-018
DRIER, BELT CONVEYOR (food prep., nec) 529.485-018
DRIER FEEDER (rubber reclaim.) 559.686-014
DRIER HELPER (chemical) 553.687-010
DRIER, LONG GOODS (food prep., nec) 523.585-022
drier-machine hand (soap & rel.) 553.685-098
drier operator (brick & tile) 573.362-010
drier operator (cement; chemical; mine & quarry) 573.382-010
DRIER OPERATOR (chemical; pharmaceut.) 553.685-042
DRIER OPERATOR (food prep., nec) 523.362-014
drier operator (laundry & rel.) 369.685-034
DRIER OPERATOR (mine & quarry) 543.682-014
Drier Operator (rubber reclaim.) 553.665-038
drier operator (smelt. & refin.) 511.565-014
drier operator (sugar & conf.) 529.682-010
DRIER OPERATOR (sugar & conf.) 529.682-022
drier operator (textile) 581.685-026
DRIER OPERATOR (utilities) 543.382-010
DRIER OPERATOR (can. & preserv.) 523.685-062
DRIER OPERATOR (can. & preserv.; dairy products) 523.682-022
DRIER OPERATOR, DRUM (food prep., nec) 529.685-098
Drier Operator, Head (plastic-synth.) 559.132-042
DRIER-OPERATOR HELPER (chemical) 553.685-058
DRIER-OPERATOR HELPER (rubber reclaim.) 553.686-030
DRIER OPERATOR I (chemical) 553.665-026
DRIER OPERATOR I (plastic-synth.) 559.562-010
DRIER OPERATOR II (chemical) 553.582-010
DRIER OPERATOR II (plastic-synth.) 553.685-046
DRIER OPERATOR III (chemical) 553.685-050
DRIER OPERATOR III (plastic-synth.) 581.685-018
DRIER OPERATOR IV (chemical) 553.685-054
DRIER OPERATOR V (chemical) 553.686-026
DRIER OPERATOR VI (chemical) 553.685-118
DRIER, SHORT GOODS (food prep., nec) 523.587-010
DRIER-TAKE-OFF TENDER (elec. equip.) 921.685-034
DRIER TENDER (can. & preserv.) 523.685-066
DRIER TENDER (fabrication, nec) 543.685-014
DRIER TENDER (grain-feed mills) 523.685-070
drier tender (knitting) 580.685-014
Drier Tender (rubber goods) 553.665-038
DRIER TENDER (smelt. & refin.) 511.565-014
drier tender (soap & rel.) 553.585-018
drier tender (textile) 581.685-022
drier tender (textile) 580.685-066
DRIER TENDER (wood prod., nec) 563.585-010
DRIER TENDER I (oils & grease) 523.685-074
Drier Tender II (oils & grease) 529.685-106
Drier Tender, Naphthalene (steel & rel.) 551.665-010
drier unloader (nonmet. min.) 921.583-010

drifter (construction) 850.662-014
DRIFTER (steel & rel.) 503.685-018
drifting-machine operator (steel & rel.) 503.685-018
Drift Miner (mine & quarry) 939.281-010
DRILL-BIT SHARPENER (electron. comp.) 603.682-030
drill doctor (any industry) 630.281-010
DRILLER (jewelry-silver.) 700.684-026
DRILLER (optical goods) 716.685-014
driller (petrol. & gas) 930.382-018
driller (petrol. & gas) 930.382-026
driller (stonework) 771.684-010
driller (stonework) 676.682-014
DRILLER AND BROACHER (clock & watch) 715.685-022
DRILLER AND DEBURRER, REFLECTOR (light. fix.) 676.686-014
DRILLER-AND-REAMER, AUTOMATIC (musical inst.) 606.382-010
DRILLER, BRAKE LINING (nonmet. min.) 676.685-010
driller, fine-diamond dies (machine tools) 770.381-018
DRILLER, HAND (any industry) 809.684-018
DRILLER, HAND (button & notion) 754.684-026
DRILLER HELPER (construction; mine & quarry) 930.666-010
driller helper (petrol. & gas) 930.684-026
DRILLER, MACHINE (construction; mine & quarry) 930.382-010
DRILLER, MACHINE (glass products) 676.685-014
driller, multiple spindle (glass products) 676.682-010
driller operator (construction; mine & quarry) 930.382-010
driller, portable (any industry) 809.684-018
Drilling Engineer (petrol. & gas) 010.061-018
drilling inspector (petrol. & gas) 930.167-010
DRILLING-MACHINE OPERATOR (mine & quarry) 930.482-010
DRILLING-MACHINE OPERATOR, AUTOMATIC (clock & watch) 606.685-030
DRILL OPERATOR, AUTOMATIC (glass products) 676.682-010
Drill Operator, Pneumatic (stonework) 676.682-014
drill-press operator (jewelry-silver.) 700.684-026
DRILL-PRESS OPERATOR (machine shop) 606.682-014
DRILL-PRESS OPERATOR, ACOUSTICAL TILE (wood prod., nec) 649.682-018
DRILL-PRESS OPERATOR, NUMERICAL CONTROL (machine shop) 606.362-010
DRILL-PRESS OPERATOR, PRINTED CIRCUIT BOARDS (electron. comp.) 676.382-010
DRILL-PRESS SET-UP OPERATOR, MULTIPLE SPINDLE (machine shop) 606.380-010
DRILL-PRESS SET-UP OPERATOR, RADIAL (machine shop) 606.380-014
DRILL-PRESS SET-UP OPERATOR, RADIAL, TOOL (machine shop) 606.380-018
DRILL-PRESS SET-UP OPERATOR, SINGLE SPINDLE (machine shop) 606.682-018
DRILL PRESS TENDER (machine shop) 606.685-026
DRILL-PUNCH OPERATOR (paper goods; print. & pub.) 649.685-034
drill-runner helper (any industry) 930.687-014
drill sergeant (military ser.) 378.227-014
drill sharpener (electron. comp.) 603.682-030
Drill Sharpener (machine shop) 603.280-038
drill-sharpener operator (any industry) 601.682-010
DRIP-BOX TENDER (grain-feed mills) 521.687-038
DRIP PUMPER (pipe lines; utilities) 953.583-010
DRIVE-IN THEATER ATTENDANT (amuse. & rec.) 349.673-010
drive-in waiter/waitress (hotel & rest.) 311.477-010
Driver (agriculture) 404.131-010
DRIVER (auto. mfg.; automotive ser.) 919.683-014
driver (domestic ser.) 359.673-010
DRIVER (motor trans.) 913.663-018
driver helper (any industry) 905.687-010
DRIVER HELPER, SALES ROUTE (retail trade; wholesale tr.) 292.667-010
DRIVER, SALES ROUTE (retail trade; wholesale tr.) 292.353-010
DRIVERS'-CASH CLERK (motor trans.) 211.462-030
DRIVER'S LICENSE EXAMINER (government ser.) 168.267-034
DRIVER, STARTING GATE (amuse. & rec.) 919.683-030
DRIVER SUPERVISOR (motor trans.) 909.137-010
DRIVER-UTILITY WORKER (auto. mfg.; automotive ser.) 919.663-018
Drive-Shaft-And-Steering-Post Repairer (automotive ser.) 620.261-010
drop-board operator (any industry) 379.362-014
drop clipper (millwork-plywood) 663.685-050
DROPHAMMER OPERATOR (aircraft mfg.; forging) 610.362-010
Drop-Hammer-Operator Helper (forging) 619.686-034
Drop-Hammer-Pile-Driver Operator (construction) 859.682-018
Drophammer Setter-Up (forging) 612.360-010
Drop-Machine Operator (bakery products) 520.682-034
dropper (beverage) 529.685-246
Dropper, Dehairing Machine (meat products) 525.685-018
DROPPER, FERMENTING CELLAR (beverage) 522.685-054
dropper, tank storage (beverage) 529.685-246
drop-pit worker (railroad equip.) 622.381-014
DROP TESTER (ordnance) 737.387-010

DROP-WIRE ALIGNER (textile) 689.685-062
DROP-WIRE BUILDER (textile) 689.687-034
DROP-WIRE HANGER (textile) 683.687-014
drop-wire stringer (textile) 689.687-034
DROSS SKIMMER (smelt. & refin.) 519.683-010
druggist (medical ser.) 074.161-010
drug-room clerk (any industry) 550.684-014
DRUM ATTENDANT (leather mfg.; tex. prod., nec) 582.685-050
Drum-Barker Operator (paper & pulp) 669.485-010
drum carrier (chemical) 559.687-050
drum chainer (petrol. refin.) 599.687-034
Drum Cleaner (beverage) 529.687-066
DRUM CLEANER (petrol. refin.) 599.687-034
DRUM DRIER (grain-feed mills) 523.682-026
DRUM-DRIER OPERATOR (chemical) 553.665-030
drum-drier operator (chemical; pharmaceut.) 553.685-042
DRUM-DRIER OPERATOR (plastic-synth.) 581.685-082
drum-dyeing-machine operator (knitting) 582.685-170
Drum Filler (beverage) 522.687-010
Drum Filler (chemical) 559.687-050
drum filler (chemical) 559.565-010
drum filler (rubber reclaim.) 914.665-010
DRUM LOADER AND UNLOADER (beverage) 522.685-058
Drummer (amuse. & rec.) 152.041-010
DRUMMER (hat & cap) 589.685-034
Drummer (leather mfg.) 589.686-022
drum operator (any industry) 699.587-010
drum plater (electroplating) 500.362-014
drum-reel cutter (tex. prod., nec) 690.682-026
drum sander (pen & pencil) 662.685-030
drum sander (woodworking) 662.682-014
drum-sander offbearer (woodworking) 662.686-014
Drum-Sander Setter (woodworking) 669.280-010
Drum-Saw Operator (saw. & plan.) 667.682-022
Drum Sealer (beverage) 529.687-066
Drum-Shell Maker (musical inst.) 730.381-042
Drum Stenciler (beverage) 920.687-178
Drum-Stock Clerk (clerical) 222.387-058
DRUM STRAIGHTENER I (any industry) 619.685-034
Drum Straightener II (any industry) 619.685-046
drum tender (leather mfg.) 582.482-018
DRUM TESTER (petrol. refin.) 599.687-038
dry boss (any industry) 358.687-010
dry-box operator (chemical) 553.685-022
Dry-Cans Back-Tender (textile) 589.686-010
DRY-CANS OPERATOR (textile) 581.685-022
DRY-CELL-ASSEMBLY-MACHINE TENDER (elec. equip.) 692.665-018
DRY-CELL TESTER (elec. equip.) 727.381-018
Dry-Chain Offbearer (saw. & plan.) 669.686-018
DRY-CHARGE-PROCESS ATTENDANT (elec. equip.) 590.685-026
DRY CLEANER (knitting) 589.685-038
DRY CLEANER (laundry & rel.) 362.382-014
DRY-CLEANER APPRENTICE (laundry & rel.) 362.382-010
dry cleaner, furniture, hand (laundry & rel.) 362.684-022
DRY CLEANER, HAND (laundry & rel.) 362.684-010
DRY-CLEANER HELPER (laundry & rel.) 362.686-010
dry-cleaning-machine operator (laundry & rel.) 362.382-014
dry-cleaning-machine-operator apprentice (laundry & rel.) 362.382-010
dry-cleaning-machine-operator helper (laundry & rel.) 362.686-010
dry-clipper tender (millwork-plywood) 663.685-050
DRY CURER (meat products) 525.687-026
DRY-END OPERATOR (plastic-synth.) 559.665-014
Dry-End Tester (paper & pulp) 539.364-010
dryer feeder (hat & cap) 581.686-022
dry-felt splicer (fabrication, nec) 692.687-010
dry folder, cloth (knitting; textile) 589.685-058
Dry-Heat-Cabinet Attendant (personal ser.) 335.677-014
Dry-Heat-Room Attendant (personal ser.) 335.677-014
DRY-HOUSE ATTENDANT (chemical) 553.585-014
DRY-HOUSE ATTENDANT (woodworking) 563.685-018
dry-house operator (chemical) 559.685-046
DRY-HOUSE TENDER (ordnance) 559.585-010
Drying-Equipment Operator (elec. equip.) 599.682-014
Drying-Machine Back-Tender (knitting; textile) 589.686-010
drying-machine operator (chemical) 529.382-030
drying-machine operator (knitting) 580.685-014
drying-machine operator (knitting) 581.686-038
drying-machine operator (laundry & rel.) 369.685-034
drying-machine operator (plastic-synth.) 581.685-018
drying-machine operator (textile) 581.685-054
DRYING-MACHINE OPERATOR, PACKAGE YARNS (textile) 581.685-026
drying-machine receiver (textile) 589.686-010
drying-machine tender (any industry) 581.685-038
drying-machine tender (knitting) 581.686-014
Drying-Machine Tender (motion picture) 976.685-018

drying machine tender (textile) 581.685-022
drying-machine tender (textile) 589.686-010
drying-machine tender (textile) 580.685-066
DRYING-MACHINE TENDER (textile) 581.685-030
DRYING-OVEN ATTENDANT (hat & cap) 581.686-022
drying-oven tender (tobacco) 523.685-118
DRYING-RACK CHANGER (boot & shoe) 581.686-026
DRYING-ROOM ATTENDANT (hat & cap) 581.687-014
DRYING-ROOM ATTENDANT (soap & rel.) 553.585-018
DRYING-ROOM ATTENDANT (tobacco) 523.587-014
drying-room operator (plastic-synth.) 581.685-018
Drying-Room Supervisor (chemical) 559.132-122
drying-tumbler operator (laundry & rel.) 369.685-034
DRYING-UNIT-FELTING-MACHINE OPERATOR (tex. prod., nec) 581.685-034
DRYING-UNIT-FELTING-MACHINE-OPERATOR HELPER (tex. prod., nec) 581.687-018
dry janitor (any industry) 358.687-010
Dry-Kiln Burner (brick & tile) 573.682-010
DRY-KILN OPERATOR (brick & tile) 573.362-010
dry-kiln operator (woodworking) 563.382-010
DRY-KILN OPERATOR HELPER (brick & tile) 573.687-014
Dry-Lumber Grader (woodworking) 669.687-030
dry-mill operator (brick & tile) 570.665-010
Dry-Mill Worker (leather mfg.) 582.685-050
dry mixer (chemical) 550.665-018
dry mixer (ordnance) 550.565-010
dry-mop maker (tex. prod., nec) 739.687-078
DRY-PAN CHARGER (brick & tile) 570.683-010
dry-pan feeder (brick & tile) 570.683-010
DRY-PAN OPERATOR (brick & tile) 570.665-010
DRY-PLACER-MACHINE OPERATOR (mine & quarry) 939.382-010
DRY-PRESS OPERATOR (brick & tile) 575.662-010
DRY-PRESS-OPERATOR HELPER (brick & tile) 575.686-010
Dry Roaster (can. & preserv.) 529.685-174
Dry Roller (leather mfg.) 583.685-094
dry-room helper (rubber reclaim.) 553.686-030
dry-room operator (chemical) 553.665-026
dry sander (stonework) 673.666-010
dry-slasher tender (textile) 681.585-010
DRY-STARCH OPERATOR (grain-feed mills) 520.362-014
DRY-STARCH OPERATOR, AUTOMATIC (grain-feed mills) 529.362-014
dry-talc racker (build. mat., nec) 549.686-014
DRY-WALL APPLICATOR (construction; mfd. bldgs.) 842.684-014
DRY-WALL APPLICATOR (construction) 842.361-030
dry-wall finisher (construction; mfd. bldgs.) 842.664-010
dry-wall installations mechanic (construction) 842.361-030
dry-wall installer (construction) 842.361-030
dry-wall nailer (construction; mfd. bldgs.) 842.684-014
DRY-WALL SPRAYER (mfd. bldgs.) 842.684-010
DUAL-HOSE CEMENTER (rubber goods) 690.685-134
DUBBING-MACHINE OPERATOR (motion picture; radio-tv broad.) 962.665-010
Dubbing-Machine Operator (recording) 194.362-010
Duck-Bill Operator (mine & quarry) 850.683-030
Duck Farmer (agriculture) 411.161-018
Duct Installer (construction; mfd. bldgs.) 869.664-014
duct layer (construction; utilities) 869.361-010
Duct-Layer Helper (construction; utilities) 821.667-010
Duct-Layer Supervisor (construction; utilities) 899.131-010
DUCT MAKER (construction; mfd. bldgs.) 809.687-010
DUDE WRANGLER (amuse. & rec.) 353.364-010
dukey rider (any industry) 932.664-010
dulite-machine bluer (heat treating) 504.682-022
Dull-Coat-Mill Operator (tex. prod., nec) 584.382-010
Duller (furniture) 742.684-010
dull shoe repairer (boot & shoe) 788.684-022
DULSER (fishing & hunt.) 447.687-010
Dumbwaiter Operator (hotel & rest.) 311.677-018
DUMPER (any industry) 921.667-018
dumper (beverage) 921.662-010
Dumper (beverage) 529.687-066
Dumper (can. & preserv.) 529.686-014
DUMPER (chemical) 922.686-010
Dumper (food prep., nec) 523.685-102
DUMPER-BAILER OPERATOR (petrol. & gas) 931.684-010
dumper-bulk system (any industry) 921.686-014
Dumper, Central-Concrete-Mixing Plant (construction) 579.665-014
Dumper, Mold Cleaner (foundry) 514.685-014
Dump Grader (construction) 869.687-026
DUMPING-MACHINE OPERATOR (can. & preserv.; wholesale tr.) 529.685-102
DUMP OPERATOR (any industry) 921.685-038
DUMP-TRUCK DRIVER (any industry) 902.683-010
Dump-Truck Driver, Off-Highway (any industry) 902.683-010

Duplicate Maker (garment) 785.361-018
DUPLICATING-MACHINE OPERATOR I (clerical) 207.682-010
DUPLICATING-MACHINE OPERATOR II (clerical) 207.682-014
duplicating-machine operator (machine shop) 605.280-018
Duplicating-Machine Servicer (any industry) 633.281-018
duplicator (any industry) 809.381-014
DUPLICATOR-PUNCH OPERATOR (any industry) 615.482-014
durable medical equipment repairer (protective dev.; retail trade) 639.281-022
DUST BOX WORKER (build. mat., nec) 574.667-010
DUST-BRUSH ASSEMBLER (house. appl.) 739.687-074
DUST-COLLECTOR ATTENDANT (mine & quarry) 511.685-022
DUST-COLLECTOR OPERATOR (smelt. & refin.) 511.482-018
DUST-COLLECTOR OPERATOR (soap & rel.) 551.685-050
DUST COLLECTOR, ORE CRUSHING (smelt. & refin.) 511.682-010
DUST COLLECTOR-TREATER (smelt. & refin.) 511.687-014
DUSTER (hat & cap) 587.685-026
duster (pottery & porc.) 574.684-010
DUSTING-AND-BRUSHING-MACHINE OPERATOR (rubber goods) 559.685-054
DUSTLESS OPERATOR (chemical) 550.685-058
DUST-MILL OPERATOR (tex. prod., nec) 581.686-030
DUST MIXER (smelt. & refin.) 510.685-010
DUST-MOP MAKER (tex. prod., nec) 739.687-078
dust operator (smelt. & refin.) 511.482-018
DUST PULLER (smelt. & refin.) 519.687-014
DUST SAMPLER (mine & quarry) 939.585-010
Dust-Truck Driver (any industry) 902.683-010
dwarf tree grower (agriculture) 405.161-010
dx board operator (any industry) 379.362-014
DYE AUTOMATION OPERATOR (textile) 582.362-014
dye-beck-reel operator (textile) 582.665-014
dye blender (chemical) 550.685-014
Dye-Boarding-Machine Operator (knitting) 589.685-010
DYED-YARN OPERATOR (textile) 582.685-058
dye feeder (textile) 582.582-010
dye-house supervisor (knitting; tex. prod., nec; textile) 582.131-014
DYE-HOUSE SUPERVISOR (leather mfg.) 582.131-010
DYE-HOUSE WORKER (leather mfg.) 582.686-010
Dyeing-Machine Back-Tender (textile) 589.686-010
dyeing-machine feeder (textile) 582.582-010
DYEING-MACHINE OPERATOR (knitting) term
dyeing-machine tender (textile) 582.685-102
Dyeing Supervisor (leather mfg.) 582.131-010
DYE-LAB TECHNICIAN (knitting) 582.384-010
dye-machine tender (textile) 582.685-130
dye-machine-tender helper (tex. prod., nec; textile) 582.686-030
dye maker (any industry) 550.684-014
dye mixer (leather mfg.) 582.482-010
Dye Mixer (photo. appar.) 550.685-090
dye-padder operator (textile) 582.685-106
DYER (button & notion) 582.687-014
DYER (chemical) 554.384-010
DYER (fabrication, nec) 599.685-034
dyer (hat & cap) 582.685-034
dyer (knitting) 582.685-170
DYER (laundry & rel.) 364.361-010
DYER (woodworking) 562.687-010
dyer and washer (leather mfg.) 582.482-010
dye-range feeder (textile) 582.582-010
DYE-RANGE OPERATOR, CLOTH (textile) 582.582-010
dyer assistant (any industry) 550.684-014
dyer assistant (knitting) 582.261-010
dyer assistant (laundry & rel.) 364.687-010
DYE-REEL OPERATOR (textile) 582.665-014
DYE-REEL-OPERATOR HELPER (textile) 582.686-014
DYER HELPER (hat & cap) 589.685-042
DYER HELPER (laundry & rel.) 364.687-010
dye-room helper (laundry & rel.) 364.687-010
dye-room helper (textile) 582.686-014
DYER, SUPERVISOR (knitting; tex. prod., nec; textile) 582.131-014
DYE-STAND LOADER (textile) 589.687-062
DYE-TANK TENDER (tex. prod., nec) 582.685-054
Dye Tester (pottery & porc.) 774.687-026
DYE-TUB OPERATOR (knitting) 582.685-170
dye-tub operator (textile) 582.665-014
DYE WEIGHER (any industry) 550.684-014
dye weigher (leather mfg.) 582.482-010
DYE-WEIGHER HELPER (any industry) 550.687-018
dye-winch operator (textile) 582.665-014
dynamic-balancer set-up worker (any industry) 809.382-010
DYNAMITE-CARTRIDGE CRIMPER (chemical) 692.685-078
DYNAMITE-PACKING-MACHINE FEEDER (chemical) 692.686-038
DYNAMITE-PACKING-MACHINE OPERATOR (chemical) 692.662-010
dynamiter (mine & quarry) 931.261-010
DYNAMITE RECLAIMER (chemical) 551.687-018

Dynamometer Assembler And Tester (office machines) 710.281-010
Dynamometer Repairer (elec. equip.) 729.281-026
Dynamometer Tester, Chassis (auto. mfg.) 806.281-010
DYNAMOMETER TESTER, MOTOR (auto. mfg.) 806.281-010
Dynamometer Tuner (automotive ser.) 620.281-066
dynamo operator (utilities)　　see GENERATOR OPERATOR
Dynamotor Repairer (any industry) 721.281-018

E

Ear-Flap Binder (hat & cap) 787.682-010
EAR-MOLD LABORATORY TECHNICIAN (plastic prod.) 777.361-010
EAR-MUFF ASSEMBLER (hat & cap) 784.687-022
EARRING MAKER (jewelry-silver.) 700.684-030
earth-auger operator (construction; utilities) 859.682-010
EARTH-BORING-MACHINE OPERATOR (construction; utilities) 859.682-010
earth burner (petrol. refin.) 573.685-014
Easter Bunny (any industry) 299.647-010
Ecclesiastical-Art-Metal Worker (jewelry-silver.; metal prod., nec) 619.260-014
ecg technician (medical ser.) 078.362-018
ECHOCARDIOGRAPH TECHNICIAN (medical ser.) 078.364-014
ECOLOGIST (profess. & kin.) term
ecologist (profess. & kin.)　　see ENVIRONMENTALIST
economic analyst (profess. & kin.) 050.067-010
ECONOMIC DEVELOPMENT COORDINATOR (government ser.) 188.117-102
Economic Officer (government ser.) 188.117-106
ECONOMIST (profess. & kin.) 050.067-010
EDDY-CURRENT INSPECTOR (steel & rel.) 619.381-014
EDGE BANDER, HAND (furniture) 762.684-038
EDGE BANDER, MACHINE (furniture; millwork-plywood) 762.685-010
EDGE-BANDING-MACHINE OFFBEARER (furniture; millwork-plywood) 762.686-010
Edge Baster (garment) 786.682-030
edge beader (boot & shoe) 690.685-174
edge blacker, machine (boot & shoe) 690.685-234
edge burnisher (boot & shoe) 690.685-146
EDGE BURNISHER, UPPERS (boot & shoe) 690.685-138
edge dyer (boot & shoe) 690.685-234
EDGE-GLUE-MACHINE TENDER (millwork-plywood) 569.685-034
Edge Gluer (millwork-plywood) 569.685-062
EDGE GRINDER (plastic prod.) 690.685-142
edge grinder, machine (glass products) 775.684-062
Edge Inker (boot & shoe) 788.684-066
Edge Inker, Heels (boot & shoe) 788.684-066
Edge Inker, Uppers (boot & shoe) 788.684-066
edge kitter (boot & shoe) 690.685-146
Edge Maker (garment) 782.684-058
edge plugger (millwork-plywood) 769.685-010
Edge Polisher (boot & shoe) 788.687-018
Edge Polisher (glass products) 775.684-058
edger (boot & shoe) 690.685-138
edger (paper goods; wood. container) 795.684-014
EDGER, AUTOMATIC (saw. & plan.) 667.682-026
EDGER, HAND (glass mfg.; glass products) 775.684-014
EDGER-MACHINE HELPER (stonework) 673.686-018
EDGER-MACHINE OPERATOR (stonework) 673.682-018
Edger Machine Setter (machine shop) 601.280-022
EDGE ROLLER (furniture) 780.684-058
Edge-Round Tender (electron. comp.) 673.685-094
EDGER, TOUCH-UP (glass products) 775.684-018
Edge Sander (woodworking) 761.682-014
EDGE SETTER (boot & shoe) 690.685-146
Edge Setter, Heel Lift (boot & shoe) 690.685-146
edge skiver (boot & shoe; rubber goods) 690.685-378
EDGE STAINER I (leather prod.) 589.685-046
EDGE STAINER II (leather prod.) 749.684-022
edge stainer, machine (boot & shoe) 690.685-234
Edge Stitcher (boot & shoe) 690.682-082
Edge Stitcher, Lockstitch (garment) 786.682-238
EDGE STRIPPER (paper goods; wood. container) 795.684-014
EDGE TRIMMER (boot & shoe) 690.685-150
edge trimmer (leather mfg.) 585.684-010
edge-trimming-machine operator (boot & shoe) 690.685-150
edging-machine catcher (optical goods) 673.686-014
EDGING-MACHINE FEEDER (glass mfg.) 673.686-022
edging-machine feeder (optical goods) 673.686-014
edging-machine operator (any industry)　　see SERGING-MACHINE OPERATOR
EDGING-MACHINE SETTER (glass products) 673.380-010
editing-machine operator (motion picture) 962.382-014
editor (radio-tv broad.) 131.267-022
EDITOR, BOOK (print. & pub.) 132.067-014

EDITOR, CITY (print. & pub.) 132.037-014
editor, continuity and script (radio-tv broad.) 132.037-010
EDITOR, DEPARTMENT (print. & pub.) 132.037-018
EDITOR, DICTIONARY (profess. & kin.) 132.067-018
Editor, Farm Journal (print. & pub.) 132.037-022
EDITOR, GREETING CARD (print. & pub.) 132.067-022
Editor, House Organ (print. & pub.) 132.037-022
EDITORIAL ASSISTANT (print. & pub.) 132.267-014
Editorial Cartoonist (print. & pub.) 141.061-010
EDITORIAL WRITER (print. & pub.) 131.067-022
editor-in-chief, newspaper (print. & pub.) 132.017-014
EDITOR, INDEX (print. & pub.) 132.367-010
Editor, Magazine (print. & pub.) 132.037-022
EDITOR, MANAGING, NEWSPAPER (print. & pub.) 132.017-010
EDITOR, MAP (profess. & kin.) 018.261-018
EDITOR, NEWS (print. & pub.) 132.067-026
EDITOR, NEWSPAPER (print. & pub.) 132.017-014
EDITOR, PUBLICATIONS (print. & pub.) 132.037-022
EDITOR, SCHOOL PHOTOGRAPH (photofinishing) 976.687-010
editor, sound (motion picture) 962.382-014
EDITOR, TECHNICAL AND SCIENTIFIC PUBLICATIONS (profess. & kin.) 132.017-018
EDITOR, TELEGRAPH (print. & pub.; radio-tv broad.) 132.267-010
Editor, Trade Journal (print. & pub.) 132.037-022
editor, wire (print. & pub.; radio-tv broad.) 132.267-010
educational/development assistant (medical ser.) 076.364-010
EDUCATIONAL RESOURCE COORDINATOR (museums) 099.167-030
EDUCATIONAL SPECIALIST (education) 099.167-022
education department registrar (museums) 238.367-034
EDUCATION SUPERVISOR, CORRECTIONAL INSTITUTION (education) 099.117-014
Education Supervisor, Penal Institution (education) 099.117-014
Education Supervisor, Youth Authority (education) 099.117-014
eeg technologist (medical ser.) 078.362-022
EFFERVESCENT-SALTS COMPOUNDER (pharmaceut.) 559.685-058
efficiency expert (profess. & kin.) 012.167-070
Egg-And-Spice Mixer (food prep., nec) 520.685-154
EGG BREAKER (any industry) 521.687-042
EGG-BREAKING-MACHINE OPERATOR (can. & preserv.) 521.685-114
EGG CANDLER (any industry) 529.687-074
Egg Grader (any industry) 529.687-074
Egg Packer (agriculture; wholesale tr.) 920.687-134
EGG PASTEURIZER (agriculture) 529.682-038
EGG PROCESSOR (pharmaceut.) 559.687-034
egg room supervisor (can. & preserv.; wholesale tr.) 529.137-042
Egg Smeller (any industry) 521.687-042
EGG WASHER, MACHINE (agriculture; wholesale tr.) 529.686-030
Eight-Section Blower (hat & cap) 680.685-046
ekg technician (medical ser.) 078.362-018
Elastic Assembler (protective dev.) 712.684-010
ELASTIC ATTACHER, CHAINSTITCH (garment) 786.682-086
ELASTIC ATTACHER, COVERSTITCH (garment) 786.682-090
ELASTIC ATTACHER, OVERLOCK (garment) 786.682-094
ELASTIC ATTACHER, ZIGZAG (garment) 786.682-098
Elastic Cutter (garment) 699.685-014
Elastic Cutter, Hand (any industry) 781.687-026
Elastic Sewer (tex. prod., nec) 787.682-066
ELASTIC-TAPE INSERTER (garment) 782.687-022
elastic-yarn twister (textile) 681.685-038
elastic-yarn-twister helper (textile) 681.685-042
ELECTION ASSISTANT (government ser.) 188.167-050
ELECTION CLERK (government ser.) 205.367-030
election supervisor (government ser.) 188.167-050
electrical and electronics development mechanic (any industry) 726.261-010
ELECTRICAL AND RADIO MOCK-UP MECHANIC (aircraft mfg.) 693.381-026
ELECTRICAL-APPLIANCE PREPARER (any industry) 827.584-010
ELECTRICAL-APPLIANCE REPAIRER (any industry) 723.381-010
ELECTRICAL-APPLIANCE SERVICER (any industry) 827.261-010
ELECTRICAL-APPLIANCE-SERVICER APPRENTICE (any industry) 827.261-014
ELECTRICAL-APPLIANCE-SERVICER SUPERVISOR (any industry) 827.131-010
electrical-appliance service supervisor (utilities) 187.167-010
ELECTRICAL ASSEMBLER (aircraft mfg.) 729.384-026
Electrical Checkout Mechanic (aircraft mfg.) 806.261-050
ELECTRICAL-CONTROL ASSEMBLER (comm. equip.; elec. equip.) 729.684-026
ELECTRICAL-DESIGN ENGINEER (profess. & kin.) 003.061-018
ELECTRICAL-DISCHARGE-MACHINE OPERATOR, PRODUCTION (machine shop) 609.482-010
ELECTRICAL-DISCHARGE-MACHINE SET-UP OPERATOR (machine shop) 609.380-010
ELECTRICAL ENGINEER (profess. & kin.) 003.061-010
electrical engineer, geophysical prospecting (profess. & kin.) 003.061-022

ELECTRICAL ENGINEER, POWER SYSTEM (utilities) 003.167-018
ELECTRICAL-EQUIPMENT TESTER (aircraft mfg.) 729.381-010
ELECTRICAL INSPECTOR (aircraft mfg.; air trans.) 825.381-026
Electrical Inspector (automotive ser.) 620.281-030
Electrical Inspector (railroad equip.) 807.381-026
ELECTRICAL-INSTALLATION SUPERVISOR (utilities) 821.131-010
ELECTRICAL-INSTRUMENT REPAIRER (any industry) 729.281-026
electrical-laboratory technician (profess. & kin.) 003.161-010
ELECTRICAL-LINE SPLICER (petrol. & gas) 728.684-014
electrical-logging operator (petrol. & gas) 010.261-014
ELECTRICAL-PROSPECTING ENGINEER (profess. & kin.) 003.061-022
electrical-prospecting operator (petrol. & gas) 010.261-014
Electrical Prospector (petrol. & gas) 024.061-026
electrical repairer (any industry) 829.261-018
Electrical Repairer, Internal Combustion Engines (automotive ser.; engine-turbine) 825.281-022
ELECTRICAL-RESEARCH ENGINEER (profess. & kin.) 003.061-026
ELECTRICAL SUPERVISOR (petrol. & gas) 826.131-010
ELECTRICAL TECHNICIAN (profess. & kin.) 003.161-010
ELECTRICAL TEST ENGINEER (profess. & kin.) 003.061-014
ELECTRICAL TESTER (utilities) term
electrical tester, battery (elec. equip.) 727.384-010
Electrical-Tests Supervisor (utilities) 184.167-218
electrical-transmission engineer (utilities) 003.167-050
Electrical-Unit Rebuilder (automotive ser.) 825.281-022
Electric-Arc-Furnace Operator (foundry; smelt. & refin.; steel & rel.) 512.362-018
electric-bath attendant (personal ser.) 335.677-014
ELECTRIC BLANKET WIRER (tex. prod., nec) 789.684-054
electric-blasting-cap assembler (ordnance) 737.687-018
Electric-Cable Diagrammer (elec. equip.) 003.281-010
ELECTRIC-CELL TENDER (chemical) 558.565-014
ELECTRIC-CONTAINER TESTER (elec. equip.) 727.687-050
electric deicer inspector (rubber goods) 729.387-010
electric-detector operator (construction) 862.687-014
ELECTRIC-DISTRIBUTION CHECKER (construction; utilities) 824.281-014
electric-distribution engineer (utilities) 003.167-046
Electric-Dragline Operator (any industry) 850.683-018
Electric-Fan Assembler (house. appl.) 723.684-010
ELECTRIC-FORK OPERATOR (agriculture) 921.685-042
Electric-Freight-Car Operator (r.r. trans.) 921.683-050
Electric-Frying-Pan Repairer (house. appl.) 723.584-010
ELECTRIC-GOLF-CART REPAIRER (amuse. & rec.; automotive ser.) 620.261-026
Electric-Heater Assembler (house. appl.) 723.684-010
Electric-Hoist Operator (mine & quarry) 921.663-026
ELECTRICIAN (construction) 824.261-010
ELECTRICIAN (mfd. bldgs.) 824.681-010
ELECTRICIAN (ship-boat mfg.) 825.381-030
ELECTRICIAN (water trans.) 825.281-014
ELECTRICIAN, AIRCRAFT (aircraft mfg.; air trans.) 825.261-018
ELECTRICIAN APPRENTICE (construction) 824.261-014
ELECTRICIAN APPRENTICE (ship-boat mfg.) 825.381-034
electrician apprentice, elevator maintenance (any industry) 825.281-034
ELECTRICIAN APPRENTICE, POWERHOUSE (utilities) 820.261-010
ELECTRICIAN (automotive ser.) 825.281-022
Electrician, Bus (automotive ser.) 825.281-022
electrician, cable-splicing (construction; tel. & tel.; utilities) 829.361-010
ELECTRICIAN, CHIEF (motion picture) 824.137-010
Electrician, Chief (water trans.) 825.281-014
electrician-constructor supervisor (utilities) 821.131-026
Electrician, Control Equipment (railroad equip.) 825.281-026
Electrician, Crane Maintenance (any industry) 829.261-018
Electrician, Deck (water trans.) 825.281-014
electrician, elevator-maintenance (any industry) 825.281-030
electrician, front (amuse. & rec.) 962.381-014
ELECTRICIAN HELPER (any industry) 829.684-022
ELECTRICIAN HELPER (ship-boat mfg.) 829.684-026
electrician helper (utilities) 821.667-010
ELECTRICIAN HELPER, AUTOMOTIVE (automotive ser.) 825.684-010
Electrician Helper, Powerhouse (utilities) 821.667-010
ELECTRICIAN, LOCOMOTIVE (railroad equip.) 825.281-026
Electrician, Machine Shop (machine shop) 829.261-018
ELECTRICIAN, MAINTENANCE (any industry) 829.261-018
electrician, marine (ship-boat mfg.) 825.381-030
electrician, master (amuse. & rec.) 962.267-010
ELECTRICIAN, OFFICE (tel. & tel.) 822.261-010
electrician, outside (ship-boat mfg.) 825.381-030
ELECTRICIAN, POWERHOUSE (utilities) 820.261-014
ELECTRICIAN, RADIO (any industry) 823.281-014
Electrician, Rectifier Maintenance (utilities) 829.261-018
Electrician, Refinery (petrol. refin.) 829.261-018
ELECTRICIAN, RESEARCH (aircraft mfg.) 726.261-014
Electrician, Second (water trans.) 825.281-014
Electrician, Ship (ship-boat mfg.) 825.381-030

Electrician, Shop (ship-boat mfg.) 825.381-030
Electrician, Sound (water trans.) 825.281-014
electrician, station, assistant (tel. & tel.) 822.261-010
ELECTRICIAN, SUBSTATION (utilities) 820.261-018
ELECTRICIAN SUPERVISOR (any industry) 829.131-014
ELECTRICIAN SUPERVISOR (ship-boat mfg.) 825.131-010
Electrician Supervisor, Airplane (air trans.) 829.131-014
Electrician Supervisor, Automotive (automotive ser.) 829.131-014
Electrician Supervisor, Locomotive (railroad equip.) 829.131-014
Electrician Supervisor, Maintenance (any industry) 829.131-014
ELECTRICIAN SUPERVISOR, SUBSTATION (utilities) 820.131-010
electrician, telephone (any industry) 822.281-018
Electrician, Third (water trans.) 825.281-014
electrician, underground (utilities) 821.361-010
electrician, wiring (auto. mfg.; vehicles, nec) 829.684-014
Electrician, Yard (ship-boat mfg.) 825.381-030
Electric-Locomotive-Crane Operator (any industry) 921.663-038
electric-meter inspector (utilities) 821.364-010
Electric-Meter-Installer Helper (utilities) 821.667-010
ELECTRIC-METER INSTALLER I (utilities) 821.361-014
ELECTRIC-METER INSTALLER II (utilities) 821.684-010
Electric-Meter Reader (utilities) 209.567-010
ELECTRIC-METER REPAIRER (utilities) 729.281-014
ELECTRIC-METER-REPAIRER APPRENTICE (utilities) 729.281-018
Electric-Meter-Repairer Helper (utilities) 821.564-010
ELECTRIC-METER TESTER (utilities) 821.381-010
Electric-Meter-Tester Helper (utilities) 821.564-010
electric-meter tester, shop (utilities) 729.281-034
ELECTRIC-MOTOR ANALYST (any industry) 721.261-010
ELECTRIC-MOTOR-AND-GENERATOR ASSEMBLER (elec. equip.) 820.361-014
ELECTRIC-MOTOR ASSEMBLER (elec. equip.) 721.684-022
ELECTRIC-MOTOR ASSEMBLER AND TESTER (any industry) 721.281-014
ELECTRIC-MOTOR-CONTROL ASSEMBLER (elec. equip.) 721.381-014
ELECTRIC-MOTOR FITTER (railroad equip.) 721.381-010
electric-motor-repair clerk (retail trade; wholesale tr.) 271.354-010
ELECTRIC-MOTOR REPAIRER (any industry) 721.281-010
ELECTRIC MOTOR REPAIRING SUPERVISOR (any industry) 721.131-010
ELECTRIC-MOTOR WINDER (elec. equip.) 721.484-010
electric-needle specialist (personal ser.) 339.371-010
ELECTRIC-ORGAN ASSEMBLER AND CHECKER (musical inst.) 730.381-022
ELECTRIC-ORGAN INSPECTOR AND REPAIRER (musical inst.) 730.281-018
electric-organ technician (any industry) 828.261-010
Electric-Pile-Driver Operator (construction) 859.682-018
ELECTRIC POWERLINE EXAMINER (utilities) 959.367-010
Electric-Power-Shovel Operator (any industry) 850.683-030
Electric-Range Assembler (elec. equip.) 827.684-010
Electric-Range Preparer (any industry) 827.584-010
Electric-Range Servicer (any industry) 827.261-010
Electric-Razor Assembler (cutlery-hrdwr.) 701.687-010
Electric-Refrigerator Preparer (any industry) 827.584-010
Electric-Refrigerator Servicer (any industry) 827.261-010
electric-repair supervisor (utilities) 820.131-010
ELECTRIC-SEALING-MACHINE OPERATOR (any industry) 690.685-154
electric-sewer-cleaning-machine operator (business ser.) 899.664-014
ELECTRIC-SIGN ASSEMBLER (fabrication, nec) 729.684-022
electric-sorting-machine operator (can. & preserv.) 521.685-238
Electric-Switch Tester (elec. equip.) 729.684-058
Electric-Tape Slitter (rubber goods) 699.682-030
ELECTRIC-TOOL REPAIRER (any industry) 729.281-022
ELECTRIC-TRACK-SWITCH MAINTAINER (r.r. trans.) 825.261-010
Electric-Truck-Crane Operator (any industry) 921.683-050
Electric-Truck Operator (any industry) 921.683-050
ELECTRIFIER OPERATOR (textile) 585.685-042
Electrocardiograph Repairer (any industry) 729.281-030
ELECTROCARDIOGRAPH TECHNICIAN (medical ser.) 078.362-018
ELECTRODE CLEANER (elec. equip.) 729.687-014
ELECTRODE-CLEANING-MACHINE OPERATOR (elec. equip.) 559.685-062
ELECTRODE TURNER-AND-FINISHER (elec. equip.) 692.682-034
ELECTROENCEPHALOGRAPHIC TECHNOLOGIST (medical ser.) 078.362-022
ELECTROFORMER (electroplating) 500.684-010
electroformer (inst. & app.) 500.684-034
ELECTROGALVANIZING-MACHINE OPERATOR (electroplating) 500.362-010
ELECTROLESS PLATER (any industry) 505.684-010
ELECTROLESS PLATER, PRINTED CIRCUIT BOARD PANELS (electron. comp.) 501.685-014
ELECTROLOGIST (personal ser.) 339.371-010
ELECTROLYSIS-AND-CORROSION-CONTROL ENGINEER (profess. & kin.) 003.167-022
electrolysis engineer (profess. & kin.) 003.167-022
electrolysis investigator (profess. & kin.) 003.167-022

electrolysis operator (personal ser.) 339.371-010
Electrolytic De-Scaler (any industry) 503.362-010
Electromagnet-Crane Operator I (any industry) 921.663-058
Electromagnet-Crane Operator II (any industry) 921.663-062
electromechanical instrument mechanic (inst. & app.) 710.381-054
ELECTROMECHANICAL TECHNICIAN (inst. & app.) 710.281-018
ELECTROMEDICAL-EQUIPMENT REPAIRER (any industry) 729.281-030
electromedical service engineer (any industry) 729.281-030
ELECTROMYOGRAPHIC TECHNICIAN (medical ser.) 078.362-038
electron-beam operator (electron. comp.) 972.382-018
Electron Gun Assembler (electron. comp.) 725.384-010
Electron Gun Inspector (electron. comp.) 726.684-022
Electronic Color Correction Operator (print. & pub.) 979.282-010
Electronic-Communications Technician (profess. & kin.) 003.161-014
ELECTRONIC-COMPONENT PROCESSOR (electron. comp.) 590.684-014
ELECTRONIC EQUIPMENT REPAIRER (comm. equip.; electron. comp.) 726.381-014
ELECTRONIC EQUIPMENT SET-UP OPERATOR (electron. comp.) 726.380-010
Electronic-Eye-Thermal-Cutting-Machine Operator (welding) 816.482-010
ELECTRONIC FUNDS TRANSFER COORDINATOR (financial) 216.362-038
electronic gluer (woodworking) 569.685-050
electronic imaging system operator (print. & pub.) 979.282-010
electronic induction hardener (heat treating) 504.685-022
ELECTRONIC INTELLIGENCE OPERATIONS SPECIALIST (military ser.) 193.382-010
ELECTRONIC MASKING SYSTEM OPERATOR (print. & pub.) 972.282-018
Electronic-Organ Installer (any industry) 828.261-010
ELECTRONIC-ORGAN TECHNICIAN (any industry) 828.261-010
Electronic Page Makeup System Operator (print. & pub.) 979.282-010
electronic paint operator (any industry) 599.682-010
Electronic-Piano Installer (any industry) 828.261-010
electronic plotting system operator (print. & pub.) 972.282-018
ELECTRONIC PREPRESS SYSTEM OPERATOR (print. & pub.) 979.282-010
ELECTRONIC-PRODUCTION-LINE-MAINTENANCE MECHANIC (electron. comp.) 629.261-022
ELECTRONIC-SALES-AND-SERVICE TECHNICIAN (profess. & kin.) 828.251-010
ELECTRONICS ASSEMBLER (electron. comp.) 726.684-018
ELECTRONICS ASSEMBLER, DEVELOPMENTAL (any industry) 726.261-010
Electronic-Scale Assembler And Tester (office machines) 710.281-010
ELECTRONIC-SCALE SUBASSEMBLER (office machines) 726.684-014
electronic scanner operator (print. & pub.) 972.282-010
ELECTRONICS-DESIGN ENGINEER (profess. & kin.) 003.061-034
ELECTRONICS ENGINEER (profess. & kin.) 003.061-030
electronics-equipment mechanic (any industry) 828.261-010
ELECTRONICS INSPECTOR (comm. equip.; electron. comp.; inst. & app.) 726.381-010
ELECTRONICS INSPECTOR (electron. comp.) 726.684-022
ELECTRONICS MECHANIC (any industry) 828.261-010
ELECTRONICS-MECHANIC APPRENTICE (any industry) 828.261-026
Electronics Mechanic, Computer (any industry) 828.261-022
electronic-sound technician (any industry) 823.261-010
ELECTRONICS-RESEARCH ENGINEER (profess. & kin.) 003.061-038
electronics specialist (any industry) 828.261-022
electronics supervisor (petrol. & gas) 710.131-034
electronics-system mechanic (any industry) 828.261-022
electronics technician (any industry) 823.281-018
electronics technician (any industry) 828.261-022
ELECTRONICS TECHNICIAN (profess. & kin.) 003.161-014
electronics-technician apprentice (any industry) 828.261-010
Electronics Technician, Nuclear Reactor (profess. & kin.) 003.161-014
ELECTRONICS-TEST ENGINEER (profess. & kin.) 003.061-042
ELECTRONICS TESTER (any industry) 726.261-018
ELECTRONICS TESTER (electron. comp.) 726.684-026
ELECTRONICS UTILITY WORKER (comm. equip.; electron. comp.) 726.364-018
ELECTRONICS WORKER (electron. comp.) 726.687-010
ELECTRO-OPTICAL ENGINEER (profess. & kin.) 023.061-010
electroplater (electroplating) 500.380-010
electroplater apprentice (electroplating) 500.380-014
electroplater, automatic (electroplating) 500.685-014
electroplater helper (electroplating) 500.686-010
Electrotype Caster (print. & pub.) 974.381-010
Electrotype Molder (print. & pub.) 974.381-010
ELECTROTYPER (print. & pub.) 974.381-010
ELECTROTYPER APPRENTICE (print. & pub.) 974.381-014
Electrotyper Helper (print. & pub.) 979.684-026
ELECTROTYPE SERVICER (print. & pub.) 659.462-010
Electro-Winning Operator (smelt. & refin.) 519.362-014
Element Setter (elec. equip.) 727.687-038
ELEMENT WINDING MACHINE TENDER (elec. equip.; inst. & app.) 724.685-010
Elephant Keeper (amuse. & rec.) 412.674-010

ELEVATING-GRADER OPERATOR (construction) 850.663-014
elevator builder (construction) 825.361-010
ELEVATOR CONSTRUCTOR (construction) 825.361-010
Elevator Constructor, Electric (construction) 825.361-010
ELEVATOR-CONSTRUCTOR HELPER (construction) 825.664-010
Elevator Constructor, Hydraulic (construction) 825.361-010
ELEVATOR-CONSTRUCTOR SUPERVISOR (construction) 825.131-014
elevator dispatcher (any industry) 388.367-010
elevator erector (construction) 825.361-010
elevator-erector helper (construction) 825.664-010
ELEVATOR EXAMINER-AND-ADJUSTER (any industry) 825.261-014
elevator inspector (any industry) 825.261-014
elevator installer (construction) 825.361-010
elevator mechanic (any industry) 825.281-030
elevator mechanic (construction) 825.361-010
ELEVATOR OPERATOR (any industry) 388.663-010
ELEVATOR OPERATOR, FREIGHT (any industry) 921.683-038
elevator operator, service (any industry) 921.683-038
ELEVATOR REPAIRER (any industry) 825.281-030
ELEVATOR-REPAIRER APPRENTICE (any industry) 825.281-034
ELEVATOR-REPAIRER HELPER (any industry) 825.684-014
elevator-repair mechanic (any industry) 825.281-030
ELEVATOR STARTER (any industry) 388.367-010
elevator supervisor (any industry) 388.367-010
elevator tender (grain-feed mills) 921.365-010
ELIGIBILITY-AND-OCCUPANCY INTERVIEWER (government ser.) 168.267-038
ELIGIBILITY WORKER (government ser.) 195.267-010
EMBALMER (personal ser.) 338.371-014
EMBALMER APPRENTICE (personal ser.) 338.371-010
embalmer assistant (personal ser.) 339.361-010
Embedder (elec. equip.) 575.684-042
EMBLEM DRAWER-IN (tex. prod., nec) 689.380-010
Emblem-Fuser Tender (garment; knitting) 583.685-046
EMBOSSER (any industry) 583.685-030
EMBOSSER (boot & shoe) 690.685-158
EMBOSSER (leather mfg.; leather prod.) 690.682-030
EMBOSSER (optical goods) 713.684-022
embosser (print. & pub.) 659.682-014
EMBOSSER (print. & pub.) 659.382-010
Embosser (print. & pub.) 652.682-030
embosser operator (clerical) 208.682-010
EMBOSSER OPERATOR (paper goods) 649.682-022
embossing-calender operator (any industry) 583.685-030
embossing clerk (tobacco) 529.567-014
embossing-machine operator (any industry) 583.685-030
embossing-machine operator (leather mfg.; leather prod.) 690.682-030
EMBOSSING-MACHINE OPERATOR (nonfer. metal) 617.685-018
EMBOSSING-MACHINE OPERATOR (ordnance) 619.685-038
EMBOSSING-MACHINE OPERATOR (tex. prod., nec) 583.685-034
EMBOSSING-MACHINE OPERATOR (wood prod., nec) 669.682-046
embossing-machine-operator helper (paper goods) 640.685-070
EMBOSSING-MACHINE-OPERATOR HELPER (plastic-synth.) 583.685-038
Embossing-Machine-Operator Helper (tex. prod., nec) 589.687-026
EMBOSSING-MACHINE OPERATOR I (clerical) 208.582-014
EMBOSSING-MACHINE OPERATOR II (clerical) 208.682-010
EMBOSSING-MACHINE TENDER (paper goods) 649.685-038
Embossing-Press Operator (elec. equip.) 652.682-030
embossing-press operator (leather mfg.; leather prod.) 690.682-030
EMBOSSING-PRESS OPERATOR (print. & pub.) 659.682-014
EMBOSSING-PRESS-OPERATOR APPRENTICE (print. & pub.) 659.682-018
EMBOSSING-PRESS OPERATOR, MOLDED GOODS (fabrication, nec) 690.682-034
EMBOSSING TOOLSETTER (ordnance) 616.260-010
EMBOSSOGRAPH OPERATOR (any industry) 652.682-014
EMBROIDERER, HAND (tex. prod., nec) 782.684-018
EMBROIDERY-MACHINE OPERATOR (any industry) 787.682-022
EMBROIDERY-MACHINE OPERATOR (garment) 786.685-018
EMBROIDERY PATTERNMAKER (retail trade; wholesale tr.) 782.361-014
Embroidery Supervisor (tex. prod., nec) 787.132-014
EMBROIDERY SUPERVISOR (tex. prod., nec) 689.130-010
Emergency-Crew Supervisor (utilities) 821.131-014
Emergency-Detail Driver (government ser.) 375.263-014
EMERGENCY MEDICAL SERVICES COORDINATOR (medical ser.) 079.117-010
EMERGENCY MEDICAL TECHNICIAN (medical ser.) 079.374-010
Emery-Wheel Molder (nonmet. min.) 575.685-010
emg technician (medical ser.) 078.362-038
employee relations administrator (profess. & kin.) 166.117-010
EMPLOYEE RELATIONS SPECIALIST (motor trans.) 166.267-042
employee-service officer (profess. & kin.) 166.117-014
EMPLOYER RELATIONS REPRESENTATIVE (profess. & kin.) 166.257-010
EMPLOYMENT-AND-CLAIMS AIDE (government ser.) 169.367-010
EMPLOYMENT CLERK (clerical) 205.362-014
Employment Counselor (government ser.) 045.107-010

EMPLOYMENT INTERVIEWER (profess. & kin.) 166.267-010
employment supervisor (profess. & kin.) 166.167-030
emt-paramedic (medical ser.) 079.364-026
Emulsification Operator (oils & grease) 558.685-062
Emulsion Operator (chemical) 559.382-034
enamel burner (paint & varnish) 553.685-082
enamel cracker (jewelry-silver.) 770.687-030
Enamel Dipper (any industry) 599.685-026
enamel drier (plumbing-heat.) 509.684-010
ENAMELER (jewelry-silver.) 740.684-018
enameler (leather mfg.) 584.687-010
ENAMELER (plumbing-heat.) 509.684-010
Enameler (pottery & porc.) 741.684-026
Enamel-Machine Operator (elec. equip.) 599.685-046
enamel pulverizer (jewelry-silver.) 770.687-030
Enamel Shader (paint & varnish) 550.381-014
Enamel Sprayer I (any industry) 741.684-026
Enamel Sprayer II (any industry) 741.687-018
ENCAPSULATOR (aircraft mfg.) 556.684-014
ENCAPSULATOR (elec. equip.; electron. comp.) 726.687-022
Enchilada Maker (food prep., nec) 520.687-046
ENDBAND CUTTER, HAND (hat & cap) 784.687-026
endbander (hat & cap) 784.687-026
endband sizer (hat & cap) 784.687-026
END FINDER, FORMING DEPARTMENT (textile) 681.687-010
END FINDER, ROVING DEPARTMENT (glass mfg.) 689.687-038
END FINDER, TWISTING DEPARTMENT (textile) 689.687-042
END FRAZER (fabrication, nec) 665.685-014
ENDING-MACHINE OPERATOR (paper goods) 641.685-042
end-lathe operator (hat & cap) 585.685-074
Endless-Bed-Drum Sander (woodworking) 662.682-014
endless-belt finisher (narrow fabrics; textile) 782.684-062
Endless-Steamer Tender (textile) 582.585-010
ENDODONTIST (medical ser.) 072.101-014
end operator (wood. container) 669.685-054
Endorsement Clerk (insurance) 203.582-066
end packer (tinware) 509.666-010
END POLISHER (clock & watch) 715.685-026
Ends-Down Checker (textile) 221.367-034
END STAPLER (wood. container) 669.685-054
END-TOUCHING-MACHINE OPERATOR (wood prod., nec) 662.686-010
end trimmer (pen & pencil) 669.685-062
end trimmer (pen & pencil) 662.685-030
end user consultant (profess. & kin.) 032.262-010
ENERGY-CONSERVATION REPRESENTATIVE (utilities) 959.367-018
ENERGY-CONTROL OFFICER (education) 199.167-018
engine assembler (engine-turbine) 806.481-014
engine buildup mechanic (aircraft mfg.) 806.381-022
ENGINE DISPATCHER (r.r. trans.) 910.367-018
Engine Emission Technician (profess. & kin.) 029.261-014
ENGINEER (profess. & kin.) term
ENGINEER (water trans.) 197.130-010
engineer, automated equipment (machinery mfg.) 638.261-010
engineer, booster and exhauster (utilities) 953.382-010
engineer, byproduct (steel & rel.) 950.362-010
engineer, chief (radio-tv broad.) 003.167-034
Engineer, Chief (water trans.) 197.130-010
Engineer, Design-And-Construction (utilities) 003.167-018
ENGINEER, EXHAUSTER (steel & rel.) 950.362-010
Engineer, First Assistant (water trans.) 197.130-010
Engineer, Fishing Vessel (water trans.) 197.130-010
engineer, gas-pumping station (utilities) 953.382-010
engineer, geophysical laboratory (profess. & kin.) 024.167-010
ENGINEER-IN-CHARGE, STUDIO OPERATIONS (radio-tv broad.) 003.167-030
ENGINEER-IN-CHARGE, TRANSMITTER (radio-tv broad.) 003.167-034
engineering aide (profess. & kin.)   see TECHNICIAN
ENGINEERING ASSISTANT, MECHANICAL EQUIPMENT (profess. & kin.) 007.161-018
engineering clerk (any industry) 229.267-010
ENGINEERING-DOCUMENT-CONTROL CLERK (aircraft mfg.; electron. comp.) 206.367-010
Engineering Geologist (profess. & kin.) 024.061-018
engineering illustrator (profess. & kin.) 017.281-034
engineering laboratory technician (aircraft mfg.) 019.281-010
Engineering Librarian (library) 100.167-026
ENGINEERING MANAGER, ELECTRONICS (profess. & kin.) 003.167-070
ENGINEERING MODEL MAKER (inst. & app.) 693.260-018
engineering-release clerk (aircraft mfg.; electron. comp.) 206.367-010
engineering technician (profess. & kin.) 007.161-026
engineering technician, parking (government ser.) 199.261-014
engineering test mechanic (aircraft mfg.) 710.361-014
engineering test pilot (aircraft mfg.) 196.263-042
ENGINEER OF SYSTEM DEVELOPMENT (utilities) 003.167-026
Engineer, Operations-And-Maintenance (utilities) 003.167-018

Engineer, Remote Control, Diesel (r.r. trans.) 910.363-018
Engineer, Second Assistant (water trans.) 197.130-010
ENGINEER, SOILS (profess. & kin.) 024.161-010
engineer, steam (ship-boat mfg.) 623.281-030
Engineer, Third Assistant (water trans.) 197.130-010
Engine-Generator Assembler (engine-turbine) 820.361-014
Engine-Head Repairer (automotive ser.) 620.261-010
Engine Inspector (automotive ser.) 620.281-030
ENGINE-LATHE SET-UP OPERATOR (machine shop) 604.362-010
ENGINE-LATHE SET-UP OPERATOR (machine shop) 604.380-018
ENGINE-LATHE SET-UP OPERATOR, TOOL (machine shop) 604.280-010
engine-lathe tender (machine shop) 604.685-026
Engine Repairer (auto. mfg.) 620.381-022
ENGINE REPAIRER, PRODUCTION (engine-turbine) 625.381-010
ENGINE REPAIRER, SERVICE (engine-turbine) 625.281-018
Engine-Repair Mechanic, Bus (automotive ser.) 620.261-010
Engine-Room Cleaner (any industry) 381.687-018
engine supervisor (r.r. trans.) 910.137-022
ENGINE TESTER (aircraft mfg.; air trans.) 621.261-014
engine tester (auto. mfg.) 806.281-010
ENGINE-TESTING SUPERVISOR (engine-turbine) 625.131-010
ENGINE TURNER (jewelry-silver.) 704.381-018
ENGRAVER (glass products) 775.381-010
engraver (glass products) 775.584-010
ENGRAVER APPRENTICE, DECORATIVE (engraving) 704.381-022
ENGRAVER, AUTOMATIC (clock & watch) 609.685-014
ENGRAVER, BLOCK (print. & pub.) 979.281-014
Engraver, Copperplate (print. & pub.) 979.381-010
Engraver, Flatware (engraving) 704.381-030
ENGRAVER, HAND, HARD METALS (engraving) 704.381-026
ENGRAVER, HAND, SOFT METALS (engraving) 704.381-030
ENGRAVER I (print. & pub.) 979.381-010
ENGRAVER II (print. & pub.) 979.684-014
Engraver, Jewelry (engraving) 704.381-030
Engraver, Letter (print. & pub.) 979.281-018
Engraver, Lettering (engraving) 704.381-030
ENGRAVER, MACHINE (print. & pub.) 979.382-014
ENGRAVER, MACHINE I (engraving) 704.682-010
ENGRAVER, MACHINE II (engraving) 704.582-010
Engraver, Optical Frames (engraving) 704.381-030
Engraver, Ornamental Design (engraving) 704.381-030
ENGRAVER, PANTOGRAPH I (engraving) 704.382-010
ENGRAVER, PANTOGRAPH II (engraving) 704.682-014
ENGRAVER, PICTURE (print. & pub.) 979.281-018
ENGRAVER, RUBBER (pen & pencil) 733.381-010
ENGRAVER, RUBBER (print. & pub.) 979.581-010
ENGRAVER, SEALS (pen & pencil) 704.381-034
engraver, signature (pen & pencil) 733.381-010
Engraver, Steel Plate (print. & pub.) 979.381-010
ENGRAVER TENDER (glass products) 673.685-050
ENGRAVER, TIRE MOLD (machine shop) 605.382-014
engraver, wood (print. & pub.) 979.281-014
engraving operator (print. & pub.) 971.381-022
engraving photographer (electron. comp.; print. & pub.) 971.382-014
ENGRAVING-PRESS OPERATOR (print. & pub.) 651.382-010
Engravings Polisher (glass products) 775.684-058
ENGRAVING SUPERVISOR (engraving) 704.131-010
ENGROSSER (profess. & kin.) 970.661-010
enologist (beverage) 183.161-014
enrober (bakery products) 524.685-026
enrober tender (sugar & conf.) 524.686-010
ENROBING-MACHINE CORDER (sugar & conf.) 524.684-018
ENROBING-MACHINE FEEDER (sugar & conf.) 524.686-010
ENROBING-MACHINE OPERATOR (bakery products) 524.685-026
ENROBING-MACHINE OPERATOR (bakery products; sugar & conf.) 524.382-014
ENTERTAINER (amuse. & rec.; motion picture; radio-tv broad.) term
enthone solder stripper (ordnance) 503.685-046
ENTOMOLOGIST (profess. & kin.) 041.061-046
entrance guard (government ser.) 205.367-038
entry clerk (laundry & rel.) 369.687-026
Entry-Driver Operator (mine & quarry) 930.683-014
Entry Examiner (clerical) 209.687-010
Entry Miner (mine & quarry) 939.281-010
envelope addresser (clerical) 209.587-010
Envelope Cutter (paper products) 699.682-018
envelope folder (paper goods) 794.687-022
ENVELOPE-FOLDING-MACHINE ADJUSTER (paper goods) 641.380-010
envelope-fold operator (paper goods) 649.685-042
ENVELOPE-MACHINE OPERATOR (paper goods) 649.685-042
Envelope-Press Operator I (print. & pub.) 651.362-010
Envelope-Press Operator II (print. & pub.) 651.362-018
Envelope-Sealing-Machine Operator (clerical) 208.685-026
envelope-stamping-machine operator (clerical) 208.685-026

ENVIRONMENTAL ANALYST (government ser.) 199.167-022
ENVIRONMENTAL ANALYST (profess. & kin.) 029.081-010
environmental-control-system installer-servicer (construction) 637.261-014
ENVIRONMENTAL ENGINEER (profess. & kin.) term
ENVIRONMENTAL EPIDEMIOLOGIST (government ser.) 041.167-010
ENVIRONMENTALIST (profess. & kin.) term
environmental planner (profess. & kin.) 001.061-018
Environmental-Research Test Technician (profess. & kin.) 003.261-014
environmental scientist (profess. & kin.) 029.081-010
environmental technician (profess. & kin.) 029.261-014
EPITAXIAL REACTOR OPERATOR (electron. comp.) 590.382-018
EPITAXIAL REACTOR TECHNICIAN (electron. comp.) 590.282-010
equalizer (saw. & plan.) 667.682-074
equalizer operator (saw. & plan.) 667.682-074
Equalizing-Saw Operator (woodworking) 667.682-022
EQUAL OPPORTUNITY OFFICER (any industry) 168.267-114
EQUAL-OPPORTUNITY REPRESENTATIVE (government ser.) 168.167-014
EQUESTRIAN (amuse. & rec.) 159.344-010
EQUIPMENT CLEANER (any industry) 599.684-010
Equipment Cleaner (paint & varnish) 559.685-110
EQUIPMENT CLEANER-AND-TESTER (smelt. & refin.) 630.584-010
equipment inspector (r.r. trans.) 910.387-014
EQUIPMENT INSPECTOR (tel. & tel.) 822.261-014
EQUIPMENT INSTALLER (any industry) 828.381-010
equipment installer (tel. & tel.) 822.361-014
EQUIPMENT INSTALLER (tel. & tel.) 822.381-010
equipment installer (tel. & tel.) 822.381-022
EQUIPMENT MECHANIC (tel. & tel.) term
EQUIPMENT MONITOR, PHOTOTYPESETTING (print. & pub.) 650.682-010
equipment processer, storage (government ser.) 929.367-010
Equipment-Records Supervisor (construction) 222.137-038
equipment scheduler (air trans.) 221.362-010
equipment-service engineer (any industry) 620.281-018
Equipment Specialist (profess. & kin.) 096.121-014
Equipment Sterilizer (dairy products) 599.684-010
equipment washer (any industry) 381.687-022
erector (engine-turbine; machinery mfg.) 638.261-014
erector (machine shop) 706.684-018
erector (ship-boat mfg.) 806.261-014
erector appentice (ship-boat mfg.) 806.261-018
erector operator (construction) 850.682-010
Escalator Constructor (construction) 825.361-010
escapement matcher (clock & watch) 715.381-018
ESCORT (any industry) 353.667-010
ESCORT (personal ser.) 359.367-010
escort, blind (personal ser.) 359.573-010
escort, patients (medical ser.) 355.677-014
ESCORT-VEHICLE DRIVER (motor trans.) 919.663-022
Escrow Clerk (financial) 249.362-014
ESCROW OFFICER (profess. & kin.) 119.367-010
ESTATE PLANNER (insurance) 186.167-010
ESTIMATOR (profess. & kin.) 169.267-038
ESTIMATOR AND DRAFTER (utilities) 019.261-014
estimator, automobile damage (business ser.; insurance) 241.267-014
Estimator, Binding (print. & pub.) 221.367-014
ESTIMATOR, JEWELRY (jewelry-silver.) 221.387-022
estimator, lumber (wood. container) 221.482-014
ESTIMATOR, PAPERBOARD BOXES (paper goods) 221.362-018
Estimator, Printing-Plate-Making (print. & pub.) 221.367-014
ESTIMATOR, PRINTING (print. & pub.) 221.367-014
ETCHED-CIRCUIT PROCESSOR (electron. comp.) 590.684-018
etcher (cutlery-hrdwr.) 500.685-010
ETCHER (electron. comp.) 590.685-078
ETCHER (engraving) 704.684-010
etcher, aircraft (aircraft mfg.) 704.381-014
etcher apprentice (print. & pub.) 971.381-010
ETCHER APPRENTICE, PHOTOENGRAVING (print. & pub.) 971.381-010
ETCHER, ELECTROLYTIC (cutlery-hrdwr.) 500.685-010
etcher, enameling (jewelry-silver.) 735.687-010
ETCHER, HAND (cutlery-hrdwr.) 704.687-014
etcher, hand (engraving) 704.684-014
ETCHER, HAND (print. & pub.) 971.261-010
ETCHER HELPER, HAND (print. & pub.) 971.687-010
ETCHER, MACHINE (cutlery-hrdwr.) 619.685-042
ETCHER, PHOTOENGRAVING (print. & pub.) 971.381-014
Etcher, Printed Circuit Boards (electron. comp.) 590.685-082
ETCHER-STRIPPER, SEMICONDUCTOR WAFERS (electron. comp.) 590.684-026
ETCH OPERATOR, SEMICONDUCTOR WAFERS (electron. comp.) 590.685-074
Ethnographer (profess. & kin.) 055.067-022
ETHNOLOGIST (profess. & kin.) 055.067-022
Ethylbenzene-Compressor Utility Operator (chemical) 559.682-066
Ethylbenzene-Converter Helper (chemical) 558.585-010

Ethylbenzene-Converter Operator (chemical) 558.362-010
Ethylbenzene-Cracking Supervisor (chemical; petrol. refin.) 559.132-078
Ethylbenzene Hydrogenator (chemical) 558.362-010
Ethylbenzene Oxidizer (chemical) 558.362-010
Ethyl Blender (petrol. refin.) 540.462-010
Ethylene-Compressor Operator (chemical) 950.382-014
Ethylene-Oxide Panelboard Operator (chemical) 559.382-018
Ethylene-Plant Helper (chemical) 558.585-010
Ethylene-Plant Operator (chemical) 558.362-010
Etymologist (profess. & kin.) 059.067-010
EVALUATOR (education) 094.267-010
EVALUATOR (nonprofit org.) 249.367-034
Evaluator, Transfer Students (education) 205.367-010
EVAPORATIVE-COOLER INSTALLER (any industry) 637.381-010
EVAPORATOR OPERATOR (can. & preserv.; dairy products; sugar & conf.) 521.382-010
EVAPORATOR OPERATOR (paper & pulp) 532.685-018
EVAPORATOR OPERATOR I (chemical) 553.382-018
EVAPORATOR OPERATOR II (chemical) 553.682-018
Evaporator Operator, Molasses (can. & preserv.) 521.382-010
Evaporator Repairer (chemical) 891.687-030
EXAMINATION PROCTOR (government ser.) 199.267-018
EXAMINER (fabrication, nec) 739.687-082
EXAMINER (glove & mit.) 789.687-042
EXAMINER (government ser.) 169.267-014
examiner (knitting) 684.687-010
EXAMINER (print. & pub.) 979.687-010
examiner (tex. prod., nec) 789.687-050
Examiner-Mender (tex. prod., nec) 787.682-030
EXAMINER, QUESTIONED DOCUMENTS (government ser.) 199.267-022
examiner-rating clerk (insurance) 214.482-018
Examining-Chair Assembler (furniture) 706.381-026
EXCAVATOR (any industry) 850.684-010
excelsior-machine feeder (saw. & plan.) 663.685-014
EXCELSIOR-MACHINE TENDER (saw. & plan.) 663.685-014
Excelsior Picker (furniture) 680.685-078
EXECUTIVE CHEF (hotel & rest.) 187.161-010
executive-chef assistant (hotel & rest.) 313.131-026
executive, community planning (nonprofit org.) 187.167-234
Executive Director, Contract Shop (nonprofit org.) 187.117-026
EXECUTIVE DIRECTOR, NURSES' ASSOCIATION (medical ser.) 075.117-034
EXECUTIVE DIRECTOR, RED CROSS (nonprofit org.) 187.117-066
EXECUTIVE DIRECTOR, SHELTERED WORKSHOP (nonprofit org.) 187.117-026
EXECUTIVE HOUSEKEEPER (any industry) 187.167-046
EXECUTIVE PILOT (any industry) 196.263-030
Executive Producer (radio-tv broad.) 159.117-010
EXECUTIVE PRODUCER, PROMOS (radio-tv broad.) 159.167-022
executive secretary (any industry) 169.167-014
Executive Secretary (profess. & kin.) 189.117-010
executive secretary, nurses' association (medical ser.) 075.117-034
executive secretary, social welfare (profess. & kin.) 195.117-010
EXECUTIVE SECRETARY, STATE BOARD OF NURSING (government ser.) 169.117-010
executive steward/stewardess (hotel & rest.) 310.137-018
EXECUTIVE TRAINEE (any industry) term
EXECUTIVE VICE PRESIDENT, CHAMBER OF COMMERCE (nonprofit org.) 187.117-030
EXERCISE PHYSIOLOGIST (medical ser.) 076.121-018
EXERCISER, HORSE (amuse. & rec.) 153.674-010
EXHAUST EQUIPMENT OPERATOR (electron. comp.) 599.382-014
exhaust operator (electron. comp.) 599.382-014
exhaust tender (any industry) 950.585-010
EXHIBIT ARTIST (museums) 149.261-010
EXHIBIT BUILDER (museums) 739.261-010
Exhibit Carpenter (museums) 739.261-010
Exhibit Cleaner (museums) 899.384-010
EXHIBIT DESIGNER (museums) 142.061-058
EXHIBIT-DISPLAY REPRESENTATIVE (any industry) 297.367-010
Exhibit Electrician (museums) 739.261-010
exhibition carver (hotel & rest.) 316.661-010
exhibition specialist (museums) 739.261-010
exhibit technician (museums) 739.261-010
EXPANDING MACHINE OPERATOR (steel & rel.) 617.685-022
EXPANSION ENVELOPE MAKER, HAND (paper goods) 794.684-018
EXPANSION-JOINT BUILDER (rubber goods) 759.664-014
expansion-joint finisher (rubber goods) 759.664-014
expediter (clerical) 221.367-042
EXPEDITER (clerical) 222.367-018
EXPEDITER CLERK (optical goods) 221.387-026
EXPEDITER, SERVICE ORDER (furniture) 222.367-070
EXPEDITION SUPERVISOR (fishing & hunt.) 461.134-010
EXPELLER OPERATOR (grain-feed mills; oils & grease) 529.685-106
Expenditure-Requisition Clerk (utilities) 216.382-022

Expense Clerk (clerical) 210.382-010
expense clerk (clerical) 216.382-034
experimental aircraft and engine mechanic, field and hangar (aircraft mfg.) 621.261-022
EXPERIMENTAL AIRCRAFT MECHANIC (aircraft mfg.) 621.261-022
EXPERIMENTAL ASSEMBLER (any industry) 739.381-026
EXPERIMENTAL-BOX TESTER (wood. container) 761.281-014
experimental-display builder (fabrication, nec) 739.361-010
Experimental Electronics Developer (aircraft mfg.) 003.161-014
Experimental Fabricator-And-Installer (metal prod., nec) 709.381-046
experimental flight test mechanic (aircraft mfg.) 621.261-022
experimental mechanic (aircraft mfg.) 693.261-014
EXPERIMENTAL MECHANIC (motor-bicycles) 600.260-014
EXPERIMENTAL MECHANIC, ELECTRICAL (motor-bicycles) 806.281-014
EXPERIMENTAL MECHANIC, OUTBOARD MOTORS (engine-turbine) 623.261-010
Experimental Mechanic, Spacecraft (aircraft mfg.) 621.261-022
Experimental Plastics Fabricator (aircraft mfg.) 754.381-018
experimental preflight mechanic (aircraft mfg.) 621.261-022
EXPERIMENTAL-ROCKET-SLED MECHANIC (aircraft mfg.) 825.281-038
experimental technician (profess. & kin.) 007.161-026
explosive-actuated-tool operator (construction)   see STUD-DRIVER OPERATOR
EXPLOSIVE HANDLER (chemical) term
Explosive Operator, Bomb (ordnance) 737.687-046
Explosive Operator, Fuse (ordnance) 737.687-046
Explosive Operator, Grenade (ordnance) 737.687-046
EXPLOSIVE OPERATOR I (ordnance) 737.687-042
EXPLOSIVE OPERATOR II (ordnance) 737.687-046
EXPLOSIVE-OPERATOR SUPERVISOR (ordnance) 694.132-010
explosives operator (chemical) 694.685-038
EXPLOSIVES-TRUCK DRIVER (ordnance) 903.683-010
Export Clerk (clerical) 214.467-010
Exporter (wholesale tr.) 185.157-018
exposure machine operator (electron. comp.) 976.684-030
EXPRESS CLERK (motor trans.; r.r. trans.) 222.367-022
Extended-Insurance Clerk (insurance) 216.382-050
extension agent (government ser.) 096.127-010
EXTENSION CLERK (utilities) 219.362-030
EXTENSION EDGER (paper goods) 641.685-046
extension-service agent (government ser.) 096.127-010
EXTENSION SERVICE SPECIALIST (government ser.) 096.127-014
extension supervisor (government ser.) 096.167-010
extension worker (government ser.) 096.127-010
EXTERMINATOR (business ser.) 389.684-010
EXTERMINATOR HELPER (any industry) 383.684-010
EXTERMINATOR HELPER, TERMITE (business ser.) 383.687-010
EXTERMINATOR, TERMITE (business ser.) 383.364-010
external-cylindrical-grinder operator (machine shop) 603.280-010
External-Grinder Tender (machine shop) 603.685-062
external grinder, tool (machine shop) 603.280-010
EXTRA (amuse. & rec.; motion picture; radio-tv broad.) 159.647-014
extraction supervisor (petrol. refin.) 549.132-030
extract operator (can. & preserv.) 521.685-262
extractor (any industry) 581.685-038
extractor (chemical) 553.665-018
extractor (hat & cap) 581.685-070
extractor (knitting) 589.485-010
EXTRACTOR-AND-WRINGER OPERATOR (chemical) 551.685-066
EXTRACTOR LOADER AND UNLOADER (chemical) 551.686-014
EXTRACTOR-MACHINE OPERATOR (can. & preserv.) 521.665-014
EXTRACTOR OPERATOR (any industry) 581.685-038
EXTRACTOR OPERATOR (beverage) 521.685-118
extractor operator (leather mfg.; tex. prod., nec) 589.685-098
EXTRACTOR OPERATOR (pharmaceut.) 551.685-058
EXTRACTOR OPERATOR (tex. prod., nec) 582.685-062
EXTRACTOR OPERATOR (textile) 581.685-042
EXTRACTOR OPERATOR (chemical) 552.682-018
EXTRACTOR OPERATOR (chemical; oils & grease) 551.685-054
EXTRACTOR-OPERATOR HELPER (chemical) 552.686-010
EXTRACTOR OPERATOR, SOLVENT PROCESS (chemical) 551.685-062
EXTRACTOR-PLANT OPERATOR (chemical; oils & grease) 559.665-018
Extractor Puller (oils & grease) 551.686-014
Extractor Tender, Raw Stock (textile) 581.685-038
extract wringer (leather mfg.; tex. prod., nec) 589.685-098
extra-gang supervisor (construction) 869.134-022
EXTRUDER OPERATOR (forging) 614.482-014
EXTRUDER OPERATOR (grain-feed mills) 520.682-018
extruder operator (rubber goods; rubber tire) 690.662-014
EXTRUDER OPERATOR (wood prod., nec) 569.685-038
Extruder-Operator Helper (forging) 619.686-034
EXTRUDER-OPERATOR HELPER (plastic prod.; plastic-synth.) 557.564-010
Extruder Operator, Horizontal (wood prod., nec) 569.685-038
Extruder Operator, Multiple (wood prod., nec) 569.685-038
EXTRUDER OPERATOR (plastic prod.; plastic-synth.) 557.382-010

Extruder Operator, Vertical (wood prod., nec) 569.685-038
EXTRUDER TENDER (rubber goods) 557.685-014
EXTRUDING-MACHINE OPERATOR (nonfer. metal) 691.382-010
extruding-machine operator (sugar & conf.) 520.682-014
EXTRUDING-MACHINE OPERATOR (tex. prod., nec) 557.565-010
extruding-press operator (nonfer. metal) 691.382-014
EXTRUDING-PRESS OPERATOR (ordnance) 614.685-010
EXTRUSION BENDER (ship-boat mfg.) 804.684-014
EXTRUSION-DIE REPAIRER (nonfer. metal) 705.381-014
EXTRUSION-PRESS ADJUSTER (elec. equip.) 614.380-010
extrusion-press operator (forging) 614.482-014
EXTRUSION-PRESS OPERATOR I (elec. equip.) 614.482-018
EXTRUSION-PRESS OPERATOR II (elec. equip.) 614.685-014
extrusion press supervisor (forging) 614.132-014
EYE-DROPPER ASSEMBLER (glass products) 739.687-086
EYEGLASS-FRAME TRUER (optical goods) 713.684-026
EYEGLASS-LENS CUTTER (optical goods) 716.682-014
Eyeglass-Lens Generator (optical goods) 716.682-014
Eyeglass-Lens Grinder (optical goods) 716.382-018
eyelet cutter (hat & cap) 686.685-038
EYELET-MACHINE OPERATOR (any industry) 699.685-018
eyelet maker (any industry) 699.685-018
EYELET-PUNCH OPERATOR (furniture) 699.685-022
eyelet riveter (any industry) 699.685-018
Eyelet-Row Marker (boot & shoe) 788.584-014
eyeletter (any industry) 699.685-018
eye specialist (medical ser.) 070.101-058

F

FABRIC-AND-ACCESSORIES ESTIMATOR (garment) 221.482-010
fabric assembler (furniture) 709.667-010
fabricating-machine operator (any industry) 616.380-018
Fabrication And Structures Development Mechanic (aircraft mfg.) 693.261-014
Fabrication Supervisor (construction) 899.131-010
Fabrication Supervisor (toy-sport equip.) 732.130-010
fabricator (plastic prod.) 754.684-010
FABRICATOR, ARTIFICIAL BREAST (protective dev.) 712.684-042
FABRICATOR-ASSEMBLER, METAL PRODUCTS (any industry) 809.381-010
FABRICATOR, FOAM RUBBER (any industry) 780.684-062
FABRICATOR, INDUSTRIAL FURNACE (machinery mfg.) 826.381-010
FABRICATOR, SHOWER DOORS AND PANELS (struct. metal) 739.381-030
Fabricator, Special Items (any industry) 804.281-010
FABRIC-COATING SUPERVISOR (tex. prod., nec) 589.130-014
fabric inspector (textile) 781.687-014
FABRIC-LAY-OUT WORKER (textile) 589.687-022
FABRIC-MACHINE OPERATOR I (furniture) 616.362-010
FABRIC-MACHINE OPERATOR II (furniture) 616.685-022
FABRIC NORMALIZER (rubber goods) 559.685-066
fabric-separator operator (rubber reclaim.) 551.365-010
FABRIC STRETCHER (furniture) 709.667-010
Face-And-Fill Packer (agriculture) 920.687-134
face cleaner (glass products) 779.687-022
face layer (millwork-plywood) 762.687-066
FACER (clock & watch) 770.582-010
facer (jewelry-silver.) 705.682-014
facer (toy-sport equip.) 761.684-010
Facer, Buffing Wheel (tex. prod., nec) 585.685-086
facer operator (woodworking) 665.682-022
Facial Operator (personal ser.) 332.271-010
FACILITIES-FLIGHT-CHECK PILOT (government ser.) 196.263-034
FACILITIES PLANNER (any industry) 019.261-018
FACILITY EXAMINER (tel. & tel.) 959.367-014
FACING BASTER, JUMPBASTING (garment) 786.682-102
Facing-Cutting-Machine Operator (garment) 686.685-066
Facing-End Trimmer (knitting) 781.687-070
facing grinder (nonmet. min.) 673.685-010
FACING-MACHINE OPERATOR (clock & watch) 604.685-014
Facing-Slitter (garment; knitting) 699.682-030
facsimile operator (print. & pub.; tel. & tel.) 193.362-010
FACTOR (financial) 186.167-082
factory engineer (profess. & kin.) 007.167-014
FACTORY HELPER (sugar & conf.) 529.686-034
FACTORY LAY-OUT ENGINEER (profess. & kin.) 012.167-018
faculty dean (education) 090.117-010
FACULTY MEMBER, COLLEGE OR UNIVERSITY (education) 090.227-010
Faculty Member, Technical Institute (education) 090.227-010
Fagoting-Machine Operator (garment) 786.682-278
FALLER I (logging) 454.384-010
FALLER II (logging) 454.684-014
Falsework Builder (construction) 860.381-042
family counselor (social ser.) 195.107-018
Family-Dinner Service Specialist (domestic ser.) 305.281-010

family physician (medical ser.) 070.101-026
FAMILY PRACTITIONER (medical ser.) 070.101-026
Fan Balancer (elec. equip.) 724.384-014
FAN-BLADE ALIGNER (elec. equip.) 706.687-018
fan-blade truer (elec. equip.) 706.687-018
Fancy Packer (retail trade; wholesale tr.) 920.587-018
Fancy Sewer (leather prod.) 783.682-014
Fancy Stitcher (boot & shoe) 690.682-082
Fancy-Stitch Marker (boot & shoe) 788.584-014
FANCY-WIRE DRAWER (jewelry-silver.) 700.381-014
Fan-Mail Clerk (amuse. & rec.) 209.362-034
farebox repairer (r.r. trans.) 710.681-018
FARE-REGISTER REPAIRER (motor trans.) 729.384-014
farm adviser (government ser.) 096.127-010
farm agent (government ser.) 096.127-010
farm butcher (agriculture) 525.664-010
farm-crew leader (agriculture) 180.167-050
FARM-EQUIPMENT-MECHANIC APPRENTICE (agric. equip.) 624.281-014
FARM-EQUIPMENT MECHANIC I (agric. equip.) 624.281-010
FARM-EQUIPMENT MECHANIC II (agric. equip.) 624.381-014
FARMER (agriculture) term
FARMER, CASH GRAIN (agriculture) 401.161-010
FARMER, CONTRACT (agriculture) term
FARMER, DIVERSIFIED CROPS (agriculture) 407.161-010
FARMER, DRY LAND (agriculture) term
FARMER, FIELD CROP (agriculture) 404.161-010
FARMER, FRUIT CROPS, BUSH AND VINE (agriculture) 403.161-014
FARMER, GENERAL (agriculture) 421.161-010
FARMER, TENANT (agriculture) term
FARMER, TREE-FRUIT-AND-NUT CROPS (agriculture) 403.161-010
FARMER, VEGETABLE (agriculture) 402.161-010
farm-labor contractor (agriculture) 409.117-010
farm laborer (agriculture) 421.687-010
FARM-MACHINE OPERATOR (agriculture) 409.683-010
Farm-Machinery-And-Equipment-Rental Clerk (business ser.) 295.467-022
FARM-MACHINERY SET-UP MECHANIC (agric. equip.) 624.381-018
FARM-MACHINE TENDER (agriculture) 409.685-010
Farm-Management Agent (government ser.) 096.127-010
farm mechanic (agric. equip.) 624.381-014
farm mechanic (agric. equip.) 624.281-010
farm-mechanic apprentice (agric. equip.) 624.281-014
farm-seed specialist (profess. & kin.) 040.361-014
FARMWORKER (agriculture) term
farmworker, animal (any industry) 410.674-010
Farmworker, Berry (agriculture) 403.687-010
Farmworker, Brooder Farm (agriculture) 411.584-010
FARMWORKER, BULBS (agriculture) 405.683-010
Farmworker, Chicken Farm (agriculture) 411.584-010
Farmworker, Cranberry (agriculture) 403.687-010
FARMWORKER, DAIRY (agriculture) 410.684-010
FARMWORKER, DIVERSIFIED CROPS I (agriculture) 407.663-010
FARMWORKER, DIVERSIFIED CROPS II (agriculture) 407.687-010
Farmworker, Egg-Producing Farm (agriculture) 411.584-010
FARMWORKER, FIELD CROP I (agriculture) 404.663-010
FARMWORKER, FIELD CROP II (agriculture) 404.687-010
FARMWORKER, FRUIT I (agriculture) 403.683-010
FARMWORKER, FRUIT II (agriculture) 403.687-010
Farmworker, Fryer Farm (agriculture) 411.584-010
Farmworker, Fur (agriculture) 410.674-010
FARMWORKER, GENERAL I (agriculture) 421.683-010
FARMWORKER, GENERAL II (agriculture) 421.687-010
FARMWORKER, GRAIN I (agriculture) 401.683-010
FARMWORKER, GRAIN II (agriculture) 401.687-010
FARMWORKER, LIVESTOCK (agriculture) 410.664-010
FARMWORKER, MACHINE (agriculture) 409.686-010
FARMWORKER, POULTRY (agriculture) 411.584-010
Farmworker, Pullet Farm (agriculture) 411.584-010
FARMWORKER, RICE (agriculture) 401.683-014
FARMWORKER, SEASONAL (agriculture) term
Farmworker, Turkey Farm (agriculture) 411.584-010
FARMWORKER, VEGETABLE I (agriculture) 402.663-010
FARMWORKER, VEGETABLE II (agriculture) 402.687-010
FASHION ARTIST (retail trade) 141.061-014
Fashion Consultant (profess. & kin.) 096.121-014
FASHION COORDINATOR (retail trade) 185.157-010
FASHION DESIGNER (profess. & kin.) 142.061-018
fashion model (garment; retail trade; wholesale tr.) 297.667-014
fashion stylist (retail trade) 185.157-010
fast-brim pouncer (hat & cap) 585.685-010
fastener (boot & shoe) 690.685-162
Fastener Attacher (any industry) 699.685-018
FASTENER, MACHINE (boot & shoe) 690.685-162
FASTENER-SEWING-MACHINE OPERATOR (any industry) 787.685-010
fastener-sewing-machine operator (garment) 786.685-010
FASTENER TECHNOLOGIST (nut & bolt) 612.260-010

FAST-FOODS WORKER (hotel & rest.) 311.472-010
Fatback Trimmer (meat products) 525.684-054
FAT-PURIFICATION WORKER (oils & grease) 551.685-070
Fats And Oils Loader (soap & rel.) 914.667-010
Feather Baler (tex. prod., nec) 920.685-010
Feather Boner (button & notion) 734.684-010
feather-crushing-machine operator (tex. prod., nec) 589.686-018
FEATHER-CURLING-MACHINE OPERATOR (tex. prod., nec) 589.686-018
FEATHER-CUTTING-MACHINE FEEDER (tex. prod., nec) 585.686-010
FEATHER-DRYING-MACHINE OPERATOR (tex. prod., nec) 581.686-034
FEATHER-DUSTER WINDER (tex. prod., nec) 734.684-014
featheredge-machine operator (boot & shoe) 690.685-166
FEATHEREDGER AND REDUCER, MACHINE (boot & shoe) 690.685-166
featherer (cutlery-hrdwr.) 701.687-030
Feather Grader (tex. prod., nec) 929.687-062
FEATHER MIXER (tex. prod., nec) 589.685-050
FEATHER RENOVATOR (laundry & rel.) 362.685-010
feather renovator (tex. prod., nec) 589.685-082
FEATHER SAWYER (toy-sport equip.) 732.685-014
FEATHER SEPARATOR (tex. prod., nec) 589.685-054
FEATHER SHAPER (button & notion) 734.684-010
FEATHER STITCHER (toy-sport equip.) 732.684-050
Feather Trimmer (button & notion) 734.684-010
FEATHER WASHER (tex. prod., nec) 582.685-066
FEATURED PLAYER (amuse. & rec.) term
FEDERAL AID COORDINATOR (government ser.) 188.167-054
Federal-Housing-Administration-Loan Auditor (insurance) 210.382-010
FEED AND FARM MANAGEMENT ADVISER (agriculture; retail trade) 096.127-018
feed-and-pellet operator (grain-feed mills) 520.685-178
FEED BLENDER (grain-feed mills) 520.685-094
feed-cup-sewing-machine operator (garment) 786.682-122
Feed-Drier Tender (grain-feed mills) 523.685-058
feed elevator worker (grain-feed mills) 920.685-058
feeder (garment; glove & mit.) 781.687-010
feeder (hat & cap) 586.686-018
feeder (nonmet. min.) 570.685-050
feeder (optical goods) 575.686-014
FEEDER (print. & pub.) 651.686-014
FEEDER-CATCHER, TOBACCO (tobacco) 529.686-038
feeder loader (grain-feed mills) 520.686-018
feeder operator (concrete prod.) 575.664-010
feeder operator (grain-feed mills) 520.685-098
Feeder Operator, Automatic (grain-feed mills) 520.685-098
FEEDER-SWITCHBOARD OPERATOR (utilities) 952.362-014
feeder tender (tex. prod., nec; textile) 680.686-018
feeder worker power-unit operator (construction; retail trade; wholesale tr.) 863.685-010
FEED GRINDER (grain-feed mills) 521.685-122
Feed Inspection Supervisor (government ser.) 168.167-090
Feed-in Tender, Dehairing Machine (meat products) 525.685-018
FEED-IN WORKER (grain-feed mills) 929.686-022
feed miller (grain-feed mills) 521.682-026
FEED MIXER (grain-feed mills) 520.685-098
FEED-MIXER HELPER (grain-feed mills) 520.686-018
Feed-Preparation Operator (mine & quarry) 511.685-050
FEED-RESEARCH AIDE (agriculture) 049.364-010
FEED WEIGHER (grain-feed mills) 920.685-058
FELLED-SEAM OPERATOR, CHAINSTITCH (garment) 786.682-106
feller (garment) 786.682-126
Feller-Buncher Operator (logging) 454.683-010
Feller, Hand (garment) 782.684-058
feller operator (logging) 454.683-010
felling-machine operator (garment) 786.682-106
FELT CARBONIZER (tex. prod., nec) 586.687-010
felt cementer (toy-sport equip.) 795.687-030
felt-coating-and-mixing supervisor (tex. prod., nec) 589.130-014
felt coverer (toy-sport equip.) 795.687-026
FELT CUTTER (ordnance) 686.685-026
FELT-CUTTING-MACHINE OPERATOR (tex. prod., nec) 686.682-018
Felt-Dyeing-Machine Tender (tex. prod., nec) 582.685-070
felter (furniture; tex. prod., nec) 680.685-054
felter, tennis balls (toy-sport equip.) 795.687-026
felt finisher (tex. prod., nec) 586.685-038
Felt-Finishing Supervisor (tex. prod., nec) 589.130-014
FELT-GOODS SUPERVISOR, NEEDLE PROCESS (tex. prod., nec) 689.130-014
FELT HANGER (build. mat., nec) 549.686-014
Felt-Hat-Flanging Operator (hat & cap) 784.684-026
Felt-Hat Inspector And Packer (hat & cap) 784.687-042
Felt-Hat-Mellowing-Machine Operator (hat & cap) 585.685-066
felt-hat-pouncing operator, hand (hat & cap) 784.687-018
FELT-HAT STEAMER (hat & cap) 582.687-018
felting-machine operator (furniture; tex. prod., nec) 680.685-054
FELTING-MACHINE OPERATOR (tex. prod., nec) 586.662-010

FELTING-MACHINE-OPERATOR HELPER (tex. prod., nec) 586.686-014
FELTMAKER AND WEIGHER (tex. prod., nec) 586.685-022
Felt-Pad Cutter (button & notion) 781.687-030
Felt-Pad Cutter (tex. prod., nec) 585.687-014
felt puller (hat & cap) 580.684-010
FELT-STRIP FINISHER (tex. prod., nec) 586.685-018
FELT-TIPPING-MACHINE TENDER (pen & pencil) 686.686-010
FELT-WASHING-MACHINE TENDER (tex. prod., nec) 582.685-070
Female Impersonator (amuse. & rec.) 159.047-018
FENCE ERECTOR (construction) 869.684-022
FENCE-ERECTOR SUPERVISOR (construction) 869.134-010
Fence-Gate Assembler (construction) 869.684-022
FENCE-MAKING MACHINE OPERATOR (metal prod., nec) 616.582-010
Fence-Post Cutter (agriculture) 454.684-026
Fence Setter (construction) 869.684-022
Fence Stretcher (construction) 869.684-022
FERMENTATION OPERATOR (beverage) 522.382-014
FERMENTATION OPERATOR (chemical) 558.682-018
Fermenter, Champagne (beverage) 522.685-062
fermenter helper (food prep., nec) 522.686-014
FERMENTER OPERATOR (pharmaceut.) 559.685-070
FERMENTER, WINE (beverage) 522.685-062
Ferris-Wheel Operator (amuse. & rec.) 342.663-010
ferruler (fabrication, nec) 739.687-014
FERRYBOAT CAPTAIN (water trans.) 197.163-010
Ferryboat Deckhand (water trans.) 911.687-022
ferryboat helper (water trans.) 911.667-010
FERRYBOAT OPERATOR (water trans.) 911.363-010
FERRYBOAT OPERATOR, CABLE (water trans.) 911.664-010
FERRYBOAT-OPERATOR HELPER (water trans.) 911.667-010
ferry operator (water trans.) 911.664-010
ferry operator (water trans.) 911.363-010
ferry-terminal agent (water trans.) 911.137-026
FERTILIZER MIXER (chemical) 550.665-018
FETTLER (brick & tile) 779.684-018
fettler (pottery & porc.) 774.684-018
fettler (nonfer. metal; smelt. & refin.; steel & rel.) 512.684-014
fiber-drier operator (textile) 581.685-046
FIBERGLASS-BONDING-MACHINE TENDER (glass mfg.) 574.665-010
FIBERGLASS-CONTAINER-WINDING OPERATOR (glass products) 579.584-010
FIBERGLASS-DOWEL-DRAWING-MACHINE OPERATOR (plastic prod.) 575.682-010
FIBERGLASS LAMINATOR (ship-boat mfg.; vehicles, nec) 806.684-054
FIBERGLASS-MACHINE OPERATOR (glass products) 574.682-010
Fiber-Heel-Piece Shaper (boot & shoe) 690.685-162
FIBER-MACHINE TENDER (glass mfg.) 575.685-030
Fiber Picker (furniture) 680.685-078
FIBER TECHNOLOGIST (profess. & kin.) 040.061-026
Fidelity-And-Surety-Bonds-Claim Adjuster (business ser.; insurance) 241.217-010
FIELD ARTILLERY CREWMEMBER (military ser.) 378.684-018
FIELD ARTILLERY OPERATIONS SPECIALIST (military ser.) 378.367-014
FIELD ARTILLERY SENIOR SERGEANT (military ser.) 378.132-010
FIELD-ASSEMBLY SUPERVISOR (mfd. bldgs.) 869.131-018
field attendant (amuse. & rec.) 349.673-010
Field Auditor (government ser.) 160.167-038
field captain (amuse. & rec.) 153.267-018
FIELD CASHIER (construction) 219.137-010
Field Clerk (clerical) 219.362-010
field clerk (utilities) 229.367-010
Field-Coil Enameler (any industry) 599.685-030
Field-Coil Repairer (elec. equip.) 721.281-018
Field-Coil Winder (any industry) 724.381-014
Field-Coil Winder (elec. equip.) 724.684-026
FIELD-CONTACT TECHNICIAN (dairy products) 162.117-026
FIELD CONTRACTOR (any industry) 162.117-022
field control inspector (government ser.) 375.267-026
field director (social ser.) 195.167-022
field engineer (machinery mfg.; machine tools) 638.261-018
FIELD ENGINEER (radio-tv broad.) 193.262-018
FIELD ENGINEER, SPECIALIST (petrol. & gas) 010.261-010
field-equipment-maintenance mechanic, farm (agric. equip.) 624.381-014
field gauger (petrol. & gas; petrol. refin.; pipe lines) 914.384-010
FIELD HAULER (agriculture) 409.683-014
field inspector (government ser.) 373.267-010
field inspector (utilities) 869.387-010
field inspector (utilities) 959.361-010
FIELD INSPECTOR, DISEASE AND INSECT CONTROL (agriculture) 408.687-010
Field-Kiln Burner (brick & tile) 573.682-010
FIELD-MAP EDITOR (profess. & kin.) 018.262-010
Field Mechanic (petrol. & gas) 629.381-014
FIELD-MECHANICAL-METER TESTER (petrol. refin.; pipe lines; utilities) 953.281-010

field operating superintendent (petrol. refin.; retail trade) 181.117-010
Field Operator (petrol. & gas) 710.381-022
field operator (petrol. & gas) 914.382-022
field-party manager (petrol. & gas) 181.167-010
FIELD RECORDER (utilities) 229.367-010
FIELD REPRESENTATIVE (business ser.; wholesale tr.) 163.267-010
FIELD REPRESENTATIVE (profess. & kin.) 189.267-010
field representative (retail trade; wholesale tr.) 168.267-026
field return repairer (inst. & app.) 710.381-050
FIELD-RING ASSEMBLER (elec. equip.) 721.484-014
field seismologist (petrol. & gas) 010.161-018
FIELD-SERVICE ENGINEER (aircraft mfg.) 002.167-014
FIELD-SERVICE ENGINEER (photo. appar.) 826.261-010
FIELD SERVICE ENGINEER (profess. & kin.) 828.261-014
FIELD-SERVICE REPRESENTATIVE (aircraft mfg.) 621.221-010
field service representative (profess. & kin.) 828.261-014
field servicer (machinery mfg.; machine tools) 638.261-018
FIELD SERVICE TECHNICIAN (machinery mfg.) 638.261-026
FIELD SERVICE TECHNICIAN, POULTRY (agriculture) 411.267-010
field supervisor (agriculture) 402.131-010
field supervisor (any industry) 899.133-010
field supervisor (clerical) 205.137-014
FIELD SUPERVISOR, BROADCAST (radio-tv broad.) 193.167-014
FIELD SUPERVISOR, OIL-WELL SERVICES (petrol. & gas) 930.131-010
FIELD SUPERVISOR, SEED PRODUCTION (agriculture) 180.167-014
field technical assistant (profess. & kin.) 828.261-014
field technician (any industry) 162.117-010
field technician (radio-tv broad.) 193.262-018
Fig-Bar-Machine Operator (bakery products) 520.682-034
FIG CAPRIFIER (agriculture) 403.687-014
Fig Sorter (agriculture; can. & preserv.; wholesale tr.) 529.687-186
FIGURE REFINISHER AND REPAIRER (retail trade) 739.381-034
Fig Washer (food prep., nec) 521.685-110
Filament-Coil Winder (electron. comp.) 724.684-026
Filament-Wound Parts Fabricator (aircraft mfg.) 754.381-018
Filbert Grower (agriculture) 403.161-010
File Clerk, Correspondence (clerical) 206.387-034
FILE CLERK I (clerical) 206.387-034
FILE CLERK II (clerical) 206.367-014
FILE CUTTER (cutlery-hrdwr.) 605.685-014
file-drawer finisher (furniture) 706.684-050
filer (any industry) 701.381-014
FILER (jewelry-silver.) 700.684-034
FILER AND SANDER (woodworking) 705.684-018
FILER, FINISH (ordnance) 705.481-010
FILER, HAND, TOOL (machine shop) 705.484-010
filer, metal patterns (foundry) 693.281-018
Filer Repairer (ordnance) 705.481-010
FILING-AND-POLISHING SUPERVISOR (ordnance) 603.137-010
Filing Writer (insurance) 203.582-066
Filler (any industry) 920.587-018
filler (beverage) 920.665-014
filler (boot & shoe) 788.684-022
filler (chemical) 559.565-010
Filler (elec. equip.; electron. comp.) 726.687-022
FILLER (fabrication, nec) 739.687-090
filler (paper & pulp) 533.685-010
FILLER (tex. prod., nec) 780.684-066
filler (tex. prod., nec) 789.687-130
filler and sander (wood prod., nec) 769.687-022
Filler And Trimmer (leather prod.) 783.687-010
filler blender (tobacco) 520.687-030
FILLER-BLOCK INSERTER-REMOVER (furniture) 652.687-018
FILLER FEEDER (tobacco) 529.686-042
filler-in tinter (any industry) 970.381-022
filler-leaf cutter, long (tobacco) 521.687-014
filler mixer (bakery products) 520.685-114
FILLER MIXER (tobacco) 520.687-030
filler opener (tobacco) 521.687-110
Filler Picker (tobacco) 521.687-098
FILLER ROOM ATTENDANT (tobacco) 522.687-022
filler shaker (tobacco) 521.687-110
FILLER-SHREDDER HELPER (tobacco) 529.687-078
FILLER SHREDDER, MACHINE (tobacco) 529.685-110
filler-shredding-machine loader (tobacco) 529.687-078
filler-sifter helper (tobacco) 529.687-078
filler sifter, machine (tobacco) 529.685-110
FILLER SPREADER (tobacco) 521.687-046
filler stemmer, hand (tobacco) 521.687-134
Filler Wiper (furniture) 742.687-010
FILLING-AND-STAPLING-MACHINE OPERATOR (fabrication, nec) 692.682-038
Filling Hauler, Weaving (textile) 929.687-030
filling inspector (glass mfg.; plastic-synth.; textile) 681.687-030
filling inspector (tex. prod., nec; textile) 681.687-026

Filling-Machine Feeder (can. & preserv.) 521.686-034
Filling-Machine Operator (any industry) 920.685-078
filling-machine operator (bakery products) 524.682-010
FILLING-MACHINE OPERATOR (nonfer. metal) 699.685-038
FILLING-MACHINE OPERATOR (pen & pencil) 733.685-014
FILLING-MACHINE SET-UP MECHANIC (food prep., nec) 920.680-010
FILLING MACHINE TENDER (bakery products) 524.685-030
filling separator (textile) 689.687-086
filling sorter and hauler (textile) 689.687-086
filling-station attendant (automotive ser.) 915.467-010
filling winder (textile) 681.685-074
Film Booker (amuse. & rec.) 191.117-014
film booker (business ser.; retail trade) 295.367-018
FILM-CASTING OPERATOR (plastic-synth.) 559.682-022
film cutter (any industry) 979.681-022
film cutter (photofinishing) 976.685-010
FILM DEVELOPER (motion picture; photofinishing) 976.382-018
FILM FLAT INSPECTOR (print. & pub.) 972.284-010
film inspector (electron. comp.) 726.384-014
Film Inspector (motion picture) 976.684-014
FILM INSPECTOR (photofinishing) 976.362-010
FILM LABORATORY TECHNICIAN (motion picture; photofinishing) 976.684-014
FILM LABORATORY TECHNICIAN I (motion picture) 976.381-010
FILM LABORATORY TECHNICIAN II (motion picture) 976.685-018
film librarian (library) 100.167-010
Film Librarian (motion picture) 222.367-026
FILM LOADER (motion picture) 962.687-014
film machine operator (photofinishing) 976.685-014
film masker (print. & pub.) 971.684-010
Film Numberer (motion picture) 976.685-018
film numberer (photofinishing) 976.687-018
FILM-OR-TAPE LIBRARIAN (clerical) 222.367-026
FILM OR VIDEOTAPE EDITOR (motion picture; radio-tv broad.) 962.262-010
film painter (print. & pub.) 971.684-010
FILM PRINTER (motion picture) 976.682-010
Film Recordist (motion picture) 962.382-010
FILM-RENTAL CLERK (business ser.; retail trade) 295.367-018
FILM-REPLACEMENT ORDERER (motion picture) 976.567-010
film sorter (photofinishing) 976.687-018
Film Splicer (motion picture) 976.684-014
FILM SPOOLER (photo. appar.) 692.685-082
film technician (motion picture; photofinishing; radio-tv broad.) 976.131-014
FILM TOUCH-UP INSPECTOR (electron. comp.) 726.684-050
FILM-VAULT SUPERVISOR (motion picture) 222.137-010
Filter-Bed Placer (construction) 869.687-026
FILTER CHANGER (beverage) 521.687-050
filter changer (plastic-synth.) 559.687-038
Filter-Cigarette-Making-Machine Operator (tobacco) 529.685-066
FILTER CLEANER (plastic-synth.) 559.687-038
Filter-Cloth Maker (tex. prod., nec) 787.682-058
filterer (plastic-synth.) 559.687-038
FILTER HELPER (chemical) 551.685-074
FILTERING-MACHINE TENDER (grain-feed mills) 521.685-138
Filter Inspector (electron. comp.) 726.684-022
filter-machine operator (beverage) 521.582-010
FILTER OPERATOR (any industry) 551.685-078
filter operator (beverage) 522.382-018
FILTER OPERATOR (beverage; sugar & conf.) 521.685-126
filter operator (chemical) 550.685-018
FILTER OPERATOR (grain-feed mills) 521.682-018
filter operator (plastic-synth.) 551.582-010
filter operator (waterworks) 954.382-014
FILTER-PLANT SUPERVISOR (smelt. & refin.) 511.135-010
FILTER-PRESS OPERATOR (any industry) 551.685-082
filter-press operator (beverage) 521.565-014
filter-press pumper (oils & grease) 559.685-146
Filter-Press Supervisor (chemical) 559.132-122
FILTER-PRESS TENDER (beverage) 521.685-130
FILTER-PRESS TENDER (beverage; chemical) 599.685-042
FILTER-PRESS TENDER, HEAD (grain-feed mills) 521.665-018
filter-pulp washer (beverage; chemical) 599.685-038
FILTER-SCREEN CLEANER (beverage) 521.687-054
FILTER-TANK OPERATOR (chemical) 551.585-010
FILTER-TANK-TENDER HELPER, HEAD (grain-feed mills) 521.685-134
FILTER TENDER (grain-feed mills) 522.665-010
FILTER TENDER, JELLY (can. & preserv.) 529.685-114
FILTER WASHER (chemical) 559.687-042
FILTER WASHER AND PRESSER (beverage; chemical) 599.685-038
FILTRATION OPERATOR, POLYETHYLENE CATALYST (chemical) 551.562-010
filtration-plant mechanic (waterworks) 630.281-038
Filtrose Crusher (chemical) 555.685-034
final-application reviewer (insurance) 209.687-018

FINAL ASSEMBLER (garment) 789.687-046
FINAL ASSEMBLER (office machines) 706.381-018
FINAL ASSEMBLER (optical goods) 713.687-018
final assembler (ordnance) 736.381-010
final assembler, boat (ship-boat mfg.) 806.684-146
Final Assembler, Brass-Wind Instruments (musical inst.) 730.684-010
Final-Block-Press Operator (chemical) 556.685-014
final cigar and box examiner (tobacco) 529.687-042
Final Cleaner (electron. comp.) 599.685-134
Final-Coat Sprayer (leather mfg.) 584.687-014
FINAL-DRESSING CUTTER (meat products) 525.684-026
final finisher (mfd. bldgs.; vehicles, nec) 869.684-026
FINAL FINISHER, FORGING DIES (machine shop) 705.484-014
Final-Finish Supervisor (mfd. bldgs.; vehicles, nec) 869.131-030
Final-Inspection Supervisor (rubber reclaim.) 559.132-058
FINAL INSPECTOR (auto. mfg.) 806.687-018
FINAL INSPECTOR (boot & shoe) 753.687-018
FINAL INSPECTOR (clock & watch) 715.381-050
Final Inspector (cutlery-hrdwr.) 701.687-026
final inspector (elec. equip.) 729.387-018
FINAL INSPECTOR (elec. equip.) 727.687-054
final inspector (foundry) 514.687-010
final inspector (furniture) 763.687-026
FINAL INSPECTOR (glass products) 779.387-010
FINAL INSPECTOR (musical inst.) 730.367-010
Final Inspector (office machines) 706.387-014
Final Inspector (optical goods) 716.381-010
Final Inspector (ordnance) 736.387-010
final inspector (rubber tire) 750.684-030
final inspector (textile) 689.685-038
final inspector (wood. container) 764.687-022
final inspector and tester (rubber goods) 729.387-014
Final Inspector, Balance Wheel (clock & watch) 715.684-094
FINAL INSPECTOR, MOTORCYLES (motor-bicycles) 806.281-018
FINAL INSPECTOR, MOVEMENT ASSEMBLY (clock & watch) 715.684-094
FINAL INSPECTOR, PAPER (paper & pulp) 539.367-010
FINAL INSPECTOR, SHUTTLE (woodworking) 769.684-022
FINAL INSPECTOR, TRUCK TRAILER (auto. mfg.) 806.361-018
Final-Rail Cutter (meat products) 525.684-026
FINAL TESTER (elec. equip.) 721.261-014
final tester (wood. container) 764.687-022
final-touch-up painter (any industry) 749.684-038
FINANCIAL-AID COUNSELOR (education) 169.267-018
FINANCIAL-AIDS OFFICER (education) 090.117-030
Financial Economist (profess. & kin.) 050.067-010
FINANCIAL PLANNER (profess. & kin.) 250.257-014
finding fastener (jewelry-silver.) 735.687-022
FINE ARTS PACKER (museums) 102.367-010
fine-chemicals operator (chemical; plastic-synth.) 559.382-046
Fine-Grade-Bulldozer Operator (any industry) 850.683-010
Fine Grader (construction) 869.664-014
Fine Grinder (rubber reclaim.) 555.685-030
Fine Patcher (fabrication, nec) 739.687-146
FINER (clock & watch) 715.684-098
Fine Sander (fabrication, nec) 761.684-030
Fine-Wire Drawer (nonfer. metal) 614.382-010
Finger-Buff Sewer (tex. prod., nec) 787.682-058
FINGER COBBLER (boot & shoe) 788.684-046
Fingerer (glove & mit.) 784.682-010
FINGER-GRIP-MACHINE OPERATOR (glass products) 673.685-054
FINGERNAIL FORMER (personal ser.) 331.674-014
FINGERPRINT CLASSIFIER (government ser.) 375.387-010
FINGERPRINT CLERK I (government ser.) 209.367-026
FINGERPRINT CLERK II (government ser.) 206.387-014
fingerprint expert (government ser.) 375.387-010
Finger Waver (personal ser.) 332.271-010
Finish Carpenter (construction) 860.381-022
finish cleaner (furniture) 763.684-034
Finish-Coat-Mill Operator (tex. prod., nec) 584.382-010
finished-cigar maker (tobacco) 790.684-014
finished-cloth checker (textile) 781.687-014
Finished-Cloth Examiner (textile) 689.685-038
Finished-Garment Inspector (garment; knitting) 789.687-070
finished-goods inspector (agric. equip.) 801.381-018
Finished-Goods Stock Clerk (clerical) 222.387-058
Finished-Hardware Erector (construction) 860.381-022
finished-leather presser (leather mfg.; leather prod.) 690.682-030
FINISHED-STOCK INSPECTOR (furniture) 763.687-026
finished-wire inspector (metal prod., nec; nonfer. metal) 691.367-010
finished-yarn examiner (glass mfg.; plastic-synth.; textile) 681.687-030
finished-yarn examiner (textile) 689.687-082
finisher (any industry) 781.687-070
finisher (any industry) 705.687-014
finisher (bakery products) 524.684-022

finisher (boot & shoe) 690.685-058
finisher (brick & tile) 779.684-042
finisher (electron. comp.) 699.682-034
FINISHER (fabrication, nec) 731.687-014
finisher (furniture; wood prod., nec) 742.684-010
finisher (furniture) 616.685-018
finisher (glass mfg.) 573.685-018
Finisher (jewelry-silver.) 705.684-022
finisher (knitting) 580.485-010
FINISHER (nonmet. min.) 775.687-010
FINISHER (plastic-synth.) 554.586-010
FINISHER (pottery & porc.) 774.684-018
finisher (pottery & porc.) 774.687-022
finisher (protective dev.) 712.381-050
finisher (recording) 500.684-014
FINISHER (steel & rel.) 613.382-014
finisher (stonework) 673.382-018
finisher (sugar & conf.) 524.382-010
FINISHER (tex. prod., nec) 789.687-050
FINISHER (toy-sport equip.) 732.584-014
FINISHER (wood. container) 749.684-026
Finisher, Accordion (musical inst.) 730.281-010
FINISHER, BRUSH (fabrication, nec) 739.684-062
FINISHER-CARD TENDER (nonmet. min.; textile) 680.685-042
Finisher, Cold Rolling (steel & rel.) 613.382-014
FINISHER, DENTURE (protective dev.) 712.381-050
FINISHER, FIBERGLASS BOAT PARTS (ship-boat mfg.) 809.684-022
Finisher, Fine-Diamond Dies (machine tools) 770.381-018
finisher, hand (any industry) 363.684-018
finisher, hand (furniture) 780.684-070
Finisher, Hand (garment) 782.684-058
Finisher, Hand (laundry & rel.) 363.681-010
FINISHER, HAND (plastic prod.) 754.684-030
FINISHER, HAND (tex. prod., nec) 789.484-014
FINISHER, HAND (toy-sport equip.) 731.587-010
Finisher, Hot Strip (steel & rel.) 613.382-014
finisher, machine (any industry) 363.682-018
finisher, machine (bakery products) 524.685-034
FINISHER, MACHINE (plastic prod.) 690.685-170
finisher, map and chart (print. & pub.) 979.684-022
Finisher, Merchant Products (steel & rel.) 613.382-014
FINISHER OPERATOR (can. & preserv.) 521.685-142
Finisher, Plate (steel & rel.) 613.382-014
finisher-polisher (protective dev.) 712.381-050
finisher, screwdown (steel & rel.) 613.382-018
Finisher, Special Stocks (ordnance) 763.381-010
finisher-tailor apprentice (garment; retail trade) 785.361-026
finisher, wallboard and plasterboard (construction; mfd. bldgs.) 842.664-010
FINISHING-AREA OPERATOR (plastic-synth.) 559.362-014
FINISHING-AREA SUPERVISOR (plastic-synth.) 559.132-022
Finishing-Compound Mixer (chemical) 550.685-106
finishing department supervisor (photofinishing) 976.137-014
finishing inspector (clock & watch) 715.381-050
FINISHING INSPECTOR (elec. equip.) 729.387-018
Finishing Inspector (steel & rel.) 619.381-010
finishing machine operator (print. & pub.) 653.382-010
finishing machine operator (print. & pub.) 653.662-010
finishing machine operator (print. & pub.) 640.682-018
finishing-machine operator, automatic (glass mfg.) 677.562-010
FINISHING-MACHINE OPERATOR (narrow fabrics) 582.682-010
FINISHING-MACHINE OPERATOR (nonmet. min.) 674.682-010
FINISHING-MACHINE OPERATOR (paper goods) 649.686-022
finishing-pan operator (chemical; smelt. & refin.) 559.685-074
finishing-powder-press operator (chemical) 557.682-010
Finishing-Range Feeder (textile) 589.686-014
finishing-range operator (textile) 589.665-014
finishing range supervisor (textile) 589.562-010
finishing supervisor (carpet & rug; textile) 589.130-010
FINISHING SUPERVISOR (elec. equip.) 692.130-014
Finishing Supervisor (foundry) 519.131-010
Finishing Supervisor (rubber goods) 559.137-014
FINISHING SUPERVISOR, PLASTIC SHEETS (plastic-synth.) 554.137-010
finishing supervisor, weld-pipe continuous (steel & rel.) 619.130-038
FINISHING TRIMMER (boot & shoe) 788.687-042
finishing tunnel operator (garment) 582.685-150
finishing wire sawyer (stonework) 677.462-014
finish inspector (any industry) 741.687-010
Finish Inspector (furniture) 763.687-026
Finish Judge (amuse. & rec.) 153.267-018
FINISH-MACHINE TENDER (pottery & porc.) 673.685-058
Finish Mender (knitting) 782.684-030
Finish-Mill Operator (cement) 570.685-046
finish mixer (paint & varnish) 550.381-014
finish molder (foundry) 518.684-018
FINISH OPENER, JEWEL HOLE (clock & watch) 673.682-022

FINISH PATCHER (furniture) 763.684-034
finish remover (furniture) 749.687-030
finish repairer (any industry) 749.684-038
finish repairer (furniture) 763.684-034
finish roller (metal prod., nec) 613.682-022
Finish Sander (woodworking) 761.687-010
Finish Specialist (museums) 763.380-010
Finnish Rubber (personal ser.) 334.677-010
fire-alarm dispatcher (government ser.) 379.162-010
fire-and-safety helper (any industry) 739.687-094
fire-apparatus sprinkler inspector (any industry) 379.687-010
FIREARMS-ASSEMBLY SUPERVISOR (ordnance) 736.131-014
firearms expert (government ser.) 199.267-010
FIRE ASSISTANT (government ser.) 169.167-022
Firebrick-And-Refractory Tile Repairer (construction) 861.381-026
FIRE CAPTAIN (government ser.) 373.134-010
Fire Captain, Marine (government ser.) 373.134-010
FIRE CHIEF (government ser.) 373.117-010
Fire Chief (saw. & plan.) 373.167-010
Fire Chief, Deputy (government ser.) 373.117-010
FIRE CHIEF'S AIDE (government ser.) 373.363-010
fire-control assistant (government ser.) 169.167-022
FIRE-CONTROL MECHANIC (government ser.) 632.261-014
fire-control technician (government ser.) 632.261-014
fire crew worker (forestry) 452.687-014
fire deputy (government ser.) 169.167-022
Fire Drier (grain-feed mills) 523.685-058
Fire Eater (amuse. & rec.) 159.647-010
FIRE-EQUIPMENT INSPECTOR (any industry) 739.484-014
FIRE-EQUIPMENT-INSPECTOR HELPER (any industry) 739.687-094
FIRE-EXTINGUISHER REPAIRER (any industry) 709.384-010
FIRE-EXTINGUISHER-SPRINKLER INSPECTOR (any industry) 379.687-010
FIRE FIGHTER (any industry) 373.364-010
fire fighter, airport (air trans.) 373.663-010
FIRE FIGHTER, CRASH, FIRE, AND RESCUE (air trans.) 373.663-010
Firefighter, Marine (any industry) 373.364-010
FIRE-FIGHTING-EQUIPMENT SPECIALIST (government ser.) 638.281-010
FIRE-HOSE CURER (rubber goods) 553.685-062
FIRE INSPECTOR (any industry) 373.367-010
FIRE INSPECTOR (government ser.) 373.267-010
Fire-Insurance-Claim Adjuster (business ser.; insurance) 241.217-010
Fire-Insurance-Claim Examiner (business ser.; insurance) 241.267-018
FIRE-INVESTIGATION LIEUTENANT (government ser.) 373.267-018
Fire Lieutenant (government ser.) 373.134-010
Fire Lieutenant, Marine (government ser.) 373.134-010
FIRE LOOKOUT (forestry) 452.367-010
fire-loss-prevention engineer (profess. & kin.) 012.167-026
FIRE MARSHAL (any industry) 373.167-018
FIRE MARSHAL (government ser.) 373.267-014
Fire Marshal, Refinery (petrol. refin.) 373.167-018
Fire Patroller (logging) 372.667-034
FIRE-PREVENTION RESEARCH ENGINEER (profess. & kin.) 012.167-022
Fireproof-Door Assembler (struct. metal) 809.681-010
FIRE-PROTECTION ENGINEER (profess. & kin.) 012.167-026
FIRE-PROTECTION ENGINEERING TECHNICIAN (profess. & kin.) 019.261-026
firer (any industry) 859.261-010
Firer (electron. comp.) 590.684-014
firer (glass products) 573.685-010
FIRER (jewelry-silver.) 590.685-034
firer (mine & quarry) 931.261-010
FIRE RANGER (forestry) 452.367-014
Firer, Automatic Stoker (any industry) 951.685-010
Firer, Bisque Kiln (pottery & porc.) 573.662-010
firer, boiler (any industry) 950.382-010
firer, boiler (any industry) 951.685-010
Firer, Diesel Locomotive (r.r. trans.) 910.363-010
fire regulator (foundry) 512.667-010
Firer, Electric Locomotive (r.r. trans.) 910.363-010
Firer, Glost Kiln (pottery & porc.) 573.662-010
FIRER HELPER (paper & pulp) 553.665-034
FIRER, HIGH PRESSURE (any industry) 951.685-010
FIRER, KILN (pottery & porc.) 573.662-010
FIRER, KILN (sugar & conf.) 523.685-078
FIRER, LOCOMOTIVE (r.r. trans.) 910.363-010
Firer, Locomotive Crane (any industry) 951.685-010
FIRER, LOW PRESSURE (any industry) 951.685-014
FIRER, MARINE (water trans.) 951.685-018
Firer, Pile Driver (any industry) 951.685-010
Firer, Portable Boiler (any industry) 951.685-010
Firer, Powerhouse (any industry) 951.685-010
FIRER, RETORT (chemical) 553.685-066
Firer, Round Kiln (pottery & porc.) 573.662-010
Firer, Stationary Boiler (any industry) 951.685-010
Firer, Steam Shovel (any industry) 951.685-010

Firer, Tunnel Kiln (pottery & porc.) 573.662-010
Firer-Watertender (water trans.) 951.685-018
FIRESETTER (elec. equip.; electron. comp.; inst. & app.) 692.360-018
Fire-Truck Driver (petrol. & gas) 905.663-014
FIRE WARDEN (forestry) 452.167-010
fire watcher (any industry) 373.367-010
Firewood Cutter (logging) 454.684-026
FIREWORKS ASSEMBLER (chemical) 737.587-014
FIREWORKS DISPLAY SPECIALIST (chemical) 969.664-010
FIREWORKS MAKER (chemical) 737.684-018
Firing-Pin Gauger (chemical) 737.687-062
FIRST-AID ATTENDANT (any industry) 354.677-010
FIRST-BREAKER FEEDER (tex. prod., nec) 680.686-014
First-Coat Operator (tex. prod., nec) 584.382-010
First-Coat Sander (woodworking) 761.687-010
First Front Ventilator (fabrication, nec) 739.384-022
FIRST HELPER (steel & rel.) 512.362-010
first helper (sugar & conf.) 529.682-018
first press operator (print. & pub.) 651.382-042
fiscal clerk (clerical) 216.382-022
FISH AND GAME WARDEN (government ser.) 379.167-010
Fish-And-Game Warden, Marine Patrol (government ser.) 379.167-010
FISH BAILER (fishing & hunt.) 914.685-010
fish-bait picker (agriculture) 413.687-010
FISH-BIN TENDER (can. & preserv.) 529.687-082
Fish-Boning-Machine Feeder (can. & preserv.) 521.686-034
FISH-CAKE MAKER (food prep., nec) 529.685-122
Fish Checker (can. & preserv.) 221.587-030
FISH CHOPPER, GANG KNIFE (can. & preserv.) 521.687-058
FISH CLEANER (can. & preserv.; fishing & hunt.) 525.684-030
FISH CLEANER MACHINE TENDER (can. & preserv.) 529.685-118
fish culturist (fishing & hunt.) 180.167-030
fish cutter (can. & preserv.; fishing & hunt.) 525.684-030
Fish-Cutting-Machine Operator (can. & preserv.) 521.686-034
fish dresser (can. & preserv.; fishing & hunt.) 525.684-030
FISH DRIER (can. & preserv.) 523.687-014
FISH-EGG PACKER (can. & preserv.) 529.687-086
FISHER (fishing & hunt.) term
fisher (fishing & hunt.) 442.684-010
Fisher, Clam (fishing & hunt.) 446.684-014
Fisher, Crab (fishing & hunt.) 441.684-014
Fisher, Dip Net (fishing & hunt.) 441.684-010
Fisher, Diver Net (fishing & hunt.) 441.684-010
FISHER, DIVING (fishing & hunt.) 443.664-010
Fisher, Eel (fishing & hunt.) 441.684-014
Fisher, Eel Spear (fishing & hunt.) 443.684-010
Fisher, Gill Net (fishing & hunt.) 441.684-010
Fisher, Hand Line (fishing & hunt.) 442.684-010
Fisher, Haul, Drag, Or Beach Seine (fishing & hunt.) 441.684-010
Fisher, Hoop Net (fishing & hunt.) 441.684-010
Fisher, Lampara Net (fishing & hunt.) 441.684-010
FISHER, LINE (fishing & hunt.) 442.684-010
Fisher, Lobster (fishing & hunt.) 441.684-014
Fisher, Mussel (fishing & hunt.) 446.684-014
FISHER, NET (fishing & hunt.) 441.684-010
Fisher, Oyster (fishing & hunt.) 446.684-014
FISHER, POT (fishing & hunt.) 441.684-014
Fisher, Pound Net Or Trap (fishing & hunt.) 441.684-010
Fisher, Purse Seine (fishing & hunt.) 441.684-010
Fisher, Quahog (fishing & hunt.) 446.684-014
Fisher, Reef Net (fishing & hunt.) 441.684-010
Fisher, Scallop (fishing & hunt.) 446.684-014
fisher, seal (fishing & hunt.) 461.684-010
FISHER, SPEAR (fishing & hunt.) 443.684-010
FISHER, SPONGE (fishing & hunt.) term
fisher, sponge hooking (fishing & hunt.) 447.684-010
Fisher, Swordfish (fishing & hunt.) 443.684-010
FISHER, TERRAPIN (fishing & hunt.) 441.684-018
Fisher, Trammel Net (fishing & hunt.) 441.684-010
fisher, trap (fishing & hunt.) 441.684-022
Fisher, Trawl Line (fishing & hunt.) 442.684-010
Fisher, Trawl Net (fishing & hunt.) 441.684-010
Fisher, Troll Line (fishing & hunt.) 442.684-010
Fisher, Trot Line (fishing & hunt.) 442.684-010
FISHER, WEIR (fishing & hunt.) 441.684-022
FISH FARMER (fishing & hunt.) 446.161-010
Fish Filleter (can. & preserv.; fishing & hunt.) 525.684-030
fish flaker (can. & preserv.) 523.687-014
Fish Flipper (can. & preserv.) 521.686-034
Fish Grader (can. & preserv.) 529.687-098
fish hatchery assistant (fishing & hunt.) 446.684-010
fish hatchery attendant (fishing & hunt.) 446.684-010
Fish Hatchery Laborer (fishing & hunt.) 446.687-014
FISH HATCHERY WORKER (fishing & hunt.) 446.684-010
Fish Housekeeper (hotel & rest.) 525.684-030

fish-house worker (can. & preserv.) 920.687-086
Fish Icer (can. & preserv.; wholesale tr.) 922.687-046
FISHING ACCESSORIES MAKER (toy-sport equip.) 619.682-018
fishing captain (fishing & hunt.) 197.133-018
FISHING-LINE-WINDING-MACHINE OPERATOR (tex. prod., nec) 689.685-066
FISHING-LURE ASSEMBLER (toy-sport equip.) 732.684-058
FISHING-REEL ASSEMBLER (toy-sport equip.) 732.684-062
FISHING-ROD ASSEMBLER (toy-sport equip.) 732.684-066
FISHING-ROD MARKER (toy-sport equip.) 732.684-070
fishing-rod trimmer (toy-sport equip.) 732.684-066
Fishing-Tackle Repairer (any industry) 732.684-122
FISHING-TOOL TECHNICIAN, OIL WELL (petrol. & gas) 930.261-010
FISH-LIVER SORTER (can. & preserv.; fishing & hunt.) 521.687-062
FISH-MACHINE FEEDER (can. & preserv.) 521.686-034
FISH-NET STRINGER (tex. prod., nec) 782.684-026
FISH PACKER (can. & preserv.) 920.687-086
Fish Pickler (can. & preserv.) 522.684-010
fish pitcher (can. & preserv.) 922.687-062
Fish Protector (government ser.) 379.167-010
FISH ROE PROCESSOR (can. & preserv.) 522.687-046
FISH ROE TECHNICIAN (can. & preserv.) 522.384-010
Fish-Skinning-Machine Feeder (can. & preserv.) 521.686-034
FISH SMOKER (can. & preserv.) 522.685-066
Fish Straightener (can. & preserv.) 521.686-034
FISH-STRINGER ASSEMBLER (toy-sport equip.) 732.684-054
fish-worm grower (agriculture) 413.161-018
Fitted-Sheet Binder (tex. prod., nec) 787.682-010
fitter (boot & shoe) 690.682-082
Fitter (construction; pipe lines) 869.664-014
fitter (fabrication, nec) 739.684-190
fitter (jewelry-silver.) 700.684-034
FITTER (machine shop) 801.381-014
fitter (machinery mfg.; machine tools) 600.281-022
fitter (retail trade; wood prod., nec) 739.684-146
fitter (retail trade) 276.257-022
fitter (ship-boat mfg.) 806.381-046
fitter, factory (garment; glove & mit.) 781.687-010
fitter, hand (metal prod., nec) 709.381-042
FITTER HELPER (any industry) 801.687-014
fitter helper (construction) 862.684-022
FITTER I (any industry) 801.261-014
FITTER II (any industry) 706.684-054
FITTER-PLACER (rubber goods) 753.687-022
Fitter-Tacker (any industry) 801.261-014
Fitter, Type-Bar-And-Segment (office machines) 706.684-026
fitter-up (leather mfg.) 629.280-010
FITTER, VENTILATED RIB (ordnance) 736.381-014
fitting maker (brick & tile) 862.684-010
Fitting-Room Inspector (boot & shoe) 788.384-010
Fitting-Room Maintenance Mechanic (boot & shoe) 639.281-018
fitting room operator (boot & shoe) 788.685-018
Fitting-Room Supervisor (boot & shoe) 788.131-010
FITTINGS FINISHER (plumbing-heat.) 619.382-014
fittings tightener (plumbing-heat.) 706.684-086
Five-Piece-Expansion Maker, Hand (paper goods) 794.684-018
five-roll-refiner batch mixer (sugar & conf.) 520.685-150
FIXED-CAPITAL CLERK (utilities) 210.382-042
fixer (any industry) 638.281-014
fixer (narrow fabrics; nonmet. min.; textile) 683.260-018
fixer (textile) 689.260-010
FIXER, BOARDING ROOM (knitting) 580.380-010
fixer supervisor (narrow fabrics) 683.130-014
FIXING-MACHINE OPERATOR (toy-sport equip.) 732.685-018
Fixture Builder (machinery mfg.) 600.281-022
Fixture Designer (furniture) 142.061-022
FIXTURE MAKER (light. fix.) 600.380-010
fixture relamper (any industry) 389.687-018
FIXTURE REPAIRER-FABRICATOR (any industry) 630.384-010
flag decorator and designer (profess. & kin.) 142.051-010
FLAGGER (amuse. & rec.) 372.667-026
FLAGGER (construction) 372.667-022
Flagsetter (construction) 861.381-038
FLAKE-CUTTER OPERATOR (wood prod., nec) 564.682-014
flake drier (soap & rel.) 553.685-098
flake-miller helper (grain-feed mills) 526.585-010
FLAKE MILLER, WHEAT AND OATS (grain-feed mills) 521.682-022
flake-or-shred-roll operator (grain-feed mills) 520.685-102
flaker (can. & preserv.) 523.687-014
flaker operator (can. & preserv.) 523.685-062
Flaker Operator (chemical) 553.685-098
FLAKER OPERATOR (chemical; smelt. & refin.) 559.685-074
flaker tender (can. & preserv.) 523.687-014
flaking-machine operator (chemical; smelt. & refin.) 559.685-074
FLAKING-ROLL OPERATOR (grain-feed mills) 520.685-102

Flame-Annealing-Machine Operator (heat treating) 504.685-014
FLAME-ANNEALING-MACHINE SETTER (heat treating) 504.360-010
flame-brazing-machine operator (welding) 813.382-014
FLAME CHANNELER (construction; mine & quarry) 930.684-010
flame-cutting-machine operator (welding) 816.482-010
Flame-Cutting-Machine-Operator Helper (welding) 819.666-010
FLAME DEGREASER (automotive ser.) 503.685-022
flame gouger (welding) 816.464-010
FLAME-HARDENING-MACHINE OPERATOR (heat treating) 504.685-014
FLAME-HARDENING-MACHINE SETTER (heat treating) 504.380-010
flame planer (welding) 816.482-010
FLAMER (boot & shoe) 788.684-050
flamer, after lasting (boot & shoe) 788.684-130
flamer-sealer (elec. equip.) 727.684-030
Flame Scarfer (welding) 816.464-010
flame-spraying-machine operator, automatic (any industry) 505.382-010
flame-spray operator (any industry) 505.380-010
flange cutter (hat & cap; tex. prod., nec) 585.685-086
FLANGER (hat & cap) 784.684-026
FLANGER (inst. & app.) 712.684-018
flanging-machine operator (hat & cap) 690.686-058
flanging-machine operator (paper goods) 641.685-046
flanging operator (hat & cap) 784.684-026
FLANGING-ROLL OPERATOR (any industry) 619.362-010
Flap-Lining Binder (hat & cap) 787.682-010
FLARE BREAKER (boot & shoe) 788.685-010
flare chalker (boot & shoe) 788.687-010
flarer (wood. container) 619.682-034
Flare Stitcher (boot & shoe) 690.682-082
FLASH-DRIER OPERATOR (chemical) 553.462-010
FLASH-DRIER OPERATOR (grain-feed mills) 529.582-014
FLASHER ADJUSTER (light. fix.) 723.684-022
Flash-Oven Operator (elec. equip.) 554.685-014
FLASH RANGING CREWMEMBER (military ser.) 378.367-018
Flash-Welding-Machine Operator (welding) 812.682-010
Flask Carrier (foundry) 519.687-022
flask fitter (foundry) 518.684-018
flat-bed-press feeder (print. & pub.) 651.686-010
flatbed-press operator (print. & pub.) 651.362-010
Flatbed Stitcher (boot & shoe) 690.682-082
FLATCAR WHACKER (saw. & plan.) 807.667-010
FLAT CLOTHIER (textile) 628.382-010
FLAT DRIER (tex. prod., nec) 581.685-078
flat folder (boot & shoe) 788.687-050
flat-folding-machine operator (textile) 689.585-014
flat-grinder operator (clock & watch) 770.682-018
flat hammerer (jewelry-silver.) 700.381-022
Flat Knitter (knitting) 685.665-014
Flat-Knitter Helper (knitting) 685.686-014
FLATLOCK-SEWING-MACHINE OPERATOR (garment) 786.682-110
flat optical element maker (optical goods) 716.280-018
FLAT POLISHER (clock & watch) 603.685-054
flat-sheet maker (plastic-synth.) 556.684-018
flat-spring assembler (furniture) 709.667-010
FLAT SURFACER, JEWEL (clock & watch) 770.685-010
flattening-machine operator (any industry) 363.682-018
FLATWARE MAKER (jewelry-silver.) 700.682-010
Flatwork Assembler (laundry & rel.) 369.687-010
Flatwork Catcher (laundry & rel.) 363.686-010
Flatwork Feeder (laundry & rel.) 363.686-010
FLATWORK FINISHER (laundry & rel.) 363.686-010
Flatwork Finisher (pottery & porc.) 774.684-018
Flatwork Finisher, Hand (laundry & rel.) 363.684-018
Flatwork Folder (laundry & rel.) 363.686-010
Flatwork Supervisor (laundry & rel.) 361.137-010
FLATWORK TIER (laundry & rel.) 361.587-010
Flatwork Washer (laundry & rel.) 361.665-010
FLAVOR EXTRACTOR (grain-feed mills) 529.685-126
flavoring-machine operator (tobacco) 522.685-030
flavoring maker (tobacco) 520.685-054
FLAVORING OIL FILTERER (beverage) 521.685-382
flavor maker (tobacco) 520.685-082
FLAVOR ROOM WORKER (dairy products) 529.685-130
Flavor-Tank Tender (dairy products) 529.685-146
fleecer (knitting) 585.665-010
FLEECE TIER (agriculture) 410.687-010
FLESHER (leather mfg.) 585.681-010
Fleshing-Machine Operator (leather mfg.) 585.685-094
Fletcher (toy-sport equip.) 732.684-010
Flexible Machining System Machinist (machine shop) 600.280-022
Flexible-Shaft Winder (metal prod., nec) 619.482-010
flexigraphic printer (plastic prod.; tex. prod., nec) 651.382-026
Flexo-Folder-Gluer-Machine Helper (paper goods) 659.686-014
Flexo-Folder-Gluer Operator (paper goods) 659.662-010
flexographic-press helper (print. & pub.) 651.585-010

FLEXOGRAPHIC-PRESS OPERATOR (paper goods; print. & pub.) 651.682-010
FLIGHT ATTENDANT, RAMP (air trans.) 352.367-014
flight-control-tower operator (government ser.) 193.162-018
FLIGHT-CREW-TIME CLERK (air trans.) 215.362-018
FLIGHT ENGINEER (air trans.) 621.261-018
flight follower (air trans.) 209.367-050
FLIGHT-INFORMATION EXPEDITER (air trans.) 912.367-010
Flight-Line Mechanic (aircraft mfg.) 621.281-014
Flight Line Service Attendant (aircraft mfg.) 621.684-010
flight mechanic (air trans.) 621.261-018
flight-operations-dispatch clerk (air trans.) 248.367-010
FLIGHT-OPERATIONS INSPECTOR (government ser.) 196.163-010
FLIGHT OPERATIONS SPECIALIST (military ser.) 248.387-010
flight physiologist (medical ser.) 070.101-030
flight security specialist (air trans.) 372.667-010
FLIGHT SURGEON (medical ser.) 070.101-030
FLIGHT-TEST DATA ACQUISITION TECHNICIAN (aircraft mfg.) 002.262-010
flipping-machine operator (rubber goods) 690.685-450
Flitch Hanger (millwork-plywood) 663.686-022
Float Builder (any industry) 869.687-010
floating-derrick operator (water trans.) 921.683-034
floating-labor-gang supervisor (any industry) 899.133-010
Floatlight-Loading Supervisor (chemical) 737.131-010
Floatlight-Powder Mixer (chemical) 737.687-090
float remover (textile) 689.685-094
Float Sander (woodworking) 662.682-010
flocculator operator (plastic-synth.) 559.582-010
FLOCKER (tex. prod., nec) 789.687-054
FLOOR AND WALL APPLIER, LIQUID (construction) 864.684-010
Floor Assembler (mfd. bldgs.) 869.684-018
FLOOR ATTENDANT (amuse. & rec.) 343.467-014
FLOOR ATTENDANT (glass mfg.) 579.687-018
FLOOR BROKER (financial) 162.167-034
Floor Cashier (clerical) 211.462-010
Floor Cleaner (any industry) 381.687-018
floor clerk (clerical) 221.387-038
Floor Clerk (hotel & rest.) 238.367-038
floor coverer (construction; retail trade) 864.481-010
floor-coverer apprentice (construction; retail trade) 864.481-014
FLOOR-COVERING LAYER (railroad equip.) 622.381-026
Floor-Coverings Estimator (retail trade; wholesale tr.) 270.357-026
floor-covering-tile layer (construction; retail trade) 864.481-010
Floor Finisher (construction) 869.664-014
Floor Finisher (mfd. bldgs.; vehicles, nec) 869.684-010
Floor Finisher (vehicles, nec) 806.684-018
Floor-Finisher Helper (construction) 869.687-026
Floor Framer (mfd. bldgs.; vehicles, nec) 869.684-010
Floor Framer (vehicles, nec) 806.684-018
floor grinder (construction) 861.381-046
floor hand (tobacco) 529.687-070
floor housekeeper (hotel & rest.; medical ser.; real estate) 321.137-010
Flooring Grader (saw. & plan.) 669.687-030
Flooring-Machine Feeder (saw. & plan.) 669.686-030
Floor Inspector (glass mfg.) 579.384-018
FLOOR LAYER (construction; retail trade) 864.481-010
FLOOR-LAYER APPRENTICE (construction; retail trade) 864.481-014
Floor-Layer Helper (construction; retail trade) 869.687-026
floorleader (print. & pub.) 653.131-010
floor molder, sweep method (foundry) 518.361-018
floor plan adjuster (financial) 241.367-038
floor-press operator (any industry) 616.682-010
floor representative (financial) 162.167-034
floor runner (water trans.) 222.567-014
Floor-Sanding-Machine Operator (construction) 869.664-014
FLOOR SERVICE WORKER, SPRING (automotive ser.) 807.684-022
FLOOR-SPACE ALLOCATOR (tobacco; wholesale tr.) 222.367-030
floor steward/stewardess (hotel & rest.) 318.137-010
Floor Supervisor (hotel & rest.) 321.137-014
FLOOR SUPERVISOR, ENDLESS-BELT-WEAVING DEPARTMENT (narrow fabrics) 683.130-010
floor trader (financial) 162.167-034
FLOOR WINDER (textile) 681.685-050
floor worker (any industry) 929.687-030
floorworker (leather mfg.) 589.686-022
FLOOR WORKER (sugar & conf.) 920.687-090
FLOOR WORKER (wood prod., nec) 739.687-098
FLOORWORKER-DISTRIBUTOR (hat & cap) 784.687-030
FLOORWORKER, LASTING (boot & shoe) 788.687-046
Floor Worker, Transfer Bay (nonfer. metal) 921.667-022
FLOOR WORKER, WELL SERVICE (petrol. & gas) 930.684-014
Floral Arranger (retail trade) 142.081-010
FLORAL DESIGNER (retail trade) 142.081-010
florist (retail trade) 142.081-010

Flotation Supervisor (smelt. & refin.) 511.135-010
FLOTATION TENDER (smelt. & refin.) 511.685-026
FLOTATION-TENDER HELPER (smelt. & refin.) 511.687-018
FLOUR BLENDER (grain-feed mills) 520.685-106
Flour-Blender Helper (bakery products) 526.686-010
FLOUR-BLENDER HELPER (grain-feed mills) 520.686-022
flour distributor (food prep., nec) 921.382-010
flour mixer (bakery products) 520.585-010
FLOUR MIXER (grain-feed mills) 520.485-010
flour-mixer helper (grain-feed mills) 520.686-022
flour tester (grain-feed mills) 526.381-018
flower arranger (button & notion) 739.684-014
flower cheniller (tex. prod., nec) 687.682-010
flower cutter (glass products) 775.381-010
Flower Grader (agriculture) 529.687-186
Flower Grower (agriculture) 405.161-014
FLOWER-MACHINE OPERATOR (tex. prod., nec) 687.682-010
FLOWER PICKER (agriculture) 405.687-010
FLOWER-POT-PRESS OPERATOR (pottery & porc.) 575.685-034
flow floor attendant (glass mfg.) 579.687-018
flow machine operator (glass mfg.) 575.382-014
Flowmeter Test And Certification Technician (inst. & app.) 710.281-022
flow-solder machine operator (comm. equip.; electron. comp.; inst. & app.; office machines) 726.362-014
Flue Cleaner (any industry) 891.687-030
flue-dust laborer (smelt. & refin.) 519.687-014
Flue-Lining Dipper (concrete prod.) 579.687-042
Flue-Tile-Press Operator (brick & tile) 575.462-010
FLUID JET CUTTER OPERATOR (aircraft mfg.) 699.382-010
FLUID-POWER MECHANIC (any industry) 600.281-010
Flume Maker (mine & quarry) 860.281-010
FLUMER (grain-feed mills) 521.686-038
FLUMER I (sugar & conf.) 922.665-010
Flume-Ride Operator (amuse. & rec.) 342.663-010
FLUMER II (sugar & conf.) 521.686-042
fluorescent lamp replacer (any industry) 389.687-018
fluoroscope operator (can. & preserv.; tobacco) 529.685-274
FLUOROSCOPE OPERATOR (nonfer. metal) 502.382-014
FLUSHER (chemical) 559.682-026
Flusher (fabrication, nec) 761.684-030
flusher (grain-feed mills) 529.687-210
Flush Tester (pottery & porc.) 774.687-026
Flux Brusher (welding) 819.666-010
FLUX MIXER (chemical) 550.584-010
FLUX-TUBE ATTENDANT (nonfer. metal; smelt. & refin.) 519.687-018
FLYER (amuse. & rec.; radio-tv broad.) 962.687-018
flyer builder (textile) 628.687-010
FLYER REPAIRER (textile) 628.687-010
FLYING-SHEAR OPERATOR (steel & rel.) 615.682-010
Fly Raiser, Lockstitch (garment) 786.682-238
Fly Setter (garment) 786.682-286
FLY TIER (toy-sport equip.) 732.684-074
fly winder (toy-sport equip.) 732.684-074
Foam Caster (nonmet. min.) 754.684-022
FOAM CHARGER (svc. ind. mach.) 827.585-010
FOAM DISPENSER (rubber goods) 554.684-014
foam fabricator (any industry) 780.684-062
FOAM-GUN OPERATOR (plastic prod.) 741.684-014
foaming machine operator (textile) 584.685-030
FOAM-MACHINE OPERATOR (plastic prod.; plastic-synth.) 559.685-078
Foam Molder (clock & watch) 754.684-022
FOCUSER (light. fix.) 725.687-018
Foil Cutter (any industry) 699.685-014
Foil Cutter (electron. comp.) 699.682-018
FOILING-MACHINE ADJUSTER (ordnance) 629.381-010
FOILING-MACHINE OPERATOR (ordnance) 692.685-086
folded-cloth taper (textile) 920.587-010
Folded-Towel-Machine Operator (paper goods) 649.685-046
folder (garment; glove & mit.) 781.687-010
folder (garment) 583.685-042
FOLDER (laundry & rel.) 369.687-018
FOLDER (narrow fabrics) 686.685-030
FOLDER (tex. prod., nec) 789.687-058
folder-and-notcher (musical inst.) 730.684-014
Folder-Gluer Operator (paper goods) 649.682-010
FOLDER, HAND (boot & shoe) 788.687-050
FOLDER, HAND (paper goods) 794.687-022
folder, hand (tex. prod., nec; textile) 589.687-014
folder inspector (any industry) 789.587-014
FOLDER, MACHINE (boot & shoe) 690.685-174
folder, machine (paper goods) 649.685-042
folder, machine (print. & pub.) 653.382-010
folder, machine (textile) 689.585-014
folder operator (clerical) 208.685-014
folder operator (knitting; textile) 589.685-058

folder operator (print. & pub.) 653.382-010
FOLDER-SEAMER, AUTOMATIC (any industry) 787.685-014
Folder-Stitcher Operator (paper goods) 649.682-010
Folder-Taper Operator (paper goods) 649.682-010
FOLDER-TIER (nonmet. min.) 759.684-034
FOLDING-MACHINE FEEDER (paper goods) 641.685-050
Folding-Machine Feeder (print. & pub.) 653.686-026
FOLDING-MACHINE FEEDER (tex. prod., nec) 920.686-018
folding-machine operator (boot & shoe) 690.685-074
folding-machine operator (boot & shoe) 690.685-174
FOLDING-MACHINE OPERATOR (clerical) 208.685-014
FOLDING-MACHINE OPERATOR (garment) 583.685-042
FOLDING-MACHINE OPERATOR (hat & cap) 690.686-034
FOLDING-MACHINE OPERATOR (knitting; textile) 589.685-058
folding-machine operator (knitting) 580.485-010
FOLDING-MACHINE OPERATOR (laundry & rel.) 369.686-010
FOLDING-MACHINE OPERATOR (leather prod.) 690.685-178
FOLDING-MACHINE OPERATOR (paper goods) 649.685-046
FOLDING-MACHINE OPERATOR (print. & pub.) 653.382-010
folding-machine operator (textile) 689.685-078
FOLDING-MACHINE OPERATOR (textile) 689.585-014
Folding-Machine Setter (print. & pub.) 653.360-018
FOLDING-MACHINE TENDER (boot & shoe) 788.685-014
fold skiver (boot & shoe) 788.685-014
foliage arranger (button & notion) 739.684-014
FOLLOW-UP CLERK (elec. equip.) 221.367-018
Fondant Cooker (sugar & conf.) 526.382-014
Fondant-Machine Operator (sugar & conf.) 521.585-018
Fondant-Puff Maker (sugar & conf.) 520.682-014
FOOD-AND-BEVERAGE CHECKER (hotel & rest.) 211.482-018
FOOD-AND-BEVERAGE CONTROLLER (hotel & rest.) 216.362-022
FOOD AND DRUG INSPECTOR (government ser.) 168.267-042
food assembler, commissary kitchen (hotel & rest.) 319.484-010
FOOD ASSEMBLER, KITCHEN (hotel & rest.) 319.484-010
FOOD CHECKER (hotel & rest.) 211.482-014
Food Demonstrator (retail trade; wholesale tr.) 297.354-010
FOOD-MANAGEMENT AIDE (government ser.) 195.367-022
FOOD MIXER (grain-feed mills) 520.687-034
Food-Mixer Assembler (house. appl.) 723.684-010
Food-Mixer Repairer (house. appl.) 723.584-010
FOOD ORDER EXPEDITER (hotel & rest.) 319.467-010
food preparer (amuse. & rec.; museums) 412.687-010
food scientist (profess. & kin.) 041.081-010
food-service agent (hotel & rest.) 906.683-010
food service coordinator (hotel & rest.) 313.131-018
FOOD-SERVICE DRIVER (hotel & rest.) 906.683-010
FOOD-SERVICE SUPERVISOR (hotel & rest.) 319.137-010
Food-Service Worker (hotel & rest.) 313.361-014
FOOD-SERVICE WORKER, HOSPITAL (medical ser.) 319.677-014
Food-Storeroom Clerk (hotel & rest.) 222.387-058
FOOD TECHNOLOGIST (profess. & kin.) 041.081-010
FOOD TESTER (any industry) 029.361-014
food-tray assembler (hotel & rest.) 319.484-010
Football Coach (amuse. & rec.) 153.227-010
Football-Pad Repairer (any industry) 732.684-122
Football Scout (amuse. & rec.) 153.117-018
Foot Cager (mine & quarry) 939.667-010
Foot Caster (glass mfg.) 772.381-018
Foot Cutter (meat products) 525.687-074
FOOT-MITER OPERATOR (wood prod., nec) 739.684-066
Foot-Piece Assembler (furniture) 706.684-082
foot specialist (medical ser.) 079.101-022
FOOT STRAIGHTENER (clock & watch) 715.687-030
foot tender (mine & quarry) 932.667-010
FOOT WORKER (chemical) 934.685-010
force dispatcher (tel. & tel.) 215.137-018
Forcer Maker (jewelry-silver.) 601.381-014
FORCE-VARIATION EQUIPMENT TENDER (rubber tire) 690.685-182
Foreclosure Clerk (financial) 249.362-014
foreign agent (any industry) 184.117-022
FOREIGN BANKNOTE TELLER-TRADER (financial) 211.362-014
FOREIGN-BROADCAST SPECIALIST (radio-tv broad.) term
Foreign-Car Mechanic (automotive ser.) 620.261-010
FOREIGN CLERK (clerical) 214.467-010
Foreign-Collection Clerk (financial) 216.362-014
Foreign Correspondent (print. & pub.; radio-tv broad.) 131.262-018
FOREIGN-EXCHANGE DEALER (financial) 186.117-082
FOREIGN-EXCHANGE-POSITION CLERK (financial) 210.367-014
foreign-exchange trader (financial) 186.117-082
Foreign-Language Stenographer (clerical) 202.362-014
FOREIGN-SERVICE OFFICER (government ser.) 188.117-106
FOREIGN-STUDENT ADVISER (education) 090.107-010
forensic artist (government ser.) 141.061-034
Forensic Pathologist (medical ser.) 070.061-010
FOREPART LASTER (boot & shoe) 690.685-186

Forepart Rasper (boot & shoe) 788.684-094
forepart reducer (boot & shoe) 690.685-166
forepart rounder (boot & shoe) 690.685-334
FOREST ECOLOGIST (profess. & kin.) 040.061-030
FOREST ENGINEER (forestry; logging) 005.167-018
FORESTER (profess. & kin.) 040.167-010
FORESTER AIDE (forestry) 452.364-010
Forest Fire Equipment Operator (government ser.) 850.683-010
FOREST-FIRE FIGHTER (forestry) 452.687-014
FOREST NURSERY SUPERVISOR (forestry) 451.137-010
FOREST-PRODUCTS GATHERER (agriculture; forestry) 453.687-010
forestry hunter (fishing & hunt.) 461.661-010
Forestry Supervisor (profess. & kin.) 040.167-010
forest technician (forestry) 452.364-010
FOREST WORKER (forestry) 452.687-014
FORGE HELPER (forging) 619.686-034
FORGE-SHOP-MACHINE REPAIRER (forging) 626.261-010
FORGE-SHOP SUPERVISOR (forging) 612.131-010
forging-die finisher (machine shop) 705.484-014
forging-die sinker (machine shop) 601.280-022
forging-machine operator (forging) 611.482-010
Forging-Press Lever Tender (forging) 612.685-010
FORGING-PRESS OPERATOR I (forging) 611.482-010
FORGING-PRESS OPERATOR II (forging) 611.685-010
Forging Press Setter-Up (forging) 612.360-010
FORGING-ROLL OPERATOR (forging) 612.682-014
Fork Assembler (motor-bicycles) 806.684-094
Fork-Lift-Truck Operator (any industry) 921.683-050
Fork Repairer (motor-bicycles) 620.684-026
Formal-Wear-Rental Clerk (retail trade) 295.357-010
Formation-Fracturing Operator (petrol. & gas) 939.462-010
Formation-Fracturing-Operator Helper (petrol. & gas) 939.684-018
FORMATION-TESTING OPERATOR (petrol. & gas) 930.261-014
Form Block Maker (aircraft mfg.) 693.281-030
FORM BUILDER (construction) 860.381-046
Form-Builder Helper (construction) 869.664-014
Form-Building Supervisor (construction) 860.131-018
FORM CLEANER (construction) term
FORM COVERER (fabrication, nec) 739.684-070
FORM DESIGNER (print. & pub.) 970.361-010
form drafter (print. & pub.) 970.361-010
former (elec. equip.) 691.685-018
former (oils & grease) 520.685-038
former (pottery & porc.) 575.685-026
FORMER, HAND (any industry) 619.361-010
FORMER HELPER, HAND (any industry) 619.684-010
former puller (oils & grease) 520.685-038
Former, Type-Bar-And-Segment (office machines) 706.684-026
Form-Finishing-Machine Operator (laundry & rel.) 363.681-010
FORM-GRADER OPERATOR (construction) 850.683-022
forming acid dumper (elec. equip.) 727.687-010
forming fixer (glass mfg.) 629.281-026
FORMING-MACHINE ADJUSTER (glass mfg.) 629.281-026
forming-machine operator (boot & shoe) 690.685-098
FORMING-MACHINE OPERATOR (button & notion) 559.665-022
FORMING-MACHINE OPERATOR (glass mfg.) 575.382-014
forming-machine operator (hat & cap) 586.685-030
forming-machine operator (ordnance) 617.585-010
Forming-Machine Operator (paper & pulp) 539.685-018
FORMING-MACHINE TENDER (glass mfg.) 575.685-038
FORMING-MACHINE UPKEEP MECHANIC (glass mfg.) 575.380-010
FORMING-MACHINE UPKEEP-MECHANIC HELPER (glass mfg.) 575.687-014
forming-mill operator (any industry) 616.685-042
forming operator (glass mfg.) 575.685-030
forming operator (wood. container) 669.685-046
forming-press operator (rubber goods; rubber tire; toy-sport equip.) 556.685-066
Forming-Press Operator I (any industry) 615.382-010
Forming-Press Operator II (any industry) 615.685-030
FORMING-PROCESS-LINE WORKER (elec. equip.) 727.687-058
FORMING-PROCESS WORKER (elec. equip.) 590.362-010
Forming-Roll Operator, Heavy Duty (any industry) 617.482-014
FORMING-ROLL OPERATOR I (any industry) 617.482-014
FORMING-ROLL OPERATOR II (any industry) 619.685-046
forming-tube selector (textile) 681.687-010
FORM MAKER, PLASTER (plastic prod.) 777.684-010
Form-Press Operator (laundry & rel.) 363.682-018
form puller (construction)   see FORM STRIPPER
form remover (construction)   see FORM STRIPPER
FORMS ANALYST (profess. & kin.) 161.267-018
form scraper (construction)   see FORM CLEANER
Form-Setter Helper (construction) 869.687-026
Form Setter, Metal Road-Forms (construction) 869.664-014
Form Setter, Steel Forms (construction) 869.664-014
Form Setter, Steel-Pan Forms (construction) 869.664-014

Form-Setter Supervisor (construction) 869.131-014
Form Stripper (concrete prod.; construction) 869.687-026
FORM STRIPPER (construction) term
form tamper (construction) 869.683-010
FORM-TAMPER OPERATOR (construction) 869.683-010
form-tamping-machine operator (construction) 869.683-010
Formula Bottler (dairy products) 520.487-014
Formula Checker (tex. prod., nec; textile) 221.387-046
FORMULA CLERK (textile) 221.367-090
Formula Figurer (paint & varnish) 216.482-022
Formula Maker (dairy products) 520.487-014
FORMULA-ROOM WORKER (dairy products) 520.487-014
formulator (chemical) 559.665-026
FORMULA WEIGHER (pen & pencil) 559.685-082
FORMULA WEIGHER (rubber goods) 550.663-010
form wrecker (construction)   see FORM STRIPPER
Fortune Cookie Maker (bakery products) 526.685-070
Fortune Teller (amuse. & rec.) 159.647-018
FORWARDER (print. & pub.) 794.687-026
FOSTER PARENT (domestic ser.) 309.677-014
FOUNDATION-DRILL OPERATOR (construction) 859.682-014
Foundation-Drill-Operator Helper (construction) 869.664-014
FOUNDATION MAKER (fabrication, nec) 739.384-014
FOUNDATION MAKER (hat & cap) 784.684-030
FOUNDRY LABORER, COREROOM (foundry) 518.687-014
FOUNDRY METALLURGIST (foundry) 011.061-010
FOUNDRY SUPERVISOR (foundry) 519.131-014
foundry technician (foundry) 011.061-010
FOUNDRY WORKER, GENERAL (foundry) 519.687-022
Fountain-Brush Assembler (pen & pencil) 733.687-010
fountain dispenser (hotel & rest.) 319.474-010
FOUNTAIN PEN TURNER (pen & pencil) 690.685-190
Fountain-Roller Assembler (pen & pencil) 733.687-010
FOUNTAIN SERVER (hotel & rest.) 319.474-010
Fourchette Sewer (glove & mit.) 784.682-010
FOUR-CORNER-STAYER-MACHINE OPERATOR (paper goods) 641.685-054
FOURDRINIER-MACHINE OPERATOR (paper & pulp; paper goods) 539.362-014
Fourdrinier-Paper-Machine Supervisor (paper & pulp) 539.132-010
FOUR-H CLUB AGENT (education) 096.127-022
Four-Horse Hitch Driver (any industry) 919.664-010
FOUR-SLIDE-MACHINE OPERATOR I (any industry) 619.382-018
FOUR-SLIDE-MACHINE OPERATOR II (any industry) 619.685-050
FOUR-SLIDE-MACHINE SETTER (any industry) 616.380-010
Fox Farmer (agriculture) 410.161-014
FOXING CUTTER, HOT KNIFE (boot & shoe; rubber goods) 751.684-022
FOXING-CUTTING-MACHINE OPERATOR, AUTOMATIC (boot & shoe) 690.682-038
FOXING PAINTER (rubber goods) 584.685-022
Fractional-Horsepower Motor Repairer (any industry) 721.281-018
fractionation operator, head (petrol. refin.) 549.132-030
fractionation supervisor (petrol. refin.) 549.132-030
frame aligner (motor-bicycles) 807.484-010
frame-and-scrap crusher (fabrication, nec) 555.685-022
Frame Assembler (mfd. bldgs.) 869.684-018
Frame Assembler (motor-bicycles) 806.684-094
frame assembler (optical goods) 713.684-014
Frame Assembler (struct. metal) 809.684-010
Frame Assembler (toy-sport equip.) 732.384-010
FRAME BANDER (textile) 628.684-014
frame bender (tex. prod., nec) 809.484-010
frame builder, silk-screen (any industry) 709.484-010
FRAME CARVER, SPINDLE (optical goods) 713.684-030
frame catcher (textile) 589.686-010
FRAME CHANGER (textile) 689.686-026
frame cleaner (textile) 680.687-014
Frame Coverer (leather prod.) 783.687-010
frame crusher (fabrication, nec) 555.685-022
FRAME FEEDER (chemical) 553.686-034
frame-gate-mortiser operator (saw. & plan.) 667.482-014
FRAME HAND (tex. prod., nec) 689.687-046
Frame Maker (leather mfg.) 860.281-010
Frame Maker (saw. & plan.) 669.380-014
Frame Nailer (wood. container) 669.682-058
frame opener (leather prod.) 222.687-042
frame-pulley-mortising-machine operator (saw. & plan.) 666.482-010
framer (fabrication, nec) 739.684-162
FRAMER (glass products; wood prod., nec) 739.684-078
framer (leather prod.) 739.684-090
framer (mfd. bldgs.; vehicles, nec) 869.684-010
framer (textile) 689.687-026
framer (wood prod., nec) 669.662-014
FRAMER (wood prod., nec) 666.684-010
FRAME REPAIRER (furniture) 763.681-010

FRAME REPAIRER (glass products) 739.684-074
FRAME REPAIRER (motor-bicycles) 807.381-018
FRAME STRAIGHTENER (motor-bicycles) 807.484-010
FRAME STRIPPER (chemical) 559.687-046
FRAME STRIPPER (soap & rel.) 559.685-086
frame stripper and crusher (soap & rel.) 555.685-062
FRAME-TABLE OPERATOR (wood prod., nec) 669.662-014
FRAME-TABLE-OPERATOR HELPER (wood prod., nec) 669.685-058
FRAME TRIMMER I (wood prod., nec) 749.684-030
FRAME TRIMMER II (wood prod., nec) 769.687-022
FRAME WIRER (tel. & tel.) 822.684-010
framing-machine tender (textile) 580.685-066
framing-mill operator (wood prod., nec) 669.662-014
framing-mill-operator helper (wood prod., nec) 669.685-058
frankfurter inspector (meat products) 529.587-014
Fraternity Adviser (education) 090.167-022
FRAZER (fabrication, nec) 664.685-022
Freelance Reporter (clerical) 202.362-010
freezer (dairy products) 529.482-010
freezer assistant (dairy products) 529.685-146
FREEZER OPERATOR (dairy products) 529.482-010
FREEZER TUNNEL OPERATOR (can. & preserv.) 523.685-082
FREEZING-MACHINE OPERATOR (pharmaceut.) 559.685-090
FREEZING-ROOM WORKER (can. & preserv.) 523.687-022
Freight-Air-Brake Fitter (railroad equip.) 862.281-022
freight and passenger agent (r.r. trans.) 910.137-038
FREIGHT-CAR CLEANER, DELTA SYSTEM (r.r. trans.) 910.687-022
freight checker (water trans.) 222.367-010
Freight Clerk (clerical) 222.387-050
freight clerk (water trans.) 248.167-010
freighter (any industry) 919.664-010
FREIGHT-LOADING SUPERVISOR (r.r. trans.) 910.137-026
freight-rate clerk (clerical) 214.362-038
Freight-Traffic Agent (air trans.; motor trans.; r.r. trans.; water trans.) 252.257-010
FREIGHT-TRAFFIC CONSULTANT (business ser.) 184.267-010
French-Binding Folder (boot & shoe) 788.684-018
french-binding folder (boot & shoe) 690.685-070
french-edge operator (paper goods) 641.685-046
french weaver (personal ser.) 782.381-022
frequency checker (textile) 221.367-034
fresh-meat grader (meat products) 529.687-106
FRESH-WORK INSPECTOR (tobacco) 529.687-090
fresh-work wrapper-layer (tobacco) 529.685-266
fret-saw operator (woodworking) 667.682-042
FRETTED-INSTRUMENT INSPECTOR (musical inst.) 730.684-034
FRETTED-INSTRUMENT MAKER, HAND (musical inst.) 730.281-022
FRETTED-INSTRUMENT REPAIRER (any industry) 730.281-026
frickertron checker (glass mfg.) 575.685-082
FRICTION-PAINT-MACHINE TENDER (fabrication, nec) 534.685-014
fried-cake maker (bakery products) 526.682-022
fringe-binder operator (carpet & rug; retail trade) 787.682-014
FRINGER (carpet & rug; tex. prod., nec) 789.687-062
Fringer (tex. prod., nec) 787.682-066
fringer, hand (tex. prod., nec) 782.684-050
FRINGING-MACHINE OPERATOR (knitting) 685.686-010
frit burner (brick & tile; pottery & porc.) 579.685-014
Frit Coater (electron. comp.) 725.684-022
frit maker (brick & tile; pottery & porc.) 570.685-098
FRIT-MIXER-AND-BURNER (brick & tile; pottery & porc.) 579.685-014
Frog Shaker (tobacco) 521.687-110
Front Desk Clerk (hotel & rest.) 238.367-038
FRONT-EDGE-TAPE SEWER, LOCKSTITCH (garment) 786.682-118
Front-Elevator Operator (hotel & rest.) 388.663-010
FRONT-END LOADER OPERATOR (any industry) 921.683-042
FRONT-END MECHANIC (automotive ser.) 620.281-038
FRONT MAKER, LOCKSTITCH (garment) 786.682-114
FRONT-SIGHT ATTACHER (ordnance) 736.684-030
front tender (textile) 582.582-010
froster (bakery products) 524.684-022
froster, machine (bakery products) 524.685-034
FROTHING-MACHINE OPERATOR (rubber goods) 550.362-010
FROZEN PIE MAKER (can. & preserv.) 529.684-010
FRUIT-BAR MAKER (sugar & conf.) 529.685-134
FRUIT-BUYING GRADER (can. & preserv.; wholesale tr.) 529.387-018
FRUIT COORDINATOR (can. & preserv.) 529.167-010
FRUIT CUTTER (sugar & conf.) 521.687-066
FRUIT DISTRIBUTOR (agriculture) 921.685-046
FRUIT-GRADER OPERATOR (agriculture; wholesale tr.) 529.665-010
fruit inspector (can. & preserv.; wholesale tr.) 529.387-018
Fruit Mixer (bakery products) 520.685-114
Fruit Packer, Face-And-Fill (agriculture; wholesale tr.) 920.687-134
Fruit Packer, Wrap-And-Place (agriculture; wholesale tr.) 920.687-134
fruit picker (agriculture) 403.687-018
FRUIT-PRESS OPERATOR (beverage; can. & preserv.) 521.685-146

Fruit Sorter

Fruit Sorter (agriculture; can. & preserv.; wholesale tr.) 529.687-186
Fruit Stuffer (sugar & conf.) 524.687-014
FRUIT WORKER (agriculture) term
Fudge-Candy Maker (sugar & conf.) 529.361-014
fuel assembler (chemical) 709.381-010
FUEL ATTENDANT (any industry) 953.362-010
fuel-cell assembler (rubber goods) 752.684-046
fuel-cell repairer (rubber goods) 759.384-010
FUEL-HOUSE ATTENDANT (saw. & plan.) 951.686-010
FUEL-INJECTION SERVICER (any industry) 625.281-022
FUEL-OIL CLERK (clerical) 222.387-018
Fuel-Oil-Delivery Driver (petrol. refin.; retail trade; wholesale tr.) 903.683-018
FUEL-SYSTEM-MAINTENANCE SUPERVISOR (any industry) 638.131-010
FUEL-SYSTEM-MAINTENANCE WORKER (any industry) 638.381-010
Fuel Tank Sealer And Tester (aircraft mfg.) 806.384-038
Full-Decator Operator (textile) 582.685-042
FULLER (textile) 586.682-010
FULLING-MACHINE OPERATOR (tex. prod., nec) 586.382-010
fulling-mill operator (textile) 586.682-010
Full-Roll Inspector (photofinishing) 976.687-014
FUMIGATOR (business ser.) 383.361-010
FUMIGATOR AND STERILIZER (furniture) 582.685-074
FUNCTIONAL TESTER, TYPEWRITERS (office machines) 706.382-010
FUND RAISER I (nonprofit org.) 293.157-010
FUND RAISER II (nonprofit org.) 293.357-014
funds transfer clerk (financial) 203.562-010
FUNERAL ATTENDANT (personal ser.) 359.677-014
funeral driver (personal ser.) 359.673-014
funeral-home attendant (personal ser.) 339.361-010
Funeral-Limousine Driver (personal ser.) 359.673-014
Fun-House Attendant (amuse. & rec.) 376.667-010
FUN-HOUSE OPERATOR (amuse. & rec.) 342.665-010
Funnel Coater (electron. comp.) 725.684-022
Funnel Setter (plastic-synth.) 557.685-026
fur beater (fur goods; laundry & rel.; retail trade; wholesale tr.) 369.685-014
FUR BLENDER (leather mfg.) 783.681-010
fur blower (hat & cap) 680.685-046
FUR BLOWER (retail trade) 369.685-010
FUR-BLOWER OPERATOR (hat & cap) 680.685-046
fur-blowing-machine attendant (hat & cap) 680.685-046
fur-blowing-machine operator (hat & cap) 680.685-046
FUR CLEANER (laundry & rel.) 362.684-014
FUR CLEANER, HAND (laundry & rel.) 362.684-018
FUR CLEANER, MACHINE (fur goods; laundry & rel.; retail trade; wholesale tr.) 369.685-014
Fur Clipper (leather mfg.) 589.686-022
FUR CUTTER (fur goods) 783.381-010
FUR-CUTTING-MACHINE OPERATOR (hat & cap) 585.685-046
FUR DESIGNER (fur goods) 142.081-014
FUR DRESSER (leather mfg.) 589.361-010
fur drummer (fur goods; laundry & rel.; retail trade; wholesale tr.) 369.685-014
fur dry-cleaner (fur goods; laundry & rel.; retail trade; wholesale tr.) 369.685-014
fur dry-cleaner (laundry & rel.) 362.684-014
fur dry-cleaner, hand (laundry & rel.) 362.684-018
fur dyer (leather mfg.) 783.681-010
FUR FARMER (agriculture) 410.161-014
fur feeder (hat & cap) 586.686-018
FUR FINISHER (fur goods) 783.381-014
Fur Finisher, Head (fur goods) 783.131-010
FUR-FLOOR WORKER (leather mfg.) 589.686-022
FUR GLAZER (fur goods) 369.684-010
FUR-GLAZING-AND-POLISHING-MACHINE OPERATOR (laundry & rel.) 369.685-022
fur glosser (fur goods) 369.684-010
fur grader (fur goods) 783.384-010
fur ironer (laundry & rel.) 369.685-022
FUR IRONER (laundry & rel.) 369.685-018
fur joiner (fur goods) 783.682-010
Fur Liner (fur goods) 783.381-014
FUR-MACHINE OPERATOR (fur goods) 783.682-010
FUR-MACHINE OPERATOR (garment) 786.682-122
fur matcher (fur goods) 783.384-010
fur mixer (hat & cap) 680.685-046
fur-mixer operator (hat & cap) 680.685-062
FURNACE-AND-WASH-EQUIPMENT OPERATOR (ordnance) 503.685-026
furnace attendant (glass mfg.) 572.382-010
FURNACE CHARGER (nonfer. metal; smelt. & refin.; steel & rel.) 512.684-014
furnace-charging-machine operator (steel & rel.) 512.683-010
FURNACE CLEANER (any industry) 891.687-014
furnace clerk (optical goods) 573.686-014
FURNACE-COMBUSTION ANALYST (glass mfg.) 572.360-010
Furnace Cooler (elec. equip.) 543.666-010
furnace feeder (heat treating) 504.685-018

FURNACE HELPER (chemical) 558.686-010
FURNACE HELPER (chemical) 553.687-014
FURNACE HELPER (heat treating) 504.686-014
FURNACE HELPER (nonfer. metal; smelt. & refin.) 512.666-010
FURNACE INSTALLER (utilities) 862.361-010
FURNACE-INSTALLER-AND-REPAIRER HELPER, HOT AIR (any industry) 869.687-030
FURNACE INSTALLER-AND-REPAIRER, HOT AIR (any industry) 869.281-010
Furnace Installer Helper (utilities) 862.684-022
Furnace Loader (elec. equip.) 543.666-010
furnace loader (heat treating) 504.685-018
Furnace Mason (construction) 861.381-026
FURNACE OPERATOR (chemical) 558.482-010
FURNACE OPERATOR (elec. equip.) 543.682-018
furnace operator (forging) 619.682-022
FURNACE OPERATOR (foundry; steel & rel.) 512.362-018
furnace operator (glass mfg.) 573.685-026
furnace operator (mine & quarry) 543.682-014
FURNACE OPERATOR (nonfer. metal) 613.462-014
FURNACE OPERATOR (nonfer. metal; smelt. & refin.) 512.362-014
FURNACE OPERATOR (petrol. refin.) 542.562-010
FURNACE OPERATOR (smelt. & refin.) 513.462-010
Furnace Operator, Oil Or Gas (foundry) 512.362-018
Furnace Packer (elec. equip.) 543.666-010
furnace repairer helper (any industry) 869.687-030
furnace-room supervisor (paint & varnish) 559.132-110
FURNACE-STOCK INSPECTOR (elec. equip.) 559.364-010
furnace tender (construction) 869.685-010
furnace tender (forging) 619.682-022
FURNACE TENDER (foundry; nonfer. metal) 512.685-010
furnace tender (foundry) 512.662-010
furnace tender (paint & varnish) 572.685-010
Furnace Unloader (elec. equip.) 543.666-010
furnace worker (any industry) 869.281-010
FURNACE WORKER (elec. equip.) 543.666-010
FUR NAILER (fur goods) 783.684-014
furnishings conservator (museums) 763.380-010
FURNITURE ASSEMBLER (furniture) 763.684-038
FURNITURE ASSEMBLER-AND-INSTALLER (retail trade) 739.684-082
furniture cleaner (furniture) 709.687-014
FURNITURE CLEANER (laundry & rel.) 362.684-022
FURNITURE DESIGNER (furniture) 142.061-022
FURNITURE FINISHER (woodworking) 763.381-010
FURNITURE-FINISHER APPRENTICE (woodworking) 763.381-014
furniture mover (motor trans.) 905.687-014
furniture-mover driver (motor trans.) 905.663-018
Furniture Packer (retail trade) 920.587-018
furniture refinisher (woodworking) 763.381-010
FURNITURE-RENTAL CONSULTANT (retail trade) 295.357-018
FURNITURE REPRODUCER (furniture) 149.281-010
FURNITURE RESTORER (museums) 763.380-010
furniture shampooer (laundry & rel.) 362.684-022
FURNITURE UPHOLSTERER (any industry) 780.381-018
FURNITURE-UPHOLSTERER APPRENTICE (any industry) 780.381-022
fur operator (fur goods) 783.682-010
FUR PLUCKER (leather mfg.) 585.681-014
Fur-Polishing-Machine Operator (laundry & rel.) 369.685-022
Fur Puller (leather mfg.) 589.686-022
fur repairer (fur goods) 783.261-010
FUR-REPAIR INSPECTOR (retail trade) 783.387-010
FURRIER (fur goods) 783.261-010
furrier (laundry & rel.) 362.684-014
fur scraper (leather mfg.) 585.681-010
fur sewer (fur goods) 783.682-010
fur sewer (fur goods) 783.381-014
FUR SORTER (fur goods) 783.384-010
FUR-STORAGE CLERK (retail trade) 369.367-010
Fur Stretcher (leather mfg.) 589.686-022
fur tailor (fur goods) 783.261-010
fur tailor (fur goods) 783.381-014
fur tinter (leather mfg.) 783.681-010
fur trapper (fishing & hunt.) 461.684-014
FUR TRIMMER (fur goods) 783.687-014
fur-trimming machine operator (hat & cap) 585.685-046
fur-vault attendant (retail trade) 369.367-010
fur weigher (hat & cap) 586.686-018
FUSE ASSEMBLER (ordnance) 737.684-022
FUSE-CUP EXPANDER (ordnance) 694.685-022
FUSE MAKER (chemical) 559.685-094
FUSING-FURNACE LOADER (optical goods) 573.686-014
Fusing-Line Inspector (optical goods) 716.687-018
FUSING-MACHINE FEEDER (garment) 583.686-014
FUSING-MACHINE TENDER (garment; knitting) 583.685-046
Fusion-Juncture Grinder (optical goods) 716.685-022

G

Gaffer (fishing & hunt.) 443.684-010
gaffer (glass mfg.) 772.381-022
Gaging-Machine Operator (ordnance) 737.685-010
Gag-Press Straightener (steel & rel.) 617.482-026
Gag Writer (profess. & kin.) 131.067-026
GALLEY STRIPPER (print. & pub.) 973.681-010
galvanizer (any industry) 503.685-030
Galvanizer, Zinc (galvanizing) 501.685-010
galvanizing dipper (galvanizing) 501.685-010
Galvanometer Assembler (elec. equip.) 729.384-010
gambling broker (amuse. & rec.) 249.587-010
GAMBLING DEALER (amuse. & rec.) 343.464-010
GAMBLING MONITOR (amuse. & rec.) 343.367-014
GAMBRELER (meat products) 525.687-030
GAMBRELER HELPER (meat products) 525.687-034
game and fish protector (government ser.) 379.167-010
GAME ATTENDANT (amuse. & rec.) 342.657-014
GAME-BIRD FARMER (agriculture) 412.161-010
GAME-FARM HELPER (agriculture) 412.684-010
GAMEKEEPER (agriculture) 169.171-010
game operator (amuse. & rec.) 342.657-014
Game Protector (government ser.) 379.167-010
game show host/hostess (radio-tv broad.) 159.147-018
game warden (government ser.) 379.167-010
GAMMA-FACILITIES OPERATOR (profess. & kin.) 015.362-014
Gang-Bore Operator (woodworking) 666.382-010
gang boss (petrol. refin.) 899.137-018
gang boss (water trans.) 911.137-018
gang-drill-press operator (machine shop) 606.380-010
Gang-Hemstitching-Machine Operator (tex. prod., nec) 787.685-018
gang leader (any industry)   see STRAW BOSS
gang-punch operator (boot & shoe) 690.685-114
gang pusher (petrol. refin.) 899.137-018
gang rider (any industry) 932.664-010
Gang-Ripsaw Operator (woodworking) 667.682-066
gang-saw operator (stonework) 670.362-010
GANG SAWYER (saw. & plan.) 667.682-030
GANG SAWYER, STONE (stonework) 670.362-010
gang supervisor, pipe lines (petrol. & gas) 862.131-022
Gang-Vibrator Operator (construction) 853.663-014
gang worker (petrol. & gas) 869.684-046
Gantry Crane Operator (any industry) 921.663-010
Garage-Door Hanger (construction) 860.381-022
garage mechanic (automotive ser.) 620.261-010
GARAGE SERVICER, INDUSTRIAL (any industry) 915.687-014
GARBAGE-COLLECTION SUPERVISOR (motor trans.) 909.137-014
GARBAGE COLLECTOR (motor trans.) 955.687-022
GARBAGE COLLECTOR DRIVER (motor trans.) 905.663-010
GARDE MANGER (hotel & rest.) 313.361-034
garde manger (water trans.) 315.381-014
gardener (any industry) 406.684-014
Gardener (domestic ser.) 301.687-018
gardener-florist (agriculture; museums) 406.684-018
GARDENER, SPECIAL EFFECTS AND INSTRUCTION MODELS (motion picture; museums) 406.381-010
garden farmer (agriculture) 402.161-010
Garden-Hose Tuber-Machine Operator (rubber goods) 690.662-014
garden worker (agriculture) 402.687-010
GARDEN WORKER (agriculture; museums) 406.684-018
GARLAND-MACHINE OPERATOR (fabrication, nec) 692.685-090
GARMENT-ALTERATION EXAMINER (retail trade) 789.687-078
garment examiner (laundry & rel.) 369.687-022
garment finisher (any industry) 782.684-058
GARMENT FITTER (retail trade) 785.361-014
GARMENT FOLDER (garment; knitting) 789.687-066
GARMENT INSPECTOR (any industry) 789.687-070
Garment Looper (knitting) 689.682-010
garment maker (garment)   see CLOTHING MAKER
garment marker (laundry & rel.) 369.687-026
Garment-Parts Cutter, Hand (garment) 781.684-074
Garment-Parts Cutter, Machine (garment) 781.684-014
Garment Ripper, Alterations (garment) 782.687-038
garment sewer, hand (any industry) 782.684-058
GARMENT SORTER (garment) 222.687-014
GARMENT STEAMER (knitting) 582.685-078
Garment-Tag Stringer (paper goods) 794.687-054
GARMENT TURNER (garment; knitting) 789.687-074
Garment Weigher (knitting) 222.387-074
GARNETTER (furniture; tex. prod., nec) 680.685-054
garnetter (textile) 680.685-050
Garnett Feeder (tex. prod., nec) 680.686-018
Garnett Fixer (tex. prod., nec) 689.260-010

garnetting-machine operator (textile) 680.685-050
Garnett-Machine-Operator Helper (tex. prod., nec) 586.686-022
GARNETT-MACHINE OPERATOR (textile) 680.685-050
GARNISHER (sugar & conf.) 524.687-014
gas analyst (petrol. refin.) 029.261-022
gas-and-oil checker (motor trans.) 915.587-010
GAS-AND-OIL SERVICER (motor trans.) 915.587-010
gas-anneal feeder (heat treating) 504.685-014
GAS-APPLIANCE SERVICER (any industry) 637.261-018
GAS-APPLIANCE-SERVICER HELPER (any industry) 637.684-010
gasateria attendant (automotive ser.) 915.477-010
GAS CHARGER (svc. ind. mach.) 827.485-010
GAS-CHECK-PAD MAKER (ordnance) 736.684-034
GAS-COMPRESSOR OPERATOR (any industry) 950.382-014
gas-cutting-machine operator (welding) 816.482-010
gas-cylinder inspector (chemical) 953.387-010
Gas-Delivery Driver (petrol. refin.; retail trade; wholesale tr.) 903.683-018
gas desulfurizer (steel & rel.) 541.362-010
GAS DISPATCHER (pipe lines; utilities) 953.167-010
GAS-DISTRIBUTION-AND-EMERGENCY CLERK (utilities) 249.367-042
gas-distribution supervisor (utilities) 862.137-018
gas-engine engineer (petrol. & gas) 950.382-022
GAS-ENGINE OPERATOR (any industry) 950.382-018
Gas-Engine Operator, Compressors (any industry) 950.382-018
Gas-Engine Operator, Generators (any industry) 950.382-018
GAS-ENGINE REPAIRER (any industry) 625.281-026
gas fitter (utilities) 953.364-010
gas-fitter helper (any industry) 637.684-010
Gas-Generator Operator (chemical) 559.382-018
Gas Inspector (mine & quarry) 168.267-074
GAS INSPECTOR (utilities) 168.264-018
Gas Inspector, Liquefied (government ser.) 168.264-018
Gasket Attacher (machinery mfg.) 795.687-014
GASKET INSPECTOR (nonmet. min.) 739.687-102
Gasket Molder (rubber goods) 556.685-066
Gasket Notcher (rubber goods) 690.680-010
GASKET SUPERVISOR (wood prod., nec) 569.130-010
GAS-LEAK INSPECTOR (pipe lines; utilities) 953.367-010
GAS-LEAK INSPECTOR HELPER (pipe lines; utilities) 953.667-010
GAS-LEAK TESTER (svc. ind. mach.) 827.584-014
gas-lift engineer (any industry) 950.382-014
GAS-MAIN FITTER (utilities) 862.361-014
GAS-MASK ASSEMBLER (protective dev.) 712.684-022
GAS-MASK INSPECTOR (protective dev.) 712.687-022
gas-meter adjuster (utilities) 710.281-022
GAS-METER CHECKER (utilities) 953.367-014
GAS-METER INSTALLER (utilities) 953.364-010
GAS-METER-INSTALLER HELPER (utilities) 953.687-010
GAS-METER MECHANIC I (utilities) 710.381-022
GAS-METER MECHANIC II (utilities) 710.684-026
GAS-METER PROVER (utilities) 710.281-022
Gas-Meter Reader (utilities) 209.567-010
gas-meter repairer (utilities) 710.684-026
GAS-METER TESTER (utilities) term
Gasoline-Dragline Operator (any industry) 850.683-018
Gasoline-Engine Assembler (engine-turbine) 806.481-014
Gasoline-Engine Inspector (engine-turbine) 806.261-010
gasoline finisher (petrol. refin.) 540.462-010
Gasoline-Locomotive-Crane Operator (any industry) 921.663-038
Gasoline-Power-Shovel Operator (any industry) 850.683-030
Gasoline-Tractor Operator (any industry) 929.683-014
Gasoline-Truck-Crane Operator (any industry) 921.663-062
Gasoline-Truck Operator (any industry) 921.683-050
gas-pit specialist (any industry) 638.381-010
GAS-PUMPING-STATION HELPER (utilities) 953.684-010
GAS-PUMPING-STATION OPERATOR (utilities) 953.382-010
GAS-PUMPING-STATION SUPERVISOR (utilities) 953.137-010
Gas-Refrigerator Servicer (any industry) 637.261-018
GAS-REGULATOR REPAIRER (petrol. refin.; pipe lines; utilities) 710.381-026
GAS-REGULATOR-REPAIRER HELPER (petrol. refin.; pipe lines; utilities) 710.384-010
Gas-Roller Operator (construction) 859.683-030
gas-scrubber operator (chemical) 551.362-010
GASSER (textile) 585.685-050
gas-station attendant (automotive ser.) 915.467-010
Gas-Stove Servicer (any industry) 637.261-018
Gas-Stove-Servicer Helper (any industry) 637.684-010
gas-substation operator (utilities) 953.382-010
gas tender (automotive ser.) 915.467-010
gas tender (steel & rel.) 519.683-014
gas tester (chemical) 549.364-010
GAS-TRANSFER OPERATOR (chemical) 914.585-010
GAS TREATER (any industry) 546.385-010
Gas-Turbine-Powerplant Mechanic (utilities) 631.261-014

Gas-Turbine-Powerplant-Mechanic Helper (utilities) 631.684-010
GAS USAGE METER CLERK (petrol. refin.; pipe lines; utilities) 216.685-010
GAS-WELDING-EQUIPMENT MECHANIC (any industry) 626.381-014
gas worker (chemical) 559.565-010
GATE AGENT (air trans.) 238.367-010
Gate Attendant (amuse. & rec.) 344.667-010
gate cutter (saw. & plan.) 667.482-014
GATE GUARD (any industry) 372.667-030
Gate Guard (r.r. trans.) 376.667-018
gatekeeper (any industry) 372.667-030
gate-mortiser operator (saw. & plan.) 667.482-014
Gate-Shear Operator I (any industry) 615.685-034
Gate-Shear Operator II (any industry) 615.682-018
gate tender (musical inst.) 690.686-042
gatherer (any industry) 787.682-078
GATHERER (glass mfg.) 575.684-026
Gathering-Machine Feeder (print. & pub.) 653.686-026
Gathering-Machine Setter (print. & pub.) 653.360-018
GAUGE-AND-WEIGH-MACHINE ADJUSTER (ordnance) 632.360-010
GAUGE-AND-WEIGH-MACHINE OPERATOR (ordnance) 737.685-010
gauge checker (machine shop) 601.281-018
Gauge Controller (clock & watch) 601.281-022
Gage Maker (machine shop) 601.281-026
GAUGE OPERATOR (fabrication, nec) 692.682-042
gauger (any industry) 609.684-010
GAUGER (beverage) 529.387-022
gauger (beverage) 529.587-010
GAUGER (clock & watch) 715.687-034
gauger (fabrication, nec) 590.685-022
GAUGER (petrol. & gas; petrol. refin.; pipe lines) 914.384-010
GAUGER (protective dev.) 712.687-018
GAUGER, CHIEF (petrol. & gas; petrol. refin.; pipe lines) 914.134-010
gauger, chief delivery (pipe lines) 914.132-022
Gauger, Delivery (pipe lines) 914.384-010
gauntlet pairer (glove & mit.) 784.687-034
gear-and-spline grinder (machine shop) 602.360-010
Gear Burnisher (machine shop) 602.482-010
Gearcase Assembler (engine-turbine) 706.481-010
Gear Cleaner (machine shop) 609.684-014
gear-coding machine operator (machine shop) 602.362-014
gear cutter (machine shop) 602.380-010
gear cutter (machine shop) 602.280-010
GEAR-CUTTING-MACHINE OPERATOR, PRODUCTION (machine shop) 602.685-010
GEAR-CUTTING-MACHINE SET-UP OPERATOR (machine shop) 602.380-010
GEAR-CUTTING-MACHINE SET-UP OPERATOR, TOOL (machine shop) 602.280-010
gear finisher (machine shop) 602.482-010
GEAR-GENERATOR SET-UP OPERATOR, SPIRAL BEVEL (machine shop) 602.382-014
GEAR-GENERATOR SET-UP OPERATOR, STRAIGHT BEVEL (machine shop) 602.382-018
gear-grinding-machine operator (machine shop) 602.382-034
GEAR HOBBER SET-UP OPERATOR (machine shop) 602.382-010
GEAR INSPECTOR (machine shop) 602.362-010
GEAR-LAPPING-MACHINE OPERATOR (machine shop) 602.482-010
gear-machine operator, general (machine shop) 602.380-010
GEAR-MILLING-MACHINE SET-UP OPERATOR (machine shop) 602.382-022
gear nicker (machine shop) 602.482-010
GEAR REPAIRER (water trans.) 623.381-010
Gear Roller (machine shop) 602.362-014
gear shaper (machine shop) 602.280-010
GEAR-SHAPER SET-UP OPERATOR (machine shop) 602.382-026
GEAR-SHAVER SET-UP OPERATOR (machine shop) 602.382-030
GEAR-SORTING-AND-INSPECTING MACHINE OPERATOR (machine shop) 602.362-014
Gear Straightener (auto. mfg.) 617.482-026
gear tester (auto. mfg.) 806.684-134
gear-tooth-grinding-machine operator (machine shop) 602.382-034
gear-tooth-lapping-machine operator (machine shop) 602.482-010
GELATIN-DYNAMITE-PACKING OPERATOR (chemical) 692.662-014
GELATIN MAKER, UTILITY (chemical) 529.382-022
Gelatin-Powder Mixer (beverage) 520.685-146
Gel-Coat Sprayer (ship-boat mfg.; toy-sport equip.) 741.684-026
GEM CUTTER (jewelry-silver.) 770.281-014
gem expert (jewelry-silver.) 199.281-010
GEMOLOGIST (jewelry-silver.) 199.281-010
GENEALOGIST (profess. & kin.) 052.067-018
General Agent (insurance) 250.257-010
GENERAL AGENT, OPERATIONS (air trans.; motor trans.; r.r. trans.) 184.167-042
General-Cargo Clerk (water trans.) 248.367-014
GENERAL CAR SUPERVISOR, YARD (r.r. trans.) 184.167-286

GENERAL CLAIMS AGENT (air trans.; motor trans.; r.r. trans.; water trans.) 186.117-030
General Extra (amuse. & rec.; motion picture; radio-tv broad.) 159.647-014
GENERAL-HANDLING SUPERVISOR (smelt. & refin.) 929.137-010
general helper (aircraft mfg.) 809.687-014
GENERAL HELPER (food prep., nec) 522.686-014
GENERAL HELPER (oils & grease) 529.687-094
GENERAL HELPER (sugar & conf.) 529.686-046
general-labor supervisor (any industry) 899.133-010
GENERAL-LEDGER BOOKKEEPER (clerical) 210.382-046
general lot attendant (automotive ser.) 915.667-014
general-maintenance helper (any industry) 899.684-022
General Manager, Broadcasting (radio-tv broad.) 184.117-062
GENERAL MANAGER, FARM (agriculture; wholesale tr.) 180.167-018
general manager, industrial organization (any industry) 189.117-022
general manager, land department (petrol. & gas) 186.117-046
GENERAL MANAGER, ROAD PRODUCTION (amuse. & rec.) 187.117-034
general matcher (textile) 582.687-022
general-office dispatcher (petrol. & gas; petrol. refin.; pipe lines) 914.167-010
GENERAL PRACTITIONER (medical ser.) 070.101-022
general production worker (can. & preserv.; food prep., nec) 529.686-070
General Scrap Worker (nonfer. metal) 519.686-010
general secretary, social welfare (profess. & kin.) 195.117-010
GENERAL SUPERINTENDENT, MILLING (grain-feed mills) 183.167-014
general superintendent, power sales and service (utilities) 163.167-022
GENERAL SUPERVISOR (any industry) 183.167-018
GENERAL SUPERVISOR (beverage) 183.167-022
general teller (financial) 211.362-018
general utility helper (sugar & conf.) 529.686-034
general utility machine operator (sugar & conf.) 529.382-014
general utility worker (utilities) 952.687-010
GENERAL WORKER, LITHOGRAPHIC (print. & pub.) 979.687-034
general worker (tex. prod., nec) 586.686-022
generating-substation-operator assistant (utilities) 952.367-014
generation-mechanic helper (utilities) 631.684-010
GENERATOR OPERATOR (utilities) term
generator operator, straight-bevel gear (machine shop) 602.382-018
generator-switchboard operator (utilities) 952.362-034
Generator Tender, Portable (construction) 869.665-010
GENETICIST (profess. & kin.) 041.061-050
GEODESIST (profess. & kin.) 024.061-014
GEODETIC COMPUTATOR (profess. & kin.) 018.167-014
Geoduck Diver (fishing & hunt.) 443.664-010
GEOGRAPHER (profess. & kin.) 029.067-010
GEOGRAPHER, PHYSICAL (profess. & kin.) 029.067-014
GEOLOGICAL AIDE (petrol. & gas) 024.267-010
Geological Engineer (profess. & kin.) 024.061-018
GEOLOGIST (profess. & kin.) 024.061-018
GEOLOGIST, PETROLEUM (petrol. & gas) 024.061-022
Geomagnetician (profess. & kin.) 024.061-030
Geomorphologist (profess. & kin.) 024.061-018
GEOPHYSICAL-LABORATORY CHIEF (profess. & kin.) 024.167-010
geophysical operator (petrol. & gas) 010.161-018
GEOPHYSICAL PROSPECTOR (petrol. & gas) 024.061-026
GEOPHYSICIST (profess. & kin.) 024.061-030
Geothermal-Powerplant Mechanic (utilities) 631.261-014
Geothermal-Powerplant-Mechanic Helper (utilities) 631.684-010
Geothermal-Powerplant Supervisor (utilities) 631.131-010
Geriatric Nurse Assistant (medical ser.) 355.674-014
Germ Drier (grain-feed mills) 523.685-058
GERMINATION WORKER (beverage) 522.585-014
GETTERER (light. fix.) 725.687-022
getterer (light. fix.) 509.685-026
GETTERING-FILAMENT-MACHINE OPERATOR (light. fix.) 509.685-026
getter operator (light. fix.) 509.685-026
Gherkin Pickler (can. & preserv.) 522.684-010
Giant-Tire Repairer (automotive ser.) 915.684-010
GIFT WRAPPER (retail trade) 299.364-014
gigger (textile) 585.685-054
GIG TENDER (textile) 585.685-054
GILDER (any industry) 749.381-010
gilder (pottery & porc.) 740.681-010
Gill-Box Fixer (textile) 689.260-010
GILL-BOX TENDER (textile) 680.685-058
Gill-Net Stringer (tex. prod., nec) 782.684-026
gill tender (textile) 680.685-058
Gimp-Buttonhole-Machine Operator (garment) 786.685-014
gimp tacker (furniture) 780.684-126
GIN CLERK (agriculture) 221.467-010
gin feeder (furniture) 680.685-078
Gin Inspector (beverage) 522.667-010
GINNER (agriculture) 429.685-010
ginner (oils & grease) 521.685-198
Gin-Pole Operator (construction) 921.663-030
Ginseng Farmer (agriculture) 404.161-010

GIRDLER (jewelry-silver.) 770.261-014
Gizzard-Skin Remover (meat products) 525.687-074
glacing-machine tender (textile) 585.685-078
Glaciologist (profess. & kin.) 024.061-030
glass artist (glass mfg.; glass products) 740.381-010
glass-bead maker (jewelry-silver.) 770.381-010
glass bender (cutlery-hrdwr.) 573.686-018
GLASS BENDER (fabrication, nec) 772.381-010
glass bender (glass mfg.) 575.685-054
glass blower (fabrication, nec) 772.381-010
GLASS BLOWER (glass mfg.) 772.381-022
glass blower (jewelry-silver.) 770.381-010
GLASS BLOWER, LABORATORY APPARATUS (glass products; inst. & app.) 772.281-010
glass blower, machine forming (glass mfg.) 575.382-014
GLASS-BLOWING-LATHE OPERATOR (glass products) 772.482-010
glass breaker (glass mfg.) 779.684-054
glass breaker (glass products) 779.687-010
glass buffer (glass mfg.) 775.684-038
GLASS-BULB-MACHINE ADJUSTER (glass mfg.) 575.360-010
GLASS-BULB-MACHINE FORMER, TUBULAR STOCK (glass mfg.) 575.382-018
GLASS-BULB SILVERER (glass products) 779.687-018
GLASS CALIBRATOR (glass products) 775.584-010
GLASS CHECKER (optical goods) 716.687-014
GLASS-CLEANING-MACHINE TENDER (glass products) 579.685-018
glass crusher (glass mfg.) 570.685-026
glass curvature gauger (cutlery-hrdwr.) 701.687-022
GLASS-CUT-OFF SUPERVISOR (glass mfg.) 677.131-010
GLASS CUT-OFF TENDER (glass mfg.) 677.685-030
GLASS CUTTER (any industry) 775.684-022
glass cutter, hand (glass mfg.) 779.684-054
GLASS CUTTER, HAND (optical goods) 716.681-014
GLASS-CUTTER HELPER (any industry) 775.687-018
GLASS CUTTER, OVAL OR CIRCULAR (glass mfg.) 779.684-022
GLASS-CUTTING-MACHINE FEEDER (glass products) 677.686-014
GLASS-CUTTING-MACHINE OPERATOR, AUTOMATIC (glass mfg.) 677.562-010
glass-cylinder flanger (inst. & app.) 712.684-018
GLASS DECORATOR (glass mfg.; glass products) 775.381-014
Glass Deposition Tender (electron. comp.) 590.685-086
GLASS DRILLER (glass mfg.) 775.687-014
Glass Enamel Mixer (paint & varnish) 550.685-078
Glass Etcher (glass mfg.; glass products) 775.381-014
glass etcher (optical goods) 716.681-022
glass-etcher helper (glass products) 779.687-038
GLASS FINISHER (glass products) 775.684-026
GLASS-FURNACE TENDER (paint & varnish) 572.685-010
glass grinder (cutlery-hrdwr.) 673.685-066
GLASS GRINDER (glass mfg.) 775.684-034
GLASS GRINDER (glass products) 775.684-030
GLASS GRINDER, LABORATORY APPARATUS (glass products; inst. & app.) 775.382-010
Glassine-Machine Tender (any industry) 920.685-078
glass inserter (woodworking) 865.684-014
GLASS INSPECTOR (any industry) 579.687-022
glass inspector (glass products) 779.687-022
GLASS INSTALLER (woodworking) 865.684-014
GLASS INSTALLER (automotive ser.) 865.684-010
GLASS-LATHE OPERATOR (electron. comp.) 674.382-010
GLASS-LINED TANK REPAIRER (beverage) 779.684-026
Glass-Loading-Equipment Tender (glass mfg.) 677.665-010
glass marker (cutlery-hrdwr.) 775.684-046
Glass-Mold Repairer (glass mfg.) 519.684-018
Glass-Novelty Maker (glass products) 770.381-010
GLASS POLISHER (glass mfg.) 775.684-038
glass-products inspector (glass mfg.) 579.687-030
glass pulverizer equipment operator (glass mfg.) 570.685-026
GLASS-RIBBON-MACHINE OPERATOR (glass mfg.) 575.362-014
GLASS-RIBBON-MACHINE-OPERATOR ASSISTANT (glass mfg.) 575.365-010
GLASS-ROLLING-MACHINE OPERATOR (glass mfg.) 575.382-022
glass sagger (glass mfg.) 575.685-054
GLASS SANDER, BELT (glass products) 775.684-042
Glass Scullion (water trans.) 318.687-014
glass setter (construction) 865.381-010
glass setter (cutlery-hrdwr.) 701.684-018
glass setter (woodworking) 865.684-014
glass smoother (glass mfg.) 775.684-038
glass technician (glass products) 006.261-010
glass technologist (glass mfg.) 772.687-010
glass technologist (glass products; inst. & app.) 772.281-010
glass technologist (glass products) 006.261-010
GLASS TINTER (glass products) 840.684-010
glass-tube bender (fabrication, nec) 772.381-010

GLASS-UNLOADING-EQUIPMENT TENDER (glass mfg.) 677.665-010
GLASS-VIAL-BENDING-CONVEYOR FEEDER (cutlery-hrdwr.) 573.686-018
glassware engraver (glass products) 775.381-010
glassware finisher (glass mfg.) 772.381-018
Glassware-Maker Demonstrator (retail trade) 297.354-010
Glass Washer And Carrier (hotel & rest.) 311.677-018
Glass Washer, Laboratory (any industry) 381.687-022
GLASS-WOOL-BLANKET-MACHINE FEEDER (glass products) 579.685-022
glassworker (construction) 865.381-010
GLASS-WORKER, PRESSED OR BLOWN (glass mfg.) 772.687-010
GLAZE HANDLER (brick & tile) 571.685-014
GLAZE MAKER (brick & tile; pottery & porc.) 570.685-098
glazer (sugar & conf.) 524.382-010
glazer (textile) 583.685-126
Glaze Sprayer (auto. mfg.) 741.684-026
GLAZE SUPERVISOR (brick & tile) 574.130-010
GLAZE SUPERVISOR (pottery & porc.) 574.132-010
Glaze Wiper (furniture) 742.687-010
glazier (automotive ser.) 865.684-010
GLAZIER (construction) 865.381-010
GLAZIER (inst. & app.) 712.684-026
GLAZIER APPRENTICE (construction) 865.381-014
glazier artist (glass products) 779.381-010
Glazier Helper (construction) 869.664-014
GLAZIER, METAL FURNITURE (furniture) 865.684-018
glazier, plate glass (construction) 865.381-010
GLAZIER, STAINED GLASS (glass products) 779.381-010
Glazier, Structural Glass (construction) 865.381-010
GLAZIER SUPERVISOR (construction) 865.131-010
GLAZING-MACHINE OPERATOR (glass mfg.) 573.685-018
Glazing-Machine Operator (leather mfg.) 583.685-094
glazing-machine operator (textile) 583.685-126
GLAZING OPERATOR, BLACK POWDER (chemical) 550.686-022
gleason-gear generator (machine shop) 602.382-014
GLOBE MOUNTER (print. & pub.) 795.684-018
glosser (sugar & conf.) 524.382-010
Glost-Kiln Drawer (pottery & porc.) 573.667-010
Glost-Kiln Placer (pottery & porc.) 573.686-026
Glost-Tile Burner (brick & tile) 573.382-018
glost-tile shader (brick & tile) 574.367-010
glost tile sorter (brick & tile) 573.687-038
GLOVE CLEANER, HAND (laundry & rel.) 362.687-010
Glove Cutter (glove & mit.; leather prod.) 781.687-030
glove finisher (glove & mit.; laundry & rel.) 363.687-010
GLOVE FORMER (glove & mit.; laundry & rel.) 363.687-010
GLOVE PAIRER (glove & mit.) 784.687-034
Glove-Parts Cutter (glove & mit.) 699.682-022
GLOVE-PARTS INSPECTOR (glove & mit.) 781.687-034
glove presser (glove & mit.; laundry & rel.) 363.687-010
GLOVE PRINTER (glove & mit.) 652.685-034
GLOVE SEWER (glove & mit.) 784.682-010
Glove Tagger (glove & mit.) 652.685-094
GLOVE TURNER (glove & mit.) 784.687-038
Glove Turner-And-Former (glove & mit.) 784.687-038
glove turner and former (glove & mit.; laundry & rel.) 363.687-010
GLOVE TURNER AND FORMER, AUTOMATIC (glove & mit.) 583.686-018
GLUCOSE-AND-SYRUP WEIGHER (sugar & conf.) 520.686-026
glue-bone crusher (chemical) 555.685-014
glue-bone drier (chemical) 553.685-022
glue-drier operator (chemical) 553.685-118
GLUED WOOD TESTER (woodworking) 762.384-010
Glue-Jointer Feeder (woodworking) 669.686-030
Glue-Jointer Operator (woodworking) 665.682-042
glue-machine feeder (leather prod.) 690.686-022
GLUE-MACHINE OPERATOR (pen & pencil) 692.685-094
GLUE MAKER, BONE (chemical) 559.382-022
GLUE-MILL OPERATOR (chemical) 559.685-098
GLUE MIXER (any industry) 550.685-062
glue mixer (chemical) 550.564-010
glue-mixer operator (wood prod., nec) 560.465-010
glue-plant operator (wood prod., nec) 560.465-010
GLUER (any industry) 795.687-014
gluer (boot & shoe) 788.687-030
gluer (print. & pub.) 795.684-022
GLUER (woodworking) 762.687-034
GLUER AND SLICER, HAND (paper goods) 794.687-030
GLUER-AND-WEDGER (woodworking) 762.687-038
GLUER, WET SUIT (plastic prod.) 795.687-018
GLUE-SIZE-MACHINE OPERATOR (furniture) 562.685-010
Glue Spreader (furniture) 795.687-014
glue spreader helper (millwork-plywood) 762.687-026
glue-spreader operator (millwork-plywood; wood prod., nec) 569.685-042
GLUE SPREADER, VENEER (millwork-plywood; wood prod., nec) 569.685-042
GLUE-SPREADING-MACHINE OPERATOR (leather prod.) 584.665-014

Gluing-Machine Adjuster (paper goods) 649.380-010
GLUING-MACHINE FEEDER (woodworking) 569.686-038
GLUING-MACHINE OFFBEARER (woodworking) 569.686-022
GLUING-MACHINE OPERATOR (rubber goods) 692.685-098
GLUING-MACHINE OPERATOR (woodworking) 569.685-046
GLUING-MACHINE OPERATOR, AUTOMATIC (print. & pub.) 641.682-014
GLUING-MACHINE OPERATOR, ELECTRONIC (woodworking) 569.685-050
GLUTEN-SETTLING TENDER (grain-feed mills) 521.685-150
Glycerin Operator (soap & rel.) 552.685-014
Glycol-Service Operator (plastic-synth.) 914.682-010
Goal Umpire (amuse. & rec.) 153.267-018
Goat Farmer (agriculture) 410.161-018
GOAT HERDER (agriculture) 410.687-014
GOAT-TRUCK DRIVER (agriculture) term
Goggles Assembler (rubber goods) 752.684-038
Gold-And-Silver Assayer (profess. & kin.) 022.281-010
gold bander, striper (pottery & porc.) 679.682-010
GOLDBEATER (metal prod., nec) 700.381-018
GOLD BURNISHER (pottery & porc.) 775.687-022
gold charmer (any industry) 749.381-010
GOLD CUTTER (metal prod., nec) 700.684-038
gold-leaf gilder (any industry) 749.381-010
gold-leaf printer (any industry) 652.682-030
gold marker (any industry) 652.682-030
GOLD-NIB GRINDER (pen & pencil) 705.682-010
Gold Plater (electron. comp.) 500.684-026
Gold Plater (electroplating) 500.380-018
GOLD RECLAIMER (metal prod., nec) 709.685-010
Goldsmith (jewelry-silver.) 700.281-010
gold stamper (any industry) 652.682-030
GOLF-BALL-COVER TREATER (toy-sport equip.) 559.685-102
Golf Ball Molder (toy-sport equip.) 556.685-066
GOLF-BALL TRIMMER (toy-sport equip.) 732.587-010
Golf-Ball Winder (toy-sport equip.) 692.685-246
golf caddie (amuse. & rec.) 341.677-010
golf-cart mechanic (amuse. & rec.; automotive ser.) 620.261-026
GOLF-CLUB ASSEMBLER (toy-sport equip.) 732.684-078
GOLF-CLUB FACER (toy-sport equip.) 761.684-010
Golf-Club Finisher (toy-sport equip.) 732.381-022
GOLF-CLUB HEAD FORMER (toy-sport equip.) 732.381-018
Golf-Club Maker (toy-sport equip.) 732.381-022
golf-club matcher (toy-sport equip.) 732.587-014
GOLF-CLUB REPAIRER (toy-sport equip.) 732.381-022
GOLF-CLUB WEIGHER (toy-sport equip.) 732.587-014
GOLF-CLUB WEIGHTER (toy-sport equip.) 732.687-026
golf-course patroller (amuse. & rec.) 379.667-010
GOLF-COURSE RANGER (amuse. & rec.) 379.667-010
Golf-Course Starter (amuse. & rec.) 341.367-010
GOLF-RANGE ATTENDANT (amuse. & rec.) 341.683-010
GOLF-SHOE-SPIKE ASSEMBLER (boot & shoe) 788.687-054
golf-stud riveter (boot & shoe) 788.687-054
GOODS LAYER (textile) 781.687-010
GOODWILL AMBASSADOR (business ser.) 293.357-018
Gore Inserter (boot & shoe) 690.682-082
Gore Stapler (boot & shoe) 690.685-162
goring cutter (boot & shoe) 788.687-042
governor assembler (elec. equip.) 609.682-022
Governor Assembler (engine-turbine) 706.481-010
GOVERNOR ASSEMBLER, HYDRAULIC (elec. equip.) 721.381-018
grade and center marker (toy-sport equip.) 732.381-014
GRADE CHECKER (construction) 850.467-010
GRADER (can. & preserv.) 529.687-098
Grader (construction) 869.687-026
grader (leather mfg.) 585.684-010
grader (leather mfg.) 589.387-010
GRADER (woodworking) 669.687-030
GRADER, DRESSED POULTRY (meat products) 529.687-102
grade recorder (education) 219.467-010
GRADER, GREEN MEAT (meat products) 529.687-106
GRADER MARKER (garment) 781.381-034
GRADER, MEAT (meat products) 525.387-010
grader operator (any industry) 850.683-010
Grader, Sausage And Wiener (meat products) 920.587-018
GRADER TENDER (agriculture) 521.685-154
Grade Tamper (construction) 869.687-026
GRADING CLERK (education) 219.467-010
grading-machine feeder (can. & preserv.) 521.685-318
GRADUATE ASSISTANT (education) 090.227-014
graduate tucker (any industry) 787.682-082
grain blender (grain-feed mills) 520.485-014
grain cleaner (grain-feed mills) 521.685-254
Grain-Cleaner-And-Transfer Operator (beverage) 521.362-014
Grain Distributor (grain-feed mills) 921.662-018
GRAIN DRIER (beverage) 523.685-086

GRAIN-DRIER OPERATOR (grain-feed mills) 523.685-090
grain-elevator agent (grain-feed mills; wholesale tr.) 162.167-010
GRAIN ELEVATOR CLERK (beverage; grain-feed mills) 222.567-010
Grain-Elevator-Motor Starter (grain-feed mills) 921.685-026
Grain-Elevator Operator (grain-feed mills) 921.662-018
Grainer (jewelry-silver.) 700.687-058
GRAINER, MACHINE (any industry) 652.686-014
grain farmer (agriculture) 401.161-010
Graining-Machine Operator (leather mfg.) 583.685-094
Graining Operator (chemical) 555.685-066
GRAINING-PRESS OPERATOR (chemical) 557.682-010
Grain Miller (beverage) 521.362-014
grain-miller helper (beverage) 521.687-082
GRAIN MIXER (grain-feed mills) 520.485-014
GRAIN PICKER (grain-feed mills) 529.687-110
GRAIN RECEIVER (grain-feed mills) 921.365-010
grain trader (financial; wholesale tr.) 162.157-010
Grain Unloader (grain-feed mills) 921.667-018
Grain Unloader, Machine (grain-feed mills) 921.685-038
GRAIN-WAFER-MACHINE OPERATOR (bakery products) 523.685-094
grain weigher (beverage; grain-feed mills) 222.567-010
Granite Carver (stonework) 771.281-014
granite cutter apprentice (stonework) 771.381-010
granite polisher apprentice (stonework)-673.382-022
Granite Polisher, Hand (stonework) 775.664-010
Granite Polisher, Machine (stonework) 673.382-018
granite sandblaster apprentice (stonework) 673.382-014
Granite Setter (construction) 861.381-038
GRANT COORDINATOR (profess. & kin.) 169.117-014
Granular Operator (chemical) 553.685-090
Granulated-Tobacco Screener (tobacco) 521.685-270
granulating blender (tobacco) 520.387-010
GRANULATING-MACHINE OPERATOR (tobacco) 521.685-158
granulator (pharmaceut.) 559.382-026
GRANULATOR-MACHINE OPERATOR (pharmaceut.) 559.382-026
granulator operator (chemical) 555.685-042
GRANULATOR OPERATOR (sugar & conf.) 523.685-098
granulator operator (tobacco) 521.685-158
GRANULATOR TENDER (steel & rel.) 519.665-010
granulizing-machine operator (food prep., nec) 521.685-078
grape crusher (beverage) 521.685-094
Grape Grower (agriculture) 403.161-014
graphic artist (profess. & kin.) 141.061-022
graphic arts technician (print. & pub.) 979.382-018
GRAPHIC DESIGNER (profess. & kin.) 141.061-018
Graphite-Disk Assembler (rubber goods) 752.684-038
graphite-mill operator (steel & rel.) 549.685-026
GRAPHITE PAN-DRIER TENDER (nonmet. min.) 549.685-014
GRAPHOLOGIST (profess. & kin.) 199.267-038
grapple operator (logging) 921.683-058
Grapple Operator Helper (logging) 921.687-022
Grapple-Yarder Operator (logging) 921.663-066
Grass Farmer (agriculture) 405.161-014
Grass-Farm Laborer (agriculture) 405.687-014
GRATED-CHEESE MAKER (dairy products) 521.685-162
grating-machine operator (dairy products) 521.685-162
gravedigger (real estate) 406.684-010
GRAVEL INSPECTOR (construction) 859.281-010
GRAVES REGISTRATION SPECIALIST (military ser.) 355.687-014
Gravity-Meter Observer (mine & quarry; petrol. & gas) 010.261-018
gravity-prospecting operator (petrol. & gas) 010.261-018
gravity-prospecting-operator helper (petrol. & gas) 939.663-010
Gravity Prospector (petrol. & gas) 024.061-026
GRAY-CLOTH TENDER, PRINTING (textile) 652.686-018
Gray Mixing Operator (tex. prod., nec) 680.850-010
gray tender (textile) 652.686-018
GREASE-AND-TALLOW PUMPER (oils & grease) 559.585-014
GREASE BUFFER (jewelry-silver.) 705.684-022
Grease-Machine Worker (smelt. & refin.) 519.565-014
GREASE MAKER (petrol. refin.) 549.682-010
GREASE MAKER, HEAD (petrol. refin.) 549.132-010
grease-press helper (oils & grease) 551.686-018
GREASER (agric. equip.) 624.684-010
greaser (any industry) 699.687-018
greaser (automotive ser.) 915.687-018
greaser (brick & tile) 575.665-014
Greaser (leather mfg.) 589.686-022
Greaser (metal prod., nec) 706.684-090
GREASER (ordnance) 736.687-010
greaser and oiler (any industry) 699.687-018
GREASE-REFINER OPERATOR (oils & grease) 551.685-086
grease remover (any industry) 503.685-030
GREASER OPERATOR (hat & cap) 582.685-082
Green-Chain Marker (saw. & plan.) 669.687-030
GREEN-CHAIN OFFBEARER (millwork-plywood) 663.686-018

Green-Chain Offbearer (saw. & plan.) 669.686-018
GREEN-COFFEE BLENDER (food prep., nec) 520.685-110
green-hide inspector (meat products) 525.687-042
Greenhouse Laborer (agriculture) 405.687-014
green house manager (agriculture) 405.131-010
Greenhouse Superintendent (agriculture) 405.131-010
Greenhouse Worker (agriculture) 405.684-014
GREEN INSPECTOR (elec. equip.) 726.367-010
Green-Lumber Grader (woodworking) 669.687-030
green-meat packer (meat products) 522.687-034
green-pipe inspector (brick & tile) 575.687-030
Green-Prize Packer (tobacco) 920.687-142
greenskeeper, head (any industry) 406.137-010
GREENSKEEPER I (any industry) 406.137-010
GREENSKEEPER II (any industry) 406.683-010
Greens Planter (motion picture) 406.381-010
GREENS TIER (wholesale tr.) 920.687-094
GREEN-TIRE INSPECTOR (rubber tire) 750.684-018
Greige-Goods Examiner (textile) 689.685-038
Greige-Goods Inspector (knitting) 789.687-070
GREIGE-GOODS MARKER (textile) 229.587-010
greige-goods worker (textile)   see GREIGE-ROOM WORKER
Greige Mender (knitting) 782.684-030
GREIGE-ROOM WORKER (textile) term
grey inspector (knitting) 684.684-010
Grid Caster (elec. equip.) 502.684-010
grid-casting-machine-operator helper (elec. equip.) 502.686-010
Grid Inspector (elec. equip.) 502.687-018
grid-pasting-machine operator (elec. equip.) 505.482-010
grinder (office machines) 690.385-010
GRINDER (plastic prod.; plastic-synth.) 555.685-026
grinder (pottery & porc.) 774.684-010
Grinder (recording) 559.686-010
GRINDER (rubber goods; rubber reclaim.) 555.685-030
grinder (ship-boat mfg.) 809.684-022
grinder-and-honer operator, automatic (cutlery-hrdwr.) 603.685-058
grinder and plater (print. & pub.) 500.381-010
Grinder, Belt (any industry) 705.684-026
Grinder, Brake Lining (nonmet. min.) 579.687-010
GRINDER, CARBON PLANT (smelt. & refin.) 544.565-010
GRINDER-CHIPPER I (any industry) 705.684-030
GRINDER-CHIPPER II (any industry) 809.684-026
grinder-dresser (any industry) 705.684-030
GRINDER, GEAR (machine shop) 602.382-034
GRINDER, HAND (button & notion) 734.687-054
grinder, hand (machine shop) 603.280-014
grinder, hand (machine shop) 603.280-022
grinder, hand (machine shop) 603.280-010
GRINDER, HAND (optical goods) 716.685-018
GRINDER, HARDBOARD (wood prod., nec) 569.682-010
GRINDER I (any industry) 705.684-026
GRINDER I (clock & watch) 603.482-030
Grinder II (any industry) 705.684-030
GRINDER II (clock & watch) 715.685-030
Grinder III (any industry) 701.381-018
Grinder IV (any industry) 809.684-026
GRINDER, LAP (clock & watch) 603.685-066
Grinder, Lead (auto. mfg.) 705.684-026
GRINDER MACHINE SETTER (machine shop) 603.380-010
GRINDER-MILL OPERATOR (smelt. & refin.) 519.485-010
grinder, needle tip (comm. equip.) 770.382-014
grinder operator (cement) 570.685-046
GRINDER OPERATOR (chemical) 555.685-034
GRINDER OPERATOR (grain-feed mills) 521.682-026
GRINDER OPERATOR (grain-feed mills) 521.685-166
grinder operator (machine shop) 603.280-038
grinder operator (paint & varnish)   see PAINT GRINDER
grinder operator (toy-sport equip.) 662.685-010
GRINDER OPERATOR, AUTOMATIC (cutlery-hrdwr.) 603.685-058
GRINDER OPERATOR, EXTERNAL, TOOL (machine shop) 603.280-010
GRINDER OPERATOR, SURFACE, TOOL (machine shop) 603.280-014
GRINDER OPERATOR, TOOL (machine shop) 603.280-018
grinder, outside diameter (clock & watch) 770.684-010
grinder, rough (any industry) 809.684-026
GRINDER SET-UP OPERATOR (machine shop) 603.382-
GRINDER SET-UP OPERATOR, CENTERLESS (machine shop) 603.382-014
Grinder Set-Up Operator, External (machine shop) 603.382-034
GRINDER SET-UP OPERATOR, GEAR, TOOL (machine shop) 602.360-010
Grinder Set-Up Operator, Internal (machine shop) 603.382-034
GRINDER SET-UP OPERATOR, INTERNAL (machine shop) 603.280-022
GRINDER SET-UP OPERATOR, JIG (machine shop) 603.280-026
Grinder Set-Up Operator, Surface (machine shop) 603.382-034
Grinder Set-Up Operator, Thread (machine shop) 603.382-034
GRINDER SET-UP OPERATOR, THREAD TOOL (machine shop) 603.260-010
GRINDER SET-UP OPERATOR, UNIVERSAL (machine shop) 603.280-030

grinder, watch parts (clock & watch) 603.482-030
Grinder, Wheel Or Disc (any industry) 705.684-026
grinding machine operator (electron. comp.) 673.382-026
grinding-machine operator (office machines) 690.385-010
GRINDING-MACHINE OPERATOR, AUTOMATIC (button & notion) 690.685-194
GRINDING-MACHINE OPERATOR, PORTABLE (r.r. trans.) 910.684-010
GRINDING MACHINE TENDER (machine shop) 603.685-062
grinding-mill operator (mine & quarry; smelt. & refin.) 939.362-014
GRINDING-MILL OPERATOR (mine & quarry; smelt. & refin.) 515.382-010
Grinding Operator (tex. prod., nec) 550.382-014
grinding operator (wood prod., nec) 662.685-026
Grinding-Room Inspector (rubber reclaim.) 559.132-058
Grinding-Room Supervisor (chemical) 559.132-122
GRINDING-WHEEL INSPECTOR (nonmet. min.) 776.487-010
GRIP (amuse. & rec.; radio-tv broad.) 962.684-014
GRIP (motion picture; radio-tv broad.) 962.687-022
GRIP ASSEMBLER (woodworking) 762.684-042
GRIP BOSS (motion picture) 962.137-010
grip checkerer, machine (ordnance) 665.685-034
gripper (toy-sport equip.) 732.684-082
Gripper Attacher (any industry) 699.685-018
GRIP WRAPPER (toy-sport equip.) 732.684-082
gristmiller (grain-feed mills) 521.682-026
Grit-Removal Operator (sanitary ser.) 955.362-010
Grit Station Attendant (sanitary ser.) 955.585-010
GRIZZLY WORKER (mine & quarry; smelt. & refin.) 933.687-010
Grocery Checker (retail trade) 211.462-014
Grocery Clerk (retail trade) 290.477-018
grocery packer (retail trade) 920.687-014
grommet-machine operator (any industry) 699.685-018
grommet maker (any industry) 699.685-018
groove-machine operator (glass mfg.; glass products) 673.682-026
GROOVER (any industry) 692.686-042
GROOVER (nonmet. min.) 673.685-062
Groover (optical goods) 713.684-018
GROOVER-AND-STRIPER OPERATOR (wood prod., nec) 669.685-102
GROOVER AND TURNER (boot & shoe) 690.685-198
groove turner (clock & watch) 715.685-014
GROOVING-LATHE TENDER (plastic prod.) 690.685-202
GROOVING-MACHINE OPERATOR (pen & pencil) 733.685-018
ground equipment mechanic (aircraft mfg.) 809.261-010
Ground Helper (tel. & tel.; utilities) 821.684-014
Ground Helper, Street Railway (r.r. trans.) 821.684-014
Grounding Engineer (utilities) 003.167-054
grounding-machine operator (paper & pulp; paper goods) 534.682-018
ground instructor, advanced (air trans.) 099.227-018
Ground Instructor, Advanced (education) 097.227-010
Ground Instructor, Basic (education) 097.227-010
Ground Instructor, Instrument (education) 097.227-010
GROUND LAYER (pottery & porc.) 574.684-010
GROUND MIXER (chemical) 550.685-066
Grounds Guard, Arboretum (any industry) 372.667-034
GROUNDSKEEPER, INDUSTRIAL-COMMERCIAL (any industry) 406.684-014
Groundskeeper, Parks And Grounds (government ser.) 406.687-010
Ground Wirer (construction) 869.664-014
ground-wood supervisor (paper & pulp) 530.132-022
group assembler (engine-turbine) 706.481-010
group burner, machine (elec. equip.) 727.662-010
Group-Contract Analyst (insurance) 169.267-034
grouper (elec. equip.) 729.687-026
GROUP LEADER (agriculture) 180.167-022
group leader (any industry)   see STRAW BOSS
GROUP LEADER (any industry) term
group leader (auto. mfg.) 806.367-010
group leader (social ser.) 195.227-010
GROUP LEADER, PRINTED CIRCUIT BOARD ASSEMBLY (electron. comp.) 726.361-014
GROUP LEADER, PRINTED CIRCUIT BOARD QUALITY CONTROL (electron. comp.) 726.361-018
group leader, river-and-harbor soundings (any industry) 911.667-018
GROUP LEADER, SEMICONDUCTOR PROCESSING (electron. comp.) 590.362-018
GROUP LEADER, SEMICONDUCTOR TESTING (electron. comp.) 726.362-010
group leader, wafer polishing (electron. comp.) 673.364-010
GROUP-SALES REPRESENTATIVE (amuse. & rec.) 259.357-010
group supervisor, yard (any industry) 899.133-010
GROUP WORKER (social ser.) 195.164-010
Grouter Helper (construction) 869.687-026
GROUT-MACHINE TENDER (smelt. & refin.) 519.685-014
Grout-Pump Operator (construction) 849.665-010
Grout Supervisor (construction) 869.131-014
grove superintendent (agriculture) 180.167-058

GROWTH-MEDIA MIXER, MUSHROOM (agriculture) 405.683-014
guard (any industry) 372.667-030
guard (business ser.) 372.667-038
guard (government ser.) 372.667-018
Guard, Captain (any industry) 372.167-014
GUARD, CHIEF (any industry) 372.167-014
Guard, Convoy (any industry) 372.667-034
Guard, Dance Hall (amuse. & rec.) 376.667-010
Guard, Deputy (government ser.) 372.667-018
GUARD, IMMIGRATION (government ser.) 372.567-014
Guard, Lieutenant (any industry) 372.167-014
Guard, Museum (museums) 372.667-034
guard, range (government ser.) 379.167-010
GUARD, SCHOOL-CROSSING (government ser.) 371.567-010
GUARD, SECURITY (any industry) 372.667-034
Guard, Sergeant (any industry) 372.167-014
Guest-History Clerk (hotel & rest.) 203.362-010
Guidance Counselor (education) 045.107-010
GUIDE (personal ser.) 353.367-010
GUIDE, ALPINE (personal ser.) 353.164-010
GUIDE-BASE WINDER, MACHINE (toy-sport equip.) 732.685-022
GUIDE, CHIEF AIRPORT (air trans.) 353.137-010
Guide, Cruise (personal ser.) 353.167-010
Guide, Delegate (personal ser.) 353.367-010
Guide, Domestic Tour (personal ser.) 353.167-010
guide escort (personal ser.) 359.367-010
GUIDE, ESTABLISHMENT (any industry) 353.367-014
guide, excursion (personal ser.) 353.167-010
Guide, Foreign Tour (personal ser.) 353.167-010
GUIDE, HUNTING AND FISHING (amuse. & rec.) 353.161-010
Guide-Installer, Type-Bar-And-Segment (office machines) 706.684-026
guide, itinerary (personal ser.) 353.167-010
GUIDE, PLANT (any industry) 353.367-018
GUIDER (fabrication, nec) 590.686-014
Guide-Rail Cleaner (textile) 699.687-014
GUIDE SETTER (steel & rel.) 613.361-010
GUIDE, SIGHTSEEING (amuse. & rec.; personal ser.) 353.363-010
guide, tour (any industry) 353.367-014
guide, tour (personal ser.) 353.167-010
GUIDE, TRAVEL (personal ser.) 353.167-010
guide, visitor (personal ser.) 353.367-010
guide winder (toy-sport equip.) 732.685-022
GUIDE WINDER (toy-sport equip.) 732.684-086
guillotine cutter (stonework) 677.685-046
Guillotine Operator (pen & pencil) 699.685-014
guillotine operator (tex. prod., nec; textile) 680.686-018
Guinea-Pig Breeder (agriculture) 410.161-010
Guitar Maker, Hand (musical inst.) 730.281-022
Guitar Repairer (any industry) 730.281-026
Gum Coater (sugar & conf.) 524.382-010
Gum Maker (sugar & conf.) 526.382-014
gummed-tape-press operator (paper goods) 640.685-050
gummer (boot & shoe) 788.687-030
Gum Mixer (textile) 550.585-018
GUM PULLER (sugar & conf.) 520.687-038
gum-rolling-machine tender (sugar & conf.) 520.682-022
GUM-SCORING-MACHINE OPERATOR (sugar & conf.) 520.682-022
Gum Sprayer (leather mfg.) 584.687-014
Guncotton Packer (chemical) 920.587-018
GUN EXAMINER (ordnance) 736.281-010
Gun Examiner And Repairer (ordnance) 736.281-010
GUNNER (grain-feed mills) 523.382-010
gun numberer (ordnance) 652.582-010
gun perforator (petrol. & gas) 931.382-010
GUN-PERFORATOR LOADER (petrol. & gas) 931.384-010
GUN-REPAIR CLERK (ordnance) 222.387-022
Gun-Sealing-Machine Operator (electron. comp.) 725.684-022
GUNSMITH (any industry) 632.281-010
GUNSMITH, BALLISTICS LABORATORY (ordnance) 609.260-010
gunstock repairer (ordnance) 761.381-038
Gunstock-Spray-Unit Adjuster (ordnance) 599.382-010
Gunstock-Spray-Unit Feeder (ordnance) 599.686-014
gun striper (any industry) 741.687-022
GUN SYNCHRONIZER (ordnance) 632.381-010
gusset folder (leather prod.) 690.685-178
Gusset Maker (paper goods) 794.684-018
gusset ripper (boot & shoe) 788.687-042
Gut Puller (meat products) 525.687-010
Gut Sorter (meat products) 525.687-010
gutter (meat products) 525.687-010
Gutter-Mouth Cutter (construction) 861.381-038
gut winder (protective dev.) 712.687-034
guyline operator (construction) 850.683-042
GYNECOLOGIST (medical ser.) 070.101-034
gypsum dry-wall systems installer (construction) 842.361-030

H

haberdasher (retail trade) 261.357-054
HACKER (brick & tile) 573.686-022
hackler (fabrication, nec) 739.684-086
HACKLER, DOLL WIGS (toy-sport equip.) 731.687-018
Hacksaw Inspector (cutlery-hrdwr.) 709.587-010
hack-saw operator (machine shop) 607.682-010
hair-and-scalp specialist (personal ser.) 339.371-014
Hair Baler (leather mfg.) 920.685-010
hair blender (fabrication, nec) 739.387-014
hair blender (fabrication, nec) 739.384-018
HAIR-BOILER OPERATOR (leather mfg.) 582.685-086
Hair-Brush-Boring-And-Filling-Machine Operator (fabrication, nec) 692.682-018
HAIR CLIPPER, POWER (leather mfg.) 789.684-022
Hair Colorist (personal ser.) 332.271-010
haircutter (personal ser.) 330.371-010
hairdresser (fabrication, nec; personal ser.) 332.361-010
hairdresser (personal ser.) 332.271-018
hair mixer (fabrication, nec) 739.387-014
Hair-Picking-Machine Operator (furniture; tex. prod., nec) 680.685-082
Hairpiece Stylist (fabrication, nec) 332.271-018
HAIR PREPARER (fabrication, nec) 739.384-018
hair-rooting-machine operator (fabrication, nec) 731.685-010
HAIR-SAMPLE MATCHER (fabrication, nec) 739.387-014
HAIR-SPINNING-MACHINE OPERATOR (leather mfg.) 689.686-030
HAIRSPRING ADJUSTER (clock & watch) 715.684-102
HAIRSPRING ASSEMBLER (clock & watch) 715.381-054
HAIRSPRING CUTTER I (clock & watch) 715.687-038
HAIRSPRING CUTTER II (clock & watch) 715.687-042
Hairspring Staker (clock & watch) 715.684-182
HAIRSPRING TRUER (clock & watch) 715.381-058
HAIRSPRING VIBRATOR (clock & watch) 715.381-062
Hairspring Winder (metal prod., nec) 616.685-070
HAIR STYLIST (personal ser.) 332.271-018
Hair Tinter (personal ser.) 332.271-010
HAIR WORKER (fabrication, nec) 739.684-086
Halal Butcher (meat products) 525.361-010
Half-Section Ironer (hat & cap) 583.685-098
Hall Cleaner (hotel & rest.) 381.687-014
hall cleaner (hotel & rest.) 323.687-018
Halver-Machine Operator (can. & preserv.) 521.685-018
Ham Boner (meat products) 525.684-010
Ham-Hock Mopper (meat products) 525.687-026
HAMMER ADJUSTER (clock & watch) 715.687-046
Hammer Driver (forging) 612.685-010
Hammerer, Tab (boot & shoe) 788.687-050
hammer heater (forging) 619.682-022
Hammer-Mill Operator (cement) 570.685-046
Hammer-Mill Operator (grain-feed mills) 521.685-122
HAMMER-MILL OPERATOR (nonmet. min.) 570.685-030
HAMMER-MILL OPERATOR (smelt. & refin.) 515.687-010
HAMMER OPERATOR (aircraft mfg.) 617.382-014
hammer repairer (forging) 626.261-010
Hammer-Shop Supervisor (forging) 612.131-010
Hammersmith (forging) 612.361-010
HAMMERSMITH (jewelry-silver.) 700.381-022
Hammersmith Helper (forging) 612.687-014
Ham Molder (meat products) 520.685-182
Hamper Maker (wood. container) 769.684-054
Hamper Maker, Machine (wood. container) 669.685-014
HAM-ROLLING-MACHINE OPERATOR (meat products) 529.685-138
Ham Sawyer (meat products) 525.684-018
hand assembler (boot & shoe) 788.684-010
Handbag Designer (leather prod.) 142.061-018
Handbag Finisher (leather prod.) 783.682-014
HANDBAG FRAMER (leather prod.) 739.684-090
Handbag-Parts Cutter (leather prod.) 699.682-022
Handbill Distributor (any industry) 230.687-010
hand blocker (glass mfg.; glass products) 673.685-026
hand-booked folder and stitcher (tex. prod., nec; textile) 589.687-014
hand carver (stonework) 771.281-014
hand clipper (any industry) 781.687-070
hand-cooper helper (wood. container) 764.687-050
hand decorator (brick & tile) 773.684-010
hand decorator (glass mfg.; glass products) 740.381-014
hand developer (photofinishing) 976.681-010
HANDER-IN (narrow fabrics; textile) 683.687-018
HAND FILER, BALANCE WHEEL (clock & watch) 715.684-106
hand finisher (leather mfg.) 584.687-010
Hand Finisher, Bowling Balls (toy-sport equip.) 690.685-038
hand folder (paper goods) 794.687-022
hand gluer (print. & pub.) 795.684-022

hand hardener (hat & cap) 784.684-034
Handhole-Machine Operator (wood. container) 665.682-030
HANDICAPPER, HARNESS RACING (amuse. & rec.) 219.267-010
hand inspector (textile) 689.387-010
Handkerchief Cutter (textile) 686.685-066
HANDKERCHIEF FOLDER (garment) 920.687-098
handkerchief ironer (laundry & rel.) 363.685-022
hand lacer (boot & shoe) 788.684-054
hand lacer (toy-sport equip.) 732.687-034
HANDLE-AND-VENT-MACHINE OPERATOR (furniture) 686.685-034
HANDLE ASSEMBLER (woodworking) 762.687-042
Handle Attacher (any industry) 690.685-014
Handle Attacher (leather prod.) 783.687-010
Handle-Bar Assembler (motor-bicycles) 806.684-094
Handle Bender (wood. container) 669.685-014
Handle Finisher (pottery & porc.) 774.684-018
Handle-Lathe Operator (woodworking) 664.382-010
HANDLE-MACHINE OPERATOR (paper goods) 649.685-050
Handle-Machine Operator (wood. container) 669.685-014
Handle Maker (leather prod.) 783.687-010
HANDLE MAKER (pottery & porc.) 575.684-030
handle maker (tex. prod., nec) 739.687-122
HANDLER (pottery & porc.) 774.684-022
Handle-Rounder Operator (woodworking) 665.682-010
Handle-Sander Operator (woodworking) 662.685-014
Handle Sewer (leather prod.) 783.682-014
handle sticker (pottery & porc.) 774.684-022
hand luggage repairer (any industry) 365.361-010
hand-miter operator (wood prod., nec) 739.684-066
Hand Molder, Meat (meat products) 520.685-174
hand packager (any industry) 920.587-018
hand painter (any industry) 740.684-026
hand pouncer (hat & cap) 784.687-018
hand roller (tobacco) 790.687-030
hands-and-dial inspector (clock & watch) 715.687-066
hand sander (fabrication, nec) 761.684-030
HANDS ASSEMBLER (clock & watch) 715.684-110
hand scraper (machine shop) 705.384-010
HAND SEWER, SHOES (boot & shoe) 788.684-054
hand shaker (tobacco) 521.687-110
hands hanger (tobacco) 529.686-010
hand shoe cutter (boot & shoe) 788.684-082
Hands Inspector (clock & watch) 715.384-022
hands parter (tex. prod., nec) 689.687-018
hand-spray operator (government ser.) 379.687-014
hands-size sorter (tobacco) 529.687-142
HAND STAMPER (any industry) 709.684-042
hand stitcher (any industry) 782.684-058
hand stitcher (toy-sport equip.) 732.684-034
hand tacker (any industry) 782.684-058
hand-tier (furniture) 780.684-106
hand trimmer (boot & shoe) 788.684-054
hand trimmer (hat & cap) 784.684-050
hand turner (fabrication, nec) 664.684-010
hand worker (paper goods) 794.687-054
Hand Worker (print. & pub.) 794.687-010
handwriting expert (government ser.) 199.267-022
hanger (meat products) 525.687-086
Hanger, Meat (meat products) 525.587-014
hanger-off (meat products) 525.687-030
HARBOR MASTER (government ser.) 375.167-026
Harbor-Police Captain (government ser.) 375.167-030
Harbor-Police Lieutenant (government ser.) 375.167-030
hardboard panel printer (furniture; wood prod., nec) 652.662-018
hard-candy batch-mixer (sugar & conf.) 520.685-046
Hard-Candy Maker (sugar & conf.) 529.361-014
hard-candy spinner (sugar & conf.) 520.682-030
HARDENER (clock & watch) 504.382-010
hardener (hat & cap) 586.685-026
HARDENER (hat & cap) 784.684-034
Hardener (oils & grease) 529.382-026
HARDENER HELPER (clock & watch) 504.686-018
hardening-machine operator (tex. prod., nec) 586.662-010
HARDENING-MACHINE OPERATOR (hat & cap) 586.685-026
hardening-machine-operator helper (tex. prod., nec) 586.686-014
HARDNESS INSPECTOR (heat treating) 504.387-010
HARDNESS TESTER (mine & quarry) 519.585-010
hardness tester (mine & quarry) 579.484-010
HARDWARE ASSEMBLER (furniture) 763.684-042
hardware assembler (leather prod.) 739.684-046
HARDWARE ASSEMBLER (wood. container) 762.687-046
HARDWARE ASSEMBLER (woodworking) 762.684-046
Hardware Installer (mfd. bldgs.; vehicles, nec) 869.684-026
Hardware Installer (struct. metal) 809.684-010
Hardware Press Operator (wood. container) 762.687-046

Hardwood-Floor Installer (construction) 860.381-022
Harmonic Tuner (musical inst.) 730.381-058
HARNESS-AND-BAG INSPECTOR (tex. prod., nec) 789.687-086
harness brusher (textile) 699.687-010
HARNESS BUILDER (textile) 683.380-010
HARNESS CLEANER (textile) 699.687-010
Harness Inspector (tex. prod., nec) 789.687-086
harness maker (elec. equip.; electron. comp.; office machines) 728.684-010
HARNESS MAKER (leather prod.; retail trade) 783.381-018
HARNESS PLACER (textile) 683.680-010
harness preparer (textile) 683.380-010
HARNESS PULLER (textile) 683.684-018
harness racer (amuse. & rec.) 153.244-014
Harness Repairer (leather prod.) 783.381-018
harness repairer (textile) 683.380-010
HARNESS RIGGER (tex. prod., nec) 789.687-082
harness tier (textile) 683.680-010
HARP-ACTION ASSEMBLER (musical inst.) 730.381-030
Harpist (amuse. & rec.) 152.041-010
HARP MAKER (musical inst.) 730.281-030
Harpooner (fishing & hunt.) 443.684-010
harpooner, fish (fishing & hunt.) 443.684-010
HARP REGULATOR (musical inst.) 730.381-026
Harp Repairer (any industry) 730.281-030
HARPSICHORD MAKER (musical inst.) 730.281-034
HARVEST CONTRACTOR (agriculture) 409.117-010
harvester (pharmaceut.) 559.687-034
HARVESTER OPERATOR (chemical) 930.683-022
harvesting manager (agriculture) 405.131-010
harvest supervisor (agriculture) 409.131-010
HARVEST WORKER, FIELD CROP (agriculture) 404.687-014
HARVEST WORKER, FRUIT (agriculture) 403.687-018
HARVEST WORKER, VEGETABLE (agriculture) 402.687-014
HASHER OPERATOR (meat products) 521.685-170
HASSOCK MAKER (tex. prod., nec) 780.687-018
Hat-And-Cap-Parts Cutter, Hand (hat & cap) 781.684-074
HAT-AND-CAP SEWER (hat & cap) 784.682-014
hat-band attacher (hat & cap) 784.684-078
hat-block bench hand (woodworking) 661.381-010
hat blocker (hat & cap) 580.684-010
HAT BLOCKER (laundry & rel.) 363.684-014
HAT-BLOCKING-MACHINE OPERATOR I (hat & cap) 580.685-026
HAT-BLOCKING-MACHINE OPERATOR II (hat & cap) 580.685-030
hat-blocking operator (hat & cap) 580.684-014
HAT-BLOCK MAKER (woodworking) 661.381-010
Hat-Body Inspector (hat & cap) 784.387-010
HAT-BODY SORTER (hat & cap) 784.587-010
HAT BRAIDER (hat & cap) 784.684-038
hat-brim-and-crown-laminating operator (hat & cap) 584.685-026
hat-brim curler (hat & cap) 784.684-014
hat-brim curler (hat & cap) 784.684-026
Hat Brusher, Machine (hat & cap) 587.685-026
Hat Buffer, Automatic (hat & cap) 585.685-014
Hat Checker (any industry) 358.677-010
hatchery helper (agriculture) 411.687-022
hatch supervisor (water trans.) 911.137-018
HATCH TENDER (water trans.) 911.667-014
HAT CONDITIONER (hat & cap) 784.687-086
Hat-Cone Inspector (hat & cap) 784.387-010
Hat Designer (hat & cap) 142.061-018
Hat-Designer Helper (hat & cap) 784.684-042
HAT FINISHER (hat & cap) 589.685-062
hat finisher (laundry & rel.) 363.684-014
HAT-FINISHING-MATERIALS PREPARER (hat & cap) 559.684-030
HAT-FORMING-MACHINE FEEDER (hat & cap) 586.686-018
HAT-FORMING-MACHINE OPERATOR (hat & cap) 586.685-030
Hat Lacer (hat & cap) 784.684-022
HAT-LINING BLOCKER (hat & cap) 583.685-050
HAT MAKER (hat & cap) 784.684-042
Hat Marker (hat & cap) 781.384-014
hat measurer (hat & cap) 784.387-010
Hat-Parts Cutter (leather prod.) 699.682-022
Hat-Parts Cutter, Machine (hat & cap) 781.684-014
Hat Sprayer (hat & cap) 741.684-026
HAT-STOCK-LAMINATING-MACHINE OPERATOR (hat & cap) 584.685-026
HATTER (hat & cap) term
HATTER (laundry & rel.) 369.384-010
hat trimmer (hat & cap) 784.684-022
HAT TRIMMER (laundry & rel.) 782.381-010
haulage boss (mine & quarry) 932.167-010
hauler (any industry) 919.664-010
hawker (retail trade) 291.457-018
Hay Farmer (agriculture) 404.161-010
HAY SORTER (toy-sport equip.) 732.686-010

HAZARDOUS-WASTE MANAGEMENT SPECIALIST (government ser.) 168.267-086
head (any industry)   see STRAW BOSS
Head Animal Trainer (amuse. & rec.) 159.224-010
HEAD-BANDER-AND-LINER OPERATOR (print. & pub.) 653.682-018
head-bone grinder (meat products) 521.687-130
head boner (meat products) 525.684-034
Head Cager (mine & quarry) 939.667-010
Head Charrer (wood. container) 764.684-014
HEAD COACH (amuse. & rec.) 153.117-010
head cook, school (hotel & rest.) 313.131-018
head counselor (profess. & kin.) 045.107-018
HEAD DOFFER (textile) 689.366-010
Header (agriculture; wholesale tr.) 920.687-134
header (nonfer. metal; smelt. & refin.) 514.584-010
Header (tex. prod., nec) 787.682-026
HEADER (water trans.) 911.137-018
HEADER (wood prod., nec) 665.682-014
HEADER (wood. container) 764.687-058
header boss (construction) 859.137-018
Header, Dock (water trans.) 911.137-018
Header, Ship (water trans.) 911.137-018
header-up (wood. container) 764.687-058
head facer (fabrication, nec) 754.684-018
HEAD-GAUGE-UNIT OPERATOR (ordnance) 619.685-054
heading-and-priming operator (ordnance) 694.685-042
heading-and-priming tool setter (ordnance) 616.360-030
Heading-Machine Operator (elec. equip.) 692.482-010
HEADING-MACHINE OPERATOR (pen & pencil) 669.685-062
HEADING MATCHER AND ASSEMBLER (wood. container) 764.687-062
heading pinner (wood. container) 764.687-062
HEADING REPAIRER (wood. container) 764.687-066
HEADING-SAW OPERATOR (saw. & plan.) 667.682-038
HEAD INSPECTOR (wood. container) 764.387-010
Head-Inspector-And-Center Marker (wood. container) 764.387-010
head kiln operator (grain-feed mills) 523.662-010
HEAD-MACHINE FEEDER (meat products) 525.686-018
Head of Stock (retail trade) 222.137-034
HEAD OPERATOR, SULFIDE (chemical) 559.132-026
head-out worker (tobacco) 920.687-110
head paper tester (paper & pulp) 539.367-010
Head-Piece Assembler (furniture) 706.684-082
head resident, dormitory (education) 045.107-038
Head Rigger (logging) 921.664-014
head rose grader (agriculture) 405.137-010
head ruler, linoprint ruling machine operator (paper goods; print. & pub.) 659.682-022
HEAD-SAW OPERATOR, INSULATION BOARD (wood prod., nec) 677.682-010
HEAD SAWYER (saw. & plan.) 667.662-010
HEAD SAWYER, AUTOMATIC (paper & pulp; saw. & plan.) 667.682-034
Head Scorer (amuse. & rec.) 153.387-014
head setter (wood. container) 764.687-058
head-stock operator (paper & pulp) 539.132-018
head switcher (r.r. trans.) 910.137-022
HEAD TRIMMER (meat products) 525.684-034
Head-Turning-Machine Operator (wood. container) 667.685-066
Head-Up Operator (wood. container) 669.682-014
Head-Up-Operator Helper (wood. container) 669.685-010
HEADWAITER/HEADWAITRESS (water trans.) 350.137-010
head well-puller (petrol. & gas) 939.131-018
HEALER (medical ser.) term
HEALTH-EQUIPMENT SERVICER (medical ser.) 359.363-010
HEALTH OFFICER, FIELD (government ser.) 168.167-018
HEALTH PHYSICIST (profess. & kin.) 015.021-010
health-physics technician (profess. & kin.) 199.167-010
health unit clerk (medical ser.) 245.362-014
HEARING-AID REPAIRER (inst. & app.) 719.381-014
HEARING AID SPECIALIST (retail trade) 276.354-010
hearing instrument specialist (retail trade) 276.354-010
HEARING OFFICER (government ser.) 119.107-010
Hearings Reporter (clerical) 202.362-010
hearing-test technician (profess. & kin.) 078.362-010
Hearse Driver (personal ser.) 359.673-014
heart specialist (medical ser.) 070.101-014
HEAT CURER (textile) 581.586-010
HEATER (forging) 619.682-022
heater, furnace (forging) 619.682-022
Heater Helper, Forge (forging) 619.686-034
HEATER HELPER (steel & rel.) 613.685-014
heater helper (steel & rel.) 542.665-010
HEATER I (steel & rel.) 613.362-010
HEATER II (steel & rel.) 542.362-010
Heater Operator (wood. container) 669.682-014
heater operator (construction) 853.683-014

Heater Operator Helper (wood. container) 669.685-010
HEATER-PLANER OPERATOR (construction) 853.683-014
heater tender (oils & grease) 523.685-034
HEATER TENDER (rubber goods; rubber reclaim.; rubber tire) 553.665-038
heater tender (rubber goods) 553.585-022
heater worker (construction) 869.685-010
HEATING-AND-AIR-CONDITIONING INSTALLER-SERVICER (construction) 637.261-014
HEATING-AND-AIR-CONDITIONING INSTALLER-SERVICER HELPER (construction) 637.664-010
heating-and-air-conditioning mechanic (construction) 637.261-014
heating-and-air-conditioning-mechanic helper (construction) 637.664-010
HEATING-AND-BLENDING SUPERVISOR (chemical) 559.132-030
heating-and-ventilating tender (any industry) 950.585-010
heating-element builder (rubber goods) 739.684-058
Heating-Element Repairer (house. appl.) 723.584-010
HEATING-ELEMENT WINDER (elec. equip.; house. appl.) 723.685-010
heating-equipment repairer (any industry) 805.361-010
heating-fixture tender (optical goods) 713.687-042
HEATING-PLANT SUPERINTENDENT (any industry) 959.131-010
Heating Technician (profess. & kin.) 007.181-010
heating worker (any industry) 869.281-010
HEAT READER (forging) 612.687-010
heat-seal operator (any industry) 690.685-154
HEAT-TRANSFER TECHNICIAN (profess. & kin.) 007.181-010
HEAT TREATER (electron. comp.) 504.686-022
heat treater (jewelry-silver.) 504.687-010
HEAT-TREATER APPRENTICE (heat treating) 504.382-018
heat treater, head (heat treating) 504.131-010
HEAT-TREATER HELPER (heat treating) 504.685-018
HEAT TREATER I (heat treating) 504.382-014
HEAT TREATER II (heat treating) 504.682-018
HEAT-TREATING BLUER (heat treating) 504.682-022
HEAT-TREAT INSPECTOR (heat treating) 504.281-010
heat-treat puller (heat treating) 504.685-018
HEAT-TREAT SUPERVISOR (heat treating) 504.131-010
heat treat worker (glass mfg.) 573.685-026
HEAT WELDER, PLASTICS (plastic prod.) 553.684-010
heavy-equipment mechanic (construction) 620.261-022
heavy-equipment operator (construction; mine & quarry) 859.683-010
heavy-equipment-operator apprentice (construction; mine & quarry) 859.683-014
HEAVY FORGER (forging) 612.361-010
HEAVY-FORGER HELPER (forging) 612.687-014
heavy-machinery assembler (engine-turbine; machinery mfg.) 638.261-014
HEAVY-MEDIA OPERATOR (mine & quarry) 541.685-010
HEDDLE CLEANER, MACHINE (textile) 689.685-070
HEDDLE-MACHINE OPERATOR (machinery mfg.) 616.685-026
HEDDLES TIER, JACQUARD LOOM (narrow fabrics; textile) 683.680-014
HEEL ATTACHER, WOOD (boot & shoe) 788.684-058
heel-boom operator (logging) 921.683-058
HEEL BREASTER, LEATHER (boot & shoe) 690.682-042
Heel Brusher (boot & shoe) 788.687-018
Heel Buffer (boot & shoe) 690.685-046
Heel Builder, Hand (boot & shoe) 788.687-030
HEEL BUILDER, MACHINE (boot & shoe) 690.685-206
Heel Burnisher (boot & shoe) 690.685-058
Heel Cementer (boot & shoe) 788.687-030
Heel Cementer, Machine (boot & shoe) 690.686-018
HEEL COMPRESSOR (boot & shoe) 690.685-210
Heel Coverer (boot & shoe) 788.687-030
Heel-Cover Softener (boot & shoe) 788.687-090
Heel-Cover Splitter (boot & shoe) 585.685-114
HEEL DIPPER (boot & shoe) 788.687-058
Heel Dipper, Insole (boot & shoe) 788.687-062
Heel-Edge Inker, Machine (boot & shoe) 690.685-234
Heel-Emery Buffer (boot & shoe) 690.685-046
Heeler, Machine (boot & shoe) 690.685-162
heel finisher (boot & shoe) 788.684-126
heel fitter, machine (boot & shoe) 690.682-046
heel former (boot & shoe) 690.685-206
HEEL GOUGER (boot & shoe) 690.685-214
Heel Grinder (wood prod., nec) 669.682-054
Heel Layer (boot & shoe) 690.685-074
Heel-Lift-Beam Cutter (boot & shoe) 699.682-022
Heel-Lift Gouger (boot & shoe) 690.685-214
Heel-Lining Paster (boot & shoe) 690.686-018
Heel Marker (boot & shoe) 788.584-014
heel molder (boot & shoe) 690.685-210
Heel Molder (rubber goods) 556.685-066
HEEL-NAILING-MACHINE OPERATOR (boot & shoe) 690.685-226
Heel-Nail Rasper (boot & shoe) 788.684-094
Heel Padder (boot & shoe) 788.687-030
HEEL PRICKER (boot & shoe) 690.685-218

Heel Reducer (boot & shoe) 690.685-166
Heel-Room Supervisor (boot & shoe) 788.131-010
Heel Sander, Rubber (boot & shoe) 690.685-046
HEEL SCORER (boot & shoe) 690.685-222
Heel-Seam Rubber (boot & shoe) 690.685-350
Heel-Seat Filler (boot & shoe) 690.685-162
HEEL-SEAT FITTER, HAND (boot & shoe) 788.684-062
HEEL-SEAT FITTER, MACHINE (boot & shoe) 690.682-046
Heel-Seat-Flap Stapler (boot & shoe) 690.685-162
HEEL-SEAT LASTER, MACHINE (boot & shoe) 690.685-230
Heel-Seat Pounder (boot & shoe) 690.685-314
Heel-Seat Sander (boot & shoe) 690.685-046
Heel-Seat Trimmer (boot & shoe) 690.685-434
Heel Slicker (boot & shoe) 690.685-046
HEEL SORTER (boot & shoe) 788.584-010
Heel Splitter (boot & shoe) 585.685-114
heel sprayer, first (boot & shoe) 788.687-034
HEEL SPRAYER, MACHINE (boot & shoe) 590.685-038
heel stainer (boot & shoe) 690.685-234
Heel-Top-Lift Splitter (boot & shoe) 585.685-114
Heel Trimmer I (boot & shoe) 690.685-434
Heel Trimmer II (boot & shoe) 690.682-086
HEEL-WASHER-STRINGING-MACHINE   OPERATOR   (rubber   goods)
    619.685-058
Heel Wheeler (boot & shoe) 690.685-058
hefter (leather mfg.) 589.387-010
helicopter dispatcher (air trans.) 912.167-010
Helicopter Mechanic (air trans.) 621.281-014
HELICOPTER PILOT (any industry) 196.263-038
Helix-Coil Winder (elec. equip.; electron. comp.) 724.684-026
Helmet Binder (hat & cap) 787.682-010
Helmet-Brim Coverer (hat & cap) 689.685-074
HELMET COVERER (hat & cap) 689.685-074
Helmet-Crown Coverer (hat & cap) 689.685-074
Helmet-Hat-Brim Cutter (hat & cap) 699.682-022
Helmet-Hat Puncher (hat & cap) 686.685-038
Helmet-Hat-Sweatband Puncher (hat & cap) 686.685-038
Helminthologist (profess. & kin.) 041.061-070
help desk representative (profess. & kin.) 032.262-010
help desk supervisor (profess. & kin.) 032.132-010
HELPER (any industry) master
Helper, Animal Laboratory (pharmaceut.) 410.674-010
helper, chicken farm (agriculture) 411.584-010
HELPER, ELECTRICAL (utilities) 821.667-010
HELPER, LIQUEFACTION-AND-REGASIFICATION (utilities) 953.584-010
HELPER, MANUFACTURING (aircraft mfg.) 809.687-014
HELPER, METAL BONDING (aircraft mfg.) 806.687-022
HELPER, METAL HANGING (mfd. bldgs.) 806.667-010
helper, patcher (steel & rel.) 861.687-014
HELPER, SHEAR OPERATOR (steel & rel.) 615.687-010
helper, steel fabrication (any industry) 619.686-022
Hem Inspector (tex. prod., nec) 789.687-114
Hem Marker (garment; retail trade; tex. prod., nec) 781.687-042
HEMMER (any industry) 787.682-026
hemmer (rubber goods) 690.686-026
HEMMER, AUTOMATIC (tex. prod., nec) 787.685-018
HEMMER, BLINDSTITCH (garment) 786.682-126
HEMMER, CHAINSTITCH (garment) 786.682-130
HEMMER, LOCKSTITCH (garment) 786.682-134
HEMMER, OVERLOCK (garment) 786.682-138
HEMMING-AND-TACKING-MACHINE OPERATOR (furniture) 787.685-022
hemodialysis technician (medical ser.) 078.362-014
hemotherapist (medical ser.) 078.261-042
Hemstitching-Machine Operator (tex. prod., nec) 787.682-058
HEMSTITCHING-MACHINE OPERATOR (garment) 786.682-142
HERBARIUM WORKER (profess. & kin.) 041.384-010
herder (agriculture) 410.687-022
Herpetologist (profess. & kin.) 041.061-090
Hide Buffer (boot & shoe) 690.685-046
hide cleaner (leather mfg.) 585.681-010
hide-cooking operator (chemical) 553.665-018
hide examiner (leather mfg.) 783.687-018
hide grader (meat products) 525.687-042
HIDE HANDLER (meat products; oils & grease) 525.687-038
HIDE INSPECTOR (leather mfg.) 783.687-018
HIDE INSPECTOR (meat products) 525.687-042
hide-measuring-machine operator (leather mfg.) 589.685-070
HIDE PULLER (meat products) 525.685-022
Hide Salter (meat products; oils & grease) 525.687-038
hide selector (meat products; oils & grease) 525.687-038
Hide Shaker (meat products; oils & grease) 525.687-038
hide sorter (leather mfg.) 589.387-010
HIDE SPLITTER (leather mfg.) 690.580-010
Hide Spreader (meat products) 525.687-038
HIDE STRETCHER, HAND (leather mfg.) 580.687-014

HIDE TRIMMER (meat products; oils & grease) 525.687-046
hide washer (meat products) 582.685-134
highballer (construction) 869.667-014
HIGH-DENSITY FINISHING OPERATOR (wood prod., nec) 539.562-010
high-density-press operator (paper & pulp) 535.685-010
High-Density-Talc-Coater Operator (wood prod., nec) 534.682-022
HIGH-ENERGY-FORMING WORKER (aircraft mfg.) 619.380-010
High-Heel Builder (boot & shoe) 690.685-206
High-Lead Yarder (logging) 921.663-066
High-Lighter (furniture) 742.684-010
High-Pressure Devulcanizer Operator (rubber reclaim.) 558.585-026
High-Pressure-Kettle Operator (chemical) 558.382-038
High-Raw-Sugar Boiler (sugar & conf.) 522.382-034
HIGH RIGGER (amuse. & rec.; radio-tv broad.) 962.664-010
High Scaler (construction) 859.261-010
high school teacher (education) 091.227-010
HIGHWAY-ADMINISTRATIVE ENGINEER (government ser.) 005.167-022
Highway Engineer (government ser.) 005.061-038
Highway Inspector (construction) 182.267-010
Highway-Landscape Architect (profess. & kin.) 001.061-018
HIGHWAY-MAINTENANCE SUPERVISOR (government ser.) 899.134-010
HIGHWAY-MAINTENANCE WORKER (government ser.) 899.684-014
HIGHWAY SUPERVISOR (construction) term
highway worker (government ser.) 899.684-014
high-wire artist (amuse. & rec.) 159.347-022
hiker (utilities) 821.361-026
hired worker (agriculture) 421.683-010
histologic technologist (medical ser.) 078.261-030
histologist (medical ser.) 041.061-054
HISTOPATHOLOGIST (medical ser.) 041.061-054
HISTORIAN (profess. & kin.) 052.067-022
HISTORIAN, DRAMATIC ARTS (profess. & kin.) 052.067-026
Historical Archeologist (profess. & kin.) 055.067-018
HISTORIC-SITE ADMINISTRATOR (museums) 102.167-014
HISTORY-CARD CLERK (utilities) 209.587-022
HISTOTECHNOLOGIST (medical ser.) 078.261-030
hitcher (any industry) 921.667-022
hobbing-machine operator (machine shop) 602.382-010
HOBBING-PRESS OPERATOR (any industry) 617.682-018
Hob Grinder (machine shop) 603.280-038
hob mill operator (machine shop) 602.685-010
Hod Carrier (construction) 869.687-026
Hoer (agriculture) 409.687-018
HOG-CONFINEMENT-SYSTEM MANAGER (agriculture) 410.161-022
Hog Grader (meat products) 525.387-010
Hog-Head Singer (meat products) 525.687-098
hog operator (rubber goods; rubber reclaim.) 555.685-030
Hog Ribber (meat products) 525.684-010
hog-room supervisor (rubber reclaim.) 559.132-058
Hog Sawyer (meat products) 525.684-018
hogshead builder (wood. container) 764.687-074
HOGSHEAD COOPER I (wood. container) 764.684-026
HOGSHEAD COOPER II (wood. container) 764.687-070
HOGSHEAD COOPER III (wood. container) 764.687-074
Hogshead Dumper (tobacco) 929.687-030
hogshead filler (tobacco) 920.687-142
hogshead hand (tobacco) 920.687-102
hogshead head-matcher (wood. container) 667.685-010
HOGSHEAD HOOPER (wood. container) 764.687-078
HOGSHEAD INSPECTOR (tobacco) 529.367-014
hogshead liner (tobacco) 920.687-110
HOGSHEAD MAT ASSEMBLER (wood. container) 764.687-082
HOGSHEAD MAT INSPECTOR (wood. container) 764.687-086
HOGSHEAD OPENER (tobacco) 920.687-102
hogshead packer (tobacco) 920.687-142
hogshead-press operator (tobacco) 920.685-062
hogshead roller (tobacco) 922.687-026
Hogshead-Stock Clerk (tobacco) 222.387-058
hogshead stripper (tobacco) 920.687-102
hogshead unpacker (tobacco) 920.687-102
hogshead wrecker (tobacco) 920.687-102
Hog Sticker (meat products) 525.684-050
Hog Stomach Preparer (meat products) 529.687-034
HOG TENDER (woodworking) 564.685-018
Hoist-Cylinder Loader (chemical) 549.587-010
HOISTING ENGINEER (any industry) 921.663-030
hoisting engineer, pile driving (construction) 859.682-018
hoisting-machine operator (any industry) 921.663-030
HOIST OPERATOR (mine & quarry) 921.663-026
HOIST OPERATOR (petrol. & gas) 932.363-010
hoist worker (agriculture) 929.687-018
Holder, Pile Driving (construction) 869.664-014
hole-digger operator (construction; utilities) 859.682-010
Hole-Digger-Truck Driver (construction; tel. & tel.; utilities) 905.663-014
Hole Puncher, Strap (boot & shoe) 690.685-114

HOLIDAY-DETECTOR OPERATOR (construction) 862.687-014
Hollow-Core Door-Frame Assembler (wood prod., nec) 762.687-022
HOLLOW-HANDLE-KNIFE ASSEMBLER (jewelry-silver.) 700.684-042
Hollow-Tile-Partition Erector (construction) 861.381-018
Holster Maker (leather prod.) 783.684-026
HOLTER SCANNING TECHNICIAN (medical ser.) 078.264-010
holter technician (medical ser.) 078.264-010
home agent (government ser.) 096.121-010
home and school visitor (profess. & kin.) 195.107-038
HOME ATTENDANT (personal ser.) 354.377-014
home-demonstration agent (government ser.) 096.121-010
Home Economics Specialist (government ser.) 096.127-014
HOME ECONOMIST (profess. & kin.) 096.121-014
Home Economist, Consumer Service (profess. & kin.) 096.121-014
home-extension agent (government ser.) 096.121-010
Home Health Aide (medical ser.) 355.674-014
home health aide (personal ser.) 354.377-014
Home Health Nurse, Licensed Practical (medical ser.) 079.374-014
HOMEMAKER (social ser.) 309.354-010
HOME-SERVICE DIRECTOR (profess. & kin.) 096.161-010
Homicide-Squad Captain (government ser.) 375.167-010
Homicide-Squad Lieutenant (government ser.) 375.167-010
Homicide-Squad Sergeant (government ser.) 375.167-010
Homogenizer Operator (dairy products) 529.382-018
hone operator (machine shop) 603.382-018
honer (machine shop) 603.482-034
HONEYCOMB DECAPPER (food prep., nec) 521.687-070
HONEY EXTRACTOR (food prep., nec) 521.685-174
HONEY GRADER-AND-BLENDER (food prep., nec) 520.361-010
honey liquefier (food prep., nec) 520.361-010
HONEY PROCESSOR (food prep., nec) 522.685-070
honey producer (agriculture) 413.161-010
honing-machine operator (machine shop) 603.382-018
HONING-MACHINE OPERATOR, PRODUCTION (machine shop) 603.482-034
honing-machine operator, semiautomatic (machine shop) 603.482-034
honing-machine operator, tool (machine shop) 603.382-022
HONING-MACHINE SET-UP OPERATOR (machine shop) 603.382-018
HONING-MACHINE SET-UP OPERATOR, TOOL (machine shop) 603.382-022
Honing-Machine Try-Out Setter (machine tools) 600.360-010
HOOD MAKER (tex. prod., nec) 804.481-010
HOOF AND SHOE INSPECTOR (amuse. & rec.) 153.287-010
Hook-And-Eye Attacher (garment) 782.684-058
Hook-And-Eye Attacher, Machine (garment) 699.685-018
hook-and-eye-sewing-machine operator (any industry) 787.685-010
hooker (any industry) 921.667-022
hooker (logging) 921.131-010
hooker (fishing & hunt.) 447.684-014
HOOKER INSPECTOR (textile) 689.685-078
HOOKER-LASTER (boot & shoe) 753.684-018
hooker operator (textile) 689.685-078
HOOKING-MACHINE OPERATOR (clock & watch) 605.685-018
HOOKING-MACHINE OPERATOR (textile) 580.685-034
hooking-machine operator (textile) 689.585-014
Hook Loader (toy-sport equip.) 599.686-014
HOOK PULLER (narrow fabrics) 683.687-022
hook tender (any industry) 921.260-010
HOOK TENDER (logging) 921.131-010
hook-up driver (motor trans.) 909.663-010
HOOP BENDER, TANK (wood. container) 619.682-026
hoop-bending-machine operator (wood. container) 619.682-026
HOOP COILER (wood. container) 617.686-010
Hoop-Coiling-Machine Operator (wood. container) 669.685-014
Hoop-Driving-Machine Operator (wood. container) 669.682-014
Hoop-Driving-Machine-Operator Helper (wood. container) 669.685-010
hooper (wood. container) 764.687-078
HOOP-FLARING-AND-COILING-MACHINE OPERATOR (wood. container) 619.682-034
Hoop-Flaring-Machine Operator (wood. container) 619.682-030
Hoop-Flaring-Machine-Operator Helper (wood. container) 619.686-014
HOOP-MAKER HELPER, MACHINE (wood. container) 619.686-014
HOOP MAKER, MACHINE (wood. container) 619.682-030
Hoop-Punch-And-Coiler Operator (wood. container) 619.682-030
Hoop-Punch-And-Coiler-Operator Helper (wood. container) 619.686-014
Hoop-Punch-Operator Helper (wood. container) 619.687-014
Hoop-Riveting-Machine Operator (wood. container) 619.682-030
Hoop-Riveting-Machine-Operator Helper (wood. container) 619.686-014
hoop-rolls operator (wood. container) 617.686-010
Hoosier Pole Hand (construction) 869.687-026
Hop Grower (agriculture) 404.161-010
HOPPER ATTENDANT (sugar & conf.) 521.685-182
HOPPER FEEDER (oils & grease) 551.686-018
HOPPER FEEDER (ordnance) 619.686-018
hopper feeder (tex. prod., nec; textile) 680.686-018

hopper feeder (tobacco) 529.686-038
hopper loader (grain-feed mills) 520.686-018
hopper operator (plastic-synth.) 556.585-010
hop separator (beverage) 521.685-178
Hops Farmworker (agriculture) 404.687-010
Hop Sorter (agriculture) 529.687-186
HOP STRAINER (beverage) 521.685-178
HOP WEIGHER (beverage) 520.687-042
horizontal-boring-drilling-and-milling-machine operator (machine shop) 606.280-014
horizontal-boring-mill operator (machine shop) 606.280-014
horizontal-drill operator (mine & quarry) 930.482-010
HORIZONTAL-EARTH-BORING-MACHINE OPERATOR (construction) 850.662-010
HORIZONTAL-EARTH-BORING-MACHINE-OPERATOR HELPER (construction) 850.684-014
Horizontal-Resaw Operator (saw. & plan.) 667.682-058
Horizontal-Stick-Turning-Machine Operator (tex. prod., nec) 689.685-146
Horse-And-Wagon Driver (any industry) 919.664-010
HORSE-RACE STARTER (amuse. & rec.) 153.267-010
HORSE-RACE TIMER (amuse. & rec.) 153.367-014
horseradish grinder (can. & preserv.) 529.685-142
HORSERADISH MAKER (can. & preserv.) 529.685-142
Horse Rancher (agriculture) 410.161-018
HORSESHOER (agriculture) 418.381-010
Horse Tender (any industry) 410.674-022
HORSE TRAINER (agriculture) 419.224-010
Horticultural Agent (government ser.) 096.127-010
HORTICULTURAL-SPECIALTY GROWER, FIELD (agriculture) 405.161-014
HORTICULTURAL-SPECIALTY GROWER, INSIDE (agriculture) 405.161-018
HORTICULTURAL THERAPIST (medical ser.) 076.124-018
HORTICULTURAL WORKER I (agriculture) 405.684-014
HORTICULTURAL WORKER II (agriculture) 405.687-014
HORTICULTURIST (profess. & kin.) 040.061-038
hose builder (rubber goods) 752.684-030
hose cementer (rubber goods) 690.685-134
HOSE-COUPLING JOINER (rubber goods) 759.687-014
HOSE CUTTER, HAND (rubber goods) 751.687-010
HOSE CUTTER, MACHINE (rubber goods) 751.686-010
hose finisher (rubber goods) 690.685-134
hose handler (railroad equip.; retail trade; wholesale tr.) 863.664-010
Hose Inspector (rubber goods) 759.684-074
HOSE INSPECTOR AND PATCHER (rubber goods) 759.364-010
HOSE MAKER (rubber goods) 752.684-030
Hose-Suspender Cutter (garment) 699.685-014
Hose Tender (any industry) 899.664-010
Hose Tester (rubber goods) 759.684-074
HOSE-TUBING BACKER (rubber goods) 559.686-018
Hose Turner (knitting) 789.687-182
HOSE WRAPPER (rubber goods) 759.684-038
Hosiery Looper (knitting) 689.682-010
HOSIERY MENDER (knitting) 782.684-030
Hospital Administrator (medical ser.) 187.117-010
HOSPITAL-ADMITTING CLERK (medical ser.) 205.362-018
Hospital Collection Clerk (medical ser.) 241.357-010
hospital-insurance clerk (medical ser.) 214.362-022
HOSPITAL-INSURANCE REPRESENTATIVE (insurance) 166.267-014
hospital librarian (library) 100.167-022
hospital-receiving clerk (medical ser.) 205.362-018
HOSPITAL-TELEVISION-RENTAL CLERK (business ser.) 295.467-018
HOST/HOSTESS (any industry) 352.667-010
HOST/HOSTESS, DANCE HALL (amuse. & rec.) 349.667-010
HOST/HOSTESS, GROUND (air trans.) 352.377-010
HOST/HOSTESS, HEAD (amuse. & rec.) 349.667-014
host/hostess, railway (r.r. trans.) 352.677-010
HOST/HOSTESS, RESTAURANT (hotel & rest.) 310.137-010
hostler (any industry) 410.131-010
hostler (any industry) 699.687-018
HOSTLER (motor trans.) 909.663-010
HOSTLER (r.r. trans.) 910.683-010
hotbed operator (steel & rel.) 613.685-034
hotbed transfer operator (steel & rel.) 613.685-034
Hot-Billet-Shear Operator (smelt. & refin.; steel & rel.) 615.685-034
hot blaster (steel & rel.) 512.382-014
HOT BOX OPERATOR (metal prod., nec) 709.685-014
Hot-Bread Baker (hotel & rest.) 313.381-010
HOT-CAR OPERATOR (steel & rel.) 519.663-014
HOT-CELL TECHNICIAN (profess. & kin.) 015.362-018
Hot-Die Picker (boot & shoe) 690.682-050
Hot-Die-Press Feeder (boot & shoe) 690.682-050
HOT-DIE-PRESS OPERATOR (boot & shoe) 690.682-050
HOTEL CLERK (hotel & rest.) 238.367-038
Hot-Food Packer (hotel & rest.) 319.484-010
hot-frame tender (textile) 580.685-066

Hot-Header Operator (forging) 612.462-010
Hot-Head-Machine Operator (laundry & rel.) 363.681-010
HOTHOUSE WORKER (chemical) 549.687-014
hot-melt-machine operator (paper & pulp; paper goods) 534.682-026
Hot-Metal Charger (steel & rel.) 512.683-010
Hot-Metal Crane Operator I (foundry; nonfer. metal; steel & rel.) 921.663-010
Hot-Metal-Crane Operator II (foundry; smelt. & refin.; steel & rel.) 921.663-042
Hot-Mill Operator (nonfer. metal) 613.462-018
Hot-Mill Supervisor (nonfer. metal) 619.132-014
Hot-Plate Plywood-Press Feeder (millwork-plywood) 569.686-026
Hot-Plate Plywood-Press Offbearer (millwork-plywood) 569.686-026
HOT-PLATE-PLYWOOD-PRESS OPERATOR (millwork-plywood) 569.685-054
hot-plate-press operator (millwork-plywood) 569.685-054
HOT-PRESS OPERATOR (nonmet. min.) 575.685-042
hot-press operator (paper & pulp) 535.685-010
hot press operator (woodworking) 569.685-050
Hot-Roll Inspector (steel & rel.) 619.381-010
hot roll laminator (electron. comp.) 554.685-034
HOT-ROOM ATTENDANT (personal ser.) 335.677-014
Hot-Sealing-Machine Operator (any industry) 920.685-074
hot stamper (any industry) 652.682-030
HOT-STONE SETTER (button & notion) 734.687-058
Hot-Strip-Mill Inspector (steel & rel.) 619.381-010
HOT-TOP LINER (steel & rel.) 709.684-046
HOT-TOP-LINER HELPER (steel & rel.) 709.687-018
HOT-WIRE GLASS-TUBE CUTTER (glass products) 772.684-014
HOT-WORT SETTLER (beverage) 521.685-186
HOUSE BUILDER (construction) 869.281-014
House Carpenter (construction) 860.381-022
HOUSECLEANER (hotel & rest.) 323.687-018
Housecleaner, Floor (hotel & rest.) 323.687-018
house detective (amuse. & rec.) 376.667-010
house detective (hotel & rest.) 376.367-018
House-Furnishings Cutter, Machine (tex. prod., nec) 781.684-014
HOUSEHOLD-APPLIANCE INSTALLER (any industry) 827.661-010
housekeeper (any industry) 381.687-014
HOUSEKEEPER (hotel & rest.; medical ser.; real estate) 321.137-010
housekeeper, administrative (any industry) 187.167-046
housekeeper, head (any industry) 187.167-046
HOUSEKEEPER, HOME (domestic ser.) 301.137-010
housekeeper, home (domestic ser.) 301.474-010
housekeeper, hospital (medical ser.) 323.687-010
house manager (any industry) 187.167-186
house model (garment; retail trade; wholesale tr.) 297.667-014
HOUSE MOVER (construction) 869.261-010
HOUSE-MOVER HELPER (construction) 869.687-034
HOUSE-MOVER SUPERVISOR (construction) 869.131-022
HOUSE OFFICER (hotel & rest.) 376.367-018
house parent (any industry) 359.677-010
HOUSE-PIPING INSPECTOR (utilities) 953.367-018
HOUSE REPAIRER (construction) 869.381-010
HOUSE SITTER (domestic ser.) 309.367-010
housesmith (construction) 801.361-014
housesmith (construction) 809.381-022
house steward/stewardess (hotel & rest.) 310.137-018
house supervisor (agriculture; wholesale tr.) 920.137-010
Housewares Demonstrator (retail trade; wholesale tr.) 297.354-010
House Worker (domestic ser.) 301.687-010
HOUSE WORKER, GENERAL (domestic ser.) 301.474-010
HOUSING-MANAGEMENT OFFICER (government ser.) 188.117-110
hub cutter (jewelry-silver.) 601.381-014
hub-cutter apprentice (jewelry-silver.) 601.381-022
huckster (retail trade) 291.457-018
HULL AND DECK REMOVER (ship-boat mfg.) 809.667-010
Hull Builder (ship-boat mfg.) 860.361-010
huller operator (can. & preserv.) 521.687-118
HULLER OPERATOR (grain-feed mills) 521.682-030
HULL INSPECTOR (ship-boat mfg.) 806.264-010
Hull Molder (ship-boat mfg.) 806.684-054
hull sorter (can. & preserv.) 521.687-086
Humane Officer (government ser.) 379.673-010
human factors specialist (profess. & kin.) 045.061-014
Human Projectile (amuse. & rec.) 159.347-018
HUMAN RESOURCE ADVISOR (profess. & kin.) 166.267-046
human resources clerk (clerical) 209.362-026
HUMIDIFIER ATTENDANT (textile; tobacco) 950.485-010
humidifier-maintenance worker (textile; tobacco) 950.485-010
HUMIDIFIER OPERATOR (wood prod., nec) 562.682-010
humid-system operator (textile; tobacco) 950.485-010
hummer operator (textile) 585.685-042
HUMORIST (profess. & kin.) 131.067-026
hunter, skin diver (fishing & hunt.) 461.664-010
hurl shaker (fabrication, nec) 692.686-062

Hybrid Tester (electron. comp.) 726.684-078
Hydrant-And-Valve Setter (construction) 869.664-014
HYDRATE-CONTROL TENDER (smelt. & refin.) 511.585-010
hydrate-thickener operator (smelt. & refin.) 511.562-010
hydraulic and mechanical assembler (machinery mfg.) 801.261-010
Hydraulic And Plumbing Development Mechanic (aircraft mfg.) 693.261-014
hydraulic and plumbing installer (aircraft mfg.) 806.381-066
Hydraulic-Barker Operator (paper & pulp; saw. & plan.) 669.485-010
HYDRAULIC-BILLET MAKER (pen & pencil) 575.685-046
HYDRAULIC BLOCKER (hat & cap) 580.685-038
HYDRAULIC-BOOM OPERATOR (smelt. & refin.) 921.683-046
Hydraulic-Brim-Flanging-Machine Operator (hat & cap) 580.685-038
hydraulic-bull-riveter operator (any industry) 800.662-010
HYDRAULIC-CHAIR ASSEMBLER (furniture) 706.684-058
hydraulic-corrugating-machine operator (nonfer. metal) 611.685-014
Hydraulic Dredge Operator (fishing & hunt.) 446.663-010
HYDRAULIC ENGINEER (profess. & kin.) 005.061-018
hydraulic-hammer operator (construction) 869.683-018
HYDRAULIC-JACK ADJUSTER (construction) 869.361-014
hydraulic-jack operator (construction; mine & quarry) 910.663-010
Hydraulic Oil-Tool Operator (petrol. & gas) 930.382-030
hydraulic operator (construction) 850.682-010
HYDRAULIC OPERATOR (nonfer. metal) 611.685-014
hydraulic-press operator (any industry) 617.260-010
hydraulic-press operator (chemical) 555.685-042
HYDRAULIC PRESS OPERATOR (construction) 616.662-010
hydraulic-press operator (hat & cap) 580.685-038
HYDRAULIC-PRESS OPERATOR (knitting) 583.685-054
HYDRAULIC-PRESS OPERATOR (millwork-plywood) 569.685-058
hydraulic-press operator (pen & pencil) 733.687-026
HYDRAULIC-PRESS OPERATOR (tex. prod., nec) 583.685-058
HYDRAULIC-PRESS OPERATOR (tobacco) 920.685-062
Hydraulic Press Operator, First Pressing (hat & cap) 580.685-038
HYDRAULIC-PRESS SERVICER (ordnance) 626.381-018
hydraulic-press tender (paper & pulp) 532.685-026
HYDRAULIC-PRESSURE-AUTO-FRETTAGE-MACHINE OPERATOR (ordnance) 694.682-014
HYDRAULIC-PRESSURE-AUTO-FRETTAGE-MACHINE-OPERATOR SUPERVISOR (ordnance) 619.130-010
Hydraulic-Punch-Press Operator (rubber goods) 690.685-290
HYDRAULIC REPAIRER (any industry) 638.281-034
HYDRAULIC-RUBBISH-COMPACTOR MECHANIC (sanitary ser.) 638.281-030
hydraulic-steam-press operator (rubber goods; rubber tire; toy-sport equip.) 556.685-066
HYDRAULIC-STRAINER OPERATOR (plastic-synth.) 551.582-010
Hydraulic Tester (air trans.) 621.281-014
Hydrochloric-Acid Operator (chemical) 551.382-010
hydrochloric-manufacturing supervisor (chemical) 558.134-022
HYDROELECTRIC-MACHINERY MECHANIC (utilities) 631.261-010
HYDROELECTRIC-MACHINERY-MECHANIC HELPER (utilities) 631.364-010
HYDROELECTRIC-PLANT MAINTAINER (utilities) 952.687-010
Hydroelectric-Powerplant Supervisor (utilities) 631.131-010
HYDROELECTRIC-STATION OPERATOR (utilities) 952.362-018
HYDROELECTRIC-STATION OPERATOR, CHIEF (utilities) 952.137-014
HYDROGENATION OPERATOR (oils & grease) 529.382-026
hydrogen braze-furnace operator (welding) 813.685-010
Hydrogen-Cell Tender (chemical) 558.382-026
Hydrogen Treater (petrol. refin.) 549.362-014
HYDROGRAPHER (waterworks) 025.264-010
hydrologic engineer (profess. & kin.) 005.061-018
HYDROLOGIST (profess. & kin.) 024.061-034
HYDROMETER CALIBRATOR (inst. & app.) 710.381-030
hydrometer finisher (inst. & app.) 710.381-030
HYDRO-PNEUMATIC TESTER (any industry) 862.687-018
Hydroponics Grower (agriculture) 405.161-014
Hydroponics Worker (agriculture) 405.684-014
Hydropulper (paper & pulp; wood prod., nec) 530.685-014
HYDRO-SPRAYER OPERATOR (agriculture) 408.662-010
Hydrostatic Tester (any industry) 862.687-018
hydrostatic tester (chemical) 953.387-010
Hypercil-Core-Transformer Assembler (elec. equip.) 820.381-014
hypertrichologist (personal ser.) 339.371-010
HYPNOTHERAPIST (profess. & kin.) 079.157-010
Hypnotist (amuse. & rec.) 159.647-010
hypnotist (profess. & kin.) 079.157-010
hypoid-gear generator (machine shop) 602.382-014

I

Ic Designer, Custom (profess. & kin.) 003.261-018
Ic Designer, Gate Arrays (profess. & kin.) 003.261-018
Ic Designer, Standard Cells (profess. & kin.) 003.261-018

Ice-Bag Assembler

Ice-Bag Assembler (rubber goods) 752.684-038
ICE-CREAM CHEF (hotel & rest.) 313.381-034
ice cream dispenser (hotel & rest.) 319.474-010
ice-cream freezer (dairy products) 529.482-010
ICE CREAM FREEZER ASSISTANT (dairy products) 529.685-146
Ice-Cream Vendor (retail trade) 291.457-018
Ice Crusher (any industry) 529.685-150
ICE CUTTER (food prep., nec) 529.685-150
ice-guard inspector (rubber goods) 729.387-010
ice-guard repairer (rubber goods) 759.684-026
Ice Guard, Skating Rink (amuse. & rec.) 376.667-010
ice-guard tester (rubber goods) 729.387-014
Ice Handler (chemical) 549.587-010
ICE MAKER (food prep., nec) 523.685-102
ICE MAKER, SKATING RINK (amuse. & rec.) 969.687-014
ice platform supervisor (food prep., nec) 299.137-022
Ice Puller (food prep., nec) 523.685-102
ICER (wholesale tr.) 922.687-046
icer, air conditioning (food prep., nec; meat products) 910.687-018
ICER, HAND (bakery products) 524.684-022
Icer Helper, Hand (bakery products) 526.686-010
ICER, MACHINE (bakery products) 524.685-034
ice seller (food prep., nec) 299.377-010
Ichthyologist (profess. & kin.) 041.061-090
ICICLE-MACHINE OPERATOR (dairy products) 920.482-010
Icing Coater (sugar & conf.) 524.684-010
icing-machine operator (bakery products) 524.685-034
Icing Maker (sugar & conf.) 526.382-014
ICING MIXER (bakery products) 520.685-114
icing spreader (bakery products) 524.684-022
IDENTIFICATION CLERK (government ser.) 209.362-022
IDENTIFICATION CLERK (clerical) 205.362-022
IDENTIFICATION OFFICER (government ser.) 377.264-010
IDENTIFIER, HORSE (amuse. & rec.) 153.387-010
IGNITER CAPPER (ordnance) 737.687-050
Ignition-And-Carburetor Mechanic (automotive ser.) 825.281-022
Ignition Specialist (air trans.) 621.281-014
ILLUMINATING ENGINEER (profess. & kin.) 003.061-046
Illuminator (profess. & kin.) 970.661-010
ILLUSTRATOR (profess. & kin.) 141.061-022
ILLUSTRATOR, MEDICAL AND SCIENTIFIC (profess. & kin.) 141.061-026
ILLUSTRATOR, SET (motion picture; radio-tv broad.) 141.061-030
image assembler (print. & pub.) 972.281-022
imager (electron. comp.) 976.684-030
imitation-marble mechanic (nonmet. min.) 556.484-010
imitator (amuse. & rec.) 159.047-018
IMMIGRATION INSPECTOR (government ser.) 168.167-022
Immigration Patrol Inspector (government ser.) 168.167-022
IMMUNOHEMATOLOGIST (medical ser.) 078.221-010
Impact Hammer Operator (forging) 610.362-010
IMPERSONATOR (amuse. & rec.) 159.047-018
IMPERSONATOR, CHARACTER (any industry) 299.647-010
Import Clerk (clerical) 214.467-010
Importer (retail trade; wholesale tr.) 185.157-018
IMPORT-EXPORT AGENT (any industry) 184.117-022
impregnating helper (elec. equip.; light. fix.) 599.685-050
IMPREGNATING-MACHINE OPERATOR (metal prod., nec) 590.362-014
impregnating-machine operator (plastic-synth.) 554.585-014
IMPREGNATING-TANK OPERATOR (any industry) 599.685-046
impregnating-tank operator (any industry) 599.685-030
Impregnation Inspector (elec. equip.) 726.367-010
IMPREGNATION OPERATOR (paper goods) 539.685-014
impregnator (any industry) 599.685-026
IMPREGNATOR (nonfer. metal; steel & rel.) 509.685-030
IMPREGNATOR (pen & pencil) 562.685-014
impregnator (plastic-synth.) 554.687-010
IMPREGNATOR AND DRIER (elec. equip.; electron. comp.) 599.682-014
IMPREGNATOR-AND-DRIER HELPER (elec. equip.; light. fix.) 599.685-050
Impregnator, Carbon Products (electron. comp.) 599.682-014
Impregnator, Electrolytic Capacitors (electron. comp.) 599.682-014
IMPREGNATOR OPERATOR (chemical) 559.685-106
impregnator operator (nonmet. min.) 579.665-010
Impresario (amuse. & rec.) 191.117-014
Impression Printer (print. & pub.) 979.381-034
Incendiaries Supervisor (chemical) 737.131-010
Incendiary-Powder Mixer (chemical) 737.687-090
INCINERATOR OPERATOR I (sanitary ser.) 955.685-010
INCINERATOR OPERATOR II (sanitary ser.) 955.362-014
INCINERATOR-PLANT-GENERAL SUPERVISOR (sanitary ser.) 184.167-046
INCINERATOR PLANT LABORER (sanitary ser.) 955.667-010
INCISING-MACHINE OPERATOR (wood prod., nec) 569.662-010
Inclined-Railway Operator (any industry) 921.663-030
income-tax-return preparer (business ser.) 219.362-070
INCOMING-FREIGHT CLERK (water trans.) 248.362-010

incubator helper (agriculture) 411.687-022
indexer (print. & pub.) 132.367-010
Indigo Mixer (textile) 550.684-014
Indigo-Vat Tender, Cloth (textile) 582.582-010
Indigo-Vat Tender, Warp (textile) 582.685-158
INDUCTION-COORDINATION POWER ENGINEER (utilities) 003.167-038
Induction-Furnace Operator (foundry) 512.362-018
INDUCTION-MACHINE OPERATOR (heat treating) 504.685-022
INDUCTION-MACHINE SETTER (heat treating) 504.380-014
Inductor Tester (electron. comp.) 726.684-078
industrial clerk (r.r. trans.) 910.667-018
INDUSTRIAL DESIGNER (profess. & kin.) 142.061-026
Industrial-Diamond Polisher (jewelry-silver.) 770.281-014
Industrial Economist (profess. & kin.) 050.067-010
Industrial Editor (print. & pub.) 132.037-022
INDUSTRIAL ENGINEER (profess. & kin.) 012.167-030
INDUSTRIAL ENGINEERING TECHNICIAN (profess. & kin.) 012.267-010
INDUSTRIAL-GAS FITTER (utilities) 862.381-014
INDUSTRIAL-GAS SERVICER (utilities) 637.261-022
INDUSTRIAL-GAS-SERVICER HELPER (utilities) 637.384-010
Industrial-Gas-Servicer Supervisor (utilities) 953.137-018
INDUSTRIAL-HEALTH ENGINEER (profess. & kin.) 012.167-034
industrial hygiene engineer (profess. & kin.) 012.167-034
INDUSTRIAL HYGIENIST (profess. & kin.) 079.161-010
Industrial-Illuminating Engineer (profess. & kin.) 003.061-046
Industrial-Locomotive Operator (any industry) 910.363-018
Industrial Occupational Analyst (profess. & kin.) 166.067-010
INDUSTRIAL-ORDER CLERK (clerical) 221.367-022
Industrial Relations Representative (government ser.) 166.167-034
Industrial Renderer (profess. & kin.) 970.281-014
industrial robot operator (aircraft mfg.) 606.382-026
INDUSTRIAL-SAFETY-AND-HEALTH TECHNICIAN (any industry) 168.161-014
industrial servicer (utilities) 862.381-014
Industrial Sociologist (profess. & kin.) 054.067-014
INDUSTRIAL THERAPIST (medical ser.) 076.167-010
INDUSTRIAL-TRUCK OPERATOR (any industry) 921.683-050
industrial x-ray operator (any industry) 199.361-010
Industrial-Yard Brake Coupler (any industry) 910.664-010
infant educator (social ser.) 195.227-018
INFANTRY INDIRECT FIRE CREWMEMBER (military ser.) 378.684-022
INFANTRY OPERATIONS SPECIALIST (military ser.) 378.367-022
INFANTRY UNIT LEADER (military ser.) 378.137-010
INFANTRY WEAPONS CREWMEMBER (military ser.) 378.684-026
Inflation Tester (rubber goods) 759.684-074
IN-FLIGHT REFUELING OPERATOR (military ser.) 912.662-010
IN-FLIGHT REFUELING SYSTEM REPAIRER (military ser.) 829.281-018
information and referral director (social ser.) 195.167-010
information broker (profess. & kin.) 109.067-010
information center specialist (profess. & kin.) 032.262-010
INFORMATION CLERK (clerical) 237.367-022
INFORMATION CLERK (motor trans.; r.r. trans.; water trans.) 237.367-018
INFORMATION CLERK, AUTOMOBILE CLUB (nonprofit org.) 237.267-010
information clerk, brokerage (financial) 237.367-046
INFORMATION CLERK-CASHIER (amuse. & rec.) 249.467-010
information manager (profess. & kin.) 109.067-010
Information Officer (government ser.) 188.117-106
information processing engineer (profess. & kin.) 033.167-010
information resources director (profess. & kin.) 109.067-010
information resources manager (profess. & kin.) 109.067-010
INFORMATION SCIENTIST (profess. & kin.) 109.067-010
information security (profess. & kin.) 033.162-010
Ingenue (amuse. & rec.) 150.047-010
ingot buggy operator (steel & rel.) 919.683-018
INGOT HEADER (nonfer. metal; smelt. & refin.) 514.584-010
Ingot Stripper I (steel & rel.) 921.663-018
Ingot Stripper II (steel & rel.) 921.663-042
Ingot Weigher (steel & rel.) 221.587-030
ingredient mixer (bakery products; dairy products) 529.684-014
INGREDIENT SCALER (bakery products; dairy products) 529.684-014
Ingredient-Scaler Helper (bakery products) 526.686-010
Initial Maker (garment) 782.684-018
injection-machine operator (meat products) 522.685-086
injection molder (plastic prod.) 556.382-014
injection molder, outer sole (boot & shoe) 690.685-406
INJECTION-MOLDING-MACHINE OFFBEARER (musical inst.) 690.686-042
INJECTION-MOLDING-MACHINE OFFBEARER (pen & pencil) 690.686-038
INJECTION-MOLDING-MACHINE OPERATOR (plastic prod.) 556.382-014
Injection-Molding-Machine Setter (plastic prod.) 556.380-010
INJECTION-MOLDING-MACHINE TENDER (plastic prod.; recording; rubber goods) 556.685-038
Injection-Wax Molder (foundry; jewelry-silver.) 549.685-038
INJECTOR ASSEMBLER (engine-turbine) 706.684-062
INKER (boot & shoe) 788.684-066
INKER (print. & pub.) 659.667-010

INKER AND OPAQUER (motion picture) 970.681-018
INKER, MACHINE (boot & shoe) 690.685-234
inking-machine tender (pen & pencil) 692.685-142
INK PRINTER (jewelry-silver.; leather prod.; plastic prod.) 652.685-038
INLAYER (print. & pub.) 977.684-014
Inlayer, Silver (plastic prod.) 692.685-070
INLETTER (ordnance) 669.682-050
inner-diameter grinder, tool (machine shop) 603.280-022
Inner-Layer Scrubber Tender (electron. comp.) 599.685-134
inner seamer (boot & shoe) 690.685-238
Inner-Tube Cutter (rubber tire) 690.685-446
INNER-TUBE INSERTER (rubber tire) 750.687-010
Inner-Tube Tester (rubber tire) 759.684-074
Inner-Tube Tuber-Machine Operator (rubber tire) 690.662-014
In-Process Inspector (electron. comp.) 726.381-010
in-Process Inspector (optical goods) 716.381-010
inseamer (boot & shoe) 690.682-078
inseam leveler (boot & shoe) 690.685-382
INSEAM TRIMMER (boot & shoe) 690.685-238
inseam-trimming-machine operator (boot & shoe) 690.685-238
INSECTICIDE MIXER (chemical) 550.685-070
Insect Sprayer, Mobile Unit (government ser.) 906.683-022
inseminator (agriculture) 418.384-010
Inserter (construction) 869.687-026
inserter (paper goods) 794.687-058
inserter (toy-sport equip.) 732.687-042
Inserter, Promotional Item (any industry) 920.587-018
INSERTING-MACHINE OPERATOR (clerical) 208.685-018
inserting-press operator (any industry) 692.685-062
INSERTION MACHINE TENDER, ELECTRONIC COMPONENTS (comm. equip.; electron. comp.; office machines) 726.685-014
insert-machine operator (paper goods; print. & pub.) 653.685-030
INSERVICE COORDINATOR, AUXILIARY PERSONNEL (medical ser.) 079.127-010
INSET CUTTER (fabrication, nec) 739.381-038
INSIDE-METER TESTER (utilities) 729.281-034
Inside-Panel Padder (furniture) 780.684-082
Inside-Plant Supervisor (tel. & tel.) 822.131-010
inside polisher (fabrication, nec) 603.685-014
inside steward/stewardess (hotel & rest.) 318.137-010
inside tester (utilities) 729.281-034
INSOLE-AND-HEEL-STIFFENER (boot & shoe) 788.687-062
insole-and-outsole preparer (boot & shoe) 788.685-018
Insole-And-Outsole Splitter (boot & shoe) 585.685-114
INSOLE BEVELER (boot & shoe) 690.685-242
insole-bottom filler (boot & shoe) 788.684-026
Insole Buffer (boot & shoe) 690.685-046
insole-cloth trimmer (boot & shoe) 690.685-246
Insole Coverer (boot & shoe) 690.685-074
Insole Cutter, Machine (boot & shoe) 699.682-022
insole filler (boot & shoe) 788.684-026
insole gemmer (boot & shoe) 690.685-246
Insole-Lip Turner (boot & shoe) 690.685-074
Insole Rasper (boot & shoe) 788.684-094
INSOLE REINFORCER (boot & shoe) 690.685-246
insole rounder (boot & shoe) 690.685-338
Insole Sander (boot & shoe) 690.685-046
Insole Tacker (boot & shoe) 690.685-162
insole-tack-puller, hand (boot & shoe) 788.687-146
Insole Taper (boot & shoe) 690.685-074
Insole Tape Stitcher, Uco (boot & shoe) 690.682-082
Insole-Toe-Snipping-Machine Operator (boot & shoe) 690.685-222
INSPECTING-MACHINE ADJUSTER (ordnance) 632.380-010
INSPECTION CLERK (fabrication, nec) 739.587-010
inspection-machine tender (textile) 689.685-038
INSPECTION SUPERVISOR (chemical; nonfer. metal) 709.137-010
Inspection Supervisor (forging) 612.131-010
INSPECTION SUPERVISOR I (ordnance) 736.131-018
INSPECTION SUPERVISOR II (ordnance) 737.134-010
INSPECTION SUPERVISOR (machine shop) 609.131-010
Inspection Supervisor (metal prod., nec; nonfer. metal) 691.130-014
Inspection Supervisor (nonfer. metal) 691.130-010
INSPECTOR (boot & shoe) 788.384-010
inspector (brick & tile) 573.687-034
INSPECTOR (build. mat., nec) 549.367-010
INSPECTOR (chemical) 709.687-022
inspector (cutlery-hrdwr.) 701.687-026
INSPECTOR (cutlery-hrdwr.) 709.587-010
INSPECTOR (elec. equip.) 727.687-062
inspector (engine-turbine) 806.261-010
inspector (fabrication, nec) 739.687-146
INSPECTOR (forging) 612.261-010

inspector (foundry) 518.684-026
inspector (furniture) 763.684-010
INSPECTOR (hat & cap) 784.387-010
INSPECTOR (hotel & rest.) 321.137-014
INSPECTOR (house. appl.) 729.387-022
INSPECTOR (jewelry-silver.) 700.687-034
INSPECTOR (laundry & rel.) 369.687-022
INSPECTOR (mfd. bldgs.) 869.687-038
inspector (mine & quarry) 779.687-026
INSPECTOR (narrow fabrics) 689.687-022
INSPECTOR (nonmet. min.) 776.667-010
inspector (nonprofit org.) 379.137-010
INSPECTOR (office machines) 710.384-014
INSPECTOR (paper & pulp) 649.487-010
INSPECTOR (pen & pencil) 733.687-042
inspector (petrol. refin.) 549.261-010
INSPECTOR (pharmaceut.) 559.387-014
inspector (photofinishing) 976.687-014
INSPECTOR (plastic prod.; plastic-synth.) 559.381-010
inspector (print. & pub.) 970.361-014
inspector (print. & pub.) 653.667-010
Inspector (protective dev.) 789.687-070
Inspector (rubber goods) 759.684-074
INSPECTOR (steel & rel.) 619.381-010
inspector (stonework) 670.384-010
INSPECTOR (sugar & conf.) 529.687-114
INSPECTOR (toy-sport equip.) 732.684-130
INSPECTOR (woodworking) 769.687-026
INSPECTOR-ADJUSTER, OFFICE-MACHINE COMPONENTS (office machines) 706.384-010
Inspector, Advanced Composit (aircraft mfg.) 806.261-046
INSPECTOR, AGRICULTURAL COMMODITIES (government ser.) 168.287-010
INSPECTOR, AIR-CARRIER (government ser.) 168.264-010
INSPECTOR, AIRCRAFT LAUNCHING AND ARRESTING SYSTEMS (government ser.) 806.264-014
INSPECTOR, ALINING (office machines) 706.687-022
INSPECTOR, ALUMINUM BOAT (ship-boat mfg.) 806.687-026
INSPECTOR AND ADJUSTER, GOLF CLUB HEAD (toy-sport equip.) 732.384-014
inspector and clerk (utilities) 821.367-010
inspector and clipper (any industry) 789.587-014
inspector and clipper (knitting) 684.684-010
inspector and counter (paper & pulp) 649.687-010
INSPECTOR AND HAND PACKAGER (plastic prod.) 559.687-074
inspector and mender (tex. prod., nec) 782.487-010
inspector and patch worker (furniture) 763.684-070
Inspector And Shaper, End Windings (elec. equip.) 724.364-010
INSPECTOR AND SORTER (leather mfg.) 589.387-010
INSPECTOR AND TESTER (agric. equip.) 624.361-010
inspector and tester (engine-turbine) 806.261-010
Inspector And Tester (rubber goods) 759.684-074
INSPECTOR AND TESTER (struct. metal) 809.687-018
inspector-and-unloader (metal prod., nec) 709.687-038
INSPECTOR, ASSEMBLIES AND INSTALLATIONS (aircraft mfg.) 806.261-030
inspector, assembly (aircraft mfg.) 806.261-030
INSPECTOR, ASSEMBLY (furniture) 669.364-010
INSPECTOR, ASSEMBLY (ordnance) 736.387-010
INSPECTOR, AUTOMATIC TYPEWRITER (office machines) 706.387-010
INSPECTOR, BALANCE-BRIDGE (clock & watch) 715.687-058
INSPECTOR, BALANCE TRUING (clock & watch) 715.687-050
INSPECTOR, BALANCE WHEEL MOTION (clock & watch) 715.687-054
INSPECTOR, BALL POINTS (nonfer. metal) 733.687-046
INSPECTOR, BARREL ASSEMBLY (clock & watch) 715.684-114
INSPECTOR, BARREL (ordnance) 736.687-014
INSPECTOR, BENCH ASSEMBLY (aircraft mfg.) 806.281-026
INSPECTOR, BICYCLE (motor-bicycles) 806.687-030
INSPECTOR, BOILER (profess. & kin.) 168.167-026
inspector, brake lining (nonmet. min.) 776.667-010
INSPECTOR, BUILDING (government ser.) 168.167-030
INSPECTOR, BULLET SLUGS (ordnance) 737.687-058
INSPECTOR, CANNED FOOD RECONDITIONING (can. & preserv.) 529.687-118
Inspector, Canvas Products (tex. prod., nec) 789.587-014
INSPECTOR, CASING (clock & watch) 715.687-062
INSPECTOR, CHIEF (elec. equip.) 729.131-010
INSPECTOR, CHIEF (foundry) 514.131-010
inspector, chief (machine shop) 609.131-010
INSPECTOR, CHIEF (ordnance) 737.137-010
INSPECTOR, CHIEF (utilities) 956.267-010

INSPECTOR, CIRCUITRY NEGATIVE (electron. comp.) 726.384-014
INSPECTOR, CLIP-ON SUNGLASSES (optical goods) 713.667-010
Inspector, Coated Fabrics (tex. prod., nec) 689.685-038
INSPECTOR, COLD WORKING (ordnance) 612.384-010
inspector, component parts (electron. comp.) 726.684-022
INSPECTOR, CONTAINER FINISHING (elec. equip.) 727.687-066
Inspector, Conveyor Line (office machines) 706.381-022
INSPECTOR, CRYSTAL (electron. comp.) 726.684-054
INSPECTOR, DIALS (clock & watch) 715.687-066
Inspector, Electrical And Electronic Installations (aircraft mfg.) 806.261-030
inspector, electrical bench (aircraft mfg.; air trans.) 825.381-026
INSPECTOR, ELECTRICAL (government ser.) 168.167-034
INSPECTOR, ELECTROMECHANICAL (inst. & app.) 729.361-010
INSPECTOR, ELEVATORS (government ser.) 168.167-038
Inspector, Engines And Components Assembly (aircraft mfg.) 806.261-030
INSPECTOR, EXHAUST EMISSIONS (auto. mfg.) 806.364-010
Inspector, Experimental Assembly (aircraft mfg.) 806.261-030
INSPECTOR, EYEGLASS (optical goods) 713.384-014
INSPECTOR, EYEGLASS FRAMES (optical goods) 713.687-022
INSPECTOR, FABRIC (any industry) 789.587-014
INSPECTOR, FABRICATION (aircraft mfg.) 806.361-022
INSPECTOR, FIBROUS WALLBOARD (wood prod., nec) 539.487-010
Inspector, Filters (auto. mfg.) 609.684-010
INSPECTOR, FILTER TIP (tobacco) 529.667-010
Inspector, Final Assembly (aircraft mfg.) 806.261-030
INSPECTOR, FINAL ASSEMBLY (pen & pencil) 733.687-050
Inspector, Final Assembly-Conveyor Line (office machines) 706.381-022
Inspector, Final Assembly - Electrical (aircraft mfg.) 806.261-030
Inspector, Final Assembly - Mechanical (aircraft mfg.) 806.261-030
inspector, finished machines and bundles (agric. equip.) 801.667-010
INSPECTOR, FINISHING (tex. prod., nec) 589.387-022
INSPECTOR, FIREARMS (ordnance) 632.381-014
INSPECTOR, FIREWORKS (chemical) 737.687-062
INSPECTOR, FLOOR (machine shop) 609.361-010
Inspector, Floor Sub-Assembly (office machines) 706.381-022
Inspector, Fuel Hose (rubber goods) 759.684-074
INSPECTOR, FURNITURE AND BEDDING (government ser.) 168.267-046
INSPECTOR, FURNITURE DECALS (furniture) 979.687-030
INSPECTOR, GAUGE AND INSTRUMENT (machine shop) 601.281-018
INSPECTOR, GENERAL (any industry) 609.684-010
INSPECTOR, GLASS OR MIRROR (glass products) 779.687-022
INSPECTOR, GOLF BALL (toy-sport equip.) 732.567-010
INSPECTOR, GOVERNMENT PROPERTY (government ser.) 168.267-050
INSPECTOR-GRADER, AGRICULTURAL ESTABLISHMENT (agriculture) 409.687-010
INSPECTOR, GRAIN MILL PRODUCTS (grain-feed mills) 529.387-026
INSPECTOR, HAIRSPRING I (clock & watch) 715.381-066
INSPECTOR, HAIRSPRING II (clock & watch) 715.684-122
INSPECTOR, HAIRSPRING TRUING (clock & watch) 715.684-118
INSPECTOR, HANDBAG FRAMES (leather prod.) 222.687-042
INSPECTOR, HEALTH CARE FACILITIES (government ser.) 168.167-042
INSPECTOR, HEATING AND REFRIGERATION (government ser.) 168.167-046
Inspector, Hot Forgings (forging) 612.261-010
INSPECTOR I (concrete prod.) 779.387-014
INSPECTOR I (fabrication, nec) 739.687-106
INSPECTOR I (furniture) 780.687-066
INSPECTOR I (nonfer. metal) 619.364-010
INSPECTOR I (ordnance) 737.387-014
INSPECTOR I (pottery & porc.) 575.687-034
INSPECTOR II (concrete prod.) 579.664-014
INSPECTOR II (fabrication, nec) 590.367-010
INSPECTOR II (furniture) 780.687-022
Inspector II (nonfer. metal) 519.686-010
INSPECTOR II (ordnance) 737.687-054
INSPECTOR II (pottery & porc.) 774.384-010
INSPECTOR III (furniture) 739.687-110
INSPECTOR III (ordnance) 737.367-010
INSPECTOR, INDUSTRIAL WASTE (government ser.) 168.267-054
inspector-in-process (optical goods) 716.687-022
INSPECTOR, INSULATION (nonfer. metal) 691.387-010
INSPECTOR, INTEGRATED CIRCUITS (electron. comp.) 726.684-058
INSPECTOR IV (ordnance) 559.387-010
inspector, jewels (clock & watch) 770.687-022
inspector, line (tel. & tel.) 822.267-010
INSPECTOR, LIVE AMMUNITION (ordnance) 736.687-018
inspector, machine-cut glass (glass mfg.) 579.687-030
Inspector, Machined Parts (aircraft mfg.) 806.361-022
Inspector, Magnetic Particle (any industry) 709.364-010
INSPECTOR, MAGNETIC PARTICLE AND PENETRANT (any industry) 709.364-010
inspector, manufactured parts (office machines) 706.381-022
INSPECTOR, MATERIAL DISPOSITION (aircraft mfg.) 806.261-034
inspector, mechanical (office machines) 706.381-022

INSPECTOR, MECHANISM (clock & watch) 715.384-014
INSPECTOR, METAL CAN (tinware) 709.367-010
INSPECTOR, METAL FABRICATING (any industry) 619.261-010
INSPECTOR, MISSILE (aircraft mfg.) 806.261-038
Inspector, Missile Final Assembly (aircraft mfg.) 806.261-038
INSPECTOR, MOTORS AND GENERATORS (elec. equip.) 721.361-010
INSPECTOR, MOTOR VEHICLES (government ser.) 168.267-058
INSPECTOR, MULTIFOCAL LENS (optical goods) 716.687-018
INSPECTOR OF DREDGING (water trans.) 850.387-010
INSPECTOR, OPEN DIE (cutlery-hrdwr.) 701.684-014
inspector, optical elements (optical goods) 716.381-010
INSPECTOR, OPTICAL INSTRUMENT (optical goods) 711.281-010
INSPECTOR, OUTSIDE PRODUCTION (aircraft mfg.) 806.261-042
inspector, outside steam-distribution (utilities) 862.361-022
Inspector-Packager (any industry) 920.587-018
INSPECTOR, PACKAGING MATERIALS (pharmaceut.) 920.387-010
inspector-packer, glass container (glass mfg.) 579.687-030
INSPECTOR-PACKER (hat & cap) 784.687-042
INSPECTOR, PAPER PRODUCTS (paper goods) 649.367-010
Inspector, Pawnshop Detail (government ser.) 375.267-030
Inspector, Penetrant (any industry) 709.364-010
INSPECTOR, PHOTOGRAPHIC EQUIPMENT (photo. appar.) 714.381-014
INSPECTOR, PICTURE FRAMES (wood prod., nec) 769.687-030
INSPECTOR, PLASTICS AND COMPOSITES (aircraft mfg.) 806.261-046
Inspector, Plastics Fabrication-Developmental (aircraft mfg.) 806.261-046
INSPECTOR, PLATING (electroplating) 500.287-010
inspector, plug seam (tobacco) 529.667-010
INSPECTOR, PLUMBING (government ser.) 168.167-050
INSPECTOR, POISING (clock & watch) 715.384-018
INSPECTOR, PRECISION (optical goods) 716.381-010
inspector, precision (photo. appar.) 714.381-014
inspector, precision electrical assembly (aircraft mfg.; air trans.) 825.381-026
inspector, precision electrical assembly (aircraft mfg.) 729.381-010
INSPECTOR, PRINTED CIRCUIT BOARDS (electron. comp.) 726.684-062
inspector, process (elec. equip.) 829.361-018
INSPECTOR, PROCESSING (aircraft mfg.) 806.381-074
INSPECTOR, PROCESSING (sugar & conf.) 529.687-226
Inspector, Production Plastic Parts (aircraft mfg.) 806.261-046
INSPECTOR, PUBLICATIONS (print. & pub.) 653.667-010
Inspector, Purchased Parts (office machines) 706.381-022
INSPECTOR, QUALITY ASSURANCE (government ser.) 168.287-014
Inspector, Radar And Electronics (aircraft mfg.) 722.381-014
inspector, rag sorting (paper & pulp) 530.687-010
INSPECTOR, RAILROAD (government ser.) 168.287-018
Inspector, Raw Quartz (electron. comp.) 726.381-010
INSPECTOR, RECEIVING (aircraft mfg.; elec. equip.; electron. comp.) 222.384-010
INSPECTOR-REPAIRER (button & notion) 734.684-018
INSPECTOR-REPAIRER (leather prod.) 783.684-018
INSPECTOR-REPAIRER, SANDSTONE (stonework) 779.684-030
INSPECTOR, RETURNED MATERIALS (auto. mfg.) 806.384-014
inspector, rough castings (machine shop) 600.281-014
INSPECTOR, RUBBER-STAMP DIE (pen & pencil) 733.687-054
INSPECTOR, SALVAGE (ordnance) 737.684-026
inspector, scales (office machines) 710.381-014
INSPECTOR, SCREEN PRINTING (print. & pub.) 979.667-010
INSPECTOR, SEMICONDUCTOR WAFER (electron. comp.) 726.684-066
INSPECTOR, SEMICONDUCTOR WAFER PROCESSING (electron. comp.) 726.384-018
INSPECTOR, SET-UP AND LAY-OUT (machine shop) 601.261-010
Inspector, Sheet Metal Parts (aircraft mfg.) 806.361-022
INSPECTOR, SHELLS (ordnance) 737.687-066
INSPECTOR, SHIPPING (agric. equip.) 801.667-010
INSPECTOR, SLIDE FASTENERS (button & notion) 734.687-062
INSPECTOR, SOLDERING (clock & watch) 715.687-070
Inspector, Station Assembly-Conveyor Line (office machines) 706.381-022
Inspector, Structural Bonding (aircraft mfg.) 806.261-046
Inspector, Structures (aircraft mfg.) 806.261-030
Inspector, Subassemblies (electron. comp.) 726.381-010
Inspector, Subassembly (aircraft mfg.) 806.261-030
INSPECTOR, SURGICAL GARMENT (protective dev.) 712.487-010
INSPECTOR, SURGICAL INSTRUMENTS (inst. & app.) 712.684-050
inspector technician (grain-feed mills) 529.387-026
INSPECTOR, TIMERS (clock & watch) 715.687-074
INSPECTOR, TIMING (clock & watch) 715.685-034
INSPECTOR, TOOL (machine shop) 601.281-022
INSPECTOR, TOYS (toy-sport equip.) 731.687-022
inspector trimmer (glove & mit.) 789.687-042
Inspector, Tubes (electron. comp.) 726.381-010
INSPECTOR, TYPE (office machines) 706.687-026
INSPECTOR, TYPEWRITER ASSEMBLY AND PARTS (office machines) 706.381-022
INSPECTOR, WATCH ASSEMBLY (clock & watch) 715.381-070
INSPECTOR, WATCH PARTS (clock & watch) 715.384-022
INSPECTOR, WATCH TRAIN (clock & watch) 715.381-074

INSPECTOR, WATER-POLLUTION CONTROL (government ser.) 168.267-090
Inspector, Weights And Measures (government ser.) 168.267-062
Inspector, Welded Parts (aircraft mfg.) 806.361-022
INSPECTOR, WHEEL AND PINION (clock & watch) 715.684-126
INSPECTOR, WIRE (metal prod., nec; nonfer. metal) 691.367-010
INSPECTOR, WIRE PRODUCTS (metal prod., nec) 709.687-026
Inspector, Wire Rope (metal prod., nec) 691.367-010
INSPECTOR, WOODWIND INSTRUMENTS (musical inst.) 730.684-038
INSPECTOR, WREATH (fabrication, nec) 739.687-118
INSTALLATION ENGINEER (profess. & kin.) term
installation helper (construction; retail trade; tex. prod., nec) 869.687-010
INSTALLATION SUPERINTENDENT, PIN-SETTING MACHINE (construction) 829.131-018
Installation Supervisor (tel. & tel.) 822.131-014
installation supervisor (tel. & tel.) 822.131-010
installation worker, draperies (retail trade) 869.484-014
installer (business ser.) 822.361-018
INSTALLER (mfd. bldgs.; vehicles, nec) 869.684-026
INSTALLER (museums) 922.687-050
installer (retail trade) 869.484-014
INSTALLER, DOOR FURRING (railroad equip.) 806.687-034
INSTALLER, ELECTRICAL, PLUMBING, MECHANICAL (ship-boat mfg.) 806.381-062
INSTALLER-INSPECTOR, FINAL (vehicles, nec) 806.684-066
INSTALLER, INTERIOR ASSEMBLIES (aircraft mfg.) 806.381-078
INSTALLER, METAL FLOORING (railroad equip.) 806.684-070
installer, molding and trim (mfd. bldgs.) 869.684-066
INSTALLER, MOVABLE BULKHEAD (railroad equip.) 806.684-074
INSTALLER, SOFT TOP (automotive ser.) 807.684-026
Installment-Account Checker (clerical) 209.687-010
INSTANTIZER OPERATOR (dairy products) 523.685-106
Instant-Powder Supervisor (dairy products) 529.131-014
INSTANT PRINT OPERATOR (print. & pub.) 979.362-010
institutional-nutrition consultant (profess. & kin.) 077.127-018
INSTITUTION LIBRARIAN (library) 100.167-022
instructional technology specialist (profess. & kin.) 149.061-010
INSTRUCTOR (boot & shoe) 788.222-010
Instructor (education) 090.227-010
instructor (textile) 789.222-010
INSTRUCTOR (textile) 689.324-010
INSTRUCTOR, APPAREL MANUFACTURE (textile) 789.222-010
Instructor, Ballroom Dancing (education) 151.027-014
Instructor, Braille (education) 094.224-018
INSTRUCTOR, BRIDGE (education) 159.227-010
INSTRUCTOR, BUSINESS EDUCATION (education) 090.222-010
INSTRUCTOR, BUS, TROLLEY, AND TAXI (motor trans.; r.r. trans.) 919.223-010
INSTRUCTOR, CORRESPONDENCE SCHOOL (education) 099.227-014
Instructor, Creeler (textile) 689.324-010
INSTRUCTOR, DANCING (education) 151.027-014
INSTRUCTOR, DECORATING (pottery & porc.) 740.221-010
instructor, dramatic arts (education) 150.027-014
INSTRUCTOR, DRIVING (education) 099.223-010
INSTRUCTOR, EXTENSION WORK (education) 090.227-018
INSTRUCTOR, FLYING I (education) 196.223-010
INSTRUCTOR, FLYING II (education) 097.227-010
INSTRUCTOR, GROUND SERVICES (air trans.) 099.227-018
Instructor, Hairspring (clock & watch) 715.221-010
Instructor, Illustration (education) 149.021-010
Instructor, Industrial Design (education) 149.021-010
instructor, kindergarten (education) 092.227-014
Instructor, Knitting (textile) 689.324-010
Instructor, Looping (textile) 689.324-010
INSTRUCTOR, MACHINE (any industry) term
INSTRUCTOR, MILITARY SCIENCE (education) 099.227-022
INSTRUCTOR, MODELING (education) 099.227-026
instructor of blind (education; medical ser.; nonprofit org.) 076.224-014
INSTRUCTOR, PAINTING (retail trade) 297.451-010
INSTRUCTOR, PHYSICAL (amuse. & rec.; education) 153.227-014
INSTRUCTOR, PHYSICAL EDUCATION (education) 099.224-010
INSTRUCTOR, PILOT (air trans.) 196.223-014
instructor, private (education) 099.227-034
Instructor, Product Inspection (textile) 689.324-010
Instructor, Programmable Controllers (education) 166.221-010
INSTRUCTOR, PSYCHIATRIC AIDE (education) 075.127-010
Instructor, Robotics (education) 166.221-010
instructor, self-improvement (education) 099.227-026
INSTRUCTOR, SPORTS (amuse. & rec.; education) 153.227-018
Instructor, Tap Dancing (education) 151.027-014
INSTRUCTOR, TECHNICAL TRAINING (education) 166.221-010
INSTRUCTOR-TRAINER, CANINE SERVICE (government ser.) 379.227-010
instructor, training (retail trade)   see SPONSOR
INSTRUCTOR, VOCATIONAL TRAINING (education) 097.221-010
Instructor, Warper (textile) 689.324-010

INSTRUCTOR, WASTEWATER-TREATMENT PLANT (sanitary ser.) 955.222-010
INSTRUCTOR, WATCH ASSEMBLY (clock & watch) 715.221-010
INSTRUCTOR, WEAVING (textile) 683.222-010
INSTRUMENT ASSEMBLER (inst. & app.) 710.684-046
INSTRUMENTATION ENGINEER (profess. & kin.) term
INSTRUMENTATION TECHNICIAN (profess. & kin.) 003.261-010
instrument calibrator (inst. & app.) 710.381-042
instrument-case finisher (leather prod.) 739.684-034
Instrument Fitter (construction) 862.281-022
INSTRUMENT INSPECTOR (inst. & app.) 710.684-050
INSTRUMENT INSPECTOR (aircraft mfg.; air trans.) 722.381-014
Instrument-Lens Generator (optical goods) 716.682-014
Instrument-Lens Grinder (optical goods) 716.382-018
instrument-lens-grinder apprentice (optical goods) 716.382-022
Instrument-Lens Inspector (optical goods) 716.381-010
instrument maker (any industry) 729.281-026
INSTRUMENT MAKER (any industry) 600.280-010
INSTRUMENT-MAKER AND REPAIRER (petrol. & gas) 600.280-014
INSTRUMENT-MAKER APPRENTICE (any industry) 600.280-018
INSTRUMENT MECHANIC (any industry) 710.281-026
INSTRUMENT MECHANIC, WEAPONS SYSTEM (inst. & app.) 711.281-014
instrument repairer (any industry) 710.281-026
instrument repairer (any industry) 729.281-026
INSTRUMENT REPAIRER (any industry) 710.261-010
INSTRUMENT REPAIRER (tel. & tel.) 722.281-010
INSTRUMENT-REPAIRER HELPER (any industry) 710.384-018
Instrument Repairer, Steam Plant (utilities) 710.281-030
instrument repair supervisor (any industry) 710.131-014
INSTRUMENT-SHOP SUPERVISOR (tel. & tel.) 722.131-010
INSTRUMENT TECHNICIAN (utilities) 710.281-030
INSTRUMENT-TECHNICIAN APPRENTICE (utilities) 710.281-042
INSTRUMENT-TECHNICIAN HELPER (utilities) 710.684-030
insulating-machine operator (any industry) 599.685-046
INSULATING-MACHINE OPERATOR (nonfer. metal) 691.682-018
INSULATION CUTTER AND FORMER (elec. equip.) 721.484-018
Insulation Installer (construction) 869.664-014
INSULATION-POWER-UNIT TENDER (construction; retail trade; wholesale tr.) 863.685-010
insulation supervisor (construction) 863.134-010
INSULATION WORKER (construction) 863.364-014
INSULATION-WORKER APPRENTICE (construction) 863.364-010
insulation worker, interior surface (construction) 863.381-010
Insulator (elec. equip.) 724.684-026
insulator apprentice (construction) 863.364-010
Insulator Cutter And Former (elec. equip.) 724.684-026
INSULATOR TESTER (utilities) 729.387-026
insurance adjustor (business ser.; insurance) 241.217-010
insurance agent (insurance) 250.257-010
insurance and benefits clerk (clerical) 205.567-010
insurance and risk manager (any industry) 186.117-066
Insurance Application Investigator (insurance) 241.267-030
INSURANCE ATTORNEY (insurance) 110.117-014
Insurance Broker (insurance) 250.257-010
INSURANCE CHECKER (insurance) 219.482-014
insurance-claim approver (business ser.; insurance) 241.267-018
insurance-claim auditor (business ser.; insurance) 241.267-018
insurance-claim representative (business ser.; insurance) 241.217-010
INSURANCE CLERK (clerical) 219.387-014
Insurance Clerk (financial) 249.362-014
INSURANCE CLERK (financial; insurance) 219.367-014
INSURANCE CLERK (medical ser.) 214.362-022
Insurance Collector (insurance) 241.367-010
insurance counsel (insurance) 110.117-014
insurance investigator (business ser.; insurance) 241.217-010
Insurance Licensing Supervisor (government ser.) 168.167-090
intake worker (social ser.) 195.107-010
Integral Tank Sealer (aircraft mfg.) 806.384-038
INTEGRATED CIRCUIT FABRICATOR (electron. comp.) 590.684-042
INTEGRATED CIRCUIT LAYOUT DESIGNER (profess. & kin.) 003.261-018
INTELLIGENCE CLERK (military ser.) 249.387-014
INTELLIGENCE RESEARCH SPECIALIST (profess. & kin.) 059.167-010
INTELLIGENCE SPECIALIST (government ser.) 059.267-010
INTELLIGENCE SPECIALIST (military ser.) 059.267-014
Intercell-Connector Placer (elec. equip.) 727.687-070
interceptor operator (business ser.) 235.662-026
inter-com installer (any industry) 829.281-022
inter-com servicer (any industry) 829.281-022
inter-fold roll cutter (pen & pencil) 640.685-066
Interior Decorator (profess. & kin.) 142.051-014
INTERIOR DESIGNER (profess. & kin.) 142.051-014
interior horticulturist (agriculture) 408.364-010
interior paneler, partition setter (mfd. bldgs.) 869.684-038
Interior Wall Assembler (mfd. bldgs.) 869.684-018

INTERLACER

INTERLACER (boot & shoe) 788.684-070
INTERLINE CLERK (motor trans.; r.r. trans.) 214.382-022
Interlocking Tower Operator (r.r. trans.) 910.362-010
intermediate-card tender (nonmet. min.; textile) 680.665-018
INTERNAL CARVER (plastic prod.) 754.381-010
INTERNAL-COMBUSTION-ENGINE INSPECTOR (engine-turbine) 806.261-010
INTERNAL-COMBUSTION-ENGINE SUBASSEMBLER (engine-turbine) 706.481-010
Internal-Grinder Tender (machine shop) 603.685-062
internal grinder, tool (machine shop) 603.280-022
internal-grinding-machine hand (machine shop) 603.280-022
internal-grinding-machine operator (machine shop) 603.280-022
internal medicine specialist (medical ser.) 070.101-042
International Banking Officer (financial) 186.267-018
International-Trade Economist (profess. & kin.) 050.067-010
INTERNIST (medical ser.) 070.101-042
Interpretative Dancer (amuse. & rec.) 151.047-010
INTERPRETER (profess. & kin.) 137.267-010
INTERPRETER, DEAF (profess. & kin.) 137.267-014
interviewer (clerical) 205.367-054
interviewer (clerical) 205.362-014
Interviewer (radio-tv broad.) 166.167-010
Inventory-Audit Clerk (clerical) 210.382-010
inventory clerk (clerical) 219.387-030
INVENTORY CLERK (clerical) 222.387-026
Inventory Clerk, Physical (clerical) 222.387-026
inventory control clerk (clerical) 219.387-030
Inventory Transcriber (business ser.) 216.482-022
Invertebrate Zoologist (profess. & kin.) 041.061-090
Inverter-And-Clipper (leather prod.) 789.687-182
Investigation Division Captain (government ser.) 375.167-014
Investigation Division Lieutenant (government ser.) 375.167-014
Investigation Division Sergeant (government ser.) 375.167-014
investigator (any industry) 376.367-014
investigator (business ser.) 376.267-022
INVESTIGATOR (clerical) 241.267-030
INVESTIGATOR (government ser.) 168.267-062
INVESTIGATOR (utilities) 376.367-022
INVESTIGATOR, CASH SHORTAGE (retail trade) 376.267-010
Investigator, Claims (government ser.) 168.267-062
investigator, communicable disease (government ser.) 168.167-018
INVESTIGATOR, DEALER ACCOUNTS (financial) 241.367-038
INVESTIGATOR, FRAUD (retail trade) 376.267-014
INVESTIGATOR, INTERNAL AFFAIRS (government ser.) 375.267-034
Investigator, Internal Revenue (government ser.) 168.267-062
INVESTIGATOR, NARCOTICS (government ser.) 375.267-018
investigator operator (business ser.) 376.367-010
INVESTIGATOR, PRIVATE (business ser.) 376.267-018
INVESTIGATOR, UTILITY-BILL COMPLAINTS (utilities) 241.267-034
INVESTIGATOR, VICE (government ser.) 375.267-022
Investigator, Welfare (government ser.) 168.267-062
INVESTMENT ANALYST (financial; insurance) 160.267-026
investment executive (financial) 250.257-018
Invoice-Classification Clerk (clerical) 210.382-030
invoice clerk (clerical) 214.382-014
INVOICE-CONTROL CLERK (clerical) 214.362-026
invoicing-machine operator (clerical) 214.482-010
inweaver (personal ser.) 782.381-022
ION EXCHANGE OPERATOR (beverage) 521.685-190
ION-EXCHANGE OPERATOR (chemical) 558.685-034
ION-EXCHANGE OPERATOR (pharmaceut.) 558.685-038
ION-EXCHANGE OPERATOR (smelt. & refin.) 558.685-030
ION IMPLANT MACHINE OPERATOR (electron. comp.) 590.382-022
IRISH-MOSS BLEACHER (fishing & hunt.) 447.687-014
IRISH-MOSS GATHERER (fishing & hunt.) 447.687-018
IRISH-MOSS OPERATOR (chemical) 529.382-030
iron-and-steel-work supervisor (construction) 809.131-018
ironer (boot & shoe) 788.684-130
IRONER (button & notion) 590.685-042
IRONER (domestic ser.) 302.687-010
ironer (glove & mit.; laundry & rel.) 363.687-010
ironer (hat & cap) 584.685-026
ironer (hat & cap) 583.685-022
ironer (knitting) 583.685-070
ironer (wood prod., nec) 739.684-098
iron erector (construction) 801.361-014
ironer, hand (any industry) 363.684-018
ironer, machine (any industry) 363.682-018
IRONER, SOCK (laundry & rel.) 363.687-014
IRON-LAUNDER OPERATOR (smelt. & refin.) 511.565-018
IRON-PLASTIC BULLET MAKER (ordnance) 590.365-010
ironworker (construction) 801.361-014
ironworker apprentice (construction) 801.361-018
ironworker apprentice, shop (any industry) 619.361-018

Ironworker Helper, Shop (any industry) 619.686-022
IRONWORKER-MACHINE OPERATOR (any industry) 615.482-018
ironworker, wire-fence erector (construction) 869.684-022
IRRADIATED-FUEL HANDLER (chemical) 921.663-034
irradiation technician (profess. & kin.) 015.362-018
Irrigating-Pump Operator (agriculture) 914.682-010
IRRIGATION ENGINEER (profess. & kin.) 005.061-022
IRRIGATION SYSTEM INSTALLER (construction) 851.383-010
IRRIGATOR, GRAVITY FLOW (agriculture) 409.687-014
IRRIGATOR, HEAD (agriculture) 409.137-010
irrigator, overhead (agriculture) 409.685-014
IRRIGATOR, SPRINKLING SYSTEM (agriculture) 409.685-014
IRRIGATOR, VALVE PIPE (agriculture) 409.684-010
Islamic Butcher (meat products) 525.361-010
Isobutylene Operator, Chief (chemical) 559.132-078
Isolation-Washer (laundry & rel.) 361.665-010
isotope-production technician (profess. & kin.) 015.362-022

J

jacker feeder (millwork-plywood; paper & pulp; saw. & plan.) 921.686-022
Jacket Changer (foundry) 519.687-022
JACKET PREPARER (print. & pub.) 221.387-030
JACKHAMMER OPERATOR (mine & quarry) 930.684-018
jackhammer-splitter operator (stonework) 677.685-042
JACK SETTER (mine & quarry) 939.684-010
jackspooler (narrow fabrics; textile) 681.685-142
Jack-Strip Assembler (comm. equip.; elec. equip.) 729.684-026
Jack-Tamp Operator (construction) 910.683-018
jacquard-lace weaver (tex. prod., nec) 683.682-026
Jacquard-Loom Fixer (textile) 683.260-018
JACQUARD-LOOM WEAVER (narrow fabrics) 683.682-022
JACQUARD-LOOM WEAVER (textile) 683.662-010
jacquard-pattern servicer (textile) 683.685-014
JACQUARD-PLATE MAKER (knitting) 685.381-010
JACQUARD-TWINE-POLISHER OPERATOR (tex. prod., nec) 583.685-062
jagger (personal ser.) 339.571-010
JAILER (government ser.) 372.367-014
JAILER, CHIEF (government ser.) 372.167-018
jail keeper (government ser.) 372.367-014
Jalousie Installer (construction) 860.381-022
JAMMER OPERATOR (logging) 921.683-054
Jammer Operator Helper (logging) 921.687-022
JANITOR (any industry) 382.664-010
janitor (any industry) 381.687-018
janitor (any industry) 381.687-014
janitor, church (nonprofit org.) 389.667-010
janitor, head (any industry) 381.137-010
Japanner (any industry) 740.684-022
japanner (leather mfg.) 584.687-010
Jawbone Breaker (meat products) 525.684-034
jeeper operator (construction) 862.687-014
Jersey Knitter (knitting) 685.665-014
jet channeler (construction; mine & quarry) 930.684-010
JET-DYEING-MACHINE TENDER (textile) 582.685-090
JET HANDLER (plastic-synth.) 557.684-010
jet-piercer operator (construction; mine & quarry) 930.684-010
JET WIPER (plastic-synth.) 557.684-014
JEWEL-BEARING BROACHER (clock & watch) 770.682-010
JEWEL-BEARING DRILLER (clock & watch) 770.682-014
JEWEL-BEARING FACER (clock & watch) 770.682-018
JEWEL-BEARING GRINDER (clock & watch) 770.685-018
JEWEL-BEARING MAKER (clock & watch) 770.381-010
JEWEL-BEARING POLISHER (clock & watch) 770.685-022
JEWEL-BEARING TURNER (clock & watch) 770.682-022
JEWEL BLOCKER AND SAWYER (clock & watch) 770.381-026
JEWEL-CORNER-BRUSHING-MACHINE OPERATOR (clock & watch) 770.685-026
JEWEL-CUPPING-MACHINE OPERATOR (clock & watch) 770.685-030
Jewel-Diameter Gauger (clock & watch) 770.687-018
JEWELER (jewelry-silver.) 700.281-010
JEWELER APPRENTICE (jewelry-silver.) 700.281-014
JEWEL GAUGER (clock & watch) 770.687-018
JEWEL GRINDER I (clock & watch) 770.685-014
JEWEL GRINDER II (clock & watch) 770.684-010
JEWEL-HOLE CORNERER (clock & watch) 770.684-014
JEWEL-HOLE DRILLER (clock & watch) 770.682-026
jewel-hole finish opener (clock & watch) 673.682-022
Jewel-Hole Gauger (clock & watch) 770.687-018
jewel-hole rough opener (clock & watch) 770.684-018
JEWEL INSERTER (clock & watch) 715.684-130
JEWEL INSPECTOR (clock & watch) 770.687-022
jewel-oliving-machine operator (clock & watch) 770.381-034
jewel polisher (clock & watch) 770.685-010

jewelry-casting-model maker (jewelry-silver.) 709.381-018
jewelry-casting-model-maker apprentice (jewelry-silver.) 709.381-022
JEWELRY COATER (jewelry-silver.) 590.685-046
Jewelry-Engraving Supervisor (engraving) 704.131-010
jewelry jobber (jewelry-silver.) 700.281-010
jewelry repairer (jewelry-silver.) 700.281-010
jewelry-repairer apprentice (jewelry-silver.) 700.281-014
jewelry setter (jewelry-silver.; optical goods) 700.381-054
Jewelry Sorter (nonprofit org.) 222.387-054
jewel sawyer (clock & watch) 770.381-026
Jewel Sorter (clock & watch) 770.687-014
JEWEL STAKER (clock & watch) 715.684-134
JEWEL STRINGER (clock & watch) 770.687-026
JEWEL STRIPPER (clock & watch) 605.685-022
JEWEL SUPERVISOR (clock & watch) 770.131-010
Jig And Fixture Builder (aircraft mfg.) 693.281-030
Jig-And-Fixture Maker (machine shop) 601.281-026
jig and form maker (plastic prod.) 754.381-014
jig-borer (machine shop) 606.280-010
JIG-BORING MACHINE OPERATOR, NUMERICAL CONTROL (machine shop) 606.382-014
JIG BUILDER (metal prod., nec) 761.684-014
JIG BUILDER (wood. container) 761.381-014
jig fitter (any industry) 801.261-014
JIG FITTER (machinery mfg.) 801.684-010
JIGGER (jewelry-silver.) 705.687-010
JIGGER (textile) 582.665-018
Jigger-Brim-Pouncing-Machine Operator (hat & cap) 585.685-010
JIGGER-CROWN-POUNCING-MACHINE OPERATOR (hat & cap) 585.685-058
jigger operator (pottery & porc.) 774.382-010
jig grinder (machine shop) 603.280-026
jig-grinding-machine operator (machine shop) 603.280-026
jig operator (textile) 582.665-018
jigsaw operator (jewelry-silver.) 700.684-046
JIGSAW OPERATOR (woodworking) 667.682-042
JIGSAWYER (jewelry-silver.) 700.684-046
JINRIKISHA DRIVER (amuse. & rec.) 349.477-010
JOB ANALYST (profess. & kin.) 166.267-018
job checker (clerical) 221.387-034
Job Compositor (print. & pub.) 973.381-010
JOB DEVELOPMENT SPECIALIST (profess. & kin.) 166.267-034
job honer (machine shop) 603.382-022
job-order clerk (clerical) 221.387-046
JOB-PRESS OPERATOR (print. & pub.) term
JOB PRINTER (print. & pub.) 973.381-018
JOB-PRINTER APPRENTICE (print. & pub.) 973.381-022
JOB PUTTER-UP AND TICKET PREPARER (boot & shoe) 788.587-010
JOB SETTER (electron. comp.) 616.380-014
JOB SETTER, HONING (machine shop) 603.280-034
JOB SETTER, SPLINE-ROLLING MACHINE (machine shop) 617.480-010
Job Setter, Thread-Rolling Machine (machine shop) 617.480-010
job spotter (clerical) 221.387-034
JOB TRACER (clerical) 221.387-034
JOCKEY (amuse. & rec.) 153.244-010
JOCKEY AGENT (amuse. & rec.) 191.117-026
JOCKEY-ROOM CUSTODIAN (amuse. & rec.) 346.667-010
JOCKEY VALET (amuse. & rec.) 346.677-010
JOGGER (print. & pub.) 651.686-018
jogger operator (paper & pulp; paper goods; print. & pub.) 649.685-066
joiner (boot & shoe) 690.682-082
joiner (boot & shoe) 690.685-074
joiner (boot & shoe) 690.685-250
JOINER (glass mfg.) 673.687-010
Joiner (glass products) 779.381-010
joiner (rubber goods) 690.686-026
JOINER (ship-boat mfg.) 860.381-050
joiner (tex. prod., nec) 787.682-066
JOINER APPRENTICE (ship-boat mfg.) 860.381-054
JOINER HELPER (ship-boat mfg.) 860.664-014
JOINT-CLEANING-AND-GROOVING-MACHINE OPERATOR (construction) 853.683-018
joint-cleaning-machine operator (construction) 853.683-018
joint creaser (print. & pub.) 977.684-018
JOINT CUTTER, MACHINE (boot & shoe) 690.685-250
jointer, machine (boot & shoe) 690.685-250
Jointer Offbearer (woodworking) 669.686-034
JOINTER OPERATOR (woodworking) 665.682-042
Jointer, Submarine Cable (tel. & tel.; utilities) 829.361-010
Joint Filler (construction) 869.687-026
Joint-Machine Operator (construction) 853.663-014
joint maker, machine (boot & shoe) 690.685-250
Joint Sander (boot & shoe) 690.685-046
joint supervisor (construction) 843.134-010
Joist Setter, Adjustable Steel (construction) 869.664-014

jollier (boot & shoe) 690.685-314
Jollier (pottery & porc.) 774.382-010
journal-box inspector (r.r. trans.) 910.387-014
Journal-Entry-Audit Clerk (clerical) 210.382-010
JOURNEY WORKER (any industry) term
Jowl Trimmer (meat products) 525.684-034
judge (amuse. & rec.) 153.267-018
JUDGE (government ser.) 111.107-010
JUGGLER (amuse. & rec.) 159.341-010
Jukebox Coin Collector (business ser.) 292.483-010
Juke-Box Servicer (business ser.) 639.281-014
JUMPBASTING-MACHINE OPERATOR (garment) 786.682-146
Jump-Iron-Machine Presser (garment) 363.682-018
jump-roll operator (saw. & plan.) 921.682-022
JUNCTION MAKER (brick & tile) 862.684-010
justice (government ser.) 111.107-010
justice-court judge (government ser.) 111.107-014
justice of the peace (government ser.) 111.107-014
Justowriter Operator (print. & pub.) 203.582-062
Jute-Bag Clipper (tex. prod., nec) 789.687-030
Jute-Bag-Cutting-Machine Operator (tex. prod., nec) 686.585-010
Jute-Bag Sewer (tex. prod., nec) 787.682-058
Juvenile (amuse. & rec.) 150.047-010
Juvenile-Court Judge (government ser.) 111.107-010

K

Kamborian Operator (boot & shoe) 690.685-174
KAPOK-AND-COTTON-MACHINE OPERATOR (tex. prod., nec) 689.685-082
Keel Assembler (ship-boat mfg.) 860.361-010
keeper, head (amuse. & rec.) 412.137-010
keg inspector (wood. container) 764.687-022
keg-lathe operator, inside (wood. container) 664.682-010
keg raiser (wood. container) 764.684-018
KEG VARNISHER (wood. container) 749.687-014
KELP CUTTER (fishing & hunt.) 447.687-022
Kennel Attendant (agriculture) 410.674-010
KENNEL MANAGER, DOG TRACK (amuse. & rec.) 349.367-010
KENO WRITER (amuse. & rec.) 343.467-022
KERFER-MACHINE OPERATOR (furniture) 667.685-042
kersey-department supervisor (tex. prod., nec) 689.130-014
kettle chipper (chemical; plastic-synth.) 559.687-062
KETTLE OPERATOR (beverage) 522.682-010
KETTLE OPERATOR (plastic-synth.) 558.382-042
kettle operator (plastic-synth.) 558.382-050
KETTLE OPERATOR (smelt. & refin.) 519.685-018
kettle operator, head (plastic-synth.) 559.132-042
KETTLE OPERATOR I (chemical) 558.382-038
Kettle Operator II (chemical) 559.682-018
Kettle-Room Helper (chemical) 559.687-050
KETTLE TENDER (any industry) term
KETTLE TENDER (beverage) 526.665-014
KETTLE TENDER (construction) 869.685-010
KETTLE TENDER (sugar & conf.) 520.685-118
kettle tender (textile) 582.685-130
kettle-tender helper (tex. prod., nec; textile) 582.686-030
KETTLE TENDER I (smelt. & refin.) 519.685-022
KETTLE TENDER II (smelt. & refin.) 511.685-030
KETTLE TENDER, PLATINUM AND PALLADIUM (smelt. & refin.) 511.685-034
KETTLE WORKER (soap & rel.) 553.685-070
Key-Bed Installer (musical inst.) 763.684-058
KEYBOARD-ACTION ASSEMBLER (musical inst.) 730.684-042
Keycase Assembler (leather prod.) 783.684-010
Key Clerk (hotel & rest.) 238.367-038
KEY CUTTER (any industry) 709.684-050
KEYING-MACHINE OPERATOR (print. & pub.) 652.685-042
keyliner (print. & pub.) 972.381-030
key maker (any industry) 709.684-050
KEYMODULE-ASSEMBLY-MACHINE TENDER (office machines) 692.685-274
KEYSEATING-MACHINE SET-UP OPERATOR (machine shop) 605.382-018
keysmith (any industry) 709.684-050
key worker (any industry) 709.684-050
Kick-Plate Installer (struct. metal) 809.684-010
KICK-PRESS OPERATOR (protective dev.) 692.685-102
KICK-PRESS OPERATOR I (any industry) 616.682-026
Kick-Press Operator II (any industry) 690.685-014
KICK PRESS SETTER (button & notion) 617.380-010
kier drier (textile) 581.685-026
Kieselguhr-Regenerator Operator (sugar & conf.) 573.685-034
KILN BURNER (brick & tile) 573.682-010
kiln burner (chemical) 563.682-010

kiln burner (pottery & porc.) 573.662-010
KILN-BURNER HELPER (brick & tile) 573.687-026
Kiln Car Unloader (brick & tile) 929.687-030
KILN CLEANER (concrete prod.) 573.687-018
KILN-DOOR BUILDER (brick & tile) 573.684-010
KILN DRAWER (brick & tile) 929.687-014
KILN DRAWER (pottery & porc.) 573.667-010
Kiln Feeder (cement) 570.685-010
kiln firer (concrete prod.) 573.462-010
kiln-firer helper (concrete prod.) 573.685-022
KILN-FURNITURE CASTER (pottery & porc.) 579.684-018
Kiln Furniture, Saw Tender (brick & tile) 677.685-034
kiln-head house operator (smelt. & refin.) 511.565-010
KILN LOADER (beverage) 523.687-018
kiln loader (beverage) 921.682-010
kiln maintenance laborer (pottery & porc.) 573.687-022
kiln operator (glass mfg.) 575.362-010
kiln operator (jewelry-silver.) 590.685-034
kiln operator (mine & quarry) 543.682-014
kiln operator (paint & varnish) 553.685-030
kiln operator (pottery & porc.) 573.662-010
KILN OPERATOR (smelt. & refin.) 513.565-010
KILN OPERATOR (steel & rel.) 509.565-010
KILN OPERATOR (woodworking) 563.382-010
KILN-OPERATOR HELPER (concrete prod.) 573.685-022
KILN-OPERATOR HELPER (smelt. & refin.) 513.587-010
KILN OPERATOR, MALT HOUSE (beverage) 523.682-030
KILN PLACER (pottery & porc.) 573.686-026
kiln repairer (brick & tile) 861.381-014
kiln setter (brick & tile) 573.684-014
kiln setter (pottery & porc.) 573.686-026
kiln-setter helper (brick & tile) 573.687-030
kiln stacker (brick & tile) 573.684-014
Kiln Stacker (woodworking) 922.687-070
kiln tender (paint & varnish) 553.685-082
KILN-TRANSFER OPERATOR (woodworking) 569.683-010
kiln unloader (chemical) 569.686-034
KILN WORKER (pottery & porc.) 573.687-022
kindergartner (any industry) 359.677-026
King Maker (sugar & conf.) 526.382-014
kinker (tinware) 703.685-010
Kiss Mixer (sugar & conf.) 520.685-122
KISS SETTER, HAND (sugar & conf.) 529.687-122
kitchen chef (hotel & rest.) 313.131-014
KITCHEN CLERK (hotel & rest.) 222.587-022
kitchen hand (hotel & rest.) 318.687-010
KITCHEN HELPER (hotel & rest.) 318.687-010
kitchen porter (hotel & rest.) 318.687-010
kitchen runner (hotel & rest.) 318.687-010
KITCHEN STEWARD/STEWARDESS (hotel & rest.) 318.137-010
KITCHEN SUPERVISOR (hotel & rest.) 319.137-030
Kitter (aircraft mfg.) 754.684-042
knee bolter (saw. & plan.) 667.685-022
Knife And Spur Grinder (saw. & plan.) 603.664-010
knife changer (paper & pulp) 564.684-010
KNIFE CHANGER (tobacco) 638.684-010
knife cutter (rubber goods) 751.684-014
Knife Glazer (jewelry-silver.) 603.685-062
Knife Grinder (any industry) 603.664-010
KNIFE GRINDER (machine shop) 603.382-038
KNIFE-MACHINE OPERATOR (textile) 584.685-030
KNIFE OPERATOR (concrete prod.) 579.382-018
KNIFE SETTER (saw. & plan.) 663.380-010
KNIFE SETTER (sugar & conf.) 638.684-014
knife setter (tobacco) 638.684-010
KNIFE SETTER, GRINDER MACHINE (paper & pulp) 564.684-010
Knit-Goods Cutter, Hand (knitting) 781.684-074
KNIT-GOODS WASHER (knitting) 582.685-094
Knitted-Cloth Examiner (knitting) 689.685-038
knitted-garment finisher (laundry & rel.) 363.684-010
knitted-goods shaper (laundry & rel.) 363.684-010
knitter (knitting) 685.665-014
knitter (knitting) 685.665-018
knitter (knitting) 684.685-010
KNITTER, FULL-FASHIONED GARMENT (knitting) 685.665-010
KNITTER, HAND (tex. prod., nec) 782.684-034
knitter helper (knitting) 685.686-014
knitter, machine (knitting) 685.665-014
knitter, machine (knitting) 685.380-010
KNITTER MECHANIC (knitting) 685.360-010
KNITTER, WIRE MESH (metal prod., nec) 616.685-030
Knitting Inspector (knitting) 684.684-010
KNITTING-MACHINE FIXER (knitting) 689.260-026
KNITTING-MACHINE FIXER, HEAD (knitting) 689.130-018
KNITTING-MACHINE OPERATOR (knitting) 685.665-014

knitting-machine operator (metal prod., nec) 616.685-030
KNITTING-MACHINE OPERATOR (tex. prod., nec) 685.685-010
knitting-machine operator, automatic (knitting) 685.380-010
knitting-machine operator, automatic (knitting) 684.685-010
KNITTING-MACHINE OPERATOR, FULL-FASHIONED HOSIERY, AUTO-
MATIC (knitting) 684.682-010
KNITTING-MACHINE OPERATOR HELPER (knitting) 685.686-014
knitting-machine operator, seamless hosiery (knitting) 684.685-010
Knitting-Machine Tender (rubber goods) 692.665-010
knitting-order distributor (knitting) 221.667-010
Knit-Tubing Dyer (textile) 582.665-014
knit-wrist cutter (glove & mit.) 686.685-018
Knobber (musical inst.) 730.684-010
knocker (oils & grease) 521.686-014
knocker-off (paper goods) 794.687-050
KNOCK-OUT HAND (plastic prod.) 754.684-034
KNOCK-UP ASSEMBLER (woodworking) 762.687-050
knot picker, cloth (carpet & rug; textile) 689.684-010
knotter (tex. prod., nec) 789.684-030
knotter, hand (tex. prod., nec) 789.684-030
KNOTTING-MACHINE OPERATOR (paper goods) 649.685-054
knotting-machine operator, portable (narrow fabrics; textile) 683.685-034
knot-tying operator (narrow fabrics; textile) 683.685-034
Knuckle-Strap Sewer (glove & mit.) 784.682-010
KNURLING-MACHINE OPERATOR (ordnance) 604.685-018
Knurling-Machine Tender (pen & pencil) 604.685-026
Kosher Cutter And Searcher (meat products) 525.361-010
KOSHER INSPECTOR (dairy products) 529.687-126

L

LABEL CODER (any industry) 920.587-014
Label Cutter (garment; knitting) 699.685-014
Label Cutter (garment) 699.682-022
Label Cutter (narrow fabrics) 585.685-062
Label Cutter (textile) 789.687-150
LABEL-CUTTING-AND-FOLDING-MACHINE OPERATOR, AUTOMATIC
(narrow fabrics) 689.685-086
LABEL DRIER (recording) 532.687-010
labeler (any industry) 920.687-126
labeler (textile) 229.587-018
Labeler, Machine (any industry) 920.685-078
Label-Fuser Tender (garment) 583.685-046
LABELING-MACHINE OPERATOR (recording) 920.685-066
label marker (any industry) 920.587-014
LABEL PINKER (narrow fabrics) 585.685-062
Label-Press Operator I (print. & pub.) 651.362-010
Label-Press Operator II (print. & pub.) 651.362-018
LABEL REMOVER (beverage) 920.687-106
Label Sewer (hat & cap) 784.682-014
Label Sewer, Hand (any industry) 782.684-058
label stamper (any industry) 652.685-098
Label Stitcher (boot & shoe) 690.682-082
Label Tacker (tex. prod., nec) 787.685-042
laboratory aide (any industry) 381.687-022
laboratory aide (pharmaceut.) 559.384-010
laboratory assistant (any industry) 381.687-022
laboratory assistant (medical ser.) 078.381-014
laboratory assistant (paper & pulp; pharmaceut.) 599.687-026
laboratory assistant (paper & pulp; paper goods) 078.381-014
LABORATORY ASSISTANT (petrol. & gas) 024.381-010
laboratory assistant (profess. & kin.) 199.364-014
LABORATORY ASSISTANT (textile) 029.381-014
laboratory assistant (textile) 689.384-010
LABORATORY ASSISTANT (utilities) 029.361-018
LABORATORY ASSISTANT, BLOOD AND PLASMA (medical ser.;
pharmaceut.) 078.687-010
LABORATORY ASSISTANT, CULTURE MEDIA (pharmaceut.) 559.384-010
LABORATORY ASSISTANT, LIAISON INSPECTION (steel & rel.) 169.167-
026
LABORATORY ASSISTANT, METALLURGICAL (steel & rel.) 011.261-022
LABORATORY CHIEF (photofinishing) 976.131-010
LABORATORY CHIEF (profess. & kin.) term
LABORATORY CLERK (clerical) 222.587-026
laboratory contact supervisor (motion picture; photofinishing; radio-tv broad.)
976.131-014
laboratory coordinator (steel & rel.) 169.167-026
laboratory-development technician (profess. & kin.) 007.161-026
LABORATORY-EQUIPMENT INSTALLER (construction) 869.381-014
laboratory helper (any industry) 381.687-022
LABORATORY HELPER (utilities) 821.564-010
laboratory inspector (petrol. refin.) 029.261-022
LABORATORY MANAGER (education) 090.164-010
laboratory manager (photofinishing) 976.131-010

laboratory-mechanic helper (ordnance) 736.387-014
LABORATORY MILLER (grain-feed mills) 521.685-194
LABORATORY-SAMPLE CARRIER (any industry) 922.687-054
laboratory sampler (petrol. refin.) 549.587-014
LABORATORY SUPERVISOR (machine shop) 706.131-010
LABORATORY SUPERVISOR (profess. & kin.) 022.137-010
laboratory technician (utilities) 579.384-014
LABORATORY TECHNICIAN, ARTIFICIAL BREEDING (agriculture) 040.361-010
LABORATORY TECHNICIAN (auto. mfg.) 019.261-030
laboratory technician (chemical; plastic-synth.) 559.382-046
laboratory technician (glass mfg.) 579.384-014
laboratory technician (petrol. refin.) 029.261-022
laboratory technician (pharmaceut.) 559.382-042
LABORATORY TECHNICIAN PHARMACEUTICAL (pharmaceut.) 559.685-170
LABORATORY TESTER (any industry) 029.261-010
laboratory tester (petrol. & gas) 024.381-010
laboratory tester (petrol. refin.) 029.261-022
LABORATORY TESTER (plastic-synth.) 022.281-018
laboratory tester (textile) 029.381-014
LABORATORY TESTER (textile) 689.384-014
laboratory test mechanic (aircraft mfg.) 002.261-014
LABORATORY WORKER (any industry) term
LABOR-CREW SUPERVISOR (construction; utilities) 899.131-010
Labor Economist (profess. & kin.) 050.067-010
LABORER (fabrication, nec) 590.687-010
LABORER (meat products) 529.687-130
LABORER (petrol. & gas) 939.687-018
LABORER (pharmaceut.) 559.686-022
LABORER (toy-sport equip.) 732.687-030
Laborer, Adjustable Steel Joist (construction) 869.664-014
LABORER, AIRPORT MAINTENANCE (air trans.) 899.687-014
LABORER, AMMUNITION ASSEMBLY I (ordnance) 737.687-070
LABORER, AMMUNITION ASSEMBLY II (ordnance) 737.687-074
LABORER, AQUATIC LIFE (fishing & hunt.) 446.687-014
Laborer, Batching Plant (construction) 869.687-026
Laborer, Beam House (leather mfg.) 589.686-026
Laborer, Bituminous Paving (construction) 869.687-026
LABORER, BOOT AND SHOE (boot & shoe) 788.687-066
Laborer, Brooder Farm (agriculture) 411.687-018
LABORER, BRUSH CLEARING (any industry) 459.687-010
laborer, building maintenance (any industry) 381.687-014
LABORER, CANVAS SHOP (tex. prod., nec) 789.687-090
LABORER, CAR BARN (r.r. trans.) 910.583-010
Laborer, Carpentry (construction) 869.664-014
Laborer, Carpentry, Dock (construction) 869.664-014
Laborer, Cement-Gun Placing (construction) 869.687-026
LABORER, CHEESEMAKING (dairy products) 529.686-050
LABORER, CHEMICAL PROCESSING (chemical) 559.687-050
Laborer, Chicken Farm (agriculture) 411.687-018
LABORER, CONCRETE-MIXING PLANT (construction) 579.665-014
Laborer, Concrete Paving (construction) 869.687-026
LABORER, CONCRETE PLANT (concrete prod.) 579.687-042
LABORER, CONSTRUCTION OR LEAK GANG (utilities) 862.684-014
LABORER, COOK HOUSE (chemical) 551.687-022
Laborer, Corrugated-Iron-Culvert Placing (construction) 869.687-026
laborer, cutting tool (cutlery-hrdwr.) 701.687-018
laborer, dairy farm (agriculture) 410.684-010
Laborer, Drying Department (leather mfg.) 589.686-026
laborer, drying department (leather mfg.) 580.687-014
Laborer, Egg-Producing Farm (agriculture) 411.687-018
Laborer, Electric Power And Transmission Line (construction; utilities) 869.687-026
LABORER, ELECTROPLATING (electroplating) 500.686-010
laborer, excavation (construction)   see DITCH DIGGER
Laborer, Filter Plant (petrol. refin.) 549.687-018
laborer, filter plant (waterworks) 954.587-010
Laborer, Fryer Farm (agriculture) 411.687-018
laborer, game farm (agriculture) 412.684-010
LABORER, GENERAL (brick & tile) 579.667-010
LABORER, GENERAL (leather mfg.) 589.686-026
LABORER, GENERAL (machine shop) 609.684-014
LABORER, GENERAL (motor trans.) 909.687-014
LABORER, GENERAL (nonfer. metal) 519.686-010
LABORER, GENERAL (paint & varnish) 559.685-110
LABORER, GENERAL (plastic prod.) 754.687-010
LABORER, GENERAL (plastic-synth.) 559.667-014
LABORER, GENERAL (rubber goods; rubber reclaim.; rubber tire) 559.686-026
LABORER, GENERAL (smelt. & refin.) 519.687-026
LABORER, GENERAL (steel & rel.) 509.687-026
LABORER, GENERAL (tex. prod., nec) 589.687-026
laborer, glue drying (chemical) 553.685-058
LABORER, GOLD LEAF (metal prod., nec) 700.687-038

laborer, golf course (any industry) 406.683-010
LABORER, GRINDING AND POLISHING (any industry) 705.687-014
Laborer, Heading (construction) 869.687-026
Laborer, Hide House (leather mfg.) 589.686-026
LABORER, HIGH-DENSITY PRESS (agriculture) 929.687-018
LABORER, HOISTING (any industry) 921.667-022
LABORER, HOT-PLATE PLYWOOD PRESS (millwork-plywood) 569.686-026
laborer, laboratory (any industry) 381.687-022
LABORER, LANDSCAPE (agriculture) 408.687-014
laborer, livestock (agriculture) 410.664-010
laborer, marine terminal (water trans.) 911.687-026
laborer, mine (mine & quarry) 939.687-014
laborer, mixing plant (construction) 579.665-014
laborer, Orchard (agriculture) 403.687-010
LABORER, PETROLEUM REFINERY (petrol. refin.) 549.687-018
LABORER, PIE BAKERY (bakery products) 529.686-054
Laborer, Pile Driving, Ground Work (construction) 869.687-026
Laborer, Pipe-Line (construction) 869.687-026
LABORER, PIPE-LINES (pipe lines) 914.687-010
Laborer, Plumbing (construction) 869.687-026
laborer, pole crew (utilities) 821.687-010
LABORER, POULTRY FARM (agriculture) 411.687-018
LABORER, POULTRY HATCHERY (agriculture) 411.687-022
LABORER, POWERHOUSE (utilities) 952.665-010
LABORER, PRESTRESSED CONCRETE (concrete prod.) 575.687-018
Laborer, Pullet Farm (agriculture) 411.687-018
LABORER, RAGS (paper & pulp) 539.587-010
Laborer, Road (construction) 869.687-026
LABORER, SALVAGE (any industry) 929.687-022
laborer, sawmill (saw. & plan.) 669.687-018
Laborer, Shaft Sinking (construction) 869.687-026
LABORER, SHELLFISH PROCESSING (can. & preserv.) 529.687-230
Laborer, Shipyard (ship-boat mfg.) 809.687-022
Laborer, Shore Dredging (construction) 869.687-026
LABORER, SOLDER MAKING (nonfer. metal) 519.667-014
LABORER, STARCH FACTORY (grain-feed mills) 529.685-154
Laborer, Steel Handling (construction) 869.687-026
Laborer, Stone Block Ramming (construction) 869.687-026
LABORER, STORES (any industry) 922.687-058
LABORER, SYRUP MACHINE (grain-feed mills) 521.687-074
LABORER, TANBARK (logging) 454.687-014
Laborer, Tan House (leather mfg.) 589.686-026
LABORER, TIN CAN (tinware) 709.686-010
LABORER, TREE TAPPING (agriculture; forestry) 453.687-014
Laborer, Turkey Farm (agriculture) 411.687-018
LABORER, VAT HOUSE (chemical) 559.686-030
laborer, vegetable farm (agriculture) 402.687-010
Laborer, Vineyard (agriculture) 403.687-010
laborer, wash-and-dye house (textile) 582.686-014
LABORER, WHARF (can. & preserv.) 922.687-062
LABORER, WOOD-PRESERVING PLANT (wood prod., nec) 561.686-010
Laborer, Wrecking And Salvaging (construction) 869.687-026
Laborer, Yard (any industry) 929.687-030
LABOR EXPEDITER (construction) 249.167-018
labor-gang supervisor (motor trans.) 929.137-018
Labor Relations Consultant (profess. & kin.) 166.167-034
labor relations representative (profess. & kin.) 166.167-034
Labor Relations Supervisor (profess. & kin.) 166.167-034
labor supervisor (chemical) 382.137-010
Lace Breaker (tex. prod., nec) 689.665-014
Lace Inspector (knitting) 689.685-038
lace-machine operator (tex. prod., nec) 683.682-026
LACE-PAPER-MACHINE OPERATOR (paper goods) 649.685-058
Lace Pinner (garment; tex. prod., nec) 782.687-026
LACER (nonmet. min.) 774.687-014
LACER (protective dev.) 789.687-094
LACER (toy-sport equip.) 732.687-034
LACER AND TIER (elec. equip.) 724.687-010
LACER I (boot & shoe) 788.687-070
LACER II (boot & shoe) 690.685-254
LACE-ROLLER OPERATOR (leather prod.) 920.685-070
Lace Separator (tex. prod., nec) 689.665-014
Lace Stripper (tex. prod., nec) 689.665-014
LACE WINDER (tex. prod., nec) 685.687-018
Lacing Cutter (plastic-synth.) 781.687-026
lacing-machine operator, jacquard cards (narrow fabrics; textile) 683.685-018
Lacing Presser (tex. prod., nec) 739.685-010
LACING-STRING CUTTER (boot & shoe) 788.687-074
Lacquer Blender (paint & varnish) 550.685-078
Lacquer Coater (plastic prod.) 599.685-074
LACQUER-DIPPING-MACHINE OPERATOR (button & notion) 509.685-034
Lacquerer (button & notion) 599.686-014
LACQUERER (clock & watch) 715.684-138
LACQUERER (jewelry-silver.) 749.684-034

Lacquerer (machine shop) 740.684-022
LACQUERER (plastic prod.) 599.685-054
Lacquer Filterer (paint & varnish) 551.685-034
lacquer-machine feeder (ordnance) 694.685-046
LACQUER MAKER (paint & varnish) 559.682-030
lacquer mixer (paint & varnish) 559.682-030
LACQUER-PIN-PRESS OPERATOR (ordnance) 737.687-078
Lacquer Polisher (fabrication, nec) 739.684-026
lacquer-press adjuster (ordnance) 632.380-018
Lacquer Shader (paint & varnish) 550.381-014
Lacquer Sizer (hat & cap) 589.687-038
Lacquer Sprayer (electron. comp.) 725.684-022
Lacquer Sprayer I (any industry) 741.684-026
Lacquer Sprayer II (any industry) 741.687-018
Ladies'-Hat Trimmer (hat & cap) 784.684-022
ladle cleaner (foundry; smelt. & refin.) 519.684-010
ladle handler (foundry) 514.684-022
LADLE LINER (foundry; smelt. & refin.) 519.684-010
Ladle-Liner Helper (foundry) 519.687-022
ladle patcher (foundry; smelt. & refin.) 519.684-010
LADLE POURER (smelt. & refin.) 514.684-014
Ladle Pusher (foundry) 519.687-022
LAGGING-MACHINE OPERATOR (nonfer. metal) 691.685-014
LAG SCREWER (furniture) 763.684-046
LAMBER (agriculture) 410.364-010
Lambskin Trimmer (leather mfg.) 585.684-010
lamina searcher (tobacco) 521.687-098
LAMINATED-PLASTIC-TABLETOP-MOLDING WRAPPER (furniture) 692.686-046
LAMINATING-MACHINE FEEDER (wood prod., nec) 569.686-042
LAMINATING-MACHINE OFFBEARER (wood prod., nec) 569.686-046
LAMINATING-MACHINE OPERATOR (furniture) 692.685-106
LAMINATING-MACHINE OPERATOR (knitting; textile) 584.682-014
laminating-machine operator (paper & pulp; paper goods) 534.682-026
Laminating-Machine-Operator Helper (textile) 584.665-010
laminating machine tender (electron. comp.) 554.685-034
LAMINATING-MACHINE TENDER (rubber goods) 554.665-014
Laminating-Press Operator (plastic prod.) 690.682-062
LAMINATION ASSEMBLER (elec. equip.; electron. comp.) 729.684-066
LAMINATION ASSEMBLER, PRINTED CIRCUIT BOARDS (electron. comp.) 726.687-026
lamination inspector (elec. equip.) 729.687-018
LAMINATION SPINNER (elec. equip.) 729.687-018
Lamination Stacker, Hand (elec. equip.; electron. comp.) 729.684-066
lamination stacker, machine (any industry) 692.682-054
Lamination Stacker, Machine (elec. equip.; electron. comp.) 729.684-066
LAMINATOR (rubber goods) 899.684-018
laminator (ship-boat mfg.; vehicles, nec) 806.684-054
LAMINATOR (tex. prod., nec) 584.685-034
LAMINATOR (wood prod., nec) 554.685-030
laminator grader (wood prod., nec) 569.686-046
LAMINATOR, HAND (furniture) 763.684-050
LAMINATOR I (leather prod.) 690.685-258
LAMINATOR II (leather prod.) 783.685-022
LAMINATOR, PREFORMS (plastic prod.) 754.684-050
LAMINATOR, PRINTED CIRCUIT BOARDS (electron. comp.) 692.685-282
lamp cleaner, street-light (utilities) 952.667-010
lamp decorator (light. fix.) 749.684-018
LAMP-SHADE ASSEMBLER (fabrication, nec) 739.684-094
LAMP-SHADE JOINER (fabrication, nec) 692.685-110
LAMP-SHADE SEWER (fabrication, nec) 787.381-010
lamp wirer (light. fix.) 723.684-014
land agent (profess. & kin.) 186.117-058
land-and-leases supervisor (petrol. & gas) 186.117-046
land department head (petrol. & gas) 186.117-046
lander (mine & quarry) 939.667-010
Landing Scaler (logging) 455.487-010
land-lease-information clerk (government ser.) 237.367-026
LAND-LEASING EXAMINER (government ser.) 237.367-026
land planner (profess. & kin.) 001.061-018
land planner (profess. & kin.) 199.167-014
LANDSCAPE ARCHITECT (profess. & kin.) 001.061-018
LANDSCAPE CONTRACTOR (construction) 182.167-014
LANDSCAPE GARDENER (agriculture) 408.161-010
landscaper (agriculture) 408.161-010
LANDSCAPE SPECIALIST (government ser.) 406.687-010
LAND SURVEYOR (profess. & kin.) 018.167-018
LANE-MARKER INSTALLER (construction) 859.684-010
Lanolin-Plant Operator (pharmaceut.) 559.382-018
lap checker (amuse. & rec.) 153.387-014
LAP CUTTER-TRUER OPERATOR (optical goods) 604.685-022
Lapel Baster (garment) 782.684-058
Lapel Padder (garment; retail trade) 785.361-022
Lapel Padder (garment) 782.684-058
LAPEL PADDER, BLINDSTITCH (garment) 786.682-150

lap hand, tool (machine shop) 705.481-014
lapidary (jewelry-silver.) 770.281-014
lap-machine tender (paper & pulp) 539.685-030
lap-machine tender (textile) 680.685-086
lapper (electron. comp.) 673.685-094
Lapper (jewelry-silver.) 700.687-058
LAPPER (textile) 689.687-090
LAPPER, HAND, TOOL (machine shop) 705.481-014
LAPPING-MACHINE OPERATOR, PRODUCTION (machine shop) 603.685-070
LAPPING-MACHINE SET-UP OPERATOR (machine shop) 603.382-026
Lapping Machine Tender (electron. comp.) 673.685-094
lap polisher (clock & watch) 603.685-054
lap regulator (textile) 680.685-094
lap winder (textile) 680.685-086
lap-winding-machine operator (textile) 680.685-094
lard maker (meat products; oils & grease) 521.685-026
LARD REFINER (meat products; oils & grease) 529.685-158
lard trimmer (meat products) 521.687-106
Lard-Tub Washer (meat products) 599.684-010
larry-car operator (any industry) 919.663-014
LARRY OPERATOR (steel & rel.) 519.683-014
Laryngologist (medical ser.) 070.101-062
laser-beam-color-scanner operator (print. & pub.) 972.282-010
Laser-Beam Cutter (welding) 815.682-010
LASER-BEAM-MACHINE OPERATOR (welding) 815.682-010
LASER-BEAM-TRIM OPERATOR (electron. comp.) 726.682-010
LASERIST (amuse. & rec.) 159.042-010
LASER TECHNICIAN (electron. comp.; inst. & app.) 019.261-034
LAST CHALKER (boot & shoe) 788.687-078
LAST CLEANER (boot & shoe) 788.687-082
Last-Code Striper (wood prod., nec) 740.684-022
last dipper (boot & shoe) 788.687-078
LASTER (boot & shoe) 753.684-022
laster, hand (boot & shoe) 788.684-010
LASTER, HAND (boot & shoe) 788.684-074
Lastex-Thread Winder (textile) 681.685-098
last greaser (boot & shoe) 788.687-078
last grinder (wood prod., nec) 662.685-018
lasting-machine operator, bed (boot & shoe) 690.682-018
LASTING-MACHINE OPERATOR, HAND METHOD (boot & shoe) 788.684-078
Lasting-Room Supervisor (boot & shoe) 788.131-010
last inserter (boot & shoe) 788.684-106
LAST IRONER (wood prod., nec) 739.684-098
LAST MARKER (wood prod., nec) 739.684-102
LAST-MODEL MAKER (wood prod., nec) 761.381-018
LAST-PATTERN GRADER (wood prod., nec) 693.382-010
Last Polisher (wood prod., nec) 761.684-026
LAST PULLER (boot & shoe) 788.687-086
LAST PUTTER-AWAY (boot & shoe; rubber goods) 922.687-066
LAST REMODELER-REPAIRER (boot & shoe; wood prod., nec) 739.684-106
LAST REPAIRER (boot & shoe; wood prod., nec) 739.684-110
LAST-REPAIRER HELPER (boot & shoe) 739.684-114
LAST SAWYER (wood prod., nec) 690.685-262
LAST SCOURER (wood prod., nec) 662.685-018
LAST TRIMMER (wood prod., nec) 669.682-054
Last Turner (wood prod., nec) 664.685-018
last waxer (boot & shoe) 788.687-078
Latex Compounder (textile) 550.585-018
Latex Dipper (rubber goods) 556.685-030
LATEXER (carpet & rug) 584.684-010
LATEXER I (protective dev.) 584.685-038
Latexer II (protective dev.) 712.684-010
Latex-Paint Shader (paint & varnish) 550.381-014
LATEX-RIBBON-MACHINE OPERATOR (rubber goods) 559.682-034
LATEX SPOOLER (rubber goods) 559.685-114
Latex-Thread-Machine Operator (rubber goods) 559.682-034
LATHE HAND (jewelry-silver.) 700.682-014
lathe hand (woodworking) 664.382-010
LATHE OPERATOR (jewelry-silver.) 770.382-010
Lathe Operator (rubber goods) 690.680-010
lathe operator (rubber goods) 690.685-322
lathe operator (stonework) 674.662-010
lathe operator (wood. container) 664.682-014
LATHE OPERATOR, CONTACT LENS (optical goods) 716.382-010
LATHE OPERATOR, NUMERICAL CONTROL (machine shop) 604.362-010
LATHER (construction) 842.361-010
LATHER APPRENTICE (construction) 842.361-014
LATHE SANDER (woodworking) 761.682-010
Lathe Set-Up Operator, Large (machine shop) 604.280-010
LATHE SPOTTER (millwork-plywood) 663.686-022
LATHE TENDER (machine shop) 604.685-026
LATHE WINDER (metal prod., nec) 619.482-010
LATRINE CLEANER (mine & quarry) 939.687-022

LAUNCH COMMANDER, HARBOR POLICE (government ser.) 375.167-030
LAUNDERER, HAND (laundry & rel.) 361.684-010
LAUNDRY-BAG-PUNCH OPERATOR (paper goods) 649.685-062
LAUNDRY CLERK (clerical) 221.387-038
LAUNDRY HAND (laundry & rel.) term
LAUNDRY LABORER (laundry & rel.) 361.687-018
LAUNDRY-MACHINE MECHANIC (laundry & rel.) 629.261-010
LAUNDRY-MACHINE TENDER (tex. prod., nec) 589.685-066
Laundry-Marker Supervisor (laundry & rel.) 361.137-010
LAUNDRY OPERATOR (laundry & rel.) 369.684-014
Laundry Operator, Finishing (laundry & rel.) 369.684-014
Laundry Operator, Wash Room (laundry & rel.) 369.684-014
LAUNDRY PRICING CLERK (laundry & rel.) 216.482-030
LAUNDRY-TUB MAKER (concrete prod.) 575.684-034
LAUNDRY WORKER, DOMESTIC (domestic ser.) 302.685-010
LAUNDRY WORKER I (any industry) 361.684-014
LAUNDRY WORKER II (any industry) 361.685-018
LAUNDRY WORKER III (any industry) 369.387-010
Lautertub Tender (beverage) 521.565-014
lavatory attendant (any industry) 358.677-018
law clerk (profess. & kin.) 119.267-026
law examiner (profess. & kin.) 110.167-010
Law Librarian (library) 100.167-026
Lawnmower Mechanic (any industry) 625.281-034
LAWN-SERVICE WORKER (agriculture) 408.684-010
LAWN-SPRINKLER INSTALLER (construction) 869.684-030
law reporter (clerical) 202.362-010
LAWYER (profess. & kin.) 110.107-010
LAWYER, ADMIRALTY (profess. & kin.) 110.117-018
LAWYER, CORPORATION (profess. & kin.) 110.117-022
LAWYER, CRIMINAL (profess. & kin.) 110.107-014
LAWYER, PATENT (profess. & kin.) 110.117-026
LAWYER, PROBATE (profess. & kin.) 110.117-030
LAWYER, REAL ESTATE (profess. & kin.) 110.117-034
LAYAWAY CLERK (retail trade) 299.467-010
LAYBOY TENDER (paper & pulp; paper goods; print. & pub.) 649.685-066
layer (boot & shoe) 690.685-074
LAYER (glass mfg.) 673.686-026
layer-off (glove & mit.; laundry & rel.) 363.687-010
layer-out (profess. & kin.) 007.261-010
Layer-Out, Plate Glass (construction) 869.664-014
layer up (any industry) 781.685-010
layer-up (knitting; textile) 589.685-058
lay-out and detail drafter (utilities) 019.261-014
layout artist (profess. & kin.) 141.061-018
Lay-Out Carpenter (construction) 860.381-022
lay-out drafter (profess. & kin.) 007.261-010
LAY-OUT FORMER (business ser.) 970.381-018
Lay-Out Helper (any industry) 801.687-014
LAY-OUT INSPECTOR (machine shop) 600.281-014
Lay-Out Inspector (any industry) 619.261-010
LAY-OUT-MACHINE OPERATOR (tex. prod., nec) 781.684-034
lay-out maker (any industry) 809.381-014
Lay-Out Supervisor (any industry) 619.130-030
LAY-OUT TECHNICIAN (optical goods) 716.381-014
LAY-OUT WORKER (jewelry-silver.) 700.381-026
lay-out worker (machine shop) 600.281-014
LAY-OUT WORKER (machine shop) 600.281-018
LAY-OUT WORKER (mfd. bldgs.) 869.684-034
LAY-OUT WORKER I (any industry) 809.281-010
LAY-OUT WORKER II (any industry) 809.381-014
lay-up operator (plastic-synth.) 690.585-014
lay-up presser (tex. prod., nec) 586.662-010
LEACHER (paper & pulp) 551.685-090
LEACHER (smelt. & refin.) 511.582-010
lead assembler (elec. equip.) 691.685-018
lead bender (elec. equip.) 691.685-018
lead blender (petrol. refin.) 540.462-010
LEAD BURNER (elec. equip.) 727.684-022
LEAD BURNER (welding) 819.281-010
LEAD-BURNER APPRENTICE (welding) 819.281-014
LEAD-BURNER HELPER (elec. equip.) 727.687-070
LEAD BURNER, MACHINE (elec. equip.) 727.662-010
LEAD-BURNER SUPERVISOR (welding) 819.131-010
LEAD CASTER (elec. equip.) 502.684-010
LEAD-CASTER HELPER (elec. equip.) 502.687-018
Lead Coater (galvanizing) 501.485-010
leader (any industry)   see SUPERVISOR
leader (any industry)   see GROUP LEADER
leader assembler (toy-sport equip.) 732.687-038
leader, print rubber (rubber goods) 652.462-010
LEADER TIER (toy-sport equip.) 732.687-038
lead fabricator (plumbing-heat.) 619.382-014
LEAD FORMER (elec. equip.) 691.685-018
LEAD FORMER (pen & pencil) 575.685-050

LEAD HAND, INSPECTING AND TESTING (electron. comp.) 726.364-010
LEAD HANDLER (ordnance) 599.687-018
Leadite Heater (construction) 869.685-010
lead janitor (any industry) 381.137-010
lead-laying-and-gluing-machine operator (pen & pencil) 692.685-094
Lead Loader (smelt. & refin.) 921.683-050
leadman, turbine assembly (engine-turbine) 600.261-010
LEAD-NITRATE PROCESSOR (chemical) 558.585-030
LEAD OPERATOR (smelt. & refin.) 630.381-018
LEAD OPERATOR, AUTOMATIC VULCANIZING (rubber goods) 690.362-010
LEAD-OXIDE-MILL TENDER (elec. equip.) 558.685-042
LEAD PONY RIDER (amuse. & rec.) 153.674-014
lead presser (pen & pencil) 575.685-050
LEAD-PRESS OPERATOR (nonfer. metal) 691.382-014
lead printer (print. & pub.) 979.130-014
LEAD RECOVERER, CONTINUOUS-NAPHTHA-TREATING PLANT (petrol. refin.) 541.685-014
lead-relay tester (utilities) 729.131-014
lead rider (agriculture) 410.137-014
LEAD-SECTION SUPERVISOR (ordnance) 619.132-010
lead-sheet cutter (nonfer. metal) 502.684-014
lead-shop operator (chemical) 558.585-030
Lead-Supply Worker (elec. equip.) 502.687-018
lead ticket-sales agent (air trans.) 238.137-022
Lead Tinner (elec. equip.) 691.685-018
Lead-Tong Worker (petrol. & gas) 930.684-026
lead welder (welding) 819.281-010
LEAD WORKER, WAFER POLISHING (electron. comp.) 673.364-010
LEAD WORKER, WAFER PRODUCTION (electron. comp.) 590.364-010
leaf binner (tobacco) 922.687-010
leaf blender (tobacco) 520.387-010
LEAF CONDITIONER (tobacco) 522.687-026
LEAF-CONDITIONER HELPER (tobacco) 522.687-030
LEAF COVERER (smelt. & refin.) 519.684-014
Leaf-Fat Scraper (meat products) 525.687-010
LEAF-SIZE PICKER (tobacco) 529.687-142
LEAF SORTER (tobacco) 529.687-134
leaf stamper (any industry) 652.682-030
leaf stemmer, hand (tobacco) 521.687-134
leaf sticker (button & notion) 734.687-090
Leaf-Sucker Operator (government ser.) 919.683-022
LEAF TIER (tobacco) 529.687-138
leaf tinner (tobacco) 922.687-010
Leak-Gang Supervisor (utilities) 862.137-010
LEAK HUNTER (beverage) 764.687-090
leak locator (pipe lines; utilities) 953.367-010
Leak Operator, Paraffin Plant (petrol. refin.) 541.682-010
Leak Patcher (meat products) 525.687-010
LEAK TESTER, SEMICONDUCTOR PACKAGES (electron. comp.) 726.685-034
lease agent (petrol. & gas) 186.117-046
LEASE BUYER (mine & quarry; petrol. & gas) 191.117-030
LEASE-OUT WORKER (textile) 683.684-022
LEASE PICKER (textile) 689.684-018
leaser (mine & quarry; petrol. & gas) 191.117-030
leases-and-land supervisor (petrol. & gas) 186.117-046
lease supervisor (petrol. & gas) 939.131-014
LEASING AGENT, OUTDOOR ADVERTISING (business ser.) 254.357-010
LEASING AGENT, RESIDENCE (real estate) 250.357-014
LEASING-MACHINE TENDER (textile) 681.685-054
Leather Baler (leather mfg.) 920.685-010
Leather-Belt-Loop Cutter (leather prod.) 690.685-266
LEATHER-BELT MAKER (leather prod.) 690.685-266
Leather-Belt Puncher (leather prod.) 690.685-266
Leather-Belt Shaper (leather prod.) 690.685-266
Leather-Cartridge-Belt Maker (leather prod.) 690.685-266
leather-case finisher (leather prod.) 739.684-034
LEATHER CLEANER (laundry & rel.) 362.684-026
LEATHER COATER (leather mfg.) 584.687-010
leather colorer (leather mfg.) 582.482-010
Leather Coverer (toy-sport equip.) 732.684-026
Leather Crafter (leather prod.) 142.061-018
Leather Cutter (glove & mit.; leather prod.) 789.382-010
LEATHER CUTTER (leather prod.) 783.684-022
leather dresser (leather mfg.) 584.687-010
LEATHER ETCHER (garment) 583.685-066
LEATHER FINISHER (laundry & rel.) 363.682-010
Leather Fitter (hat & cap) 784.682-014
Leather Flanger (hat & cap) 690.686-058
leather grader (boot & shoe) 788.387-010
LEATHER GRADER (glove & mit.) 784.387-014
leather leveler (leather mfg.) 690.686-054
Leather-Novelty-Parts Cutter (leather prod.) 699.682-022
leather patcher (leather mfg.) 585.687-022

leather-piece inspector

leather-piece inspector (glove & mit.) 781.687-034
leather polisher (leather mfg.) 583.685-094
leather pourer (leather mfg.) 584.687-014
leather repairer (boot & shoe) 788.684-022
leather repairer (leather mfg.) 585.687-022
leather sander (leather mfg.) 585.685-018
LEATHER SOFTENER (boot & shoe) 788.687-090
Leather Softener, Drum (leather mfg.) 582.482-010
leather sorter (glove & mit.) 784.387-014
leather sorter (leather mfg.) 589.387-010
leather sprayer (leather mfg.) 584.687-014
LEATHER STAMPER (leather prod.) 781.381-018
leather-stripping-machine operator (leather prod.) 585.685-038
LEATHER TOOLER (furniture) 763.684-054
leather tooler (leather prod.) 781.381-018
LEATHER WORKER (leather prod.) 783.684-026
Leather Worker (protective dev.) 712.684-010
Lecturer (education) 090.227-010
legal aid (profess. & kin.) 119.267-026
legal assistant (profess. & kin.) 119.267-026
legal assistant (profess. & kin.) 119.267-022
LEGAL INVESTIGATOR (profess. & kin.) 119.267-022
LEGAL SECRETARY (clerical) 201.362-010
Legal Stenographer (clerical) 202.362-014
Legal Transcriber (clerical) 203.582-058
Leg Assembler (toy-sport equip.) 732.384-010
LEGEND MAKER (fabrication, nec) 979.684-018
Legger-Press Operator (laundry & rel.) 363.682-018
legislative advocate (profess. & kin.) 165.017-010
Legislative Aide (government ser.) 199.267-034
LEGISLATIVE ASSISTANT (government ser.) 169.167-066
Leg Skinner (meat products) 525.684-046
lehr attendant (glass mfg.) 573.685-026
Lehr Cutter (glass mfg.) 779.684-054
lehr operator (glass mfg.) 573.685-026
lehr stripper (glass mfg.) 573.685-026
LEHR TENDER (glass mfg.) 573.685-026
lei maker (retail trade) 291.454-010
LEI SELLER (retail trade) 291.454-010
Lemon Grower (agriculture) 403.161-010
length control tester (knitting) 684.684-014
leno sewer (carpet & rug; retail trade) 787.682-014
lens assorter (optical goods) 716.687-026
lens assorter (optical goods) 716.687-022
LENS-BLANK GAUGER (optical goods) 716.687-026
LENS-BLOCK GAUGER (optical goods) 716.687-030
lens cutter (optical goods) 716.682-010
Lens-Edge Grinder, Machine (optical goods) 716.685-022
LENS EXAMINER (optical goods) 716.687-022
LENS-FABRICATING-MACHINE TENDER (optical goods) 716.685-022
Lens-Generating-Machine Tender (optical goods) 716.685-022
lens grinder (optical goods) 716.382-018
lens-grinder apprentice (optical goods) 716.382-022
lens grinder, rough (optical goods) 673.685-074
LENS HARDENER (optical goods) 573.685-030
LENS INSERTER (optical goods) 713.687-026
lens inspector (optical goods) 716.687-022
lens inspector (optical goods) 716.381-010
LENS MATCHER (optical goods) 713.687-030
lens molder (glass mfg.) 575.685-054
LENS-MOLDING-EQUIPMENT OPERATOR (glass mfg.) 575.685-054
LENS-MOLD SETTER (optical goods) 713.381-010
Lens Mounter I (optical goods) 690.685-014
LENS MOUNTER II (optical goods) 713.681-010
LENS POLISHER, HAND (optical goods) 716.681-018
letter carrier (government ser.) 230.367-010
letterer (any industry) 979.684-034
letterer (any industry) 970.381-026
Letterer (garment) 787.682-022
LETTERER (machinery mfg.) 979.681-010
LETTERER (profess. & kin.) 970.661-014
lettering-machine operator (any industry) 652.682-030
LETTER-OF-CREDIT CLERK (financial) 219.367-050
LETTER-OF-CREDIT DOCUMENT EXAMINER (financial) 169.267-042
letter-stamping-machine operator (clerical) 208.685-026
Lettuce Trimmer (agriculture) 920.687-134
levee superintendent (construction) 851.137-010
leveler (boot & shoe) 690.685-382
Leveler Helper (wood. container) 669.685-010
LEVELER I (wood. container) 764.687-094
Leveler II (wood. container) 669.682-014
LEVEL-GLASS-FORMING-MACHINE OPERATOR (cutlery-hrdwr.) 679.665-010
LEVEL-GLASS-VIAL FILLER (cutlery-hrdwr.) 692.685-114
leveling-machine operator (boot & shoe) 690.685-382

LEVEL-VIAL CURVATURE GAUGER (cutlery-hrdwr.) 701.687-022
LEVEL-VIAL INSIDE GRINDER (cutlery-hrdwr.) 673.685-066
LEVEL-VIAL INSPECTOR-AND-TESTER (cutlery-hrdwr.) 701.687-026
LEVEL-VIAL MARKER (cutlery-hrdwr.) 775.684-046
LEVEL-VIAL SEALER (cutlery-hrdwr.) 779.684-034
LEVEL-VIAL SETTER (cutlery-hrdwr.) 701.684-018
LEVER MILLER (clock & watch) 605.685-026
LEVERS-LACE MACHINE OPERATOR (tex. prod., nec) 683.682-026
LEVER TENDER (forging) 612.685-010
lexicographer (profess. & kin.) 132.067-018
LIAISON ENGINEER (aircraft mfg.) 012.167-038
liaison officer (nonprofit org.) 187.167-198
LIBRARIAN (library) 100.127-014
librarian (radio-tv broad.) 100.367-022
librarian, head (library) 100.117-010
librarian, school (library) 100.167-030
LIBRARIAN, SPECIAL COLLECTIONS (library) 100.267-014
LIBRARIAN, SPECIAL LIBRARY (library) 100.167-026
LIBRARY ASSISTANT (library) 249.367-046
library assistant (library) 100.367-018
library attendant (library) 249.367-046
library clerk (library) 249.367-046
Library Clerk, Art Department (library) 249.367-046
LIBRARY CLERK, TALKING BOOKS (library) 209.387-026
LIBRARY CONSULTANT (library) 100.117-014
LIBRARY DIRECTOR (library) 100.117-010
library helper (library) 249.367-046
LIBRARY TECHNICAL ASSISTANT (library) 100.367-018
library technician (library) 100.367-018
LIBRETTIST (profess. & kin.) 131.067-030
LICENSE CLERK (government ser.) 205.367-034
LICENSE INSPECTOR (government ser.) 168.267-066
Lidder (agriculture; wholesale tr.) 920.687-134
Lidder (any industry) 920.587-018
Lidding-Machine Operator (any industry) 669.682-058
lie-detection examiner (profess. & kin.) 199.267-026
Lieutenant, Ballistics (government ser.) 199.267-010
LIFEGUARD (amuse. & rec.) 379.667-014
life-line attendant (any industry) 899.664-010
Life Tester, Outboard Motors (engine-turbine) 623.261-014
lift builder, whole (boot & shoe) 690.685-206
LIFT-SLAB OPERATOR (construction) 869.662-010
Lift-Truck Operator (water trans.) 911.663-014
LIGHT AIR DEFENSE ARTILLERY CREWMEMBER (military ser.) 378.684-030
LIGHT-BULB ASSEMBLER (light. fix.) 692.685-118
light-bulb replacer (any industry) 389.687-018
Light-Bulb Tester (elec. equip.; light. fix.) 729.684-058
light cleaner (any industry) 389.687-018
Light-Fixture Cleaner (any industry) 381.687-014
LIGHT-FIXTURE SERVICER (any industry) 389.687-018
LIGHTING-EQUIPMENT OPERATOR (amuse. & rec.) 962.381-014
Lightning-Rod Erector (construction) 869.664-014
light-oil operator (steel & rel.) 549.382-018
LIGHTOUT EXAMINER (beverage) 529.687-146
lights inspector (beverage) 529.687-058
LIGHT TECHNICIAN (motion picture; radio-tv broad.) 962.362-014
Limber (logging) 454.687-010
lime burner (concrete prod.) 573.462-010
lime hide inspector (leather prod.) 585.687-010
LIME-KILN OPERATOR (concrete prod.) 573.462-010
LIME-KILN OPERATOR (paper & pulp) 559.685-118
lime mixer (concrete prod.) 570.685-034
LIME MIXER TENDER (steel & rel.) 514.685-022
lime-plant operator (concrete prod.) 570.685-034
Limer (chemical; leather mfg.) 582.482-014
Limer (grain-feed mills) 520.685-098
limerock tower loader (paper & pulp) 559.666-010
LIME SLAKER (concrete prod.) 570.685-034
lime slaker (paper & pulp) 559.685-118
LIME-SLUDGE KILN OPERATOR (paper & pulp) 553.685-074
LIME-SLUDGE MIXER (paper & pulp) 550.585-026
Lime Trimmer (leather mfg.) 585.684-010
Lime-Vat Tender (meat products) 582.685-126
Limnologist (profess. & kin.) 041.061-022
Limousine Rental Clerk (automotive ser.) 295.467-026
line-and-frame poler (utilities; wood prod., nec) 959.684-010
line assembler, aircraft (aircraft mfg.) 806.361-014
Line Cleaner (beverage; dairy products) 599.684-010
Line-Construction Supervisor (utilities) 821.131-014
line decorator (pottery & porc.) 740.681-010
LINE ERECTOR (construction; utilities) 821.361-018
LINE-ERECTOR APPRENTICE (construction; utilities) 821.361-030
line inspector (electron. comp.) 726.684-022
LINE INSPECTOR (tel. & tel.) 822.267-010

line inspector (utilities) 003.167-014
LINE INSTALLER-REPAIRER (tel. & tel.) 822.381-014
Line Installer-Repairer, City (tel. & tel.) 822.381-014
LINE INSTALLER, STREET RAILWAY (r.r. trans.) 821.361-022
line installer, trolley (r.r. trans.) 821.361-022
LINE MAINTAINER (any industry) 821.261-014
Line Maintainer, District (any industry) 821.261-014
Line Maintainer, Section (tel. & tel.) 822.381-014
LINE MOVER (railroad equip.) 921.664-010
linen checker (hotel & rest.; medical ser.) 222.387-030
linen clerk (hotel & rest.; medical ser.) 222.387-030
LINEN CONTROLLER (laundry & rel.) 299.357-010
linen-exchange attendant (hotel & rest.; medical ser.) 222.387-030
LINEN GRADER (laundry & rel.) 361.687-022
LINEN-ROOM ATTENDANT (hotel & rest.; medical ser.) 222.387-030
linen-room houseperson (hotel & rest.; medical ser.) 222.387-030
LINEN-ROOM SUPERVISOR (laundry & rel.) 222.137-014
Linen-Room Worker (hotel & rest.) 323.687-018
LINEN-SUPPLY LOAD-BUILDER (laundry & rel.) 920.687-118
Linen-Supply-Room Worker (laundry & rel.) 361.687-018
line operator (beverage) 920.687-042
LINE-OUT WORKER I (tobacco) 920.687-110
LINE-OUT WORKER II (tobacco) 920.687-114
LINER (glove & mit.) 784.687-046
liner (machinery mfg.) 759.684-050
LINER (pottery & porc.) 740.681-010
LINER ASSEMBLER (nonfer. metal) 613.667-010
LINE REPAIRER (utilities) 821.361-026
Line Repairer, Tower (utilities) 821.361-026
line rider (petrol. & gas; petrol. refin.; pipe lines) 869.564-010
LINER INSERTER (tobacco) 929.687-026
LINER-MACHINE OPERATOR (paper goods) 641.685-058
LINER-MACHINE-OPERATOR HELPER (paper goods) 641.686-022
LINER REPLACER (mine & quarry; smelt. & refin.) 801.664-010
LINER REROLL TENDER (rubber goods; rubber tire) 554.685-022
liner-roll changer (rubber goods; rubber tire) 554.686-018
Liner Sheeter (any industry) 699.682-018
LINE-SERVICE ATTENDANT (air trans.) 912.687-010
line servicer (utilities) 821.361-026
LINES TENDER (water trans.) 911.687-026
line supervisor (smelt. & refin.) 511.130-010
LINE SUPERVISOR (tel. & tel.) 822.131-018
LINE SUPERVISOR (utilities) 821.131-014
Line Supervisor, Tower (utilities) 821.131-014
line supply (any industry) 929.687-030
LINE TENDER, FLAKEBOARD (wood prod., nec) 569.382-010
Line Umpire (amuse. & rec.) 153.267-018
LINE-UP EXAMINER (print. & pub.) 979.381-014
line-up-machine operator (elec. equip.) 706.687-018
LINE-UP WORKER (auto. mfg.) 221.367-026
LINE WALKER (petrol. & gas; petrol. refin.; pipe lines) 869.564-010
LINGO CLEANER (textile) 683.687-026
linguist (profess. & kin.) 059.067-014
LINGUIST (profess. & kin.) term
LINING BASTER, JUMPBASTING (garment) 786.682-154
lining brusher (laundry & rel.) 362.687-014
LINING CEMENTER (hat & cap) 795.687-022
lining cleaner (laundry & rel.) 362.687-014
Lining Closer (boot & shoe) 690.682-082
Lining Cutter, Machine (boot & shoe) 699.682-022
LINING FELLER, BLINDSTITCH (garment) 786.682-158
Lining Finisher (garment) 782.684-058
Lining Finisher (laundry & rel.) 783.381-014
LINING INSERTER (toy-sport equip.) 732.687-042
Lining Inspector (boot & shoe) 788.384-010
Lining Ironer (boot & shoe) 788.684-130
LINING-MACHINE OPERATOR (concrete prod.) 575.565-010
lining-machine tender (any industry) 692.685-062
Lining Maker (hat & cap) 784.682-010
Lining Maker, Hand (jewelry-silver.) 739.687-138
LINING MAKER, LOCKSTITCH (garment) 786.682-162
Lining Marker (boot & shoe) 788.584-014
Lining-Parts Sewer (leather prod.) 783.682-014
Lining Presser (garment; laundry & rel.) 363.684-018
Lining Presser (laundry & rel.) 363.682-018
lining printer (hat & cap) 651.682-022
Lining Repairer (boot & shoe) 788.381-010
LINING SCRUBBER (laundry & rel.) 362.687-014
LINING SETTER, LOCKSTITCH (garment) 786.682-166
Lining Sewer (tex. prod., nec) 787.682-066
lining stamper (boot & shoe) 690.685-398
Lining Stitcher (boot & shoe) 690.682-082
Lining-Strap Closer (boot & shoe) 690.682-082
lining stuffer (toy-sport equip.) 732.687-042
Lining Vamper (boot & shoe) 690.682-082

LINK-AND-LINK-KNITTING-MACHINE OPERATOR (knitting) 685.380-010
Link Assembler (jewelry-silver.) 735.687-014
LINKER (jewelry-silver.) 735.687-014
LINKER (meat products) 529.687-150
linker-up (jewelry-silver.) 735.687-014
link-fabric-machine operator (furniture) 616.685-022
LINKING-MACHINE OPERATOR (meat products) 529.685-162
link-wire-machine operator (furniture) 616.362-010
link-wire-fabric-machine tender (furniture) 616.685-022
Linoleum Cutter (retail trade) 929.381-010
Linoleum-Floor Layer (construction; retail trade) 864.481-010
Linoleum Layer (construction; retail trade) 864.481-010
Linoleum-Tile-Floor Layer (construction; retail trade) 864.481-010
linotype-maintenance-mechanic apprentice (print. & pub.) 627.261-018
LINOTYPE OPERATOR (print. & pub.) 650.582-010
linseed-oil-mill tender (oils & grease) 559.685-122
LINSEED-OIL-PRESS TENDER (oils & grease) 559.685-122
LINSEED-OIL REFINER (oils & grease) 559.382-030
linter (oils & grease) 521.685-198
Linter-Drier Operator (chemical) 553.685-034
LINTER-SAW SHARPENER (oils & grease) 603.682-018
LINTER TENDER (oils & grease) 521.685-198
linting-machine operator (textile) 680.685-050
Lip-And-Gate Builder (glass mfg.) 861.381-026
Lipcoat Sprayer (any industry) 741.687-018
LIP CUTTER AND SCORER (boot & shoe) 690.685-270
LIP-OF-SHANK CUTTER (boot & shoe) 690.685-274
Lipstick Molder (pharmaceut.) 556.687-022
LIQUEFACTION-AND-REGASIFICATION-PLANT OPERATOR (utilities) 953.362-014
LIQUEFACTION-PLANT OPERATOR (chemical) 559.362-018
liquefier (chemical) 559.362-018
liquid-chlorine operator (chemical) 559.362-018
Liquid Compounder I (pharmaceut.) 559.382-042
Liquid Compounder II (pharmaceut.) 550.685-090
LIQUID-FERTILIZER SERVICER (agriculture) 906.683-014
Liquid-Hydrogen-Plant Operator (chemical) 552.362-014
liquid loader (any industry) 914.667-010
LIQUID-SUGAR FORTIFIER (sugar & conf.) 520.585-022
LIQUID-SUGAR MELTER (sugar & conf.) 520.382-014
LIQUOR BLENDER (beverage) 522.382-018
LIQUOR-BRIDGE OPERATOR (sugar & conf.) 521.565-010
LIQUOR-BRIDGE-OPERATOR HELPER (sugar & conf.) 521.687-078
liquor-gallery operator (sugar & conf.) 521.565-010
LIQUOR-GRINDING-MILL OPERATOR (sugar & conf.) 521.685-202
LIQUOR INSPECTOR (beverage) 522.667-010
liquor maker (paint & varnish) 553.685-026
liquor runner (sugar & conf.) 521.565-010
Liquor-Store Stock Clerk (retail trade) 299.367-014
LITERARY AGENT (business ser.) 191.117-034
LITHOGRAPHED-PLATE INSPECTOR (tinware) 651.687-010
lithographer apprentice (print. & pub.) 972.382-010
lithographer retoucher (print. & pub.) 972.281-010
lithographic-camera operator (print. & pub.) 972.382-014
LITHOGRAPHIC PLATEMAKER (print. & pub.) 972.381-010
LITHOGRAPHIC-PLATE-MAKER APPRENTICE (print. & pub.) 972.381-014
Lithographic-Press Feeder (print. & pub.) 651.686-010
lithographic-press operator (print. & pub.) 651.382-042
lithographic-press operator apprentice (print. & pub.) 651.382-046
lithographic-press-plate-maker apprentice, photomechanical (print. & pub.) 972.381-014
Lithographic Proofer (print. & pub.) 651.582-010
LITHOGRAPHIC-PROOFER APPRENTICE (print. & pub.) 651.582-014
lithographic retoucher apprentice (print. & pub.) 972.281-018
LITHOGRAPH-PRESS OPERATOR, TINWARE (tinware) 651.382-014
Liver Trimmer (meat products) 525.684-038
Livestock Agent (government ser.) 096.127-010
livestock breeder (agriculture) 410.161-018
Livestock Counter (agriculture) 221.587-030
livestock farmer (agriculture) 410.161-018
LIVESTOCK RANCHER (agriculture) 410.161-018
LIVESTOCK-YARD ATTENDANT (any industry) 410.674-018
load blocker (glass mfg.; glass products) 673.685-030
Load-Chain Welding-Machine Repairer (forging) 626.261-010
LOAD CHECKER (utilities) 952.367-010
load clerk (any industry) 929.687-058
LOAD DISPATCHER (utilities) 952.167-014
Load Dispatcher, Local (utilities) 952.167-014
loader (construction)   see WHEELER
LOADER (mfd. bldgs.) 921.687-018
loader (mine & quarry) 932.687-010
Loader (mine & quarry) 939.687-014
loader and unloader (any industry) 929.687-030
LOADER-DEMOLDER (furniture) 556.684-030
loader-head operator (any industry) 921.683-014

LOADER HELPER (any industry) 914.687-014
Loader Helper, Sorting Yard (logging) 921.687-022
LOADER I (any industry) 914.667-010
Loader II (any industry) 929.687-030
loader, machine (mine & quarry) 932.683-014
LOADER, MAGAZINE GRINDER (paper & pulp) 530.686-014
LOADER, MALT HOUSE (beverage) 921.682-010
loader operator (any industry) 921.683-042
loader operator (mine & quarry) 932.683-018
LOADER, SEMICONDUCTOR DIES (electron. comp.) 726.687-030
LOADER-UNLOADER, SCREEN-PRINTING MACHINE (textile) 652.686-022
loading checker (clerical) 222.687-030
Loading Checker (steel & rel.) 509.687-026
LOADING INSPECTOR (r.r. trans.) 910.667-018
LOADING-MACHINE ADJUSTER (ordnance) 632.360-014
LOADING-MACHINE OPERATOR (mine & quarry) 932.683-014
LOADING-MACHINE OPERATOR (ordnance) 694.685-026
loading-machine operator (ordnance) 694.665-010
LOADING-MACHINE-OPERATOR HELPER (mine & quarry) 939.686-010
LOADING-MACHINE TOOL-SETTER (ordnance) 694.260-010
LOADING-RACK SUPERVISOR (petrol. refin.) 914.137-014
LOADING-SHOVEL OILER (mine & quarry) 932.667-014
loading supervisor (petrol. refin.) 549.137-018
LOADING-UNIT OPERATOR (ordnance) 694.685-030
Loading-Unit Operator, Crimping (ordnance) 694.685-030
Loading-Unit Operator, Powder Charging (ordnance) 694.685-030
Loading-Unit Operator, Seating (ordnance) 694.685-030
loading-unit plate filler (ordnance) 737.685-014
LOADING-UNIT TOOL-SETTER (ordnance) 632.380-014
load mixer (leather mfg.) 584.687-010
LOAD-OUT SUPERVISOR (mine & quarry) 921.133-014
load-out worker (tobacco) 922.687-026
load tallier (wood prod., nec) 221.167-022
LOAD TESTER (metal prod., nec) 616.685-034
LOAD-TEST MECHANIC (aircraft mfg.) 929.382-010
Loan-Application Clerk (financial) 205.367-022
Loan-Approval Agent (government ser.) 205.367-022
loan clerk (clerical) 205.367-022
loan closer (clerical) 219.362-038
Loan Counselor (education) 169.267-018
LOAN INTERVIEWER, MORTGAGE (financial) 241.367-018
loan officer (financial) 241.367-018
LOAN OFFICER (financial; insurance) 186.267-018
LOAN REVIEW ANALYST (financial) 186.267-022
loan-servicing officer (financial) 186.167-078
LOBBYIST (profess. & kin.) 165.017-010
Local Announcer (radio-tv broad.) 159.147-010
Local-Collection Clerk (financial) 216.362-014
LOCATION-AND-MEASUREMENT TECHNICIAN (clock & watch) 715.381-078
Location-And-Measurement Technician, Tool Room (clock & watch) 715.381-078
LOCATION MANAGER (motion picture; radio-tv broad.) 191.167-018
Lock-And-Dam Equipment Repairer (water trans.) 899.281-010
LOCK ASSEMBLER (cutlery-hrdwr.) 706.684-074
LOCK ASSEMBLER (furniture) 706.684-070
LOCK-CORNER-MACHINE OPERATOR (woodworking) 665.382-014
locker attendant (personal ser.) 358.677-014
LOCKER-PLANT ATTENDANT (retail trade; wholesale tr.) 922.684-010
LOCKER-ROOM ATTENDANT (personal ser.) 358.677-014
locker-room clerk (personal ser.) 358.677-014
LOCKET MAKER (jewelry-silver.) 700.381-030
lock expert (any industry) 709.281-010
LOCK INSTALLER (furniture) 706.684-078
LOCK MAINTENANCE SUPERVISOR (construction) 899.131-014
LOCK OPERATOR (water trans.) 911.362-010
LOCKSMITH (any industry) 709.281-010
LOCKSMITH APPRENTICE (any industry) 709.281-014
lock-stitch channeler (boot & shoe) 690.685-086
Lockstitcher (boot & shoe) 690.682-078
LOCKSTITCH-MACHINE OPERATOR (garment) 786.682-170
LOCKSTITCH-SEWING-MACHINE OPERATOR, COMPLETE GARMENT (garment) 786.682-174
LOCK TENDER, CHIEF OPERATOR (water trans.) 911.131-014
Lock Tender I (construction) 869.665-010
LOCK TENDER II (construction) 850.663-018
LOCOMOTIVE-CRANE OPERATOR (any industry) 921.663-038
Locomotive-Crane-Operator Helper (any industry) 921.667-022
locomotive engineer (r.r. trans.) 910.363-018
LOCOMOTIVE ENGINEER (r.r. trans.) 910.363-014
Locomotive Engineer, Diesel (r.r. trans.) 910.363-014
Locomotive Engineer, Electric (r.r. trans.) 910.363-014
Locomotive Engineer, Gasoline (any industry) 910.363-018
Locomotive-Engine Supervisor (any industry) 910.137-022

LOCOMOTIVE INSPECTOR (railroad equip.) 622.281-010
LOCOMOTIVE LUBRICATING-SYSTEMS CLERK (r.r. trans.) 221.367-030
LOCOMOTIVE OPERATOR HELPER (r.r. trans.) 910.367-022
Locomotive Repairer, Diesel (railroad equip.) 625.281-010
loft and lie inspector and adjuster (toy-sport equip.) 732.384-014
loft patternmaker (aircraft mfg.) 777.281-018
loft patternmaker (machine tools) 777.381-038
loft rigger (ship-boat mfg.) 806.261-014
LOFT WORKER (ship-boat mfg.) 661.281-010
LOFT WORKER APPRENTICE (ship-boat mfg.) 661.281-014
Loft Worker, Concrete-Mixing Plant (construction) 579.665-014
LOFT WORKER, HEAD (ship-boat mfg.) 661.131-010
Loft Worker, Pile Driving (construction) 869.687-026
log-chain feeder (millwork-plywood; paper & pulp; saw. & plan.) 921.686-022
LOG-CHIPPER OPERATOR (logging) 564.662-010
log clerk (radio-tv broad.) 249.387-010
LOG COOKER (wood. container) 562.665-010
log culler (saw. & plan.) 667.687-014
LOG-CUT-OFF SAWYER, AUTOMATIC (saw. & plan.) 667.682-090
log-deck tender (saw. & plan.) 921.685-014
LOGGER (logging) term
LOGGER, ALL-ROUND (logging) 454.684-018
Logging-Arch Operator (logging) 929.663-010
Logging Contractor (logging) 183.167-038
LOGGING-EQUIPMENT MECHANIC (logging) 620.281-042
LOGGING-OPERATIONS INSPECTOR (forestry; logging) 168.267-070
LOGGING-TRACTOR OPERATOR (forestry; logging; saw. & plan.) 929.663-010
Logging-Tractor Operator, Swamp (logging) 929.663-010
LOG GRADER (logging; saw. & plan.) 455.367-010
log handler (saw. & plan.) 677.687-010
LOG-HAUL CHAIN FEEDER (paper & pulp; saw. & plan.) 921.686-018
log hauler (logging) 904.683-010
Log Hooker (millwork-plywood; saw. & plan.) 921.667-022
LOG INSPECTOR (saw. & plan.) 667.687-014
LOGISTICS ENGINEER (profess. & kin.) 019.167-010
logistics specialist (profess. & kin.) 019.167-010
LOG LOADER (logging) 921.683-058
LOG LOADER HELPER (logging) 921.687-022
LOG MARKER (logging) 455.687-010
LOG MARKER (logging; millwork-plywood) 454.687-018
log operations coordinator (radio-tv broad.) 199.382-010
LOG PEELER (saw. & plan.) 569.684-010
Log Rider (saw. & plan.) 921.686-022
LOG ROLLER (saw. & plan.) 677.687-010
LOG SCALER (logging; millwork-plywood; paper & pulp; saw. & plan.) 455.487-010
LOG SORTER (logging) 455.684-010
Log-Stacker Operator (logging; saw. & plan.) 929.663-010
LOG-TRUCK DRIVER (logging) 904.683-010
LOG WASHER (saw. & plan.) 569.687-014
LOG-YARD CRANE OPERATOR (saw. & plan.) term
Log-Yard Derrick Operator (saw. & plan.) 921.663-022
Loin Boner (meat products) 525.684-010
Loin Trimmer (meat products) 525.684-054
lollypop-machine operator (sugar & conf.) 529.685-234
lollypop maker (sugar & conf.) 529.685-234
LONG-CHAIN BEAMER (textile) 681.685-058
long-chain-dyeing-machine operator (textile) 582.685-158
long-chain-quiller tender (textile) 681.685-070
Long-Distance Operator (tel. & tel.) 235.462-010
long-filler-cigar roller, machine (tobacco) 529.685-266
long-goods drier (food prep., nec) 523.585-022
LONG-GOODS HELPER, MACHINE (food prep., nec) 529.686-062
Long-Haul-Sleeper Driver (any industry) 904.383-010
Longitudinal-Float Operator (construction) 853.663-014
Long-Line Teamster (any industry) 919.664-010
longseam-machine operator (garment) 786.685-026
long-wall-mining-machine helper (mine & quarry) 930.666-014
LONG-WALL-MINING-MACHINE TENDER (mine & quarry) 930.665-010
LONG-WALL SHEAR OPERATOR (mine & quarry) 930.662-010
Loom Blower (textile) 699.687-014
LOOM CHANGEOVER OPERATOR (carpet & rug) 683.687-030
LOOM CHANGER (textile) 683.360-010
loom doffer (textile) 689.686-058
loom fixer (carpet & rug) 628.281-010
LOOM FIXER (narrow fabrics; nonmet. min.; textile) 683.260-018
LOOM-FIXER SUPERVISOR (narrow fabrics) 683.130-014
loom helper (metal prod., nec) 616.687-014
loom inspector (carpet & rug; textile) 683.684-034
loom operator apprentice (nonmet. min.; textile) 683.682-042
loom operator (furniture) 692.685-262
loom operator (nonmet. min.; textile) 683.682-038
Loom Operator (rubber goods) 692.665-010
loom operator (tex. prod., nec) 685.685-010

loom repairer (narrow fabrics; nonmet. min.; textile) 683.260-018
Loom Setter, Fourdrinier (metal prod., nec) 616.360-014
LOOM SETTER, WIRE WEAVING (metal prod., nec) 616.360-014
LOOM STARTER (textile) 683.360-014
Loom-Stop Checker (textile) 221.367-034
LOOM-WINDER TENDER (textile) 681.685-062
Loop-Drier Operator (textile) 581.685-030
LOOPER (knitting) 689.682-010
LOOPER (musical inst.) 730.685-010
Looper (smelt. & refin.) 519.565-014
looper (wood. container) 692.685-258
Looping Inspector (knitting) 684.684-010
Loop-Machine Operator (wood. container) 669.685-014
loop tender (fabrication, nec) 590.686-010
LOOSE-END FINDER, BOBBIN (knitting) 681.687-014
loose-hand packer (tobacco) 920.687-142
loss-claim clerk (insurance) 205.367-018
loss-control technician (insurance) 168.167-078
loss-prevention research engineer (profess. & kin.) 012.167-022
LOST-AND-FOUND CLERK (clerical) 222.367-034
LOST-CHARGE-CARD CLERK (clerical) 209.367-034
LOT ATTENDANT (retail trade) 915.583-010
lot boss (any industry) 410.131-010
lot caller (retail trade; wholesale tr.) 294.667-010
LOUNGE-CAR ATTENDANT (r.r. trans.) 291.457-014
Louver-Door Assembler (wood prod., nec) 762.687-022
Louver-Mortiser Operator (saw. & plan.) 665.482-014
Low-Chloride Soda Operator (chemical) 558.685-062
LOWERATOR OPERATOR (fabrication, nec) 922.686-014
Lower-in Supervisor (construction) 899.131-010
Low-Heel Builder (boot & shoe) 690.685-206
Low-Pressure-Kettle Operator (chemical) 558.382-038
Low-Raw-Sugar Cutter (sugar & conf.) 521.682-010
LOZENGE-DOUGH MIXER (sugar & conf.) 520.685-122
LOZENGE MAKER (sugar & conf.) 529.682-026
Lozenge-Maker Helper (sugar & conf.) 529.686-034
l-tacker (tex. prod., nec) 787.685-026
L-Type-Ruling-Machine Operator (print. & pub.) 659.682-022
LUBRICATING-MACHINE TENDER (ordnance) 509.685-038
LUBRICATION-EQUIPMENT SERVICER (any industry) 630.381-022
LUBRICATION SERVICER (automotive ser.) 915.687-018
lubrication technician (automotive ser.) 915.687-018
lubricator (any industry) 699.687-018
LUBRICATOR-GRANULATOR (nonfer. metal; steel & rel.) 509.685-042
Lug-Breaker-And-Wire-Puller (elec. equip.) 727.687-058
luggage checker (air trans.; motor trans.) 357.477-010
LUGGAGE MAKER (leather prod.) 783.381-022
LUGGAGE REPAIRER (any industry) 365.361-010
Lugger (agriculture) 929.687-030
Lugger (elec. equip.) 691.685-018
Lumber-Carrier Driver (saw. & plan.) 921.683-070
Lumber Checker (woodworking) 221.587-030
LUMBER ESTIMATOR (wood. container) 221.482-014
lumber guider (saw. & plan.) 669.687-018
LUMBER HANDLER (woodworking) 922.687-070
lumber inspector (woodworking) 669.687-030
lumber piler (woodworking) 922.687-070
lumber-piler operator (woodworking) 569.685-066
lumber puller (woodworking) 922.687-074
lumber racker (woodworking) 922.687-070
Lumber Salvager (any industry) 929.687-022
LUMBER SCALER (woodworking) 221.487-010
LUMBER SORTER (woodworking) 922.687-074
lumber sorter, machine (saw. & plan.) 921.685-054
lumber stacker (woodworking) 922.687-070
lumber sticker (woodworking) 922.687-070
LUMBER STRAIGHTENER (saw. & plan.) 669.687-018
lumber tallier (woodworking) 221.487-010
Lumber-Yard Worker (woodworking) 929.687-030
LUMITE INJECTOR (boot & shoe) 690.685-278
lumper (can. & preserv.) 922.687-062
lumper (stonework) 679.664-010
LUMPIA WRAPPER MAKER (food prep., nec) 526.684-014
LUMP INSPECTOR (tobacco) 790.687-018
lump receiver (tobacco) 790.687-018
LUNCH-TRUCK DRIVER (hotel & rest.) 292.463-010
lunch-truck operator (hotel & rest.) 292.463-010
Lunch-Wagon Operator (hotel & rest.) 292.463-010
Lung Splitter (meat products) 525.684-038
lurer (hat & cap) 784.684-062
LUSTER APPLICATOR (glass mfg.; glass products) 740.381-014
lusterer (textile) 584.685-014
luster repairer (boot & shoe) 788.687-038
luter (steel & rel.) 543.687-014
LYE-PEEL OPERATOR (can. & preserv.) 521.685-206

LYE TREATER (chemical; soap & rel.) 551.685-094
LYRICIST (profess. & kin.) 131.067-034
lyric writer (profess. & kin.) 131.067-034

M

macaroni-press operator (chemical) 557.682-010
Macerator Operator (chemical) 550.665-010
machine adjuster (print. & pub.) 653.360-010
Machine Adjuster (tobacco) 638.281-014
MACHINE ADJUSTER (any industry) term
machine-adjuster helper (any industry) 638.684-018
MACHINE-ADJUSTER LEADER (ordnance) 619.137-010
Machine-Adjuster Leader, Bullet Assembly (ordnance) 619.137-010
Machine-Adjuster Leader, Cannelure And Finish (ordnance) 619.137-010
Machine-Adjuster Leader, Case Trim (ordnance) 619.137-010
Machine-Adjuster Leader, Primer Assembly (ordnance) 619.137-010
machine assembler (boot & shoe) 690.685-010
MACHINE ASSEMBLER (machinery mfg.) 638.361-010
machine assembler (paper goods) 649.685-010
MACHINE-ASSEMBLER SUPERVISOR (machinery mfg.) 638.131-014
machine boss (mine & quarry) 939.137-018
machine brusher (any industry) 699.687-014
MACHINE BUILDER (machinery mfg.; machine tools) 600.281-022
machine captain (bakery products) 520.682-034
machine-casting operator and adjuster (ordnance) 502.382-010
MACHINE-CASTINGS PLASTERER (foundry) 519.687-030
MACHINE CLEANER (any industry) 699.687-014
MACHINE-CLOTHING REPLACER (paper & pulp) 629.361-010
MACHINE FEEDER (any industry) 699.686-010
MACHINE FEEDER (clock & watch) 715.686-014
MACHINE FEEDER (welding) 819.686-010
MACHINE FEEDER, RAW STOCK (tex. prod., nec; textile) 680.686-018
MACHINE FIXER (carpet & rug) 628.281-010
MACHINE FIXER (textile) 689.260-010
MACHINE HELPER (any industry) 619.687-014
machine helper (construction) 579.665-014
MACHINE HELPER (tex. prod., nec) 586.686-022
MACHINE HELPER (welding) 819.666-010
machine helper (welding) 819.686-010
machine hostler (any industry) 699.687-018
machine line molder (foundry) 518.682-010
Machine-Load Clerk (any industry) 221.382-018
MACHINE-MADE-SHOE UNIT WORKER (boot & shoe) 753.584-010
machine-maintenance servicer (any industry) 638.281-014
MACHINE MOLDER (foundry) 518.682-010
Machine Molder, Roll-Over (foundry) 518.682-010
Machine Molder, Squeeze (foundry) 518.682-010
Machine Mover (construction) 921.260-010
Machine-Operations Inspector (any industry) 619.261-010
Machine-Operations Supervisor (any industry) 619.130-030
machine operator (print. & pub.) 653.662-010
machine operator, all around (machine shop) 600.380-018
MACHINE OPERATOR, CENTRIFUGAL-CONTROL SWITCHES (elec. equip.) 609.682-022
MACHINE OPERATOR, CERAMICS (pottery & porc.) 679.685-010
machine operator, general (machine shop) 600.380-018
MACHINE OPERATOR, GENERAL (paper goods) 649.685-070
machine-operator helper (any industry) 699.587-014
MACHINE OPERATOR I (any industry) 616.380-018
MACHINE OPERATOR II (any industry) 619.685-062
machine operator, packaging (any industry) 920.685-078
machine operator technician (electron. comp.) 679.362-010
machine overhauler (any industry) 638.281-014
MACHINE-PACK ASSEMBLER (ordnance) 920.687-122
machine pack-shaker lubricator (ordnance) 694.685-018
machine printer, hose (rubber goods) 690.685-042
Machine Rebuilder (forging) 626.261-010
machine repairer (any industry) 638.281-014
machine repairer (grain-feed mills) 629.281-030
machine repairer (machine shop) 600.280-042
machine repairer (textile) 689.260-010
MACHINE REPAIRER, MAINTENANCE (any industry) 638.261-030
machine riveter (furniture) 616.685-058
machine rubber (any industry) 699.687-014
MACHINE RUNNER (mine & quarry) term
Machinery Crater (machinery mfg.) 920.684-010
MACHINERY ERECTOR (engine-turbine; machinery mfg.) 638.261-014
Machinery Erector (ship-boat mfg.) 921.260-010
MACHINE SETTER (any industry) 616.360-022
MACHINE SETTER (button & notion) 690.380-010
MACHINE SETTER (clock & watch) 600.380-022
MACHINE SETTER (machine shop) 600.360-014
MACHINE SETTER (nonmet. min.) 692.260-010

MACHINE SETTER

MACHINE SETTER (woodworking) 669.280-010
MACHINE SETTER-AND-REPAIRER (plastic prod.) 690.380-014
Machine Setter, Automatic (clock & watch) 600.380-022
Machine Setter, Hand (clock & watch) 600.380-022
Machine Setter, Semiautomatic (clock & watch) 600.380-022
Machine Setter, Sheet Metal (any industry) 616.360-022
MACHINE SET-UP OPERATOR (machine shop) 600.380-018
MACHINE SET-UP OPERATOR, PAPER GOODS (paper goods) 649.380-010
machine-shop apprentice (machine shop) 600.280-026
machine shop production worker (machine shop) 609.685-018
MACHINE-SHOP SUPERVISOR, PRODUCTION (machine shop) 609.130-010
MACHINE-SHOP SUPERVISOR, TOOL (machine shop) 600.130-010
machine sizer (hat & cap) 589.687-038
MACHINE SNELLER (toy-sport equip.) 732.685-026
machine specialist (machine shop) 600.380-018
machine sprayer (any industry) 599.686-014
MACHINE-STOPPAGE-FREQUENCY CHECKER (textile) 221.367-034
machine stuffer, automatic (furniture) 780.684-054
machine supervisor (any industry) 619.130-030
MACHINE-TANK OPERATOR (wood. container) 667.662-014
MACHINE TESTER (machinery mfg.) 629.382-010
MACHINE TESTER (office machines) 706.387-014
Machine Tool Fixture Builder (aircraft mfg.) 693.281-030
machine-tool operator, general (machine shop) 601.280-054
machine tracer (boot & shoe) 690.685-282
MACHINE TRY-OUT SETTER (machine tools) 600.360-010
MACHINING-AND-ASSEMBLY SUPERVISOR (elec. equip.) 619.131-010
machinist (machine shop) 600.380-018
machinist (machine shop) 601.280-054
MACHINIST (machine shop) 600.280-022
machinist (railroad equip.) 622.381-014
MACHINIST APPRENTICE (machine shop) 600.280-026
machinist apprentice (railroad equip.) 622.381-022
machinist apprentice (utilities) 631.261-018
MACHINIST APPRENTICE, AUTOMOTIVE (automotive ser.) 600.280-030
MACHINIST APPRENTICE, COMPOSING ROOM (print. & pub.) 627.261-014
MACHINIST APPRENTICE, LINOTYPE (print. & pub.) 627.261-018
MACHINIST APPRENTICE, MARINE ENGINE (ship-boat mfg.) 623.281-018
MACHINIST APPRENTICE, OUTSIDE (ship-boat mfg.) 623.281-022
MACHINIST APPRENTICE, WOOD (woodworking) 669.380-010
MACHINIST, AUTOMOTIVE (automotive ser.) 600.280-034
machinist, bench (machinery mfg.; machine tools) 600.281-022
machinist, brake (automotive ser.) 620.682-010
MACHINIST, EXPERIMENTAL (machine shop) 600.260-022
machinist, first-class (machine shop) 600.280-022
machinist, general (machine shop) 600.280-022
machinist, general maintenance (machine shop) 600.280-042
machinist helper (railroad equip.) 622.684-014
machinist helper, marine (ship-boat mfg.) 623.687-010
MACHINIST HELPER, OUTSIDE (ship-boat mfg.) 623.687-010
machinist, installation (ship-boat mfg.) 623.281-030
machinist, job setter (machine shop) 600.360-014
MACHINIST, LINOTYPE (print. & pub.) 627.261-022
MACHINIST, MARINE ENGINE (ship-boat mfg.) 623.281-026
MACHINIST, MOTION-PICTURE EQUIPMENT (motion picture; photo. appar.) 714.281-018
MACHINIST, OUTSIDE (ship-boat mfg.) 623.281-030
MACHINIST SUPERVISOR, OUTSIDE (ship-boat mfg.) 623.131-010
MACHINIST, WOOD (woodworking) 669.380-014
made-to-measure tailor (garment; personal ser.; retail trade) 785.261-014
made-to-measure-tailor apprentice (garment; personal ser.; retail trade) 785.261-022
Magazine-Delivery Driver (wholesale tr.) 292.363-010
magazine filler (textile) 683.686-010
magazine hand (textile) 689.686-038
MAGAZINE KEEPER (clerical) 222.367-038
magazine loader (paper & pulp) 530.686-014
MAGAZINE REPAIRER (print. & pub.) 653.685-022
MAGAZINE SUPERVISOR (chemical; ordnance) 222.137-018
MAGICIAN (amuse. & rec.) 159.041-010
MAGISTRATE (government ser.) 111.107-014
MAGNESIUM-MILL OPERATOR (nonfer. metal) 607.686-010
Magnetic Prospector (petrol. & gas) 024.061-026
magnetic-resonance imaging technologist (medical ser.) 078.362-058
MAGNETIC-TAPE-COMPOSER OPERATOR (print. & pub.) 203.382-018
MAGNETIC-TAPE WINDER (recording) 726.685-010
Magnetic-Thermal-Cutting-Machine Operator (welding) 816.482-010
Magnetometer Operator (mine & quarry; petrol. & gas) 010.261-018
MAGNETO REPAIRER (any industry) 721.281-022
Magnet Placer (steel & rel.) 921.667-022
MAGNET-VALVE ASSEMBLER (elec. equip.) 724.684-034
maid (any industry) 323.687-014
MAIL CARRIER (government ser.) 230.367-010

MAIL CENSOR (government ser.) 243.367-010
MAIL CLERK (clerical) 209.687-026
Mail Clerk, Bills (clerical) 209.687-026
MAIL-DISTRIBUTION-SCHEME EXAMINER (government ser.) 239.367-018
MAILER (print. & pub.) 222.587-030
MAILER APPRENTICE (print. & pub.) 222.587-032
MAIL HANDLER (government ser.) 209.687-014
Mailing-List Compiler (clerical) 209.387-014
MAILING-MACHINE OPERATOR (print. & pub.) 208.462-010
Mail-Order Biller (retail trade; wholesale tr.) 214.382-014
Mail-Order Clerk (clerical) 249.362-026
Mail-Order Sorter (retail trade) 222.387-038
MAIL-PROCESSING-EQUIPMENT MECHANIC (government ser.) 633.261-014
mailroom clerk (clerical) 209.687-026
MAILROOM SUPERVISOR (clerical) 209.137-010
MAILROOM SUPERVISOR (print. & pub.) 222.137-022
mail sorter (clerical) 209.687-026
Mail Sorter (r.r. trans.) 222.687-022
Mail-Truck Driver (any industry) 906.683-022
Main-Galley Scullion (water trans.) 318.687-014
main-line assembler (agric. equip.) 801.684-022
MAINS-AND-SERVICE SUPERVISOR (utilities) 862.137-010
Mainspring-Barrel-Assembly Cleaner (clock & watch) 715.687-126
MAINSPRING FORMER, ARBOR END (clock & watch) 715.687-078
MAINSPRING FORMER, BRACE END (clock & watch) 715.687-082
Mainspring-Reverse Winder (clock & watch) 715.685-038
Mainspring-Strip Gauger (clock & watch) 715.384-022
Mainspring-Strip Inspector (clock & watch) 715.384-022
mainspring-torque tester (clock & watch) 715.685-066
MAINSPRING WINDER AND OILER (clock & watch) 715.685-038
mainspring-winding-machine operator (clock & watch) 715.685-038
Mainstreaming Facilitator (education) 094.267-010
MAINTAINABILITY ENGINEER (profess. & kin.) 019.081-010
maintainer, central office (tel. & tel.) 822.381-022
maintainer, equipment (tel. & tel.) 822.381-022
maintainer, plant (tel. & tel.) 822.381-022
Maintainer, Sewer-And-Waterworks (construction) 862.281-022
maintenance advisor (any industry) 638.131-022
maintenance-and-utilities supervisor (any industry) 899.131-018
maintenance associate (any industry) 899.261-014
Maintenance Carpenter (museums) 899.384-010
maintenance chief (tel. & tel.) 822.131-010
maintenance clerk (clerical) 239.367-014
maintenance-crew supervisor (pipe lines) 869.134-018
MAINTENANCE DATA ANALYST (military ser.) 221.367-038
maintenance engineer (any industry) 828.261-022
maintenance engineer (any industry) 950.382-026
maintenance engineer (any industry) 382.664-010
maintenance engineer, oil field (any industry) 638.131-026
maintenance inspector (pipe lines; utilities) 953.367-010
maintenance inspector (r.r. trans.) 910.367-030
MAINTENANCE INSPECTOR (tel. & tel.) 822.261-018
MAINTENANCE MACHINIST (machine shop) 600.280-042
MAINTENANCE MECHANIC (any industry) 638.281-014
MAINTENANCE MECHANIC (construction; petrol. & gas; pipe lines) 620.281-046
MAINTENANCE MECHANIC (grain-feed mills) 629.281-030
MAINTENANCE MECHANIC (leather mfg.) 629.280-010
MAINTENANCE MECHANIC, COMPRESSED-GAS PLANT (chemical) 630.261-010
maintenance mechanic, elevators (any industry) 825.281-030
MAINTENANCE MECHANIC, ENGINE (water trans.) 623.281-034
maintenance mechanic helper (any industry) 899.684-022
MAINTENANCE-MECHANIC HELPER (any industry) 638.684-018
MAINTENANCE MECHANIC HELPER (construction; petrol. & gas; pipe lines) 620.664-014
Maintenance Mechanic, Record Processing Equipment (recording) 638.281-014
MAINTENANCE-MECHANIC SUPERVISOR (any industry) 638.131-022
MAINTENANCE MECHANIC, TELEPHONE (any industry) 822.281-018
maintenance-of-way supervisor (r.r. trans.) 184.167-234
maintenance-planning clerk (air trans.) 221.362-010
MAINTENANCE REPAIRER, BUILDING (any industry) 899.381-010
MAINTENANCE-REPAIRER HELPER, INDUSTRIAL (any industry) 899.684-022
MAINTENANCE REPAIRER, INDUSTRIAL (any industry) 899.261-014
maintenance supervisor (any industry) 638.131-022
MAINTENANCE SUPERVISOR (any industry) 891.137-010
maintenance supervisor (tel. & tel.) 822.131-014
MAINTENANCE SUPERVISOR (utilities) 184.167-050
maintenance supervisor (waterworks) 899.130-010
Maintenance Supervisor, Electrical (utilities) 184.167-050
MAINTENANCE SUPERVISOR, FIRE-FIGHTING-EQUIPMENT (government ser.) 638.131-018
Maintenance Supervisor, Mechanical (utilities) 184.167-050

MAINTENANCE SUPERVISOR, MOBILE BATTERY EQUIPMENT (mine & quarry) 638.131-034
MAINTENANCE WORKER (any industry) term
maintenance worker (museums) 899.384-010
maintenance worker, house trailer (retail trade) 899.484-010
MAINTENANCE WORKER, MUNICIPAL (government ser.) 899.684-046
maintenance worker, swimming pool (any industry) 891.684-018
major-appliance-servicer apprentice, electrical (any industry) 827.261-014
MAJOR-ASSEMBLY INSPECTOR (agric. equip.) 801.381-018
maker (boot & shoe) 690.682-082
make-ready apprentice (print. & pub.) 651.362-022
make-ready mechanic (automotive ser.; retail trade) 806.361-026
make-ready worker (print. & pub.) 651.384-010
maker-up, folding (tex. prod., nec; textile) 589.687-014
MAKE-UP ARRANGER (print. & pub.) 973.381-026
MAKE-UP ARTIST (amuse. & rec.; motion picture; radio-tv broad.) 333.071-010
makeup editor (print. & pub.) 132.067-026
Make-Up Market Worker, Truck Garden (agriculture) 920.687-134
MAKE-UP OPERATOR (chemical) 559.382-034
MAKE-UP OPERATOR HELPER (chemical) 550.587-010
MAKING-LINE WORKER (boot & shoe) 753.687-026
making-machine catcher (tobacco) 529.666-014
making-machine operator, filter (tobacco) 529.685-066
Male Impersonator (amuse. & rec.) 159.047-018
mallet-and-die cutter (any industry) 781.687-030
malted-milk masher (dairy products) 526.485-010
malted-milk mixer (dairy products) 521.685-222
malter operator (textile) 582.685-046
MALT-HOUSE OPERATOR (beverage) 522.685-074
malt loader (beverage) 921.682-010
MALT ROASTER (beverage) 526.682-026
MALT-SPECIFICATIONS-CONTROL ASSISTANT (beverage) 022.261-014
Mammal Keeper (amuse. & rec.) 412.674-010
Mammalogist (profess. & kin.) 041.061-090
MANAGEMENT AIDE (social ser.) 195.367-014
MANAGEMENT ANALYST (profess. & kin.) 161.167-010
MANAGEMENT TRAINEE (any industry) 189.167-018
manager (any industry)   see SUPERVISOR
manager, administrative services (any industry) 169.167-034
MANAGER, ADVERTISING (any industry) 164.117-010
MANAGER, ADVERTISING (print. & pub.) 163.167-010
MANAGER, ADVERTISING AGENCY (business ser.) 164.117-014
MANAGER, AERIAL PLANTING AND CULTIVATION (agriculture) 180.167-062
MANAGER, AGRICULTURAL-LABOR CAMP (profess. & kin.) 187.167-050
MANAGER, AIRPORT (air trans.) 184.117-026
Manager, Airport-Property-And-Development (air trans.) 184.117-026
MANAGER, ANIMAL SHELTER (nonprofit org.) 187.167-218
Manager, Apartment House (hotel & rest.) 320.137-014
MANAGER, APARTMENT HOUSE (real estate) 186.167-018
MANAGER, AQUATIC FACILITY (amuse. & rec.) 187.167-054
manager, area (any industry) 183.117-010
MANAGER, AREA DEVELOPMENT (utilities) 184.117-030
MANAGER, ARMORED TRANSPORT SERVICE (business ser.) 372.167-022
MANAGER, ATHLETE (amuse. & rec.) 153.117-014
manager, athletic team (amuse. & rec.) 153.117-010
MANAGER, AUTOMOBILE SERVICE STATION (retail trade) 185.167-014
MANAGER, AUTOMOTIVE SERVICES (any industry) 184.117-034
MANAGER, AUTO SPECIALTY SERVICES (automotive ser.) 185.167-074
Manager, Aviation And Space (nonprofit org.) 187.167-042
MANAGER, BAKERY (bakery products) 189.117-046
Manager, Banquet (hotel & rest.) 187.167-106
MANAGER, BAR (hotel & rest.) term
MANAGER, BARBER OR BEAUTY SHOP (personal ser.) 187.167-058
Manager, Beer Parlor (hotel & rest.) 187.167-126
MANAGER, BENEFITS (profess. & kin.) 166.167-018
MANAGER, BOARDING HOUSE (hotel & rest.) 320.137-010
MANAGER, BOWLING ALLEY (amuse. & rec.) 187.167-222
Manager, Boxer (amuse. & rec.) 153.117-014
MANAGER, BRANCH (any industry) 183.117-010
Manager, Branch Bank (financial) 186.167-086
MANAGER, BRANCH OPERATION EVALUATION (hotel & rest.) 187.167-062
MANAGER, BRANCH STORE (laundry & rel.) 369.467-010
MANAGER, BROKERAGE OFFICE (financial) 186.117-034
manager, building (any industry) 187.167-190
MANAGER, BULK PLANT (petrol. refin.; retail trade) 181.117-010
manager, business promotion (hotel & rest.) 163.117-018
MANAGER, BUS TRANSPORTATION (motor trans.) 184.167-054
Manager, Cafeteria Or Lunchroom (hotel & rest.) 187.167-106
MANAGER, CAMP (amuse. & rec.) 329.161-010
MANAGER, CAMP (construction; logging) 187.167-066
MANAGER, CARDROOM (amuse. & rec.) 343.137-010
MANAGER, CARGO-AND-RAMP-SERVICES (air trans.) 184.167-058

MANAGER, CAR INSPECTION AND REPAIR (r.r. trans.) 184.117-086
MANAGER, CASINO (amuse. & rec.) 187.167-070
Manager, Catering (hotel & rest.) 187.167-106
MANAGER, CEMETERY (real estate) 187.167-074
manager, chamber of commerce (nonprofit org.) 187.117-030
Manager, Chicken Hatchery (agriculture) 180.167-046
MANAGER, CHRISTMAS-TREE FARM (forestry) 180.117-010
MANAGER, CIRCULATION (print. & pub.) 163.167-014
MANAGER, CITY (government ser.) 188.117-114
Manager, City Circulation (print. & pub.) 163.167-014
Manager, Classified Advertising (print. & pub.) 163.167-010
manager, club (hotel & rest.) 187.167-126
Manager, Cocktail Lounge (hotel & rest.) 187.167-126
Manager, Conmmercial Bank (financial) 186.167-086
Manager, Commerical Sales (utilities) 163.167-022
Manager, Commissary Service (air trans.) 184.167-082
MANAGER, COMMUNICATIONS STATION (tel. & tel.) 184.167-062
MANAGER, COMPENSATION (profess. & kin.) 166.167-022
MANAGER, COMPUTER OPERATIONS (profess. & kin.) 169.167-082
Manager, Construction Industries (nonprofit org.) 187.167-042
MANAGER, CONTRACTS (petrol. & gas; petrol. refin.; pipe lines) 163.117-010
Manager, Contracts-And-Titles (petrol. & gas) 186.167-038
MANAGER, CONVENTION (hotel & rest.) 187.167-078
manager, county (government ser.) 188.117-114
MANAGER, CREDIT AND COLLECTION (any industry) 169.167-086
Manager, Credit Card Operations (any industry) 169.167-086
Manager, Credit Union (financial) 186.167-086
MANAGER, CUSTOMER SERVICE (tel. & tel.) 168.167-058
MANAGER, CUSTOMER SERVICES (business ser.; retail trade) 187.167-082
MANAGER, CUSTOMER TECHNICAL SERVICES (profess. & kin.) 189.117-018
MANAGER, DAIRY FARM (agriculture) 180.167-026
Manager, Dance Floor (amuse. & rec.) 187.117-042
MANAGER, DANCE STUDIO (education) 187.167-086
MANAGER, DATA PROCESSING (profess. & kin.) 169.167-030
MANAGER, DENTAL LABORATORY (protective dev.) 187.167-090
MANAGER, DEPARTMENT (any industry) 189.167-022
MANAGER, DEPARTMENT (retail trade) 299.137-010
MANAGER, DEPARTMENT STORE (retail trade) 185.117-010
MANAGER, DISPLAY (retail trade) 142.031-014
Manager, Display Advertising (print. & pub.) 163.167-010
MANAGER, DISTRIBUTION WAREHOUSE (wholesale tr.) 185.167-018
Manager, District (any industry) 183.117-010
Manager, Divisional Leasing (petrol. & gas) 186.117-046
manager, division (any industry) 183.117-010
Manager, Domestic Trade (nonprofit org.) 187.167-042
Manager, Duck Hatchery (agriculture) 180.167-046
MANAGER, DUDE RANCH (amuse. & rec.) 187.167-094
MANAGER, EDUCATION AND TRAINING (education) 166.167-026
manager, electric distribution department (utilities) 184.167-150
manager, employee benefits (profess. & kin.) 166.167-018
manager, employee services (profess. & kin.) 166.167-018
MANAGER, EMPLOYEE WELFARE (profess. & kin.) 166.117-014
MANAGER, EMPLOYMENT (profess. & kin.) 166.167-030
MANAGER, EMPLOYMENT AGENCY (profess. & kin.) 187.167-098
manager, equipment (amuse. & rec.) 969.367-010
MANAGER, EXCHANGE FLOOR (financial) 186.117-086
MANAGER, EXPORT (any industry) 163.117-014
MANAGER, FACILITATING SERVICES (any industry) term
manager, factory (any industry) 183.117-014
Manager, Farm Underwriters (insurance) 186.167-034
MANAGER, FAST FOOD SERVICES (retail trade; wholesale tr.) 185.137-010
MANAGER, FIELD PARTY, GEOPHYSICAL PROSPECTING (petrol. & gas) 181.167-010
Manager, Field Underwriters (insurance) 186.167-034
Manager, Finance Company (financial) 186.167-086
MANAGER, FINANCIAL INSTITUTION (financial) 186.167-086
MANAGER, FISH-AND-GAME CLUB (amuse. & rec.) 187.167-102
MANAGER, FISH HATCHERY (fishing & hunt.) 180.167-030
MANAGER, FLIGHT CONTROL (air trans.) 184.167-066
Manager, Flight Dispatching (air trans.) 184.167-082
MANAGER, FLIGHT KITCHEN (hotel & rest.) 319.137-014
MANAGER, FLIGHT OPERATIONS (air trans.) 184.117-038
MANAGER, FLIGHT-RESERVATIONS (air trans.) 184.167-070
Manager, Flight Service (air trans.) 184.167-082
manager, floor (retail trade) 299.137-010
manager, floor operations (financial) 186.117-086
manager, floor services (financial) 186.117-086
Manager, Food And Beverage (hotel & rest.) 187.167-106
MANAGER, FOOD CONCESSION (hotel & rest.) 185.167-022
MANAGER, FOOD PROCESSING PLANT (can. & preserv.) 183.167-026
manager, food production (hotel & rest.) 187.161-010
MANAGER, FOOD SERVICE (hotel & rest.; personal ser.) 187.167-106

Manager For Health, Safety, And Environment (government ser.) 188.117-134
MANAGER, FORMS ANALYSIS (profess. & kin.) 161.167-014
MANAGER, FRONT OFFICE (hotel & rest.) 187.137-018
manager, funeral home (personal ser.) 187.167-030
Manager, Game-Animal Farm (agriculture) 180.167-034
Manager, Game-Bird Farm (agriculture) 180.167-034
MANAGER, GAME BREEDING FARM (agriculture) 180.167-034
MANAGER, GAME PRESERVE (agriculture) 180.167-038
manager, general (any industry) 189.117-022
manager, general (any industry) 183.117-014
manager, general (hotel & rest.) 187.117-038
MANAGER, GOLF CLUB (amuse. & rec.) 187.167-114
Manager, Governmental Program (government ser.) 189.167-030
manager, grain elevator (grain-feed mills; wholesale tr.) 162.167-010
manager, guest house (hotel & rest.) 320.137-010
MANAGER, GUN CLUB (amuse. & rec.) 187.167-118
MANAGER, HANDICRAFT-OR-HOBBY SHOP (amuse. & rec.) 187.161-014
MANAGER, HARBOR DEPARTMENT (water trans.) 184.117-042
MANAGER, HEALTH CLUB (personal ser.) 339.137-010
Manager, Hotel (hotel & rest.) 320.137-014
MANAGER, HOTEL OR MOTEL (hotel & rest.) 187.117-038
MANAGER, HOTEL RECREATIONAL FACILITIES (amuse. & rec.) 187.167-122
manager, house (amuse. & rec.) 187.167-154
manager, household (domestic ser.) 301.137-010
MANAGER, HOUSING PROJECT (profess. & kin.) 186.167-030
manager, human resources (profess. & kin.) 166.117-018
Manager, Hydroponics Nursery (agriculture) 180.167-042
Manager, Ice-Skating Rink (amuse. & rec.) 187.167-146
MANAGER, INDUSTRIAL CAFETERIA (hotel & rest.) 319.137-018
Manager, Industrial Development (r.r. trans.) 186.117-042
MANAGER, INDUSTRIAL ORGANIZATION (any industry) 189.117-022
Manager, Industrial Sales (utilities) 163.167-022
Manager, Insurance Agency (insurance) 186.167-034
MANAGER, INSURANCE OFFICE (insurance) 186.167-034
MANAGER, INTERNAL SECURITY (business ser.) 376.137-010
MANAGER, IRRIGATION DISTRICT (waterworks) 184.117-046
manager, kitchen (hotel & rest.) 319.137-030
MANAGER, LABOR RELATIONS (profess. & kin.) 166.167-034
manager, land department (petrol. & gas) 186.117-046
MANAGER, LAND DEVELOPMENT (real estate) 186.117-042
MANAGER, LAND LEASES-AND-RENTALS (petrol. & gas) 186.167-038
MANAGER, LAND SURVEYING (profess. & kin.) 018.167-022
MANAGER, LAUNDROMAT (laundry & rel.) 369.167-010
MANAGER, LEASING (petrol. & gas) 186.117-046
MANAGER, LIQUOR ESTABLISHMENT (hotel & rest.) 187.167-126
Manager, Local (any industry) 183.117-010
Manager, Local Advertising (print. & pub.) 163.167-010
MANAGER, LODGING FACILITIES (hotel & rest.) 320.137-014
MANAGER, MACHINERY-OR-EQUIPMENT, RENTAL AND LEASING (any industry) 185.167-026
Manager, Marina (hotel & rest.) 320.137-014
MANAGER, MARINA DRY DOCK (amuse. & rec.; water trans.) 187.167-226
Manager, Marine Life Hatchery (fishing & hunt.) 180.167-030
MANAGER, MARINE SERVICE (ship-boat mfg.) 187.167-130
MANAGER, MARKET (retail trade; wholesale tr.) 186.167-042
manager, material control (profess. & kin.) 162.167-022
MANAGER, MEAT SALES AND STORAGE (retail trade; wholesale tr.) 185.167-030
MANAGER, MERCHANDISE (retail trade; wholesale tr.) 185.167-034
Manager, Mortgage Company (financial) 186.167-086
Manager, Motel (hotel & rest.) 320.137-014
manager, motor hotel (hotel & rest.) 187.117-038
manager, motor inn (hotel & rest.) 187.117-038
MANAGER, MUTUEL DEPARTMENT (amuse. & rec.) 187.167-134
Manager, National Advertising (print. & pub.) 163.167-010
Manager, Natural-Gas Utilization (petrol. & gas) 163.117-010
Manager, Newspaper Circulation (print. & pub.) 163.167-014
Manager, Night Club (hotel & rest.) 187.167-126
MANAGER, NURSERY (agriculture; retail trade; wholesale tr.) 180.167-042
MANAGER, OFFICE (any industry) 169.167-034
MANAGER, OFFICE (government ser.) 188.167-058
manager of student placement service (education) 166.167-014
manager, oil-well services (petrol. & gas) 010.167-018
manager, operating and occupancy (retail trade) 189.167-014
MANAGER, OPERATIONS (air trans.; motor trans.; r.r. trans.; water trans.) 184.117-050
Manager, Options Exchange Floor (financial) 186.117-086
MANAGER, ORCHARD (agriculture) 180.167-066
MANAGER, PARTS (retail trade; wholesale tr.) 185.167-038
Manager, Passenger Service (air trans.) 184.167-082
MANAGER, PERSONNEL (profess. & kin.) 166.117-018
manager, personnel services (profess. & kin.) 166.167-018
manager, plant (any industry) 183.117-010
manager, plant (any industry) 183.117-014

MANAGER, POOL (amuse. & rec.) 153.137-010
MANAGER, POULTRY HATCHERY (agriculture) 180.167-046
MANAGER, PROCUREMENT SERVICES (profess. & kin.) 162.167-022
manager, product development (any industry) 189.117-014
manager, production (agriculture) 180.167-058
manager, production (any industry) 183.117-014
manager, production (profess. & kin.) 012.167-070
MANAGER, PRODUCTION (radio-tv broad.) 184.162-010
MANAGER, PRODUCTION, SEED CORN (agriculture) 180.161-010
MANAGER, PROFESSIONAL EQUIPMENT SALES-AND-SERVICE (business ser.) 185.167-042
manager, program (radio-tv broad.) 184.167-030
MANAGER, PROMOTION (hotel & rest.) 163.117-018
MANAGER, PROPERTY (real estate) 186.167-046
Manager, Prorate (tel. & tel.) 822.131-014
manager, public service (radio-tv broad.) 184.117-010
manager, public utility, rural (utilities) 184.167-162
MANAGER, QUALITY CONTROL (profess. & kin.) 012.167-014
manager, range (amuse. & rec.) 187.167-118
manager, rates and schedules (air trans.; motor trans.; water trans.) 184.117-066
MANAGER, REAL-ESTATE FIRM (real estate) 186.167-066
MANAGER, RECORDS ANALYSIS (profess. & kin.) 161.167-018
MANAGER, RECREATION ESTABLISHMENT (amuse. & rec.) 187.117-042
MANAGER, RECREATION FACILITY (amuse. & rec.) 187.167-230
manager, regional (agriculture) 180.161-010
Manager, Regional (any industry) 183.117-010
MANAGER, REGIONAL (motor trans.) 184.117-054
MANAGER, REGULATED PROGRAM (government ser.) 168.167-090
MANAGER, REPORTS ANALYSIS (profess. & kin.) 161.167-022
manager, research and development (any industry) 189.117-014
MANAGER, RESERVATIONS (hotel & rest.) 238.137-010
Manager, Reservations-And-Ticketing (air trans.) 184.167-082
Manager, Resident (any industry) 382.664-010
manager, resident (hotel & rest.) 187.117-038
Manager, Residential Sales (utilities) 163.167-022
Manager, Restaurant Or Coffee Shop (hotel & rest.) 187.167-106
Manager, Retail Nursery (agriculture; retail trade) 180.167-042
MANAGER, RETAIL STORE (retail trade) 185.167-046
Manager, Roller-Skating Rink (amuse. & rec.) 187.167-146
Manager, Rooming House (hotel & rest.) 320.137-010
MANAGER, SALES (any industry) 163.167-018
manager, sales (hotel & rest.) 163.117-018
MANAGER, SALES (laundry & rel.) 187.167-138
Manager, Savings Bank (financial) 186.167-086
MANAGER, SCHEDULE PLANNING (air trans.) 184.117-058
manager, school lunch program (hotel & rest.) 187.167-026
Manager, Self-Service Gasoline Station (retail trade) 185.167-014
manager, service (automotive ser.) 620.261-018
manager, service (hotel & rest.) 329.137-010
manager, service (tel. & tel.) 822.131-014
manager, service (wholesale tr.) 187.167-142
MANAGER, SERVICE DEPARTMENT (wholesale tr.) 187.167-142
MANAGER, SERVICE ESTABLISHMENT (any industry) term
Manager, Shellfish Hatchery (fishing & hunt.) 180.167-030
MANAGER, SKATING RINK (amuse. & rec.) 187.167-146
MANAGER, SOLID-WASTE-DISPOSAL (government ser.) 184.167-078
MANAGER, SOUND EFFECTS (radio-tv broad.) 962.167-010
MANAGER, STAGE (amuse. & rec.) 159.167-018
MANAGER, STATION (air trans.) 184.167-082
MANAGER, STATION (radio-tv broad.) 184.117-062
Manager, Stock Exchange Floor (financial) 186.117-086
manager, stockroom (clerical) 222.137-034
manager, stockroom (retail trade; wholesale tr.) 185.167-038
MANAGER, STORAGE GARAGE (automotive ser.) 187.167-150
manager, student union (education) 090.167-022
manager, surplus property (government ser.) 188.117-122
Manager, Tavern (hotel & rest.) 187.167-126
manager, technical and scientific publications (profess. & kin.) 132.017-018
MANAGER, TELEGRAPH OFFICE (tel. & tel.) 184.167-086
MANAGER, TEXTILE CONVERSION (business ser.; wholesale tr.) 185.167-050
MANAGER, THEATER (amuse. & rec.) 187.167-154
manager, theatrical production (amuse. & rec.) 191.117-038
manager, tire service (automotive ser.) 915.134-010
Manager, Titles-And-Land-Records (petrol. & gas) 186.167-038
MANAGER, TITLE SEARCH (real estate) 186.167-090
MANAGER, TOBACCO WAREHOUSE (wholesale tr.) 185.167-054
manager, touring (amuse. & rec.) 191.117-038
MANAGER, TOURING PRODUCTION (amuse. & rec.) 191.117-038
Manager, Tourist Camp (hotel & rest.) 320.137-014
manager, town (government ser.) 188.117-114
MANAGER, TRAFFIC (air trans.; motor trans.; water trans.) 184.117-066
MANAGER, TRAFFIC (any industry) 184.167-094
MANAGER, TRAFFIC (radio-tv broad.) 184.167-090
MANAGER, TRAFFIC I (motor trans.) 184.167-102

MANAGER, TRAFFIC I (tel. & tel.) 184.167-098
MANAGER, TRAFFIC II (motor trans.) 237.367-030
MANAGER, TRAFFIC II (tel. & tel.) 184.167-106
Manager, Trailer Park (hotel & rest.) 320.137-014
manager, transportation (any industry) 184.167-226
MANAGER, TRAVEL AGENCY (business ser.; retail trade) 187.167-158
MANAGER, TRUCK TERMINAL (motor trans.) 184.167-110
Manager, Trust Company (financial) 186.167-086
Manager, Tumor Registry (medical ser.) 079.362-018
Manager, Turkey Hatchery (agriculture) 180.167-046
MANAGER, UTILITY SALES AND SERVICE (utilities) 163.167-022
MANAGER, VEHICLE LEASING AND RENTAL (automotive ser.) 187.167-162
manager, vending department (svc. ind. mach.) 637.131-010
MANAGER, WAREHOUSE (any industry) 184.167-114
manager, water department (waterworks) 184.117-046
manager, welfare (profess. & kin.) 166.117-014
MANAGER, WINTER SPORTS (amuse. & rec.) 187.167-166
MANAGER, WORLD TRADE AND MARITIME DIVISION (nonprofit org.) 187.167-170
Manager, Wrestler (amuse. & rec.) 153.117-014
managing editor (radio-tv broad.) 132.132-010
managing editor (print. & pub.) 132.017-010
Mandrel Cleaner (plastic prod.) 690.685-438
mandrel-press hand (textile) 652.385-010
Mandrel Puller (plastic prod.) 690.685-438
Mangle Back-Tender (textile) 589.686-010
Mangle Catcher (textile) 589.686-010
mangle doffer (textile) 583.686-022
mangle operator, garments (knitting) 583.685-070
MANGLE-PRESS CATCHER (textile) 583.686-022
MANGLER (knitting) 583.685-070
mangler (textile) 584.685-042
MANGLE TENDER (textile) 584.685-042
mangle tender, cloth (knitting) 580.485-010
manhole-and-underground-steam-line inspector (utilities) 862.361-022
MANICURIST (personal ser.) 331.674-010
Manifest Clerk (air trans.; motor trans.; r.r. trans.; water trans.) 214.362-014
manifold operator (chemical) 559.565-010
MANIPULATOR (steel & rel.) 613.682-010
MANIPULATOR OPERATOR (forging) 612.683-010
MANNEQUIN-MOLD MAKER (fabrication, nec) 739.381-046
MANNEQUIN MOUNTER (fabrication, nec) 739.684-118
MANNEQUIN SANDER AND FINISHER (fabrication, nec) 739.684-122
MANNEQUIN WIG MAKER (fabrication, nec) 739.381-042
MANOMETER TECHNICIAN (smelt. & refin.) 519.387-010
MANUAL-ARTS THERAPIST (medical ser.) 076.124-010
manual hardener (hat & cap) 784.684-034
MANUAL-PLATE FILLER (ordnance) 737.687-082
MANUAL WINDER (musical inst.) 730.684-046
manufacturers' agent (wholesale tr.) 279.157-010
MANUFACTURERS' REPRESENTATIVE (wholesale tr.) 279.157-010
MANUFACTURER'S SERVICE REPRESENTATIVE (machinery mfg.; machine tools) 638.261-018
manufacturing engineer, chief (any industry) 189.117-014
MANUFACTURING ENGINEER (profess. & kin.) 012.167-042
MANUGRAPHER (fabrication, nec) 970.681-022
Manuscript Reader (print. & pub.) 132.267-014
MAP-AND-CHART MOUNTER (print. & pub.) 979.684-022
MAP CLERK (insurance) 209.587-030
Map Colorer (print. & pub.) 970.681-014
Maple-Products Maker (food prep., nec) 523.382-014
MAPLE-SYRUP MAKER (food prep., nec) 523.382-014
Map Librarian (library) 100.167-026
map maker (profess. & kin.) 018.261-010
mapper (profess. & kin.) 018.261-010
Marble Carver (stonework) 771.281-014
Marble Cleaner (any industry) 381.687-014
marble coper (stonework) 771.384-010
Marble-Cutter Operator (stonework) 677.462-010
MARBLE FINISHER (construction) 861.664-010
marble helper (construction) 861.664-010
marbleizing-machine tender (fabrication, nec) 559.665-034
MARBLE-MACHINE TENDER (glass mfg.) 575.685-058
marble mason helper (construction) 861.664-010
marble mechanic helper (construction) 861.664-010
Marble Polisher, Hand (stonework) 775.664-010
Marble Polisher, Machine (stonework) 673.382-018
MARBLE SETTER (construction) 861.381-030
marble setter helper (construction) 861.664-010
Marceller (personal ser.) 332.271-010
MARGIN CLERK I (financial) 216.362-042
MARGIN CLERK II (financial) 216.382-046
margin trimmer (boot & shoe) 690.685-150
margin trimmer (boot & shoe) 690.685-238

Marine Biologist (profess. & kin.) 041.061-022
MARINE-CARGO SURVEYOR (business ser.) 168.267-094
marine clerk (water trans.) 222.367-010
Marine Driller (construction) 899.261-010
marine-electrician apprentice (ship-boat mfg.) 825.381-034
MARINE ENGINEER (profess. & kin.) 014.061-014
marine engineer (water trans.) 197.130-010
marine-engine-installation-and-repairer apprentice (ship-boat mfg.) 623.281-018
marine-engine mechanic (ship-boat mfg.) 623.281-026
marine erector (ship-boat mfg.) 623.281-030
Marine-Insurance-Claim Adjuster (business ser.; insurance) 241.217-010
Marine-Insurance-Claim Examiner (business ser.; insurance) 241.267-018
marine machinist (ship-boat mfg.) 623.281-030
marine-machinist apprentice (ship-boat mfg.) 623.281-022
MARINE OILER (water trans.) 911.584-010
Marine-Radio Installer-And-Servicer (any industry) 823.281-014
MARINE RAILWAY OPERATOR (ship-boat mfg.) 921.662-022
Marine-Service-Station Attendant (water trans.) 915.477-010
MARINE-SERVICES TECHNICIAN (ship-boat mfg.) 806.261-026
MARINE SURVEYOR (profess. & kin.) 014.167-010
marker (electron. comp.) 652.685-110
MARKER (garment; retail trade; tex. prod., nec) 781.687-042
MARKER (laundry & rel.) 369.687-026
marker (logging) 455.687-010
MARKER (ordnance) 652.582-010
MARKER (retail trade; wholesale tr.) 209.587-034
Marker (steel & rel.) 509.687-026
marker (woodworking) 761.684-022
marker assembler (pen & pencil) 733.687-010
MARKER, COMPANY (tobacco) 529.567-014
marker, delivery (clerical) 222.587-038
MARKER, HAND (boot & shoe) 788.584-014
marker, hand (textile) 229.587-010
MARKER I (any industry) 781.384-014
MARKER II (any industry) 920.687-126
MARKER, MACHINE (boot & shoe) 690.685-282
MARKER MACHINE ATTENDANT (glass mfg.) 579.685-070
MARKER, SEMICONDUCTOR WAFERS (electron. comp.) 920.587-026
marker, shipments (any industry) 920.687-178
Market-Basket Maker I (wood. container) 669.685-014
Market-Basket Maker II (wood. container) 769.684-054
marketing engineer (profess. & kin.) see SALES ENGINEER
MARKET-RESEARCH ANALYST I (profess. & kin.) 050.067-014
Market-Research Analyst II (profess. & kin.) 045.107-030
marking clerk (retail trade; wholesale tr.) 209.587-034
MARKING-MACHINE OPERATOR (knitting; tex. prod., nec) 652.685-050
MARKING-MACHINE OPERATOR (textile) 652.685-046
MARKING-MACHINE TENDER (boot & shoe; leather prod.) 783.685-026
MARKING STITCHER (garment) 781.687-046
MARKSMANSHIP INSTRUCTOR (military ser.) 378.227-010
MARK-UP DESIGNER (glass mfg.) 775.684-050
MARQUETRY WORKER (furniture) 761.281-018
MARSHALL (amuse. & rec.) 153.384-010
Marsh-Buggy Operator (construction) 929.683-014
marshmallow-machine worker (bakery products) 524.682-010
Marshmallow Maker (sugar & conf.) 526.382-014
Marshmallow Packer (sugar & conf.) 529.686-034
Marshmallow Runner (sugar & conf.) 520.682-010
marzipan maker (sugar & conf.) 529.361-010
marzipan molder (sugar & conf.) 520.684-010
MASHER (beverage) 522.482-010
mash-feed-mixer operator (grain-feed mills) 520.685-098
MASH-FILTER-CLOTH CHANGER (beverage) 529.667-014
MASH-FILTER OPERATOR (beverage) 521.565-014
mash-filter-press operator (beverage) 521.565-014
mash-floor operator (food prep., nec) 522.685-078
MASH GRINDER (dairy products) 520.685-130
MASH-TUB-COOKER OPERATOR (beverage) 522.382-022
mask designer (profess. & kin.) 003.261-018
MASKER (any industry) 749.687-018
MASKER (clock & watch) 715.687-086
MASKER (electron. comp.) 726.687-034
Mask Former (electron. comp.) 725.685-010
MASKING-MACHINE FEEDER (plastic-synth.) 920.586-010
MASKING-MACHINE OPERATOR (plastic-synth.) 554.682-014
mask inspector (electron. comp.) 726.384-022
MASON (construction) term
MASON HELPER (construction) term
Masonry Inspector (construction) 182.267-010
MASSEUR/MASSEUSE (personal ser.) 334.374-010
MASTER (water trans.) term
Master, Bays, Sounds, And Lakes (water trans.) 197.167-010
Master, Coastal Waters (water trans.) 197.167-010
Master, Coastwise Yacht (water trans.) 197.133-014
master control engineer (radio-tv broad.) 194.262-022

MASTER CONTROL OPERATOR (radio-tv broad.) 194.262-022
Master, Great Lakes (water trans.) 197.167-010
master hypnotist (profess. & kin.) 079.157-010
Master, Ocean (water trans.) 197.167-010
Master, Ocean Yacht (water trans.) 197.133-014
MASTER, PASSENGER BARGE (water trans.) 197.163-014
master-pattern maker (boot & shoe) 788.281-010
Master Rigger (air trans.) 912.684-010
MASTER, RIVERBOAT (water trans.) 197.163-018
Master-Sheet Clerk (insurance) 203.582-066
MASTER, SHIP (water trans.) 197.167-010
Master, Steam Yacht (water trans.) 197.133-014
MASTER, YACHT (water trans.) 197.133-014
MATCHBOOK ASSEMBLER (fabrication, nec) 649.685-074
Matcher (garment) 781.687-042
matcher (garment; glove & mit.) 781.687-010
matcher (laundry & rel.) 369.687-010
MATCHER, LEATHER PARTS (leather prod.) 783.687-022
MATCH-UP WORKER (garment) 782.684-038
MAT CUTTER (wood prod., nec) 739.684-126
Mate, Chief (water trans.) 197.133-022
Mate, First (water trans.) 197.133-022
MATE, FISHING VESSEL (fishing & hunt.) 197.133-018
Mate, Fourth (water trans.) 197.133-022
Mate, Relief (water trans.) 197.133-022
MATERIAL ASSEMBLER (furniture) 781.684-066
MATERIAL ASSEMBLER (hat & cap) 784.687-050
MATERIAL CLERK (clerical) 222.387-034
material combiner (boot & shoe) 788.687-030
material control expediter (clerical) 221.167-014
MATERIAL COORDINATOR (clerical) 221.167-014
MATERIAL-CREW SUPERVISOR (construction; mfd. bldgs.) 921.137-014
material cutter (fabrication, nec) 690.485-010
MATERIAL EXPEDITER (clerical) 221.367-042
MATERIAL HANDLER (any industry) 929.687-030
MATERIAL-HANDLING SUPERVISOR (any industry) 921.133-018
Material Hauler (construction) 869.687-026
MATERIAL INSPECTOR (wood. container) 764.387-014
MATERIAL LISTER (construction) 229.387-010
MATERIAL MIXER (plastic prod.) 550.685-130
material planning and acquisition analyst (aircraft mfg.) 012.167-082
MATERIAL PREPARATION WORKER (electron. comp.) 590.684-030
Material Review Board Representative, Quality Control (aircraft mfg.) 806.261-034
MATERIAL SCHEDULER (aircraft mfg.) 012.167-082
MATERIALS ENGINEER (profess. & kin.) 019.061-014
materials-handling coordinator (nonfer. metal) 222.167-010
materials inspector (mine & quarry) 579.484-010
materials-make-up operator (chemical) 559.382-034
MATERIALS SCIENTIST (profess. & kin.) 029.081-014
Material Stockkeeper, Yard (petrol. & gas) 222.387-058
Mate, Second (water trans.) 197.133-022
MATE, SHIP (water trans.) 197.133-022
Mate, Third (water trans.) 197.133-022
MATHEMATICAL TECHNICIAN (profess. & kin.) 020.162-010
MATHEMATICIAN (profess. & kin.) 020.067-014
Mathematician, Applied (profess. & kin.) 020.067-014
Mathematician, Research (profess. & kin.) 020.067-014
mathematics improvement teacher (education) 099.227-042
MAT INSPECTOR (concrete prod.) 575.687-022
MAT-MACHINE OPERATOR (concrete prod.) 579.662-010
Mat-Machine Tender (wood. container) 669.685-014
MAT-MAKING MACHINE TENDER (furniture) 692.685-122
MAT PACKER (concrete prod.) 579.686-014
MAT PUNCHER (rubber goods) 690.685-286
MAT REPAIRER (rubber goods) 759.684-042
MATRIX-BATH ATTENDANT (recording) 500.384-014
MATRIX-DRIER TENDER (paper & pulp) 532.585-010
matrix inspector (recording) 194.387-010
MATRIX INSPECTOR (machinery mfg.) 654.687-010
MATRIX PLATER (recording) 500.384-010
MATRIX WORKER (recording) 500.684-014
mat selector (glass mfg.) 689.687-038
MAT SEWER (oils & grease) 529.687-154
Matte Cutter (motion picture) 976.684-010
MAT TESTER (concrete prod.) 579.387-010
Matting Inspector (rubber goods) 759.684-074
MATTING-PRESS TENDER (rubber goods) 556.685-042
MATTRESS-FILLING-MACHINE TENDER (furniture) 780.685-010
MATTRESS FINISHER (furniture) 780.684-070
Mattress Inspector (rubber goods) 759.684-074
MATTRESS MAKER (furniture) 780.684-074
Mattress Packer (furniture) 920.587-018
MATTRESS-SPRING ENCASER (furniture) 780.687-030

MATTRESS STRIPPER (furniture) 780.687-026
MATURITY CHECKER (can. & preserv.) 529.485-022
Matzo-Forming-Machine Operator (bakery products) 520.682-034
Mayonnaise Mixer (food prep., nec) 520.685-154
meal cook (oils & grease) 523.685-034
MEAL-GRINDER TENDER (grain-feed mills) 521.685-210
meal temperer (oils & grease) 523.685-034
measurement superintendent (petrol. & gas; pipe lines) 184.167-190
measurer (leather mfg.) 589.685-070
measurer (mine & quarry) 679.567-010
MEASURER (retail trade) 869.367-014
MEASURER (struct. metal) 869.487-010
measurer, machine (garment; textile) 589.685-022
MEASURING-MACHINE OPERATOR (leather mfg.) 589.685-070
measuring-machine tender (textile) 689.685-078
measuring percher-and-inspector (garment; textile) 589.685-022
Meat And Poultry Specialist Supervisor (government ser.) 168.167-090
MEAT BLENDER (can. & preserv.) 529.685-166
meat carver (hotel & rest.) 316.661-010
MEAT CLERK (retail trade) 222.684-010
Meat Counter Clerk (retail trade) 290.477-018
meat cutter (hotel & rest.) 316.681-010
MEAT CUTTER (retail trade; wholesale tr.) 316.684-018
MEAT-CUTTER APPRENTICE (retail trade; wholesale tr.) 316.684-022
Meat-Cutting-Block Repairer (any industry) 860.281-010
MEAT DRESSER (agriculture) 525.664-010
MEAT-GRADING-MACHINE OPERATOR (can. & preserv.) 521.685-218
MEAT GRINDER (meat products) 521.685-214
Meat Inspector (retail trade; wholesale tr.) 316.684-018
meat smoker (meat products) 525.682-010
Meat Stock Clerk (retail trade) 299.367-014
Meat Wrapper (retail trade) 920.587-018
mechanic (mine & quarry) 630.281-022
MECHANIC, AIRCRAFT RIGGING AND CONTROLS (aircraft mfg.) 806.261-050
mechanical adjuster (any industry) 638.281-014
mechanical artist (print. & pub.) 972.381-030
MECHANICAL-DESIGN ENGINEER, FACILITIES (profess. & kin.) 007.061-018
MECHANICAL-DESIGN ENGINEER, PRODUCTS (profess. & kin.) 007.061-022
mechanical design technician (profess. & kin.) 007.161-018
MECHANICAL ENGINEER (profess. & kin.) 007.061-014
MECHANICAL-ENGINEERING TECHNICIAN (profess. & kin.) 007.161-026
mechanical inspector (agric. equip.) 624.361-010
mechanical inspector (electron. comp.) 726.682-018
MECHANICAL INSPECTOR (petrol. refin.) 549.261-010
MECHANICAL-MAINTENANCE SUPERVISOR (any industry) 638.131-026
mechanical-meter tester (petrol. refin.; pipe lines; utilities) 953.281-010
MECHANICAL OXIDIZER (fabrication, nec) 590.662-014
mechanical-press operator (chemical) 555.685-042
MECHANICAL RESEARCH ENGINEER (profess. & kin.) 007.161-022
MECHANICAL-SHOVEL OPERATOR (mine & quarry) 932.683-018
mechanical-spreader operator (construction) 853.663-010
mechanical striper (any industry) 741.687-022
mechanical technician (any industry) 600.280-010
mechanical technician (profess. & kin.) 007.161-026
MECHANICAL TECHNICIAN, LABORATORY (clock & watch) 715.261-010
MECHANICAL-TEST TECHNICIAN (inst. & app.) 869.261-014
MECHANICAL-UNIT REPAIRER (automotive ser.; railroad equip.) 620.381-018
mechanic, chief (automotive ser.) 620.131-014
Mechanic, Electrical Operational Test (aircraft mfg.) 806.261-050
MECHANIC, ENDLESS TRACK VEHICLE (automotive ser.) 620.381-014
Mechanic, Experimental Structural Assembly (aircraft mfg.) 693.261-014
Mechanic, Field-Service (aircraft mfg.) 621.281-014
Mechanic, General Operational Test (aircraft mfg.) 806.261-050
mechanic helper (any industry) 630.684-022
mechanic helper (automotive ser.) 620.684-014
mechanic helper (construction; petrol. & gas; pipe lines) 620.664-014
MECHANIC, INDUSTRIAL TRUCK (any industry) 620.281-050
mechanic, marine engine (water trans.) 197.130-010
mechanic, trouble-shooting (automotive ser.) 620.261-018
MECHANISM ASSEMBLER (clock & watch) 715.684-142
media center director, school (library) 100.167-030
MEDIA CLERK (business ser.) 247.382-010
media coordinator (radio-tv broad.) 199.382-010
MEDIA DIRECTOR (profess. & kin.) 164.117-018
MEDIA SPECIALIST, SCHOOL LIBRARY (library) 100.167-030
mediator (profess. & kin.) 169.207-010
Medical Anthropologist (profess. & kin.) 055.067-014
Medical-Apparatus Model Maker (inst. & app.) 693.260-018
MEDICAL ASSISTANT (medical ser.) 079.362-010
medical clerk (medical ser.) 205.362-018
MEDICAL COORDINATOR, PESTICIDE USE (government ser.) 041.067-010

metal-tile lather

metal-tile lather (construction) 860.381-010
Metal-Tile Setter (construction; retail trade) 861.381-034
metal-trim erector (construction) 809.381-022
METAL-WASHING-MACHINE OPERATOR (svc. ind. mach.) 503.685-034
Metal-Window-Screen Assembler (struct. metal) 809.681-010
metal worker (automotive ser.) 807.381-010
METEOROLOGICAL-EQUIPMENT REPAIRER (any industry) 823.281-018
meteorological technician (profess. & kin.) 025.267-014
METEOROLOGIST (profess. & kin.) 025.062-010
meter-and-service-line inspector (utilities) 953.367-014
Meter Assembler (photo. appar.) 714.684-010
Meter Attendant (government ser.) 375.587-010
meter-changes records clerk (utilities) 209.587-022
meter inspector (petrol. refin.; pipe lines; utilities) 953.281-010
METER INSPECTOR (utilities) 710.384-022
meter installer (utilities) 953.364-010
Meter Installer-And-Remover (utilities) 821.361-014
METER READER (utilities; waterworks) 209.567-010
METER READER, CHIEF (utilities; waterworks) 209.137-014
meter-record clerk (utilities) 209.587-022
METER REPAIRER (any industry) 710.281-034
meter repairer (utilities) 729.281-014
meter-repairer apprentice (utilities) 729.281-018
METER-REPAIRER HELPER (any industry) 710.684-034
meter shop superintendent (utilities) 184.167-194
meter tester (utilities) 710.381-022
meter tester (utilities) 821.381-010
Meter Tester, Demand Meters (utilities) 821.381-010
Meter Tester, Polyphase (utilities) 821.381-010
Meter Tester, Primary (utilities) 821.381-010
Meter Tester, Single Phase (utilities) 821.381-010
methods analyst, data processing (profess. & kin.) 033.167-010
methods-and-procedures analyst (profess. & kin.) 012.167-070
Methods-Study Analyst (profess. & kin.) 012.267-014
METROLOGIST (profess. & kin.) 012.067-010
metropolitan editor (print. & pub.) 132.037-014
MEXICAN-FOOD-MACHINE TENDER (food prep., nec) 524.685-038
MEXICAN FOOD MAKER, HAND (food prep., nec) 520.687-046
MICA INSPECTOR (mine & quarry) 779.687-026
MICA-LAMINATING-MACHINE FEEDER (mine & quarry) 579.686-018
Mica-Parts Sprayer (electron. comp.) 741.687-018
MICA PATCHER (mine & quarry) 579.687-026
MICA-PLATE LAYER (mine & quarry) 579.685-026
MICA-PLATE LAYER, HAND (mine & quarry) 579.684-022
MICA SIZER (mine & quarry) 779.687-030
MICA SPLITTER (mine & quarry) 779.681-010
MICA-WASHER GLUER (mine & quarry) 729.687-022
MICROBIOLOGIST (profess. & kin.) 041.061-058
MICROBIOLOGY TECHNOLOGIST (medical ser.; pharmaceut.) 078.261-014
MICROCOMPUTER SUPPORT SPECIALIST (profess. & kin.) 039.264-010
microelectronics processor (electron. comp.) 726.684-034
MICROELECTRONICS TECHNICIAN (electron. comp.) 590.362-022
MICROFICHE DUPLICATOR (business ser.) 976.381-014
MICROFILM-CAMERA OPERATOR (business ser.) 976.682-022
MICROFILM MOUNTER (clerical) 208.685-022
MICROFILM PROCESSOR (business ser.) 976.385-010
Micrographics-Services Supervisor (clerical) 207.137-010
microgrinder operator (tex. prod., nec) 586.685-018
micromatic-hone operator (machine shop) 603.685-070
Micropaleontologist (profess. & kin.) 024.061-042
MICROPHONE-BOOM OPERATOR (motion picture; radio-tv broad.) 962.384-010
Microwave Engineer (radio-tv broad.) 193.262-018
MIDDLE-CARD TENDER (nonmet. min.; textile) 680.665-018
Middle Stitcher (toy-sport equip.) 732.684-050
MIGRANT LEADER (agriculture) 180.167-050
MIGRANT WORKER (agriculture) term
Milanese-Knitting-Machine Operator (knitting) 685.665-018
Mileage Clerk (r.r. trans.) 216.382-062
MILK DRIVER (dairy products) 905.483-010
MILKER, MACHINE (agriculture) 410.685-010
milk hauler (dairy products) 905.483-010
milking-machine operator (agriculture) 410.685-010
MILKING-SYSTEM INSTALLER (agric. equip.; retail trade) 809.381-018
milk-of-lime slaker (concrete prod.) 570.685-034
MILK-POWDER GRINDER (dairy products) 521.685-222
MILK RECEIVER (dairy products) 222.585-010
MILK-RECEIVER, TANK TRUCK (dairy products) 222.485-010
MILK SAMPLER (agriculture) 410.357-010
MILL-AND-COAL-TRANSPORT OPERATOR (utilities) 544.665-010
MILL ATTENDANT I (chemical) 555.565-010
MILL ATTENDANT II (chemical) 555.685-038
mill attendant (leather mfg.; tex. prod., nec) 582.685-050
mill attendant (mine & quarry; smelt. & refin.) 939.362-014
Milled-Lumber Grader (woodworking) 669.687-030

milled-rice broker (grain-feed mills) 162.167-018
MILLED-RUBBER TENDER (rubber goods; rubber tire) 553.685-078
MILLER (any industry) term
MILLER (beverage) 521.585-014
MILLER (cement) 570.685-046
MILLER (mine & quarry) 570.685-038
MILLER, DISTILLERY (beverage) 521.362-014
miller, first (grain-feed mills) 521.130-010
miller, head (grain-feed mills) 521.130-010
MILLER, HEAD, ASSISTANT, WET PROCESS (grain-feed mills) 629.684-014
MILLER, HEAD, WET PROCESS (grain-feed mills) 629.261-014
MILLER HELPER, DISTILLERY (beverage) 521.687-082
MILLER I (chemical) 570.685-042
MILLER II (chemical) 555.682-010
Miller, Kiln-Dried Salt (chemical) 555.682-010
Miller, Rod-Mill (cement) 570.685-046
MILLER SUPERVISOR (grain-feed mills) 521.130-010
MILLER, WET PROCESS (grain-feed mills) 521.662-010
MILLER, WOOD FLOUR (woodworking) 564.682-018
MILL FEEDER (grain-feed mills) 520.685-134
MILL HAND (any industry) term
MILL HAND (grain-feed mills) term
MILL HAND, PLATE MILL (steel & rel.) 613.667-014
MILL HELPER (nonfer. metal) 502.684-014
MILLINER (retail trade) 784.261-010
milling-machine operator (machine shop) 605.282-018
milling-machine operator, gear (machine shop) 602.382-022
MILLING-MACHINE SET-UP OPERATOR I (machine shop) 605.280-010
MILLING-MACHINE SET-UP OPERATOR II (machine shop) 605.282-010
MILLING-MACHINE SET-UP OPERATOR, NUMERICAL CONTROL (machine shop) 605.380-010
MILLING-MACHINE TENDER (machine shop) 605.685-030
milling-planer operator (machine shop) 605.282-018
milling superintendent (grain-feed mills) 183.167-014
MILLING SUPERVISOR (brick & tile) 570.132-014
mill laborer (woodworking) 769.687-054
MILL-LABOR SUPERVISOR (smelt. & refin.) 519.131-014
MILL OPERATOR (any industry) 599.685-058
mill operator (bakery products) 520.585-010
MILL OPERATOR (brick & tile; pottery & porc.) 570.382-010
mill operator (chemical) 555.685-034
mill operator (grain-feed mills) 521.130-010
mill operator (grain-feed mills) 521.682-026
MILL OPERATOR (grain-feed mills) 521.685-226
mill operator (utilities) 544.665-010
mill operator, head (plastic-synth.) 559.132-042
MILL-OPERATOR HELPER (any industry) 599.686-010
MILL OPERATOR, ROLLS (any industry) 613.682-030
MILL PLATFORM SUPERVISOR (sugar & conf.) 521.132-010
Mill Recorder (nonfer. metal) 221.382-018
MILL RECORDER, COMPUTERIZED MILL (steel & rel.) 221.367-046
mill-roll operator (plastic-synth.) 554.682-018
MILL-ROLL REWINDER (plastic-synth.) 690.585-010
millroom supervisor (any industry) 921.137-010
Millroom Supervisor (mfd. bldgs.; vehicles, nec) 869.131-030
Millroom Supervisor (rubber goods) 559.137-014
Millroom Supervisor (rubber reclaim.) 559.132-058
Millroom Supervisor (rubber tire) 750.130-010
MILL STENCILER (steel & rel.) 659.685-026
MILL SUPERVISOR (nonmet. min.) 559.132-034
MILL SUPERVISOR (smelt. & refin.) 515.130-010
Mill Tender, Break-Down (rubber goods; rubber tire) 550.685-102
Mill Tender, Warm-Up (rubber goods; rubber tire) 550.685-102
Mill Tender, Washing (rubber goods; rubber tire) 550.685-102
MILL WORKER (any industry) term
MILLWRIGHT (any industry) 638.281-018
MILLWRIGHT APPRENTICE (any industry) 638.281-022
MILLWRIGHT HELPER (any industry) 638.484-010
MILLWRIGHT SUPERVISOR (any industry) 638.131-030
MIME (amuse. & rec.) 159.047-022
mimic (amuse. & rec.) 159.047-018
MINCEMEAT MAKER (can. & preserv.) 520.485-018
mincing-machine operator (meat products) 521.685-170
Mind Reader (amuse. & rec.) 159.647-018
mine captain (mine & quarry) 939.137-018
MINE-CAR REPAIRER (mine & quarry) 622.381-030
Mine Electrician (mine & quarry) 824.261-010
MINE INSPECTOR (mine & quarry) 168.267-074
Mine Inspector, Federal (government ser.) 168.267-074
Mine Inspector, State (government ser.) 168.267-074
Mine-Machinery Mechanic (mine & quarry) 620.261-022
MINER (construction) 850.381-010
MINERALOGIST (profess. & kin.) 024.061-038
Mineral-Wool-Insulation Supervisor (construction) 863.134-010

Miner Helper (construction) 869.687-026
MINER I (mine & quarry) 939.281-010
MINER II (mine & quarry) term
Miner, Pick (mine & quarry) 939.281-010
MINER, PLACER (mine & quarry) 939.684-014
MINE SUPERINTENDENT (mine & quarry) 181.117-014
MINGLER OPERATOR (sugar & conf.) 520.665-010
miniature-model maker (auto. mfg.) 693.380-014
miniature-set builder (motion picture) 962.381-018
MINIATURE-SET CONSTRUCTOR (motion picture) 962.381-018
Miniature Set Designer (motion picture; radio-tv broad.) 142.061-046
MINING ENGINEER (mine & quarry) 010.061-014
mining-machine operator (mine & quarry)   see MACHINE RUNNER
minister (profess. & kin.) 120.107-010
Mink Farmer (agriculture) 410.161-014
Mint-Lozenge Mixer (sugar & conf.) 520.685-122
Mint-Machine Operator (sugar & conf.) 521.685-102
Mint-Wafer Depositor (sugar & conf.) 529.682-018
MIRROR-FINISHING-MACHINE OPERATOR (jewelry-silver.) 603.682-022
mirror inspector (glass products) 779.687-022
MIRROR INSTALLER (construction) 865.361-010
MIRROR-MACHINE FEEDER (glass products) 579.686-022
mirror silverer (glass products) 574.684-014
MIRROR SPECIALIST (glass products; wood prod., nec) 779.684-038
misdraw hand (textile) 683.384-010
Missile-Control Pilot (aircraft mfg.) 196.263-026
MISSILE FACILITIES REPAIRER (military ser.) 828.281-018
Missile Inspector, Preflight (aircraft mfg.) 806.261-038
Missionary (profess. & kin.) 120.107-010
miter cutter (glass products) 775.381-010
MITER GRINDER OPERATOR (glass mfg.; glass products) 673.682-026
Miter Sawyer (woodworking) 667.682-086
Mitten Stitcher (glove & mit.) 784.682-014
MIX-CRUSHER OPERATOR (elec. equip.) 544.585-010
mixer (any industry) 550.684-018
MIXER (brick & tile) 579.685-074
mixer (build. mat., nec; nonmet. min.) 550.382-030
mixer (chemical; pharmaceut.) 550.685-090
MIXER (food prep., nec) 520.685-138
MIXER (glass mfg.) 570.685-054
MIXER (hat & cap) 680.685-062
MIXER (nonfer. metal; steel & rel.) 510.685-018
MIXER (nonmet. min.) 570.685-050
MIXER (paint & varnish) 550.685-078
mixer (pottery & porc.) 570.685-086
MIXER-AND-BLENDER (food prep., nec) 520.685-154
mixer-and-scaler (grain-feed mills) 520.485-010
MIXER, CHILI POWDER (food prep., nec) 520.685-158
MIXER, DIAMOND POWDER (nonmet. min.) 570.484-010
MIXER, DRY-FOOD PRODUCTS (food prep., nec) 520.685-162
MIXER, FOAM RUBBER (rubber goods) 550.685-086
Mixer, Hand, Cement Gun (construction) 869.687-026
MIXER HELPER (build. mat.) 550.686-026
mixer helper (build. mat., nec; nonmet. min.) 550.686-038
MIXER HELPER (concrete prod.) 530.384-010
mixer helper (construction) 579.665-014
MIXER I (chemical) 559.665-026
MIXER I (tex. prod., nec) 550.685-074
MIXER II (chemical) 737.687-090
MIXER II (tex. prod., nec) 789.687-098
mixer-machine feeder (grain-feed mills) 520.686-018
MIXER OPERATOR (beverage) 520.685-146
Mixer Operator (brick & tile) 570.382-010
MIXER OPERATOR (chemical; electron. comp.) 550.685-082
MIXER OPERATOR (concrete prod.) 570.685-058
mixer operator (concrete prod.) 579.682-010
mixer operator (fabrication, nec) 550.665-014
mixer operator (grain-feed mills) 520.485-010
mixer operator (motion picture; radio-tv broad.; recording) 194.262-018
mixer operator (nonmet. min.) 570.485-010
mixer operator (smelt. & refin.; steel & rel.) 570.685-070
MIXER OPERATOR (sugar & conf.) 520.685-150
MIXER OPERATOR, CARBON PASTE (elec. equip.; smelt. & refin.) 540.585-010
MIXER OPERATOR HELPER, HOT METAL (steel & rel.) 509.566-010
MIXER OPERATOR, HOT METAL (steel & rel.) 509.362-010
MIXER OPERATOR I (chemical) 550.382-018
MIXER OPERATOR II (chemical) 550.685-142
Mixer Operator, Raw Salt (chemical) 520.685-142
MIXER OPERATOR, SNACK FOODS (food prep., nec) 520.685-230
Mixer Operator, Tablets (chemical) 520.685-142
Mixer Operator, Vacuum-Pan Salt (chemical) 520.685-142
mixer, pigment (leather mfg.; plastic-synth.; tex. prod., nec) 550.381-010
Mixer Tender (cement) 570.685-010
mixer tender (construction) 579.665-014

mixer tender (smelt. & refin.) 510.685-022
MIXER TENDER, BOARD (concrete prod.) 570.685-062
MIXER, WET POUR (concrete prod.) 579.682-010
MIXER, WHIPPED TOPPING (food prep., nec) 520.385-010
mix-house operator (glass mfg.) 570.685-054
MIX-HOUSE TENDER (smelt. & refin.) 510.685-014
mixing-and-dispensing supervisor (chemical) 559.132-030
mixing-and-molding-machine operator (pen & pencil) 570.685-066
mixing-house operator (chemical) 550.382-018
mixing-machine attendant (bakery products) 520.685-234
mixing-machine attendant (bakery products) 520.685-010
MIXING-MACHINE FEEDER (chemical) 550.686-030
MIXING-MACHINE OPERATOR (any industry) 550.382-022
MIXING-MACHINE OPERATOR (can. & preserv.) 520.685-166
MIXING-MACHINE OPERATOR (fabrication, nec) 680.685-066
MIXING-MACHINE OPERATOR (food prep., nec) 520.665-014
mixing-machine operator (hat & cap) 680.685-062
MIXING-MACHINE OPERATOR (plastic prod.; plastic-synth.) 550.685-134
MIXING-MACHINE TENDER (chemical; pharmaceut.) 550.685-090
MIXING-MACHINE TENDER (wood prod., nec) 560.585-010
Mixing-Machine Tender, Cork Gasket (wood prod., nec) 560.585-010
Mixing-Machine Tender, Cork Rod (wood prod., nec) 560.585-010
Mixing-Pan Tender (smelt. & refin.) 510.685-014
mixing-plant dumper (construction) 579.665-014
mixing-plant operator (chemical) 550.585-030
MIXING-ROLL OPERATOR (fabrication, nec) 590.662-018
MIXING SUPERVISOR (plastic prod.) 550.135-014
Mixing Supervisor (tex. prod., nec) 589.130-014
MIXING-TANK OPERATOR (oils & grease) 520.685-170
Mix Maker (dairy products) 529.382-018
Mix-Mill Tender (rubber goods; rubber tire) 550.685-102
mobile-crane operator (any industry) 921.663-062
MOBILE-HOME-LOT UTILITY WORKER (retail trade) 899.484-010
MOBILE-LOUNGE DRIVER (motor trans.) 913.663-014
moccasin sewer (boot & shoe) 788.684-054
mock-up assembler (vehicles, nec) 693.381-018
MOCK-UP BUILDER (aircraft mfg.) 693.361-014
MOCK-UP BUILDER (vehicles, nec) 693.381-018
MODEL-AND-MOLD MAKER (brick & tile) 777.381-014
MODEL-AND-MOLD MAKER, PLASTER (concrete prod.) 777.381-018
MODEL, ARTISTS' (any industry) 961.667-010
MODEL BUILDER (furniture) 709.381-014
Model Builder, Display (aircraft mfg.) 693.261-018
Model Builder, Wind Tunnel (aircraft mfg.) 693.261-018
Model Dresser (retail trade) 298.081-010
modeler (boot & shoe) 788.684-082
MODELER (brick & tile) 777.081-010
modeler (pottery & porc.) 777.281-014
MODEL (garment; retail trade; wholesale tr.) 297.667-014
MODEL MAKER (aircraft mfg.) 693.261-018
MODEL MAKER (auto. mfg.) 693.380-014
model maker (boot & shoe) 788.281-010
MODEL MAKER (clock & watch) 693.380-010
model maker (fabrication, nec) 739.361-010
model maker (house. appl.; light. fix.) 600.280-054
MODEL MAKER (pottery & porc.) 777.281-014
MODEL MAKER (toy-sport equip.) 731.280-014
model maker (wood prod., nec) 761.381-018
MODEL-MAKER APPRENTICE (jewelry-silver.) 709.381-022
MODEL MAKER, FIBERGLASS (concrete prod.) 777.381-010
MODEL MAKER, FIREARMS (ordnance) 600.260-018
MODEL MAKER, FLUORESCENT LIGHTING (light. fix.) 723.361-010
MODEL MAKER I (any industry) 777.261-010
MODEL MAKER I (jewelry-silver.) 700.281-018
MODEL MAKER II (any industry) term
MODEL MAKER II (jewelry-silver.) 709.381-018
Model Maker, Plaster (concrete prod.) 777.381-018
model maker, plaster and plastic (aircraft mfg.) 777.281-018
model maker, plastic (machine shop) 601.381-030
MODEL MAKER, SCALE (office machines) 710.361-010
Model Maker, Sheet-Metal (any industry) 804.281-010
MODEL MAKER, WOOD (any industry) 661.380-010
MODEL, PHOTOGRAPHERS' (any industry) 961.367-010
model-set artist (motion picture) 962.381-018
mogul feeder (sugar & conf.) 520.686-030
mogul operator (sugar & conf.) 520.682-026
MOHEL (profess. & kin.) 129.271-010
MOISTURE-CONDITIONER OPERATOR (paper & pulp) 532.685-022
MOISTURE-MACHINE TENDER (tobacco) 529.685-170
MOISTURE-METER OPERATOR (tobacco) 529.687-162
MOISTURE TESTER (woodworking) 563.687-014
moisture-test puller (tobacco) 529.587-022
MOLASSES AND CARAMEL OPERATOR (grain-feed mills) 526.382-022
Molasses-Feed Mixer (grain-feed mills) 520.685-098
MOLASSES PREPARER (food prep., nec) 522.685-078

mold-car operator (steel & rel.) 514.362-010
mold carrier (tobacco) 790.687-022
mold changer (glass mfg.) 575.687-014
Mold Changer (rubber tire) 629.684-010
Mold Checker (foundry) 518.687-010
Mold Clamper (foundry) 519.687-022
mold cleaner (glass mfg.) 579.685-030
MOLD CLEANER (rubber goods) 556.687-018
MOLD CLEANER (toy-sport equip.) 732.687-046
MOLD CLOSER (foundry) 518.684-018
Mold-Closer Helper (foundry) 519.687-022
MOLD DRESSER (any industry) 519.684-018
mold dresser (rubber tire) 709.381-026
Molded-Goods Inspector-Trimmer (rubber goods) 759.684-074
molded-grid-and-parts inspector (elec. equip.) 727.687-074
MOLDED-PARTS INSPECTOR (elec. equip.) 727.687-074
MOLDED-RUBBER-GOODS CUTTER (rubber goods) 690.685-290
molder (aircraft mfg.) 502.381-014
MOLDER (aircraft mfg.; concrete prod.; foundry) 518.361-010
molder (boot & shoe) 690.682-070
MOLDER (hat & cap) 580.685-042
molder (jewelry-silver.) 502.381-010
molder (nonmet. min.) 575.685-010
MOLDER (optical goods) 575.381-010
molder (pharmaceut.) 556.685-026
molder (plastic prod.) 556.685-022
molder (plastic prod.) 556.382-014
molder (plastic prod.) 777.684-010
molder (protective dev.) 712.684-034
molder (tex. prod., nec) 692.685-286
molder (toy-sport equip.) 732.687-070
MOLDER APPRENTICE (aircraft mfg.; concrete prod.; foundry) 518.361-014
MOLDER, AUTOMOBILE CARPETS (tex. prod., nec) 692.685-286
Molder, Bench (concrete prod.; foundry) 518.361-010
MOLDER, BENCH (jewelry-silver.) 518.381-022
molder, closed molds (aircraft mfg.) 502.381-014
Molder Feeder (woodworking) 669.686-030
MOLDER, FIBERGLASS LUGGAGE (leather prod.) 575.685-066
Molder, Fitting (foundry) 518.682-010
Molder, Floor (foundry) 518.361-010
MOLDER, FOAM RUBBER (rubber goods) 556.685-046
MOLDER, HAND (brick & tile; elec. equip.) 575.684-042
molder, hand (sugar & conf.) 520.687-018
Molder Helper (foundry) 519.687-022
MOLDER HELPER (optical goods) 575.686-014
Molder Helper, Machine (foundry) 519.687-022
MOLDER, INFLATED BALL (toy-sport equip.) 732.687-054
MOLDER, LABELS (boot & shoe) 690.685-294
MOLDER, LEAD INGOT (ordnance) 502.685-010
molder, machine (brick & tile) 575.662-010
MOLDER, MACHINE (pharmaceut.) 556.685-050
MOLDER-MACHINE TENDER (nonmet. min.) 575.685-062
MOLDER, MEAT (meat products) 520.685-174
Molder Offbearer (woodworking) 669.686-034
molder operator (plastic prod.) 556.685-090
MOLDER OPERATOR (woodworking) 665.682-018
MOLDER, PATTERN (foundry) 693.381-022
MOLDER, PIPE COVERING (plastic prod.) 556.665-018
MOLDER, PUNCH (aircraft mfg.) 502.381-014
molder, resin (aircraft mfg.) 556.684-014
Molder Setter (woodworking) 669.280-010
MOLDER, SHOE PARTS (boot & shoe) 788.687-094
MOLDER, SHOULDER PAD (garment) 789.684-026
MOLDER, SWEEP (foundry) 518.361-018
MOLDER, TOILET PRODUCTS (pharmaceut.) 556.687-022
molder-trimmer (tex. prod., nec) 692.685-286
molder, vacuum (plastic prod.) 556.685-082
MOLDER, WAX (petrol. refin.) 549.685-018
MOLDER, WAX BALL (toy-sport equip.) 732.687-058
Mold Filler (dairy products) 529.685-030
Mold Filler (metal prod., nec) 700.687-038
MOLD FILLER (toy-sport equip.) 556.687-030
Mold Filler (wood prod., nec) 569.685-030
MOLD FILLER AND DRAINER (boot & shoe) 753.687-030
MOLD FILLER, PLASTIC DOLLS (toy-sport equip.) 731.687-026
MOLD-FILLING OPERATOR (plastic-synth.) 556.684-018
mold finisher (foundry) 518.684-018
MOLD FINISHER (machine shop) 705.684-038
mold finisher (ship-boat mfg.) 809.687-026
mold-forms builder (brick & tile; concrete prod.) 860.381-034
Mold Hoister (wood prod., nec) 569.685-030
MOLDING CUTTER (woodworking) 663.685-018
Molding Fitter (fabrication, nec) 739.684-190
Molding-Machine Operator (bakery products) 520.685-086
molding-machine operator (fabrication, nec) 549.662-010

MOLDING-MACHINE OPERATOR (sugar & conf.) 520.682-026
MOLDING-MACHINE OPERATOR (toy-sport equip.) 575.682-014
Molding-Machine-Operator Helper (bakery products) 526.686-010
MOLDING-MACHINE-OPERATOR HELPER (sugar & conf.) 520.686-030
MOLDING-MACHINE TENDER (paper & pulp) 539.685-018
MOLDING-MACHINE TENDER (pen & pencil) 570.685-066
molding-press operator (rubber goods; rubber tire; toy-sport equip.) 556.685-066
Molding-Room Supervisor (optical goods) 716.130-010
MOLDING SANDER (woodworking) 662.682-010
MOLDING SUPERVISOR (plastic prod.) 556.130-018
MOLD-INSERT CHANGER (boot & shoe) 753.687-034
mold inspector (plastic-synth.) 556.684-010
MOLD LAMINATOR (concrete prod.; ship-boat mfg.) 806.684-086
mold loft worker (ship-boat mfg.) 661.281-010
Mold Maker (construction) 869.687-026
mold maker (fabrication, nec) 739.381-046
mold maker (hat & cap) 784.361-010
mold maker (jewelry-silver.) 559.684-018
MOLD MAKER (nonmet. min.) 777.684-014
MOLD MAKER (pottery & porc.) 777.684-018
MOLD MAKER (smelt. & refin.) 518.664-010
MOLD-MAKER APPRENTICE (jewelry-silver.) 700.381-038
MOLD MAKER, DIE-CASTING AND PLASTIC MOLDING (machine shop) 601.280-030
MOLD-MAKER HELPER (jewelry-silver.) 700.687-050
MOLD-MAKER HELPER (smelt. & refin.) 518.687-018
MOLD MAKER I (jewelry-silver.) 700.381-034
MOLD MAKER II (jewelry-silver.) 777.381-022
Mold Maker, Plaster (concrete prod.) 777.381-018
mold maker, plastic molds (machine shop) 601.280-030
MOLD MAKER, TERRA COTTA (brick & tile) 575.684-038
Mold-Making Supervisor (foundry) 519.131-010
Mold Mover (toy-sport equip.) 929.687-030
MOLD OPERATOR (elec. equip.) 729.684-030
MOLD PARTER (plastic-synth.) 556.587-010
Mold Picker (rubber goods) 222.387-058
MOLD POLISHER (glass mfg.) 579.685-030
MOLD PREPARER (ship-boat mfg.) 809.687-026
MOLD PRESSER (tobacco) 790.687-022
Mold-Press Operator (glass mfg.) 575.382-014
Mold-Release Worker (chemical) 590.464-010
Mold Remover (dairy products) 529.685-030
mold repairer (any industry) 519.684-018
Mold Repairer, Die-Casting And Plastic Molding (machine shop) 601.280-030
MOLD SETTER (elec. equip.) 502.684-018
MOLD SETTER (inst. & app.; office machines; plastic prod.; recording) 556.380-010
mold setter (optical goods) 713.381-010
MOLD SHEET CLEANER (metal prod., nec) 700.687-046
Mold Sprayer (wood prod., nec) 569.685-030
Mold Stacker (foundry) 519.687-022
MOLD STAMPER (machine shop) 709.684-054
MOLD STAMPER AND REPAIRER (rubber tire) 709.381-026
mold stripper (plastic prod.; rubber goods) 556.686-018
mold stripper (plastic-synth.) 556.686-014
MOLD STRIPPER (toy-sport equip.) 732.687-050
MOLD WORKER (steel & rel.) 514.567-010
Molybdenum-Flotation Operator (smelt. & refin.) 511.685-026
Molybdenum-Leaching-Plant Operator (smelt. & refin.) 511.582-010
MOLYBDENUM-STEAMER OPERATOR (smelt. & refin.) 511.485-010
MONEY COUNTER (amuse. & rec.) 211.467-014
Money-Order Clerk (tel. & tel.) 249.362-010
money position officer (financial; insurance) 186.167-054
money-room teller (amuse. & rec.) 211.467-014
monitor (tel. & tel.) 239.367-026
MONITOR-AND-STORAGE-BIN TENDER (grain-feed mills) 521.685-230
MONITOR CAR OPERATOR (mine & quarry) 939.682-010
monitor chief (tel. & tel.) 239.137-022
Monkey Breeder (agriculture) 410.161-010
Monkey Keeper (amuse. & rec.) 412.674-010
MONOGRAM-AND-LETTER PASTER (tex. prod., nec) 789.687-102
monogram-machine operator (any industry) 787.682-022
MONOMER-PURIFICATION OPERATOR (chemical) 552.362-010
Monomer-Recovery Supervisor (plastic-synth.) 559.132-042
Mononitrotoluene Operator (chemical) 558.382-046
MONORAIL CRANE OPERATOR (any industry) 921.663-042
Monorail Operator (amuse. & rec.) 342.663-010
monotype caster (machinery mfg.; print. & pub.) 654.382-010
MONOTYPE-KEYBOARD OPERATOR (machinery mfg.; print. & pub.) 650.582-014
monotype operator (machinery mfg.; print. & pub.) 650.582-014
Monument Carver (stonework) 771.281-014
MONUMENT SETTER (construction) 861.361-014
Monument Stonecutter (stonework) 771.381-014

MOP-HANDLE ASSEMBLER (tex. prod., nec) 739.687-122
Mophead Sewer (tex. prod., nec) 787.682-066
MOPHEAD TRIMMER-AND-WRAPPER (tex. prod., nec) 789.687-106
mop-machine operator (tex. prod., nec) 739.685-026
MOP MAKER (tex. prod., nec) 739.685-026
mopper (any industry) 381.687-014
morals-squad police officer (government ser.) 375.267-022
MORGUE ATTENDANT (medical ser.) 355.667-010
Mortar Mixer (concrete prod.; construction) 869.687-026
MORTGAGE-ACCOUNTING CLERK (clerical) 216.362-026
MORTGAGE CLERK (financial) 249.362-014
MORTGAGE-CLOSING CLERK (clerical) 219.362-038
MORTGAGE LOAN CLOSER (financial) 249.362-018
MORTGAGE-LOAN-COMPUTATION CLERK (insurance) 210.382-050
Mortgage-Loan Officer (financial; insurance) 186.267-018
Mortgage Loan Originator (financial) 186.267-018
MORTGAGE LOAN PROCESSOR (financial) 249.362-022
Mortgage-Papers-Assignment-And-Assembly Clerk (insurance) 203.582-066
mortician (personal ser.) 187.167-030
MORTICIAN INVESTIGATOR (government ser.) 168.267-078
MORTISING-MACHINE OPERATOR (woodworking) 665.482-014
MORTUARY BEAUTICIAN (personal ser.) 339.361-010
MOSAICIST (profess. & kin.) 018.261-022
MOSAIC WORKER (glass products; nonmet. min.) 779.381-014
moshgiach (hotel & rest.) 319.137-026
MOSQUITO SPRAYER (government ser.) 379.687-014
Moss Picker (agriculture) 453.687-010
Motel Cleaner (hotel & rest.) 323.687-014
motel clerk (hotel & rest.) 238.367-038
MOTHER REPAIRER (recording) 705.684-042
mother tester (recording) 194.387-010
motion-picture-camera repairer (motion picture; photo. appar.) 714.281-018
motion-picture commentator (motion picture) 150.147-010
MOTION-PICTURE PROJECTIONIST (amuse. & rec.; motion picture) 960.362-010
Motion-Study Analyst (profess. & kin.) 012.267-010
moto-mix operator (construction) 900.683-010
Motor Analyst (automotive ser.) 620.261-014
motor-and-generator assembler (elec. equip.) 820.361-014
motor-and-generator-brush cutter (elec. equip.) 721.684-014
MOTOR-AND-GENERATOR-BRUSH MAKER (elec. equip.) 724.684-038
motor assembler (any industry) 721.281-014
Motor Assembler (automotive ser.) 620.261-010
motor assembler (railroad equip.) 721.381-010
Motor-Assembly Supervisor (agric. equip.) 801.137-010
MOTORBOAT MECHANIC (engine-turbine; ship-boat mfg.) 623.281-038
MOTORBOAT-MECHANIC HELPER (engine-turbine; ship-boat mfg.) 623.684-010
Motorboat Mechanic, Inboard (ship-boat mfg.) 623.281-038
Motorboat Mechanic, Inboard/Outboard (ship-boat mfg.) 623.281-038
MOTORBOAT OPERATOR (any industry) 911.663-010
motor boss (mine & quarry) 932.167-010
Motor Checker (clock & watch) 715.684-094
Motor-Coach Driver (motor trans.) 913.463-010
MOTORCYCLE ASSEMBLER (motor-bicycles) 806.684-090
Motorcycle-Engine Assembler (engine-turbine) 806.481-014
motorcycle mechanic (automotive ser.) 620.281-054
Motorcycle Police Officer (government ser.) 375.263-014
MOTORCYCLE RACER (amuse. & rec.) 153.243-014
MOTORCYCLE REPAIRER (automotive ser.) 620.281-054
MOTORCYCLE SUBASSEMBLER (motor-bicycles) 806.684-094
MOTORCYCLE SUBASSEMBLY REPAIRER (motor-bicycles) 620.684-026
MOTORCYCLE TESTER (motor-bicycles) 620.384-010
Motor-Equipment Captain (government ser.) 375.167-018
Motor-Equipment Lieutenant (government ser.) 375.167-018
Motor-Equipment Sergeant (government ser.) 375.167-018
Motor-Express Clerk (motor trans.) 222.367-022
Motor-Generator-Set Operator (chemical) 952.362-038
Motor Grader, Fine Grade (construction) 850.663-022
MOTOR-GRADER OPERATOR (construction) 850.663-022
Motor Grader, Rough Grade (construction) 850.663-022
motor-inspection mechanic (automotive ser.) 620.281-030
Motorized-Squad Captain (government ser.) 375.163-010
Motorized-Squad Lieutenant (government ser.) 375.163-010
Motorized-Squad Sergeant (government ser.) 375.163-010
motor-lodge clerk (hotel & rest.) 238.367-038
MOTOR OPERATOR (r.r. trans.) 910.683-014
motor overhauler (railroad equip.) 721.381-010
motor-patrol operator (construction) 850.663-022
MOTOR POLARIZER (clock & watch) 715.687-090
Motor-Pool Clerk (clerical) 203.362-010
MOTOR-POWER CONNECTOR (motion picture) 962.684-018
MOTOR-ROOM CONTROLLER (utilities) 820.662-010
Motor-Scooter Repairer (automotive ser.) 620.281-054
motor-transport inspector (government ser.) 168.267-058

Motor-Vehicle-Escort Driver (business ser.) 906.683-022
motor-vehicle inspector (government ser.) 379.364-010
MOTOR-VEHICLE-LIGHT ASSEMBLER (light. fix.) 729.684-034
motor vehicles supervisor (any industry) 184.167-226
MOTTLE-LAY-UP OPERATOR (plastic-synth.) 690.585-014
mottle line operator (fabrication, nec) 559.665-034
MOTTLER-MACHINE FEEDER (fabrication, nec) 550.686-034
MOTTLER OPERATOR (fabrication, nec) 550.665-022
Mounted Police Officer (government ser.) 375.263-014
mounter (fabrication, nec) 739.684-170
mounter (furniture) 763.684-042
mounter (print. & pub.) 979.682-010
MOUNTER, AUTOMATIC (photofinishing) 976.685-022
Mounter, Brass-Wind Instruments (musical inst.) 730.684-010
Mounter, Clarinets (musical inst.) 730.684-010
MOUNTER, CLOCK AND WATCH HANDS (clock & watch) 715.687-094
Mounter, Flutes And Piccolos (musical inst.) 730.684-010
MOUNTER, HAND (light. fix.) 725.684-014
MOUNTER, HAND (photofinishing) 976.684-018
MOUNTER I (light. fix.) 692.686-050
MOUNTER II (light. fix.) 692.685-126
Mounter, Keyed Instruments (musical inst.) 730.684-010
Mounter, Saxophones (musical inst.) 730.684-010
MOUNTER, SMOKING PIPE (fabrication, nec) 739.684-130
Mounter, Sousaphones (musical inst.) 730.684-010
Mounter, Trombones (musical inst.) 730.684-010
Mounter, Trumpets And Cornets (musical inst.) 730.684-010
Mounting Inspector (photofinishing) 976.687-014
mounting-machine operator (paint & varnish; print. & pub.) 641.685-030
Mouse Breeder (agriculture) 410.161-010
MOUTHPIECE MAKER (musical inst.) 730.685-014
mover (hotel & rest.) 323.687-018
Movie Critic (print. & pub.; radio-tv broad.) 131.067-018
muck boss (mine & quarry) 939.137-018
Mucker (construction) 869.687-026
Mucker (mine & quarry) 939.687-014
Mucker, Cofferdam (construction) 869.687-026
mucker operator (construction) 850.683-026
MUCKING-MACHINE OPERATOR (construction) 850.683-026
mucking-machine operator (mine & quarry) 932.683-018
mud-analysis-well-logging captain (petrol. & gas) 010.131-010
mud-analysis-well-logging operator (petrol. & gas) 010.281-022
mud-analysis-well-logging supervisor, district (petrol. & gas) 010.167-014
MUD BOSS (smelt. & refin.) 519.585-014
mud engineer (petrol. & gas) 010.167-014
mud grinder (smelt. & refin.; steel & rel.) 570.685-070
Mud-Jack Nozzle Worker (construction) 869.687-026
mud-logging superintendent (petrol. & gas) 010.167-014
mud-mill operator (smelt. & refin.; steel & rel.) 570.685-070
MUD-MILL TENDER (smelt. & refin.) 519.685-026
MUD-MIXER HELPER (steel & rel.) 549.687-022
MUD-MIXER OPERATOR (smelt. & refin.; steel & rel.) 570.685-070
MUD-PLANT OPERATOR (petrol. & gas) 930.685-010
Mud Trucker (steel & rel.) 902.683-010
muffler fringer (knitting) 685.686-010
MUFFLER INSTALLER (automotive ser.) 807.664-010
Muff Winder (textile) 681.685-154
Mule Driver (any industry) 919.664-010
Mule Tender (any industry) 410.674-022
muller (hat & cap) 784.687-086
multicut-line operator (glass mfg.) 677.562-010
multifocal-button assembler (optical goods) 713.684-034
Multifocal-Button Countersink Grinder (optical goods) 716.685-022
Multifocal-Button Generator (optical goods) 716.682-014
Multifocal-Button Grinder (optical goods) 716.382-018
Multifocal-Button Inspector (optical goods) 716.687-018
MULTIFOCAL-LENS ASSEMBLER (optical goods) 713.684-034
multifold operator (paper goods) 649.685-046
MULTINEEDLE-CHAINSTITCH-MACHINE OPERATOR (garment) 786.682-178
multineedle shirrer (garment) 786.682-178
MULTI-OPERATION-FORMING-MACHINE OPERATOR I (any industry) 616.360-026
MULTI-OPERATION-FORMING-MACHINE OPERATOR II (any industry) 616.685-042
MULTI-OPERATION-FORMING-MACHINE SETTER (any industry) 616.260-014
MULTI-OPERATION-MACHINE OPERATOR (any industry) 612.462-010
Multiple-Cut-Off-Saw Operator (millwork-plywood; wood. container) 667.682-022
MULTIPLE-DRUM SANDER (woodworking) 662.682-014
MULTIPLE-DRUM-SANDER HELPER (woodworking) 662.686-014
multiple-effect evaporator operator (chemical) 553.382-018
multiple-knife-edge-trimmer operator (print. & pub.) 640.685-010
Multiple-Needle Stitcher (boot & shoe) 690.682-082

multiple-pressure-riveter operator (any industry) 800.662-010
Multiple-Punch-Press Operator I (any industry) 615.382-010
Multiple-Punch-Press Operator II (any industry) 615.685-030
Multiple-Resaw Operator (wood. container) 667.682-058
multiple-slide operator (any industry) 619.382-018
multiple-spindle-drilling-machine operator (machine shop) 606.380-010
Multiple-Spindle-Router Operator (woodworking) 665.682-030
multiple-tube-winding-machine operator (textile) 681.685-046
Multiple-Wire Sawyer (stonework) 677.462-014
Multiplex-Machine Operator (tel. & tel.) 203.582-050
multi-punch operator (any industry) 615.482-038
MULTI-PURPOSE MACHINE OPERATOR (furniture) 669.382-022
multi-slide-machine tender (any industry) 619.685-050
Municipal-Court Judge (government ser.) 111.107-010
MUNICIPAL-SERVICES SUPERVISOR (government ser.) term
MUNITIONS HANDLER (ordnance) 929.687-034
Munitions-Handler Supervisor (ordnance) 922.137-018
Munitions Worker (government ser.) 632.261-018
MUSEUM ATTENDANT (museums) 109.367-010
museum craft worker (museums) 739.261-010
MUSEUM INTERN (museums) term
museum preparator (museums) 102.381-010
museum service scheduler (museums) 238.367-034
MUSEUM TECHNICIAN (museums) 102.381-010
Mushroom Grower (agriculture) 405.161-018
Mushroom-Growing Supervisor (agriculture) 405.131-010
Mushroom Laborer (agriculture) 405.687-014
Mushroom Packer (agriculture) 920.687-134
Mushroom-Press Operator (laundry & rel.) 363.682-018
Mushroom Sorter-Grader (can. & preserv.) 529.687-186
Mushroom-Spawn Maker (profess. & kin.) 041.061-062
musical director (motion picture; radio-tv broad.) 152.047-018
MUSICAL-STRING MAKER (musical inst.) 730.684-050
music autographer (print. & pub.) 970.581-010
MUSIC COPYIST (print. & pub.) 209.582-010
Music Critic (print. & pub.; radio-tv broad.) 131.067-018
music department head (motion picture; radio-tv broad.) 152.047-018
music director (radio-tv broad.) 100.367-022
MUSIC ENGRAVER (print. & pub.) 972.681-010
MUSIC GRAPHER (print. & pub.) 970.581-010
MUSICIAN, INSTRUMENTAL (amuse. & rec.) 152.041-010
music instructor (education) 152.021-010
MUSIC LIBRARIAN (radio-tv broad.) 100.367-022
MUSIC LIBRARIAN, INTERNATIONAL BROADCAST (radio-tv broad.) 100.367-026
music mixer (motion picture; radio-tv broad.; recording) 194.262-018
MUSIC SUPERVISOR (education) 099.167-026
MUSIC THERAPIST (medical ser.) 076.127-014
music typographer (print. & pub.) 209.582-010
Muskrat Trapper (fishing & hunt.) 461.684-014
Mustard Mixer (food prep., nec) 520.685-154
mutton puncher (agriculture) 410.687-022
mutuel cashier (amuse. & rec.) 211.467-018
mutuel clerk (amuse. & rec.) 211.467-022
MVA-REACTOR OPERATOR (chemical) 558.685-046
MVA-REACTOR OPERATOR, HEAD (chemical) 559.362-022
MYCOLOGIST (profess. & kin.) 041.061-062

N

NAIL-ASSEMBLY-MACHINE OPERATOR (steel & rel.) 616.682-030
nailer (boot & shoe) 690.685-162
NAILER (tinware) 739.687-126
NAILER, HAND (any industry) 762.684-050
nailer, machine (any industry) 669.682-058
nailhead puncher (garment; tex. prod., nec) 789.685-010
Nailhead Setter (garment; tex. prod., nec) 789.685-010
NAILING-MACHINE OPERATOR (any industry) 669.682-058
NAILING-MACHINE OPERATOR, AUTOMATIC (any industry) 669.685-066
nail-machine operator (steel & rel.) 616.460-010
NAIL-MAKING-MACHINE SETTER (steel & rel.) 616.460-010
NAIL-MAKING-MACHINE TENDER (steel & rel.) 617.665-010
NAIL-POLISH-BRUSH-MACHINE FEEDER, AUTOMATIC (fabrication, nec) 692.686-054
nail puller (boot & shoe) 690.685-410
Nail Welter (boot & shoe) 690.685-162
NAME-PLATE STAMPER (any industry) 652.685-054
name-plate-stamping-machine operator (clerical) 208.582-014
NAPHTHALENE OPERATOR (steel & rel.) 551.665-010
NAPHTHALENE-OPERATOR HELPER (steel & rel.) 551.687-026
Naphthalene-Still Operator (chemical) 552.462-010
Naphtha-Plant Treater (petrol. refin.) 549.362-014
NAPHTHA-WASHING-SYSTEM OPERATOR (plastic-synth.) 559.382-038
Naphthol-Soaping-Machine Operator (textile) 582.685-030

Napkin-Band Wrapper (paper goods) 920.687-026
Napkin-Machine Operator (paper goods) 649.685-046
napper (tex. prod., nec; textile) 585.685-070
Napper Grinder (textile) 680.380-010
napper operator (tex. prod., nec; textile) 585.685-070
NAPPER TENDER (knitting) 585.665-010
NAPPER TENDER (tex. prod., nec; textile) 585.685-070
narcotics investigator (government ser.) 375.267-018
Narrator (amuse. & rec.) 139.167-010
NARRATOR (motion picture) 150.147-010
NARROW-FABRIC CALENDERER (narrow fabrics) 583.685-074
Narrow-Fabric-Loom Fixer (narrow fabrics) 683.260-018
National Editor (print. & pub.) 132.037-014
national insurance officer (nonprofit org.) 187.167-198
NATURAL-GAS-TREATING-UNIT OPERATOR (petrol. & gas) 549.382-010
NATURALIST (profess. & kin.) term
naturopathic physician (medical ser.) 079.101-014
naval designer (profess. & kin.) 001.061-014
NAVIGATOR (air trans.) 196.167-014
Neck Cutter (light. fix.) 692.685-118
NECKER (jewelry-silver.) 692.686-058
Neck Feller (garment) 782.684-058
Neck Fitter (musical inst.) 730.684-010
neck pinner (meat products) 525.687-050
NECK SKEWER (meat products) 525.687-050
NECKTIE-CENTRALIZING-MACHINE OPERATOR I (garment) 786.682-186
NECKTIE-CENTRALIZING-MACHINE OPERATOR II (garment) 786.682-190
NECKTIE OPERATOR, POCKETS AND PIECES (garment) 786.682-182
necktie stitcher (garment) 786.682-186
Necktie Turner (garment) 789.687-182
NEEDLE-BAR MOLDER (carpet & rug) 556.684-022
NEEDLE-BOARD REPAIRER (tex. prod., nec) 739.684-134
NEEDLE-CONTROL CHENILLER (tex. prod., nec) 687.685-010
NEEDLE-FELT-MAKING-MACHINE OPERATOR (tex. prod., nec) 689.362-010
NEEDLE GRINDER (button & notion) 734.584-010
needle grinder (comm. equip.) 770.382-014
NEEDLE LEADER (button & notion) 502.684-022
NEEDLE-LOOM OPERATOR (tex. prod., nec) 689.662-010
Needle-Loom-Operator Helper (tex. prod., nec) 586.686-022
NEEDLE-LOOM SETTER (tex. prod., nec) 689.360-010
NEEDLE-LOOM TENDER (tex. prod., nec) 689.685-090
NEEDLEMAKER (button & notion) 619.280-010
needle molder (button & notion) 502.684-022
NEEDLE POLISHER (button & notion) 705.684-046
NEEDLE-PUNCH-MACHINE OPERATOR (textile) 689.682-014
NEEDLE-PUNCH-MACHINE-OPERATOR HELPER (textile) 689.686-034
needle-punch operator (carpet & rug; tex. prod., nec) 687.682-014
needle setter (tex. prod., nec) 739.684-134
NEEDLE STRAIGHTENER (knitting) 628.684-018
NEEDLE-TRADE WORKER (garment) term
needle-valve operator (waterworks) 954.382-018
needleworker (any industry) 782.684-058
negative assembler (print. & pub.) 971.381-050
negative checker (print. & pub.) 971.684-010
Negative Developer (motion picture; photofinishing) 976.382-018
Negative Notcher (motion picture) 976.684-010
Negative Spotter (photofinishing) 970.381-034
negative turner (print. & pub.) 971.381-050
negative-turner apprentice (print. & pub.) 971.381-054
NEMATOLOGIST (profess. & kin.) 041.061-066
NEON-SIGN SERVICER (fabrication, nec) 824.281-018
NEON-TUBE PUMPER (fabrication, nec) 824.684-010
nerve specialist (medical ser.) 070.101-050
NESTING OPERATOR, NUMERICAL CONTROL (aircraft mfg.) 007.362-010
net checker-hanger (laundry & rel.) 361.687-010
net finisher (tex. prod., nec) 582.685-054
net hanger (tex. prod., nec) 782.684-026
NET MAKER (tex. prod., nec) 789.684-030
NET REPAIRER (fishing & hunt.) 449.664-010
Net Sorter (laundry & rel.) 361.687-018
NETTING INSPECTOR (tex. prod., nec) 782.487-010
netting machine operator (tex. prod., nec) 685.685-010
NET WASHER (rubber goods) 599.687-022
Network Announcer (radio-tv broad.) 159.147-010
NETWORK CONTROL OPERATOR (any industry) 031.262-014
network-relay tester (utilities) 729.281-038
NEUROLOGIST (medical ser.) 070.101-050
Neuropathologist (medical ser.) 070.061-010
Neurosurgeon (medical ser.) 070.101-094
neutralizer (any industry) 503.685-030
neutralizer (chemical) 558.685-050
NEUTRALIZER (grain-feed mills) 522.685-082
neutralizer (optical goods) 716.687-026

NEUTRALIZER (soap & rel.) 558.585-034
Neverslip Stitcher (boot & shoe) 690.682-082
new-account interviewer (clerical) 205.367-014
new-business clerk (insurance) 209.687-018
NEW-CAR GET-READY MECHANIC (automotive ser.; retail trade) 806.361-026
NEW-CAR INSPECTOR (motor trans.) 919.363-010
News Agent (r.r. trans.) 291.457-014
News Analyst (radio-tv broad.) 131.067-010
News Anchor (radio-tv broad.) 131.262-010
NEWS ASSISTANT (radio-tv broad.) 209.367-038
NEWSCASTER (radio-tv broad.) 131.262-010
news information resource manager (library) 100.167-038
NEWS LIBRARIAN (library) 100.167-038
news library director (library) 100.167-038
NEWSPAPER CARRIER (retail trade) 292.457-010
newspaper deliverer (retail trade) 292.457-010
NEWSPAPER-DELIVERY DRIVER (wholesale tr.) 292.363-010
newspaper library manager (library) 100.167-038
newspaper-press-operator apprentice (print. & pub.) 651.362-034
newsperson (print. & pub.; radio-tv broad.) 131.262-018
newsperson (radio-tv broad.) 131.262-010
NEWSWRITER (print. & pub.; radio-tv broad.) 131.262-014
nib adjuster (pen & pencil) 733.687-042
Nib Assembler (pen & pencil) 733.685-010
NIBBLER OPERATOR (any industry) 615.685-026
NIB FINISHER (pen & pencil) 705.684-050
NIB INSPECTOR (pen & pencil) 733.687-058
Nickel Cleaner (any industry) 709.687-010
NICKEL-PLANT OPERATOR (smelt. & refin.) 519.362-010
Nickel Plater (electron. comp.) 500.684-026
Nickel Plater (electroplating) 500.380-010
NICKER (boot & shoe) 690.685-298
nicker and breaker (nonfer. metal) 614.684-014
NICKING-MACHINE OPERATOR (cutlery-hrdwr.) 609.682-026
nick setter (cutlery-hrdwr.) 609.682-026
NIGHT AUDITOR (hotel & rest.) 210.382-054
Night Baker (hotel & rest.) 313.381-010
night cleaner (any industry) 599.684-010
night cleaner (hotel & rest.) 323.687-018
night-clerk auditor (hotel & rest.) 210.382-054
Night-Court Magistrate (government ser.) 111.107-014
Night Guard (any industry) 372.667-034
NIGHT-PATROL INSPECTOR (fabrication, nec) 824.683-010
nipper (any industry) 932.664-010
Nipple-Machine Operator (machine shop) 604.682-014
NITRATING-ACID MIXER (chemical) 550.585-030
NITRATOR OPERATOR (chemical) 558.382-046
nitric-acid-concentrator operator (chemical) 559.682-062
NITROCELLULOSE OPERATOR (chemical) 553.684-014
NITROGLYCERIN DISTRIBUTOR (chemical) 559.664-010
NITROGLYCERIN NEUTRALIZER (chemical) 558.685-050
Nitroglycerin-Nitrator Operator, Batch (chemical) 558.382-046
NITROGLYCERIN-SEPARATOR OPERATOR (chemical) 551.685-102
NITROGLYCERIN SUPERVISOR (chemical) 559.132-038
Nock Applier (toy-sport equip.) 795.687-014
NODULIZER (cement) 579.685-034
Noise-Abatement Engineer (profess. & kin.) 019.081-018
NONDESTRUCTIVE TESTER (profess. & kin.) 011.261-018
NOODLE-CATALYST MAKER (chemical) 559.685-126
NOODLE MAKER (food prep., nec) 529.385-010
NOODLE-PRESS OPERATOR (food prep., nec) 520.662-010
normalizer (heat treating) 504.682-010
normalizing-equipment tender (rubber goods) 559.685-066
Notched-Blade Loader (cutlery-hrdwr.) 701.687-018
notcher (glass products) 673.685-070
NOTCH GRINDER (glass products) 673.685-070
Notching-Press Operator (any industry) 615.682-014
Notch-Machine Operator (rubber goods) 690.680-010
NOTEREADER (clerical) 203.582-078
Nougat-Candy Maker (sugar & conf.) 529.361-014
Nougat-Candy-Maker Helper (sugar & conf.) 520.685-050
Nougat Cutter, Machine (sugar & conf.) 521.685-102
Novelty-Balloon Assembler And Packer (rubber goods) 920.587-018
novelty-candy maker (fabrication, nec) 739.684-010
novelty-candy maker (sugar & conf.) 520.687-018
Novelty-Chain Maker (jewelry-silver.) 700.684-022
novelty dipper (dairy products) 529.482-014
novelty maker (paper goods) 794.684-022
NOVELTY MAKER I (dairy products) 529.482-014
NOVELTY MAKER II (dairy products) 529.482-018
Novelty-Printing-Machine Operator (textile) 652.382-010
Novelty-Twister Tender (textile) 681.685-130
NOVELTY WORKER (dairy products) 524.686-014
NOZZLE-AND-SLEEVE WORKER (nonfer. metal) 514.684-018

NOZZLE TENDER (nonfer. metal) 512.685-014
Nozzle Worker (mine & quarry) 939.684-014
Nub-Card Tender (textile) 680.686-018
NUCLEAR-CRITICALITY SAFETY ENGINEER (profess. & kin.) 015.067-010
Nuclear-Decontamination Research Specialist (profess. & kin.) 015.021-010
NUCLEAR ENGINEER (profess. & kin.) 015.061-014
NUCLEAR-FUELS RECLAMATION ENGINEER (profess. & kin.) 015.061-026
NUCLEAR-FUELS RESEARCH ENGINEER (profess. & kin.) 015.061-030
Nuclear Logging Engineer (petrol. & gas) 010.261-022
NUCLEAR MEDICAL TECHNOLOGIST (medical ser.) 078.361-018
nuclear plant control operator (utilities) 952.362-022
Nuclear-Plant-Instrument Technician (utilities) 710.281-030
NUCLEAR-PLANT TECHNICAL ADVISOR (utilities) 015.167-010
Nuclear-Powerplant Mechanic (utilities) 631.261-014
Nuclear-Powerplant-Mechanic Helper (utilities) 631.684-010
Nuclear-Powerplant Supervisor (utilities) 631.131-010
NUCLEAR-TEST-REACTOR PROGRAM COORDINATOR (profess. & kin.) 015.167-014
Nuclear-Waste-Process Operator (any industry) 955.382-014
Nuclear Weapons Mechanical Specialist (government ser.) 632.261-018
NUMBERER AND WIRER (textile) 689.587-010
NUMERICAL-CONTROL DRILL OPERATOR, PRINTED CIRCUIT BOARDS (electron. comp.) 606.382-018
Numerical Control Machine Machinist (machine shop) 600.280-022
NUMERICAL-CONTROL-MACHINE OPERATOR (machine shop) 609.362-010
NUMERICAL CONTROL MACHINE SET-UP OPERATOR (machine shop) 609.360-010
NUMERICAL-CONTROL ROUTER OPERATOR (aircraft mfg.; electron. comp.) 605.382-046
Numerical-Control-Wire-Preparation-Machine-Tender (aircraft mfg.) 728.685-010
NUMISMATIST (profess. & kin.) term
nurse (medical ser.)   see NURSE, PROFESSIONAL
nurse aide (medical ser.) 355.674-014
NURSE ANESTHETIST (medical ser.) 075.371-010
NURSE ASSISTANT (medical ser.) 355.674-014
nurse, certified (medical ser.)   see NURSE, PROFESSIONAL
nurse, children's (domestic ser.) 301.677-010
Nurse, College (medical ser.) 075.124-010
NURSE, CONSULTANT (medical ser.) 075.127-014
nurse, first aid (any industry) 354.677-010
NURSE, GENERAL DUTY (medical ser.) 075.364-010
NURSE, HEAD (medical ser.) 075.137-014
Nurse, Infants' (domestic ser.) 301.677-010
NURSE, INFECTION CONTROL (medical ser.) 075.127-034
NURSE, INSTRUCTOR (medical ser.) 075.124-018
nurse, licensed (medical ser.)   see NURSE, PROFESSIONAL
NURSE, LICENSED PRACTICAL (medical ser.) 079.374-014
NURSE-MIDWIFE (medical ser.) 075.264-014
NURSE, OFFICE (medical ser.) 075.374-010
NURSE, PRACTICAL (medical ser.) 354.374-010
NURSE PRACTITIONER (medical ser.) 075.264-010
NURSE, PRIVATE DUTY (medical ser.) 075.374-018
NURSE, PROFESSIONAL (medical ser.) term
nurse, registered (medical ser.)   see NURSE, PROFESSIONAL
Nursery Laborer (agriculture) 405.687-014
NURSERY SCHOOL ATTENDANT (any industry) 359.677-018
NURSE, SCHOOL (medical ser.) 075.124-010
nurse, special (medical ser.) 075.374-018
nurse, staff (medical ser.) 075.364-010
NURSE, STAFF, COMMUNITY HEALTH (medical ser.) 075.124-014
nurse, staff, industrial (medical ser.) 075.374-022
NURSE, STAFF, OCCUPATIONAL HEALTH NURSING (medical ser.) 075.374-022
NURSE, SUPERVISOR (medical ser.) 075.167-010
NURSE, SUPERVISOR, COMMUNITY-HEALTH NURSING (medical ser.) 075.127-026
NURSE, SUPERVISOR, EVENING-OR-NIGHT (medical ser.) 075.127-030
nurse supervisor, industrial nursing (medical ser.) 075.137-010
NURSE, SUPERVISOR, OCCUPATIONAL HEALTH NURSING (medical ser.) 075.137-010
Nursing Home Administrator (medical ser.) 187.117-010
NUT-AND-BOLT ASSEMBLER (nut & bolt) 929.587-010
NUT CHOPPER (can. & preserv.; food prep., nec; sugar & conf.) 521.686-046
nut-dehydrator operator (can. & preserv.) 523.685-066
NUT FORMER (nut & bolt) 612.462-014
NUT GRINDER (can. & preserv.) 521.685-234
Nut Orchardist (agriculture) 403.161-010
nut picker (can. & preserv.) 521.687-086
NUT-PROCESS HELPER (can. & preserv.) 529.486-010
nutrition aide (government ser.) 195.367-022
nutrition consultant (any industry) 199.251-010

nutrition educator (personal ser.) 359.367-014
Nutritionist (profess. & kin.) 096.121-014
Nutritionist, Public Health (government ser.) 077.127-010
NUT ROASTER (can. & preserv.) 529.685-174
Nut-Roaster Helper (can. & preserv.) 529.486-010
nut sifter (can. & preserv.) 521.687-086
Nut Sorter (agriculture) 529.687-186
NUT SORTER (can. & preserv.) 521.687-086
NUT-SORTER OPERATOR (can. & preserv.) 521.685-238
NUT STEAMER (can. & preserv.) 521.687-090
nutter-up (nut & bolt) 929.587-010
NYLON-HOT-WIRE CUTTER (tex. prod., nec) 781.684-038

O

Oak Tanner (leather mfg.) 582.482-018
observer (tel. & tel.) 239.367-026
OBSERVER, ELECTRICAL PROSPECTING (petrol. & gas) 010.261-014
OBSERVER, GRAVITY PROSPECTING (petrol. & gas) 010.261-018
observer helper (petrol. & gas) 939.364-010
OBSERVER HELPER, GRAVITY PROSPECTING (petrol. & gas) 939.663-010
OBSERVER HELPER, SEISMIC PROSPECTING (petrol. & gas) 939.364-010
OBSERVER, SEISMIC PROSPECTING (petrol. & gas) 010.161-018
OBSTETRICIAN (medical ser.) 070.101-054
OCCUPATIONAL ANALYST (profess. & kin.) 166.067-010
occupational-safety-and-health-compliance officer (government ser.) 168.167-062
OCCUPATIONAL-SAFETY-AND-HEALTH INSPECTOR (government ser.) 168.167-062
OCCUPATIONAL THERAPIST (medical ser.) 076.121-010
OCCUPATIONAL THERAPY AIDE (medical ser.) 355.377-010
OCCUPATIONAL THERAPY ASSISTANT (medical ser.) 076.364-010
OCEANOGRAPHER, ASSISTANT (military ser.) 025.267-010
Oceanographer, Geological (profess. & kin.) 024.061-018
Oceanographer, Physical (profess. & kin.) 024.061-030
Octave Tuner (musical inst.) 730.381-058
ocularist (optical goods) 713.261-014
ocularist, glass (optical goods) 713.261-010
oculist (medical ser.) 070.101-058
ODD BUNDLE WORKER (tobacco) 529.687-166
odd-job worker (domestic ser.) 301.687-010
ODD-PIECE CHECKER (knitting) 221.587-018
ODD-SHOE EXAMINER (boot & shoe) 788.667-010
Offal Baler (leather mfg.) 920.685-010
OFFAL ICER, POULTRY (meat products) 525.687-054
OFFAL SEPARATOR (meat products) 525.684-038
OFFBEARER, PIPE SMOKING MACHINE (fabrication, nec) 563.686-018
OFFBEARER, SEWER PIPE (brick & tile) 579.686-026
Office Auditor (government ser.) 160.167-038
office automation analyst (profess. & kin.) 032.262-010
Office-Chair Assembler (furniture) 709.684-014
office clerk, routine (clerical) 209.562-010
OFFICE COPY SELECTOR (print. & pub.) 249.687-010
office-equipment mechanic (any industry) 633.281-018
OFFICE HELPER (clerical) 239.567-010
office-machine inspector (any industry) 633.281-018
Office-Machine-Repair-Shop Supervisor (any industry) 633.131-010
OFFICE-MACHINE SERVICER (any industry) 633.281-018
OFFICE-MACHINE-SERVICER APPRENTICE (any industry) 633.281-022
OFFICE-MACHINE-SERVICE SUPERVISOR (any industry) 633.131-010
office manager (financial) 186.117-034
office-planning representative (any industry) 019.261-018
OFFICE SUPERVISOR, ANIMAL HOSPITAL (nonprofit org.) 249.137-010
OFFSET-DUPLICATING-MACHINE OPERATOR (clerical) 207.682-018
OFFSET-DUPLICATING-MACHINE OPERATOR (print. & pub.) 651.682-014
offset-duplicating machine operator, instant print (print. & pub.) 979.362-010
OFFSET-PRESS-OPERATOR APPRENTICE (print. & pub.) 651.382-046
offset press operator, helper (print. & pub.) 651.685-026
OFFSET-PRESS OPERATOR I (print. & pub.) 651.382-042
OFFSET-PRESS OPERATOR II (print. & pub.) 651.685-018
Offset-Proof-Press Operator (print. & pub.) 651.582-010
OIL BOILER (tex. prod., nec) 543.362-010
OIL-BURNER-SERVICER-AND-INSTALLER (any industry) 862.281-018
OIL-BURNER-SERVICER-AND-INSTALLER HELPER (any industry) 862.687-022
OIL DIPPER (woodworking) 769.684-026
oil dispatcher (petrol. & gas; petrol. refin.; pipe lines) 914.167-014
Oil Dispenser (can. & preserv.) 529.685-190
oil-distributor tender (construction) 853.665-010
OILER (any industry) 699.687-018
oiler (any industry) 950.685-014
oiler (any industry) 921.667-022

oiler (automotive ser.) 915.687-018
OILER (clock & watch) 715.684-146
oiler (mine & quarry) 850.684-018
oiler (water trans.) 911.584-010
oiler and greaser (any industry) 699.687-018
oiler and packer, gun parts (ordnance) 736.687-010
Oil-Expeller (grain-feed mills; oils & grease) 529.685-106
Oil-Expeller (meat products) 529.685-202
Oil Extractor (machine shop) 609.684-014
OIL-FIELD EQUIPMENT MECHANIC (petrol. & gas) 629.381-014
OIL-FIELD EQUIPMENT MECHANIC SUPERVISOR (petrol. & gas) 629.131-014
Oil-Field-Pipe-Line Supervisor (petrol. & gas) 862.131-022
Oil-House Attendant (clerical) 222.387-058
Oiling-Machine Operator (leather mfg.; tex. prod., nec) 582.685-050
OILING-MACHINE OPERATOR (paper & pulp; paper goods) 534.685-018
Oiling-Machine Operator (steel & rel.) 599.685-074
Oil-Paint Shader (paint & varnish) 550.381-014
OIL-PIPE INSPECTOR (petrol. & gas) 930.267-010
OIL-PIPE-INSPECTOR HELPER (petrol. & gas) 930.364-010
OIL PUMPER (petrol. & gas) 914.382-010
oil-pump-station operator, chief (pipe lines) 914.132-014
Oil-Rag Washer (any industry) 361.685-018
OIL-RECOVERY-UNIT OPERATOR (petrol. refin.) 549.382-014
OIL-SEAL ASSEMBLER (leather prod.) 739.684-138
OILSEED-MEAT PRESSER (oils & grease) 521.685-242
OIL-SPOT WASHER (tex. prod., nec; textile) 689.687-050
Oil Sprayer (construction) 869.687-026
oil sprayer (construction) 853.663-018
Oil Sprayer (leather mfg.) 584.687-014
oil-spreader operator (construction) 853.663-018
oil-spreader-truck operator (construction) 853.663-018
oil tester (petrol. refin.) 029.261-022
oil-well-electrical-wall-sampling-device operator (petrol. & gas) 931.361-010
oil-well-fishing-tool operator (petrol. & gas) 930.261-010
oil-well formation tester (petrol. & gas) 930.261-014
oil-well gun-perforator operator (petrol. & gas) 931.382-010
oil-well-logging engineer (petrol. & gas) 010.261-022
oil-well pumper (petrol. & gas) 914.382-010
OIL-WELL-SERVICE OPERATOR (petrol. & gas) 939.462-010
OIL-WELL-SERVICE-OPERATOR HELPER (petrol. & gas) 939.684-018
OIL-WELL-SERVICES SUPERVISOR (petrol. & gas) 939.132-014
oil-well shooter (petrol. & gas) 931.361-014
oil-well-sounding-device operator (petrol. & gas) 930.361-010
oil winterizer (oils & grease) 521.685-374
Ointment-Mill Tender (pharmaceut.) 550.685-090
Oleo-Hasher-And-Renderer (oils & grease) 529.685-158
OLIVE BRINE TESTER (can. & preserv.) 522.584-010
OLIVING-MACHINE OPERATOR (clock & watch) 770.381-034
One-Piece-Expansion Maker, Hand (paper goods) 794.684-018
Onion Farmer (agriculture) 402.161-010
Onion-Harvesting Supervisor (agriculture) 409.131-010
OPAQUER (protective dev.) 712.684-030
OPEN-DEVELOPER OPERATOR (textile) 582.685-098
OPENER (rubber goods) 559.686-034
OPENER I (hat & cap) 784.687-054
OPENER II (hat & cap) 589.686-030
OPENER TENDER (textile) 680.685-070
OPENER-VERIFIER-PACKER, CUSTOMS (government ser.) 168.387-010
Open-Hearth Door-Liner (steel & rel.) 861.381-026
open-hearth-furnace laborer (steel & rel.) 512.687-014
open-hearth-furnace operator (steel & rel.) 512.362-010
open-hearth-furnace-operator helper (steel & rel.) 512.684-010
Opening-Machine Cleaner (textile) 699.687-014
opening-machine tender (textile) 680.685-070
Open-Shank Coverer (boot & shoe) 690.685-074
open-tenter operator (textile) 580.685-066
Operating-Cost Clerk (clerical) 216.382-034
operating engineer (any industry) 950.362-014
operating engineer (any industry) 950.382-026
OPERATING ENGINEER (construction; mine & quarry) 859.683-010
OPERATING-ENGINEER APPRENTICE (construction; mine & quarry) 859.683-014
operating-engineer apprentice, stationary (any industry) 950.382-030
operating-room technician (medical ser.) 079.374-022
OPERATING-TABLE ASSEMBLER (furniture) 706.381-026
operations agent (air trans.) 912.367-014
OPERATIONS AND INTELLIGENCE ASSISTANT (military ser.) 378.367-026
operations chief (tel. & tel.) 822.131-010
operations clerk (financial) 216.362-046
operations clerk (financial) 216.482-034
operations inspector (government ser.) 168.264-010
operations manager (air trans.; motor trans.; r.r. trans.; water trans.) 184.117-050
OPERATIONS MANAGER (motor trans.) 184.167-118

operations manager (retail trade) 185.117-014
OPERATIONS MANAGER (tel. & tel.) 184.117-070
OPERATIONS OFFICER (financial) 186.137-014
operations officer (government ser.) 375.137-014
Operations Officer, Branch Office (financial) 186.137-014
Operations Officer, Trust Department (financial) 186.137-014
OPERATIONS-RESEARCH ANALYST (profess. & kin.) 020.067-018
operations supervisor (government ser.) 185.167-066
OPERATIONS SUPERVISOR, NUCLEAR POWER PLANT (utilities) 952.132-010
Operations Technician (tel. & tel.) 822.281-010
operative supervisor (motion picture) 962.134-010
OPERATOR, AUTOMATED PROCESS (electron. comp.) 590.382-010
OPERATOR, CATALYST CONCENTRATION (plastic-synth.) 550.382-026
OPERATOR, CAVITY PUMP (elec. equip.) 729.682-010
operator, circuit (any industry) 379.362-014
Operator, Coating Furnace (cutlery-hrdwr.) 554.685-014
operator, control room (petrol. refin.) 546.382-010
operator, direct wire (any industry) 379.362-014
operator, lights (motion picture; radio-tv broad.) 962.362-014
OPERATOR, PREFINISH (millwork-plywood) 562.685-018
Operator, Scales (plastic-synth.) 929.687-062
Ophthalmic-Lens Inspector (optical goods) 716.381-010
OPHTHALMIC PHOTOGRAPHER (medical ser.) 143.362-014
OPHTHALMIC TECHNICIAN (medical ser.) 078.361-038
ophthalmic-technician apprentice (optical goods; retail trade) 716.280-010
OPHTHALMOLOGIST (medical ser.) 070.101-058
Optical-Brightener Maker (chemical) 559.682-018
Optical-Brightener-Maker Helper (chemical) 550.687-010
optical designer (profess. & kin.) 019.061-018
OPTICAL-EFFECTS-CAMERA OPERATOR (motion picture) 143.260-010
OPTICAL-EFFECTS LAYOUT PERSON (motion picture) 962.361-010
optical-effects-line-up person (motion picture) 962.361-010
OPTICAL-ELEMENT COATER (optical goods) 716.382-014
OPTICAL ENGINEER (profess. & kin.) 019.061-018
OPTICAL-GLASS ETCHER (optical goods) 716.681-022
optical-glass inspector (optical goods) 716.687-034
OPTICAL-GLASS SILVERER (optical goods) 574.484-010
OPTICAL-INSTRUMENT ASSEMBLER (optical goods) 711.381-010
optical mechanic (optical goods; retail trade) 716.280-014
optical-mechanic apprentice (optical goods; retail trade) 716.280-010
optical model maker and tester (optical goods) 716.280-018
optical technician (optical goods) 716.382-018
OPTICIAN (optical goods; retail trade) 716.280-014
OPTICIAN (optical goods) 716.280-018
OPTICIAN APPRENTICE (optical goods; retail trade) 716.280-010
OPTICIAN APPRENTICE, DISPENSING (optical goods; retail trade) 299.361-014
Optician, Contact-Lens Dispensing (optical goods; retail trade) 299.361-010
OPTICIAN, DISPENSING II (optical goods) 299.361-010
OPTOMECHANICAL TECHNICIAN (optical goods; photo. appar.) 007.161-030
OPTOMETRIC ASSISTANT (profess. & kin.) 079.364-014
OPTOMETRIST (medical ser.) 079.101-018
ORAL AND MAXILLOFACIAL SURGEON (medical ser.) 072.101-018
ORAL PATHOLOGIST (medical ser.) 072.061-010
oral surgeon (medical ser.) 072.101-018
Orange Grower (agriculture) 403.161-010
Orange-Peel Operator I (any industry) 921.663-058
Orange-Peel Operator II (any industry) 921.663-062
Orange-Picking Supervisor (agriculture) 409.131-010
Orange Washer (agriculture; can. & preserv.; wholesale tr.) 529.685-258
orchardist (agriculture) 403.161-010
Orchard Pruner (agriculture) 408.684-018
orchestra leader (profess. & kin.) 152.047-014
ORCHESTRATOR (profess. & kin.) 152.067-022
Orchid Grower (agriculture) 405.161-018
Orchid Superintendent (agriculture) 405.131-010
Orchid Worker (agriculture) 405.684-014
ORDER CALLER (clerical) 209.667-014
order checker (clerical) 222.687-030
order checker (clerical) 222.687-018
order clerk (clerical) 214.382-014
ORDER CLERK (clerical) 249.362-026
order clerk (radio-tv broad.; tel. & tel.; utilities; waterworks) 239.362-014
Order Clerk (utilities) 203.362-010
ORDER CLERK, FOOD AND BEVERAGE (hotel & rest.) 209.567-014
ORDER-CONTROL CLERK, BLOOD BANK (medical ser.; nonprofit org.) 245.367-022
ORDER-DEPARTMENT SUPERVISOR (any industry) 169.167-038
order-desk caller (clerical) 209.667-014
ORDER DETAILER (clerical) 221.387-046
ORDER DISPATCHER, CHIEF (utilities) 959.137-018
Order Filler (any industry) 922.687-058
order filler (clerical) 249.362-026

ORDER FILLER (retail trade; wholesale tr.) 222.487-014
order filler, bakery products (bakery products) 222.487-010
ORDER FILLER, LINSEED OIL (oils & grease) 920.686-022
ordering-box operator (tobacco) 522.682-014
ORDERING-MACHINE OPERATOR (tobacco) 522.682-014
ORDERLY (medical ser.) 355.674-018
order picker (any industry) 922.687-058
ORDER RUNNER (meat products) 525.687-058
order taker (clerical) 249.362-026
ORDINARY SEAMAN (water trans.) 911.687-030
ORDNANCE ARTIFICER (government ser.) 632.261-018
ORDNANCE-ARTIFICER HELPER (government ser.) 632.684-010
ORDNANCE ENGINEER (chemical; ordnance) 019.061-022
ORDNANCE TRUCK INSTALLATION MECHANIC (ordnance) 806.684-098
ore crusher (smelt. & refin.) 515.685-014
ore grader (mine & quarry) 939.167-010
ore sampler (mine & quarry) 579.484-010
Organ Grinder (amuse. & rec.) 159.647-010
organ installer (musical inst.) 730.381-046
Organist (amuse. & rec.) 152.041-010
Organ-Pipe Finisher (musical inst.) 730.381-038
ORGAN-PIPE MAKER, METAL (musical inst.) 709.381-030
ORGAN-PIPE VOICER (musical inst.) 730.381-038
organ transplant coordinator (medical ser.) 079.151-010
Organ Tuner, Electronic (any industry) 828.261-010
ORIENTAL-RUG REPAIRER (any industry) 782.381-014
ORIENTAL-RUG STRETCHER (any industry) 580.687-010
ORIENTATION AND MOBILITY THERAPIST FOR THE BLIND (education; medical ser.; nonprofit org.) 076.224-014
Orientation And Mobility Instructor (education) 076.224-014
orientation therapist for blind (education; medical ser.; nonprofit org.) 076.224-014
orientor (education; medical ser.; nonprofit org.) 076.224-014
Ornamental-Brick Installer (construction; retail trade) 863.684-014
Ornamental-Bronze Worker (construction) 809.381-022
ornamental-iron erector (construction) 809.381-022
ORNAMENTAL-IRON WORKER (construction) 809.381-022
ORNAMENTAL-IRON-WORKER APPRENTICE (construction) 809.381-026
Ornamental-Iron-Worker Helper (construction) 869.664-014
ORNAMENTAL-MACHINE OPERATOR (wood prod., nec) 690.682-054
ornamental-metal-erector apprentice (construction) 809.381-026
ornamental-metal-fabricator apprentice (metal prod., nec) 619.260-010
ORNAMENTAL-METALWORK DESIGNER (struct. metal) 142.061-034
ORNAMENTAL-METAL WORKER (metal prod., nec) 619.260-014
ORNAMENTAL-METAL-WORKER APPRENTICE (metal prod., nec) 619.260-010
ORNAMENTAL-METAL-WORKER HELPER (metal prod., nec) 619.484-010
Ornamental-Plaster Sticker (construction) 842.361-018
Ornamental-Rail Installer (construction) 809.381-022
ornamenter (bakery products; sugar & conf.) 524.684-014
ornamenter, hand (wood prod., nec) 769.381-010
ORNAMENT MAKER, HAND (fabrication, nec) 739.687-130
ORNAMENT SETTER (garment; tex. prod., nec) 789.685-010
Ornament Stapler (boot & shoe) 690.685-162
Ornithologist (profess. & kin.) 041.061-090
ORTHODONTIC BAND MAKER (protective dev.) 712.381-026
ORTHODONTIC TECHNICIAN (protective dev.) 712.381-030
ORTHODONTIST (medical ser.) 072.101-022
ORTHOPEDIC ASSISTANT (medical ser.) 078.664-010
ORTHOPEDIC-BOOT-AND-SHOE DESIGNER AND MAKER (boot & shoe; protective dev.) 788.261-010
orthopedic cast specialist (medical ser.) 078.664-010
orthopedic-shoe fitter (retail trade) 276.257-018
Orthopedic Surgeon (medical ser.) 070.101-094
ORTHOPTIST (medical ser.) 079.371-014
ORTHOTICS ASSISTANT (medical ser.) 078.361-022
Orthotics-Prosthetics Assistant (medical ser.) 078.361-022
Orthotics-Prosthetics Technician (protective dev.) 712.381-034
ORTHOTICS TECHNICIAN (protective dev.) 712.381-034
ORTHOTIST (medical ser.) 078.261-018
Orthotist-Prosthetist (medical ser.) 078.261-018
oscillograph technician (utilities) 710.281-030
osteopath (medical ser.) 071.101-010
OSTEOPATHIC PHYSICIAN (medical ser.) 071.101-010
OTOLARYNGOLOGIST (medical ser.) 070.101-062
Otologist (medical ser.) 070.101-062
otorhinolaryngologist (medical ser.) 070.101-062
out-and-out cigar maker, hand (tobacco) 790.684-014
Outboard-Motor Assembler (engine-turbine) 806.481-014
outboard-motorboat rigger (retail trade; ship-boat mfg.) 806.464-010
OUTBOARD-MOTOR INSPECTOR (engine-turbine) 806.687-042
OUTBOARD-MOTOR MECHANIC (engine-turbine; ship-boat mfg.) 623.281-042
OUTBOARD-MOTOR TESTER (engine-turbine) 623.261-014
Outdoor-Illuminating Engineer (profess. & kin.) 003.061-046

outer-diameter grinder, tool (machine shop) 603.280-010
OUTFITTER, CABIN (ship-boat mfg.) 806.684-102
outfitter (ship-boat mfg.) 623.281-030
outgoing inspector (retail trade) 789.687-078
Outlaw-Loan-Record Clerk (clerical) 209.687-010
Out-Of-Town Collection Clerk (financial) 216.362-014
OUTPATIENT-ADMITTING CLERK (medical ser.) 205.362-030
Outpatient Receptionist (medical ser.) 237.367-038
Outreach Librarian (library) 100.127-014
outsewer (garment) 786.682-166
outside collector (clerical) 241.367-010
outside contact clerk (radio-tv broad.; tel. & tel.; utilities; waterworks) 239.362-014
OUTSIDE CUTTER, HAND (boot & shoe) 788.684-082
outside-installation machinist (ship-boat mfg.) 623.281-030
outside-installer apprentice (ship-boat mfg.) 623.281-022
outside marker (boot & shoe) 690.685-398
OUTSIDE-PLANT ENGINEER (tel. & tel.) 003.167-042
Outside-Plant Supervisor (tel. & tel.) 822.131-010
OUTSIDE PROPERTY AGENT (motion picture) 162.157-030
outside repairer, special (ordnance) 761.381-038
outside rigger (ship-boat mfg.) 806.261-014
Outside Trucker (any industry) 929.687-030
outsole beveler (boot & shoe) 690.685-166
Outsole Cementer, Machine (boot & shoe) 690.686-018
OUTSOLE CUTTER, AUTOMATIC (rubber goods) 690.462-010
Outsole Cutter, Hand (rubber goods) 751.684-014
Outsole Cutter, Machine (boot & shoe) 699.682-022
OUTSOLE FLEXER (boot & shoe) 583.686-026
outsole leveler (boot & shoe) 690.685-382
Outsole Molder (rubber goods) 556.685-066
outsole or insole molder (boot & shoe) 690.682-070
outsole paraffiner (boot & shoe) 788.687-010
OUTSOLE SCHEDULER (boot & shoe) 221.587-022
outsole skiver (boot & shoe) 690.685-166
Outsole Tacker (boot & shoe) 690.685-162
outsole trimmer (boot & shoe) 690.685-150
oven attendant (plastic-synth.) 556.585-014
OVEN CURING ATTENDANT (aircraft mfg.; electron. comp.) 590.685-090
OVEN DAUBER (steel & rel.) 543.687-014
oven-drier tender (textile) 581.685-026
OVEN-EQUIPMENT REPAIRER (steel & rel.) 630.261-014
OVEN-HEATER HELPER (steel & rel.) 542.665-010
OVEN OPERATOR (fabrication, nec) 590.665-010
OVEN OPERATOR (grain-feed mills) 526.585-010
OVEN OPERATOR, AUTOMATIC (bakery products) 526.685-070
OVEN-PRESS TENDER I (nonmet. min.) 573.685-042
OVEN-PRESS TENDER II (nonmet. min.) 573.685-046
oven roaster (can. & preserv.) 529.685-174
Oven Stripper (any industry) 929.687-030
OVEN TENDER (bakery products) 526.685-030
OVEN TENDER (elec. equip.) 543.685-018
OVEN TENDER (glass mfg.) 573.585-010
oven tender (hotel & rest.) 313.381-010
OVEN TENDER (ordnance) 534.565-010
OVEN TENDER (paint & varnish) 553.685-082
Oven Tender, Bagels (bakery products) 526.685-030
Oven Unloader (any industry) 929.687-030
Overall Washer (laundry & rel.) 361.665-010
overcasting-machine operator (any industry)   see SERGING-MACHINE OP-ERATOR
OVERCOILER (clock & watch) 715.684-150
overedge-machine operator (any industry)   see SERGING-MACHINE OP-ERATOR
OVEREDGE SEWER (any industry) 787.682-034
Overhaul and Repair Mechanic (aircraft mfg.) 621.281-014
OVERHAULER (textile) 628.261-010
OVERHAULER HELPER (textile) 628.664-010
Overhead Cleaner (any industry) 381.687-018
OVERHEAD CLEANER MAINTAINER (textile) 628.684-022
OVERHEAD CRANE OPERATOR (any industry) 921.663-010
Overhead-Distribution Engineer (utilities) 003.167-046
overland driver (auto. mfg.) 806.283-014
overlay operator (carpet & rug; tex. prod., nec) 687.682-014
OVERLAY PLASTICIAN (ship-boat mfg.) 806.684-106
overlock-machine operator (any industry)   see SERGING-MACHINE OP-ERATOR
OVERLOCK-MACHINE OPERATOR, COMPLETE GARMENT (garment) 786.682-198
OVERLOCK SEWING MACHINE OPERATOR (garment) 786.682-194
overlooker (paper & pulp) 649.687-010
overseaming-machine operator (any industry)   see SERGING-MACHINE OPERATOR
overseer (any industry)   see SUPERVISOR
overseer (any industry) 899.133-010

overseer (textile) 789.222-010
overseer, kosher kitchen (hotel & rest.) 319.137-026
Over-Short-And-Damaged Clerk (clerical) 241.367-014
overshot operator (tobacco) 522.685-030
overweaver (personal ser.) 782.381-022
oxide-furnace tender (paint & varnish) 558.685-054
OXIDIZED-FINISH PLATER (any industry) 599.685-062
OXIDIZER (jewelry-silver.) 700.684-054
OXYGEN-FURNACE OPERATOR (steel & rel.) 512.382-010
OXYGEN-PLANT OPERATOR (chemical) 552.362-014
Oyster-Bed Laborer (fishing & hunt.) 446.687-014
Oyster-Bed Worker (fishing & hunt.) 446.684-014
oyster culturist (fishing & hunt.) 446.161-014
Oyster Dredge Operator (fishing & hunt.) 446.663-010
Oyster Dredger (fishing & hunt.) 446.684-014
OYSTER FLOATER (fishing & hunt.) 449.687-010
Oyster Grower (fishing & hunt.) 446.161-014
Oyster Picker (fishing & hunt.) 446.684-014
Oyster Preparer (hotel & rest.) 311.674-014
Oyster Shucker (can. & preserv.) 521.687-122
Oyster Tonger (fishing & hunt.) 446.684-014
Oyster Unloader (fishing & hunt.) 446.684-014
Oyster Washer (can. & preserv.) 529.685-214
Oyster Worker (fishing & hunt.) 446.684-014

P

Pace Analyst (profess. & kin.) 012.267-010
pacer (any industry)   see STRAW BOSS
PACE SETTER (agriculture) term
package clerk (hotel & rest.) 324.577-010
PACKAGE CRIMPER (textile) 589.686-034
PACKAGE DESIGNER (profess. & kin.) 142.081-018
package drier (textile) 581.685-026
PACKAGE-DYEING-MACHINE OPERATOR (textile) 582.685-102
package dyer (textile) 582.685-102
package-dye-stand loader (textile) 589.687-062
Package-Lift Operator (any industry) 921.683-050
package opener (ordnance) 222.387-022
packager and strapper (any industry) 929.687-058
PACKAGER, HAND (any industry) 920.587-018
PACKAGER, HEAD (saw. & plan.) 667.682-046
PACKAGER, MACHINE (any industry) 920.685-078
Packager, Meat (meat products) 920.587-018
PACKAGE SEALER, MACHINE (any industry) 920.685-074
package winder (tex. prod., nec; textile) 681.685-154
PACKAGING ENGINEER (profess. & kin.) 019.187-010
packaging inspector (pharmaceut.) 920.387-010
Packaging-Line Attendant (any industry) 920.587-018
Packaging-Machine-Supplies Distributor (tobacco) 929.687-030
packaging operator (tobacco) 920.685-050
PACKAGING SUPERVISOR (any industry) 920.132-010
Packaging Supervisor (oils & grease) 529.137-030
PACKAGING TECHNICIAN (paper goods) 739.281-010
packer (agriculture) 920.687-134
PACKER (ordnance) 929.684-010
PACKER (tobacco) 920.687-130
packer (tobacco) 920.687-142
PACKER, AGRICULTURAL PRODUCE (agriculture) 920.687-134
PACKER, DENTURE (protective dev.) 712.684-034
Packer, Dried Beef (meat products) 920.587-018
Packer, Foamed-in-Place (any industry) 920.587-018
PACKER-FUSER (chemical) 737.687-094
Packerhead-Machine Operator (concrete prod.) 575.665-010
PACKER, INSULATION (concrete prod.) 579.685-038
packer operator (paper goods) 649.682-042
PACKER OPERATOR, AUTOMATIC (tobacco) 920.685-082
Packer, Sausage And Wiener (meat products) 920.587-018
packing-and-final-assembly supervisor (protective dev.) 712.137-014
packing-and-shipping clerk (clerical) 222.587-018
packing-and-stamping machine operator (tobacco) 920.685-098
packing checker (clerical) 222.687-030
PACKING-FLOOR WORKER (tobacco) 920.686-026
PACKING-HOUSE SUPERVISOR (agriculture; wholesale tr.) 920.137-010
packing inspector (boot & shoe) 753.687-018
PACKING-LINE WORKER (rubber goods) 753.687-038
PACKING-MACHINE CAN FEEDER (tobacco) 920.686-030
Packing-Machine Feeder (tobacco) 529.686-038
packing-machine inspector (tobacco) 920.665-010
packing-machine inspector (tobacco) 920.667-010
PACKING-MACHINE-PILOT CAN ROUTER (tobacco) 920.685-086
packing-machine relief-operator-and-salvager (tobacco)   see RELIEF WORKER
Packing-Machine Tender (any industry) 920.685-078

packing presser (tobacco) 920.686-050
Packing-Room Inspector (boot & shoe) 788.384-010
packing-shed supervisor (agriculture; wholesale tr.) 920.137-010
pack-press operator (elec. equip.) 726.684-010
PACK-ROOM OPERATOR (plastic-synth.) 559.684-010
pack-train driver (any industry) 919.687-022
Pad Assembler (jewelry-silver.) 739.687-138
Pad Attacher (any industry) 795.687-014
PAD CUTTER (plastic prod.) 690.685-302
pad cutter and assembler (leather prod.) 780.381-030
padded-box sewer (furniture) 787.685-022
PADDED-PRODUCTS FINISHER (rubber goods) 752.684-034
Padded-Products Inspector-Trimmer (rubber goods) 759.684-074
padder (textile) 589.687-030
PADDER, CUSHION (furniture) 780.684-078
PADDING GLUER (furniture) 780.687-034
Padding-Machine Operator (tex. prod., nec) 584.685-018
padding-machine operator (textile) 587.685-018
PADDING-MACHINE OPERATOR (textile) 582.685-106
Paddle-Dyeing-Machine Operator (knitting) 582.685-170
PADDOCK JUDGE (amuse. & rec.) 153.167-010
PAD-EXTRACTOR TENDER (knitting) 589.485-010
PAD HAND (leather prod.) 780.381-030
PAD-MACHINE FEEDER (saw. & plan.) 920.686-034
PAD-MACHINE OFFBEARER (saw. & plan.) 569.686-030
pad maker (furniture) 780.685-014
pad maker (optical goods) 739.687-154
pad maker (protective dev.) 689.685-130
PAD MAKER (textile) 589.687-030
pad tufter (furniture) 780.687-050
pad tufter (furniture) 687.684-014
Page (hotel & rest.) 324.677-010
page (hotel & rest.) 352.677-018
PAGE (library) 249.687-014
PAGE (radio-tv broad.) 353.367-022
PAGER (machinery mfg.) 654.687-014
Pagination System Operator (print. & pub.) 979.282-010
PAIL BAILER (tinware) 703.685-010
pail tester (tinware) 703.685-014
paint and table edger (furniture) 740.687-022
PAINT-BRUSH MAKER (fabrication, nec) 733.684-010
Paint Cleaner (any industry) 381.687-014
paint-coating-machine operator (any industry) 599.685-046
paint-coating-machine operator (paper goods; wood prod., nec) 534.682-022
Paint-Crew Supervisor (government ser.) 869.137-010
Paint Dipper (any industry) 599.685-026
PAINTER (button & notion) 740.381-018
PAINTER (construction) 840.381-010
PAINTER (jewelry-silver.) 735.687-018
PAINTER (profess. & kin.) 144.061-010
PAINTER, AIRBRUSH (any industry) 741.684-018
Painter, Aircraft (aircraft mfg.; air trans.) 845.381-014
Painter, Aircraft-Production (aircraft mfg.) 845.381-014
PAINTER AND GRADER, CORK (toy-sport equip.) 732.687-062
PAINTER, ANIMATED CARTOONS (motion picture; radio-tv broad.) 970.681-026
PAINTER APPRENTICE, SHIPYARD (ship-boat mfg.) 840.381-014
PAINTER APPRENTICE, TRANSPORTATION EQUIPMENT (aircraft mfg.; air trans.; automotive ser.) 845.381-010
Painter, Automotive (automotive ser.) 845.381-014
Painter, Barrel (petrol. refin.) 741.687-018
Painter, Battery Brand And Vent Plug (elec. equip.) 740.687-018
Painter, Blackwall Tire (rubber tire) 741.687-018
PAINTER, BOTTOM (boot & shoe) 788.687-098
PAINTER, BRUSH (any industry) 740.684-022
Painter, Chassis (auto. mfg.) 741.687-018
PAINTER, CLOCK AND WATCH HANDS (clock & watch) 715.687-098
Painter, Decorative-Commercial Aircraft (aircraft mfg.) 845.381-014
PAINTER, DEPILATORY (meat products) 525.687-062
Painter, Drum (any industry) 740.684-022
Painter, Electric Motor (any industry) 741.687-018
PAINTER, ELECTROSTATIC (any industry) 599.682-010
PAINTER, EMBOSSED OR IMPRESSED LETTERING (any industry) 740.687-018
painter, hand (any industry) 740.684-022
PAINTER, HAND (any industry) 970.381-022
Painter Helper (construction) 869.687-026
PAINTER HELPER, AUTOMOTIVE (automotive ser.) 845.684-014
PAINTER HELPER, SHIPYARD (ship-boat mfg.) 840.687-010
PAINTER HELPER, SIGN (any industry) 970.664-010
PAINTER HELPER, SPRAY (any industry) 741.687-014
Painter, Insignia (aircraft mfg.; auto. mfg.) 741.684-026
Painter, Interior Finish (construction) 840.381-010
Painter, Maintenance (any industry) 840.381-010
Painter, Mannequin (fabrication, nec) 740.684-022

PAINTER, MIRROR (glass products) 741.684-022
Painter, Ordnance (ordnance) 741.684-026
PAINTER, PANEL EDGE (furniture) 740.687-022
PAINTER, PLATE (print. & pub.) 970.681-030
painter, railroad car (r.r. trans.) 845.681-010
painter, rough (any industry) 741.687-018
Painter, Rough (construction) 869.664-014
PAINTER, RUG TOUCH-UP (laundry & rel.) 364.381-010
painter, set (motion picture) 840.681-010
PAINTER, SHIPYARD (ship-boat mfg.) 840.381-018
PAINTER, SIGN (any industry) 970.381-026
Painter, Sign, Maintenance (r.r. trans.) 970.381-026
PAINTER, SKI EDGE (toy-sport equip.) 749.687-022
PAINTER, SPRAY I (any industry) 741.684-026
PAINTER, SPRAY II (any industry) 741.687-018
Painter, Spring (furniture; metal prod., nec) 599.685-026
PAINTER, STAGE SETTINGS (motion picture) 840.681-010
Pairter, Structural Steel (construction) 869.664-014
PAINTER, TOUCH-UP (any industry) 749.684-038
PAINTER, TRANSPORTATION EQUIPMENT (aircraft mfg.; air trans.; automotive ser.) 845.381-014
PAINTER, TUMBLING BARREL (any industry) 599.685-070
PAINT GRINDER (paint & varnish) term
paint grinder, roller mill (paint & varnish) 555.682-014
paint grinder, stone mill (paint & varnish) 555.682-022
PAINTING-MACHINE OPERATOR (any industry) 599.685-074
painting-machine operator (pen & pencil) 692.685-054
paintings conservator (profess. & kin.) 102.261-014
PAINTINGS RESTORER (profess. & kin.) 102.261-014
PAINT-LINE OPERATOR (toy-sport equip.) 599.685-066
Paint Maker (paint & varnish) 550.685-078
PAINT MIXER, HAND (any industry) 550.684-018
PAINT MIXER, MACHINE (any industry) 550.485-018
PAINT POURER (fabrication, nec) 652.687-022
PAINT-ROLLER ASSEMBLER (fabrication, nec) 739.687-134
PAINT-ROLLER-COVER-MACHINE SETTER (fabrication, nec) 692.682-046
PAINT-ROLLER COVERMAKER (fabrication, nec) 739.684-142
PAINT-ROLLER WINDER (fabrication, nec) 739.685-030
paint sprayer (glass products) 741.684-022
PAINT-SPRAYER OPERATOR, AUTOMATIC (any industry) 599.382-010
PAINT SPRAYER, SANDBLASTER (concrete prod.) 845.381-018
paint-spraying-machine-operator helper (any industry) 741.687-014
PAINT-SPRAY INSPECTOR (any industry) 741.687-010
PAINT-SPRAY TENDER (glass products) 574.685-014
Paint Stocker (aircraft mfg.) 222.387-058
PAINT STRIPPER (petrol. refin.) 599.685-130
Paint-Stripping-Machine Operator (construction) 869.664-014
paint tinter (paint & varnish) 550.381-014
PAINT TRIMMER, PIPE BOWLS (fabrication, nec) 749.684-050
PAIRER (knitting) 684.687-010
PAIRER (tex. prod., nec) 789.687-110
pairer-inspector (knitting) 684.687-010
Pairer, Odds (knitting) 684.687-010
Pairer, Substandard (knitting) 684.687-010
PAIRING-MACHINE OPERATOR (nonfer. metal) 691.685-022
Paleobotanist (profess. & kin.) 024.061-042
PALEONTOLOGICAL HELPER (profess. & kin.) 024.364-010
PALEONTOLOGIST (profess. & kin.) 024.061-042
PALLBEARER (personal ser.) 359.687-010
PALLET ASSEMBLER (clock & watch) 715.684-154
PALLETIZER (nonfer. metal) 929.687-054
PALLETIZER OPERATOR I (any industry) 921.682-014
Palletizer Operator II (any industry) 920.685-078
PALLET RECTIFIER (clock & watch) 715.684-158
PALLET-STONE INSERTER (clock & watch) 715.381-082
PALLET-STONE POSITIONER (clock & watch) 715.381-086
Palm-And-Back Forger (glove & mit.) 784.682-010
Palmist (amuse. & rec.) 159.647-018
Pamphlet Distributor (any industry) 230.687-010
Panama-Hat Blocker (hat & cap) 580.684-014
Panama-Hat Flanger (hat & cap) 784.684-026
Panama-Hat-Hydraulic-Press Operator (hat & cap) 580.685-038
Panama-Hat Smearer (hat & cap) 589.687-038
pan devulcanizer (rubber reclaim.) 550.685-022
pan-devulcanizer helper (rubber reclaim.) 553.686-014
panel assembler (furniture) 706.684-082
panel assembler and wirer (elec. equip.; machinery mfg.) 826.361-010
panelboard assembler (elec. equip.) 721.381-014
PANELBOARD OPERATOR (chemical) 950.562-010
PANELBOARD OPERATOR (mine & quarry; smelt. & refin.) 939.362-014
PANELBOARD OPERATOR (textile) 582.362-010
Panel Coverer (fabrication, nec) 780.684-026
panel coverer (furniture) 780.684-086
PANEL COVERER, METAL FURNITURE (furniture) 780.684-082
PANEL CUTTER (furniture) 761.684-050

PANEL EDGE SEALER (millwork-plywood) 769.685-010
Panel Finisher (paint & varnish) 741.684-026
Panel Fitter (fabrication, nec) 739.684-190
panel gluer (woodworking) 569.685-050
PANEL INSTALLER (mfd. bldgs.) 869.684-038
Panel-Instrument Repairer (any industry) 710.281-026
PANEL LAMINATOR (struct. metal) 809.684-042
PANEL-LAY-UP WORKER (woodworking) 761.684-018
PANEL-MACHINE OPERATOR (paper goods) 640.685-038
PANEL-MACHINE SETTER (paper goods) 640.360-010
panel-machine tender (paper goods) 649.685-038
Panel Maker (fabrication, nec) 762.687-034
PANEL MAKER (furniture) 780.684-086
Panel Maker (woodworking) 762.684-050
Panel-Raiser Operator (saw. & plan.) 665.682-034
Panel Sewer (tex. prod., nec) 787.682-066
PAN GREASER, MACHINE (bakery products) 526.685-034
PAN HELPER (chemical) 551.585-018
pan operator (chemical; smelt. & refin.) 559.685-074
pan operator (sugar & conf.) 524.382-010
pan reclaim processor (rubber reclaim.) 550.685-022
pan shaker (oils & grease) 521.685-242
pan shoveler (oils & grease) 521.685-242
pan shover (oils & grease) 521.685-242
PANTOGRAPHER (print. & pub.) 979.382-022
PANTOGRAPH-MACHINE SET-UP OPERATOR (machine shop) 605.382-022
pantograph operator (print. & pub.) 979.381-010
PANTOGRAPH SETTER (print. & pub.) 979.380-010
pantomimist (amuse. & rec.) 159.047-022
Pantry Attendant (r.r. trans.) 311.477-022
PANTRY GOODS MAKER (hotel & rest.) 317.684-014
Pantry Goods Maker Helper (hotel & rest.) 317.687-010
Pantry Steward/Stewardess (hotel & rest.) 318.137-010
PANTRY WORKER (sugar & conf.) 520.487-018
Pants Busheler (retail trade) 785.261-010
pants closer (garment) 786.682-202
PANTS OUTSEAMER, CHAINSTITCH (garment) 786.682-202
Pants Presser (any industry) 363.682-018
Pants Presser, Automatic (laundry & rel.) 363.685-014
Pantyhose-Crotch-Closing-Machine Operator (knitting) 787.682-074
Pan Washer, Hand (sugar & conf.) 529.686-034
PAPERBACK-MACHINE OPERATOR (metal prod., nec) 616.685-046
Paper-Bag Inspector (paper goods) 649.367-010
PAPER-BAG-PRESS OPERATOR (paper goods) 641.686-026
Paper Baler (paper goods) 920.685-010
Paperboard Sheeter (paper products) 699.682-018
paper coater (paper & pulp; paper goods) 534.682-018
PAPER COATER (paper & pulp; paper goods) 534.685-022
PAPER-COATING-MACHINE OPERATOR (photo. appar.) 534.582-010
PAPER-CONE-DRYING-MACHINE OPERATOR (paper goods) 532.686-014
PAPER-CONE GRADER (paper goods) 649.687-014
PAPER-CONE-MACHINE TENDER (paper goods) 641.685-062
Paper-Cone Maker (electron. comp.) 795.687-014
PAPER-CONTROL CLERK (water trans.) 219.367-022
PAPER-CORE-MACHINE OPERATOR (paper goods) 640.685-042
paper-cup-handle-machine operator (paper goods) 649.685-050
PAPER-CUP-MACHINE OPERATOR (paper goods) 649.685-078
paper cutter (print. & pub.) 640.682-018
Paper Cutter (any industry) 690.685-122
PAPER CUTTER (beverage) 640.565-010
Paper Cutter, Hand (any industry) 690.685-122
paper-cutting-machine operator (beverage) 640.565-010
paper finisher (fabrication, nec) 739.684-122
PAPERHANGER (concrete prod.) 574.585-010
PAPERHANGER (construction) 841.381-010
Paperhanger, Pipe (construction) 869.687-026
PAPER INSERTER (glass mfg.) 920.687-138
Paper Latcher (construction) 869.687-026
paper layer (fabrication, nec) 794.684-026
paper-machine operator (paper & pulp; paper goods) 539.362-014
PAPER-NOVELTY MAKER (paper goods) 794.684-022
PAPER-PATTERN FOLDER (paper goods) 794.687-034
PAPER-PATTERN INSPECTOR (paper goods) 649.687-018
PAPER-PROCESSING-MACHINE HELPER (paper & pulp; paper goods) 534.686-010
paper reeler (paper goods) 640.685-046
PAPER-REEL OPERATOR (paper goods) 640.685-046
Paper Sheeter (any industry) 699.682-018
Paper Slitter (elec. equip.; paper & pulp; paper goods) 699.682-030
PAPER SORTER AND COUNTER (paper & pulp) 649.687-010
Paper Spooler (construction) 869.687-026
PAPER STRIPPER (paper goods; print. & pub.) 922.687-078
Paper Tester (paper & pulp) 539.364-010
paper-tube cutter (paper goods) 640.685-034

Paper-Tube Grader (paper goods) 649.687-014
paper-tube sawyer (paper goods) 640.685-034
paper twister (tex. prod., nec) 681.685-134
Paper-Wrapping-Machine Operator (nonfer. metal) 691.682-018
Papeterie-Table Assembler (paper goods) 920.687-026
PAPIER MACHE MOLDER (fabrication, nec) 794.684-026
Parachute-Accessories Attacher (tex. prod., nec) 787.682-058
Parachute-Crown Sewer (tex. prod., nec) 787.682-058
Parachute-Cushion Installer (tex. prod., nec) 787.682-058
PARACHUTE FOLDER (tex. prod., nec) 789.684-034
parachute-harness rigger (tex. prod., nec) 789.687-082
PARACHUTE INSPECTOR (tex. prod., nec) 789.687-114
PARACHUTE-LINE TIER (tex. prod., nec) 789.687-118
PARACHUTE MARKER (tex. prod., nec) 789.587-018
PARACHUTE MENDER (tex. prod., nec) 789.684-038
parachute packer (air trans.) 912.684-010
Parachute-Panel Joiner (tex. prod., nec) 787.682-058
PARACHUTE RIGGER (air trans.) 912.684-010
Parachute Taper (tex. prod., nec) 787.682-010
Parachutist (amuse. & rec.) 159.347-018
Paradichlorobenzene-Machine Operator (chemical) 555.685-034
PARADICHLOROBENZENE TENDER (chemical) 556.685-054
paradi tender (chemical) 556.685-054
PARAFFIN-MACHINE OPERATOR (paper goods) 534.685-026
PARAFFIN-PLANT OPERATOR (petrol. refin.) 541.682-010
PARAFFIN-PLANT-SWEATER OPERATOR (petrol. refin.) 543.682-022
PARALEGAL (profess. & kin.) 119.267-026
PARAMEDIC (medical ser.) 079.364-026
para operator (chemical) 556.685-054
PARASITOLOGIST (profess. & kin.) 041.061-070
parboiler (can. & preserv.) 526.382-026
Parcel-Post Carrier (government ser.) 230.367-010
PARCEL POST CLERK (clerical) 222.387-038
Parcel-Post Order-Clerk (clerical) 222.387-038
parcel post packer (clerical) 222.387-038
parcel post weigher (clerical) 222.387-038
parent trainer (social ser.) 195.227-018
parimutuel cashier (amuse. & rec.) 211.467-018
parimutuel clerk (amuse. & rec.) 211.467-022
PARIMUTUEL-TICKET CASHIER (amuse. & rec.) 211.467-018
PARIMUTUEL-TICKET CHECKER (amuse. & rec.) 219.587-010
PARIMUTUEL-TICKET SELLER (amuse. & rec.) 211.467-022
PARK AIDE (government ser.) 249.367-082
Park Guard (amuse. & rec.) 372.667-034
PARKING ANALYST (government ser.) 199.261-014
parking attendant (automotive ser.) 915.473-010
parking enforcement agent (government ser.) 375.587-010
PARKING ENFORCEMENT OFFICER (government ser.) 375.587-010
PARKING-LOT ATTENDANT (automotive ser.) 915.473-010
parking-lot chauffeur (automotive ser.) 915.473-010
PARKING LOT SIGNALER (automotive ser.) 915.667-014
Parking-Meter-Coin Collector (business ser.) 292.687-010
PARKING-METER SERVICER (government ser.) 710.384-026
parking-station attendant (automotive ser.) 915.473-010
Park-Landscape Architect (profess. & kin.) 001.061-018
PARK NATURALIST (government ser.) 049.127-010
PARK RANGER (government ser.) 169.167-042
PARK SUPERINTENDENT (government ser.) 188.167-062
park technician (government ser.) 249.367-082
park worker (government ser.) 406.687-010
PARLOR CHAPERONE (hotel & rest.) 352.667-014
Parole Officer (profess. & kin.) 195.107-046
parter (plastic-synth.) 556.587-010
Partition Assembler (mfd. bldgs.; vehicles, nec) 762.684-014
PARTITION ASSEMBLER (wood. container) 762.687-054
PARTITION-ASSEMBLY-MACHINE OPERATOR (any industry) 649.582-010
PARTITION-MAKING-MACHINE OPERATOR (paper goods) 649.685-082
Partition Notcher (wood. container) 669.382-010
partition-slotter helper (paper goods) 640.686-014
PART MAKER (jewelry-silver.) 739.687-138
Part Maker (fabrication, nec) 739.384-022
Partridge Farmer (agriculture) 412.161-010
parts assembler (furniture) 763.684-038
parts caster, hand (elec. equip.) 502.684-010
parts-casting-machine operator (elec. equip.) 502.482-014
PARTS CATALOGER (any industry) 229.267-010
PARTS CLERK (clerical) 222.367-042
parts clerk (retail trade; wholesale tr.) 279.357-062
Parts Clerk, Automobile Repair (clerical) 222.367-042
Parts Clerk, Plant Maintenance (clerical) 222.367-042
Parts Counter-Weigher (clock & watch; electron. comp.; office machines) 221.587-030
parts data writer (any industry) 229.267-010
parts inspector (any industry) 609.684-010

parts inspector (furniture) 763.684-070
PARTS LISTER (electron. comp.) 229.367-014
parts mechanic (any industry) 600.280-010
PARTS-ORDER-AND-STOCK CLERK (clerical) 249.367-058
parts picker (any industry) 922.687-058
PARTS REMOVER (clock & watch) 715.687-102
PARTS SALVAGER (any industry) 638.281-026
PASSEMENTERIE WORKER (tex. prod., nec) 782.684-050
passenger agent (any industry) 238.367-026
PASSENGER ATTENDANT (water trans.) 350.677-014
passenger-booking clerk (any industry) 238.367-026
Passenger-Car-Cleaning Supervisor (r.r. trans.) 910.137-014
Passenger-Car Inspector (r.r. trans.) 910.387-014
passenger-car scrubber (railroad equip.) 845.684-010
passenger-car-upholsterer apprentice (automotive ser.) 780.381-014
Passenger-Interline Clerk (air trans.) 214.382-022
PASSENGER REPRESENTATIVE (r.r. trans.) 910.367-026
PASSENGER SERVICE REPRESENTATIVE (air trans.) 359.677-022
PASSENGER SERVICE REPRESENTATIVE I (r.r. trans.) 352.677-010
PASSENGER SERVICE REPRESENTATIVE II (r.r. trans.) 910.677-010
Passenger-Tire Inspector (rubber tire) 750.684-030
Passenger Traffic Agent (air trans.; motor trans.; r.r. trans.; water trans.) 252.257-010
passer (hat & cap) 784.387-010
passer (leather mfg.) 589.387-010
passing boss (mine & quarry) 932.167-010
PASSPORT-APPLICATION EXAMINER (government ser.) 169.267-030
past-due-accounts clerk (clerical) 241.357-010
paste-make-up-artist apprentice (print. & pub.) 979.381-022
paste-mill operator (chemical) 559.685-098
PASTE MIXER (chemical) 550.585-034
Paste Mixer (paint & varnish) 550.685-078
Paste Mixer, Liquid (elec. equip.) 550.585-034
paster (boot & shoe) 788.687-030
PASTER (brick & tile) 773.684-014
paster (fabrication, nec) 692.685-110
paster (steel & rel.) 543.687-014
paster (tex. prod., nec) 789.687-102
PASTER, HAND OR MACHINE (leather prod.) 783.687-026
PASTER, HAT LINING (hat & cap) 692.686-070
paster operator (paper & pulp; paper goods) 534.682-026
PASTER, SCREEN PRINTING (textile) 652.687-026
PASTER SUPERVISOR (brick & tile) 773.131-010
Paste Thinner (paint & varnish) 550.585-038
PASTE-UP ARTIST (print. & pub.) 972.381-030
PASTE-UP COPY-CAMERA OPERATOR APPRENTICE (print. & pub.) 979.381-022
PASTEURIZER (beverage; can. & preserv.) 523.685-110
pasteurizer (food prep., nec) 522.685-070
PASTEURIZER (oils & grease) 523.585-026
Pasteurizer Helper (dairy products) 529.686-026
Pasteurizer Operator (dairy products) 529.382-018
Pasteurizing Supervisor (dairy products) 529.131-014
paste worker (sugar & conf.) 520.687-018
PASTING INSPECTOR (brick & tile) 773.687-010
PASTING-MACHINE OFFBEARER (elec. equip.) 509.686-014
PASTING-MACHINE OPERATOR (elec. equip.) 505.482-010
Pastor (profess. & kin.) 120.107-010
PASTORAL ASSISTANT (nonprofit org.) 129.107-026
PASTRY CHEF (hotel & rest.) 313.131-022
PASTRY CHEF (water trans.) 315.131-014
pastry decorator (bakery products) 524.381-010
pastry helper (hotel & rest.) 313.687-010
Pastry Mixer (bakery products) 520.685-234
patch developer (textile) 582.685-110
PATCH DRILLER (fabrication, nec) 739.687-142
patcher (any industry) 932.664-010
patcher (automotive ser.) 750.684-038
patcher (beverage) 764.687-090
PATCHER (fabrication, nec) 739.687-146
PATCHER (house. appl.) 723.687-010
PATCHER (leather mfg.) 585.687-022
PATCHER (pottery & porc.) 774.684-046
PATCHER (steel & rel.) 861.684-014
patcher (tobacco) 790.684-018
PATCHER (woodworking) 769.684-030
PATCHER, BOWLING BALL (toy-sport equip.) 759.684-046
PATCHER HELPER (steel & rel.) 861.687-014
patcher, plastic boat (ship-boat mfg.) 807.684-014
patcher-wood welder (ordnance) 761.684-042
PATCH FINISHER (textile) 582.684-010
PATCHING-MACHINE OPERATOR (laundry & rel.) 361.685-022
PATCH-MACHINE OPERATOR (paper goods) 641.685-066
PATCH SANDER (stonework) 775.684-054
patch setter (woodworking) 769.684-030

PATCH WASHER (textile) 582.685-110
PATCH WORKER (agriculture) 381.687-030
PATCH WORKER (tobacco) 790.684-018
PATENT AGENT (profess. & kin.) 119.167-014
patent attorney (profess. & kin.) 110.117-026
patent-button machine operator, automatic (garment; hat & cap) 699.685-010
Patent Clerk (government ser.) 119.267-026
patented-hogshead assembler (wood. container) 764.687-070
Patent-Leather Sorter (leather mfg.) 589.387-010
PATHOLOGIST (medical ser.) 070.061-010
patient-insurance clerk (medical ser.) 214.362-022
PATIENT-RESOURCES-AND-REIMBURSEMENT AGENT (government ser.) 195.267-018
patient's librarian (library) 100.167-022
patrol commander (government ser.) 375.167-034
PATROL CONDUCTOR (government ser.) 372.677-010
Patrol Driver (government ser.) 375.263-014
patrol guard (any industry) 372.667-034
PATROL JUDGE (amuse. & rec.) 153.267-014
PATROLLER (knitting) 685.687-022
PATROLLER (r.r. trans.) 376.667-018
patrol officer (government ser.) 375.263-014
patrol sergeant (government ser.) 375.133-010
pattern-and-chain maker (knitting) 685.360-010
PATTERN ASSEMBLER (knitting) 685.685-014
Pattern Carrier (foundry) 519.687-022
PATTERN-CHAIN MAKER SUPERVISOR (textile) 683.132-010
pattern changer and repairer (textile) 683.685-014
PATTERN CHART-WRITER (paper goods) 789.381-014
Pattern Cleaner (foundry) 519.687-022
pattern cutter (any industry) 775.684-022
pattern data operator (aircraft mfg.) 007.362-010
pattern designer (profess. & kin.) 142.061-014
Pattern-Drum Maker (knitting) 685.684-010
PATTERN DUPLICATOR (textile) 683.685-026
PATTERN GATER (foundry) 801.684-014
pattern generator operator (electron. comp.) 976.382-038
PATTERN GRADER-CUTTER (garment) 781.381-022
PATTERN-GRADER SUPERVISOR (wood prod., nec) 693.132-010
PATTERN HAND (woodworking) 652.687-030
pattern hanger (textile) 683.685-014
PATTERN-LEASE INSPECTOR (textile) 683.384-010
patternmaker (brick & tile; concrete prod.) 860.381-034
PATTERNMAKER (engraving) 751.381-010
PATTERNMAKER (fabrication, nec) 772.381-014
PATTERNMAKER (furniture) 709.381-034
PATTERNMAKER (furniture; garment; tex. prod., nec) 781.361-014
PATTERNMAKER (furniture) 661.280-010
PATTERNMAKER (glass products) 779.584-010
PATTERNMAKER (hat & cap) 784.361-010
patternmaker (knitting) 685.381-010
PATTERNMAKER (metal prod., nec) 693.281-014
patternmaker (pottery & porc.) 777.281-014
PATTERNMAKER (stonework) 703.381-010
PATTERNMAKER, ACOUSTICAL TILE (wood prod., nec) 649.685-086
PATTERNMAKER, ALL-AROUND (foundry; plastic prod.) 693.280-014
PATTERNMAKER APPRENTICE, METAL (foundry) 600.280-046
PATTERNMAKER APPRENTICE, WOOD (foundry) 661.281-018
patternmaker, bench (foundry) 693.281-018
PATTERNMAKER, ENVELOPE (paper goods) 649.361-010
patternmaker, hand (foundry) 693.281-018
PATTERNMAKER, METAL (foundry) 600.280-050
PATTERNMAKER, METAL, BENCH (foundry) 693.281-018
PATTERNMAKER, PLASTER (aircraft mfg.) 777.281-018
patternmaker, plaster and plastic (aircraft mfg.) 777.281-018
PATTERNMAKER, PLASTICS (plastic prod.) 754.381-014
patternmaker, pressure cast (foundry) 777.381-034
PATTERNMAKER, SAMPLE (cutlery-hrdwr.) 693.281-022
PATTERNMAKER, WOOD (foundry) 661.281-022
pattern marker (any industry) 781.384-014
PATTERN MARKER I (woodworking) 761.381-022
PATTERN MARKER II (woodworking) 761.684-010
pattern-perforating-machine operator (tex. prod., nec) 781.684-042
pattern puncher (knitting) 685.684-010
pattern-punching-machine operator (any industry) 781.684-058
Pattern-Room Attendant (foundry) 222.387-058
PATTERN RULER (tex. prod., nec) 794.687-038
pattern setter (foundry) 518.380-010
Pattern Setter (foundry) 661.281-022
PATTERN-SHOP SUPERVISOR (foundry) 693.131-010
PATTERN WHEEL MAKER (knitting) 685.684-010
pavement curer (construction)   see CONCRETE CURER
pavement-joint-cleaning-machine operator (construction) 853.683-018
Pavilion Cutter (jewelry-silver.) 770.261-010
Paving-Bed Maker (construction) 869.687-026

Paving-Block Cutter I (stonework) 677.685-046
Paving-Block Cutter II (stonework) 771.684-010
paving-form mover (construction)   see FORM STRIPPER
paving-machine operator, asphalt or bituminous (construction) 853.663-010
Paving Rammer (construction) 869.687-026
PAWNBROKER (retail trade) 191.157-010
Pay Agent (clerical) 215.362-022
PAYMASTER OF PURSES (amuse. & rec.) 211.367-010
Payroll Auditor (insurance) 160.167-054
PAYROLL CLERK (clerical) 215.382-014
payroll clerk, chief (clerical) 215.137-014
PAY-STATION ATTENDANT (tel. & tel.) 237.367-034
pay-station collector (business ser.; tel. & tel.) 292.687-010
pbx installer (tel. & tel.) 822.381-018
pbx operator (clerical) 235.662-022
pbx repairer (tel. & tel.) 822.281-022
Peach Grower (agriculture) 403.161-010
Peach Harvesting Supervisor (agriculture) 409.131-010
Peach Sorter (agriculture; can. & preserv.; wholesale tr.) 529.687-186
PEANUT BLANCHER (can. & preserv.) 521.685-246
PEANUT-BUTTER MAKER (can. & preserv.; food prep., nec) 529.685-178
Peanut Farmer (agriculture) 404.161-010
Peanut Roaster (can. & preserv.) 529.685-174
Peanut Sorter (can. & preserv.) 521.687-086
pearl dipper (jewelry-silver.) 770.687-010
Pearl Diver (fishing & hunt.) 443.664-010
PEARLER (clock & watch) 715.684-162
pearl-glue drier (chemical) 553.685-118
PEARL-GLUE OPERATOR (chemical) 550.685-094
Pearl Hand (jewelry-silver.) 735.687-034
pearl maker (jewelry-silver.) 770.687-010
pearl peeler (jewelry-silver.) 735.381-014
PEARL RESTORER (jewelry-silver.) 735.381-014
Pearl Stringer (jewelry-silver.) 735.684-010
Pear Packer (agriculture; wholesale tr.) 920.687-134
Pebble-Mill Operator (chemical; paint & varnish) 599.685-058
Pecan Grower (agriculture) 403.161-010
Pecan-Mallow Dipper (sugar & conf.) 524.684-010
pedal assembler (musical inst.) 730.684-090
peddler (amuse. & rec.) 291.457-022
peddler (retail trade) 291.357-010
PEDDLER (retail trade) 291.457-018
PEDIATRIC DENTIST (medical ser.) 072.101-026
PEDIATRICIAN (medical ser.) 070.101-066
Pediatric Nurse Practitioner (medical ser.) 075.264-010
pedigree researcher (clerical) 249.387-018
PEDIGREE TRACER (clerical) 249.387-018
perodontist (medical ser.) 072.101-026
PEELED-POTATO INSPECTOR (food prep., nec) 521.687-094
Peeler (can. & preserv.) 529.686-014
peeler (paper goods) 794.687-050
Peel Oven Tender (bakery products) 526.685-030
PEGGER (boot & shoe) 788.687-102
PEGGER, DOBBY LOOMS (narrow fabrics; textile) 689.687-054
pelletizer (cement) 579.685-034
pelletizer (plastic prod.; plastic-synth.) 556.685-058
pelletizer tender (chemical) 550.685-058
pellet-machine operator (plastic prod.; plastic-synth.) 556.685-058
PELLET-MILL OPERATOR (grain-feed mills) 520.685-178
Pellet Operator (grain-feed mills) 520.682-018
Pellet-Post Inspector (chemical) 737.687-062
Pellet-Preparation Operator (electron. comp.) 590.684-014
PELLET-PRESS OPERATOR (chemical) 555.685-042
PELLET-PRESS OPERATOR (ordnance) 694.685-034
pellet-press operator (smelt. & refin.) 519.685-010
PELOTA MAKER (toy-sport equip.) 732.684-090
PELTER (agriculture) 410.687-018
pelt inspector (meat products) 525.687-042
pelt salter (meat products; oils & grease) 525.687-038
pelt scraper (leather mfg.) 585.681-010
pelt shearer (hat & cap) 585.685-046
PEN-AND-PENCIL REPAIRER (any industry) 733.684-014
Pen Assembler (pen & pencil) 733.687-010
PENCIL INSPECTOR (pen & pencil) 733.687-062
pencil sorter (pen & pencil) 733.687-062
pencil striper (any industry) 741.687-022
Penologist (profess. & kin.) 054.067-014
pen-point smoother (pen & pencil) 733.685-026
pen-ruler operator (paper goods; print. & pub.) 659.682-022
Pensionholder-Information Clerk (insurance) 249.262-010
Pepper Pickler (can. & preserv.) 522.684-010
percher (textile) 689.685-038
perch-machine inspector (textile) 689.685-038
PERCOLATOR OPERATOR (grain-feed mills) 523.682-034
PERCUSSION-INSTRUMENT REPAIRER (any industry) 730.381-042

Percussion-Welding-Machine Operator (welding) 812.682-010
Per Diem Clerk (r.r. trans.) 214.382-022
Perfect-Binder Feeder-Offbearer (print. & pub.) 653.686-026
Perfect-Binder Setter (print. & pub.) 653.360-018
PERFORATING-MACHINE OPERATOR (hat & cap) 686.685-038
PERFORATING-MACHINE OPERATOR (print. & pub.) 649.685-090
perforating-machine operator (wood prod., nec) 569.662-010
Perforator (boot & shoe) 690.685-114
perforator (hat & cap) 686.685-038
PERFORATOR (tex. prod., nec) 781.684-042
perforator operator (hat & cap) 686.685-038
perforator operator (print. & pub.) 203.582-062
PERFORATOR OPERATOR, OIL WELL (petrol. & gas) 931.382-010
PERFORATOR TYPIST (clerical) 203.582-038
Performance-Test Inspector (welding) 819.281-018
performer (amuse. & rec.; motion picture; radio-tv broad.)   see ENTER-
TAINER
Perfume And Toilet Water Maker (pharmaceut.) 550.685-090
perfume compounder (pharmaceut.; soap & rel.) 550.685-046
PERFUMER (chemical) 022.161-018
PERFUSIONIST (medical ser.) 078.362-034
PERIODONTIST (medical ser.) 072.101-030
PERISHABLE-FREIGHT INSPECTOR (r.r. trans.) 910.667-022
PERISHABLE-FRUIT INSPECTOR (wholesale tr.) 910.387-010
PERMANENT-MOLD SUPERVISOR (foundry; nonfer. metal) 514.130-010
Permanent Waver (personal ser.) 332.271-010
Permastone Dresser (construction) 869.664-014
permit agent (any industry) 191.117-046
PERMIT AGENT, GEOPHYSICAL PROSPECTING (petrol. & gas) 191.117-
042
personal agent (amuse. & rec.) 191.117-010
PERSONAL ATTENDANT (domestic ser.) 309.674-014
personal attendant (personal ser.) 358.677-014
personal manager (amuse. & rec.) 191.117-010
PERSONAL PROPERTY ASSESSOR (government ser.) 191.367-010
PERSONAL SHOPPER (retail trade) 296.357-010
Personal Trust Officer (financial) 186.117-074
personnel administrator (profess. & kin.) 166.167-018
personnel analyst (profess. & kin.) 166.267-018
PERSONNEL CLERK (clerical) 209.362-026
personnel interviewer (profess. & kin.) 166.267-010
personnel monitor (profess. & kin.) 199.167-010
PERSONNEL QUALITY ASSURANCE AUDITOR (electron. comp.) 168.367-
022
personnel records clerk (clerical) 209.362-026
PERSONNEL RECRUITER (profess. & kin.) 166.267-038
PERSONNEL SCHEDULER (clerical) 215.367-014
Persulfate Make-Up Operator (chemical) 559.382-034
Pest-Control Pilot (agriculture) 196.263-010
pest-control worker (agriculture) 408.381-010
pest control worker (business ser.) 389.684-010
pest control worker helper (any industry) 383.684-010
PESTICIDE-CONTROL INSPECTOR (government ser.) 168.267-098
Petal Cutter (button & notion) 781.687-030
Petal Shaper, Hand (button & notion) 739.684-014
PETROLEUM ENGINEER (petrol. & gas) 010.061-018
PETROLEUM INSPECTOR (business ser.) 222.367-046
PETROLEUM-INSPECTOR SUPERVISOR (business ser.) 222.137-026
Petroleum Products District Supervisor (government ser.) 168.167-090
Petroleum Products Inspection Supervisor (government ser.) 188.117-134
PETROLOGIST (profess. & kin.) 024.061-046
Pet Shop Attendant (retail trade) 410.674-010
PEWTER CASTER (jewelry-silver.) 502.384-010
PEWTERER (jewelry-silver.) 700.261-010
PEWTER FINISHER (jewelry-silver.) 700.281-026
PHARMACEUTICAL-COMPOUNDING   SUPERVISOR   (pharmaceut.)
559.131-010
PHARMACEUTICAL DETAILER (wholesale tr.) 262.157-010
PHARMACEUTICAL OPERATOR (pharmaceut.) 559.382-042
PHARMACIST (medical ser.) 074.161-010
PHARMACIST ASSISTANT (military ser.) 074.381-010
Pharmacist, Hospital (medical ser.) 074.161-010
PHARMACOLOGIST (profess. & kin.) 041.061-074
pharmacy clerk (medical ser.) 074.382-010
Pharmacy Stock Clerk (retail trade) 299.367-014
PHARMACY TECHNICIAN (medical ser.) 074.382-010
Pheasant Farmer (agriculture) 412.161-010
PHERESIS SPECIALIST (medical ser.) 078.261-042
philatelic consultant (retail trade) 299.387-014
PHILATELIST (profess. & kin.) term
PHILOLOGIST (profess. & kin.) 059.067-010
PHLEBOTOMIST (medical ser.) 079.364-022
phone-book deliverer (business ser.) 230.667-014
phone-circuit operator (any industry) 193.262-034
PHONOGRAPH-CARTRIDGE ASSEMBLER (comm. equip.) 720.684-014

PHONOGRAPH-NEEDLE-TIP MAKER (comm. equip.) 770.382-014
PHOSPHORIC-ACID OPERATOR (chemical) 558.582-010
PHOTO CHECKER AND ASSEMBLER (photofinishing) 976.687-014
PHOTOCOMPOSING-MACHINE OPERATOR (print. & pub.) 650.582-018
PHOTOCOMPOSING-PERFORATOR-MACHINE OPERATOR (print. & pub.) 203.582-042
PHOTOCOMPOSITION-KEYBOARD OPERATOR (print. & pub.) 203.582-046
PHOTOCOPYING-MACHINE OPERATOR (clerical) 207.685-014
photocopy operator (any industry) 976.382-022
PHOTOENGRAVER (print. & pub.) 971.381-022
PHOTOENGRAVER APPRENTICE (print. & pub.) 971.381-026
PHOTOENGRAVING FINISHER (print. & pub.) 971.381-030
Photoengraving Helper (print. & pub.) 979.684-026
PHOTOENGRAVING PRINTER (print. & pub.) 971.381-034
PHOTOENGRAVING PROOFER (print. & pub.) 971.381-038
PHOTOENGRAVING-PROOFER APPRENTICE (print. & pub.) 971.381-040
PHOTOFINISHING LABORATORY WORKER (photofinishing) 976.687-018
photo-finish photographer (amuse. & rec.) 143.382-014
Photoflash-Powder Mixer (chemical) 737.687-090
Photogeologist (profess. & kin.) 024.061-018
PHOTOGRAMMETRIC ENGINEER (profess. & kin.) 018.167-026
PHOTOGRAMMETRIST (profess. & kin.) 018.261-026
photograph enlarger (photofinishing) 976.381-018
PHOTOGRAPHER (amuse. & rec.) 143.457-010
PHOTOGRAPHER, AERIAL (profess. & kin.) 143.062-014
PHOTOGRAPHER, APPRENTICE (profess. & kin.) 143.062-018
PHOTOGRAPHER APPRENTICE, LITHOGRAPHIC (print. & pub.) 972.382-010
PHOTOGRAPHER, FINISH (amuse. & rec.) 143.382-014
PHOTOGRAPHER HELPER (any industry) 976.667-010
PHOTOGRAPHER, LITHOGRAPHIC (print. & pub.) 972.382-014
Photographer, Motion Picture (profess. & kin.) 143.062-022
photographer, news (print. & pub.; radio-tv broad.) 143.062-034
PHOTOGRAPHER, PHOTOENGRAVING (electron. comp.; print. & pub.) 971.382-014
PHOTOGRAPHER, SCIENTIFIC (profess. & kin.) 143.062-026
PHOTOGRAPHER, STILL (profess. & kin.) 143.062-030
PHOTOGRAPH FINISHER (photofinishing) 976.487-010
PHOTOGRAPHIC ALIGNER, SEMICONDUCTOR WAFERS (electron. comp.) 976.382-030
Photographic Double (amuse. & rec.) 961.364-010
PHOTOGRAPHIC ENGINEER (profess. & kin.) 019.081-014
PHOTOGRAPHIC-EQUIPMENT-MAINTENANCE TECHNICIAN (photo. appar.) 714.281-026
PHOTOGRAPHIC EQUIPMENT TECHNICIAN (photo. appar.) 714.281-022
photographic-laboratory supervisor (photofinishing) 976.131-010
PHOTOGRAPHIC-MACHINE OPERATOR (clerical) 207.685-018
Photographic-Paper-Coating-Machine Operator (photo. appar.) 534.582-010
PHOTOGRAPHIC-PLATE MAKER (electron. comp.) 714.381-018
photographic-process attendant (electron. comp.) 714.381-018
PHOTOGRAPHIC PROCESSOR, SEMICONDUCTOR WAFERS (electron. comp.) 976.685-038
Photo-Graphics Librarian (library) 100.167-038
photograph printer (photofinishing) 976.682-014
photograph restorer (profess. & kin.) 970.281-010
PHOTOGRAPH RETOUCHER (photofinishing) 970.281-018
PHOTOJOURNALIST (print. & pub.; radio-tv broad.) 143.062-034
PHOTOLETTERING-MACHINE OPERATOR (print. & pub.) 652.585-010
photolithographer (print. & pub.) 972.382-014
photolithographer apprentice (print. & pub.) 972.382-010
photolithographic process worker (print. & pub.) 972.382-014
photolith operator (any industry) 976.361-010
photolith operator (print. & pub.) 971.381-022
PHOTO MASK CLEANER (electron. comp.) 590.684-034
PHOTO MASK INSPECTOR (electron. comp.) 726.384-022
PHOTO MASK MAKER, ELECTRON-BEAM (electron. comp.) 972.382-018
PHOTO MASK PATTERN GENERATOR (electron. comp.) 976.382-038
PHOTO MASK PROCESSOR (electron. comp.) 976.384-014
PHOTO MASK TECHNICIAN, ELECTRON-BEAM (electron. comp.) 972.382-022
photo-optical instrumentation engineer (profess. & kin.) 019.081-014
PHOTO-OPTICS TECHNICIAN (profess. & kin.) 029.280-010
photo printer (electron. comp.) 976.684-030
PHOTORADIO OPERATOR (print. & pub.; tel. & tel.) 193.362-010
PHOTORESIST LAMINATOR, PRINTED CIRCUIT BOARD (electron. comp.) 554.685-034
photoresist printer (electron. comp.) 976.684-030
PHOTOSTAT OPERATOR (any industry) 976.382-022
PHOTOSTAT-OPERATOR HELPER (any industry) 979.687-014
PHOTO TECHNICIAN (electron. comp.) 976.384-010
phototypesetter (print. & pub.) 650.582-022
PHOTOTYPESETTER OPERATOR (print. & pub.) 650.582-022
Phrenologist (amuse. & rec.) 159.647-010
Phthalic-Acid Purifier (chemical) 559.685-010

PHYSIATRIST (medical ser.) 070.101-070
PHYSICAL-INTEGRATION PRACTITIONER (medical ser.) 076.264-010
physical-laboratory assistant (profess. & kin.) 011.261-010
physical medicine specialist (medical ser.) 070.101-070
physical tester (profess. & kin.) 011.361-010
physical-testing supervisor (profess. & kin.) 011.161-010
PHYSICAL THERAPIST (education; medical ser.) 076.121-014
PHYSICAL THERAPIST ASSISTANT (medical ser.) 076.224-010
PHYSICAL THERAPY AIDE (medical ser.) 355.354-010
Physical Therapy Aide, Hydrotherapy (medical ser.) 355.354-010
Physical Therapy Aide, Transport (medical ser.) 355.354-010
physical therapy assistant (medical ser.) 076.224-010
physical therapy technician (medical ser.) 076.224-010
PHYSICIAN ASSISTANT (medical ser.) 079.364-018
physician, general practice (medical ser.) 070.101-022
PHYSICIAN, HEAD (medical ser.) 070.101-074
physician, industrial (medical ser.) 070.101-078
PHYSICIAN, OCCUPATIONAL (medical ser.) 070.101-078
PHYSICIAN, RESEARCH (medical ser.) term
PHYSICIST (profess. & kin.) 023.061-014
Physicist, Acoustics (profess. & kin.) 023.061-014
Physicist, Astrophysics (profess. & kin.) 023.061-014
Physicist, Atomic, Electronic And Molecular (profess. & kin.) 023.061-014
Physicist, Cryogenics (profess. & kin.) 023.061-014
Physicist, Electricity And Magnetism (profess. & kin.) 023.061-014
Physicist, Fluids (profess. & kin.) 023.061-014
Physicist, Light And Optics (profess. & kin.) 023.061-014
Physicist, Nuclear (profess. & kin.) 023.061-014
Physicist, Plasma (profess. & kin.) 023.061-014
Physicist, Solid Earth (profess. & kin.) 023.061-014
Physicist, Solid State (profess. & kin.) 023.061-014
PHYSICIST, THEORETICAL (profess. & kin.) 023.067-010
Physicist, Thermodynamics (profess. & kin.) 023.061-014
Physiognomist (amuse. & rec.) 159.647-010
PHYSIOLOGIST (profess. & kin.) 041.061-078
physiotherapist (education; medical ser.) 076.121-014
Pianist (amuse. & rec.) 152.041-010
Piano-And-Organ Refinisher (woodworking) 763.381-010
Piano Bench Assembler (musical inst.) 763.684-058
PIANO CASE AND BENCH ASSEMBLER (musical inst.) 763.684-058
Piano-Case Maker (musical inst.) 660.280-010
piano-machine operator (narrow fabrics; textile) 683.582-010
PIANO REGULATOR-INSPECTOR (musical inst.) 730.681-010
Piano-Sounding-Board Matcher (musical inst.) 761.684-018
PIANO STRINGER (musical inst.) 730.684-054
PIANO TECHNICIAN (any industry) 730.281-038
PIANO TUNER (any industry) 730.361-010
PICKED-EDGE SEWING-MACHINE OPERATOR (garment) 786.682-206
picker (nonfer. metal) 509.686-018
picker (nonmet. min.) 739.687-102
picker (optical goods) 573.686-014
PICKER (saw. & plan.) 669.687-022
picker (textile) 680.685-074
PICKER (tobacco) 521.687-098
picker-box operator (oils & grease) 520.565-010
Picker Feeder (nonmet. min.) 570.686-018
Picker Feeder (tex. prod., nec; textile) 680.686-018
PICKER-MACHINE OPERATOR (furniture) 680.685-078
PICKER TENDER (textile) 680.685-074
Picket, Labor Union (nonprofit org.) 299.687-014
picking-belt operator (can. & preserv.) 521.687-086
PICKING-MACHINE OPERATOR (any industry) 680.685-082
Picking-Machine-Operator Helper (tex. prod., nec) 586.686-022
PICKING-TABLE WORKER (sugar & conf.) 521.687-102
pickle maker (can. & preserv.) 522.684-010
pickle processor (can. & preserv.) 522.684-010
PICKLE PUMPER (meat products) 522.685-086
pickler (any industry) 503.685-030
PICKLER (can. & preserv.) 522.684-010
Pickler (leather mfg.) 582.482-014
PICKLER (meat products) 522.687-034
PICKLER, CONTINUOUS PICKLING LINE (any industry) 503.362-010
PICKLER HELPER, CONTINUOUS PICKLING LINE (any industry) 503.686-010
pickler operator (any industry) 503.362-010
pickle-water-pump operator (meat products) 522.685-086
Pickling-Drum Operator (meat products) 582.685-126
pickling grader (meat products) 529.687-106
pickling operator (any industry) 503.685-030
pickling-solution maker (can. & preserv.) 522.685-018
PICKLING SOLUTION MAKER (meat products) 522.485-010
pickling-tank operator (any industry) 503.685-030
PICK-PULLING-MACHINE OPERATOR (textile) 689.685-094
PICK REMOVER (textile) 689.687-058
Pick-Up Driver (motor trans.) 906.683-022

PICK-UP OPERATOR (textile) 689.685-098
PICTURE FRAMER (retail trade; wood prod., nec) 739.684-146
Pie Bottomer (bakery products) 526.685-038
piece-dyeing-machine tender (textile) 582.665-014
piece-dye worker (textile) 582.665-014
Piece-Goods Packer (textile) 920.587-018
Piece Hand (textile) 681.685-154
piece marker, small arms (ordnance) 652.582-010
piece-meat trimmer (meat products) 521.687-106
Piece Presser (garment) 363.684-018
piecer-up (garment; glove & mit.) 781.687-010
piece trimmer (meat products) 521.687-106
pie chef (hotel & rest.) 313.361-038
Pie-Crimping-Machine Operator (bakery products) 526.685-038
Pie-Crust Mixer (bakery products) 520.685-234
Pie-Dough Roller (bakery products) 526.685-038
Pie Filler (bakery products) 526.685-038
Pie-Filling Mixer (bakery products) 520.685-114
Pie Icer (bakery products) 524.684-022
Pie Icer, Machine (bakery products) 524.685-034
PIE MAKER (hotel & rest.) 313.361-038
PIE MAKER, MACHINE (bakery products) 526.685-038
piercer operator (nonfer. metal) 613.482-014
PIERCING-MACHINE OPERATOR (nonfer. metal) 613.482-014
PIERCING-MILL OPERATOR (steel & rel.) 613.685-018
pier hand (water trans.) 911.364-014
pier hand helper (water trans.) 911.687-010
Pie Topper (bakery products) 526.685-038
PIG-MACHINE OPERATOR (steel & rel.) 514.362-010
PIG-MACHINE-OPERATOR HELPER (steel & rel.) 514.667-014
Pigment And Lacquer Mixer (chemical) 550.685-106
pigment blender (chemical) 550.685-014
PIGMENT FURNACE TENDER (chemical) 553.685-086
Pigment Mixer (paint & varnish) 550.685-078
Pigment Presser (chemical) 551.685-082
PIGMENT PROCESSOR (chemical; paint & varnish) 559.685-130
PIGMENT PUMPER (rubber reclaim.) 914.665-010
pigment supplier (rubber reclaim.) 914.665-010
pigment weigher (fabrication, nec) 590.487-010
Pigskin Trimmer (meat products) 525.687-046
PILE DRIVER (construction) term
PILE-DRIVER OPERATOR (construction) 859.682-018
Pile-Driver Operator, Barge Mounted (construction) 859.682-018
Pile-Driving Setter (construction) 869.664-014
Pile-Fabric Knitter (knitting) 685.665-014
pile operator (profess. & kin.) 015.362-014
pill coater (pharmaceut.) 554.382-010
PILLING-MACHINE OPERATOR (plastic prod.; plastic-synth.) 556.685-058
Pillow-And-Cushion-Department Supervisor (tex. prod., nec) 789.132-010
Pillowcase Cleaner (tex. prod., nec) 689.687-050
pillowcase cutter (tex. prod., nec) 686.685-014
Pillowcase Folder (tex. prod., nec) 589.687-014
Pillowcase Sewer (tex. prod., nec) 787.682-026
Pillowcase Sewer, Automatic (tex. prod., nec) 787.685-014
PILLOWCASE TURNER (tex. prod., nec) 583.685-078
pillow cleaner (laundry & rel.) 362.685-010
PILLOW CLEANER (tex. prod., nec) 789.687-122
Pillow Filler (tex. prod., nec) 780.684-066
pilot (air trans.) 196.263-014
pilot (textile) 582.685-130
Pilot-Boat Deckhand (water trans.) 911.687-022
pilot-can router (tobacco) 920.685-086
PILOT-CONTROL OPERATOR (chemical; plastic-synth.) 559.382-046
PILOT-CONTROL-OPERATOR HELPER (chemical; plastic-synth.) 559.664-014
PILOT, HIGHWAY PATROL (government ser.) 375.163-014
pilot-plant-operator helper (chemical; plastic-synth.) 559.664-014
Pilot-Plant Research-Technician (petrol. refin.) 008.261-010
pilot-plant technician (chemical; plastic-synth.) 559.382-046
PILOT, SHIP (water trans.) 197.133-026
Pilot, Steam Yacht (water trans.) 197.133-026
PILOT, SUBMERSIBLE (any industry) 029.383-010
Pilot, Tank Vessel (water trans.) 197.133-026
Pin Attacher (button & notion) 692.685-206
Pinball-Machine Repairer (business ser.) 639.281-014
Pin Cleaner (textile) 699.687-014
pin-drafting-machine operator (textile) 680.685-058
Pin-Feather-Machine Operator (tex. prod., nec) 589.685-054
PIN-GAME-MACHINE INSPECTOR (svc. ind. mach.) 729.381-014
Pin Inserter (any industry) 920.685-034
Pin Inserter (clock & watch) 715.684-182
PIN INSERTER, REGULATOR (clock & watch) 715.684-166
Pinion Inspector (clock & watch) 715.384-022
PINION POLISHER (clock & watch) 715.685-042
Pinion Staker (clock & watch) 715.684-182

pinker (boot & shoe; garment) 686.685-042
PINKING-MACHINE OPERATOR (boot & shoe; garment) 686.685-042
PINKING-MACHINE OPERATOR (button & notion) 692.685-130
pin-machine operator (furniture) 763.684-046
pin-machine tender (textile) 680.685-058
pinmaker (button & notion) 609.482-014
PIN MAKER (pottery & porc.) 575.686-018
pinner (cutlery-hrdwr.) 701.687-010
PINNER (garment; tex. prod., nec) 782.687-026
pinner (medical ser.) 712.687-014
Pinner (metal prod., nec) 706.684-090
PINNER (tex. prod., nec) 782.684-054
pinner, jewel bearing (clock & watch) 770.682-010
PINNER, PRINTED CIRCUIT BOARDS (electron. comp.) 699.685-046
PIN-OR-CLIP FASTENER (jewelry-silver.) 735.687-022
Pin Puller (smelt. & refin.) 630.684-010
PINSETTER ADJUSTER, AUTOMATIC (toy-sport equip.) 829.381-010
PINSETTER MECHANIC, AUTOMATIC (any industry) 638.261-022
PINSETTER-MECHANIC HELPER (any industry) 829.667-014
Pin Sorter And Bagger (laundry & rel.) 361.687-018
pin-tenter operator (textile) 580.685-066
Pin-Ticket-Machine Operator (any industry) 652.685-098
Pin Worker (laundry & rel.) 361.687-018
PIPE-AND-TANK FABRICATOR (wood. container) 669.380-018
Pipe-And-Test Supervisor (construction) 899.131-010
Pipe-Bending-Machine Operator (construction) 617.482-010
PIPE BUFFER (construction) 705.684-054
Pipe Caulker (construction) 869.664-014
PIPE CHANGER (mine & quarry) 891.564-010
PIPE-CLEANING-AND-PRIMING-MACHINE   OPERATOR   (construction) 862.662-010
Pipe-Cleaning-Machine Operator (construction) 862.662-010
Pipe Coater (steel & rel.) 740.684-022
PIPE COVERER AND INSULATOR (ship-boat mfg.) 863.381-014
PIPE CUTTER (construction) term
PIPE CUTTER (mfd. bldgs.) 862.682-010
Piped-Buttonhole-Machine Operator (garment) 786.685-022
PIPED-POCKET-MACHINE OPERATOR (garment) 786.685-022
PIPE FINISHER (brick & tile) 779.684-042
PIPE FITTER (construction) 862.281-022
PIPE FITTER (ship-boat mfg.) 862.261-010
pipe fitter (utilities) 862.361-014
Pipe Fitter, Ammonia (construction) 862.281-022
PIPE-FITTER APPRENTICE (construction) 862.281-026
PIPE FITTER, DIESEL ENGINE I (engine-turbine) 862.361-018
PIPE FITTER, DIESEL ENGINE II (engine-turbine) 862.381-022
Pipe Fitter, Fire-Sprinkler Systems (construction) 862.281-022
PIPE-FITTER HELPER (construction) 862.684-022
PIPE-FITTER HELPER (ship-boat mfg.) 862.684-018
Pipe Fitter, Gas Pipe (construction) 862.281-022
Pipe Fitter, Maintenance (any industry) 862.281-022
pipe fitter, marine (ship-boat mfg.) 862.261-010
Pipe Fitter, Plastic Pipe (construction) 862.281-022
Pipe Fitter, Soft Copper (construction) 862.281-022
Pipe Fitter, Street Service (utilities) 862.361-014
PIPE-FITTER SUPERVISOR (construction) 862.131-010
PIPE-FITTER SUPERVISOR (ship-boat mfg.) 862.131-014
Pipe-Fitter Supervisor, Maintenance (any industry) 862.131-010
Pipe Fitter, Welding (construction) 862.281-022
Pipe-Fittings Molder (brick & tile) 575.684-042
pipe inspector (construction) 862.687-010
pipe inspector (petrol. & gas) 930.267-010
PIPE INSTALLER (construction; utilities) 869.381-018
pipe jeeper (construction) 862.687-010
Pipe Layer (construction) 869.664-014
Pipe-Layer Helper (construction) 869.687-026
Pipe-Laying Supervisor (construction) 899.131-010
PIPE-LINE-CONSTRUCTION INSPECTOR (construction) 869.367-018
pipe-line gauger (petrol. & gas; petrol. refin.; pipe lines) 914.384-010
Pipe-Line Inspector (construction) 182.267-010
pipe-line maintenance supervisor (pipe lines) 869.134-018
PIPELINER (pipe lines) 899.684-026
Pipe-Line Superintendent, District (pipe lines) 184.167-198
Pipe-Line Superintendent, Division (pipe lines) 184.167-198
PIPE-LINE SUPERVISOR (construction) term
Pipe-Line Worker (construction) 869.664-014
Pipe-Machine Operator (construction) 869.687-026
PIPE-ORGAN BUILDER (musical inst.) 730.281-042
PIPE-ORGAN INSTALLER (musical inst.) 730.381-046
PIPE-ORGAN TUNER AND REPAIRER (any industry) 730.361-014
pipe processor (steel & rel.) 619.662-014
pipe puller (petrol. & gas) 930.382-030
piper (engine-turbine) 862.361-018
PIPE RACKER (fabrication, nec) 749.687-034
Pipe Racker (petrol. & gas) 930.684-026

PIPE-SMOKER-MACHINE OPERATOR (fabrication, nec) 739.687-150
pipe smoking machine operator (fabrication, nec) 563.686-018
pipe steamer (garment) 789.687-166
PIPE STEM ALIGNER (fabrication, nec) 739.687-210
PIPE STEM REPAIRER (fabrication, nec) 739.684-186
PIPE STRIPPER (concrete prod.) 575.687-026
PIPE TESTER (petrol. & gas) 930.382-014
PIPE THREADER, HAND (construction) term
Pipe-Threading-Machine Operator (machine shop) 604.682-014
pipe-thread inspector (petrol. & gas) 862.381-038
Pipe Washer (dairy products) 599.684-010
PIPE-WRAPPING-MACHINE OPERATOR (construction; pipe lines) 862.682-014
Piping Blocker (boot & shoe) 699.685-014
Piping-Cutting-Machine Operator (garment) 686.685-066
Pirn Winder (textile) 681.685-154
Piston-Cup Inspector (rubber goods) 759.684-074
PISTON MAKER (musical inst.) 730.681-014
pit boss (amuse. & rec.) 153.167-014
pit car repairer (mine & quarry) 622.381-030
PITCH FILLER (any industry) 619.687-018
Pitch Flaker (chemical) 559.685-074
Pitching Coach (amuse. & rec.) 153.227-010
PITCH WORKER (optical goods) 551.666-010
pit-furnace melter (foundry; steel & rel.) 512.362-018
pit inspector (railroad equip.) 622.281-010
PIT STEWARD (amuse. & rec.) 153.167-014
PIT SUPERVISOR (mine & quarry) 939.137-014
pit tanner (leather mfg.) 582.482-018
Pit-Worker, Power Shovel (any industry) 921.667-022
pivot-end polisher (clock & watch) 715.685-026
Pivot Polisher (clock & watch) 715.685-042
placement interviewer (profess. & kin.) 166.267-010
PLACER (insurance) 239.267-010
Placer Miner, Hydraulic (mine & quarry) 939.684-014
Placing Judge (amuse. & rec.) 153.267-014
plain-clothes officer (government ser.) 375.267-010
plain-goods hemmer (any industry) 787.682-026
plaiter (textile) 589.685-074
PLAN CHECKER (government ser.) 168.267-102
Planer-Chain Offbearer (saw. & plan.) 669.686-018
planer feeder (saw. & plan.) 665.686-014
Planer Feeder (woodworking) 669.686-030
Planer-Mill Grader (saw. & plan.) 669.687-030
Planer Offbearer (woodworking) 669.686-034
PLANER OPERATOR (elec. equip.) 675.682-014
planer operator (saw. & plan.) 665.482-018
PLANER OPERATOR (woodworking) 665.682-022
Planer Setter (woodworking) 669.280-010
PLANER SET-UP OPERATOR, TOOL (machine shop) 605.282-014
PLANER, STONE (stonework) 675.682-018
Planer-Type Milling-Machine Operator, Numerical Control (machine shop) 605.380-010
PLANER-TYPE-MILLING-MACHINE SET-UP OPERATOR (machine shop) 605.282-018
Planetarium Sky Show Technician (museums) 739.261-010
PLANETARIUM TECHNICIAN (museums) 962.261-010
PLANIMETER OPERATOR (government ser.) 219.387-022
PLANING-MACHINE OPERATOR (clock & watch) 605.685-034
planing-machine operator (stonework) 675.682-018
planing machine operator (woodworking) 665.682-022
PLANISHER (jewelry-silver.) 700.687-054
planishing-hammer operator (aircraft mfg.) 617.382-014
PLANISHING-PRESS OPERATOR (plastic-synth.) 690.682-058
planner, chief (profess. & kin.) 012.167-050
PLANNER, PROGRAM SERVICES (government ser.) 188.167-110
planning assistant (profess. & kin.) 199.364-010
planning-division superintendent (utilities) 184.167-210
planning engineer (profess. & kin.) 012.167-018
planning engineer (utilities) 003.167-026
PLANNING ENGINEER, CENTRAL OFFICE FACILITIES (tel. & tel.) 003.061-050
planning supervisor (profess. & kin.) 012.167-050
PLANT BREEDER (profess. & kin.) 041.061-082
PLANT-CARE WORKER (agriculture) 408.364-010
plant chief (tel. & tel.) 184.117-082
plant clerk (clerical) 221.382-018
Plant Cytologist (profess. & kin.) 041.061-042
Plant Ecologist (profess. & kin.) 041.061-038
PLANT ENGINEER (profess. & kin.) 007.167-014
PLANTER (agriculture) term
plant machinist (utilities) 631.261-010
plant-maintenance worker (any industry) 899.261-014
PLANT OPERATOR (concrete prod.; construction) 570.682-014
PLANT OPERATOR, CHANNEL PROCESS (chemical) 542.685-010

PLANT OPERATOR, FURNACE PROCESS (chemical) 559.362-026
plant-operator helper (chemical) 542.685-018
Plant Packer (agriculture) 920.687-134
PLANT PATHOLOGIST (profess. & kin.) 041.061-086
Plant Physiologist (profess. & kin.) 041.061-078
PLANT PROPAGATOR (agriculture) 405.361-010
Plant-Protection Supervisor (any industry) 372.167-014
plant superintendent (pipe lines) 914.132-010
plant superintendent, industrial organization (any industry) 189.117-022
plant supervisor (any industry) 183.117-014
PLANT SUPERVISOR (grain-feed mills) 529.132-014
plant supervisor (petrol. refin.) 542.130-010
Plant Taxonomist (profess. & kin.) 041.061-038
plant tender (agriculture) 408.364-010
plant tour guide (any industry) 353.367-018
Plant Wrapper (agriculture) 920.687-134
Plaque Maker (nonmet. min.) 779.684-046
Plasma-Cutting-Machine Operator (welding) 816.482-010
PLASMA ETCHER, PRINTED CIRCUIT BOARDS (electron. comp.) 590.685-094
Plaster-Block Layer (construction) 861.381-018
PLASTER-DIE MAKER (pottery & porc.) 774.684-026
PLASTERER (construction) 842.361-018
PLASTERER (furniture) 749.687-026
PLASTERER APPRENTICE (construction) 842.361-022
Plasterer, Finish (construction) 842.361-018
Plasterer Helper (construction) 869.687-026
Plasterer, Maintenance (construction) 842.361-018
PLASTERER, MOLDING (concrete prod.; construction) 842.361-026
plasterer, ornamental (concrete prod.; construction) 842.361-026
Plasterer, Rough (construction) 842.361-018
plasterer, spot (furniture) 749.687-026
Plasterer, Spray Gun (construction) 842.361-018
plasterer, stucco (construction) 842.381-014
PLASTER-MACHINE TENDER (construction) 842.665-010
PLASTER MAKER (nonmet. min.) 779.684-046
PLASTER MIXER, MACHINE (concrete prod.) 570.382-014
PLASTER MOLDER I (foundry) 777.381-034
PLASTER MOLDER II (foundry) 518.484-010
Plaster-of-Paris Molder (elec. equip.) 729.684-030
PLASTER-PATTERN CASTER (machine tools) 777.381-038
plaster whittler (hat & cap) 784.361-010
plastic ball buffer (toy-sport equip.) 690.685-038
PLASTIC-CARD GRADER, CARDROOM (amuse. & rec.) 343.687-010
PLASTIC-DESIGN APPLIER (boot & shoe) 690.686-046
PLASTIC DUPLICATOR (machine tools) 754.684-038
Plastic-Extruding-Machine Operator (nonfer. metal) 691.382-010
plastic-eye technician (optical goods) 713.261-014
PLASTIC-FIXTURE BUILDER (machine shop) 601.381-030
Plastic-Frame Inserter (optical goods) 713.681-010
plastic insert molder (boot & shoe) 788.687-094
plastic installer (foundry) 849.484-010
PLASTIC-JOINT MAKER (brick & tile) 590.687-014
plastic-machine folder (boot & shoe) 690.685-070
PLASTIC MOLDER (fabrication, nec) 779.684-050
Plastic Outfitter (ship-boat mfg.) 806.684-146
Plastic-Panel Installer (construction; retail trade) 863.684-014
Plastic Parts Fabricator (aircraft mfg.) 754.381-018
Plastic Parts Fabricator-Trimmer (aircraft mfg.) 754.684-042
plastic-press molder (plastic prod.) 556.685-022
PLASTIC ROLLER (plastic prod.) 690.685-498
plastics bench mechanic (aircraft mfg.; plastic prod.) 754.381-018
PLASTICS FABRICATOR (aircraft mfg.; plastic prod.) 754.381-018
plastics fabricator and assembler (aircraft mfg.; plastic prod.) 754.381-018
Plastic-Sheeting Cutter (plastic prod.) 699.682-026
Plastic-Sign Fabricator (plastic prod.) 754.381-018
Plastics Plater (plastic prod.) 500.380-010
PLASTICS REPAIRER (plastic prod.) 754.684-046
Plastics Rework And Repair Mechanic (aircraft mfg.) 754.381-018
PLASTICS-SEASONER OPERATOR (plastic-synth.) 553.665-042
plastics-sheet-finishing-press operator (plastic-synth.) 690.682-058
PLASTICS-SPREADING-MACHINE OPERATOR (plastic-synth.) 554.382-014
Plastic Surgeon (medical ser.) 070.101-094
PLASTICS WORKER (aircraft mfg.) 754.684-042
Plastic-Tile Layer (construction; retail trade) 861.381-034
PLASTIC TOOL MAKER (machine shop) 601.381-026
PLASTIC-TOP ASSEMBLER (furniture) 763.684-062
Plastic-Top Installer (furniture) 763.684-050
Plastic-Tubing-Insulation Supervisor (nonfer. metal) 691.130-010
plastic-welding-machine operator (any industry) 690.685-154
Plate-And-Frame-Filter Operator (any industry) 551.685-082
plate-and-weld inspector (any industry) 619.261-010
PLATE ASSEMBLER, SMALL BATTERY (elec. equip.) 727.684-026
Plate Boner (meat products) 525.684-010
plate colorer (print. & pub.) 970.681-030

PLATE CONDITIONER (steel & rel.) 819.664-010
Plate-Drying-Machine Tender (elec. equip.) 590.685-026
plate embosser (clerical) 208.582-014
plate embosser (clerical) 208.682-010
plate filler (ordnance) 737.685-014
plate fin assembler (svc. ind. mach.) 706.684-010
PLATE FINISHER (print. & pub.) 659.360-010
plate finisher, photoengraving (print. & pub.) 971.381-030
PLATE FORMER (elec. equip.) 500.684-018
PLATE GAUGER (print. & pub.) 979.687-018
Plate-Glass Installer (construction) 865.381-010
PLATE GRAINER (print. & pub.) 972.682-010
PLATE-GRAINER APPRENTICE (print. & pub.) 972.682-014
plate grouper, machine (elec. equip.) 692.382-014
Plate Inspector (clock & watch) 715.384-022
PLATE INSPECTOR (print. & pub.) 972.687-010
Plate Inspector (steel & rel.) 619.381-010
platemaker (print. & pub.) 972.381-010
PLATEMAKER, SEMICONDUCTOR PACKAGES (electron. comp.) 972.384-014
Plate Maker, Zinc (print. & pub.) 971.381-022
PLATE MOLDER (pen & pencil; print. & pub.) 556.582-010
plate mounter (paper goods) 659.684-010
PLATEN BUILDER-UP (print. & pub.) 651.384-010
platen-drier operator (millwork-plywood) 563.685-026
PLATEN GRINDER (office machines) 690.385-010
platen operator, metal bond (aircraft mfg.) 553.382-026
PLATEN-PRESS FEEDER (print. & pub.) 651.685-022
PLATEN-PRESS OPERATOR (paper goods) 649.682-026
PLATEN-PRESS OPERATOR (print. & pub.) 651.362-018
PLATEN-PRESS-OPERATOR APPRENTICE (print. & pub.) 651.362-022
plate preparer (print. & pub.) 972.682-010
plate printer (print. & pub.) 651.382-030
Plate-Put-in Worker (elec. equip.) 727.687-058
plater (agriculture) 418.381-010
PLATER (electroplating) 500.380-010
PLATER (inst. & app.) 500.684-034
plater (paper & pulp) 649.686-026
PLATER APPRENTICE (electroplating) 500.380-014
PLATER, BARREL (electroplating) 500.362-014
plater helper (any industry) 599.685-062
plater helper (electroplating) 500.686-010
PLATER, HOT DIP (galvanizing) 501.685-010
plater, machine (electroplating) 500.362-014
Plate Roller (any industry) 613.662-022
PLATER, PRINTED CIRCUIT BOARD PANELS (electron. comp.) 500.684-026
plater production (electroplating) 500.685-014
PLATER, SEMICONDUCTOR WAFERS AND COMPONENTS (electron. comp.) 500.684-030
plater supervisor (electroplating) 500.131-010
PLATE SETTER, FLEXOGRAPHIC PRESS (print. & pub.) 659.381-010
plate-shear operator (any industry) 615.682-018
plate-shop helper (any industry) 619.686-022
plate-shop inspector (any industry) 619.261-010
PLATE SLITTER-AND-INSPECTOR (elec. equip.) 727.685-010
PLATE STACKER, HAND (elec. equip.) 729.687-026
plate stacker, machine (any industry) 692.682-054
PLATE STACKER, MACHINE (elec. equip.) 692.382-014
PLATE-TAKE-OUT WORKER (elec. equip.) 500.687-010
Plate Washer (elec. equip.) 727.687-058
plate-worker helper (any industry) 801.687-014
PLATE WORKER (paper & pulp) 535.685-010
plate worker (plastic prod.) 690.682-062
PLATFORM ATTENDANT (food prep., nec) 299.377-010
platform beater (boot & shoe) 690.685-470
Platform Cementer (boot & shoe) 690.686-018
platform inspector (can. & preserv.; wholesale tr.) 529.387-018
Platform Loader (any industry) 929.687-030
Platform Presser (boot & shoe) 690.685-074
Platform Stapler (boot & shoe) 690.685-162
Platform Stitcher (boot & shoe) 690.682-078
Platform Supervisor (any industry) 922.137-018
platform-worker (glass mfg.) 575.687-010
platform worker (wood prod., nec) 561.665-010
plating-department helper (electroplating) 500.686-010
PLATING EQUIPMENT TENDER (electroplating) 500.685-014
plating inspector (amuse. & rec.) 153.287-010
PLATING-MACHINE OPERATOR (paper & pulp) 649.686-026
plating-press operator (leather mfg.; leather prod.) 690.682-030
Plating Stripper (electroplating) 500.380-010
Plating-Tank Cleaner (electron. comp.) 891.687-022
plating-tank-operator apprentice (electroplating) 500.380-014
plating-tank operator (electroplating) 500.380-010
Platinumsmith (jewelry-silver.) 700.281-010

playback operator (petrol. & gas) 194.382-010
Player-Manager (amuse. & rec.) 153.117-010
PLAYER-PIANO TECHNICIAN (musical inst.) 730.381-050
PLAYGROUND-EQUIPMENT ERECTOR (retail trade) 801.684-018
PLAYROOM ATTENDANT (any industry) 359.677-026
PLAYWRIGHT (profess. & kin.) 131.067-038
pleater (any industry) 787.682-082
PLEATER (tex. prod., nec) 787.685-026
PLEATER (textile) 589.685-074
PLEATER, HAND (tex. prod., nec) 583.684-010
PLEATING-MACHINE OPERATOR (any industry) 583.685-082
pleating-machine operator (knitting; textile) 589.685-086
PLEAT PATTERNMAKER (garment; tex. prod., nec) 781.484-010
Pleat Presser (laundry & rel.) 363.681-010
PLEAT TAPER (tex. prod., nec) 789.487-014
plier worker (jewelry-silver.) 735.687-014
Plisse-Machine Operator (textile) 652.382-010
Plisse-Machine Operator Helper (textile) 652.686-010
PLODDER OPERATOR (soap & rel.) 556.682-018
plodding-machine operator (soap & rel.) 556.682-018
plotter (motion picture) 962.361-010
PLOW-AND-BORING-MACHINE TENDER (saw. & plan.) 665.685-018
plow holder (construction) 850.663-014
plow shaker (construction) 850.663-014
plug-and-mold finisher (concrete prod.; ship-boat mfg.) 806.684-086
Plug Assembler (elec. equip.) 729.687-010
Plug Builder (ship-boat mfg.) 661.281-010
PLUG CUTTER (pen & pencil) 690.685-306
plug-cutter (tobacco) 529.685-182
plug-cutting-and-wrapping-machine operator (tobacco) 529.685-182
PLUG-CUTTING-MACHINE OPERATOR (tobacco) 529.685-182
plug-drill operator (mine & quarry) 930.684-018
PLUGGER (steel & rel.) 613.687-010
PLUGGER (wood. container) 764.687-098
PLUGGING-MACHINE OPERATOR (woodworking) 669.682-062
plug maker (plastic prod.) 754.381-014
plug-making operator (tobacco) 529.685-062
PLUG-OVERWRAP-MACHINE TENDER (tobacco) 529.685-186
PLUG SHAPER, HAND (tobacco) 520.687-050
PLUG SHAPER, MACHINE (tobacco) 520.686-034
PLUG SORTER (woodworking) 769.687-034
Plug Stitcher (boot & shoe) 690.682-078
PLUG WIRER (elec. equip.) 726.687-014
PLUMBER (construction) 862.381-030
PLUMBER (mfd. bldgs.) 862.681-010
PLUMBER APPRENTICE (construction) 862.381-034
Plumber Helper (construction) 869.664-014
Plumber, Maintenance (any industry) 862.381-030
plumber, pipe fitting (construction) 862.281-022
PLUMBER SUPERVISOR (construction) 862.131-018
Plumber Supervisor, Maintenance (construction) 862.131-018
PLUMBING ASSEMBLER-INSTALLER (mfd. bldgs.) 862.684-026
PLUMBING-HARDWARE ASSEMBLER (plumbing-heat.) 706.684-086
Plum Packer (agriculture; wholesale tr.) 920.687-134
Plunger-Machine Operator (paper goods) 649.685-042
PLUSH WEAVER (textile) 683.682-030
Plycor Operator (woodworking) 569.685-046
ply cutter (rubber tire) 690.682-022
ply splicer (rubber tire) 759.684-058
Plywood Builder (millwork-plywood) 762.687-026
Plywood Patcher (millwork-plywood) 769.684-030
PLYWOOD-SCARFER TENDER (millwork-plywood) 665.685-022
Plywood-Stock Grader (millwork-plywood) 569.687-034
Pneumatic-Drum Sander (woodworking) 761.682-014
PNEUMATIC-HOIST OPERATOR (construction; mfd. bldgs.) 921.663-046
PNEUMATIC JACKETER (nonfer. metal) 691.667-010
PNEUMATIC-JACK OPERATOR (petrol. & gas) 939.667-010
pneumatic-press operator (any industry)   see AIR-PRESS OPERATOR
pneumatic-systems operator (food prep., nec) 921.382-010
Pneumatic Tester (any industry) 862.687-018
pneumatic-tool operator (construction)   see AIR-TOOL OPERATOR
PNEUMATIC-TOOL OPERATOR (ship-boat mfg.) 809.381-030
PNEUMATIC-TOOL REPAIRER (any industry) 630.281-010
Pneumatic-Tube Fitter (construction) 862.281-022
pneumatic-tube operator (clerical) 239.687-014
PNEUMATIC-TUBE REPAIRER (any industry) 630.281-014
POACHER OPERATOR (chemical) 551.685-106
Poacher-Wringer Operator (chemical) 551.685-162
Pocket-And-Pulley-Machine Operator (saw. & plan.) 667.482-014
Pocket Assembler (toy-sport equip.) 732.384-010
Pocketbook Framer (leather prod.) 739.684-090
pocket builder (rubber tire) 750.684-010
Pocket Creaser (garment; knitting) 583.685-042
POCKET CUTTER (saw. & plan.) 667.482-014
POCKETED-SPRING ASSEMBLER (furniture) 780.684-090

pocketed-spring-machine operator (furniture) 616.685-050
Pocket-Flap-Creasing-Machine Operator (garment) 583.685-042
Pocket-Grinder Operator (paper & pulp) 530.662-014
POCKET-MACHINE OPERATOR (furniture) 616.685-050
pocket maker (garment) 786.682-210
Pocket Marker (garment) 781.687-042
Pocket Presser (garment) 363.684-018
Pocket-Secretary Assembler (leather prod.) 783.684-010
POCKET SETTER, LOCKSTITCH (garment) 786.682-210
PODIATRIC ASSISTANT (medical ser.) 079.374-018
Podiatric Surgeon (medical ser.) 079.101-022
PODIATRIST (medical ser.) 079.101-022
Podiatrist, Orthopedic (medical ser.) 079.101-022
Podopediatrician (medical ser.) 079.101-022
POET (profess. & kin.) 131.067-042
Pointer, Caulker, And Cleaner (construction) 869.664-014
POINTING-MACHINE OPERATOR (plastic prod.; rubber goods) 690.685-310
poiser, balance (clock & watch) 715.681-010
poker-in (steel & rel.) 512.683-010
polarity tester (elec. equip.) 727.687-054
pole classifier (wood prod., nec) 561.587-010
POLE FRAMER (utilities; wood prod., nec) 959.684-010
Pole Framer, Machine (wood prod., nec) 669.662-014
Pole-Incisor Operator (wood prod., nec) 569.662-010
POLE INSPECTOR (utilities) 869.387-010
POLE INSPECTOR (wood prod., nec) 561.587-010
pole peeler (saw. & plan.; wood prod., nec) 663.682-014
pole-peeler helper (wood prod., nec) 665.686-010
POLE-PEELING-MACHINE OPERATOR (saw. & plan.; wood prod., nec) 663.682-014
POLE-PEELING-MACHINE-OPERATOR HELPER (wood prod., nec) 665.686-010
poler (millwork-plywood; paper & pulp; saw. & plan.) 921.686-022
Pole-Sander Operator (woodworking) 662.685-014
pole setter (utilities) 821.687-010
pole shaver (saw. & plan.; wood prod., nec) 663.682-014
pole-shaver helper (wood prod., nec) 665.686-010
pole tester (utilities) 869.387-010
Pole-Truck Driver (construction; tel. & tel.; utilities) 904.383-010
POLEYARD SUPERVISOR (utilities) 929.137-014
POLICE-ACADEMY INSTRUCTOR (government ser.) 375.227-010
POLICE ACADEMY PROGRAM COORDINATOR (government ser.) 375.167-054
POLICE AIDE (government ser.) 243.362-014
POLICE ARTIST (government ser.) 141.061-034
POLICE CAPTAIN, PRECINCT (government ser.) 375.167-034
police captain, senior (government ser.) 375.267-026
police chemist (profess. & kin.) 029.261-026
POLICE CHIEF (government ser.) 375.117-010
Police Chief, Deputy (government ser.) 375.267-026
POLICE CLERK (government ser.) 375.362-010
POLICE COMMISSIONER I (government ser.) 188.117-118
Police Commissioner II (government ser.) 375.117-010
police-department secretary (government ser.) 375.137-022
police inspector, chief (government ser.) 375.117-010
POLICE INSPECTOR I (government ser.) 375.267-026
POLICE INSPECTOR II (government ser.) 375.267-030
police judge (government ser.) 111.107-014
police justice (government ser.) 111.107-014
POLICE LIEUTENANT, COMMUNITY RELATIONS (government ser.) 375.137-018
POLICE LIEUTENANT, PATROL (government ser.) 375.167-038
Police Lieutenant, Precinct (government ser.) 375.167-034
police magistrate (government ser.) 111.107-014
POLICE OFFICER, BOOKING (government ser.) 375.367-018
POLICE OFFICER, CRIME PREVENTION (government ser.) 375.264-010
POLICE OFFICER, IDENTIFICATION AND RECORDS (government ser.) 375.384-010
POLICE OFFICER I (government ser.) 375.263-014
POLICE OFFICER II (government ser.) 375.367-010
POLICE OFFICER III (government ser.) 375.267-038
POLICE OFFICER, SAFETY INSTRUCTION (government ser.) 375.267-042
police radio dispatcher (government ser.) 379.362-010
POLICE SERGEANT, PRECINCT I (government ser.) 375.133-010
Police Sergeant, Precinct II (government ser.) 375.167-034
Police Sergeant, Radio Patrol (government ser.) 375.133-010
Police Stenographer (government ser.) 202.362-014
POLICE SURGEON (government ser.) 070.101-082
policy-cancellation clerk (insurance) 203.382-014
POLICY-CHANGE CLERK (insurance) 219.362-042
Policy Checker (insurance) 219.482-014
POLICYHOLDER-INFORMATION CLERK (insurance) 249.262-010
Policy-Issue Clerk (insurance) 203.362-010
policy-issue supervisor (insurance) 219.132-022
Policy-Loan Calculator (insurance) 216.382-050

policy rater (insurance) 214.482-022
POLICY-VALUE CALCULATOR (insurance) 216.382-050
Policy Writer (insurance) 203.582-066
POLISHER (any industry) 705.684-058
polisher (boot & shoe) 690.685-046
polisher (boot & shoe) 690.685-058
POLISHER (button & notion) 599.685-078
POLISHER (clock & watch) 715.682-018
polisher (fabrication, nec) 739.684-026
POLISHER (glass mfg.; glass products) 775.684-058
POLISHER (jewelry-silver.) 700.687-058
polisher (sugar & conf.) 524.382-010
POLISHER (woodworking) 761.684-026
Polisher, Aluminum (any industry) 705.684-058
Polisher And Buffer I (any industry) 705.684-014
POLISHER AND BUFFER II (any industry) 705.684-062
polisher and sander (wood prod., nec) 662.685-026
POLISHER APPRENTICE (any industry) 705.684-066
POLISHER, BALANCE SCREWHEAD (clock & watch) 715.685-046
Polisher, Brass (any industry) 705.684-058
Polisher, Bronze (any industry) 705.684-058
POLISHER, DIAL (clock & watch) 715.684-170
POLISHER, EYEGLASS FRAMES (optical goods) 713.684-038
polisher, hand (stonework) 775.664-010
POLISHER, IMPLANT (optical goods) 713.687-034
Polisher, Numeral (clock & watch) 715.684-170
POLISHER, SAND (jewelry-silver.) 705.684-070
Polisher, Zinc (any industry) 705.684-058
POLISHING-MACHINE OPERATOR (any industry) 603.682-026
polishing-machine operator (stonework) 673.382-018
POLISHING-MACHINE-OPERATOR HELPER (any industry) 603.686-010
polishing-machine operator, semiautomatic (jewelry-silver.) 603.682-022
POLISHING MACHINE TENDER (electron. comp.) 673.685-094
POLISHING-PAD MOUNTER (optical goods) 739.687-154
polishing-wheel repairer (any industry) 739.684-030
POLISHING-WHEEL SETTER (any industry) 776.684-014
Political Officer (government ser.) 188.117-106
POLITICAL SCIENTIST (profess. & kin.) 051.067-010
poll clerk (government ser.) 205.367-030
POLLUTION-CONTROL ENGINEER (profess. & kin.) 019.081-018
POLLUTION-CONTROL TECHNICIAN (profess. & kin.) 029.261-014
poly-area supervisor (plastic-synth.) 559.132-042
Polyethylene-Bag-Machine Operator (paper goods) 649.685-014
Polyethylene Combiner (paper goods) 534.682-026
POLYGRAPH EXAMINER (profess. & kin.) 199.267-026
POLYMERIZATION HELPER (plastic-synth.) 558.585-038
POLYMERIZATION-KETTLE OPERATOR (plastic-synth.) 558.382-050
POLYMERIZATION OPERATOR (chemical; plastic-synth.) term
POLYMERIZATION-OVEN OPERATOR (plastic-synth.) 556.585-014
Polymerization Supervisor (plastic-synth.) 559.132-042
Polymer Operator (plastic-synth.) 559.382-018
POLY-PACKER AND HEAT-SEALER (protective dev.) 920.686-038
POLYSILICON PREPARATION WORKER (electron. comp.) 590.684-038
POLYSOMNOGRAPHIC TECHNICIAN (medical ser.) 078.362-042
polysomnographic technologist (medical ser.) 078.362-042
POLYSTYRENE-BEAD MOLDER (plastic prod.) 556.382-018
POLYSTYRENE-MOLDING-MACHINE TENDER (plastic prod.) 556.685-062
POMPOM MAKER (knitting) 789.687-126
pondsaw operator (paper & pulp; saw. & plan.) 667.685-034
Pond Scaler (paper & pulp; saw. & plan.) 455.487-010
POND TENDER (chemical) 939.685-010
POND WORKER (millwork-plywood; paper & pulp; saw. & plan.) 921.686-022
Pony-Cylinder-Press Feeder (print. & pub.) 651.686-010
Pony-Cylinder-Press Operator (print. & pub.) 651.362-010
PONY EDGER (saw. & plan.) 667.682-050
Pony-Ride Attendant (amuse. & rec.) 349.674-010
Pony-Roll Finisher (paper & pulp) 920.685-090
pony winder (paper goods) 640.685-058
Pool-Hall Inspector (government ser.) 375.263-014
pooling operator (medical ser.; pharmaceut.) 599.687-026
poolroom attendant (amuse. & rec.) 340.477-010
pool servicer (any industry) 891.684-018
POPCORN-CANDY MAKER (sugar & conf.) 526.685-042
popcorn maker (sugar & conf.) 526.685-026
popped-corn oven attendant (sugar & conf.) 526.685-026
porcelain-buildup assistant (protective dev.) 712.684-030
PORCELAIN-ENAMELING SUPERVISOR (any industry) 590.131-010
Porcelain-Enamel Installer (construction; retail trade) 863.684-014
PORCELAIN-ENAMEL LABORER (any industry) 509.687-014
PORCELAIN-ENAMEL REPAIRER (any industry) 741.684-030
Porcelain-Enamel Sprayer (any industry) 741.684-026
porcelain finisher (protective dev.) 712.664-010
Porcelain Slusher (any industry) 599.685-026
porcelain waxer (protective dev.) 712.664-010

portable grinder operator (any industry) 705.684-030
Portable Grout-Mixer Operator (concrete prod.; construction) 869.687-026
PORTABLE SAWYER (railroad equip.) 899.684-030
Port Captain (water trans.) 184.167-182
port drier (textile) 581.685-026
PORT ENGINEER (ship-boat mfg.; water trans.) 014.167-014
PORTER (air trans.; motor trans.; r.r. trans.) 357.677-010
porter (any industry) 381.687-014
porter, baggage (air trans.; motor trans.; r.r. trans.) 357.677-010
PORTER, BAGGAGE (hotel & rest.) 324.477-010
porter, bath (personal ser.) 335.677-014
porter, head (any industry) 381.137-010
Porter, Lobby (hotel & rest.) 323.687-018
porter, luggage (hotel & rest.) 324.477-010
PORTER, MARINA (water trans.) 329.677-010
porter, pullman (r.r. trans.) 351.677-010
PORTER, SAMPLE CASE (wholesale tr.) 299.687-010
PORTER, USED-CAR LOT (retail trade; wholesale tr.) 915.687-022
portfolio administrator (financial; insurance) 186.167-054
PORT PURSER (water trans.) 166.167-038
portrait photographer apprentice (profess. & kin.) 143.062-018
PORT-TRAFFIC MANAGER (water trans.) 184.167-122
port warden (government ser.) 375.167-026
Position Classifier (government ser.) 166.267-018
position clerk (financial) 210.367-014
Positive Developer (motion picture; photofinishing) 976.382-018
positive printer operator (motion picture) 976.682-010
postage-machine operator (clerical) 208.685-026
postal clerk (clerical) 209.687-026
postal clerk (government ser.) 243.367-014
Postal Inspector (government ser.) 168.267-062
Postbed Stitcher (boot & shoe) 690.682-082
Post-Form Remover (elec. equip.) 727.687-070
post-hole digger (construction; utilities) 859.682-010
POSTMASTER (government ser.) 188.167-066
POST-OFFICE CLERK (government ser.) 243.367-014
post-office supervisor (government ser.) 243.137-010
Post-Wave Assembler (electron. comp.) 726.684-070
Pot Annealer (heat treating) 504.682-010
Potash Flaker (chemical) 559.685-074
potato-chip cooker machine (food prep., nec) 526.685-046
POTATO-CHIP FRIER (food prep., nec) 526.685-046
POTATO-CHIP-PROCESSING SUPERVISOR (food prep., nec) 526.137-010
POTATO-CHIP SORTER (food prep., nec) 526.687-010
Potato Grader (agriculture; wholesale tr.) 529.687-186
POTATO-PANCAKE FRIER (food prep., nec) 526.685-050
POTATO-PEELING-MACHINE OPERATOR (food prep., nec) 521.685-250
potato-seed cutter (agriculture) 404.686-010
Potato Sorter (agriculture; wholesale tr.) 529.687-186
potato spotter (food prep., nec) 521.687-094
POT BUILDER (chemical) 826.684-022
Potdevin Cementer, Machine (boot & shoe) 690.686-018
POT FIRER (chemical) 553.582-014
Pot-Holder Binder (tex. prod., nec) 787.682-010
POTLINE MONITOR (smelt. & refin.) 512.467-010
POT LINER (smelt. & refin.) 519.664-014
POT-LINING SUPERVISOR (smelt. & refin.) 519.134-010
Pot Maker (brick & tile) 575.684-042
pot maker (pottery & porc.) 774.381-010
pot maker (pottery & porc.) 774.382-010
pot-press operator (pottery & porc.) 575.685-034
pot puncher (smelt. & refin.) 512.685-018
POT-ROOM SUPERVISOR (smelt. & refin.) 512.135-010
pot runner (galvanizing) 501.685-010
POT TENDER (smelt. & refin.) 512.685-018
Potter (electron. comp.) 726.687-022
Potter (pottery & porc.) 774.382-010
POTTERY-MACHINE OPERATOR (pottery & porc.) 774.382-010
Pottery Striper (pottery & porc.) 741.687-022
Pouch-Making-Machine Operator (tobacco) 920.685-098
POULTICE-MACHINE OPERATOR (pharmaceut.) 692.685-134
poultry-and-fish butcher (hotel & rest.) 316.684-010
POULTRY BONER (meat products) 525.687-066
POULTRY BREEDER (agriculture) 411.161-014
poultry culler (agriculture) 411.687-010
POULTRY DEBEAKER (agriculture) 411.687-026
POULTRY DRESSER (agriculture; meat products) 525.687-070
POULTRY-DRESSING WORKER (meat products) 525.687-082
POULTRY EVISCERATOR (meat products) 525.687-074
POULTRY FARMER (agriculture) 411.161-018
Poultry Farmer, Egg (agriculture) 411.161-018
Poultry Farmer, Meat (agriculture) 411.161-018
Poultry-Feed-Mixer Operator (grain-feed mills) 520.685-098
Poultry Feed Supervisor (grain-feed mills) 529.132-054
POULTRY HANGER (meat products) 525.687-078

poultry helper (agriculture) 411.584-010
POULTRY INSEMINATOR (agriculture) 411.384-010
POULTRY KILLER (meat products) 525.684-042
Poultry Picker (meat products) 525.687-070
POULTRY-PICKING MACHINE TENDER (meat products) 525.685-026
Poultry Scalder (meat products) 525.687-070
POULTRY SCIENTIST (profess. & kin.) 040.061-042
Poultry Specialist Supervisor (government ser.) 168.167-090
POULTRY TENDER (agriculture) 411.364-014
POULTRY VACCINATOR (agriculture) 411.684-014
pouncer (hat & cap) 784.687-018
pouncer (hat & cap) 585.685-074
pouncer, machine (hat & cap) 585.685-074
POUNCING-LATHE OPERATOR (hat & cap) 585.685-074
pouncing-machine operator (hat & cap) 585.685-074
pouncing-machine operator (hat & cap) 585.685-058
POUNDER (boot & shoe) 690.685-314
POURED-CONCRETE-WALL TECHNICIAN (construction) 869.261-018
poured-pipe maker (concrete prod.) 779.684-014
POURER (fabrication, nec) 739.687-158
pourer (leather mfg.) 584.687-010
pourer (leather mfg.) 584.687-014
pourer (plastic prod.) 754.684-022
pourer (pottery & porc.) 575.684-014
POURER (rubber goods) 556.687-026
pourer (smelt. & refin.) 514.682-010
Pourer, Buggy Ladle (foundry) 514.684-022
Pourer, Bull Ladle (foundry) 514.684-022
Pourer, Crane Ladle (foundry) 514.684-022
Pourer, Crucible (foundry) 514.684-022
POURER, METAL (foundry) 514.684-022
powder-actuated-tool operator (construction)   STUD-DRIVER OPERATOR
POWDER-AND-PRIMER-CANNING LEADER (ordnance) 737.137-014
POWDER BLENDER AND POURER (chemical) 550.485-022
powder carrier (any industry) 859.687-010
Powder Compounder (pharmaceut.) 550.685-090
POWDER-CUTTING OPERATOR (chemical) 559.685-134
Powdered-Sugar-Pulverizer Operator (sugar & conf.) 521.585-018
POWDERER (hat & cap) 784.687-058
Powder Gilder (wood prod., nec) 763.381-010
Powder Guard (construction) 372.667-034
POWDER-LINE REPAIRER (chemical) 629.261-018
POWDER LOADER (mine & quarry) 931.667-010
POWDER-MILL OPERATOR (sugar & conf.) 521.585-018
Powder Mixer (chemical) 550.685-090
powder monkey (clerical) 222.367-038
powder nipper (clerical) 222.367-038
powder operator (can. & preserv.; dairy products) 523.682-022
powder-press operator (chemical) 556.685-014
powder-press operator (chemical) 557.682-010
powder shoveler (chemical) 692.686-038
POWDER-TRUCK DRIVER (ordnance) 903.683-014
Powder Trucker (chemical; ordnance) 929.687-030
POWDER WORKER, TNT (ordnance) 737.684-030
POWER-BARKER OPERATOR (paper & pulp; saw. & plan.) 669.485-010
power-brake operator (any industry) 617.360-010
POWER-CHISEL OPERATOR (cutlery-hrdwr.) 701.687-030
power-cleaner operator (any industry) 389.683-010
power-cutting-machine operator (tex. prod., nec) 686.682-018
power dispatcher (utilities) 952.167-014
POWER-DISTRIBUTION ENGINEER (utilities) 003.167-046
POWER-DRIVEN-BRUSH MAKER (fabrication, nec) 692.682-050
POWERED BRIDGE SPECIALIST (military ser.) 378.683-014
power engineer (utilities) 952.382-018
power engineer (utilities) 003.167-018
power equipment mechanic (government ser.) 620.281-014
power-grader operator (construction) 850.663-022
power-hammer operator (aircraft mfg.) 617.382-014
Power-Hammer Operator (boot & shoe) 690.685-350
power hammer repairer (forging) 626.261-010
powerhouse attendant (chemical) 952.362-038
powerhouse engineer (utilities) 952.382-018
POWERHOUSE HELPER (chemical) 550.685-098
POWERHOUSE MECHANIC (utilities) 631.261-014
POWERHOUSE-MECHANIC APPRENTICE (utilities) 631.261-018
POWERHOUSE-MECHANIC HELPER (utilities) 631.684-010
POWERHOUSE-MECHANIC SUPERVISOR (utilities) 631.131-010
powerhouse oiler (any industry) 950.685-014
power-line inspector (utilities) 821.367-010
power-nut-runner operator (any industry) 699.685-026
POWER OPERATOR (tel. & tel.) 952.382-014
power-panel assembler (elec. equip.) 721.381-014
power-plant assistant (utilities) 952.367-014
power-plant engineer (utilities) 952.382-018
power-plant operator (any industry) 950.382-026

POWER-PLANT OPERATOR (utilities) 952.382-018
power-plant-operator apprentice (any industry) 950.382-030
power-press operator (any industry) 699.682-022
POWER-PRESS OPERATOR (any industry) term
power-press supervisor (jewelry-silver.) 615.130-010
POWER-PRESS TENDER (any industry) 617.685-026
POWER-REACTOR OPERATOR (utilities) 952.362-022
POWER-SAW MECHANIC (any industry) 625.281-030
power-saw operator (machine shop) 607.682-010
power-saw operator (wood. container) 667.662-014
powersaw supervisor (logging) 454.134-010
POWER-SCREWDRIVER OPERATOR (any industry) 699.685-026
power-shear operator (any industry) 615.682-018
power-shear operator (any industry) 615.685-034
POWER-SHOVEL OPERATOR (any industry) 850.683-030
Power-Shovel-Operator Helper (any industry) 921.667-022
Power-Sweeper Operator (any industry) 919.683-022
power-switchboard operator (utilities) 952.362-026
Power-Tool Assembler (house. appl.) 723.684-010
power-tool repairer (any industry) 729.281-022
Power-Transformer Assembler (elec. equip.) 820.381-014
POWER-TRANSFORMER REPAIRER (utilities) 821.361-034
Power-Transformer-Repair Supervisor (utilities) 829.131-014
POWER-TRANSMISSION ENGINEER (utilities) 003.167-050
power washer (any industry) 503.685-030
preacher (profess. & kin.) 120.107-010
PREASSEMBLER AND INSPECTOR (musical inst.) 730.684-058
PREASSEMBLER, PRINTED CIRCUIT BOARD (electron. comp.) 726.687-038
Preboarder (knitting) 589.685-010
PRECAST MOLDER (concrete prod.) 579.685-042
precast worker (concrete prod.) 579.685-042
precinct captain (government ser.) 375.167-034
PRECIPITATE WASHER (chemical) 551.685-110
Precipitation Equipment Tender (chemical) 558.685-062
PRECIPITATOR I (smelt. & refin.) 511.685-038
PRECIPITATOR II (smelt. & refin.) 511.685-042
Precipitator Operator (chemical) 558.682-014
PRECIPITATOR OPERATOR (smelt. & refin.) term
PRECIPITATOR SUPERVISOR (smelt. & refin.; steel & rel.) 511.132-010
PRECISE WINDER (textile) 681.685-066
PRECISION ASSEMBLER (aircraft mfg.) 806.381-082
PRECISION ASSEMBLER, BENCH (aircraft mfg.) 706.381-050
precision filer, hand (machine shop) 705.484-010
precision grinder (machine shop) 603.280-018
precision grinder (machine shop) 603.280-022
precision grinder, external (machine shop) 603.280-010
precision grinder, surface (machine shop) 603.280-014
precision grinder, universal (machine shop) 603.280-030
precision-honing-machine operator (machine shop) 603.382-022
precision inspector (machine shop) 601.281-022
precision-instrument and tool maker (any industry) 600.280-010
precision jig grinder (machine shop) 603.280-026
precision lap hand (machine shop) 705.481-014
precision-lathe operator (machine shop) 604.280-010
PRECISION-LENS CENTERER AND EDGER (optical goods) 716.462-010
PRECISION-LENS GENERATOR (optical goods) 716.682-014
PRECISION-LENS GRINDER (optical goods) 716.382-018
PRECISION-LENS-GRINDER APPRENTICE (optical goods) 716.382-022
PRECISION-LENS POLISHER (optical goods) 716.682-018
precision lens technician (optical goods) 716.280-018
precision-mechanical-instrument maker (any industry) 600.280-010
precision-mechanical-instrument-maker apprentice (any industry) 600.280-018
PRECISION-OPTICAL WORKER (optical goods) term
precision-thread-grinder operator (machine shop) 603.260-010
PREDATORY-ANIMAL HUNTER (fishing & hunt.) 461.661-010
prefitter (furniture) 763.684-026
PREFITTER, DOORS (woodworking) 666.582-010
preformer, impregnated fabrics (plastic prod.) 754.684-050
Preforming-Machine Operator (electron. comp.) 590.684-014
PREFORM-MACHINE OPERATOR (button & notion) 556.380-014
preform-machine operator (plastic prod.; plastic-synth.) 556.685-058
PREFORM PLATE MAKER (ship-boat mfg.) 751.684-026
prehemmer (tex. prod., nec) 781.684-034
Preliminary-Block-Press Operator (chemical) 556.685-014
premium-cancellation clerk (insurance) 203.382-014
premium-card-cancellation clerk (insurance) 203.382-014
Premium-Note Interest-Calculator Clerk (insurance) 216.482-022
Premix Operator, Concentrate (grain-feed mills) 523.685-022
preparation center coordinator (hotel & rest.) 313.131-018
Preparation-Plant Repairer (mine & quarry) 630.281-022
PREPARATION-ROOM WORKER (nonmet. min.) 570.686-018
PREPARATION SUPERVISOR (can. & preserv.) 529.137-010
Preparation Supervisor, Canning (can. & preserv.) 529.137-010
Preparation Supervisor, Freezing (can. & preserv.) 529.137-010

PREPARER (jewelry-silver.) 700.687-062
preparer (leather mfg.) 585.684-010
PREPARER, MAKING DEPARTMENT (jewelry-silver.) 700.684-058
PREPARER, SAMPLES AND REPAIRS (jewelry-silver.) 700.684-062
PREPAROLE-COUNSELING AIDE (government ser.) 195.367-026
PREPLEATER (tex. prod., nec) 686.685-046
Prescription Clerk, Frames (optical goods) 222.367-050
PRESCRIPTION CLERK, LENS-AND-FRAMES (optical goods) 222.367-050
Prescription Clerk, Lenses (optical goods) 222.367-050
PRESERVATION INSPECTOR, MARINE EQUIPMENT (government ser.) 929.367-010
preservationist (profess. & kin.) 055.381-010
PRESERVATIVE FILLER, MACHINE (can. & preserv.) 529.685-190
presetter operator (textile) 587.685-018
PRESIDENT (any industry) 189.117-026
President, Business School (education) 090.117-034
President, College Or University (education) 090.117-034
President, Commercial Bank (financial) 186.117-054
President, Credit Union (financial) 186.117-054
PRESIDENT, EDUCATIONAL INSTITUTION (education) 090.117-034
President, Finance Company (financial) 186.117-054
PRESIDENT, FINANCIAL INSTITUTION (financial) 186.117-054
President, Mortgage Company (financial) 186.117-054
President, Savings Bank (financial) 186.117-054
President, Trust Company (financial) 186.117-054
press-and-blow-machine tender (glass mfg.) 575.685-038
PRESS-BOX CUSTODIAN (amuse. & rec.) 344.677-010
press-brake operator (any industry) 619.685-026
press-brake operator (any industry) 617.360-010
PRESS BREAKER (wood prod., nec) 569.686-050
PRESS BUCKER (any industry) 920.686-042
presser (boot & shoe) 788.684-130
PRESSER (glass mfg.) 575.685-074
presser (hat & cap) 580.685-038
presser (hat & cap) 584.685-026
PRESSER (print. & pub.) 977.684-018
PRESSER (rubber goods) 690.685-318
PRESSER (soap & rel.) 559.685-142
PRESSER, ALL-AROUND (laundry & rel.) 363.682-014
presser-and-blocker, knitted goods (laundry & rel.) 363.684-010
presser-and-shaper, knitted goods (laundry & rel.) 363.684-010
PRESSER, AUTOMATIC (laundry & rel.) 363.685-014
PRESSER, BUFFING WHEEL (tex. prod., nec) 583.685-090
presser, cotton ginning (agriculture) 920.685-114
Presser, First (hat & cap) 583.685-110
PRESSER, FORM (any industry) 363.685-018
PRESSER, HAND (any industry) 363.684-018
PRESSER, HANDKERCHIEF (laundry & rel.) 363.685-022
presser, leather garments (laundry & rel.) 363.682-010
PRESSER, MACHINE (any industry) 363.682-018
Presser, Second (hat & cap) 583.685-110
PRESS FEEDER (knitting; textile) 583.686-030
PRESS FEEDER (print. & pub.) term
PRESS FEEDER (tinware) 652.685-058
PRESS FEEDER, BROOMCORN (agriculture) 429.686-010
press hand (forging) 611.685-010
PRESS HAND (knitting) 583.687-010
PRESS-HAND SUPERVISOR (jewelry-silver.) 615.130-010
press helper (forging) 619.686-034
PRESS HELPER (plastic prod.) 651.586-010
pressing-machine operator (any industry) 363.685-018
pressing machine operator (any industry) 363.682-018
pressing machine operator (knitting) 583.685-070
PRESS MACHINE FEEDER (tobacco) 529.686-066
PRESS-MACHINE OPERATOR (fabrication, nec) 590.665-014
PRESS OFFBEARER (brick & tile) 579.686-030
press operator (any industry) 920.685-010
Press Operator (beverage) 521.685-118
PRESS OPERATOR (brick & tile) 575.682-018
press operator (chemical) 556.685-078
press operator (forging) 611.685-010
PRESS OPERATOR (laundry & rel.) 363.685-010
Press Operator (meat products) 529.685-202
PRESS OPERATOR (mine & quarry) 575.685-070
press operator (nonfer. metal) 691.382-014
PRESS OPERATOR (oils & grease) 551.685-114
PRESS OPERATOR (plastic prod.) 690.682-062
press operator (plastic-synth.) 690.682-058
press operator (pottery & porc.) 575.685-026
press operator (print. & pub.) 651.362-010
PRESS OPERATOR (print. & pub.) term
PRESS OPERATOR (protective dev.) 686.685-050
PRESS OPERATOR (rubber reclaim.) 559.685-138
PRESS OPERATOR (textile) 583.685-086
press operator, automatic (laundry & rel.) 363.685-014

press operator, automatic (tobacco) 920.685-082
PRESS OPERATOR, CARBON BLOCKS (smelt. & refin.) 514.682-014
Press Operator, Carbon Products (elec. equip.) 556.682-014
press operator, carcass (toy-sport equip.) 732.687-054
PRESS OPERATOR, HARDBOARD (wood prod., nec) 569.682-014
PRESS OPERATOR, HEAVY DUTY (any industry) 617.260-010
PRESS OPERATOR I (chemical) 559.665-030
PRESS OPERATOR II (chemical) 551.685-118
press operator, instant print shop (print. & pub.) 979.362-010
PRESS OPERATOR, MEAT (meat products) 520.685-182
Press Operator, Paraffin Plant (petrol. refin.) 541.682-010
PRESS OPERATOR, PIERCE AND SHAVE (clock & watch) 715.685-050
press operator, wax ball (toy-sport equip.) 732.687-058
PRESS-PIPE INSPECTOR (brick & tile) 575.687-030
press-plate maker (print. & pub.) 972.381-026
PRESS PULLER (grain-feed mills) 529.687-170
press reader (business ser.) 249.387-022
PRESSROOM WORKER, FAT (oils & grease) 559.685-146
press-service reader (business ser.) 249.387-022
PRESS SETTER (nonfer. metal; steel & rel.) 617.480-014
Press Smith (forging) 612.361-010
Press-Smith Helper (forging) 612.687-014
PRESS SUPERVISOR (brick & tile) 575.130-010
PRESS TENDER (food prep., nec) 520.685-186
press tender (print. & pub.) 651.686-018
PRESS TENDER (rubber goods; rubber tire; toy-sport equip.) 556.685-066
Press Tender, Head, Feed House (grain-feed mills) 521.665-018
Press Tender, Incendiary Grenade (chemical) 694.685-038
Press Tender, Long Goods (food prep., nec) 520.685-186
PRESS TENDER, PYROTECHNICS (chemical) 694.685-038
Press Tender, Short Goods (food prep., nec) 520.685-186
Press Tender, Smoke Signal (chemical) 694.685-038
Press Tender, Star Signal (chemical) 694.685-038
PRESSURE CONTROLLER (utilities) 953.362-018
pressure-control supervisor (utilities) 953.137-014
PRESSURE SEALER-AND-TESTER (aircraft mfg.) 806.384-038
PRESSURE SUPERVISOR (utilities) 953.137-014
PRESSURE-TANK OPERATOR (chemical) 523.385-010
PRESSURE-TEST OPERATOR (ordnance) 737.387-018
Pressurization Mechanic (aircraft mfg.) 806.384-038
Pressurization Mechanic, Air Controls (aircraft mfg.) 806.384-038
Pressurizer (aircraft mfg.) 806.384-038
PRETZEL COOKER (bakery products) 526.685-054
Pretzel-Dough Mixer (bakery products) 520.685-234
Pretzel-Stick-Machine Operator (bakery products) 520.685-190
PRETZEL TWISTER (bakery products) 520.587-010
PRETZEL-TWISTING-MACHINE OPERATOR (bakery products) 520.685-190
PREVENTIVE MAINTENANCE COORDINATOR (any industry) 169.167-074
Pre-Wave Assembler (electron. comp.) 726.684-070
Price Checker (clerical) 209.687-010
Price Economist (profess. & kin.) 050.067-010
price marker (retail trade; wholesale tr.) 209.587-034
pricer (laundry & rel.) 216.482-030
pricer-bagger (photofinishing) 976.687-018
PRICER, MESSAGE AND DELIVERY SERVICE (business ser.) 214.467-014
pricer-sorter (nonprofit org.) 222.387-054
priest (profess. & kin.) 120.107-010
priller (clerical) 222.367-038
primary care nurse practitioner (medical ser.) 075.264-010
Primary Connector, Armature (elec. equip.) 724.684-014
primary-crusher operator (any industry) 570.685-022
primer-and-powder-canning leader (ordnance) 737.137-014
primer assembler (ordnance) 694.685-010
PRIMER ASSEMBLER (ordnance) 737.687-098
PRIMER BOXER (ordnance) 737.587-018
PRIMER CHARGER (ordnance) 737.687-102
PRIMER-CHARGING TOOL SETTER (ordnance) 694.360-010
PRIMER EXPEDITOR AND DRIER (chemical) 553.385-014
PRIMER-INSERTING-MACHINE ADJUSTER (ordnance) 632.360-018
PRIMER-INSERTING-MACHINE OPERATOR (ordnance) 694.685-042
PRIMER INSPECTOR (ordnance) 737.687-106
PRIMER-POWDER BLENDER, DRY (ordnance) 550.565-010
PRIMER-POWDER BLENDER, WET (chemical) 550.582-010
primer-press operator (ordnance) 694.685-010
Primer Sprayer (aircraft mfg.; auto. mfg.) 741.684-026
PRIMER SUPERVISOR (ordnance) 737.132-010
PRIMER-WATERPROOFING-MACHINE ADJUSTER (ordnance) 632.380-018
PRIMER-WATERPROOFING-MACHINE OPERATOR (ordnance) 694.685-046
priming-machine operator (ordnance) 694.685-042
PRIMING-MIXTURE CARRIER (ordnance) 922.587-010
PRIMING-POWDER-PREMIX BLENDER (chemical) 550.684-022
principal (any industry)   see SUPERVISOR
PRINCIPAL (education) 099.117-018

principal librarian (library) 100.127-010
print applier (any industry) 749.684-010
Print-Color Matcher (tex. prod., nec) 550.382-014
Print-Color Mixer (tex. prod., nec) 550.382-014
print-color operator (tex. prod., nec) 550.382-014
PRINT CONTROLLER (photofinishing) 976.360-010
print cutter (photofinishing) 976.685-010
Print Decorator (pottery & porc.) 749.684-010
PRINT DEVELOPER, AUTOMATIC (photofinishing) 976.685-026
PRINTED CIRCUIT BOARD ASSEMBLER, HAND (electron. comp.) 726.684-070
PRINTED CIRCUIT BOARD COMPONENT TESTER, CHEMICAL (electron. comp.) 726.684-074
PRINTED CIRCUIT BOARD COMPONENT TESTER, PRE-ASSEMBLY (electron. comp.) 726.684-078
PRINTED CIRCUIT BOARD INSPECTOR, PRE-ASSEMBLY (electron. comp.) 726.684-082
PRINTED CIRCUIT DESIGNER (profess. & kin.) 003.261-022
Printed-Forms Proofreader (clerical) 209.687-010
printer (any industry) 652.382-010
printer (boot & shoe) 690.685-158
PRINTER (glass products) 979.681-014
printer (leather mfg.; leather prod.) 690.682-030
PRINTER (pen & pencil) 652.685-062
PRINTER (print. & pub.) 979.382-018
printer (print. & pub.) 973.381-018
printer (sugar & conf.) 526.687-014
printer (tex. prod., nec) 652.685-022
PRINTER, FLOOR COVERING (fabrication, nec) 652.685-066
PRINTER, FLOOR COVERING, ASSISTANT (fabrication, nec) 652.687-038
PRINTER, MACHINE (hat & cap) 652.685-070
Printer Maintainer (tel. & tel.) 822.281-010
PRINTER OPERATOR, BLACK-AND-WHITE (photofinishing) 976.682-014
PRINTER, PLASTIC (plastic prod.; tex. prod., nec) 651.382-026
printer's devil (print. & pub.) 973.381-022
PRINTER-SLOTTER HELPER (paper goods) 659.686-014
PRINTER-SLOTTER OPERATOR (paper goods) 659.662-010
printer, small print shop (print. & pub.) 979.382-018
print finisher (photofinishing) 976.487-010
printing-equipment mechanic (print. & pub.) 627.261-010
printing-equipment-mechanic apprentice (print. & pub.) 627.261-014
printing-machine operator (any industry) 652.382-010
PRINTING-MACHINE OPERATOR, FOLDING RULES (cutlery-hrdwr.) 652.685-074
PRINTING-MACHINE OPERATOR, TAPE RULES (cutlery-hrdwr.) 652.662-010
Printing-Plate Clerk (print. & pub.) 222.387-058
printing-plate router (print. & pub.) 979.682-026
PRINTING-ROLLER HANDLER (textile) 652.385-010
PRINTING-ROLLER POLISHER (machine shop) 603.382-030
PRINTING SCREEN ASSEMBLER (electron. comp.) 979.684-042
Printing Supervisor (tex. prod., nec) 589.130-014
PRINT INSPECTOR (photofinishing) 976.687-022
PRINT INSPECTOR (pottery & porc.) 774.687-018
PRINT-LINE FEEDER (furniture) 652.686-026
PRINT-LINE INSPECTOR (furniture) 652.687-034
PRINT-LINE OPERATOR (furniture; wood prod., nec) 652.662-018
print-line supervisor (furniture; wood prod., nec) 652.662-018
PRINT-LINE TAILER (furniture) 652.686-030
PRINTMAKER (profess. & kin.) 144.061-014
PRINT-SHOP HELPER (print. & pub.) 979.684-026
PRINT WASHER (photofinishing) 976.684-022
Prism Inspector (optical goods) 716.381-010
PRISONER-CLASSIFICATION INTERVIEWER (profess. & kin.) 166.267-022
prison librarian (library) 100.167-022
PRIVATE-BRANCH-EXCHANGE INSTALLER (tel. & tel.) 822.381-018
Private-Branch-Exchange Installer, Mobile Radio (tel. & tel.) 822.381-018
private-branch-exchange operator (clerical) 235.662-022
PRIVATE-BRANCH-EXCHANGE REPAIRER (tel. & tel.) 822.281-022
PRIVATE-BRANCH-EXCHANGE SERVICE ADVISER (tel. & tel.) 235.222-010
Private-Branch-Exchange Teletypewriter (tel. & tel.) 822.381-018
private pilot (any industry) 196.263-030
PRIZE COORDINATOR (radio-tv broad.) 162.167-026
prize jacker (tobacco) 920.685-062
PRIZER (tobacco) 920.687-142
Probate Judge (government ser.) 111.107-010
PROBATION-AND-PAROLE OFFICER (profess. & kin.) 195.107-046
Probation Officer (profess. & kin.) 195.107-046
PROBE TEST EQUIPMENT TECHNICIAN, SEMICONDUCTOR WAFERS (electron. comp.) 729.360-010
PROCESS-AREA SUPERVISOR (plastic-synth.) 559.132-042
process artist (print. & pub.) 972.281-010
process attendant (elec. equip.) 590.362-010
process-camera operator (print. & pub.) 972.382-014

progress clerk

progress clerk (clerical) 221.167-018
PROGRESS CLERK (construction) 221.362-022
PROGRESSIVE ASSEMBLER AND FITTER (agric. equip.) 801.684-022
Progressive-Die Maker (machine shop) 601.281-010
PROJECT-CREW WORKER (any industry) 891.687-018
project development coordinator (profess. & kin.) 033.162-018
PROJECT DIRECTOR (profess. & kin.) 189.117-030
PROJECT ENGINEER (profess. & kin.) 019.167-014
projection-camera operator (photofinishing) 976.381-018
projectionist (amuse. & rec.; motion picture) 960.362-010
projectionist (any industry) 960.382-010
PROJECTION PRINTER (photofinishing) 976.381-018
Projection-Welding-Machine Operator (welding) 812.682-010
project manager (profess. & kin.) 189.117-030
PROJECT MANAGER, ENVIRONMENTAL RESEARCH (profess. & kin.) 029.167-014
Projector Assembler (photo. appar.) 714.684-010
prom burn-off operator (electron. comp.) 726.685-062
promotor, group-ticket sales (amuse. & rec.) 259.357-010
PROMPTER (amuse. & rec.) 152.367-010
Pronger (jewelry-silver.) 735.687-034
proof clerk (financial) 217.382-010
PROOF-COIN COLLECTOR (government ser.) 709.687-030
proofer (print. & pub.) 651.582-010
proofer apprentice (print. & pub.) 651.582-014
proofer apprentice (print. & pub.) 971.381-040
Proofer, Black And White (print. & pub.) 971.381-038
Proofer, Color (print. & pub.) 971.381-038
PROOFER, PREPRESS (print. & pub.) 972.381-034
Proofing-Machine Operator (print. & pub.) 652.382-010
PROOF INSPECTOR (ordnance) 736.384-010
proof-load mechanic (aircraft mfg.) 929.382-010
PROOF-MACHINE OPERATOR (financial) 217.382-010
PROOF-MACHINE-OPERATOR SUPERVISOR (financial) 217.132-010
proof-plate maker (print. & pub.) 971.381-034
PROOF-PRESS OPERATOR (print. & pub.) 651.582-010
proofreader (clerical) 209.687-010
PROOFREADER (print. & pub.) 209.387-030
proof runner (print. & pub.) 239.677-010
PROOFSHEET CORRECTOR (print. & pub.) 973.381-030
proof sorter (photofinishing) 976.687-018
PROOF TECHNICIAN (ordnance) 199.171-010
PROOF-TECHNICIAN HELPER (ordnance) 736.387-014
proof tester (ordnance) 736.384-010
PROP ATTENDANT (amuse. & rec.) 962.684-022
PROPELLANT-CHARGE LOADER (ordnance) 737.487-010
PROPELLANT-CHARGE-ZONE ASSEMBLER (ordnance) 737.687-110
Propeller Inspector (ship-boat mfg.) 609.361-010
Property-And-Equipment Clerk (petrol. & gas) 222.387-026
PROPERTY-ASSESSMENT MONITOR (government ser.) 241.367-042
PROPERTY CLERK (government ser.) 222.367-054
PROPERTY COORDINATOR (amuse. & rec.; radio-tv broad.) 962.167-018
property custodian (government ser.) 222.367-054
PROPERTY CUSTODIAN (motion picture) 222.387-042
PROPERTY-DISPOSAL OFFICER (any industry) 163.167-026
property handler (motion picture; radio-tv broad.) 962.687-022
property investor (business ser.; real estate) 189.157-010
Property-Loss-Insurance-Claim Adjuster (clerical) 241.217-010
Property Manager (government ser.) 186.117-042
PROPERTY-UTILIZATION OFFICER (government ser.) 188.117-122
PROP MAKER (amuse. & rec.; motion picture) 962.281-010
proposition player (amuse. & rec.) 343.367-010
Proprietor-Manager, Retail Automotive Service (retail trade) 185.167-014
PROPULSION-MOTOR-AND-GENERATOR REPAIRER (automotive ser.) 721.281-026
prosecuting attorney (government ser.) 110.117-010
prosecutor (government ser.) 110.117-010
PROSPECTING DRILLER (petrol. & gas) 930.382-018
Prospecting-Driller Helper (petrol. & gas) 939.364-010
PROSPECTOR (any industry) 024.284-010
prosthetic dentist (medical ser.) 072.101-034
PROSTHETICS ASSISTANT (medical ser.) 078.361-026
PROSTHETICS TECHNICIAN (protective dev.) 712.381-038
PROSTHETIST (medical ser.) 078.261-022
PROSTHODONTIST (medical ser.) 072.101-034
protection chief, industrial plant (any industry) 189.167-050
PROTECTION ENGINEER (utilities) 003.167-054
protective-clothing-and-equipment specialist (profess. & kin.) 142.061-038
PROTECTIVE-CLOTHING ISSUER (chemical) 222.687-046
PROTECTIVE OFFICER (government ser.) 372.363-010
PROTECTIVE-SIGNAL INSTALLER (business ser.) 822.361-018
PROTECTIVE-SIGNAL-INSTALLER HELPER (business ser.) 822.664-010
PROTECTIVE-SIGNAL OPERATOR (any industry) 379.362-014
PROTECTIVE-SIGNAL REPAIRER (business ser.) 822.361-022
PROTECTIVE-SIGNAL-REPAIRER HELPER (business ser.) 822.684-014

PROTECTIVE-SIGNAL SUPERINTENDENT (business ser.) 822.131-022
PROTECTOR-PLATE ATTACHER (cutlery-hrdwr.) 692.685-138
prototype assembler, electronics (any industry) 726.261-010
PROTOTYPE-DEICER ASSEMBLER (rubber goods) 759.261-010
prototype-machine operator (engraving) 704.382-010
prototype machinist (machine shop) 600.260-022
Protozoologist (profess. & kin.) 041.061-070
prover (print. & pub.) 971.381-038
Provider (steel & rel.) 221.387-046
provost (education) 090.117-010
Prune Washer (food prep., nec) 521.685-110
PSYCHIATRIC AIDE (medical ser.) 355.377-014
psychiatric attendant (medical ser.) 355.377-014
PSYCHIATRIC TECHNICIAN (medical ser.) 079.374-026
PSYCHIATRIST (medical ser.) 070.107-014
PSYCHIC READER (amuse. & rec.) 159.647-018
Psychological Anthropologist (profess. & kin.) 055.067-010
Psychological Stress Evaluator (profess. & kin.) 199.267-026
PSYCHOLOGIST, CHIEF (profess. & kin.) 045.107-046
psychologist, clinical (profess. & kin.) 045.107-022
Psychologist, Comparative (profess. & kin.) 045.061-018 *
PSYCHOLOGIST, COUNSELING (profess. & kin.) 045.107-026
PSYCHOLOGIST, DEVELOPMENTAL (profess. & kin.) 045.061-010
PSYCHOLOGIST, EDUCATIONAL (profess. & kin.) 045.067-010
PSYCHOLOGIST, ENGINEERING (profess. & kin.) 045.061-014
PSYCHOLOGIST, EXPERIMENTAL (profess. & kin.) 045.061-018
PSYCHOLOGIST, INDUSTRIAL-ORGANIZATIONAL (profess. & kin.) 045.107-030
Psychologist, Military Personnel (profess. & kin.) 045.107-030
Psychologist, Personnel (profess. & kin.) 045.107-030
Psychologist, Physiological (profess. & kin.) 045.061-018
PSYCHOLOGIST, SCHOOL (profess. & kin.) 045.107-034
PSYCHOLOGIST, SOCIAL (profess. & kin.) 045.067-014
PSYCHOMETRIST (profess. & kin.) 045.067-018
public-address announcer (amuse. & rec.) 159.347-010
PUBLIC-ADDRESS SERVICER (any industry) 823.261-010
public-address-system operator (any industry) 823.261-010
Public Affairs Officer (government ser.) 188.117-106
publications-distribution clerk (clerical) 222.587-018
public-bath attendant (personal ser.) 335.677-014
Public Finance Specialist (government ser.) 160.162-022
PUBLIC-HEALTH DENTIST (medical ser.) 072.101-038
PUBLIC HEALTH EDUCATOR (profess. & kin.) 079.117-014
public-health engineer (profess. & kin.) 005.061-030
public-health engineer (profess. & kin.)   see ENVIRONMENTAL ENGINEER
PUBLIC-HEALTH MICROBIOLOGIST (government ser.) 041.261-010
public-health nurse (medical ser.) 075.124-014
PUBLIC HEALTH PHYSICIAN (government ser.) 070.101-046
PUBLIC HEALTH REGISTRAR (government ser.) 169.167-046
PUBLIC HEALTH SERVICE OFFICER (government ser.) 187.117-050
public improvement inspector (utilities) 859.267-010
Public Information Officer (profess. & kin.) 165.167-014
public interviewer (clerical) 205.367-054
public-relations player (amuse. & rec.) 343.367-010
public-relations practitioner (profess. & kin.) 165.167-014
PUBLIC-RELATIONS REPRESENTATIVE (profess. & kin.) 165.167-014
PUBLIC-SAFETY OFFICER (government ser.) 379.263-014
Public Stenographer (clerical) 202.362-014
Public Utilities Complaint Analyst Supervisor (government ser.) 168.167-090
PUBLIC-UTILITIES ENGINEER (profess. & kin.) term
public-works commissioner (government ser.) 188.117-030
PUBLISHER (print. & pub.) term
puddler (concrete prod.) 530.384-010
Puddler, Pile Driving (construction) 869.687-026
puffer (laundry & rel.) 363.687-018
PUFF IRONER (laundry & rel.) 363.687-018
Puff-Iron Operator I (laundry & rel.) 363.681-010
Puff-Iron Operator II (laundry & rel.) 363.682-018
pugger helper (brick & tile; pottery & porc.) 570.685-074
pugg maker (hat & cap) 690.686-034
Pug Mill Operator (brick & tile; pottery & porc.) 575.382-010
Pug-Mill Operator (cement) 570.685-046
PUG-MILL OPERATOR (smelt. & refin.) 510.685-022
PUG-MILL-OPERATOR HELPER (brick & tile; pottery & porc.) 570.685-074
Pullboat Engineer (logging) 921.663-066
PULLER AND LASTER, MACHINE (boot & shoe) 788.684-086
puller (button & notion) 734.687-074
Puller (foundry) 514.685-014
Puller (laundry & rel.) 361.686-010
PULLER, MACHINE (leather mfg.) 589.685-078
PULLER OVER, MACHINE (boot & shoe) 788.684-090
PULLER-THROUGH (glove & mit.) 782.687-030
PULLEY MAINTAINER (mine & quarry) 630.687-010
PULLEY-MORTISER OPERATOR (saw. & plan.) 666.482-010

pulling-machine operator (petrol. & gas) 930.382-030
Pullman Attendant (r.r. trans.) 315.381-018
pullman clerk (r.r. trans.) 215.167-010
PULL-OUT OPERATOR (fabrication, nec) 739.687-162
pull-out operator (plastic-synth.) 559.584-010
Pull-Socket Assembler (elec. equip.; light. fix.) 729.687-010
Pull-Through Hooker (meat products) 525.685-018
PULMONARY-FUNCTION TECHNICIAN (medical ser.) 078.262-010
pulmonary-function technologist (medical ser.) 078.262-010
PULP-AND-PAPER TESTER (paper & pulp) 539.364-010
pulp drier (wood prod., nec) 532.685-010
PULP-DRIER FIRER (sugar & conf.) 523.585-030
PULPER (paper & pulp; wood prod., nec) 530.685-014
PULPER, SYNTHETIC SOIL BLOCKS (paper & pulp) 530.582-010
PULPER TENDER (can. & preserv.) 521.685-262
PULP GRINDER AND BLENDER (paper & pulp; wood prod., nec) 530.682-010
pulping-machine operator (chemical) 555.685-010
pulp-machine operator (paper & pulp) 539.685-030
pulp-making-plant operator (paper & pulp; paper goods) 532.686-010
PULP PILER (logging) 922.687-082
PULP-PRESS TENDER (paper & pulp) 532.685-026
PULP-PRESS TENDER (sugar & conf.) 521.685-258
PULP-REFINER OPERATOR (paper & pulp) 530.382-010
pulp roller (logging) 922.687-082
pulp-screen operator (chemical) 551.685-106
Pulp Tester (paper & pulp) 539.364-010
Pulpwood Cutter (logging) 454.684-026
Pulpwood Scaler (paper & pulp) 455.487-010
pulverizer (brick & tile; pottery & porc.) 570.685-098
PULVERIZER (chemical) 555.685-046
PULVERIZER (jewelry-silver.) 770.687-030
PULVERIZER (meat products) 521.685-266
pulverizer (plastic prod.; plastic-synth.) 555.685-026
PULVERIZER-MILL OPERATOR (rubber goods; rubber reclaim.) 555.382-010
pulverizer operator (steel & rel.) 544.582-010
pulverizer tender (chemical) 555.685-034
PULVERIZING-AND-SIFTING OPERATOR (chemical) 550.485-026
Pulvi-Mixer Operator (construction) 859.683-026
Pump-And-Blower Attendant (sanitary ser.) 955.585-010
Pump-And-Blower Operator (sanitary ser.) 955.362-010
pump-and-still operator (steel & rel.) 559.382-010
pump-and-tank servicer (any industry) 620.281-018
Pump Assembler (machinery mfg.) 801.361-010
PUMPER (any industry) 914.682-010
pumper (chemical) 559.565-010
pumper (petrol. & gas) 541.382-014
pumper (petrol. & gas) 914.382-010
PUMPER (petrol. refin.) 549.360-010
PUMPER, BREWERY (beverage) 914.665-014
PUMP ERECTOR (construction) 637.281-010
Pump-Erector Helper (construction) 869.664-014
PUMPER-GAUGER (chemical; petrol. refin.; pipe lines) 914.382-014
PUMPER-GAUGER APPRENTICE (chemical; petrol. refin.; pipe lines) 914.382-018
Pumper, Hand (meat products) 522.685-086
PUMPER, HEAD (petrol. & gas) 914.382-022
PUMPER HELPER (any industry) 914.687-018
PUMPER HELPER (petrol. refin.) 549.684-010
pumphouse operator, chief (chemical) 559.132-138
pumping-plant operator (waterworks) 954.382-010
pump installation and servicer (construction) 637.281-010
PUMP INSTALLER (any industry) 630.684-018
pump-machine operator (any industry) 914.682-010
PUMP MECHANIC (paper & pulp) 629.281-034
pump operator (any industry) 914.682-010
pump operator (petrol. refin.) 549.362-010
pump operator, brine well (chemical) 559.685-026
PUMP OPERATOR, BYPRODUCTS (steel & rel.) 541.362-014
PUMP-PRESS OPERATOR (paper & pulp) 539.685-022
pump repairer (any industry) 630.281-018
pump-room operator (utilities) 952.362-010
pump runner (any industry) 914.682-010
PUMP SERVICER (any industry) 630.281-018
PUMP-SERVICER HELPER (any industry) 630.684-022
PUMP-SERVICER SUPERVISOR (any industry) 630.131-010
pump-station operator (pipe lines) 914.362-018
PUMP-STATION OPERATOR, WATERWORKS (waterworks) 954.382-010
pump tender (any industry) 914.682-010
Pump Tender (construction) 869.665-010
pump tender (steel & rel.) 541.362-014
PUMP TENDER, CEMENT BASED MATERIALS (concrete prod.; construction) 849.665-010
PUMP TESTER (plastic-synth.) 557.564-014

PUNCHBOARD ASSEMBLER I (paper goods) 794.687-042
PUNCHBOARD ASSEMBLER II (paper goods) 794.687-046
PUNCHBOARD-FILLING-MACHINE OPERATOR (paper goods) 649.685-094
punchboard inserter (paper goods) 794.687-042
punchboard stuffer (paper goods) 794.687-042
puncher (agriculture) 410.674-014
puncher (boot & shoe) 690.685-162
puncher (boot & shoe) 690.685-114
puncher (leather prod.) 690.685-266
puncher (optical goods) 713.687-014
Puncher (saw. & plan.) 669.687-030
PUNCHER (tex. prod., nec) 689.582-010
PUNCHER (woodworking) 663.685-022
puncher and fastener (boot & shoe) 690.685-162
Punch Finisher (machine shop) 601.381-010
punching-machine operator (hat & cap) 686.685-038
Punch-Press Feeder (any industry) 699.686-010
Punch-Press Offbearer (any industry) 699.686-010
PUNCH-PRESS OPERATOR (fabrication, nec) 692.665-014
punch press operator (glass mfg.) 575.685-054
PUNCH PRESS OPERATOR (wood prod., nec) 669.685-106
PUNCH-PRESS OPERATOR, AUTOMATIC (any industry) 615.482-026
Punch-Press-Operator Helper (any industry) 619.687-014
PUNCH-PRESS OPERATOR I (any industry) 615.382-010
PUNCH-PRESS OPERATOR II (any industry) 615.685-030
PUNCH-PRESS OPERATOR III (any industry) 615.682-014
Punch-Press Operator IV (any industry) 617.685-026
PUNCH-PRESS SETTER (any industry) 619.380-014
Punch-Press Supervisor (any industry) 619.130-030
PUPPETEER (amuse. & rec.) 159.041-014
purchase-order checker (clerical) 214.362-026
PURCHASE-PRICE ANALYST (profess. & kin.) 162.167-030
purchaser, automotive parts (clerical) 249.367-058
purchase-request editor (clerical) 249.367-066
PURCHASING AGENT (profess. & kin.) 162.157-038
PURCHASING-AND-CLAIMS SUPERVISOR (water trans.) 248.137-014
purchasing-and-fiscal clerk (clerical) 249.367-066
purchasing clerk (clerical) 249.367-066
purchasing-contracting clerk (clerical) 249.367-066
pure-culture operator (food prep., nec) 522.685-090
purification operator (chemical) 552.362-022
purification operator (chemical) 552.462-010
Purification Operator (petrol. refin.) 549.260-010
PURIFICATION-OPERATOR HELPER (chemical) 551.465-010
Purification-Operator Helper (petrol. refin.) 542.362-014
PURIFICATION OPERATOR I (chemical) 551.685-122
PURIFICATION OPERATOR II (chemical) 551.362-010
Purifier (grain-feed mills) 521.685-030
purifying-plant operator (waterworks) 954.382-014
Purse Framer (leather prod.) 739.684-090
PURSER (water trans.) 197.167-014
push-bench-operator helper (nonfer. metal; steel & rel.) 614.686-010
Push-Button-Switch Assembler (elec. equip.) 729.687-010
PUSH-CONNECTOR ASSEMBLER (house. appl.) 706.687-030
pusher (any industry)　　　see STRAW BOSS
pusher (dairy products) 529.685-030
pusher (steel & rel.) 504.665-014
PUSHER OPERATOR (steel & rel.) 519.663-018
pusher runner (steel & rel.) 512.683-010
push-up machine operator (boot & shoe) 690.685-206
PUT-IN-BEAT ADJUSTER (clock & watch) 715.684-174
putter-in (dairy products) 529.685-030
putter-out, machine (leather mfg.; tex. prod., nec) 589.685-098
putty-and-patch worker (furniture) 763.684-070
PUTTY GLAZER (any industry) 749.684-042
Putty Maker (paint & varnish) 550.685-078
PUTTY MIXER AND APPLIER (wood. container) 769.687-038
Putty Remover (fabrication, nec) 761.684-030
PUTTY TINTER-MAKER (paint & varnish) 559.482-014
PUZZLE ASSEMBLER (toy-sport equip.) 731.687-030
PYRIDINE OPERATOR (steel & rel.) 552.382-010
pyridine-recovery operator (steel & rel.) 552.382-010
pyroglazer (glass mfg.; glass products) 740.381-010
pyrometer operator (ordnance) 619.662-010
pyrotechnic assembler (chemical) 737.587-014
Pyrotechnic-Loading Supervisor (chemical) 737.131-010
Pyrotechnic Mixer (chemical) 737.687-090

Q

quad stayer (paper goods) 641.685-054
Quail Farmer (agriculture) 412.161-010
QUALITY ASSURANCE ANALYST (profess. & kin.) 033.262-010

quality assurance calibrator

quality assurance calibrator (aircraft mfg.) 019.281-010
QUALITY ASSURANCE COORDINATOR (medical ser.) 075.167-014
QUALITY ASSURANCE GROUP LEADER (auto. mfg.) 806.367-014
QUALITY ASSURANCE MONITOR (auto. mfg.) 806.367-018
Quality Assurance Monitor, Body (auto. mfg.) 806.367-018
Quality Assurance Monitor, Chassis (auto. mfg.) 806.367-018
Quality Assurance Monitor, Final (auto. mfg.) 806.367-018
Quality Assurance Monitor, Trim (auto. mfg.) 806.367-018
QUALITY ASSURANCE SUPERVISOR (auto. mfg.) 806.137-022
Quality Assurance Supervisor (office machines) 726.130-010
Quality Assurance Supervisor, Body (auto. mfg.) 806.137-022
Quality Assurance Supervisor, Chassis (auto. mfg.) 806.137-022
Quality Assurance Supervisor, Final (auto. mfg.) 806.137-022
Quality Assurance Supervisor, Trim (auto. mfg.) 806.137-022
quality auditor (elec. equip.) 727.381-022
quality-control-assembly-test technician (any industry) 726.261-018
QUALITY-CONTROL CHECKER (garment) 789.387-010
QUALITY CONTROL CHECKER, TEXTURING PROCESS (textile) 681.387-010
QUALITY-CONTROL CLERK (pharmaceut.) 229.587-014
QUALITY-CONTROL COORDINATOR (pharmaceut.) 168.167-066
QUALITY-CONTROL ENGINEER (profess. & kin.) 012.167-054
QUALITY-CONTROL INSPECTOR (bakery products) 529.367-018
quality control inspector (comm. equip.; electron. comp.; inst. & app.) 726.381-010
QUALITY-CONTROL INSPECTOR (cutlery-hrdwr.) 701.261-010
QUALITY CONTROL INSPECTOR (furniture; millwork-plywood) 569.687-030
QUALITY-CONTROL INSPECTOR (glass mfg.) 579.367-010
QUALITY-CONTROL INSPECTOR (light. fix.) 725.687-026
quality-control inspector (paper goods) 649.367-010
quality-control inspector (paper goods) 652.687-042
quality control inspector (print. & pub.) 653.667-010
QUALITY-CONTROL INSPECTOR (recording) 194.387-010
QUALITY-CONTROL INSPECTOR (rubber tire) 750.367-010
QUALITY CONTROL INSPECTOR (sugar & conf.) 529.367-034
quality-control-inspector, heading (wood. container) 764.387-010
quality-control projectionist (photofinishing) 976.362-010
quality-control supervisor (machine shop) 609.131-010
QUALITY-CONTROL SUPERVISOR (plastic prod.) 559.134-010
QUALITY-CONTROL SUPERVISOR (plastic-synth.) 559.131-014
quality-control technician (beverage) 029.361-010
QUALITY-CONTROL TECHNICIAN (beverage) 529.367-022
QUALITY-CONTROL TECHNICIAN (can. & preserv.; food prep., nec) 529.387-030
QUALITY CONTROL TECHNICIAN (concrete prod.) 579.364-010
QUALITY CONTROL TECHNICIAN (glass mfg.) 579.367-014
QUALITY CONTROL TECHNICIAN (photofinishing) 976.267-010
QUALITY CONTROL TECHNICIAN (profess. & kin.) 012.261-014
QUALITY-CONTROL TECHNICIAN (svc. ind. mach.) 637.684-014
QUALITY-CONTROL TECHNICIAN, INKED RIBBONS (pen & pencil) 733.364-010
QUALITY-CONTROL TESTER (fabrication, nec) 543.684-010
QUALITY-CONTROL TESTER (knitting) 684.384-010
QUALITY-CONTROL TESTER (paper goods; plastic-synth.) 559.367-010
QUALITY-CONTROL TESTER (wood prod., nec) 569.384-010
QUALITY TECHNICIAN, FIBERGLASS (glass mfg.) 579.384-014
quality worker (auto. mfg.) 806.684-010
Quantometer Operator (smelt. & refin.) 519.387-010
QUARRY PLUG-AND-FEATHER DRILLER (mine & quarry) 930.684-022
QUARRY SUPERVISOR, DIMENSION STONE (mine & quarry) 930.134-010
QUARRY SUPERVISOR, OPEN PIT (mine & quarry) 939.131-010
QUARRY WORKER (mine & quarry) 939.667-014
quarter doper (boot & shoe) 788.687-038
quarter folder (boot & shoe) 690.685-070
Quarter Former (boot & shoe) 690.685-098
Quarter Inspector (boot & shoe) 788.384-010
Quarter-Lining Smoother (boot & shoe) 690.685-350
Quarter-Lining Stitcher (boot & shoe) 690.682-082
QUARTERMASTER (water trans.) 911.363-014
Quarter-Section Ironer (hat & cap) 583.685-098
Quebracho Tanner (leather mfg.) 582.482-018
Queen Producer (agriculture) 413.161-010
Quick-Mixer Operator (sugar & conf.) 520.685-074
quick print operator (print. & pub.) 979.362-010
QUICK SKETCH ARTIST (amuse. & rec.) 149.041-010
QUILL-BUNCHER-AND-SORTER (tex. prod., nec) 734.687-066
Quill Changer (narrow fabrics) 689.686-038
quill cleaner (textile) 689.686-014
quill cleaner, hand (textile) 689.687-014
quill-cleaning-machine operator (textile) 689.686-014
quiller (textile) 681.685-074
quiller hand (textile) 681.685-074
Quiller-Machine Fixer (textile) 689.260-010
QUILLER OPERATOR (textile) 681.685-070

quiller tender (textile) 681.685-074
QUILLING-MACHINE OPERATOR, AUTOMATIC (textile) 681.685-074
quill inspector (glass mfg.; plastic-synth.; textile) 681.687-030
quill-machine tender (textile) 681.685-070
Quill-Picking-Machine Operator (tex. prod., nec) 589.685-054
quill skinner (textile) 689.686-014
quill stripper (textile) 689.686-014
Quill Winder (narrow fabrics) 681.685-154
QUILTER FIXER (tex. prod., nec) 689.260-014
quilting-machine helper (tex. prod., nec) 689.686-010
QUILTING-MACHINE OPERATOR (glove & mit.; tex. prod., nec) 689.685-106
QUILTING-MACHINE OPERATOR (tex. prod., nec) 584.382-014
Quilt Sewer (tex. prod., nec) 787.682-066
Quilt Sewer, Hand (tex. prod., nec) 782.684-018
QUILT STUFFER (tex. prod., nec) 789.687-130
QUILT STUFFER, MACHINE (tex. prod., nec) 689.685-102
quirk sander (boot & shoe) 662.685-042
quote clerk (financial) 237.367-046

R

rabbi (profess. & kin.) 120.107-010
Rabbit Breeder (agriculture) 410.161-010
Rabbit Dresser (meat products) 525.687-010
Rabbit Flesher (leather mfg.) 585.681-010
RABBLE-FURNACE TENDER (chemical) 553.685-090
racing-board marker (amuse. & rec.) 249.587-010
RACING SECRETARY AND HANDICAPPER (amuse. & rec.) 153.167-018
Rack Carrier (paper goods) 929.687-030
Rack Cleaner (electroplating) 500.686-010
Rack Cleaner (textile) 699.687-014
RACKER (amuse. & rec.) 340.477-010
Racker (any industry) 929.687-030
RACKER (bakery products) 524.687-018
racker (beverage) 920.665-014
RACKER (clock & watch) 715.687-106
Racker (electroplating) 500.686-010
racker (furniture) 780.684-090
racker (hat & cap) 784.387-010
RACKER (jewelry-silver.) 735.687-026
RACKER (paper goods) 659.687-010
racker (photofinishing) 976.687-018
Racker (saw. & plan.) 922.687-074
Racker (steel & rel.) 509.687-026
racker (tobacco) 529.687-090
RACKER (toy-sport equip.) 749.587-010
racker (woodworking) 922.687-074
RACKER, OCTAVE BOARD (musical inst.) 730.684-062
RACKER, SILK-SCREEN PRINTING (any industry) 659.687-014
RACKET STRINGER (toy-sport equip.) 732.684-094
Rack Loader (elec. equip.) 727.687-070
RACK LOADER (fabrication, nec) 590.687-018
RACK LOADER I (tobacco) 529.686-074
Rack Loader II (tobacco) 529.686-038
RACK-ROOM WORKER (beverage) 920.665-014
Radar Mechanic (any industry) 828.261-022
radiagraph operator (welding) 816.482-010
RADIAL-ARM-SAW OPERATOR (woodworking) 667.682-054
Radial-Drill Operator (stonework) 676.682-014
RADIATION MONITOR (profess. & kin.) 199.167-010
RADIATION-PROTECTION ENGINEER (profess. & kin.) 015.137-010
RADIATION-PROTECTION SPECIALIST (government ser.) 168.261-010
RADIATION-THERAPY TECHNOLOGIST (medical ser.) 078.361-034
radiator repairer (automotive ser.) 620.381-010
RADIOACTIVITY-INSTRUMENT MAINTENANCE TECHNICIAN (petrol. & gas) 828.281-022
radioactivity technician (petrol. & gas) 828.281-022
radio and radar technician (aircraft mfg.; air trans.) 823.261-026
Radio-And-Television-Cabinet Inspector (furniture) 763.687-026
Radio Announcer (radio-tv broad.) 159.147-010
radio board operator-announcer (radio-tv broad.) 159.147-010
radio-communications mechanic (any industry) 823.281-014
Radio-Division Captain (government ser.) 193.167-018
Radio-Division Lieutenant (government ser.) 193.167-018
radiographer (medical ser.) 078.362-026
radiographer, angiogram (medical ser.) 078.362-046
RADIOGRAPHER (any industry) 199.361-010
radiographer, cardiac catheterization (medical ser.) 078.362-050
Radio Installer (tel. & tel.) 822.381-018
Radio Installer, Automobile (automotive ser.) 806.684-038
RADIO-INTELLIGENCE OPERATOR (government ser.) 193.362-014
RADIO INTERFERENCE INVESTIGATOR (electron. comp.) 823.261-014
radio-interference trouble shooter (electron. comp.) 823.261-014

RADIOISOTOPE-PRODUCTION OPERATOR (profess. & kin.) 015.362-022
RADIOLOGICAL-EQUIPMENT SPECIALIST (medical ser.) 719.261-014
radiologic electronic specialist (medical ser.) 719.261-014
RADIOLOGIC TECHNOLOGIST (medical ser.) 078.362-026
RADIOLOGIC TECHNOLOGIST, CHIEF (medical ser.) 078.162-010
Radiologic Technologist, Mammogram (medical ser.) 078.362-026
RADIOLOGIST (medical ser.) 070.101-090
RADIOLOGY ADMINISTRATOR (medical ser.) 187.117-062
RADIO MECHANIC (any industry) 823.261-018
radio mechanic (any industry) 823.281-014
RADIO-MESSAGE ROUTER (tel. & tel.) 235.387-010
RADIO OFFICER (water trans.) 193.262-022
radio operator (water trans.) 193.262-022
radio operator, ground (aircraft mfg.) 193.262-026
RADIOPHARMACIST (medical ser.) 074.161-014
radiophone operator (any industry) 193.262-034
radio-photo technician (print. & pub.; tel. & tel.) 193.362-010
Radio Police Officer (government ser.) 375.263-014
Radio Producer (radio-tv broad.) 159.117-010
RADIO REPAIRER (any industry) 720.281-010
Radio Repairer, Domestic (any industry) 720.281-010
RADIO STATION OPERATOR (aircraft mfg.) 193.262-026
radiotelegraphist (tel. & tel.) 193.262-030
RADIOTELEGRAPH OPERATOR (tel. & tel.) 193.262-030
Radiotelegraph Operator-Servicer (any industry) 823.281-014
RADIOTELEPHONE OPERATOR (any industry) 193.262-034
radiotelephone-technical operator (any industry) 193.262-034
RADIUS CORNER MACHINE OPERATOR (glass products) 673.685-098
radius grinder (nonmet. min.) 673.685-010
RAFTER (logging) 455.664-010
RAFTER-CUTTING-MACHINE OPERATOR (mfd. bldgs.) 669.382-014
Rag Baler (laundry & rel.) 920.685-010
RAG-CUTTING-MACHINE FEEDER (paper & pulp; tex. prod., nec) 530.666-010
RAG-CUTTING-MACHINE TENDER (paper & pulp; tex. prod., nec) 530.665-014
RAG INSPECTOR (paper & pulp) 530.687-010
Rag Sorter (any industry) 929.687-022
RAG SORTER AND CUTTER (tex. prod., nec) 789.687-134
Rag Washer (laundry & rel.) 361.665-010
rag-willow operator (paper & pulp) 533.685-030
Rail Assembler (toy-sport equip.) 732.384-010
Rail-Car Operator (logging) 919.663-014
rail-doweling-machine operator (saw. & plan.) 669.682-042
Rail-Express Clerk (r.r. trans.) 222.367-022
Rail-Flaw-Detector-Car Operator (r.r. trans.) 910.363-014
RAIL-FLAW-DETECTOR OPERATOR (r.r. trans.) 910.263-010
rail gang supervisor (construction) 869.134-022
Rail Inspector (steel & rel.) 619.381-010
railroad-car-cleaning supervisor (r.r. trans.) 910.137-014
railroad-car inspector (railroad equip.) 910.667-010
RAILROAD-CAR INSPECTOR (r.r. trans.) 910.387-014
RAILROAD-CAR LETTERER (r.r. trans.) 845.681-010
railroad-car loader (mine & quarry) 932.687-010
railroad-car retarder operator (r.r. trans.) 910.382-010
RAILROAD-CAR-TRUCK BUILDER (railroad equip.) 806.684-114
RAILROAD-CONSTRUCTION DIRECTOR (r.r. trans.) 182.167-018
railroad-crane operator (any industry) 921.663-038
RAILROAD ENGINEER (profess. & kin.) 005.061-026
RAILROAD-MAINTENANCE CLERK (r.r. trans.) 221.362-026
Railroad Operator (amuse. & rec.) 342.663-010
RAILROAD SUPERVISOR (construction) term
railroad supervisor of engines (r.r. trans.) 910.137-034
RAILROAD WHEELS AND AXLE INSPECTOR (railroad equip.) 622.381-034
Rail Splitter (logging) 454.684-022
RAIL-TRACTOR OPERATOR (steel & rel.) 919.683-018
RAILWAY-EQUIPMENT OPERATOR (r.r. trans.) 859.683-018
Raimann-Machine Operator (millwork-plywood) 669.685-098
RAISED PRINTER (print. & pub.) 652.686-034
raise driller (mine & quarry) 930.683-026
Raise Miner (mine & quarry) 939.281-010
raiser (machinery mfg.) 979.681-010
raiser (wood. container) 764.684-018
raiser helper (wood. container) 764.687-038
Raisin-Separator Operator (sugar & conf.) 529.686-034
Raisin Washer (food prep., nec) 521.685-110
RAKER (carpet & rug) 789.687-138
RAKER, BUFFING WHEEL (tex. prod., nec) 589.684-010
ram-die maker (pottery & porc.) 774.684-026
RAM-PRESS OPERATOR (pottery & porc.) 575.682-022
ramrod (agriculture) 410.137-014
ranch hand, livestock (agriculture) 410.664-010
ranch manager (agriculture; wholesale tr.) 180.167-018
ranch rider (agriculture) 410.674-014

rand butter (boot & shoe) 690.685-474
rand-butting-machine operator (boot & shoe) 690.685-474
Rand Cementer (boot & shoe) 690.686-018
Rand Sewer (boot & shoe) 690.682-082
Rand Tacker (boot & shoe) 690.685-162
Range Conservationist (profess. & kin.) 040.061-046
range feeder (textile) 589.686-014
range-management specialist (profess. & kin.) 040.061-046
RANGE MANAGER (profess. & kin.) 040.061-046
range master (amuse. & rec.) 187.167-118
range operator (textile) 589.562-010
ranger (government ser.) 169.167-042
ranger aide (government ser.) 249.367-082
rapid-extractor operator (any industry) 581.685-038
Rapid-Outsole Stitcher (boot & shoe) 690.682-078
Rapier-Insertion Loom Fixer (textile) 683.260-018
rapper (smelt. & refin.) 511.687-014
Raschel-Knitting-Machine Operator (knitting) 685.665-018
Raspberry Checker (can. & preserv.) 529.687-186
Raspberry Grower (agriculture) 403.161-014
RASPER (boot & shoe) 788.684-094
rasper-machine operator (boot & shoe) 690.685-046
Rat Breeder (agriculture) 410.161-010
Rate Analyst (government ser.) 160.267-014
RATE ANALYST, FREIGHT (air trans.; motor trans.; r.r. trans.; water trans.) 214.267-010
rate-and-cost analyst (utilities) 216.137-010
rate clerk (clerical) 214.362-038
RATE CLERK, PASSENGER (motor trans.) 214.362-030
Rate Engineer (profess. & kin.) 160.162-026
rate inserter (insurance) 214.482-022
rate marker (tel. & tel.) 214.587-010
RATER (insurance) 214.482-022
RATE REVIEWER (utilities) 214.387-014
RATER, TRAVEL ACCOMMODATIONS (profess. & kin.) 168.367-014
RATE SUPERVISOR (clerical) 214.137-018
rating clerk (insurance) 214.482-022
Rattan Worker (furniture) 763.684-078
Rattan Worker (wood. container) 769.684-054
Rattlesnake Farmer (agriculture) 413.161-014
RAVELER (knitting) 782.687-034
Raw-Calender Operator (tex. prod., nec) 584.685-010
RAW-CHEESE WORKER (dairy products) 529.686-078
RAW-FINISH-MILL Operator (cement) 570.685-046
RAWHIDE-BONE ROLLER (leather prod.) 789.684-042
Raw-Hide Trimmer (leather mfg.) 585.684-010
RAW-JUICE WEIGHER (sugar & conf.) 529.685-194
RAW SAMPLER (smelt. & refin.) 519.484-014
RAW SHELLFISH PREPARER (hotel & rest.) 311.674-014
RAW-SILK GRADER (textile) 689.687-062
RAW-STOCK-DRIER TENDER (textile) 581.685-046
Raw-Stock-Dyeing-Machine Tender (textile) 582.685-102
RAW-STOCK-MACHINE LOADER (textile) 582.686-018
reactor-kettle operator (plastic-synth.) 558.382-042
reactor operator (chemical) 558.685-062
reactor operator (chemical) 559.382-018
reactor operator (chemical) 558.382-022
Reactor Operator (smelt. & refin.) 513.362-010
reactor operator (utilities) 952.362-022
REACTOR OPERATOR, TEST-AND-RESEARCH (profess. & kin.) 015.362-026
reactor-service operator (profess. & kin.) 015.362-014
READER (business ser.) 249.387-022
READER (motion picture; radio-tv broad.) 131.087-014
Readers'-Advisory-Service Librarian (library) 100.127-014
reading improvement teacher (education) 099.227-042
ready-mix-truck driver (construction) 900.683-010
REAGENT TENDER (smelt. & refin.) 511.685-046
REAGENT TENDER HELPER (smelt. & refin.) 511.686-010
REAL-ESTATE AGENT (profess. & kin.) 186.117-058
real-estate agent (real estate) 250.357-018
Real-Estate Broker (real estate) 250.357-018
REAL-ESTATE CLERK (clerical) 219.362-046
Real-Estate-Utilization Officer (government ser.) 188.117-122
Reamer (clock & watch) 606.685-030
REAMER (construction) term
reamer (fabrication, nec) 739.687-014
REAMER, CENTER HOLE (clock & watch) 715.687-110
REAMER, HAND (machine shop) 709.684-058
Reamer Operator (machine shop) 606.682-014
REAMING-MACHINE TENDER (nonfer. metal) 606.685-034
rebeamer (textile) 681.585-010
rebrander (boot & shoe) 753.687-014
REBRANDER (rubber goods) 559.685-150
rebut-machine tail offbearer (saw. & plan.) 667.686-018

RECEIPT-AND-REPORT CLERK (water trans.) 216.382-054
receiver, bulk system (any industry) 921.685-026
RECEIVER-DISPATCHER (nonprofit org.) 239.367-022
RECEIVER, FERMENTING CELLARS (beverage) 522.662-010
Receiver Setter (construction) 869.664-014
RECEIVING-BARN CUSTODIAN (amuse. & rec.) 349.367-014
RECEIVING CHECKER (clerical) 222.687-018
receiving checker (laundry & rel.) 369.687-026
Receiving Clerk (clerical) 222.387-050
receiving-distribution-station operator (utilities) 952.362-026
receiving inspector (clerical) 222.687-018
Receiving Inspector (inst. & app.) 729.361-010
Receiving, Marking, And Washing Supervisor (laundry & rel.) '61.137-010
receiving-room clerk (hotel & rest.) 324.577-010
Receiving Supervisor (clerical) 222.137-030
Receiving-Tank Operator (sugar & conf.) 529.585-014
Receiving Weigher (clerical) 222.387-074
reception clerk (clerical) 237.367-038
reception clerk (clerical) 237.367-010
reception interviewer (clerical) 205.362-014
receptionist (any industry) 352.667-010
RECEPTIONIST (clerical) 237.367-038
RECEPTIONIST, AIRLINE LOUNGE (air trans.) 352.677-014
Receptionist, Doctor's Office (medical ser.) 237.367-038
recessing-machine operator (clock & watch) 605.685-038
Rechecker (textile) 689.685-038
Reciprocating-Drill Operator (any industry) 850.683-034
reclaimer (any industry) 929.687-022
RECLAMATION KETTLE TENDER, METAL (smelt. & refin.) 512.685-022
RECLAMATION SUPERVISOR (nonfer. metal) 512.132-014
reclamation supervisor (petrol. refin.) 929.131-010
RECLAMATION WORKER (wholesale tr.) 621.684-014
recoater (woodworking) 763.381-010
recoil spring winder (metal prod., nec) 616.685-070
RECONNAISSANCE CREWMEMBER (military ser.) 378.367-030
RECONSIGNMENT CLERK (clerical) 209.367-042
record-changer adjuster (comm. equip.) 720.684-010
RECORD-CHANGER ASSEMBLER (comm. equip.) 720.687-010
RECORD-CHANGER TESTER (comm. equip.) 720.687-014
record clerk (clerical) 216.382-062
Record Clerk (hotel & rest.) 203.582-066
RECORD CLERK (textile) 206.387-022
RECORDER (knitting) 221.587-026
RECORDER (steel & rel.) 221.367-050
recorder, gravity prospecting (petrol. & gas) 010.261-018
recorder helper, gravity prospecting (petrol. & gas) 939.663-010
recorder helper, seismograph (petrol. & gas) 939.364-010
RECORDING ENGINEER (radio-tv broad.; recording) 194.362-010
recordings librarian (library) 100.167-010
RECORDING STUDIO SET-UP WORKER (recording) 962.664-014
RECORDIST (motion picture) 962.382-010
RECORDIST, CHIEF (motion picture) 962.134-010
RECORD-PRESS TENDER (recording) 556.685-070
RECORDS-MANAGEMENT ANALYST (profess. & kin.) 161.267-022
records-section supervisor (clerical) 206.137-010
RECORD TESTER (recording) 194.387-014
RECOVERY OPERATOR (chemical) 558.682-022
RECOVERY OPERATOR (paper & pulp) 552.362-018
RECOVERY OPERATOR (smelt. & refin.) 519.582-010
RECOVERY-OPERATOR HELPER (smelt. & refin.) 519.485-014
recovery-unit operator (plastic-synth.) 558.682-010
RECREATION AIDE (social ser.) 195.367-030
RECREATIONAL THERAPIST (medical ser.) 076.124-014
RECREATION-FACILITY ATTENDANT (amuse. & rec.) 341.367-010
RECREATION LEADER (social ser.) 195.227-014
recreation specialist (profess. & kin.) 187.167-238
RECREATION SUPERVISOR (profess. & kin.) 187.167-238
RECRUITER (military ser.) 166.267-026
RECRUIT INSTRUCTOR (military ser.) 378.227-014
recruitment clerk (government ser.) 205.362-010
Rectangular-Tank Cooper (wood. container) 764.684-030
RECTIFICATION PRINTER (any industry) 976.682-018
Rectifier Operator (chemical) 952.362-038
Rectifying Attendant (beverage) 522.382-018
rectifying operator (chemical) 552.362-022
Rector (profess. & kin.) 120.107-010
redcap (air trans.; motor trans.; r.r. trans.) 357.677-010
REDEYE GUNNER (military ser.) 378.682-010
redistribution-and-marketing officer (any industry) 163.167-026
RED-LEAD BURNER (paint & varnish) 558.685-054
Red-Mud Thickener Operator (smelt. & refin.) 511.485-014
Redraw Operator (textile) 681.685-154
REDRYING-MACHINE OPERATOR (tobacco) 522.662-014
reducer (paint & varnish) 550.585-038
REDUCING-MACHINE OPERATOR (optical goods) 614.685-018

REDUCING-SALON ATTENDANT (personal ser.) 359.567-010
REDUCTION-FURNACE OPERATOR (chemical) 553.682-022
REDUCTION-FURNACE-OPERATOR HELPER (chemical; oils & grease) 559.686-038
REDUCTION-PLANT SUPERVISOR (smelt. & refin.) 512.130-010
REDYE HAND (knitting) 789.687-142
reed cleaner (textile) 699.687-010
reed cleaner (textile) 628.484-010
Reeding-Machine Operator (hat & cap) 784.682-014
REED MAKER (machinery mfg.) 709.381-038
reed maker (textile) 628.484-010
reed polisher (textile) 628.484-010
REED-PRESS FEEDER (wood prod., nec) 669.686-022
REED REPAIRER (textile) 628.484-010
Reed Worker (furniture) 763.684-078
Reefer Engineer (water trans.) 950.362-014
reel assembler (toy-sport equip.) 732.684-062
REEL ASSEMBLER (woodworking) 762.484-010
REEL-BLADE-BENDER FURNACE TENDER (agric. equip.) 504.685-030
reel cutter (paper goods) 640.685-046
REELER (build. mat., nec) 549.685-022
REELER (paper goods) 640.685-054
reeler (tex. prod., nec) 681.685-034
reeler (textile) 681.685-078
REELER (woodworking) 769.684-054
reeler operator (steel & rel.) 613.682-014
Reel Fabricator (agric. equip.) 706.684-042
reel-film inspector (photofinishing) 976.362-010
Reeling-And-Tubing-Machine Operator (textile) 689.685-046
REELING-MACHINE OPERATOR (steel & rel.) 613.682-014
reeling-machine operator (textile) 689.685-042
REELING-MACHINE OPERATOR (textile) 681.685-078
reel operator (paper goods) 640.685-046
Reel Oven Tender (bakery products) 526.685-070
reel slitter (tex. prod., nec) 690.682-026
Reel Tender (nonfer. metal) 691.685-030
reel tender (textile) 681.685-078
reexaminer (knitting) 684.687-014
referee (amuse. & rec.) 153.267-018
referee (amuse. & rec.) 153.167-014
referee (government ser.) 119.107-010
Referee (profess. & kin.) 169.107-010
Reference Librarian (library) 100.127-014
REFERRAL-AND-INFORMATION AIDE (government ser.) 237.367-042
referral clerk (clerical) 205.367-062
REFERRAL CLERK, TEMPROARY-HELP AGENCY (clerical) 205.367-062
REFINED-SYRUP OPERATOR (sugar & conf.) 520.485-022
REFINER (protective dev.) 712.684-038
refiner bleacher (oils & grease) 559.685-146
REFINERY OPERATOR (grain-feed mills) 521.362-018
refinery operator (oils & grease) 559.382-030
REFINERY OPERATOR (petrol. refin.) 549.260-010
Refinery Operator, Alkylation (petrol. refin.) 549.260-010
REFINERY OPERATOR, ASSISTANT (grain-feed mills) 521.462-010
Refinery Operator, Coking (petrol. refin.) 549.260-010
Refinery Operator, Cracking Unit (petrol. refin.) 549.260-010
Refinery Operator, Crude Unit (petrol. refin.) 549.260-010
Refinery Operator, Gas Plant (petrol. refin.) 549.260-010
REFINERY OPERATOR HELPER (petrol. refin.) 542.362-014
Refinery Operator Helper, Cracking Unit (petrol. refin.) 542.362-014
Refinery Operator Helper, Crude Unit (petrol. refin.) 542.362-014
Refinery Operator, Light-Ends Recovery (petrol. refin.) 549.260-010
Refinery Operator, Polymerization Plant (petrol. refin.) 549.260-010
Refinery Operator, Reforming Unit (petrol. refin.) 549.260-010
Refinery Operator, Vapor Recovery Unit (petrol. refin.) 549.260-010
Refinery Operator, Visbreaking (petrol. refin.) 549.260-010
Refinery Supervisor (oils & grease) 529.137-030
REFINING-MACHINE OPERATOR (oils & grease) 529.685-198
REFINING-MACHINE OPERATOR (sugar & conf.) 521.682-034
refining-still operator (chemical) 552.682-010
refinisher (furniture) 763.684-034
refinisher (woodworking) 763.381-010
REFLOW OPERATOR (electron. comp.) 726.685-038
REFRACTORY-GRINDER OPERATOR (brick & tile) 677.682-014
REFRACTORY MIXER (steel & rel.) 570.685-078
refractory specialist (glass mfg.) 579.664-010
Refrigerated-Cargo Clerk (water trans.) 248.367-014
REFRIGERATING ENGINEER (any industry) 950.362-014
REFRIGERATING ENGINEER, HEAD (any industry) 950.131-010
Refrigerating Technician (profess. & kin.) 007.181-010
REFRIGERATION MECHANIC (any industry) 637.261-026
REFRIGERATION MECHANIC (svc. ind. mach.) 827.361-014
refrigeration-mechanic apprentice (construction) 862.281-026
REFRIGERATION-MECHANIC HELPER (any industry) 637.687-014
Refrigeration Operator (chemical) 559.362-018

refrigeration operator, head (any industry) 950.131-010
refrigeration supervisor (any industry) 950.131-010
Refrigeration-System Installer (any industry) 637.261-026
REFRIGERATION UNIT REPAIRER (svc. ind. mach.) 637.381-014
Refrigerator Cabinetmaker (svc. ind. mach.) 660.280-010
refrigerator-car icer (food prep., nec; meat products) 910.687-018
Refrigerator Crater (svc. ind. mach.) 920.684-010
REFRIGERATOR GLAZIER (svc. ind. mach.) 865.684-022
Refrigerator-Room Clerk (clerical) 222.387-058
REFRIGERATOR TESTER (svc. ind. mach.) 827.384-010
regeneration operator (chemical) 558.585-018
REGENERATOR OPERATOR (sugar & conf.) 573.685-034
regional coordinator for aging (government ser.) 188.117-058
regional extension-service specialist (government ser.) 096.167-010
REGIONAL SUPERINTENDENT, RAILROAD CAR INSPECTION AND RE-
    PAIR (r.r. trans.) 184.117-090
REGISTERED REPRESENTATIVE (financial) 250.257-018
REGISTER REPAIRER (r.r. trans.) 710.681-018
REGISTRAR (government ser.) 205.367-038
REGISTRAR, COLLEGE OR UNIVERSITY (education) 090.167-030
REGISTRAR, MUSEUM (museums) 102.167-018
registrar, nurses' registry (medical ser.) 187.167-034
REGISTRATION CLERK (government ser.) 205.367-042
REGISTRATION CLERK (library) 249.365-010
REGISTRATION SPECIALIST, AGRICULTURAL CHEMICALS (govern-
    ment ser.) 168.267-106
Regrinder Operator (plastic prod.) 555.685-026
regrind mill operator (cement; smelt. & refin.) 519.685-030
regulation supervisor (utilities) 953.137-014
regulator assembler (elec. equip.) 724.684-030
Regulator Assembler (inst. & app.) 710.684-046
REGULATOR INSPECTOR (utilities) 820.361-018
REGULATORY ADMINISTRATOR (tel. & tel.) 168.167-070
REHABILITATION CENTER MANAGER (government ser.) 195.167-038
REHABILITATION CLERK (nonprofit org.) 205.367-046
rehabilitation officer (nonprofit org.) 187.167-198
rehabilitation technician (personal ser.) 365.131-010
REHABILITATION THERAPIST (profess. & kin.) term
Reindeer Rancher (agriculture) 410.161-018
Reinforced-Concrete Inspector (construction) 182.267-010
reinforcing-bar setter (construction) 801.684-026
reinforcing-iron worker (construction) 801.684-026
Reinforcing-Iron-Worker Helper (construction) 869.687-026
REINFORCING-METAL WORKER (construction) 801.684-026
reinforcing-steel erector (construction) 801.684-026
REINFORCING-STEEL-MACHINE OPERATOR (construction) 859.683-022
reinforcing-steel placer (construction) 801.684-026
reinforcing-steel setter (construction) 801.684-026
reinforcing-steel worker (construction) 801.684-026
Reinforcing-Steel Worker, Wire Mesh (construction) 869.687-026
reinspector (boot & shoe) 753.687-018
REINSPECTOR (knitting) 684.687-014
reinstatement clerk (insurance) 219.362-050
REINSURANCE CLERK (insurance) 219.482-018
rejected-items clerk (financial) 216.382-058
REJECT OPENER (tobacco) 790.687-026
reject opener and filler (tobacco) 790.687-026
relaster (boot & shoe) 788.684-106
Relay Adjuster (elec. equip.) 724.381-010
Relay Assembler (elec. equip.) 729.684-026
Relay Checker (elec. equip.) 724.381-010
Relay Engineer (utilities) 003.167-054
RELAY-RECORD CLERK (utilities) 221.367-054
Relay Repairer (elec. equip.) 729.684-038
RELAY-SHOP SUPERVISOR (utilities) 729.131-014
relay-shop tester (utilities) 729.281-038
RELAY TECHNICIAN (utilities) 821.261-018
Relay Tester (electron. comp.) 726.684-078
RELAY TESTER (utilities) 729.281-038
Relay-Tester Helper (utilities) 821.564-010
release and technical records clerk (aircraft mfg.; electron. comp.) 206.367-010
RELIABILITY ENGINEER (profess. & kin.) 019.061-026
reliability inspector (clock & watch) 715.685-034
relief clerk (retail trade)   see SALESPERSON, CONTINGENT
RELIEF-MAP MODELER (any industry) 777.381-042
RELIEF WORKER (tobacco) term
RELISH BLENDER (can. & preserv.) 520.685-194
relish maker (can. & preserv.) 520.685-194
RELOCATION COMMISSIONER (government ser.) 188.167-070
Remelt-Centrifugal Operator (sugar & conf.) 521.682-010
REMELTER (elec. equip.; machinery mfg.; print. & pub.) 502.685-014
REMELT-FURNACE EXPEDITER (nonfer. metal) 512.132-018
remelt operator (foundry; nonfer. metal) 512.685-010
Remelt-Pan-Tank Operator (sugar & conf.) 529.585-014
Remelt-Sugar Boiler (sugar & conf.) 522.382-034

Remelt-Sugar Cutter (sugar & conf.) 521.682-010
remittance clerk (utilities) 211.462-034
Remittance-On-Farm-Rental-And-Soil-Conservation Auditor (insurance)
    210.382-010
REMNANTS CUTTER (textile) 789.687-150
REMNANT SORTER (textile) 789.687-146
remodeler (boot & shoe; wood prod., nec) 739.684-106
Remote-Control Assembler (engine-turbine) 706.481-010
remover (boot & shoe) 690.685-046
renderer (profess. & kin.) 970.281-014
RENDERING-EQUIPMENT TENDER (meat products) 529.685-202
Renovation-Plant Supervisor (ordnance) 694.132-010
renovator (museums) 899.384-010
RENOVATOR-MACHINE OPERATOR (tex. prod., nec) 589.685-082
rental agent (real estate) 250.357-014
rental clerk, furniture (retail trade) 295.357-018
rental clerk, tool-and-equipment (business ser.; retail trade) 295.357-014
RENTAL MANAGER, PUBLIC EVENTS FACILITIES (business ser.)
    186.117-062
Rent And Miscellaneous Remittance Clerk (insurance) 216.482-010
REPACK-ROOM WORKER (beverage) 920.687-146
repair clerk (boot & shoe) 221.387-014
repairer (any industry) 632.281-010
repairer (beverage) 764.687-090
REPAIRER (boot & shoe) 753.684-026
repairer (fabrication, nec) 739.687-146
REPAIRER (furniture) 709.684-062
repairer (hat & cap) 784.387-010
repairer (house. appl.) 723.584-010
REPAIRER (mine & quarry) 630.281-022
REPAIRER (smelt. & refin.) 630.281-026
repairer (tex. prod., nec; textile) 681.687-026
Repairer And Checker (ordnance) 761.381-034
REPAIRER, ART OBJECTS (any industry) 779.381-018
REPAIRER, ASSEMBLED WOOD PRODUCTS (woodworking) 769.684-038
Repairer, Assembly Line (motor-bicycles) 620.684-026
REPAIRER, AUTO CLOCKS (clock & watch) 715.584-014
Repairer, Cylinder Heads (welding) 819.384-010
Repairer, Electric Motors (elec. equip.) 721.684-022
Repairer, Evaporator (chemical) 630.261-018
REPAIRER, FINISHED METAL (any industry) 809.684-034
REPAIRER, GENERAL (auto. mfg.) 806.684-118
REPAIRER, GYROSCOPE (inst. & app.) 710.381-054
Repairer, Hairspring (clock & watch) 715.281-010
REPAIRER, HANDTOOLS (cutlery-hrdwr.) 701.381-010
REPAIRER, HEAVY (auto. mfg.) 620.381-022
REPAIRER HELPER (smelt. & refin.) 630.664-010
REPAIRER I (chemical) 630.261-018
REPAIRER II (chemical) 630.684-026
REPAIRER, KILN CAR (brick & tile) 861.684-022
REPAIRER, MANUFACTURED BUILDINGS (mfd. bldgs.; vehicles, nec)
    869.384-010
Repairer, Mirror And Picture Frame (wood prod., nec) 769.684-038
REPAIRER, PENS AND PENCILS (pen & pencil) 733.384-010
REPAIRER, PROBE TEST CARD, SEMICONDUCTOR WAFERS (electron.
    comp.) 726.361-022
Repairer, Pump (chemical) 630.261-018
REPAIRER, RECREATIONAL VEHICLE (vehicles, nec) 869.261-022
Repairer, Resistance-Welding Machines (welding) 626.361-010
Repairer, Sash And Door (wood prod., nec) 769.684-038
REPAIRER, SHOE STICKS (rubber goods) 619.685-074
Repairer, Still (chemical) 630.261-018
REPAIRER, SWITCHGEAR (comm. equip.; elec. equip.) 729.684-038
REPAIRER, TYPEWRITER (office machines) 706.381-030
REPAIRER, VENEER SHEET (furniture) 769.684-058
Repairer, Watchcases (clock & watch) 715.281-010
REPAIRER, WELDING, BRAZING, AND BURNING MACHINES (welding)
    626.361-010
REPAIRER, WELDING EQUIPMENT (welding) 626.384-010
REPAIRER, WELDING SYSTEMS AND EQUIPMENT (welding) 626.261-
    014
Repairer, Wood Furniture (furniture) 769.684-038
repair helper (any industry) 638.684-018
repair mechanic (any industry) 638.281-014
REPAIR OPERATOR (garment) 786.682-214
REPAIR-ORDER CLERK (clerical) 221.382-022
repair-service clerk (clerical) 221.367-070
Repair Supervisor (toy-sport equip.) 732.130-010
repair weaver (personal ser.) 782.381-022
REPEAT CHIEF (print. & pub.) 970.361-014
repeater attendant (tel. & tel.) 822.261-026
repeater operator (textile) 683.685-026
REPEAT-PHOTOCOMPOSING-MACHINE OPERATOR (print. & pub.)
    971.382-018
report checker (clerical) 209.687-010

report clerk (clerical) 216.382-062
REPORTER (print. & pub.; radio-tv broad.) 131.262-018
REPORTS ANALYST (profess. & kin.) 161.267-026
REPOSSESSOR (clerical) 241.367-022
Representative, Government Relations (profess. & kin.) 189.117-010
REPRESENTATIVE, PERSONAL SERVICE (tel. & tel.) 236.252-010
reprint sorter (photofinishing) 976.687-018
REPRODUCTION ORDER PROCESSOR (clerical) 221.367-058
REPRODUCTION TECHNICIAN (any industry) 976.361-010
REPTILE FARMER (agriculture) 413.161-014
RERECORDING MIXER (motion picture; radio-tv broad.) 194.362-014
reroller, hand (tobacco) 790.684-018
reroll tender (rubber goods; rubber tire) 554.685-022
Resaw Feeder (woodworking) 669.686-030
resaw-machine operator (woodworking) 667.682-058
RESAW OPERATOR (woodworking) 667.682-058
resawyer (woodworking) 667.682-058
RESEARCH ANALYST (insurance) 169.267-034
research assembler (photo. appar.) 714.281-010
Research Assistant (education) 090.227-010
research assistant (profess. & kin.) 199.364-014
RESEARCH ASSISTANT I (profess. & kin.) 109.267-010
RESEARCH ASSISTANT II (profess. & kin.) 199.267-034
RESEARCH ASSOCIATE (museums) 109.067-014
RESEARCH ASSOCIATE (profess. & kin.) term
RESEARCH-CONTRACTS SUPERVISOR (government ser.) 162.117-030
Research Director (profess. & kin.) 189.117-010
RESEARCH ENGINEER (profess. & kin.) master
research engineer, geophysical laboratory (profess. & kin.) 024.167-010
RESEARCH ENGINEER, MARINE EQUIPMENT (profess. & kin.) 014.061-018
RESEARCH ENGINEER, MINING-AND-OIL-WELL EQUIPMENT (mine & quarry; petrol. & gas) 010.061-022
RESEARCH ENGINEER, NUCLEAR EQUIPMENT (profess. & kin.) 015.061-018
researcher (profess. & kin.) 199.267-034
Research-Home Economist (profess. & kin.) 096.121-014
research-manufacturing operator (chemical; plastic-synth.) 559.382-046
RESEARCH MECHANIC (aircraft mfg.) 002.261-014
research mechanic (photo. appar.) 714.281-010
research nutritionist (profess. & kin.) 077.061-010
RESEARCH SUBJECT (any industry) 359.677-030
research-test-engine evaluator (petrol. refin.) 010.261-026
research-test-engine operator (petrol. refin.) 029.261-018
RESEARCH WORKER, ENCYCLOPEDIA (profess. & kin.) 109.267-014
research worker, kitchen (hotel & rest.) 310.267-010
RESEARCH WORKER, SOCIAL WELFARE (profess. & kin.) 054.067-010
reservation clerk (any industry) 238.367-026
RESERVATION CLERK (clerical) 238.362-014
Reservation Clerk (hotel & rest.) 238.367-038
RESERVATION CLERK (r.r. trans.) 238.367-014
RESERVATIONS AGENT (air trans.) 238.367-018
RESERVE OFFICER (financial; insurance) 186.167-054
reserve operator (garment) 786.682-262
RESERVE OPERATOR (tobacco) 529.685-206
RESERVES CLERK (financial) 216.362-034
reservoir caretaker (waterworks) 954.382-018
Reservoir Engineer (petrol. & gas) 010.061-018
Reshipping Clerk (clerical) 222.387-050
RESIDENCE COUNSELOR (education) 045.107-038
RESIDENCE SUPERVISOR (any industry) 187.167-186
resident care aide (medical ser.) 355.377-018
Residential Building Inspector (government ser.) 168.167-030
RESIN COATER (wood prod., nec) 562.687-014
Resin Compounder, Batch Lot (plastic-synth.) 550.685-134
Resin Filterer (paint & varnish) 551.685-082
resin maker (plastic-synth.) 558.382-050
Resin Worker (meat products) 525.687-094
resist coater-developer (electron. comp.) 976.685-038
Resistor Inspector (electron. comp.) 726.684-022
Resistor Tester (elec. equip.) 729.684-058
Resistor Tester (electron. comp.) 726.684-078
Resistor Winder (elec. equip.; electron. comp.) 724.684-026
resizer operator (woodworking) 667.682-058
Resource Agent (government ser.) 096.127-010
RESOURCE-RECOVERY ENGINEER (government ser.) 019.167-018
RESPIRATORY THERAPIST (medical ser.) 076.361-014
RESPIRATORY-THERAPY AIDE (medical ser.) 355.674-022
restoration technician (protective dev.) 712.381-038
RESTORER, CERAMIC (museums) 102.361-014
RESTORER, LACE AND TEXTILES (museums) 102.361-010
RESTORER, PAPER-AND-PRINTS (library; museums) 109.361-010
RESTRICTIVE-PREPARATION OPERATOR (ordnance) 559.685-154
Restrike Hammer Operator (forging) 610.362-010
RESTROOM ATTENDANT (any industry) 358.677-018

Retaining-Room Cutter (meat products) 525.684-026
Retanned-Leather Roller (leather mfg.) 583.685-094
retanner (leather mfg.) 582.482-018
retarder operator (r.r. trans.) 910.382-010
reticle printer (inst. & app.; optical goods) 976.684-034
RETIREMENT OFFICER (government ser.) 166.267-030
RETORT-CONDENSER ATTENDANT (chemical) 552.685-022
retort engineer (wood prod., nec) 561.362-010
Retort Feeder, Ground Bone (chemical) 553.686-010
retort forker (chemical) 569.686-034
Retort-Kiln Burner (brick & tile) 573.682-010
Retort Loader (chemical) 929.687-030
RETORT-LOAD EXPEDITER (wood prod., nec) 221.167-022
RETORT OPERATOR (can. & preserv.) 526.682-034
retort operator (woodworking) 562.665-014
RETORT-OR-CONDENSER PRESS OPERATOR (brick & tile) 575.382-026
RETORT UNLOADER (chemical) 569.686-034
retoucher (any industry) 740.684-026
retoucher (furniture) 763.684-034
retoucher (photofinishing) 970.281-018
RETOUCHER, PHOTOENGRAVING (print. & pub.) 970.381-030
Retouching Operator (hat & cap) 589.687-038
retreader (automotive ser.) 750.684-022
retread-mold operator (rubber tire) 553.685-102
RETREAD SUPERVISOR (rubber tire) 750.132-010
retrimmer (meat products) 521.687-106
Return Checker (laundry & rel.) 369.687-014
RETURNED-CASE INSPECTOR (beverage) 929.687-038
Returned-Goods Inspector (tex. prod., nec) 789.587-014
Returned-Goods Receiving Clerk (clerical) 222.387-050
returned-goods repairer (welding) 813.684-014
RETURNED-GOODS SORTER (textile) 922.687-086
RETURNED-ITEM CLERK (financial) 216.382-058
RETURNED-TELEPHONE-EQUIPMENT APPRAISER (comm. equip.) 222.387-046
Returner (agriculture) 920.687-074
returner, lasts (boot & shoe; rubber goods) 922.687-066
returning officer (government ser.) 205.367-030
returns clerk (boot & shoe) 221.387-014
returns clerk (clerical) 209.587-042
RETURN-TO-FACTORY CLERK (clerical) 209.587-042
REVENUE AGENT (government ser.) 160.167-050
REVENUE OFFICER (government ser.) 188.167-074
REVENUE-SETTLEMENTS ADMINISTRATOR (tel. & tel.) 184.117-074
revenue-stamp clerk (clerical) 219.487-010
Revenue-Stamp Cutter (beverage) 640.565-010
Reversal-Print Inspector (photofinishing) 976.687-014
Reverser (tex. prod., nec) 789.687-182
REVERSER (toy-sport equip.) 732.687-066
Reversing-Mill Roller (steel & rel.) 613.662-018
REVIEWER (insurance) 209.687-018
REVIEWING OFFICER, DRIVER'S LICENSE (government ser.) 168.167-074
REVISING CLERK (motor trans.; r.r. trans.) 214.382-026
REVIVAL CLERK (insurance) 219.362-050
revolving field assembler (elec. equip.) 721.684-026
reweaver (personal ser.) 782.381-022
rewinder (any industry) 699.587-010
rewinder (metal prod., nec) 920.685-102
Rewinder (motion picture) 976.685-018
rewinder (paper goods) 640.685-058
rewinder (tex. prod., nec; textile) 681.685-154
REWINDER OPERATOR (paper goods) 640.685-058
rewinder-operator helper (any industry) 699.587-010
reworker (electron. comp.) 726.684-090
REWORKER, PRINTED CIRCUIT BOARD (electron. comp.) 726.684-090
Rework Machine Operator (plastic prod.) 605.685-054
rewriter (print. & pub.; radio-tv broad.) 131.262-014
Rheostat Assembler (elec. equip.) 729.684-026
Rhinestone Setter (garment; tex. prod., nec) 789.685-010
Rhinestone Setter (jewelry-silver.) 735.687-034
Rhinologist (medical ser.) 070.101-062
Rib Bender (musical inst.) 569.685-014
ribber (meat products) 525.684-010
Ribbon Blocker (narrow fabrics) 689.685-014
Ribbon Cutter (garment) 699.685-014
Ribbon Cutter (hat & cap) 784.687-050
RIBBON CUTTER (narrow fabrics) 781.687-050
Rib Boner (meat products) 525.684-010
RIBBON-HANKING-MACHINE OPERATOR (paper goods) 640.385-010
RIBBON INKER (pen & pencil) 692.685-142
RIBBON-LAP-MACHINE TENDER (textile) 680.685-086
Ribbon-Sweatband Operator (hat & cap) 784.682-014
Ribbon Weaver (narrow fabrics) 683.682-046
RIBBON WINDER (pen & pencil) 733.685-022
Rib-Cloth Knitter (knitting) 685.665-014

rib matcher and fitter (ordnance) 736.381-014
rib-stiffener and heel-dipper (boot & shoe) 788.687-062
Rib-Trim Separator (knitting) 789.687-030
RICE CLEANING MACHINE TENDER (grain-feed mills) 521.665-022
Rice-Drier Operator (grain-feed mills) 523.685-090
Rice Farmer (agriculture) 401.161-010
rickshaw driver (amuse. & rec.) 349.477-010
RIDDLER OPERATOR (tobacco) 521.685-270
RIDE ATTENDANT (amuse. & rec.) 342.677-010
RIDE OPERATOR (amuse. & rec.) 342.663-010
rider (agriculture) 410.674-014
Riding Double (amuse. & rec.) 961.364-010
RIDING-SILKS CUSTODIAN (amuse. & rec.) 346.677-014
Riffler Tender (paper & pulp) 533.685-022
Rifle-Case Repairer (leather prod.) 783.684-026
rigger (amuse. & rec.) 962.684-010
RIGGER (any industry) 921.260-010
RIGGER (construction) 869.683-014
rigger (fishing & hunt.) 449.664-010
RIGGER (logging) 921.664-014
RIGGER (radio-tv broad.) 823.281-022
RIGGER (ship-boat mfg.) 806.261-014
RIGGER (tex. prod., nec) 789.684-046
RIGGER APPRENTICE (ship-boat mfg.) 806.261-018
rigger, chief (radio-tv broad.; tel. & tel.) 823.131-014
RIGGER HELPER (any industry) 921.687-026
RIGGER HELPER (ship-boat mfg.) 806.684-122
RIGGER SUPERVISOR (radio-tv broad.; tel. & tel.) 823.131-014
RIGGER, THIRD (logging) 921.687-030
Rigging-Loft Repairer (ship-boat mfg.) 806.684-122
RIGGING SLINGER (logging) 921.364-010
RIGGING SUPERVISOR (construction) 921.130-010
RIGHT-OF-WAY AGENT (any industry) 191.117-046
Right-of-Way Inspector (r.r. trans.) 376.667-018
RIGHT-OF-WAY SUPERVISOR (any industry) 191.117-050
right-of-way supervisor (construction) 869.133-010
rig operator (petrol. & gas) 930.382-030
rim-fire charger operator (ordnance) 694.685-050
RIM-FIRE-PRIMING OPERATOR (ordnance) 694.685-050
RIM-FIRE-PRIMING TOOL SETTER (ordnance) 632.380-022
Rim-Roller Setter (auto. mfg.) 616.260-014
Rim-Strip Tuber-Machine Operator (rubber tire) 690.662-014
RIM-TURNING FINISHER (clock & watch) 604.685-030
Ring Attacher (tex. prod., nec) 787.685-026
Ring-Barker Operator (saw. & plan.) 669.485-010
RING CONDUCTOR (amuse. & rec.) 159.367-010
Ring Facer (agriculture) 920.687-134
Ring-Grinder Operator (paper & pulp) 530.662-014
Ring Maker (chemical) 844.681-010
ring maker (jewelry-silver.) 700.684-010
RING MAKER (jewelry-silver.) 700.381-042
RING-MAKING-MACHINE OPERATOR (paper goods) 649.685-098
Ring Packer (agriculture; wholesale tr.) 920.687-134
RING-ROLLING-MACHINE OPERATOR (rubber goods) 690.682-066
Ring Sewer (tex. prod., nec) 789.687-090
ring-shear operator (any industry) 615.482-030
RING STAMPER (jewelry-silver.) 700.684-066
ring striker (jewelry-silver.) 700.684-066
RIP-AND-GROOVE-MACHINE OPERATOR (furniture) 667.682-062
RIPENING-ROOM ATTENDANT (plastic-synth.) 559.682-038
ripening-room hand (plastic-synth.) 559.585-018
Ripening-Room Operator (plastic-synth.) 559.585-018
rip-machine operator (any industry) 699.682-030
RIPPER (furniture) 617.685-030
RIPPER (garment; retail trade; tex. prod., nec) 782.687-038
ripper (leather mfg.) 585.684-010
ripper operator (tobacco) 529.685-090
Riprap Placer (construction) 869.687-026
Ripsaw Grader (woodworking) 667.382-010
Ripsaw Matcher (woodworking) 667.682-066
RIPSAW OPERATOR (woodworking) 667.682-066
ripsawyer (woodworking) 667.682-066
RISK AND INSURANCE MANAGER (any industry) 186.117-066
ritual circumciser (profess. & kin.) 129.271-010
RIVER (logging) 454.684-022
RIVER-AND-HARBOR SUPERVISOR (construction) term
riverboat captain (water trans.) 197.163-018
River-Crossing Supervisor (construction) 899.131-010
river tester (engine-turbine) 623.261-010
rivet bucker (any industry) 800.687-010
rivet catcher (any industry) 800.687-010
riveter (boot & shoe) 690.685-162
RIVETER (light. fix.) 616.685-054
RIVETER (railroad equip.) 800.684-010
Riveter, Automobile Brakes (automotive ser.) 620.685-010

RIVETER, HAND (any industry) 709.684-066
RIVETER, HAND (garment) 789.687-154
RIVETER HELPER (any industry) 800.687-010
RIVETER, HYDRAULIC (any industry) 800.662-010
RIVETER, PNEUMATIC (any industry) 800.684-014
Riveter, Portable Machine (any industry) 800.662-010
RIVETER, PORTABLE PINCH (any industry) 800.682-010
rivet-hammer-machine operator (furniture) 616.685-058
RIVET HEATER (heat treating) 504.485-010
Rivet Heater, Electric (heat treating) 504.485-010
Rivet Heater, Gas (heat treating) 504.485-010
rivet-hole-machine operator (garment) 686.685-054
RIVET-HOLE PUNCHER (garment) 686.685-054
RIVETING MACHINE OPERATOR (aircraft mfg.) 806.380-010
RIVETING-MACHINE OPERATOR (furniture) 616.685-058
RIVETING-MACHINE OPERATOR I (any industry) 699.482-010
RIVETING-MACHINE OPERATOR II (any industry) 699.685-030
Riveting Machine Operator, Programmed Control (aircraft mfg.) 806.380-010
Riveting Machine Operator, Tape Control (aircraft mfg.) 806.380-010
Rivet Maker (nut & bolt) 612.462-010
Rivet Spinner (any industry) 699.685-030
rivet sticker (any industry) 800.687-010
ROADABILITY-MACHINE OPERATOR (auto. mfg.) 806.383-010
Road Clerk (r.r. trans.) 221.362-026
Road Engineer, Freight (r.r. trans.) 910.363-014
Road Engineer, Passenger (r.r. trans.) 910.363-014
Road-Freight Firer (r.r. trans.) 910.363-010
road grader (construction) 850.663-022
road-hogger operator (construction) 850.663-022
Road Manager (amuse. & rec.) 191.117-038
ROAD-MIXER OPERATOR (construction) 859.683-026
road-oil distributor (construction) 853.663-018
ROAD-OILING-TRUCK DRIVER (construction) 853.663-018
Road-Passenger Firer (r.r. trans.) 910.363-010
ROAD-ROLLER OPERATOR (construction) 859.683-030
Road-Roller Operator, Hot Mix (construction) 859.683-030
ROADS SUPERVISOR (government ser.) 188.167-078
ROAD SUPERVISOR (motor trans.) 913.133-010
ROAD SUPERVISOR OF ENGINES (r.r. trans.) 910.137-034
road tester (auto. mfg.) 806.283-014
roaster (can. & preserv.) 529.685-174
roaster (cement; chemical; mine & quarry) 573.382-010
ROASTER, GRAIN (grain-feed mills) 523.585-034
roaster helper (sugar & conf.) 523.666-010
Roaster Supervisor (smelt. & refin.) 513.132-010
roast tier (meat products) 525.687-118
ROBOTIC MACHINE OPERATOR (aircraft mfg.) 606.382-026
robotic machine tender, production (machine shop) 609.685-018
robot technician (machinery mfg.) 638.261-026
Rockboard Lather (construction) 842.361-010
ROCK BREAKER (retail trade; stonework) 770.687-034
Rock Contractor (mine & quarry) 939.281-010
ROCK-DRILL OPERATOR I (construction) 850.683-034
ROCK-DRILL OPERATOR II (construction) 850.662-014
ROCK-DUST SPRAYER (mine & quarry) 939.687-026
Rocket-Assembly Operator (chemical) 590.464-010
Rocket-Control Technician (profess. & kin.) 003.261-010
ROCKET-ENGINE-COMPONENT MECHANIC (aircraft mfg.) 621.281-030
Rocket-Engine Mechanic, Liquid (aircraft mfg.) 693.261-022
ROCKET-MOTOR MECHANIC (aircraft mfg.) 693.261-022
ROCKET-TEST-FIRE WORKER (ordnance) 806.384-022
rock splitter (mine & quarry) 930.684-022
ROCK SPLITTER (stonework) 771.684-010
ROD-AND-TUBE STRAIGHTENER (plastic-synth.) 559.587-010
Rod-Bending-Machine Operator I (any industry) 617.482-010
Rod-Bending-Machine Operator II (any industry) 617.685-010
RODDING-ANODE WORKER (smelt. & refin.) 519.687-034
Rod-Drawing Supervisor (nonfer. metal; steel & rel.) 614.132-010
Rodent Exterminator (business ser.) 389.684-010
RODEO PERFORMER (amuse. & rec.) 159.344-014
Rod Inspector (construction) 182.267-010
Rod-Machine Operator (paper & pulp) 533.685-022
Rod-Mill Operator (any industry) 599.685-058
ROD-MILL TENDER (cement; smelt. & refin.) 519.685-030
ROD-PULLER AND COILER (nonfer. metal) 619.685-078
ROD TAPE OPERATOR (electron. comp.) 726.685-042
roll attendant (any industry) 570.685-022
ROLL BUILDER (rubber goods) 759.484-010
ROLL BUILDER (steel & rel.) 801.664-018
roll-calender tender (tex. prod., nec; textile) 583.685-026
roll changer (rubber goods; rubber tire) 554.665-010
roll-coating-machine operator (carpet & rug; tex. prod., nec) 584.562-010
roll-contour grinder (rubber reclaim.) 629.682-010
ROLL COVERER, BURLAP (textile) 929.687-042

ROLL CUTTER

ROLL CUTTER (rubber goods) 690.685-322
roll-cutting operator (any industry) 699.682-030
roll-dough divider (bakery products) 520.685-086
Roll-Edge Stitcher, Hand (furniture) 780.684-070
Rolled-Gold Plater (jewelry-silver.) 813.482-010
Rolled-Ham Lacer (meat products) 529.687-034
Rolled-Oats-Mill Operator (grain-feed mills) 521.685-122
Rolled-Seat Trimmer (boot & shoe) 690.685-434
roll-embosser operator (paper goods) 649.682-022
ROLLER (jewelry-silver.) 613.682-018
roller (jewelry-silver.) 735.687-042
ROLLER (ship-boat mfg.) 806.687-046
roller (textile) 689.685-046
roller (tobacco) 922.687-026
roller-bearing assembler (machinery mfg.; motor-bicycles) 706.687-034
ROLLER-BEARING INSPECTOR (machinery mfg.; motor-bicycles) 706.687-034
Roller, Billet Mill (steel & rel.) 613.362-014
Roller, Blooming Mill (steel & rel.) 613.362-014
ROLLER CHECKER (textile) 682.684-010
ROLLER CLEANER (textile) 680.687-014
Roller-Coaster Operator (amuse. & rec.) 342.663-010
ROLLER COVERER (textile) 628.682-010
Roller-Die-Cutting-Machine Operator (rubber goods) 690.685-290
roller embosser (any industry) 583.685-030
ROLLER ENGRAVER, HAND (print. & pub.) 979.681-018
ROLLER, GOLD LEAF (metal prod., nec) 709.685-018
Roller Hand (recording) 559.686-010
ROLLER, HAND (tobacco) 790.684-022
ROLLER I (sugar & conf.) 520.684-014
Roller II (sugar & conf.) 524.687-014
Roller Inspector (textile) 979.381-026
roller inspector and mender (textile) 979.381-026
ROLLER-LEVELER OPERATOR (steel & rel.) 613.685-022
ROLLER-MACHINE OPERATOR (leather mfg.) 583.685-094
ROLLER-MACHINE OPERATOR (metal prod., nec) 611.482-014
ROLLER MAKER (print. & pub.) 759.664-018
ROLLER MAKER (rubber goods) 690.685-502
roller maker (textile) 628.682-010
roller, merchant mill (steel & rel.) 613.130-014
roller-mill operator (grain-feed mills) 521.682-026
ROLLER-MILL OPERATOR (paint & varnish) 555.682-014
Roller-Mill Tender (pharmaceut.) 550.685-090
roller operator (construction) 859.683-030
ROLLER OPERATOR (hat & cap) 580.685-046
roller operator (metal prod., nec) 611.482-014
roller operator (sugar & conf.) 520.685-198
roller operator (tobacco) 521.685-330
ROLLER OPERATOR (toy-sport equip.) 652.685-078
roller painter (print. & pub.) 971.684-014
Roller, Plate Mill (steel & rel.) 613.130-018
roller, pneumatic (construction) 859.683-030
roller-presser operator (knitting; textile) 583.686-030
ROLLER, PRIMARY MILL (steel & rel.) 613.362-014
roller printer (print. & pub.) 971.685-010
roller printer (textile) 652.582-014
ROLLER-PRINT TENDER (print. & pub.) 971.685-010
ROLLER REPAIRER (textile) 979.381-026
roller-shop worker (textile) 628.682-010
ROLLER-SKATE ASSEMBLER (toy-sport equip.) 732.684-098
ROLLER-SKATE REPAIRER (any industry) 732.684-102
Roller, Slabbing Mill (steel & rel.) 613.362-014
Roller Stainer (leather prod.) 749.684-022
Roller Staker (clock & watch) 715.684-182
ROLLER-STITCHER (boot & shoe) 753.684-030
roller, structural mill (steel & rel.) 613.130-018
roller tender (grain-feed mills) 521.685-210
ROLLER VARNISHER (print. & pub.) 979.682-022
ROLL EXAMINER (paper & pulp) 640.687-010
Roll Filler (leather mfg.) 629.280-010
ROLL FINISHER (paper & pulp) 920.685-090
roll forger (forging) 612.682-014
roll former (any industry) 619.362-014
ROLL-FORMING-MACHINE OPERATOR I (any industry) 617.482-018
ROLL-FORMING-MACHINE OPERATOR II (any industry) 617.685-034
ROLL-FORMING-MACHINE SET-UP MECHANIC (any industry) 613.360-010
Roll-Forming Supervisor (any industry) 619.130-030
Roll Grinder (rubber goods) 690.680-010
ROLL GRINDER (rubber reclaim.) 629.682-010
Roll Grinder Operator (machine shop) 603.280-010
Roll Guider, Mold Goods (fabrication, nec) 590.686-014
Roll Icer (bakery products) 524.684-022
Roll Icer, Machine (bakery products) 524.685-034
ROLLING ATTENDANT (steel & rel.) 613.662-010

ROLLING-DOWN-MACHINE OPERATOR (knitting; textile) 589.685-086
rolling-machine operator (forging) 612.682-014
ROLLING-MACHINE OPERATOR (paper goods) 640.685-070
ROLLING-MACHINE OPERATOR (sugar & conf.) 520.685-198
rolling-machine operator (textile) 689.685-046
ROLLING-MACHINE OPERATOR (textile) 585.685-078
Rolling-Machine Operator, Automatic (any industry) 619.685-082
ROLLING-MACHINE TENDER (knitting) 689.685-114
ROLLING-MILL OPERATOR (nonfer. metal) 613.462-018
ROLLING-MILL-OPERATOR HELPER (nonfer. metal) 613.685-026
rolling-mill plugger (steel & rel.) 613.687-010
rolling supervisor, continuous-pipe mill (steel & rel.) 619.130-022
rolling-up-machine operator (knitting) 580.485-010
ROLL INSPECTOR (plastic-synth.) 554.587-010
roll-machine attendant (soap & rel.) 553.685-098
roll-machine operator (bakery products) 520.685-086
roll-mill operator (any industry) 616.685-042
roll molder (rubber goods) 559.482-010
roll operator (construction) 859.683-030
roll operator (grain-feed mills) 520.685-102
roll operator (grain-feed mills; oils & grease) 529.685-106
ROLL OPERATOR (plastic-synth.) 554.682-018
Roll-Operator Helper (any industry) 619.687-014
ROLL OPERATOR I (any industry) 619.362-014
ROLL OPERATOR II (any industry) term
Roll Operator, Sheet Metal (any industry) 619.362-014
ROLL-OR-TAPE-EDGE-MACHINE OPERATOR (furniture) 787.682-038
roll-over loader (optical goods) 713.687-026
ROLL-OVER-PRESS OPERATOR (optical goods) 690.685-326
roll picker (textile) 680.687-014
roll-press operator (leather mfg.; tex. prod., nec) 589.685-098
ROLL RECLAIMER (paper goods) 640.685-062
Roll Repairer (smelt. & refin.) 630.281-026
Rolls Baker (hotel & rest.) 313.381-010
roll setter (print. & pub.) 651.686-022
roll setter (steel & rel.) 613.360-014
roll setter, pipe mill (steel & rel.) 613.360-014
ROLL-SHEETING CUTTER (tex. prod., nec) 699.682-026
roll skinner (paper & pulp) 539.686-010
ROLL-SLICING-MACHINE TENDER (pen & pencil) 640.685-066
ROLL TENDER (chemical) 559.362-030
ROLL TENDER (print. & pub.) 651.686-022
ROLL-TENSION TESTER (plastic-synth.) 559.584-010
roll tester (textile) 652.685-090
ROLL-THREADER OPERATOR (nut & bolt) 619.462-010
ROLL-TUBE SETTER (steel & rel.) 613.360-014
ROLL TURNER (knitting) 689.685-110
ROLL-UP-GUIDER OPERATOR (fabrication, nec) 590.685-050
roll-up helper (fabrication, nec) 739.587-010
roll-up operator (fabrication, nec) 590.665-018
Roll Weigher (paper & pulp; paper goods; plastic-synth.) 222.387-074
roll winder (build. mat., nec) 549.685-022
roll winder (paper goods) 640.685-058
roll wrapper (paper & pulp) 920.685-090
ROOF ASSEMBLER I (mfd. bldgs.) 869.684-042
Roof Assembler II (mfd. bldgs.) 869.684-018
ROOF BOLTER (mine & quarry) 930.683-026
ROOF-CEMENT-AND-PAINT MAKER (build. mat., nec; nonmet. min.) 550.382-030
ROOF-CEMENT-AND-PAINT-MAKER HELPER (build. mat., nec; nonmet. min.) 550.686-038
ROOFER (construction) 866.381-010
ROOFER APPLICATOR (construction) 866.684-010
ROOFER APPRENTICE (construction) 866.381-014
Roofer, Gypsum (construction) 866.381-010
Roofer Helper (construction) 869.687-026
Roofer Helper, Vinyl Coating (construction) 869.687-026
Roofer, Metal (construction) 804.281-010
Roofer, Vinyl Coating (construction) 869.664-014
ROOF FITTER (railroad equip.) 806.684-126
Roof Framer (mfd. bldgs.; vehicles, nec) 869.684-010
ROOFING-MACHINE OPERATOR (build. mat., nec) 554.682-022
ROOFING-MACHINE TENDER (nonmet. min.) 590.685-098
ROOFING SUPERVISOR (construction) 866.131-010
Roofing-Tile Burner (brick & tile) 573.682-010
Roofing-Tile Sorter (brick & tile) 573.687-034
Roof-Panel Hanger (mfd. bldgs.; vehicles, nec) 809.684-030
Roof-Promenade-Tile Setter (construction) 861.381-054
ROOF-TRUSS-MACHINE TENDER (mfd. bldgs.) 669.685-070
room boss (mine & quarry) 939.137-018
Room Clerk (hotel & rest.) 238.367-038
Rooming-House Inspector (government ser.) 168.267-066
Room Service Assistant (hotel & rest.) 311.677-018
ROOM-SERVICE CLERK (hotel & rest.) 324.577-010
ROOTER OPERATOR (fabrication, nec) 731.685-010

ROPE CLEANER (textile) 699.687-022
rope-coiling-machine operator (tex. prod., nec) 681.685-086
ROPE-LAYING-MACHINE OPERATOR (tex. prod., nec) 681.685-086
ROPE-MACHINE SETTER (tex. prod., nec) 681.380-010
ROPE MAKER, MACHINE (nonmet. min.) 681.685-082
ROPE-MAKER, ROPEWALK (tex. prod., nec) 681.682-014
Roper (agriculture) 929.687-030
roper (hat & cap) 580.684-010
roper (meat products) 529.687-150
rope rider (any industry) 932.664-010
roper operator (plastic-synth.) 559.562-010
ROPE-SILICA-MACHINE OPERATOR (textile) 582.685-114
rope-twisting-machine operator (tex. prod., nec) 681.685-086
Rose-Farm Laborer (agriculture) 405.687-014
Roping Machine Tender (button & notion) 739.685-058
Rose-Farm Laborer (agriculture) 405.687-014
Rose Grader (agriculture) 409.687-010
Rose Grower (agriculture) 405.161-014
ROSIN-BARREL FILLER (chemical) 920.687-150
rotary-bar operator (steel & rel.) 619.682-042
ROTARY CUTTER (boot & shoe) 585.685-082
ROTARY-CUTTER FEEDER (paper & pulp) 640.686-010
ROTARY-CUTTER OPERATOR (rubber goods) 551.585-022
ROTARY DERRICK OPERATOR (petrol. & gas) 930.382-022
ROTARY-DRIER FEEDER (chemical) 553.686-038
rotary-drier operator (chemical) 553.685-050
rotary-drier operator (smelt. & refin.) 511.565-014
ROTARY DRILLER (petrol. & gas) 930.382-026
ROTARY-DRILLER HELPER (petrol. & gas) 930.684-026
Rotary Driller, Marine Operations (petrol. & gas) 930.382-026
rotary driller, prospecting (petrol. & gas) 930.382-018
Rotary-Drill Operator (construction; mine & quarry) 930.382-010
rotary-drill-rig operator (construction) 859.362-010
Rotary-Drum Dyer (knitting) 582.685-170
Rotary-Dump Operator (mine & quarry; steel & rel.) 921.685-038
ROTARY-ENGINE ASSEMBLER (engine-turbine) 801.261-018
Rotary-Envelope-Machine Operator (paper goods) 649.685-042
rotary-filter operator (paper & pulp) 533.682-010
rotary-furnace operator (foundry; steel & rel.) 512.362-018
ROTARY-FURNACE TENDER (chemical) 553.685-094
ROTARY-HEAD-MILLING-MACHINE SET-UP OPERATOR (machine shop) 605.382-030
rotary helper (petrol. & gas) 930.684-026
ROTARY-KILN OPERATOR (cement; chemical; mine & quarry) 573.382-010
Rotary-Kiln Operator (concrete prod.) 573.462-010
ROTARY-KILN OPERATOR (smelt. & refin.) 513.682-010
Rotary-Machine Operator (bakery products) 520.682-034
Rotary-Peel Oven Tender (bakery products) 526.685-030
Rotary Planer Set-Up Operator (machine shop) 605.282-014
Rotary Preformer (plastic prod.; plastic-synth.) 556.685-058
rotary profile-shaper operator, automatic (woodworking) 665.682-026
Rotary Pump Operator (electron. comp.) 599.382-014
ROTARY-RIG ENGINE OPERATOR (petrol. & gas) 950.382-022
Rotary-Rock-Drilling-Machine Operator (any industry) 850.683-034
rotary-saw operator (stonework) 677.462-014
ROTARY-SCREEN-PRINTING-MACHINE OPERATOR (textile) 652.582-014
ROTARY-SHEAR OPERATOR (any industry) 615.482-030
rotary-slicing-machine operator (millwork-plywood) 664.662-010
rotary-soil-stabilizer operator (construction) 859.683-026
rotary-surface grinder (machine shop) 603.280-014
Rotary-Swaging-Machine Operator (forging) 612.682-014
rotary-veneer-machine operator (millwork-plywood) 664.662-010
rotating field assembler (elec. equip.) 721.684-026
ROTOGRAVURE-PRESS OPERATOR (print. & pub.) 651.362-026
roto-mixer operator (construction) 859.683-026
rotor-and-armature bander (any industry) 724.684-010
ROTOR ASSEMBLER (clock & watch) 715.687-114
Rotor Balancer (elec. equip.) 724.384-014
ROTOR CASTING-MACHINE OPERATOR (elec. equip.) 502.482-018
rotor-lamination inspector (elec. equip.) 729.687-018
Rotor Winder (elec. equip.) 721.484-010
ROUGE MIXER (optical goods) 570.685-082
Rouge Mixer (pharmaceut.) 550.685-090
rouge presser (pharmaceut.) 556.685-026
ROUGE SIFTER AND MILLER (optical goods) 579.685-046
ROUGH-AND-TRUEING-MACHINE OPERATOR (toy-sport equip.) 690.685-330
roughener (boot & shoe) 690.685-046
Rougher (glass products) 775.684-010
ROUGHER (steel & rel.) 613.362-018
Rougher, Bar Mill (steel & rel.) 613.362-018
Rougher For Cement (boot & shoe) 690.685-046
Rougher, Hot-Strip Mill (steel & rel.) 613.362-018
Rougher, Merchant Mill (steel & rel.) 613.362-018
ROUGHER OPERATOR (steel & rel.) 613.662-014
Rough-Lumber Grader (woodworking) 669.687-030

roughneck (petrol. & gas) 930.684-026
roughneck (petrol. & gas) 869.684-046
ROUGH OPENER, JEWEL HOLE (clock & watch) 770.684-018
Rough Patcher (concrete prod.) 579.687-042
Rough Patcher (fabrication, nec) 739.687-146
ROUGH PLANER TENDER (woodworking) 665.665-010
ROUGH-RICE GRADER (grain-feed mills) 529.367-026
ROUGH-RICE TENDER (grain-feed mills) 521.685-274
ROUGH-ROUNDER, MACHINE (boot & shoe) 690.685-334
Rough Sander (fabrication, nec) 761.684-030
Roulette Dealer (amuse. & rec.) 343.464-010
Round Boner (meat products) 525.684-010
ROUND-CORNER-CUTTER OPERATOR (paper goods) 640.685-074
round-cutter operator (hat & cap; tex. prod., nec) 585.685-086
rounder (boot & shoe) 690.685-334
ROUNDER (boot & shoe) 690.685-338
rounder (hat & cap; tex. prod., nec) 585.685-086
rounder (print. & pub.) 653.685-026
rounder and backer (print. & pub.) 653.685-026
ROUNDER, HAND (hat & cap) 784.684-050
ROUNDING-AND-BACKING-MACHINE OPERATOR (print. & pub.) 653.685-026
Rounding-Machine Operator (hat & cap) 699.682-022
ROUNDING-MACHINE OPERATOR (hat & cap; tex. prod., nec) 585.685-086
rounding-machine operator (wood. container) 667.685-066
ROUNDING-MACHINE TENDER (pen & pencil) 663.685-026
round-kiln drawer (pottery & porc.) 573.667-010
ROUND-UP-RING HAND (concrete prod.) 579.587-010
roustabout (leather mfg.) 589.686-026
roustabout (petrol. & gas) 939.687-018
ROUSTABOUT (petrol. & gas) 869.684-046
roustabout, head (petrol. & gas) 862.131-022
ROUTE AIDE (tel. & tel.) 239.687-010
route clerk (clerical) 222.687-022
ROUTE-DELIVERY CLERK (clerical) 222.587-034
route driver (retail trade; wholesale tr.) 292.353-010
route driver, coin machines (business ser.) 292.483-010
route driver helper (retail trade; wholesale tr.) 292.667-010
ROUTER (clerical) 222.587-038
router (clerical) 222.687-022
ROUTER (print. & pub.) 979.682-026
Route Returner (clerical) 222.387-050
ROUTER MACHINE OPERATOR (plastic prod.) 605.685-054
ROUTER OPERATOR (any industry) 605.382-034
ROUTER OPERATOR (stonework) 676.462-010
ROUTER OPERATOR (woodworking) 665.682-030
ROUTER OPERATOR, HAND (aircraft mfg.; railroad equip.) 806.684-150
Router Operator, Pin (aircraft mfg.) 605.382-034
Router Operator, Radial (aircraft mfg.) 605.382-034
ROUTER, PRINTED CIRCUIT BOARDS (electron. comp.) 605.682-034
Router Setter (woodworking) 669.280-010
ROUTER SET-UP OPERATOR, NUMERICAL CONTROL (machine shop) 605.360-010
ROUTER TENDER (furniture) 665.685-042
route supervisor (retail trade; wholesale tr.) 292.137-014
ROUTE SUPERVISOR (tel. & tel.) 239.137-018
ROUTING CLERK (clerical) 222.687-022
routing clerk (clerical) 222.587-038
ROUTING CLERK (nonprofit org.) 249.367-070
ROUTING-EQUIPMENT TENDER (grain-feed mills) 521.685-278
routing-machine operator (woodworking) 665.682-030
roving changer (textile) 689.686-026
roving-frame tender (textile) 681.685-106
roving selector (glass mfg.) 689.687-038
ROVING SIZER (textile) 680.367-010
Roving Stock Handler (textile) 929.687-030
roving technician (textile) 589.384-010
roving tender (textile) 680.685-098
roving tester, laboratory (textile) 689.384-014
ROVING-WEIGHT GAUGER (textile) 680.687-018
ROVING WINDER, FIBERGLASS (textile) 681.485-010
row boss (agriculture) 180.167-022
ROW BOSS, HOEING (agriculture) 409.137-014
rubber (furniture) 742.687-010
RUBBER (furniture; wood prod., nec) 742.684-010
RUBBER (personal ser.) 334.677-010
rubber (personal ser.) 334.374-010
RUBBER AND PLASTICS WORKER (military ser.) 891.684-014
rubber and pounder (boot & shoe) 690.685-350
Rubber Attacher (toy-sport equip.) 795.687-014
rubber ball finisher (toy-sport equip.) 690.685-038
rubber-calender helper (rubber goods; rubber tire) 554.686-018
Rubber Compounder (plastic-synth.; rubber goods; rubber tire) 929.687-062
Rubber-Compounder Supervisor (rubber goods) 559.137-014
Rubber-Compounder Supervisor (rubber reclaim.) 559.132-058

Rubber-Compounder Supervisor

Rubber-Compounder Supervisor (rubber tire) 750.130-010
rubber coverer (textile) 681.685-038
rubber-covering-machine operator (textile) 681.685-038
rubber curer (rubber goods; rubber reclaim.; rubber tire) 553.665-038
RUBBER CUTTER (rubber goods; rubber tire) 559.685-158
rubber cutter (stonework) 771.281-010
rubber cutter and shape carver (stonework) 673.382-010
RUBBER-CUTTING-MACHINE TENDER (rubber goods) 690.685-342
Rubber-Flap Cutter (rubber goods; rubber tire) 690.685-446
Rubber-Flap Tuber-Machine Operator (rubber tire) 690.662-014
Rubber-Gasket Inspector-Trimmer (rubber goods) 759.684-074
RUBBER-GOODS ASSEMBLER (rubber goods) 752.684-038
RUBBER-GOODS CUTTER-FINISHER (rubber goods) 690.680-010
Rubber-Goods Finisher (rubber goods) 759.684-074
rubber-goods finisher (rubber goods) 690.680-010
RUBBER-GOODS INSPECTOR-TESTER (rubber goods) 759.684-074
Rubber-Goods Inspector-Trimmer (rubber goods; rubber reclaim.; rubber tire) 759.684-074
RUBBER-GOODS REPAIRER (any industry) 759.684-054
RUBBER-GOODS TESTER (elec. equip.; utilities) 759.381-010
Rubber-Goods Tester, Water (rubber goods; rubber tire) 759.684-074
Rubber-Heel-And-Sole Press Tender (rubber goods) 556.685-066
rubber insulator (machinery mfg.) 759.684-050
RUBBERIZING MECHANIC (any industry) 630.281-030
RUBBER LINER (machinery mfg.) 759.684-050
RUBBER-MILL OPERATOR (plastic-synth.) 559.682-042
RUBBER-MILL TENDER (plastic-synth.; rubber goods; rubber reclaim.; rubber tire) 550.685-102
RUBBER MOLDER (fabrication, nec) 556.684-026
RUBBER-MOLD MAKER (jewelry-silver.) 559.684-018
rubber-off (jewelry-silver.) 700.687-058
RUBBER-PRINTING-MACHINE OPERATOR (rubber goods) 652.462-010
RUBBER-ROLLER GRINDER (pen & pencil) 690.686-050
rubber-stamp assembler (pen & pencil) 733.684-018
RUBBER-STAMP MAKER (pen & pencil) 733.381-014
RUBBER TESTER (rubber goods; rubber tire) 559.381-014
RUBBER-THREAD SPOOLER (toy-sport equip.) 681.685-090
Rubber-Tile-Floor Layer (construction; retail trade) 864.481-010
rubber-tubing backer (rubber goods) 559.686-018
RUBBER-TUBING SPLICER (rubber goods) 752.684-042
rubbing-bed operator (stonework) 673.685-014
rubbish-collection supervisor (motor trans.) 909.137-014
ruching-machine operator (any industry) 787.682-082
ruffer (boot & shoe) 690.685-046
ruffler (any industry) 787.682-078
ruffler (tex. prod., nec) 787.685-038
Ruffling Hemmer, Automatic (tex. prod., nec) 787.685-018
RUG-BACKING STENCILER (carpet & rug) 781.687-054
RUG BRAIDER, HAND (carpet & rug) 782.687-042
RUG CLEANER (carpet & rug) 689.687-066
RUG CLEANER, HAND (laundry & rel.) 369.384-014
RUG-CLEANER HELPER (laundry & rel.) 362.686-014
RUG CLEANER, MACHINE (laundry & rel.) 361.682-010
RUG CLIPPER (carpet & rug) 781.684-046
RUG CUTTER (carpet & rug) 686.662-010
rug cutter (carpet & rug) 781.684-046
rug cutter (carpet & rug) 781.684-010
RUG CUTTER (fabrication, nec) 590.687-022
RUG-CUTTER HELPER (carpet & rug) 686.686-014
Rug Designer (carpet & rug) 142.061-014
RUG-DRYING-MACHINE OPERATOR (carpet & rug) 581.685-050
RUG-DRY-ROOM ATTENDANT (laundry & rel.) 369.685-026
RUG-DYER HELPER (laundry & rel.) 364.687-014
RUG DYER I (laundry & rel.) 364.361-014
RUG DYER II (laundry & rel.) 364.684-010
RUG-FRAME MOUNTER (carpet & rug) 687.464-010
RUG HOOKER (carpet & rug) 687.684-010
Rug Hooker, Hand (carpet & rug) 687.684-010
Rug Inspector (fabrication, nec) 590.367-010
RUG INSPECTOR (laundry & rel.) 369.687-030
RUG INSPECTOR (tex. prod., nec) 585.685-090
RUG-INSPECTOR HELPER (carpet & rug) 789.687-158
RUG-INSPECTOR HELPER (tex. prod., nec) 589.686-038
RUG INSPECTOR I (carpet & rug) 689.667-010
RUG INSPECTOR II (carpet & rug) 789.587-022
RUG MEASURER (laundry & rel.; retail trade) 369.367-014
Rug Mender (carpet & rug) 782.684-042
rug-receiving clerk (laundry & rel.; retail trade) 369.367-014
rug renovator (laundry & rel.) 369.384-014
RUG REPAIRER (laundry & rel.) 782.381-018
RUG-SAMPLE BEVELER (carpet & rug) 781.684-050
rug scratcher (carpet & rug) 789.687-138
rug scrubber (laundry & rel.) 369.384-014
RUG SETTER, AXMINSTER (carpet & rug) 681.682-018
Rug Setter, Six-Quarter Machine (carpet & rug) 681.682-018

Rug Setter, Three-Quarter Machine (carpet & rug) 681.682-018
Rug Setter, Velvet (carpet & rug) 681.682-018
rug shampooer (laundry & rel.) 369.384-014
rug stretcher (any industry) 580.687-010
Rug-Underlay-Machine Operator (rubber goods) 559.682-050
rug washer (laundry & rel.) 369.384-014
RULING-MACHINE SET-UP OPERATOR (paper goods; print. & pub.) 659.682-022
Rump Sawyer (meat products) 525.684-018
Run-Boat Operator (water trans.) 911.663-010
Runner (financial) 239.567-010
Runner (hotel & rest.) 311.677-018
runner (hotel & rest.) 324.577-010
runner (library) 249.687-014
runner (water trans.) 222.567-014
RUNNING RIGGER (ship-boat mfg.) 806.684-142
runstitching-machine operator (garment) 786.685-026
RURAL MAIL CARRIER (government ser.) 230.363-010
Rural-Service Engineer (utilities) 003.167-046
Rural Sociologist (profess. & kin.) 054.067-014
Russet-Leather Sorter (leather mfg.) 589.387-010
Russet Repairer (boot & shoe) 788.684-022
Russian Rubber (personal ser.) 334.677-010
Rust Proofer (auto. mfg.) 599.685-026
rust proofer (automotive ser.) 843.684-014

S

sack-cleaning hand (textile) 689.687-010
SACK-DEPARTMENT SUPERVISOR (grain-feed mills) 229.137-010
Sack Keeper (clerical) 222.387-058
sack mender (any industry) 782.687-046
SACK REPAIRER (any industry) 782.687-046
Sack Sewer, Hand (any industry) 920.587-018
Sack Sewer, Machine (any industry) 920.685-078
Sack Sorter (any industry) 929.687-022
Sack Stenciler (any industry) 920.687-178
SADDLE-AND-SIDE WIRE STITCHER (print. & pub.) 692.685-146
Saddle-Lining Stitcher (boot & shoe) 690.682-082
SADDLE MAKER (leather prod.) 783.381-026
Saddler (leather prod.; retail trade) 783.381-026
Saddle Stitcher (boot & shoe) 690.682-082
Saddle-Stitching-Machine Feeder-Offbearer (print. & pub.) 653.686-026
Saddle-Stitching-Machine Operator (print. & pub.) 653.662-010
SAFE-AND-VAULT SERVICE MECHANIC (business ser.; wholesale tr.) 869.381-022
SAFE-DEPOSIT-BOX RENTAL CLERK (financial) 295.367-022
safe deposit manager (financial) 295.137-010
safe repairer (business ser.; wholesale tr.) 869.381-022
SAFETY-CLOTHING-AND-EQUIPMENT DEVELOPER (profess. & kin.) 142.061-038
SAFETY COORDINATOR (motor trans.) 909.127-010
Safety Director (nonprofit org.) 187.167-214
safety engineer (insurance) 168.167-078
SAFETY ENGINEER (profess. & kin.) 012.061-014
safety engineer, elevators (government ser.) 168.167-038
SAFETY ENGINEER, MINES (mine & quarry) 010.061-026
safety-engineer, pressure vessels (profess. & kin.) 168.167-026
safety-equipment tester (elec. equip.; utilities) 759.381-010
safety-grooving-machine operator (construction) 853.683-018
SAFETY INSPECTOR (any industry) 168.264-014
SAFETY INSPECTOR (insurance) 168.167-078
safety inspector (mine & quarry) 168.267-074
SAFETY INSPECTOR (utilities) 821.367-014
SAFETY INSPECTOR, TRUCK (automotive ser.; motor trans.) 919.687-018
SAFETY-LAMP KEEPER (mine & quarry) 729.684-042
SAFETY MANAGER (medical ser.) 168.167-086
SAFETY MANAGER (profess. & kin.) 012.167-058
Safety-Net Maker (tex. prod., nec) 789.684-030
SAFETY-PIN-ASSEMBLING-MACHINE OPERATOR (button & notion) 616.482-010
safety-sealer (build. mat., nec) 550.686-026
Safety-Stitch-Machine Operator (garment) 786.682-194
safety technician (any industry) 168.264-014
sagger filler (pottery & porc.) 573.686-026
Sagger Former (pottery & porc.) 774.381-010
SAGGER MAKER (pottery & porc.) 774.684-030
SAGGER PREPARER (pottery & porc.) 570.685-086
sagger soak (pottery & porc.) 570.685-086
SAIL CUTTER (tex. prod., nec) 781.384-018
Sail Finisher, Hand (tex. prod., nec) 789.484-014
Sail Finisher, Machine (tex. prod., nec) 787.682-058
SAIL-LAY-OUT WORKER (tex. prod., nec) 781.381-030
Sailmaker (ship-boat mfg.; tex. prod., nec) 739.381-010

SAILOR (water trans.) term
sailor-merchant mariner (water trans.)　　see SAILOR
SAILOR, PLEASURE CRAFT (water trans.) 911.664-014
sail, tent, and awning-maker apprentice (ship-boat mfg.; tex. prod., nec) 739.381-014
Salad Counter Attendant (hotel & rest.) 311.677-014
Salad Maker (hotel & rest.) 317.684-014
SALAD MAKER (water trans.) 317.384-010
sales agent (retail trade; wholesale tr.)　　see SALES REPRESENTATIVE
SALES AGENT, BUSINESS SERVICES (business ser.) 251.357-010
Sales Agent, Casualty Insurance (insurance) 250.257-010
sales agent, credit services (business ser.) 250.357-026
sales agent, exterminating service (business ser.) 251.357-018
SALES AGENT, FINANCIAL-REPORT SERVICE (business ser.) 250.357-026
Sales Agent, Fire Insurance (insurance) 250.257-010
Sales Agent, Food-Vending Service (wholesale tr.) 251.357-010
SALES AGENT, INSURANCE (insurance) 250.257-010
Sales Agent, Life Insurance (insurance) 250.257-010
Sales Agent, Marine Insurance (insurance) 250.257-010
SALES AGENT, PEST CONTROL SERVICE (business ser.) 251.357-018
Sales Agent, Protective Service (business ser.) 251.357-010
SALES AGENT, PSYCHOLOGICAL TESTS AND INDUSTRIAL RELATIONS (business ser.; print. & pub.) 251.257-014
SALES AGENT, REAL ESTATE (real estate) 250.357-018
Sales Agent, Trading Stamps (business ser.) 251.357-010
sales associate (retail trade; wholesale tr.)　　see SALES REPRESENTATIVE
sales associate, garage service (automotive ser.) 620.261-018
SALES ATTENDANT (retail trade) 299.677-010
SALES ATTENDANT, BUILDING MATERIALS (retail trade) 299.677-014
SALES CLERK (retail trade) 290.477-014
Sales Clerk, Fish (retail trade) 290.477-018
SALES CLERK, FOOD (retail trade) 290.477-018
Sales Clerk, Fresh Poultry (retail trade) 316.684-010
Sales-Correspondence Clerk (clerical) 209.362-034
SALES CORRESPONDENT (clerical) 221.367-062
SALES ENGINEER (profess. & kin.) master
SALES ENGINEER, AERONAUTICAL PRODUCTS (aircraft mfg.) 002.151-010
SALES ENGINEER, AGRICULTURAL EQUIPMENT (profess. & kin.) 013.151-010
SALES ENGINEER, CERAMIC PRODUCTS (profess. & kin.) 006.151-010
SALES-ENGINEER, ELECTRICAL PRODUCTS (profess. & kin.) 003.151-010
SALES-ENGINEER, ELECTRONICS PRODUCTS AND SYSTEMS (profess. & kin.) 003.151-014
SALES ENGINEER, MARINE EQUIPMENT (profess. & kin.) 014.151-010
SALES ENGINEER, MECHANICAL EQUIPMENT (utilities) 007.151-010
SALES ENGINEER, MINING-AND-OIL-WELL EQUIPMENT AND SERVICES (mine & quarry; petrol. & gas) 010.151-010
SALES ENGINEER, NUCLEAR EQUIPMENT (profess. & kin.) 015.151-010
SALES EXHIBITOR (nonprofit org.) 279.357-010
SALESPERSON (retail trade; wholesale tr.) master
salesperson apprentice, meats (retail trade; wholesale tr.) 316.684-022
SALESPERSON, ART OBJECTS (retail trade) 277.457-010
SALESPERSON, AUTOMOBILE ACCESSORIES (retail trade; wholesale tr.) 273.357-030
SALESPERSON, AUTOMOBILES (retail trade) 273.353-010
SALESPERSON, BOOKS (retail trade) 277.357-034
SALESPERSON, BURIAL NEEDS (retail trade) 279.357-042
Salesperson, Burial Plots (retail trade) 279.357-042
salesperson, cemetery (retail trade) 279.357-042
Salesperson, Children's Shoes (retail trade) 261.357-062
Salesperson, China And Glassware (retail trade; wholesale tr.) 270.357-018
SALESPERSON, CHINA AND SILVERWARE (retail trade; wholesale tr.) 270.357-018
SALESPERSON, CONTINGENT (retail trade) term
SALESPERSON, CORSETS (retail trade) 261.354-010
SALESPERSON, COSMETICS AND TOILETRIES (retail trade) 262.357-018
SALESPERSON, CURTAINS AND DRAPERIES (retail trade) 270.357-022
Salesperson, Custom Draperies (retail trade) 270.357-022
SALESPERSON-DEMONSTRATOR, PARTY PLAN (retail trade) 279.357-038
SALESPERSON, ELECTRIC MOTORS (retail trade; wholesale tr.) 271.354-010
Salesperson, Fashion Accessories (retail trade) 261.357-066
SALESPERSON, FLOOR COVERINGS (retail trade; wholesale tr.) 270.357-026
SALESPERSON, FLORIST SUPPLIES (wholesale tr.) 275.357-054
SALESPERSON, FLOWERS (retail trade) 260.357-026
SALESPERSON, FLYING SQUAD (retail trade) 279.357-046
SALESPERSON, FURNITURE (retail trade) 270.357-030
SALESPERSON, FURS (retail trade) 261.357-042

SALESPERSON, GENERAL HARDWARE (retail trade; wholesale tr.) 279.357-050
SALESPERSON, GENERAL MERCHANDISE (retail trade; wholesale tr.) 279.357-054
Salesperson, Grave Coverings And Markers (retail trade) 279.357-042
Salesperson, Handbags (retail trade) 261.357-066
salesperson, hearing aids (retail trade) 276.354-010
SALESPERSON, HORTICULTURAL AND NURSERY PRODUCTS (retail trade; wholesale tr.) 272.357-022
Salesperson, Hosiery (retail trade) 261.357-066
SALESPERSON, HOUSEHOLD APPLIANCES (retail trade) 270.357-034
SALESPERSON, INFANTS' AND CHILDREN'S WEAR (retail trade) 261.357-046
SALESPERSON, JEWELRY (retail trade) 279.357-058
salesperson, ladies' wear (retail trade) 261.357-066
SALESPERSON, LEATHER-AND-SUEDE APPAREL-AND-ACCESSORIES (retail trade) 261.357-074
Salesperson, Lingerie (retail trade) 261.357-066
salesperson, meats (retail trade; wholesale tr.) 316.684-018
SALESPERSON, MEN'S AND BOYS' CLOTHING (retail trade) 261.357-050
SALESPERSON, MEN'S FURNISHINGS (retail trade) 261.357-054
Salesperson, Men's Hats (retail trade) 261.357-054
Salesperson, Men's Shoes (retail trade) 261.357-062
SALESPERSON, MILLINERY (retail trade) 261.357-058
SALESPERSON, MUSICAL INSTRUMENTS AND ACCESSORIES (retail trade) 277.357-038
Salesperson, Neckties (retail trade) 261.357-054
Salesperson, New Cars (retail trade) 273.353-010
SALESPERSON, ORTHOPEDIC SHOES (retail trade) 276.257-018
Salesperson, Paint (retail trade; wholesale tr.) 279.357-050
SALESPERSON, PARTS (retail trade; wholesale tr.) 279.357-062
salesperson, part time (retail trade)　　see SALESPERSON, CONTINGENT
SALESPERSON, PETS AND PET SUPPLIES (retail trade) 277.357-042
SALESPERSON, PHONOGRAPH RECORDS AND TAPE RECORDINGS (retail trade) 277.357-046
SALESPERSON, PHOTOGRAPHIC SUPPLIES AND EQUIPMENT (retail trade; wholesale tr.) 277.357-050
SALESPERSON, PIANOS AND ORGANS (retail trade) 277.354-010
salesperson, recreational vehicles (retail trade) 273.357-034
salesperson, relief (retail trade)　　see SALESPERSON, CONTINGENT
SALESPERSON, SEWING MACHINES (retail trade) 270.352-010
SALESPERSON, SHEET MUSIC (retail trade) 277.357-054
SALESPERSON, SHOES (retail trade) 261.357-062
Salesperson, Silverware (retail trade) 270.357-018
SALESPERSON, SPORTING GOODS (retail trade) 277.357-058
SALESPERSON, STAMPS OR COINS (retail trade; wholesale tr.) 277.357-062
SALESPERSON, STEREO EQUIPMENT (retail trade) 270.357-038
SALESPERSON, SURGICAL APPLIANCES (retail trade) 276.257-022
Salesperson, Terrazzo Tiles (retail trade; wholesale tr.) 270.357-026
SALESPERSON, TOY TRAINS AND ACCESSORIES (retail trade) 277.357-066
SALESPERSON, TRAILERS AND MOTOR HOMES (retail trade) 273.357-034
Salesperson, Used Cars (retail trade) 273.353-010
salesperson, utility staff (retail trade) 279.357-046
Salesperson, Wall Coverings (retail trade; wholesale tr.) 279.357-050
SALESPERSON, WIGS (personal ser.; retail trade) 261.351-010
SALESPERSON, WOMEN'S APPAREL AND ACCESSORIES (retail trade) 261.357-066
Salesperson, Women's Dresses (retail trade) 261.357-066
salesperson, women's hats (retail trade) 261.357-058
Salesperson, Women's Shoes (retail trade) 261.357-062
Salesperson, Women's Sportswear (retail trade) 261.357-066
SALESPERSON, YARD GOODS (retail trade) 261.357-070
sales promotion director (any industry) 164.117-010
SALES-PROMOTION REPRESENTATIVE (wholesale tr.) 269.357-018
Sales-Record Clerk (clerical) 216.382-062
sales representative (air trans.; motor trans.; r.r. trans.; water trans.) 252.257-010
sales representative (construction) 250.157-010
sales representative (insurance) 166.167-046
SALES REPRESENTATIVE (motor trans.) 250.357-022
SALES REPRESENTATIVE (retail trade; wholesale tr.) master
SALES REPRESENTATIVE, ABRASIVES (wholesale tr.) 274.357-010
Sales Representative, Adding Machines (wholesale tr.) 275.357-034
Sales Representative, Addressing Machines (wholesale tr.) 275.357-034
SALES REPRESENTATIVE, ADVERTISING (print. & pub.) 254.357-014

SALES REPRESENTATIVE, AIRCRAFT (retail trade; wholesale tr.) 273.253-010

SALES REPRESENTATIVE, AIRCRAFT EQUIPMENT AND PARTS (wholesale tr.) 273.357-010

SALES REPRESENTATIVE, ANIMAL-FEED PRODUCTS (wholesale tr.) 272.357-010

SALES REPRESENTATIVE, APPAREL TRIMMINGS (wholesale tr.) 261.357-010

SALES REPRESENTATIVE, ARCHITECTURAL AND ENGINEERING SUPPLIES (wholesale tr.) 276.357-010

SALES REPRESENTATIVE, AUDIOVISUAL PROGRAM PRODUCTIONS (motion picture) 259.157-010

Sales Representative, Automobile Parts And Supplies (wholesale tr.) 273.357-022

SALES REPRESENTATIVE, AUTOMOTIVE-LEASING (business ser.) 273.357-014

SALES REPRESENTATIVE, BARBER AND BEAUTY EQUIPMENT AND SUPPLIES (wholesale tr.) 275.357-010

SALES REPRESENTATIVE, BOATS AND MARINE SUPPLIES (retail trade; wholesale tr.) 273.357-018

Sales Representative, Bookkeeping-And-Accounting Machines (wholesale tr.) 275.357-034

SALES REPRESENTATIVE, BOTTLES AND BOTTLING EQUIPMENT (wholesale tr.) 274.357-014

Sales Representative, Bottles And Jars (wholesale tr.) 274.357-014

Sales Representative, Bottling Equipment (wholesale tr.) 274.357-014

SALES REPRESENTATIVE, BUILDING EQUIPMENT AND SUPPLIES (wholesale tr.) 274.357-018

Sales Representative, Business Courses (education) 259.257-010

Sales Representative, Calculating Machines (wholesale tr.) 275.357-034

SALES REPRESENTATIVE, CANVAS PRODUCTS (wholesale tr.) 261.357-014

Sales Representative, Cash Registers (wholesale tr.) 275.357-034

Sales Representative, Cattle-And-Poultry Feed Supplements (wholesale tr.) 272.357-010

Sales Representative, Check-Endorsing-And-Signing Machines (wholesale tr.) 275.357-034

SALES REPRESENTATIVE, CHEMICALS AND DRUGS (wholesale tr.) 262.357-010

Sales Representative, Church Furniture (wholesale tr.) 275.357-014

SALES REPRESENTATIVE, CHURCH FURNITURE AND RELIGIOUS SUPPLIES (wholesale tr.) 275.357-014

Sales Representative, Classified Advertising (print. & pub.) 254.357-014

SALES REPRESENTATIVE, COMMERCIAL EQUIPMENT AND SUPPLIES (wholesale tr.) 275.357-018

SALES REPRESENTATIVE, COMMUNICATION EQUIPMENT (wholesale tr.) 271.257-010

SALES REPRESENTATIVE, COMPUTERS AND EDP SYSTEMS (wholesale tr.) 275.257-010

SALES REPRESENTATIVE, CONSTRUCTION MACHINERY (wholesale tr.) 274.357-022

SALES REPRESENTATIVE, CONTAINERS (wholesale tr.) 274.357-026

SALES REPRESENTATIVE, CORDAGE (wholesale tr.) 275.357-022

Sales Representative, Correspondence Courses (education) 259.257-010

SALES REPRESENTATIVE, DAIRY SUPPLIES (wholesale tr.) 274.357-030

SALES REPRESENTATIVE, DANCING INSTRUCTIONS (education) 259.357-014

SALES REPRESENTATIVE, DATA PROCESSING SERVICES (business ser.) 251.157-014

SALES REPRESENTATIVE, DENTAL AND MEDICAL EQUIPMENT AND SUPPLIES (wholesale tr.) 276.257-010

Sales Representative, Dental Equipment And Supplies (wholesale tr.) 276.257-010

Sales Representative, Dental Prosthetics (wholesale tr.) 276.257-010

Sales Representative, Dictating Machines (wholesale tr.) 275.357-034

Sales Representative, Display Advertising (print. & pub.) 254.357-014

SALES REPRESENTATIVE, DOOR-TO-DOOR (retail trade) 291.357-010

Sales Representative, Duplicating Machines (wholesale tr.) 275.357-034

SALES REPRESENTATIVE, EDUCATION COURSES (education) 259.257-010

Sales Representative, Electric Service (utilities) 253.357-010

SALES REPRESENTATIVE, ELECTRONICS PARTS (wholesale tr.) 271.357-010

SALES REPRESENTATIVE, ELECTROPLATING (wholesale tr.) 259.257-014

SALES REPRESENTATIVE, ELEVATORS, ESCALATORS, AND DUMBWAITERS (wholesale tr.) 274.157-010

Sales Representative, Envelope (wholesale tr.) 279.357-026

SALES REPRESENTATIVE, FARM AND GARDEN EQUIPMENT AND SUPPLIES (wholesale tr.) 272.357-014

Sales Representative, Flour And Cereals (wholesale tr.) 260.357-014

SALES REPRESENTATIVE, FOOD PRODUCTS (wholesale tr.) 260.357-014

SALES REPRESENTATIVE, FOOTWEAR (wholesale tr.) 261.357-018

SALES REPRESENTATIVE, FOUNDRY AND MACHINE SHOP PRODUCTS (wholesale tr.) 274.257-010

SALES REPRESENTATIVE, FRANCHISE (business ser.) 251.357-022

SALES REPRESENTATIVE, FUELS (retail trade; wholesale tr.) 269.357-010

sales representative, funeral equipment (wholesale tr.) 275.357-030

Sales Representative, Gas Service (utilities) 253.357-010

SALES REPRESENTATIVE, GENERAL MERCHANDISE (wholesale tr.) 279.357-014

Sales Representative, Girls' Apparel (wholesale tr.) 261.357-038

SALES REPRESENTATIVE, GRAPHIC ART (business ser.) 254.251-010

Sales Representative, Groceries (wholesale tr.) 260.357-014

SALES REPRESENTATIVE, HARDWARE SUPPLIES (wholesale tr.) 274.357-034

sales representative, heavy equipment (wholesale tr.) 274.357-022

SALES REPRESENTATIVE, HERBICIDE SERVICE (business ser.) 251.357-026

SALES REPRESENTATIVE, HOBBIES AND CRAFTS (retail trade; wholesale tr.) 277.357-010

SALES REPRESENTATIVE, HOME FURNISHINGS (wholesale tr.) 270.357-010

SALES REPRESENTATIVE, HOTEL AND RESTAURANT EQUIPMENT AND SUPPLIES (wholesale tr.) 275.357-026

SALES REPRESENTATIVE, HOTEL SERVICES (hotel & rest.) 259.157-014

SALES REPRESENTATIVE, HOUSEHOLD APPLIANCES (wholesale tr.) 270.357-014

Sales Representative, Industrial Lubricants (wholesale tr.) 269.357-014

SALES REPRESENTATIVE, INDUSTRIAL MACHINERY (wholesale tr.) 274.357-038

SALES REPRESENTATIVE, INDUSTRIAL RUBBER GOODS (wholesale tr.) 274.357-042

SALES REPRESENTATIVE, JEWELRY (wholesale tr.) 279.357-018

SALES REPRESENTATIVE, LEATHER GOODS (wholesale tr.) 279.357-022

SALES REPRESENTATIVE, LIVESTOCK (wholesale tr.) 260.257-010

SALES REPRESENTATIVE, LUBRICATING EQUIPMENT (wholesale tr.) 274.357-046

SALES REPRESENTATIVE, MALT LIQUORS (wholesale tr.) 260.357-018

Sales Representative, Marine Supplies (retail trade; wholesale tr.) 273.357-018

SALES REPRESENTATIVE, MATERIAL-HANDLING EQUIPMENT (wholesale tr.) 274.357-050

Sales Representative, Meats (wholesale tr.) 260.357-014

SALES REPRESENTATIVE, MEN'S AND BOYS' APPAREL (wholesale tr.) 261.357-022

Sales Representative, Metals (wholesale tr.) 274.357-054

SALES REPRESENTATIVE, MORTICIAN SUPPLIES (wholesale tr.) 275.357-030

SALES REPRESENTATIVE, MOTOR VEHICLES AND SUPPLIES (wholesale tr.) 273.357-022

SALES REPRESENTATIVE, MUSICAL INSTRUMENTS AND ACCESSORIES (wholesale tr.) 277.357-014

SALES REPRESENTATIVE, NOVELTIES (wholesale tr.) 277.357-018

SALES REPRESENTATIVE, OFFICE MACHINES (retail trade; wholesale tr.) 275.357-034

Sales Representative, Oilfield Supplies (wholesale tr.) 274.357-058

SALES REPRESENTATIVE, OILFIELD SUPPLIES AND EQUIPMENT (wholesale tr.) 274.357-058

Sales Representative, Oil-Well Equipment Rentals (wholesale tr.) 274.357-058

Sales Representative, Oil-Well Services (wholesale tr.) 274.357-058

SALES REPRESENTATIVE, PAPER AND PAPER PRODUCTS (wholesale tr.) 279.357-026

SALES REPRESENTATIVE, PETROLEUM PRODUCTS (wholesale tr.) 269.357-014

SALES REPRESENTATIVE, PLASTIC PRODUCTS (wholesale tr.) 279.357-030

Sales Representative, Playground Equipment (wholesale tr.) 277.357-026

SALES REPRESENTATIVE, POULTRY EQUIPMENT AND SUPPLIES (retail trade; wholesale tr.) 272.357-018

SALES REPRESENTATIVE, PRECISION INSTRUMENTS (wholesale tr.) 276.357-014

SALES REPRESENTATIVE, PRESSURE-SENSITIVE TAPE (wholesale tr.) 275.357-038

SALES REPRESENTATIVE, PRINTING (wholesale tr.) 254.357-018

Sales Representative, Printing Paper (wholesale tr.) 279.357-026

SALES REPRESENTATIVE, PRINTING SUPPLIES (wholesale tr.) 274.357-062

Sales Representative, Prosthetic And Orthotic Appliances (wholesale tr.) 276.257-010

SALES REPRESENTATIVE, PUBLICATIONS (wholesale tr.) 277.357-022

SALES REPRESENTATIVE, PUBLIC UTILITIES (tel. & tel.; utilities) 253.357-010

SALES REPRESENTATIVE, RADIO AND TELEVISION TIME (radio-tv broad.) 259.357-018

SALES REPRESENTATIVE, RADIOGRAPHIC-INSPECTION EQUIPMENT AND SERVICES (wholesale tr.) 271.352-010

SALES REPRESENTATIVE, RAILROAD EQUIPMENT AND SUPPLIES (wholesale tr.) 273.357-026

Sales Representative, Raw Fibers (wholesale tr.) 261.357-030

SALES REPRESENTATIVE, RECREATION AND SPORTING GOODS (wholesale tr.) 277.357-026

Sales Representative, Religious Supplies (wholesale tr.) 275.357-014

Sales Representative, Rural Power (utilities) 253.357-010
SALES REPRESENTATIVE, SAFETY APPAREL AND EQUIPMENT (wholesale tr.) 261.357-026
SALES REPRESENTATIVE, SCHOOL EQUIPMENT AND SUPPLIES (wholesale tr.) 275.357-042
SALES REPRESENTATIVE, SECURITY SYSTEMS (business ser.) 259.257-022
SALES REPRESENTATIVE, SHIPPING SERVICES (motor trans.) 252.357-014
SALES REPRESENTATIVE, SHOE LEATHER AND FINDINGS (wholesale tr.) 275.357-046
SALES REPRESENTATIVE, SIGNS (fabrication, nec) 254.357-022
SALES REPRESENTATIVE, SIGNS AND DISPLAYS (fabrication, nec) 254.257-010
Sales Representative, Sporting Goods (wholesale tr.) 277.357-026
Sales Representative, Stenographic Machines (wholesale tr.) 275.357-034
Sales Representative, Telephone And Telegraph Services (tel. & tel.) 253.357-010
SALES REPRESENTATIVE, TELEPHONE SERVICES (tel. & tel.) 253.257-010
SALES REPRESENTATIVE, TELEVISION CABLE SERVICE (radio-tv broad.) 259.357-022
SALES REPRESENTATIVE, TEXTILE DESIGNS (wholesale tr.) 274.357-066
SALES REPRESENTATIVE, TEXTILE MACHINERY (wholesale tr.) 274.357-070
SALES REPRESENTATIVE, TEXTILES (wholesale tr.) 261.357-030
SALES REPRESENTATIVE, TOBACCO PRODUCTS AND SMOKING SUPPLIES (retail trade; wholesale tr.) 260.357-022
SALES REPRESENTATIVE, TOILET PREPARATIONS (wholesale tr.) 262.357-014
Sales Representative, Toys And Games (retail trade; wholesale tr.) 277.357-026
Sales Representative, Typewriters (wholesale tr.) 275.357-034
SALES REPRESENTATIVE, ULTRASONIC EQUIPMENT (wholesale tr.) 271.352-014
sales representative, undertaker supplies (wholesale tr.) 275.357-030
SALES REPRESENTATIVE, UNIFORMS (retail trade; wholesale tr.) 261.357-034
SALES REPRESENTATIVE, UPHOLSTERY AND FURNITURE REPAIR (retail trade) 259.357-026
SALES REPRESENTATIVE, VENDING AND COIN MACHINES (wholesale tr.) 275.357-050
SALES REPRESENTATIVE, VETERINARIAN SUPPLIES (wholesale tr.) 276.357-018
SALES REPRESENTATIVE, VIDEOTAPE (wholesale tr.) 271.357-014
SALES REPRESENTATIVE, WATER-SOFTENING EQUIPMENT (retail trade; wholesale tr.) 279.357-034
SALES REPRESENTATIVE, WATER-TREATMENT CHEMICALS (wholesale tr.) 262.357-022
SALES REPRESENTATIVE, WEATHER-FORECASTING SERVICE (business ser.) 259.357-030
SALES REPRESENTATIVE, WEIGHING AND FORCE-MEASUREMENT INSTRUMENTS (wholesale tr.) 276.257-014
SALES REPRESENTATIVE, WELDING EQUIPMENT (wholesale tr.) 274.357-074
SALES REPRESENTATIVE, WIRE ROPE (wholesale tr.) 274.357-078
SALES REPRESENTATIVE, WOMEN'S AND GIRLS' APPAREL (wholesale tr.) 261.357-038
Sales Representative, Women's Apparel (wholesale tr.) 261.357-038
SALES REPRESENTATIVE, WRITING AND MARKING PENS (wholesale tr.) 277.357-030
SALES REPRESENTATIVE, FINANCIAL SERVICES (financial) 250.257-022
sales-review clerk (insurance) 209.687-018
SALES-SERVICE PROMOTER (any industry) 165.167-010
SALES-SERVICE REPRESENTATIVE, MILKING MACHINES (retail trade) 299.251-010
sales-service supervisor (clerical) 249.137-026
Sales-Slip Sorter (clerical) 209.687-022
SALES SUPERVISOR, MALT LIQUORS (wholesale tr.) 299.137-014
salicylic-acid blender (chemical) 555.685-046
Salt-Bellies Overhauler (meat products) 525.687-026
Salt Cutter (chemical) 551.685-026
salter (meat products) 525.687-026
salt operator (soap & rel.) 551.685-030
Salt-Plant Operator (chemical) 558.685-062
salt spreader (meat products; oils & grease) 525.687-038
SALT WASHER (chemical) 551.685-126
Salt Washer, Harvesting Station (chemical) 551.685-126
Salt Washer, Processing Station (chemical) 551.685-126
Salvage Clerk (clerical) 222.387-058
salvage clerk (pen & pencil) 733.384-010
salvage cutter (welding) 816.684-010
salvage diver (any industry) 379.384-010
SALVAGE ENGINEER (machinery mfg.) 600.131-014
Salvage Grinder (sugar & conf.) 521.686-018
salvage inspector (auto. mfg.) 806.384-014

SALVAGE INSPECTOR (can. & preserv.) 529.687-174
SALVAGE INSPECTOR (railroad equip.) 622.381-038
salvage inspector, wood parts (ordnance) 769.387-010
SALVAGE-MACHINE OPERATOR (ordnance) 694.382-010
salvage-machine operator (ordnance) 737.684-026
salvage painter (any industry) 740.684-026
salvager (any industry) 929.687-022
SALVAGER (optical goods) 713.687-038
SALVAGER (petrol. refin.) 709.684-070
SALVAGER (utilities) 729.687-030
salvage repairer (petrol. refin.) 709.684-070
Salvage Repairer I (utilities) 829.261-018
SALVAGE REPAIRER II (utilities) 729.384-018
SALVAGER HELPER (petrol. refin.) 709.687-034
SALVAGER I (ordnance) 737.687-114
SALVAGER II (ordnance) 737.687-118
Salvager, Inserts (nonfer. metal) 509.686-018
SALVAGE SUPERVISOR (paint & varnish) 559.137-010
Salvage Winder (textile) 681.685-154
SALVAGE WINDER AND INSPECTOR (paper goods) 649.685-102
salvage worker (furniture) 709.684-062
SALVAGE WORKER (nonfer. metal) 619.387-010
SAMPLE-BOOK MAKER (paper goods) 659.685-014
sample carrier (smelt. & refin.) 519.484-014
SAMPLE CHECKER (carpet & rug; textile) 229.687-010
SAMPLE CLERK (furniture) 221.382-026
SAMPLE CLERK (plastic prod.) 222.387-066
SAMPLE CLERK (textile) 789.587-026
SAMPLE CLERK, HANDKERCHIEF (garment) 920.587-022
SAMPLE CLERK, PAPER (paper & pulp; paper goods) 209.587-046
SAMPLE COLLECTOR (chemical) 550.587-014
SAMPLE-COLOR MAKER (paint & varnish) 550.584-014
sample cutter (boot & shoe) 788.684-082
SAMPLE CUTTER (furniture) 781.684-070
Sample Cutter (garment; textile) 699.685-014
SAMPLE DISPLAY PREPARER (knitting) 222.687-026
Sample Distributor (any industry) 230.687-010
Sample Driller (tobacco) 529.587-022
sample dyer (laundry & rel.) 364.361-010
sample finisher (carpet & rug) 781.684-050
sample gatherer (any industry) 922.687-054
SAMPLE MAKER (boot & shoe) 690.685-506
Sample Maker (carpet & rug) 687.684-010
sample maker (garment) 785.361-018
sample maker (ordnance) 600.260-018
SAMPLE MAKER, APPLIANCES (house. appl.; light. fix.) 600.280-054
SAMPLE MAKER, HAND (paper goods) 794.684-030
SAMPLE MAKER I (jewelry-silver.) 700.381-046
SAMPLE MAKER II (jewelry-silver.) 735.381-018
sample maker, original (garment) 785.361-018
SAMPLE MAKER, VENEER (millwork-plywood) 769.684-042
Sample Mounter (any industry) 795.687-014
Sample Processor (carpet & rug) 787.682-010
sample puller (tobacco) 529.587-022
sampler (agriculture) 410.357-010
sampler (agriculture; textile) 922.687-042
sampler (any industry) 922.687-054
SAMPLER (beverage) 529.687-178
SAMPLER (elec. equip.) 549.587-018
SAMPLER (mine & quarry) 579.484-010
sampler (nonfer. metal; steel & rel.) 509.584-010
SAMPLER (oils & grease) 529.387-034
SAMPLER (petrol. refin.) 549.587-014
SAMPLER (steel & rel.) 599.684-014
SAMPLER, FIRST (smelt. & refin.) 619.682-038
SAMPLER, HEAD (smelt. & refin.) 519.130-014
SAMPLE-ROOM SUPERVISOR (textile) 299.137-018
Sampler, Ovens (steel & rel.) 599.684-014
sampler, pickup (beverage) 529.687-178
Sampler, Radioactive Waste (chemical) 922.687-054
SAMPLER-TESTER (nonmet. min.) 579.585-010
SAMPLER, WOOL (wholesale tr.) 222.587-042
SAMPLE SAWYER (brick & tile) 677.685-034
SAMPLE SELECTOR (tex. prod., nec) 789.387-014
sample sewer (garment) 785.361-018
SAMPLE SHOE INSPECTOR AND REWORKER (boot & shoe) 788.684-098
sample steamer (textile) 582.685-110
SAMPLE STITCHER (garment) 785.361-018
sample supervisor (textile) 299.137-018
sample tailor (garment) 785.361-018
SAMPLE-TAKER OPERATOR (petrol. & gas) 931.361-010
SAMPLE TESTER (chemical) 553.364-010
sample tester (electroplating) 500.287-010
SAMPLE TESTER-GRINDER (mine & quarry) 519.585-018
SAMPLE WASHER (petrol. & gas) 939.687-030

Sample Weaver (textile) 683.682-038
SAMPLE WORKER (any industry) 920.687-154
Sampling Inspector (office machines) 706.387-014
Sand-And-Gravel-Plant Operator (construction) 570.682-014
SANDBLASTER (any industry) 503.687-010
Sandblaster, Glass (glass mfg.; glass products) 775.381-014
SANDBLASTER, STONE (stonework) 673.382-010
SANDBLASTER, STONE APPRENTICE (stonework) 673.382-014
SANDBLAST OPERATOR (ordnance) 503.685-038
sandblast operator (stonework) 673.382-010
SANDBLAST-OR-SHOTBLAST-EQUIPMENT TENDER (any industry) 503.685-042
sand caster (jewelry-silver.) 518.381-022
sand-caster apprentice (jewelry-silver.) 518.381-010
sand-cleaning-machine operator (waterworks) 954.587-010
sand conditioner, machine (foundry) 570.682-018
SAND-CUTTER OPERATOR (foundry) 570.683-014
sand-cutting-machine operator (foundry) 570.683-014
sander (automotive ser.) 845.684-014
sander (boot & shoe) 690.685-046
SANDER (fabrication, nec) 761.684-030
sander (glass products) 775.684-042
sander (hat & cap) 585.685-014
sander (textile) 581.685-010
SANDER (toy-sport equip.) 690.685-346
Sander (wood. container) 669.682-014
SANDER-AND-BUFFER (musical inst.) 730.684-066
sander and filer (woodworking) 705.684-018
sander and polisher (boot & shoe) 690.685-046
SANDER, HAND (woodworking) 761.687-010
Sander Helper (wood. container) 669.685-010
SANDER, MACHINE (woodworking) 761.682-014
SANDER, PORTABLE MACHINE (woodworking) 761.684-034
Sander Setter (woodworking) 669.280-010
sander-up (pottery & porc.) 573.687-010
Sander, Wooden Pencils (pen & pencil) 662.685-014
SAND FILLER (mine & quarry) 939.687-034
SANDFILL OPERATOR (mine & quarry) 939.485-010
Sandfill Operator, Surface (mine & quarry) 939.485-010
Sandfill Operator, Underground (mine & quarry) 939.485-010
SAND HOG (construction) term
SANDING-MACHINE BUFFER (wood prod., nec) 662.685-022
SANDING-MACHINE OPERATOR (sugar & conf.) 524.665-010
sanding machine operator (textile) 581.685-010
Sanding-Machine Operator Helper (sugar & conf.) 529.686-034
sanding-machine tender, automatic (woodworking) 662.685-038
SANDING-MACHINE TENDER (wood prod., nec) 662.685-026
SAND-MILL GRINDER (paint & varnish) 555.682-018
sand mill operator (foundry) 570.682-018
Sand-Mill Operator, Core-Sand (foundry) 570.682-018
Sand-Mill Operator, Facing-Sand (foundry) 570.682-018
Sand-Mill Operator, Molding-Sand (foundry) 570.682-018
SAND MIXER, MACHINE (foundry) 570.682-018
sand-mixer operator (foundry) 570.683-014
sand molder (aircraft mfg.; concrete prod.; foundry) 518.361-010
sand-molder apprentice (aircraft mfg.; concrete prod.; foundry) 518.361-014
SAND PLANT ATTENDANT (concrete prod.; mine & quarry) 934.685-014
Sand-Screener Operator (foundry) 519.687-022
Sand Shoveler (foundry) 519.687-022
SAND-SLINGER OPERATOR (foundry) 518.683-010
Sandstone Splitter (mine & quarry) 930.684-022
sand-system operator (foundry) 570.682-018
sand technologist (foundry) 777.381-046
SAND TESTER (foundry) 777.381-046
Sand Wheeler (foundry) 519.687-022
SANDWICH-BOARD CARRIER (any industry) 299.687-014
sandwich-counter attendant (hotel & rest.) 317.664-010
SANDWICH-MACHINE OPERATOR (dairy products) 529.685-210
SANDWICH MAKER (hotel & rest.) 317.664-010
sandwich seller (r.r. trans.) 291.457-014
SANITARIAN (any industry) 529.137-014
sanitarian (government ser.) 379.687-014
SANITARIAN (profess. & kin.) 079.117-018
SANITARY ENGINEER (profess. & kin.) 005.061-030
Sanitary Inspector (government ser.) 168.267-042
SANITARY LANDFILL OPERATOR (sanitary ser.) 955.463-010
SANITARY-LANDFILL SUPERVISOR (sanitary ser.) 955.133-010
SANITARY-NAPKIN-MACHINE TENDER (protective dev.) 692.685-150
SANITATION INSPECTOR (government ser.) 168.267-110
sanitation supervisor (any industry) 529.137-014
Sanitizer (boot & shoe) 788.687-122
sanitor (any industry) 381.687-018
Santa Claus (any industry) 299.647-010
Santa's Helper (any industry) 299.647-010
SAPPHIRE-STYLUS GRINDER (comm. equip.) 770.381-038

Sash Assembler (woodworking) 762.687-050
Sash-Clamp Operator (saw. & plan.) 669.685-030
Sash-Gang-Saw Operator (saw. & plan.) 667.682-030
Sash Maker (saw. & plan.) 669.380-014
Sash Repairer (railroad equip.) 807.381-026
SATELLITE-INSTRUCTION FACILITATOR (education) 249.367-086
satellite-project site monitor (education) 249.367-086
Satin Finisher (furniture; wood prod., nec) 742.684-010
SATURATION-EQUIPMENT OPERATOR (fabrication, nec) 582.665-022
saturator (chemical) 551.382-010
saturator (tex. prod., nec) 584.382-010
SATURATOR OPERATOR (chemical; steel & rel.) 558.362-018
SATURATOR TENDER (build. mat., nec) 582.685-118
sauce maker (beverage) 520.485-026
SAUSAGE INSPECTOR (meat products) 529.587-014
sausage linker (meat products) 529.687-150
SAUSAGE MAKER (meat products) 520.685-202
SAUSAGE-MEAT TRIMMER (meat products) 521.687-106
SAUSAGE MIXER (meat products) 520.685-206
sausage stuffer (meat products) 520.685-210
SAVE-ALL OPERATOR (paper & pulp) 533.685-018
saw boss (logging) 454.134-010
Sawdust Drier (electroplating) 500.686-010
saw-dust machine operator (fur goods; laundry & rel.; retail trade; wholesale tr.) 369.685-014
sawdust-machine operator (laundry & rel.) 362.684-014
SAW-EDGE FUSER, CIRCULAR (cutlery-hrdwr.) 701.684-026
SAW FILER (any industry) 701.381-014
saw filer (oils & grease) 603.682-018
Saw-Handle Assembler (woodworking) 762.687-042
SAW MAKER (cutlery-hrdwr.) 601.381-034
saw maker (stonework) 701.684-022
saw mechanic (cutlery-hrdwr.) 601.381-034
Sawmill-Relief Worker (saw. & plan.) 667.687-018
SAWMILL WORKER (saw. & plan.) 667.687-018
Saw Offbearer (woodworking) 669.686-034
SAW OPERATOR (aircraft mfg.) 607.382-014
SAW OPERATOR (brick & tile) 677.685-054
saw operator (electron. comp.) 726.682-026
SAW OPERATOR (electron. comp.) 726.682-026
SAW OPERATOR, SEMICONDUCTOR WAFERS (electron. comp.) 726.685-046
SAW SETTER (stonework) 701.684-022
Sawsmith (cutlery-hrdwr.) 601.381-034
Sawyer (can. & preserv.) 525.687-126
sawyer (food prep., nec) 521.685-342
sawyer (jewelry-silver.) 770.382-010
sawyer (jewelry-silver.) 700.682-014
SAWYER (plastic prod.; plastic-synth.) 690.482-010
SAWYER (stonework) term
SAWYER, CORK SLABS (wood prod., nec) 667.685-046
SAWYER I (nonmet. min.) 677.686-010
SAWYER II (nonmet. min.) 677.685-038
SAWYER, OPTICAL GLASS (optical goods) 677.382-014
Saxophone Assembler (musical inst.) 730.381-018
Scaffold Builder (construction; ship-boat mfg.) 860.381-042
Scaffold Builder, Metal (construction) 801.361-014
scaffold worker (wood prod., nec) 561.665-010
SCAGLIOLA MECHANIC (nonmet. min.) 556.484-010
Scalder (can. & preserv.) 521.685-206
Scalder (meat products) 525.685-018
Scaler (r.r. trans.) 222.387-074
scale-and-skip-car operator (steel & rel.) 921.683-062
SCALE ASSEMBLY SET-UP WORKER (office machines) 710.360-010
scale clerk (agriculture) 221.467-010
scale clerk (clerical) 221.587-030
SCALE MECHANIC (any industry) 633.281-026
SCALE OPERATOR (chemical) 555.687-010
SCALE-RECLAMATION TENDER (smelt. & refin.) 515.585-010
SCALER-PACKER (meat products) 929.687-046
Scaler, Sliced Bacon (meat products) 920.587-018
Scale Shooter (forging) 619.686-034
scale-tank operator (oils & grease) 529.485-026
scaling-machine operator (bakery products) 526.682-010
SCALING MACHINE OPERATOR (can. & preserv.) 521.685-386
SCALLOP CUTTER, MACHINE (tex. prod., nec) 686.685-058
Scallop Dredger (fishing & hunt.) 446.684-014
Scallop Raker (fishing & hunt.) 446.684-014
Scallop Shucker (can. & preserv.) 521.687-122
SCALPER OPERATOR (nonfer. metal) 605.682-022
scalp-machine operator (nonfer. metal) 605.682-022
scalp specialist (personal ser.) 339.371-014
SCALP-TREATMENT OPERATOR (personal ser.) 339.371-014
SCANNER (profess. & kin.) 015.384-010
SCANNER OPERATOR (print. & pub.) 972.282-010

Scanner Supervisor (print. & pub.) 972.137-010
scarfer (boot & shoe) 585.685-110
scarfer (boot & shoe; rubber goods) 690.685-378
scarfer operator (millwork-plywood) 665.685-022
SCARF GLUER (millwork-plywood) 762.684-054
SCARFING MACHINE OPERATOR (steel & rel.) 816.682-010
Scarifier Operator (any industry) 850.683-010
scenario writer (motion picture; radio-tv broad.) 131.067-050
Scenic Artist (motion picture; radio-tv broad.) 144.061-010
scenic designer (amuse. & rec.) 142.061-050
schedule clerk (utilities) 959.167-010
schedule clerk (clerical) 221.167-018
schedule clerk (print. & pub.) 247.387-014
schedule clerk (r.r. trans.) 219.462-014
SCHEDULE MAKER (motor trans.) 913.167-018
scheduler (auto. mfg.) 221.367-026
scheduler (clerical) 221.167-018
SCHEDULER (museums) 238.367-034
scheduler (paper goods) 221.162-010
scheduler (profess. & kin.) 012.167-050
scheduler and planner (clerical) 215.367-014
scheduler, conveyor (auto. mfg.) 221.367-026
SCHEDULER, MAINTENANCE (clerical) 221.367-066
scheme examiner (government ser.) 239.367-018
Scholarship Counselor (education) 169.267-018
school adjustment counselor (profess. & kin.) 195.107-038
SCHOOL BUS MONITOR (government ser.) 372.667-042
school examiner (education) 099.167-010
SCHOOL-PLANT CONSULTANT (education) 001.167-010
SCHOOL SECRETARY (education) 201.362-022
Science Center, Display Builder (museums) 739.261-010
SCIENTIFIC GLASS BLOWER (glass products) 006.261-010
SCIENTIFIC HELPER (profess. & kin.) 199.364-014
SCIENTIFIC LINGUIST (profess. & kin.) 059.067-014
SCIENTIST (profess. & kin.) term
scientologist (profess. & kin.) 199.207-010
scientology auditor (profess. & kin.) 199.207-010
Scissors Grinder (any industry) 701.381-018
SCOOPING-MACHINE TENDER (furniture) 665.685-026
scoop-machine operator (button & notion) 692.685-270
SCOREBOARD OPERATOR (amuse. & rec.) 349.665-010
SCORER (amuse. & rec.) 153.387-014
SCORER (paper goods) 641.685-070
Scorer, Double (paper goods) 641.685-070
SCORER HELPER (paper goods) 641.686-030
Scorer, Single (paper goods) 641.685-070
scoring-machine-operator helper (paper goods) 641.686-030
scourer (boot & shoe) 690.685-046
scourer (pottery & porc.) 774.684-010
scouring-machine operator (carpet & rug; textile) 589.662-010
SCOURING-TRAIN OPERATOR (carpet & rug; textile) 589.662-010
Scouring-Train Operator, Chief (carpet & rug; textile) 589.662-010
SCOUT (agriculture) 408.381-010
SCOUT (petrol. & gas) 010.267-010
SCOUT, PROFESSIONAL SPORTS (amuse. & rec.) 153.117-018
scow captain (water trans.) 911.137-010
Scow Deckhand (water trans.) 911.687-022
scow-derrick operator (water trans.) 921.683-034
Scrap Baler (nonfer. metal; steel & rel.) 920.685-010
SCRAP BALLER (nonfer. metal; steel & rel.) 509.685-046
Scrap Breaker (steel & rel.) 509.687-026
Scrap-Bunch Maker (tobacco) 529.685-038
Scrap Burner (any industry) 929.687-022
scrap burner (welding) 816.684-010
Scrap-Crane Operator I (steel & rel.) 921.663-010
Scrap-Crane Operator II (steel & rel.) 921.663-042
scrap crusher (fabrication, nec) 555.685-022
scrap cutter (welding) 816.684-010
scrap cutter, machine (tobacco) 529.685-110
SCRAPER (jewelry-silver.) 700.687-066
scraper (machine shop) 705.384-010
scraper (mine & quarry) 939.687-014
scraper (pottery & porc.) 774.684-010
scraper burrer (clock & watch) 715.684-042
scraper, hand (furniture) 761.684-038
SCRAPER, HAND (machine shop) 705.384-010
SCRAPER-LOADER OPERATOR (mine & quarry) 921.663-050
Scraper, Meat (meat products) 525.587-014
SCRAPER OPERATOR (construction) 850.683-038
Scraper Operator (mine & quarry) 850.683-010
scraper tender (furniture) 665.685-026
scrap-filler-cigar roller, machine (tobacco) 529.685-270
SCRAP HANDLER (any industry) 509.685-050
SCRAPPER (paper goods) 794.687-050
Scrapper (sugar & conf.) 529.686-034

scrap picker (tobacco) 521.687-098
scrap preparer (tobacco) 520.687-030
Scrap Sawyer (saw. & plan.) 667.685-022
SCRAP SEPARATOR (food prep., nec) 529.587-018
Scrap-Shear Operator (any industry) 615.685-034
Scrap Sorter (any industry) 929.687-022
SCRAP SORTER (boot & shoe) 788.687-106
SCRAP SORTER (nonfer. metal) 509.686-018
Scrap Sorter (tobacco) 521.687-098
Scrap Stripper, Hand (tobacco) 521.687-134
Scrap-Tire Shearer (rubber reclaim.) 690.685-386
Scrap Wheeler (machine shop) 929.687-030
scratch brusher (clock & watch) 715.687-022
Scratch Brusher (jewelry-silver.) 700.687-058
scratcher (hat & cap) 585.685-014
scratcher, metal patterns (foundry) 693.281-018
SCRATCHER TENDER (fabrication, nec) 555.685-050
Scratch Polisher (glass products) 775.684-058
Screed Operator (construction) 853.663-014
SCREEN-AND-CYCLONE REPAIRER (mine & quarry) 630.664-014
SCREEN CLEANER (wood prod., nec) 569.687-018
Screen Coach (profess. & kin.) 150.027-010
screen cutter and trimmer (metal prod., nec) 709.684-074
screener (any industry) 979.684-034
Screener (electron. comp.) 725.685-010
SCREENER-AND-BLENDER OPERATOR (steel & rel.) 549.685-026
SCREENER OPERATOR (any industry) 599.685-082
SCREENER-PERFUMER (soap & rel.) 559.685-162
Screen-Frame Enameler (struct. metal) 599.685-026
SCREEN HANDLER (paper & pulp) 539.685-026
screening representative (air trans.) 372.667-010
Screen Installer (struct. metal) 809.684-010
SCREEN-MACHINE OPERATOR (tex. prod., nec) 559.682-070
SCREEN MAKER (paper goods) 739.684-150
SCREEN MAKER, PHOTOGRAPHIC PROCESS (any industry) 979.384-010
SCREEN MAKER, TEXTILE (textile) 971.381-046
Screen Operator (cement) 921.662-018
SCREEN OPERATOR (chemical) 551.685-130
SCREEN OPERATOR (smelt. & refin.) 511.685-050
SCREEN PRINTER (any industry) 979.684-034
screen printer (any industry) 979.685-010
SCREEN PRINTER (textile) 979.684-030
SCREEN PRINTER HELPER (any industry) 979.687-022
Screen Printer, Printed Circuit Boards (electron. comp.) 979.684-034
SCREEN-PRINTING-EQUIPMENT SETTER (paper goods) 979.360-010
SCREEN-PRINTING-MACHINE OPERATOR (textile) 652.682-018
SCREEN-PRINTING-MACHINE-OPERATOR HELPER (textile) 652.686-038
Screen-Printing-Machine Tender, Printed Circuit Boards (electron. comp.) 979.685-010
SCREEN REPAIRER, CRUSHER (mine & quarry) 630.684-030
Screen Roller (woodworking) 762.687-058
screen-room operator (paper & pulp) 533.685-022
SCREEN-ROOM OPERATOR (sugar & conf.) 521.685-282
screen stretcher (electron. comp.) 979.684-042
Screen Supervisor (smelt. & refin.) 511.135-010
SCREEN TACKER (saw. & plan.) 762.687-058
SCREEN TENDER (paper & pulp) 533.685-022
SCREEN TENDER (paper & pulp; wood prod., nec) 534.665-010
SCREEN TENDER, CHIPS (paper & pulp) 533.685-026
SCREEN-TENDER HELPER (paper & pulp) 533.687-010
Screen-Vent Binder (hat & cap) 787.682-010
screen washer (paper & pulp) 533.687-010
SCREEN WRITER (motion picture; radio-tv broad.) 131.067-050
SCREWDOWN OPERATOR (steel & rel.) 613.382-018
SCREW-EYE ASSEMBLER (ordnance) 737.687-122
SCREWHEAD POLISHER (clock & watch) 715.381-090
screwhead polisher (clock & watch) 715.685-046
screwhead stoner and polisher (clock & watch) 603.685-082
Screw Inspector (clock & watch) 715.384-022
Screw-Machine Adjuster, Automatic (ordnance) 638.261-030
screw-machine operator (machine shop) 604.280-014
SCREW-MACHINE OPERATOR, MULTIPLE SPINDLE (machine shop) 604.382-010
SCREW-MACHINE OPERATOR, SINGLE SPINDLE (machine shop) 604.382-010
SCREW-MACHINE OPERATOR, SWISS-TYPE (clock & watch) 604.682-010
Screw-Machine Repairer (machine shop) 638.261-030
screw-machine setter (machine shop) 604.280-014
SCREW-MACHINE SET-UP OPERATOR (machine shop) 604.380-022
SCREW-MACHINE SET-UP OPERATOR, MULTIPLE SPINDLE (machine shop) 604.280-014
SCREW-MACHINE SET-UP OPERATOR, SINGLE SPINDLE (machine shop) 604.280-018
SCREW-MACHINE SET-UP OPERATOR, SWISS-TYPE (clock & watch) 604.260-010
Screw-Machine Set-Up Operator, Tool (machine shop) 604.280-022

SCREW-MACHINE TENDER (machine shop) 604.685-034
SCREWMAKER, AUTOMATIC (clock & watch) 609.682-030
SCREW REMOVER (boot & shoe) 788.684-102
SCREW SUPERVISOR (clock & watch) 609.130-014
scriber (electron. comp.) 726.685-046
SCRIBING-MACHINE OPERATOR (cutlery-hrdwr.) 605.685-042
script artist (profess. & kin.) 970.661-010
script reader (motion picture; radio-tv broad.) 131.087-014
SCRIPT READER (radio-tv broad.) 131.267-022
SCRIPT SUPERVISOR (motion picture; radio-tv broad.) 201.362-026
script writer (motion picture; radio-tv broad.) 131.067-050
SCROLL ASSEMBLER (office machines) 710.584-010
SCROLL-MACHINE OPERATOR (struct. metal) 616.685-062
scroll-saw operator (woodworking) 667.682-010
scroll-saw operator (woodworking) 667.682-042
scrubber (any industry) 381.687-014
scrubber (any industry) 381.687-018
scrubber (glass mfg.; glass products) 673.685-026
SCRUBBER MACHINE TENDER (electron. comp.) 599.685-134
scrubber-system attendant (any industry) 950.585-010
Scrubbing-Machine Operator (any industry) 381.687-014
SCRUBBING-MACHINE OPERATOR (tex. prod., nec) 582.685-122
SCUBA DIVER (any industry) 379.384-010
scudding inspector (leather mfg.) 585.687-010
SCULLION (water trans.) 318.687-014
Scullion Chief (water trans.) 318.687-014
SCULPTOR (profess. & kin.) 144.061-018
sculptor (stonework) 771.281-014
SCUTCHER TENDER (textile) 589.685-090
sea-foam-kiss maker (sugar & conf.) 529.687-122
Sealant Mixer (aircraft mfg.) 550.685-062
Seal Driver (fishing & hunt.) 461.684-010
SEALER (elec. equip.) 727.684-030
SEALER (fishing & hunt.) 461.684-010
Sealer (light. fix.) 692.685-118
SEALER (office machines) 710.684-038
sealer, aircraft (aircraft mfg.) 806.384-038
sealer and stripper (brick & tile) 573.684-010
SEALER, DRY CELL (elec. equip.) 692.685-158
sealer operator (elec. equip.) 692.685-158
SEALER, SEMICONDUCTOR PACKAGES (electron. comp.) 726.687-042
SEAL-EXTRUSION OPERATOR (elec. equip.) 692.685-154
SEALING-AND-CANCELING-MACHINE OPERATOR (clerical) 208.685-026
SEALING-MACHINE OPERATOR (light. fix.) 692.685-162
SEALING-MACHINE OPERATOR (paper goods) 641.685-074
Seal Killer (fishing & hunt.) 461.684-010
SEAL MIXER (elec. equip.) 540.687-010
seal-mixing operator (elec. equip.) 540.687-010
Seal Skinner (fishing & hunt.) 461.684-010
seam checker (beverage; can. & preserv.) 920.687-050
seamer (boot & shoe) 690.682-082
Seamer (knitting) 787.682-074
Seamer (metal prod., nec) 709.684-074
seamer (rubber goods) 690.686-026
seamer (tex. prod., nec) 787.682-066
Seamer, Elastic Band (knitting) 787.682-074
Seamer, Pantyhose (knitting) 787.682-074
SEAM HAMMERER (musical inst.) 730.684-070
Seaming Inspector (knitting) 684.684-010
Seaming-Machine Operator (tinware) 619.685-046
SEAMLESS-HOSIERY KNITTER (knitting) 684.685-010
seamless sizer (knitting) 684.684-014
seamless-tube drawer (nonfer. metal; steel & rel.) 614.685-022
seamless-tube-mill operator (steel & rel.) 619.682-042
SEAMLESS-TUBE ROLLER (steel & rel.) 619.682-042
Seam Presser (garment) 363.684-018
SEAM PRESSER (hat & cap) 583.685-098
Seam-Press Operator (boot & shoe) 690.685-350
seam roller (boot & shoe) 690.685-350
SEAM-RUBBING-MACHINE OPERATOR (boot & shoe) 690.685-350
Seam-Stay Stitcher (boot & shoe) 690.682-082
SEAM STEAMER (garment) 789.687-166
Seam Taper, Machine (boot & shoe) 690.685-414
searcher (tobacco) 521.687-098
seasoner, hand (leather mfg.) 584.687-010
SEASONING MIXER (chemical) 550.685-106
SEASONING MIXER (meat products) 520.687-054
Seasoning Sprayer (leather mfg.) 584.687-014
Seat Assembler (furniture) 709.684-014
Seat Installer (construction) 869.664-014
SEAT JOINER, CHAINSTITCH (garment) 786.682-218
Seat Maker (furniture) 780.684-134
Seat-Pack Inspector (tex. prod., nec) 789.687-086
seat padder (furniture) 780.684-078
seat scooper, machine (furniture) 665.685-026

Seat Trimmer (boot & shoe) 690.685-434
SECOND (amuse. & rec.) 346.677-018
Secondary Connector, Armature (elec. equip.) 724.684-014
second assistant engineer (water trans.) 623.281-034
Second-Calender Operator (tex. prod., nec) 584.685-010
SECOND COOK AND BAKER (water trans.) 315.381-026
SECOND CUTTER (glass mfg.) 779.684-054
Second Facing Baster (garment) 786.682-102
SECOND-FLOOR OPERATOR (plastic-synth.) 557.685-022
SECOND HAND (textile) term
second hand, paper machine (paper & pulp) 534.662-010
SECOND HELPER (steel & rel.) 512.684-010
second loader (logging) 921.687-022
Second Operator (chemical) 552.685-030
SECOND OPERATOR, MILL TENDER (chemical) 555.685-054
second press operator (print. & pub.) 651.685-026
Second-Ride-Fare Collector (amuse. & rec.) 211.467-030
second rigger (logging) 921.664-014
seconds grader (textile) 689.387-010
SECONDS HANDLER (knitting) 782.687-050
Seconds Inspector (garment; knitting) 789.687-070
seconds inspector (textile) 689.387-010
Second Steward/Stewardess, Night (water trans.) 350.137-022
secretarial stenographer (clerical) 201.362-030
SECRETARY (clerical) 201.362-030
SECRETARY, BOARD-OF-EDUCATION (education) 169.267-022
SECRETARY OF POLICE (government ser.) 375.137-022
SECRETARY OF STATE (government ser.) 188.167-082
secretary to board of commissioners (government ser.) 375.137-022
secret-code expert (government ser.) 199.267-014
SECTIONAL-BELT-MOLD ASSEMBLER (rubber goods) 752.685-010
SECTIONAL CENTER MANAGER, POSTAL SERVICE (government ser.) 188.167-086
section beamer (knitting; narrow fabrics; nonmet. min.; textile) 681.685-018
section beamer (textile) 681.685-058
section chief (any industry)   see SUPERVISOR
section chief (clerical)   see SUPERVISOR
Section-Crews-Activities Clerk (r.r. trans.) 221.362-026
section-gang worker (r.r. trans.) 910.684-014
SECTION HAND (textile) term
section head (clerical)   see SUPERVISOR
section leader (any industry)   see SUPERVISOR
SECTION LEADER AND MACHINE SETTER (textile) 689.260-018
Section Leader And Machine Setter, Cards (textile) 689.260-018
Section Leader And Machine Setter, Drawing And Combers (textile) 689.260-018
Section Leader And Machine Setter, Opening And Picking (textile) 689.260-018
SECTION LEADER AND MACHINE SETTER, POLISHING (textile) 689.260-022
Section Leader And Machine Setter, Roving Frames (textile) 689.260-018
Section Leader And Machine Setter, Spinning (textile) 689.260-018
Section Leader All Machine Setter, Winding And Twisting (textile) 689.260-018
SECTION LEADER, SCREEN PRINTING (textile) 652.260-010
Section Maintainer (tel. & tel.) 822.261-022
section manager (print. & pub.) 653.131-010
SECTION-PLOTTER OPERATOR (petrol. & gas) 194.382-010
section-plotter operator (petrol. & gas) 010.161-018
SECTION SUPERVISOR (mine & quarry) 939.137-018
section warper (knitting; narrow fabrics; nonmet. min.; textile) 681.685-018
section weaver (personal ser.) 782.381-022
securities analyst (financial; insurance) 160.267-026
securities auditor (financial) 216.367-014
securities broker (financial) 250.257-018
SECURITIES CLERK (clerical) 210.382-062
SECURITIES CLERK (financial) 219.362-054
securities-research analyst (financial; insurance) 160.267-026
Securities Supervisor (financial) 219.132-014
SECURITIES TRADER (financial) 162.167-038
security agent (business ser.) 376.367-010
Security Chief, Museum (museums) 372.167-014
security clerk (clerical) 205.362-022
SECURITY CONSULTANT (business ser.; personal ser.) 189.167-054
security guard (business ser.) 372.667-038
security inspector (government ser.) 372.363-010
security manager (any industry) 189.167-050
SECURITY OFFICER (any industry) 189.167-034
security officer (hotel & rest.) 376.367-018
security technician (government ser.) 372.363-010
SEED ANALYST (profess. & kin.) 040.361-014
Seed And Havana-Scrap Preparer (tobacco) 520.687-030
seed cleaner (agriculture; oils & grease) 599.665-010
SEED-CLEANER OPERATOR (agriculture; oils & grease) 599.665-010
seed-cleaning-machine operator (agriculture; oils & grease) 599.665-010

Seed-Cone Picker (forestry) 453.687-010
SEED CORE OPERATOR (electron. comp.) 679.384-010
SEED CUTTER (agriculture) 404.686-010
Seed Grower (agriculture) 405.161-014
SEEDLING PULLER (forestry) 451.687-018
SEEDLING SORTER (forestry) 451.687-022
Seed Packer (agriculture) 920.687-134
SEED PELLETER (agriculture) 599.685-126
SEED-POTATO ARRANGER (agriculture) 404.685-010
Seed Sorter (agriculture) 529.687-186
SEED-YEAST OPERATOR (food prep., nec) 522.685-090
Segregator (agriculture; wholesale tr.) 929.687-030
Seismic Prospector (petrol. & gas) 024.061-026
seismograph-operator helper (petrol. & gas) 939.364-010
SEISMOLOGIST (profess. & kin.) 024.061-050
SELECTOR (fabrication, nec) 739.687-166
SELECTOR (glass mfg.) 579.687-030
selector (hat & cap) 784.387-010
selector (meat products; oils & grease) 525.687-046
selector (tobacco) 529.687-134
selector (tobacco) 529.687-090
Selenium-Plant Operator (smelt. & refin.) 511.685-054
Self-Propelled Dredge Operator (fishing & hunt.) 446.663-010
Self-Rising-Flour Mixer (grain-feed mills) 520.485-010
SELF-SEALING-FUEL-TANK BUILDER (rubber goods) 752.684-046
SELF-SEALING-FUEL-TANK REPAIRER (rubber goods) 759.384-010
SELF-SERVICE-LAUNDRY-AND-DRY-CLEANING ATTENDANT (laundry
& rel.) 369.677-010
SELVAGE-MACHINE OPERATOR (textile) 681.685-094
semiautomatic-stitcher operator (paper goods) 649.685-114
semiautomatic-taper operator (paper goods) 649.685-126
SEMICONDUCTOR PROCESSOR (electron. comp.) 590.684-022
semi-truck driver (any industry) 904.383-010
Senior Animal Trainer (amuse. & rec.) 159.224-010
SENIOR-COMMISSARY AGENT (air trans.) 922.137-010
SENIOR ENLISTED ADVISOR (military ser.) 166.167-042
senior gate agent (air trans.) 238.137-018
senior librarian (library) 100.127-010
senior passenger agent (air trans.) 238.137-022
senior radio operator (air trans.; business ser.) 193.162-022
SENIOR RESERVATIONS AGENT (air trans.) 238.137-014
Senior Service Aide (social ser.) 195.367-010
SENIOR TECHNICIAN, CONTROLS (pipe lines) 828.261-018
senior ticket-sales agent (air trans.) 238.137-022
SENSITIZED-PAPER TESTER (photo. appar.) 714.667-010
sensitizer (photo. appar.) 534.582-010
Sensitometrist (motion picture) 976.381-010
separator (chemical) 551.685-102
separator (laundry & rel.) 361.687-014
separator (saw. & plan.) 921.682-022
separator (woodworking) 922.687-074
Separator Inserter (elec. equip.) 727.687-038
separator-machine operator (any industry) 599.685-082
SEPARATOR OPERATOR (button & notion) 692.685-166
SEPARATOR OPERATOR (chemical) 559.685-166
Separator Operator (dairy products) 529.382-018
SEPARATOR OPERATOR (grain-feed mills) 521.382-014
SEPARATOR OPERATOR, SHELLFISH MEATS (can. & preserv.) 521.685-
286
Separator Tender I (grain-feed mills) 521.685-254
SEPARATOR TENDER II (grain-feed mills) 521.685-290
SEPTIC-TANK INSTALLER (construction) 851.663-010
Septic-Tank Servicer (construction) 869.664-014
SEQUENCING-MACHINE OPERATOR (electron. comp.) 726.382-010
SEQUINS STRINGER (plastic prod.) 754.687-014
sequins winder (plastic prod.) 920.686-046
sergeant (government ser.) 375.133-010
serger (any industry)　　see SERGING-MACHINE OPERATOR
SERGING-MACHINE OPERATOR (any industry) term
SERGING-MACHINE OPERATOR, AUTOMATIC (any industry) 787.685-030
server (hotel & rest.) 311.477-026
server (hotel & rest.) 311.477-030
server (hotel & rest.) 311.677-014
service aide (nonprofit org.) 239.367-022
service attendant, cafeteria (hotel & rest.) 311.677-010
SERVICE ATTENDANT, SLEEPING CAR (r.r. trans.) 351.677-010
service auditor (business ser.) 376.267-022
Service-Bar Cashier (hotel & rest.) 211.462-010
Service Bartender (hotel & rest.) 312.474-010
service-car operator (any industry) 388.663-010
service center manager (air trans.; motor trans.; r.r. trans.) 184.167-042
service-center supervisor (tel. & tel.) 822.131-014
service-claims inspector (auto. mfg.) 806.384-014
SERVICE CLERK (clerical) 221.367-070
service coordinator (air trans.) 912.367-014

Service Correspondent (clerical) 221.367-062
service-crew supervisor (smelt. & refin.) 630.134-010
Service-Crew Supervisor (utilities) 862.137-010
service dismantler (auto. mfg.) 806.384-014
service engineer (construction; petrol. & gas; pipe lines) 620.281-046
service engineer (machinery mfg.; machine tools) 638.261-018
SERVICE-ESTABLISHMENT ATTENDANT (laundry & rel.; personal ser.)
369.477-014
service inspector (motor trans.; r.r. trans.) 168.167-082
service inspector (r.r. trans.) 168.267-030
service inspector (utilities) 821.131-010
Service Investigator (tel. & tel.; utilities) 241.367-014
SERVICE MANAGER (automotive ser.) 185.167-058
SERVICE MANAGER (retail trade) 185.164-010
SERVICE MECHANIC (auto. mfg.) 807.381-022
SERVICE MECHANIC, COMPRESSED-GAS EQUIPMENT (chemical)
630.281-034
SERVICE-MECHANIC HELPER, COMPRESSED-GAS EQUIPMENT (chemical) 630.664-018
SERVICE OBSERVER (tel. & tel.) 239.367-026
SERVICE OBSERVER, CHIEF (tel. & tel.) 239.137-022
service officer (nonprofit org.) 187.167-198
service-order dispatcher (clerical) 221.367-070
service-order dispatcher, chief (utilities) 959.137-014
Service-Parts Driver (automotive ser.) 906.683-022
servicer (any industry) 929.687-030
servicer, coin machines (business ser.) 292.483-010
SERVICE REPRESENTATIVE (auto. mfg.) 191.167-022
service representative (machinery mfg.; machine tools) 638.261-018
service representative (radio-tv broad.; tel. & tel.; utilities; waterworks)
239.362-014
SERVICE REPRESENTATIVE (utilities; waterworks) 959.574-010
SERVICE REPRESENTATIVE, ELEVATORS, ESCALATORS, AND
DUMBWAITERS (wholesale tr.) 259.257-018
SERVICE RESTORER, EMERGENCY (r.r. trans.) 821.261-022
Servicer, Travel Trailers (vehicles, nec) 869.384-010
SERVICES CLERK (water trans.) 214.387-018
services engineer (tel. & tel.) 003.187-018
service-station attendant (automotive ser.) 915.467-010
service supervisor (hotel & rest.) 329.137-010
service supervisor (wholesale tr.) 187.167-142
SERVICE SUPERVISOR I (utilities) 953.137-018
SERVICE SUPERVISOR II (utilities) 821.131-018
SERVICE SUPERVISOR III (utilities) 184.167-126
SERVICE SUPERVISOR, LEASED MACHINERY AND EQUIPMENT (any
industry) 183.167-030
SERVICE TECHNICIAN, COMPUTERIZED-PHOTOFINISHING EQUIP-
MENT (photofinishing) 714.281-030
service tester (utilities) 821.381-014
Service-Transformer-Repair Supervisor (utilities) 829.131-014
SERVICE-UNIT OPERATOR, OIL WELL (petrol. & gas) 930.361-010
service worker (any industry)　　see MAINTENANCE WORKER
service writer (automotive ser.) 620.261-018
SET DECORATOR (motion picture; radio-tv broad.) 142.061-042
SET DESIGNER (amuse. & rec.) 142.061-050
SET DESIGNER (motion picture; radio-tv broad.) 142.061-046
set electrician, assistant chief (motion picture; radio-tv broad.) 962.362-014
SET-KEY DRIVER (clock & watch) 715.687-118
set-making-machine operator (print. & pub.) 653.382-014
set-model builder (motion picture) 962.381-018
Set-Off Blocker (hat & cap) 580.684-014
Set-Off-Press Operator (hat & cap) 583.685-018
set rider (any industry) 932.664-010
SET-STAFF FITTER (clock & watch) 715.684-178
setter (boot & shoe) 690.685-074
SETTER (brick & tile) 573.684-014
setter (construction) 861.361-014
setter (stonework) 679.664-010
setter (wood. container) 761.381-014
Setter, Automatic-Spinning-And-Beading-Lathe (any industry) 604.360-010
SETTER, AUTOMATIC-SPINNING LATHE (any industry) 604.360-010
SETTER, COLD-ROLLING MACHINE (machine shop) 617.682-022
SETTER HELPER (brick & tile) 573.687-030
setter-in (pottery & porc.) 573.686-026
SETTER, INDUCTION-HEATING EQUIPMENT (welding) 813.360-014
SETTER, JUICE PACKAGING MACHINES (can. & preserv.) 920.380-010
setter, machine (leather mfg.; tex. prod., nec) 589.685-098
SETTER, MOLDING-AND-COREMAKING MACHINES (foundry) 518.380-
010
setter-off (chemical) 969.664-010
setter, plastics-molding machine (inst. & app.; office machines; plastic prod.;
recording) 556.380-010
setter-up (chemical) 969.664-010
setter-up (wood. container) 764.684-018
setter-up, silk-screen frame (any industry) 709.484-010

setting-up-and-windlass-machine operator (wood. container) 764.684-018
setting-up-and-windlass-machine-operator helper (wood. container) 764.687-038
SETTLEMENT CLERK (smelt. & refin.) 214.382-030
settlement technician (insurance) 209.382-014
set-up and charger (jewelry-silver.) 700.687-026
SET-UP MECHANIC (pen & pencil) 692.380-010
SET-UP MECHANIC, AUTOMATIC LINE (pen & pencil) 692.380-014
Set-Up Mechanic, Coating Machines (pen & pencil) 692.380-010
SET-UP MECHANIC, COIL-WINDING MACHINES (elec. equip.) 724.360-010
SET-UP MECHANIC, CROWN ASSEMBLY MACHINE (any industry) 692.362-010
Set-Up Mechanic, Heading Machines (pen & pencil) 692.380-010
Set-Up Mechanic, Stamping Machines (pen & pencil) 692.380-010
set-up-operator, tool (machine shop) 601.280-054
SET-UP WORKER (clock & watch) 715.660-010
setup worker, electronics (comm. equip.; electron. comp.) 726.364-018
SEWAGE-DISPOSAL WORKER (sanitary ser.) 955.687-010
sewage-plant attendant (sanitary ser.) 955.585-010
sewage-plant operator (sanitary ser.) 955.362-010
sewage plant supervisor (sanitary ser.) 955.130-010
sewer (boot & shoe) 690.685-162
sewer (boot & shoe) 690.682-082
Sewer-And-Cutter, Finger-Buff Material (tex. prod., nec) 787.685-014
SEWER AND INSPECTOR (knitting) 684.682-014
SEWER-AND-WATERWORKS SUPERVISOR (construction) term
SEWER, HAND (any industry) 782.684-058
sewer, hand (tex. prod., nec) 782.684-050
Sewer, Head (agriculture) 920.687-022
Sewer, Linen Room (hotel & rest.) 787.682-030
SEWER-LINE PHOTO-INSPECTOR (sanitary ser.) 851.362-010
SEWER-LINE REPAIRER (sanitary ser.) 869.664-018
SEWER-LINE REPAIRER, TELE-GROUT (sanitary ser.) 851.262-010
SEWER-PIPE CLEANER (business ser.) 899.664-014
Sewer-Pipe-Press Operator (brick & tile) 575.462-010
Sewer-Pipe Sorter (brick & tile) 573.687-034
Sewer Tapper (construction) 869.664-014
Sewing-Department Supervisor (leather prod.) 783.132-010
Sewing Inspector (laundry & rel.) 369.687-022
sewing-machine adjuster (any industry) 639.281-018
SEWING-MACHINE ASSEMBLER (machinery mfg.) 706.381-034
Sewing-Machine Attachment Tester (machinery mfg.) 709.382-010
SEWING-MACHINE OPERATOR (any industry) 787.682-046
SEWING-MACHINE OPERATOR (furniture) 780.682-010
SEWING-MACHINE OPERATOR (knitting) 787.682-074
SEWING-MACHINE OPERATOR (knitting; protective dev.) 787.682-050
SEWING MACHINE OPERATOR (leather prod.) 783.682-014
SEWING-MACHINE OPERATOR (toy-sport equip.) 787.682-054
SEWING-MACHINE OPERATOR, AUTOMATIC (any industry) master
sewing-machine operator, carpet and rugs (carpet & rug; retail trade) 787.682-014
SEWING MACHINE OPERATOR I (tex. prod., nec) 787.682-066
SEWING-MACHINE OPERATOR II (tex. prod., nec) 787.682-058
SEWING-MACHINE OPERATOR, PAPER BAGS (paper goods) 787.685-054
Sewing-Machine Operator, Plastic Zipper (button & notion) 787.685-034
SEWING-MACHINE OPERATOR, REGULAR EQUIPMENT (any industry) master
SEWING-MACHINE OPERATOR, SEMIAUTOMATIC (garment) 786.685-030
SEWING-MACHINE OPERATOR, SPECIAL EQUIPMENT (furniture) 689.685-118
SEWING-MACHINE OPERATOR, ZIPPER (button & notion) 787.685-034
SEWING-MACHINE REPAIRER (any industry) 639.281-018
SEWING-MACHINE-REPAIRER HELPER (any industry) 639.684-010
SEWING-MACHINE TESTER (machinery mfg.) 709.382-010
Sewing Room Grip (motion picture) 962.687-022
SEWING SUPERVISOR (any industry) 787.132-010
sew-out operator (garment) 786.682-166
SEXTON (nonprofit org.) 389.667-010
SHACKLER (meat products) 525.687-086
Shactor (meat products) 525.361-010
SHACTOR HELPER (meat products) 525.687-090
shade-and-quality checker (textile) 582.387-010
shade classifier (brick & tile) 574.367-010
SHADE-CLOTH FINISHER (furniture) 585.687-026
SHADE MATCHER (textile) 582.687-022
shader (paint & varnish) 550.381-014
shader and folder (textile) 781.687-014
shader and toner (wood prod., nec) 749.684-030
shadowgraph operator (any industry) 699.384-010
SHADOWGRAPH-SCALE OPERATOR (ordnance) 737.687-126
Shadowgraph-Weight Operator (toy-sport equip.) 929.687-062
Shafting Cleaner (any industry) 699.687-014
Shaft Inspector (house. appl.) 729.384-022
SHAFT MECHANIC (mine & quarry) 899.684-034

shaft repairer (mine & quarry) 899.684-034
Shaft Sinker (mine & quarry) 939.281-010
shaft tender (mine & quarry) 899.684-034
SHAKE BACKBOARD NOTCHER (saw. & plan.) 663.685-030
Shake Feeder (saw. & plan.) 669.686-030
Shake-Out Worker (foundry) 519.687-022
Shake Packer (saw. & plan.) 920.687-158
SHAKER (hat & cap) 589.685-094
SHAKER (knitting) 589.687-058
SHAKER (tobacco) 521.687-110
Shaker, Flatwork (laundry & rel.) 363.686-010
shaker operator (steel & rel.) 541.665-010
SHAKER-PLATE OPERATOR (ordnance) 737.685-014
SHAKER REPAIRER (grain-feed mills) 769.664-010
shaker-screen operator (chemical) 551.685-130
SHAKER TENDER (concrete prod.; mine & quarry) 934.685-018
SHAKER TENDER (steel & rel.) 541.665-010
SHAKER WASHER (grain-feed mills) 521.687-114
SHAKER, WEARING APPAREL (laundry & rel.) 361.687-026
SHAKE SAWYER (saw. & plan.) 667.682-070
Shake Splitter (logging) 454.684-022
SHALE PLANER OPERATOR (mine & quarry) 930.663-010
SHALE PLANER OPERATOR HELPER (mine & quarry) 930.667-010
Shampooer (personal ser.) 332.271-010
Shank Beveler (boot & shoe) 690.685-166
Shank Boner (meat products) 525.684-010
Shank Burnisher (boot & shoe) 690.685-058
Shank Cementer, Hand (boot & shoe) 788.687-030
shanker (boot & shoe) 788.687-118
SHANK INSPECTOR (boot & shoe) 788.687-110
shank paperer (boot & shoe) 788.687-114
shank picker (boot & shoe) 788.687-110
SHANK-PIECE TACKER (boot & shoe) 788.687-118
Shank Sander (boot & shoe) 690.685-046
Shank Sander (fabrication, nec) 761.684-030
shank sorter (boot & shoe) 788.687-110
Shank Stapler (boot & shoe) 690.685-162
Shank Stitcher (boot & shoe) 690.682-082
shank tacker (boot & shoe) 788.687-118
SHANK TAPER (boot & shoe) 788.687-114
SHANK THREADER (fabrication, nec) 739.685-034
shank turner (fabrication, nec) 664.685-022
Shape-Brick Molder (brick & tile) 575.684-042
shape carver (stonework) 771.281-010
shape hand (tobacco) 520.687-050
shaper (button & notion) 734.684-010
shaper (jewelry-silver.) 700.684-034
shaper (ordnance) 761.381-038
shaper (pottery & porc.) 774.684-018
shaper (stonework) 673.382-010
SHAPER AND PRESSER (garment) 583.685-102
SHAPER, BASEBALL GLOVE (toy-sport equip.) 732.684-106
SHAPER, HAND (furniture) 761.684-038
shaper machine hand (machine shop) 605.382-038
shaper operator (machine shop) 605.382-038
SHAPER OPERATOR (woodworking) 665.682-034
Shaper Setter (woodworking) 669.280-010
SHAPER SET-UP OPERATOR, TOOL (machine shop) 605.382-038
shaping-machine operator (machine shop) 605.382-038
SHAPING-MACHINE OPERATOR (plastic prod.) 690.685-354
SHAPING MACHINE TENDER (furniture) 665.685-046
shaping-machine tender (pen & pencil) 663.685-026
SHARECROPPER (agriculture) term
sharpener (oils & grease) 603.682-018
Sharples-Machine Operator (oils & grease) 529.685-198
shaver (boot & shoe) 690.685-434
shaver (boot & shoe; leather prod.) 585.685-114
shaver (hat & cap) 585.685-046
SHAVER (laundry & rel.) 362.687-018
SHAVER (meat products) 525.687-094
SHAVING-MACHINE OPERATOR (leather mfg.) 585.685-094
Shear Assembler (cutlery-hrdwr.) 701.687-010
shearer (any industry) 699.685-014
shearer (hat & cap) 585.685-046
shearer (leather mfg.) 585.685-098
shearer (leather mfg.) 585.685-126
SHEARER AND TRIMMER, WIRE SCREEN AND FABRIC (metal prod., nec) 709.684-074
shearer, printed circuit boards (electron. comp.) 615.685-046
shearer, screen measurer and trimmer (metal prod., nec) 709.684-074
SHEAR-GRINDER OPERATOR (textile) 628.382-014
SHEAR-GRINDER-OPERATOR HELPER (textile) 628.687-014
SHEARING-MACHINE FEEDER (leather mfg.) 585.685-098
SHEARING-MACHINE OPERATOR (carpet & rug; textile) 585.685-102
Shearing-Machine Operator (leather mfg.) 585.685-094

shearing-machine operator (print. & pub.) 640.685-010
shear operator (carpet & rug; textile) 585.685-102
Shear Operator, Automatic I (any industry) 615.682-018
Shear Operator, Automatic II (any industry) 699.686-010
Shear-Operator Helper (any industry) 619.687-014
SHEAR OPERATOR I (any industry) 615.682-018
SHEAR OPERATOR II (any industry) 615.685-034
SHEAR SETTER (any industry) 615.380-010
shear tender (textile) 585.685-026
Sheather (construction) 860.381-042
shed boss (agriculture) 404.131-014
SHED WORKER (agriculture) term
Sheep Boner (meat products) 525.684-010
sheep clipper (agriculture) 410.684-014
SHEEP HERDER (agriculture) 410.687-022
Sheep Or Calf Grader (meat products) 525.387-010
Sheep Rancher (agriculture) 410.161-018
SHEEP SHEARER (agriculture) 410.684-014
SHEEPSKIN PICKLER (meat products) 582.685-126
Sheep Sticker (meat products) 525.684-050
Sheet Cleaner (tex. prod., nec) 689.687-050
sheet-combining operator (plastic-synth.) 690.682-058
Sheet Cutter I (tex. prod., nec) 699.685-014
Sheet Cutter II (tex. prod., nec) 787.685-014
sheet-cutting operator (tex. prod., nec) 686.585-010
sheeter (paper goods) 640.685-046
sheeter helper (paper & pulp; paper goods; print. & pub.) 649.685-066
Sheeter-Machine Operator (paper goods) 659.685-014
sheeter operator (any industry) 699.682-018
Sheeter Operator (paper & pulp) 649.682-022
SHEETER OPERATOR (plastic-synth.) 690.382-010
sheeter-waxer operator (paper goods) 534.482-010
Sheet Folder (tex. prod., nec) 589.687-014
Sheet Hanger (smelt. & refin.) 519.565-014
Sheeting Puller (construction) 869.687-026
Sheet Inspector (tex. prod., nec) 789.587-014
sheet metal assembler (aircraft mfg.) 806.384-034
Sheet-Metal-Fabricating-Machine Operator (any industry) 616.380-
Sheet-Metal Installer (any industry) 804.281-010
Sheet-Metal Lay-Out Worker (any industry) 809.281-010
sheet-metal mechanic (any industry) 804.281-010
SHEET-METAL-PATTERN CUTTER (musical inst.) 730.684-074
Sheet-Metal Production Worker (any industry) 619.685-062
Sheet-Metal-Shop Helper (any industry) 619.686-022
Sheet-Metal-Shop Supervisor (any industry) 809.130-014
SHEET-METAL WORKER (any industry) 804.281-010
SHEET-METAL-WORKER APPRENTICE (any industry) 804.281-014
Sheet-Metal Worker, Maintenance (any industry) 804.281-010
SHEET-MILL SUPERVISOR (nonfer. metal) 619.132-014
Sheet-Pile-Driver Operator (construction) 859.682-018
Sheet-Pile-Hammer Operator (construction) 869.687-026
SHEETROCK APPLICATOR (mfd. bldgs.) 869.684-050
sheetrock installer (construction; mfd. bldgs.) 842.684-014
sheetrock taper (construction; mfd. bldgs.) 842.664-010
Sheet Sewer (tex. prod., nec) 787.682-026
Sheet Straightener (plastic-synth.) 690.682-058
sheet taker (paper & pulp) 539.686-010
Sheet Tester (steel & rel.) 011.361-010
SHEET TURNER (millwork-plywood) 762.687-062
SHEET WRITER (amuse. & rec.) 211.467-026
shelf-drier operator (chemical) 553.685-106
SHELLACKER (ordnance) 737.687-130
Shellac Polisher (fabrication, nec) 739.684-026
SHELL ASSEMBLER (ordnance) 737.684-038
Shell-Core-And-Molding Supervisor (foundry) 519.131-010
Shell Coremaker (foundry) 518.685-026
Sheller (mfd. bldgs.; vehicles, nec) 869.684-010
SHELLER I (can. & preserv.) 521.687-118
SHELLER II (can. & preserv.) 521.685-294
SHELLFISH-BED WORKER (fishing & hunt.) 446.684-014
Shellfish Checker (can. & preserv.) 529.687-230
SHELLFISH DREDGE OPERATOR (fishing & hunt.) 446.663-010
SHELLFISH GROWER (fishing & hunt.) 446.161-014
shellfish harvester (fishing & hunt.) 446.663-010
Shellfish Packer (can. & preserv.) 529.687-230
SHELLFISH-PROCESSING-MACHINE TENDER (can. & preserv.) 529.685-214
SHELLFISH SHUCKER (can. & preserv.) 521.687-122
Shellfish Sorter (can. & preserv.) 529.687-230
Shellfish Weigher (can. & preserv.) 529.687-230
shell-freezing-machine operator (pharmaceut.) 559.685-090
SHELL-GRADER (button & notion) 734.687-070
shell-house operator (chemical) 649.682-030
SHELL-MACHINE OPERATOR (chemical) 649.682-030
Shell Maker, Lockstitch (garment) 786.682-174

shell mold bonder (foundry) 518.685-030
SHELL-MOLD-BONDING-MACHINE OPERATOR (foundry) 518.685-030
SHELL MOLDER (foundry) 518.685-026
shell-press operator (plastic-synth.) 690.682-058
shell-reprint operator (ordnance) 659.685-018
SHELL-SHOP SUPERVISOR (ordnance) 619.132-018
SHELL-SIEVE OPERATOR (ordnance) 694.585-010
shell sorter (button & notion) 734.687-070
shell-trim operator (ordnance) 609.685-026
shell-trim tool setter (ordnance) 609.280-010
Shelter Management Officer (government ser.) 188.117-022
shelver (library) 249.687-014
shelving clerk (library) 249.687-014
SHELVING SUPERVISOR (library) 109.137-010
shepherd (agriculture) 410.687-022
SHERIFF, DEPUTY (government ser.) 377.263-010
shield operator (construction) 850.682-010
SHIELD RUNNER (construction) 850.682-010
shift adjuster (smelt. & refin.) 511.130-010
shift boss (mine & quarry) 939.137-018
shifter (construction) 859.137-018
SHIFT SUPERINTENDENT, CAUSTIC CRESYLATE (chemical) 552.132-010
SHIFT SUPERVISOR, FILM PROCESSING (print. & pub.) 979.132-010
shift supervisor, melting (glass mfg.) 579.137-026
shill (amuse. & rec.) 343.367-010
Shingle-Bolt Cutter (logging) 454.684-022
Shingle-Machine Supervisor (build. mat., nec) 590.130-018
SHINGLE PACKER (saw. & plan.) 920.687-158
SHINGLE SAWYER (saw. & plan.) 667.485-010
SHINGLE TRIMMER (saw. & plan.) 667.685-050
shingle weaver (saw. & plan.) 920.687-158
ship boss (water trans.) 911.137-018
SHIPFITTER (ship-boat mfg.) 806.381-046
SHIPFITTER APPRENTICE (ship-boat mfg.) 806.381-050
SHIPFITTER HELPER (ship-boat mfg.) 806.687-050
ship officer (water trans.) 197.133-022
SHIPPING AND RECEIVING CLERK (clerical) 222.387-050
SHIPPING-AND-RECEIVING SUPERVISOR (clerical) 222.137-030
SHIPPING-AND-RECEIVING WEIGHER (clerical) 222.387-074
SHIPPING CHECKER (clerical) 222.687-030
Shipping Clerk (clerical) 222.387-050
Shipping Hand (chemical) 559.687-050
SHIPPING-ORDER CLERK (clerical) 219.367-030
shipping-room supervisor (rubber reclaim.) 559.132-058
Shipping Supervisor (clerical) 222.137-030
Shipping Weigher (clerical) 222.387-074
ship purser (water trans.) 197.167-014
SHIP RUNNER (water trans.) 222.567-014
ship's captain (water trans.) 197.167-010
Ship's Doctor (medical ser.) 070.101-022
ship surveyor (profess. & kin.) 014.167-010
SHIPWRIGHT (ship-boat mfg.) 860.381-058
SHIPWRIGHT APPRENTICE (ship-boat mfg.) 860.381-062
SHIPWRIGHT HELPER (ship-boat mfg.) 860.664-018
Shipwright Supervisor (ship-boat mfg.) 891.131-010
SHIRRING-MACHINE OPERATOR (any industry) 787.682-078
SHIRRING-MACHINE OPERATOR, AUTOMATIC (tex. prod., nec) 787.685-038
shirring tender (meat products) 525.685-014
Shirt-Collar-And-Cuff Presser (laundry & rel.) 363.685-026
Shirt Creaser (garment) 583.685-042
Shirt Finisher (garment) 363.682-018
Shirt Folder (garment; knitting) 789.687-066
Shirt Folder I (laundry & rel.) 369.687-018
Shirt Folder II (laundry & rel.) 363.685-026
SHIRT-FOLDING-MACHINE OPERATOR (garment; laundry & rel.) 369.685-030
Shirt-Ironer Supervisor (laundry & rel.) 361.137-010
Shirt Marker (garment) 781.384-014
SHIRT PRESSER (laundry & rel.) 363.685-026
Shirt Presser, Automatic (laundry & rel.) 363.685-014
Shirt Sorter (garment) 222.687-014
Shirt Turner (garment; knitting) 789.687-074
Shochet (meat products) 525.361-010
Shoder Filler (metal prod., nec) 700.687-038
SHOE CLEANER (boot & shoe) 788.687-122
SHOE COVERER (boot & shoe) 788.687-126
shoe cutter (boot & shoe) 788.684-082
Shoe Designer (boot & shoe) 142.061-018
shoe dresser (boot & shoe) 788.687-038
Shoe-Dressing Maker (chemical) 559.665-026
SHOE DYER (personal ser.) 364.684-014
shoe hammerer (boot & shoe) 690.685-350
shoe handler (boot & shoe) 920.687-166

shoe ironer (boot & shoe) 788.687-158
shoelace tipper (narrow fabrics) 686.685-062
SHOELACE-TIPPING-MACHINE OPERATOR (narrow fabrics) 686.685-062
SHOE-LAY-OUT PLANNER (boot & shoe) 012.187-014
shoemaker (personal ser.) 365.361-014
SHOEMAKER, CUSTOM (boot & shoe) 788.381-014
SHOE PACKER (boot & shoe) 920.687-166
Shoe-Parts Cutter (boot & shoe) 699.682-022
shoe planner (boot & shoe) 012.187-014
shoe polisher (personal ser.) 366.677-010
shoe repairer (boot & shoe) 788.684-022
shoe repairer (boot & shoe) 788.381-010
SHOE REPAIRER (personal ser.) 365.361-014
SHOE-REPAIRER HELPER (personal ser.) 365.674-010
SHOE-REPAIR SUPERVISOR (personal ser.) 365.131-010
SHOE SHINER (personal ser.) 366.677-010
shoe singer (boot & shoe) 788.684-050
shoe stitcher, odd (boot & shoe) 788.381-010
shoe tinter (personal ser.) 364.684-014
SHOE TURNER (boot & shoe) 788.687-130
shook splicer (woodworking) 669.685-042
shooter (any industry) 859.261-010
shooter (grain-feed mills) 523.382-010
shooter (mine & quarry) 931.261-010
shooter (ordnance) 736.384-010
SHOOTER (petrol. & gas) 931.361-014
Shooter Helper, Seismograph (petrol. & gas) 939.364-010
SHOOTER, SEISMOGRAPH (petrol. & gas) 931.361-018
shooter's helper (any industry) 859.687-010
Shooter, Water Well (construction) 859.261-010
Shooting Gallery Operator (amuse. & rec.) 342.657-014
shop blacksmith (mine & quarry) 622.381-030
Shop Clerk (clerical) 219.362-010
shop clerk (clerical) 222.367-042
shop cooper (wood. container) 764.684-022
SHOP ESTIMATOR (automotive ser.) 807.267-010
Shop Mechanic (any industry) 804.281-010
shop mechanic (construction; petrol. & gas; pipe lines) 620.281-046
shop mechanic (machine shop) 600.280-042
shop-mechanic helper (construction; petrol. & gas; pipe lines) 620.664-014
shopper's aid (retail trade) 296.357-010
shopping inspector (business ser.) 376.267-022
SHOPPING INVESTIGATOR (business ser.) 376.267-022
shop repairer (tel. & tel.) 722.281-010
SHOP STEWARD (any industry) term
shop superintendent (motor trans.) 184.167-170
shop supervisor (any industry) 638.131-026
shop supervisor (any industry) 809.130-014
SHOP SUPERVISOR (struct. metal) 619.131-014
SHOP TAILOR (garment; retail trade) 785.361-022
SHOP TAILOR APPRENTICE (garment; retail trade) 785.361-026
shop teacher (education) 091.221-010
SHORE HAND, DREDGE OR BARGE (construction; mine & quarry) 939.667-018
Shorer (construction) 869.664-014
shore-working supervisor (construction) 862.134-010
shortage worker (knitting) 221.587-018
Shortening Mixer (oils & grease) 520.685-070
short-filler-bunch-machine operator (tobacco) 529.685-038
SHORTHAND REPORTER (clerical) 202.362-010
short-log-bolter operator (saw. & plan.) 667.685-022
short piece handler (textile) 689.686-058
Shorts Sifter (tobacco) 521.685-270
SHOT BAGGER (ordnance) 920.687-170
SHOTBLAST-EQUIPMENT OPERATOR (foundry) 503.362-014
Shotblaster (any industry) 503.687-010
shot-blast tender (any industry) 503.685-042
SHOT-COAT TENDER (concrete prod.) 575.665-018
shot-core-drill operator (any industry) 930.682-010
shot-core-drill-operator helper (any industry) 930.687-014
SHOT DROPPER (ordnance) 502.362-010
shot firer (mine & quarry) 931.261-010
SHOT-GRINDER OPERATOR (ordnance) 603.685-074
SHOTGUN-SHELL-ASSEMBLY-MACHINE ADJUSTER (ordnance) 616.360-030
SHOTGUN-SHELL-ASSEMBLY-MACHINE OPERATOR (ordnance) 694.385-010
SHOTGUN-SHELL-LOADING-MACHINE OPERATOR (ordnance) 694.665-010
SHOTGUN-SHELL-REPRINTING-UNIT OPERATOR (ordnance) 659.685-018
shot-hole driller (petrol. & gas) 930.382-018
shot-hole shooter (petrol. & gas) 931.361-018
shot lighter (mine & quarry) 931.261-010
shot packer (ordnance) 920.687-170
SHOT-PEENING OPERATOR (aircraft mfg.) 617.280-010

Shot-Peen Operator (any industry) 503.685-042
SHOT POLISHER AND INSPECTOR (ordnance) 509.485-014
shot-tube-machine tender (ordnance) 920.685-018
SHOT-TUBE-MACHINE TENDER (paper goods) 649.685-106
Shoulder Boner (meat products) 525.684-010
SHOULDER JOINER, LOCKSTITCH (garment) 786.682-222
Shoulder Puncher (meat products) 525.684-046
Shoulder Sawyer (meat products) 525.684-018
Shoveler (mine & quarry) 939.687-014
Shovel-Handle Assembler (woodworking) 762.687-042
Shovel-Loader Operator (logging) 921.683-058
shovel operator (mine & quarry) 932.683-018
show-card writer (any industry) 970.281-022
Showcase Trimmer (retail trade) 298.081-010
Shower Attendant (personal ser.) 335.677-014
Shower-Enclosure Installer (construction) 865.381-010
shower room attendant (any industry) 358.687-010
SHOW GIRL (amuse. & rec.) 159.647-022
SHOW-HORSE DRIVER (amuse. & rec.) 159.344-018
SHOW HOST/HOSTESS (radio-tv broad.) 159.147-018
Show Inspector (government ser.) 375.263-014
Showplace Manager (amuse. & rec.) 191.117-014
shredded-filler cigar-maker, machine (tobacco) 529.685-270
shredded-filler-cutter operator (tobacco) 529.685-110
SHREDDED-FILLER HOPPER-FEEDER (tobacco) 529.687-182
shredded-filler-machine wrapper-layer (tobacco) 529.685-270
shredder (any industry) 680.685-082
SHREDDER OPERATOR (plastic-synth.) 555.685-058
shredder operator (smelt. & refin.) 515.687-010
shredder picker (tex. prod., nec; textile) 680.686-018
SHREDDER TENDER (chemical) 555.665-010
SHREDDER TENDER, PEAT (agriculture) 599.685-086
SHREDDING-FLOOR-EQUIPMENT OPERATOR (plastic-synth.) 559.382-050
shredding-machine-knife changer (tobacco) 638.684-010
shredding-machine operator (tobacco) 521.685-338
shredding-machine tender (saw. & plan.) 663.685-014
Shrimp Blancher (can. & preserv.) 529.685-214
SHRIMP-PEELING-MACHINE OPERATOR (can. & preserv.) 521.682-038
Shrimp-Peeling-Machine Tender (can. & preserv.) 529.685-214
Shrimp Pond Laborer (fishing & hunt.) 446.687-014
shrinker (textile) 587.685-018
SHRINKING-MACHINE OPERATOR (hat & cap) 586.685-034
SHRINK-PIT OPERATOR (ordnance) 619.662-010
SHRINK-PIT SUPERVISOR (ordnance) 619.131-018
SHROUDER (meat products) 525.587-010
Shroud-Line Tier (tex. prod., nec) 789.687-118
Shroud-Web Inspector (tex. prod., nec) 789.687-114
Shrub Grower (agriculture) 405.161-014
shucker (can. & preserv.) 521.687-122
shuttle-bus driver (motor trans.) 913.663-018
SHUTTLE-CAR OPERATOR (mine & quarry) 932.683-022
shuttlecock assembler (toy-sport equip.) 732.685-018
Shuttlecock-Feather Trimmer (toy-sport equip.) 699.685-014
shuttle filler (textile) 689.686-038
SHUTTLE FIXER (textile) 628.684-026
SHUTTLE HAND (textile) 689.686-038
shuttle inspector (textile) 628.684-026
SHUTTLE INSPECTOR (woodworking) 769.684-046
shuttleless-loom weaver (narrow fabrics) 683.665-010
shuttle repairer (textile) 628.684-026
SHUTTLER (tex. prod., nec) 689.687-070
shuttler (tex. prod., nec) 789.684-054
SHUTTLE SPOTTER (woodworking) 664.685-026
shuttle threader (textile) 689.686-038
Side Boss (logging) 459.133-010
Side Framer (mfd. bldgs.; vehicles, nec) 869.684-010
Side Framer (vehicles, nec) 806.684-018
Side Gluer (musical inst.) 763.684-058
Side Guider (fabrication, nec) 590.686-014
sidehand (steel & rel.) 615.687-010
side hemmer (tex. prod., nec) 787.685-018
SIDE LASTER, CEMENT (boot & shoe) 690.685-358
SIDE LASTER, STAPLE (boot & shoe) 690.685-362
Side Laster, Tack (boot & shoe) 690.685-362
Side-Panel Hanger (mfd. bldgs.; vehicles, nec) 809.684-030
Side-Panel Padder (furniture) 780.684-082
side-piece coverer (furniture) 780.684-082
SIDER (construction; mfd. bldgs.; retail trade) 863.684-014
SIDER (mfd. bldgs.) 860.684-014
SIDEROGRAPHER (print. & pub.) 979.381-030
Side-Seam-Envelope-Machine Operator (paper goods) 649.685-042
Side-Seam Tender (welding) 819.685-010
Side-Shearing-Machine Operator (chemical) 930.683-014
Side-Show Entertainer (amuse. & rec.) 159.647-010
Side Splitter (meat products) 525.684-018

side stapler (boot & shoe) 690.685-362
Side-Stitcher (furniture) 780.684-070
Side-Stitching-Machine Feeder-Offbearer (print. & pub.) 653.686-026
Side-Stitching-Machine Operator (print. & pub.) 653.662-010
side trimmer (boot & shoe) 690.685-238
siding applicator (construction; mfd. bldgs.; retail trade) 863.684-014
Siding-Coreboard Inspector (paper & pulp; wood prod., nec) 539.667-010
SIDING STAPLER (millwork-plywood) 762.684-058
SIEVE-GRADER TENDER (can. & preserv.) 521.665-026
SIEVE MAKER (grain-feed mills) 529.684-018
Sieve Repairer (grain-feed mills) 529.684-018
SIFTER (pharmaceut.) 551.687-030
sifter and miller (optical goods) 579.685-046
sifter operator (grain-feed mills) 521.685-030
SIGHT-EFFECTS SPECIALIST (amuse. & rec.) 962.267-010
sighter (ordnance) 736.684-042
SIGHT MOUNTER (ordnance) 736.481-010
Sightseeing-Boat Operator (water trans.) 911.663-010
signaler (any industry) 921.667-022
SIGNALER (construction) 869.667-014
signal inspector (r.r. trans.) 822.281-026
SIGNAL MAINTAINER (r.r. trans.) 822.281-026
SIGNAL MAINTAINER HELPER (r.r. trans.) 822.684-018
signal repairer (r.r. trans.) 822.281-026
SIGNAL SUPERVISOR (r.r. trans.) 822.131-026
signal timer (any industry) 379.362-014
signal-tower operator (r.r. trans.) 910.362-010
SIGN ERECTOR-AND-REPAIRER (fabrication, nec) 869.361-018
SIGN ERECTOR I (fabrication, nec) 869.381-026
SIGN ERECTOR II (fabrication, nec) 869.684-054
sign hanger (fabrication, nec) 869.381-026
Sign Maker (fabrication, nec) 869.381-026
sign poster (any industry) 299.667-010
sign printer (any industry) 659.682-026
SIGN WRITER, HAND (any industry) 970.281-022
SIGN WRITER, MACHINE (any industry) 659.682-026
Silent Bit Extra (amuse. & rec.; motion picture; radio-tv broad.) 159.647-014
SILHOUETTE ARTIST (amuse. & rec.) 149.051-010
Silica-Dry-Press Helper (brick & tile) 575.686-010
Silica-Dry-Press Operator (brick & tile) 575.662-010
SILICA-FILTER OPERATOR (beverage) 521.582-010
Silica-Mixer Operator (brick & tile) 570.382-010
SILICA-SPRAY MIXER (smelt. & refin.) 570.685-090
Silicator (chemical) 741.687-018
Silk Beamer (textile) 681.685-058
Silk Brusher (textile) 585.685-070
Silk-Crepe-Machine Operator (textile) 583.685-030
Silk Examiner (textile) 689.685-038
SILK FINISHER (laundry & rel.) 363.681-010
Silk Folder (textile) 689.585-014
Silk-Lining Cutter, Machine (boot & shoe; hat & cap; leather prod.) 699.682-022
Silk Presser I (garment) 363.684-018
Silk Presser II (garment) 363.682-018
SILK-SCREEN CUTTER (any industry) 979.681-022
Silk Screener (optical goods) 920.685-078
SILK-SCREEN ETCHER (engraving) 704.684-014
SILK-SCREEN-FRAME ASSEMBLER (any industry) 709.484-010
Silk-Screen-Layout Drafter (any industry) 979.681-022
silk-screen maker (any industry) 979.681-022
silk-screen operator (any industry) 979.684-034
silk-screen painter (any industry) 979.684-034
Silk-Screen Printer (electron. comp.) 979.684-034
silk-screen printer (textile) 979.684-030
SILK-SCREEN PRINTER, MACHINE (any industry) 979.685-010
SILK-SCREEN REPAIRER (any industry) 979.684-038
Silk Spotter (laundry & rel.) 362.381-010
SILK SPREADER (textile) 680.685-090
silk-top-hat-body maker (hat & cap) 784.684-074
Silo Erector (construction) 861.381-018
SILO OPERATOR (tobacco) 529.682-030
SILO TENDER (cement) 579.685-050
SILVERER (glass products) 574.684-014
silverer (optical goods) 574.484-010
SILVERING APPLICATOR (glass products) 574.582-010
Silver Plater (electroplating) 500.380-010
Silversmith I (jewelry-silver.) 700.281-010
SILVERSMITH II (jewelry-silver.) 700.281-022
SILVER-SOLUTION MIXER (chemical) 550.684-026
SILVER SPRAY WORKER (recording) 500.684-022
SILVER STRIPPER, MACHINE (glass products) 579.685-054
SILVERWARE ASSEMBLER (jewelry-silver.) 700.684-070
Silverware Washer (water trans.) 318.687-014
SILVER WRAPPER (hotel & rest.) 318.687-018
SILVICULTURIST (profess. & kin.) 040.061-050

singeing-torch operator (boot & shoe) 788.684-050
SINGER (amuse. & rec.; motion picture; radio-tv broad.) 152.047-022
SINGER (hat & cap) 784.687-062
SINGER (meat products) 525.687-098
SINGER (narrow fabrics) 585.687-030
SINGER (textile) 585.685-106
singer and unloader (boot & shoe) 788.684-050
Singer Back-Tender (textile) 589.686-010
SINGE WINDER (textile) 681.585-018
SINGING MESSENGER (business ser.) 230.647-010
Single-Beam Clicker (boot & shoe; hat & cap; leather prod.) 699.682-022
Single-Corner Cutter (paper goods) 640.685-030
Single-Ending-Machine Operator (paper goods) 641.685-042
Single-End Sewer (paper goods) 787.686-010
Single-End-Trimming-And-Boring-Machine Operator (woodworking) 669.682-038
Single-Facing-Corrugating-Machine Operator (paper goods) 641.562-010
Single-Fold-Machine Operator (paper goods) 649.685-046
single-needle operator (garment) 786.682-170
Single-Needle Stitcher (boot & shoe) 690.682-082
Single-Pass-Soil-Stabilizer Operator (construction) 859.683-026
single-pointed operator (comm. equip.) 770.382-014
Single-Stroke Preformer (plastic prod.; plastic-synth.) 556.685-058
single-wire-saw operator (stonework) 677.462-014
SINK CUTTER (stonework) 677.682-018
sinker puller (millwork-plywood; paper & pulp; saw. & plan.) 921.686-022
SINKER WINDER (toy-sport equip.) 732.685-030
SINTER FEEDER (steel & rel.) 513.685-010
SINTERING-PRESS OPERATOR (nonfer. metal; steel & rel.) 617.685-038
SINTER-MACHINE OPERATOR (smelt. & refin.; steel & rel.) 510.685-026
siphoner (any industry) 914.682-010
SIPHON OPERATOR (medical ser.; pharmaceut.) 599.687-026
S-Iron Worker (wood prod., nec) 563.687-010
sisal operator (furniture) 780.687-042
Sisal Picker (furniture) 680.685-078
site planner (profess. & kin.) 001.061-018
Six-Horse Hitch Driver (any industry) 919.664-010
six-pack-loader operator (beverage) 920.685-042
six-pack packer (beverage) 920.685-042
Six-Section Blower (hat & cap) 680.685-046
size cutter (hat & cap) 585.685-122
SIZE MAKER (paper & pulp) 550.682-010
Size Maker (textile) 550.585-018
sizer (button & notion) 739.687-178
sizer (hat & cap) 784.684-054
sizer (hat & cap) 586.685-034
sizer (hat & cap) 589.687-038
sizer (jewelry-silver.) 700.684-010
SIZER (knitting) 684.684-014
sizer (optical goods) 716.687-026
SIZER (textile) 582.687-026
sizer (textile) 582.562-010
sizer grader (woodworking) 669.687-030
SIZER, HAND (hat & cap) 784.684-054
sizer helper (textile) 582.686-026
SIZER, MACHINE (hat & cap) 784.684-058
SIZER, MACHINE (optical goods) 716.360-010
size tester (knitting) 684.684-014
sizing brusher (hat & cap) 589.687-038
sizing end-bander (hat & cap) 784.687-026
SIZING-MACHINE-AND-DRIER OPERATOR (tex. prod., nec) 582.665-026
Sizing-Machine-And-Drier-Operator Helper (tex. prod., nec) 586.686-022
sizing-machine operator (any industry) 599.685-046
sizing-machine operator (can. & preserv.) 521.685-318
SIZING-MACHINE OPERATOR (nonmet. min.) 554.685-026
SIZING-MACHINE OPERATOR (ordnance) 649.582-014
SIZING-MACHINE TENDER (clock & watch) 690.685-366
SIZING-MACHINE TENDER (pen & pencil) 662.685-030
SIZING-MACHINE TENDER (textile) 584.665-018
sizing sponger (hat & cap) 589.687-038
Sizing Sprayer (furniture) 741.687-018
SKATE-SHOP ATTENDANT (amuse. & rec.) 341.464-010
Skein Drier (plastic-synth.) 581.685-018
SKEINER (narrow fabrics) 681.685-102
skein inspector (textile) 689.687-082
skein-mercerizing-machine operator (textile) 584.685-054
skein reeler (textile) 681.685-078
Skein Washer (plastic-synth.) 582.685-162
SKEIN WINDER (elec. equip.) 721.484-022
skein winder (narrow fabrics) 681.685-102
SKEIN WINDER (textile) 681.685-098
skein winder (textile) 681.685-078
SKEIN-WINDING OPERATOR (any industry) 559.687-054
SKEIN-YARN DRIER (textile) 581.685-054
SKEIN-YARN DYER (textile) 582.685-130

SKEIN-YARN-DYER HELPER (textile) 582.686-022
SKELP PROCESSOR (steel & rel.) 619.662-014
sketcher (machinery mfg.) 979.681-010
Sketch Liner (pottery & porc.) 970.381-022
sketch maker (motion picture; radio-tv broad.) 141.061-030
SKETCH MAKER I (print. & pub.) 979.381-034
SKETCH MAKER II (print. & pub.) 972.381-018
SKETCH MAKER, PHOTOENGRAVING (print. & pub.) 970.281-026
SKI BASE TRIMMER (toy-sport equip.) 732.684-110
SKI-BINDING FITTER-AND-REPAIRER (toy-sport equip.) 732.364-014
Skidder Operator (forestry; logging) 929.663-010
Skid-Grapple Operator (logging) 929.663-010
skid-machine operator (machine shop) 605.382-014
SKIFF OPERATOR (fishing & hunt.) 441.683-010
ski-lift operator (amuse. & rec.) 341.665-010
SKI MAKER, WOOD (toy-sport equip.) 761.381-026
Skimmer (foundry) 519.687-022
SKIMMER, REVERBERATORY (smelt. & refin.) 511.687-022
Skimmer-Scoop Operator (any industry) 850.683-030
SKI MOLDER (toy-sport equip.) 732.684-114
skin bundler (meat products) 525.687-102
Skin Carver (furniture) 761.281-010
skin-drying-room attendant (hat & cap) 581.686-022
SKIN FORMER (rubber goods) 752.684-050
SKIN GRADER (meat products) 525.687-102
SKIN-LAP BONDER (aircraft mfg.) 806.684-130
SKIN LIFTER, BACON (meat products) 521.687-126
skinner (any industry) 919.664-010
SKINNER (meat products) 525.684-046
skinner (paper & pulp) 539.686-010
skinner, pelts (agriculture) 410.687-018
SKINNING-MACHINE FEEDER (meat products) 525.686-022
SKIN-PEELING-MACHINE OPERATOR (meat products) 525.685-030
skin specialist (medical ser.) 070.101-018
SKI PATROLLER (amuse. & rec.) 379.664-010
Skip-Hoist Operator (any industry) 921.663-030
SKIP OPERATOR (steel & rel.) 921.683-062
skipper (fishing & hunt.) 197.133-010
skipper (water trans.)   see MASTER
Skip Tender, Concrete Mixing Or Batch Plant (construction) 869.687-026
skip tender (mine & quarry) 939.667-010
SKIP TRACER (clerical) 241.367-026
SKI REPAIRER, PRODUCTION (toy-sport equip.) 732.684-118
skirt clipper (furniture) 780.687-070
SKIRT PANEL ASSEMBLER (furniture) 780.687-070
SKI TOPPER (toy-sport equip.) 692.685-170
SKI-TOP TRIMMER (plastic prod.) 690.685-370
SKI-TOW OPERATOR (amuse. & rec.) 341.665-010
SKIVER (leather prod.) 690.685-374
skiver (rubber goods; rubber reclaim.) 690.685-386
SKIVER, BLOCKERS (boot & shoe) 585.685-110
Skiver, Box-Toe (boot & shoe) 690.685-378
Skiver, Counter (boot & shoe) 690.685-378
Skiver, Flare (boot & shoe) 690.685-378
Skiver, Hand (leather prod.) 690.685-374
Skiver, Heel Tap (boot & shoe) 690.685-378
SKIVER, MACHINE (boot & shoe; rubber goods) 690.685-378
skiver-machine operator (hat & cap) 690.686-010
Skiver, Sock Linings (boot & shoe) 690.685-378
Skiver, Tuck (boot & shoe) 690.685-378
Skiver, Uppers Or Linings (boot & shoe) 690.685-378
Skiver, Welt-End (boot & shoe) 690.685-378
skiving-machine operator (boot & shoe; rubber goods) 690.685-378
SKIVING-MACHINE OPERATOR (ordnance) 664.682-018
Skoog-Machine Operator (millwork-plywood) 669.685-098
SKULL GRINDER (meat products) 521.687-130
Skycap (air trans.) 357.677-010
Sky-Line Yarder (logging) 921.663-066
SLABBER (soap & rel.) 559.686-042
Slabber, Light (soap & rel.) 559.686-042
slabbing-machine operator (soap & rel.) 559.686-042
SLAB-CONDITIONER SUPERVISOR (nonfer. metal) 609.132-010
SLAB-DEPILER OPERATOR (steel & rel.) 504.665-010
SLAB GRINDER (stonework) 673.682-030
Slab Inspector (rubber reclaim.) 759.684-074
slab lifting engineer (construction) 869.662-010
slab lifting supervisor (construction) 869.662-010
slab-miller operator (machine shop) 605.282-018
Slab-Off Mill Tender (rubber goods; rubber tire) 550.685-102
Slab Picker (saw. & plan.) 929.687-030
Slab Polisher (stonework) 673.682-030
slab worker (sugar & conf.) 520.684-014
Slack Cooper (wood. container) 764.684-022
slackline operator (construction) 850.683-042
Slack-Line Yarder (logging) 921.663-066

slag expander (steel & rel.) 519.665-010
Slag Scraper (welding) 819.666-010
Slag Worker (foundry) 519.687-022
slasher (boot & shoe) 690.685-470
SLASHER (plastic-synth.) 690.665-010
SLASHER OPERATOR (paper & pulp; saw. & plan.) 667.685-054
slasher sawyer (paper & pulp; saw. & plan.) 667.685-054
SLASHER TENDER (textile) 582.562-010
SLASHER-TENDER HELPER (textile) 582.686-026
SLAT-BASKET MAKER HELPER, MACHINE (wood. container) 669.686-026
SLAT-BASKET MAKER, MACHINE (wood. container) 669.685-074
Slat-Basket-Top Maker (wood. container) 669.685-014
Slate Cutter (stonework) 676.682-014
Slate-Cutter Operator (stonework) 677.462-010
SLATE MIXER (build. mat., nec) 570.685-094
Slate Roofer (construction) 866.381-010
Slate Splitter (stonework) 771.684-010
slate trimmer (stonework) 670.685-010
slat grader (meat products) 589.387-018
slat pickler (meat products) 582.685-126
SLAT TWISTER (furniture) 616.685-066
slaughter-and-butcher apprentice (meat products) 525.381-010
SLAUGHTERER, RELIGIOUS RITUAL (meat products) 525.361-010
Sleeping-Bag Filler (tex. prod., nec) 780.684-066
Sleeping Room Cleaner (hotel & rest.) 323.687-014
Sleeve Baster (garment) 782.684-058
Sleeve-Bottom Feller (garment) 782.684-058
sleeve machine operator (any industry) 652.682-010
Sleeve-Machine Tender (elec. equip.) 692.685-046
sleeve maker (nonmet. min.) 776.684-010
SLEEVE MAKER, LOCKSTITCH (garment) 786.682-226
Sleever (elec. equip.) 691.685-018
SLEEVER (paper goods) 641.686-034
Sleeve Separator (knitting) 789.687-030
SLEEVE SETTER, LOCKSTITCH (garment) 786.682-230
SLEEVE SETTER, OVERLOCK (garment) 786.682-234
Sleeve Setter, Safety-Stitch (garment) 786.682-234
Sleeve Tailor (garment; retail trade) 785.361-022
Sleeve Turner (garment; knitting) 789.687-074
sleeve wheel maker (nonmet. min.) 776.684-010
slice-cutting-machine operator (tobacco) 521.685-298
slice-cutting-machine-operator helper (tobacco) 521.686-054
SLICE-PLUG-CUTTER OPERATOR (tobacco) 521.685-298
SLICE-PLUG-CUTTER-OPERATOR HELPER (tobacco) 521.686-054
Slicer (construction) 869.687-026
slicer (textile) 686.685-066
Slicer-Machine Operator (can. & preserv.) 521.685-018
slicing-machine feeder (sugar & conf.) 521.685-102
SLICING-MACHINE OPERATOR (bakery products) 521.685-302
SLICING-MACHINE OPERATOR (button & notion) 692.685-174
SLICING-MACHINE OPERATOR (dairy products; meat products) 521.685-306
SLICING-MACHINE TENDER (furniture) 663.685-034
SLICING-MACHINE TENDER (wood prod., nec) 663.686-026
SLICKER (hat & cap) 784.684-062
SLIDE-FASTENER-CHAIN ASSEMBLER (button & notion) 734.687-074
SLIDE-FASTENER REPAIRER (button & notion) 734.684-022
slide-forming-machine operator (any industry) 619.382-018
slide-forming-machine tender (any industry) 619.685-050
SLIDE-MACHINE TENDER (fabrication, nec) 641.685-078
SLIDER ASSEMBLER (button & notion; garment) 734.687-078
slider attacher (button & notion; garment) 734.687-078
SLIDING-JOINT MAKER (musical inst.) 730.684-078
SLIME-PLANT-OPERATOR HELPER (smelt. & refin.) 511.685-058
SLIME-PLANT OPERATOR I (smelt. & refin.) 510.685-030
SLIME-PLANT OPERATOR II (smelt. & refin.) 511.685-054
Slimer (can. & preserv.; fishing & hunt.) 525.684-030
slinger (any industry) 921.260-010
SLINGER, SEQUINS (plastic prod.) 692.685-178
SLIPCOVER CUTTER (retail trade; tex. prod., nec) 780.381-034
Slip-Cover Estimator (retail trade) 299.364-010
SLIP-COVER SEWER (tex. prod., nec) 780.682-014
slip feeder (millwork-plywood; paper & pulp; saw. & plan.) 921.686-022
SLIP LASTER (boot & shoe) 788.684-106
slip mixer (brick & tile; pottery & porc.) 570.482-010
slip mixer (brick & tile; pottery & porc.) 570.482-010
slip mixer (cement) 570.685-010
SLIP-SEAT COVERER (furniture) 780.684-094
slipstitch-machine operator (garment) 786.682-190
slip tender (r.r. trans.) 919.682-010
slit-roll inspector (plastic-synth.) 554.587-010
SLITTER (knitting) 781.684-054
slitter (textile) 686.685-066
Slitter-And-Cutter Operator (paper & pulp; paper goods) 649.682-038
slitter-and-rewinder (any industry) 699.587-010

slitter-and-rewinder-machine operator (any industry) 699.682-030
SLITTER-CREASER-SLOTTER HELPER (paper goods) 649.686-030
SLITTER-CREASER-SLOTTER OPERATOR (paper goods) 649.682-034
slitter helper (any industry) 699.587-010
slitter operator (plastic-synth.) 690.382-010
Slitter, Processed Film (photofinishing) 976.684-026
SLITTER-SCORER-CUT-OFF OPERATOR (paper goods) 649.682-038
SLITTER SERVICE AND SETTER (tinware) 615.280-010
slitter sheeter operator (any industry) 699.682-018
slitting-machine coiler (nonfer. metal; steel & rel.) 613.685-010
slitting-machine feeder (tobacco) 529.685-090
slitting-machine operator (rubber goods; rubber reclaim.) 690.685-386
SLITTING-MACHINE-OPERATOR HELPER I (any industry) 699.587-010
Slitting-Machine-Operator Helper II (any industry) 619.687-014
SLITTING-MACHINE OPERATOR I (any industry) 699.682-030
SLITTING-MACHINE OPERATOR II (any industry) 615.662-010
sliver chopper (textile) 680.685-102
sliver former (glass mfg.) 575.685-030
sliver handler (glass mfg.) 575.685-030
SLIVER-LAP-MACHINE TENDER (textile) 680.685-094
Sliver-Machine Operator (can. & preserv.) 521.685-018
Slope-Hoist Operator (mine & quarry) 921.663-026
SLOT ROUTER (furniture) 763.684-066
SLOT-TAG INSERTER (clerical) 222.567-018
SLOTTER OPERATOR (paper goods) 640.685-078
SLOTTER-OPERATOR HELPER (paper goods) 640.686-014
slubber (textile) 680.685-098
Slubber Doffer (textile) 689.686-022
slubber-frame changer (textile) 689.686-026
slubber hand (textile) 680.685-098
SLUBBER TENDER (textile) 680.685-098
slub picker (carpet & rug; textile) 689.684-010
Sludge-Control Attendant (sanitary ser.) 955.585-010
Sludge-Control Operator (sanitary ser.) 955.362-010
sludge-filter operator (any industry) 551.685-078
Sludge-Filtration Attendant (sanitary ser.) 955.585-010
Sludge-Filtration Operator (sanitary ser.) 955.362-010
slug-furnace operator (forging) 619.682-022
slugger (tex. prod., nec) 782.684-026
SLUG-PRESS OPERATOR (elec. equip.) 556.685-074
sluice tender (mine & quarry) 939.684-014
slumber-room attendant (personal ser.) 335.677-010
SLUNK-SKIN CURER (meat products) 525.687-106
Slunk Skinner (meat products) 525.684-046
slurry blender (cement) 570.685-010
SLURRY-CONTROL TENDER (smelt. & refin.) 510.465-014
SLURRY MIXER (ordnance) 539.362-018
slurry-plant operator (smelt. & refin.) 570.685-090
slurry-tank tender (cement) 570.685-010
slush caster (jewelry-silver.) 502.381-010
slusher (any industry) 741.684-030
slusher (plastic prod.) 777.684-010
slusher operator (mine & quarry) 921.663-050
slusher operator (paper & pulp; wood prod., nec) 530.685-014
small-appliance repairer (any industry) 723.381-010
SMALL-ENGINE MECHANIC (any industry) 625.281-034
small kick-press operator (pen & pencil) 733.687-014
Small-Parts-Shaper Operator (woodworking) 665.682-034
small-piece cutter (garment) 781.684-062
small press operator (pen & pencil) 733.687-014
Small-Stock Facer (meat products) 525.684-046
SMASH HAND (narrow fabrics; textile) 683.684-026
smearer (hat & cap) 589.687-038
smearer (leather prod.) 589.687-034
smeller (can. & preserv.) 529.687-118
SMELTERY WORKER (smelt. & refin.) term
smocker (fabrication, nec) 780.684-042
Smocking-Machine Operator (garment) 786.682-178
SMOKE AND FLAME SPECIALIST (military ser.) 378.682-014
SMOKED MEAT PREPARER (meat products) 525.587-014
smoke eater (forestry) 452.687-014
smokehouse attendant (meat products) 525.682-010
SMOKE JUMPER (forestry) 452.364-014
SMOKE JUMPER SUPERVISOR (forestry) 452.134-010
SMOKER (meat products) 525.682-010
SMOKE-ROOM OPERATOR (hat & cap) 784.687-066
SMOKE TESTER (smelt. & refin.) 012.281-010
SMOKING-PIPE DRILLER AND THREADER (fabrication, nec) 669.685-078
SMOKING-PIPE LINER (fabrication, nec) 739.687-170
SMOKING-PIPE MAKER (fabrication, nec) 761.381-030
SMOKING-PIPE REPAIRER (any industry) 739.484-018
SMOKING-TOBACCO-CUTTER OPERATOR (tobacco) 521.685-310
Smoking-Tobacco Packer, Hand (tobacco) 920.687-130
Smoking-Tobacco-Packing-Machine Hand (tobacco) 920.685-098
Smooth And Burr Worker, Composites (aircraft mfg.) 754.684-042

Smoother (glass products) 775.684-010
SMOOTHER (hat & cap) 784.684-066
SMOOTHER (pen & pencil) 733.685-026
smoothing-machine operator (boot & shoe) 690.685-350
smooth plater (leather mfg.; leather prod.) 690.682-030
smutter (grain-feed mills) 521.685-254
snagger (foundry) 705.684-074
SNAG GRINDER (foundry) 705.684-074
SNAILER (clock & watch) 603.685-078
Snake Charmer (amuse. & rec.) 159.647-010
Snaker (logging) 919.664-010
Snap Attacher (any industry) 699.685-018
Snap-Fastener-Machine Operator (any industry) 699.685-018
snapper-on (tinware) 703.685-010
Snath-Handle Assembler (woodworking) 762.687-042
Sneller, Hand (toy-sport equip.) 732.687-038
snipper (boot & shoe) 690.685-298
snipper (leather mfg.) 585.684-010
Snout Puller (meat products) 525.684-034
SNOWMAKER (amuse. & rec.) 969.685-010
Snow-Plow Operator, Truck (government ser.) 899.684-014
Snow-Plow Tractor Operator (government ser.) 899.684-014
Snow Ranger (government ser.) 169.167-042
snow remover (government ser.) 955.687-014
SNOW-REMOVING SUPERVISOR (government ser.) 955.137-010
SNOW SHOVELER (government ser.) 955.687-014
SNUFF-BOX FINISHER (tobacco) 920.687-174
SNUFF-CONTAINER INSPECTOR (tobacco) 920.667-014
Snuff Drier (tobacco) 523.685-118
SNUFF GRINDER AND SCREENER (tobacco) 521.685-314
SNUFF-PACKING-MACHINE OPERATOR (tobacco) 920.685-094
Soaker (textile) 587.685-018
SOAKER, HIDES (meat products) 582.685-134
Soaker, Meat (meat products) 525.587-014
soaker-soda worker (beverage) 529.685-226
soaking-pit operator (nonfer. metal) 613.462-014
soaking-room operator (plastic-synth.) 551.687-034
soap boiler (soap & rel.) 559.382-054
SOAP CHIPPER (soap & rel.) 555.686-014
SOAP-DRIER OPERATOR (soap & rel.) 553.685-098
soaper (rubber goods) 599.687-010
SOAP GRINDER (soap & rel.) 555.685-062
SOAPING-DEPARTMENT SUPERVISOR (textile) 582.132-014
Soaping-Machine Back-Tender (textile) 589.686-010
SOAP INSPECTOR (soap & rel.) 559.687-058
SOAP MAKER (soap & rel.) 559.382-054
Soap Mixer (textile) 550.585-018
soap-press feeder (soap & rel.) 559.685-142
soap slabber (soap & rel.) 559.685-142
soap slabber (soap & rel.) 559.686-042
Soap Worker (nonfer. metal) 519.686-010
Soccer Ball Assembler (toy-sport equip.) 732.684-026
Social Ecologist (profess. & kin.) 054.067-014
SOCIAL GROUP WORKER (social ser.) 195.107-022
Social Problems Specialist (profess. & kin.) 054.067-014
SOCIAL SECRETARY (clerical) 201.162-010
SOCIAL-SERVICES AIDE (social ser.) 195.367-034
social service worker (social ser.) 195.107-010
SOCIAL-WORK CONSULTANT (profess. & kin.) term
Social-Work Consultant, Casework (social ser.) 195.107-010
SOCIAL WORKER (profess. & kin.) term
social worker, clinical (profess. & kin.) 195.107-034
social worker, clinical (profess. & kin.) 195.107-030
SOCIAL WORKER, DELINQUENCY PREVENTION (social ser.) 195.107-026
social worker, health services (profess. & kin.) 195.107-030
SOCIAL WORKER, MEDICAL (profess. & kin.) 195.107-030
social worker, mental (profess. & kin.) 195.107-034
SOCIAL WORKER, PSYCHIATRIC (profess. & kin.) 195.107-034
SOCIAL WORKER, SCHOOL (profess. & kin.) 195.107-038
social work unit supervisor (social ser.) 195.137-010
SOCIOLOGIST (profess. & kin.) 054.067-014
sock-and-stocking ironer (laundry & rel.) 363.687-014
SOCK BOARDER (knitting) 589.686-042
sock drier (laundry & rel.) 363.687-014
Socket Assembler (electron. comp.) 726.684-070
SOCKET PULLER (musical inst.) 730.682-010
Sock Examiner (knitting) 684.684-010
sock folder (laundry & rel.) 363.687-014
Sock Knitter (knitting) 684.685-010
sock-knitting-machine operator (knitting) 684.685-010
Sock Liner (boot & shoe) 788.687-030
Sock-Lining And Heel-Pad Embosser (boot & shoe) 690.685-158
Sock-Lining Examiner (boot & shoe) 788.384-010
Sock-Lining Stitcher (boot & shoe) 690.682-082
soda clerk (hotel & rest.) 319.474-010

SODA-COLUMN OPERATOR (chemical) 558.382-054
SODA DIALYZER (plastic-synth.) 551.685-134
soda dispenser (hotel & rest.) 319.474-010
Soda-Drier Feeder (chemical) 553.686-038
Soda-Dry-House Operator (chemical) 559.685-046
Soda Flaker (chemical) 559.685-074
soda jerker (hotel & rest.) 319.474-010
SODA-ROOM OPERATOR (beverage) 559.682-046
SODA-ROOM OPERATOR (plastic-synth.) 551.687-034
soda worker (beverage) 529.685-226
Sodium-Chlorite Operator (chemical) 559.382-018
Sodium-Methylate Operator (chemical) 558.685-062
Sofa-Cover Inspector (furniture) 789.687-038
Sofa Inspector (furniture) 763.687-026
SOFTBALL CORE MOLDER (toy-sport equip.) 732.687-070
Softball Winder (toy-sport equip.) 692.685-246
SOFT CRAB SHEDDER (fishing & hunt.) 446.684-018
Soft-Drink-Powder Mixer (beverage) 520.685-146
softener (hat & cap) 589.685-034
softener (leather mfg.; tex. prod., nec) 582.685-050
Soft-Hat Binder (hat & cap) 787.682-010
soft-iron inspector (foundry) 514.687-010
Soft-Mud Molder (brick & tile) 575.684-042
Soft-Sugar Boiler (sugar & conf.) 522.382-034
Soft-Sugar Cutter (sugar & conf.) 521.682-010
SOFT-SUGAR OPERATOR, HEAD (sugar & conf.) 521.565-018
SOFT-TILE SETTER (construction; retail trade) 861.381-034
soft tooling technician (electron. comp.) 609.262-010
SOFTWARE ENGINEER (profess. & kin.) 030.062-010
soft-work-cigar-machine operator (tobacco) 529.685-270
SOIL CONSERVATIONIST (profess. & kin.) 040.061-054
SOIL-CONSERVATION TECHNICIAN (profess. & kin.) 040.261-010
soiled linen distributor (laundry & rel.) 361.687-014
Soil Fertility Expert (profess. & kin.) 040.061-058
Soils Analyst (profess. & kin.) 029.081-010
SOIL SCIENTIST (profess. & kin.) 040.061-058
SOLAR-ENERGY-SYSTEM INSTALLER (any industry) 637.261-030
SOLAR-ENERGY-SYSTEM-INSTALLER HELPER (any industry) 637.687-018
SOLAR-ENERGY-SYSTEMS DESIGNER (profess. & kin.) 007.161-038
SOLAR-FABRICATION TECHNICIAN (machine shop) 809.381-034
Solder Cream Maker (nonfer. metal) 519.667-014
SOLDER DEPOSIT OPERATOR (electron. comp.) 726.684-094
SOLDERER (clock & watch) 715.685-058
SOLDERER (jewelry-silver.) 700.381-050
SOLDERER-ASSEMBLER (welding) 813.684-014
Solderer, Assembly Repair (welding) 813.684-014
SOLDERER, BARREL RIBS (ordnance) 736.684-038
SOLDERER-DIPPER (welding) 813.684-018
solderer, electronic (welding) 813.382-010
solderer, furnace (welding) 813.482-010
Solderer, Induction (welding) 813.382-010
SOLDERER, PRODUCTION LINE (welding) 813.684-022
SOLDERER, SILVER (welding) term
SOLDERER, TORCH I (welding) 813.684-026
Solderer, Torch II (welding) 813.684-010
SOLDERER, ULTRASONIC, HAND (welding) 813.684-030
Soldering-Machine Feeder (welding) 819.686-010
Soldering-Machine Operator (welding) 813.382-014
soldering-machine operator, automatic (welding) 813.382-014
Soldering-Machine-Operator Helper (welding) 819.666-010
SOLDER-LEVELER, PRINTED CIRCUIT BOARDS (electron. comp.) 726.685-050
Solder Sprayer (any industry) 505.684-014
sole beater (boot & shoe) 690.685-470
sole blacker (boot & shoe) 690.685-234
Sole Buffer (boot & shoe) 690.685-046
SOLE-CONFORMING-MACHINE OPERATOR (boot & shoe) 690.682-070
sole cutter (boot & shoe) 788.685-018
Sole-Cutting-Machine Operator (boot & shoe) 699.682-022
sole dyer (boot & shoe) 690.685-234
Sole-Edge Inker, Machine (boot & shoe) 690.685-234
Sole Layer (boot & shoe) 690.685-074
Sole Layer, Hand (boot & shoe) 788.687-030
Sole-Leather-Cutting-Machine Operator (boot & shoe) 699.682-022
SOLE LEVELER, MACHINE (boot & shoe) 690.685-382
sole-leveling-machine operator (boot & shoe) 690.685-382
sole-molding-machine operator (boot & shoe) 690.682-070
sole pretrimmer (boot & shoe) 690.685-150
Sole Rougher (boot & shoe) 690.685-046
sole rounder (boot & shoe) 690.685-338
sole rounder (boot & shoe) 690.685-334
sole-rounding-machine operator (boot & shoe) 690.685-338
SOLE SCRAPER (boot & shoe) 788.687-134
SOLE SEWER, HAND (boot & shoe) 788.684-110

Sole Splitter (boot & shoe) 585.685-114
sole stainer (boot & shoe) 788.687-098
Sole Stapler, Welt (boot & shoe) 690.685-162
Sole Stitcher (boot & shoe) 690.682-078
sole stitcher, hand (boot & shoe) 788.684-110
Sole-Stock Cutter (leather prod.) 585.685-038
Sole Trimmer (boot & shoe) 690.682-086
Sole Wetter (boot & shoe) 788.687-090
solicitor (retail trade) 291.357-010
solicitor, city or state (government ser.) 110.117-010
solicitor, patent (profess. & kin.) 110.117-026
solid center winder (toy-sport equip.) 692.685-246
Solid-Die Cutter (paper goods) 699.682-022
solid-fiber-paster operator (paper & pulp; paper goods) 534.682-026
solid-glass-rod-dowel-machine operator (plastic prod.) 575.682-010
Solid State Tester (electron. comp.) 726.684-026
Solid-Tire Finisher (rubber tire) 750.684-034
Solid-Tire Tuber-Machine Operator (rubber tire) 690.662-014
solid waste facility operator (sanitary ser.) 955.463-010
solid waste facility supervisor (sanitary ser.) 955.133-010
solution-make-up operator (chemical) 559.382-034
solution mixer (photofinishing) 550.485-010
Solution Mixer (plastic-synth.) 550.685-134
SOLUTIONS OPERATOR (plastic-synth.) 550.382-034
solvent-plant operator (chemical) 551.685-062
Solvent-Plant Treater (petrol. refin.) 549.362-014
Solvent Recoverer (plastic-synth.) 552.685-026
solvent-station attendant (rubber reclaim.) 914.665-010
sommelier (hotel & rest.) 310.357-010
SONG PLUGGER (recording) 165.157-010
song writer (profess. & kin.) 131.067-034
SORTER (boot & shoe) 753.587-010
SORTER (brick & tile) 573.687-034
SORTER (button & notion) 734.687-082
Sorter (can. & preserv.) 529.686-014
SORTER (clerical) 209.687-022
SORTER (jewelry-silver.) 735.687-030
Sorter (machine shop) 609.684-014
sorter (mine & quarry; smelt. & refin.) 933.687-010
SORTER (office machines) 706.587-014
sorter (paper & pulp) 649.687-010
Sorter (plastic-synth.) 681.687-018
Sorter (tex. prod., nec) 789.687-146
SORTER, AGRICULTURAL PRODUCE (agriculture; can. & preserv.; wholesale tr.) 529.687-186
sorter, food products (agriculture; can. & preserv.; wholesale tr.) 529.687-186
Sorter-Grader (can. & preserv.) 529.687-186
SORTER I (wood prod., nec) 569.687-022
SORTER II (wood prod., nec) 769.687-042
sorter, laundry articles (laundry & rel.) 361.687-014
Sorter-Lumber Straightener (saw. & plan.) 669.687-018
SORTER, MACHINE (button & notion) 692.685-182
SORTER OPERATOR (saw. & plan.) 921.685-054
sorter-packer (photofinishing) 976.687-018
SORTER-PRICER (nonprofit org.) 222.387-054
SORTER, UPHOLSTERY PARTS (furniture) 780.587-010
Sorting-And-Folding Supervisor (laundry & rel.) 361.137-010
SORTING-GRAPPLE OPERATOR (logging) 921.683-066
sorting-machine attendant (can. & preserv.) 521.685-318
SORTING-MACHINE OPERATOR (can. & preserv.) 521.685-318
SORTING-MACHINE OPERATOR (paper goods) 649.665-010
SORTING SUPERVISOR (brick & tile) 920.137-014
SOUND CONTROLLER (amuse. & rec.) 194.262-014
SOUND CUTTER (motion picture) 962.382-014
sound-effects supervisor (radio-tv broad.) 962.167-010
SOUND-EFFECTS TECHNICIAN (radio-tv broad.) 962.281-014
sound engineer, audio control (radio-tv broad.) 194.262-010
SOUNDER (any industry) 911.667-018
sound installation worker (motion picture) 194.381-010
SOUND MIXER (motion picture; radio-tv broad.; recording) 194.262-018
SOUND RANGING CREWMEMBER (military ser.) 378.362-010
sound recording technician (radio-tv broad.; recording) 194.362-010
SOUND TECHNICIAN (any industry) 829.281-022
Sound-Truck Operator (any industry) 823.261-010
Sour-Bleaching Pleater (textile) 589.685-074
SOUS CHEF (hotel & rest.) 313.131-026
SOUS CHEF (water trans.) 315.137-014
SOUVENIR AND NOVELTY MAKER (metal prod., nec) 739.381-050
souvenir assembler (metal prod., nec) 739.381-050
Soybean Grower (agriculture) 401.161-010
Soyfreeze Operator (food prep., nec) 529.685-290
SPACE-AND-STORAGE CLERK (ordnance) 219.387-026
space clerk (print. & pub.) 247.387-018
Spacer, Type-Bar-And-Segment (office machines) 706.684-026
SPACE SCHEDULER (clerical) 238.367-022

Space Vehicle Inspector, Preflight (aircraft mfg.) 806.261-038
SPAGHETTI-MACHINE OPERATOR (plastic prod.) 690.682-074
spaghetti press helper (food prep., nec) 529.686-062
Spanisher (leather prod.) 781.381-018
SPANNER (tex. prod., nec) 689.687-074
spare hand, carding (textile) 689.685-166
spare-parts clerk (clerical) 222.367-042
Spareribs Trimmer (meat products) 525.684-054
Spares Rework Mechanic (aircraft mfg.) 621.281-014
Spares Scheduler (clerical) 221.167-018
sparker and patcher (elec. equip.; nonfer. metal) 728.684-018
SPARK-PLUG ASSEMBLER (elec. equip.) 729.684-046
SPARK TESTER (elec. equip.) 727.687-078
SPARK TESTER (elec. equip.; nonfer. metal) 728.684-018
SPAR-MACHINE OPERATOR (wood prod., nec) 664.682-022
SPAR-MACHINE-OPERATOR HELPER (wood prod., nec) 664.685-030
Speaking-Unit Assembler (comm. equip.; elec. equip.) 729.684-026
spearer (fishing & hunt.) 443.684-010
Special Ability Extra (amuse. & rec.; motion picture; radio-tv broad.) 159.647-014
SPECIAL AGENT (government ser.) 375.167-042
SPECIAL AGENT (insurance) 166.167-046
SPECIAL AGENT (r.r. trans.) 372.267-010
SPECIAL AGENT, CUSTOMS (government ser.) 188.167-090
Special Agent, FBI (government ser.) 375.167-042
SPECIAL AGENT, GROUP INSURANCE (insurance) 169.167-050
SPECIAL AGENT-IN-CHARGE (r.r. trans.) 376.167-010
Special Agent, IRS (government ser.) 375.167-042
Special Agent, Secret Service (government ser.) 375.167-042
SPECIAL-CERTIFICATE DICTATOR (insurance) 209.382-014
Special-Delivery Carrier (government ser.) 230.367-010
SPECIAL-DELIVERY DRIVER (any industry) term
Special-Distribution Clerk (government ser.) 209.687-014
SPECIAL EFFECTS SPECIALIST (amuse. & rec.; motion picture; radio-tv broad.) 962.281-018
special-gas-and-electric service investigator (utilities) 959.361-010
special inspecting-and-testing supervisor (utilities) 820.131-010
Specialist (financial) 162.167-034
SPECIALIST-IN-CHARGE, EXTENSION SERVICE (government ser.) 096.167-014
Special-Lining Applier (any industry) 741.687-018
special loan officer (financial) 186.167-078
special-machine operator (nonfer. metal) 509.382-014
special officer (hotel & rest.) 376.367-018
Special Officer, Automat (hotel & rest.) 376.667-014
special police officer (any industry) 372.667-034
SPECIAL PROCEDURES TECHNOLOGIST, ANGIOGRAM (medical ser.) 078.362-046
SPECIAL PROCEDURES TECHNOLOGIST, CARDIAC CATHETERIZA-TION (medical ser.) 078.362-050
SPECIAL PROCEDURES TECHNOLOGIST, CT SCAN (medical ser.) 078.362-054
SPECIAL PROCEDURES TECHNOLOGIST, MAGNETIC RESONANCE IM-AGING (MRI) (medical ser.) 078.362-058
special-service representative (tel. & tel.) 253.157-010
special shopper (retail trade) 296.357-010
SPECIAL TESTER (tobacco) 529.487-010
SPECIALTIES OPERATOR (chemical) 559.582-014
Special-Trackwork Blacksmith (r.r. trans.) 610.381-010
SPECIALTY CHEF (hotel & rest.) term
Specialty Molder (plastic prod.) 556.665-018
Specialty-Transformer Assembler (elec. equip.) 820.381-014
specialty trimmer (hat & cap) 784.684-078
special vascular imaging technologist (medical ser.) 078.362-050
SPECIFICATION WRITER (profess. & kin.) 019.267-010
Specimen Boss (mine & quarry) 939.137-018
spectrographer (profess. & kin.) 011.281-014
spectrographic analyst (profess. & kin.) 011.281-014
SPECTROSCOPIST (profess. & kin.) 011.281-014
speech clinician (profess. & kin.) 076.107-010
SPEECH PATHOLOGIST (profess. & kin.) 076.107-010
speech therapist (profess. & kin.) 076.107-010
SPEED-BELT-SANDER TENDER (woodworking) 662.685-034
Speedboat Operator (amuse. & rec.) 342.663-010
speeder-frame changer (textile) 689.686-026
SPEEDER TENDER (textile) 681.685-106
SPEED OPERATOR (steel & rel.) 613.362-022
spent-grain dryer (beverage) 523.685-086
spice blender (food prep., nec) 520.585-026
SPICE CLEANER (food prep., nec) 521.685-322
SPICE FUMIGATOR (food prep., nec) 529.685-218
spice grinder (food prep., nec) 521.685-326
spice-grinding-mill operator (food prep., nec) 521.685-326
SPICE MILLER (food prep., nec) 521.685-326
Spice Miller, Hammer Mill (food prep., nec) 521.685-326

Spice Miller, Rolling Mill (food prep., nec) 521.685-326
SPICE MIXER (can. & preserv.) 520.687-062
SPICE MIXER (food prep., nec) 520.585-026
spice mixer (meat products) 520.687-054
SPIDER ASSEMBLER (elec. equip.) 721.684-026
spieler (amuse. & rec.; personal ser.) 353.363-010
spieler (amuse. & rec.) 342.657-010
SPIKE-MACHINE FEEDER (steel & rel.) 612.666-010
SPIKE-MACHINE HEATER (steel & rel.) 619.686-026
SPIKE-MACHINE OPERATOR (steel & rel.) 612.662-010
SPIKEMAKING SUPERVISOR (steel & rel.) 612.130-010
SPINDLE CARVER (woodworking) 761.682-018
SPINDLE PLUMBER (textile) 628.684-030
spindler (button & notion) 740.687-010
SPINDLE REPAIRER (textile) 628.684-042
Spindle Sander (woodworking) 761.682-014
spindle setter (textile) 628.684-030
spindle tester (textile) 628.684-030
SPINNER (jewelry-silver.) 700.684-074
spinner (nonmet. min.; textile) 682.685-010
SPINNER (plastic-synth.) 557.685-026
SPINNER (sugar & conf.) 520.682-030
Spinner, Box (plastic-synth.) 557.685-026
Spinner, Cap Frame (textile) 682.685-010
spinner, concrete pipe (concrete prod.) 575.664-010
Spinner, Continuous (plastic-synth.) 557.685-026
spinnerette cleaner (plastic-synth.) 557.684-010
SPINNER, FRAME (nonmet. min.; textile) 682.685-010
SPINNER, HAND (any industry) 619.362-018
Spinner Helper (sugar & conf.) 529.686-034
SPINNER, HYDRAULIC (any industry) 619.362-022
spinner, iron (elec. equip.) 729.687-018
SPINNER, MULE (nonmet. min.; textile) 682.685-014
Spinner, Open-End (textile) 682.685-010
Spinner, Ring Frame (textile) 682.685-010
SPINNING-BATH PATROLLER (plastic-synth.) 557.685-030
Spinning Doffer (textile) 689.686-022
spinning-frame changer (textile) 689.686-026
Spinning-Frame Fixer (textile) 689.260-010
spinning-frame tender (nonmet. min.; textile) 682.685-010
spinning-lathe operator (any industry) 619.362-018
SPINNING-LATHE OPERATOR, AUTOMATIC (any industry) 619.685-082
spinning-lathe-operator, hydraulic (any industry) 619.362-022
SPINNING-MACHINE TENDER (tex. prod., nec) 681.685-110
spinning operator (plastic-synth.) 557.685-026
SPINNING-ROOM WORKER (plastic-synth.) term
SPIN-TABLE OPERATOR (toy-sport equip.) 732.687-074
spin-tank tender (plastic-synth.) 559.585-018
SPIRAL BINDER (paper goods; print. & pub.) 653.685-030
spiral-bind operator (paper goods; print. & pub.) 653.685-030
spiral-gear generator (machine shop) 602.382-014
SPIRAL-MACHINE OPERATOR (paper goods) 692.685-186
SPIRAL RUNNER (mine & quarry) 934.685-022
SPIRAL SPRING WINDER (metal prod., nec) 616.685-070
SPIRAL-TUBE WINDER (paper goods) 640.682-022
SPIRAL-TUBE-WINDER HELPER (paper goods) 640.687-014
SPIRAL WEAVER (metal prod., nec) 616.685-074
spiral winder (fabrication, nec) 739.685-030
spiral-winding-machine helper (paper goods) 640.687-014
SPLASH-LINE OPERATOR (fabrication, nec) 559.665-034
splicer (construction; tel. & tel.; utilities) 829.361-010
SPLICER (fabrication, nec) 692.687-010
splicer (narrow fabrics; textile) 782.684-062
SPLICER (photofinishing) 976.684-026
SPLICER (protective dev.) 759.684-070
splicer (rubber goods) 752.684-042
SPLICER (rubber tire) 759.684-058
splicer (tex. prod., nec) 689.682-018
splicer apprentice (construction; tel. & tel.; utilities) 829.361-014
splicer-machine operator (woodworking) 669.685-042
splicer matcher (millwork-plywood) 769.687-046
SPLICER OPERATOR (millwork-plywood) 569.685-062
SPLICING-MACHINE OPERATOR (tex. prod., nec) 689.682-018
SPLICING-MACHINE OPERATOR, AUTOMATIC (tex. prod., nec) 689.685-122
Splicing Supervisor (metal prod., nec) 691.130-014
Spliner (struct. metal) 809.684-010
split-leather mosser (leather mfg.) 584.687-010
splitter (boot & shoe; leather prod.) 585.685-114
splitter (concrete prod.) 677.685-050
splitter (jewelry-silver.) 770.381-014
splitter (mine & quarry) 779.681-010
splitter (woodworking) 667.682-058
SPLITTER, HAND (button & notion) 734.687-086
Splitter, Head (meat products) 525.684-034

SPLITTER, MACHINE (boot & shoe; leather prod.) 585.685-114
splitter operator (any industry) 699.682-030
SPLITTER OPERATOR (stonework) 677.685-042
SPLITTER TENDER (saw. & plan.) 663.685-038
SPLITTING-MACHINE FEEDER (leather mfg.) 690.686-054
SPLITTING-MACHINE OPERATOR (rubber goods; rubber reclaim.) 690.685-386
SPLITTING-MACHINE OPERATOR (stonework) 677.685-046
SPLITTING-MACHINE-OPERATOR HELPER (stonework) 677.666-010
SPLITTING-MACHINE TENDER (wood prod., nec) 663.685-042
SPOILAGE WORKER (tinware) 709.587-014
Spoke Maker (toy-sport equip.) 617.665-010
SPONGE BUFFER (plastic prod.) 690.685-390
SPONGE CLIPPER (fishing & hunt.; wholesale tr.) 447.687-026
Sponge Diver (fishing & hunt.) 443.664-010
SPONGE HOOKER (fishing & hunt.) 447.684-010
Sponge Packer (wholesale tr.) 920.587-018
SPONGE-PRESS OPERATOR (rubber goods) 559.682-050
Sponger (leather mfg.) 589.685-098
sponger (pottery & porc.) 774.684-018
sponger (textile) 587.685-018
SPONSOR (retail trade) term
spool cleaner, hand (textile) 689.687-014
spooler (narrow fabrics; textile) 681.685-142
Spooler (narrow fabrics; tex. prod., nec) 689.685-014
spooler (pen & pencil) 733.685-022
spooler (tex. prod., nec; textile) 681.685-154
spooler (tex. prod., nec) 681.685-114
spooler (textile) 681.685-098
Spooler And Coiler (nonfer. metal) 691.685-030
SPOOLER OPERATOR, AUTOMATIC (textile) 681.686-018
spooler, rubber strand (rubber goods) 559.685-114
SPOOLER, SEQUINS (plastic prod.) 920.686-046
SPOOLING-MACHINE OPERATOR (metal prod., nec; nonfer. metal) 691.685-026
SPOOLING-MACHINE OPERATOR (tex. prod., nec) 681.685-114
Spooling Supervisor (metal prod., nec) 691.130-014
SPOOL MAKER (paper goods) 641.685-082
spool salvager (glass mfg.; plastic-synth.; textile) 922.687-018
Spool Sander (woodworking) 761.682-014
SPOOL WINDER (nonfer. metal) 619.485-010
spool winder (textile) 681.685-122
Spool Winder (textile) 681.685-154
Sports Announcer (radio-tv broad.) 159.147-010
Sports-Bookmaker (amuse. & rec.) 187.167-014
Sports Cartoonist (print. & pub.) 141.061-010
SPORTS-EQUIPMENT REPAIRER (any industry) 732.684-122
SPORT-SHOE-SPIKE ASSEMBLER (boot & shoe) 690.685-394
SPOT CLEANER (garment; knitting) 582.684-014
Spot Cutter (any industry) 699.682-018
spot-machine operator (any industry) 692.685-062
spot picker (fabrication, nec) 739.667-010
SPOT PICKER, MOLDED GOODS (fabrication, nec) 739.667-010
spot sprayer (any industry) 749.684-038
Spotter (any industry) 215.362-022
spotter (automotive ser.) 915.473-010
spotter (business ser.) 376.267-022
spotter (fabrication, nec) 739.687-182
SPOTTER (glass mfg.) 772.687-014
SPOTTER I (laundry & rel.) 361.684-018
SPOTTER II (laundry & rel.) 362.381-010
SPOTTER (machine tools) 770.381-042
SPOTTER, PHOTOGRAPHIC (photofinishing) 970.381-034
spot washer (tex. prod., nec; textile) 689.687-050
Spot Welder (welding) 819.685-010
spot welder, body assembly (welding) 810.664-010
spot welder, line (welding) 810.664-010
Spout Positioner (any industry) 921.667-018
SPOUT TENDER I (chemical) 932.664-014
SPOUT TENDER I (chemical) 921.685-058
SPOUT WORKER (smelt. & refin.) 514.667-018
spragger (mine & quarry) 932.683-010
Spray Blender (any industry) 550.684-018
Spray Cementer (leather prod.) 741.687-018
spray drier (chemical) 553.685-054
SPRAY-DRIER OPERATOR (brick & tile) 573.382-014
Spray-Drier-Operator Helper (chemical) 553.687-010
spray dyer (laundry & rel.) 364.684-018
sprayer (any industry) 505.685-014
sprayer (boot & shoe) 590.685-038
Sprayer (boot & shoe) 741.687-018
Sprayer (foundry) 514.685-014
sprayer, automatic spray machine (brick & tile; pottery & porc.) 574.682-014
Sprayer, Auto Parts (auto. mfg.) 741.684-026
SPRAYER, HAND (agriculture) 408.684-014

SPRAYER, HAND (leather mfg.) 584.687-014
sprayer helper (any industry) 741.687-014
sprayer, insecticide (government ser.) 379.687-014
SPRAYER, LEATHER (laundry & rel.) 364.684-018
Sprayer, Light Bulbs (elec. equip.; light. fix.) 599.686-014
SPRAYER, MACHINE (leather mfg.) 599.685-094
SPRAYER OPERATOR (smelt. & refin.) 505.682-010
Sprayer, Railroad Car (r.r. trans.) 741.684-026
spray-gun operator (any industry) 741.684-026
SPRAY-GUN REPAIRER (any industry) 630.381-026
SPRAY-GUN-REPAIRER HELPER (any industry) 630.684-034
spray-gun sizer (hat & cap) 589.687-038
SPRAY-MACHINE LOADER (brick & tile; pottery & porc.) 574.686-010
SPRAY-MACHINE OPERATOR (brick & tile; pottery & porc.) 574.682-014
spray-machine operator (any industry) 599.382-010
spray-machine operator (any industry) 599.685-074
spray-machine operator (leather mfg.) 599.685-094
SPRAY-MACHINE OPERATOR (textile) 582.685-138
SPRAY-MACHINE TENDER (tinware) 599.685-090
Spray-Painter, Machine (wood prod., nec) 599.685-074
SPRAY-PAINTING-MACHINE OPERATOR (any industry) 741.685-010
Spray Stainer (leather prod.) 749.684-022
Spray Supervisor (agriculture) 408.131-010
SPRAY-UNIT FEEDER (any industry) 599.686-014
SPREADER (hat & cap) 581.687-022
SPREADER (plastic-synth.) 554.687-010
spreader box operator (construction) 853.663-022
SPREADER I (any industry) 781.687-058
SPREADER II (any industry) term
SPREADER, MACHINE (any industry) 781.685-010
spreader machine tender (rubber goods; rubber tire) 554.362-010
Spreader Operator (construction) 853.663-014
SPREADER OPERATOR, AUTOMATIC (tobacco) 529.685-222
spreading-machine operator (bakery products) 524.682-010
SPREADING-MACHINE OPERATOR (chemical) 559.685-170
spreading-machine operator (textile) 680.685-090
sprigger (tobacco) 521.687-134
SPRING ASSEMBLER (furniture) 780.684-098
SPRING ASSEMBLER (metal prod., nec) 706.684-090
Spring-Assembler Supervisor (furniture) 616.130-022
spring bender (metal prod., nec) 617.482-022
Spring Bender (protective dev.) 712.684-010
SPRING CLIPPER (furniture) 780.684-102
SPRING COILER (metal prod., nec) 616.485-014
Spring Coiler, Hand (metal prod., nec) 619.482-010
SPRING COILING MACHINE SETTER (metal prod., nec) 616.260-018
SPRING COVERER (furniture) 780.687-038
Spring Crater (furniture) 920.685-078
spring encaser (furniture) 780.687-030
SPRINGER (furniture) 780.684-106
SPRING FITTER (metal prod., nec) 709.684-078
spring-fitter helper (automotive ser.) 620.584-010
SPRING FORMER, HAND (metal prod., nec) 709.381-042
SPRING FORMER, MACHINE (metal prod., nec) 617.482-022
SPRING INSPECTOR I (metal prod., nec) 616.361-010
SPRING INSPECTOR II (metal prod., nec) 709.687-038
SPRING LAYER (clock & watch) 715.687-122
SPRING MAKER (metal prod., nec) 616.280-010
spring-maker helper, hand (automotive ser.) 620.584-010
SPRING-MANUFACTURING SET-UP TECHNICIAN (clock & watch) 619.280-018
SPRING REPAIRER, HAND (automotive ser.) 619.380-018
SPRING-REPAIRER HELPER, HAND (automotive ser.) 620.584-010
SPRING SALVAGE WORKER (metal prod., nec) 610.684-014
spring setter (furniture) 780.684-106
spring tacker (furniture) 780.684-106
SPRING TESTER I (metal prod., nec) 612.685-014
SPRING TESTER II (metal prod., nec) 709.687-042
spring tier (furniture) 780.684-106
spring upholsterer (furniture) 780.684-106
Sprinkler-And-Irrigation-System Installer (construction) 862.281-022
SPRINKLER-IRRIGATION-EQUIPMENT MECHANIC (agric. equip.) 624.361-014
Sprinkler-Truck Driver (any industry) 906.683-022
Sprue-Cutting-Press Operator (foundry) 615.685-030
Sprue Knocker (foundry) 519.687-022
spudder (fabrication, nec; paper & pulp) 569.687-026
SPUN-PASTE-MACHINE OPERATOR (elec. equip.) 692.685-190
squad leader (government ser.) 377.137-014
squad sergeant (government ser.) 375.133-010
Square-Shear Operator I (any industry) 615.682-018
Square-Shear Operator II (any industry) 615.685-034
SQUARING-MACHINE OPERATOR (clock & watch) 605.685-046
SQUEAK, RATTLE, AND LEAK REPAIRER (automotive ser.) 620.364-010
Squeegee Finisher (construction) 869.687-026

Squeegee-Machine Tender (glass mfg.) 979.685-010
squeegeer and former (plastic prod.) 754.684-050
SQUEEGEE TENDER (rubber tire) 750.685-010
SQUEEZER OPERATOR (wood. container) 669.685-082
squirt-machine operator (boot & shoe) 690.685-278
stabilizer operator (construction) 859.683-026
stabilizing-machine operator (construction) 859.683-026
STABLE ATTENDANT (any industry) 410.674-022
stable manager (any industry) 410.131-010
STAB SETTER AND DRILLER (cutlery-hrdwr.) 709.684-082
stack clerk (library) 249.687-014
stacker (any industry) 929.687-030
stacker (beverage) 920.665-014
stacker (elec. equip.) 729.687-026
Stacker (furniture) 569.685-066
STACKER (leather prod.) 222.587-046
stacker (print. & pub.) 651.686-018
stacker (woodworking) 569.685-066
STACKER-AND-SORTER OPERATOR (saw. & plan.) 921.682-018
stacker attendant (any industry) 921.683-014
STACKER, MACHINE (woodworking) 569.685-066
Stacker Operator (any industry) 921.683-014
stacker operator (brick & tile) 579.685-058
Stacker-Straightener (saw. & plan.) 669.687-018
STACKER TENDER (millwork-plywood) 921.685-062
stacking assembler (elec. equip.; electron. comp.) 729.684-066
STACKING-MACHINE OPERATOR I (any industry) 692.682-054
STACKING-MACHINE OPERATOR II (any industry) 739.685-038
stack matcher (textile) 582.687-022
stack puller (sugar & conf.) 520.686-030
Stack Supervisor (smelt. & refin.) 511.132-010
staffing clerk (clerical) 205.367-062
STAFF TOXICOLOGIST (government ser.) 041.061-094
STAGE HAND (amuse. & rec.) term
stage manager (radio-tv broad.) 962.167-014
STAGER (print. & pub.) 971.684-014
STAGE TECHNICIAN (amuse. & rec.) 962.261-014
stage technician (amuse. & rec.)   see STAGE HAND
STAIN APPLICATOR (wood prod., nec) 561.585-010
Stain Dipper (furniture) 599.685-026
STAINED GLASS ARTIST (profess. & kin.) 142.061-054
STAINER (fabrication, nec) 739.687-174
STAINER (furniture; wood prod., nec) 742.684-014
STAINER (leather prod.) 589.687-034
STAINING-MACHINE OPERATOR (tex. prod., nec) 582.685-142
Stain Maker (paint & varnish) 550.585-038
Stain Remover (construction) 869.687-026
Stain Wiper (furniture) 742.687-010
Stair Builder (construction) 860.381-022
STAKER (clock & watch) 715.684-182
STAKER, MACHINE (leather mfg.) 580.685-050
Staker, Surveying (any industry) 869.567-010
stakes player (amuse. & rec.) 343.367-010
staking-machine operator (clock & watch) 715.684-182
staking-press operator (clock & watch) 715.684-182
Stallion Keeper (agriculture) 410.674-022
STAMP ANALYST (retail trade) 299.387-014
STAMP CLASSIFIER (retail trade) 299.387-018
stamp cutter (beverage) 640.565-010
stamper (any industry) 920.687-126
Stamper (any industry) 920.587-018
Stamper (any industry) 652.682-030
stamper (beverage) 920.665-014
stamper (boot & shoe) 690.685-158
STAMPER (button & notion) 734.685-010
STAMPER (chemical) 556.685-078
stamper (hat & cap) 580.685-042
stamper blocker (hat & cap) 580.685-026
STAMPER I (tex. prod., nec) 781.687-062
STAMPER II (tex. prod., nec) 652.685-082
STAMPER, MACHINE (pottery & porc.) 652.682-022
stamping-die maker, bench (machine shop) 601.281-010
STAMPING-MACHINE OPERATOR (boot & shoe) 690.685-398
Stamping-Machine Operator (clerical) 208.685-026
STAMPING-MACHINE OPERATOR (pen & pencil) 692.685-194
STAMPING-MILL TENDER (smelt. & refin.) 515.685-018
STAMPING-PRESS OPERATOR (any industry) 652.682-030
Stamping-Press Operator (any industry) 617.685-026
stamp maker (pen & pencil) 733.381-014
STAMP MOUNTER (pen & pencil) 733.684-018
STAMP-PAD FINISHER (pen & pencil) 733.687-066
STAMP-PAD MAKER (pen & pencil) 733.687-070
Stamp Presser (beverage) 920.687-042
stamp-press operator (chemical) 556.685-078
Standard-Practice Analyst (profess. & kin.) 131.267-026

standards analyst (profess. & kin.) 007.267-010
STANDARDS ENGINEER (profess. & kin.) 012.061-018
standards laboratory technician (aircraft mfg.; electron. comp.) 019.281-010
Stand-By (motion picture) 358.677-010
Stand Grinder (foundry) 705.684-074
STAND-IN (motion picture; radio-tv broad.) 961.667-014
STANDPIPE TENDER (steel & rel.) 519.665-014
STAPLE CUTTER (textile) 680.685-102
Staple-Fiber-Machine Tender (glass mfg.) 575.685-030
Staple Fiber Washer (plastic-synth.) 582.685-162
staple laster (boot & shoe) 690.685-362
STAPLE-PROCESSING-MACHINE OPERATOR (textile) 680.585-014
stapler (boot & shoe) 690.685-162
Stapler, Coil Unit (furniture) 780.687-042
STAPLER, HAND (furniture) 780.687-042
STAPLER, MACHINE (furniture) 692.685-198
Staple-Shear Operator (steel & rel.) 615.682-018
STAPLING-MACHINE OPERATOR (any industry) 692.685-202
starch and prosize mixer (paper & pulp) 550.682-010
starch crab (sugar & conf.) 529.682-018
Starch Dumper (sugar & conf.) 520.686-030
STARCHER (button & notion) 739.687-178
starcher (textile) 582.687-026
starcher-and-tenter-range feeder (textile) 589.665-014
STARCHMAKER (grain-feed mills) 520.485-030
STARCHMAKER (sugar & conf.) 526.687-014
Starch-Mangle Tender (textile) 584.685-042
Starch Presser (grain-feed mills) 521.687-038
STARCH-TREATING ASSISTANT (grain-feed mills) 520.665-018
starter (amuse. & rec.) 153.267-010
STARTER (amuse. & rec.) 153.667-010
starter (any industry) 388.367-010
starter (hat & cap) 784.684-058
starter (hat & cap) 586.685-034
Starter Adjuster (elec. equip.; light. fix.) 724.381-010
Starter-Cup-Powder Mixer (chemical) 737.687-090
starter, weaving (textile) 683.360-014
Starting-Sheet-Tank Operator (smelt. & refin.) 519.362-014
State Editor (print. & pub.) 132.037-014
STATE-HIGHWAY POLICE OFFICER (government ser.) 375.263-018
STATEMENT CLERK (financial) 214.362-046
state's attorney (government ser.) 110.117-010
State-Surplus-Commodity-And-Property Representative (government ser.) 188.117-122
state trooper (government ser.) 375.263-018
STATIC BALANCER (any industry) 724.384-014
STATION AGENT I (r.r. trans.) 910.137-038
Station Agent II (r.r. trans.) 211.467-030
STATIONARY ENGINEER (any industry) 950.382-026
STATIONARY-ENGINEER APPRENTICE (any industry) 950.382-030
stationary engineer, refrigeration (any industry) 950.362-014
STATIONARY-ENGINEER SUPERVISOR (any industry) 950.131-014
station attendant (automotive ser.) 915.477-010
station chief (pipe lines) 914.132-014
STATION ENGINEER, CHIEF (pipe lines) 914.132-014
STATION ENGINEER, MAIN LINE (pipe lines) 914.362-018
Station Engineer, Operating Chief (pipe lines) 914.132-014
Station Installer (tel. & tel.) 822.261-022
STATION INSTALLER-AND-REPAIRER (tel. & tel.) 822.261-022
STATION MANAGER (r.r. trans.) 184.167-130
station mechanic (any industry) 805.361-010
station mechanic (any industry) 823.281-014
station mechanic (utilities) 631.261-014
station-mechanic apprentice (utilities) 631.261-018
station mechanic helper (utilities) 631.684-010
station operator (government ser.) 379.362-010
station operator (pipe lines) 914.362-018
Station Patroller (r.r. trans.) 376.667-018
Station Repairer (tel. & tel.) 822.261-022
STATIONS-RELATIONS-CONTACT REPRESENTATIVE (radio-tv broad.) 184.167-134
station supervisor (any industry) 950.131-014
station telegrapher (r.r. trans.) 236.562-014
STATISTICAL CLERK (clerical) 216.382-062
STATISTICAL CLERK, ADVERTISING (retail trade) 216.382-066
STATISTICAL-MACHINE SERVICER (any industry) 633.281-030
Statistical Typist (clerical) 203.582-066
Statistician (radio-tv broad.) 216.382-062
statistician (utilities) 216.137-010
Statistician, Analytical (profess. & kin.) 020.167-026
STATISTICIAN, APPLIED (profess. & kin.) 020.167-026
Statistician, Engineering And Physical Science (profess. & kin.) 020.167-026
STATISTICIAN, MATHEMATICAL (profess. & kin.) 020.067-022
statistician, theoretical (profess. & kin.) 020.067-022
statler operator (glass products) 677.686-014

Stator Connector

Stator Connector (elec. equip.) 721.684-018
Stator Repairer (any industry) 721.281-018
Stator Tester (elec. equip.) 724.364-010
Stator Winder (elec. equip.) 721.484-010
statue maker (profess. & kin.) 144.061-018
Stave-Block Splitter (logging) 454.684-022
STAVE-BOLT EQUALIZER (saw. & plan.) 667.682-074
stave grader (wood. container) 764.387-014
stave inspector (wood. container) 764.387-014
stave inspector and culler (wood. container) 764.687-054
STAVE JOINTER (wood. container) 665.685-030
STAVE-LOG-CUT-OFF SAW OPERATOR (saw. & plan.) 667.682-078
STAVE-LOG-RIPSAW OPERATOR (saw. & plan.) 667.685-058
STAVE-MACHINE TENDER (wood. container) 663.685-046
stave matcher (wood. container) 764.687-054
STAVE-PLANER TENDER (saw. & plan.) 665.686-014
STAVE-SAW OPERATOR (wood. container) 667.685-062
stave steamer (woodworking) 562.665-014
stayer (boot & shoe) 690.685-414
stayer (boot & shoe) 690.682-082
stayer (garment; protective dev.) 789.687-018
staying-machine operator (paper goods) 641.685-054
STEAK SAUCE MAKER (can. & preserv.) 529.484-010
STEAK TENDERIZER, MACHINE (meat products) 529.686-082
steam blocker (hat & cap) 580.685-026
Steam-Bone-Press Tender (chemical) 555.685-014
STEAM-BOX OPERATOR (woodworking) 562.665-014
steam-box tender (tobacco) 522.682-014
steam-brush operator (textile) 587.685-010
STEAM CLEANER (automotive ser.) 915.687-026
Steam Cleaner (furniture) 780.687-058
steam cleaner, machine (laundry & rel.) 361.665-010
STEAM-CLEANING-MACHINE OPERATOR (construction) 891.685-010
Steam-Clean-Machine Operator (forging) 915.687-026
steam conditioner, filling (textile) 587.685-022
STEAM-CONDITIONER OPERATOR (tobacco) 522.685-094
STEAM-DISTRIBUTION SUPERVISOR (utilities) 862.137-014
steam drier (can. & preserv.; grain-feed mills) 523.685-058
steam-drier operator (textile) 581.685-054
STEAM-DRIER TENDER (carpet & rug) 581.685-058
STEAMER (beverage) 529.685-226
Steamer (hat & cap) 784.687-078
STEAMER (meat products) 525.687-110
STEAMER (tex. prod., nec) 789.687-170
steamer (textile) 587.685-022
steamer (tobacco) 522.682-014
steamer and shaper (toy-sport equip.) 732.684-106
STEAMER-BLOCKER (hat & cap; knitting) 784.684-070
Steamer, Gum Candy (sugar & conf.) 529.686-034
steamer operator (can. & preserv.) 521.687-090
steamer operator (can. & preserv.) 526.382-026
STEAMER TENDER (textile) 582.685-146
steam finisher (hat & cap) 784.687-010
Steam Fitter (construction) 862.281-022
steam-fitter apprentice (construction) 862.281-026
Steam-Fitter Helper (construction) 862.684-022
Steam-Fitter Supervisor (construction) 862.131-010
Steam-Fitter Supervisor, Maintenance (any industry) 862.131-010
steam flattener (any industry) 363.682-018
steam-frame operator (textile) 580.685-066
Steam-Generating-Powerplant Mechanic (utilities) 631.261-014
Steam-Generating-Powerplant-Mechanic Helper (utilities) 631.684-010
Steam Gigger (textile) 585.685-054
Steam Hammer Operator (forging) 610.362-010
steam hand (knitting) 582.685-078
Steam-Hoist Operator (mine & quarry) 921.663-026
STEAMING-CABINET TENDER (garment) 582.685-150
steaming-machine operator (knitting) 580.685-014
Steam-Iron Assembler (house. appl.) 723.684-010
Steam-Meter Reader (utilities) 209.567-010
STEAM-OVEN OPERATOR (can. & preserv.) 526.382-026
Steam-Pan Sponger (textile) 587.685-018
Steam-Pile-Driver Operator (construction) 859.682-018
Steam-Plant Records Clerk (utilities) 216.382-062
steam-power-plant operator (any industry) 950.382-010
Steam-Powerplant Supervisor (utilities) 631.131-010
steam presser (any industry) 363.682-018
steam-press operator (any industry) 363.682-018
STEAM-PRESS TENDER (textile) 583.685-106
STEAM-PRESS TENDER I (rubber goods) 553.665-046
STEAM-PRESS TENDER II (rubber goods) 553.665-050
steam-pressure-chamber operator (tobacco) 522.685-102
Steam-Room Attendant (personal ser.) 335.677-014
STEAM SERVICE INSPECTOR (utilities) 862.361-022
steam setter (textile) 680.685-026

steam-station supervisor (any industry) 950.131-014
steamtable attendant (hotel & rest.) 311.677-014
Steamtable Attendant, Railroad (r.r. trans.) 311.677-014
Steamtable Worker (hotel & rest.) 311.677-018
STEAM-TANK OPERATOR (nonmet. min.) 573.683-010
STEAM-TUNNEL FEEDER (saw. & plan.) 562.686-010
steam-tunnel feeder (woodworking) 562.665-014
steam-vat tender (wood. container) 562.665-010
STEEL-BARREL REAMER (wood. container) 703.687-022
STEEL-BOX-TOE INSERTER (boot & shoe) 788.687-138
STEEL-DIE PRINTER (print. & pub.) 651.382-030
Steel-Door Setter (construction) 809.381-022
steel-erecting pusher (construction) 809.131-018
steel erector (construction) 801.361-014
steel-erector apprentice (construction) 801.361-018
steel fabricating supervisor (any industry) 809.130-014
steel-floor-pan-placing supervisor (construction) 869.131-026
steel inspector (steel & rel.) 619.381-010
STEEL-PAN-FORM-PLACING SUPERVISOR (construction) 869.131-026
STEEL-PLATE CAULKER (any industry) 843.684-010
STEEL-POST INSTALLER (utilities) 821.687-010
STEEL-POST-INSTALLER SUPERVISOR (utilities) 821.131-022
STEEL POURER (steel & rel.) 502.664-014
STEEL-POURER HELPER (steel & rel.) 502.664-018
steel-rule die maker (paper goods) 739.381-018
steel-rule-die-maker apprentice (paper goods) 739.381-022
Steel-Rule Inspector (cutlery-hrdwr.) 709.587-010
steel sampler (nonfer. metal; steel & rel.) 509.584-010
Steel-Sash Erector (construction) 809.381-022
STEEL-SHOT-HEADER OPERATOR (ordnance) 611.682-010
Steel-Spar Operator (logging) 921.663-066
STEEL-TIE ADJUSTER, AUTOMATIC (paper goods) 649.685-110
Steel-Wheel Engraver (glass products) 775.381-010
STEEL-WOOL-MACHINE OPERATOR (nonmet. min.) 605.482-010
steeper (beverage) 522.685-114
steeping-press operator (plastic-synth.) 551.687-034
STEEPING-PRESS TENDER (plastic-synth.) 551.685-138
STEEPLE JACK (construction) 869.381-030
STEEP TENDER (grain-feed mills) 522.465-010
stem assembler (fabrication, nec) 739.687-014
stem-cleaning-machine feeder (tobacco) 521.685-362
STEM-DRYER MAINTAINER (tobacco) 529.685-230
stem frazer (fabrication, nec) 665.685-014
STEMHOLE BORER (fabrication, nec) 666.685-010
Stemhole-Borer-And-Topper (fabrication, nec) 666.685-010
Stem-Lead Former (electron. comp.) 725.384-010
STEMMER, HAND (tobacco) 521.687-134
STEMMER, MACHINE (tobacco) 521.685-334
STEM MOUNTER (light. fix.) 725.684-018
stem-mounting-machine operator (light. fix.) 692.686-050
STEM-PROCESSING-MACHINE OPERATOR (fabrication, nec) 739.685-042
STEM-ROLLER-OR-CRUSHER OPERATOR (tobacco) 521.685-330
stem setter (fabrication, nec) 739.687-014
STEM SIZER (fabrication, nec) 692.686-062
stem-threshing-machine operator (tobacco) 521.685-362
stencil cutter (any industry) 979.681-022
Stencil Cutter (clerical) 203.582-066
STENCIL CUTTER (railroad equip.) 970.381-038
STENCIL CUTTER (stonework) 771.281-010
Stencil Cutter, Machine (any industry) 920.685-078
STENCILER (any industry) 920.687-178
Stenciler (carpet & rug) 741.684-026
Stenciler (furniture) 749.684-014
STENCILER (garment; tex. prod., nec) 781.687-066
Stenciling-Machine Tender (glass mfg.; glass products) 979.685-010
STENCIL INSPECTOR (pen & pencil) 733.687-074
STENCIL-MACHINE OPERATOR (textile) 652.685-086
STENCIL MAKER (carpet & rug) 979.381-038
Stencil Maker (engraving) 704.381-026
stencil sprayer (leather mfg.) 584.687-014
STENOCAPTIONER (radio-tv broad.) 202.382-010
STENOGRAPHER (clerical) 202.362-014
STENOGRAPHER, PRINT SHOP (print. & pub.) 202.362-018
stenotype-machine operator (clerical) 202.362-022
STENOTYPE OPERATOR (clerical) 202.362-022
steno-typist (clerical) 202.362-022
STEP-AND-REPEAT REDUCTION CAMERA OPERATOR (electron. comp.) 976.382-034
Step Finisher (construction) 844.364-010
stereo operator (profess. & kin.) 018.281-010
STEREO-PLOTTER OPERATOR (profess. & kin.) 018.281-010
stereoptic projection topographer (profess. & kin.) 018.281-010
Stereotype Caster (print. & pub.) 974.382-014
Stereotype Molder (print. & pub.) 974.382-014
STEREOTYPER (print. & pub.) 974.382-014

STEREOTYPER APPRENTICE (print. & pub.) 974.382-010
Stereotyper Helper (print. & pub.) 979.684-026
STERILE-PRODUCTS PROCESSOR (pharmaceut.) 559.682-054
STERILIZER (beverage) 920.687-182
STERILIZER (medical ser.; pharmaceut.; protective dev.) 599.585-010
sterilizer (tex. prod., nec) 589.685-082
sterilizer operator (beverage) 920.687-182
STERILIZER OPERATOR (dairy products) 523.685-114
sterilizer operator (furniture) 582.685-074
Stevedore, Dock (water trans.) 922.687-090
Stevedore, Front (water trans.) 922.687-090
Stevedore, Hold (water trans.) 922.687-090
STEVEDORE I (water trans.) 911.663-014
STEVEDORE II (water trans.) 922.687-090
Stevedoring Superintendent, Container Handling (water trans.) 911.137-022
stevedoring supervisor (water trans.) 911.137-018
STEWARD/STEWARDESS (hotel & rest.) 310.137-018
STEWARD/STEWARDESS (water trans.) 350.677-022
STEWARD/STEWARDESS, BANQUET (hotel & rest.) 310.137-022
STEWARD/STEWARDESS, BATH (water trans.) 350.677-018
STEWARD/STEWARDESS, CHIEF, CARGO VESSEL (water trans.) 350.137-014
STEWARD/STEWARDESS, CHIEF, PASSENGER SHIP (water trans.) 350.137-018
Steward/Stewardess, Club Car (r.r. trans.) 310.137-026
Steward/Stewardess, Deck (water trans.) 350.677-022
steward/stewardess, dining room (water trans.) 350.677-030
Steward/Stewardess, Economy Class (water trans.) 350.137-022
Steward/Stewardess, Lounge (water trans.) 350.677-022
Steward/Stewardess, Night (water trans.) 350.677-022
STEWARD/STEWARDESS, RAILROAD DINING CAR (r.r. trans.) 310.137-026
Steward/Stewardess, Room (water trans.) 350.677-022
STEWARD/STEWARDESS, SECOND (water trans.) 350.137-022
Steward/Stewardess, Second Class (water trans.) 350.137-022
Steward/Stewardess, Smoke Room (water trans.) 350.677-022
STEWARD/STEWARDESS, THIRD (water trans.) 350.137-026
Steward/Stewardess, Third Class (water trans.) 350.137-022
Steward/Stewardess, Tourist Class (water trans.) 350.137-022
STEWARD/STEWARDESS, WINE (water trans.) 350.677-026
STEWARD, RACETRACK (amuse. & rec.) 153.117-022
stick-candy puller (sugar & conf.) 520.682-030
Sticker (bakery products) 524.687-018
STICKER (button & notion) 734.687-090
sticker (dairy products) 524.686-014
STICKER (hat & cap) 784.687-070
sticker (meat products) 525.684-042
sticker (pottery & porc.) 774.684-022
STICKER (saw. & plan.) 563.686-010
sticker (stonework) 779.684-058
STICKER, ANIMAL (meat products) 525.684-050
sticker-on (hat & cap) 784.687-070
STICKER-ON (nonmet. min.) 774.684-034
stick feeder (tobacco) 529.686-074
Stick Inserter (dairy products) 529.685-030
stick roller (sugar & conf.) 520.684-014
stick spinner (sugar & conf.) 520.682-030
STIFFENER (hat & cap) 589.687-038
Stiff-Leg Derrick Operator (wood prod., nec) 921.663-022
stiff-neck loader (logging) 921.683-054
stiff-straw-hat washer (hat & cap) 784.687-078
Still And Tank Inspector (petrol. refin.) 549.261-010
Still Cleaner, Tube (petrol. refin.) 891.687-030
STILL OPERATOR (agriculture; can. & preserv.) 522.685-098
STILL OPERATOR (any industry) term
STILL OPERATOR (build. mat., nec) 543.682-026
STILL OPERATOR, BATCH OR CONTINUOUS (chemical) 552.362-022
Still Operator, Brandy (beverage) 522.382-026
Still Operator, Gin (beverage) 522.382-026
STILL-OPERATOR HELPER (chemical) 552.685-030
STILL OPERATOR I (beverage) 522.382-030
STILL OPERATOR II (beverage) 522.382-026
Still Operator, Whisky (beverage) 522.382-026
STILL-PUMP OPERATOR (petrol. refin.) 549.362-010
still runner (beverage) 522.382-026
STILL TENDER (any industry) 552.685-026
still tender (chemical) 552.682-010
STITCH-BONDING-MACHINE TENDER (textile) 689.685-126
STITCH-BONDING-MACHINE-TENDER HELPER (textile) 689.686-042
stitchdown-thread laster (boot & shoe) 788.684-114
stitchdown-thread-lasting-machine operator (boot & shoe) 788.684-114
stitcher (boot & shoe) 690.682-082
stitcher (boot & shoe) 690.682-078
stitcher (glove & mit.; tex. prod., nec) 689.685-106
STITCHER (tex. prod., nec) 689.682-022

Stitcher Feeder (wood. container) 669.686-030
stitcher, hand (furniture) 780.684-070
STITCHER, HAND (print. & pub.) 977.684-022
stitcher, hand (toy-sport equip.) 732.684-050
STITCHER, MACHINE (boot & shoe) term
stitcher operator (print. & pub.) 653.662-010
STITCHER OPERATOR (paper goods) 649.685-114
stitcher operator (print. & pub.) 692.685-146
Stitcher Operator (wood. container) 669.685-014
stitcher operator (woodworking) 669.685-042
Stitcher Set-Up Operator, Automatic (paper goods) 649.380-010
STITCHER, SPECIAL MACHINE (boot & shoe) 690.682-078
STITCHER, STANDARD MACHINE (boot & shoe) 690.682-082
STITCHER, TAPE-CONTROLLED MACHINE (boot & shoe) 690.685-494
Stitcher, Utility (boot & shoe) 690.682-082
stitch fudger (boot & shoe) 690.685-482
STITCHING-MACHINE OPERATOR (print. & pub.) 653.662-010
stitching-machine operator (boot & shoe) 690.682-082
stitching-machine operator (wood. container) 669.662-010
STITCHING-MACHINE OPERATOR (wood. container) 669.685-086
Stitching-Machine Setter (print. & pub.) 653.360-018
stitch marker (boot & shoe) 690.685-282
Stitch Separator (boot & shoe) 690.685-482
stitch wheeler (boot & shoe) 690.685-482
stock blender (textile) 680.685-070
stock-broker (financial) 250.257-018
stock chaser (clerical) 221.367-042
stock checker (clerical) 222.387-058
STOCK CHECKER, APPAREL (retail trade) 299.667-014
STOCK CHECKERER I (ordnance) 761.381-034
STOCK CHECKERER II (ordnance) 665.685-034
STOCK CLERK (retail trade) 299.367-014
STOCK CLERK (clerical) 222.387-058
Stock Clerk, Makeup (motion picture) 222.387-042
stock clerk, self-service store (retail trade) 299.367-014
stock clipper (agriculture) 410.684-014
STOCK-CONTROL CLERK (clerical) 219.387-030
STOCK-CONTROL SUPERVISOR (clerical) 222.137-038
Stock-Crane Operator (steel & rel.) 921.663-042
stock cutter (rubber goods) 751.684-014
STOCK CUTTER (saw. & plan.) 667.482-018
stock cutter (textile) 680.685-102
stock-drier tender (textile) 581.685-046
STOCK FITTER (boot & shoe) 788.685-018
STOCK GRADER (woodworking) 667.382-010
stock grinder (paint & varnish)   see PAINT GRINDER
STOCKING-AND-BOX-SHOP SUPERVISOR (ordnance) 769.137-010
STOCKING INSPECTOR (knitting) 684.684-010
STOCKLAYER (boot & shoe) 753.687-042
STOCK MAKER, CUSTOM (ordnance) 761.381-038
Stock Mixer (textile) 929.687-062
Stock Mixer (nonmet. min.) 570.686-018
stock order lister (clerical) 219.387-030
STOCK-PARTS FABRICATOR (ship-boat mfg.) 769.684-050
STOCK-PARTS INSPECTOR (furniture) 763.684-070
STOCK PATCHER (ordnance) 761.684-042
STOCK-PATCH SAWYER (woodworking) 667.682-082
Stock Pitcher (paper & pulp) 539.587-010
Stock-Preparation Supervisor (rubber goods) 559.137-014
Stock-Preparation Supervisor (rubber tire) 750.130-010
STOCK PREPARER (plastic prod.) 751.387-010
stock-record clerk (clerical) 222.387-034
stock repairer (ordnance) 761.684-042
stock roller (rubber tire) 759.684-058
stockroom clerk (clerical) 222.387-058
stockroom supervisor (clerical) 222.137-034
stock-saw operator (saw. & plan.) 667.482-018
stock selector (any industry) 922.687-058
STOCK SHAPER (ordnance) 761.684-046
STOCK SHEETS CLEANER-INSPECTOR (glass products) 779.687-034
stock supervisor (any industry) 921.133-018
STOCK SUPERVISOR (clerical) 222.137-034
stock-transfer clerk (financial) 216.362-046
STOCK-TRANSFER CLERK, HEAD (financial) 216.137-014
stock-transfer technician (financial) 216.362-046
Stock Turner (ordnance) 664.685-018
stogie maker, hand (tobacco) 790.684-014
Stogie Packer (tobacco) 790.687-014
stoker (any industry) 951.685-010
STOKER ERECTOR-AND-SERVICER (any industry) 637.281-014
stoker-installation mechanic (any industry) 637.281-014
Stone-And-Concrete Washer (construction) 869.687-026
stone-and-plate-preparer apprentice (print. & pub.) 972.682-014
stone banker (stonework) 679.664-010
STONE CARVER (stonework) 771.281-014

STONE CLEANER (beverage) 529.687-190
stonecutter (grain-feed mills) 629.261-014
stonecutter (jewelry-silver.) 770.281-014
STONECUTTER APPRENTICE, HAND (stonework) 771.381-010
stonecutter, assistant (grain-feed mills) 629.684-014
STONECUTTER, HAND (stonework) 771.381-014
STONECUTTER, MACHINE (stonework) 677.682-022
stone dresser (stonework) 771.381-014
STONE DRILLER (stonework) 676.682-014
STONE-DRILLER HELPER (stonework) 676.686-010
stone finisher (stonework) 775.664-010
stone finisher (stonework) 673.382-018
stone finisher (stonework)   see STONE MECHANIC
Stone Gluer (jewelry-silver.) 735.687-034
STONE GRADER (mine & quarry) 679.567-010
STONE GRADER (stonework) 670.384-010
stone-grinder operator (paint & varnish) 555.682-022
stone hand (print. & pub.) 973.381-026
STONE-LATHE OPERATOR (stonework) 674.662-010
Stone-Lathe Polisher (stonework) 674.662-010
STONE LAYOUT MARKER (stonework) 670.587-010
STONEMASON (construction) 861.381-038
STONEMASON APPRENTICE (construction) 861.381-042
Stonemason Helper (construction) 869.687-026
STONEMASON SUPERVISOR (construction) 861.131-018
STONE MECHANIC (stonework) term
STONE-MILL OPERATOR (paint & varnish) 555.682-022
stone operator (optical goods) 673.685-074
Stone Polisher (construction) 869.664-014
STONE POLISHER, HAND (stonework) 775.664-010
STONE POLISHER, MACHINE (stonework) 673.382-018
STONE POLISHER, MACHINE APPRENTICE (stonework) 673.382-022
STONER (jewelry-silver.) 735.684-014
STONER AND POLISHER, BEVEL FACE (clock & watch) 603.685-082
STONE RENOVATOR (construction) term
STONE REPAIRER (stonework) 779.684-058
STONER, HAND (clock & watch) 715.584-018
stone rigger (construction) 861.381-042
STONE ROUGHER (optical goods) 673.685-074
stone rubber (stonework) 775.664-010
stone sawyer (stonework) 670.362-010
Stone Setter (construction) 861.381-038
STONE SETTER (jewelry-silver.) 735.687-034
STONE SETTER (jewelry-silver.; optical goods) 700.381-054
stone-setter apprentice (construction) 861.381-042
STONE-SETTER APPRENTICE (jewelry-silver.; optical goods) 700.381-058
Stone Setter, Metal Optical Frames (optical goods) 700.381-054
STONE SPLITTER (concrete prod.) 677.685-050
stone splitter (stonework) 677.685-042
STONE-SPREADER OPERATOR (construction) 853.663-022
STONE TRIMMER (stonework) 670.685-010
Stone Unloader (construction) 869.687-026
stoneworker (stonework) 771.381-014
STOP ATTACHER (button & notion) 692.685-206
STOPBOARD ASSEMBLER (musical inst.) 730.684-082
Stope Miner (mine & quarry) 939.281-010
Stopper Grinder (glass mfg.) 775.684-034
STOPPER MAKER (steel & rel.) 519.684-022
STOPPER-MAKER HELPER (steel & rel.) 519.687-038
stopper-rod maker (steel & rel.) 519.684-022
STOPPING BUILDER (mine & quarry) 869.684-058
storage-battery charger (any industry) 727.381-014
STORAGE BATTERY INSPECTOR AND TESTER (elec. equip.) 727.381-022
storage-bin adjuster (grain-feed mills) 521.685-230
storage brine worker (can. & preserv.) 522.584-010
STORAGE-FACILITY RENTAL CLERK (business ser.; retail trade) 295.367-026
Storage-Garage Attendant (automotive ser.) 915.473-010
storage laborer (can. & preserv.) 522.584-010
Storage-Receipt Poster (clerical) 203.362-010
storage-wharfage clerk (water trans.) 248.362-010
Store Cashier (clerical) 211.462-010
Store Detective (retail trade) 376.367-014
storekeeper (any industry) 184.167-114
storekeeper (clerical) 222.387-058
storekeeper (personal ser.) 339.687-010
STOREKEEPER (water trans.) 222.387-062
Storekeeper, Deck (water trans.) 222.387-062
Storekeeper, Engineering (water trans.) 222.387-062
Storekeeper, Steward (water trans.) 222.387-062
store manager (retail trade) 185.167-046
storeroom clerk (clerical) 222.387-058
storeroom food-checker (hotel & rest.) 222.587-022
storeroom keeper (clerical) 222.387-058
storeroom supervisor (clerical) 222.137-034

stores clerk (clerical) 222.387-058
story analyst (motion picture; radio-tv broad.) 131.087-014
STORY EDITOR (motion picture; radio-tv broad.) 132.037-026
STOVE-BOTTOM WORKER (fabrication, nec) 590.667-010
STOVE-CARRIAGE OPERATOR (fabrication, nec) 590.662-022
STOVE REFINISHER (any industry) 749.684-046
STOVE TENDER (steel & rel.) 512.382-014
straddle buggy operator (any industry) 921.683-070
STRADDLE-TRUCK OPERATOR (any industry) 921.683-070
straight cutter (any industry) 699.685-014
straight cutter (any industry) 775.684-022
Straight Cutter, Machine (tex. prod., nec) 699.682-030
Straightedge-Machine-Operator Helper (glass mfg.; glass products) 673.686-010
straight edger (glass mfg.; glass products) 673.685-078
straight edger (jewelry-silver.) 705.682-014
straightener (any industry) 617.482-026
straightener (knitting) 628.684-018
straightener-and-aligner (motor-bicycles) 807.484-010
Straightener, Gun Parts (ordnance) 709.484-014
STRAIGHTENER, HAND (any industry) 709.484-014
straightener, torch (any industry) 709.684-086
Straightening-Machine Feeder (any industry) 699.686-010
straightening-machine operator (any industry) 613.662-022
Straightening-Press Operator (plastic prod.) 690.682-062
Straightening-Press-Operator Helper (any industry) 619.687-014
Straightening-Press Operator I (any industry) 615.382-010
STRAIGHTENING-PRESS OPERATOR II (any industry) 617.482-026
STRAIGHTENING-ROLL OPERATOR (any industry) 613.662-022
Straight-Knife Cutter, Machine (any industry) 781.684-014
STRAIGHT-LINE EDGER (glass mfg.; glass products) 673.685-078
STRAIGHT-LINE-PRESS SETTER (ordnance) 616.360-034
STRAIGHT-PIN-MAKING-MACHINE OPERATOR (button & notion) 609.482-014
straight ruling machine operator (paper goods; print. & pub.) 659.682-022
straight-slicing-machine operator (millwork-plywood) 663.682-018
straight-tooth-gear-generator operator (machine shop) 602.382-018
Strainer (paint & varnish) 559.685-110
strainer cleaner (chemical) 559.687-042
strainer-mill operator (rubber reclaim.) 551.365-010
STRAINER TENDER (rubber reclaim.) 551.365-010
STRAND-AND-BINDER CONTROLLER (nonmet. min.) 680.685-106
Strand Buncher, Fine Wire (elec. equip.; light. fix.) 616.682-034
strander (steel & rel.) 613.686-010
strander operator (elec. equip.; light. fix.; metal prod., nec; nonfer. metal) 616.682-034
STRAND-FORMING-MACHINE OPERATOR (tex. prod., nec) 681.685-118
strand galvanizer (galvanizing) 501.485-010
STRANDING-MACHINE OPERATOR (elec. equip.; light. fix.; metal prod., nec; nonfer. metal) 616.682-034
STRANDING-MACHINE-OPERATOR HELPER (nonfer. metal) 616.687-010
Stranding Supervisor (metal prod., nec) 691.130-014
strand-machine operator (elec. equip.; metal prod., nec; nonfer. metal) 616.682-034
STRAP BUCKLER, MACHINE (garment) 689.665-010
Strap Cutter (garment) 699.685-014
STRAP-CUTTING-MACHINE OPERATOR (rubber goods) 690.685-402
STRAP-FOLDING-MACHINE OPERATOR (rubber goods) 554.485-014
STRAP-MACHINE OPERATOR (paper goods) 534.682-034
Strap-Machine Operator, Automatic (garment) 787.685-014
strap-making-machine operator (paper goods) 534.682-034
Strap Nailer (wood. container) 669.682-058
Strapper (glove & mit.) 784.682-010
strapper (wood. container) 692.682-058
Strapper And Buffer (woodworking) 705.684-014
STRAPPING-MACHINE OPERATOR (wood. container) 692.682-058
Strapping-Machine Tender (brick & tile) 920.685-106
Strap Recesser (wood. container) 669.382-010
Strap Setter (smelt. & refin.) 630.684-010
Strap Stitcher (boot & shoe) 690.682-082
STRATIGRAPHER (profess. & kin.) 024.061-054
Strawberry Grower (agriculture) 403.161-014
STRAW BOSS (any industry) term
Strawhat Blocker (hat & cap) 580.684-014
strawhat-blocking operator (hat & cap) 580.684-014
Straw-Hat-Brim-Cutter Operator (hat & cap) 585.685-086
straw-hat-brim-raiser operator (hat & cap) 784.687-010
STRAW-HAT BRUSHER (hat & cap) 784.687-074
straw-hat finishing operator (hat & cap) 784.687-010
Straw-Hat-Hydraulic-Press Operator (hat & cap) 580.685-038
Strawhat Inspector And Packer (hat & cap) 784.687-042
Straw-Hat-Machine Operator (hat & cap) 784.682-014
STRAW-HAT-PLUNGER OPERATOR (hat & cap) 583.685-114
straw-hat presser (hat & cap) 583.685-114
STRAW HAT PRESSER, MACHINE (hat & cap) 583.685-110
Strawhat Sizer (hat & cap) 589.687-038

STRAW-HAT-WASHER OPERATOR (hat & cap) 784.687-078
streaker (sugar & conf.) 524.684-018
streaker-off, hand (leather mfg.) 584.687-010
STREETCAR OPERATOR (r.r. trans.) 913.463-014
STREETCAR REPAIRER (railroad equip.) 807.381-026
STREETCAR-REPAIRER HELPER (railroad equip.) 807.687-014
Streetcar Sandbox And Lifeguard-Unit Repairer (railroad equip.) 807.381-026
STREET CLEANER (government ser.) 955.687-018
street-light changer-and-renewer (utilities) 952.667-010
STREET-LIGHT CLEANER (utilities) 952.667-010
street-light inspector (utilities) 952.667-010
street-light repairer (utilities) 824.381-010
STREET-LIGHT REPAIRER (utilities) 729.381-018
STREET-LIGHT-REPAIRER HELPER (utilities) 729.684-050
STREET-LIGHT SERVICER (utilities) 824.381-010
STREET-LIGHT-SERVICER HELPER (utilities) 824.664-010
STREET-LIGHT-SERVICER SUPERVISOR (utilities) 824.137-014
STREET-OPENINGS INSPECTOR (utilities) 859.267-010
street sweeper (government ser.) 955.687-018
STREET-SWEEPER OPERATOR (government ser.) 919.683-022
STRESS ANALYST (aircraft mfg.) 002.061-030
STRESS ANALYST (profess. & kin.) 007.061-042
stress technician (medical ser.) 078.362-062
STRESS TEST TECHNICIAN (medical ser.) 078.362-062
STRETCH-BOX TENDER (textile) 680.685-110
STRETCHER (hat & cap) 580.685-054
STRETCHER (jewelry-silver.) 700.684-078
stretcher (textile) 652.687-026
stretcher (textile) 781.687-014
stretcher and drier (hat & cap) 581.687-022
STRETCHER-DRIER OPERATOR (laundry & rel.) 363.687-022
STRETCHER-LEVELER OPERATOR (nonfer. metal) 619.582-010
STRETCHER-LEVELER-OPERATOR HELPER (nonfer. metal) 619.686-030
stretcher operator (laundry & rel.) 363.687-022
STRETCHING-MACHINE OPERATOR (tex. prod., nec) 580.685-058
Stretching-Machine Tender, Frame (leather mfg.) 580.685-050
Stretching-Press Operator (any industry) 615.382-010
STRETCH-MACHINE OPERATOR (plastic prod.) 559.682-058
Stretch-Press Operator (any industry) 617.260-010
STRICKLER ATTENDANT (fabrication, nec) 652.665-014
STRIKE-OFF-MACHINE OPERATOR (textile) 652.685-090
Strike-Off-Machine Operator (construction) 853.663-014
STRIKE-OUT-MACHINE OPERATOR (textile) 587.685-030
strike-plate attacher (cutlery-hrdwr.) 692.685-138
striker (forging) 610.684-010
striker (water trans.) 911.584-010
striker-out, machine (leather mfg.; tex. prod., nec) 589.685-098
string cutter (boot & shoe) 788.687-074
Stringed-Instrument Assembler (musical inst.) 730.684-010
STRINGER (jewelry-silver.) 509.687-018
STRINGER (paper goods) 794.687-054
stringer (sugar & conf.) 524.684-018
STRINGER-MACHINE TENDER (protective dev.) 692.485-010
Stringer-Up, Soldering Machine (jewelry-silver.) 509.687-018
string-glue-and-printing-machine operator (tex. prod., nec) 689.685-138
Stringing-Machine Operator (paper goods) 649.685-054
STRINGING-MACHINE TENDER (tex. prod., nec) 689.585-018
STRING LASTER (boot & shoe) 690.685-406
string picker (carpet & rug; textile) 689.684-010
STRING-TOP SEALER (paper goods) 641.685-086
STRING-WINDING-MACHINE OPERATOR (musical inst.) 692.682-062
strip cleaner (any industry) 503.362-010
STRIP-CUTTING-MACHINE OPERATOR (textile) 686.685-066
STRIP-CUTTING-MACHINE OPERATOR (tobacco) 521.685-338
STRIPE MATCHER (knitting) 689.662-014
Striper (furniture) 749.684-014
STRIPER (paper goods) 651.682-018
STRIPER, HAND (any industry) 740.484-010
STRIPER, MACHINE (motor-bicycles) 749.686-010
STRIPER, SPRAY GUN (any industry) 741.687-022
strip feeder (tobacco) 529.685-222
STRIPING-MACHINE OPERATOR (nonfer. metal) 652.682-026
Strip-Machine Tender (fabrication, nec) 590.685-022
STRIP-METAL-PUNCH-AND-STRAIGHTENER OPERATOR (wood. container) 615.685-038
strip-mine supervisor (mine & quarry) 939.137-014
STRIPPER (any industry) term
stripper (boot & shoe; leather prod.) 585.685-114
stripper (chemical) 559.687-046
STRIPPER (furniture) 749.687-030
stripper (garment; protective dev.) 789.687-018
STRIPPER (glass mfg.) 673.666-014
Stripper (mine & quarry) 939.687-014
STRIPPER (plastic prod.; rubber goods) 556.686-018
STRIPPER (print. & pub.) 971.381-050

Stripper (smelt. & refin.) 519.565-014
stripper-and-opaquer apprentice (print. & pub.) 971.381-054
stripper and printer (print. & pub.) 971.381-034
STRIPPER AND TAPER (rubber goods) 899.684-038
STRIPPER APPRENTICE (print. & pub.) 971.381-054
stripper, black and white (print. & pub.) 972.381-022
Stripper, Black And White (print. & pub.) 971.381-050
Stripper, Color (print. & pub.) 971.381-050
STRIPPER-CUTTER, MACHINE (food prep., nec) 521.685-342
STRIPPER-ETCHER, PRINTED CIRCUIT BOARDS (electron. comp.) 590.685-082
Stripper, Latex (rubber goods) 556.686-018
STRIPPER, LITHOGRAPHIC I (print. & pub.) 972.281-022
STRIPPER, LITHOGRAPHIC II (print. & pub.) 972.381-022
stripper-machine operator (sugar & conf.) 521.685-102
stripper-opaquer (print. & pub.) 972.381-022
stripper, preliminary (plastic-synth.) 556.686-014
Stripper, Printed Circuit Boards (electron. comp.) 590.685-082
Stripper, Soft Plastic (plastic prod.) 556.686-018
Stripper Truck Operator (smelt. & refin.) 921.683-050
stripping-and-booking-machine operator (tobacco) 521.685-334
STRIPPING CUTTER AND WINDER (boot & shoe) 585.685-118
stripping-machine operator (paper goods) 641.685-034
STRIPPING-MACHINE OPERATOR (paper goods) 641.685-090
STRIPPING-SHOVEL OILER (mine & quarry) 850.684-018
STRIPPING-SHOVEL OPERATOR (mine & quarry) 850.663-026
STRIP POLISHER (stonework) 673.685-082
STRIP PRESSER (boot & shoe) 583.685-118
STRIP ROLLER (metal prod., nec) 613.682-022
strip shader (textile) 582.687-022
Strip-Stamp Straightener (beverage) 920.687-042
STRIP-TANK TENDER (ordnance) 503.685-046
Strip-Tease Dancer (amuse. & rec.) 151.047-010
stroboroma operator (textile) 689.364-010
STROBOSCOPE OPERATOR (textile) 689.364-010
strobotac operator (textile) 689.364-010
STROKE-BELT-SANDER OPERATOR (woodworking) 662.682-018
stroker (sugar & conf.) 524.684-018
stroller rental clerk (retail trade) 295.367-014
STRONG-NITRIC OPERATOR (chemical) 559.682-062
STRUCTURAL ENGINEER (construction) 005.061-034
structural inspector (any industry) 619.261-010
structural-iron erector (construction) 801.361-014
structural-iron worker (construction) 801.361-014
structural-metal-fabricator apprentice (any industry) 619.361-018
STRUCTURAL-MILL SUPERVISOR (nonfer. metal) 619.132-022
structural-shop helper (any industry) 619.686-022
Structural-Steel-Equipment Erector (construction) 801.361-014
structural-steel erector (construction) 801.361-014
Structural-Steel Inspector (construction) 182.267-010
Structural-Steel Lay-Out Worker (any industry) 809.281-010
Structural-Steel-Shop Supervisor (any industry) 809.130-014
STRUCTURAL-STEEL WORKER (construction) 801.361-014
STRUCTURAL-STEEL-WORKER APPRENTICE (construction) 801.361-018
Structural-Steel-Worker Helper (construction) 869.687-026
structural test mechanic (aircraft mfg.) 710.361-014
structures assembler (aircraft mfg.) 806.381-026
STUBBER (retail trade) 222.687-034
STUCCO MASON (construction) 842.381-014
stucco worker (construction) 842.381-014
STUDDER, HAIRSPRING (clock & watch) 715.684-186
Stud Driver (smelt. & refin.) 630.684-010
STUD-DRIVER OPERATOR (construction) term
student-activities adviser (education) 090.167-022
student-union consultant (education) 090.167-022
Studio-Couch-Frame Builder (furniture) 762.684-066
studio engineer (motion picture; radio-tv broad.; recording) 194.262-018
studio technician (motion picture; radio-tv broad.; recording) 194.262-018
studio technician-video operator (radio-tv broad.) 194.382-018
stud setter (garment; tex. prod., nec) 789.685-010
stuffed-casing tier (meat products) 529.687-034
Stuffed-Toy Joiner (toy-sport equip.) 731.687-034
STUFFER (meat products) 520.685-210
STUFFER (tex. prod., nec) 780.687-046
stuffer (tex. prod., nec) 780.684-066
STUFFER (toy-sport equip.) 731.685-014
stuffer, machine (leather mfg.; tex. prod., nec) 582.685-050
stuffer, vertical hydraulic (plastic prod.; plastic-synth.) 557.382-010
STUFFING-MACHINE OPERATOR (furniture) 780.685-014
stuffing-machine operator (paper goods) 649.685-094
STUFFING-MACHINE OPERATOR (toy-sport equip.) 732.685-034
STULL INSTALLER (concrete prod.) 869.684-062
stummel selector (fabrication, nec) 739.687-166
stumper (hat & cap) 784.684-058
stumper (hat & cap) 586.685-034

stumper-feller

stumper-feller (logging) 454.684-014
STUNNER, ANIMAL (meat products) 525.687-114
STUNT PERFORMER (amuse. & rec.; motion picture; radio-tv broad.) 159.341-014
Styrene-Continuous-Still Utility Operator (chemical) 559.682-066
Styrene-Dehydration-Reactor Operator (chemical) 558.685-062
STYRENE OPERATOR (chemical) term
Styrene Operator, Chief (chemical; petrol. refin.) 559.132-078
subassembler (agric. equip.) 706.684-042
SUBASSEMBLER (elec. equip.) 729.684-054
SUBASSEMBLER (machinery mfg.) 706.381-038
SUBASSEMBLER (office machines) 706.684-094
subassembler (ordnance) 736.684-014
Subassembly Supervisor (mfd. bldgs.; vehicles, nec) 869.131-030
Subgrade-Roller Operator (construction) 859.683-030
Subgrader Operator (construction) 850.663-022
Subgrade Tester (construction) 869.687-026
subject, scientific research (any industry) 359.677-030
SUBLIMER (chemical) 542.685-014
submarine operator (metal prod., nec) 617.482-022
submarine worker (any industry) 899.261-010
subscription clerk (print. & pub.) 209.362-010
SUBSCRIPTION CREW LEADER (retail trade) 291.157-010
subsorter (laundry & rel.) 369.687-014
SUBSTANCE ABUSE COUNSELOR (profess. & kin.) 045.107-058
Substation Engineer (utilities) 003.167-046
SUBSTATION INSPECTOR (utilities) 952.261-010
Substation Inspector, Automatic (utilities) 952.261-010
SUBSTATION OPERATOR (utilities) 952.362-026
SUBSTATION OPERATOR APPRENTICE (utilities) 952.362-030
Substation Operator, Automatic (utilities) 952.362-026
SUBSTATION OPERATOR, CHIEF (utilities) 952.131-010
Substation Operator, Conversion (utilities) 952.362-026
Substation Operator, Distribution (r.r. trans.; utilities) 952.362-026
SUBSTATION-OPERATOR HELPER (utilities) 952.687-014
Substation Operator Helper, Generator (utilities) 952.367-014
Substation Operator, Generation (utilities) 952.362-026
Substation Operator, Transforming (utilities) 952.362-026
subtitle writer (motion picture; radio-tv broad.) 203.362-026
subwarehouse supervisor (beverage) 520.382-010
SUCKER-MACHINE OPERATOR (sugar & conf.) 529.685-234
suction-dredge-dumping supervisor (construction) 862.134-010
SUCTION-DREDGE-PIPE-LINE-PLACING SUPERVISOR (construction) 862.134-010
Suction-Drum-Drier Operator (textile) 581.685-030
suction-machine operator (textile) 581.685-042
Suction Operator (agriculture) 921.662-018
SUCTION-PLATE-CARRIER CLEANER (tobacco) 529.687-194
suction-plate roller, hand (tobacco) 790.684-022
suction roller (tobacco) 790.684-022
sueding-and-buffing-machine operator (boot & shoe) 753.684-010
Sueding-Machine Tender (textile) 585.685-070
Sueding-Wheel Operator (leather mfg.) 585.685-018
SUGAR BOILER (sugar & conf.) 522.382-034
Sugarcane Planter (agriculture) 404.161-010
SUGAR-CHIPPER-MACHINE OPERATOR (grain-feed mills) 521.685-354
Sugar-Coating Hand (sugar & conf.) 529.686-034
SUGAR CONTROLLER (sugar & conf.) 529.565-010
SUGAR DRIER (grain-feed mills) 523.665-010
sugar drier (sugar & conf.) 523.685-098
sugar-end supervisor (sugar & conf.) 529.130-034
sugar grinder (grain-feed mills) 521.685-354
SUGAR GRINDER (sugar & conf.) 521.685-346
SUGAR PRESSER (grain-feed mills) 521.685-350
SUGAR-REPROCESS OPERATOR, HEAD (sugar & conf.) 529.137-018
Sugar Trucker (grain-feed mills) 929.687-030
Sugar-Wafer-Machine Operator (bakery products) 526.685-066
SUGGESTION CLERK (clerical) 209.387-034
suit attendant (personal ser.) 358.677-014
Suit Finisher (garment; retail trade) 785.361-022
suit maker (rubber goods) 795.684-026
SULFATE DRIER-MACHINE OPERATOR (steel & rel.) 551.685-142
sulfate operator (chemical; steel & rel.) 558.362-018
Sulfonation Equipment Operator (chemical) 559.682-018
Sulfonator Operator (chemical) 559.382-018
Sulfur Burner (chemical) 553.685-094
Sulfur-Chloride Operator (chemical) 558.382-030
Sulfur Feeder (chemical) 553.686-038
sulfuric-acid-plant operator (chemical) 558.585-018
SULKY DRIVER (amuse. & rec.) 153.244-014
Sumac Tanner (leather mfg.) 582.482-018
SUMATRA OPENER (tobacco) 529.687-198
SUNGLASS-CLIP ATTACHER (optical goods) 713.687-042
SUPERCALENDER OPERATOR (paper & pulp) 534.682-038
Supercalender-Operator Helper (paper & pulp) 534.686-010

SUPERCARGO (water trans.) 248.167-010
Supercharger Mechanic (air trans.) 621.281-014
SUPERCHARGER-REPAIR SUPERVISOR (air trans.) 621.131-010
SUPERINTENDENT (agriculture; can. & preserv.) 180.167-054
superintendent (any industry) 189.167-022
superintendent, airport (air trans.) 184.117-026
Superintendent, Airport-Buildings-Maintenance (air trans.) 184.117-026
Superintendent, Airport-Facilities-Repair-And-Maintenance (air trans.) 184.117-026
SUPERINTENDENT, AMMUNITION STORAGE (ordnance) 189.167-038
superintendent, automotive (any industry) 184.167-226
Superintendent, Board Mill (paper & pulp) 539.132-010
SUPERINTENDENT, BUILDING (any industry) 187.167-190
superintendent, building (any industry) 382.664-010
superintendent, camp (profess. & kin.) 187.167-050
SUPERINTENDENT, CAR CONSTRUCTION (railroad equip.) 183.167-034
superintendent, cemetery (real estate) 187.167-074
Superintendent, Circus (amuse. & rec.) 187.117-034
superintendent, city plant (utilities) 184.167-154
SUPERINTENDENT, COLD STORAGE (any industry) 184.167-142
superintendent, colliery (mine & quarry) 181.117-014
SUPERINTENDENT, COMMISSARY (water trans.) 184.117-078
SUPERINTENDENT, COMMUNICATIONS (tel. & tel.) 184.117-082
SUPERINTENDENT, COMPRESSOR STATIONS (pipe lines) 184.167-146
SUPERINTENDENT, CONCRETE-MIXING PLANT (construction) 182.167-022
SUPERINTENDENT, CONSTRUCTION (construction) 182.167-026
Superintendent, Container Terminal (water trans.) 184.167-214
SUPERINTENDENT, DISTRIBUTION I (utilities) 184.167-150
SUPERINTENDENT, DISTRIBUTION II (utilities) 184.167-154
SUPERINTENDENT, DIVISION (motor trans.; r.r. trans.) 184.167-158
superintendent, drilling (petrol. & gas) 930.130-010
SUPERINTENDENT, DRILLING AND PRODUCTION (petrol. & gas) 181.167-014
superintendent, drivers (motor trans.) 913.133-010
superintendent, dyeing (knitting; tex. prod., nec; textile) 582.131-014
superintendent, electrical department (r.r. trans.) 184.167-202
SUPERINTENDENT, ELECTRIC POWER (utilities) 184.167-162
superintendent, factory (any industry) 183.117-014
superintendent, fish hatchery (fishing & hunt.) 180.167-030
superintendent, gas distribution (utilities) 184.167-154
superintendent, general (any industry) 183.117-014
SUPERINTENDENT, GENERATING PLANT (utilities) 184.167-166
superintendent, geophysical laboratory (profess. & kin.) 024.167-010
SUPERINTENDENT, GRAIN ELEVATOR (beverage; grain-feed mills) 529.137-022
SUPERINTENDENT, GREENS (amuse. & rec.) 406.137-014
SUPERINTENDENT, HORTICULTURE (museums) 180.161-014
superintendent, house (hotel & rest.) 329.137-010
SUPERINTENDENT, INDUSTRIES, CORRECTIONAL FACILITY (government ser.) 188.167-094
superintendent, institution (any industry) 187.117-018
superintendent, job (construction) 182.167-026
SUPERINTENDENT, LABOR UTILIZATION (any industry) 189.167-042
superintendent, land department (petrol. & gas) 186.117-046
superintendent, landfill operations (government ser.) 184.167-078
SUPERINTENDENT, LAUNDRY (laundry & rel.) 187.167-194
SUPERINTENDENT, LOCAL (utilities) 952.137-018
SUPERINTENDENT, LOGGING (logging) 183.167-038
SUPERINTENDENT, MAINTENANCE (air trans.) 184.167-174
SUPERINTENDENT, MAINTENANCE (any industry) 189.167-046
SUPERINTENDENT, MAINTENANCE (motor trans.) 184.167-170
superintendent, maintenance, airports (air trans.) 899.137-010
SUPERINTENDENT, MAINTENANCE OF EQUIPMENT (motor trans.; r.r. trans.) 184.167-178
SUPERINTENDENT, MAINTENANCE OF WAY (r.r. trans.) 182.167-030
SUPERINTENDENT, MARINE (water trans.) 184.167-182
SUPERINTENDENT, MARINE OIL TERMINAL (water trans.) 184.167-186
Superintendent, Materials-And-Apparatus Tests (utilities) 184.167-218
SUPERINTENDENT, MEASUREMENT (petrol. & gas; pipe lines) 184.167-190
superintendent, mechanical (profess. & kin.) 007.167-014
superintendent, menagerie (amuse. & rec.) 412.137-010
SUPERINTENDENT, METERS (utilities) 184.167-194
Superintendent, Meter Tests (utilities) 184.167-218
superintendent, mill (any industry) 183.117-014
superintendent, nonselling (retail trade) 189.167-014
SUPERINTENDENT OF GENERATION (utilities) 184.167-138
Superintendent, Oil-Field Drilling (petrol. & gas) 181.167-014
SUPERINTENDENT, OIL-WELL SERVICES (petrol. & gas) 010.167-018
superintendent, operating (retail trade) 189.167-014
superintendent, operations (utilities) 184.167-138
superintendent, operations division (utilities) 184.167-154
Superintendent, Overhead Distribution (utilities) 184.167-150
Superintendent, Pier (water trans.) 184.167-214

SUPERINTENDENT, PIPE-LINES (pipe lines) 184.167-198
superintendent, plant (any industry) 183.117-014
SUPERINTENDENT, PLANT PROTECTION (any industry) 189.167-050
superintendent, police (government ser.) 375.117-010
SUPERINTENDENT, POWER (r.r. trans.) 184.167-202
superintendent, pressure (petrol. & gas; petrol. refin.; pipe lines) 914.167-010
SUPERINTENDENT, PRODUCTION (agriculture) 180.167-058
Superintendent, Production (petrol. & gas) 181.167-014
superintendent, quarry (mine & quarry) 181.117-014
SUPERINTENDENT, RADIO COMMUNICATIONS (government ser.) 193.167-018
SUPERINTENDENT, RECREATION (government ser.) 187.117-054
Superintendent, Refuse Disposal (government ser.) 188.167-098
Superintendent, Research-And-Fault-Analysis Tests (utilities) 184.167-218
SUPERINTENDENT, SALES (construction) 250.157-010
SUPERINTENDENT, SANITATION (government ser.) 188.167-098
superintendent, scheduling (petrol. & gas; petrol. refin.; pipe lines) 184.167-038
SUPERINTENDENT, SCHOOLS (education) 099.117-022
SUPERINTENDENT, SEED MILL (agriculture) 599.137-010
SUPERINTENDENT, SERVICE (hotel & rest.) 329.137-010
superintendent, service (utilities) 953.137-018
superintendent, service establishment (any industry) see MANAGER, SERVICE ESTABLISHMENT
Superintendent, Sewage-Treatment (government ser.) 188.167-098
Superintendent, Station-And-Protection-System Tests (utilities) 184.167-218
SUPERINTENDENT, STATIONS (motor trans.; r.r. trans.) 184.167-206
SUPERINTENDENT, STEVEDORING (water trans.) 911.137-022
superintendent, storage area (any industry) 184.167-114
SUPERINTENDENT, SYSTEM OPERATION (utilities) 184.167-210
SUPERINTENDENT, TERMINAL (water trans.) 184.167-214
SUPERINTENDENT, TESTS (utilities) 184.167-218
SUPERINTENDENT, TRACK (construction) 899.137-014
SUPERINTENDENT, TRANSMISSION (utilities) 184.167-222
SUPERINTENDENT, TRANSPORTATION (any industry) 184.167-226
Superintendent, Underground Distribution (utilities) 184.167-150
superintendent, warehouse (any industry) 184.167-114
SUPERINTENDENT, WATER-AND-SEWER SYSTEMS (waterworks) 184.161-014
Superior-Court Judge (government ser.) 111.107-010
Supermarket Stock Clerk (retail trade) 299.367-014
SUPERVISING AIRPLANE PILOT (government ser.) 196.163-014
Supervising Chef (hotel & rest.) 313.131-026
supervising-chef assistant (hotel & rest.) 313.131-026
Supervising Editor, Feature (motion picture; radio-tv broad.) 962.132-010
Supervising Editor, News Reel (radio-tv broad.) 962.132-010
Supervising Editor, Trailer (motion picture; radio-tv broad.) 962.132-010
SUPERVISING FILM EDITOR (motion picture; radio-tv broad.) 962.132-010
supervising librarian (library) 100.127-010
SUPERVISOR (any industry) master
SUPERVISOR (boot & shoe) 788.131-010
SUPERVISOR (brick & tile) 570.132-022
SUPERVISOR (cement) 579.137-010
SUPERVISOR (clerical) master
SUPERVISOR (clock & watch) 715.131-010
SUPERVISOR (comm. equip.) 619.130-046
SUPERVISOR (cutlery-hrdwr.) 615.130-014
SUPERVISOR (electroplating) 500.131-010
SUPERVISOR (food prep., nec) 529.132-110
SUPERVISOR (glove & mit.) 784.132-010
SUPERVISOR (government ser.) 188.137-010
SUPERVISOR (jewelry-silver.) 700.130-010
SUPERVISOR (jewelry-silver.; plastic prod.) 700.131-010
SUPERVISOR (knitting) 684.137-010
SUPERVISOR (leather prod.) 783.132-010
SUPERVISOR (metal prod., nec) 700.131-014
SUPERVISOR (mine & quarry) 570.137-010
supervisor (motor trans.) 909.127-010
SUPERVISOR (musical inst.) 730.131-010
SUPERVISOR (nonfer. metal) 691.130-010
SUPERVISOR (nut & bolt) 616.130-010
SUPERVISOR (office machines) 706.131-014
SUPERVISOR (oils & grease) 529.137-030
SUPERVISOR (optical goods) 716.130-010
SUPERVISOR (ordnance) 737.137-018
SUPERVISOR (plastic prod.) 690.130-018
SUPERVISOR (plumbing-heat.) 609.130-018
supervisor (print. & pub.) 653.131-010
SUPERVISOR (rubber reclaim.) 559.132-058
SUPERVISOR (rubber tire) 750.130-010
SUPERVISOR (stonework) 679.130-010
SUPERVISOR (struct. metal) 617.130-010
SUPERVISOR (sugar & conf.) 920.137-018
SUPERVISOR (tobacco) 529.137-026
SUPERVISOR (toy-sport equip.) 732.130-010
SUPERVISOR, ABATTOIR (meat products) 525.131-010

SUPERVISOR, ACCOUNTING CLERKS (clerical) 216.132-010
SUPERVISOR, ACCOUNTS RECEIVABLE (utilities; waterworks) 214.137-022
SUPERVISOR, ACOUSTICAL TILE CARPENTERS (construction) 860.131-010
SUPERVISOR, ADJUSTABLE-STEEL-JOIST-SETTING (construction) 869.134-014
Supervisor, Adult Education (education) 099.117-026
SUPERVISOR, ADVERTISING-DISPATCH CLERKS (print. & pub.) 247.137-010
SUPERVISOR, ADVERTISING-MATERIAL DISTRIBUTORS (business ser.) 230.137-010
SUPERVISOR, AGENCY APPOINTMENTS (insurance) 209.137-018
Supervisor, Agricultural Education (education) 099.117-026
SUPERVISOR, AIR-CONDITIONING INSTALLER (any industry) 827.131-018
SUPERVISOR, AIRCRAFT CLEANING (air trans.) 891.137-014
SUPERVISOR, AIRCRAFT MAINTENANCE (air trans.) 621.131-014
SUPERVISOR, AIRPLANE-FLIGHT ATTENDANT (air trans.) 352.137-010
SUPERVISOR, ALTERATION WORKROOM (retail trade) 785.131-010
SUPERVISOR, ALUMINUM BOAT ASSEMBLY (ship-boat mfg.) 806.131-010
SUPERVISOR, ALUMINUM FABRICATION (ship-boat mfg.) 619.130-014
SUPERVISOR, ALUM PLANT (chemical) 559.132-062
Supervisor, Ammunition-Loading (ordnance) 737.137-018
SUPERVISOR, ANIMAL CRUELTY INVESTIGATION (nonprofit org.) 379.137-010
SUPERVISOR, ANIMAL MAINTENANCE (pharmaceut.) 410.137-018
Supervisor, Anodizing (electroplating) 500.131-010
SUPERVISOR, AREA (agriculture) 401.137-010
SUPERVISOR, ARTIFICIAL BREAST FABRICATION (protective dev.) 712.134-010
SUPERVISOR, ARTIFICIAL BREEDING RANCH (agriculture) 410.131-014
SUPERVISOR, ARTIST, SUSPECT (government ser.) 970.131-014
SUPERVISOR, ASBESTOS-CEMENT SHEET (nonmet. min.) 679.130-018
SUPERVISOR, ASBESTOS PIPE (nonmet. min.) 679.130-014
SUPERVISOR, ASBESTOS REMOVAL (construction) 869.134-026
SUPERVISOR, ASBESTOS TEXTILE (nonmet. min.) 579.137-014
SUPERVISOR, ASPHALT PAVING (construction) 853.133-010
Supervisor, Assembling (rubber goods) 759.137-010
SUPERVISOR, ASSEMBLY (agric. equip.) 801.137-010
Supervisor, Assembly (electron. comp.) 726.134-010
SUPERVISOR, ASSEMBLY (motor-bicycles) 806.131-014
SUPERVISOR, ASSEMBLY (pen & pencil) 733.137-010
SUPERVISOR, ASSEMBLY (woodworking) 769.137-014
SUPERVISOR, ASSEMBLY-AND-PACKING (cutlery-hrdwr.) 701.137-010
SUPERVISOR, ASSEMBLY DEPARTMENT (struct. metal) 809.130-010
SUPERVISOR, ASSEMBLY I (office machines) 710.137-010
Supervisor, Assembly II (office machines) 706.131-014
supervisor, assembly Line (house. appl.) 723.131-010
Supervisor, Assembly Line (inst. & app.) 710.131-042
SUPERVISOR, ASSEMBLY ROOM (fabrication, nec) 739.134-010
SUPERVISOR, ASSEMBLY ROOM (furniture) 669.130-010
Supervisor, Assembly Room (print. & pub.) 653.131-010
SUPERVISOR, ASSEMBLY STOCK (clerical) 222.137-042
SUPERVISOR, AUDIT CLERKS (clerical) 210.132-010
supervisor, automatic cutting machines (glass mfg.) 677.131-010
SUPERVISOR, AUTOMATIC MACHINES (clock & watch) 609.130-022
SUPERVISOR, AUTOMOBILE BODY REPAIR (automotive ser.) 807.137-010
SUPERVISOR, AVIONICS SHOP (air trans.) 823.131-018
Supervisor, Backfilling (construction) 850.137-014
Supervisor, Back Shop (hat & cap) 784.130-010
Supervisor, Bakery Sanitation (bakery products) 529.137-014
Supervisor, Baking (steel & rel.) 549.137-010
Supervisor, Barrel Assembly (wood. container) 764.134-010
Supervisor, Battery Assembly (elec. equip.) 727.130-010
SUPERVISOR, BEAM DEPARTMENT (leather mfg.) 589.134-010
SUPERVISOR, BEATER ROOM (paper & pulp) 530.132-014
SUPERVISOR, BEEHIVE KILN (chemical) 563.137-010
SUPERVISOR, BEET END (sugar & conf.) 529.132-018
SUPERVISOR, BELT-AND-LINK ASSEMBLY (ordnance) 737.137-022
Supervisor, Benzene-Refining (petrol. refin.) 549.132-030
SUPERVISOR, BILLPOSTING (business ser.) 841.137-010
SUPERVISOR, BINDERY (print. & pub.) 653.131-010
SUPERVISOR, BIT AND SHANK DEPARTMENT (fabrication, nec) 739.130-010
SUPERVISOR, BLAST FURNACE (smelt. & refin.) 512.132-022
SUPERVISOR, BLAST FURNACE (steel & rel.) 519.132-010
SUPERVISOR, BLAST-FURNACE-AUXILIARIES (steel & rel.) 519.132-014
Supervisor, Blasting (mine & quarry) 939.137-014
SUPERVISOR, BLEACH (chemical) 559.137-018
Supervisor, Bleach Plant (paper & pulp) 539.132-014
SUPERVISOR, BLOOD-DONOR RECRUITERS (medical ser.) 293.137-010
SUPERVISOR, BLOOMING MILL (steel & rel.) 613.130-010

SUPERVISOR, BLUEPRINTING-AND-PHOTOCOPY (any industry) 979.130-010
Supervisor, Boarding (knitting) 684.137-010
SUPERVISOR, BOARD MILL (concrete prod.) 579.130-010
SUPERVISOR, BOATBUILDERS, WOOD (ship-boat mfg.) 860.131-014
SUPERVISOR, BOAT OUTFITTING (ship-boat mfg.) 806.131-018
Supervisor, Body Assembly (auto. mfg.) 806.134-010
Supervisor, Body Department (hat & cap) 784.130-010
SUPERVISOR, BOILERMAKING (struct. metal) 805.131-010
Supervisor, Boilermaking Shop (struct. metal) 805.131-010
SUPERVISOR, BOILER REPAIR (any industry) 805.137-010
SUPERVISOR, BONDING (textile) 589.137-014
SUPERVISOR, BONE PLANT (chemical) 559.132-066
Supervisor, Border Department (furniture) 780.137-010
SUPERVISOR, BOTTLE-HOUSE CLEANERS (beverage) 529.132-022
Supervisor, Bottle Machines (glass mfg.) 575.130-018
Supervisor, Braid Department (hat & cap) 784.130-010
Supervisor, Braiding (nonmet. min.) 692.130-022
SUPERVISOR, BRAKE REPAIR (r.r. trans.) 622.137-010
SUPERVISOR, BREW HOUSE (beverage) 529.132-026
SUPERVISOR, BRIAR SHOP (fabrication, nec) 761.130-010
SUPERVISOR, BRIDGES AND BUILDINGS (r.r. trans.) 182.167-034
SUPERVISOR, BRINE (chemical) 558.134-010
SUPERVISOR, BRINEYARD (can. & preserv.) 522.134-010
Supervisor, Broadloom (carpet & rug) 687.132-010
Supervisor, Brooder Farm (agriculture) 411.131-010
SUPERVISOR, BROOMMAKING (fabrication, nec) 692.130-026
Supervisor, Buffing-And-Pasting (leather mfg.) 589.130-030
supervisor, building maintenance (any industry) 381.137-010
SUPERVISOR, BURLING AND JOINING (textile) 689.132-010
SUPERVISOR, BURNING, FORMING, AND ASSEMBLY (elec. equip.) 727.130-010
SUPERVISOR, BYPRODUCTS (steel & rel.) 542.132-010
SUPERVISOR, CAB (motor trans.) 913.133-014
Supervisor, Calcining (smelt. & refin.) 519.130-026
SUPERVISOR, CALENDERING (paper & pulp) 534.132-010
Supervisor, Calibration (inst. & app.) 710.131-042
Supervisor, Camp Department (tex. prod., nec) 787.132-010
SUPERVISOR, CANAL-EQUIPMENT MAINTENANCE (waterworks) 899.130-010
SUPERVISOR, CANDLE MAKING (fabrication, nec) 590.132-010
SUPERVISOR, CANDY (sugar & conf.) 529.130-010
Supervisor, Canvas Products (tex. prod., nec) 789.132-018
Supervisor, Capacitor Processing (electron. comp.) 590.130-010
SUPERVISOR, CAP-AND-HAT PRODUCTION (hat & cap) 784.130-010
SUPERVISOR, CAR AND YARD (r.r. trans.) 622.137-014
SUPERVISOR, CARBON ELECTRODES (steel & rel.) 549.137-010
SUPERVISOR, CARBON-PAPER-COATING (pen & pencil) 534.137-010
SUPERVISOR, CARDING (textile) 680.130-010
SUPERVISOR, CARDROOM (amuse. & rec.) 343.137-014
SUPERVISOR, CAR INSTALLATIONS (railroad equip.) 806.137-010
Supervisor, Car-Loading-And-Unloading (motor trans.) 929.137-018
SUPERVISOR, CARPENTERS (construction) 860.131-018
SUPERVISOR, CARTOGRAPHY (profess. & kin.) 018.131-010
SUPERVISOR, CARTON AND CAN SUPPLY (beverage) 920.132-014
Supervisor, Case Loading (beverage) 922.137-018
SUPERVISOR, CASHIERS (hotel & rest.; retail trade) 211.137-010
SUPERVISOR, CASTING-AND-PASTING (elec. equip.) 502.130-010
SUPERVISOR, CD-AREA (chemical) 559.132-070
SUPERVISOR, CELLARS (beverage) 914.132-018
SUPERVISOR, CELL-EFFICIENCY (chemical) 558.134-018
Supervisor, Cell Maintenance (smelt. & refin.) 630.134-010
SUPERVISOR, CELL OPERATION (smelt. & refin.) 519.132-018
SUPERVISOR, CELL ROOM (chemical) 558.134-014
SUPERVISOR, CEMETERY WORKERS (real estate) 406.134-010
SUPERVISOR, CENTRAL SUPPLY (medical ser.) 381.137-014
SUPERVISOR, CEREAL (grain-feed mills) 529.132-030
SUPERVISOR, CHANNEL PROCESS (chemical) 559.137-022
SUPERVISOR, CHAR HOUSE (sugar & conf.) 523.132-010
Supervisor, Chassis Assembly (auto. mfg.) 806.134-010
SUPERVISOR, CHEMICAL (plastic-synth.) 558.132-010
Supervisor, Chicken Hatchery (agriculture) 411.137-010
SUPERVISOR, CHIMNEY CONSTRUCTION (construction) 801.131-010
supervisor, chipping (chemical; saw. & plan.) 564.132-010
Supervisor, Chlorine-Liquefaction (chemical) 559.132-106
SUPERVISOR, CHOCOLATE-AND-COCOA PROCESSING (sugar & conf.) 529.130-014
SUPERVISOR, CHRISTMAS-TREE FARM (forestry) 451.137-014
Supervisor, Cigarette-Filter Making Department (tobacco) 529.137-026
Supervisor, Cigarette-Making Department (tobacco) 529.137-026
Supervisor, Cigarette-Packing Department (tobacco) 529.137-026
SUPERVISOR, CIGAR MAKING, HAND (tobacco) 790.134-010
SUPERVISOR, CIGAR-MAKING MACHINE (tobacco) 529.132-034
Supervisor, Cigar Processing (tobacco) 529.137-026
SUPERVISOR, CIGAR TOBACCO PROCESSING (tobacco) 529.137-034

SUPERVISOR, CIRCUS (amuse. & rec.) 969.137-010
SUPERVISOR, CLAIMS (insurance) 241.137-010
Supervisor, Clam-Bed (fishing & hunt.) 446.133-010
SUPERVISOR, CLASSIFIED ADVERTISING (print. & pub.) 247.137-014
SUPERVISOR, CLAY PREPARATION (pottery & porc.) 570.130-010
SUPERVISOR, CLAY SHOP (pottery & porc.) 774.130-010
SUPERVISOR, CLEANING (beverage; can. & preserv.; dairy products; food prep., nec) 699.137-010
Supervisor, Cleaning And Annealing (steel & rel.) 619.130-018
SUPERVISOR, CLOTH WINDING (tex. prod., nec) 689.130-022
supervisor, coal handling (any industry) 921.137-010
SUPERVISOR, COAL HANDLING (steel & rel.) 549.132-018
SUPERVISOR, COATING (photo. appar.) 534.130-010
SUPERVISOR, COATING (plastic-synth.) 554.137-014
SUPERVISOR, COFFEE (food prep., nec) 529.130-018
Supervisor, Coil And Armature Inspection (elec. equip.) 721.131-014
supervisor, coil springs (metal prod., nec) 619.130-026
Supervisor, Coil Winding (elec. equip.; electron. comp.) 724.130-010
SUPERVISOR, COIL WINDING (elec. equip.) 724.131-010
SUPERVISOR, COIN-MACHINE (svc. ind. mach.) 706.130-010
SUPERVISOR, COKE HANDLING (steel & rel.) 549.132-022
SUPERVISOR, COLD ROLLING (steel & rel.) 619.130-018
Supervisor, Color Making (chemical) 559.132-054
supervisor, color making (chemical) 559.132-122
SUPERVISOR, COLOR-PASTE MIXING (textile) 550.135-010
Supervisor, Commercial Fish Hatchery (fishing & hunt.) 446.134-010
SUPERVISOR, COMMISSARY PRODUCTION (hotel & rest.) 319.137-022
SUPERVISOR, COMMUNICATIONS-AND-SIGNALS (r.r. trans.) 184.167-290
SUPERVISOR, COMPONENT ASSEMBLER (mfd. bldgs.) 762.134-010
SUPERVISOR, COMPOSING-ROOM (print. & pub.) 973.137-010
SUPERVISOR, COMPOUNDING-AND-FINISHING (chemical) 550.137-010
SUPERVISOR, COMPRESSED YEAST (food prep., nec) 520.132-014
SUPERVISOR, COMPUTER OPERATIONS (clerical) 213.132-010
SUPERVISOR, CONCRETE BLOCK PLANT (concrete prod.) 579.130-014
SUPERVISOR, CONCRETE PIPE PLANT (concrete prod.) 579.130-018
SUPERVISOR, CONCRETE-STONE FABRICATING (concrete prod.) 575.131-010
SUPERVISOR, CONCRETE-STONE FINISHING (concrete prod.) 775.131-010
SUPERVISOR, CONDITIONING YARD (steel & rel.) 619.134-010
SUPERVISOR, CONTACT AND SERVICE CLERKS (utilities) 249.137-014
Supervisor, Contact Lens (optical goods) 716.130-010
SUPERVISOR, CONTINGENTS (retail trade) 205.367-050
SUPERVISOR, CONTINUOUS-WELD-PIPE MILL (steel & rel.) 619.130-022
SUPERVISOR, CONTRACT-SHELTERED WORKSHOP (nonprofit org.) 187.134-010
SUPERVISOR, COOK HOUSE (chemical) 559.132-074
SUPERVISOR, COOK ROOM (can. & preserv.) 529.132-038
SUPERVISOR, COOLER SERVICE (svc. ind. mach.) 637.131-010
SUPERVISOR, COOPERAGE SHOP (wood. container) 764.134-010
SUPERVISOR, CORDUROY CUTTING (textile) 585.130-010
SUPERVISOR, CORE DRILLING (construction) 850.137-010
SUPERVISOR, COREMAKER (paper & pulp) 640.132-010
Supervisor, Core Shop (toy-sport equip.) 692.132-018
SUPERVISOR, CORNCOB PIPE MANUFACTURING (fabrication, nec) 739.132-010
SUPERVISOR, CORRESPONDENCE SECTION (insurance) 249.137-018
SUPERVISOR, COSTUMING (motion picture; radio-tv broad.) 962.137-018
supervisor, counseling and guidance (education) 045.117-010
SUPERVISOR, COVERING AND LINING (fabrication, nec) 780.134-010
Supervisor, Crack-Off (glass mfg.) 775.130-010
SUPERVISOR, CREDIT AND LOAN COLLECTIONS (clerical) 241.137-010
Supervisor, Culvert Laying (construction) 859.137-010
SUPERVISOR, CURED-MEAT PACKING (meat products) 529.135-014
SUPERVISOR, CURED MEATS (meat products) 525.132-010
SUPERVISOR, CURING ROOM (tobacco) 529.137-038
SUPERVISOR, CUSTOMER-COMPLAINT SERVICE (clerical) 241.137-014
SUPERVISOR, CUSTOMER RECORDS DIVISION (utilities) 249.137-022
SUPERVISOR, CUSTOMER SERVICES (motor trans.) 248.137-018
SUPERVISOR, CUTTING AND BONING (meat products) 525.131-014
SUPERVISOR, CUTTING-AND-SEWING DEPARTMENT (furniture) 780.131-010
Supervisor, Cutting-And-Sewing Room (furniture) 780.137-010
SUPERVISOR, CUTTING AND SPLICING (motion picture; photofinishing) 976.134-010
SUPERVISOR, CUTTING DEPARTMENT (any industry) 781.134-010
Supervisor, Cutting Department (furniture) 780.131-010
SUPERVISOR, CUTTING DEPARTMENT (pen & pencil) 669.130-014
Supervisor, Cytogenetic Laboratory (medical ser.) 078.261-026
Supervisor, Cytology (medical ser.) 078.281-010
SUPERVISOR, DAIRY FARM (agriculture) 410.131-018
SUPERVISOR, DAIRY PROCESSING (dairy products) 529.131-014
Supervisor, Dairy Sanitation (dairy products) 529.137-014
supervisor, data processing (clerical) 213.132-010

Supervisor, Decaling (pottery & porc.) 749.131-010
SUPERVISOR, DECORATING (glass mfg.) 652.130-010
SUPERVISOR, DECORATING (pottery & porc.) 749.131-010
SUPERVISOR, DEHYDROGENATION (chemical; petrol. refin.) 559.132-078
SUPERVISOR, DELIVERY DEPARTMENT (tel. & tel.) 230.137-014
SUPERVISOR, DENTAL LABORATORY (protective dev.) 712.131-010
Supervisor, Denture Department (protective dev.) 712.131-010
SUPERVISOR, DETASSELING CREW (agriculture) 401.137-014
SUPERVISOR, DIALS (clock & watch) 715.131-014
SUPERVISOR, DIAMOND FINISHING (jewelry-silver.) 770.131-014
SUPERVISOR, DIE CASTING (foundry; smelt. & refin.) 514.130-014
SUPERVISOR, DIMENSION WAREHOUSE (furniture) 769.134-010
SUPERVISOR, DISPLAY FABRICATION (fabrication, nec) 739.134-014
Supervisor, Ditching (construction) 850.137-014
Supervisor, DIVERSIFIED CROPS (agriculture) 407.131-010
SUPERVISOR, DOCK (petrol. refin.; pipe lines) 914.137-018
Supervisor, Dock (steel & rel.) 921.137-010
SUPERVISOR, DOG LICENSE OFFICER (nonprofit org.) 379.137-014
SUPERVISOR, DOPING (construction) 843.134-010
SUPERVISOR, DRAFTING AND PRINTED CIRCUIT DESIGN (profess. & kin.) 003.131-010
Supervisor, Drapery Hanging (motion picture) 962.137-022
SUPERVISOR, DRAWING (nonfer. metal; steel & rel.) 614.132-010
Supervisor, Drawing (textile) 680.130-010
Supervisor, Drawing-in Department (textile) 681.130-010
SUPERVISOR, DRIED YEAST (food prep., nec) 529.132-042
Supervisor, Drilling And Shooting (mine & quarry) 939.137-014
SUPERVISOR, DRY-CELL ASSEMBLY (elec. equip.) 727.137-010
SUPERVISOR, DRY CLEANING (laundry & rel.) 369.137-010
SUPERVISOR, DRYING (millwork-plywood) 563.135-010
Supervisor, Drying-And-Softening (leather mfg.) 589.130-030
SUPERVISOR, DRYING AND WINDING (plastic-synth.) 559.134-014
SUPERVISOR, DRY PASTE (chemical) 559.132-082
SUPERVISOR, DRY-STARCH (grain-feed mills) 529.132-046
SUPERVISOR, DRY-WALL APPLICATION (construction) 842.131-010
Supervisor, Dumping (construction) 859.137-010
Supervisor, Dyeing And Finishing Department (fabrication, nec) 739.137-018
SUPERVISOR, EDGING (glass products) 673.130-010
SUPERVISOR, EDUCATION (education) 099.117-026
supervisor, education and custody (government ser.) 375.367-010
SUPERVISOR, EGG PROCESSING (can. & preserv.; wholesale tr.) 529.137-042
Supervisor, Egg-Producing Farm (agriculture) 411.131-010
SUPERVISOR, ELECTRICAL ASSEMBLIES (elec. equip.; machinery mfg.) 826.131-014
SUPERVISOR, ELECTRICAL ASSEMBLY (elec. equip.) 729.130-010
SUPERVISOR, ELECTRICAL REPAIR AND TELEPHONE LINE MAINTENANCE (utilities) 829.131-022
Supervisor, Electric Motor Testing (elec. equip.) 721.131-014
Supervisor, Electrolytic Tinning (nonfer. metal) 500.131-010
SUPERVISOR, ELECTRONIC COILS (elec. equip.; electron. comp.) 724.130-010
SUPERVISOR, ELECTRONIC CONTROLS REPAIRER (engine-turbine) 828.131-010
Supervisor, Electronics Assembly (electron. comp.; office machines) 726.130-010
Supervisor, Electronics Inspection (electron. comp.) 726.130-010
SUPERVISOR, ELECTRONICS PROCESSING (electron. comp.) 590.130-010
SUPERVISOR, ELECTRONICS PRODUCTION (comm. equip.; electron. comp.) 726.130-010
SUPERVISOR, ELECTRONICS SYSTEMS MAINTENANCE (any industry) 828.161-010
Supervisor, Electronics Testing (electron. comp.) 726.130-010
supervisor, electronic testing (electron. comp.) 726.131-018
Supervisor, Electron-Tube Processing (electron. comp.) 590.130-010
SUPERVISOR, ELECTROTYPING AND STEREOTYPING (print. & pub.) 974.131-010
Supervisor, Elementary Education (education) 099.117-026
SUPERVISOR, ENDLESS TRACK VEHICLE (automotive ser.) 620.131-010
supervisor, energy conservation representative (utilities) 959.137-022
Supervisor, Engine Assembly (auto. mfg.) 806.130-010
SUPERVISOR, ENGINE ASSEMBLY (engine-turbine) 806.130-010
SUPERVISOR, ENGINE-REPAIR (engine-turbine) 625.131-014
supervisor, engraving (furniture) 652.132-010
SUPERVISOR, ENGRAVING (pen & pencil) 704.131-014
Supervisor, Enrobing (sugar & conf.) 529.130-010
SUPERVISOR, EPOXY FABRICATION (brick & tile) 579.134-014
SUPERVISOR, ERECTION SHOP (railroad equip.) 806.131-022
SUPERVISOR, ESTERS-AND-EMULSIFIERS (chemical) 559.132-086
SUPERVISOR, ESTIMATOR AND DRAFTER (utilities) 019.161-010
SUPERVISOR, EVAPORATOR (chemical) 559.137-026
supervisor, excavating (construction) 859.137-010
SUPERVISOR, EXTERMINATION (business ser.) 389.134-010
SUPERVISOR, EXTRUDING DEPARTMENT (plastic prod.) 557.130-010
SUPERVISOR, EXTRUSION (forging) 614.132-014

Supervisor, Extrusion (steel & rel.) 549.137-010
Supervisor, Fabrication (office machines) 706.131-014
SUPERVISOR, FABRICATION (wood prod., nec) 769.130-010
SUPERVISOR, FABRICATION AND ASSEMBLY (toy-sport equip.) 809.131-010
SUPERVISOR, FABRICATION DEPARTMENT (light. fix.) 723.132-010
SUPERVISOR, FACEPIECE LINE (protective dev.) 712.137-010
SUPERVISOR, FARM-EQUIPMENT MAINTENANCE (agric. equip.) 624.131-010
SUPERVISOR, FEED HOUSE (grain-feed mills) 529.132-050
SUPERVISOR, FEED MILL (grain-feed mills) 529.132-054
SUPERVISOR, FELLING-BUCKING (logging) 454.134-010
Supervisor, Felting (tex. prod., nec) 586.130-010
SUPERVISOR, FENCE MANUFACTURE (metal prod., nec) 617.130-014
SUPERVISOR, FERMENTING CELLARS (beverage) 529.132-058
SUPERVISOR, FERRY TERMINAL (water trans.) 911.137-026
SUPERVISOR, FERTILIZER (chemical) 559.132-090
SUPERVISOR, FERTILIZER PROCESSING (chemical) 559.130-014
SUPERVISOR, FIBERGLASS BOAT ASSEMBLY (ship-boat mfg.) 806.134-014
Supervisor, Fiberglass-Ship-Component Assembly (ship-boat mfg.) 806.134-014
SUPERVISOR, FIBER-LOCKING (textile) 689.132-014
Supervisor, Field Assembly-And-Erection (struct. metal) 805.131-010
SUPERVISOR, FIELD-CROP FARMING (agriculture) 404.131-010
SUPERVISOR, FIELD-PIPE-LINES (pipe lines) 914.132-022
SUPERVISOR, FILES (clerical) 206.137-010
SUPERVISOR, FILLING-AND-PACKING (paint & varnish) 920.137-022
SUPERVISOR, FILM PROCESSING (motion picture; photofinishing; radio-tv broad.) 976.131-010
SUPERVISOR, FILM PROCESSING (photofinishing) 976.132-010
Supervisor, Filter Assembly (elec. equip.; electron. comp.) 724.130-010
SUPERVISOR, FILTRATION (sugar & conf.) 529.130-022
Supervisor, Final (electron. comp.) 726.134-010
Supervisor, Final Assembly (auto. mfg.) 806.134-010
SUPERVISOR, FINAL ASSEMBLY AND PACKING (protective dev.) 712.137-014
Supervisor, Fine Grading (construction) 859.137-010
Supervisor, Finish-End (furniture) 669.130-022
Supervisor, Finishing (carpet & rug) 687.132-010
SUPERVISOR, FINISHING (fabrication, nec) 749.134-010
SUPERVISOR, FINISHING (furniture) 742.134-010
SUPERVISOR, FINISHING (glass mfg.) 775.130-010
Supervisor, Finishing (nonmet. min.) 692.130-022
Supervisor, Finishing (toy-sport equip.) 692.132-018
SUPERVISOR, FINISHING-AND-SHIPPING (steel & rel.) 619.132-026
Supervisor, Finishing/Binding (print. & pub.) 653.131-010
supervisor, finishing department (beverage) 529.132-098
Supervisor, Finishing Department (furniture) 780.137-010
Supervisor, Finishing Department (garment) 786.132-010
Supervisor, Finishing Department (hat & cap) 784.130-010
SUPERVISOR, FINISHING DEPARTMENT (nonmet. min.) 679.137-010
SUPERVISOR, FINISHING DEPARTMENT (pen & pencil) 733.137-014
SUPERVISOR, FINISHING DEPARTMENT (photofinishing) 976.137-014
SUPERVISOR, FINISHING ROOM (leather mfg.) 589.130-018
SUPERVISOR, FINISHING ROOM (print. & pub.) 979.137-010
SUPERVISOR, FIREWORKS ASSEMBLY (chemical) 737.131-010
SUPERVISOR, FISH BAIT PROCESSING (toy-sport equip.) 550.132-014
SUPERVISOR, FISH HATCHERY (fishing & hunt.) 446.134-010
SUPERVISOR, FISH PROCESSING (can. & preserv.) 525.134-010
SUPERVISOR, FITTING (any industry) 801.131-014
SUPERVISOR, FLAME CUTTING (steel & rel.) 819.132-010
Supervisor, Fleshing (leather mfg.) 589.130-022
supervisor, floor assembly (elec. equip.) 619.131-010
Supervisor, Flushing (chemical) 559.132-054
SUPERVISOR, FOAM CUTTING (tex. prod., nec) 690.130-022
SUPERVISOR, FOOD CHECKERS AND CASHIERS (hotel & rest.) 211.137-014
SUPERVISOR, FORCE ADJUSTMENT (tel. & tel.) 215.137-018
Supervisor, Forming And Tempering (metal prod., nec) 616.130-018
SUPERVISOR, FORMING DEPARTMENT I (glass mfg.) 575.130-018
SUPERVISOR, FORMING DEPARTMENT II (glass mfg.) 579.130-022
Supervisor, Frame Assembly (motor-bicycles) 806.131-014
SUPERVISOR, FRAME SAMPLE AND PATTERN (furniture) 661.137-010
SUPERVISOR, FRAMING MILL (wood prod., nec) 669.130-018
SUPERVISOR, FRUIT GRADING (wholesale tr.) 529.137-046
Supervisor, Fryer Farm (agriculture) 411.131-010
Supervisor, Fulling (tex. prod., nec) 586.130-010
supervisor, functional testing (electron. comp.) 726.131-018
SUPERVISOR, FUR DRESSING (leather mfg.) 589.130-022
Supervisor, Fur-Floor Worker (leather mfg.) 589.130-022
supervisor, furnace (glass mfg.) 579.137-026
SUPERVISOR, FURNACE PROCESS (chemical) 559.132-094
supervisor, furnace room (glass mfg.) 579.137-026
SUPERVISOR, FURNITURE ASSEMBLY (furniture) 763.134-014
SUPERVISOR, FURRIER SHOP (fur goods) 783.131-010

Supervisor, Fusing Room (optical goods) 716.130-010
SUPERVISOR, GAME FARM (agriculture) 412.131-010
SUPERVISOR, GARAGE (automotive ser.) 620.131-014
SUPERVISOR, GARMENT MANUFACTURING (garment) 786.132-010
SUPERVISOR, GAS METER REPAIR (utilities) 710.131-010
SUPERVISOR, GATE SERVICES (air trans.) 238.137-018
SUPERVISOR, GEAR REPAIR (water trans.) 623.131-014
SUPERVISOR, GELATIN PLANT (chemical) 559.137-030
supervisor, general (mine & quarry) 181.167-018
SUPERVISOR, GLAZING DEPARTMENT (textile) 582.130-010
SUPERVISOR, GLUE SPECIALTY (chemical) 559.137-034
Supervisor, Gluing (woodworking) 769.137-014
SUPERVISOR, GLYCERIN (soap & rel.) 559.132-098
Supervisor, Gold Department (protective dev.) 712.131-010
SUPERVISOR, GRADING (construction) 859.137-010
SUPERVISOR, GRAIN AND YEAST PLANTS (beverage) 529.132-062
Supervisor, Graphite (steel & rel.) 549.137-010
supervisor, grease making (petrol. refin.) 549.132-010
SUPERVISOR, GREASE REFINING (oils & grease) 553.132-010
SUPERVISOR, GREEN END DEPARTMENT (millwork-plywood) 663.132-010
Supervisor, Grid-Casting-And-Pasting (elec. equip.) 502.130-010
SUPERVISOR, GRINDING (any industry) 603.130-010
Supervisor, Grinding (glass mfg.) 775.130-010
Supervisor, Grinding (paint & varnish) 559.132-114
supervisor, grinding (smelt. & refin.) 515.130-010
Supervisor, Grinding And Polishing (optical goods) 716.130-010
SUPERVISOR, GRINDING AND SPRAYING (struct. metal) 809.134-010
supervisor, grips (motion picture) 962.137-010
supervisor, groundwood mill (paper & pulp) 530.132-022
supervisor, grove (agriculture) 403.131-010
SUPERVISOR, HAIRSPRING FABRICATION (clock & watch) 715.131-018
SUPERVISOR, HAND SILVERING (glass products) 574.134-010
Supervisor, Hand Workers (jewelry-silver.; plastic prod.) 700.131-010
Supervisor, Hanging-And-Trimming (leather mfg.) 589.130-030
SUPERVISOR, HARDBOARD (wood prod., nec) 539.130-010
Supervisor, Hard Candy (sugar & conf.) 529.130-010
supervisor, hardening (heat treating) 504.131-010
Supervisor, Harvest-Hat Department (hat & cap) 784.130-010
SUPERVISOR, HARVESTING (chemical) 939.137-022
Supervisor, Heading (wood. container) 764.134-010
SUPERVISOR, HEARING-AID ASSEMBLY (protective dev.) 726.131-014
supervisor, heat treating (heat treating) 504.131-010
SUPERVISOR, HIDE HOUSE (leather mfg.) 922.137-014
Supervisor, Histology (medical ser.) 078.261-030
SUPERVISOR, HISTORIC SITES (government ser.) 102.117-010
Supervisor, Home Economics (education) 099.117-026
SUPERVISOR, HOME-ENERGY CONSULTANT (utilities) 959.137-022
SUPERVISOR, HOME RESTORATION SERVICE (any industry) 389.137-010
SUPERVISOR, HORTICULTURAL-SPECIALTY FARMING (agriculture) 405.131-010
SUPERVISOR, HOSPITALITY HOUSE (amuse. & rec.) 359.137-010
SUPERVISOR, HOT-DIP PLATING (galvanizing) 501.137-010
SUPERVISOR, HOT-DIP-TINNING (steel & rel.) 501.130-010
SUPERVISOR, HOT-STRIP MILL (steel & rel.) 613.132-010
SUPERVISOR, HOT-WOUND SPRING PRODUCTION (metal prod., nec) 619.130-026
SUPERVISOR, HOUSECLEANER (hotel & rest.) 323.137-010
SUPERVISOR, HYDROCHLORIC AREA (chemical) 558.134-022
SUPERVISOR I (button & notion) 692.130-018
SUPERVISOR I (chemical) 559.132-054
SUPERVISOR I (fabrication, nec) 739.131-010
SUPERVISOR I (nonmet. min.) 779.131-010
SUPERVISOR I (protective dev.) 692.137-014
SUPERVISOR I (rubber goods) 759.137-010
SUPERVISOR I (tex. prod., nec) 789.132-014
SUPERVISOR, ICE HOUSE (food prep., nec) 523.137-010
SUPERVISOR, ICE STORAGE, SALE, AND DELIVERY (food prep., nec) 299.137-022
SUPERVISOR, IDENTIFICATION AND COMMUNICATIONS (government ser.) 377.134-010
SUPERVISOR II (button & notion) 734.131-010
SUPERVISOR II (chemical) 550.132-010
SUPERVISOR II (fabrication, nec) 739.131-014
SUPERVISOR II (nonmet. min.) 579.132-010
SUPERVISOR II (protective dev.) 789.134-014
SUPERVISOR II (rubber goods) 559.137-014
SUPERVISOR II (tex. prod., nec) 789.134-010
SUPERVISOR III (button & notion) 690.130-010
SUPERVISOR III (fabrication, nec) 549.132-014
SUPERVISOR III (nonmet. min.) 575.130-014
SUPERVISOR III (tex. prod., nec) 789.132-018
SUPERVISOR, INCINERATOR PLANT (sanitary ser.) 955.131-010
supervisor, in-circuit testing (electron. comp.) 726.131-018
Supervisor, Incising (wood prod., nec) 561.131-010

Supervisor, Industrial Arts Education (education) 099.117-026
supervisor, industrial garment (laundry & rel.) 222.137-014
SUPERVISOR, INSECT AND DISEASE INSPECTION (agriculture) 408.137-010
SUPERVISOR, INSECTICIDE (chemical) 559.132-102
Supervisor, Inspect, Clean-Up, And Wrap (furniture) 920.137-026
Supervisor, Inspecting (knitting) 685.130-010
Supervisor, Inspecting (optical goods) 716.130-010
SUPERVISOR, INSPECTING (paper goods) 979.137-014
SUPERVISOR, INSPECTION (agric. equip.) 801.137-014
SUPERVISOR, INSPECTION (aircraft mfg.) 806.131-038
SUPERVISOR, INSPECTION (clock & watch) 715.131-022
SUPERVISOR, INSPECTION (glass mfg.) 579.134-010
Supervisor, Inspection (inst. & app.) 710.131-042
Supervisor, Inspection (office machines) 706.131-014
SUPERVISOR, INSPECTION (pen & pencil) 733.137-018
SUPERVISOR, INSPECTION (plastic-synth.) 559.137-038
SUPERVISOR, INSPECTION (sugar & conf.) 529.137-074
SUPERVISOR, INSPECTION AND TESTING (elec. equip.) 721.131-014
SUPERVISOR, INSPECTION AND TESTING (motor-bicycles) 806.131-026
Supervisor, Inspection Department (garment) 786.132-010
Supervisor, Inspection Room (sugar & conf.) 920.137-018
SUPERVISOR, INSTANT POTATO PROCESSING (food prep., nec) 529.137-078
SUPERVISOR, INSTRUMENT ASSEMBLY (electron. comp.; inst. & app.) 710.131-038
SUPERVISOR, INSTRUMENT MAINTENANCE (any industry) 710.131-014
SUPERVISOR, INSTRUMENT MECHANICS (utilities) 710.131-018
SUPERVISOR, INSTRUMENT REPAIR (any industry) 710.131-022
SUPERVISOR, INSULATION (construction) 863.131-010
SUPERVISOR, INSULATION (nonmet. min.) 590.130-014
Supervisor, Integrated Circuit Manufacturing (electron. comp.) 590.130-010
Supervisor, Intermediates (chemical) 559.132-054
supervisor, ironworking (construction) 801.134-010
supervisor, irrigation (agriculture) 409.137-010
SUPERVISOR IV (nonmet. min.) 692.132-010
SUPERVISOR IV (tex. prod., nec) 789.132-010
SUPERVISOR, JANITORIAL SERVICES (any industry) 381.137-010
SUPERVISOR, JEWELRY DEPARTMENT (jewelry-silver.) 700.131-014
SUPERVISOR, JOINERS (ship-boat mfg.) 860.131-022
supervisor, kashruth (hotel & rest.) 319.137-026
SUPERVISOR, KENNEL (nonprofit org.) 410.134-018
SUPERVISOR, KEYMODULE ASSEMBLY (office machines) 692.130-038
Supervisor, Knitting I (knitting) 684.137-010
SUPERVISOR, KNITTING II (knitting) 685.130-010
SUPERVISOR, KOSHER DIETARY SERVICE (hotel & rest.) 319.137-026
SUPERVISOR, LABORATORY (textile) 689.134-026
SUPERVISOR, LABORATORY ANIMAL FACILITY (agriculture) 418.137-010
SUPERVISOR, LABOR GANG (any industry) 899.133-010
SUPERVISOR, LABOR GANG (construction) 850.137-010
SUPERVISOR, LACE TEARING (tex. prod., nec) 689.134-014
SUPERVISOR, LAMP SHADES (fabrication, nec) 739.137-014
SUPERVISOR, LANDSCAPE (museums; waterworks) 406.134-014
SUPERVISOR, LAST-MODEL DEPARTMENT (wood prod., nec) 761.131-010
SUPERVISOR, LATHING (construction) 842.131-014
SUPERVISOR, LAUNDRY (laundry & rel.) 361.137-010
supervisor, layout (print. & pub.) 979.131-010
Supervisor, Lead Burning (elec. equip.) 727.130-010
SUPERVISOR, LEAD REFINERY (smelt. & refin.) 519.130-018
Supervisor, Leaf-Spring Fabrication (metal prod., nec) 616.130-018
Supervisor, Leaf-Spring Repair (metal prod., nec) 616.130-018
SUPERVISOR, LENDING ACTIVITIES (financial) 249.137-034
Supervisor, Lens Generating (optical goods) 716.130-010
SUPERVISOR, LIME (concrete prod.) 579.132-014
SUPERVISOR, LINE (any industry) 619.130-030
SUPERVISOR, LINE DEPARTMENT (r.r. trans.) 825.137-010
SUPERVISOR, LIQUEFACTION-AND-REGASIFICATION (utilities) 953.132-010
SUPERVISOR, LIQUEFACTION (chemical) 559.132-106
SUPERVISOR, LIQUID YEAST (food prep., nec) 529.132-066
SUPERVISOR, LIQUOR STORES AND AGENCIES (government ser.) 185.167-062
SUPERVISOR, LITHARGE (paint & varnish) 559.132-110
SUPERVISOR, LIVESTOCK-YARD (any industry) 410.134-010
SUPERVISOR, LOADING AND UNLOADING (any industry) 922.137-018
Supervisor, Loading (any industry) 922.137-018
supervisor, loading (construction; mfd. bldgs.) 921.137-014
SUPERVISOR, LOCOMOTIVE (r.r. trans.) 910.137-010
SUPERVISOR, LOGGING (logging) 459.133-010
SUPERVISOR, LOG SORTING (logging; millwork-plywood) 455.134-010
Supervisor, Long Goods (food prep., nec) 529.132-110
Supervisor, Looping I (knitting) 684.137-010
Supervisor, Looping II (knitting) 685.130-010

Supervisor, Lost And Found (air trans.; motor trans.) 241.137-014
SUPERVISOR, LUBRICATION (any industry) 699.131-010
SUPERVISOR, LUMP ROOM (tobacco) 520.137-010
SUPERVISOR, MACHINE SETTER (any industry) 619.130-034
Supervisor, Machine Workers (jewelry-silver.; plastic prod.) 700.131-010
SUPERVISOR, MACHINING (woodworking) 669.130-022
SUPERVISOR, MAIL CARRIERS (government ser.) 230.137-018
SUPERVISOR, MAILS (government ser.) 243.137-010
SUPERVISOR, MAINSPRING FABRICATION (clock & watch) 715.131-026
SUPERVISOR, MAINTENANCE (chemical) 382.137-010
SUPERVISOR, MAINTENANCE (petrol. refin.) 899.137-018
Supervisor, Maintenance And Custodians (education) 381.137-010
SUPERVISOR, MAJOR APPLIANCE ASSEMBLY (house. appl.) 827.131-014
SUPERVISOR, MALTED MILK (dairy products) 529.132-070
SUPERVISOR, MALT HOUSE (beverage) 522.132-010
SUPERVISOR, MANUFACTURED BUILDINGS (mfd. bldgs.; vehicles, nec) 869.131-030
SUPERVISOR, MAPLE PRODUCTS (food prep., nec) 529.137-050
SUPERVISOR, MAPPING (petrol. & gas; pipe lines) 018.167-030
SUPERVISOR, MARBLE (construction) 861.131-022
SUPERVISOR, MARINA SALES AND SERVICE (retail trade) 299.137-026
SUPERVISOR, MARKING ROOM (retail trade) 209.137-026
SUPERVISOR, MATRIX (recording) 500.134-010
SUPERVISOR, MATTRESS AND BOXSPRINGS (furniture) 780.137-010
Supervisor Mechanic, Boilermaking (struct. metal) 805.131-010
SUPERVISOR, MELT HOUSE (sugar & conf.) 522.130-010
Supervisor, Mending I (knitting) 684.137-010
Supervisor, Mending II (knitting) 685.130-010
SUPERVISOR, MERCHANT-MILL ROLLING AND FINISHING (steel & rel.) 613.130-014
SUPERVISOR, METAL CANS (tinware) 703.132-010
SUPERVISOR, METAL FABRICATING (any industry) 809.130-014
SUPERVISOR, METAL FURNITURE ASSEMBLY (furniture) 709.134-010
Supervisor, Metal Furniture Fabrication (furniture) 619.130-030
SUPERVISOR, METAL HANGING (mfd. bldgs.) 809.134-014
SUPERVISOR, METALIZING (any industry) 505.130-010
SUPERVISOR, METALLURGICAL-AND-QUALITY-CONTROL-TESTING (profess. & kin.) 011.161-010
supervisor, metal placing (construction) 801.134-010
SUPERVISOR, METER-AND-REGULATOR SHOP (petrol. refin.; utilities) 710.137-014
SUPERVISOR, METER REPAIR SHOP (utilities) 710.131-026
SUPERVISOR, METER SHOP (waterworks) 710.131-030
Supervisor, Microbiology Technologists (medical ser.) 078.261-014
SUPERVISOR, MICROFILM DUPLICATING UNIT (business ser.) 976.131-018
SUPERVISOR, MICROWAVE (radio-tv broad.) 003.167-058
SUPERVISOR, MILL (tex. prod., nec) 589.130-026
SUPERVISOR, MILL HOUSE (grain-feed mills) 529.132-074
SUPERVISOR, MINE (mine & quarry) 181.167-018
SUPERVISOR, MIRROR FABRICATION (glass products) 679.137-014
SUPERVISOR, MIRROR MANUFACTURING DEPARTMENT (glass products) 579.131-010
SUPERVISOR, MIXING (tex. prod., nec) 680.135-010
SUPERVISOR, MIXING (textile) 680.130-014
Supervisor, Mixing (paint & varnish) 559.132-114
SUPERVISOR, MIXING PLACE (construction) 853.137-010
SUPERVISOR, MODEL MAKING (clock & watch) 693.130-010
Supervisor, Model Making (toy-sport equip.) 731.131-010
Supervisor, Modern Languages (education) 099.117-026
SUPERVISOR, MOLD CLEANING AND STORAGE (glass mfg.) 579.137-018
SUPERVISOR, MOLD CONSTRUCTION (concrete prod.) 860.131-026
Supervisor, Molding (nonmet. min.) 679.130-014
SUPERVISOR, MOLD MAKING (glass mfg.) 609.131-014
SUPERVISOR, MOLD-MAKING PLASTICS SHEETS (plastic-synth.) 579.137-022
SUPERVISOR, MOLD SHOP (glass mfg.) 609.131-018
SUPERVISOR, MOLD SHOP (pottery & porc.) 777.131-010
SUPERVISOR, MOLD YARD (steel & rel.) 519.137-010
SUPERVISOR, MONEY-ROOM (amuse. & rec.) 211.137-018
SUPERVISOR, MOTION-PICTURE EQUIPMENT (motion picture; photo. appar.) 714.131-010
Supervisor, Motorcycle And Wheel Assembly (motor-bicycles) 806.131-014
SUPERVISOR, MOTORCYCLE REPAIR SHOP (automotive ser.) 620.131-018
Supervisor, Motor Vehicle Assembly (auto. mfg.) 806.134-010
Supervisor, Multifocal Lens (optical goods) 716.130-010
SUPERVISOR, NATURAL-GAS-FIELD PROCESSING (petrol. & gas; pipe lines) 549.131-010
SUPERVISOR, NATURAL-GAS PLANT (petrol. refin.) 542.130-010
SUPERVISOR, NET MAKING (toy-sport equip.) 789.132-022
SUPERVISOR, NETWORK CONTROL OPERATORS (any industry) 031.132-010
Supervisor, Newspaper Deliveries (wholesale tr.) 292.137-014
SUPERVISOR, NUT PROCESSING (can. & preserv.) 529.130-026

SUPERVISOR, NUTRITIONAL YEAST (food prep., nec) 529.132-078
SUPERVISOR OF COMMUNICATIONS (any industry) 184.167-230
Supervisor, Offset-Plate Preparation (print. & pub.) 972.137-010
supervisor of guidance and testing (education) 045.117-010
supervisor of research (education) 045.117-010
SUPERVISOR OF SALES (business ser.) 185.157-014
SUPERVISOR OF WAY (r.r. trans.) 184.167-234
SUPERVISOR, OPEN-HEARTH STOCKYARD (steel & rel.) 922.137-022
Supervisor, Opening And Picking (textile) 680.130-010
SUPERVISOR, OPERATIONS (utilities) 952.137-026
SUPERVISOR, OPTICAL INSTRUMENTS (inst. & app.) 711.137-010
supervisor, orchard (agriculture) 403.131-010
SUPERVISOR, ORDER TAKERS (clerical) 249.137-026
SUPERVISOR, ORDNANCE TRUCK INSTALLATION (ordnance) 806.137-014
supervisor, ore dressing (smelt. & refin.) 515.130-010
SUPERVISOR, ORNAMENTAL IRONWORKING (construction) 809.131-014
SUPERVISOR, OVENS (steel & rel.) 542.132-014
Supervisor, Oyster Farm (fishing & hunt.) 446.133-010
SUPERVISOR, PACKING (boot & shoe) 788.137-010
Supervisor, Packing (glass products) 920.137-026
SUPERVISOR, PACKING (sugar & conf.) 920.130-010
SUPERVISOR, PACKING AND WRAPPING (any industry) 920.137-026
SUPERVISOR, PACKING ROOM (leather mfg.) 589.137-010
SUPERVISOR, PAINT (paint & varnish) 559.132-114
SUPERVISOR, PAINT DEPARTMENT (any industry) 749.131-014
SUPERVISOR, PAINTING (construction) 840.131-010
SUPERVISOR, PAINTING DEPARTMENT (pen & pencil) 692.137-010
SUPERVISOR, PAINTING, SHIPYARD (ship-boat mfg.) 840.131-014
SUPERVISOR, PAINT ROLLER COVERS (fabrication, nec) 692.130-030
Supervisor, Pairing And Inspecting (knitting) 684.137-010
SUPERVISOR, PAPER COATING (paper & pulp; paper goods) 534.132-014
SUPERVISOR, PAPER MACHINE (paper & pulp) 539.132-010
SUPERVISOR, PAPER PRODUCTS (paper goods) 649.130-010
SUPERVISOR, PAPER TESTING (paper & pulp; paper goods) 539.134-010
SUPERVISOR, PARACHUTE MANUFACTURING (tex. prod., nec) 789.132-026
SUPERVISOR, PARKING LOT (automotive ser.) 915.133-010
Supervisor, Partial Denture Department (protective dev.) 712.131-010
SUPERVISOR, PARTICLEBOARD (wood prod., nec) 569.132-010
SUPERVISOR, PASTE MIXING (chemical) 550.137-014
SUPERVISOR, PASTE PLANT (steel & rel.) 549.132-026
Supervisor, Patching (construction) 853.133-010
Supervisor, Patching Department (fabrication, nec) 739.137-018
SUPERVISOR, PATTERN MARKING (garment) 781.131-010
SUPERVISOR, PAYROLL (clerical) 215.137-014
supervisor, permits, easements, and right-of-way (any industry) 191.117-050
SUPERVISOR, PERSONNEL CLERKS (clerical) 209.132-010
SUPERVISOR, PHOSPHATIC FERTILIZER (chemical) 558.130-010
SUPERVISOR, PHOSPHORIC ACID (chemical) 558.132-014
SUPERVISOR, PHOSPHORUS PROCESSING (chemical) 559.132-118
Supervisor, Photocomposition (print. & pub.) 650.132-010
SUPERVISOR, PHOTOENGRAVING (print. & pub.) 971.131-010
Supervisor, Photostat (any industry) 979.130-010
SUPERVISOR, PICKING (tobacco) 521.137-010
SUPERVISOR, PICKING CREW (agriculture) 409.131-010
SUPERVISOR, PIG-MACHINE (steel & rel.) 514.137-010
SUPERVISOR, PIGMENT MAKING (chemical) 559.132-122
SUPERVISOR, PILE DRIVING (construction) 859.137-014
SUPERVISOR, PIPE FINISHING (steel & rel.) 619.130-038
SUPERVISOR, PIPE JOINTS (brick & tile) 590.134-010
SUPERVISOR, PIPE-LINE MAINTENANCE (pipe lines) 869.134-018
SUPERVISOR, PIPE-LINES (petrol. & gas) 862.131-022
SUPERVISOR, PIPE MANUFACTURE (fabrication, nec) 739.137-018
SUPERVISOR, PIT-AND-AUXILIARIES (steel & rel.) 514.137-014
SUPERVISOR, PLASTERING (construction) 842.131-018
SUPERVISOR, PLASTICS (toy-sport equip.) 556.130-014
SUPERVISOR, PLASTIC SHEETS (plastic prod.) 557.130-014
SUPERVISOR, PLASTICS PRODUCTION (boot & shoe; inst. & app.; plastic prod.; plastic-synth.) 556.130-010
Supervisor, Plate Forming (elec. equip.) 727.130-010
SUPERVISOR, PLATE HEATING, ROLLING, AND FINISHING (steel & rel.) 619.132-030
Supervisor, Plate Pasting (elec. equip.) 502.130-010
SUPERVISOR, PLATING AND POINT ASSEMBLY (pen & pencil) 733.130-010
SUPERVISOR, PLEATING (tex. prod., nec) 583.137-010
Supervisor, Pole Yard (wood prod., nec) 669.130-018
SUPERVISOR, POLICY-CHANGE CLERKS (insurance) 219.132-010
Supervisor, Polishing (glass mfg.) 775.130-010
SUPERVISOR, POND (chemical) 939.130-010
Supervisor, Porcelain Department (protective dev.) 712.131-010
Supervisor, Post-Wave (electron. comp.) 726.134-010
SUPERVISOR, POULTRY FARM (agriculture) 411.131-010
SUPERVISOR, POULTRY HATCHERY (agriculture) 411.137-010

SUPERVISOR, POULTRY PROCESSING (meat products) 525.134-014
Supervisor, Powder-And-Primer-Canning (ordnance) 737.137-018
SUPERVISOR, POWDERED METAL (nonfer. metal; steel & rel.) 509.130-010
SUPERVISOR, POWDERED SUGAR (sugar & conf.) 521.130-014
SUPERVISOR, POWER-REACTOR (chemical) 509.130-014
SUPERVISOR, PRECAST AND PRESTRESSED CONCRETE (concrete prod.) 575.131-014
Supervisor, Precision Optical Elements (optical goods) 716.130-010
supervisor, prep (print. & pub.) 972.137-010
SUPERVISOR, PREPARATION DEPARTMENT (textile) 681.130-010
SUPERVISOR, PREPARATION PLANT (mine & quarry) 549.137-014
SUPERVISOR, PREPRESS (print. & pub.) 972.137-010
SUPERVISOR, PRESSING DEPARTMENT (garment) 583.132-010
SUPERVISOR, PRESS ROOM (print. & pub.) 651.130-010
Supervisor, Pre-Wave (electron. comp.) 726.134-010
SUPERVISOR, PRINTED CIRCUIT BOARD ASSEMBLY (electron. comp.) 726.134-010
Supervisor, Printed Circuit Board Processing (electron. comp.) 590.130-010
SUPERVISOR, PRINTED CIRCUIT BOARD TESTING (electron. comp.) 726.131-018
Supervisor, Printing (rubber goods) 759.137-010
SUPERVISOR, PRINTING AND STAMPING (jewelry-silver.; leather prod.) 652.130-014
Supervisor, Printing Department (print. & pub.) 979.130-014
SUPERVISOR, PRINT LINE (furniture) 652.132-010
SUPERVISOR, PRINT SHOP (print. & pub.) 979.130-014
SUPERVISOR, PROCESSING (chemical) 551.130-010
SUPERVISOR, PROCESSING (sugar & conf.) 529.137-082
Supervisor, Process Testing (electron. comp.) 590.130-010
SUPERVISOR, PRODUCT INSPECTION (textile) 689.134-018
SUPERVISOR, PRODUCTION (paper goods) 979.137-018
SUPERVISOR, PRODUCTION (petrol. & gas) 939.131-014
SUPERVISOR, PRODUCTION (tex. prod., nec) 589.135-010
supervisor, production (tex. prod., nec) 689.130-010
SUPERVISOR, PRODUCTION CLERKS (clerical) 221.137-014
SUPERVISOR, PRODUCTION CONTROL (clerical) 221.137-018
SUPERVISOR, PRODUCTION DEPARTMENT (aircraft mfg.) 806.131-042
Supervisor, Propellant-Charge-Loading (ordnance) 737.137-018
SUPERVISOR, PROPERTIES (motion picture) 962.137-026
SUPERVISOR, PROP-MAKING (motion picture) 962.137-022
SUPERVISOR, PROTECTIVE-SIGNAL OPERATIONS (business ser.) 379.137-022
SUPERVISOR, PUBLICATIONS PRODUCTION (print. & pub.) 979.131-010
supervisor, publications (profess. & kin.) 132.017-018
supervisor, public-health nursing (medical ser.) 075.127-026
SUPERVISOR, PUBLIC MESSAGE SERVICE (tel. & tel.) 239.137-026
Supervisor, Pullet Farm (agriculture) 411.131-010
SUPERVISOR, PULP HOUSE (sugar & conf.) 529.130-030
SUPERVISOR, PULP PLANT (paper & pulp) 539.132-014
SUPERVISOR, PUMPING (smelt. & refin.) 914.131-010
SUPERVISOR, PUMPING STATION (waterworks) 954.130-010
SUPERVISOR, PUNCH-AND-ASSEMBLY DEPARTMENT (elec. equip.) 619.130-042
SUPERVISOR, PURIFICATION (petrol. refin.) 549.132-030
SUPERVISOR, PUTTY AND CALKING (paint & varnish) 559.137-042
Supervisor, Pyrotechnic-Loading (ordnance) 737.137-018
Supervisor, Quality Control (electron. comp.) 726.134-010
SUPERVISOR, QUALITY CONTROL (furniture) 763.134-010
SUPERVISOR, QUALITY CONTROL (photofinishing) 976.131-022
SUPERVISOR, QUILTING (textile) 689.134-022
SUPERVISOR, RADIO INTERFERENCE (electron. comp.) 823.131-022
SUPERVISOR, RAG ROOM (paper & pulp) 539.137-010
SUPERVISOR, RAILROAD CAR REPAIR (railroad equip.) 622.131-010
SUPERVISOR, REACTOR FUELING (chemical) 929.132-010
SUPERVISOR, READY-MIXED FOOD PREPARATION (food prep., nec) 529.137-054
SUPERVISOR, REAL-ESTATE OFFICE (real estate) 249.137-030
SUPERVISOR, RECEIVING AND PROCESSING (glass mfg.) 579.137-026
SUPERVISOR, RECLAMATION (mine & quarry) 850.133-010
SUPERVISOR, RECLAMATION (wholesale tr.) 621.137-010
SUPERVISOR, RECORD PRESS (recording) 559.130-018
supervisor, records change (insurance) 219.132-010
SUPERVISOR, REFINING (chemical) 559.132-126
SUPERVISOR, REFINING (sugar & conf.) 529.130-034
SUPERVISOR, REFRACTORY PRODUCTS (brick & tile) 579.134-018
SUPERVISOR, REINFORCED-STEEL-PLACING (construction) 801.134-010
Supervisor, Remelt (sugar & conf.) 522.130-010
SUPERVISOR, REPULPING (paper & pulp) 539.132-018
SUPERVISOR, RESEARCH DAIRY FARM (agriculture) 410.134-022
SUPERVISOR, RESEARCH KENNEL (agriculture) 418.137-014
supervisor, research shop (petrol. & gas) 710.131-034
SUPERVISOR, REVERBERATORY FURNACE (smelt. & refin.) 519.130-022
Supervisor, Rework (inst. & app.) 710.131-042
SUPERVISOR, RICE MILLING (grain-feed mills) 521.131-010

SUPERVISOR, RIDE ASSEMBLY (amuse. & rec.) 801.131-018
SUPERVISOR, RIDES (amuse. & rec.) 342.137-010
SUPERVISOR, RIGGER (ship-boat mfg.) 806.131-030
SUPERVISOR, RIGHT-OF-WAY MAINTENANCE (utilities) 859.133-010
SUPERVISOR, RIPRAP PLACING (construction) 850.137-018
Supervisor, Riveting (construction) 809.131-018
SUPERVISOR, ROCKET PROPELLANT PLANT (ordnance) 559.137-046
supervisor, rod placing (construction) 801.134-010
Supervisor, Roe Processing (can. & preserv.) 529.137-062
SUPERVISOR, ROLLER PRINTING (textile) 652.130-018
SUPERVISOR, ROLLER SHOP (textile) 979.131-014
supervisor, rolling room (tobacco) 520.137-010
SUPERVISOR, ROLL SHOP (steel & rel.) 604.130-010
SUPERVISOR, ROOFING PLANT (build. mat., nec) 590.130-018
SUPERVISOR, ROSE-GRADING (agriculture) 405.137-010
Supervisor, Rough-End (furniture) 669.130-022
Supervisor, Rough Grading (construction) 859.137-010
SUPERVISOR, ROUNDHOUSE (railroad equip.) 622.131-014
SUPERVISOR, ROUTE SALES-DELIVERY DRIVERS (retail trade; wholesale tr.) 292.137-014
Supervisor, Roving (textile) 680.130-010
SUPERVISOR, ROVING DEPARTMENT (textile) 689.130-026
Supervisor, Rubber Covering (textile) 681.130-014
SUPERVISOR, RUBBER STAMPS AND DIES (pen & pencil) 733.131-010
SUPERVISOR, RUG CLEANING (laundry & rel.) 369.137-014
Supervisor, Ruling (paper products; print. & pub.) 653.131-010
SUPERVISOR, SAFETY DEPOSIT (financial) 295.137-010
SUPERVISOR, SALVAGE (petrol. refin.) 929.131-010
SUPERVISOR, SAMPLE (plastic-synth.) 754.137-010
SUPERVISOR, SAMPLE PREPARATION (textile) 979.137-022
SUPERVISOR, SANDBLASTER (ship-boat mfg.) 503.137-010
Supervisor, Sanding (toy-sport equip.) 692.132-018
SUPERVISOR, SANDING (woodworking) 662.132-010
Supervisor, Sanding Department (fabrication, nec) 739.137-018
SUPERVISOR, SAWING AND ASSEMBLY (furniture) 669.132-010
SUPERVISOR, SAWMILL (saw. & plan.) 669.130-026
SUPERVISOR, SCENIC ARTS (motion picture; radio-tv broad.) 149.031-010
SUPERVISOR, SCOURING PADS (nonmet. min.) 759.135-010
SUPERVISOR, SCRAP PREPARATION (steel & rel.) 519.137-014
SUPERVISOR, SCREEN MAKING (textile) 971.131-014
SUPERVISOR, SCREEN PRINTING (textile) 652.137-014
Supervisor, Seaming (knitting) 684.137-010
Supervisor, Seat Assembly (auto. mfg.) 806.134-010
SUPERVISOR, SECURITIES VAULT (financial) 216.132-014
Supervisor, Self-Service Store (government ser.) 185.167-062
Supervisor, Semiconductor Wafer Manufacturing (electron. comp.) 590.130-010
SUPERVISOR, SEWER MAINTENANCE (government ser.) 851.137-014
SUPERVISOR, SEWER SYSTEM (waterworks) 184.167-238
SUPERVISOR, SEWING DEPARTMENT (carpet & rug) 689.137-010
Supervisor, Sewing Department (furniture) 780.131-010
Supervisor, Sewing Department (hat & cap) 784.130-010
SUPERVISOR, SEWING ROOM (fabrication, nec) 787.132-014
Supervisor, Sewing Room (garment) 786.132-010
Supervisor, Shaving-And-Splitting (leather mfg.) 589.130-030
SUPERVISOR, SHEARING (any industry) 615.132-010
Supervisor, Shearing (leather mfg.) 589.130-022
SUPERVISOR, SHED WORKERS (agriculture) 404.131-014
SUPERVISOR, SHEET MANUFACTURING (smelt. & refin.) 500.132-010
SUPERVISOR, SHELLFISH FARMING (fishing & hunt.) 446.133-010
SUPERVISOR, SHIPFITTERS (ship-boat mfg.) 806.131-034
supervisor, ship maintenance services (ship-boat mfg.) 891.131-010
Supervisor, Shipping (bakery products) 922.137-018
SUPERVISOR, SHIPPING (chemical) 550.137-018
Supervisor, Shipping (plastic-synth.) 690.130-014
Supervisor, Shipping Room (beverage) 922.137-018
SUPERVISOR, SHIPPING TRACK (railroad equip.) 806.137-018
SUPERVISOR, SHOP (fabrication, nec) 692.130-042
SUPERVISOR, SHOP (petrol. & gas) 710.131-034
Supervisor, Short Goods (food prep., nec) 529.132-110
SUPERVISOR, SHOW OPERATIONS (amuse. & rec.) 969.137-014
Supervisor, Shrimp Pond (fishing & hunt.) 446.133-010
SUPERVISOR, SHUTTLE FITTING (woodworking) 669.130-030
SUPERVISOR, SHUTTLE PREPARATION (woodworking) 669.130-034
SUPERVISOR, SHUTTLE VENEERING (woodworking) 669.130-038
SUPERVISOR, SIGN SHOP (fabrication, nec) 970.137-010
SUPERVISOR, SILK-SCREEN CUTTING AND PRINTING (any industry) 979.131-018
SUPERVISOR, SILVERING DEPARTMENT (glass products) 574.132-014
SUPERVISOR, SINTERING PLANT (smelt. & refin.) 519.130-026
SUPERVISOR, SKI PRODUCTION (toy-sport equip.) 692.132-018
Supervisor, Slashing Department (textile) 681.130-010
SUPERVISOR, SLATE SPLITTING (stonework) 771.137-010
Supervisor, Sleeping-Bag Department (tex. prod., nec) 787.132-010
SUPERVISOR, SLITTING-AND-SHIPPING (plastic-synth.) 690.130-014
SUPERVISOR, SMALL APPLIANCE ASSEMBLY (house. appl.) 723.131-010

SUPERVISOR, SMOKE CONTROL (steel & rel.) 861.134-010
SUPERVISOR, SOAKERS (beverage) 529.132-082
SUPERVISOR, SOAKING PITS (steel & rel.) 509.132-010
SUPERVISOR, SOFT SUGAR (sugar & conf.) 529.130-038
Supervisor, Soldering (office machines) 706.131-014
SUPERVISOR, SOLDER MAKING (nonfer. metal) 519.132-022
SUPERVISOR, SOUND TECHNICIAN (business ser.) 823.131-026
SUPERVISOR, SPECIAL EDUCATION (education) 094.167-010
Supervisor, Special Effects (motion picture) 962.137-022
SUPERVISOR, SPECIAL SERVICES (education) 169.267-026
SUPERVISOR, SPECIALTY FOOD PRODUCTS (can. & preserv.; meat products) 529.137-062
SUPERVISOR, SPECIALTY MANUFACTURING (steel & rel.) 616.130-014
SUPERVISOR, SPECIALTY PLANT (petrol. refin.) 549.137-018
SUPERVISOR, SPINNING (textile) 682.130-010
SUPERVISOR, SPINNING AND WINDING (plastic-synth.) 689.130-038
SUPERVISOR, SPLIT AND DRUM ROOM (leather mfg.) 589.132-014
SUPERVISOR, SPLIT LEATHER DEPARTMENT (leather mfg.) 589.130-030
SUPERVISOR, SPRAY, LAWN AND TREE SERVICE (agriculture) 408.131-010
SUPERVISOR, SPRING PRODUCTION (metal prod., nec) 616.130-018
SUPERVISOR, SPRING-UP (furniture) 780.134-014
Supervisor, Stage Carpentry (motion picture) 962.137-022
SUPERVISOR, STATEMENT CLERKS (financial) 214.137-014
SUPERVISOR, STAVE CUTTING (wood. container) 667.137-010
Supervisor, Stave Finishing (wood. container) 764.134-010
SUPERVISOR, STEEL DIVISION (furniture) 616.130-022
SUPERVISOR, STEFFEN HOUSE (sugar & conf.) 529.132-086
SUPERVISOR, STENO POOL (clerical) 202.132-010
SUPERVISOR, STITCHING DEPARTMENT (tex. prod., nec) 787.132-018
SUPERVISOR, STOCK RANCH (agriculture) 410.131-022
Supervisor, Stripping (print. & pub.) 972.137-010
SUPERVISOR, STRUCTURAL ROLLING-AND-FINISHING (steel & rel.) 613.130-018
SUPERVISOR, STRUCTURAL-STEEL ERECTION (construction) 809.131-018
Supervisor, Stuffed-Toy Shells (toy-sport equip.) 787.132-010
SUPERVISOR, SUGAR HOUSE (grain-feed mills) 529.132-090
SUPERVISOR, SUGAR REFINERY (grain-feed mills) 529.132-094
SUPERVISOR, SULFURIC-ACID PLANT (chemical) 558.132-018
Supervisor, Sunglasses (optical goods) 716.130-010
SUPERVISOR, SURGICAL GARMENT ASSEMBLY (protective dev.) 712.132-010
SUPERVISOR, SURVEY WORKERS (clerical) 205.137-014
SUPERVISOR, SWIMMING-POOL MAINTENANCE (construction) 869.131-038
SUPERVISOR, SYRUP SHED (sugar & conf.) 529.137-058
SUPERVISOR, TANK CLEANING (paint & varnish) 559.137-050
Supervisor, Tank Cleaning (petrol. refin.) 899.137-018
SUPERVISOR, TANK CLEANING (water trans.) 891.137-018
SUPERVISOR, TANK HOUSE (meat products) 525.132-014
SUPERVISOR, TANK STORAGE (beverage) 529.132-098
SUPERVISOR, TAN ROOM (leather mfg.) 582.132-018
SUPERVISOR, TAPING (construction) 842.134-010
SUPERVISOR, TAR DISTILLATION (chemical) 542.130-014
SUPERVISOR, TEA AND SPICE (food prep., nec) 529.132-102
SUPERVISOR, TELECOMMUNICATOR (government ser.) 379.132-010
SUPERVISOR, TELEGRAPHIC-TYPEWRITER OPERATORS (clerical) 203.132-010
Supervisor, Telephone-Answering-Service (business ser.) 235.137-010
SUPERVISOR, TELEPHONE CLERKS (tel. & tel.) 239.132-010
SUPERVISOR, TELEPHONE INFORMATION (motor trans.) 237.137-010
Supervisor, Television-Chassis Repair (comm. equip.) 726.130-010
SUPERVISOR, TELLERS (utilities) 211.137-022
SUPERVISOR, TERMINAL OPERATIONS (motor trans.) 184.167-242
SUPERVISOR, TERRAZZO (construction) 861.131-026
Supervisor, Test And Inspection (elec. equip.; electron. comp.) 724.130-010
Supervisor, Testing (electron. comp.) 726.134-010
Supervisor, Testing (rubber goods) 759.137-010
SUPERVISOR, THERMOSTATIC CONTROLS (inst. & app.) 710.131-042
Supervisor, Thinning-Tinting (paint & varnish) 559.132-114
Supervisor, THRESHING DEPARTMENT (tobacco) 521.132-014
Supervisor, Throwing Department (textile) 681.130-014
SUPERVISOR, TICKET SALES (air trans.) 238.137-022
Supervisor, Tie Yard (wood prod., nec) 669.130-018
SUPERVISOR, TILE-AND-MOTTLE (fabrication, nec) 559.130-022
SUPERVISOR, TOILET-AND-LAUNDRY SOAP (soap & rel.) 559.132-130
SUPERVISOR, TOWER (petrol. refin.) 549.130-010
SUPERVISOR, TOY ASSEMBLY (toy-sport equip.) 731.131-010
SUPERVISOR, TOY PARTS FORMER (toy-sport equip.) 692.130-034
Supervisor, Trade And Industrial Education (education) 099.117-026
SUPERVISOR, TRAIN OPERATIONS (r.r. trans.) 184.167-294
SUPERVISOR, TRANSCRIBING OPERATORS (clerical) 203.132-014
Supervisor, Transferring And Boxing (knitting) 684.137-010
Supervisor, Transmission And Fork Assembly (motor-bicycles) 806.131-014

SUPERVISOR, TRAVEL-INFORMATION CENTER (government ser.) 237.137-014
Supervisor, Travel Trailer (vehicles, nec) 869.131-030
SUPERVISOR, TREATING AND PUMPING (petrol. refin.) 549.132-034
SUPERVISOR, TREE-FRUIT-AND-NUT FARMING (agriculture) 403.131-010
SUPERVISOR, TREE-TRIMMING (utilities) 408.137-014
Supervisor, Trim Assembly (auto. mfg.) 806.134-010
Supervisor, Truck-Trailer Assembly (auto. mfg.) 806.134-010
SUPERVISOR, TRUST ACCOUNTS (financial) 219.132-014
SUPERVISOR, TUBING (textile) 689.137-014
SUPERVISOR, TUFTING (carpet & rug) 687.132-010
SUPERVISOR, TUMBLERS (ordnance) 599.132-010
SUPERVISOR, TUMBLING AND ROLLING (clock & watch) 715.131-030
SUPERVISOR, TUNNEL HEADING (construction) 859.137-018
Supervisor, Turkey Farm (agriculture) 411.131-010
Supervisor, Turkey Hatchery (agriculture) 411.137-010
Supervisor, Twisting Department (textile) 681.130-014
Supervisor, Type-Bar-And-Segment (office machines) 706.131-014
SUPERVISOR, TYPE-DISK QUALITY CONTROL (machinery mfg.) 979.137-026
SUPERVISOR, TYPE PHOTOGRAPHY (machinery mfg.) 976.131-026
SUPERVISOR, TYPESETTING (print. & pub.) 650.132-010
SUPERVISOR, UNDERWRITING CLERKS (insurance) 219.132-022
Supervisor, Unloading (any industry) 922.137-018
Supervisor, Unwrapping Room (sugar & conf.) 920.137-018
Supervisor, Upholstering (motion picture) 962.137-022
SUPERVISOR, UPHOLSTERY DEPARTMENT (any industry) 780.131-014
SUPERVISOR, URANIUM PROCESSING (smelt. & refin.) 519.130-030
SUPERVISOR V (nonmet. min.) 692.132-014
SUPERVISOR V (tex. prod., nec) 586.130-010
SUPERVISOR, VACUUM METALIZING (any industry) 505.130-014
SUPERVISOR, VARNISH (paint & varnish) 559.132-134
SUPERVISOR, VAT HOUSE (chemical; leather mfg.) 582.132-022
SUPERVISOR, VEGETABLE FARMING (agriculture) 402.131-010
SUPERVISOR, VENDOR QUALITY (any industry) 012.167-062
SUPERVISOR, VENEER (millwork-plywood) 569.135-010
SUPERVISOR VI (nonmet. min.) 692.130-022
SUPERVISOR VI (tex. prod., nec) 589.132-010
SUPERVISOR, VINE-FRUIT FARMING (agriculture) 403.131-014
SUPERVISOR, VOLUNTEER SERVICES (profess. & kin.) 187.137-014
SUPERVISOR, WALL MIRROR DEPARTMENT (glass products) 739.137-022
Supervisor, Warping Department (textile) 681.130-010
SUPERVISOR, WASH HOUSE (beverage) 529.132-106
SUPERVISOR, WATERPROOFING (construction) 843.137-010
SUPERVISOR, WATER SOFTENER SERVICE (business ser.) 862.134-014
SUPERVISOR, WATER TREATMENT PLANT (waterworks) 954.132-010
SUPERVISOR, WATERWORKS (waterworks) 184.167-246
SUPERVISOR, WEAVING (carpet & rug) 689.130-030
SUPERVISOR, WEBBING (tex. prod., nec) 789.137-014
Supervisor, Weights and Measures, Gas And Oil Inspection (government ser.) 168.167-090
SUPERVISOR, WELDING EQUIPMENT REPAIRER (welding) 626.137-010
SUPERVISOR, WET END (wood prod., nec) 539.131-010
SUPERVISOR, WET POUR (concrete prod.) 575.137-014
SUPERVISOR, WET ROOM (paper & pulp) 539.130-014
SUPERVISOR, WHEEL SHOP (railroad equip.) 622.131-018
SUPERVISOR, WHIPPED TOPPING (dairy products) 529.137-066
SUPERVISOR, WHITE SUGAR (sugar & conf.) 529.130-042
SUPERVISOR, WINDING AND TWISTING DEPARTMENT (textile) 681.130-014
Supervisor, Winding Department (textile) 681.130-014
SUPERVISOR, WIRE-ROPE FABRICATION (metal prod., nec) 691.130-014
SUPERVISOR, WOOD-CREW (saw. & plan.) 669.137-010
SUPERVISOR, WOOD ROOM (paper & pulp) 530.132-018
SUPERVISOR, WOOL-SHEARING (agriculture) 410.134-014
SUPERVISOR, WORD PROCESSING (clerical) 203.137-010
Supervisor, Wrapping Room (sugar & conf.) 920.137-018
SUPERVISOR, YARD (beverage) 529.137-070
SUPERVISOR, YARN PREPARATION (textile) 689.130-034
supervisory park ranger (government ser.) 188.167-062
SUPERVISORY WASTEWATER-TREATMENT-PLANT OPERATOR (sanitary ser.) 955.130-010
SUPPLIES PACKER (any industry) 919.687-022
supply clerk (clerical) 222.387-058
SUPPLY CLERK (personal ser.) 339.687-010
SUPPLY CONTROLLER (concrete prod.) 570.382-018
Supply Representative, Dry Gas (petrol. & gas; petrol. refin.; pipe lines) 163.117-010
supply representative, petroleum products (petrol. & gas; petrol. refin.; pipe lines) 163.117-010
supply-room clerk (clerical) 222.387-058
supply service worker (hotel & rest.) 319.484-010
Suppository Molder (pharmaceut.) 556.687-022

SUPPOSITORY-MOLDING-MACHINE OPERATOR (pharmaceut.) 556.686-022
Suppression-Crew Leader (forestry) 452.687-014
Supreme-Court Justice (government ser.) 111.107-010
Surface Carpenter (construction) 860.381-042
surface grinder (machine shop) 603.280-014
Surface-Grinder Tender (machine shop) 603.685-062
surface-grinding-machine hand (machine shop) 603.280-014
Surface-Lay-Out Technician (optical goods) 716.381-014
SURFACE-PLATE FINISHER (stonework) 775.281-010
surface-plate inspector (machine shop) 601.281-022
surface printer (paper goods) 652.662-014
surfacer operator (stonework) 677.682-022
SURFACE SUPERVISOR (mine & quarry) 932.132-014
surfacing-machine operator (stonework) 677.682-022
SURFBOARD MAKER (toy-sport equip.) 732.684-126
SURGEON (medical ser.) 070.101-094
Surgeon Assistant (medical ser.) 079.364-018
surgeon, chief (government ser.) 070.101-082
surgical-appliance fitter (retail trade) 276.257-022
SURGICAL-DRESSING MAKER (protective dev.) 689.685-130
SURGICAL-ELASTIC KNITTER, HAND FRAME (protective dev.) 685.382-010
SURGICAL-FORCEPS FABRICATOR (inst. & app.) 712.684-054
surgical orderly (medical ser.) 079.374-022
Surgical Pathologist (medical ser.) 070.061-010
SURGICAL TECHNICIAN (medical ser.) 079.374-022
surplus-property disposal agent (any industry) 163.167-026
surplus sales officer (any industry) 163.167-026
SURVEILLANCE-SYSTEM MONITOR (government ser.) 379.367-010
Survey Compiler (clerical) 209.387-014
survey hand (textile) 221.367-034
SURVEYOR ASSISTANT, INSTRUMENTS (profess. & kin.) 018.167-034
SURVEYOR, GEODETIC (profess. & kin.) 018.167-038
SURVEYOR, GEOPHYSICAL PROSPECTING (petrol. & gas) 018.167-042
SURVEYOR HELPER (any industry) 869.567-010
Surveyor Helper, Chain (any industry) 869.567-010
Surveyor Helper, Rod (any industry) 869.567-010
surveyor, hydrographic (profess. & kin.) 018.167-046
SURVEYOR, MARINE (profess. & kin.) 018.167-046
SURVEYOR, MINE (profess. & kin.) 018.161-010
SURVEYOR, OIL-WELL DIRECTIONAL (petrol. & gas) 010.261-022
SURVEY WORKER (clerical) 205.367-054
SURVIVAL-EQUIPMENT REPAIRER (government ser.) 739.381-054
SURVIVAL SPECIALIST (military ser.) 378.227-018
Suspender Cutter (garment) 686.685-066
Suspension-Cord Tier (tex. prod., nec) 789.687-118
suture gauger (protective dev.) 712.687-018
suture measurer (protective dev.) 712.687-018
SUTURE POLISHER (protective dev.) 712.687-030
SUTURE WINDER, HAND (protective dev.) 712.687-034
swabber (leather mfg.) 584.687-010
Swabber (petrol. & gas) 930.363-010
SWAGER OPERATOR (pen & pencil) 616.685-078
SWAGE TENDER (ordnance) 617.685-042
swage toolsetter (ordnance) 617.360-014
Swaging-And-Plastic Supervisor (metal prod., nec) 691.130-014
SWAGING-MACHINE ADJUSTER (ordnance) 617.360-014
SWAGING-MACHINE OPERATOR (ordnance) 617.585-010
swamper (any industry) 459.687-010
swamper (any industry) 932.664-010
swamper (saw. & plan.) 667.687-018
SWATCH CHECKER (textile) 683.260-022
SWATCH CLERK (garment) 222.587-050
SWEATBAND-CUTTING-MACHINE OPERATOR (hat & cap) 690.686-062
Sweatband-Decorating-Machine Operator (hat & cap) 583.685-030
sweatband drummer (hat & cap) 583.686-010
SWEATBAND FLANGER (hat & cap) 690.686-058
Sweatband Maker (hat & cap) 699.685-018
sweatband perforator (hat & cap) 686.685-038
Sweatband Printer (hat & cap) 652.682-030
SWEATBAND SEPARATOR (hat & cap) 585.685-122
SWEATBAND SHAPER (hat & cap) 784.687-090
sweat-box attendant (personal ser.) 335.677-014
sweater operator (petrol. refin.) 543.682-022
swedger (elec. equip.) 724.684-030
SWEDGER (jewelry-silver.) 735.687-038
sweeper (any industry) 381.687-018
sweeper (any industry) 381.687-014
SWEEPER-BRUSH MAKER, MACHINE (fabrication, nec) 692.682-066
SWEEPER-CLEANER, INDUSTRIAL (any industry) 389.683-010
Sweeper Operator, Highways (construction) 919.683-022
SWEEPING-COMPOUND BLENDER (chemical) 550.685-110
SWEEP-PRESS OPERATOR (clock & watch) 616.685-082
Sweet-Dough Mixer (bakery products) 520.685-234

SWEET-GOODS-MACHINE OPERATOR (bakery products) 520.685-214
Sweet-Pickled-Fruit Maker (can. & preserv.) 522.684-010
Sweet-Pickle Maker (can. & preserv.) 522.684-010
SWEET-POTATO DISINTEGRATOR (can. & preserv.) 521.685-358
swift tender (textile) 681.685-098
Swimming Coach (amuse. & rec.) 153.227-010
SWIMMING POOL INSTALLER-AND-SERVICER (construction) 869.463-010
SWIMMING-POOL SERVICER (any industry) 891.684-018
Swine Rancher (agriculture) 410.161-018
swing-folding-machine operator (knitting; textile) 589.685-086
swing-frame-grinder operator (foundry) 705.684-074
swing grinder (foundry) 705.684-074
Swinging-Cut-Off-Saw Operator (woodworking) 667.682-022
Swing-Ride Operator (amuse. & rec.) 342.663-010
swing tender (textile) 589.686-010
SWING-TYPE-LATHE OPERATOR (woodworking) 664.382-010
Switch Adjuster (elec. equip.) 724.381-010
Switchboard Assembler (comm. equip.; elec. equip.) 729.381-022
switchboard contact assembler (elec. equip.; light. fix.) 729.687-010
SWITCHBOARD OPERATOR (chemical) 952.362-038
switchboard operator (clerical) 235.662-022
switchboard operator (tel. & tel.) 235.462-010
SWITCHBOARD OPERATOR (utilities) 952.362-034
SWITCHBOARD OPERATOR ASSISTANT (utilities) 952.367-014
switchboard-operator helper (utilities) 952.367-014
SWITCHBOARD OPERATOR, POLICE DISTRICT (government ser.) 235.562-014
SWITCHBOX ASSEMBLER I (comm. equip.) 722.687-010
Switchbox Assembler II (comm. equip.; elec. equip.) 729.684-026
switch-house operator (mine & quarry; smelt. & refin.) 939.362-014
Switching Clerk (r.r. trans.) 222.387-014
switching operator (radio-tv broad.) 962.162-010
SWITCH INSPECTOR (utilities) 952.381-010
switchpanel mounter (svc. ind. mach.) 731.684-010
SWITCH REPAIRER (r.r. trans.) 622.684-018
SWITCH TENDER (r.r. trans.) 910.667-026
SWITCHYARD WORKER (r.r. trans.) term
Sword Swallower (amuse. & rec.) 159.647-010
SYMBOL STAMPER, SEMICONDUCTOR PACKAGES (electron. comp.) 652.685-110
Synchro Assembler (photo. appar.) 714.684-010
Synchro-Unit Assembler (elec. equip.) 721.381-014
synthetic department supervisor (pharmaceut.) 559.130-010
SYNTHETIC-FILAMENT EXTRUDER (plastic-synth.) 557.565-014
SYNTHETIC-GEM-PRESS OPERATOR (jewelry-silver.) 575.685-078
synthetic-resin operator (plastic-synth.) 558.382-050
SYNTHETIC-STAPLE EXTRUDER (plastic-synth.) 557.665-010
Syrup Blender (beverage) 520.485-026
Syrup Crystallizer (sugar & conf.) 529.686-034
syruper (can. & preserv.) 529.685-190
Syruper, Machine (can. & preserv.) 529.685-190
Syrup Filterer (beverage) 520.485-026
syrup-kettle operator (plastic-synth.) 558.382-050
SYRUP MAKER (beverage) 520.485-026
SYRUP MAKER (sugar & conf.) 529.482-022
SYRUP-MIXER ASSISTANT (grain-feed mills) 520.687-058
SYRUP MIXER (grain-feed mills) 529.462-010
system dispatcher (utilities) 952.167-014
system operator (print. & pub.) 979.282-010
system operator, chief (utilities) 952.137-010
system operator (utilities) 952.167-014
system-planning engineer (utilities) 003.167-026
SYSTEMS ANALYST (profess. & kin.) 030.167-014
systems analyst (profess. & kin.) 161.167-010
systems checkout mechanic (aircraft mfg.) 806.261-050
systems inspector (comm. equip.; electron. comp.; inst. & app.) 726.381-010
Systems Manager (print. & pub.) 972.137-010
SYSTEMS PROGRAMMER (profess. & kin.) 030.162-022
Systems-Testing-Laboratory Technician (profess. & kin.) 003.161-014
TABBER (paper goods) 794.687-058
TAB-CARD-PRESS OPERATOR (print. & pub.) 651.382-034
Table-And-Desk Finisher (furniture) 709.687-014
table and slab depiler (steel & rel.) 504.665-010
Table Assembler, Metal (furniture) 709.684-014
table attendant (amuse. & rec.) 340.477-010
table attendant, cafeteria (hotel & rest.) 311.677-010
TABLE-COVER FOLDER (tex. prod., nec) 920.687-186
Table-Cut-Off-Saw Operator (woodworking) 667.682-022
table draper (garment; tex. prod., nec) 782.687-026
Table Filler (sugar & conf.) 529.686-034
TABLE HAND (tobacco) 521.687-138
table inspector (textile) 689.387-010
table inspector (tobacco) 529.687-090
TABLE OPERATOR (nonfer. metal; steel & rel.) 613.682-026

Table Operator (steel & rel.) 919.683-018
tabler (tex. prod., nec) 781.684-034
Table Setter (hotel & rest.) 311.677-018
tablet coater (pharmaceut.) 554.382-010
TABLE TENDER (smelt. & refin.) 511.685-062
Table Tender, Sludge (smelt. & refin.) 511.685-062
TABLET-MACHINE OPERATOR (dairy products) 529.685-238
tablet-machine operator (plastic prod.; plastic-synth.) 556.685-058
TABLET-MAKING-MACHINE OPERATOR (paper goods) 649.682-042
TABLET-MAKING-MACHINE-OPERATOR HELPER (paper goods) 649.685-130
TABLE-TOP TILE SETTER (brick & tile) 763.684-074
TABLET TESTER (pharmaceut.) 559.667-010
Table Worker (any industry) 920.587-018
TABLE WORKER (boot & shoe) 788.687-142
TABLE WORKER (fabrication, nec) 739.687-182
TABLE WORKER (leather prod.) 783.687-030
table worker (paper goods) 794.687-022
table worker (print. & pub.) 653.685-010
table worker (tex. prod., nec) 734.687-014
table worker, sewing (any industry) 782.684-058
TAB-MACHINE OPERATOR (nonmet. min.) 754.685-010
Tabular Typist (clerical) 203.582-066
tabulating clerk (clerical) 216.382-062
tacker (boot & shoe) 690.685-162
Tacker (elec. equip.) 787.685-042
tacker (fabrication, nec) 739.684-162
Tacker (garment) 782.684-058
Tacker (plastic prod.) 690.685-438
tacker (welding) 810.684-010
Tacker, Elastic Band (knitting) 787.682-074
TACKING-MACHINE OPERATOR (any industry) 787.685-042
TACKING-MACHINE OPERATOR (garment) 786.685-034
Tacking-Stitch Remover (textile) 689.686-050
TACK PULLER (boot & shoe) 788.687-146
TACK PULLER, MACHINE (boot & shoe) 690.685-410
Taco Maker (food prep., nec) 520.687-046
Taffy-Candy Maker (sugar & conf.) 529.361-014
Taffy Puller (sugar & conf.) 520.685-046
Tag-And-Label Cutter (print. & pub.) 699.682-018
Tagger (forestry) 920.687-046
tagger (laundry & rel.) 369.687-026
tagger (paper goods) 794.687-058
tagger (textile) 229.587-018
TAG-MACHINE OPERATOR (paper goods) 649.685-118
tag-meter operator (tobacco) 529.687-162
TAG-PRESS OPERATOR (paper goods) 649.682-046
tail-end rider (any industry) 932.664-010
TAILER (mine & quarry) 930.666-014
tailer (woodworking) 669.686-034
tailing hand (textile) 689.686-014
Tailing-Machine Operator (textile) 681.685-154
TAILINGS-DAM LABORER (smelt. & refin.) 511.687-026
Tailings-Dam Pumper (smelt. & refin.) 914.682-010
TAILINGS MACHINERY TENDER (smelt. & refin.) term
Tailing-Thickener Operator (smelt. & refin.) 511.485-014
tailor (garment; personal ser.; retail trade) 785.261-014
TAILOR APPRENTICE, ALTERATION (garment; personal ser.; retail trade) 785.261-018
TAILOR APPRENTICE, CUSTOM (garment; personal ser.; retail trade) 785.261-022
Tailor, Men's Ready-To-Wear Garment (retail trade) 785.261-010
Tailor, Women's-Garment Alteration (retail trade) 785.261-010
take-away attendant (textile) 589.686-010
Take-Down Inspector (photofinishing) 976.687-014
TAKE-DOWN SORTER (photofinishing) 976.665-010
taker-off (tex. prod., nec) 589.686-046
Taker-Off, Braker Machine (tex. prod., nec) 589.686-046
Taker-Off, Drying Kiln (tex. prod., nec) 589.686-046
TAKER-OFF, HEMP FIBER (tex. prod., nec) 589.686-046
Taker-Off, Scutcher Machine (tex. prod., nec) 589.686-046
TAKE-UP OPERATOR (plastic-synth.) 557.685-034
Take-Up Supervisor (construction) 899.131-010
talent (radio-tv broad.) 159.147-018
talent agent (amuse. & rec.) 191.117-010
talent director (motion picture; radio-tv broad.) 159.267-010
talk show host/hostess (radio-tv broad.) 159.147-018
TALLIER (clerical) 221.587-030
Tallow Pumper (meat products) 529.685-202
TAMALE-MACHINE FEEDER (food prep., nec) 520.686-038
Tamale Maker (food prep., nec) 520.687-046
tamper operator (construction) 869.683-018
TAMPING-MACHINE OPERATOR (construction) 869.683-018
Tamping-Machine Operator (elec. equip.) 692.482-010
Tamping-Machine Operator (r.r. trans.) 859.683-018

tamping-machine operator, road forms (construction) 869.683-010
tanbark peeler (logging) 454.687-014
Tandem-Mill Operator (nonfer. metal) 613.462-018
Tandem-Mill Roller (steel & rel.) 613.662-018
Tandem-Taping-And-Paper-Wrapping-Machine Operator (nonfer. metal) 691.682-018
tangled-yarn-spool straightener (tex. prod., nec; textile) 681.687-026
Tankage-Grinder Operator (meat products) 529.685-202
TANKAGE SUPERVISOR (construction) 869.131-034
TANK AND AMPHIBIAN TRACTOR OPERATIONS CHIEF (military ser.) 620.137-010
tank-and-batch operator (glass mfg.) 572.382-010
TANK ASSEMBLER (wood. container) 764.684-030
Tank-Bottom Assembler (wood. container) 764.684-030
tank builder (petrol. & gas) 801.361-022
TANK BUILDER AND ERECTOR (construction) 860.381-066
tank-builder helper (petrol. & gas) 801.687-018
tank-builder supervisor (construction) 869.131-034
TANK CALIBRATOR (business ser.) 229.387-014
Tank-Car Cleaner (petrol. refin.) 891.687-022
TANK-CAR INSPECTOR (chemical) 622.684-022
TANK-CAR INSPECTOR (petrol. refin.) 910.384-010
tank-car loader (any industry) 914.667-010
Tank-Car Repairer (railroad equip.) 622.381-014
Tank Charger (meat products) 529.685-202
tank charger (oils & grease) 921.685-030
TANK CLEANER (any industry) 891.687-022
TANK CLEANER (chemical; plastic-synth.) 559.687-062
Tank Cleaner (elec. equip.) 727.687-058
TANK CLEANER (paint & varnish) 559.684-022
tank cooper (wood. container) 764.684-030
TANK CREWMEMBER (military ser.) 378.683-018
TANK ERECTOR (construction) 860.381-070
TANKER (wood prod., nec) 561.665-010
TANK-FARM ATTENDANT (chemical) 559.665-038
tank-farm gauger (petrol. & gas; petrol. refin.; pipe lines) 914.384-010
Tank-Furnace Operator (glass mfg.) 572.382-010
TANK-HOUSE OPERATOR (smelt. & refin.) 519.362-014
TANK-HOUSE-OPERATOR HELPER (smelt. & refin.) 519.565-014
Tank Insulator, Rubber (machinery mfg.) 759.684-050
tank maker, wood (construction) 860.381-066
tank operator (fabrication, nec) 582.665-022
TANK PUMPER, PANELBOARD (beverage) 529.685-242
tank refinisher (beverage) 779.684-026
tankroom supervisor (paint & varnish) 559.132-134
TANKROOM TENDER (plastic-synth.) 559.585-018
TANK SETTER (petrol. & gas) 801.361-022
TANK-SETTER HELPER (petrol. & gas) 801.687-018
Tank-Shop Supervisor (any industry) 809.130-014
Tank-Stave Assembler (wood. container) 764.684-030
TANK TENDER (smelt. & refin.) 509.685-054
TANK TENDER (sugar & conf.) 529.585-014
TANK-TRUCK DRIVER (petrol. refin.; retail trade; wholesale tr.) 903.683-018
Tank Worker (plastic-synth.) 550.685-034
tanned-hide-cutter, machine (leather prod.) 585.685-038
tanner (leather mfg.) 582.482-018
tanner (leather mfg.) 589.361-010
TANNER, ROTARY DRUM, CONTINUOUS PROCESS (leather mfg.) 582.482-014
tannery gummer (leather mfg.) 584.687-010
TANNING-DRUM OPERATOR (leather mfg.) 582.482-018
TANNING-SOLUTION MAKER (chemical) 550.682-014
Tanning Supervisor (leather mfg.) 582.131-010
Tanning-Wheel Filler (leather mfg.) 582.685-050
TAP-AND-DIE-MAKER TECHNICIAN (clock & watch) 601.280-034
Tap Dancer (amuse. & rec.) 151.047-010
tape armorer (nonfer. metal) 691.685-010
tape calender (nonmet. min.) 583.585-010
TAPE COATER (nonmet. min.) 692.685-210
Tape Control Skin-Or-Spar-Mill Operator (machine shop) 605.380-010
Tape Cutter (garment; knitting) 699.682-030
Tape Cutter (garment) 699.685-014
Tape-Cutting-Machine Operator (garment; tex. prod., nec) 686.685-066
tape duplicator (radio-tv broad.; recording) 194.382-014
TAPE-FASTENER-MACHINE OPERATOR (paper goods) 649.685-122
TAPE-FOLDING-MACHINE OPERATOR (rubber goods; tex. prod., nec) 689.685-134
Tape Keller Operator (machine shop) 605.380-010
TAPE LIBRARIAN (clerical) 206.367-018
tape machine tailer (millwork-plywood) 569.686-054
TAPE-MAKING-MACHINE OPERATOR (tex. prod., nec) 689.685-138
taper (any industry) 787.682-010
taper (any industry) 749.687-018
taper (boot & shoe) 690.685-414
taper (boot & shoe) 690.685-074

TAPER (construction; mfd. bldgs.) 842.664-010
taper (textile) 920.587-010
taper (textile) 628.684-014
taper and bedder (construction; mfd. bldgs.) 842.664-010
taper and floater (construction; mfd. bldgs.) 842.664-010
TAPE-RECORDER REPAIRER (any industry) 720.281-014
Tape-Recording-Machine Operator (radio-tv broad.; recording) 194.362-010
TAPER, MACHINE (boot & shoe) 690.685-414
TAPER, MACHINE (fabrication, nec) 692.685-214
TAPER OPERATOR (paper goods) 649.685-126
TAPER, PRINTED CIRCUIT LAYOUT (electron. comp.) 017.684-010
tape-sewing-machine operator (print. & pub.) 653.685-014
Tape Stitcher (boot & shoe) 690.682-082
TAPE STRINGER (garment; knitting) 782.687-054
TAPE TRANSFERRER (radio-tv broad.; recording) 194.382-014
Tape Weaver (narrow fabrics; nonmet. min.) 683.682-046
Tape Winder (narrow fabrics; nonmet. min.) 689.685-014
Taping Machine Operator (tex. prod., nec) 787.682-066
Tap-Out Operator (wood. container) 669.682-014
TAPPER (beverage) 529.685-246
TAPPER (nonfer. metal; smelt. & refin.) 514.664-014
TAPPER, BALANCE-WHEEL SCREW HOLE (clock & watch) 715.682-022
TAPPER, BIT (fabrication, nec) 739.685-046
TAPPER, HAND (ordnance) 737.687-134
Tapper I (clock & watch) 604.685-026
TAPPER II (clock & watch) 715.685-062
Tapper Operator (machine shop) 606.682-014
TAPPER OPERATOR (nut & bolt) 606.682-022
TAPPER, SHANK (fabrication, nec) 739.685-050
TAPPER SUPERVISOR (smelt. & refin.) 514.134-010
Tapping-Machine Operator (construction) 869.664-014
Tapping-Machine Operator, Automatic (clock & watch) 606.685-030
Tapping-Machine Operator, Automatic (nut & bolt) 619.365-010
TAPROOM ATTENDANT (amuse. & rec.) 312.677-010
tar-and-ammonia pump operator (steel & rel.) 541.362-014
tar chaser (steel & rel.) 549.687-010
TARE WEIGHER (meat products; sugar & conf.; tobacco) 221.587-034
TARGET AIRCRAFT TECHNICIAN (military ser.) 378.281-010
TARGETEER (ordnance) 736.684-042
Target-Face Maker (toy-sport equip.) 979.684-034
TARGET TRIMMER (toy-sport equip.) 732.687-078
Tar Heater (construction) 869.685-010
Tar-Heater Operator (chemical) 552.462-010
Tar Heat-Exchanger Cleaner (petrol. refin.) 891.687-030
TARIFF INSPECTOR (r.r. trans.) 214.362-034
TARIFF PUBLISHING AGENT (business ser.) 184.167-250
TARRING-MACHINE OPERATOR (tex. prod., nec) 584.685-046
tar runner (steel & rel.) 549.687-010
TASSEL-MAKING-MACHINE OPERATOR (tex. prod., nec) 689.685-142
TASTER (food prep., nec) 529.281-010
TATTOO ARTIST (personal ser.) 339.571-010
tattooer (personal ser.) 339.571-010
tattooist (personal ser.) 339.571-010
Tavern Inspector (government ser.) 168.267-066
tawer (leather mfg.) 582.482-018
tax agent (profess. & kin.) 110.117-038
Tax Analyst (government ser.) 160.167-038
TAX ATTORNEY (profess. & kin.) 110.117-038
TAX CLERK (clerical) 219.487-010
Tax Clerk (financial) 249.362-014
Tax Economist (profess. & kin.) 050.067-010
Tax Examiner (government ser.) 160.167-038
tax form preparer (business ser.) 219.362-070
TAXICAB COORDINATOR (motor trans.) 215.367-018
TAXICAB STARTER (motor trans.) 913.367-010
TAXIDERMIST (profess. & kin.) 199.261-010
TAXI DRIVER (motor trans.) 913.463-018
TAXIMETER REPAIRER (automotive ser.) 710.281-038
TAXI SERVICER (motor trans.) 915.687-030
TAX PREPARER (business ser.) 219.362-070
Tax-Record Clerk (utilities) 216.482-010
tax representative (profess. & kin.) 110.117-038
Tax Searcher (real estate) 209.367-046
tc operator (chemical) 559.682-062
Tea-Bag-Machine Tender (food prep., nec) 920.685-078
Tea Blender (food prep., nec) 520.585-026
TEACHER (museums) 099.227-038
TEACHER, ADULT EDUCATION (education) 099.227-030
TEACHER, ADVENTURE EDUCATION (education) 099.224-014
teacher aide, clerical (education) 249.367-074
TEACHER AIDE I (education) 099.327-010
TEACHER AIDE II (education) 249.367-074
TEACHER, ART (education) 149.021-010
teacher assistant (education) 099.327-010
Teacher, Ballet (education) 151.027-014

Teacher, Child Development Center (education) 092.227-018
Teacher, Citizenship (education) 099.227-030
teacher, dancing (education) 151.027-014
Teacher, Day Care Center (education) 092.227-018
TEACHER, DRAMA (education) 150.027-014
teacher, dramatics (education) 150.027-014
teacher, driver education (education) 099.223-010
Teacher, Early Childhood Development (education) 092.227-018
TEACHER, ELEMENTARY SCHOOL (education) 092.227-010
TEACHER, EMOTIONALLY IMPAIRED (education) 094.227-010
TEACHER, HEARING IMPAIRED (education) 094.224-010
TEACHER, HOME (education) term
TEACHER, HOME THERAPY (social ser.) 195.227-018
TEACHER, INDUSTRIAL ARTS (education) 091.221-010
Teacher, Instrumental (education) 152.021-010
Teacher, Junior College (education) 090.227-010
TEACHER, KINDERGARTEN (education) 092.227-014
TEACHER, LEARNING DISABLED (education) 094.227-030
Teacher, Lip Reading (education) 094.224-010
TEACHER, MENTALLY IMPAIRED (education) 094.227-022
TEACHER, MUSIC (education) 152.021-010
Teacher, Nursery School (education) 092.227-018
teacher, physical education (education) 099.224-010
TEACHER, PHYSICALLY IMPAIRED (education) 094.224-014
TEACHER, PRESCHOOL (education) 092.227-018
teacher, private (education) 099.227-034
teacher, public health (profess. & kin.) 079.117-014
TEACHER, RESOURCE (education) 099.227-042
TEACHER, SECONDARY SCHOOL (education) 091.227-010
teacher selection specialist (education) 099.167-010
teacher, theater arts (education) 150.027-014
TEACHER, VISUALLY IMPAIRED (education) 094.224-018
Teacher, Vocal (education) 152.021-010
teacher, vocational training (education) 097.221-010
TEACHER, VOCATIONAL TRAINING (education) 094.227-026
Teaching Assistant (education) 090.227-010
Tea-Leaf Reader (amuse. & rec.) 159.647-018
team coordinator (auto. mfg.) 806.367-014
team coordinator (auto. mfg.) 806.367-010
team driver (any industry) 919.664-010
team leader (auto. mfg.) 806.134-010
team leader (auto. mfg.) 806.367-014
team member (auto. mfg.) 806.684-010
TEAMSTER (any industry) 919.664-010
tear-down matcher (textile) 582.687-022
tearer (garment) 781.687-018
tearer, press clipping (business ser.) 249.587-014
tear-up worker, spring (automotive ser.) 620.584-010
Tea Taster (food prep., nec) 529.281-010
technical aide, flight test data (aircraft mfg.) 002.262-010
technical aide (profess. & kin.)   see TECHNICIAN
technical assistant (pharmaceut.) 559.384-010
technical assistant (profess. & kin.)   see TECHNICIAN
TECHNICAL COORDINATOR (government ser.) 209.132-014
TECHNICAL DIRECTOR, CHEMICAL PLANT (profess. & kin.) 008.167-010
TECHNICAL ILLUSTRATOR (profess. & kin.) 017.281-034
technical-maintenance technician (photo. appar.) 714.281-026
technical manager, chemical plant (profess. & kin.) 008.167-010
technical operations specialist (profess. & kin.) 033.162-018
TECHNICAL OPERATOR (petrol. & gas) 930.167-010
Technical Operator, Grain Preparation (chemical) 590.464-010
technical release analyst (any industry) 229.267-010
technical specialist (museums) 962.261-010
technical specialist, aircraft systems (aircraft mfg.) 621.221-010
Technical Stenographer (clerical) 202.362-014
TECHNICAL SUPPORT SPECIALIST (profess. & kin.) 033.162-018
TECHNICAL TESTING ENGINEER (motion picture) 194.381-010
TECHNICAL TRAINING COORDINATOR (education) 166.167-054
technician (glass mfg.) 579.367-014
TECHNICIAN (profess. & kin.) term
technician, automated equipment (machinery mfg.) 638.261-010
technician, automatic (tel. & tel.) 822.281-010
TECHNICIAN, NEWS GATHERING (radio-tv broad.) 194.362-022
technician-photographer/editor (radio-tv broad.) 194.362-022
TECHNICIAN, PLANT AND MAINTENANCE (radio-tv broad.) 822.281-030
TECHNICIAN, SEMICONDUCTOR DEVELOPMENT (profess. & kin.) 003.161-018
TECHNICIAN, SUBMARINE CABLE EQUIPMENT (tel. & tel.) 822.281-034
technician, terminal and repeater (tel. & tel.) 822.261-026
technician, test systems (any industry) 726.261-018
technologist, biochemistry (medical ser.) 078.261-010
Tectonophysicist (profess. & kin.) 024.061-030
TELECINE OPERATOR (radio-tv broad.) 194.362-018
TELECOMMUNICATOR (government ser.) 379.362-018
Telegram Messenger (tel. & tel.) 230.663-010

telegraph-equipment maintainer (tel. & tel.) 822.281-010
TELEGRAPHER (r.r. trans.) 236.562-010
TELEGRAPHER AGENT (r.r. trans.) 236.562-014
Telegraphic-Instrument Supervisor (tel. & tel.) 722.131-010
Telegraphic-Service Dispatcher (tel. & tel.) 959.167-010
Telegraphic-Typewriter Installer (tel. & tel.) 822.381-010
TELEGRAPHIC-TYPEWRITER OPERATOR (clerical) 203.582-050
telegraphic-typewriter operator, chief (clerical) 203.132-010
Telegraphic-Typewriter Repairer (tel. & tel.) 822.281-010
telegraph operator, automatic (clerical) 203.582-050
TELEGRAPH-PLANT MAINTAINER (tel. & tel.) 822.381-022
Telegraph-Repeater Installer (tel. & tel.) 822.381-010
Telegraph-Repeater Technician (tel. & tel.) 822.261-026
TELEGRAPH-SERVICE RATER (tel. & tel.) 214.587-010
telemarketer (any industry) 299.357-014
telemetry technician (medical ser.) 078.367-010
Telephone Ad-Taker (print. & pub.) 247.367-010
TELEPHONE-ANSWERING-SERVICE OPERATOR (business ser.) 235.662-026
TELEPHONE CLERK, TELEGRAPH OFFICE (tel. & tel.) 239.362-010
Telephone Coin-Box Collector (tel. & tel.) 236.567-010
Telephone-Diaphragm Assembler (comm. equip.; elec. equip.) 729.684-026
TELEPHONE-DIRECTORY DELIVERER (business ser.) 230.667-014
TELEPHONE-DIRECTORY-DISTRIBUTOR DRIVER (business ser.) 906.683-018
telephone-information clerk (financial) 237.367-046
Telephone-Instrument Supervisor (tel. & tel.) 722.131-010
telephone-interceptor operator (business ser.) 235.662-026
TELEPHONE OPERATOR (clerical) 235.662-022
telephone operator (tel. & tel.) 235.462-010
TELEPHONE OPERATOR, CHIEF (clerical) 235.137-010
Telephone-Order Clerk (clerical) 249.362-026
Telephone-Order Clerk, Drive-in (hotel & rest.) 209.567-014
Telephone-Order Clerk, Room Service (hotel & rest.) 209.567-014
Telephone-Order Dispatcher (clerical) 249.362-026
telephone-plant power operator (tel. & tel.) 952.382-014
TELEPHONE-QUOTATION CLERK (financial) 237.367-046
telephoner (r.r. trans.) 236.562-010
telephone repairer (tel. & tel.) 822.281-022
telephone-sales agent (air trans.) 238.367-018
telephone sales representative (any industry) 299.357-014
TELEPHONE SOLICITOR (any industry) 299.357-014
telephone supervisor (tel. & tel.) 239.132-010
telephone-switchboard operator (clerical) 235.662-022
Telephone-Switch Repairer (comm. equip.; elec. equip.) 729.684-038
telephoto engineer (print. & pub.; tel. & tel.) 193.362-010
Telephoto Installer (tel. & tel.) 822.381-018
telephoto operator (print. & pub.) 239.382-010
Teleprinter Installer (tel. & tel.) 822.381-018
teleticketing agent (air trans.) 248.382-010
Teletype Installer (tel. & tel.) 822.381-010
teletypesetter monitor (print. & pub.) 650.685-010
teletype-telegrapher (r.r. trans.) 236.562-010
TELEVISION-AND-RADIO REPAIRER (any industry) 720.281-018
Television Announcer (radio-tv broad.) 159.147-010
Television-Cabinet Finisher (woodworking) 763.381-010
TELEVISION INSTALLER (any industry) 823.361-010
television-picture-tube rebuilder (electron. comp.) 725.381-010
Television Producer (radio-tv broad.) 159.117-010
Television-Receiver Analyzer (electron. comp.) 726.261-018
television repairer (any industry) 720.281-018
TELEVISION-SCHEDULE COORDINATOR (radio-tv broad.) 199.382-010
TELEVISION TECHNICIAN (radio-tv broad.) 194.062-010
Television-Tube Inspector (glass mfg.) 579.384-018
TELLER (financial) 211.362-018
TELLER (utilities) 211.462-034
TELLER, HEAD (financial) 211.132-010
TELLER, VAULT (financial) 211.382-010
Tempeh Maker (food prep., nec) 529.685-290
TEMPERATURE-CONTROL INSPECTOR (plastic-synth.) 559.467-010
TEMPERATURE INSPECTOR (meat products) 529.687-202
TEMPERATURE REGULATOR, PYROMETER (foundry) 512.667-010
TEMPERER (heat treating) 504.682-026
temperer (leather mfg.; tex. prod., nec) 582.685-050
tempering-kiln tender (heat treating) 504.685-018
tempering-machine operator (sugar & conf.) 523.682-010
Temper-Mill Roller (steel & rel.) 613.662-018
TEMPLATE CUTTER (cutlery-hrdwr.) 703.684-018
Template Inspector (any industry) 619.261-010
TEMPLATE MAKER (any industry) 601.381-038
TEMPLATE MAKER, EXTRUSION DIE (machine shop) 601.280-038
TEMPLATE MAKER, TRACK (any industry) 809.484-014
TEMPLATE REPRODUCTION TECHNICIAN (aircraft mfg.) 976.381-022
Template-Storage Clerk (clerical) 222.387-058
Temple-Meat Cutter (meat products) 525.684-034

templer, head (meat products) 525.684-034
tenant relations coordinator (social ser.) 195.167-014
tenderizer tender (millwork-plywood) 669.685-038
TENNIS-BALL-COVER CEMENTER (toy-sport equip.) 795.687-030
TENNIS-BALL COVERER, HAND (toy-sport equip.) 795.687-026
Tennis Coach (amuse. & rec.) 153.227-010
Tennis-Court Attendant (amuse. & rec.) 341.367-010
Tennis-Net Maker (tex. prod., nec) 789.684-030
Tennis-Racket Repairer (any industry) 732.684-122
Tenoner Offbearer (woodworking) 669.686-034
TENONER OPERATOR (wood prod., nec) 677.682-026
TENONER OPERATOR (woodworking) 669.382-018
tension checker (textile) 683.687-034
TENSIONING-MACHINE OPERATOR (concrete prod.) 616.665-010
tension machine operator (paper goods) 649.685-070
Tension Regulator (print. & pub.) 651.362-030
Tent Assembler (tex. prod., nec) 787.682-058
Tenter-Frame Back-Tender (textile) 589.686-010
Tenter-Frame Feeder (textile) 589.686-014
TENTER-FRAME OPERATOR (textile) 580.685-066
tentering-machine off-bearer (textile) 589.686-010
tentering-machine operator (textile) 580.685-066
Tent Finisher (tex. prod., nec) 789.484-014
Tentmaker (tex. prod., nec) 739.381-010
Terminal-Block Assembler (elec. equip.) 729.687-010
terminal gauger (petrol. & gas; petrol. refin.; pipe lines) 914.384-010
terminal-gauger supervisor (pipe lines) 914.132-022
TERMINAL-MAKEUP OPERATOR (print. & pub.) 208.382-010
terminal manager (motor trans.) 184.167-110
terminal superintendent (petrol. refin.; retail trade) 181.117-010
TERMINAL SUPERINTENDENT (r.r. trans.) 184.167-254
terminal supervisor (chemical) 559.132-138
terminal supervisor (petrol. refin.; pipe lines) 914.137-018
termination clerk (insurance) 203.382-014
termite treater (business ser.) 383.364-010
termite-treater helper (business ser.) 383.687-010
Terra-Cotta Mason (construction) 861.381-018
TERRAZZO FINISHER (construction) 861.664-014
terrazzo helper (construction) 861.664-014
terrazzo mechanic helper (construction) 861.664-014
Terrazzo Polisher (construction) 861.381-046
TERRAZZO-TILE MAKER (brick & tile) 575.684-046
TERRAZZO WORKER (construction) 861.381-046
TERRAZZO-WORKER APPRENTICE (construction) 861.381-050
terrazzo worker helper (construction) 861.664-014
Terry-Cloth Cutter, Hand (tex. prod., nec) 781.684-074
Terry Cloth Cutter, Machine (tex. prod., nec) 781.684-014
test assembler (nonfer. metal; steel & rel.) 509.584-010
test-bore helper (any industry) 930.687-014
test borer (any industry) 930.682-010
test-boring crew chief (construction) 850.137-010
test carrier (nonfer. metal; steel & rel.) 509.584-010
Test Cell Technician (aircraft mfg.) 621.261-014
test clerk (education) 219.467-010
TEST-DEPARTMENT HELPER (comm. equip.; elec. equip.) 729.664-010
TEST-DESK SUPERVISOR (tel. & tel.) 822.131-030
TEST DRIVER I (auto. mfg.) 806.283-014
TEST DRIVER II (auto. mfg.) 806.283-010
TEST ENGINEER (profess. & kin.) master
TEST ENGINEER, AGRICULTURAL EQUIPMENT (profess. & kin.) 013.061-022
TEST ENGINEER, MARINE EQUIPMENT (profess. & kin.) 014.061-022
TEST ENGINEER, MECHANICAL EQUIPMENT (profess. & kin.) 007.161-034
TEST ENGINEER, MINING-AND-OILFIELD EQUIPMENT (mine & quarry; petrol. & gas) 010.061-030
TEST ENGINEER, NUCLEAR EQUIPMENT (profess. & kin.) 015.061-022
TEST-ENGINE EVALUATOR (petrol. refin.) 010.261-026
TEST-ENGINE OPERATOR (petrol. refin.) 029.261-018
test equipment certification technician (aircraft mfg.) 019.281-010
TEST EQUIPMENT MECHANIC (aircraft mfg.) 710.361-014
tester (agric. equip.) 624.361-010
Tester (cutlery-hrdwr.) 701.687-026
tester (mine & quarry) 579.484-010
TESTER (musical inst.) 730.684-086
TESTER (petrol. refin.) 029.261-022
TESTER (pottery & porc.) 774.687-026
TESTER (profess. & kin.) 011.361-010
TESTER (rubber goods) 899.487-010
tester (woodworking) 762.384-010
TESTER AND INSPECTOR, LAMPS (light. fix.) 723.687-014
tester, armature or fields (elec. equip.) 724.384-010
TESTER, COMPRESSED GASES (chemical) 549.364-010
TESTER, CONVERTIBLE SOFA BEDSPRING (furniture) 780.684-110
tester, electrical accessories (aircraft mfg.) 729.381-010

TESTER, ELECTRICAL CONTINUITY (elec. equip.; house. appl.; light. fix.) 729.684-058
TESTER, ELECTRONIC SCALE (office machines) 710.381-046
tester, equipment (tel. & tel.) 822.261-026
TESTER, FOOD PRODUCTS (any industry) 199.251-010
tester helper (any industry) 381.687-022
TESTER, MOTORS AND CONTROLS (elec. equip.) 721.281-030
TESTER OPERATOR (nonfer. metal) 614.684-014
tester operator (tobacco) 529.387-014
TESTER-OPERATOR HELPER (nonfer. metal) 614.686-014
Tester, Printed Circuit Boards (electron. comp.) 726.684-026
TESTER, REGULATOR (protective dev.; toy-sport equip.) 710.387-010
tester, rocket engine (aircraft mfg.) 806.261-022
TESTER, ROCKET MOTOR (aircraft mfg.) 806.261-022
TESTER, SEMICONDUCTOR PACKAGES (electron. comp.) 726.685-054
TESTER, SEMICONDUCTOR WAFERS (electron. comp.) 726.684-102
TESTER, SOUND (machinery mfg.) 706.382-014
tester, systems (any industry) 726.261-018
tester, vibrator equipment (machinery mfg.) 825.361-014
TESTER, WAFER SUBSTRATE (electron. comp.) 726.684-106
TESTER, WASTE DISPOSAL LEAKAGE (house. appl.) 723.687-018
test examiner (clerical) 249.367-078
TEST FIXTURE ASSEMBLER (electron. comp.) 726.684-098
TEST FIXTURE DESIGNER (electron. comp.) 726.364-014
test-hole driller (any industry) 930.682-010
TESTING AND ANALYSIS DEPARTMENT SUPERVISOR (can. & preserv.) 523.131-010
TESTING-AND-REGULATING CHIEF (tel. & tel.) 184.167-258
TESTING-AND-REGULATING TECHNICIAN (tel. & tel.) 822.261-026
testing-machine operator (profess. & kin.) 011.361-010
TESTING-MACHINE OPERATOR (tex. prod., nec) 586.685-038
TESTING-MACHINE OPERATOR (tinware) 703.685-014
testing-tool operator (petrol. & gas) 930.261-014
Test-Kitchen-Home Economist (profess. & kin.) 096.121-014
TEST PILOT (aircraft mfg.) 196.263-042
TEST PREPARER (nonfer. metal; steel & rel.) 509.584-010
test puller (tobacco) 529.587-022
test rack operator (railroad equip.) 622.382-010
Test Rider (motor-bicycles) 806.281-018
TEST-SKEIN WINDER (glass mfg.) 575.685-082
TEST TECHNICIAN (agric. equip.) 019.261-022
TEST TECHNICIAN (clerical) 249.367-078
test technician (elec. equip.) 727.381-022
test technician (any industry) 726.261-018
TEST TECHNICIAN (profess. & kin.) 019.161-014
TEST TECHNICIAN, SEMICONDUCTOR PROCESSING EQUIPMENT (electron. comp.) 590.262-014
TEST WORKER (foundry) 519.687-042
Tetryl-Blender Operator (chemical) 550.665-010
Tetryl-Boiling-Tub Operator (chemical) 551.685-014
TETRYL-DISSOLVER OPERATOR (chemical) 550.685-114
Tetryl-Nitrator Operator (chemical) 558.382-046
TETRYL-SCREEN OPERATOR (chemical) 551.685-146
tetryl-wringer operator (chemical) 551.685-162
TEXTILE ENGINEER (profess. & kin.) term
textile-scrap salvager (tex. prod., nec) 789.687-010
textile stylist (profess. & kin.) 142.061-014
TEXTURING-MACHINE FIXER (textile) 628.684-046
THAW-SHED HEATER TENDER (steel & rel.) 543.685-022
Theater Coach (profess. & kin.) 150.027-010
theater projectionist (amuse. & rec.; motion picture) 960.362-010
theatrical performer (amuse. & rec.; motion picture; radio-tv broad.) see ENTERTAINER
theatrical-scenic designer (amuse. & rec.) 142.061-050
Theatrical Variety Agent (amuse. & rec.) 191.117-014
therapeutic recreation worker (medical ser.) 076.124-014
therapist for blind (education; medical ser.; nonprofit org.) 076.224-014
THERMAL CUTTER, HAND I (welding) 816.464-010
THERMAL CUTTER, HAND II (welding) 816.684-010
Thermal-Cutter Helper (welding) 819.687-014
THERMAL-CUTTING-MACHINE OPERATOR (welding) 816.482-010
Thermal-Cutting-Tracer-Machine Operator (welding) 816.482-010
THERMAL MOLDER (rubber goods) 553.585-022
THERMAL-SURFACING-MACHINE OPERATOR (stonework) 679.685-018
Thermite-Bomb Loader (ordnance) 737.684-014
thermo-cementing-folder operator (boot & shoe) 690.685-070
Thermodynamics Engineer (aircraft mfg.) 002.061-010
Thermoelectric-Heat-Sealing-Machine Operator (tex. prod., nec) 754.684-010
thermograph operator (print. & pub.) 652.686-034
THERMOMETER MAKER (inst. & app.) 710.681-026
THERMOMETER PRODUCTION WORKER (inst. & app.) 710.685-014
THERMOMETER TESTER (inst. & app.) 710.384-018
THERMOSCREW OPERATOR (can. & preserv.) 526.685-058
Thermospray Operator (any industry) 505.380-010
Thermostat Assembler (inst. & app.) 710.684-046

THERMOSTAT-ASSEMBLY-MACHINE TENDER, AUTOMATIC (inst. & app.) 692.685-218
THERMOSTAT REPAIRER (inst. & app.) 710.381-050
THICKENER OPERATOR (smelt. & refin.) 511.485-014
Thimble-Press Operator (smelt. & refin.) 519.664-010
THINNER (paint & varnish) 550.585-038
Thinner Sprayer (auto. mfg.) 741.684-026
third assistant engineer (water trans.) 623.281-034
Third-Calender Operator (tex. prod., nec) 584.685-010
THIRD DRY-CELL-ASSEMBLING-MACHINE TENDER (elec. equip.) 692.686-066
THIRD HELPER (steel & rel.) 512.687-014
THIRD-RAIL INSTALLER (r.r. trans.) 825.381-038
Thorough Bred Horse Farm Manager (agriculture) 410.161-018
THRASHER FEEDER (paper & pulp) 533.685-030
THREAD CUTTER (any industry) 789.684-050
thread cutter (garment) 782.684-038
THREAD-CUTTER TENDER (tex. prod., nec) 689.665-014
thread drawer (tex. prod., nec) 789.687-174
thread dresser (textile) 681.682-010
THREADER (knitting) 685.680-010
THREADER (tex. prod., nec) 689.687-078
thread-grinder, tool (machine shop) 603.260-010
THREADING-MACHINE FEEDER, AUTOMATIC I (machine shop) 604.666-010
Threading-Machine Feeder, Automatic II (machine shop) 609.684-014
THREADING-MACHINE OPERATOR (machine shop) 604.682-014
THREADING-MACHINE OPERATOR (ordnance) 604.685-038
THREADING-MACHINE SETTER (machine shop) 609.380-014
THREADING-MACHINE TENDER (carpet & rug) 683.685-030
THREAD INSPECTOR (petrol. & gas) 862.381-038
THREAD INSPECTOR (plastic-synth.) 681.687-018
THREAD LASTER (boot & shoe) 788.684-114
Thread-Machine Operator (rubber goods) 559.682-034
THREAD MARKER (garment) 782.687-058
THREAD-MILLING-MACHINE SET-UP OPERATOR (machine shop) 605.382-042
thread puller (textile) 689.687-058
THREAD-PULLING-MACHINE ATTENDANT (garment) 689.686-046
THREAD SEPARATOR (tex. prod., nec) 789.687-174
thread singer (textile) 585.685-050
thread spooler (toy-sport equip.) 681.685-090
thread weaver (personal ser.) 782.381-022
THREAD WINDER, AUTOMATIC (textile) 681.685-122
three-dimensional-map modeler (any industry) 777.381-042
THRESHER, BROOMCORN (agriculture) 429.685-014
THRESHING-MACHINE OPERATOR (tobacco) 521.685-362
THRILL PERFORMER (amuse. & rec.) 159.347-018
THROWER (pottery & porc.) 774.381-010
THROW-OUT CLERK (retail trade) 241.367-030
Thumb Sewer (glove & mit.) 784.682-010
Ticker Installer (tel. & tel.) 822.381-010
ticket agent (air trans.) 248.382-010
TICKET AGENT (any industry) 238.367-026
TICKET BROKER (amuse. & rec.) 259.357-034
TICKET-CHOPPER ASSEMBLER (furniture) 739.684-154
ticket clerk (any industry) 238.367-026
ticket clerk (clerical) 211.462-010
ticket counter (amuse. & rec.) 219.587-010
TICKET-DISPENSER CHANGER (amuse. & rec.) 349.680-010
TICKETER (any industry) 652.685-098
ticketer (clerical) 221.387-046
TICKETER (textile) 229.587-018
TICKETING CLERK (air trans.) 248.382-010
ticket maker (any industry) 652.685-098
ticket maker (retail trade; wholesale tr.) 209.587-034
TICKET MARKER (wholesale tr.) 216.567-010
ticket printer (any industry) 652.685-098
TICKET PRINTER AND TAGGER (garment) 652.685-094
TICKET PULLER (tobacco) 221.687-014
ticket sales instructor (air trans.) 099.227-018
TICKET SCHEDULER (boot & shoe) 221.587-038
ticket seller (any industry) 238.367-026
TICKET SELLER (clerical) 211.467-030
ticket stamper (textile) 229.587-018
TICKET TAKER (amuse. & rec.) 344.667-010
TICKET TAKER, FERRYBOAT (water trans.) 911.677-010
TICKET WORKER (tobacco) 221.482-018
tick sewer (furniture) 780.682-010
Tie-Back Sewer, Automatic (tex. prod., nec) 787.685-014
TIE BINDER (garment) 920.687-190
tie fastener (paper goods) 649.685-122
Tie Handler (wood prod., nec) 561.686-010
TIE INSPECTOR (saw. & plan.) 669.687-026
Tie-Knitter Helper (knitting) 685.686-014

tie-mill operator (wood prod., nec) 669.682-010
tie-out worker (agriculture) 920.687-074
TIE PRESSER (knitting) 789.687-178
Tie Presser (laundry & rel.) 363.681-010
tie puller (any industry) 920.685-010
tier (garment; glove & mit.) 781.687-010
TIER (meat products) 525.687-118
TIER-AND-DETONATOR (mine & quarry) 931.664-010
Tier-Lift-Truck Operator (any industry) 921.683-050
Tier, Meat (meat products) 525.587-014
tie-tape-machine operator (paper goods) 649.685-122
TIE-UP WORKER (office machines) 710.687-034
tiger-machine operator (textile) 587.685-030
Tight Cooper (wood. container) 764.684-022
TIGHTENING-MACHINE OPERATOR (paper goods) 640.685-082
tight-rope walker (amuse. & rec.) 159.347-022
Tile-And-Terra-Cotta Roofer (construction) 866.381-010
tile classifier (brick & tile) 574.367-010
TILE-CONDUIT LAYER (construction) 861.381-062
TILE DECORATOR (brick & tile) 773.381-010
tile edger (brick & tile) 779.684-018
TILE FINISHER (construction) 861.664-018
tile fitter (construction) 861.381-054
TILE GRINDER (brick & tile) 679.685-022
Tile Inspector (fabrication, nec) 590.367-010
Tile Installer (mfd. bldgs.; vehicles, nec) 869.684-026
tile layer (construction) 861.381-054
Tile-Machine Operator (wood prod., nec) 539.562-010
tile mason (construction) 861.381-054
tile mechanic helper (construction) 861.664-018
Tile-Molder, Hand (brick & tile) 575.684-042
tile paster (brick & tile) 773.684-014
TILE-POWER-SHEAR OPERATOR (fabrication, nec) 692.685-222
TILE SETTER (construction) 861.381-054
tile setter (construction; retail trade) 861.381-034
TILE SETTER (mfd. bldgs.) 861.684-018
TILE SETTER APPRENTICE (construction) 861.381-058
tile setter helper (construction) 861.664-018
Tile Setter Supervisor (construction) 861.131-010
TILE SHADER (brick & tile) 574.367-010
TILE SORTER (brick & tile) 573.687-038
Tile Sprayer (brick & tile) 741.687-018
Tilting-Furnace Operator, Oil Or Gas (foundry) 512.362-018
tilting-head band-sawyer (woodworking) 667.682-010
Tilting-Saw Operator (woodworking) 667.682-022
Tilting-Table Operator (steel & rel.) 613.682-026
Tilt-Wall Supervisor (construction) 869.131-014
timber cruiser (forestry; logging) 459.387-010
Timber Cutter (mine & quarry) 667.682-022
TIMBER FRAMER (mine & quarry) 869.381-034
TIMBER-FRAMER HELPER (mine & quarry) 869.687-042
Timber-Incisor Operator (wood prod., nec) 569.662-010
Timbering Supervisor (construction) 860.131-018
TIMBER PACKER (saw. & plan.) 922.687-094
timber repairer (mine & quarry) 869.381-034
Timber Setter (construction) 860.381-042
TIMBER-SIZER OPERATOR (saw. & plan.) 665.482-018
Timber Sprinkler (mine & quarry) 741.687-018
timber supervisor (logging) 454.134-010
timber-treating-tank operator (wood prod., nec) 561.362-010
timber trimmer (paper & pulp; saw. & plan.) 667.685-034
Time-Analysis Clerk (clerical) 216.382-062
Time Checker (clerical) 215.362-022
Time-Clock Repairer (clock & watch) 715.281-010
Time Clock Repairer (elec. equip.) 829.261-018
TIMEKEEPER (clerical) 215.362-022
timekeeper supervisor (clerical) 215.137-014
Timer (amuse. & rec.) 153.387-014
timer (clock & watch) 715.685-034
Timer (motion picture) 976.381-010
Time-Signal Wirer (tel. & tel.) 822.381-010
time-study analyst (profess. & kin.) 012.167-070
Time-Study Analyst (profess. & kin.) 012.267-010
TIME-STUDY ENGINEER (profess. & kin.) 012.167-070
TIMING ADJUSTER (clock & watch) 715.681-010
timing-machine operator (clock & watch) 715.685-034
tin-can feeder (tobacco) 920.686-030
TIN-CONTAINER STRIGHTENER (tobacco) 709.687-046
Tin Dipper (galvanizing) 501.685-010
Tinner, Automatic (galvanizing) 501.362-010
Tinner Operator, Connecting Rods (auto. mfg.) 599.685-026
TINNING-EQUIPMENT TENDER (elec. equip.) 501.685-014
TINNING-MACHINE SET-UP OPERATOR (print. & pub.) 653.682-022
Tin Plater (electroplating) 500.380-010
TIN RECOVERY WORKER (smelt. & refin.) 512.382-018

TIN ROLLER, HOT MILL (steel & rel.) 613.360-018
TINSEL-MACHINE OPERATOR (fabrication, nec) 692.685-226
Tinsmith (any industry) 804.281-010
TIN STACKER (tinware) 922.687-098
TINTER (paint & varnish) 550.381-014
tinter, photograph (photofinishing) 970.381-010
tin-tie-machine operator, automatic (paper goods) 649.685-110
tint layer (print. & pub.) 970.681-010
TIN-WHIZ-MACHINE OPERATOR (textile) 582.685-154
TIP BANDER (pen & pencil) 733.685-030
tip-banding-machine operator (pen & pencil) 733.685-030
Tip Burnisher (boot & shoe) 690.685-058
tip cementer (boot & shoe) 788.685-014
TIP FINISHER (boot & shoe) 690.685-418
TIP INSERTER (woodworking) 669.682-066
TIP-LENGTH CHECKER (tobacco) 529.467-010
Tip Maker (hat & cap) 784.682-014
TIP-OUT WORKER (concrete prod.) 575.687-038
tipper (agriculture; meat products) 525.687-070
Tipper (glove & mit.) 784.682-010
tipper (hat & cap) 580.685-062
tipper (hat & cap) 580.685-026
tipper (jewelry-silver.) 705.682-014
tipper (pen & pencil) 733.685-034
TIPPER (print. & pub.) 795.684-022
Tipping-Machine Operator (fabrication, nec) 787.685-010
tipping-machine operator (hat & cap) 580.685-062
TIPPING-MACHINE OPERATOR (pen & pencil) 733.685-034
tipping-machine operator (pen & pencil) 686.686-010
tipping-machine operator, automatic (narrow fabrics) 686.685-062
TIPPLE OPERATOR (saw. & plan.) 921.662-026
Tipple Repairer (mine & quarry) 630.281-022
tipple supervisor (mine & quarry) 549.137-014
TIPPLE TENDER (grain-feed mills) 521.685-366
TIPPLE TENDER (millwork-plywood) 669.685-090
tipple worker (any industry) 921.685-038
TIP PRINTER (hat & cap) 651.682-022
Tip Puncher (boot & shoe) 690.685-114
Tip Sewer (glove & mit.) 787.685-042
Tip Stitcher (boot & shoe) 690.682-082
TIP STRETCHER (hat & cap) 580.685-062
tip tester (tobacco) 529.467-010
tip tightener (pen & pencil) 733.687-014
TIRE ADJUSTER (retail trade) 241.367-034
tire-and-tube repairer (automotive ser.) 915.684-010
tire-and-tube servicer (automotive ser.) 915.684-010
tire assembler (fabrication, nec) 739.684-158
TIRE BALANCER (rubber tire) 750.687-014
TIRE-BLADDER MAKER (rubber tire) 750.684-042
TIRE BUFFER (automotive ser.) 690.685-422
Tire Buffer (rubber tire) 759.684-022
TIRE BUILDER (automotive ser.) 750.684-022
TIRE BUILDER (rubber tire) term
TIRE BUILDER, AUTOMOBILE (rubber tire) 750.384-010
Tire Builder, Heavy Service (rubber tire) 750.384-010
Tire-Building Supervisor (rubber tire) 750.130-010
Tire Changer (automotive ser.) 915.684-010
Tire Changer, Aircraft (air trans.) 915.684-010
Tire Changer, Road Service (automotive ser.) 915.684-010
TIRE CLASSIFIER (rubber tire) 750.387-010
Tire Debeader (rubber reclaim.) 690.685-386
Tire-Fabric-Impregnating-Range Back-Tender (tex. prod., nec) 589.686-010
TIRE-FABRIC-IMPREGNATING-RANGE OPERATOR, CHIEF (tex. prod., nec) 589.662-014
Tire-Fabric-Impregnating-Range Tender (tex. prod., nec) 589.685-026
Tire-Fabric Inspector (tex. prod., nec) 689.685-038
Tire-Finishing Supervisor (rubber tire) 750.130-010
tire fixer (automotive ser.) 915.684-010
TIRE GROOVER (automotive ser.) 750.684-026
TIRE INSPECTOR (automotive ser.) 750.687-018
TIRE INSPECTOR (rubber tire) 750.684-030
Tire Mold Engraver, Numerical Control (machine shop) 605.382-014
TIRE MOLDER (rubber tire) 553.685-102
TIRE MOUNTER (fabrication, nec) 739.684-158
tire rebuilder (automotive ser.) 750.684-022
TIRE RECAPPER (automotive ser.) 750.685-014
TIRE-REGROOVING-MACHINE OPERATOR (automotive ser.) 690.662-010
TIRE REPAIRER (automotive ser.) 915.684-010
TIRE REPAIRER (rubber tire) 750.681-010
Tire-Room Supervisor (rubber tire) 750.130-010
tire servicer (automotive ser.) 915.684-010
TIRE-SERVICE SUPERVISOR (automotive ser.) 915.134-010
TIRE SETTER (toy-sport equip.) 731.685-018
TIRE SORTER (rubber tire) 750.687-022
tire spotter (rubber tire) 750.687-014

TIRE TECHNICIAN (rubber tire) 750.382-010
TIRE TRIMMER, HAND (rubber tire) 750.684-034
Tire Trucker (rubber tire) 929.687-030
TIRE VULCANIZER (automotive ser.) 750.684-038
Tire Wrapper (automotive ser.; rubber tire) 920.685-078
Tissue Inserter (knitting) 920.687-062
tissue technologist (medical ser.) 078.261-030
title abstractor (profess. & kin.) 119.267-010
Title Artist (motion picture; radio-tv broad.) 141.061-022
TITLE ATTORNEY (profess. & kin.) 110.117-042
TITLE CLERK (petrol. & gas; petrol. refin.; pipe lines) 162.267-010
Title Clerk, Automobile (clerical) 203.582-066
TITLE EXAMINER (profess. & kin.) 119.287-010
title examiner (profess. & kin.) 110.117-042
TITLE SEARCHER (real estate) 209.367-046
TITLE SUPERVISOR (profess. & kin.) 119.167-018
titrator (textile) 582.587-010
TNT-LINE SUPERVISOR (chemical) 559.131-018
Toaster-Element Repairer (house. appl.) 723.584-010
Toaster Operator (tobacco) 523.685-118
Tobacco Baler (tobacco) 920.685-010
TOBACCO BLENDER (retail trade) 790.381-010
Tobacco-Checkout Clerk (wholesale tr.) 222.687-030
tobacco cleaner (tobacco) 521.685-270
TOBACCO-CLOTH RECLAIMER (tex. prod., nec) 589.686-050
tobacco conditioner (tobacco) 522.687-026
TOBACCO CURER (agriculture) 523.682-038
tobacco curer (tobacco) 522.687-026
tobacco cutter (tobacco) 521.685-338
tobacco cutter (tobacco) 521.685-310
tobacco cutter (tobacco) 521.685-298
tobacco dipper (tobacco) 522.687-026
TOBACCO-DRIER OPERATOR (tobacco) 523.685-118
tobacco drying-machine operator (tobacco) 522.662-014
Tobacco Farmworker (agriculture) 404.687-010
tobacco flavorer (tobacco) 522.685-030
Tobacco Grader (agriculture) 409.687-010
Tobacco Grower (agriculture) 404.161-010
Tobacco Packer (agriculture) 920.687-134
TOBACCO-PACKING-MACHINE OPERATOR (tobacco) 920.685-098
tobacco roller (tobacco) 790.687-030
TOBACCO-SAMPLE PULLER (tobacco) 529.587-022
Tobacco-Scrap Sifter (tobacco) 521.685-270
tobacco shaker (tobacco) 521.687-110
tobacco-sieve operator (tobacco) 521.685-270
tobacco sprayer (tobacco) 522.687-042
Tobacco-Stem-Drier Operator (tobacco) 523.685-118
tobacco stemmer, machine (tobacco) 521.685-334
tobacco stripper, hand (tobacco) 521.687-134
tobacco-stripping-machine operator (tobacco) 521.685-334
TOBACCO-WAREHOUSE AGENT (business ser.) 259.357-038
Tobacco Weigher (clerical) 222.387-074
toe and heel laster (boot & shoe) 690.682-018
TOE-CLOSING-MACHINE TENDER (knitting) 787.685-046
TOE FORMER, STITCHDOWNS (boot & shoe) 690.685-426
TOE LASTER, AUTOMATIC (boot & shoe) 690.685-430
toe laster, automatic (boot & shoe) 690.685-426
Toe-Lining Closer (boot & shoe) 690.682-082
Toe Pounder (boot & shoe) 690.685-314
Toe Puller (meat products) 525.687-094
TOE PUNCHER (knitting) 689.685-162
Toe Sewer (knitting) 787.682-074
Toe Stapler (boot & shoe) 690.685-162
Toe Stripper (wood prod., nec) 669.682-054
Tofu Maker (food prep., nec) 529.685-290
TOGGLE-PRESS FOLDER-AND-FEEDER (boot & shoe) 690.686-066
toggle-press operator (any industry) 617.260-010
toggler (leather mfg.) 589.686-026
toilet attendant (any industry) 358.677-018
Toll-Bridge Attendant (government ser.) 211.462-038
TOLL COLLECTOR (government ser.) 211.462-038
Toll-Line Repairer (tel. & tel.) 822.381-014
Toll Repairer, Central Office (tel. & tel.) 822.281-014
Tomato Grader (wholesale tr.) 529.687-186
Tomato-Paste Maker (can. & preserv.) 521.382-010
Tomato-Pulper Operator (can. & preserv.) 521.685-262
tombstone setter (construction) 861.361-014
tonal regulator (any industry) 730.361-010
Ton-Container Filler (chemical) 559.565-010
Ton-Container Shipper (chemical) 549.587-010
Ton-Cylinder Inspector (chemical) 953.387-010
tone artist (print. & pub.) 972.281-010
tone-artist apprentice (print. & pub.) 972.281-018
TONE CABINET ASSEMBLER (musical inst.) 730.684-090
TONE REGULATOR (musical inst.) 730.684-094

Tongue-And-Groove-Machine Feeder (woodworking) 669.686-030
TONGUE-AND-GROOVE-MACHINE OPERATOR (woodworking) 669.662-018
Tongue-And-Groove-Machine Setter (woodworking) 669.280-010
Tongue And Quarter Stitcher (boot & shoe) 690.682-082
Tongue Cutter (meat products) 525.684-034
Tongue-Lining Stitcher (boot & shoe) 690.682-082
TONGUE PRESSER (boot & shoe) 788.685-022
Tongue Stitcher (boot & shoe) 690.682-082
TONNAGE-COMPILATION CLERK (water trans.) 248.387-014
tonsorial artist (personal ser.) 330.371-010
tool-and-die inspector (machine shop) 601.281-022
TOOL-AND-DIE MAKER (machine shop) 601.260-010
TOOL-AND-DIE-MAKER APPRENTICE (machine shop) 601.260-014
Tool-And-Die Repairer (machine shop) 601.260-010
TOOL-AND-DIE SUPERVISOR (machine shop) 601.130-010
TOOL-AND-EQUIPMENT-RENTAL CLERK (business ser.; retail trade) 295.357-014
tool-and-gauge inspector (machine shop) 601.281-022
tool-and-machine maintainer (any industry) 638.281-014
tool-and-production planner (profess. & kin.) 012.167-050
Tool Bender, Hand (any industry) 619.361-010
TOOL BUILDER (aircraft mfg.) 693.281-030
Tool Chaser (any industry) 922.687-058
tool clerk (clerical) 222.367-062
TOOL-CRIB ATTENDANT (clerical) 222.367-062
TOOL-CRIB SUPERVISOR (clerical) 222.137-046
TOOL DESIGN CHECKER (aircraft mfg.) 007.267-014
TOOL DESIGNER (profess. & kin.) 007.061-026
TOOL-DESIGNER APPRENTICE (profess. & kin.) 007.061-030
tool-drawing checker (aircraft mfg.) 007.267-014
TOOL DRESSER (any industry) 601.682-010
Tool-Dresser (forging) 610.381-010
tool dresser (machine shop) 603.280-038
tooler (leather prod.) 781.381-018
TOOL FILER (pottery & porc.) 701.684-030
tool filer, hand (machine shop) 705.484-010
TOOL, GAUGE, AND FIXTURE REPAIRER (auto. mfg.) 601.281-030
tool grinder (machine shop) 603.382-038
tool grinder (machine shop) 603.280-038
TOOL GRINDER I (any industry) 701.381-018
TOOL GRINDER II (any industry) 603.664-010
TOOL-GRINDER OPERATOR (machine shop) 603.280-038
tool-grinding-machine operator (machine shop) 603.280-038
TOOLING COORDINATOR, PRODUCTION ENGINEERING (aircraft mfg.) 169.167-054
tooling inspector (machine shop) 601.281-022
tooling reproduction technician (aircraft mfg.) 976.381-022
Tool Liaison (aircraft mfg.) 012.167-038
TOOL-MACHINE SET-UP OPERATOR (machine shop) 601.280-054
TOOL-MAINTENANCE WORKER (office machines) 701.384-010
TOOL MAKER (machine shop) 601.280-042
TOOL-MAKER APPRENTICE (machine shop) 601.280-058
TOOL MAKER, BENCH (machine shop) 601.281-026
Tool Marker (machine shop) 609.684-014
TOOL PLANNER (any industry) 012.167-074
tool procurement coordinator (aircraft mfg.) 169.167-054
tool programmer (any industry) 007.167-018
TOOL PROGRAMMER, NUMERICAL CONTROL (any industry) 007.167-018
TOOL PROGRAMMER, NUMERICAL CONTROL (electron. comp.) 609.262-010
TOOL PUSHER (petrol. & gas) 930.130-010
Tool Pusher, Shallow-Exploratory Drilling (petrol. & gas) 930.130-010
Tool Repairer (machine shop) 601.280-042
Tool Repairer, Bench (machine shop) 601.281-026
TOOL REPAIRER (smelt. & refin.) 519.684-026
tool-room gear-machine operator (machine shop) 602.280-010
tool-room-lathe operator (machine shop) 604.280-010
tool setter (button & notion) 617.380-010
tool setter (jewelry-silver.) 615.130-010
tool sharpener (any industry) 603.664-010
tool sharpener (any industry) 701.381-018
tool sharpener (machine shop) 603.280-038
Tool Straightener (any industry) 709.484-014
Tooth-Brush-Boring-And-Filling-Machine Operator (fabrication, nec) 692.682-018
TOOTH CLERK (protective dev.) 222.687-038
TOOTH CUTTER (clock & watch) 605.685-050
Tooth Cutter, Clutch (clock & watch) 605.685-050
Tooth Cutter, Contact Wheel (clock & watch) 605.682-026
TOOTH CUTTER, ESCAPE WHEEL (clock & watch) 605.682-026
Tooth Cutter, Hobbing Machine (clock & watch) 605.685-050
Tooth Cutter, Pinion (clock & watch) 605.685-050
Tooth Cutter, Spur (clock & watch) 605.685-050

TOOTH INSPECTOR (protective dev.) 712.687-038
TOOTH POLISHER (clock & watch) 715.682-026
top-and-seat-cover fitter (automotive ser.) 780.384-010
top-bottom-attaching-machine operator (garment; hat & cap) 699.685-010
Top Cager (mine & quarry) 939.667-010
Top Case Assembler (musical inst.) 763.684-058
top cleaner (textile) 680.687-014
Top-Collar Baster (garment) 782.684-058
Top-Collar Maker (garment; retail trade) 785.361-022
Top Coverer (fabrication, nec) 780.684-026
TOP-DYEING-MACHINE LOADER (tex. prod., nec; textile) 582.686-030
Top-Dyeing-Machine Tender (textile) 582.685-102
Top-Edge Beveler (any industry) 705.687-014
top flavor attendant (tobacco) 520.687-026
TOP FORMER (boot & shoe) 788.685-026
Top-Frame Coverer (fabrication, nec) 780.684-026
Top-Frame Fitter (fabrication, nec) 739.684-190
Top-Frame Maker (fabrication, nec) 739.684-190
TOP-HAT-BODY MAKER (hat & cap) 784.684-074
top icer (wholesale tr.) 922.687-046
Top Installer (automotive ser.) 780.381-010
top ironer (boot & shoe) 788.685-026
top-lift and automatic-window repairer (automotive ser.) 825.381-014
Top-Lift Compressor (boot & shoe) 690.685-210
Top-Lift Cutter (boot & shoe) 699.682-022
Top-Lift Nailer (boot & shoe) 690.685-162
Top-Lift Scourer (boot & shoe) 690.685-046
Top-Lift Trimmer (boot & shoe) 690.685-434
topline-beading-machine tender (boot & shoe) 788.685-014
topographic computator (profess. & kin.) 018.167-014
topper (fabrication, nec) 761.684-030
topper (furniture) 780.685-018
TOPPER (knitting) 685.687-026
Topper Packer (agriculture) 920.687-134
Topper-Press Operator (laundry & rel.) 363.682-018
Topper-Press Operator, Automatic (laundry & rel.) 363.682-018
Toppiece Chopper (boot & shoe) 699.685-014
Toppiece Cutter (boot & shoe) 699.682-022
TOP POLISHER (stonework) 673.662-010
TOP-PRECIPITATOR OPERATOR (smelt. & refin.) 511.465-010
TOP-PRECIPITATOR-OPERATOR HELPER (smelt. & refin.) 511.586-010
TOP SCREW (agriculture) 410.137-014
Topside Inspector (optical goods) 716.687-018
Top Steep Tender (grain-feed mills) 522.465-010
Top Stitcher (boot & shoe) 690.682-082
Top Stitcher (hat & cap) 784.682-014
Top Stitcher (toy-sport equip.) 732.684-050
TOPSTITCHER, LOCKSTITCH (garment) 786.682-238
TOPSTITCHER, ZIGZAG (garment) 786.682-242
Top-Stop Attacher (button & notion) 692.685-206
Top Taper, Machine (boot & shoe) 690.685-414
top-tile decorator (brick & tile) 773.684-010
Top Trimmer I (boot & shoe) 690.685-434
Top Trimmer II (boot & shoe) 690.682-086
top waddy (agriculture) 410.137-014
torch brazer (welding) 813.684-010
torch cutter (welding) 816.464-010
TORCH-STRAIGHTENER-AND HEATER (any industry) 709.684-086
torpedo shooter (petrol. & gas) 931.361-014
Torpedo Specialist (government ser.) 632.261-018
TORQUE TESTER (clock & watch) 715.685-066
TORSION SPRING COILING MACHINE SETTER (metal prod., nec) 616.260-022
Tortilla Maker (food prep., nec) 529.685-078
toter (any industry) 919.664-010
TOUCH-UP CARVER (fabrication, nec) 761.684-054
touch-up finisher, metal (automotive ser.) 807.381-010
touch-up inspector, printed circuit boards (electron. comp.) 726.684-062
TOUCH-UP PAINTER, HAND (any industry) 740.684-026
TOUCH-UP SCREENER, PRINTED CIRCUIT BOARD ASSEMBLY (electron. comp.) 726.684-110
touch-up worker (office machines) 706.587-010
Tour Agent (motor trans.) 252.152-010
touring counselor (nonprofit org.) 238.167-014
tourist-camp attendant (hotel & rest.) 329.467-010
TOURIST-INFORMATION ASSISTANT (government ser.) 237.367-050
tow-car driver (automotive ser.) 919.663-026
Towel Bander (paper goods) 920.687-026
TOWEL-CABINET REPAIRER (business ser.) 709.364-014
Towel Folder (tex. prod., nec) 589.687-014
Towel Inspector (tex. prod., nec) 789.587-014
TOWEL INSPECTOR (textile) 652.686-042
Towel-Rack Assembler (woodworking) 762.687-070
towel-rolling-machine operator (laundry & rel.) 361.685-014
Towel Sewer (tex. prod., nec) 787.682-026

TOWER ATTENDANT (paper & pulp) 559.666-010
TOWER-CRANE OPERATOR (construction) 921.663-054
tower-dragline operator (construction) 850.683-042
TOWER ERECTOR (construction; utilities) 821.361-038
TOWER ERECTOR HELPER (construction; utilities) 821.684-014
TOWER-EXCAVATOR OPERATOR (construction) 850.683-042
TOWER HELPER (chemical) 558.385-014
Tower-Hoist Operator (mine & quarry) 921.663-026
TOWER-LOADER OPERATOR (water trans.) 921.683-074
TOWER OPERATOR (r.r. trans.) 910.362-010
TOWER OPERATOR (soap & rel.) 559.362-034
TOWER OPERATOR I (chemical) term
Tower Operator II (chemical) 558.685-062
Tower Supervisor (construction) 809.131-018
Tower-Truck Driver (tel. & tel.; utilities) 905.663-014
Tower-Whirler Operator (any industry) 921.663-010
Tow Feeder (tex. prod., nec) 680.686-014
TOWN CLERK (government ser.) 243.367-018
town planner (profess. & kin.) 199.167-014
Tow Picker (furniture) 680.685-078
Tow-Picker Operator (furniture) 680.685-082
TOW-TRUCK OPERATOR (automotive ser.) 919.663-026
TOXICOLOGIST (pharmaceut.) 022.081-010
TOXIC OPERATOR (chemical) term
TOY ASSEMBLER (retail trade) 731.684-018
TOY ASSEMBLER (toy-sport equip.) 731.687-034
Toy Assembler, Plastic (toy-sport equip.) 731.687-034
Toy Assembler, Wood (toy-sport equip.) 731.687-034
Toy-Department Manager (retail trade) 299.137-010
TOY-ELECTRIC-TRAIN REPAIRER (retail trade) 731.684-022
Toy Sorter (sugar & conf.) 529.686-034
toy stuffer (toy-sport equip.) 731.685-014
tracer (clerical) 241.367-026
TRACER (construction; stonework) 779.381-022
tracer (medical ser.) 078.384-010
tracer-bullet assembly-machine tool setter (ordnance) 616.360-034
TRACER-BULLET-CHARGING-MACHINE OPERATOR (ordnance) 694.382-014
TRACER-BULLET-SECTION SUPERVISOR (ordnance) 694.131-010
Tracer Clerk (clerical) 241.367-014
tracer-controlled-milling-machine operator (machine shop) 605.280-018
tracer-lathe set-up operator (machine shop) 604.280-010
TRACER-POWDER BLENDER (chemical) 550.585-042
Tracing-Lathe Set-Up Operator (machine shop) 604.380-018
Track-Broom Operator (r.r. trans.) 859.683-018
track-grinder operator (r.r. trans.) 910.684-010
track inspector (r.r. trans.) 910.367-030
track laborer (r.r. trans.) 910.684-014
TRACK LAMINATING MACHINE TENDER (inst. & app.) 692.685-290
Track Layer (construction) 869.687-026
track layer, head (construction) 869.134-022
track-laying-machine operator (construction; mine & quarry) 910.663-010
TRACK-LAYING SUPERVISOR (construction) 869.134-022
track leader (construction) 869.134-022
Track-Liner Operator (construction) 910.683-018
TRACKMOBILE OPERATOR (any industry) 919.683-026
TRACK-MOVING-MACHINE OPERATOR (construction; mine & quarry) 910.663-010
TRACK OILER (r.r. trans.) 910.687-026
TRACK REPAIRER (r.r. trans.) 910.684-014
Track-Repairer Helper (construction) 869.687-026
TRACK SUPERVISOR (grain-feed mills) 921.132-010
track supervisor (r.r. trans.) 910.367-030
TRACK-SURFACING-MACHINE OPERATOR (construction) 910.683-018
Track-Template-Thermal-Cutting-Machine Operator (welding) 816.482-010
tractor-crane engineer (any industry) 921.663-058
TRACTOR-CRANE OPERATOR (any industry) 921.663-058
Tractor-Drill Operator (construction; mine & quarry) 930.382-010
TRACTOR MECHANIC (automotive ser.) 620.281-058
TRACTOR-MECHANIC HELPER (automotive ser.) 620.684-030
TRACTOR OPERATOR (any industry) 929.683-014
Tractor Operator (water trans.) 911.663-014
Tractor Operator, Battery (mine & quarry) 929.683-014
Tractor Operator, Laser Leveling (any industry) 929.683-014
tractor-sweeper driver (government ser.) 919.683-022
TRACTOR-TRAILER-TRUCK DRIVER (any industry) 904.383-010
TRADE MARKER (fabrication, nec) 690.685-510
trader (financial) 162.167-034
trader (financial) 162.167-038
Trade-Show Representative (any industry) 297.367-010
TRAFFIC AGENT (air trans.; motor trans.; r.r. trans.; water trans.) 252.257-010
TRAFFIC CHECKER (government ser.) 205.367-058
traffic chief (tel. & tel.) 184.167-106
TRAFFIC CLERK (radio-tv broad.) 209.382-022

TRAFFIC CLERK (business ser.) 221.367-078
TRAFFIC CLERK (clerical) 214.587-014
traffic controller, cable (tel. & tel.) 239.137-026
traffic-control operator (r.r. trans.) 184.167-262
traffic control signaler (construction) 372.667-022
Traffic-Court Magistrate (government ser.) 111.107-014
Traffic Engineer (government ser.) 005.061-038
traffic engineer (radio-tv broad.) 003.187-014
Traffic Enumerator (clerical) 216.382-062
TRAFFIC INSPECTOR (motor trans.; r.r. trans.) 184.163-010
TRAFFIC LIEUTENANT (government ser.) 375.167-046
Traffic-Maintenance Officer (government ser.) 869.137-010
TRAFFIC-MAINTENANCE SUPERVISOR (government ser.) 869.137-010
traffic manager (radio-tv broad.) 209.382-022
traffic officer (government ser.) 375.263-014
Traffic Police Officer (government ser.) 375.263-014
TRAFFIC-RATE CLERK (clerical) 214.362-038
TRAFFIC-SAFETY ADMINISTRATOR (government ser.) 188.167-102
TRAFFIC SERGEANT (government ser.) 375.137-026
Traffic-Signal Repairer (utilities) 824.381-010
Traffic-Signal Supervisor, Maintenance (government ser.) 869.137-010
Traffic-Sign Erection Supervisor (government ser.) 869.137-010
traffic superintendent (tel. & tel.) 184.167-106
traffic supervisor (any industry) 921.133-018
TRAFFIC TECHNICIAN (government ser.) 199.267-030
trailer (any industry) 932.664-010
TRAILER ASSEMBLER I (auto. mfg.) 806.381-058
TRAILER ASSEMBLER II (auto. mfg.) 806.684-082
trailer assembler, paneling (auto. mfg.) 806.684-082
Trailer-Body Assembler (auto. mfg.) 806.381-058
Trailer Chief (photofinishing) 976.131-010
TRAILER-RENTAL CLERK (automotive ser.) 295.467-022
trailer-sections assembler (auto. mfg.) 806.684-082
Trailer Steerer (logging) 904.683-010
Trailer-Tank-Truck Driver (petrol. refin.; retail trade; wholesale tr.) 903.683-018
trailer-truck driver (any industry) 904.383-010
TRAIN CLERK (r.r. trans.) 219.462-014
train conductor (any industry) 932.664-010
TRAIN DISPATCHER (r.r. trans.) 184.167-262
TRAIN DISPATCHER, ASSISTANT CHIEF (r.r. trans.) 910.167-014
TRAINEE (any industry) term
TRAINEE ENGINEER (profess. & kin.) term
training administrator (education) 166.167-026
training instructor (education) 166.227-010
TRAINING REPRESENTATIVE (education) 166.227-010
training specialist (education) 166.221-010
TRAINING TECHNICIAN (can. & preserv.) 522.264-010
Train Operator (amuse. & rec.) 342.663-010
trammer (any industry) 919.663-014
Tram Operator (amuse. & rec.) 353.363-010
transcriber (profess. & kin.) 152.067-010
TRANSCRIBING-MACHINE OPERATOR (clerical) 203.582-058
transcribing operator, head (clerical) 203.132-014
transcripter (profess. & kin.) 152.067-010
transfer and line-up worker (auto. mfg.) 221.367-026
transfer-and-pumphouse operator (chemical) 559.665-038
TRANSFER-AND-PUMPHOUSE OPERATOR, CHIEF (chemical) 559.132-138
TRANSFER-CAR OPERATOR (brick & tile) 921.683-078
TRANSFER-CAR OPERATOR, DRIER (nonmet. min.) 921.583-010
TRANSFER CLERK (financial) 216.362-046
TRANSFER CONTROLLER (saw. & plan.) 921.682-022
Transfer Engineer (logging) 921.663-030
transfer-iron operator (knitting; tex. prod., nec) 659.685-022
transfer knitter (knitting) 685.665-010
TRANSFER-MACHINE OPERATOR (knitting; tex. prod., nec) 659.685-022
TRANSFER-MACHINE OPERATOR (machine shop) 609.685-022
TRANSFER OPERATOR (paper & pulp) 921.685-066
TRANSFER OPERATOR (print. & pub.) 651.382-038
transfer operator (woodworking) 569.683-010
TRANSFERRER (clock & watch) 715.684-190
TRANSFERRER (print. & pub.) 972.381-026
TRANSFER-TABLE OPERATOR (railroad equip.; r.r. trans.) 910.683-022
Transfer-Table Operator (steel & rel.) 613.682-026
TRANSFER-TABLE OPERATOR HELPER (railroad equip.; r.r. trans.) 910.667-030
transformer assembler (any industry) 724.381-018
transformer assembler (utilities) 821.361-034
TRANSFORMER ASSEMBLER I (elec. equip.) 820.381-014
TRANSFORMER ASSEMBLER II (elec. equip.) 820.684-010
TRANSFORMER ASSEMBLY SUPERVISOR (elec. equip.) 820.137-010
Transformer-Coil Winder (elec. equip.; electron. comp.) 724.684-026
Transformer-Coil Winder (utilities) 829.261-018
Transformer-Core Assembler (elec. equip.) 729.684-066

Transformer Inspector (elec. equip.) 829.361-018
Transformer Molder (elec. equip.) 729.684-030
transformer rebuilder (any industry) 724.381-018
TRANSFORMER REPAIRER (any industry) 724.381-018
TRANSFORMER SHOP SUPERVISOR (any industry) 724.131-014
TRANSFORMER-STOCK CLERK (utilities) 222.587-054
Transformer Tester (elec. equip.) 721.281-030
Transformer Tester (electron. comp.) 726.684-078
TRANSFORMER TESTER (utilities) 724.281-010
transit clerk (financial) 217.382-010
transit-mix operator (construction) 900.683-010
transit-operations supervisor (motor trans.) 913.167-014
TRANSLATOR (profess. & kin.) 137.267-018
translator, deaf (profess. & kin.) 137.267-014
Transliterator (profess. & kin.) 137.267-018
transmission-and-coordination engineer (utilities) 003.167-050
TRANSMISSION-AND-PROTECTION ENGINEER (tel. & tel.) 003.167-066
Transmission Assembler (motor-bicycles) 806.684-094
transmission engineer (radio-tv broad.) 003.167-030
transmission engineer (tel. & tel.) 003.167-066
transmission-line engineer (utilities) 003.167-050
Transmission-Maintenance Supervisor (tel. & tel.) 822.131-014
TRANSMISSION MECHANIC (automotive ser.) 620.281-062
Transmission Repairer (auto. mfg.) 620.381-022
Transmission Repairer (motor-bicycles) 620.684-026
TRANSMISSION TESTER (auto. mfg.) 806.684-134
TRANSMISSION TESTER (tel. & tel.) 822.361-026
Transmitter Assembler (elec. equip.) 721.381-014
transmitter engineer (radio-tv broad.) 003.167-034
transmitter engineer (radio-tv broad.) 193.262-038
TRANSMITTER OPERATOR (radio-tv broad.) 193.262-038
Transmitter Tester (electron. comp.) 726.261-018
TRANSPLANT COORDINATOR (medical ser.) 079.151-010
TRANSPLANTER, ORCHID (agriculture) 405.687-018
TRANSPORTATION AGENT (air trans.) 912.367-014
transportation clerk (hotel & rest.) 238.367-030
transportation consultant (business ser.) 184.267-010
transportation department head (any industry) 184.167-226
transportation-department supervisor (automotive ser.) 620.131-014
Transportation Director (nonprofit org.) 187.167-214
TRANSPORTATION ENGINEER (profess. & kin.) 005.061-038
TRANSPORTATION-EQUIPMENT-MAINTENANCE WORKER (museums) 899.384-010
transportation inspector (motor trans.; r.r. trans.) 184.163-010
TRANSPORTATION INSPECTOR (motor trans.; r.r. trans.) 168.167-082
TRANSPORTATION-MAINTENANCE SUPERVISOR (any industry) 184.167-266
transportation-museum helper (museums) 899.384-010
Transportation Planning Engineer (government ser.) 005.061-038
Transport Driver (motor trans.) 904.383-010
TRANSPORTER, PATIENTS (medical ser.) 355.677-014
Transport Pilot (air trans.) 196.263-014
trapeze artist (amuse. & rec.) 159.247-014
trapeze performer (amuse. & rec.) 159.247-014
TRAPPER, ANIMAL (fishing & hunt.) 461.684-014
TRAPPER, BIRD (fishing & hunt.) 461.684-018
trash-collection supervisor (motor trans.) 909.137-014
trash collector (any industry) 381.687-018
trash collector (any industry) 929.687-022
Trash Collector (motor trans.) 955.687-022
trauma coordinator (medical ser.) 079.117-010
TRAVEL AGENT (business ser.; motor trans.; retail trade) 252.152-010
travel clerk (clerical) 238.362-014
TRAVEL CLERK (government ser.) 238.167-010
TRAVEL CLERK (hotel & rest.) 238.367-030
travel clerk (motor trans.; r.r. trans.; water trans.) 237.367-018
travel counselor (business ser.; motor trans.; retail trade) 252.152-010
TRAVEL COUNSELOR, AUTOMOBILE CLUB (nonprofit org.) 238.167-014
TRAVELER CHANGER (textile) 682.687-010
traveling cleaner, maintenance (textile) 628.684-022
traveling clerk (nonprofit org.) 238.167-014
traveling-crane operator (any industry) 921.663-010
Traveling-Freight-And-Passenger Agent (air trans.; motor trans.; r.r. trans.; water trans.) 252.257-010
Traveling-Maintenance Supervisor (any industry) 638.131-026
traveling-plant operator (construction) 859.683-026
Travel-Ticketing Reviewer (nonprofit org.) 238.167-014
TRAVERSE-ROD ASSEMBLER (furniture) 739.687-186
TRAWL NET MAKER (tex. prod., nec) 789.381-018
TRAY-CASTING-MACHINE OPERATOR (dairy products) 520.685-218
TRAY DRIER (knitting) 581.686-038
TRAY-DRIER OPERATOR (chemical) 553.665-054
TRAY FILLER (tobacco) 920.686-050
Tray-Line Supervisor (medical ser.) 319.137-010
tray packer (tobacco) 920.686-050

tray setter (hotel & rest.) 319.484-010
tray thickener operator (smelt. & refin.) 511.562-010
tray worker (medical ser.) 319.677-014
Treadle-Cut-Off-Saw Operator (woodworking) 667.682-022
Treadmill Inspector (agric. equip.) 624.361-010
Tread-Tuber-Machine Operator (rubber tire) 690.662-014
TREASURER (profess. & kin.) 161.117-018
TREASURER, FINANCIAL INSTITUTION (financial) 186.117-070
Treasurer, Savings Bank (financial) 186.117-070
treasury representative (profess. & kin.) 161.117-018
TREATER (any industry) 582.687-030
treater (petrol. & gas) 541.382-014
TREATER (petrol. refin.) 549.362-014
treater (textile) 589.665-014
TREATER HELPER (petrol. refin.) 549.685-030
treating and pumping supervisor (petrol. refin.) 549.132-034
TREATING ENGINEER (wood prod., nec) 561.362-010
TREATING-ENGINEER HELPER (wood prod., nec) 561.685-010
TREATING INSPECTOR (wood prod., nec) 569.367-010
treating-plant operator (petrol. refin.) 549.362-014
TREATING-PLANT OPERATOR (wood prod., nec) 563.662-010
treating-plant operator (wood prod., nec) 561.362-010
TREATING-PLANT SUPERVISOR (wood prod., nec) 561.131-010
TREATMENT-PLANT MECHANIC (waterworks) 630.281-038
TREE CUTTER (agriculture; logging) 454.684-026
TREE DRILLER (boot & shoe) 788.684-118
Tree Loader, Meat (meat products) 525.587-014
TREE PLANTER (forestry) 452.687-018
TREE PRUNER (agriculture) 408.684-018
tree puller (forestry) 451.687-018
treer (boot & shoe) 788.687-122
Tree-Service Supervisor (agriculture) 408.131-010
TREE-SHEAR OPERATOR (logging) 454.683-010
tree sorter (forestry) 451.687-022
TREE SURGEON (agriculture) 408.181-010
Tree-Surgeon Helper I (agriculture) 408.684-018
TREE-SURGEON HELPER II (agriculture) 408.687-018
TREE TRIMMER (tel. & tel.; utilities) 408.664-010
TREE-TRIMMER HELPER (utilities) 408.667-010
tree trimmer helper, line clearance (utilities) 408.667-010
tree trimmer, line clearance (tel. & tel.; utilities) 408.664-010
tree-trimming-line technician (tel. & tel.; utilities) 408.664-010
Tree Wrapper (agriculture) 920.687-134
trench backfiller (construction)   see DITCH DIGGER
trench digger (construction)   see DITCH DIGGER
Trench Trimmer, Fine (construction) 869.687-026
trichologist (personal ser.) 339.371-014
Tricot-Knitting-Machine Operator (knitting) 685.665-018
tricot-warper tender (knitting; narrow fabrics; nonmet. min.; textile) 681.685-018
trim and burr operator (ordnance) 609.685-026
TRIM ATTACHER (cutlery-hrdwr.) 692.685-230
Trim-Crew Supervisor (mfd. bldgs.) 869.131-018
trim die maker (machine shop) 601.280-014
Trim Inspector (auto. mfg.) 806.687-018
Trim Installer (ship-boat mfg.) 806.684-146
TRIM-MACHINE ADJUSTER (ordnance) 609.280-010
TRIM-MACHINE OPERATOR (ordnance) 609.685-026
trimmer (aircraft mfg.) 693.261-010
trimmer (any industry) 789.687-070
trimmer (any industry) 782.684-058
trimmer (any industry) 920.687-038
trimmer (boot & shoe) 690.685-434
Trimmer (can. & preserv.) 529.686-014
trimmer (fabrication, nec) 664.685-022
Trimmer (forestry) 920.687-046
TRIMMER (hat & cap) 784.684-078
trimmer (hat & cap) 784.387-010
TRIMMER (jewelry-silver.) 705.682-014
TRIMMER (mfd. bldgs.) 869.684-066
Trimmer (mine & quarry) 939.687-014
trimmer (pen & pencil) 662.685-030
TRIMMER (plastic prod.) 690.482-014
trimmer (tex. prod., nec) 789.687-050
trimmer and reinforcer (boot & shoe) 690.685-246
trimmer and sorter (leather mfg.) 585.684-010
Trimmer, Buffing Wheel (tex. prod., nec) 585.685-086
TRIMMER, HAND (any industry) 781.687-070
TRIMMER, HAND (boot & shoe) 788.687-150
TRIMMER, HAND (leather mfg.) 585.684-010
TRIMMER, HAND (paper goods) 794.687-062
trimmer, hand (rubber goods) 751.684-014
TRIMMER HELPER (saw. & plan.) 667.686-018
Trimmer Loader (saw. & plan.) 669.687-018
TRIMMER, MACHINE (garment; knitting) 781.682-010

TRIMMER, MACHINE (leather mfg.) 585.685-126
trimmer, machine (toy-sport equip.) 732.685-038
TRIMMER, MACHINE I (boot & shoe) 690.685-434
TRIMMER, MACHINE II (boot & shoe) 690.682-086
trimmer maker (machine shop) 601.280-014
TRIMMER, MEAT (meat products) 525.684-054
TRIMMER OPERATOR (nut & bolt) 619.462-014
trimmer operator (woodworking) 667.682-022
trimmer operator, three knife (print. & pub.) 640.685-010
trimmer, press clippings (business ser.) 249.587-014
TRIMMER, PRINTED CIRCUIT BOARD PANELS (electron. comp.) 699.685-054
TRIMMER SAWYER (saw. & plan.) 667.682-094
Trimmer-Sorter (can. & preserv.) 529.687-186
Trimmer Tailer (saw. & plan.) 669.687-018
TRIMMING ASSEMBLER (furniture) 780.684-114
Trimming Cutter (garment) 699.682-022
Trimming Cutter, Machine (boot & shoe) 699.682-022
Trimming-Department Blocker (hat & cap) 580.684-014
Trimming Finisher (garment) 782.684-058
Trimming Inspector (hat & cap) 784.387-010
trimming-machine operator (any industry) 789.684-050
TRIMMING-MACHINE OPERATOR (button & notion) 690.682-090
TRIMMING-MACHINE OPERATOR (garment; knitting) 583.685-122
trimming-machine operator (paper goods) 640.685-034
trimming-machine operator (rubber goods; rubber reclaim.) 690.685-386
TRIMMING-MACHINE OPERATOR (toy-sport equip.) 732.685-038
TRIMMING MACHINE SET-UP OPERATOR (fabrication, nec) 664.382-018
Trimming-Press Operator (forging) 615.685-030
TRIMMING SEWER, AUTOMATIC (garment; tex. prod., nec) 787.685-050
Trimming Supervisor (tex. prod., nec) 589.130-014
Trim Mounter (toy-sport equip.) 732.384-010
Trim Mounter I (optical goods) 713.684-022
Trim Mounter II (optical goods) 713.681-010
trim operator (tex. prod., nec) 699.682-026
trim preparer (hat & cap) 784.687-050
trim sawyer (saw. & plan.) 667.482-018
Trim Setter (construction) 860.381-022
trim-setter helper (forging) 619.686-034
TRIM-STENCIL MAKER (any industry) 781.684-058
TRIPE COOKER (meat products) 526.685-062
TRIP FOLLOWER (air trans.) 209.367-050
TRIPLE-AIR-VALVE TESTER (railroad equip.) 622.382-010
Triple-Drum Operator (logging) 921.663-066
Tripod-Drill Operator (mine & quarry) 930.684-018
tripoler (fabrication, nec) 739.684-026
trip rider (any industry) 932.664-010
trolley-car operator (r.r. trans.) 913.463-014
TROLLEY CLEANER (meat products) 529.687-206
Trolley-Coach Driver (motor trans.) 913.463-010
TROLLEY OPERATOR (bakery products) 524.565-010
TROLLEY-WIRE INSTALLER (mine & quarry) 821.684-022
TROMBONE-SLIDE ASSEMBLER (musical inst.) 730.381-054
TROMMEL TENDER (smelt. & refin.) 511.685-066
tromper (agriculture) 920.687-198
TROPHY ASSEMBLER (jewelry-silver.) 735.684-018
trouble dispatcher (utilities) 959.167-010
trouble dispatcher (utilities) 952.167-010
TROUBLE LOCATOR, TEST DESK (tel. & tel.) 822.361-030
trouble shooter (any industry)   se MAINTENANCE WORKER
trouble shooter (any industry) 726.261-018
TROUBLE SHOOTER I (utilities) 952.364-010
TROUBLE SHOOTER II (utilities) 821.261-026
trouble shooter, radio (any industry) 720.281-010
Trout Farmer (fishing & hunt.) 446.161-010
truant officer (education) 168.367-010
TRUCK-BODY BUILDER (auto. mfg.; automotive ser.) 807.281-010
TRUCK-CRANE OPERATOR (any industry) 921.663-062
Truck-Crane-Operator Helper (any industry) 921.667-022
TRUCK DRIVER (any industry) term
Truck Driver, Flatbed (logging) 905.663-014
TRUCK DRIVER, HEAVY (any industry) 905.663-014
TRUCK-DRIVER HELPER (any industry) 905.687-010
TRUCK DRIVER, LIGHT (any industry) 906.683-022
truck driver, sales route (retail trade; wholesale tr.) 292.353-010
Trucker, Hand (any industry) 929.687-030
trucker helper (any industry) 905.687-010
Truck Farmer (agriculture) 402.161-010
Truck-Headlight Assembler (light. fix.) 729.684-034
TRUCKLOAD CHECKER (construction) 222.367-066
truck loader (any industry) 914.667-010
TRUCK LOADER, OVERHEAD CRANE (nonfer. metal) 921.663-070
Truck Mechanic (automotive ser.) 620.261-010
Truck-Mechanic Helper (automotive ser.) 620.684-014
truck operator (any industry)   see TRUCK DRIVER

Truck-Rental Clerk

Truck-Rental Clerk (automotive ser.) 295.467-022
truck repairer (any industry) 620.281-050
Truck-Repair-Service Estimator (automotive ser.) 620.261-018
TRUCK SUPERVISOR (motor trans.) 909.137-018
Truck-Tire Inspector (rubber tire) 750.684-030
Truck Washer (dairy products) 919.687-014
TRUER (metal prod., nec) 616.484-010
Truer (optical goods) 716.682-014
TRUER, PINION AND WHEEL (clock & watch) 715.684-194
Trunk Repairer (any industry) 365.361-010
Truss Assembler (protective dev.) 712.684-010
TRUSS ASSEMBLER (saw. & plan.) 762.684-062
Truss Driver (wood. container) 669.682-014
Truss-Driver Helper (wood. container) 669.685-010
Truss Puller (wood. container) 669.682-014
Truss-Puller Helper (wood. container) 669.685-010
trust administrator (financial) 186.117-074
TRUST OFFICER (financial) 186.117-074
TRUST OPERATIONS ASSISTANT (financial) 219.362-074
TRUST-VAULT CLERK (financial) 216.367-014
Try-on Baster (garment) 785.261-014
tub attendant (personal ser.) 335.677-014
TUBBER (jewelry-silver.) 599.685-098
tub chucker (wood. container) 664.685-014
TUBE-AND-MANIFOLD BUILDER (rubber goods) 759.684-062
tube-and-rod straightener (plastic-synth.) 559.587-010
TUBE ASSEMBLER, CATHODE RAY (electron. comp.) 725.684-022
TUBE ASSEMBLER, ELECTRON (electron. comp.) 725.384-010
tube backer (rubber goods) 559.686-018
TUBE BALANCER (rubber tire) 750.684-046
tube bender-assembler (aircraft mfg.) 806.381-034
TUBE BENDER, BRASS-WIND INSTRUMENTS (musical inst.) 617.382-010
TUBE BENDER, HAND I (any industry) 709.684-090
TUBE BENDER, HAND II (any industry) 709.687-050
Tube-Bending-Machine Operator I (any industry) 617.482-010
Tube-Bending-Machine Operator II (any industry) 617.685-010
TUBE BUILDER, AIRPLANE (rubber tire) 750.384-014
TUBE-BUILDING-MACHINE OPERATOR (rubber goods) 559.685-174
TUBE CLEANER (any industry) 891.687-030
TUBE CLEANER (textile) 589.687-042
TUBE-CLEANING OPERATOR (foundry) 514.685-026
tube clerk (clerical) 239.687-014
tube closing machine operator (glass mfg.) 573.685-018
TUBE COATER (metal prod., nec) 599.685-102
Tube-Component Assembler (electron. comp.) 725.384-010
tube coremaker (foundry) 518.685-018
TUBE COVERER (textile) 589.687-046
tube cutter (paper goods) 640.685-034
tube depatcher (rubber reclaim.) 559.687-066
tube dispatcher (clerical) 239.687-014
TUBE DRAWER (nonfer. metal; steel & rel.) 614.685-022
tube-draw helper (nonfer. metal; steel & rel.) 614.686-010
Tube-Drawing Supervisor (nonfer. metal; steel & rel.) 614.132-010
tube filler (any industry) 619.687-018
Tube-Filling-Machine Operator (can. & preserv.; chemical) 920.685-078
tube finishing machine operator (glass mfg.) 573.685-018
Tube Fitter (electron. comp.) 725.384-010
TUBE HANDLER (textile) 582.686-034
Tube Inspector (electron. comp.) 726.684-022
Tube Inspector (paper goods) 649.367-010
tube-machine operator (nonfer. metal) 691.382-010
TUBE-MACHINE OPERATOR (paper goods) 641.662-014
tube-machine operator (pottery & porc.) 575.685-026
TUBE-MACHINE-OPERATOR HELPER (paper goods) 641.686-038
tube maker (nonmet. min.) 692.685-234
tube maker (paper goods) 641.662-014
tube-making-machine operator (paper goods) 641.662-014
Tube-Mill Operator (cement) 570.685-046
TUBE MOLDER, FIBERGLASS (plastic prod.) 690.685-438
TUBE OPERATOR (clerical) 239.687-014
Tube Packer (rubber tire) 920.587-018
tube puller (petrol. & gas) 930.382-030
tuber (rubber tire) 750.687-010
tuber (textile) 689.685-046
TUBE REBUILDER (electron. comp.) 725.381-010
TUBE REPAIRER (rubber tire) 750.684-050
Tuber Feeder (nonfer. metal) 691.685-030
tuber helper (paper goods) 641.686-038
TUBER-MACHINE CUTTER (rubber goods; rubber tire) 690.685-446
TUBER-MACHINE OPERATOR (rubber goods; rubber tire) 690.662-014
TUBER-MACHINE-OPERATOR HELPER (rubber goods; rubber tire) 690.686-070
tube roller (hat & cap) 690.686-034
Tube Roller (plastic prod.) 690.685-438
tube roller (steel & rel.) 619.682-042

Tube-Room Supervisor (rubber tire) 750.130-010
tuber operator (plastic prod.; plastic-synth.) 557.382-010
tuber operator (rubber reclaim.) 551.365-010
TUBE SIZER-AND-CUTTER OPERATOR (ordnance) 640.685-086
TUBE SORTER (rubber reclaim.) 559.687-066
TUBE SPLICER (rubber tire) 690.685-442
tube-station attendant (clerical) 239.687-014
Tube Tester (electron. comp.) 726.684-026
Tube-Test Technician (electron. comp.) 726.261-018
Tube-Trailer Filler (chemical) 559.565-010
tube turner (knitting) 689.685-110
Tube Winder (any industry) 681.685-154
TUBE WINDER, HAND (nonmet. min.) 692.685-234
tubing drier (textile) 581.685-030
Tubing Inspector (steel & rel.) 619.381-010
TUBING-MACHINE OPERATOR (nonfer. metal; steel & rel.) 613.685-030
TUBING-MACHINE TENDER (clock & watch) 715.685-070
Tubing-Machine Tender (elec. equip.) 692.685-046
Tubing-Mill Operator I (any industry) 616.685-042
Tubing-Mill Operator II (any industry) 616.360-026
Tubing-Mill Setter (any industry) 616.260-014
Tub Operator (chemical) 559.682-018
tub rider (any industry) 932.664-010
tub turner (wood. container) 669.682-018
Tubular-Products Fabricator (any industry) 809.381-010
TUBULAR-SPLITTING-MACHINE TENDER (knitting) 686.685-070
Tub Washer (textile) 599.687-030
Tuck-And-Insole Cementer (boot & shoe) 690.686-018
TUCKING-MACHINE OPERATOR (any industry) 787.682-082
Tuck Pointer (construction) 869.664-014
TUFTER (furniture) 687.684-014
TUFTER, HAND (furniture) 780.687-050
tufter operator (furniture) 687.684-014
Tufting-Machine Fixer (carpet & rug) 689.260-010
TUFTING-MACHINE OPERATOR (carpet & rug; textile) 687.685-018
TUFTING-MACHINE OPERATOR (furniture) 687.685-014
TUFTING-MACHINE OPERATOR, SINGLE-NEEDLE (carpet & rug) 687.685-022
TUFT-MACHINE OPERATOR (carpet & rug; tex. prod., nec) 687.682-014
TUGBOAT CAPTAIN (water trans.) 197.133-030
Tugboat Deckhand (water trans.) 911.687-022
Tugboat Engineer (water trans.) 197.130-010
TUGBOAT MATE (water trans.) 197.133-034
Tugger Operator (mine & quarry) 921.663-026
tumbler (amuse. & rec.) 159.247-010
TUMBLER (clock & watch) 599.685-106
tumbler-drier operator (laundry & rel.) 369.685-034
tumbler-dyeing-machine operator (knitting) 582.685-170
TUMBLER-MACHINE OPERATOR (rubber goods) 559.685-178
tumbler-machine operator (tex. prod., nec) 582.685-066
TUMBLER OPERATOR (any industry) 599.685-110
TUMBLER OPERATOR (chemical) 550.685-118
TUMBLER OPERATOR (laundry & rel.) 369.685-034
tumbler operator (laundry & rel.) 361.685-010
TUMBLER OPERATOR (rubber goods) 553.585-026
tumbler plater (electroplating) 500.362-014
Tumbler-Switch Assembler (elec. equip.) 729.687-010
TUMBLER TENDER (food prep., nec) 520.685-222
TUMBLER TENDER (knitting) 581.685-062
TUMOR REGISTRAR (medical ser.) 079.362-018
tuner (any industry) 730.361-010
TUNER, PERCUSSION (musical inst.) 730.381-058
TUNE-UP MECHANIC (automotive ser.) 620.281-066
Tung-Nut Grower (agriculture) 403.161-010
TUNGSTEN REFINER (smelt. & refin.) 511.382-010
tunnel-drier operator (chemical) 553.582-010
TUNNEL-ELASTIC OPERATOR, CHAINSTITCH (garment) 786.682-246
TUNNEL-ELASTIC OPERATOR, LOCKSTITCH (garment) 786.682-250
TUNNEL-ELASTIC OPERATOR, ZIGZAG (garment) 786.682-254
Tunnel-Form-Placing Supervisor (construction) 869.131-014
Tunnel-Heading Inspector (construction) 182.267-010
tunneling-machine operator (construction) 850.662-010
Tunnel-Kiln Drawer (pottery & porc.) 573.667-010
TUNNEL-KILN OPERATOR (brick & tile) 573.382-018
Tunnel-Kiln Repairer (brick & tile; pottery & porc.) 861.381-014
Tunnel Miner (mine & quarry) 939.281-010
TUNNEL WORKER (construction) term
turbinated-bone grinder (meat products) 521.687-130
TURBINE ATTENDANT (utilities) 952.567-010
TURBINE-BLADE ASSEMBLER (engine-turbine) 600.380-026
Turbine Inspector (engine-turbine) 609.361-010
TURBINE OPERATOR (utilities) 952.362-042
TURBINE OPERATOR, HEAD (utilities) 952.137-022
TURBINE SUBASSEMBLER (engine-turbine) 706.381-042
turbogenerator operator (utilities) 952.362-042

Turkey Cleaner (meat products) 525.687-074
Turkey Dresser (meat products) 525.687-070
Turkey Farmer (agriculture) 411.161-018
TURKEY-ROLL MAKER (meat products) 525.684-058
Turkish-Line Attendant (tobacco) 520.685-026
Turkish Rubber (personal ser.) 334.677-010
TURNER (any industry) 789.687-182
turner (brick & tile) 579.686-026
TURNER (can. & preserv.) 522.687-038
TURNER (fabrication, nec) 669.685-094
turner (knitting) 689.685-110
TURNER (pottery & porc.) 774.684-038
turner (stonework) 674.662-010
turner (tex. prod., nec) 689.685-146
turner (toy-sport equip.) 732.687-066
Turner (woodworking) 669.686-030
turner and former, automatic (glove & mit.) 583.686-018
TURNER, MACHINE (clock & watch) 770.685-034
turner-machine operator (wood. container) 667.685-066
turner-splitter-machine operator (rubber goods; rubber reclaim.) 690.685-386
TURNING-AND-BEADING-MACHINE OPERATOR (button & notion) 679.685-026
TURNING LATHE TENDER (furniture) 664.685-034
turning-machine operator (hat & cap) 690.686-034
turning-machine operator (knitting) 689.685-110
TURNING-MACHINE OPERATOR (tex. prod., nec) 689.685-146
TURNING-MACHINE OPERATOR (wood. container) 667.685-066
TURNING-MACHINE-OPERATOR HELPER (wood. container) 667.686-022
TURNING MACHINE SET-UP OPERATOR (fabrication, nec) 669.382-026
TURNING-SANDER TENDER (woodworking) 662.685-038
turn keeper (mine & quarry) 932.167-010
turnkey (government ser.) 372.367-014
turn-machine operator (hat & cap) 585.685-074
turn-out worker (glass mfg.) 579.687-018
Turnstile Attendant (amuse. & rec.) 344.667-010
Turnstile Collector (water trans.) 211.462-018
Turret Lathe Operator, Numerical Control (machine shop) 604.362-010
TURRET-LATHE OPERATOR, TUMBLE TAILSTOCK (clock & watch) 604.685-042
TURRET-LATHE SET-UP OPERATOR (machine shop) 604.380-026
TURRET-LATHE SET-UP OPERATOR, TOOL (machine shop) 604.280-022
Turret-Lathe Set-Up Operator, Tool, Vertical (machine shop) 604.280-022
turret-lathe tender (machine shop) 604.685-026
TURRET-PUNCH-PRESS OPERATOR (any industry) 615.482-038
TURRET-PUNCH-PRESS OPERATOR, TAPE-CONTROL (any industry) 615.685-042
TUTOR (education) 099.227-034
Tuyere Fitter (steel & rel.) 862.281-022
Twenty-One Dealer (amuse. & rec.) 343.464-010
Twin-Beam Clicker (boot & shoe; hat & cap; leather prod.) 699.682-022
twine operator (tex. prod., nec) 689.685-138
Twine-Reeling-Machine Operator (tex. prod., nec) 681.685-078
Twine Winder (tex. prod., nec) 681.685-154
TWISTER (tex. prod., nec) 681.685-126
Twister Doffer (textile) 689.686-022
TWISTER, HAND (tobacco) 790.687-030
TWISTER TENDER (glass mfg.; nonmet. min.; plastic-synth.; textile) 681.685-130
TWISTER TENDER, PAPER (tex. prod., nec) 681.685-134
twisthand (tex. prod., nec) 683.682-026
twisting-frame changer (textile) 689.686-026
Twisting-Frame Fixer (textile) 689.260-010
TWISTING-MACHINE OPERATOR (any industry) 619.485-014
TWISTING-MACHINE OPERATOR (comm. equip.; elec. equip.) 691.686-010
TWISTING-MACHINE OPERATOR (fabrication, nec) 692.682-070
Twisting-Press Operator (forging) 611.685-010
twisting-tube selector (textile) 689.687-042
twist maker (tobacco) 790.687-030
Twist Packer (tobacco) 920.687-130
TWITCHELL OPERATOR (chemical) 558.585-042
Two-Stage, Steel-Bender Annealer (toy-sport equip.) 617.685-010
tying-in-machine operator (narrow fabrics; textile) 683.685-034
Tying-Machine Operator (any industry) 920.685-078
TYING-MACHINE OPERATOR (paper goods; tex. prod., nec) 929.685-014
TYING-MACHINE OPERATOR, LUMBER (woodworking) 929.685-018
type caster (machinery mfg.; print. & pub.) 654.382-010
TYPE-CASTING MACHINE OPERATOR (print. & pub.) 654.582-010
TYPE-COPY EXAMINER (machinery mfg.) 979.687-026
TYPE COPYIST (machinery mfg.) 970.381-042
TYPE-PROOF REPRODUCER (machinery mfg.) 652.685-106
TYPE-ROLLING-MACHINE OPERATOR (office machines) 619.382-022
TYPESETTER (print. & pub.) term
typesetter (print. & pub.) 973.381-010
typesetter (print. & pub.) 650.582-018
typesetter (print. & pub.) 652.585-010

typesetter apprentice (print. & pub.) 973.381-014
TYPESETTER-PERFORATOR OPERATOR (print. & pub.) 203.582-062
TYPESETTING-MACHINE TENDER (print. & pub.) 650.685-010
TYPE-SOLDERING-MACHINE TENDER (office machines) 706.685-010
Typewriter Operator, Automatic (clerical) 203.582-038
typewriter-ribbon winder (pen & pencil) 733.685-022
Typewriter Servicer (any industry) 633.281-018
Typing Checker (clerical) 209.687-010
TYPING-ELEMENT-MACHINE OPERATOR (office machines) 616.382-018
TYPING SECTION CHIEF (clerical) 203.137-014
TYPIST (clerical) 203.582-066
typographer (print. & pub.) 973.381-010

U

Ultrasonic Cleaner (any industry) 503.685-030
ULTRASONIC-SEAMING-MACHINE OPERATOR (garment) 786.682-258
ULTRASONIC-SEAMING-MACHINE OPERATOR, SEMIAUTOMATIC (garment) 786.685-038
ULTRASONIC TESTER (any industry) 739.281-014
ULTRASONIC TESTER (chemical) 709.687-054
ULTRASOUND TECHNOLOGIST (medical ser.) 078.364-010
UMBRELLA FINISHER (fabrication, nec) 739.687-190
UMBRELLA REPAIRER (any industry) 369.684-018
UMBRELLA TIPPER, HAND (fabrication, nec) 739.684-162
UMBRELLA TIPPER, MACHINE (fabrication, nec) 739.685-054
UMPIRE (amuse. & rec.) 153.267-018
Umpire (profess. & kin.) 169.107-010
UNATTENDED-GROUND-SENSOR SPECIALIST (military ser.) 378.382-018
unbundler (leather mfg.) 585.684-010
UNCLAIMED PROPERTY OFFICER (government ser.) 188.167-106
uncrater (any industry) 827.584-010
Underbaster (garment) 786.682-102
UNDERCOATER (automotive ser.) 843.684-014
Undercoat Sprayer (aircraft mfg.; auto. mfg.) 741.687-018
Undercollar Baster (garment; retail trade) 785.361-022
Undercollar Maker (garment; retail trade) 785.361-022
undercover agent (business ser.) 376.267-018
undercover agent (motor trans.; r.r. trans.) 168.167-082
undercover agent (retail trade) 376.367-026
undercover operator (business ser.) 376.267-018
UNDERCOVER OPERATOR (retail trade) 376.367-026
undercutter (mine & quarry) 930.683-014
Underground-Distribution Engineer (utilities) 003.167-046
Underground Repairer (utilities) 829.261-018
Underground Supervisor (utilities) 829.131-010
Underlay Stitcher (boot & shoe) 690.682-082
Underpresser, Hand (garment) 363.684-018
undertaker (personal ser.) 187.167-030
undertaker assistant (personal ser.) 359.677-014
UNDERWATER HUNTER-TRAPPER (fishing & hunt.) 461.664-010
Underwriter, Direct Endorsement (financial) 186.267-026
UNDERWRITER (insurance) 169.267-046
UNDERWRITER, MORTGAGE LOAN (financial) 186.267-026
underwriting analyst (insurance) 219.367-038
UNDERWRITING CLERK (insurance) 219.367-038
Unemployment-Insurance-Hearing Officer (government ser.) 119.107-010
unhairing inspector (leather mfg.) 585.687-010
Unhairing-Machine Operator (leather mfg.) 585.685-094
uniform attendant (hotel & rest.; medical ser.) 222.387-030
Uniform-Cap Operator (hat & cap) 784.684-018
uniformer (boot & shoe) 788.687-034
uniform-force captain (government ser.) 375.167-034
unit assembler (machinery mfg.) 706.684-038
UNIT CLERK (medical ser.) 245.362-014
united states attorney (government ser.) 110.117-010
UNIT OPERATOR (chemical) 542.685-018
unit tender (chemical) 558.382-026
universal grinder, tool (machine shop) 603.280-030
universal-saw operator (woodworking) 667.682-086
university dean (education) 090.117-010
UNLEAVENED-DOUGH MIXER (bakery products) 520.685-226
unloading checker (clerical) 222.687-018
UNSCRAMBLER (can. & preserv.) 921.685-070
Unstacker (woodworking) 569.685-066
upfitter (furniture) 763.684-042
UPHOLSTERER (aircraft mfg.) 780.384-014
upholsterer (any industry) 780.381-018
upholsterer (furniture) 780.684-046
Upholsterer (r.r. trans.) 780.381-018
upholsterer apprentice (any industry) 780.381-022
upholsterer apprentice (automotive ser.) 780.381-014
UPHOLSTERER, ASSEMBLY LINE (furniture) 780.684-134
UPHOLSTERER HELPER (any industry) 780.687-054

upholsterer helper

upholsterer helper (furniture) 780.684-010
UPHOLSTERER, INSIDE (furniture) 780.381-038
UPHOLSTERER, LIMOUSINE AND HEARSE (auto. mfg.) 780.381-026
UPHOLSTERER, OUTSIDE (furniture) 780.684-118
upholstery and drapery measurer (retail trade) 299.364-010
upholstery bundler (furniture) 780.587-010
UPHOLSTERY CLEANER (furniture) 780.687-058
Upholstery Cutter, Machine (furniture) 781.684-014
Upholstery Estimator (retail trade) 299.387-010
upholstery handler (furniture) 780.587-010
UPHOLSTERY REPAIRER (furniture) 780.684-122
Upholstery Restorer (museums) 763.380-010
UPHOLSTERY SEWER (any industry) 780.682-018
UPHOLSTERY TRIMMER (furniture) 780.684-126
upkeep mechanic (glass mfg.) 575.380-010
UPPER-AND-BOTTOM LACER, HAND (boot & shoe) 788.684-122
Upper Cutter, Machine (boot & shoe) 699.682-022
upper cutter-out (boot & shoe) 788.684-082
Upper Doubler (boot & shoe) 788.687-030
upper edger (boot & shoe) 690.685-138
Upper Inspector (boot & shoe) 788.384-010
upper-leather cutter (boot & shoe) 788.684-082
UPPER-LEATHER SORTER (boot & shoe) 788.387-010
Upper-Lining Cementer (boot & shoe) 690.686-018
upper marker (boot & shoe) 788.584-014
Upper Muller (boot & shoe) 788.687-090
upper shaper (boot & shoe) 788.685-026
upper stamper (boot & shoe) 690.685-398
Upper Stitcher (boot & shoe) 690.682-082
Upper Trimmer (boot & shoe) 690.685-434
UPSETTER (forging) 611.662-010
Upsetter Helper (forging) 619.686-034
Upsetter Setter-Up (forging) 612.360-010
Upset-Welding-Machine Operator (welding) 812.682-010
UPTWISTER TENDER (textile) 681.685-138
uptwist spinner (textile) 681.685-138
Urban Anthropologist (profess. & kin.) 055.067-010
URBAN PLANNER (profess. & kin.) 199.167-014
Urban Sociologist (profess. & kin.) 054.067-014
UROLOGIST (medical ser.) 070.101-098
used-car conditioner (retail trade) 620.684-034
used-car-lot attendant (retail trade; wholesale tr.) 915.687-022
USED-CAR RENOVATOR (retail trade) 620.684-034
USER REPRESENTATIVE, INTERNATIONAL ACCOUNTING (profess. & kin.) 189.117-038
USER SUPPORT ANALYST (profess. & kin.) 032.262-010
USER SUPPORT ANALYST SUPERVISOR (profess. & kin.) 032.132-010
USHER (amuse. & rec.) 344.677-014
usher (personal ser.) 359.677-014
USHER, HEAD (amuse. & rec.) 344.137-010
UTILITIES-AND-MAINTENANCE SUPERVISOR (any industry) 899.131-018
utilities operator (sanitary ser.) 955.362-010
UTILITIES SERVICE INVESTIGATOR (utilities) 821.364-010
Utility Assembler (motor-bicycles) 806.684-090
UTILITY BAG ASSEMBLER (leather prod.) 783.684-030
Utility-Bill-Collection Clerk (utilities) 241.357-010
Utility-Bill Collector (clerical) 241.367-010
UTILITY CLERK (utilities) 239.367-034
utility hand (tobacco)   see RELIEF WORKER
Utility Hand (water trans.) 318.687-014
Utility Inspector (office machines) 706.387-014
Utility Inspector (utilities) 953.367-018
UTILITY OPERATOR (garment) 786.682-262
UTILITY OPERATOR (saw. & plan.) 669.682-070
UTILITY OPERATOR I (chemical) 559.682-066
UTILITY OPERATOR II (chemical) 709.684-094
UTILITY OPERATOR III (chemical) 549.685-042
utility repairer (any industry) 899.261-014
UTILITY SUPERVISOR, BOAT AND PLANT (ship-boat mfg.) 899.131-022
UTILITY TENDER, CARDING (textile) 689.685-166
UTILITY-TRACTOR OPERATOR (construction) 850.683-046
utility worker (any industry) 929.687-030
UTILITY WORKER (mfd. bldgs.; vehicles, nec) 869.684-074
UTILITY WORKER (sugar & conf.) 529.686-086
UTILITY WORKER, CLOTH PRINTING (textile) 652.586-010
UTILITY WORKER, EXTRUSION (nonfer. metal) 691.685-030
UTILITY WORKER, FILM PROCESSING (photofinishing) 976.685-030
UTILITY WORKER, FORGE (forging) 612.684-010
UTILITY WORKER, LINE ASSEMBLY (auto. mfg.) 806.367-010
UTILITY WORKER, MERCHANT MILL (steel & rel.) 801.664-014
UTILITY WORKER, MOLDING (plastic prod.) 559.684-026
UTILITY WORKER, PRODUCTION (pharmaceut.) 559.684-034
UTILITY WORKER, ROLLER SHOP (textile) 628.684-034
utility worker, virus (pharmaceut.) 559.684-034
UTILITY WORKER, WOOLEN MILL (textile) 689.686-050

UTILIZATION COORDINATOR (radio-tv broad.) 169.167-078
UTILIZATION ENGINEER (utilities) 007.061-034
UTILIZATION-REVIEW COORDINATOR (medical ser.) 079.267-010
utilization supervisor (utilities) 187.167-010

V

VACUUM-APPLICATOR OPERATOR (fabrication, nec) 692.685-238
VACUUM-BOTTLE ASSEMBLER (glass products) 739.687-194
VACUUM CASTER (foundry) 514.582-010
vacuum cleaner (any industry) 381.687-018
vacuum-cleaner operator (any industry) 389.683-010
VACUUM CLEANER REPAIRER (any industry) 723.381-014
Vacuum-Cleaner Repairer (house. appl.) 723.584-010
VACUUM-CONDITIONER OPERATOR (tobacco) 522.685-102
Vacuum-Cooker Operator (sugar & conf.) 526.382-014
VACUUM DRIER OPERATOR (can. & preserv.) 523.685-122
VACUUM-DRIER OPERATOR (tex. prod., nec) 581.685-066
VACUUM-DRIER TENDER (chemical) 553.685-106
vacuum-drum-drier operator (chemical; pharmaceut.) 553.685-042
Vacuum-Evaporation Operator (electron. comp.) 590.684-014
vacuum-extractor operator (textile) 581.685-042
vacuum-filter operator (any industry) 551.685-078
vacuum-forming-machine operator (plastic prod.) 553.685-014
vacuum-frame operator (any industry) 976.361-010
VACUUM-METALIZER OPERATOR (any industry) 505.685-018
vacuum-pan operator (chemical) 553.382-018
VACUUM-PAN OPERATOR I (chemical) 551.685-150
VACUUM-PAN OPERATOR II (chemical) 551.685-154
VACUUM-PAN OPERATOR III (chemical) 559.585-022
VACUUM PLASTIC-FORMING-MACHINE OPERATOR (plastic prod.) 556.685-082
Vacuum-Spindle Sander (furniture) 761.682-010
VACUUM-TANK TENDER (textile) 689.665-018
VACUUM TESTER, CANS (can. & preserv.) 920.687-194
Vacuum Worker (hotel & rest.) 323.687-018
Valance Shirrer (tex. prod., nec) 787.685-038
Valet Manager (hotel & rest.) 369.137-010
Valuation Engineer (profess. & kin.) 160.162-026
VALUE ENGINEER (aircraft mfg.) 002.167-010
Valve Assembler (inst. & app.) 710.684-046
VALVE GRINDER (machine shop) 706.684-098
valve inspector-and-assembler (chemical) 630.381-030
valve inspector (chemical) 630.381-030
valve lapper (machine shop) 706.684-098
Valve Liner, Rubber (machinery mfg.) 759.684-050
Valve Maker I (musical inst.) 730.381-018
VALVE MAKER II (musical inst.) 730.681-018
VALVE REPAIRER (chemical) 630.381-030
valve repairer, reclamation (petrol. refin.) 709.684-070
Valve Steamer (chemical) 549.587-010
VALVING-MACHINE OPERATOR (paper goods) 641.685-094
vamp-and-whole-shoe cutter, hand (boot & shoe) 788.684-082
VAMP CREASER (boot & shoe) 788.687-154
vamper (boot & shoe) 690.682-078
Vamp Marker (boot & shoe) 690.685-282
Vamp Presser (boot & shoe) 690.685-350
Vamp Stitcher (boot & shoe) 690.682-082
VAMP-STRAP IRONER (boot & shoe) 788.687-158
Vamp Wetter (boot & shoe) 788.687-090
VAN DRIVER (motor trans.) 905.663-018
van driver (motor trans.) 913.663-018
VAN-DRIVER HELPER (motor trans.) 905.687-014
van helper (motor trans.) 905.687-014
Vanilla-Chocolate-Coin Counter (sugar & conf.) 529.686-034
vapor coater (any industry) 505.685-018
variety-lathe operator (woodworking) 664.382-010
VARIETY-SAW OPERATOR (woodworking) 667.682-086
VARITYPE OPERATOR (clerical) 203.382-026
varnish blender (paint & varnish) 553.382-022
Varnish-Cambric-Covering-Machine Operator (nonfer. metal) 691.682-018
varnish cooker (paint & varnish) 553.382-022
Varnish Dipper (furniture) 599.685-026
Varnisher (construction) 840.381-010
VARNISHER (fabrication, nec) 569.685-070
Varnisher (hat & cap) 589.687-038
Varnisher-Plasticoater (fabrication, nec) 534.682-018
Varnish Filterer I (paint & varnish) 551.685-034
Varnish Filterer II (paint & varnish) 551.685-082
Varnishing-Machine Operator (elec. equip.) 599.685-046
VARNISHING-MACHINE OPERATOR (print. & pub.) 534.685-030
VARNISHING-UNIT OPERATOR (ordnance) 737.687-138
VARNISHING-UNIT TOOL SETTER (ordnance) 632.380-026
VARNISH INSPECTOR (paint & varnish) 559.584-014

VARNISH MAKER (paint & varnish) 553.382-022
VARNISH-MAKER HELPER (paint & varnish) 553.686-042
varnish melter (paint & varnish) 553.382-022
Varnish Thinner (paint & varnish) 550.585-038
vat overhauler (meat products) 522.687-034
vat packer (meat products) 522.687-034
Vat Tender (chemical) 582.482-014
vat tender (textile) 582.665-014
VAULT CASHIER (business ser.) 222.137-050
vault custodian (financial) 216.367-014
VAULT CUSTODIAN (laundry & rel.) 369.587-010
vault mechanic (business ser.; wholesale tr.) 869.381-022
vault supervisor (business ser.) 222.137-050
VAULT WORKER (business ser.) 222.587-058
V-BELT BUILDER (rubber goods) 759.684-066
V-BELT COVERER (rubber goods) 690.685-450
V-BELT CURER (rubber goods) 553.682-026
V-BELT FINISHER (rubber goods) 690.685-454
V-Belt Inspector (rubber goods) 759.684-074
v-belt mold assembler and curer (rubber goods) 752.685-010
V-BELT SKIVER (rubber goods) 690.685-458
V-Block Saw Operator (electron. comp.) 677.382-018
VECTOR CONTROL ASSISTANT (government ser.) 049.364-014
vegetable grower (agriculture) 402.161-010
Vegetable Scullion (water trans.) 318.687-014
Vegetable Sorter (agriculture; can. & preserv.; wholesale tr.) 529.687-186
Vegetable Vendor (retail trade) 291.457-018
vegetable worker (agriculture) 402.687-010
Vehicle-Fare Collector (motor trans.; water trans.) 211.462-038
VEHICLE-FUEL-SYSTEMS CONVERTER (automotive ser.) 620.281-070
vehicle-safety inspector (government ser.) 379.364-010
Vehicle Unloader (any industry) 929.687-030
vein pumper (meat products) 522.685-086
Velvet Steamer (laundry & rel.) 363.681-010
Velvet Weaver (carpet & rug) 683.682-010
vending-enterprises supervisor (government ser.) 185.167-066
VENDING-MACHINE ASSEMBLER (svc. ind. mach.) 706.684-102
VENDING-MACHINE ATTENDANT (hotel & rest.) 319.464-014
Vending-Machine Coin Collector (business ser.) 292.483-010
vending-machine repairer (svc. ind. mach.) 639.281-014
VENDING-STAND SUPERVISOR (government ser.) 185.167-066
VENDOR (amuse. & rec.) 291.457-022
vendor (retail trade) 291.457-018
vendor (r.r. trans.) 291.457-014
VENEER CLIPPER (millwork-plywood) 663.685-050
VENEER-CLIPPER HELPER (millwork-plywood) 663.686-030
veneer cutter (millwork-plywood) 663.685-050
VENEER DRIER (millwork-plywood) 563.685-022
VENEER-DRIER FEEDER (millwork-plywood) 563.686-014
veneer-drier tailer (millwork-plywood) 563.685-022
veneer-edge bander (furniture) 762.684-038
veneer-glue-jointer feedback (millwork-plywood) 665.686-018
veneer gluer (millwork-plywood; wood prod., nec) 569.685-042
VENEER GRADER (millwork-plywood) 569.687-034
veneer joiner (millwork-plywood) 569.685-074
VENEER JOINTER (millwork-plywood) 665.682-038
VENEER-JOINTER HELPER (millwork-plywood) 665.686-018
VENEER-JOINTER OFFBEARER (millwork-plywood) 665.686-022
veneer-jointer returner (millwork-plywood) 665.686-018
VENEER-LATHE OPERATOR (millwork-plywood) 664.662-010
Veneer Marker (woodworking) 761.684-022
Veneer Matcher (furniture) 769.687-046
VENEER MATCHER (millwork-plywood) 769.687-046
veneer-press operator (millwork-plywood) 569.685-054
VENEER REDRIER (millwork-plywood) 563.685-026
VENEER REPAIRER, MACHINE (millwork-plywood) 669.685-098
Veneer Sander (woodworking) 662.682-014
VENEER-SLICING-MACHINE OPERATOR (millwork-plywood) 663.682-018
Veneer Sorter (millwork-plywood) 921.685-054
veneer splicer (millwork-plywood) 569.685-062
Veneer Stacker (millwork-plywood) 569.687-010
VENEER STAPLER (ship-boat mfg.) 869.684-078
VENEER-STOCK GRADER (wood. container) 769.687-050
VENEER-STOCK LAYER (millwork-plywood) 762.687-066
VENEER TAPER (millwork-plywood) 569.685-074
VENEER-TAPING-MACHINE OFFBEARER (millwork-plywood) 569.686-054
veneer-taping-machine operator (millwork-plywood) 569.685-074
veneer trimmer (millwork-plywood) 663.685-
VENETIAN-BLIND ASSEMBLER (furniture; retail trade) 739.684-166
VENETIAN-BLIND CLEANER AND REPAIRER (any industry) 739.687-198
VENETIAN-BLIND INSTALLER (furniture; retail trade) 869.484-018
Venetian-Blind-Tape Cutter (furniture) 781.687-026
VENTILATION EQUIPMENT TENDER (any industry) 950.585-010
ventilation mechanic (any industry) 950.585-010
ventilation worker (mine & quarry) 869.684-058

VENTILATOR (fabrication, nec) 739.384-022
VENTRILOQUIST (amuse. & rec.) 159.044-010
verger (nonprofit org.) 389.667-010
vermin exterminator (business ser.) 389.684-010
Vertical-Kiln Operator (concrete prod.) 573.462-010
Vertical-Mill Operator (cement) 570.685-046
Vertical-Roll Operator (any industry) 619.362-014
Vertical-Shade Assembler (furniture) 739.684-166
Vertical-Stretching-Machine Operator (tex. prod., nec) 580.685-058
Vessel Liner (steel & rel.) 861.381-026
vessel ventilation system operator (chemical) 950.562-010
Vest Busheler (retail trade) 785.261-010
Vest-Front Presser (garment) 363.682-018
Vest Presser (garment) 363.684-018
Vest Tailor (garment; retail trade) 785.361-022
veterans' claims representative (nonprofit org.) 187.167-198
VETERANS CONTACT REPRESENTATIVE (nonprofit org.) 187.167-198
veterans' coordinator (education) 169.267-026
veterans' counselor (nonprofit org.) 187.167-198
veterans' service officer (nonprofit org.) 187.167-198
VETERINARIAN, LABORATORY ANIMAL CARE (medical ser.) 073.061-010
VETERINARIAN (medical ser.) 073.101-010
VETERINARIAN, POULTRY (agriculture) 073.101-014
Veterinarian, Public Health (government ser.) 073.101-010
VETERINARY ANATOMIST (profess. & kin.) 073.061-014
veterinary assistant (medical ser.) 079.361-014
Veterinary Bacteriologist (profess. & kin.) 073.061-018
VETERINARY EPIDEMIOLOGIST (profess. & kin.) 073.061-022
Veterinary-Hospital Attendant (medical ser.) 410.674-010
VETERINARY LIVESTOCK INSPECTOR (government ser.) 073.161-010
VETERINARY MEAT-INSPECTOR (government ser.) 073.264-010
veterinary medical officer (government ser.) 073.264-010
VETERINARY MICROBIOLOGIST (profess. & kin.) 073.061-018
Veterinary Milk-Specialist (government ser.) 073.264-010
VETERINARY PARASITOLOGIST (profess. & kin.) 073.061-026
VETERINARY PATHOLOGIST (medical ser.) 073.061-030
VETERINARY PHARMACOLOGIST (profess. & kin.) 073.061-034
VETERINARY PHYSIOLOGIST (profess. & kin.) 073.061-038
Veterinary-Poultry Inspector (government ser.) 073.264-010
Veterinary Radiologist (medical ser.) 073.101-010
VETERINARY TECHNICIAN (medical ser.) 079.361-014
Veterinary Virologist (profess. & kin.) 073.061-018
VETERINARY VIRUS-SERUM INSPECTOR (government ser.) 073.261-010
Vial Gauger (cutlery-hrdwr.) 701.687-026
Vibrating-Screed Operator (construction) 853.663-014
vibrating-screen operator (chemical) 551.685-130
Vibration Technician (profess. & kin.) 003.261-010
Vibrator Assembler (machinery mfg.) 706.361-010
VIBRATOR-EQUIPMENT TESTER (machinery mfg.) 825.361-014
VICE PRESIDENT (any industry) 189.117-034
Vice President, Commercial Bank (financial) 186.117-078
VICE PRESIDENT, FINANCIAL INSTITUTION (financial) 186.117-078
vice president for institutional research (education) 090.167-018
vice president for instruction (education) 090.117-010
vice president, industrial relations (profess. & kin.) 166.117-010
Vice President, Lending (financial) 186.117-078
vice president of student affairs (education) 090.117-018
vice-squad police officer (government ser.) 375.267-022
video engineer (radio-tv broad.) 194.282-010
Video Installer (tel. & tel.) 822.381-018
VIDEO OPERATOR (radio-tv broad.) 194.282-010
videotape engineer (radio-tv broad.) 194.382-018
VIDEOTAPE OPERATOR (radio-tv broad.) 194.382-018
Videotape-Recording Engineer (radio-tv broad.) 194.362-010
Vinegar Maker (beverage) 183.161-014
VINEGAR MAKER (food prep., nec) 522.382-038
VINE PRUNER (agriculture) 403.687-022
Viner Mechanic (agric. equip.) 624.281-010
Vineyard Supervisor (agriculture) 403.131-014
Vinyl Dipper (rubber goods) 599.685-026
Violinist (amuse. & rec.) 152.041-010
VIOLIN MAKER, HAND (musical inst.) 730.281-046
VIOLIN REPAIRER (any industry) 730.281-050
Violin Restorer (musical inst.) 730.281-046
Virginia-Line Attendant (tobacco) 520.685-026
Virologist (profess. & kin.) 041.061-058
Viscera Washer (meat products) 525.684-038
Viscose-Cellar Attendant (plastic-synth.) 559.682-038
vise hand (machinery mfg.; machine tools) 600.281-022
Visiting Professor (education) 090.227-010
visiting-student counselor (education) 090.107-010
visiting teacher (profess. & kin.) 195.107-038
VISUAL-INFORMATION SPECIALIST (profess. & kin.) term
Vocational Adviser (education) 045.107-010

VOCATIONAL REHABILITATION CONSULTANT (government ser.) 094.117-018
VOCATIONAL-REHABILITATION COUNSELOR (government ser.) 045.107-042
VOICE PATHOLOGIST (profess. & kin.) 076.104-010
voicer (musical inst.) 730.381-038
Volcanologist (profess. & kin.) 024.061-030
Volleyball Assembler (toy-sport equip.) 732.684-026
Voltage-Regulator Assembler (elec. equip.) 721.381-014
VOLTAGE TESTER (utilities) 821.381-014
volumetric weigher (ordnance) 920.687-170
volunteer coordinator (social ser.) 187.167-022
volunteer services assistant (profess. & kin.) 187.137-014
Vortex Operator (sugar & conf.) 520.585-018
VOTATOR-MACHINE OPERATOR (meat products; oils & grease) 529.685-250
Voting-Machine Repairer (government ser.) 828.261-022
VOUCHER CLERK (r.r. trans.) 219.362-066
VULCAN CREWMEMBER (military ser.) 378.663-010
VULCANIZED-FIBER-UNIT OPERATOR (paper goods) 539.565-010
VULCANIZER (boot & shoe) 690.685-462
vulcanizer operator (rubber goods; rubber reclaim.; rubber tire) 553.665-038
Vulcanizer, Rubber Plate (pen & pencil; print. & pub.) 556.582-010
VULCANIZING-PRESS OPERATOR (boot & shoe) 690.685-466

W

WAD-BLANKING-PRESS ADJUSTER (ordnance) 690.360-010
WAD-COMPRESSOR OPERATOR-ADJUSTER (ordnance) 535.482-010
WADER-BOOT-TOP ASSEMBLER (rubber goods) 795.684-026
WAD IMPREGNATOR (ordnance) 590.685-054
WAD LUBRICATOR (ordnance) 590.685-058
WAD-PRINTING-MACHINE OPERATOR (ordnance) 652.685-102
WAFER ABRADING MACHINE TENDER (electron. comp.) 673.685-102
Wafer-Batter Mixer (bakery products) 520.685-010
WAFER BREAKER, SEMICONDUCTORS (electron. comp.) 726.687-046
wafer-cell-battery assembler (elec. equip.) 727.687-082
WAFER CLEANER (electron. comp.) 590.685-102
Wafer Cutter (bakery products) 521.685-302
wafer etcher (electron. comp.) 590.685-078
wafer fab operator (electron. comp.) 590.684-042
WAFER-LINE WORKER (elec. equip.) 727.687-082
WAFER-MACHINE OPERATOR (bakery products) 526.685-066
WAFER-MACHINE OPERATOR (elec. equip.) 692.662-018
WAFER MOUNTER (electron. comp.) 726.685-058
wafer polisher (electron. comp.) 673.685-094
wafer slicer (electron. comp.) 677.382-018
waffle baker (bakery products) 526.685-066
waffle-machine operator (bakery products) 526.685-066
wage and salary administrator (profess. & kin.) 166.167-022
wage worker (agriculture)   see FARMWORKER, SEASONAL
Wagon-Drill Operator (construction; mine & quarry) 930.382-010
Wagon Driver (any industry) 919.664-010
WAISTBAND SETTER, LOCKSTITCH (garment) 786.682-266
WAISTLINE JOINER, LOCKSTITCH (garment) 786.682-270
WAISTLINE JOINER, OVERLOCK (garment) 786.682-274
WAIST PLEATER (tex. prod., nec) 583.684-014
Waist Presser (garment) 363.684-018
WAITER/WAITRESS (water trans.) 350.677-030
WAITER/WAITRESS, BANQUET, HEAD (hotel & rest.) 311.137-014
Waiter/Waitress, Banquet (hotel & rest.) 311.477-026
WAITER/WAITRESS, BAR (hotel & rest.) 311.477-018
WAITER/WAITRESS, BUFFET (hotel & rest.) 311.674-018
Waiter/Waitress, Cabin Class (water trans.) 350.677-030
waiter/waitress, cafeteria (hotel & rest.) 311.677-010
WAITER/WAITRESS, CAPTAIN (hotel & rest.) 311.137-018
WAITER/WAITRESS, CLUB (hotel & rest.) 352.677-018
waiter/waitress, cocktail lounge (hotel & rest.) 311.477-018
waiter/waitress, counter (hotel & rest.) 311.477-014
WAITER/WAITRESS, DINING CAR (r.r. trans.) 311.477-022
Waiter/Waitress, Economy Class (water trans.) 350.677-030
Waiter/Waitress, First Class (water trans.) 350.677-030
WAITER/WAITRESS, FORMAL (hotel & rest.) 311.477-026
WAITER/WAITRESS, HEAD (hotel & rest.) 311.137-022
waiter/waitress, head (hotel & rest.) 310.137-010
WAITER/WAITRESS, INFORMAL (hotel & rest.) 311.477-030
WAITER/WAITRESS, ROOM SERVICE (hotel & rest.) 311.477-034
Waiter/Waitress, Second Class (water trans.) 350.677-030
WAITER/WAITRESS, TAKE OUT (hotel & rest.) 311.477-038
Waiter/Waitress, Tavern (hotel & rest.) 311.477-018
Waiter/Waitress, Third Class (water trans.) 350.677-030
Waiter/Waitress, Tourist Class (water trans.) 350.677-030
Walking-Dragline Oiler (mine & quarry) 850.684-018
Walking-Dragline Operator (any industry) 850.683-018

walk-through operator (amuse. & rec.) 342.665-010
wall attendant (amuse. & rec.) 249.587-010
WALLCOVERING TEXTURER (paper goods) 749.684-054
Wall-Crane Operator (foundry) 921.663-010
Wallet Assembler (leather prod.) 783.684-010
wallpaper cleaner (any industry) 381.687-026
wallpaper-embosser helper (paper goods) 640.685-070
WALLPAPER INSPECTOR (paper goods) 652.687-042
WALLPAPER INSPECTOR AND SHIPPER (paper goods) 652.687-046
WALLPAPER-PRINTER HELPER (paper goods) 652.687-050
WALLPAPER PRINTER I (paper goods) 652.662-014
Wallpaper Printer II (paper goods) 979.684-034
Wallpaper Remover, Steam (construction) 869.687-026
wall washer (any industry) 381.687-026
Wall Washer (construction) 869.687-026
Walnut-Dehydrator Operator (can. & preserv.) 523.685-066
Walnut Grower (agriculture) 403.161-010
Warble-Saw Operator (woodworking) 669.382-010
ward attendant (medical ser.) 355.377-014
ward clerk (medical ser.) 245.362-014
Warden (government ser.) 187.117-018
wardrobe draper (motion picture; radio-tv broad.) 346.374-010
WARDROBE-SPECIALTY WORKER (motion picture; radio-tv broad.) 969.381-010
WARDROBE SUPERVISOR (amuse. & rec.) 346.361-010
Ward Supervisor (medical ser.) 355.377-014
WARE CLEANER (pottery & porc.) 774.687-022
WARE DRESSER (pottery & porc.) 774.684-042
WARE FINISHER (glass mfg.) 772.381-018
WARE FORMER (pottery & porc.) term
Warehouse Checker (clerical) 222.687-010
Warehouse Cutter (glass mfg.) 779.684-054
Warehouse Guard (any industry) 372.667-034
Warehouse-Record Clerk (clerical) 222.387-034
warehouse supervisor (any industry) 184.167-114
warehouse supervisor (any industry) 921.133-018
WAREHOUSE SUPERVISOR (any industry) 929.137-022
warehouse supervisor (clerical) 222.137-034
WAREHOUSE SUPERVISOR (motor trans.) 929.137-018
WAREHOUSE TRAFFIC SUPERVISOR (wholesale tr.) 922.137-026
warehouse worker (any industry) 922.687-058
WARE SERVER (glass mfg.) 652.686-046
Wares Sorter (nonprofit org.) 222.387-054
WARE TESTER (glass mfg.) 579.384-018
Ware Washer (pottery & porc.) 599.687-030
WARM-IN WORKER (glass mfg.) 772.684-018
Warp-Bleaching-Vat Tender (textile) 582.685-158
warp changer (textile) 683.360-010
warp clamper (textile) 681.686-010
WARP COILER (textile) 582.686-038
warp drawer (textile) 683.684-014
warp dresser (textile) 681.682-010
WARP-DYEING-VAT TENDER (textile) 582.685-158
WARPER (narrow fabrics) 681.685-146
warper tender (knitting; narrow fabrics; nonmet. min.; textile) 681.685-018
warper tender (textile) 681.682-010
warp hanger (textile) 681.686-010
warp hanger (textile) 683.680-010
warping-mill operator (textile) 681.682-010
Warp-Knitter Helper (knitting) 685.686-014
WARP-KNITTING-MACHINE OPERATOR (knitting) 685.665-018
warp placer (textile) 681.686-010
Warp-Scouring-Vat Tender (textile) 582.685-158
WARP SPOOLER (narrow fabrics; textile) 681.685-142
Warp-Spool Slasher (narrow fabrics) 582.562-010
warp starter (textile) 683.360-014
warp starter (textile) 683.684-018
WARP-TENSION TESTER (textile) 683.687-034
warp tier (textile) 683.680-010
warp trucker (textile) 681.686-010
warp-tying-machine knotter (narrow fabrics; textile) 683.685-034
WARP-TYING-MACHINE TENDER (narrow fabrics; textile) 683.685-034
WARP-YARN SORTER (textile) 681.687-022
washateria attendant (laundry & rel.) 369.677-010
wash-barrel leader (ordnance) 599.132-010
wash-box operator (mine & quarry) 541.382-010
wash-box operator (mine & quarry; smelt. & refin.) 939.362-014
Wash-Clothes Presser (laundry & rel.) 363.682-018
Washcloth Folder (tex. prod., nec) 589.687-014
Washcoat Wiper (furniture) 742.687-010
wash driller (any industry) 930.682-010
wash-driller helper (any industry) 930.687-014
WASHER (any industry) 599.687-030
WASHER (clock & watch) 715.687-126
washer (garment; knitting) 582.684-014

WASHER (grain-feed mills) 529.687-210
WASHER (optical goods) 713.684-042
WASHER (pen & pencil) 733.687-078
WASHER (plastic-synth.) 582.685-162
WASHER, AGRICULTURAL PRODUCE (agriculture; can. & preserv.; sugar & conf.; wholesale tr.) 529.685-258
washer-and-capper-machine operator (elec. equip.) 692.685-042
WASHER-AND-CRUSHER TENDER (mine & quarry) 939.685-014
Washer, Blanket (laundry & rel.) 361.665-010
WASHER, CARCASS (meat products) 525.687-122
Washer Cutter (rubber goods) 690.680-010
washer driver (automotive ser.; retail trade) 919.663-010
Washer-Dryer Preparer (any industry) 827.584-010
WASHER ENGINEER (paper & pulp) 533.685-034
WASHER-ENGINEER HELPER (paper & pulp) 533.686-014
WASHER, HAND (laundry & rel.) 361.687-030
Washer Helper, Machine (laundry & rel.) 361.686-010
WASHER, MACHINE (any industry) 599.685-114
WASHER, MACHINE (laundry & rel.) 361.665-010
Washer, Meat (meat products) 525.587-014
washer-off (jewelry-silver.) 735.687-010
washer operator (mine & quarry) 541.382-010
washery boss (mine & quarry) 549.137-014
WASH HELPER (chemical) 559.665-042
WASH-HOUSE WORKER (beverage) 529.685-254
WASHING-AND-SCREENING PLANT SUPERVISOR (construction) 570.132-018
Washing-And-Waxing-Machine Operator (agriculture; wholesale tr.) 529.685-258
Washing-Machine Assembler (house. appl.) 827.684-010
WASHING-MACHINE LOADER-AND-PULLER (laundry & rel.) 361.686-010
Washing-Machine Loader I (laundry & rel.) 361.686-010
Washing-Machine Loader II (laundry & rel.) 361.687-018
WASHING-MACHINE OPERATOR (any industry) 599.685-118
Washing-Machine Operator (leather mfg.) 582.685-050
washing-machine operator (pharmaceut.) 559.685-022
washing-machine operator (rubber reclaim.) 559.685-138
washing-machine operator (textile) 582.685-030
Washing-Machine Servicer (any industry) 827.261-010
Washing-Machine Striper (elec. equip.) 741.687-022
washing-tub operator (chemical) 551.685-014
WASH-MILL OPERATOR (chemical) 559.485-010
wash-oil-cooler operator (steel & rel.) 549.382-018
WASH-OIL-PUMP OPERATOR (steel & rel.) 549.382-018
WASH-OIL-PUMP OPERATOR HELPER (steel & rel.) 549.685-034
WASH OPERATOR (chemical) 559.662-014
washroom attendant (any industry) 358.677-018
WASHROOM CLEANER (sugar & conf.) 529.687-214
WASHROOM OPERATOR (sugar & conf.) 529.665-014
Washroom Supervisor (laundry & rel.) 361.137-010
WASH-TANK TENDER (chemical) 559.685-182
wash-test checker (textile) 587.384-010
waste baler (any industry) 920.685-010
WASTE CHOPPER (tex. prod., nec) 689.686-054
waste chopper (textile) 680.685-102
waste collector (any industry) 929.687-022
waste collector (any industry) 381.687-018
waste-cotton cleaner (tex. prod., nec; textile) 680.685-114
WASTE-DISPOSAL ATTENDANT (any industry) 955.383-010
waste duster (tex. prod., nec; textile) 680.685-114
waste filling remover (textile) 689.685-094
WASTE HAND (textile) term
waste-house operator (chemical) 551.687-018
WASTE-MACHINE OFFBEARER (tex. prod., nec) 680.686-022
waste-machine operator (textile) 680.685-050
WASTE-MACHINE TENDER (tex. prod., nec; textile) 680.685-114
WASTE-MANAGEMENT ENGINEER, RADIOACTIVE MATERIALS (profess. & kin.) 005.061-042
WASTE-PAPER-HAMMERMILL OPERATOR (paper & pulp) 530.686-018
WASTE SALVAGER (garment) 781.684-062
WASTE-TREATMENT OPERATOR (chemical) 955.382-014
WASTEWATER-TREATMENT-PLANT ATTENDANT (sanitary ser.) 955.585-010
WASTEWATER-TREATMENT-PLANT OPERATOR (sanitary ser.) 955.362-010
watch adjuster (clock & watch) 715.281-010
WATCH-AND-CLOCK-REPAIR CLERK (retail trade) 299.367-018
WATCH ASSEMBLER (clock & watch) 715.381-094
watch-assembly inspector (clock & watch) 715.381-050
Watch Balance Assembly Manufacturing Supervisor (clock & watch) 609.130-026
WATCH-BAND ASSEMBLER (jewelry-silver.) 700.684-082
watch commander (government ser.) 377.137-014
WATCH-CRYSTAL EDGE GRINDER (glass products) 775.684-062
WATCH-CRYSTAL MOLDER (glass products) 772.684-022

watch-dial maker (clock & watch) 715.381-046
watch-dial printer (clock & watch) 715.684-190
Watch-Dial Stoner (clock & watch) 715.684-170
Watch Electrician (tel. & tel.) 829.261-018
watch engineer (any industry) 950.131-014
watch engineer (any industry) 950.382-026
WATCHER, AUTOMAT (tex. prod., nec) 689.685-150
Watcher, Automat, Frame Goods (tex. prod., nec) 689.685-150
Watcher, Automat, Long Goods (tex. prod., nec) 689.685-150
watcher, lookout tower (forestry) 452.367-010
WATCHER, PANTOGRAPH (tex. prod., nec) 689.685-154
watchguard (any industry) 372.667-034
watch guard, gate (any industry) 372.667-030
Watchguard, Racetrack (amuse. & rec.) 372.667-034
watch-hairspring assembler (clock & watch) 715.381-054
Watch Hairspring Manufacturing Supervisor (clock & watch) 609.130-026
watch inspector, final movement (clock & watch) 715.381-050
watchmaker (clock & watch) 715.281-010
watchmaker apprentice (clock & watch) 715.281-014
WATCH MANUFACTURING SUPERVISOR (clock & watch) 609.130-026
Watch Metal Dial Manufacturing Supervisor (clock & watch) 609.130-026
WATCH REPAIRER (clock & watch) 715.281-010
WATCH REPAIRER APPRENTICE (clock & watch) 715.281-014
Watchstander (water trans.) 911.364-010
watch supervisor (air trans.; business ser.) 193.162-022
WATER-AND-SEWER-SYSTEMS SUPERVISOR (waterworks) 862.137-018
Water Chaser (logging) 921.667-014
water-control-station engineer (waterworks) 954.382-014
WATER CONTROL SUPERVISOR (waterworks) 184.167-270
WATER-FILTER CLEANER (waterworks) 954.587-010
water filterer (waterworks) 954.382-014
water-filterer helper (waterworks) 954.587-010
Water Hauler (logging) 905.663-014
Water-Jet Loom Fixer (textile) 683.260-018
WATER LEAK REPAIRER (auto. mfg.) 807.684-034
water-maintenance supervisor (waterworks) 862.137-018
Water-Mangle Tender (textile) 584.685-042
Watermelon-Harvesting Supervisor (agriculture) 409.131-010
Watermelon Inspector (agriculture) 409.687-010
WATER-METER INSTALLER (waterworks) 954.564-010
Water-Meter Reader (waterworks) 209.567-010
water-plant-pump operator (waterworks) 954.382-010
water-plant-pump-operator supervisor (waterworks) 954.130-010
Waterproof-Bag-Cutting-Machine Operator (tex. prod., nec) 686.585-010
Waterproof-Bag Sewer (tex. prod., nec) 787.682-058
Waterproof-Coating-Machine Tender (paper goods) 534.682-018
Waterproofer (boot & shoe) 741.687-018
Waterproofer (construction) 869.664-014
Waterproofer Helper (construction) 869.687-026
Waterproofing-Machine Operator (textile) 589.665-014
Waterproofing Mixer (textile) 550.585-018
waterproof-material folder (tex. prod., nec) 789.687-058
Water-Pump Assembler (engine-turbine) 706.481-010
Water-Pumping-Station Engineer (any industry) 950.382-026
Water-Pump Servicer (any industry) 630.281-018
water purifier (waterworks) 954.382-014
Water Quality Analyst (profess. & kin.) 029.081-010
Water Quality-Control Engineer (profess. & kin.) 019.081-018
WATER-QUALITY TESTER (paper & pulp) 539.367-014
WATER REGULATOR AND VALVE REPAIRER (waterworks) 862.684-030
Water Router Operator (aircraft mfg.) 699.382-010
Water Server (hotel & rest.) 311.677-018
WATER-SERVICE DISPATCHER (waterworks) 954.367-010
water-service supervisor (waterworks) 862.137-018
WATERSHED TENDER (waterworks) 954.382-018
Water-Ski Assembler (toy-sport equip.) 732.684-014
WATER-SOFTENER SERVICER-AND-INSTALLER (business ser.) 862.684-034
water sponger (textile) 587.685-018
water supervisor (waterworks) 862.137-018
Water-Taxi Driver (water trans.) 911.663-010
WATER TENDER (any industry) 599.685-122
water tender (waterworks) 954.362-010
Water-Treatment-Plant Engineer (profess. & kin.) 005.061-030
water-treatment-plant mechanic (waterworks) 630.281-038
WATER-TREATMENT-PLANT OPERATOR (chemical) 551.485-010
WATER-TREATMENT-PLANT OPERATOR (waterworks) 954.382-014
Water-Truck Driver I (construction; petrol. & gas) 904.383-010
WATER-TRUCK DRIVER II (construction; petrol. & gas) 905.683-010
WATERWAY TRAFFIC CHECKER (water trans.) 248.367-030
water-well driller (construction) 859.362-010
WAVE-SOLDERING MACHINE OPERATOR (comm. equip.; electron. comp.; inst. & app.; office machines) 726.362-014
WAVE-SOLDER OFFBEARER (electron. comp.) 726.686-010
WAX-BALL KNOCK-OUT WORKER (toy-sport equip.) 732.687-082

WAX BLEACHER (chemical) 551.685-158
WAX BLENDER (fabrication, nec) 550.585-046
wax-coating-machine tender (paper goods) 534.482-010
Waxed-Bag-Machine Operator (paper goods) 649.685-014
WAXER (glass products) 779.687-038
waxer (hat & cap) 582.685-082
waxer (protective dev.) 712.381-046
WAXER, FLOOR (any industry) 381.687-034
waxer operator (paper goods) 534.482-010
Waxer Tender (motion picture) 976.685-018
Wax Impregnator (electron. comp.) 599.682-014
Waxing-Machine Operator (elec. equip.) 599.685-046
WAXING-MACHINE OPERATOR (paper goods) 534.482-010
Waxing-Machine-Operator Helper (paper goods) 534.686-010
WAX-MACHINE OPERATOR (textile) 584.685-050
WAX MOLDER (foundry; jewelry-silver.) 549.685-038
WAX-PATTERN ASSEMBLER (foundry) 518.684-022
WAX-PATTERN COATER (foundry) 518.687-022
WAX-PATTERN REPAIRER (foundry) 518.684-026
WAX-POT TENDER (foundry) 553.685-110
WAX POURER (chemical) 737.685-018
wax pumper (petrol. refin.) 541.682-010
Wax-Room Supervisor (foundry) 519.131-010
Wax Treater (petrol. refin.) 549.362-014
Waybill Clerk (air trans.; motor trans.; r.r. trans.; water trans.) 214.362-014
WAY INSPECTOR (r.r. trans.) 910.367-030
ways operator (ship-boat mfg.) 921.662-022
Wearing-Apparel Assembler (laundry & rel.) 369.687-010
Wearing-Apparel Finisher, Hand (laundry & rel.) 363.684-018
Wearing-Apparel Folder (laundry & rel.) 369.687-018
wearing-apparel presser (laundry & rel.) 363.685-010
Weasand Rodder (meat products) 525.687-010
WEATHER CLERK (air trans.) 248.362-014
weather forcaster (profess. & kin.) 025.062-010
WEATHER OBSERVER (profess. & kin.) 025.267-014
WEATHERSTRIP-MACHINE OPERATOR (rubber goods) 690.382-014
Weather Stripper (construction) 860.381-022
WEAVE-DEFECT-CHARTING CLERK (textile) 221.587-042
weaver (boot & shoe) 788.684-070
WEAVER (carpet & rug) 683.682-034
WEAVER (fabrication, nec) 739.684-170
weaver (furniture) 763.684-018
weaver (furniture) 692.685-262
WEAVER (nonmet. min.; textile) 683.682-038
WEAVER (wood. container) 769.684-054
WEAVER APPRENTICE (nonmet. min.; textile) 683.682-042
WEAVER, AXMINSTER (carpet & rug) 683.685-038
WEAVER, BENCH LOOM (metal prod., nec) 616.681-010
weaver, broadloom (nonmet. min.; textile) 683.682-038
Weaver, Dobby Loom (textile) 683.682-038
WEAVER, HAND (narrow fabrics; textile) 782.684-062
WEAVER, HAND (personal ser.) 782.381-022
WEAVER, HAND LOOM (carpet & rug; textile) 683.684-030
WEAVER, NARROW FABRICS (narrow fabrics; nonmet. min.) 683.682-046
WEAVER, NEEDLE LOOM (narrow fabrics) 683.665-010
WEAVE-ROOM SUPERVISOR (carpet & rug) 683.130-018
Weaver, Rapier-Insertion Loom (textile) 683.682-030
WEAVER, TIRE CORD (tex. prod., nec) 683.682-050
Weaver, Wire Loom (textile) 683.682-030
WEAVING INSPECTOR (carpet & rug; textile) 683.684-034
weaving-machine operator (metal prod., nec) 616.685-046
WEAVING SUPERVISOR (nonmet. min.; textile) 683.130-022
Webbing Seamer, Pound Net (tex. prod., nec) 782.684-026
WEBBING TACKER (furniture) 780.684-130
Webb Layer (wood. container) 669.685-014
web-machine tender (paper & pulp) 539.686-010
WEB-PRESS OPERATOR (print. & pub.) 651.362-030
WEB-PRESS-OPERATOR APPRENTICE (print. & pub.) 651.362-034
web-press-operator assistant (print. & pub.) 651.585-010
Web Sizer (textile) 680.687-018
web worker (fishing & hunt.) 449.664-010
WEDDING CONSULTANT (retail trade) 299.357-018
wedger-and-gluer (woodworking) 762.687-038
WEDGER, MACHINE (cutlery-hrdwr.) 701.687-034
web-press-operator helper, offset (print. & pub.) 651.685-026
weed-cooking operator (chemical) 529.382-030
WEEDER-THINNER (agriculture) 409.687-018
WEED INSPECTOR (agriculture) 408.381-014
weft maker (fabrication, nec) 739.684-170
WEFT STRAIGHTENER (textile) 580.682-010
weigh and charge worker (rubber reclaim.) 558.666-010
weigher (clerical) 221.587-030
Weigher (recording) 559.686-010
WEIGHER (toy-sport equip.) 732.687-086
WEIGHER, ALLOY (nonfer. metal) 509.687-022

Weigher-And-Charger (fabrication, nec) 929.687-062
WEIGHER-AND-CRUSHER (smelt. & refin.) 515.567-010
WEIGHER AND GRADER (chemical) 559.567-014
WEIGHER AND MIXER (chemical) 550.685-122
WEIGHER-BULKER (chemical) 550.582-014
WEIGHER OPERATOR (chemical) 559.687-070
Weigher, Packing (any industry) 929.687-062
WEIGHER, PRODUCTION (any industry) 929.687-062
weigh-station inspector (government ser.) 168.267-058
WEIGHT ANALYST (profess. & kin.) 020.167-030
weight-and-test-bar clerk (foundry) 221.387-042
WEIGH-TANK OPERATOR (oils & grease) 529.485-026
Weight Calculator (ship-boat mfg.) 216.482-022
Weight Caller (clerical) 209.667-014
weight clerk (clerical) 221.587-030
Weight-Count Operator (electron. comp.) 590.684-014
weight engineer (profess. & kin.) 020.167-030
weighter (toy-sport equip.) 732.687-026
WEIGHT GUESSER (amuse. & rec.) 342.357-010
weight recorder (clerical) 222.387-074
WEIGHT-REDUCTION SPECIALIST (personal ser.) 359.367-014
WEIGHT TESTER (paper & pulp) 539.485-010
weight tester (toy-sport equip.) 732.687-086
WEIGHT-YARDAGE CHECKER (textile) 589.487-010
welcome-wagon host/hostess (business ser.) 293.357-018
Welder, Acetylene (welding) 811.684-014
WELDER APPRENTICE, ARC (welding) 810.384-010
WELDER APPRENTICE, COMBINATION (welding) 819.384-008
WELDER APPRENTICE, GAS (welding) 811.684-010
WELDER, ARC (welding) 810.384-014
WELDER-ASSEMBLER (machinery mfg.) 819.381-010
Welder, Boilermaker (struct. metal) 810.384-014
Welder, Carbon Arc (welding) 810.384-014
WELDER, CERTIFIED (welding) term
WELDER, COMBINATION (welding) 819.384-010
WELDER, EXPERIMENTAL (welding) 819.281-022
WELDER, EXPLOSION (welding) 814.684-010
WELDER-FITTER (welding) 819.361-010
WELDER-FITTER APPRENTICE (welding) 819.361-014
Welder-Fitter, Arc (welding) 819.361-010
Welder-Fitter, Gas (welding) 819.361-010
welder-fitter helper (any industry) 801.687-014
Welder, Flux-Cored Arc (welding) 810.384-014
WELDER, GAS (welding) 811.684-014
welder, gas, automatic (welding) 811.482-010
Welder, Gas-Metal Arc (welding) 810.384-014
Welder, Gas-Tungsten Arc (welding) 810.384-014
WELDER, GUN (welding) 810.664-010
Welder, Hand, Submerged Arc (welding) 810.384-014
WELDER HELPER (welding) 819.687-014
Welder, Oxyacetylene (welding) 811.684-014
Welder, Oxyhydrogen (welding) 811.684-014
Welder, Pipe Making (steel & rel.) 616.360-026
Welder, Plasma Arc (welding) 810.384-014
welder, plastic (plastic prod.) 553.684-010
WELDER, PRODUCTION LINE (welding) 819.684-010
Welder, Production Line, Arc (welding) 819.684-010
Welder, Production Line, Combination (welding) 819.684-010
Welder, Production Line, Gas (welding) 819.684-010
Welder, Repair (welding) 819.384-010
WELDER SETTER, ELECTRON-BEAM MACHINE (welding) 815.380-010
WELDER SETTER, RESISTANCE MACHINE (welding) 812.360-010
Welder, Shielded-Metal Arc (welding) 810.384-014
Welder, Structural Repair (welding) 819.361-010
WELDER, TACK (welding) 810.684-010
Welder, Tool And Die (welding) 819.361-010
WELDING ENGINEER (profess. & kin.) 011.061-026
Welding-Machine Assembler (elec. equip.) 826.361-010
Welding-Machine Feeder (welding) 819.686-010
WELDING-MACHINE OPERATOR, ARC (welding) 810.382-010
Welding-Machine Operator, Electro-Gas (welding) 810.382-010
WELDING-MACHINE OPERATOR, ELECTRON BEAM (welding) 815.382-010
WELDING-MACHINE OPERATOR, ELECTROSLAG (welding) 815.382-014
WELDING-MACHINE OPERATOR, FRICTION (welding) 814.382-010
WELDING-MACHINE OPERATOR, GAS (welding) 811.482-010
Welding-Machine Operator, Gas-Metal Arc (welding) 810.382-010
Welding-Machine Operator, Gas-Tungsten Arc (welding) 810.382-010
Welding-Machine-Operator Helper, Arc (welding) 819.666-010
Welding-Machine-Operator Helper, Gas (welding) 819.666-010
Welding-Machine Operator, Plasma Arc (welding) 810.382-010
WELDING-MACHINE OPERATOR, RESISTANCE (welding) 812.682-010
Welding-Machine Operator, Submerged Arc (welding) 810.382-010
WELDING-MACHINE OPERATOR, THERMIT (welding) 815.682-014
WELDING-MACHINE OPERATOR, ULTRASONIC (welding) 814.682-010

WELDING-MACHINE TENDER (welding) 819.685-010
WELDING-ROD COATER (elec. equip.) 505.382-014
WELDING SUPERVISOR (welding) 819.131-014
Welding Supervisor, Electric-Weld Pipe Mill (welding) 819.131-014
WELDING TECHNICIAN (profess. & kin.) 011.261-014
welding tester (welding) 819.281-018
WELD INSPECTOR (elec. equip.) 724.685-014
WELD INSPECTOR I (welding) 819.281-018
WELD INSPECTOR II (welding) 819.687-010
WELFARE DIRECTOR (government ser.) 188.117-126
well cleaner (petrol. & gas) 930.363-010
Well Digger (construction) 869.687-026
well driller (petrol. & gas) 930.382-026
WELL-DRILL OPERATOR (construction) 859.362-010
Well-Drill Operator, Cable Tool (construction) 859.362-010
Well-Drill-Operator Helper, Cable Tool (construction) 869.664-014
Well-Drill-Operator Helper, Rotary Drill (construction) 869.664-014
Well-Drill Operator, Rotary Drill (construction) 859.362-010
WELL-LOGGING CAPTAIN, MUD ANALYSIS (petrol. & gas) 010.131-010
WELL-LOGGING OPERATOR, MUD ANALYSIS (petrol. & gas) 010.281-022
WELL-POINT PUMPING SUPERVISOR (construction) 862.132-010
WELL-POINT SETTER (construction) term
WELL PULLER (petrol. & gas) 930.382-030
WELL PULLER, HEAD (petrol. & gas) 939.131-018
Well-Reactivator Operator (construction) 859.362-010
well shooter (petrol. & gas) 931.361-014
WELT BEATER (boot & shoe) 690.685-470
WELT-BUTTER, HAND (boot & shoe) 788.687-162
WELT BUTTER, MACHINE (boot & shoe) 690.685-474
WELT CUTTER (boot & shoe) 690.685-478
welt cutter (hat & cap) 686.685-074
welt-edge rounder (hat & cap) 784.684-050
welter (boot & shoe) 690.682-078
Welting Stitcher, Front (boot & shoe) 690.682-082
welt-insole channeler (boot & shoe) 690.685-086
welt maker (boot & shoe) 690.685-478
welt-pocket-machine operator (garment) 786.685-022
Welt Rougher (boot & shoe) 690.685-046
Welt Sewer (furniture) 780.682-018
Welt-Sole Layer (boot & shoe) 690.685-074
Welt-Strip Cementer, Machine (boot & shoe) 690.686-018
Welt Treater (boot & shoe) 788.687-090
welt trimmer (boot & shoe) 690.685-238
WELT-TRIMMING-MACHINE OPERATOR (hat & cap) 686.685-074
WELT WHEELER (boot & shoe) 690.685-482
western-felt-hat blocker (hat & cap) 580.685-026
Western-Saddle Maker (leather prod.) 783.381-026
WET-AND-DRY-SUGAR-BIN OPERATOR (sugar & conf.) 529.665-018
Wet-Char Conveyor Tender (sugar & conf.) 529.685-050
wet cleaner, machine (laundry & rel.) 361.665-010
WET-COTTON FEEDER (textile) 581.686-042
wet-crown-blocking operator (hat & cap) 580.685-026
WET-END HELPER (wood prod., nec) 534.685-034
WET-END OPERATOR I (plastic-synth.) 559.685-186
WET-END OPERATOR II (plastic-synth.) 559.685-190
Wet-End Tester (paper & pulp) 539.364-010
wet finisher, wool (textile) 586.682-010
WET INSPECTOR, OPTICAL GLASS (optical goods) 716.687-034
WET-MACHINE TENDER (paper & pulp) 539.685-030
wet-milling-wheel operator (leather mfg.; tex. prod., nec) 582.685-050
wet mixer (brick & tile; pottery & porc.) 570.482-010
wet mixer (chemical) 550.582-010
WET MIXER (chemical) 550.685-126
WET-MIX OPERATOR (chemical) 558.382-058
wet-mix operator (pharmaceut.) 559.382-026
Wet-Pan Mixer (smelt. & refin.; steel & rel.) 570.685-070
WET-PLANT OPERATOR (smelt. & refin.) 519.665-018
wet-press tender (paper & pulp) 539.686-010
Wet Roaster (can. & preserv.) 529.685-174
Wet Roller (leather mfg.) 583.685-094
Wet Trimmer (leather mfg.) 585.684-010
wet washer, machine (laundry & rel.) 361.665-010
WHARF ATTENDANT (amuse. & rec.) 342.667-010
wharf hand (can. & preserv.) 922.687-062
wharf hand (water trans.) 911.364-014
wharf helper (water trans.) 911.687-010
WHARFINGER (water trans.) 184.387-010
WHARFINGER, CHIEF (water trans.) 184.167-274
wharf operator (water trans.) 911.364-014
WHARF TENDER (steel & rel.) 542.667-010
wharf tender (water trans.) 911.364-014
wharf tender, head (petrol. refin.; pipe lines) 914.137-018
wharf-tender helper (water trans.) 911.687-010
WHARF WORKER (water trans.) 921.667-026

WHEAT CLEANER (grain-feed mills) 529.685-262
Wheat Grower (agriculture) 401.161-010
wheel-alignment mechanic (automotive ser.) 620.281-038
wheel and axle inspector (railroad equip.) 622.381-034
WHEEL-AND-CASTER REPAIRER (any industry) 630.684-038
WHEEL ASSEMBLER (mfd. bldgs.; vehicles, nec) 809.684-038
wheel assembler (motor-bicycles) 706.684-106
Wheel Assembler, Baby Carriage (toy-sport equip.) 731.687-034
wheelbarrow pusher (construction)   see WHEELER
wheel blocker (knitting) 685.684-010
wheelchair and baby-stroller rental clerk (retail trade) 295.367-014
wheelchair repairer (protective dev.; retail trade) 639.281-022
WHEEL CUTTER (clock & watch) 605.682-030
wheel engraver (glass products) 775.381-010
Wheeler (chemical) 559.687-050
WHEELER (construction) term
Wheel Filler (auto. mfg.) 749.684-042
Wheel Fitter (railroad equip.) 622.381-014
WHEEL INSPECTOR (r.r. trans.) 806.387-014
Wheel Inspector (steel & rel.) 619.381-010
Wheel Installer (mfd. bldgs.; vehicles, nec) 869.684-010
WHEEL LACER AND TRUER (motor-bicycles) 706.684-106
wheel loader operator (any industry) 921.683-042
WHEEL-MILL OPERATOR (chemical) 555.685-066
WHEEL-PRESS CLERK (railroad equip.) 221.587-046
Wheel-Press Operator (railroad equip.) 616.682-010
wheel setter (any industry) 776.684-014
wheel truer (motor-bicycles) 706.684-106
WHEEL-TRUING MACHINE TENDER (motor-bicycles) 706.685-014
WHEELWRIGHT (automotive ser.) 706.381-046
Whip Operator (amuse. & rec.) 342.663-010
WHIPPED-TOPPING FINISHER (oils & grease) 529.682-034
whipper-beater (sugar & conf.) 520.685-050
whirling-machine operator (textile) 585.685-022
Whisky Filterer (beverage) 522.382-018
Whisky Inspector (beverage) 522.667-010
Whisky-Proof Reader (beverage) 522.382-018
Whisky-Regauger (beverage) 522.382-018
White-Kid Buffer (leather mfg.) 585.685-018
white-metal corrosion proofer (any industry) 500.682-010
White Mixing Operator (tex. prod., nec) 680.685-010
Whitener (wood prod., nec) 763.381-010
whiteprinting-machine operator (any industry) 979.682-014
White-Shoe Examiner (boot & shoe) 788.384-010
WHITE-SHOE RAGGER (boot & shoe) 788.687-166
White-Sidewall-Tire Buffer (rubber tire) 759.684-022
White-Sugar Boiler (sugar & conf.) 522.382-034
White-Sugar Centrifugal Operator (sugar & conf.) 521.682-010
White-Sugar-Pan-Tank Operator (sugar & conf.) 529.585-014
White-Sugar-Syrup Operator (sugar & conf.) 529.585-014
White Washer (construction) 869.687-026
White-Washer Piler (textile) 589.686-010
white-work cleaner (engraving) 704.687-010
WHITING-MACHINE OPERATOR (wood prod., nec) 562.485-010
whittling-room operator (hat & cap) 784.361-010
WHIZZER (hat & cap) 581.685-070
whizzer operator I (hat & cap) 581.685-070
WHOLESALER I (wholesale tr.) 185.167-070
WHOLESALER II (wholesale tr.) 185.157-018
WICK-AND-BASE ASSEMBLER (fabrication, nec) 739.687-202
wick cutter (fabrication, nec) 739.687-050
WICKER, MOLDED CANDLES (fabrication, nec) 692.685-242
WICKER WORKER (furniture) 763.684-078
wicker worker (wood. container) 769.684-054
wick tender (fabrication, nec) 692.685-242
wide-cloth folder (textile) 689.685-050
Wide-Piece-Goods Inspector (fabrication, nec) 590.367-010
WIDTH STRIPPER (boot & shoe) 690.685-486
width stripper (leather prod.) 585.685-038
Wig Comber (toy-sport equip.) 731.687-018
WIG DRESSER (fabrication, nec; personal ser.) 332.361-010
WIG MAKER (fabrication, nec) 739.381-058
Wig Stylist (personal ser.) 261.351-010
WILDLIFE AGENT, REGIONAL (government ser.) 379.137-018
Wildlife Biologist (profess. & kin.) 041.061-030
WILDLIFE CONTROL AGENT (government ser.) 379.267-010
will-call clerk (retail trade) 299.467-010
willower (any industry) 680.685-082
willow-machine operator (tex. prod., nec; textile) 680.685-114
willow-machine tender (tex. prod., nec; textile) 680.685-114
Willow Worker (furniture) 763.684-078
Willow Worker (wood. container) 769.684-054
Wilton Weaver (carpet & rug) 683.682-014
WINCH DRIVER (water trans.) 921.683-082
Wincher (any industry) 921.667-018

Wincher (wood prod., nec) 561.686-010
winch operator (petrol. & gas) 932.363-010
Winch Operator (water trans.) 911.663-014
WINDER (clock & watch) 715.687-130
winder (fabrication, nec) 739.684-018
winder (garment; knitting) 583.685-122
winder (paper goods) 640.682-022
winder (pen & pencil) 640.685-018
winder (tex. prod., nec; textile) 681.685-154
winder (tex. prod., nec) 681.685-114
WINDER (toy-sport equip.) 692.685-246
Winder Fixer (textile) 689.260-010
winder, gammeter (toy-sport equip.) 692.685-246
WINDER HELPER (paper & pulp) 539.687-010
winder helper (paper goods) 640.687-014
winder operator (build. mat.) 549.685-022
WINDER OPERATOR (fabrication, nec) 590.665-018
winder operator (nonmet. min.) 692.685-234
WINDER OPERATOR, AUTOMATIC (textile) 681.685-150
WIND-GENERATING-ELECTRIC-POWER INSTALLER (construction; utilities) 821.381-018
WINDING INSPECTOR (house. appl.) 729.384-022
WINDING INSPECTOR AND TESTER (elec. equip.) 724.364-010
WINDING-LATHE OPERATOR (ordnance) 619.685-086
winding-machine operator (tex. prod., nec; textile) 681.685-154
winding-machine operator (textile) 689.685-046
WINDING-MACHINE OPERATOR (concrete prod.) 619.665-010
winding-machine operator (tex. prod., nec) 681.685-114
WINDING-RACK OPERATOR (tex. prod., nec) 581.685-074
Winding-Rack-Operator Helper (tex. prod., nec) 589.687-010
WIND-INSTRUMENT REPAIRER (any industry) 730.281-054
windlace-machine operator (rubber goods) 690.382-014
Window Assembler (saw. & plan.) 865.684-014
Window Dresser (retail trade) 298.081-010
window-glass cutter off (glass mfg.) 677.685-030
Window Installer (mfd. bldgs.; vehicles, nec) 809.684-030
Window Installer (ship-boat mfg.) 806.684-146
window-machine operator (paper goods) 641.685-066
WINDOW REPAIRER (any industry) 899.684-042
Window-Shade-Cloth Sewer (furniture) 787.682-026
WINDOW-SHADE CUTTER AND MOUNTER (furniture) 692.685-250
Window-Shade Estimator (retail trade) 299.364-010
window-shade-ring coverer (furniture) 692.685-254
WINDOW-SHADE-RING SEWER (furniture) 692.685-254
window washer (any industry) 389.687-014
windshield installer (automotive ser.) 865.684-010
Windshield Installer (ship-boat mfg.) 806.684-146
Windshield-Wiper Repairer (automotive ser.) 825.281-022
Windshield-Wiper Repairer (railroad equip.) 620.381-018
WIND TUNNEL MECHANIC (aircraft mfg.) 869.261-026
wind-up operator (rubber goods; rubber tire) 554.686-018
wine-bottle inspector (beverage) 529.687-014
Wine-Cellar Stock Clerk (hotel & rest.) 222.387-058
WINE MAKER (beverage) 183.161-014
WINE PASTEURIZER (beverage) 523.685-126
WINERY WORKER (beverage) 521.685-370
WINE STEWARD/STEWARDESS (hotel & rest.) 310.357-010
WING-MAILER-MACHINE OPERATOR (print. & pub.) 208.685-034
WINK-CUTTER OPERATOR (rubber goods) 557.382-014
WINTERIZER (oils & grease) 521.685-374
wiper (any industry) 699.687-014
wiper (fabrication, nec) 739.687-058
WIPER (furniture) 742.687-010
WIPER (light. fix.) 723.687-022
wiper-blender (furniture) 742.687-010
Wiping-Rag Washer (tex. prod., nec) 361.685-018
wire-and-repeater technician (tel. & tel.) 822.261-026
WIRE-BASKET MAKER (metal prod., nec) 709.687-062
Wire Bender (elec. equip.) 727.687-022
WIRE BENDER (furniture) 709.687-058
Wire Bender (wood. container) 669.686-014
Wire Bender, Hand (any industry) 709.687-050
WIRE-BORDER ASSEMBLER (furniture) 780.685-018
Wire-Bound-Box-Machine Helper (wood. container) 669.686-014
Wire-Bound-Box-Machine Operator (wood. container) 669.662-010
Wire-Brush-Boring-And-Filling-Machine Operator (fabrication, nec) 692.682-018
Wire Brusher (any industry) 705.687-014
wire-brushing-machine operator (button & notion) 603.685-050
wire-brush maker (elec. equip.) 724.684-038
WIRE BRUSH OPERATOR (fabrication, nec) 761.684-058
WIRE CHARGER (elec. equip.) 614.586-010
wire chief (tel. & tel.) 822.131-010
WIRE-COATING OPERATOR, METAL (galvanizing) 501.485-010
WIRE COILER (house. appl.) 724.362-010

WIRE COINER (button & notion) 616.685-086
Wire Cutter (elec. equip.) 691.685-018
WIRE CUTTER (svc. ind. mach.) 731.687-038
WIRE DRAWER (clock & watch) 614.382-014
WIRE DRAWER (jewelry-silver.) 735.687-042
WIRE DRAWER (nonfer. metal) 614.382-010
WIRE DRAWING MACHINE OPERATOR (inst. & app.; jewelry-silver.) 614.382-018
WIRE-DRAWING-MACHINE TENDER (nonfer. metal) 614.685-026
Wire-Drawing-Machine Tender (welding) 819.685-010
Wire-Drawing Supervisor (nonfer. metal; steel & rel.) 614.132-010
wire-draw operator (nonfer. metal) 614.382-010
wire dropper (textile) 683.687-014
wired-sweatband cutter (hat & cap) 585.685-122
wire-fence builder (construction) 869.684-022
Wire-Fence Erector (construction) 869.684-022
WIRE-FRAME DIPPER (button & notion) 734.684-026
WIRE-FRAME-LAMP-SHADE MAKER (fabrication, nec) 709.684-098
WIRE-FRAME MAKER (button & notion) 734.481-010
wire galvanizer (galvanizing) 501.485-010
WIRE HARNESS ASSEMBLER (elec. equip.; electron. comp.; office machines) 728.684-010
WIRE INSERTER (hat & cap) 784.687-082
wire-loop-machine operator (metal prod., nec) 616.682-014
Wire-Machine Operator (hat & cap) 784.682-014
WIRE-MESH-FILTER FABRICATOR (metal prod., nec) 709.381-046
WIRE-PHOTO OPERATOR, NEWS (print. & pub.) 239.382-010
WIRE PREPARATION MACHINE TENDER (any industry) 728.685-010
wire-preparation worker (elec. equip.; electron. comp.) 728.684-022
wirer (auto. mfg.; vehicles, nec) 829.684-014
wirer (construction) 824.261-010
wirer (elec. equip.; electron. comp.; office machines) 728.684-010
WIRER (office machines) 729.281-042
wirer (tel. & tel.) 722.381-010
WIRER, CABLE (comm. equip.; elec. equip.) 729.381-022
WIRE REPAIRER (carpet & rug) 628.684-038
wirer helper (any industry) 829.684-022
Wirer Helper (utilities) 821.667-010
Wirer, Maintenance (utilities) 829.261-018
WIRE-ROPE-SLING MAKER (metal prod., nec) 709.684-102
Wirer, Passenger Car (railroad equip.) 825.281-026
WIRER, STREET LIGHT (utilities) 821.684-018
WIRER, SUBASSEMBLIES (office machines) 729.684-062
Wire Saw Operator (electron. comp.) 677.382-018
wire-saw operator (stonework) 677.462-014
WIRE SAWYER (stonework) 677.462-014
WIRE SETTER (glass mfg.) 579.665-018
Wire-Shape Maker (hat & cap) 784.684-030
wire-spiral binder (paper goods; print. & pub.) 653.685-030
Wire-Spring-Relay Adjuster (elec. equip.) 724.381-010
wire stitcher, hand (furniture) 780.687-042
wire-stitcher, machine (furniture) 692.685-198
wire-stitcher operator (any industry) 692.685-202
Wire Stockkeeper (metal prod., nec) 222.387-058
Wire-Straightening-Machine Operator (any industry) 613.662-022
Wire Stripper (elec. equip.) 691.685-018
wire-taping-machine operator (nonfer. metal) 691.682-018
WIRE THREADER (clock & watch) 604.686-010
Wire Tinner (galvanizing) 501.485-010
WIRE-TRANSFER CLERK (financial) 203.562-010
WIRE-TURNING-MACHINE OPERATOR (wood. container) 692.685-258
WIRE WALKER (amuse. & rec.) 159.347-022
wire weaver (metal prod., nec) 616.382-014
WIRE WEAVER, CLOTH (metal prod., nec) 616.382-014
WIRE-WEAVER HELPER (metal prod., nec) 616.687-014
wire winder (rubber goods) 690.685-490
WIRE-WINDING-MACHINE OPERATOR (wood. container) 619.685-090
WIRE-WINDING-MACHINE TENDER (rubber goods) 690.685-490
WIREWORKER (elec. equip.; electron. comp.) 728.684-022
WIREWORKER SUPERVISOR (utilities) 821.131-026
WIRE-WRAPPING-MACHINE OPERATOR (electron. comp.) 726.682-014
WIRE-WRAPPING-MACHINE OPERATOR (office machines) 692.662-022
Wiring Inspector (elec. equip.) 829.361-018
Wiring-Machine Operator (paper goods) 649.685-054
Wolf Hunter (fishing & hunt.) 461.661-010
Women's-Activities Adviser (education) 090.167-022
Women's Garment Fitter (retail trade) 785.361-014
Women's Leather-Belt Maker (leather prod.) 690.685-266
Wood And Hardware Outfitter (ship-boat mfg.) 806.684-146
wood barker (fabrication, nec; paper & pulp) 569.687-026
Wood Buffer (musical inst.) 761.684-026
wood carver, hand (woodworking) 761.281-010
WOOD-CARVING-MACHINE OPERATOR (woodworking) 665.382-018
WOOD CAULKER (ship-boat mfg.) 843.384-010
Wood-Club-Neck Whipper (toy-sport equip.) 732.684-082

X

x-ray consultant (any industry) 729.281-046
X-Ray-Control-Equipment Repairer (any industry) 710.281-026
X-Ray-Developing-Machine Operator (medical ser.) 976.685-014
x-ray equipment servicer (any industry) 729.281-046
X-RAY-EQUIPMENT TESTER (any industry) 729.281-046
X-RAY INSPECTOR (can. & preserv.; tobacco) 529.685-274
x-ray service engineer (any industry) 729.281-046
X-Ray Technician (any industry) 199.361-010
X-ray Technician, Printed Circuit Boards (electron. comp.) 726.684-062
x-ray technologist (medical ser.) 078.362-026

Y

Yardage Caller (textile) 209.667-014
YARDAGE-CONTROL CLERK (carpet & rug) 221.587-050
YARDAGE-CONTROL OPERATOR, FORMING (glass mfg.) 575.662-014
YARDAGE ESTIMATOR (garment) 221.484-010
yardage-machine operator (textile) 689.685-078
yardage-tufting-machine operator (carpet & rug; textile) 687.685-018
yard boss (any industry)   see YARD SUPERVISOR
YARD CLERK (r.r. trans.) 209.367-054
YARD COUPLER (r.r. trans.) 910.664-010
YARD ENGINEER (r.r. trans.) 910.363-018
Yarder (concrete prod.) 579.687-042
yarder operator (logging) 921.663-066
yarding-and-folding-machine operator (textile) 689.685-078
YARDING ENGINEER (logging) 921.663-066
yarding supervisor (logging) 459.133-010
yarding supervisor (logging) 183.167-038
YARD INSPECTOR (ship-boat mfg.) 869.281-018
YARD LABORER (paper & pulp) 922.687-102
yard-labor supervisor (any industry) 899.133-010
YARD MANAGER (any industry) 910.137-046
YARD MANAGER (r.r. trans.) 184.167-278
Yard Patroller (r.r. trans.) 376.667-018
yard pipe grader (brick & tile) 573.687-034
Yard Pumper (any industry) 914.682-010
yard rigger (any industry) 921.260-010
yard salesperson (retail trade) 299.677-014
yard spotter (motor trans.) 909.663-010
YARD SUPERVISOR (any industry) term
YARD SUPERVISOR (construction) 229.137-014
YARD SUPERVISOR (forestry) 922.137-030
yard supervisor (r.r. trans.) 910.137-022
YARD SUPERVISOR (smelt. & refin.) 929.137-026
YARD SUPERVISOR (woodworking) 929.133-010
YARD SUPERVISOR, BUILDING MATERIALS OR LUMBER (retail trade; wholesale tr.) 929.137-030
YARD SUPERVISOR, COTTON GIN (agriculture) 929.137-034
YARD WORKER (agriculture) 929.583-010
yard worker (brick & tile) 579.667-010
YARD WORKER (domestic ser.) 301.687-018
YARD WORKER (ship-boat mfg.) 921.683-086
YARD WORKER, USED BUILDING MATERIALS (retail trade) 922.667-010
Yarn-Bleaching-Machine Operator (textile) 582.685-102
YARN CLEANER (tex. prod., nec; textile) 681.687-026
yarn conditioner (textile) 587.685-022
yarn-dry-room worker (textile) 581.685-054
yarn dyer (textile) 582.685-130
YARN EXAMINER (glass mfg.; plastic-synth.; textile) 681.687-030
YARN EXAMINER, SKEINS (textile) 689.687-082

yarn inspector (glass mfg.; plastic-synth.; textile) 681.687-030
yarn inspector (textile) 689.687-082
YARN-MERCERIZER-OPERATOR HELPER (textile) 584.686-010
YARN-MERCERIZER OPERATOR I (textile) 584.685-054
YARN-MERCERIZER OPERATOR II (textile) 584.685-058
YARN-POLISHING-MACHINE OPERATOR (textile) 583.685-126
yarn salvager (tex. prod., nec; textile) 681.687-026
YARN SORTER (textile) 689.687-086
yarn tester (textile) 689.384-014
Yarn-Texturing Machine Fixer (textile) 689.260-010
YARN-TEXTURING-MACHINE OPERATOR (plastic-synth.) 589.685-102
YARN-TEXTURING-MACHINE OPERATOR I (textile) 681.685-158
YARN-TEXTURING-MACHINE OPERATOR II (textile) 689.685-158
Yarn-Weight-And-Strength Tester (textile) 689.384-014
YARN WINDER (tex. prod., nec; textile) 681.685-154
yeast-cake cutter (food prep., nec) 529.665-022
YEAST-CULTURE DEVELOPER (beverage) 022.381-010
yeast-culture operator (food prep., nec) 522.685-090
YEAST-CUTTING-AND-WRAPPING-MACHINE OPERATOR (food prep., nec) 529.665-022
YEAST DISTILLER (beverage) 522.362-010
Yeast-Drier Operator, Drum (food prep., nec) 529.685-098
YEAST-FERMENTATION ATTENDANT (food prep., nec) 522.685-110
yeast maker (beverage) 522.362-010
Yeast Pumper (beverage) 914.665-014
YEAST PUSHER (beverage) 522.665-014
yeast stacker (food prep., nec) 522.686-014
YEAST WASHER (food prep., nec) 529.685-278
YEOMAN (water trans.) term
yield clerk (clerical) 221.382-010
YIELD-LOSS INSPECTOR (grain-feed mills) 529.367-030
Yoke Presser (laundry & rel.) 363.685-026
Yolk Spray Drier (can. & preserv.) 523.682-022
YOUNG-ADULT LIBRARIAN (library) 100.167-034
Youth Agent (education) 096.127-022
Youth Nutritional Monitor (social ser.) 195.367-010

Z

zanjero (waterworks) 954.362-010
ZIGZAG-MACHINE OPERATOR (garment) 786.682-278
Zig-Zag-Spring-Machine Operator (metal prod., nec) 616.682-022
Zig-Zag Stitcher (boot & shoe) 690.682-082
ZINC-CHLORIDE OPERATOR (smelt. & refin.) 511.385-010
Zinc Etcher (print. & pub.) 971.381-014
zinc-plate grainer (print. & pub.) 972.682-010
ZINC-PLATING-MACHINE OPERATOR (electroplating) 500.485-010
ZIPPER CUTTER (button & notion) 616.685-090
zipper ironer (button & notion) 590.685-042
zipper joiner (button & notion) 734.687-074
zipper-lining folder (leather prod.) 690.685-178
ZIPPER-MACHINE OPERATOR (button & notion) 692.685-270
zipper measurer (button & notion) 734.687-094
zipper repairer (button & notion) 734.684-022
ZIPPER SETTER (any industry) 787.682-086
ZIPPER SETTER, CHAINSTITCH (garment) 786.682-282
ZIPPER SETTER, LOCKSTITCH (garment) 786.682-286
zipper-slide attacher (button & notion; garment) 734.687-078
ZIPPER TRIMMER, HAND (button & notion) 734.687-094
ZIPPER TRIMMER, MACHINE (button & notion) 692.685-266
zoo caretaker (amuse. & rec.) 412.674-010
ZOOLOGIST (profess. & kin.) 041.061-090
ZOO VETERINARIAN (medical ser.) 073.101-018